O9-AIG-842

Group
0 (VIII A)

						2
						He
						4.003

Group III A	Group IV A	Group V A	Group VI A	Group VII A	
5	6	7	8	9	10
B	**C**	**N**	**O**	**F**	**Ne**
10.81	12.01	14.01	16.00	19.00	20.18
13	14	15	16	17	18
Al	**Si**	**P**	**S**	**Cl**	**Ar**
26.98	28.09	30.97	32.07	35.45	39.95

Group I B	Group II B

28	29	30	31	32	33	34	35	36
Ni	**Cu**	**Zn**	**Ga**	**Ge**	**As**	**Se**	**Br**	**Kr**
58.69	63.55	65.39	69.72	72.59	74.92	78.96	79.90	83.80
46	47	48	49	50	51	52	53	54
Pd	**Ag**	**Cd**	**In**	**Sn**	**Sb**	**Te**	**I**	**Xe**
106.4	107.9	112.4	114.8	118.7	121.8	127.6	126.9	131.3
78	79	80	81	82	83	84	85	86
Pt	**Au**	**Hg**	**Tl**	**Pb**	**Bi**	**Po**	**At**	**Rn**
195.1	197.0	200.6	204.4	207.2	209.0	(210)	(210)	(222)

64	65	66	67	68	69	70	71
Gd	**Tb**	**Dy**	**Ho**	**Er**	**Tm**	**Yb**	**Lu**
157.3	158.9	162.5	164.9	167.3	168.9	173.0	175.0
96	97	98	99	100	101	102	103
Cm	**Bk**	**Cf**	**Es**	**Fm**	**Md**	**No**	**Lr**
(247)	(247)	(249)	(254)	(253)	(256)	(254)	(257)

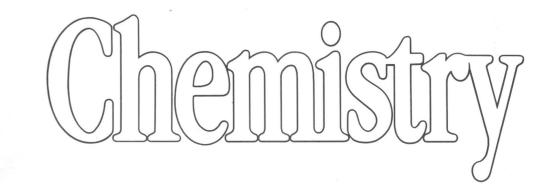

Table of Contents

Reference Section

Features at a Glance

Preface

Chemistry: A Second Course has been written for students who have already taken an introductory chemistry course. Thus we assume a familiarity with the conversion-factor method, chemical equations, and the mole concept. Should students require a quick review of these topics, they are covered briefly in the opening chapter.

Chemistry is a very relevant subject. A knowledge of chemistry helps us to interpret and understand some of the larger environmental issues of the day, such as the destruction of the ozone layer and the build-up of the greenhouse effect. It can also help us in making decisions about the many chemical products we use around the home and at work. To be able to make informed judgements concerning the use of these products, we often need to understand some of the basic principles of chemistry. Introducing the student to these basic principles is one of the main goals of this text.

After explaining the foundations and applications of important chemical concepts, we point out how these principles are important to everyday life. And in stressing the connection between science, technology, and society, we hope to lead the student to the conclusion that the major issues and decisions facing society, at least those that involve science and technology, can only be solved by a society that is scientifically literate.

Since chemical knowledge is not static, we show that our explanations and models are continually being modified to match our increasing awareness of the factors that affect the different chemical events. Above all, chemistry is concerned with trying to understand how things work. It is a human endeavor, of men and women seeking answers. As in other disciplines, however, agreement does not always proceed smoothly and without incident. This theme is raised several times in the text.

Features of This Text

CONCEPT DEVELOPMENT

Wherever possible, we have started each chapter with an explanation of the concepts being covered. With an overview of this kind, students are better able to work through the material ahead. We also believe that it is important, when introducing new ideas, for students to understand the how and the why. At the same time we point out how concepts introduced apply to our lives. To reinforce this we have established a very strong art program consisting of diagrams, graphs, and photographs.

After covering the main concepts, and relating them to students' lives, we introduce both conceptual and numerical problems. These are solved in a step-by-step fashion under the framework of worked examples. The examples are solved by systematic methods to show that there are patterns to problem solving. As well, we have ensured that these examples start from the simple case and move to the more complex case.

To help the students master the problem types, we identify each step in the solution, and often incorporate a graph or table in the problem-solving method. Examples of this latter innovation can be seen in context below:

	[HI]	$[H_2]$	$[I_2]$
Initial	0.100		
Change	$-2x$	$+x$	$+x$
Equilibrium	$(0.100 - 2x)$	x	x

In sections relating to reaction rates and equilibrium, data is arranged in special tables for easy analysis.

$$N_{2\,(g)} + 3\,H_{2\,(g)} \longrightarrow 2\,NH_{3\,(g)}$$

In sections relating to oxidation and reduction, we use a helpful "ticker tape" diagram to show how oxidation states of elements change during redox reactions.

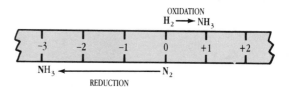

Throughout the text we use SI units, and as a result students do not have to convert from one system of units to another. In conforming to the new IUPAC Thermochemistry Tables, we have adopted their approved Standard Ambient Temperature and Pressure of 298 K and 100 kPa. This recent change should make pressure calculations simpler.

Developing a well-balanced knowledge of chemistry involves not only understanding the major principles of the discipline, but also requires an appreciation of the physical and chemical properties of the chemicals involved. Chemical formulas are not just symbols; they represent real materials that you can see, feel, or smell. In *Chemistry: A First Course* we introduced the properties of many of the common elements and compounds. We continue to do so in this text. Where possible, we describe the physical and chemical properties and uses of the more interesting compounds. You'll notice this particularly in the the organic chemistry chapters.

Each chapter contains short articles that relate closely to the principles being studied in the chapter. Most of these articles show an important or interesting application. Some are historical accounts of chemists who made major contributions to the field. These are not dull date-filled biographies, but instead are portrayals of scientists as real people. Other articles relate STS ISSUES. The more than 50 such articles, and the additional more lengthy articles found in the *"Issues in Chemical Technology"* section of our Teacher's Resource Book, provide the most comprehensive coverage of Science, Technology, and Society available.

Superconductors

In 1911 a Dutch scientist, Heinke Onnes, noticed that when metals are cooled to near absolute zero, they lose all resistance to electricity, and become almost perfect electrical conductors, or superconductors. Thirty years later, scientists discovered alloys of the element niobium that became superconductors at 15 K (−258 °C) — a temperature that could be reached by cooling with liquid helium. The discovery, however, had only limited practical use because of the high cost of the liquid gas. Although research continued, most researchers came to believe that the superconductors could not exist at higher temperatures.

Making Diamonds

Diamonds were obtained from stream beds in India in prehistoric times and have been discovered in many parts of the world including South America and the Soviet Union. However, comes from South Africa.

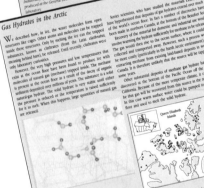

Figure 4.14
Industrially-synthesized diamonds produced at the General Electric research laboratory.

Gas Hydrates in the Arctic

We described how, in ice, the water molecules form open structures like cages. Other atoms and molecules can be trapped within these structures. Only by melting the ice can the trapped substances, known as clathrates, from the Latin *clathratus*, meaning latticed work, be released. Until recently, clathrates were only laboratory curiosities.

Figure 4.54
The structure of methane gas hydrate.

Figure 4.55
Methane gas hydrates have been found at a large number of sites in Canada's Arctic.

John Polanyi and the Nature of Chemical Reactions

John Polanyi was born in Berlin, Germany in 1929, and he received his Ph. D. in chemistry at the University of Manchester, in England. He worked at the National Research Laboratories in Ottawa and then at Princeton University, New Jersey, where he studied visible and ultraviolet light emissions during certain chemical reactions.

He obtained a post at the University of Toronto in 1956 and he decided to look at the infrared light emission from reactions, the field of *infrared chemiluminescence*. Polanyi chose to examine the reaction between hydrogen atoms and chlorine molecules (shown below) because a text on his bookshelf had a complete set of theoretical data on the hydrogen chloride molecule.

$$H + Cl_2 \rightarrow HCl + Cl$$

Figure 6.35
a) Graduate student Ken Cashion working in lab.
b) A reaction chamber similar to those used in Polanyi's experiments.
c) John Polanyi, 1986 Nobel prize winner.

The Chlorofluorocarbon Problem

When they were first prepared and studied, the chlorofluorocarbons (CFCs) appeared to be the answer to concerns about chemical toxicity. This family of compounds, having a carbon chain bonded to chlorine and fluorine atoms, were stable, non-toxic, and nonflammable.

TABLE 6.5	*The Most Important Chlorofluorocarbons*		
Trade Name	Formula		
CFC 11	$CFCl_3$	aerosols, foams
CFC 12	CF_2Cl_2	aerosols, foams
CFC 113	$C_2F_3Cl_3$	cleaning electronics
Halon 1211	CF_2ClBr	fire extinguishers
Halon 1301	CF_3Br	fire extinguishers
Halon 2402	$C_2F_4Br_2$	fire extinguishers
Halothane	C_2HF_3ClBr	inhalation anesthetic

Figure 6.44
The chlorofluorocarbon Freon-12 is used in automobile air conditioners.

Harriet Brooks — Pioneer Canadian Nuclear Scientist

Figure 13.3
Harriet Brooks (1876-1933). A Canadian pioneer researcher who worked with Ernest Rutherford.

Consumer Beware

A knowledge of chemistry can help you make informed decisions in your life. An example of the importance of chemistry was described by Joseph Hesse, a high school teacher, in the magazine *Chem Matters*. He recounted how a salesperson representing a company that sold water distillers visited his parents house.

$$Fe_{(s)} \rightarrow Fe^{3+}_{(aq)} + 3e^-$$
$$2 H_2O_{(l)} + 2e^- \rightarrow H_{2(g)} + 2 OH^-_{(aq)}$$
$$Fe^{3+}_{(aq)} + 3 OH^-_{(aq)} \rightarrow Fe(OH)_{3(s)}$$

Figure 12.22
The precipitator that was supposed to indicate ions in solution. In fact, it was an electrolytic cell.

INDUSTRIAL CHEMISTRY	Our chemical industry is a key part of the Canadian economy. In *Chemistry: A First Course*, we devoted an entire chapter to explaining the significant features of industrial chemistry, and we looked at the industrial preparation of a number of elements and compounds. In this text we continue with this theme by looking at the industrial synthesis of ammonia, the extraction techniques for copper and zinc, the corrosion process, the petroleum industry, and the Canadian nuclear industry.
THE INTERNATIONAL OUTLOOK	Although we have provided many Canadian examples in this text, it is important to realize what is happening in the rest of the world. Therefore, we have examined significant events elsewhere, such as the Chernobyl nuclear disaster and the use of herbicides in Vietnam.
EVERYDAY CHEMISTRY	As students acquire a knowledge of how and why chemical reactions happen, they can start to understand common phenomena: how detergents work, the molecular basis of sight, the chemical basis of photography, and many others.
	Plastics are a key part of our lives and we examine how the molecular structure relates to the physical properties of these materials. We also show how the shape, size, and polarity of molecules relates to the odour, taste, or toxicity of a compound.
SOCIETAL ISSUES	With a knowledge of chemical principles, we have a better understanding of some of the problems that face us today. In this text and in the supporting materials we look at many of the major issues. Students are asked to prepare reports on many of these or to involve their peers in classroom discussions. In addition, the Teacher's Resource Book provides forms for the evaluation of radio, television, and newspaper articles on science. This helps to bring the issues of the day into the classroom and to give the students an opportunity not only to examine the issues but also the quality of the reporting.
THE NATURE OF SCIENCE	In keeping with the recommendations of the Science Council of Canada, we have tried to portray science in a realistic way. For example, the feature on Canadian chemist John Polanyi reflects the complex combination of chance, intuition, intellect, and perseverence that led him to the Nobel Prize. We also show how science, technology, and economics are linked: how the discovery of the Haber process for ammonia was an economic disaster for Chile, and how World War II had a dramatic effect on the synthetic rubber industry. We use the case of Fritz Haber to show the moral and ethical dilemmas that can face a scientist.
THE HANDLING OF DATA	Data tables that appear in each chapter are used to illustrate general trends when developing a concept. Much more comprehensive data tables have been included as appendixes. By so doing it is hoped that both teachers and students will be able to develop their own extra testing assignments.

The Comprehensive Package

Whereas this text provides the basis for a successful second course in chemistry, Addison-Wesley provides a wide range of supplementary course material. These support materials have been developed in response to the needs of the Canadian teaching community and offer something for both the experienced teacher and those who are just starting their careers in the teaching of chemistry. A brief description of each of these supplements follows:

THE TEACHER'S RESOURCE BOOK

The Teacher's Resource Book for Chemistry: A Second Course is divided into the following sections:

A TEACHER'S NOTES In the Teacher's Notes we expand on the material covered in the Student Edition, providing extra information that may be worked into class discussions. We also provide suggestions for demonstrations that would be beneficial for explaining certain concepts in the course.

B ANSWERS TO CHAPTER-ENDING PROBLEMS This section provides answers to all of the chapter-ending problems in the Student Edition.

C SELECTED POSTABLE SOLUTIONS In this section we provide complete solutions for selected problems in the text. These solutions can be posted or be distributed to students who would like to see detailed solutions to problems.

D MULTIPLE-CHOICE TESTS Short multiple-choice tests are provided for teachers to give to students after studying each chapter. The tests can be photocopied directly from the book and distributed to a class.

E TEACHER'S NOTES TO THE LABS In this section we provide suggestions to assist the teacher in preparing for the laboratory exercises. Possible answers to the questions in the students' manual are included at the end of each lab.

F ISSUES IN CHEMISTRY This section applies abstract ideas in chemistry to concrete situations. We look at both natural and technological chemistry, and we provide suggestions for class discussions and debates.

G CAREERS In this section we look at contemporary careers involving chemistry, and we provide teachers with suggestions for encouraging their students to consider pursuing careers in this field.

The Laboratory Book

This procedure-based laboratory manual serves to complement and explain the ideas covered in *Chemistry: A Second Course*. Each lab includes a discussion of the purpose of the lab, a list of apparatus and materials, and a detailed set of procedures. Questions are also included at the end of each lab in order to test the student's comprehension.

The Learning Cycles Approach To Labs

This lab book follows a guided enquiry approach and allows students to investigate some of the fundamental principles of chemistry in a more open-ended fashion.

Acknowledgements

No project of this dimension could have been successfully completed without the assistance of reviewers, who countless times steered us in the right direction. It is fitting, therefore, that we acknowledge the contribution made by the following:

Sudhir Abhyankar, *Sir Wilfred Grenfell College, Newfoundland*
Peter Carmicheal, *Madonna High School, Ontario*
Ted Farion, *Jasper Place Composite High School, Alberta*
Art Frankel, *Saunders Secondary School, Ontario*
Fred Gainer, *J. Percy Page Composite High School, Alberta*
Joe Hammill, *Hill Park Secondary School, Ontario*
Roy Harrison, *Mountain Secondary School, British Columbia*
Hugh Hossack, *Burnaby North Secondary School, British Columbia*
Len Jones, *Eastdale Collegiate and Vocational Institute, Ontario*
Robert Killam, *Eastview Secondary School, Ontario*
Art Last, *Athabasca University, Alberta*
John Li, *The Woodlands School, Ontario*
Harold Magel, *Kelowna Secondary School, British Columbia*
Bob Milburn, *Humberview School, Ontario*
L. Nakashima, *Magee Secondary School, British Columbia*
Graham Ruxton, *Belmont Secondary School, British Columbia*
Milan Sanader, *Holy Name of Mary High School, Ontario*
Peter Sutherland, *Stephenville Central High, Newfoundland*
Kevin Toope, *Booth Memorial Regional High, Newfoundland*
Michael Webb, *York University, Ontario*

We are grateful for the enthusiastic support of Addison-Wesley Publishers, particularly the tireless efforts of Ron Doleman, who initiated the project and encouraged us throughout its long gestation, and the advice and counsel of Fred Di Gasparro, who guided the manuscript through the production phase. Many thanks also go to Vicky Troup, who managed the developmental editing of manuscript, Shirley Tessier, who tracked down many hard-to-get photos, and Cindy Kantor, who maintained the many revisions on the computer.

Finally, we would like to express our gratitude to Marelene Rayner-Canham, Germaine Fisher, Peter Le Couteur, and Wilhemina Raap. Without their constant support and encouragement, this task would not have been possible.

A Review of Basic Principles

Chemistry, more than any other science, builds upon previous knowledge. As you proceed into this second-level chemistry course, you will still need the basic concepts of chemistry that you learned in an introductory course. Chemistry is about chemical reactions, so we will review the types of reactions. Then we will concentrate on the quantitative skills of problem solving. Wherever possible, we have used the conversion-factor method in problem solving. Therefore it is particularly important to review the principles involved in this method. Finally, we will use these concepts in calculations as they apply to chemical reactions.

Reaction Types   *1.1*

We can divide reactions into four main classes. Each of these classes can be subdivided into two or more similar types of reactions.

Combination Reactions

Combination reactions take place when two or more simple substances combine together to produce a more complex substance. We can represent this process as

$$\textbf{A} + \textbf{B} \longrightarrow \textbf{AB}$$

where A and B may be atoms or molecules. This class of reaction can be subdivided into four main types.

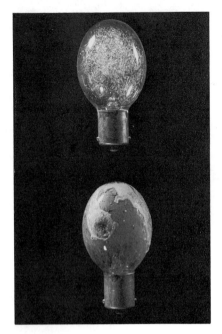

Figure 1.1
A flashbulb before and after firing. An electric current ignites the combination reaction between magnesium wire and pure oxygen.

Figure 1.2
The Pont du Gard, in France. Calcium hydroxide cement, used by ancient Romans to hold the blocks together, has combined with carbon dioxide to produce strong calcium carbonate.

Combination Reactions of Elements The simplest type of combination reaction involves two elements that react together to form a single compound. Magnesium, for example, will burn vigorously in oxygen to form magnesium oxide:

$$2\ Mg_{(s)} + O_{2(g)} \longrightarrow 2\ MgO_{(s)}$$

Combination Reactions that Produce Acids Often two simple compounds will combine to produce a more complex compound. Many non-metal oxides, for example, are acidic and will combine with water to form acids. Sulfur dioxide will react readily with water to form sulfurous acid:

$$SO_{2(g)} + H_2O_{(\ell)} \longrightarrow H_2SO_{3(aq)}$$

Combination Reactions that Produce Hydroxides Most metal oxides are basic oxides: they will react with acids to produce salts and water. Some of these oxides, particularly those of the elements in Groups IA and IIA of the Periodic Table, will combine with water to produce hydroxides. Calcium oxide, for example, will combine with water to produce calcium hydroxide. If enough water is added, the calcium hydroxide will dissolve, forming a solution known as *limewater*:

$$CaO_{(s)} + H_2O_{(\ell)} \longrightarrow Ca(OH)_{2(aq)}$$

Combination Reactions that Produce Salts Although a base will react with an acid to form a salt, we would not classify this reaction as a combination reaction because water is also produced, whether the base is an oxide or a hydroxide. Nonetheless, we can imagine that it might be possible for a basic oxide to react with an acidic oxide to form a salt only. Such a reaction would be a combination reaction because no water would be produced. An example of such a reaction would be the combination of calcium oxide with silicon dioxide to produce calcium silicate:

$$CaO_{(s)} + SiO_{2(s)} \longrightarrow CaSiO_{3(s)}$$

Decomposition Reactions

A decomposition reaction takes place when a compound breaks down to produce two or more simpler substances. Often decomposition reactions occur as a result of heating. These reactions are known as **thermal decomposition** reactions. We can represent the process as

$$AB \longrightarrow A + B$$

The classification used for decomposition reactions is similar to that for combination reactions, although most decomposition reactions are not simply combination reactions in reverse.

Decomposition Reactions that Produce Elements Thermal decomposition reactions that produce elements are uncommon. But mercury(II) oxide will decompose on heating to produce mercury metal and oxygen gas:

$$2\ HgO_{(s)} \xrightarrow{\Delta} 2\ Hg_{(\ell)} + O_{2\,(g)}$$

Figure 1.3

a) Joseph Priestly (1733-1804) discovered that the decomposition of mercury(II) oxide produced oxygen gas. b) Priestly's lab equipment shown on commemorative envelope.

Much more common are decomposition reactions that use electrical energy to break down compounds into their elements. All of the metals in Groups IA and IIA, as well as aluminum and some other metals, are manufactured using reactions of this type.

$$2\ Al_2O_{3\,(s)} \xrightarrow[\text{current}]{\text{electric}} 4\ Al_{(\ell)} + 3\ O_{2\,(g)}$$

Decomposition of Acids Although many acids are formed in combination reactions between acidic oxides and water, most of these reactions cannot be reversed; it is quite uncommon for acids to decompose and produce both an acidic oxide and water. However, when a solution of sulfurous acid is heated, sulfur dioxide gas will be produced:

$$H_2SO_{3\,(aq)} \xrightarrow{\Delta} SO_{2\,(g)} + H_2O_{(g)}$$

Decomposition of Hydroxides Most hydroxides, except those of the alkali metals, will decompose to produce the metal oxide and water. Copper(II) hydroxide, for example, will readily decompose when heated to produce copper(II) oxide and water:

$$Cu(OH)_{2\,(s)} \xrightarrow{\Delta} CuO_{(s)} + H_2O_{(g)}$$

Decomposition of Salts A number of salts may be decomposed. Sometimes these reactions will produce an acidic oxide and a basic oxide. Solid calcium carbonate will decompose when heated to produce solid calcium oxide and gaseous carbon dioxide:

$$CaCO_{3\,(s)} \xrightarrow{\Delta} CaO_{(s)} + CO_{2\,(g)}$$

Other salts may decompose to produce a variety of products. Potassium chlorate will undergo thermal decomposition to yield potassium chloride and oxygen gas:

$$2\,KClO_{3\,(s)} \xrightarrow{\Delta} 2\,KCl_{(s)} + 3\,O_{2\,(g)}$$

Most nitrates, except those of the alkali metals, will decompose to produce a metal oxide, nitrogen dioxide gas, and oxygen:

$$2\,Pb(NO_3)_{2\,(s)} \xrightarrow{\Delta} 2\,PbO_{(s)} + 4\,NO_{2\,(g)} + O_{2\,(g)}$$

Figure 1.4
A major fire in the harbour of Texas City, Texas, 1947. The decomposition of a ship's cargo of ammonium nitrate fertilizer produced dinitrogen oxide gas and steam so violently it destroyed much of the city.

Single Displacement Reactions

In a single displacement reaction one element replaces another element in a compound. We can represent this process as

$$A + BC \longrightarrow AB + C$$

This class can be subdivided into reactions of two types.

TABLE 1.1	*The Activity Series*
Lithium	
Potassium	
Barium	These metals displace
Calcium	hydrogen from water.
Sodium	
Magnesium	
Aluminum	
Zinc	
Iron	These metals displace
Nickel	hydrogen from acids.
Tin	
Lead	
Hydrogen	
Copper	
Mercury	These metals do not displace
Silver	hydrogen from acids or water.
Gold	

Single Displacement of One Metal by Another Many metals will displace hydrogen from acids:

$$\mathbf{Zn_{(s)} + H_2SO_{4\,(aq)} \longrightarrow ZnSO_{4\,(aq)} + H_{2\,(g)}}$$

In this reaction zinc takes the place of hydrogen in the sulfuric acid; the hydrogen that was in the acid is released as a gas.

We can usually predict whether this type of reaction will occur by referring to the **activity series**. This series lists the metals, and hydrogen, in order of reactivity; any element in the series will displace ions of an element below it from an aqueous solution. Thus we can see, for example, that lead will displace hydrogen from an acid, while copper will not. Also, zinc will displace copper metal from a solution of any of its salts:

$$\mathbf{Zn_{(s)} + CuSO_{4\,(aq)} \longrightarrow ZnSO_{4\,(aq)} + Cu_{(s)}}$$

The metals that are very high in the activity series are particularly reactive, and will displace hydrogen from both water and acids. Potassium reacts vigorously with water to produce hydrogen gas and potassium hydroxide. The heat produced by the reaction causes the hydrogen gas to catch fire.

$$\mathbf{2\ K_{(s)} + 2\ H_2O_{(\ell)} \longrightarrow 2\ KOH_{(aq)} + H_{2\,(g)}}$$

Figure 1.5
In this single displacement reaction, sodium reacts vigorously with water to produce sodium hydroxide and hydrogen gas.

TABLE 1.2	*The Halogen Displacement Series*
Fluorine	A specific halogen will
Chlorine	displace any halide
Bromine	ion that appears below it.
Iodine	

Single Displacement of One Halogen by Another The halogens provide us further examples of displacement reactions. Fluorine, the most reactive halogen, will displace any of the other halides from an aqueous solution of one of its salts. Chlorine will displace bromine or iodine from bromides or iodides:

$$\mathbf{Cl_{2\,(g)} + 2\ NaBr_{(aq)} \longrightarrow 2\ NaCl_{(aq)} + Br_{2\,(aq)}}$$

A series similar to the activity series exists for the halogens (Table 1.2).

Double Displacement Reactions

Double displacement reactions *always involve ionic compounds*, in which the cation of one compound changes place with the cation of a second compound. In other words the positive ions exchange negative partners.

This group of reactions, which can be subdivided into three types, can be represented by the following equation:

$$AB + CD \longrightarrow AD + CB$$

Double Displacement to Produce a Precipitate In many cases double displacement reactions result from the mixing of solutions of two different ionic compounds. The exchange of partners often produces an ionic compound that is insoluble in water. The reaction between sodium chloride and silver nitrate is a good example of this type of reaction:

$$NaCl_{(aq)} + AgNO_{3\,(aq)} \longrightarrow NaNO_{3\,(aq)} + AgCl_{(s)}$$

Both sodium chloride and silver nitrate are soluble in water. When solutions of the two salts are mixed, silver ions and chloride ions combine to form a precipitate of silver chloride. The sodium ions and nitrate ions remain in solution as aqueous sodium nitrate.

The silver chloride precipitate could have resulted from the reaction between silver nitrate and any other ionic chloride that is soluble in water. Because of this fact, we can use this reaction as an indicator for the presence of chloride ions in solution.

To help us identify precipitates, and to predict whether a precipitate is likely to form when solutions are mixed, we can make use of a number of solubility rules. These rules, summarized in Table 1.3, simply indicate which ionic compounds are soluble in water and which are insoluble.

TABLE 1.3 *Solubility Rules*

Soluble Compounds	Exceptions
Nitrates	None
Na^+, K^+, NH_4^+ compounds	None
Halides (Cl^-, Br^-, I^-)	Except Ag^+, Hg_2^{2+}, Cu^+, Pb^{2+}
Sulfates (SO_4^{2-})	Except Ca^{2+}, Sr^{2+}, Ba^{2+}, Pb^{2+}, Hg_2^{2+}, Ag^+

Insoluble Compounds	Exceptions
Sulfides (S^{2-})	Except NH_4^+, Group IA, and IIA ions
Carbonates (CO_3^{2-})	Except NH_4^+ and Group IA ions
Phosphates (PO_4^{3-})	Except NH_4^+ and Group IA ions
Hydroxides (OH^-)	Except NH_4^+, Group IA ions, and Ba^{2+}

Figure 1.6

Mining phosphate rock in Lakeland, Florida. The double displacement reaction between phosphate rock and sulfuric acid is used to make phosphoric acid.

Double Displacement to Produce a Gas   Sometimes a double displacement reaction will occur because one of the products of the reaction is a gas. For example, hydrogen sulfide gas is formed when an acid (such as hydrochloric acid), is added to a sulfide (such as iron(II) sulfide):

$$FeS_{(s)} + 2\ HCl_{(aq)} \longrightarrow FeCl_{2\,(aq)} + H_2S_{(g)}$$

Double displacement may also take place if one of the products of a reaction decomposes to produce a gas. For example, carbon dioxide gas is released when an acid is added to a carbonate:

$$Na_2CO_{3\,(aq)} + 2\ HCl_{(aq)} \longrightarrow 2\ NaCl_{(aq)} + CO_{2\,(g)} + H_2O_{(\ell)}$$

We can classify this reaction as a double displacement if we consider that it takes place in two stages:

$$Na_2CO_{3\,(aq)} + 2\ HCl_{(aq)} \longrightarrow 2\ NaCl_{(aq)} + H_2CO_{3\,(aq)}$$
$$H_2CO_{3\,(aq)} \longrightarrow CO_{2\,(g)} + H_2O_{(\ell)}$$

In the first stage the sodium ions and hydrogen ions exchange partners; the products are sodium chloride and carbonic acid. In the second stage the carbonic acid decomposes to produce carbon dioxide and water.

Sulfur dioxide gas and ammonia gas are also produced in reactions of this type. When an acid is added to a sulfite, sulfurous acid is produced, which then decomposes to sulfur dioxide and water:

$$Na_2SO_{3\,(aq)} + 2\ HCl_{(aq)} \longrightarrow 2\ NaCl_{(aq)} + H_2SO_{3\,(aq)}$$
$$H_2SO_{3\,(aq)} \longrightarrow SO_{2\,(g)} + H_2O_{(\ell)}$$

When a base, such as sodium hydroxide, is added to an ammonium salt, a double displacement reaction takes place to produce ammonium hydroxide and a sodium salt. The ammonium hydroxide subsequently decomposes to form ammonia gas and water:

$$NH_4Cl_{(aq)} + NaOH_{(aq)} \longrightarrow NaCl_{(aq)} + NH_4OH_{(aq)}$$
$$NH_4OH_{(aq)} \longrightarrow NH_{3\,(g)} + H_2O_{(\ell)}$$

Double Displacement to Produce Water   Both types of double displacement reactions we have discussed involve the removal of ions from solution. In the first type a solid ionic compound is formed. In the second type a covalently-bonded gas is formed. The reactions we will now discuss also involve the removal of ions from solution, this time by the formation of covalently-bonded water molecules.

This type of reaction is called a **neutralization** reaction, which involves the reaction of an acid with a base to produce salt plus water. For example, nitric acid reacts with potassium hydroxide to produce potassium nitrate and water:

$$HNO_{3\,(aq)} + KOH_{(aq)} \longrightarrow KNO_{3\,(aq)} + H_2O_{(\ell)}$$

Such a reaction, in which the acid is neutralized by the base, would also be classed as a double displacement reaction because the hydrogen and potassium ions exchange partners. A similar neutralization reaction takes place when carbon dioxide is added to sodium hydroxide solution:

$$2\ NaOH_{(aq)} + CO_{2\,(g)} \longrightarrow Na_2CO_{3\,(aq)} + H_2O_{(\ell)}$$

We can argue that this is a double displacement reaction if we assume that the carbon dioxide first dissolves in the aqueous solution to produce carbonic acid, which in turn reacts with the sodium hydroxide.

EXAMPLE **1.1** Classify each of these reactions as a combination, decomposition, single displacement, or double displacement:

a) $Fe_{(s)} + S_{(s)} \longrightarrow FeS_{(s)}$

b) $Pb(NO_3)_{2\,(aq)} + H_2S_{(g)} \longrightarrow PbS_{(s)} + 2\ HNO_{3\,(aq)}$

c) $2\ HCl_{(aq)} + Ba(OH)_{2\,(aq)} \longrightarrow BaCl_{2\,(aq)} + 2\ H_2O_{(\ell)}$

SOLUTION a) This is a reaction between two elements to form a compound. It is therefore a combination reaction.

b) In this reaction the hydrogen from the hydrogen sulfide and the lead(II) ions from the lead(II) nitrate exchange negative ions. A precipitate of lead(II) sulfide is formed. The reaction is therefore a double displacement reaction.

c) In this reaction the hydrogen ions and the barium ions exchange negative partners indicating that the reaction is of the double displacement type. However, since a salt and water are formed, we can be more specific and call it a neutralization reaction.

EXAMPLE **1.2** Use the activity series (Table 1.1) and the halogen displacement series (Table 1.2) to determine whether or not single displacement reactions will occur in the following cases:

a) $Zn_{(s)} + Pb(NO_3)_{2\,(aq)} \longrightarrow$

b) $Br_{2\,(aq)} + MgI_{2\,(aq)} \longrightarrow$

SOLUTION a) Zinc is more reactive than lead, and so will displace lead ions from the solution. The products of the reaction will be lead metal and zinc nitrate solution.

$$Zn_{(s)} + Pb(NO_3)_{2\,(aq)} \longrightarrow Zn(NO_3)_{2\,(aq)} + Pb_{(s)}$$

b) Bromine is more reactive than iodine, and so will displace iodide ions from the solution. The products of the reaction will be iodine and magnesium bromide solution.

$$Br_{2\,(aq)} + MgI_{2\,(aq)} \longrightarrow I_{2\,(aq)} + MgBr_{2\,(aq)}$$

EXAMPLE   *1.3*   Identify the products, if any, of the following reactions:

a) $Cu_{(s)} + SnSO_{4(aq)} \longrightarrow$

b) $Fe_2(SO_4)_{3(aq)} + NaOH_{(aq)} \longrightarrow$

SOLUTION

a) To make it easier for us to determine the products of a reaction we will first classify the reaction type. This reaction between a metal and a salt is a single displacement reaction.

Using Table 1.1 we can determine whether this reaction will take place. The table shows that tin is more reactive than copper. Copper metal will not displace tin(II) ions from the solution of tin(II) sulfate. Therefore, there will be no reaction.

b) Since there are two ionic solutions, the reaction is a double displacement reaction. Although one of the compounds is a base, the other is not an acid. Therefore, this is not a neutralization reaction.

Since we would not expect a gas to result from the reaction of sodium hydroxide with a sulfate, we must conclude that if this reaction occurs, a precipitate would be formed. We can see from Table 1.3 that all sodium compounds are soluble in water. Many hydroxides, including that of iron(III), however, are insoluble. However, a reaction can take place between iron(III) sulfate and sodium hydroxide to produce sodium sulfate solution and iron(III) hydroxide.

$$Fe_2(SO_4)_{3(aq)} + 6\,NaOH_{(aq)} \longrightarrow 3\,Na_2SO_{4(aq)} + 2\,Fe(OH)_{3(s)}$$

Figure 1.7

Coal-fired electrical generating station at Marmion Lake, Ontario. Much of our electrical energy comes from the combustion reaction of coal or oil with oxygen.

Combustion Reactions

Sometimes reactions will not fit neatly into one or other of the four classes we have discussed. For example, **combustion** is a term used to describe chemical reactions in which substances react with oxygen producing heat and light. We have already seen that magnesium will burn in oxygen to produce magnesium oxide. This combustion reaction is also a combination reaction.

There are other combustion reactions, however, that are not combination reactions. These exceptions are usually reactions of organic compounds such as methane gas, CH_4, that contain carbon and hydrogen. In these cases the products of combustion are carbon dioxide and water:

$$CH_{4(g)} + 2\,O_{2(g)} \longrightarrow CO_{2(g)} + 2\,H_2O_{(g)}$$

We will consider combustion reactions in Chapter 5, which deals with energy changes in chemical reactions.

QUESTIONS

1. Classify each of the following reactions as a combination, decomposition, single displacement, or double displacement:

a) $CuCl_{2\,(aq)} + Na_2S_{(aq)} \longrightarrow CuS_{(s)} + 2\,NaCl_{(aq)}$

b) $Fe_3O_{4\,(s)} + 4\,H_{2\,(g)} \longrightarrow 3\,Fe_{(s)} + 4\,H_2O_{(g)}$

2. Use the activity series (Table 1.1) or the halogen displacement series (Table 1.2) to determine whether or not single displacement reactions will occur in the following cases:

a) $H_{2\,(g)} + MgO_{(s)} \longrightarrow$ c) $Cu_{(s)} + AgNO_{3\,(aq)} \longrightarrow$

b) $Cl_{2\,(aq)} + NaI_{(aq)} \longrightarrow$

3. Identify the products, if any, of the following reactions:

a) $Al_{(s)} + HCl_{(aq)} \longrightarrow$

b) $Pb(NO_3)_{2\,(aq)} + K_2CO_{3\,(aq)} \longrightarrow$

The Conversion-Factor Method

1.2

In many problems we may need to convert from one unit of measure to another. For example, when solving problems that involve aqueous solutions, we may need to convert from millilitres to litres. In these and other problems, we can make use of a conversion factor as an aid to arriving at a correct solution.

A **conversion factor** is a ratio that relates two quantities that are expressed in different units, and that is numerically equal to one. Consider the following relation between millilitres and litres:

$$1000\,mL = 1\,L$$

If we divide both sides of the above expression by 1 L, we find that

$$\frac{1000\,mL}{1\,L} = \frac{1\,L}{1\,L}$$

which reduces to $\dfrac{1000\,mL}{1\,L} = 1$

The ratio on the left, and its inverted form (which is also equal to one), are conversion factors that we can use to convert litres to millilitres or millilitres to litres. The value of any quantity multiplied by one of these factors will be unaltered because they both have a numerical value of one.

EXAMPLE   *1.4*   Convert 265 mL to litres.

SOLUTION   To solve this problem we multiply 265 mL by a conversion factor that relates millilitres to litres. Two such factors are

$$\frac{1000\,mL}{1\,L} \quad \text{and} \quad \frac{1\,L}{1000\,mL}$$

In order to cancel the mL we choose the conversion factor on the right.

$$\text{Number of litres} = 265\,\text{mL} \times \frac{1\,\text{L}}{1000\,\text{mL}}$$

$$= 0.265\,\text{L}$$

The use of conversion factors extends beyond simple unit conversions. If, for example, we wish to determine the density of a substance, we must measure both the mass and the volume of the sample. The density, which is the mass per unit volume, is given by the relationship:

$$\textbf{Density} = \frac{\textbf{Mass}}{\textbf{Volume}}$$

From this expression we get two conversion factors

$$\frac{\textbf{Volume}}{\textbf{Mass}} \quad \text{and} \quad \frac{\textbf{Mass}}{\textbf{Volume}}$$

In solving density problems, the appropriate choice of conversion factors must be made.

EXAMPLE   **1.5**   The density of lead is $11.3\,\text{g}\cdot\text{cm}^{-3}$. Calculate the mass of $50.0\,\text{cm}^3$ of the metal.

SOLUTION   We solve this problem by using the density of lead as a conversion factor. The mass of $50.0\,\text{cm}^3$ of lead is given by

$$\text{Mass of Pb} = \text{Volume of Pb} \times \frac{\text{Mass of Pb}}{\text{Volume of Pb}}$$

$$= 50.0\,\text{cm}^3\,\text{Pb} \times \frac{11.3\,\text{g Pb}}{1\,\text{cm}^3\,\text{Pb}}$$

$$= 565\,\text{g Pb}$$

The use of conversion factors assumes a specific degree of accuracy, designated by the number of significant figures in the measured values. A discussion of this follows, in Section 1.3.

Conversion Factors and Chemical Equations

Another type of conversion factor, called an **equation factor**, is derived from the balanced chemical equation. The equation factor is a ratio comparing moles of reactants to reactants, reactants to products, and products to products.

EXAMPLE   **1.6**   The following equation represents the decomposition of solid mercury(II) oxide to its constituent elements: liquid mercury and oxygen gas.

$$2\,\text{HgO}_{(s)} \xrightarrow{\;\Delta\;} 2\,\text{Hg}_{(\ell)} + \text{O}_{2\,(g)}$$

What are the equation factors comparing mercury(II) oxide and each of the products?

SOLUTION   From the balanced equation, we see there are 2 moles of mercury(II) oxide for every 2 moles of liquid mercury. Therefore, the equation factors are

$$\frac{2 \text{ mol HgO}}{2 \text{ mol Hg}} \quad \text{and} \quad \frac{2 \text{ mol Hg}}{2 \text{ mol HgO}}$$

Similarly, for the comparison of mercury(II) oxide to oxygen gas, the equation factors are

$$\frac{2 \text{ mol HgO}}{1 \text{ mol O}_2} \quad \text{and} \quad \frac{1 \text{ mol O}_2}{2 \text{ mol HgO}}$$

QUESTIONS

4. Perform the following conversions:
   a) 2347 g to kg
   b) 0.769 cm to mm
   c) 1.35 L to mL
   d) 129 mm to m
   e) 0.25 kg to mg

5. The density of ether is $0.71 \text{ g} \cdot \text{mL}^{-1}$. What volume does $1.8 \times 10^3 \text{ g}$ of ether occupy?

6. The following equation represents the combination reaction involving zinc metal and fluorine gas to produce zinc fluoride:

$$Zn_{(s)} + F_{2(g)} \longrightarrow ZnF_{2(s)}$$

What are the equation factors relating the reactant fluorine gas to the product zinc fluoride?

Significant Figures

1.3   Scientific experiments involve making measurements. When these measurements are recorded, it is important that their precision be clearly indicated. We do this by using the appropriate number of significant figures.

All measurements consist of a number of digits about which we are certain, and a final digit that has been estimated and about which there is some uncertainty. If we examine Figure 1.8, we can be certain that the measuring cylinder contains between 15 mL and 16 mL of liquid. We can estimate that the volume is 15.7 mL, but we are not quite certain about the 7; the volume could be 15.6 mL or 15.8 mL.

We could, however, record the volume as 15.7 mL, and it would be understood that what we mean is 15.7 ± 0.1 mL. In this way, we would use three significant figures—the 1 and 5, which are certain, and the 7, about which we are somewhat uncertain. Adding any further digits to the recorded measurement, after the 7, would be totally meaningless. The three significant figures clearly indicate the precision of the measurement.

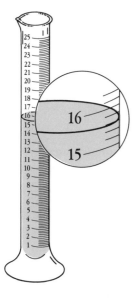

Figure 1.8
A measuring cylinder graduated in units of millilitres.

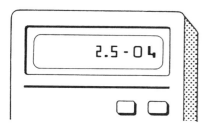

Figure 1.9
A calculator can convert a number to scientific notation, but may not necessarily show the correct number of significant figures.

Zero as a Significant Figure

When numbers are written in decimal notation, all of the figures from 0 to 9 can be used as part of a measurement. The zero, however, unlike all of the other figures, is also used to indicate the magnitude of the number. Thus, in the number 0.000 250, the zeros to the left of the 2 are used only to indicate the position of the decimal point and would not be significant if this were a measurement. The final zero, on the other hand, would be part of the measurement and would be significant. There would be three signficant figures.

It is particularly difficult to determine how many significant figures are present in numbers such as 2500. Here the zeros are again required in order to indicate magnitude, but we have no way of knowing whether or not they are significant. We can avoid this confusion by recording our measurements in scientific notation. If we do this, zeros are no longer used to indicate the magnitude of a number. Like all of the other digits they are used as part of measurements only.

Scientific Notation

A number written in scientific notation consists of a number that has the decimal point after the first digit from the left, multiplied by 10, which is raised to a power. The value of the number and the precision of the measurement are indicated by the first part of the expression. The exponent, or power of ten, indicates its magnitude. Any zeros included in the number will be part of the measurement, and so will be significant.

To convert from decimal to scientific notation, we move the decimal point until it immediately follows the first digit of the number. The value of the exponent is determined by counting the number of places that the decimal point is moved, to the right or the left. If the number is greater than 10, the decimal must be moved to the left, and the exponent will be positive. On the other hand, if the number is less than 1, the decimal must be moved to the right, and the exponent will be negative. The number 0.000 250 is equal to 2.50 divided by 10 000 (or 10^4). It can be represented as

$$0.000\,250 = \frac{2.50}{10\,000} = \frac{2.50}{10^4} = 2.50 \times 10^{-4}$$

To convert 0.000 250 to scientific notation, we must move the decimal point four places to the right, obtaining 2.50. We multiply the 2.50 by 10^{-4} to indicate its correct magnitude.

EXAMPLE   *1.7*   Convert the following numbers to scientific notation, and determine the number of significant figures in each.
a) 650.0   b) 0.003 050

SOLUTION a) Moving the decimal point two places to the left gives 6.500×10^2. Both of the zeros are significant because the measurement was to the nearest tenth—that is 650.0 ± 0.1. Therefore, there are four significant figures.

b) Moving the decimal point three places to the right gives 3.050×10^{-3}. Both of the zeros that are now included in the number are part of the measurement and are significant. There are four significant figures.

Significant Figures in Calculations

When we carry out calculations involving measured values, we must remember that the precision of the answer is determined by the precision of the measurements. The number of significant figures in the answer is determined differently, however, in different types of calculations. The rules for multiplication and division are different from those for addition and subtraction.

Multiplication and Division For multiplication and division we examine the precision of each measurement in the calculation. The answer to the calculation will have the same number of significant figures as the measurement with the *fewest significant figures*.

EXAMPLE *1.8* A block of iron measures 12.5 cm by 4.2 cm by 3.7 cm. It has a mass of 1529.5 g. Determine the density of the iron in $g \cdot cm^{-3}$.

SOLUTION First we determine the volume of the iron block.

$$\text{Volume of Fe} = 12.5 \, \text{cm} \times 4.2 \, \text{cm} \times 3.7 \, \text{cm}$$
$$= 194.25 \, \text{cm}^3$$

Examination shows that two of the measurements have only two significant figures. Therefore, our answer for the volume of the iron can have only two significant figures. We should round off the $194.25 \, \text{cm}^3$ and use scientific notation to give $1.9 \times 10^2 \, \text{cm}^3$.

Since the density of the iron is the mass per cubic centimetre:

$$\text{Density of Fe} = \frac{1529.5 \, \text{g Fe}}{1.9 \times 10^2 \, \text{cm}^3 \, \text{Fe}}$$
$$= 8.05 \, \text{g} \cdot \text{cm}^{-3}$$

Now we must round off our answer to two significant figures. In this case we round up, showing the density of iron to be $8.1 \, \text{g} \cdot \text{cm}^{-3}$.

In Example 1.8 and in many problems that involve measured quantities, we must round off the numerical answer that we obtain so that it is given to the correct number of significant figures. When we do this we must take account of the value of the digits that are being discarded. The rules for rounding off are:

1. **If the first nonsignificant digit is less than 5, it is dropped, and the last significant digit is left unaltered.**
2. **If the first nonsignificant digit is 5 or greater, it is dropped, and the last significant digit is increased by one.**

Addition and Subtraction   When we are carrying out calculations that involve addition and subtraction, we are concerned with the number of places after the decimal point for each measurement. Our answer should have the same number of places after the decimal as the measurement with the *fewest number of decimal places.*

EXAMPLE   *1.9*   A 6.23 mL sample of a solution was added from a burette to a beaker that already contained 95.4 mL of water. What was the total volume of liquid in the beaker?

SOLUTION   The first measurement was precise to a hundredth of a millilitre, but the second was precise only to a tenth of a millilitre. Adding the two together will produce an answer that can only be precise to a tenth of a millilitre:

$$
\begin{array}{r}
95.4\ \text{mL} \\
+\ 6.23\ \text{mL} \\
\hline
101.6\ \text{mL}
\end{array}
$$

Notice that even though each of the measurements had only three significant figures, the calculated value for the total volume has four. Nonetheless, it is only as precise as the least precise measurement.

Exact Numbers

An exact number is different from a measurement. A measurement always has a number of significant figures determined by the precision of the measuring instrument. By contrast, an exact number has no uncertainty. If, for example, we count 32 people in a class, then we know that there are not 31.9 or 32.1, but exactly 32 people. We could calculate an average height for the class by measuring each person's height to the nearest tenth of a centimetre, adding the results together, and dividing by 32. We would *not determine* the number of significant figures by looking at the number of digits in the exact number, 32.

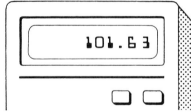

Figure 1.10
A calculator may not necessarily show the correct number of significant figures even in a simple arithmetic operation.

QUESTIONS

7. How many significant figures are in each of the following measurements?
   a) 3.96 g   b) 207.0 mL
8. Convert the following numbers from decimal to scientific notation, and identify the number of significant figures:
   a) 0.003 940   b) 249.0

9. Round off the following numbers to four significant figures:
   a) 349.451   b) 149.27   c) 2.1473

10. The density of lead is $11.35 \, \text{g} \cdot \text{cm}^{-3}$. What is the mass of a block of lead with dimensions 11.3 cm by 12.5 cm by 2.4 cm?

11. A 3.735 g sample of salt is dissolved in 50.0 g of water in a beaker of mass 87.32 g. What is the total mass of the beaker and contents?

The Mole Concept 1.4

Figure 1.11
Amadeo Avogadro (1776-1856).

If we go into a stationery store to buy a box of typing paper, we will find that the box contains 500 sheets, or one *ream* of paper. A ream, then, is the unit that is used to denote a particular amount of paper.

In the laboratory we have to work with much larger numbers of atoms and molecules. We therefore need a unit, similar to the ream but much larger. This unit is the **mole**. One mole consists of 6.02×10^{23} atoms or molecules of a substance. The number 6.02×10^{23} is known as Avogadro's Number (symbol N), named after the Italian chemist Amadeo Avogadro.

We often need to know the relationship between the mass of a substance and the number of moles it contains. If we measure the mass, in grams, of one mole of any element, we find that it has the same numerical value as the atomic mass of the element. For example, one mole of copper, atomic mass 63.55 u, has a mass of 63.55 g. The mass of one mole of an element is called the **molar mass**. It has units of $\text{g} \cdot \text{mol}^{-1}$. We can use the molar mass as a conversion factor when converting from moles to mass and vice versa.

EXAMPLE   *1.10*   Calculate the mass of 1.50 mol of chromium.

                    SOLUTION   From the Periodic Table we see that the atomic mass of chromium is 52.00 u. Thus the molar mass is $52.00 \, \text{g} \cdot \text{mol}^{-1}$, which we use as a conversion factor.

$$\frac{52.00 \, \text{g Cr}}{1 \, \text{mol Cr}}$$

The mass of chromium is therefore

3 significant figures   4 significant figures

$$1.50 \times \frac{5.200}{1}$$

exact number

$$\text{Mass of Cr} = 1.50 \, \text{mol Cr} \times \frac{52.00 \, \text{g Cr}}{1 \, \text{mol Cr}}$$

$$= 78.0 \, \text{g Cr}$$

(Notice that the number of significant figures in the answer is not determined by the number "1" in "1 mol Cr.")

We can determine the molar mass of a compound by adding the atomic masses of all of the atoms or ions in a molecule or formula unit of the compound, and expressing the answer in grams. Thus the molar mass of magnesium chloride, $MgCl_2$, would be

$$[24.31 + (2 \times 35.45)] \, g \cdot mol^{-1} = 95.21 \, g \cdot mol^{-1}$$

We can use the molar masses of compounds in the same way as those of elements.

EXAMPLE   **1.11** Calculate the number of moles in 35.0 g of copper(II) sulfate pentahydrate.

SOLUTION In order to determine the number of moles of copper(II) sulfate penta-hydrate, we must first calculate the molar mass of the compound. To do this we need to know the correct formula, $CuSO_4 \cdot 5H_2O$.

$$
\begin{aligned}
1 \times (\text{Mass of one mole of Cu}) &= \ 1 \times 63.55 \, g = \ \ 63.55 \, g \\
1 \times (\text{Mass of one mole of S}) &= \ 1 \times 32.07 \, g = \ \ 32.07 \, g \\
9 \times (\text{Mass of one mole of O}) &= \ 9 \times 16.00 \, g = 144.0 \ \ g \\
10 \times (\text{Mass of one mole of H}) &= 10 \times 1.008 \, g = \ \ 10.08 \, g \\
\text{Mass of one mole of } CuSO_4 \cdot 5H_2O &= \overline{249.7 \ \ g}
\end{aligned}
$$

Using molar mass as a conversion factor, we can now find the number of moles of copper(II) sulfate pentahydrate.

Number of moles $CuSO_4 \cdot 5H_2O$

$$= 35.0 \, g \ CuSO_4 \cdot 5H_2O \times \frac{1 \, mol \ CuSO_4 \cdot 5H_2O}{249.7 \, g \ CuSO_4 \cdot 5H_2O}$$

$$= 0.140 \, mol \ CuSO_4 \cdot 5H_2O$$

The Mole Method

To aid us further in conversions involving moles, we use a technique called the **mole method**. It is essentially a three-step process and can be used to solve a problem in which we wish to solve any of the following:

a) The mass of a specified reactant that must be used in order to convert a given mass of another reactant completely into products;

b) The mass of a particular product formed in a given reaction from a specified mass of one or more reactants;

c) The mass of each reactant required in order to produce a given mass of product.

For example, in category a) above, we may want to calculate the mass of substance B that will combine with a given mass of substance A. In this case the three steps would involve

1. Conversion of the given mass of substance A to the number of moles of A, using the molar mass of A as the conversion factor

(Mass of A $\longrightarrow$ Moles of A)

2. Use of an equation factor to determine the number of moles of substance B that are required from the number of moles of substance A determined in Step 1

(Moles of A $\longrightarrow$ Moles of B)

3. Conversion of the number of moles of substance B found in Step 2 to the corresponding mass, using the molar mass of B as the conversion factor

(Moles of B $\longrightarrow$ Mass of B)

Use of the mole method can be best illustrated by the following simple stoichiometric problem. As well, a modified version of the mole method can be used to solve problems involving the ideal gas equation and solution concentrations.

EXAMPLE   *1.12*   As shown in the following equation, one mole of lead combines with one mole of sulfur to produce one mole of lead(II) sulfide. If we perform the same reaction, but with only 50.0 g of lead, how much sulfur do we need?

$$Pb_{(s)} + S_{(s)} \longrightarrow PbS_{(s)}$$

SOLUTION   **STRATEGY**

We know that we have 50.0 g of lead (Substance A), therefore we use this data to calculate the number of moles of lead. We then use the number of moles of lead to calculate the number of moles of sulfur (Substance B). Thus, our overall strategy will be

1. **Mass of A $\longrightarrow$ Moles of A**
2. **Moles of A $\longrightarrow$ Moles of B**
3. **Moles of B $\longrightarrow$ Mass of B**

STEP 1:   Number of moles of Pb = $50.0\,g\,Pb \times \dfrac{1\,mol\,Pb}{207.2\,g\,Pb}$

$$= 0.241\,mol\,Pb$$

STEP 2:   The equation factors that relate the number of moles of lead used to the number of moles of sulfur used come from the ratio of the coefficients in the balanced equation.

$$\frac{1\,mol\,Pb}{1\,mol\,S} \quad and \quad \frac{1\,mol\,S}{1\,mol\,Pb}$$

Since we want to calculate the number of moles of S, we use the second equation factor.

$$\text{Number of moles of S} = \text{Number of moles of Pb used} \times \frac{1 \text{ mol S}}{1 \text{ mol Pb}}$$

$$= 0.241 \text{ mol Pb} \times \frac{1 \text{ mol S}}{1 \text{ mol Pb}}$$

$$= 0.241 \text{ mol S}$$

STEP 3:   Mass of S $= 0.241 \text{ mol S} \times \dfrac{32.07 \text{ g S}}{1 \text{ mol S}}$

$$= 7.73 \text{ g S}$$

QUESTIONS

12. How many moles of carbon dioxide are present in 66.0 g of the compound?

13. Calculate the molar masses of the following:
   a) $Ca_3(PO_4)_2$ b) KNO_2 c) $Na_2CO_3 \cdot 10H_2O$

14. Calculate the mass of 0.150 mol of lead.

15. How many moles of potassium dichromate are present in 50.0 g of the compound?

16. Water can be decomposed by an electric current according to the equation

$$2 H_2O_{(\ell)} \longrightarrow 2 H_{2(g)} + O_{2(g)}$$

If 10.0 g of water produces 1.11 g of hydrogen, what mass of oxygen will also be produced?

17. Sulfuric acid is formed when sulfur trioxide combines with water:

$$SO_{3(g)} + H_2O_{(\ell)} \longrightarrow H_2SO_{4(\ell)}$$

What mass of sulfur trioxide and what mass of water are needed to produce 20.0 g of sulfuric acid?

Solution Concentrations

1.5 A **solution** is formed when a **solute** dissolves in a **solvent**. While solutes and solvents can be any of the three phases of matter, the most common solutions are those formed when a solid or liquid solute dissolves in a liquid solvent. Very often this liquid solvent is water, which is able to dissolve a large number of ionic compounds as well as many covalently-bonded compounds such as sugar and alcohol. Solutions in which water is the solvent are called **aqueous solutions**.

The **concentration** of a solution is a measure of the quantity of solute that is dissolved in a particular quantity of solvent. The units that are used to measure these quantities will depend upon the purpose for which the solution is being used.

Molar Concentration

We often determine solution concentrations by measuring the mass of solute that is dissolved in a specific volume of solution. Using this information we can calculate the number of moles of solute dissolved in one litre of solution, or the **molar concentration**. This information is particularly useful when we wish to calculate the volume of a solution that should be measured to obtain a specific number of moles of solute for an experiment.

EXAMPLE   *1.13*   A sample of anhydrous sodium carbonate, Na_2CO_3, with a mass of 5.674 g is dissolved in water in a volumetric flask. More water is added until the volume of solution is 250.0 mL. What is the molar concentration of the solution?

SOLUTION

> *STRATEGY*
>
> We use a modified version of the mole method to find the molar concentration of the solution of Na_2CO_3.
>
> 1. Mass of $Na_2CO_3 \longrightarrow$ Moles of Na_2CO_3
> 2. Moles of $Na_2CO_3 \longrightarrow$ Molar concentration of Na_2CO_3 solution

STEP 1: We must first determine the number of moles of sodium carbonate that were added to the flask:

$$\text{Moles of } Na_2CO_3 = 5.674 \text{ g } Na_2CO_3 \times \frac{1 \text{ mol } Na_2CO_3}{105.99 \text{ g } Na_2CO_3}$$

$$= 5.353 \times 10^{-2} \text{ mol } Na_2CO_3$$

STEP 2: This number of moles is dissolved in 250.0 mL (0.2500 L) of solution. The molar concentration is the number of moles of solute that are dissolved in one litre of solution.

$$\text{Molar concentration of } Na_2CO_3 = \frac{5.353 \times 10^{-2} \text{ mol } Na_2CO_3}{0.2500 \text{ L}}$$

$$= 2.141 \times 10^{-1} \text{ mol·L}^{-1} Na_2CO_3$$

If we examine the second step of Example 1.13, we can see that we are able to determine the molar concentration of the solution if we know the number of moles of solute that are dissolved in a known volume of solution. The relationship between these three variables can be expressed as:

Figure 1.12
A volumetric flask is used to prepare a solution of known concentration. These flasks are available in sizes ranging from 1.00 mL to 2.00 L.

$$\textbf{Molar concentration (mol·L}^{-1}\textbf{)} = \frac{\textbf{Moles of solute (mol)}}{\textbf{Volume of solution (L)}}$$

We can use this relationship as a conversion factor to determine either the number of moles of solute or the volume of solution.

EXAMPLE	*1.14*	What volume of a 2.00 mol·L^{-1} sulfuric acid solution would contain 0.275 moles of this acid?

SOLUTION We can solve this problem by treating the molar concentration as a conversion factor. Since we want moles to cancel, we use the inverted form of molar concentration.

$$\frac{\text{Volume of solution (L)}}{\text{Moles of solute (mol)}}$$

The volume of 2.00 mol·L^{-1} sulfuric acid required is therefore

$$\text{Volume of } H_2SO_4 = 0.275 \text{ mol } H_2SO_4 \times \frac{1\,L}{2.00 \text{ mol } H_2SO_4}$$
$$= 1.38 \times 10^{-1}\,L, \text{ or } 138\,mL\ H_2SO_4$$

Diluting Solutions

A **standard solution** is prepared by dissolving a precise mass of solute in a precise volume of solution. From this we can prepare a solution of lower concentration by diluting the standard solution with water. We can also calculate the molar concentration of the diluted solution provided that we know its final volume.

EXAMPLE	*1.15*	A 50.00 mL solution of sodium chloride with a molar concentration of 0.360 mol·L^{-1} is diluted to 250.0 mL by adding water. What is the molar concentration of the resulting solution?

SOLUTION

STRATEGY

We use a variation of the mole method to find the change in concentration from our original solution of sodium chloride (Solution A) to our new solution of sodium chloride (Solution B).

1. **Molar concentration of Solution A** $\longrightarrow$ Moles of A
2. Moles of A $\longrightarrow$ **Molar concentration of Solution B**

STEP 1:   After converting 50.00 mL to litres we use molar concentration as a conversion factor to find the number of moles of NaCl. The number of moles of NaCl is therefore

$$\text{Moles of NaCl} = 5.000 \times 10^{-2}\,L\ NaCl \times \frac{0.360 \text{ mol NaCl}}{1\,L\ NaCl}$$
$$= 1.80 \times 10^{-2} \text{ mol NaCl}$$

STEP 2:   After dilution this number of moles is dissolved in 250.0 mL of solution. The new molar concentration is therefore:

$$\text{Molar concentration of NaCl} = \frac{1.80 \times 10^{-2}\,\text{mol NaCl}}{0.2500\,\text{L}}$$
$$= 7.20 \times 10^{-2}\,\text{mol} \cdot \text{L}^{-1}\,\text{NaCl}$$

QUESTIONS

18. A sample of potassium dichromate, $K_2Cr_2O_7$, with a mass of 13.26 g is dissolved in enough water to produce 250.0 mL of solution. Calculate the molar concentration of the solution.

19. How many moles of hydrochloric acid are contained in 350.0 mL of a 2.50 mol$\cdot$L^{-1} solution of the acid?

20. A 20.00 mL sample of a 1.350 mol$\cdot$L^{-1} potassium bromide solution is diluted to 250.0 mL by adding water. Calculate the molar concentration of the diluted solution.

The Ideal Gas Equation

1.6

So far, we have reviewed methods for obtaining the number of moles of a substance from its measured mass, and the number of moles of solute in a solution of known concentration. Many chemical reactions, however, involve substances that are in the gas phase. We must also be able to determine the number of moles of a gaseous compound from a knowledge of its volume, pressure, and temperature. We do this by using the **ideal gas equation**

$$PV = nRT$$

where R is a constant, known as the **universal gas constant**. The equation tells us that pressure, P, times volume, V, is equal to this constant value R times n moles of gaseous material at Kelvin temperature T.

We can determine the value of R experimentally by measuring P, V, and T for a sample of gas that contains a known number of moles of molecules. The value of R is:

$$\frac{PV}{nT} = R = 8.314\,\text{kPa}\cdot\text{L}\cdot\text{mol}^{-1}\cdot\text{K}^{-1}$$

Figure 1.13
The kelvin is named after British physicist Lord Kelvin (1824-1907).

We can use the ideal gas equation to determine any one of the variables from a knowledge of the other three.

| *EXAMPLE* | *1.16* | Calculate the volume occupied by 3.56 g of carbon dioxide gas at 25 °C and 98.5 kPa. |

SOLUTION

STRATEGY

The mole method can be used when dealing with gases, such as carbon dioxide.

1. Mass of Gas $\longrightarrow$ Moles of Gas
2. Moles of Gas $\longrightarrow$ Volume of Gas

STEP 1: The molar mass of carbon dioxide gas is $44.01\,\text{g·mol}^{-1}$.

$$\text{Moles of CO}_2 = 3.56\,\text{g CO}_2 \times \frac{1\,\text{mol CO}_2}{44.01\,\text{g CO}_2}$$
$$= 8.09 \times 10^{-2}\,\text{mol CO}_2$$

STEP 2: We rearrange the ideal gas equation to determine the volume of the gas:

$$V = \frac{nRT}{P}$$

Substituting known values into this equation, we find

$$V = \frac{8.09 \times 10^{-2}\,\text{mol} \times 8.314\,\text{kPa·L·mol}^{-1}\text{·K}^{-1} \times 298\,\text{K}}{98.5\,\text{kPa}}$$
$$= 2.03\,\text{L}$$

| *EXAMPLE* | *1.17* | A 5.00 L container is filled with oxygen gas at a pressure of 110.0 kPa and a temperature of 19 °C. Calculate the mass of oxygen in the container. |

SOLUTION

STRATEGY

We use the volume of oxygen gas as our starting point.

1. Volume of Gas $\longrightarrow$ Moles of Gas
2. Moles of Gas $\longrightarrow$ Mass of Gas

STEP 1: We rearrange the ideal gas equation to determine the number of moles of the gas:

$$n = \frac{PV}{RT}$$
$$= \frac{110.0\,\text{kPa} \times 5.00\,\text{L}}{8.314\,\text{kPa·L·mol}^{-1}\text{·K}^{-1} \times 292\,\text{K}}$$
$$= 0.227\,\text{mol}$$

STEP 2:   The molar mass of oxygen gas is $32.00\,\text{g}\cdot\text{mol}^{-1}$. The mass of O_2 is therefore

$$\text{Mass of } O_2 = 0.227 \text{ mol } O_2 \times \frac{32.00\,\text{g } O_2}{1 \text{ mol } O_2}$$

$$= 7.26\,\text{g } O_2$$

EXAMPLE　　**1.18**　A bulb with a volume of 225 mL contains 0.580 g of an unknown gaseous compound. The pressure is measured as 145.0 kPa at a temperature of 25 °C. What is the molar mass of the compound?

SOLUTION　　*STRATEGY*

1. Volume of Gas ⟶ Moles of Gas
2. Moles of Gas ⟶ Molar Mass of Gas

STEP 1:   After converting 225 mL to litres we apply the ideal gas equation to determine the number of moles of the gas:

$$n = \frac{PV}{RT}$$

$$= \frac{145.0\,\text{kPa} \times 0.225\,\text{L}}{8.314\,\text{kPa}\cdot\text{L}\cdot\text{mol}^{-1}\cdot\text{K}^{-1} \times 298\,\text{K}}$$

$$= 1.32 \times 10^{-2} \text{ mol}$$

STEP 2:   Knowing that 0.580 g is equivalent to 1.32×10^{-2} mol of the gas, we can calculate the molar mass:

$$\text{Molar mass of gas} = \frac{0.580\,\text{g}}{1.32 \times 10^{-2} \text{ mol}}$$

$$= 44.0\,\text{g}\cdot\text{mol}^{-1}$$

QUESTIONS

21. Calculate the volume of 36.0 g of steam at 115 °C and 110.0 kPa pressure.

22. What mass of nitrogen dioxide gas would be required to fill a 200.0 mL gas jar at a pressure of 98.6 kPa and a temperature of 22 °C?

23. A 1.50 g sample of a gas has a volume of 615 mL at a pressure of 95.0 kPa and a temperature of 27 °C. What is the molar mass of the gas?

Calculations Involving Reactions

A balanced equation allows us to calculate the quantities of reactants and products involved in a reaction — whether we measure masses of substances that are solids, or volumes of substances that are solutions or gases. Calculations that make use of a balanced equation are known as **stoichiometric calculations**. The common feature of all stoichiometric calculations is the use of the mole relationships indicated in a balanced equation.

Mole-Mole Calculations

The simplest stoichiometric problems are those where the quantities of reactants and products are measured in moles. In such cases we need only use a balanced equation to determine the number of moles of one species that will react with, or be produced from, a definite number of moles of another species.

EXAMPLE   *1.19*   Nitrogen monoxide gas may be prepared by reacting copper metal with dilute nitric acid:

$$3\,Cu_{(s)} + 8\,HNO_{3\,(aq)} \longrightarrow 3\,Cu(NO_3)_{2\,(aq)} + 2\,NO_{(g)} + 4\,H_2O_{(\ell)}$$

Determine the maximum number of moles of nitrogen monoxide that could be obtained from the reaction of 0.75 mol of copper with an excess of nitric acid.

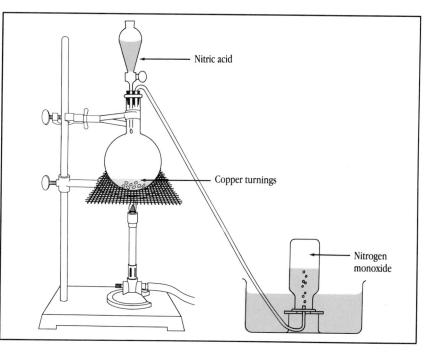

Figure 1.14

Nitrogen monoxide can be prepared by adding nitric acid to copper turnings and warming gently. The gas is collected over water.

Nitric acid

Copper turnings

Nitrogen monoxide

SOLUTION The balanced equation indicates that the complete reaction of three moles of copper will produce two moles of nitrogen monoxide. The two equation factors relating the two substances are

$$\frac{3 \text{ mol Cu}}{2 \text{ mol NO}} \quad \text{and} \quad \frac{2 \text{ mol NO}}{3 \text{ mol Cu}}$$

The amount of nitrogen monoxide that could be obtained from 0.75 mol of copper is therefore

$$\text{Moles of NO} = 0.75 \text{ mol Cu} \times \frac{2 \text{ mol NO}}{3 \text{ mol Cu}}$$

$$= 0.50 \text{ mol NO}$$

Mass-Mass Calculations

When we carry out a chemical reaction, we generally measure solids by their masses. If we calculate the numbers of moles from the measured masses, we can use the balanced equation to determine the numbers of moles of the other species that take part in the reaction. We can then calculate their masses.

EXAMPLE   **1.20** Given the following balanced equation

$$3 \text{ Cu}_{(s)} + 8 \text{ HNO}_{3\,(aq)} \longrightarrow 3 \text{ Cu(NO}_3)_{2\,(aq)} + 2 \text{ NO}_{(g)} + 4 \text{ H}_2\text{O}_{(\ell)}$$

determine the mass of copper(II) nitrate that would be formed from the complete reaction of 35.5 g of copper with an excess of nitric acid.

SOLUTION

STRATEGY

Our strategy is to use the known mass of copper (Substance A) to find the equivalent number of moles. We can then calculate the number of moles and the mass of copper(II) nitrate (Substance B).

1. Mass of A $\longrightarrow$ Moles of A
2. Moles of A $\longrightarrow$ Moles of B
3. Moles of B $\longrightarrow$ Mass of B

STEP 1: We determine the number of moles of copper used in the reaction:

$$\text{Moles of Cu} = 35.5 \text{ g Cu} \times \frac{1 \text{ mol Cu}}{63.55 \text{ g Cu}}$$

$$= 0.559 \text{ mol Cu}$$

STEP 2: From the balanced equation we determine that three moles of copper will produce three moles of copper(II) nitrate. This provides us with the following equation factor:

$$\frac{3 \text{ mol Cu(NO}_3)_2}{3 \text{ mol Cu}}$$

The number of moles of copper(II) nitrate produced in this reaction is therefore

$$\text{Moles of } Cu(NO_3)_2 = 0.559 \text{ mol Cu} \times \frac{3 \text{ mol } Cu(NO_3)_2}{3 \text{ mol Cu}}$$

$$= 0.559 \text{ mol } Cu(NO_3)_2$$

STEP 3: $\text{Mass of } Cu(NO_3)_2 = 0.559 \text{ mol } Cu(NO_3)_2 \times \dfrac{187.57 \text{ g } Cu(NO_3)_2}{1 \text{ mol } Cu(NO_3)_2}$

$$= 105 \text{ g } Cu(NO_3)_2$$

Calculations Involving Aqueous Solutions

When one or more of the reactants or products of a reaction is in aqueous solution, we normally measure the solution volume and concentration rather than the mass. We can determine the number of moles of the aqueous compound from this information, and use the balanced equation to calculate the quantities of other reactants to use or products to expect.

EXAMPLE   **1.21**   Given the following balanced equation

$$3 \, Cu_{(s)} + 8 \, HNO_{3\,(aq)} \longrightarrow 3 \, Cu(NO_3)_{2\,(aq)} + 2 \, NO_{(g)} + 4 \, H_2O_{(\ell)}$$

determine the volume of $2.50 \text{ mol} \cdot L^{-1}$ nitric acid that would be required to react with 15.5 g of copper.

SOLUTION

STRATEGY

We use the known mass of the reactant copper (Substance A) to find the equivalent number of moles. We can then calculate the moles and volume of the other reactant, nitric acid (Substance B).

1. Mass of A $\longrightarrow$ Moles of A
2. Moles of A $\longrightarrow$ Moles of B
3. Moles of B $\longrightarrow$ Volume of B

STEP 1:   We determine the number of moles of copper used in the reaction:

$$\text{Moles of Cu} = 15.5 \text{ g Cu} \times \frac{1 \text{ mol Cu}}{63.55 \text{ g Cu}}$$

$$= 0.244 \text{ mol Cu}$$

STEP 2:   From the balanced equation we determine that three moles of copper will react with eight moles of nitric acid. The number of moles of nitric acid required is

$$\text{Moles of } HNO_3 = 0.244 \text{ mol Cu} \times \frac{8 \text{ mol } HNO_3}{3 \text{ mol Cu}}$$

$$= 0.651 \text{ mol } HNO_3$$

STEP 3:   Using the molar concentration $(2.50 \text{ mol} \cdot \text{L}^{-1})$ as a conversion factor, we can now find the volume of acid that contains 0.651 mol HNO_3:

$$\text{Volume of } HNO_3 = 0.651 \text{ mol } HNO_3 \times \frac{1 \text{ L}}{2.50 \text{ mol } HNO_3}$$

$$= 0.260 \text{ L, or } 260 \text{ mL}$$

Calculations Involving Gases

In some reactions a product or reactant may be a gas. In such cases the quantity of material would be determined by measuring or calculating the gas volume at the specific temperature and pressure of the experiment. The ideal gas equation is used to relate this information to the number of moles of the gas.

EXAMPLE   *1.22*   Given the balanced equation

$$3 \, Cu_{(s)} + 8 \, HNO_{3\,(aq)} \longrightarrow 3 \, Cu(NO_3)_{2(aq)} + 2 \, NO_{(g)} + 4 \, H_2O_{(\ell)}$$

determine the mass of copper that would be required to react to produce 4.00 L of nitrogen monoxide at 102.5 kPa and 22 °C.

SOLUTION   *STRATEGY*

Using our data on the product, nitrogen monoxide (Gas A), we use the ideal gas equation to find the equivalent number of moles. We can then calculate moles and mass of the reactant copper (Substance B).

1. Volume of Gas A ⟶ Moles of Gas A
2. Moles of Gas A ⟶ Moles of B
3. Moles of B ⟶ Mass of B

STEP 1:   To determine the number of moles of nitrogen monoxide, we rearrange the ideal gas to obtain:

$$n = \frac{PV}{RT}$$

$$n_{NO} = \frac{102.5 \text{ kPa} \times 4.00 \text{ L}}{8.314 \text{ kPa} \cdot \text{L} \cdot \text{mol}^{-1} \cdot \text{K}^{-1} \times 295 \text{ K}}$$

$$= 0.167 \text{ mol NO}$$

STEP 2:   The balanced equation shows that three moles of copper will produce two moles of nitrogen monoxide. The number of moles of copper is therefore

$$\text{Moles of Cu} = 0.167 \text{ mol NO} \times \frac{3 \text{ mol Cu}}{2 \text{ mol NO}}$$

$$= 0.251 \text{ mol Cu}$$

STEP 3:   The mass of copper is therefore

$$\text{Mass of Cu} = 0.251 \text{ mol Cu} \times \frac{63.55 \text{ g Cu}}{1 \text{ mol Cu}}$$

$$= 16.0 \text{ g Cu}$$

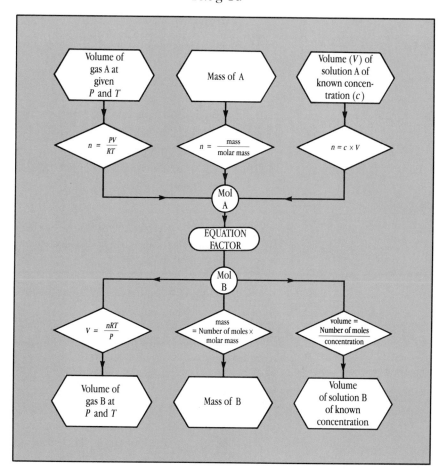

Figure 1.15

A summary of the mole method approach to solving problems.

Limiting Reagents

If we were to prepare nitrogen monoxide in the laboratory from copper and nitric acid, we would normally make sure that we measured the correct mass of copper to produce the volume of gas that we wanted. We would then add a measured excess of nitric acid. The amount of copper would determine the amount of nitrogen monoxide produced. In this case, copper would be called the **limiting reagent**.

If we react measured quantities of two substances, we can calculate the number of moles of each reagent used. We can then use the balanced equation to determine which material is the limiting reagent. The quantity of product formed will depend upon the amount of the limiting reagent.

1.23   Copper reacts with dilute nitric acid according to the equation:

$$3\,Cu_{(s)} + 8\,HNO_{3\,(aq)} \longrightarrow 3\,Cu(NO_3)_{2\,(aq)} + 2\,NO_{(g)} + 4\,H_2O_{(\ell)}$$

A 200.0 mL sample of 2.00 mol·L^{-1} nitric acid is added to 30.48 g of copper. Determine which reactant is the limiting reagent. What volume of nitrogen monoxide, measured at 99.5 kPa and 20 °C, would be produced?

SOLUTION

STRATEGY

After finding the number of moles of each reagent, we determine the limiting reagent (A): either nitric acid or copper. From this we can find the volume of nitrogen monoxide gas (B).

1. Determine the number of moles of each reactant.
2. Use the equation factor to find the limiting reagent.
3. Moles of limiting reagent (A) ⟶ Moles of gas (B)
4. Moles of gas (B) ⟶ Volume of gas (B)

STEP 1:   After converting the volume of acid to litres, we use the molar concentration of the acid as a conversion factor to determine the number of moles of acid:

$$\text{Moles of } HNO_3 = 0.2000\,L\,HNO_3 \times \frac{2.00\,\text{mol } HNO_3}{1\,L\,HNO_3}$$

$$= 0.400\,\text{mol } HNO_3$$

We determine the number of moles of copper from the mass given:

$$\text{Moles of } Cu = 30.48\,g \times \frac{1\,\text{mol } Cu}{63.55\,g\,Cu}$$

$$= 0.4796\,\text{mol } Cu$$

STEP 2:   We determine the limiting reagent by comparing the relative numbers of moles of copper and nitric acid used in the experiment with those required by the balanced equation.

The equation factor that we get from the balanced equation is

$$\frac{8\,\text{mol } HNO_3}{3\,\text{mol } Cu}$$

The number of moles of nitric acid required to react with the 0.4796 mol of copper used in this experiment would be

$$\text{Moles of } HNO_3 = 0.4796\,\text{mol } Cu \times \frac{8\,\text{mol } HNO_3}{3\,\text{mol } Cu}$$

$$= 1.279\,\text{mol } HNO_3$$

Although this amount of nitric acid is required by 0.4796 moles of copper, only 0.400 mol of nitric acid are actually used in the experiment. There is not enough acid to react with all of the copper. The nitric acid is the limiting reagent.

STEP 3: The amount of the limiting reagent, nitric acid, determines the amount of nitrogen monoxide produced. From the balanced equation we see that eight moles of nitric acid will produce two moles of nitrogen monoxide. The number of moles of nitrogen monoxide produced is

$$\text{Moles of NO} = 0.400 \text{ mol HNO}_3 \times \frac{2 \text{ mol NO}}{8 \text{ mol HNO}_3}$$

$$= 0.100 \text{ mol NO}$$

STEP 4: We can now determine the volume of the nitrogen monoxide by rearranging the ideal gas equation.

$$V = \frac{nRT}{P}$$

$$V_{NO} = \frac{0.100 \text{ mol} \times 8.314 \text{ kPa·L·mol}^{-1} \cdot \text{K}^{-1} \times 293 \text{ K}}{99.5 \text{ kPa}}$$

$$= 2.45 \text{ L NO}$$

Percent Yield

When we carry out stoichiometric calculations to determine the quantity of product that will be formed in a reaction, we assume that we will obtain the maximum possible yield. What we are calculating is in fact the **theoretical yield** of the reaction. If we actually carry out a reaction in the laboratory, we often find that we obtain less than this theoretical yield. What we obtain is the **actual yield**. The **percent yield** is given by the expression:

$$\textbf{Percent Yield} = \frac{\textbf{Actual yield}}{\textbf{Theoretical yield}} \times \textbf{100\%}$$

EXAMPLE **1.24** Copper(II) oxide may be reduced to copper by heating it in a stream of hydrogen gas:

$$\text{CuO}_{(s)} + \text{H}_{2\,(g)} \longrightarrow \text{Cu}_{(s)} + \text{H}_2\text{O}_{(g)}$$

In an experiment 13.65 g of copper(II) oxide produces 10.75 g of copper metal. What is the percent yield?

SOLUTION The number of moles of copper(II) oxide is

$$\text{Moles of CuO} = 13.65 \text{ g CuO} \times \frac{1 \text{ mol CuO}}{79.55 \text{ g CuO}}$$

$$= 0.1716 \text{ mol CuO}$$

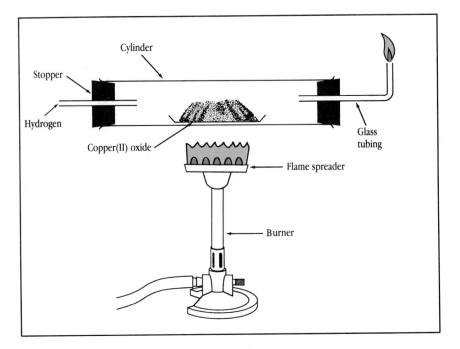

Figure 1.16
Copper(II) oxide can be reduced to copper metal using this apparatus.

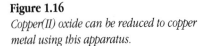

We use the correct equation factor to determine the number of moles of copper:

$$\text{Moles of Cu} = 0.1716 \text{ mol CuO} \times \frac{1 \text{ mol Cu}}{1 \text{ mol CuO}}$$

$$= 0.1716 \text{ mol Cu}$$

The mass of copper (theoretical yield) is

$$\text{Mass of Cu} = 0.1716 \text{ mol} \times \frac{63.55 \text{ g Cu}}{1 \text{ mol Cu}}$$

$$= 10.91 \text{ g Cu}$$

We can now determine the percent yield:

$$\text{Percent yield} = \frac{10.75 \text{ g Cu}}{10.91 \text{ g Cu}} \times 100\%$$

$$= 98.53\%$$

QUESTIONS

24. In the manufacture of nitric acid, one of the important steps is the reaction of ammonia with oxygen:

$$4\,NH_{3\,(g)} + 5\,O_{2\,(g)} \longrightarrow 4\,NO_{(g)} + 6\,H_2O_{(g)}$$

a) How many moles of nitrogen monoxide would be produced from the reaction of 0.875 mol of ammonia?

b) How many moles of oxygen gas would be required to completely react with 2.65 mol of ammonia?

c) How many moles of ammonia were used if 8.83 mol of water is produced?

25. Iron can be produced from the reaction of iron(III) oxide with carbon monoxide:

$$Fe_2O_{3(s)} + 3\,CO_{(g)} \longrightarrow 2\,Fe_{(s)} + 3\,CO_{2(g)}$$

a) What mass of iron can be produced from 14.7 mol of iron(III) oxide?

b) What mass of iron can be produced from 14.7 g of iron(III) oxide?

26. Zinc metal reacts with hydrochloric acid to produce zinc chloride and hydrogen gas:

$$Zn_{(s)} + 2\,HCl_{(aq)} \longrightarrow ZnCl_{2(aq)} + H_{2(g)}$$

a) Calculate the minimum volume of $0.200\ mol \cdot L^{-1}$ hydrochloric acid necessary to react completely with 1.22 g of zinc.

b) What volume of hydrogen gas, measured at 100 kPa and 20 °C, is produced from this 1.22 g of zinc?

27. "Red lead" is an oxide of lead that has the formula Pb_3O_4. When boiled with dilute nitric acid, the red lead reacts to produce lead(II) nitrate and lead(IV) oxide:

$$Pb_3O_{4(s)} + 4\,HNO_{3(aq)} \longrightarrow 2\,Pb(NO_3)_{2(aq)} + PbO_{2(s)} + 2\,H_2O_{(\ell)}$$

a) How many moles of lead(II) nitrate would be produced from the complete reaction of 0.46 mol of red lead with an excess of nitric acid?

b) What volume of $2.50\ mol \cdot L^{-1}$ nitric acid would be required to react with 15.85 g of red lead?

c) What mass of red lead would be required to react to produce 14.75 g of lead(IV) oxide?

d) What is the percent yield if 11.25 g of red lead reacts with an excess of nitric acid to produce 3.85 g of lead(IV) oxide?

28. Ammonia can be produced in the laboratory by heating ammonium chloride and calcium hydroxide together:

$$2\,NH_4Cl_{(s)} + Ca(OH)_{2(s)} \longrightarrow CaCl_{2(s)} + 2\,NH_{3(g)} + 2\,H_2O_{(g)}$$

An 8.15 g sample of ammonium chloride is mixed with 7.48 g of calcium hydroxide and heated.

a) Determine which of the two reactants is the limiting reagent.

b) Calculate the maximum volume of dry ammonia gas that could be produced in the reaction, measured at a temperature of 23 °C and a pressure of 102.5 kPa.

Summary

- Chemical reactions can be classified into four main types: combination reactions, decomposition reactions, single displacement reactions, and double displacement reactions.

- Many problems can be solved by using conversion factors: ratios that relate two quantities expressed in different units.

- It is important that the precision of all measurements is clearly indicated by using the correct number of significant figures. Particular rules apply when adding and subtracting or when multiplying and dividing measured values.

- The amount of material is measured in moles, where one mole of any substance contains a fixed number, 6.02×10^{23}, of atoms or molecules.

- The molar mass of an element or compound is expressed in $g \cdot mol^{-1}$

- The mole method is essentially a three-step process used to solve a problem in which we wish to solve the following:
  a) The mass of a specified reactant that must be used in order to convert a given mass of another reactant into products;
  b) The mass of a particular product formed in a given reaction from a specified mass of one or more reactants;
  c) The mass of each reactant required in order to produce a given mass of product.

- A solution is formed when a solute dissolves in a solvent. The concentration of a solution is a measure of the mass of solute that is dissolved in a particular volume of solution.

- The ideal gas equation indicates the relationship between the pressure, volume, temperature, and number of moles of a gas.

- The coefficients in a balanced equation indicate the relationship between the numbers of moles of each species involved in the reaction. The balanced equation allows quantities of reactants and products, whether solids, liquids, or gases, to be calculated. Calculations of this type are known as stoichiometric calculations.

KEY WORDS

activity series	conversion factor
actual yield	decomposition reaction
aqueous solution	double displacement reaction
combination reaction	equation factor
combustion	ideal gas equation
combustion reaction	limiting reagent
concentration	molar concentration

molar mass
mole
mole method
neutralization
percent yield
single displacement reaction
solute
solution
solvent
standard solution
stoichiometric calculation
theoretical yield
thermal decomposition
universal gas constant

ANSWERS TO SECTION QUESTIONS

1. a) double displacement b) single displacement
2. a) no reaction b) reaction c) reaction
3. a) hydrogen gas + aluminum chloride solution
   b) lead carbonate precipitate + potassium nitrate solution
4. a) 2.347 kg c) 1.35×10^3 mL e) 2.5×10^5 mg
   b) 7.69 mm d) 0.129 m
5. 2.5 L
6. $\frac{1 \text{ mol } F_2}{1 \text{ mol } ZnF_2}, \frac{1 \text{ mol } ZnF_2}{1 \text{ mol } F_2}$
7. a) 3 b) 4
8. a) 3.940×10^{-3}, 4 significant figures
   b) 2.490×10^2, 4 significant figures
9. a) 349.5 b) 149.3 c) 2.147
10. 3.9×10^3 g
11. 141.1 g
12. 1.50 mol
13. a) $310.18\, g \cdot mol^{-1}$ b) $85.11\, g \cdot mol^{-1}$ c) $286.19\, g \cdot mol^{-1}$
14. 31.1 g
15. 0.170 mol
16. 8.88 g $O_{2(g)}$
17. 16.3 g $SO_{3(g)}$, 3.68 g $H_2O_{(\ell)}$
18. $1.803 \times 10^{-1}\, mol \cdot L^{-1}$
19. 0.875 mol
20. $0.1080\, mol \cdot L^{-1}$
21. 58.7 L
22. 0.370 g
23. $64.1\, g \cdot mol^{-1}$
24. a) 0.875 mol b) 3.31 mol c) 5.89 mol
25. a) 1.64×10^3 g b) 10.3 g
26. a) 187 mL b) 456 mL
27. a) 0.92 mol b) 37.0 mL c) 42.27 g d) 98.1 %
28. a) NH_4Cl b) 3.65 L

1. How does a combination reaction differ from a single displacement reaction?
2. What is thermal decomposition?
3. Can hydrogen gas be used to displace lead from lead oxide? Explain.
4. As a safety precaution, sodium metal is stored in oil. Use the activity series to explain this practice.
5. In double displacement reactions, normally only one product is insoluble. What is unusual in the reaction between iron(III) sulfate and barium hydroxide?
6. Under what circumstances is the figure zero significant?
7. A farmer counts the number of cows in his field and finds that there are 11. Explain why it would be incorrect to say that this value is accurate to two significant figures.
8. Explain the relationship between the mass and the number of moles of an element.
9. What is a solute?
10. Explain how you would prepare 250.0 mL of 0.100 mol·L^{-1} sodium carbonate solution from a sample of solid sodium carbonate.
11. Explain how you would prepare 250.0 mL of 0.100 mol·L^{-1} hydrochloric acid from a solution of the acid that has a concentration of 2.00 mol·L^{-1}.
12. Identify each of the symbols in the ideal gas equation, $PV = nRT$.
13. What information can we obtain from a balanced chemical equation?
14. What one feature do all stoichiometric calculations have in common?
15. What is a limiting reagent?

Reaction Types

16. Classify each of the following reactions as a combination, decomposition, single displacement, or double displacement:
    a) $Ca_{(s)} + Br_{2(\ell)} \longrightarrow CaBr_{2(s)}$
    b) $2\,Al_{(s)} + 3\,CuSO_{4\,(aq)} \longrightarrow Al_2(SO_4)_{3\,(aq)} + 3\,Cu_{(s)}$
    c) $CdCl_{2\,(aq)} + H_2S_{(g)} \longrightarrow CdS_{(s)} + 2\,HCl_{(aq)}$
    d) $2\,NaNO_{3\,(s)} \longrightarrow 2\,NaNO_{2\,(s)} + O_{2\,(g)}$
17. Which of the following reactions are neutralization reactions:
    a) $2\,HCl_{(aq)} + Zn_{(s)} \longrightarrow ZnCl_{2\,(aq)} + H_{2\,(g)}$
    b) $2\,HCl_{(aq)} + ZnO_{(s)} \longrightarrow ZnCl_{2\,(aq)} + H_2O_{(\ell)}$
    c) $2\,HCl_{(aq)} + ZnCO_{3\,(s)} \longrightarrow ZnCl_{2\,(aq)} + CO_{2\,(g)} + H_2O_{(\ell)}$
    d) $2\,HCl_{(aq)} + Zn(OH)_{2\,(s)} \longrightarrow ZnCl_{2\,(aq)} + 2\,H_2O_{(\ell)}$
18. Identify the products of the following double displacement reactions, then balance each equation.

a) $AgNO_{3\,(aq)} + K_2CO_{3\,(aq)} \longrightarrow$

b) $BaCl_{2\,(aq)} + Na_2SO_{4\,(aq)} \longrightarrow$

c) $Al_2(SO_4)_{3\,(aq)} + NH_4OH_{(aq)} \longrightarrow$

19. Use the activity series to determine whether the following single displacement reactions will take place. Complete and balance the equations for each reaction that will occur.

a) $Ca_{(s)} + HCl_{(aq)} \longrightarrow$

b) $Mg_{(s)} + Pb(NO_3)_{2\,(aq)} \longrightarrow$

c) $Fe_{(s)} + ZnCl_{2\,(aq)} \longrightarrow$

The Conversion-Factor Method

20. Convert the following:

a) 434 cm to m   d) 245 mL to L

b) 2425 g to kg   e) 3689 mm to m

c) 1674 mm to cm

21. Convert the density measurement of $0.554\,g \cdot mL^{-1}$ to the following:

a) $g \cdot L^{-1}$ b) $kg \cdot L^{-1}$ c) $kg \cdot m^{-3}$ (Remember: $1\,L = 10^3\,cm^3$)

22. When we combine sodium sulfide solution with hydrochloric acid, the double displacement reaction produces sodium chloride solution and hydrogen sulfide gas.

$$Na_2S_{(aq)} + 2\,HCl_{(aq)} \longrightarrow 2\,NaCl_{(aq)} + H_2S_{(g)}$$

What are the equation factors relating to the following species:

a) sodium sulfide and sodium chloride

b) hydrochloric acid and hydrogen sulfide

c) the reactants

23. The density of dry air is $1.205 \times 10^{-3}\,g \cdot mL^{-1}$ at a temperature of $20\,°C$ and a pressure of $100.0\,kPa$. Calculate the mass of $25.0\,L$ of dry air at this temperature and pressure.

Significant Figures

24. How many significant figures are in each of the following measurements?

a) 2.465 mg   b) 18.0 mL   c) 0.0860 L   d) 250.00 m

25. Convert the following measurements to scientific notation, and identify the number of significant figures:

a) 0.008 40 g   b) 365.0 s   c) 20.00 mL   d) 0.237 g

26. A 2.3684 g sample of ammonium chloride is dissolved in 25.00 mL of water. A specific volume of this solution is removed, which has a mass of 14.811 g. What is the mass of the remaining solution? (Remember: density of water is $1.00\,g \cdot mL^{-1}$.)

27. A small ingot of gold has a mass of 28.35 g. What is the total mass of five such ingots?

The Mole Concept

28. Determine the molar mass of the following compounds:

   a) N_2H_4 b) $(NH_4)_2SO_4$ c) $Pb(ClO_4)_2$

29. Calculate the mass of 0.250 mol of each of the following compounds:

   a) $Ca(BrO_3)_2 \cdot H_2O$

   b) $CrCl_3$

   c) $(CH_3CO_2)_2Cr$

30. Determine the number of moles of each of the following:

   a) 18.7 g of $CaCO_3$

   b) 23.9 g of $K_2Cr_2O_7$

   c) 143.8 g of lead(II) hydroxide

31. Determine the mass of the following:

   a) 2.37 mol of $NaHCO_3$

   b) 1.46 mol of NH_4BrO_3

   c) 0.459 mol of mercury(II) iodide

Solution Concentrations

32. Calculate the molar concentration of a solution that contains 2.76 g of sodium chromate, Na_2CrO_4, in 250.0 mL of solution.

33. What mass of potassium carbonate, K_2CO_3, must be weighed out to prepare 125.0 mL of a 0.0500 mol·L⁻¹ solution of the salt?

34. How many moles of sulfuric acid, H_2SO_4, are contained in 25.00 mL of 2.00 mol·L⁻¹ solution?

35. a) What volume of 1.5 mol·L⁻¹ nitric acid, $HNO_{3(aq)}$, would contain 0.470 mol of the acid?

   b) What volume of 0.500 mol·L⁻¹ potassium iodate, $KIO_{3(aq)}$, would contain 0.675 mol of the salt?

36. How many moles of silver nitrate, $AgNO_3$, are contained in 18.00 mL of a 0.150 ml·L⁻¹ solution of the salt?

37. A 25.00 mL sample of 0.250 mol·L⁻¹ sodium sulfate solution, $Na_2SO_{4(aq)}$, is diluted to 100 mL. What is the molar concentration of the diluted solution?

The Ideal Gas Equation

38. How many moles of hydrogen would be necessary to fill a 5.00 L container at a pressure of 105.0 kPa and a temperature of 24 °C?

39. What mass of carbon dioxide would be contained in a 15.0 L bottle, if the pressure were 95.0 kPa and the temperature 27 °C?

40. A 0.582 g sample of a gas has a volume of 0.520 L at 25 °C and 99.3 kPa. What is the molar mass of the gas?

41. What would be the volume of 10.00 g of sulfur dioxide gas at a pressure of 102.0 kPa and a temperature of 18.0 °C?

Calculations Involving Reactions

42. Concentrated nitric acid will react with bismuth according to the equation:

$$Bi_{(s)} + 6\,HNO_{3\,(aq)} \longrightarrow Bi(NO_3)_{3\,(aq)} + 3\,NO_{2\,(g)} + 3\,H_2O_{(\ell)}$$

a) How many moles of bismuth would react completely with 2.50 mol of nitric acid?

b) How many moles of bismuth would be required to react with an excess of nitric acid to produce 1.60 mol of NO_2 gas?

43. Carbon dioxide can be produced by adding dilute nitric acid to potassium carbonate:

$$K_2CO_{3\,(aq)} + 2\,HNO_{3\,(aq)} \longrightarrow 2\,KNO_{3\,(aq)} + CO_{2\,(g)} + H_2O_{(\ell)}$$

a) What mass of potassium nitrate would be produced from the complete reaction of 1.38 g of potassium carbonate?

b) What volume of 2.00 mol·L^{-1} nitric acid would be required to react with 2.47 g of potassium carbonate?

c) What volume of carbon dioxide, measured at 20 °C and 100.0 kPa, would be produced from the reaction of 24.0 g of potassium carbonate with an excess of nitric acid?

44. Copper metal will react with concentrated sulfuric acid to produce sulfur dioxide gas:

$$2\,H_2SO_{4\,(aq)} + Cu_{(s)} \longrightarrow CuSO_{4\,(aq)} + SO_{2\,(g)} + 2\,H_2O_{(\ell)}$$

a) What mass of copper would be required to react to produce 0.125 mol of sulfur dioxide gas?

b) What volume of 15.0 mol·L^{-1} sulfuric acid would be required to react with 21.4 g of copper?

c) What volume of sulfur dioxide, measured at 19 °C and 98.0 kPa, would be produced from the reaction of 15.0 g of copper with an excess of sulfuric acid?

45. Given the balanced equation for the reaction between hydrazine, N_2H_4, and hydrogen peroxide, H_2O_2,

$$N_2H_{4\,(\ell)} + 2\,H_2O_{2\,(\ell)} \longrightarrow N_{2\,(g)} + 4\,H_2O_{(\ell)}$$

What volume of nitrogen gas, measured at 21 °C and 95.0 kPa, would be obtained from the reaction of 25.0 mL hydrazine (density 1.00 g·mL^{-1}) with an excess of hydrogen peroxide solution?

46. Nitric acid can be prepared from the reaction between nitrogen dioxide and water:

$$3\,NO_{2\,(g)} + H_2O_{(\ell)} \longrightarrow 2\,HNO_{3\,(aq)} + NO_{(g)}$$

What would be the molar concentration of the nitric acid produced if 12.0 L of nitrogen dioxide, measured at 23 °C and 102.0 kPa, was reacted with enough water to produce 2.50 L of solution?

47. Hydrogen chloride gas can be prepared by reacting sodium chloride with concentrated sulfuric acid:

$$H_2SO_{4\,(\ell)} + NaCl_{(s)} \longrightarrow HCl_{(g)} + NaHSO_{4\,(s)}$$

Calculate the volume of hydrogen chloride, measured at 18 °C and 103.0 kPa, that would be produced from the reaction of 5.00 g of sodium chloride with an excess of sulfuric acid.

48. Zinc will react with dilute hydrochloric acid to produce hydrogen gas:

$$Zn_{(s)} + 2\,HCl_{(aq)} \longrightarrow H_{2\,(g)} + ZnCl_{2\,(aq)}$$

a) What mass of zinc would need to react to produce 3.0 L of hydrogen gas at 20 °C and 95.0 kPa?
b) What volume of 1.50 mol·L⁻¹ hydrochloric acid would be required to react completely with 13.9 g of zinc?

49. Aluminum metal can displace silver from a solution of silver nitrate. In an experiment 0.270 g of aluminum is added to 40.0 mL of 1.00 mol·L⁻¹ silver nitrate solution.
a) Write a balanced equation for the reaction.
b) Determine which of the reactants is the limiting reagent.
c) What is the theoretical yield of silver?
d) The mass of silver collected in the experiment was 2.98 g. Calculate the percent yield.

50. Barium bromate is precipitated when bromine is added to a hot concentrated solution of barium hydroxide:

$$6\,Br_{2\,(\ell)} + 6\,Ba(OH)_{2\,(aq)} \longrightarrow Ba(BrO_3)_{2\,(s)} + 5\,BaBr_{2\,(aq)} + 6\,H_2O_{(\ell)}$$

In an experiment 9.00 g of bromine was added to 20.00 mL of 3.00 mol·L⁻¹ barium hydroxide solution. A 3.59 g sample of barium bromate was obtained. Determine the limiting reagent, the theoretical yield of barium bromate, and the percent yield.

51. Silver nitrate solution reacts with calcium chloride solution:

$$2\,AgNO_{3\,(aq)} + CaCl_{2\,(aq)} \longrightarrow Ca(NO_3)_{2\,(aq)} + 2\,AgCl_{(s)}$$

A 10.8 g sample of silver nitrate and a 7.02 g sample of calcium chloride are mixed with 250 mL of water.
a) What mass of silver chloride is formed?
b) What mass of the excess reagent remains in solution?

MISCELLANEOUS PROBLEMS   **52.** a) How much water must be added to 15.00 mL of 2.000 mol·L⁻¹ hydrochloric acid to dilute it to 0.350 mol·L⁻¹?
b) If another 50.00 mL of water is added to the diluted solution above, calculate the molar concentration of the resulting solution.

53. A 25.00 mL sample of 2.000 mol·L^{-1} hydrochloric acid is added to 35.00 mL of 0.5000 mol·L^{-1} hydrochloric acid. What is the final molar concentration of 60.00 mL of acid solution?

54. The pressure of a 50.00 mL sample of nitrogen gas is 98.6 kPa at 20 °C.
   a) What will be the pressure if the volume is reduced to 40.00 mL, and the temperature increased to 25 °C?
   b) What will be the new volume if the pressure is then increased to 150 kPa?

55. Nitrogen monoxide gas will react with hydrogen gas, under specific conditions, to produce ammonia gas and water. Write a balanced equation for this reaction. What volume of hydrogen gas, measured at the same temperature and pressure, would react with 15.0 mL of nitrogen monoxide? What volume of ammonia would be produced?

56. Write an equation for the neutralization of the acid HX by sodium hydroxide solution. In an experiment exactly 30.20 mL of 0.100 mol·L^{-1} sodium hydroxide neutralizes 0.314 g of the acid. What is the molar mass of the acid?

57. A 0.300 L sample of 0.100 mol·L^{-1} iron(III) chloride solution is mixed with 0.100 L of 0.200 mol·L^{-1} sodium hydroxide solution. A precipitate of iron(III) hydroxide is formed.
   a) Write a balanced equation for the reaction.
   b) Determine which of the reactants is the limiting reagent.
   c) What is the theoretical yield of iron(III) hydroxide?
   d) Determine the percent yield if the actual mass of iron(III) hydroxide was 0.600 g.

58. A 20.0 mL sample of hydrogen gas is reacted with 20.0 mL of oxygen gas to produce steam. Write an equation for this reaction.
   a) Which reagent is the limiting reagent?
   b) Determine the volume of steam, measured at the same temperature and pressure, that would be produced.

59. Nitrogen monoxide may be made by heating an aqueous solution of iron(III) sulfate with a mixture of nitric acid and sulfuric acid:

$$6 \, FeSO_{4\,(aq)} + 2 \, HNO_{3\,(aq)} + 3 \, H_2SO_{4\,(aq)} \longrightarrow$$
$$3 \, Fe_2(SO_4)_{3\,(aq)} + 2 \, NO_{(g)} + 4 \, H_2O_{(\ell)}$$

In an experiment 7.694 g of iron (II) sulfate heptahydrate, $FeSO_4 \cdot 7H_2O$, is reacted with an excess of sulfuric acid and nitric acid.

   a) What mass of iron(III) sulfate, $Fe_2(SO_4)_3$, would be produced?
   b) What is the maximum volume of nitrogen monoxide, measured at 23 °C and 99.5 kPa that could be produced?
   c) Calculate the percent yield if the actual volume of nitrogen monoxide obtained was 195 mL.

60. Bromic acid will oxidize sulfur dioxide to sulfuric acid:

$$2\ HBrO_{3\,(aq)} + 5\ SO_{2\,(g)} + 4\ H_2O_{(\ell)} \longrightarrow Br_{2\,(aq)} + 5\ H_2SO_{4\,(aq)}$$

In an experiment 0.100 L of 0.200 mol·L^{-1} bromic acid is reacted with 0.100 L of a solution of sulfur dioxide.

a) What volume of sulfur dioxide measured at 23 °C and 98.7 kPa would need to be dissolved in the aqueous solution to react with all of the bromic acid?

b) What is the maximum number of moles of sulfuric acid that could be produced?

c) Calculate the percent yield of sulfuric acid if the concentration of the acid solution produced was found to be 0.230 mol·L^{-1}.

Chemical Bonding

In order to understand chemical processes we must understand the nature of chemical bonding. In this chapter we will review a number of simple concepts on atomic structure and then look at the different types of bonding in detail. Finally we will examine the crystal structures of metals and ionic compounds.

Atomic Theory *2.1* Atoms are made up of a large number of particles, the most important of which are the **proton**, the **neutron**, and the **electron**. Protons and neutrons are located in the atomic **nucleus**; electrons in the outer regions of the atom. Protons and neutrons are equal in mass, as Table 2.1 shows, and account for almost all of the mass of an atom.

TABLE 2.1 *The Three Main Particles that Make up the Atom*

Particle	Relative Mass	Relative Charge
proton	1	+1
neutron	1	0
electron	0.0005	−1

Since protons and electrons have equal but opposite charges, it follows that in an electrically neutral atom the number of electrons will equal the number of protons. The number of protons in the nucleus of an atom is known as the **atomic number** of the atom. It is the atomic number that determines the identity of the element.

The number of neutrons in the nucleus is usually greater than the number of protons, although in lighter atoms there are sometimes equal numbers of the two particles. Atoms having fewer neutrons than protons are rare. The total number of protons and neutrons in the nucleus of an atom is known as the **mass number**.

Mass number = Number of protons + Number of neutrons

TABLE 2.2 *Composition of the Most Common Atoms of Various Elements*

Element	Number of Protons (Atomic Number)	Number of Electrons	Number of Neutrons	Total Number of Protons & Neutrons (Mass number)
Hydrogen, H	1	1	0	1
Carbon, C	6	6	6	12
Oxygen, O	8	8	8	16
Copper, Cu	29	29	34	63
Lead, Pb	82	82	126	208

EXAMPLE   *2.1*   A neutral atom of a particular element has an atomic number of 35 and a mass number of 80. Identify this element and state how many protons, electrons, and neutrons it contains.

SOLUTION   The Periodic Table tells us that the element that has an atomic number of 35 is bromine, Br.

Number of protons = Atomic number = 35
Number of electrons in the neutral atom = Number of protons = 35
Number of neutrons + Number of protons = Mass number = 80
Number of neutrons = 80 − 35 = 45

Figure 2.1
Deuterium (^2_1H) is a less common isotope of hydrogen, and can be found in compounds such as deuterium oxide (heavy water).

Although different atoms of a particular element will always have the same number of protons, they may have slightly different numbers of neutrons. Such atoms are known as **isotopes**. Isotopes therefore have the same atomic number but different mass numbers. The following representation is often used to distinguish between different isotopes, where X represents the chemical symbol for the element, A is the mass number, and Z is the atomic number.

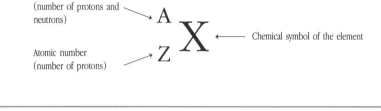

Mass number (number of protons and neutrons)

Atomic number (number of protons)

Chemical symbol of the element

$$^A_Z X$$

EXAMPLE   *2.2*

Three common isotopes of lead are lead-206, lead-207, and lead-208. How many protons, electrons, and neutrons does each isotope possess?

SOLUTION

Since the number of protons is given by the atomic number, we can see that for each isotope of lead the number of protons is 82. The number of electrons is also 82. To determine how many neutrons each atom contains, we write

Number of neutrons = Mass number − Atomic number

Therefore, the number of neutrons in $^{206}_{82}Pb$ is $206 − 82 = 124$
The number of neutrons in $^{207}_{82}Pb$ is $207 − 82 = 125$
The number of neutrons in $^{208}_{82}Pb$ is $208 − 82 = 126$

The Bohr Model

Although most of the mass of an atom is concentrated in the nucleus, the electrons are largely responsible for the chemical behaviour. Knowing the **electron configuration** of an atom — that is, the arrangement of electrons around the nucleus — will help us to understand this behaviour.

The earliest **quantum model** of the atom to describe the arrangement of electrons was developed by Danish physicist and Nobel Prize winner, Niels Bohr. Bohr proposed that electrons could possess only specific quantities of energy. Each quantity corresponded to an electron occupying an **energy level** located at a particular distance from the nucleus. Bohr identified each energy level using an integer, **n**, called the **principal quantum number**. This number could have any whole-number value ranging from one to infinity. Figure 2.3 shows a schematic representation of some of the energy levels of the hydrogen atom. Notice that the energy levels are closer together as *n* increases.

Figure 2.2
Niels Bohr (1885-1962) devised the first quantum model of the atom.

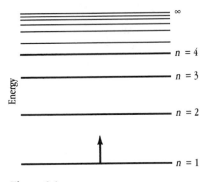

Figure 2.3

The principal energy levels of the hydrogen atom come closer together as ***n*** *increases from 1 to infinity.*

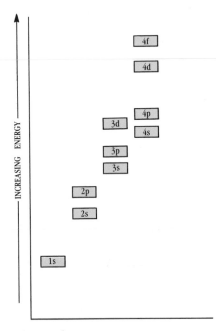

Figure 2.4

A schematic representation of the energy sublevels for ***n*** *= 1 to* ***n*** *= 4. The energy of sublevel 4**s** is lower than that of sublevel 3**d**.*

In Figure 2.3 the single electron of hydrogen is represented by an arrow (↑). The electron normally remains in the lowest energy level, identified by principal quantum number, $n = 1$. When it is in this lowest energy level, the electron is said to be in the **ground state**. If energy is added to the atom, the electron may absorb the appropriate amount of energy to move to one of the higher energy levels. It is then said to be in an **excited state**. The electron can fall back to lower energy levels by emitting energy in the form of light.

Bohr proposed that the electron configurations of atoms with more than one electron follow the pattern set up for the hydrogen atom, and that there are two rules that apply as additional electrons are added into the different energy levels:

1. Additional electrons always occupy the lowest available energy level.
2. The maximum number of electrons that can be placed in any particular energy level is given by the formula:

Maximum number of electrons = $2n^2$

Thus in the first energy level, for which $n = 1$, there may be $2(1)^2 = 2$ electrons. In the second level, for which $n = 2$, there may be $2(2)^2 = 8$ electrons. In the third level, for which $n = 3$, there may be $2(3)^2 = 18$ electrons, and so forth.

Arnold Sommerfeld, a Prussian physicist, extended the work of Bohr to show that each of the principal energy levels (except the first) is split into two or more **sublevels** having slightly different energies. These sublevels can be identified using a **secondary quantum number**, *l*. While this quantum number can have numerical values, it is more common for the sublevels to be described by the letters *s*, *p*, *d*, and *f*, where the *s* sublevel has the lowest energy, followed by the *p*, then the *d*, and finally the *f*. Figure 2.4 shows a representation of all of the energy sublevels for values of *n* from 1 to 4.

Notice that the number of sublevels in any given energy level corresponds to the value of *n*. Thus when $n = 2$, there are two sublevels, the 2*s* and 2*p*; when $n = 3$, there are three, the 3*s*, 3*p*, and 3*d*, and so on. Also, the energy levels are closer together as the value of *n* increases, and the energy of sublevel 4*s* is lower than that of sublevel 3*d*. This means that sublevel 4*s* will be filled with electrons before sublevel 3*d*. As we will see, overlapping of energy levels also occurs at higher values of *n*.

Just as the number of electrons occupying a particular principal energy level is limited to $2n^2$, there is also a limit to the number of electrons that can be placed in each of the *s*, *p*, *d*, and *f* sublevels. An *s* sublevel can hold just two electrons; a *p* sublevel can hold six; a *d* sublevel can hold a maximum of ten electrons; and an *f* sublevel can hold 14. In other words each successive sublevel can hold four more electrons than the preceding one.

TABLE 2.3   *Assignment of Electrons in Energy Sublevels*

Principal Energy level, n	Sublevel, l	Maximum Number of Electrons	
1	$1s$	2	$(2n^2 = 2)$
2	$2s$	2	
	$2p$	6	$(2n^2 = 8)$
3	$3s$	2	
	$3p$	6	
	$3d$	10	$(2n^2 = 18)$
4	$4s$	2	
	$4p$	6	
	$4d$	10	
	$4f$	14	$(2n^2 = 32)$

In chemist's shorthand the number of electrons in an energy sublevel of an atom is represented by a subscript to the right of the symbol representing the secondary quantum number. For example, the configuration $2s^2$ means that there are *two* electrons in the **s** sublevel when $n = 2$. By following this convention and using a helpful memory aid known as the *diagonal rule* (Figure 2.5), we can now write electron configurations for many of the elements.

Figure 2.5

The diagonal rule, used for predicting the order of filling sublevels:
a) The orbital symbols are written in the pattern shown;
b) Diagonal arrows are drawn from lower left to upper right;
*c) The head of one arrow is joined to the tail of the next. This gives the sequence of orbital filling; i.e., 1**s**, 2**s**, 2**p**, 3**s**, etc.*

a)

1s	2s	3s	4s	5s	6s	7s	8s	—
	2p	3p	4p	5p	6p	7p	—	—
		3d	4d	5d	6d	—	—	—
			4f	5f	—	—	—	—
				—	—	—	—	—

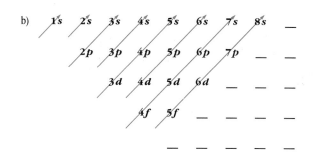

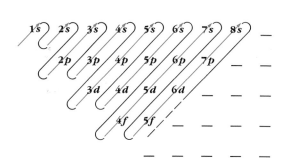

EXAMPLE 2.3

Write the electron configurations for the following:

a) phosphorus   b) bromine

SOLUTION

a) The atomic number for phosphorus is 15. Therefore, it will have 15 electrons. Applying the diagonal rule as shown in Figure 2.5, and using Table 2.3 to tell us how many electrons we can assign to each energy sublevel, will show that the configuration is $1s^22s^22p^63s^23p^3$.

b) The atomic number for bromine is 35. Figure 2.5 shows us that we must fill the $4s$ sublevel before the $3d$, because of its lower energy. The $4p$ sublevel is filled after the $3d$. Therefore, the configuration is $1s^22s^22p^63s^23p^64s^23d^{10}4p^5$.

Figure 2.6 shows the order in which the sublevels are filled as we read across the Periodic Table, from left to right. Notice that for all of the elements in Groups IA and IIA, s sublevels are being filled; p sublevels are

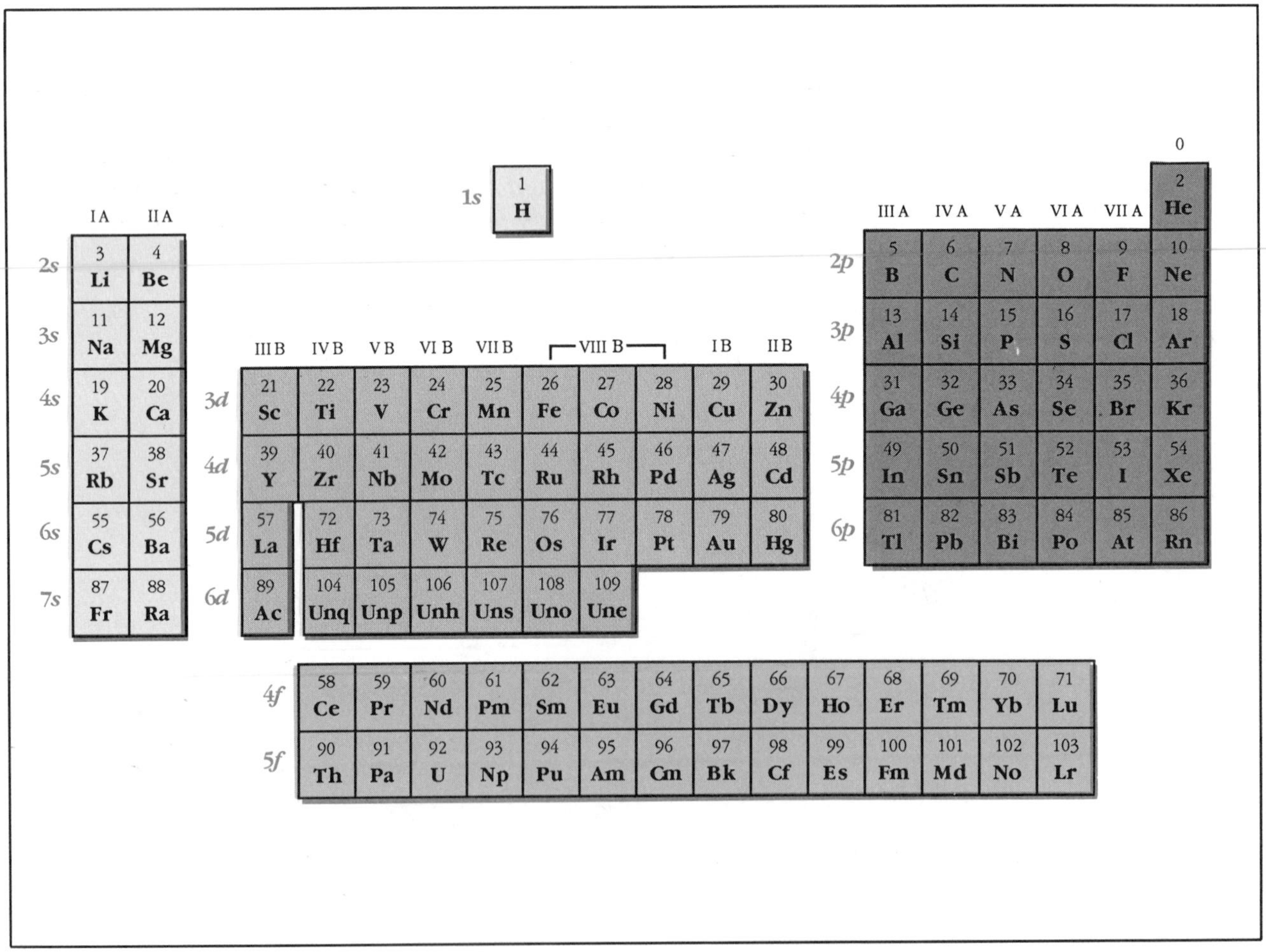

Figure 2.6

The relationship between the position of elements in the Periodic Table and the sublevel being filled with electrons. To find the sequence of orbitals filled, read across the period.

being filled for all elements from Group IIIA through to the noble gases. For energy levels $n = 4$ and upwards, the **s** sublevels have lower energy than the previous **d** sublevels, and are filled first.

The Probability Model

Although the Bohr model of the atom is very useful for determining basic electron configurations, it is not adequate to account for all experimental evidence. A probability, or quantum mechanical, model must be used that treats the electron as a wave rather than as a particle.

The idea that moving electrons could be considered as waves, similar to X-rays or to visible light, was first suggested by French physicist Louis de Broglie in 1924. De Broglie developed a formula for calculating the wavelength associated with particles in motion such as electrons. His ideas were subsequently confirmed by experiments that showed that a beam of electrons could be bent, or diffracted, by passing it through a crystal in just the same way that light is diffracted by passing it through a glass prism.

De Broglie's idea was taken a step further by German physicist Werner Heisenberg, who realized that the dual particle and wave nature of the electron made it impossible to determine both its position and energy at the same time. Any attempt to measure one of these properties would automatically interfere with, and alter, the other. This observation, known as the **Heisenberg uncertainty principle**, limits the strict application of the Bohr model. It means that if we know the energy of an electron, as we do when it is in a particular energy level, then we cannot know its position in space. We cannot say, as Bohr's theory did, that it is located at a fixed distance from the nucleus. Instead, we must make use of a mathematical equation, developed by Austrian physicist Erwin Schrodinger, that describes the behaviour of the electron as a wave. A solution to the wave equation indicates where the probability of finding the electron is high, and where it is low, for any energy level.

The Schrodinger wave equation is highly complex, and can be solved, exactly, only for one-electron systems. It does, however, produce the same principal and secondary quantum numbers that we have been using. It also gives more information about the way the electrons are arranged. In particular the model suggests that the electrons contained in energy sublevels occupy **orbitals**. Orbitals are volumes of space where the probability of finding the electron is high. Each orbital may contain a maximum of two electrons. Thus each **s** sublevel, which may contain two electrons, consists of just one **s** orbital; each **p** sublevel, which may contain up to six electrons, consists of three **p** orbitals; and each **d** sublevel, containing a maximum of ten electrons, consists of five orbitals.

As Figure 2.8 shows, all the electrons contained in a particular sublevel of a neutral atom will have the same energy, no matter which of the

Figure 2.7
Erwin Schrödinger (1887-1961) devised the equation that relates the wave properties of the electron to a set of quantum numbers.

available orbitals they occupy. All of the electrons contained in the $3p$ orbitals of calcium, for example, will have the same energy.

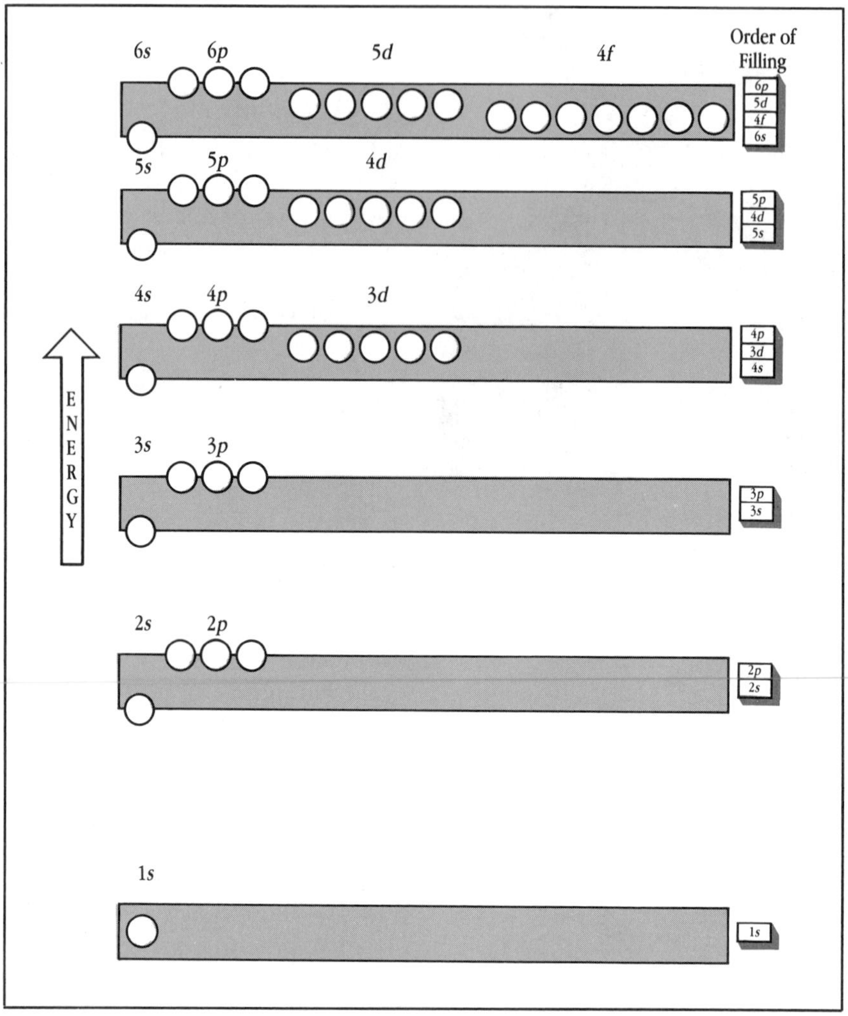

Figure 2.8

A schematic representation of the orbital energies, up to $6p$.

Distinguishing one orbital from another in the same sublevel requires a third quantum number, the **magnetic quantum number**, m_l.

The probability model was able to explain almost all of the experimental evidence related to electron configurations. However, in 1924 two German physicists, Otto Stern and Walther Gerlach, found some unexpected results when they passed a stream of hydrogen atoms through a magnetic field. They observed that the magnetic field caused the stream to split in two. The only way to account for the observation was to postulate that electrons possessed a spin and that an electron could spin clockwise or counterclockwise. In a sample of hydrogen atoms, half of the atoms would possess a clockwise spin, and the other half a counterclockwise spin. Interaction with a magnetic field would cause each spin to be deflected in a different direction. To distinguish between electrons with opposite spins, we must introduce a fourth quantum number, the **spin quantum number**, m_s. This quantum number can have two values, usually assigned as $+1/2$ or $-1/2$.

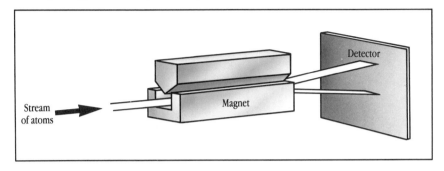

Figure 2.9

In the Stern-Gerlach experiment, a stream of hydrogen atoms is split in two by a magnetic field. This is evidence of the two possible electron spins.

We can now write electron configurations for the elements based on the probability model rather than on the Bohr theory. However, the rules that we use are very similar to those that Bohr proposed:

1. **The Aufbau principle** is identical to the first of Bohr's rules: each additional electron that is added to an electron configuration will occupy the lowest available energy level.

2. **The Pauli exclusion principle** states that no two electrons within an atom may have the same set of four quantum numbers. The principle has the same effect as Bohr's second rule. It indicates that each orbital may hold a maximum of two electrons and that these two electrons must be spinning in opposite directions.

3. **Hund's rule** follows from experimental findings and is concerned with the filling of an orbital set. The rule states that electrons must be distributed among orbitals of equal energy in such a way that as many electrons remain unpaired as possible. Thus, if there are three electrons in a set of orbitals, they must be placed into separate orbitals, and must have the same value for the spin quantum number.

We can use the four quantum numbers in much the same way as your postal code is used to define your address. The six digits in this alphanumeric code correspond to a specific mailing zone — representing the province, region (urban or rural), and a designated number of homes on one side of the street. Similarly, the four quantum numbers delineate the "region" in which an electron is likely to be found.

The electron configurations of different atoms can be represented in detail by incorporating the four quantum numbers into an *orbital diagram* such as that shown below. Each pair of electrons occupying an orbital is represented in the diagram by a pair of arrows that are shown pointing in opposite directions. This corresponds to the fourth quantum number; here we use arrows pointing up and down to represent the values of $+1/2$ and $-1/2$. The three different p orbitals and five different d orbitals are distinguishable in the diagram as separate boxes.

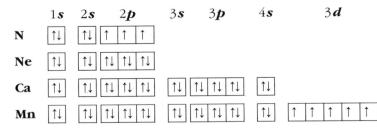

If we examine the electron configuration of nitrogen, we can see that, following the Aufbau principle, the first two electrons have been placed into the 1s orbital. The second two electrons have been placed into the 2s orbital, and, applying Hund's rule, the remaining three electrons have been placed, one each, into the three 2p orbitals. The arrows representing these three electrons are all pointing in the same direction, indicating that the electrons are all spinning in the same direction. In accordance with the Pauli exclusion principle, no orbital has more than two electrons, and, where an orbital is filled, the two electrons have opposite spins.

The electron configuration for calcium, which has 20 electrons, is also shown. Once again, we must follow the Aufbau principle. Electrons are placed in orbitals from 1s through to 3p. The remaining two electrons are placed into the 4s orbital, because this has lower energy than the 3d orbitals. The configuration for manganese, which includes five electrons spinning in the same direction in each of five d orbitals, illustrates the application of Hund's rule.

EXAMPLE   *2.4*   Draw an orbital diagram to show the (ground-state) electron configuration of a titanium atom.

SOLUTION   A titanium atom has 22 electrons. We apply the Aufbau principle and place the first two electrons in the 1s orbital. According to the Pauli exclusion principle, this orbital is now filled. The next eight electrons fill the 2s orbital and the three 2p orbitals. The 3s and 3p orbitals will accommodate a further eight electrons; the 4s orbital, which has the next lowest energy, can receive two more. The last two electrons must be placed in the 3d sublevel. We follow Hund's rule and place them, with the same spin, in two separate orbitals.

The electron configuration of titanium is therefore:

$$1s^2 2s^2 2p^6 3s^2 3p^6 4s^2 3d^2$$

The orbital diagram is:

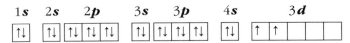

Unfortunately, simple predictions of electron configurations do not always match experimental findings. For example, we would predict the electron configuration of chromium to be $1s^22s^22p^63s^23p^64s^23d^4$. In fact it is $1s^22s^22p^63s^23p^64s^13d^5$. We can devise an explanation for this and other exceptions, but in this text we will use examples that strictly follow our three rules for electron configurations.

Shapes of Orbitals

As well as giving us information about the different electronic energy levels, the equations that are part of the quantum mechanical model of the atom also tell us about the shapes of the different orbitals. Remember that an orbital is simply a volume of space where the probability of finding the electron is high. This means that we can visualize particular orbitals as volumes of negative charge that have particular shapes and sizes.

When electrons occupy an **s** orbital, the volume of space in which they will most probably be found is spherical in shape, with the nucleus of the atom at the centre of the sphere (Figure 2.10). The size of the sphere will depend upon the principal quantum number. As this number increases, so does the average radius of the **s** orbital. A 3**s** orbital is larger than a 2**s** orbital which, in turn, is larger than a 1**s** orbital.

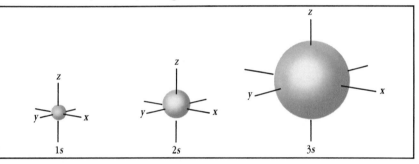

Figure 2.10
*The shapes and sizes of **s** orbitals. The size of the orbital increases as the principal quantum number increases.*

The **p** orbitals are shaped rather like dumb-bells (Figure 2.11). Since each of the three **p** orbitals lies along one of the three coordinate axes, the orbitals are known as p_x, p_y, and p_z.

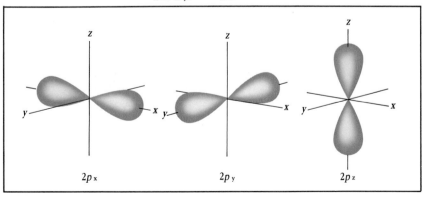

Figure 2.11
*The shapes of the three 2**p** orbitals.*

The shapes of the orbitals become more complex as the secondary quantum number increases. As you can see from Figure 2.12, one of the five $3d$ orbitals lies on the x and y axes ($d_{x^2-y^2}$), another is on the z axis (d_{z^2}), and the three remaining orbitals lie in a plane between two axes (d_{xy}, d_{xz}, d_{yz}).

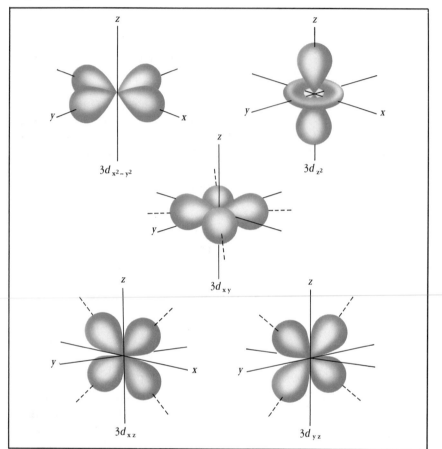

Figure 2.12
The shapes of the five 3d orbitals.

QUESTIONS

1. The nucleus of an atom of uranium contains 92 protons and 146 neutrons. What are the atomic number and mass number of the atom?

2. Two common isotopes of copper are copper-63 and copper-65. How many protons, neutrons, and electrons does each of these isotopes possess?

3. Write ground-state electron configurations of these elements:
   a) fluorine   b) scandium   c) krypton

4. Draw orbital diagrams to show the ground-state electron configurations of these elements:
   a) sodium   b) phosphorus   c) iron

Another View

Stephen Leacock, in his essay "Common Sense and the Universe," provides us with a rather different image of the structure of the atom, likening the protons and electrons to Irishmen swinging shillelaghs (clubs) at high speed . . .

Figure 2.13
Canadian author Stephen Leacock (1869-1944).

"Imagine to yourself an Irishman whirling a shillelagh around his head with the rapidity and dexterity known only in Tipperary or Donegal. If you come anywhere near, you'll get hit with the shillelagh. Now make it go faster; faster still; get it going so fast that you can't tell which is Irishman and which is shillelagh. The whole combination has turned into a green blur. If you shoot a bullet at it, it will probably go through, as there is mostly nothing there. Yet if you go up against it, it won't hit you now, because the shillelagh is going so fast that you will seem to come against a solid surface. Now make the Irishman smaller and the shillelagh longer. In fact, you don't need the Irishman at all; just his force, his Irish determination, so to speak. Just keep that, the *disturbance*. And you don't need the shillelagh either, just the *field of force* that it sweeps. There! Now put in two Irishmen and two shillelaghs and reduce them in the same way to one solid body — at least it seems solid but you can shoot bullets through it anywhere now. What you have now is a hydrogen atom, one proton and one electron flying around as a *disturbance* in space. Put in more Irishmen and more shillelaghs — or, rather, more protons and electrons — and you get other kinds of atoms. Put in a whole lot — eleven protons, eleven electrons; that is a sodium atom. Bunch the atoms together into combinations called molecules, themselves flying round — and there you are! That's solid matter, and nothing in it at all except disturbance. You're standing on it right now: the molecules are beating against your feet. But there is nothing there, and nothing in your feet. This may help you to understand how "waves," ripples of disturbance — for instance, the disturbance you call radio — go right through all matter, indeed right through *you*, as if you weren't there. You see, you aren't."

Periodic Properties of the Elements

<u>2.2</u> A knowledge of the electron configurations of the elements is essential to the understanding of chemical behaviour and chemical bonding. In particular we need to know about the electrons that are in the outermost energy level of atoms of different elements. The ease with which electrons are gained or lost from this energy level determines what types of compounds, if any, the elements will form.

The electrons that are contained in the outermost principal energy level of an atom are often called the **valence electrons**. Table 2.4 shows the electron configurations of a number of elements. The valence electrons are shown in bold type.

TABLE 2.4   *Electron Configurations of Some Common Elements*

Element	Atomic Number	Electron Configuration
Carbon, C	6	$1s^2 \mathbf{2s^2 2p^2}$
Sodium, Na	11	$1s^2 2s^2 2p^6 \mathbf{3s^1}$
Silicon, Si	14	$1s^2 2s^2 2p^6 \mathbf{3s^2 3p^2}$
Chlorine, Cl	17	$1s^2 2s^2 2p^6 \mathbf{3s^2 3p^5}$
Potassium, K	19	$1s^2 2s^2 2p^6 3s^2 3p^6 \mathbf{4s^1}$
Bromine, Br	35	$1s^2 2s^2 2p^6 3s^2 3p^6 \mathbf{4s^2} 3d^{10} \mathbf{4p^5}$

Valence Electrons and the Periodic Table

The electron configurations that are listed in Table 2.4 can be grouped in pairs: sodium and potassium both have one valence electron ($n\mathbf{s^1}$); carbon and silicon both have four valence electrons ($n\mathbf{s^2} n\mathbf{p^2}$); and chlorine and bromine both have seven valence electrons ($n\mathbf{s^2} n\mathbf{p^5}$). If we examine the Periodic Table, we see that sodium and potassium are in Group IA, carbon and silicon are both in Group IVA, and chlorine and bromine are both in Group VIIA. If we were to write out the electron configurations of other elements, we would confirm that elements in the same group of the Periodic Table have the same number of valence electrons and that, for Groups IA through VIIA, the number of valence electrons corresponds to the group number (Figure 2.14).

Except for helium, the outermost principal energy level of each of the noble gases has the configuration $n\mathbf{s^2} n\mathbf{p^6}$. These elements can therefore be

Figure 2.14

The first four periods of the Periodic Table, showing the electron configurations of the outermost energy levels.

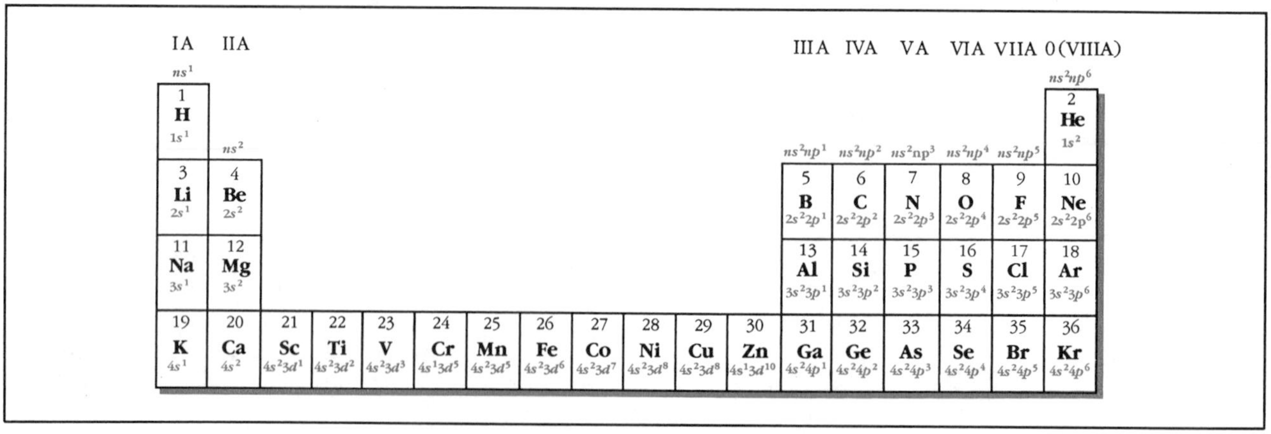

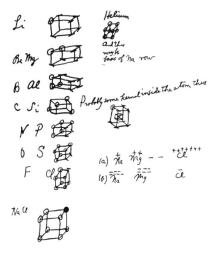

Figure 2.15
Notes made by Gilbert N. Lewis on the arrangement of electrons around the atomic nucleus. In these diagrams, he shows the electrons at corners of cubes.

considered to have eight valence electrons each, and for this reason the noble gas group is often referred to as Group VIIIA.

An alternative view regards the valence level as the level beyond the last one that is completely filled. In the case of the typical noble gas neon, both $2s$ and $2p$ sublevels are filled. Since there are no electrons in the next principal energy level (level 3) neon is said to have no valence electrons and to be in Group 0.

Electron-Dot Formulas

The chemical properties of an element depend largely upon the number of valence electrons. This is why elements possessing the same number of valence electrons and appearing in the same group of the Periodic Table have similar chemical properties. In fact valence electrons are so important to the formation of molecules and ions that we can often use a shorthand system for depicting electron configurations that show only these electrons. First developed by Gilbert N. Lewis, the system is known as the **Lewis formula**, or **electron-dot formula**, method. Its principles are as follows:

1. The symbol for the element is used to represent the nucleus and core (non-valence) electrons.
2. The symbol is assumed to have four sides (as if it were sitting in a square); dots are drawn on each of the four sides to represent the valence electrons.
3. When distributing electrons, the dots are first placed one to a side.
4. No more than two electrons can be placed on any one side.

EXAMPLE   **2.5**   Write an electron-dot formula for a neutral atom of the following elements:
a) nitrogen   b) potassium   c) bromine

SOLUTION   a) Nitrogen, in Group VA, has a total of seven electrons. Two of these are in the first energy level; five are in the outermost (valence) energy level.

$$\cdot \overset{\displaystyle \cdot}{\underset{\displaystyle \cdot}{N}} :$$

b) Potassium is in Group IA, so this atom has one valence electron.

$$\mathbf{K} \cdot$$

c) Bromine is in Group VIIA, so this atom has seven valence electrons.

$$: \overset{\displaystyle \cdot}{\underset{\displaystyle \cdot \cdot}{\mathbf{Br}}} :$$

Ionization Energy

In Section 2.1 we noted that the single electron of hydrogen is in the ground state when it occupies the lowest possible energy level. It will be in an excited state if it absorbs energy and moves to a higher energy level. The same is true of the electrons of other atoms. If sufficient energy is added, an electron can be completely removed from an atom. Normally this will be an electron that is already in the outermost valence energy level. The atom, by definition, is now an ion.

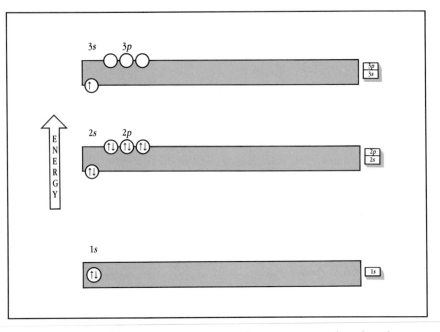

Figure 2.16

An energy level diagram showing the ground-state electron configuration of the neutral sodium atom. The first ionization energy is the quantity of energy needed to remove the 3s electron.

If we take a sodium atom as an example, we can see that the electron that is most easily removed is the single valence electron occupying the 3**s** orbital. The amount of energy required to remove this electron can be measured experimentally using gaseous sodium atoms. This energy is known as the **first ionization energy** of the element.

$$\text{Na}_{(g)} + \text{energy} \longrightarrow \text{Na}^+_{(g)} + e^-$$

An inspection of Figure 2.17 shows that ionization energy varies periodically; the elements that have the highest ionization energies are the noble gases, while the elements with the lowest are the alkali metals. Ionization energy increases going across a period from left to right and decreases going down a group. The elements that have relatively low ionization energies are metals; those with high ionization energies are nonmetals.

As we go down a group, both the nuclear charge and the number of electrons between the nucleus and the valence electrons increase. In addition, the distance between the nucleus and the outermost electrons becomes greater. Each of these factors will have an effect on the magnitude of the ionization energy.

We would expect that an increased nuclear charge would result in a greater attraction for a valence electron, and would cause a higher ionization energy. However, as we go down a group, valence electrons are increasingly shielded from the nuclear charge by a growing number of

Figure 2.17

The first ionization energies of the elements are represented by the height of the bars. The values increase across a period and decrease down a group.

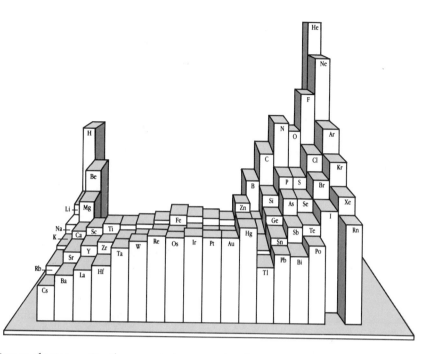

inner electrons. Furthermore, the attraction between a positive charge and a negative charge decreases sharply with distance. Both the shielding effect and the effect of increasing distance between valence electrons and the nucleus, tend to lower the ionization energy. The experimental evidence that ionization energy decreases as we go down a group clearly indicates that the effect of increasing nuclear charge is outweighed by the other two effects.

As we go across a period of the Periodic Table from left to right, the effect of increasing nuclear charge becomes more important. Since all elements in a particular period have the same number of non-valence electrons, there is little change in the shielding effect. In addition, the distance between the nucleus and the valence electrons decreases from left to right. As a result, ionization energies increase as we go across a period from Group IA to Group 0. If we examine Table 2.5, however, we can see that there are some deviations from this trend. For example, both aluminum and sulfur have lower ionization energies than the previous element in the period.

TABLE 2.5	*First Ionization Energies for the Elements of the Third Row of the Periodic Table ($MJ \cdot mol^{-1}$)*						
Na	Mg	Al	Si	P	S	Cl	Ar
0.50	0.74	0.58	0.79	1.01	1.00	1.25	1.52

In order to explain the low ionization energy of aluminum we must remember that electrons in p sublevels are slightly farther from the nucleus, on average, than those in s sublevels. Slightly less energy is therefore required to remove these electrons from such an atom. This means the ionization energy of aluminum $(1s^2 2s^2 2p^6 3s^2 3p^1)$ will be slightly less than that of magnesium $(1s^2 2s^2 2p^6 3s^2)$.

We can account for the ionization energy of sulfur if we compare its electron configuration with that of phosphorus.

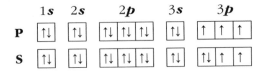

Each of the three $3p$ orbitals of phosphorus contains a single electron. All three $3p$ electrons are spinning in the same direction. This configuration, in which the sublevel is half-filled, is especially stable, and a relatively large amount of energy is therefore required to remove an electron. The result is that the ionization energy for sulfur is lower than that for phosphorus.

TABLE 2.6 *Factors that Affect Ionization Energy*
Nuclear charge. Ionization energy increases with increasing nuclear charge.
Shielding effect. Ionization energy decreases as the number of electrons between the nucleus and the valence electrons increases.
Radius. Ionization energy decreases as the distance between the nucleus and the valence electrons increases.
Sublevel. Less energy is required to remove an electron from a p sublevel than from an s sublevel. Additional energy is required to remove an electron from a half-filled sublevel.

Multiple Ionization Energies

If an atom that has already lost one electron absorbs more energy, other electrons will become excited. If this energy is sufficient, further electrons may be removed. The energy required to remove a second electron from an atom is called the **second ionization energy**, the amount to remove a third electron, the **third ionization energy**, and so on.

When one electron is removed from an element, and a positive ion is formed, the remaining electrons become more firmly held. This is because the nucleus of the atom, with one fewer electron to attract, can exert a greater net force on those that remain. As a result the second ionization energy for any element would be higher than the first.

Electron Affinity

Electrons may not only be lost from an atom, they may also be gained. The energy released when a neutral gaseous atom gains an additional electron is known as the **electron affinity**. However, this quantity is much more difficult to measure experimentally than the ionization energy, so data are somewhat unreliable. What the data show is that metal elements have very little attraction for additional electrons, while nonmetal elements (except for the noble gases) have high electron affinities. In general then, elements that have low ionization energies also have low electron affinities; those whose ionization energy is high also have high electron affinities.

The trends in electron affinities can be explained in much the same way as the trends in ionization energy. The electron affinity will be high if the gain of an electron or electrons results in an ion with an electron configuration that is of lower energy than the neutral atom. In the case of the halogens (Group VIIA), for example, the gain of one electron will produce an ion with a more stable noble-gas electron configuration. As we go down the halogen group, the shielding effect becomes larger and the distance of the valence electrons from the nucleus becomes greater. The result is that there is less attraction for the added electron as we move towards the bottom of the group. The electron affinity consequently becomes lower as we move from fluorine to iodine.

Electronegativity

A further quantity known as electronegativity was introduced by the American scientist Linus Pauling, winner of the Nobel Prize for Chemistry in 1954. Unlike ionization energy and electron affinity, which can be measured directly from individual atoms, this quantity is a relative measure based on a variety of experimental results.

The **electronegativity** of an element is a measure of the ability of an atom in a molecule to attract shared electron pairs to itself. Electronegativity is a different idea from electron affinity. It is concerned with comparing the electron-attracting properties of elements when they are competing for the same electrons rather than with the energy involved in the capture of an isolated electron by a neutral atom. Different chemists have used different criteria to devise scales of electronegativity; Figure 2.18 shows Pauling's values for the main group elements. Note that the values are shown without units.

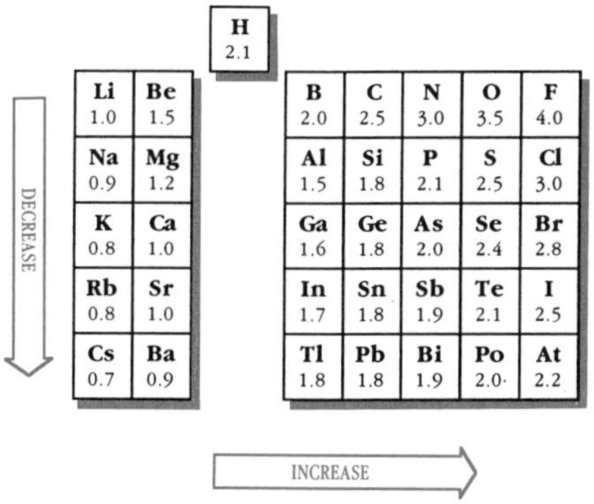

Electronegativities vary in much the same way as ionization energies. The values increase going across a period from left to right, and decrease going down a group.

Bonding Types, Ionization Energy, and Electronegativity

A knowledge of ionization energies and electronegativities is very useful when we wish to consider what type of bonding (metallic, ionic, or

Figure 2.18
Electronegativity values for the elements in the main groups of the Periodic Table, as assigned by Linus Pauling.

covalent) is likely to take place between any two atoms. In fact we can conveniently group bonding types according to the magnitudes of these quantities.

TABLE 2.7 *Bonding Types*			
		Second Atom	
		Low Electronegativity and Low Ionization Energy	High Electronegativity and High Ionization Energy
First Atom	Low Electronegativity and Low Ionization Energy	Metallic	Ionic
	High Electronegativity and High Ionization Energy	Ionic	Covalent

1. **Metallic bonding** is likely to occur when both atoms have low ionization energies and low electronegativities.
2. Predominantly **ionic bonding** is likely to occur when one atom has a low ionization energy and low electronegativity while the other has a high ionization energy and high electronegativity.
3. Predominantly **covalent bonding** is likely to occur when both atoms have high electronegativities and high ionization energies.

QUESTIONS

5. Write an electron-dot formula for a neutral atom of each of these elements:
   a) oxygen   b) silicon   c) calcium
6. Explain why the second element in each of the following pairs has the lower first ionization energy.
   a) sodium, rubidium   b) chlorine, sodium   c) argon, potassium
7. What type of bonding is most likely to occur between the following pairs of atoms? Give reasons for your answer.
   a) potassium and bromine   c) aluminum and aluminum
   b) chlorine and chlorine   d) carbon and oxygen

Metallic Bonding

2.3   Bonds formed between elements involve either the loss, gain, or sharing of valence electrons. Metal atoms have low ionization energies and low electronegativities. This means that they can *lose* electrons easily, forming positive ions, but are unlikely to *gain* electrons to form negative ions.

The simplest model we can construct for metallic bonding shows the metal as a regular array of positive metal ions, packed closely together like marbles in a box. The valence electrons are no longer restricted to a single atom, but are **delocalized**, forming a "sea" of electrons that holds the metal ions together. The delocalized electrons are mobile and are able to move throughout the metal structure.

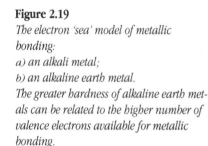 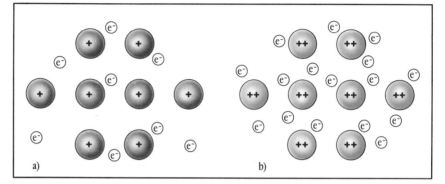

Figure 2.19

The electron 'sea' model of metallic bonding:
a) an alkali metal;
b) an alkaline earth metal.
The greater hardness of alkaline earth metals can be related to the higher number of valence electrons available for metallic bonding.

This model accounts for many of the physical properties of metals. For example, a metal can be bent, hammered out of shape, or stretched because the atoms are not restricted to one position by a fixed bond. The positive ions roll past one another quite easily under pressure: the sea of electrons moving with them preserves the bonding.

The electrons in this sea can move from one end of a piece of metal to the other. Metals, therefore, are good electrical and heat conductors. Heat is simply motion at the atomic or molecular level. If one end of a metal rod is heated, the positive metal ions at that end start to vibrate more rapidly. As this vibration is transmitted to ions nearby, heat is conducted through the rod. The mobile electrons are able to transmit the heat energy through the material very rapidly.

Our model also accounts for the characteristic shiny surfaces of metals. When light strikes a metal, surface valence electrons absorb energy and oscillate back and forth with the same frequency as the incident light. The oscillating electrons then re-emit the energy as light waves of exactly the same frequency. Thus we see the emitted light as a reflection of the original.

We should note of course that not all metals are the same. All have different melting points, and some are much harder than others and exhibit greater strength. The alkali metals, for example, may be easily cut with a knife, while many of the transition elements, such as chromium and nickel, are very hard and tough. Clearly the atoms of some metals are held in place much more firmly than others. If we compare the hardness of many different metals, it becomes apparent that this property is related to the number of valence electrons that are available for bonding. The alkaline earth metals have two valence electrons and are harder than the alkali metals, which have only one. The transition elements are the hardest of the metals because the electrons contained in the *d* orbitals are also delocalized.

Metal Crystal Structures

In our model of metallic bonding we picture the metal atoms to be closely packed in neat, repeating layers. Such an arrangement is called a **crystal lattice**. When we examine these lattices, we find they consist of repeated patterns, much as a wall is made up by the stacking of bricks. The smallest packing unit for a crystal is called a **unit cell**. Fortunately, there are only a few common ways of packing atoms (and molecules and ions) together.

The simplest unit cell is constructed by placing a second layer of atoms directly over the first (Figure 2.20). This **simple cubic packing** is extremely rare for metals, but as we will see, it is important for ionic compounds.

Figure 2.20

Simple cubic packing:
a) the first layer of atoms; the next layer is placed directly over the first;
b) the arrangement of atoms;
c) a cubic unit of the crystal lattice.

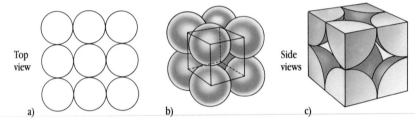

Simple cubic packing leaves large empty spaces between the atoms. If the second layer is placed over the spaces in the first layer, this produces a more compact arrangement. The third layer is then placed over the spaces in the second layer, but also directly over the first layer (Figure 2.21). This **body-centred cubic** arrangement is found in many metals, such as sodium and iron.

Figure 2.21

Body-centred cubic packing:
a) the upper and lower layers are arranged directly over each other; the middle layer fits between the spaces;
b) the arrangement of atoms;
c) a cubic unit of the crystal lattice.

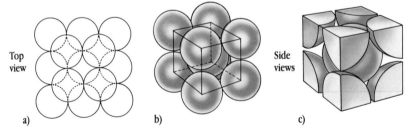

The second common arrangement for metals is even more compact than body-centred cubic. To construct this pattern, we must alter the first layer so that the base consists of four spheres in a square with a fifth sphere in the middle. When subsequent layers are superimposed, the arrangement is the one shown in Figure 2.22. Calcium, copper, and gold are three metals whose atoms assume this **face-centred cubic** pattern (also called cubic close packing).

Figure 2.22
Face-centred cubic packing:
a) the upper and lower layers contain a fifth, central atom; the middle layer occupies the spaces left by these two layers;
b) the arrangement of atoms;
c) a cubic unit of the crystal lattice.

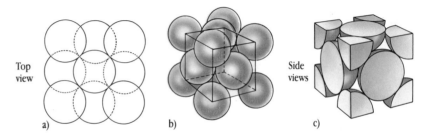

Top view

Side views

a)   b)   c)

The other possible close packing arrangement, called hexagonal close packing, is also common in nature, but it is more difficult to visualize. Unfortunately, there is no easy method of predicting which packing method a particular metallic element will adopt. When we discuss ionic crystals, we will see that the same principles of packing apply to these compounds as well.

Alloys

The physical properties of pure metals can be altered significantly by combining them with other metals (or sometimes with carbon or small quantities of other nonmetals) to form **alloys**. Usually the alloying elements will be added to the pure metal while it is molten.

If the atoms of the added metal are similar in size to those of the original pure metal, they will be dispersed throughout the metal crystals in place of the original atoms when the mixture solidifies. Such alloys are known as **substitutional alloys** (Figure 2.24a).

Sometimes the atoms of the alloying substance are so small that they will fit into the spaces between atoms of the pure metal crystal. Alloys with this structure are called **interstitial alloys** (Figure 2.24b). Steel, for example, is the interstitial alloy produced by adding carbon to iron.

Figure 2.23
The Atomium, in Brussels, Belgium. This enormous representation of face-centred cubic structure was built for the 1958 World's Fair.

Figure 2.24
a) Substitutional alloys.
b) Interstitial alloys.

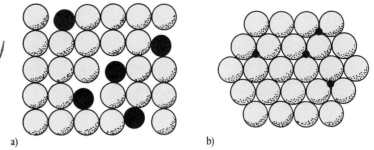

a)   b)

Both types of alloys are usually harder and stronger than pure metals because of two different factors:

1. The added metal may provide additional valence electrons, causing an increase in the hardness and strength of the alloy. This is what happens when small amounts of copper and manganese are added to aluminum to produce the alloy known as "duralumin."

Figure 2.25
Some examples of pewter drinking utensils from the 18th and 19th centuries. This alloy can have a range of compositions with about 85% tin, 5% antimony, and the remainder being copper and zinc.

2. The atoms of the alloying metal, because they are a different size, may interfere with the slipping of layers of atoms within the metal. Brass, an alloy of copper and zinc, is considerably harder than pure copper of this reason. The degree of hardness increases with the amount of zinc added. In the case of steel, the dissolved carbon atoms make it more difficult for layers of iron atoms to move smoothly over one another, thereby increasing the hardness of the material.

TABLE 2.8   *Common Alloys*

Name	% Composition	Properties	Uses
brass	Cu 70–85, Zn 15–30	harder than pure copper	plumbing fixtures
bronze	Cu 70–95, Sn 1–18, Zn 0–25	harder than brass corrosion resistant	machinery, statues
dental amalgam	Hg 50–55, Ag 23–35, Sn 1–15, Zn 1–20, Cu 5–30	soft on mixing, hardens quickly	dental fillings
duralumin	Al 94.4, Cu 4.0, Mg 0.8, Mn 0.8	lightweight, durable, harder & stronger than pure aluminum	stuctures, aircraft bodies & other vehicles
gold, 18-carat	Au 75, Ag 10–20, Cu 5–15	harder than pure 24-carat gold	jewellery
nickel coins	Ni 75, Cu 25	corrosion resistant	coinage
solder	Pb 35–70, Sn 30–65	low melting point	electronic parts & plumbing
steel	Fe 99, C 1	hard, durable	steel structures, rails, etc.
steel, stainless	Fe 65–85, Cr 12–20, Ni 2–15, Mn 1–2, C 0.1–1, Si 0.5–1,	corrosion resistant, hard	chemical equipment, cutlery, tools
sterling silver	Ag 92.5, Cu 7.5	durable, harder than pure silver	silverware & jewellery

The properties of alloys can be very different from those of pure metals, and can change markedly with small changes in composition. Alloys are very important materials and are widely used in almost all industries (Table 2.8). In fact most of the metals in use today are alloys rather than pure metals. Consequently, there is a great deal of research and development in an effort to understand more fully the structure and properties of alloys, and to develop new alloys with physical properties tailored to specific purposes.

Ionic Bonding   ## 2.4

A very large number of compounds are formed between the metal elements, which have low ionization energies, and the nonmetal elements (except the noble gases), which have high electronegativities. These compounds are formed when the valence electrons are removed from a metal atom and are added to the valence energy level of a nonmetal. The result is that the metal atoms form positive ions that have completely empty valence levels, while the nonmetal atoms form negative ions whose valence energy levels contain eight electrons. In either case the ion will have the same stable electron configuration as one of the noble gases.

We can illustrate this process by considering the reaction between sodium metal and chlorine gas, which results in the formation of the salt sodium chloride:

$$2\ Na_{(s)}\ +\ Cl_{2(g)}\ \longrightarrow\ 2\ NaCl_{(s)}$$

Each sodium atom loses an electron, forming a sodium ion:

$$Na\cdot\ \longrightarrow\ [Na]^+\ +\ e^-$$

Each chlorine atom gains an electron, forming a chloride ion:

$$:\!\overset{\cdot\cdot}{\underset{\cdot\cdot}{Cl}}\!\cdot\ +\ e^-\ \longrightarrow\ \left[:\!\overset{\cdot\cdot}{\underset{\cdot\cdot}{Cl}}\!:\right]^-$$

Figure 2.26
Ionic crystals of sodium chloride magnified 17 times.

Positively-charged sodium ions are attracted to negatively-charged chloride ions, and form solid sodium chloride:

$$[Na]^+\ +\ \left[:\!\overset{\cdot\cdot}{\underset{\cdot\cdot}{Cl}}\!:\right]^-\ \longrightarrow\ [Na]^+\!\left[:\!\overset{\cdot\cdot}{\underset{\cdot\cdot}{Cl}}\!:\right]^-$$

The electron configuration of the sodium ion is now $1s^2 2s^2 2p^6$, which is the same as that of neon. The sodium is said to be **isoelectronic** with neon. The electron configuration of the chloride ion is now $1s^2 2s^2 2p^6 3s^2 3p^6$, which is the same as that of argon, showing that the chloride ion is isoelectronic with argon.

When magnesium burns in oxygen to form magnesium oxide, the magnesium atoms must each lose two valence electrons to achieve the same stable electron configuration as the neon atom. Oxygen atoms must each gain two electrons to form a similar stable configuration.

Figure 2.27
The Montreal apartment block Habitat has a cube-on-cube crystalline regularity.

$$\cdot Mg\cdot\ +\ \cdot\overset{\cdot\cdot}{\underset{\cdot\cdot}{O}}\!:\ \longrightarrow\ [Mg]^{2+}\!\left[:\!\overset{\cdot\cdot}{\underset{\cdot\cdot}{O}}\!:\right]^{2-}$$

Notice that all the electrons lost by the metal atom must be gained by the nonmetal atom.

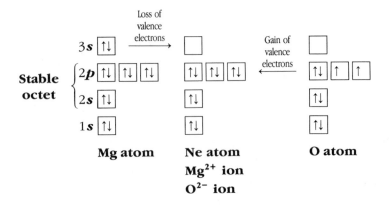

Figure 2.28
When magnesium loses its valence electrons and oxygen gains two valence electrons, both acquire the stable electron configuration of neon.

EXAMPLE   *2.6*   a) Predict the formula of the compound formed between magnesium and nitrogen.
b) Draw the electron-dot formula of this compound.

SOLUTION   a) Magnesium will have two valence electrons since it is in Group IIA of the Periodic Table. Nitrogen, which is in Group VA, will have five valence electrons. Each magnesium atom will lose two electrons to form a Mg^{2+} ion. Each nitrogen atom will gain three electrons to form a N^{3-} ion. In order that the number of electrons lost by the magnesium atoms is equal to the number gained by the nitrogen, two nitrogen atoms are required for every three magnesium atoms. The unit formula for magnesium nitride is therefore Mg_3N_2.

b) By forming Mg^{2+}, a magnesium atom empties its valence level. By gaining three electrons and forming N^{3-}, a nitrogen atom fills its valence level. The electron-dot formula for magnesium nitride will therefore be

$$[Mg]^{2+} \left[:\!\overset{..}{\underset{..}{N}}\!: \right]^{3-} [Mg]^{2+} \left[:\!\overset{..}{\underset{..}{N}}\!: \right]^{3-} [Mg]^{2+}$$

QUESTIONS

8. Write the electron configuration for each of the following:
   a) Mg^{2+} b) F^- c) Al^{3+} d) S^{2-}

9. Write chemical formulas and electron-dot formulas for the compounds formed between these elements:
   a) calcium and oxygen
   b) sodium and fluorine
   c) aluminum and oxygen

10. Which of the following pairs are isoelectronic?

a) F^- and Mg^{2+}

b) Al^{3+} and P^{3-}

c) Li^+ and He

Crystal Packing of Ions

2.5

If we examine an ionic compound, we find that the ions are not located randomly, but are arranged in a highly-ordered crystal structure. Solid sodium chloride, for example, consists of a three-dimensional array of positive and negative ions. The equal numbers of sodium and chloride ions are arranged so that each ion is as close to as many ions of the opposite charge as possible.

Just as in the case of the metals, the ions that make up a crystal of sodium chloride, or any other ionic salt, can be considered to be spheres that are packed together as closely as possible. The difference between the structures of ionic salts and those of metals is that the salts are made of two different types of ions of opposite charges and usually of quite different sizes. In addition, there is no sea of electrons.

Atomic and Ionic Sizes

If we examine the elements in a particular row of the Periodic Table, we find a gradual decrease in atomic size as we move from left to right. We can account for this trend if we think carefully about the atomic structures and electron configurations of the different elements. Sodium and chlorine are at opposite ends of the third row (Figure 2.29). Both have third principal energy levels that are partly filled: the electron configuration of the outermost energy level of sodium is $3s^1$, that of chlorine is $3s^2 3p^5$.

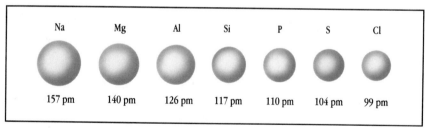

Na	Mg	Al	Si	P	S	Cl
157 pm	140 pm	126 pm	117 pm	110 pm	104 pm	99 pm

Figure 2.29

Atomic radii decrease as we move from left to right across a period. Radii are measured in picometres (pm).

The sodium nucleus contains 11 protons; the nucleus of chlorine contains 17 protons. The valence electrons of chlorine are therefore attracted by six more protons and are held more strongly. The chlorine atom, as a consequence, is smaller than the sodium atom.

When a metal atom has formed a positive ion, the protons in the nucleus of the atom have fewer electrons to attract. The result is that these electrons are attracted closer to the nucleus and the ion becomes smaller than the atom. *Sodium ions,* for example, have only half the diameter of *sodium*

Superconductors

In 1911 a Dutch scientist, Heinke Omnes, noticed that when metals are cooled to near absolute zero, they lose all resistance to electricity, and become almost perfect electrical conductors, or *superconductors*. Thirty years later, scientists discovered alloys of the element niobium that became superconductors at 15 K ($-258\,°C$) — a temperature that could be reached by cooling with liquid helium. The discovery, however, had only limited practical use because of the high cost of the liquid gas. Although research continued, most researchers came to believe that the superconductors could not exist at higher temperatures.

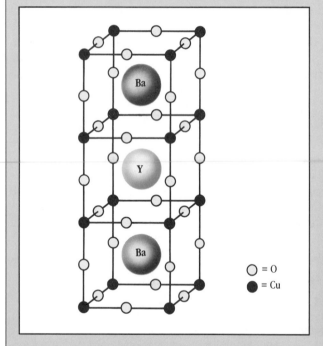

Figure 2.30
The ion packing in a superconductor.

There was a great deal of excitement in 1986, when J. Georg Bednorz and K. Alex Müller, working for IBM in Zurich, Switzerland, discovered that a complex oxide of copper, barium, and lanthanum became a superconducting material at 35 K. By the end of that year many researchers were preparing and testing a variety of oxides and early in 1987 a material was discovered that became a superconductor when cooled to 98 K using inexpensive liquid nitrogen. Bednorz and Müller were awarded the Nobel Prize in 1987, in recognition of their breakthrough.

Although there are many applications for materials that are superconductors when cooled by liquid nitrogen, a great deal of research is now taking place to find materials that are superconductors at room temperature. Such materials would revolutionize many areas of technology.

A great deal of energy is lost when electricity is transmitted over long distances between generating plant and consumer. Transmission through a superconducting material would produce enormous savings. The use of superconducting materials in the construction of computer chips would speed up computers a hundred, maybe a thousand, times. Transportation could be revolutionized by the application of the unique magnetic properties of superconductors. A magnet close to a superconductor induces an electric current in the material. This in turn produces an opposite magnetic field, and thus the material floats just above the magnet. Such a system is already in use in Japan to lift an entire train off the tracks and allow it to move forward on a cushion of air at speeds of up to $500\,km\cdot h^{-1}$.

Figure 2.31
A Japanese prototype train uses a magnetic field to float above the tracks. Superconductors would enhance its efficiency.

The superconductors that have been recently discovered are not expensive materials. In fact small discs of the ceramic material can be prepared in a school laboratory for only a few dollars. The challenge is to find the combination of starting materials that will produce a room-temperature superconductor.

Figure 2.32

a) Positive ions formed by metals are smaller than corresponding neutral atoms.

b) Negative ions formed by nonmetals are larger than corresponding neutral atoms.

atoms. The opposite effect occurs when negative ions are formed from nonmetal atoms. In these cases the nuclear charge must attract an increased number of electrons, and so each is attracted less strongly than in the neutral atom. As well, the additional electrons cause an increase in the forces of repulsion between the negative charges. The result of both of these effects is that the electron cloud expands in size and the negative ions become larger than their parent atoms.

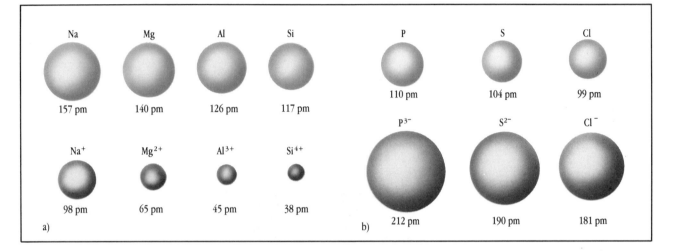

Crystal Structures

In Section 2.3 we saw metal atoms are packed in crystal lattices. The ions in ionic compounds pack in similar lattices. Like metals, the smallest repeating unit is called the unit cell.

Generally, anions are much larger than cations. In ionic compounds then, the arrangement of the ions is usually determined by the packing of the anions. The cations can be considered to fit in the spaces between.

Figure 2.33

The packing of ions in sodium chloride. The small spheres are sodium ions; the large spheres are chloride ions.

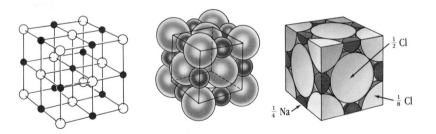

Figure 2.33 shows the structure of common salt, sodium chloride. The larger spheres represent chloride ions, and you can see how their arrangement matches that of the face-centred cube. The sodium ions fit in the spaces between the chloride ions.

In the case of cesium chloride, however, the cations and anions are of similar size. The simple cubic arrangement has very large holes in the centre of the cubes. The chloride ions adopt this simple cubic structure while a cesium cation fits into the centre of each cube (Figure 2.34). Each cesium ion is surrounded by eight chloride ions. Each chloride ion is surrounded by eight cesium ions of the neighbouring unit cells.

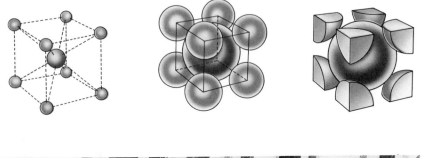

Figure 2.34
The packing of ions in cesium chloride. The larger spheres represent the chloride ions, which make up the cubic structure.

Figure 2.35
The arrangement of ions in the sodium chloride lattice is displayed in the print 'Cubic Space Divisions' by M. C. Escher.

Figure 2.36

The central mechanism of an X-ray crystallography instrument, used to determine the molecular structure of a compound.

The substances we have considered illustrate two fairly common crystal structures. There are many others, however, and they are not always cubic. When greater differences exist between the sizes of the ions making up a compound, when the ratio of positive to negative ions differs from our examples, or when the formulas of compounds are more complex, different crystal structures will result.

Much of what we know about crystal structure has been determined experimentally by **X-ray crystallography**, in which a sample of a crystalline compound is placed in the path of a beam of X-rays. The sample may be a single crystal or a "powder" of many very small crystals. Some of the X-rays are **reflected** by different planes of ions within the crystals; others are diffracted, or bent, as they pass between layers of ions. The emerging X-rays interfere with each other to produce a **diffraction pattern**. Using modern computer methods, we can determine the arrangement of atoms in the crystal.

Figure 2.37

This computer-generated representation of trinitrotoluene (TNT) was found using X-ray crystallography.

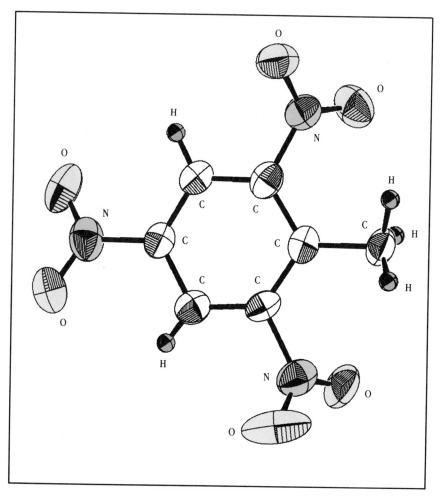

Dorothy Crowfoot Hodgkin — Crystallographer

Dorothy Crowfoot Hodgkin was born in Eygpt in 1910, where her British father was an inspector for the Ministry of Education. By the age of ten she was already keenly interested in chemistry and began to study the shapes and symmetry of the crystals she grew from simple salt solutions. At her small country high school in Suffolk, England, she was allowed to study chemistry with the boys — something almost unheard of at the time. Eventually she went to Oxford University to study for a degree in chemistry, spending even her vacations at work in the laboratories.

When Hodgkin completed her degree, she joined the Cavendish laboratory at Cambridge University and became interested in the application of crystallography to complex organic molecules. She was only 23 years old when she and fellow crystallographer J.D. Bernal published the first X-ray diffraction photograph of a protein. Soon afterward Oxford University gave her a lectureship in chemistry and later awarded her a doctorate. She married, continued her research, and by the time she was 32 she was directing a team that was using X-ray crystallography to determine the structure of penicillin; four years later they succeeded. Hodgkin, who by now had three children, moved on to determine the structure of vitamin B_{12} — a major project that began in 1948 and took nine years to complete.

In the midst of all her research she continued as director of Oxford's crystallography laboratory, receiving many honorary degrees and travelling widely to give lectures.

Figure 2.38
Dorothy Crowfoot Hodgkin (1910-) was awarded the Nobel Prize for the determination of the structure of vitamin B_{12}.

Covalent Bonding

2.6 Elements with high electronegativities can only form negative ions in chemical reactions if the ionization energy of the other reactant is low. If the second element also has a high electronegativity, and a correspondingly high ionization energy, ion formation cannot take place because there is insufficient energy available in the process to produce positive ions from either element. Instead, atoms that both have high electronegativities bond by *sharing* electrons. The shared electrons are considered to belong simultaneously to the valence energy levels of both atoms. A shared pair of electrons constitutes a **covalent bond**.

We can illustrate this process by considering the bonding between two chlorine atoms combining to form a chlorine molecule. Each chlorine atom has the electron configuration $1s^2 2s^2 2p^6 3s^2 3p^5$. There are thus seven valence electrons, represented by the electron dot formula:

$$:\ddot{\text{Cl}}\cdot$$

When two chlorine atoms form a bond, each atom contributes one electron to the bond; the shared pair of electrons occupy a volume of space that lies mostly between the two nuclei. Since the shared pair of electrons belong simultaneously to both atoms, each can be considered to have eight electrons in its valence energy level. That energy level is now filled. We can represent the formation of the bond by using an electron-dot formula:

$$:\ddot{\text{Cl}}\cdot + \cdot\ddot{\text{Cl}}: \longrightarrow :\ddot{\text{Cl}}:\ddot{\text{Cl}}:$$

We can also use a solid line to represent the bonding pair of electrons in the molecule. In this case the chlorine molecule would be written as follows:

$$:\ddot{\text{Cl}}-\ddot{\text{Cl}}:$$

The Octet Rule

By forming a covalent bond, each atom in a chlorine molecule acquires a filled valence energy level. Other nonmetal elements bond in the same way. In fact, as a rule, the atoms in almost all covalently-bonded species acquire, by sharing, a filled valence energy level. For elements other than hydrogen, this valence level contains eight electrons — an "octet" of electrons. For this reason the rule, developed by the same Gilbert N. Lewis who invented the electron-dot formula, is often referred to as the **octet rule**:

> **Atoms other than hydrogen tend to form bonds until they are surrounded by eight valence electrons.**

The octet rule is a very useful one to remember when we are writing formulas for molecules. However, the rule does have its limitations. For example, the elements in the third and subsequent rows of the Periodic Table form compounds whose valence energy levels contain *more than* eight electrons. We shall deal with these compounds after we have considered the electron-dot formulas of molecules that do obey the octet rule. In order for the octet rule to be obeyed, a nonmetal element will normally form a number of covalent bonds equal to

> **8 – the number of valence electrons**

When two covalent bonds exist between a pair of atoms, the bonds are usually referred to as a **double bond**. Double bonds are quite common in covalently-bonded compounds. Sometimes two atoms will need to share six electrons and form a **triple bond**.

EXAMPLE   2.7   Draw an electron-dot formula to represent the formation of a nitrogen molecule, N_2, from two nitrogen atoms.

SOLUTION   Nitrogen is in Group VA of the Periodic Table, therefore it has five valence electrons:

$$:\overset{\cdot}{\underset{\cdot}{N}}\cdot$$

This leaves it with three electrons less than the noble-gas configuration. Thus three covalent bonds are expected.

$$:\overset{\cdot}{\underset{\cdot}{N}}\cdot + \cdot\overset{\cdot}{\underset{\cdot}{N}}: \longrightarrow :N:::N: \quad \text{or} \quad :N\equiv N:$$

A triple bond exists between the two nitrogen atoms that form a nitrogen molecule.

Polar Covalent Bonds

The valence electrons that make up a covalent bond between atoms of the same element will be shared equally, since such atoms are identical and have equal attractions for electrons. When compounds are formed between different elements, with different electronegativities, the bonding valence electrons will be attracted more towards one atom than the other. The difference in electronegativity between the two elements will indicate which atom has the greater share of the bonding electrons.

When a molecule of water is formed, the two hydrogen atoms each share a pair of valence electrons with the oxygen atom.

$$\text{H}\cdot + \cdot\overset{\cdot\cdot}{\underset{\cdot\cdot}{O}}\cdot + \cdot\text{H} \longrightarrow \text{H}:\overset{\cdot\cdot}{\underset{\cdot\cdot}{O}}:\text{H}$$

If we examine the electronegativity values contained in Figure 2.18, we see that hydrogen has been assigned the value 2.1, while oxygen has been assigned the value 3.5. Remember that the electronegativity of an element is simply a measure of its tendency to attract shared electron pairs from other elements to which it is bonded. The higher the assigned electronegativity value, the greater the attraction the element has for shared electrons. Since the value for oxygen is almost double that for hydrogen, it follows that oxygen atoms have a considerable tendency to attract shared electrons away from hydrogen atoms. The bonds between oxygen and hydrogen atoms in water thus consist of pairs of electrons that are more strongly attracted toward the oxygen atom. Within the molecule, the oxygen atom acquires a partial negative charge, and the hydrogen atoms a partial positive charge.

$$\overset{\delta^+}{\text{H}}-\overset{\overset{\delta^-}{\cdot\cdot}}{\underset{\cdot\cdot}{\text{O}}}-\overset{\delta^+}{\text{H}}$$

The Oxygen Problem

Electron-dot structures are extremely useful for understanding the concept of covalent bonding. However, experimental evidence for bonding in some compounds cannot be satisfactorily explained by the rules governing electron-dot formulas. We cannot depict oxygen, for example, by an electron-dot structure that correctly reflects the observed properties of the molecule.

A covalent bond vibrates at an energy level that corresponds to the infrared portion of the spectrum. From studying a large number of compounds, it is known that the stronger the bond, the shorter the corresponding wavelength. Spectroscopic studies on the oxygen molecule have shown that the energy of the bond between the two oxygen atoms matches that of a double bond.

Only molecules containing unpaired electrons will be attracted by a magnetic field. If we pour liquid oxygen between the poles of a very strong magnet, we find that the oxygen sticks to the pole caps. Other more sophisticated measurements confirm that each oxygen molecule contains two unpaired electrons.

When we attempt to construct an electron-dot structure for the oxygen molecule, we find it is impossible to satisfy all our requirements. We are faced with two alternatives: we can draw a structure with a double bond, but no unpaired electrons; or, we can draw a structure with two unpaired electrons and a single bond.

$$:\ddot{O}::\ddot{O}: \qquad :\dot{O}:\dot{O}:$$

This does not mean that electron-dot structures are useless. They are really the only simple way to introduce bonding concepts. Just because the model will not work in one case does not give us reason to throw out the whole concept. We can explain the bonding in the oxygen molecule by extending the probability model of the atom to molecules. This involves the construction of molecular orbitals. When we do this for the oxygen molecule, the representation matches perfectly our observed properties of oxygen. Unfortunately, the complexity of the model makes it of little use in conveying simple ideas of bonding.

Figure 2.39

a) Liquid nitrogen is poured between the poles of a strong magnet. It flows straight through.

b) Liquid oxygen is poured between the poles of a strong magnet. It is held in the magnetic field.

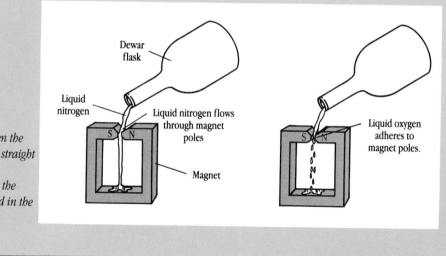

Because of this partial charge, the bonds are said to be **polar covalent**. As an alternative, we can say that the bond has **ionic character**. The degree of ionic character depends upon the difference in electronegativity between the two atoms that form the bond.

Electron-Dot Formulas of More Complex Molecules

Drawing electron-dot formulas of more complex molecules is not particularly difficult, but to avoid mistakes it will help to adopt the following approach:

1. Identify the central atom (or atoms) in the molecule; that is, identify the atom to which all of the other atoms are bonded. Often, the central atom will be the one that is least electronegative — for example, silicon in silicon tetrafluoride (SiF_4), or sulfur in sulfonyl chloride ($SOCl_2$). But we must exercise caution here because there are many exceptions. In compounds that contain hydrogen, for example, the hydrogen is never the central atom, even though it may often be the least electronegative.
2. Draw an electron-dot formula for the molecule, joining atoms to the central atom with single bonds — that is, with one shared pair of electrons. Solid lines may be used to represent these bonds.
3. Determine the number of bonds in the molecule by comparing the total number of valence electrons in the molecule with the number that would be present if each atom in the molecule independently acquired a filled valence level. Each pair of electrons in this difference represents a bond.
4. Add to the electron-dot formula any double or triple bonds that may be required to give the number of bonds indicated in Step 3.
5. Complete the structure by drawing in dots to represent the remaining unshared electron pairs in the molecule. Remember that hydrogen atoms require only two electrons to fill the valence energy level.

EXAMPLE   2.8   How many bonds must be present in a sulfur dioxide, SO_2, molecule?

SOLUTION   Both sulfur and oxygen have six valence electrons. The total number of electrons in SO_2 is therefore 18. If each of the two oxygen atoms and the sulfur atom independently acquired an octet of electrons, the total would be 24. The difference between 18 and 24 is 6. This means there must be *three bonds* in the molecule.

EXAMPLE   2.9   Draw an electron-dot formula for carbon tetrachloride, CCl_4.

SOLUTION   1. Since carbon is less electronegative than chlorine (Figure 2.18) we can consider that carbon is the central atom in the carbon tetrachloride molecule.
2. The structure of the molecule is therefore

3. Each chlorine atom has seven valence electrons; the carbon atom has four. Therefore, the total number of valence electrons in the molecule is 32. If each atom had a full octet of valence electrons, the total would be 40. The difference of eight electrons corresponds to the presence of four bonds in the molecule.

4. The structure we have drawn satisfies this requirement. No further bonds need to be added.

5. We can now distribute the remaining valence electrons so that each of the atoms is surrounded by an octet of electrons.

EXAMPLE   *2.10*   Draw an electron-dot formula for carbon dioxide, CO_2.

     SOLUTION   1. Carbon is less electronegative than oxygen, and is the central atom.

2. The structure of the molecule is therefore

$$O—C—O$$

3. The total number of valence electrons is 16; and, if each atom independently acquired a complete octet, the number would be 24. The difference of eight electrons indicates the presence of four bonds.

$$O=C=O$$

4. We can now distribute the remaining valence electrons so that each of the atoms is surrounded by an octet of electrons.

Coordinate Covalent Bonds

We have up to this point drawn electron-dot formulas for a number of molecules in which each of the combining atoms contributes one electron to each bond. Sometimes, however, a bond will be formed when both of the electrons are contributed by one atom. Such a bond is called a **coordinate covalent bond**. The idea of the coordinate covalent bond was first suggested by British chemist Nevil Sidgwick in 1923. For example, the compound nitrogen trifluoride, NF_3, would have this electron-dot formula:

$$\begin{array}{c} :\!\ddot{F}\!: \\ :\!\ddot{F}\!:\!\ddot{N}\!: \\ :\!\ddot{F}\!: \end{array}$$

We can see that nitrogen forms three covalent bonds, one with each of the fluorine atoms. A single pair of non-bonding electrons is present on

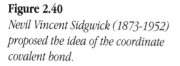

Figure 2.40
Nevil Vincent Sidgwick (1873-1952) proposed the idea of the coordinate covalent bond.

the nitrogen atom, which now has a complete octet. A further atom could be bonded to the central nitrogen atom provided that both of the electrons forming the bond came from the nitrogen. We can consider this to be the case in nitrosyl trifluoride, NOF_3.

The difference between the total number of valence electrons in NOF_3 and the number that each atom would possess if it independently acquired an octet is eight. There are therefore four bonds in the molecule. We would draw the electron-dot formula for NOF_3 as

In this molecule the bond between the nitrogen atom and the oxygen atom is a coordinate covalent bond; both of the electrons forming the bond are provided by the nitrogen atom.

We may continue to replace the bonding pairs of electrons in the molecule by solid lines. Sometimes when this is done, the coordinate covalent bond is represented by an arrow to indicate the contribution of an entire electron pair to a bond. However, once the coordinate bond is formed, it is no different from any other covalent bond. We will therefore represent both ordinary and coordinate covalent bonds by solid lines between the bonding atoms.

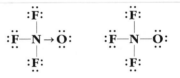

EXAMPLE　　*2.11*　Draw an electron-dot formula for sulfur trioxide, SO_3.

SOLUTION　　1. Sulfur is less electronegative than oxygen. The sulfur atom will therefore be the central atom.

2. The structure of the molecule is therefore

3. Each of the four atoms contributes six valence electrons to the structure. The total is 24. If each atom were to independently acquire an octet of electrons, the total would be 32. The difference of eight indicates that there are four bonds in the molecule.

4. We therefore need to add one further bond between the central sulfur atom and one of the oxygen atoms.

5. We can now distribute the remaining electrons so that each atom acquires a filled valence energy level.

One of the bonds between sulfur and oxygen is a double bond, the other two are coordinate covalent bonds.

Resonance Structures

In the electron-dot formula for sulfur trioxide, any one of the three oxygen atoms in the molecule could have been bonded to the sulfur atom with a double bond. We could have drawn three electron-dot formulas that were identical except for the position of the double bond. Alternative structures such as these are sometimes referred to as **resonance** structures. There are a number of molecules like sulfur trioxide where it is possible to draw more than one electron-dot formula while leaving the atoms themselves in the same positions. These structures differ only in the position of the double (or triple) bonds. The true structure of such molecules is believed to lie between those of the different resonance forms. In the case of sulfur trioxide, for example, all three of the sulfur-oxygen bonds have been found by experiment to be identical. The pair of electrons constituting the double bond is actually delocalized over all three bonds.

Electron-Dot Formulas of Polyatomic Ions

Many ions are not simply charged atoms, but are charged *groups* of atoms. Two familiar, negatively-charged groups are the sulfate ion, SO_4^{2-} and the nitrate ion, NO_3^-. The atoms within the charged group are bonded together covalently. The additional electrons that give the ions their overall negative charge are included in the electron pool, shared between the individual atoms. If we wish to represent these ions with electron-dot formulas, we must include these additional electrons in the computed total number of valence electrons. The negative charge is possessed by the entire ion, and is represented by writing the electron-dot formula inside square brackets; the net charge is written outside the brackets as a superscript.

_2.12_ Draw an electron-dot formula for the sulfate ion, SO_4^{2-}.

SOLUTION 1. The sulfur atom is most likely to be the central atom.
2. The structure of the ion is therefore

3. Each of the five atoms contributes six valence electrons to the structure, giving a total of 30. We must, however, add a further two electrons because the ion has a charge of -2. The total number of electrons available to the structure is therefore 32. If each of the five atoms independently acquired an octet of valence electrons, the total would be 40. The difference of eight electrons represents the presence of four bonds in the ion.
4. No further bonds need to be added to the skeletal structure. We can now add the remaining electrons so that each of the atoms acquires an octet.

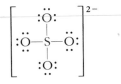

Each of the four bonds is a coordinate covalent bond. Since sulfur, with six valence electrons, can form only three coordinate covalent bonds, the electron pair forming the fourth must result from the addition of two electrons to the negatively charged ion. We should remember, however, that once the ion is formed, all the electrons are identical. Also, all single bonds, regular or coordinate, are the same.

The ammonium ion, NH_4^+, is an example of a positively-charged polyatomic ion, the overall positive charge resulting from the loss of an electron from the pool of valence electrons. We must take this loss into account when writing the structural formula.

We can imagine that the ammonium ion is formed when an ammonia molecule, NH_3, reacts with a hydrogen ion, H^+. When the positively-charged hydrogen ion bonds to the nitrogen atom, it brings no electrons with it. The bond is a coordinate covalent bond in which both electrons originate from the lone pair of electrons on the nitrogen atom. Once formed, this bond is identical with all three of the other bonds in the ion.

The entire ion possesses the positive charge.

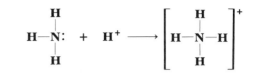

Expansion of the Valence Level

Elements of the third and subsequent rows of the Periodic Table are able to form molecules in which the central atom is surrounded by more than the normal octet of valence electrons. The expansion is possible because the elements make use of unfilled **d** orbitals for bonding. In the case of phosphorus and sulfur, if sufficient energy is available in the bonding process, some of the valence electrons may absorb energy and become excited into the vacant $3d$ orbitals. In this way each of the valence electrons may occupy an orbital by itself, and so may form a bond. Phosphorus, which has five valence electrons, may form as many as five bonds; sulfur, which has six, may form as many as six bonds.

A number of the noble gases, from argon through to radon, also have empty **d** orbitals that are close in energy to the valence energy level. Linus Pauling predicted in 1933 that these elements also might form compounds by expanding the valence level. Approximately thirty years later, Neil Bartlett prepared the first compound of xenon — xenon tetrafluoride (XeF_4) — at the University of British Columbia. Since then a number of compounds of krypton and xenon have been produced, further showing that Pauling was right.

Further Exceptions to the Octet Rule

The great majority of molecules and polyatomic ions either obey the octet rule or have central atoms with an expanded valence level. A few, however, do not. These exceptions may be divided into two groups.

Molecules with an Odd Number of Valence Electrons Atoms, ions, and molecules that have orbitals containing single unpaired electrons are attracted by a magnetic field; they are **paramagnetic**. The strength of the attraction is directly proportional to the number of unpaired electrons.

Nitrogen monoxide, NO, and nitrogen dioxide, NO_2, are two molecules that have been found to be paramagnetic. In each case the degree of paramagnetism corresponds to a single unpaired electron. Our electron-dot formulas for these molecules must reflect the experimental data. Indeed if we attempt to draw an electron-dot formula for either of these oxides of nitrogen, we find that the total number of valence electrons in each of the molecules is *odd*.

Valence electrons in NO = 5 + 6 = 11
Valence electrons in NO$_2$ = 5 + 6 + 6 = 17

Figure 2.41

A magnetic susceptibility balance. This sensitive balance can be used to determine if a compound is paramagnetic.

Consequently, it is impossible to draw electron-dot formulas in which each of the atoms obeys the octet rule. No matter how hard we may try, there will always be a single, unpaired electron.

$$:\ddot{N}::\ddot{O}. \quad \text{or} \quad :\ddot{N}::\ddot{O}:$$

Even though the electron-dot formulas do not obey the octet rule, they are consistent with experimental results.

EXAMPLE   *2.13*   Draw an electron-dot formula for nitrogen dioxide, NO_2.

SOLUTION   **1.** Nitrogen, the less electronegative of the two elements, will be the central atom.

2. The structure of the molecule is therefore

$$O—N—O$$

3. Each of the oxygen atoms contributes six valence electrons to the structure; the nitrogen atom contributes five. Therefore, the total number of valence electrons is 17. If each of the atoms independently acquired an octet of valence electrons, the total would be 24. The difference of seven electrons represents the presence of three bonds. Quite clearly, when there is an odd total number of valence electrons in the molecule, we cannot draw a structure that obeys the octet rule.

4. We can draw a number of possible structures for NO_2, each of which has a single, unpaired electron. The following electron-dot formula is consistent with experimental evidence:

$$:\ddot{O}—\dot{N}=\ddot{O}.$$

Molecules with Insufficient Valence Electrons   Beryllium, the first element in Group IIA of the Periodic Table, has only two valence electrons; boron, the first element in Group IIIA, has three. We might expect that these two elements would behave in the same way as other members of their groups and form ionic compounds. However, the ionization energies of the two elements are too high for this to occur. Instead, both form covalent compounds that have a relatively high degree of ionic character.

When these covalent molecules are formed, the beryllium and boron atoms contribute each of their valence electrons to form bonds. Beryllium is thus able to form just two bonds, boron three. Experimental evidence indicates that neither element acquires an octet of electrons as a result of this bonding. Although we can draw electron-dot formulas that obey the octet rule, we must reflect this experimental evidence.

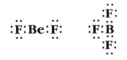

In each case there are too few electrons surrounding the central atom for the octet rule to be obeyed. The molecules are said to be **electron deficient**.

The ionic character of the compounds is reflected in the fact that all of the bonds are *polar*. In beryllium difluoride and boron trifluoride, the fluorine atoms carry a partial negative charge; the central atoms carry a partial positive charge.

QUESTIONS

11. Draw electron-dot formulas to represent the structure of these molecules and ions:
  a) fluorine, F_2
  b) sulfur dichloride, SCl_2
  c) methanal, CH_2O (carbon is the central atom)
  d) the nitrate ion, NO_3^-
  e) phosphorus pentafluoride, PF_5

The Bonding Continuum

2.7

In this chapter we have considered metallic bonding, ionic bonding, and covalent bonding. We have used the relative magnitudes of electronegativity and ionization energy to predict the type of bonding that is most likely to be present in a substance. The magnitudes of these quantities do not change dramatically between one strictly-defined group of elements called metals and a second group called nonmetals. Instead, there is a gradual increase in the magnitude of each going across a period from left to right, and a gradual decrease going down a group. These gradual changes are matched by a gradual change in the type of bonding we find in elements and compounds as we move down and across the Periodic Table.

Bonding in Elements

As we have seen, the metals, lying to the left of the Periodic Table, form large crystals made of regular three-dimensional arrays of metal atoms. The valence electrons are delocalized — that is, they are free to move throughout the crystal rather than being restricted to any particular atom. Atoms of the nonmetal elements, in contrast, share valence electrons to form covalent bonds. The electrons that make up these bonds are restricted to, or are localized in, a volume of space that lies largely between the nuclei of the bonding atoms.

As we move across any period of the Table, from left to right, the ionization energy gradually increases and the bonding between atoms of the same element becomes gradually less metallic and more covalent. However, there are a number of elements, often called **semimetals**, in which the bonding is part-way between the two.

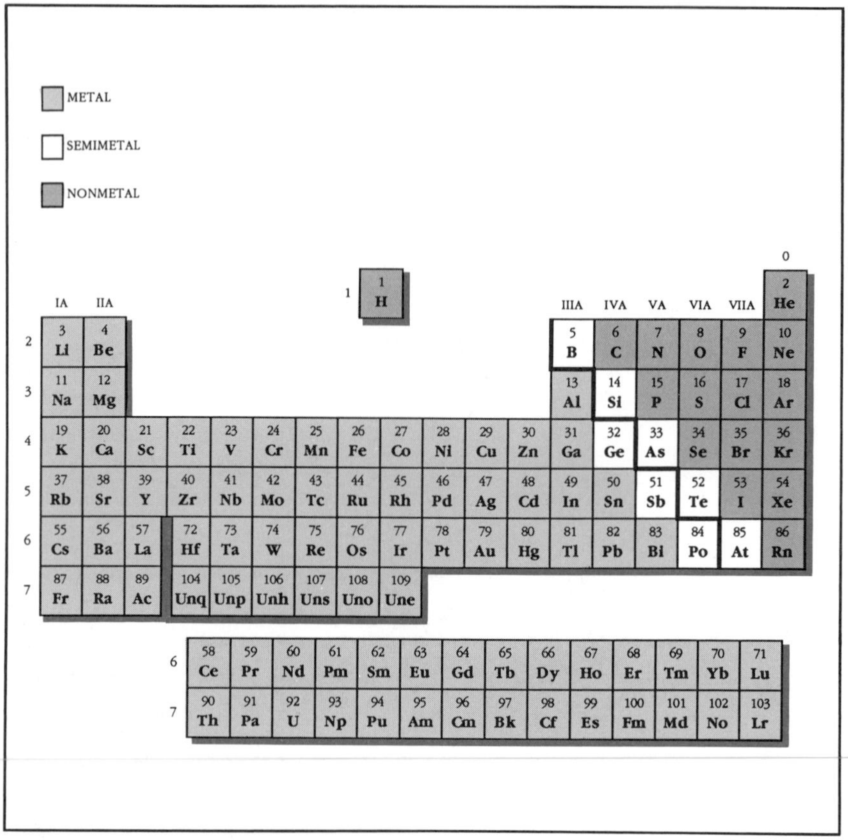

Figure 2.42

The Periodic Table showing the positions of the metals, semimetals, and nonmetals.

The element germanium is one of the best examples. Germanium is metallic in appearance but brittle. In its chemistry it behaves more like the nonmetal elements and forms compounds in which the bonding is mainly covalent. The element conducts electricity much better than solid non-metals such as sulfur, but considerably less well than the true metals. In fact the electrical properties of germanium and the other semimetals are unique; while the electrical conductivity of metals normally *decreases* as the temperature rises, that of the semimetals *increases*.

Germanium was unknown in 1869 when Dmitri Mendeléev proposed the Periodic Table. He was forced to leave a gap underneath silicon, in Group IVA, in order that the Group VA element arsenic appear below phosphorus, which it resembles. Mendeléev was so convinced that an element existed to fill the gap that he set out a list of its physical and chemical properties based upon the Periodic Law, which states that elements arranged in order of increasing atomic mass show a periodic repetition of properties. The discovery of germanium some 15 years later, and the fact that its properties were almost identical to those predicted by Mendeléev, did much to secure widespread acceptance of this law (though not all of his predictions were as accurate).

Semiconductors and the Microchip

The semimetal elements, such as silicon and germanium, and compounds such as gallium arsenide, GaAs, are known as *semiconductors*. Extremely pure crystals of these substances will not conduct electricity at room temperature, but they can be made to do so by raising the temperature or by adding very small amounts of impurities. The conduction of electricity by crystals containing impurities is the basis of transistor and microchip design.

Pure crystals of semiconductors such as germanium and silicon (Group IVA) consist of a giant, three-dimensional array of atoms similar to the arrays of atoms making up metal crystals. Unlike metals, however, the valence electrons are not delocalized. Instead, they are restricted to covalent bonds, which hold the structure together (Figure 2.43a). As a result, no electrons are free to move through the crystal and electricity is not conducted.

Atoms of impurities such as arsenic (Group VA) or boron (Group IIIA) can be used to replace atoms of germanium or silicon (Group IVA) in the crystal. In the case of arsenic, which has five valence electrons ($4s^2 4p^3$), the result is that one extra electron is included in the structure for each arsenic atom present (Figure 2.43b). Since these additional electrons are able to move through the crystal, it will now conduct electricity. Boron, on the other hand, has only three valence electrons ($2s^2 2p^1$). This means that one electron is missing from the structure for each boron atom substituted. In this case "positive holes" result (Figure 2.43c). Valence electrons are able to move to fill these holes, but when they do they leave a new hole in the position that they left behind. Because of this displacement of electrons, the positive holes appear to move around and the crystal conducts electricity. The addition of impurities to pure samples of a semiconductor is known as *doping*. Crystals doped with elements such as arsenic, which provide additional electrons, are known as *n-type semiconductors* (Figure 2.43b); those doped with elements such as boron, which produce positive holes, are known as *p-type semiconductors* (Figure 2.43c).

If a semiconductor is manufactured in such a way that a region containing a p-type impurity joins on to one containing an n-type impurity, the junction of the two areas — a *p–n junction* — will conduct electricity in one direction, but not in the other. This property is the principle of the *transistor*, invented in 1948 by a research group from the United States, headed by physicist William Shockley. The transistor replaced large glass diode tubes in radios, televisions, and other electronic equipment and allowed the development of much smaller and longer lasting radios and televisions.

After many years of research, it is now possible to form many p–n junctions on one tiny wafer of a semiconductor crystal. Silicon is most widely used for this purpose because the pure crystals are relatively cheap to produce and because silicon dioxide, which will insulate one part of the crystal from another, can easily be formed on the surface. Circular wafers of silicon are now being produced that are 0.125 mm thick and 15 cm in diameter. Since each transistor occupies only 1×10^{-3} mm^2, more than 17 000 000 transistors can be placed onto one such wafer. The result is the *silicon microchip* — many transistors on pieces of a silicon wafer.

Silicon is not the only semiconductor material that can be used for the production of microchips. One other material of growing importance is the compound gallium arsenide, GaAs. This compound, manufactured by a number of companies around the world, including Cominco at their zinc operations in British Columbia, has a number of advantages over silicon. Gallium arsenide chips are able to operate at a lower voltage over a much wider temperature range. In addition, the electrons are able to move through the material much faster; the material is therefore likely to be used extensively in computers, where high speed is of particular importance.

Figure 2.43

A pure semiconductor and two 'impure' semiconductors.

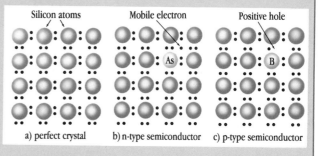

a) perfect crystal   b) n-type semiconductor   c) p-type semiconductor

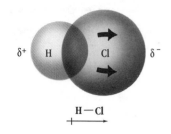

$$\delta^+ \quad \quad \quad \delta^-$$
$$H \quad \quad Cl$$

$$H-Cl$$

Figure 2.44

Hydrogen chloride is a polar molecule. The chlorine attracts the electrons, giving it a partial negative charge.

Bonding in Compounds

When two nonmetal atoms of the same element bond together, the electrons will be equally shared, and the bond will be purely covalent. When two nonmetal atoms of different elements bond together, however, one of the atoms usually attracts electrons to a greater extent than the other. As a result, the bond will be polar; one of the atoms will have a partial negative charge, the other a partial positive charge (Figure 2.44).

The degree of polarity of the bond, or the extent to which it has ionic character, will depend upon the difference in electronegativity between the two atoms forming the bond. Figure 2.45 shows the relationship between these two quantities.

Pauling developed the concept of electronegativity on experimental evidence that the bond in chlorine monofluoride, ClF, was stronger than the bond in either Cl_2 or F_2. He proposed that the Cl—F bond was polar and that fluorine exerted the greater attractive force on the bonding electron pair. The unequal charge distribution strengthens the bond.

$$\overset{\delta^+}{Cl}-\overset{\delta^-}{F}$$

If we refer to the electronegativity values in Figure 2.18, we can see that the difference in electronegativity between chlorine and hydrogen is $3.0 - 2.1 = 0.9$ units. From Figure 2.45 we can see that the proportion of ionic character in the hydrogen chloride bond will therefore be about 20 %.

The proportion of ionic character in covalent bonds reaches 25 % when the difference in electronegativity is just over one unit. When the difference becomes 1.7 units, two elements will form a bond which has 50 % ionic character. Such a bond would be halfway between a pure covalent bond and a pure ionic bond. When the difference in electronegativity between two elements is greater than 1.7 units, the bonding will be largely ionic.

We can see that the only "pure" covalent bonds will be those between two atoms of the same element. Bonds between atoms of different nonmetal elements will always have some *ionic* character. Conversely, bonds between metals and nonmetals, which we usually refer to as being ionic, will actually always have at least a small proportion of *covalent* character. Thus in ionic solids the valence electrons of the metal atoms are never *completely* removed by the nonmetal atoms.

The compounds of aluminum can be used to illustrate this point. As Table 2.9 indicates, the difference in electronegativity between aluminum and fluorine is 2.5 units; while the bonding in aluminum fluoride is about 80% ionic in character, in the remainder of the halides it is mainly covalent. The bonding in aluminum iodide, in fact, has less ionic character than water.

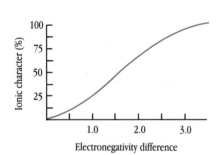

Figure 2.45

The relationship between the electronegativity difference and the degree of ionic character of a bond.

TABLE 2.9	*Bonding in Aluminum Halides*	
Compound	Electronegativity Difference	Proportion of Ionic Character
AlF_3	2.5 units	80 %
$AlCl_3$	1.5 units	40 %
$AlBr_3$	1.3 units	35 %
AlI_3	1.0 units	23 %

It is clearly very difficult to classify all compounds as either ionic or covalent; many, if not most, have bonding that is actually somewhere in between. Nonetheless, such a classification is often useful, if only an approximation. As a general rule we classify all compounds formed between metals and nonmetals as being ionic, and all compounds formed between nonmetals and nonmetals (or semimetals) as being covalent.

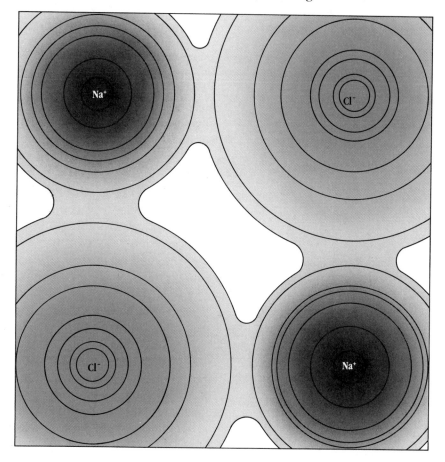

Figure 2.46
An electron probability diagram for sodium chloride. The more intense the colour, the greater the probability of finding the electrons. Even in this ionic solid there is a very slight sharing of electrons.

2.14 Since magnesium is a metal and iodine is a nonmetal, we classify the bonding in magnesium iodide as ionic. Using Figure 2.45, determine the degree of ionic character of the magnesium-iodine bond.

SOLUTION From Figure 2.18 we see that the electronegativity of iodine is 2.5 and that of magnesium is 1.2. The electronegativity difference between these two atoms is

$$2.5 - 1.2 = 1.3$$

Using Figure 2.45, we can see that an electronegativity of 1.3 corresponds to about 35% ionic character.

QUESTIONS

12. Classify each of the following elements as a metal, semimetal, or nonmetal:

a) boron   b) sulfur   c) zinc   d) tellurium

13. Using the Periodic Table, arrange the following bonds in order of increasing polarity: Cl—Cl   Cl—Na   Cl—N.

14. Using Figures 2.18 and 2.45 determine the percent ionic character ot the following bonds:

a) K—Br   b) C—S   c) P—F   d) Cs—I

Summary

- Atoms consist of a nucleus — containing protons and neutrons — and electrons, which occupy successive energy levels outside the nucleus. The chemistry of an element is largely determined by the number and arrangement of the electrons.

- The electron configuration of an element indicates which orbitals contain electrons. Electron configurations follow three rules: the Aufbau principle, the Pauli exclusion principle, and Hund's rule.

- The electrons in the outermost principal energy level are called valence electrons. In an electron-dot formula for a neutral atom the number of valence electrons is represented by dots placed around the chemical symbol for the element.

- Ionization energy is the energy necessary to remove the outermost valence electron from a neutral atom.

- Electronegativity is a measure of the tendency of an element to attract shared electron pairs from other elements in a compound.

- The elements can be divided into three groups: metals, semimetals, and nonmetals. Metals have low ionization energies and appear on the left of the Periodic Table. Metal crystals consist of close-packed, regular arrays of metal atoms; the valence electrons are delocalized.

- Semimetals have properties in common with each of the other two groups. The semimetals consist of a regular array of atoms similar to the structure of metals, except that the valence electrons are not delocalized.

- Nonmetals have high ionization energies and appear on the right of the Periodic Table. They may exist as separate, covalently-bonded molecules.

- Compounds that are formed between metals and nonmetals are generally ionic. Ionic compounds are solid crystals that consist of close-packed regular arrays of positive and negative ions held in the crystal lattice.

- Compounds formed between nonmetal elements are generally covalent; valence electrons are shared in a bond between two atoms.

- A coordinate covalent bond is formed when both electrons that make up the bond are provided by one atom.

- Very often the atoms in covalent molecules are surrounded by an octet of valence electrons, but elements of the third and subsequent rows of the Periodic Table may form molecules in which the central atom is surrounded by more than eight electrons.

- The degree to which an ionic compound is purely ionic, or a covalent compound is purely covalent, depends upon the relative electronegativities of the atoms forming the compound.

KEY WORDS

alloy	ionic character
atomic number	isoelectronic
Aufbau principle	isotopes
body-centered cubic	Lewis formula
coordinate covalent bond	magnetic quantum number
covalent bond	mass number
crystal lattice	metallic bond
delocalized	neutron
diffraction pattern	nucleus
double bond	octet rule
electron	orbital
electron affinity	paramagnetic
electron configuration	Pauli exclusion principle
electron deficient	polar covalent bond
electron-dot formula	principal quantum number
electronegativity	proton
energy level	quantum model
excited state	reflected
face-centred cubic	resonance
first ionization energy	second ionization energy
ground state	secondary quantum number
Heisenberg uncertainty principle	semimetal
Hund's rule	shielding effect
interstitial alloy	simple cubic packing
ionic bond	spin quantum number

sublevel
substitutional alloy
third ionization energy
triple bond

unit cell
valence electron
X-ray crystallography

---

1. Atomic number 92; mass number 238

2. $^{63}_{29}$Cu: 29 protons, 34 neutrons, 29 electrons
$^{65}_{29}$Cu: 29 protons, 36 neutrons, 29 electrons

3. a) $1s^2 2s^2 2p^5$
   b) $1s^2 2s^2 2p^6 3s^2 3p^6 4s^2 3d^1$
   c) $1s^2 2s^2 2p^6 3s^2 3p^6 4s^2 3d^{10} 4p^6$

4.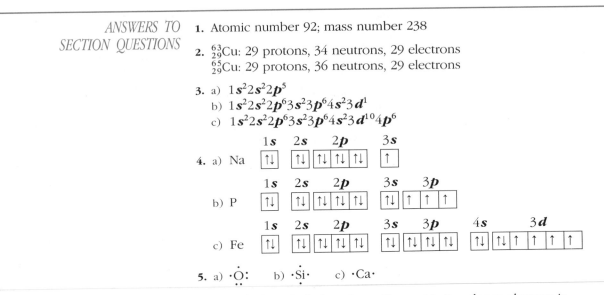

5. a) $\cdot \ddot{\underset{\cdot\cdot}{O}}{:}$ b) $\cdot \overset{\cdot}{Si} \cdot$ c) $\cdot Ca \cdot$

6. a) Rubidium is farther down Group IA; its valence electron is
   farther from the nucleus and is shielded by a greater number
   of non-valence electrons. These two effects outweigh
   the effect of a greater nuclear charge.
   b) Sodium is at the left-hand side of period 3; chlorine is at the
   right-hand side. Both elements have the same number of
   non-valence electrons, therefore there is little difference in the
   shielding effect. Sodium atoms are larger and so the valence
   electron is farther from the nucleus.
   c) Potassium has one more electron than argon. In addition,
   potassium atoms are larger. The extra electron is in a new,
   higher energy level. Less energy is therefore required to
   remove it from the atom.

7. a) metal + nonmetal: ionic
   b) nonmetal + nonmetal: covalent
   c) metal + metal: metallic
   d) nonmetal + nonmetal: covalent

8. a) $1s^2 2s^2 2p^6$
   b) $1s^2 2s^2 2p^6$
   c) $1s^2 2s^2 2p^6$
   d) $1s^2 2s^2 2p^6 3s^2 3p^6$

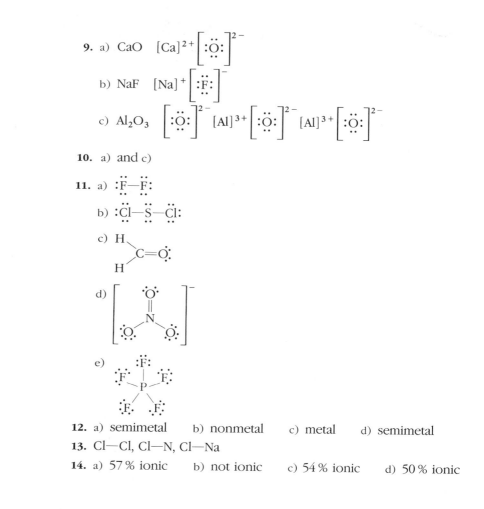

9. a) CaO $[Ca]^{2+}\left[:\ddot{O}:\right]^{2-}$

b) NaF $[Na]^{+}\left[:\ddot{F}:\right]^{-}$

c) Al_2O_3 $\left[:\ddot{O}:\right]^{2-}[Al]^{3+}\left[:\ddot{O}:\right]^{2-}[Al]^{3+}\left[:\ddot{O}:\right]^{2-}$

10. a) and c)

11. a) $:\ddot{F}-\ddot{F}:$

b) $:\ddot{Cl}-\ddot{S}-\ddot{Cl}:$

c) $\begin{matrix} H \\ \\ H \end{matrix}$ C=$\ddot{O}:$

d)

e)

12. a) semimetal   b) nonmetal   c) metal   d) semimetal

13. Cl—Cl, Cl—N, Cl—Na

14. a) 57 % ionic   b) not ionic   c) 54 % ionic   d) 50 % ionic

---

COMPREHENSION QUESTIONS

1. What are isotopes? Give at least three examples.

2. Explain the modifications made to the Bohr model that led to the probability model of the atom.

3. What is the Pauli exclusion principle?

4. Explain the term orbital.

5. What information does the secondary quantum number, l, tell us about an orbital?

6. The ground-state electron configuration of a phosphorus atom is $1s^2 2s^2 2p^6 3s^2 3p^3$. What does this statement mean?

7. What feature of their ground-state electron configurations distinguishes the transition elements from other elements?

8. Explain the trend in first ionization energies in Group IA from lithium to cesium.

9. Consider the following table of ionization energies ($MJ \cdot mol^{-1}$):

Element	1st I.E.	2nd I.E.	3rd I.E.	4th I.E.
1	2.18	4.20	6.30	8.61
2	0.52	4.83	7.24	10.29
3	0.61	1.89	2.84	12.18
4	0.44	3.26	4.65	6.20
5	0.62	1.16	5.25	7.56

a) Which two of the five elements are likely to be in the same group of the Periodic Table? Which group is this?

b) Which one element of the five is most likely to be a Group IIA element?

10. Consider the valence-level electron configurations of the following five elements:

Element	s orbital	p orbitals
1	↑↓	↑↓ ↑↓ ↑↓
2	↑	
3	↑↓	
4	↑↓	↑ ↑
5	↑↓	↑↓ ↑↓ ↑

a) Which element is most likely to react with element 2 to form an ionic compound?

b) Which two of the elements would be most likely to form covalent bonds between their own atoms?

c) Which two elements are most likely to be metals?

11. Explain briefly, in your own words, how the "electron sea" model of metallic bonding accounts for the typical physical properties of metals.

12. Which is the harder metal: zinc or potassium? Explain your answer.

13. Explain the difference between interstitial and substitutional alloys.

14. Why is steel used as reinforcing in concrete rather than iron? (Your reasons should include a chemical explanation for the difference in properties between steel and iron.)

15. A typical sample of 18-carat gold contains only about 75% gold. Why is this preferable to pure gold for use as jewellery?

16. Explain the difference between the body-centred cubic and face-centred cubic arrangement of metallic packing.

17. Explain the term isoelectronic. Give an example of three pairs of ions or atoms that are isoelectronic, using the period from lithium to neon.

18. Why are sodium ions much smaller than sodium atoms, yet chloride ions much larger than chlorine atoms?

19. Would you expect the ionic compound magnesium sulfide, MgS, to have a crystal structure of the sodium chloride type? Give reasons for your answer.

20. Compare the bonding in hydrogen fluoride with that in sodium fluoride. Account for differences in terms of differences in ionization energy and electronegativity.

21. Explain the term polar bond.

22. How are coordinate covalent bonds formed? How do they differ from regular covalent bonds?

PROBLEMS   *Atomic Theory*

23. What are the numbers of neutrons, protons, and electrons in an atom of
    a) $^{19}_{9}F$ c) $^{41}_{19}K$ e) $^{74}_{33}As$
    b) $^{18}_{8}O$ d) $^{238}_{92}U$ f) $^{133}_{55}Cs$

24. Write symbols of the type $^{A}_{Z}X$ for atoms that have a) 60 neutrons and a mass number of 107, b) 6 protons and a mass number of 13, and c) 12 neutrons and a mass number of 33.

25. What is the atomic number and mass number of a copper atom that contains 34 neutrons?

26. What is the atomic number and mass number of an atom that contains 48 neutrons and 36 protons? Which element is this?

27. Which of the following are isotopes:

$$^{17}_{9}F \quad ^{17}_{8}O \quad ^{18}_{7}N \quad ^{18}_{9}F \quad ^{14}_{7}N$$

28. Which of the following is an isotope of $^{12}_{6}C$:

$$^{17}_{7}N \quad ^{14}_{6}C \quad ^{12}_{5}B \quad ^{17}_{9}F$$

29. For $n = 1$ we have one orbital; for $n = 2$ we have four orbitals. How many orbitals would you expect there to be in principal energy level $n = 6$?

30. What is the maximum number of electrons allowed in the principal energy level for which $n = 4$?

31. Write the ground-state electron configurations for the following:
    a) boron   b) sodium   c) chlorine   d) calcium   e) strontium

32. Draw orbital diagrams to show the ground-state electron configurations of the following:
    a) lithium   b) nitrogen   c) argon   d) zinc

33. Identify the elements that have electron configurations corresponding to the following orbital diagrams.

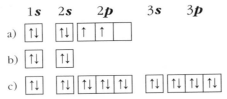

34. How many electrons are in the outermost (valence) energy level of these elements?
    a) aluminum   c) bromine   e) xenon
    b) selenium   d) carbon   f) arsenic

35. Name the elements that have the following electron configurations:
    a) $1s^2 2s^2 2p^6 3s^2 3p^5$
    b) $1s^2 2s^2 2p^6 3s^2 3p^6 4s^2 3d^2$
    c) $1s^2 2s^2 2p^6 3s^2 3p^6 4s^2 3d^8$

Periodic Properties of the Elements

36. Draw electron-dot formulas for neutral atoms of these elements:
    a) potassium   b) boron   c) arsenic   d) sulfur   e) fluorine

37. Which atom of the following pairs has the lower first ionization energy? Explain briefly.
    a) lithium and potassium   b) lithium and fluorine

38. What type of bonding is most likely to occur between the following pairs of atoms?
    a) magnesium and sulfur   d) bromine and bromine
    b) potassium and oxygen   e) copper and copper
    c) chlorine and sulfur

Ionic Bonding

39. Write the electron configuration for each of the following:
    a) Cl^- b) Mg^{2+} c) F^- d) Na^+

40. Draw an orbital diagram for each of the following:
    a) S^{2-} b) Al^{3+} c) N^{3-} d) Ca^{2+}

41. Name three ions that could have the electron configuration $1s^2 2s^2 2p^6 3s^2 3p^6$.

42. Name three ions that would be isoelectronic with Al^{3+}.

43. Draw electron-dot formulas for the following ions:
    a) Mg^{2+} b) Cl^- c) P^{3-}

44. Predict the formula of the compound formed between each of the following pairs of elements:
    a) calcium and phosphorus
    b) aluminum and sulfur
    c) magnesium and iodine

45. Draw an electron-dot formula to represent the formation of the following compounds from their elements:
  a) aluminum fluoride   b) sodium sulfide

Covalent Bonding

46. Draw an electron-dot formula for each of the following molecules:
  a) Br_2 b) PH_3 c) HI d) H_2S e) NCl_3 f) SiH_4

47. For each of the following molecules identify which of the atoms (if any) will have a partial positive charge and which a partial negative charge.
  a) HCl b) PCl_3 c) CF_4 d) OF_2 e) NCl_3

48. Draw an electron-dot formula for each of the following molecules and ions:
  a) SO_2 b) HCN c) SO_4^{2-} d) ClO_2^- e) NO^+

The Bonding Continuum

49. Classify each of the following as a metal, semimetal, or nonmetal:
  a) mercury   c) carbon   e) indium
  b) palladium   d) antimony   f) barium

50. Using Figures 2.18 and 2.45, determine the degree of ionic character of the following bonds:
  a) Be—F   b) Sr—Cl   c) H—O   d) Mg—S

51. Using electronegativity values, list the following bonds in order of decreasing polarity:
  a) S—O   b) N—O   c) P—O   d) O—Cl

MISCELLANEOUS PROBLEMS

52. Naturally-occurring copper consists of two isotopes: copper-63, with an atomic mass of 62.93 u; and copper-65, with an atomic mass of 64.93 u. The average atomic mass of a copper atom is 63.55 u. From this information calculate the percentage of copper-63 in copper.

53. Consider the three elements nitrogen, phosphorus, and oxygen. Write them in increasing order of the following:
  a) atomic size
  b) ionic size
  c) electron affinity
  d) first ionization energy
  e) electronegativity

54. Draw all the resonance structures for the carbonate ion, CO_3^{2-}.

55. Which of the following molecules or ions have an atom with an expanded octet?
  a) SF_2 b) SF_4 c) SF_6

56. Phosphorus forms both PCl_3 and PCl_5. Predict whether nitrogen, with the same number of valence electrons as phosphorus, would form NCl_3 and NCl_5.

57. Which of the following are paramagnetic:
a) Cl   b) Cl_2 c) Cl_2O d) ClO_2

58. Draw electron-dot formulas for the following:
a) LiCl   b) $BeCl_2$ c) BCl_3 d) CCl_4

59. In each of the compounds in Question 58, determine the degree of ionic character of the bonds involved (using Figures 2.18 and 2.45).

SUGGESTED PROJECTS

1. This chapter mentioned several famous scientists whose research contributed to our understanding of the structure of the atom. Write a short biography on one of them. Your local public library would be a good source of material for this project.

2. Build models of three common packing arrangements using spheres of the same size. Although you can use marbles or ping-pong balls, you may find that the easiest model-building spheres are polystyrene balls available from craft and hobby shops. These can be joined together with glue and are normally easily handled once the glue has dried. Make a model, using appropriate sized spheres of any or all of these structures:
a) simple cubic packing
b) body-centred cubic packing
c) face-centred cubic packing

3. Report to the class on the various types of steel made in Canada. Explain the percent composition of these steels, what the different properties are, and how this leads to different uses.

4. Build a model of a NaCl or a CsCl crystal. For this model you should use heavy wire joining the spheres so that you can see the arrangement of positive ions around negative ions and negative ions around positive ions. You will need two sizes of spheres: the larger sphere for the anion in NaCl, and the cation in CsCl.

The Shapes of Molecules

In this chapter we develop a model that will allow us to predict molecular shapes from a knowledge of electron-dot formulas. The model is an aid to assist us in understanding molecular structure. Bear in mind that modifications will often have to be made to account for differences between our initial predictions and experimental evidence.

An Introduction to VSEPR Theory

3.1 We already know how to represent the bonding in covalent compounds using electron-dot formulas. These formulas, however, are two-dimensional representations while real molecules exist in three dimensions. Although the electron-dot formulas do not represent the actual shapes of molecules, they can be used to predict shapes by using the **valence-shell electron-pair repulsion (VSEPR) theory**, developed by Canadian chemist Ronald Gillespie. This theory can be stated as follows:

> **The pairs of electrons that surround the core of the central atom in a molecule repel each other and arrange themselves in space in such a way that they are as far apart as possible.**

Once we have determined (using an electron-dot formula) how many pairs of electrons surround the core of the central atom, we can readily work out the shape of the molecule by using elementary geometry. We can also use the theory to determine the shapes of covalently-bonded ions.

Molecules in which the octet rule is obeyed always contain central atoms whose valence energy level contains eight electrons. In many cases only single bonds are present, and the eight electrons are present as four separate pairs. VSEPR theory tells us that the electron pairs surrounding a central atom repel each other because all pairs are negatively charged. Therefore they will try to arrange themselves as far apart as possible.

If we imagine a central atom at the centre of a sphere, surrounded by four pairs of electrons, then each of the four pairs of electrons will occupy a volume of space that is directed towards a point on the surface of the sphere (Figure 3.2a). For the electron pairs to be as far apart as possible, these four points will be at the corners of a regular tetrahedron (Figure 3.2b) with the central atom at the centre. If the electron pairs are bonding pairs, then the atoms to which they are joined will also be aligned in the same directions.

Figure 3.1
Ronald Gillespie (1924-) has been the foremost developer of VSEPR theory, used to predict molecular shapes.

Figure 3.2
a) Four pairs of electrons in an atom are arranged tetrahedrally.
b) Bonds to other atoms form along the direction of the electron pairs.

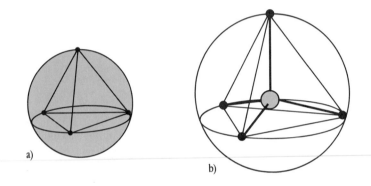

Molecular Models

To use VSEPR theory requires a knowledge of both electron-dot formulas and geometry. The capacity to "think" in three dimensions is also helpful. Perspective drawings make this easier, but it is even better to have one of the commercially available sets of **molecular models**.

There are several types of available models, two of which — the ball-and-stick and the space-filling models — are particularly useful to students. In ball-and-stick models, atoms are represented by plastic balls with holes drilled in them at specific angles to each other. Bonds are represented by rods (wood, plastic, or metal springs) inserted into the holes to join the "atoms" together. The rods are often cut in lengths that are proportional to common bond lengths. This kind of model will give us a good idea of the angles between the bonds, but not of the relative sizes of the atoms.

Space-filling models are exact-scale models and therefore do indicate the relative sizes of the atoms. Each atom is represented by a plastic ball, proportional to the size of the atom. Bonds are not directly represented, but each atom has an appropriate number of flat faces and connectors, which allow us to join them together. But these models do not tell us much about bond angles and bond lengths.

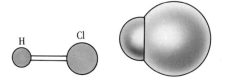

Figure 3.3

Diffferent models of a hydrogen chloride molecule:

a) a ball-and-stick model;

b) a space-filling model.

Figure 3.4

a) In a methane molecule, the hydrogen atoms are arranged tetrahedrally.

b) A ball-and-stick model of methane.

c) A space-filling model.

To be useful, models need not be particularly elaborate. Balloons, styrofoam balls, even gumdrops and toothpicks, are often sufficient. We will use the ball-and-stick model more often, since we concentrate on the bond angles within molecules.

A Central Atom Surrounded by Four Bonding Pairs

Methane is an example of a compound in which all four pairs of electrons surrounding the core of the central atom are bonded to other atoms. In this case there are bonded atoms at each corner of the regular tetrahedron (Figure 3.4a) so the molecule itself is **tetrahedral** in shape. If we were to measure the angles between the bonds we would find that all of the **bond angles** are 109.5°.

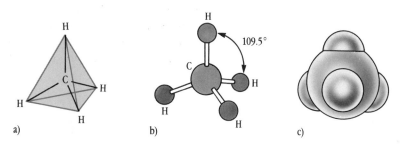

a)   b)   c)

A Central Atom Surrounded by Three Bonding Pairs and One Non-Bonding Pair

Whenever four pairs of electrons surround a central atom, they will *always* arrange themselves tetrahedrally. But the actual shape of the molecule will depend upon how many of the electron pairs are **bonding pairs** and how many are **non-bonding pairs**. By *shape*, we mean the arrangement of the atoms within the molecule.

For instance, we can represent the ammonia molecule by the following electron-dot formula:

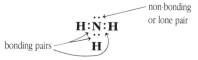

The central nitrogen atom is surrounded by four pairs of electrons. We expect these four pairs to be arranged tetrahedrally. However, only three of the four pairs actually represent bonds between two types of atoms. These pairs are bonding pairs. The remaining pair of electrons is a non-bonding pair, or "lone pair."

In the ammonia molecule the nitrogen atom lies directly above the centre of a triangular plane, defined by the three hydrogen atoms. The four atoms form a pyramid with a triangular base and with the nitrogen atom at the apex (Figure 3.5a). Molecules with this shape are said to be **trigonal pyramidal** (or triangular pyramidal).

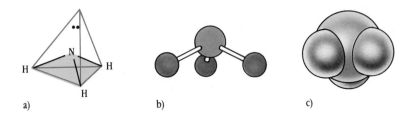

Figure 3.5

a) The trigonal pyramidal shape of an ammonia molecule

b) The ball-and-stick model of ammonia.

c) A space-filling model.

a)   b)   c)

We would expect the bond angles in the ammonia molecule to be the same as those in the methane molecule, since both are derived from the same orientation of electron pairs in space. However, experimental evidence indicates that the bond angles in ammonia, and other similar pyramidal molecules, are slightly less than expected. This appears to result from the repulsion by the non-bonding pair of electrons, which requires slightly more space than a bonding pair. We must adjust our model to account for this experimental evidence (Figure 3.6).

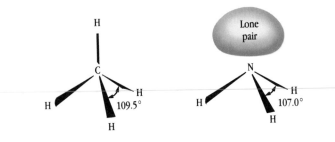

Figure 3.6

The presence of a non-bonding pair of electrons on the central atom reduces the bond angles from 109.5° to 107.0°.

A Central Atom Surrounded by Two Bonding Pairs and Two Non-Bonding Pairs

We can represent the water molecule by either of the following structures:

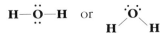

An application of VSEPR theory will help us determine the actual shape of the water molecule.

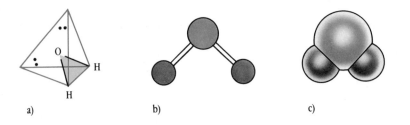

Figure 3.7

a) The shape of a water molecule.

b) A ball-and-stick model of water.

c) A space-filling model.

a)   b)   c)

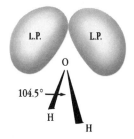

Figure 3.8
The presence of two non-bonding pairs of electrons on the central atom reduces the bond angle from 109.5° to 104.5°.

The central oxygen atom is surrounded by four pairs of electrons. Once again these four pairs will be arranged tetrahedrally; however, only two of the four pairs are actually bonding pairs. In this case the two hydrogen atoms are at two of the corners of a regular tetrahedron (Figure 3.7a). The shape of the molecule is itself **bent**, or **v-shaped**. Since water molecules have two non-bonding pairs, we might expect that the bond angle would be even more reduced than they are in ammonia. This is, in fact, the case. The measured bond angle in the water molecule is 104.5°.

EXAMPLE   *3.1*   Predict the geometry of a) hydrogen sulfide, H_2S, and b) boron tetrafluoride ion, BF_4^-.

SOLUTION   a) Sulfur is in Group VIA, so it has six valence electrons. The hydrogen atoms have one valence electron each. The structure for hydrogen sulfide can be represented as

$$H-\overset{..}{\underset{..}{S}}-H$$

The central sulfur atom is surrounded by four pairs of electrons. Two of these pairs are bonding pairs, the other two are non-bonding pairs. The four pairs of electrons will be arranged tetrahedrally; but, the hydrogen sulfide molecule will be bent, like a water molecule.

b) Boron, Group IIIA, has three valence electrons. The fluorine atoms have seven valence electrons each. Since the ion has an overall charge of −1, there must be one extra valence electron in the total. The number of valence electrons is thus

$$3 + (4 \times 7) + 1 = 32$$

If each atom independently acquired an octet of valence electrons, the total would be 40. The difference of eight electrons ($40 - 32 = 8$) represents four bonds. The structure for boron tetrafluoride ion is therefore

$$\left[\begin{array}{c} :\overset{..}{F}: \\ | \\ :\overset{..}{\underset{..}{F}}-B-\overset{..}{\underset{..}{F}}: \\ | \\ :\overset{..}{\underset{..}{F}}: \end{array}\right]^-$$

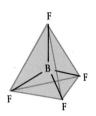

The central boron atom is surrounded by four bonding pairs of electrons. The four pairs of electrons and the four fluorine atoms will be arranged tetrahedrally; the boron tetrafluoride ion will be tetrahedral.

QUESTIONS

1. Draw electron-dot formulas for and predict the shape of the following molecules:
   a) carbon tetrachloride   b) nitrogen trifluoride
2. Use VSEPR theory to predict the shape of these molecules:
   a) dichlorine oxide   b) PH_4^+
3. Why would the bond angle be distorted from the expected 109.5° in dichlorine oxide?

Shapes of More Complex Molecules and Ions

3.2

When explaining covalent bonding, we saw that there are exceptions to the octet rule. Now we will proceed to analyze the shape of molecules and ions in which the rule is not obeyed.

A Central Atom with an Expanded Valence Level

Elements from the third and subsequent rows of the Periodic Table are able to make use of vacant **d** orbitals to expand their valence levels. By this means, the central atom in some compounds may be surrounded by more than four pairs of electrons. For example, in phosphorus pentafluoride, PF_5, the central phosphorus atom is surrounded by five bonded pairs of electrons.

How will these five pairs be arranged in space so that they will be as far apart as possible? If we apply VSEPR theory, we arrive at the orientation shown in Figure 3.9. The result is consistent with experimental evidence.

We can see that three pairs of electrons lie in a plane with the phosphorus atom at the centre. If these three pairs are to be as far apart as possible, they will be oriented 120° apart, rather like a three-bladed propeller. One of the remaining pairs will be positioned directly above the

Figure 3.9

a) Five pairs of electrons arranged at two corners of a trigonal bipyramid.

b) Bonds to other atoms form along the direction of the electron pairs.

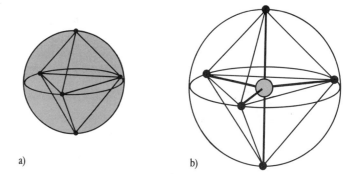

a)   b)

centre of this plane; the other will be positioned directly below the centre. Each of these pairs of electrons is a bonding pair and so the five fluorine atoms of the PF_5 molecule will have the same orientation as the electron pairs. This molecular shape is called **trigonal bipyramidal** (or triangular bipyramidal), since it consists of two pyramids sharing the same triangular base.

Many other molecules and ions contain central atoms that are surrounded by five pairs of electrons. Unlike the electron pairs in phosphorus pentafluoride, however, not all of these are *bonding* pairs. In these cases the electrons will be oriented in the same trigonal bipyramidal arrangement, but the shapes of the molecules will be different. A discussion on the shapes of these molecules and ions is beyond the scope of this text.

When we consider the compound sulfur hexafluoride, SF_6, we can see that the central atom is surrounded by six pairs of electrons.

If these six pairs are arranged according to VSEPR theory, we find that the sulfur atom is at the centre of a square plane (Figure 3.10b), with one electron pair directly above this plane and another pair directly below.

Figure 3.10

a) Six electron pairs arranged at the corners of an octahedron.

b) Bonds to other atoms form along the direction of the electron pairs.

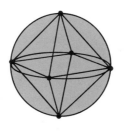

a)

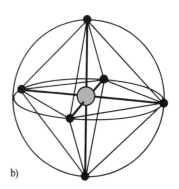

b)

Each of the six pairs of electrons in sulfur hexafluoride is a bonding pair; hence the six fluoride atoms will have the same orientation as the bonding electron pairs. The shape of the molecule is said to be **octahedral**, since each of the bonded fluorine atoms is at one corner of a regular octahedron. All of the bond angles are 90°.

Figure 3.11

a) The complex instrumentation of a jetstream aircraft and b) a Hercules aircraft are used to detect sulfur hexafluoride, which is used to trace the path of sulfur dioxide emissions.

A Central Atom with an Incomplete Octet of Valence Electrons

Both beryllium and boron form covalently-bonded compounds in which the central atom is surrounded by fewer than eight electrons. The basic structures of the compounds beryllium difluoride, BeF_2, and boron trifluoride, BF_3, can be shown as follows:

$$:\overset{..}{\underset{..}{F}}—Be—\overset{..}{\underset{..}{F}}: \quad \text{and} \quad \overset{\displaystyle :\overset{..}{F}:}{\underset{\displaystyle :\overset{..}{F}:}{}}\!\!>B—\overset{..}{\underset{..}{F}}:$$

For the two bonding pairs of electrons in beryllium difluoride to be as far apart as possible, they must be arranged on opposite sides of the central atom. All three atoms will therefore be oriented in a straight line and the bond angle will be 180°. Molecules with this shape are said to be **linear**.

Figure 3.12

a) Two electron pairs arranged linearly.
b) Bonds to other atoms form along the same direction, giving a linear molecule.

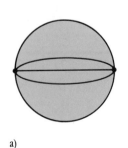

a)

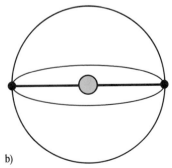

b)

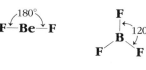

Figure 3.13

The bond angles in beryllium difluoride and boron trifluoride.

The central atom of boron trifluoride is surrounded by three pairs of electrons. These three pairs will be oriented 120° apart in the same plane as the boron atom (Figure 3.14b). Since each is a bonding pair, the three bonded fluorine atoms will be positioned at the points of an equilateral triangle, with the boron atom in the centre. Molecules with this shape are said to be **trigonal planar** (or triangular planar).

Figure 3.14

a) Three electron pairs arranged at the corners of a triangular plane.

b) Bonds to other atoms form a trigonal planar molecule.

c) Ball-and-stick and space-filling models for boron trifluoride.

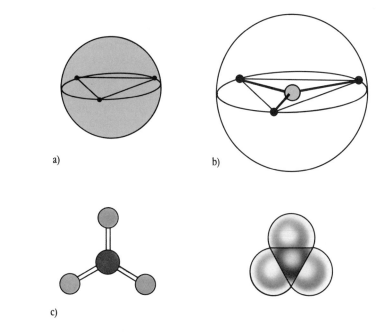

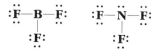

A Structural Comparison

The effect of a non-bonding pair of electrons on the shape of a molecule can be seen very clearly by comparing boron trifluoride, BF_3, and nitrogen trifluoride, NF_3. The molecules have similar formulas, but as we have seen, boron, in boron trifluoride, does not have a complete octet of electrons.

The three electron pairs around the boron atom are arranged in a trigonal planar shape; since each is a bonding pair, the molecule itself is trigonal planar. The four pairs of electrons around the nitrogen atom are arranged tetrahedrally: one of these pairs is a non-bonding pair and therefore the shape of nitrogen trifluoride, like that of ammonia, is trigonal pyramidal.

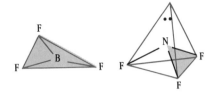

Figure 3.15
The shapes of boron trifluoride and nitrogen trifluoride.

The non-bonding pair of electrons in the nitrogen trifluoride molecule repels the three bonding pairs. This causes them to move down and out of the plane. As a result, boron trifluoride and nitrogen trifluoride have quite different shapes although their formulas are similar. For us to predict the shape of a molecule accurately, we must be sure of the electron-dot formula, and we must know how many pairs of electrons surround the central atom.

Shapes of Molecules and Ions with Double or Triple Bonds

So far we have applied VSEPR theory to molecules and ions that contain only single bonds. By extending the theory, we can also use it successfully to predict the shapes of compounds that contain double or triple bonds. The modification that we must make is simply to treat double or triple bonds as if they were single pairs of electrons. If we treat carbon dioxide, CO_2, and hydrogen cyanide, HCN, in this way, we can see in each case that the central atom is surrounded by just two "groups" of electrons:

$$\ddot{O}=C=\ddot{O}: \qquad H—C≡N:$$

Both of these structures therefore resemble that of beryllium difluoride. In each case the two groups of electrons will arrange themselves on opposite sides of the central atom, and the molecules will be linear.

EXAMPLE　　　*3.2*　Predict the geometry of a) nitrate ion, NO_3^- and b) nitrite ion, NO_2^-.

　　SOLUTION　a) We can represent the nitrate ion by a structure in which there are two coordinate covalent bonds and one double bond between the nitrogen atom and the three oxygen atoms.

The three "groups" of electrons surrounding the central nitrogen atom will be oriented 120° apart in a plane. Since all of these electrons are bonding electrons, the ion will be trigonal planar in shape.

b) The nitrite ion can be shown as follows:

The central nitrogen atom is surrounded by three "groups" of electrons. VSEPR theory would indicate that these would be oriented 120°

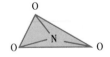

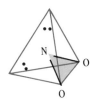

apart in a plane. Since there are only two bonding groups, the shape of the ion is bent, like the shape of the water molecule but with a bond angle of 120°.

Table 3.1 contains a summary of the different molecular shapes we have considered. Notice once again that to predict the shape of a molecule with confidence, it is essential first of all to draw the correct electron-dot formula. The number of electron pairs around the central atom can then be determined and their orientations worked out using VSEPR theory. The general shape of the molecule depends upon how many of the electron pairs are bonding pairs and how many are non-bonding, or lone pairs.

TABLE 3.1   *Shapes of Molecules and Ions*

Number of Electron Pairs around Central Atom	Orientation of Electron Pairs	Number of Bonding and Lone Pairs	Bond Angles	Shape	
2	linear	2BP, 0LP	180°	linear	
3	triangular planar	3BP, 0LP	120°	trigonal planar	
4	tetrahedral	4BP, 0LP	109.5°	tetrahedral	
		3BP, 1LP	< 109.5°	trigonal pyramidal	
		2BP, 2LP	< 109.5°	v-shaped	
5	trigonal bipyramidal	5BP, 0LP	120° & 90°	trigonal bipyramidal	
6	octahedral	6BP, 0LP	90°	octahedral	

QUESTIONS

4. Draw electron-dot formulas for, and predict the shape of the following:
   a) phosphorus pentachloride   b) the carbonate ion
5. Use VSEPR theory to predict the shape of the following compounds:
   a) carbon disulfide   b) sulfur dioxide
6. What effect would you expect the lone electron pair on the central sulfur atom in sulfur dioxide to have on the bond angle of the molecule?

Network Solids

In Section 2.3 and Section 2.5 we saw that metals and ionic compounds form crystals, which consist of regular three-dimensional arrays of atoms or ions. So far we have only considered covalently-bonded atoms as they exist in individual molecules. However, it is also possible for covalently-bonded substances to consist of atoms bonded together in giant arrays. Graphite and diamond, for example, are two forms of carbon that contain covalent bonds. Silicon forms a large variety of covalently-bonded silicate compounds. These giant structures in which atoms are covalently bonded together in continuous two- or three-dimensional arrays are often referred to as **network solids**.

Two Allotropes of Carbon

Some nonmetal elements exist in different physical forms called **allotropes**. Although they have quite different physical properties, they yield exactly the same products in their chemical reactions.

Carbon exists as two different allotropes: graphite (a slippery black powder that is the only nonmetallic substance to conduct electricity) and diamond (a colourless crystal that is the hardest naturally-occurring substance). It is difficult to believe from appearance alone that both consist of pure carbon, and that the only difference between them is the way in which the carbon atoms are bonded together; yet both graphite and diamond will burn in oxygen to produce carbon dioxide.

$$C_{(s)} + O_{2\,(g)} \longrightarrow CO_{2\,(g)}$$

In graphite each carbon atom is bonded to three other carbon atoms, forming one double bond and two single bonds:

Figure 3.16

a) Graphite and b) diamond are allotropes of carbon.

a)

b)

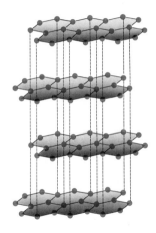

Figure 3.17

Graphite consists of flat layers of carbon atoms, with weak attracting forces between the layers.

If we apply VSEPR theory, remembering that the electrons forming a double bond are treated as a "group," we can see that the three groups of electrons surrounding the carbon atom will be arranged in a trigonal planar (or triangular planar) orientation, with a bond angle of 120°. Since every carbon atom in the graphite structure is bonded in the same way, a two-dimensional layer is formed in which the carbon atoms are arranged in a series of regular hexagons. (The inside angle of a regular hexagon is 120°.)

Solid graphite consists of a number of layers, one on top of another. Although there are weak attractions between the layers, there are no bonds, and the layers can readily slide past each other (Figure 3.17). Graphite is therefore soft and slippery to the touch. For this reason it is often used as a lubricant.

Each of the three bonds between a carbon atom and its three neighbours is identical. The fourth pair of electrons that forms the double bond is not restricted to a single location within the structure. Instead it is delocalized. As a result the structure gains stability and, because delocalized electrons are free to move, graphite will conduct electricity.

In diamond each carbon atom is bonded to four other carbon atoms, forming four single bonds:

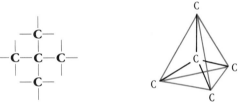

There are four pairs of electrons surrounding the carbon atom, which (according to VSEPR theory) will be tetrahedrally arranged. Since these are all bonding pairs, each carbon atom in the crystal is at the centre of a tetrahedron with another carbon atom at each corner. The bond angles are 109.5°. Since the bonding pattern is repeated for every carbon atom, this results is a three-dimensional network solid (Figure 3.18). If we examine the network closely, we see that there are several planes of atoms within the crystal. It is the reflection of light by these planes that gives diamonds their brilliant sparkle. A diamond cutter can enhance this property by cleaving stones along the planes to use the diamond in jewellery settings. The hardness is derived from the three-dimensional array of strong covalent bonds.

There are no double bonds in diamond and no delocalized electrons. Diamond will not conduct electricity.

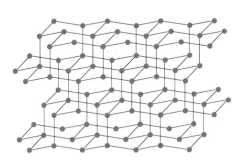

Figure 3.18

Diamond consists of a giant three-dimensional network solid. Each carbon atom is covalently bonded to four other carbon atoms.

Silica and The Silicates

Silicon is the second most abundant element of the earth's crust, 25.7 % by mass. It combines with the most abundant element, oxygen (49.5 % by

Figure 3.19
Quartz crystals.

Figure 3.20

a) The electron-dot formula of a silica molecule.

b) Oxygen atoms are arranged tetrahedrally around the central silicon atom.

c) These tetrahedrons link together to form quartz.

mass), to form silicon dioxide, SiO_2 — commonly called *silica*. Further reaction with metal compounds will produce metal silicates. Most of the earth's rocks consist of silica or silicates.

Quartz (Figure 3.20c) is the principal component of common sand and the most common form of silica. This substance is another example of a covalently-bonded network solid, in which every silicon atom is bonded to four different oxygen atoms. An entire quartz structure consists of one giant molecule.

VSEPR theory tells us that each silicon atom will be bonded tetrahedrally to the four oxygen atoms. Each oxygen atom is in turn bonded to another silicon atom, thus linking the tetrahedra together into a giant, three-dimensional network.

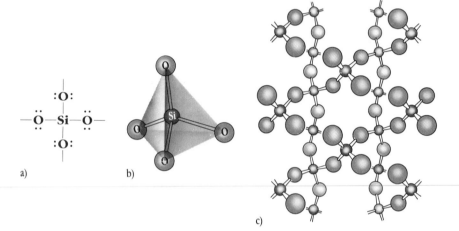

a)   b)

c)

Silicate minerals are formed when a proportion of the oxygen atoms are bonded to only one silicon atom rather than two. The bonding requirements of these oxygen atoms are satisfied by the addition of electrons from metal atoms thereby creating negatively-charged silicate ions and positively-charged metal ions. Depending upon the proportion of oxygen atoms that are bonded to only one silicon atom, a large number of structures may be formed. These include three-dimensional networks, two-dimensional sheets, one-dimensional chains, and separate negatively-charged ionic groups of silicon and oxygen atoms.

The simplest silicate unit is a $4-$ ion consisting of one silicon atom bonded to four oxygen atoms (SiO_4^{4-}). No oxygen atoms are shared, and compounds such as magnesium silicate (Mg_2SiO_4), containing this ion, are not network solids but merely crystals made up of a regular array of positive metal ions and negative SiO_4^{4-} silicate ions.

Slightly larger silicate ions are formed when three, four, or six SiO_4^{4-} tetrahedra join together to form rings. Crystals of the gemstone *emerald* consist of silicate ions of this type combined with positive beryllium and aluminum ions.

Two-dimensional silicate sheets are formed when three of the four oxygen atoms bonded to each silicon atom are bonded to other silicon atoms, while the fourth carries a negative charge. Depending upon the particular metal ions present in the structure and the way in which the sheets are separated, the result might be a *mica* or a *clay*. In mica, like the graphite allotrope of carbon, the bonds are in two dimensional layers, or sheets. Because there are only very weak attractions between the different sheets, mica flakes easily.

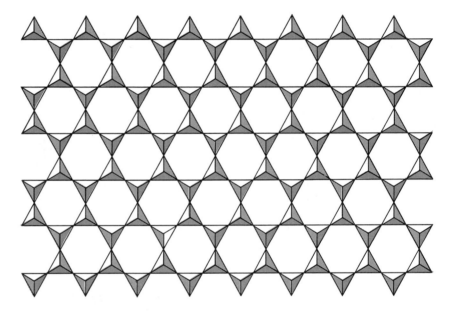

Figure 3.21

If silicate ions join to form a two-dimensional network, a layered mineral such as mica is formed.

If only one or two of the oxygen atoms that are bonded to each silicon atom are bonded to other silicon atoms, with the remainder carrying a negative charge, silicate clusters consisting of endless one-dimensional chains are formed. Different forms of asbestos, all containing calcium and magnesium ions in addition to the repeating silicate units, have structures of this type. Asbestos is fibrous and stringy because the atoms are only bonded in a chain.

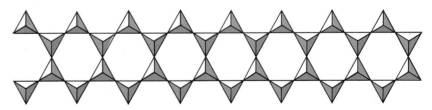

Figure 3.22

If silicate ions join to form chains, a fibrous asbestos type compound is formed.

a)

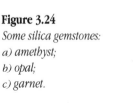

b)

Figure 3.23
*a) In asbestos the fibres contain long dou-
ble chains of silicate units.*
b) Mica contains layers of silcate units.

Figure 3.24
Some silica gemstones:
a) amethyst;
b) opal;
c) garnet.

Quartz itself can contain foreign metal ions. For example, aluminum ions may replace silicon atoms in the quartz structure. Because aluminum has only three valence electrons, while silicon has four, one of the four oxygen atoms around an aluminum ion will have to carry a negative charge. This requires the inclusion of other positive metal ions to balance the charge. The result is a quartz-like network solid containing a variety of positive metal ions. Some of these foreign ions add colour to the normally colourless quartz. Well-formed coloured quartz, without flaws, is often cut and polished to produce semiprecious stones for jewellery. Some examples are given in Table 3.2.

TABLE 3.2 *Some Common Precious and Semiprecious Silicates*

Stone	Major Foreign Constituents	Colour
Amethyst	Fe, Mn	clear purple
Emerald	Al, Be, Cr	clear green
Garnet	Al, Fe, Mg	clear dark red, green, brown, or yellow
Onyx	Fe, Mn	banded black, green, or brown
Opal	H_2O	pearly with a wide range of colours
Topaz	Al, F	clear wine, straw yellow

a)   c)

b)

Asbestos and Its Hazards

Asbestos has been used around the world for many centuries. Over 4000 years ago the material was mixed with clay to add strength to pottery. The ancient Greeks used the material for wicks in their lamps.

Behind many modern applications of asbestos are its properties of reinforcement and fire-resistance. Until recently, asbestos was added to cement to increase strength to finished concrete products. It was also widely incorporated into buildings as a fire-proofing and insulating agent. Asbestos was used in the manufacture of clutch and brake linings for the automobile industry, and for the manufacture of fire resistant blankets, papers, and tiles. It has also been used to make floor tiles as well as filters for the soft drink, wine, beer, and water purification industries.

Asbestos has been mined in Quebec for over a hundred years, continuing as the major source of the material in Canada, although there are also mines in British Columbia, the Yukon, Ontario, and Newfoundland. When asbestos production was at its peak, Canada was the world's second largest producer. Since the late 1970s, however, widespread fears of health hazards associated with asbestos have resulted in a drastic cut in production and a severe economic impact upon those areas of the country that were dependent on the industry.

Asbestos is not a single material but a group of silicate minerals that are fibrous as a result of a one-dimensional structure of the networks. Asbestos from different mines always has a slightly different compositions, but all forms have been found to cause health problems. Workers exposed to asbestos fibres over a prolonged period have been found to suffer from *asbestosis* — a severe scarring of the lungs that makes breathing very difficult. Many have also developed lung cancer, particularly those who also smoke tobacco products.

There is still much debate about whether some forms of asbestos are safer than others and about whether there is any safe level of exposure to the fibres. The Canadian asbestos industry is mounting a campaign to persuade potential users that the material is safe if used with the right precautions. In the meantime large amounts of money are being spent, particularly in the United States, on the removal of the material from public buildings. Research teams are working to develop substitutes for asbestos in the very many areas in which it was used.

Figure 3.25
An open pit asbestos mine in Thetford Mines, Quebec.

Figure 3.26
Asbestos fibres lodged in the respiratory tract and surrounded by spherical white cells. The cells attempt to engulf the fibres and transport them from the lungs.

QUESTIONS

7. Graphite is soft and slippery and used as a lubricant while its allotrope, diamond, is extremely hard and used as a cutting tool. Explain how the internal bonding in graphite and in carbon accounts for these differences.

8. Different silicate structural forms depend on the attachment of oxygen atoms to other silicon atoms. Of the four oxygen atoms around a silicon atom, how many will be bonded to another silicon atom when forming the following:
   a) a two-dimensional sheet
   b) a long chain
   c) an individual silicate unit

Hybridization Theory

3.4

VSEPR theory enables us to predict correctly the shapes of many molecules and ions. Once the shape has been established, however, we must still explain the bonding in terms of electron orbitals. To do this we must keep in mind the following:

1. Bonding occurs along the axis of the orbitals involved.
2. A covalent bond is formed when orbitals of two atoms overlap (Figure 3.27). The two overlapping orbitals must share two electrons.
3. When a covalent bond is formed, the probability of finding an electron between the nuclei of the two bonding atoms increases. It is the attraction of the positive nuclei for the negative electrons between them that constitutes the bond.

Figure 3.27

In the formation of a hydrogen chloride molecule, the 1s orbitals of two hydrogen atoms overlap to form a covalent bond.

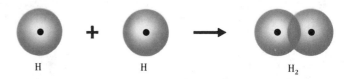

The concept of overlapping orbitals is a simplified, theoretical approach that must be modified to be consistent with experimental evidence. According to the quantum mechanical model of the atom, the *p* orbitals are at 90° to each other. Because bonding occurs along the direction of orbitals, we would expect bonding involving these orbitals to result in 90° angles. As we saw in our discussion of VSEPR theory, this value is quite uncommon. Instead we more often find bond angles of 109.5° and 120°. One model used to explain these observations is **hybridization theory**, which proposes that atomic orbitals combine to form new **hybrid orbitals**. The hydrids then overlap with orbitals of other atoms to form covalent bonds. The bond angles depend upon the mix of orbitals in the hybrid.

Hybrid orbitals can be generated mathematically by combining the wave functions of the Schrödinger equation for specific atomic orbitals. For example, combining the wave function for one *p* orbital with the wave function for an *s* orbital will define two identical *sp* hybrid orbitals 180° apart (Figure 3.28).

Figure 3.28

The combining of one **p** *orbital and an* **s** *orbital forms two identical* **sp** *hybrid orbitals, each of which can hold two electrons.*

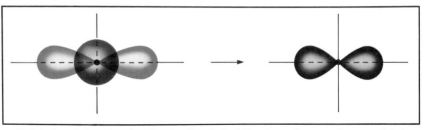

Orbital mixing is the basis for hybridization theory. By combining different orbital wave functions, each of the known simple geometries can be obtained. In this text we will only deal with combinations of *s* and *p* orbitals. These combinations and their corresponding geometries are listed in Table 3.3.

TABLE 3.3 *Simple Hybrid Orbitals*

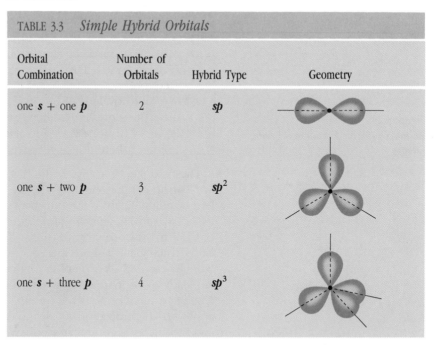

Orbital Combination	Number of Orbitals	Hybrid Type	Geometry
one *s* + one *p*	2	*sp*	
one *s* + two *p*	3	*sp²*	
one *s* + three *p*	4	*sp³*	

Let us now turn to a practical example and use hybridization theory to understand the bonding in methane, CH_4. The bond angles in methane are 109.5° and all four bonds are equivalent. According to Table 3.3 we must assume that four *sp³* hybrid orbitals are involved.

It is easier to picture the bonding if we work with individual atoms and follow the bonding through a series of hypothetical steps. We start with the central carbon atom. The ground-state electron configuration of a carbon atom is $1s^2 2s^2 2p^2$. The valence level contains two electrons in the $2s$ orbital and two electrons in the $2p$ orbitals. When a carbon atom forms four single bonds, one of the electrons in the $2s$ orbital is "promoted" to the empty $2p$ orbital. The $2s$ orbital and three $2p$ orbitals then combine to produce four equivalent sp^3 hybrid orbitals. Hund's rule tells us that the four electrons of the carbon atom will each occupy a different orbital, but the spins will be parallel. The sp^3 notation indicates the number and type of orbitals in the hybrid set: in this case, one s and three p orbitals. The number of electrons in the orbitals is not indicated.

The four hybrid orbitals have identical shape and identical energy. To minimize overlapping, the orbitals are arranged tetrahedrally in space, which means that the angles between them are 109.5°. Their formation can be compared to the production of four cans of pink paint from one can of red paint mixed with three cans of white paint. The total number of cans will remain the same, but all four will now contain paint of the same colour (Figure 3.29).

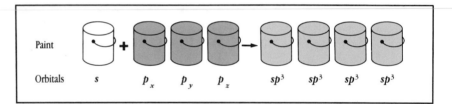

Figure 3.29
An analogy for the formation of hybrid orbitals.

The next step is to apply the basic principles of orbital bonding. Each sp^3 hybrid orbital contains a single electron, which is available for covalent bonding. Each of the four hydrogen atoms possesses one electron in its $1s$ orbital. The carbon atom, then, can form one bond along the axis of each hybrid orbital with one hydrogen atom. In the process, each hybrid orbital gains a share in a second electron. The configuration of overlapping sp^3 and $1s$ orbitals in methane is shown in Figure 3.30. The overlap leads to an increase in electron density between the two atoms. This type of covalent bond is referred to as a **sigma (σ) bond**. We can, in fact, apply sp^3 hybridization to all molecules that contain only single bonds and in which the central atom obeys the octet rule. The only variation will be in the number of electrons provided by the central atom.

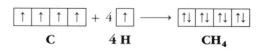

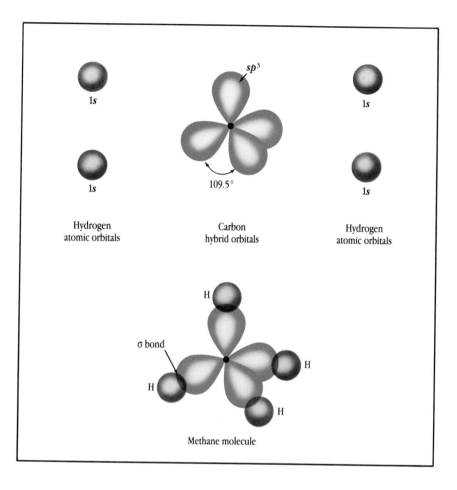

Figure 3.30
*The tetrahedral shape of the methane molecule can be explained by the use of **sp³** hybrid orbitals of the electrons in the central carbon atom.*

EXAMPLE

3.3 Use hybridization theory to account for the bonding and shape of the ammonia molecule. Remember that the bond angles approximate those of a tetrahedron.

SOLUTION The central atom of ammonia, NH_3, is nitrogen. The ground-state electron configuration of a nitrogen atom is $1s^2 2s^2 2p^3$. There are five valence electrons. To form bonds at tetrahedral angles, the $2s$ and three $2p$ orbitals must hybridize to form four **sp³** orbitals. One hybrid orbital will be filled; the remaining three will contain just one electron each.

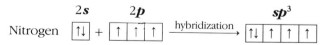

The four **sp³** hybrid orbitals will be arranged tetrahedrally. The three half-filled orbitals will each overlap with the $1s$ orbital of a hydrogen atom to form a sigma bond. The fourth hybrid orbital will contain a non-bonding pair of electrons. This model is consistent with the observed trigonal pyramidal shape of the molecule.

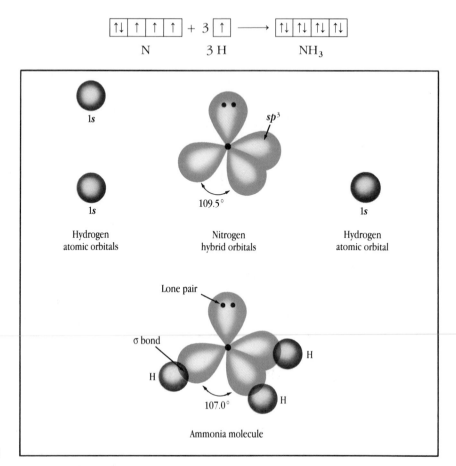

Figure 3.31
The trigonal pyramidal shape of the ammonia molecule can be explained by the use of three ***sp³*** *orbitals and one lone pair.*

Hybridization Theory and Electron-Deficient Molecules

To explain the bonding in electron-deficient molecules, we must apply the same principles as before. The geometry of the molecule is matched with the appropriate set of hybrid orbitals. We can use boron trifluoride, BF_3, as an example. This molecule is known to have bond angles of $120°$. The corresponding set of hybrid orbitals is sp^2. We therefore take the two $2s$ electrons and the single $2p$ electron of boron and place each one in an sp^2 hybrid orbital.

The three equivalent orbitals, now $120°$ apart, can form sigma bonds with the half-filled p orbital of each fluorine atom.

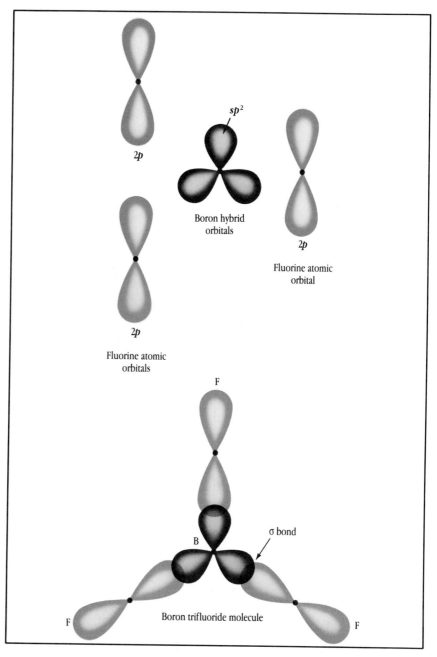

Figure 3.32

In the boron trifluoride molecule, three ***sp²*** *hybrid orbitals account for its trigonal planar shape.*

It should be understood that valence-level orbitals are not hybridized unless they are needed for bonding. In boron trifluoride, for instance, there is an empty 2**p** orbital. Also, only the hybridization of valence-level electrons of the central atom is considered. We will assume that the electrons on the non-central atom remain unhybridized.

3.4 Use hybridization theory to account for the bonding in the beryllium difluoride molecule. The molecule is known to be linear.

SOLUTION To form bonds at 180° angles, the valence electrons of the central beryllium atom must be **sp** hybridized. The beryllium atom has two valence electrons, both in the **2s** orbital. We form two **sp** hybrids, each containing one electron.

The hybridized atom can now form sigma bonds with the two fluorine atoms. The resulting molecule will have a linear shape, as observed.

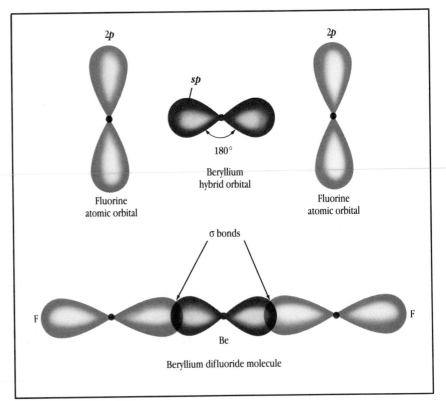

Figure 3.33
*The formation of two **sp** hybrid orbitals accounts for the linear shape of beryllium difluoride molecule.*

Figure 3.34
The bond angles in ethene.

Hybridization Theory and Double Bonds

The molecule ethene, C_2H_4, is observed to be a planar molecule with bond angles that are close to 120°. This is the shape that we would predict from VSEPR theory, since the electron-dot formula for the molecule shows that each carbon atom forms two single and one double bond. Each is therefore surrounded by three "groups" of electrons.

We can account for the bonding and shape of this molecule using hybridization theory if, for each carbon atom, we construct three **sp²** hybrid orbitals from the 2**s** orbital and two of the 2**p** orbitals. This will leave one 2**p** orbital containing a single electron. The **sp²** orbitals will be 120° apart in a plane.

A bond between the two carbon atoms is formed when one **sp²** orbital from each carbon atom overlaps the other. The remaining **sp²** hybrid orbitals each overlap the 1**s** orbital of a hydrogen atom and form sigma bonds. Each carbon atom is surrounded by three other atoms arranged 120° apart in a plane.

A second bond between the two carbon atoms is formed because the remaining **p** orbitals on each carbon atom are now lying parallel to each other and are able to overlap sideways. The resulting extra bond between the two carbon atoms is known as a **pi (π) bond**. There is now a double bond between the carbon atoms. The formation of the double bond requires the two ends of the molecule to become aligned and form a planar molecule.

Figure 3.35

In the ethene molecule a sigma bond is formed between each pair of bonded atoms. There is also a pi bond between the two carbon atoms.

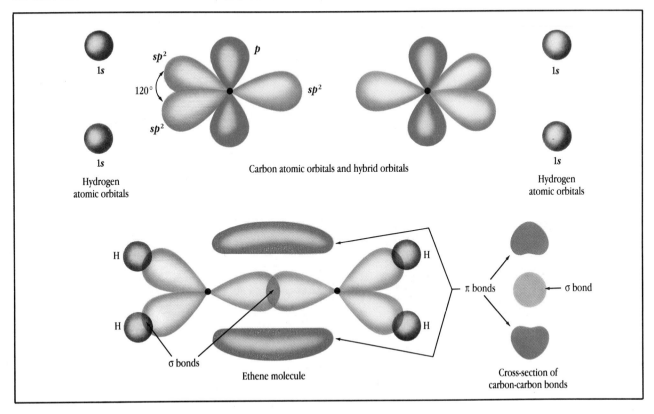

As Figure 3.35 shows, hybridization theory describes a double bond as consisting of two different types of bonds. The initial single bond between the two carbon atoms in C_2H_4 is formed by the overlap of an sp^2 hybrid orbital from each. The second bond between the two carbon atoms is formed by the overlap of two $2p$ orbitals.

Hybridization theory also provides a description of a *triple* bond. In this case two pi bonds are formed in addition to the sigma bond.

EXAMPLE   **3.5**   Use hybridization theory to account for the bonding and shape of ethyne, C_2H_2.

SOLUTION   Ethyne is observed to be a linear molecule, as we would predict using VSEPR theory.

$$H-C\equiv C-H$$

Each carbon atom must be sp hybridized. For each carbon atom, we can construct two sp hybrid orbitals by combining the $2s$ and one of the $2p$ orbitals. In each case two p orbitals will remain. Each orbital will contain one electron. The two sp hybrid orbitals will be 180° apart.

Figure 3.36

The triple bond in ethyne results from the formation of two pi bonds and sigma bond.

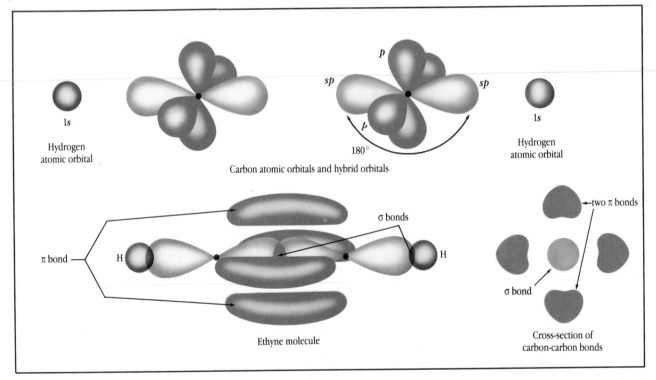

A sigma bond will be formed between the two carbon atoms as a result of an overlap of an sp orbital from each. The remaining sp orbitals each overlap the $1s$ orbital of a hydrogen atom to form a single covalent bond.

Interaction of the remaining **p** orbitals on the carbon atoms will produce two pi bonds at right angles to each other. The linear shape of the resulting molecule is consistent with the observed geometry.

Hybridization Theory and Expansion of the Valence Level

Hybrid orbitals can be constructed to account for the formation of molecules and ions with expanded valence levels. In these cases not only **s** and **p** orbitals but also **d** orbitals are involved. Hybrids such as **sp³d** and **sp³d²** must be constructed to account for cases in which the central atom forms five or six bonds.

Limitations of Hybridization Theory

In chemistry a theory often provides a way of picturing events at the microscopic level of the molecule. Provided that the image is useful and enables us to understand chemical phenomena, the theory itself is valuable even if it has flaws and limitations. In the case of hybridization theory, we encounter two problems.

The first is that the theory is not very predictive. If we already know the molecular shape, we can propose the hybrid orbitals involved. For example, the bond angle in the water molecule is 104.5°. This angle is close to the bond angle of a tetrahedral arrangement. Therefore, according to hybridization theory, the orbitals must be **sp³** hybridized. Sulfur, selenium, and tellurium are in the same Periodic group (Group VIA) as oxygen and also form analogous compounds: hydrogen sulfide (H_2S), hydrogen selenide (H_2Se), and hydrogen telluride (H_2Te). These compounds have bond angles of 92°, 91°, and 89.5° respectively. Here we would have to suggest that unhybridized **p** orbitals are being used. Thus it is necessary to have some idea of the geometry of the molecule used before we can suggest the type of hybridization, if any.

The second problem is specific to the water molecule. According to hybridization theory, the oxygen atom is **sp³** hybridized. Two of the hybrid orbitals are used for bonding to the hydrogen atoms, the other two are occupied by the lone pairs. Evidence from spectroscopic measurements now suggests that each lone pair is quite different. It is suggested that one is in the 2**s** orbital and the other is in a 2**p** orbital, which is quite contrary to hybridization theory.

Despite these flaws, hybridization theory does provide some useful insights into bonding in simple molecules, particularly in the field of organic chemistry.

QUESTIONS

9. What is the hybridization of each carbon atom in the following compounds:

    a) CCl_4 b) C_2Cl_4 c) C_2Cl_2

10. Compare the hybridization of the central atom in BF_3 and in BF_4^-.

Summary

- We can predict the shapes of covalent molecules by using VSEPR theory. The theory states that the pairs of electrons that surround the central atom repel each other, and will be oriented in space so as to be as far away from each other as possible.

- Four pairs of electrons surrounding a central atom will be arranged tetrahedrally in space. But the actual shape of a molecule depends on how many of these pairs are bonding pairs and how many are non-bonding.

- When all four pairs of electrons surrounding a central atom are bonding pairs, the resulting molecule will be tetrahedral in shape. When three of the four pairs are bonding pairs, the molecule will be trigonal pyramidal. When two pairs are bonding pairs, the molecule will be bent, or v-shaped.

- VSEPR theory may be applied to molecules and ions in which the central atom has an expanded valence level. The presence of five bonding pairs of electrons around a central atom produces a molecule that is trigonal bipyramidal in shape. The presence of six pairs produces an octahedral molecule.

- VSEPR theory may be applied to electron-deficient molecules. The presence of only three pairs of bonding electrons around a central atom produces a trigonal planar molecule. The presence of two pairs produces a linear molecule.

- When applying VSEPR theory, double and triple bonds in molecules and ions are treated as if they are single pairs of electrons.

- Giant structures in which atoms are covalently bonded together in continuous two- and three-dimensional arrays are called network solids.

- Pure carbon has two different forms, or allotropes, both of which are network solids: graphite and diamond.

- Silicon, the second most abundant element in the earth's crust, bonds with oxygen to form a wide range of network solids that may also contain a variety of other elements.

- Hybridization theory uses the concept of hybrid orbitals to describe the bonding in molecules and ions for which the shapes are already known. The electron orbitals of the central atom combine, or hybridize.

- Hybridization theory describes a double bond as consisting to two different kinds of bond: a sigma (σ) bond that lies along the axis joining the two bonding atoms, and a pi (π) bond made up of two parts that lie above and below this axis.

KEY WORDS

allotrope	octahedral
bent	pi (π) bond
bond angle	sigma (σ) bond
bonding pair	tetrahedral
hybrid orbital	trigonal planar
hybridization theory	trigonal bipyramidal
linear	trigonal pyramidal
molecular model	v-shaped
network solid	VSEPR theory
non-bonding pair	

ANSWERS TO SECTION QUESTIONS

1. a)

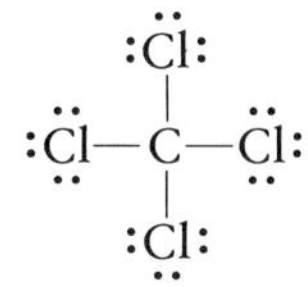

:Cl—C—Cl: tetrahedral

b) 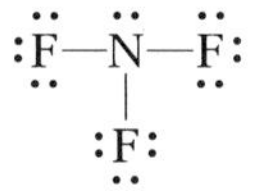 :F—N—F: trigonal pyramidal

2. a) bent   b) tetrahedral

3. The central oxygen atom is surrounded by two bonding and two non-bonding pairs of electrons. The repulsion between the bonding and non-bonding pairs will reduce the Cl—O—Cl bond angle.

4. a)

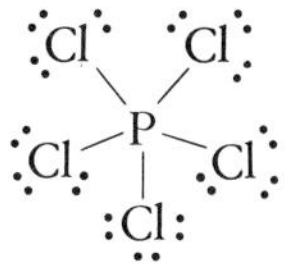

trigonal bipyramidal

b)

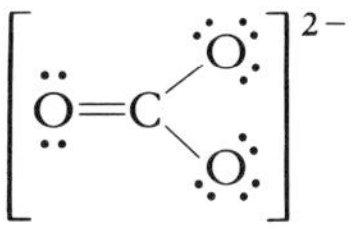

trigonal planar

5. a) linear   b) bent

6. Because lone pairs tend to occupy more space than bonding pairs, we would expect the bond angle to be slightly less than 120°. (Experimental results show the bond angle in sulfur dioxide to be 119.5°.)

7. Carbon atoms in graphite are arranged in layers. There are no bonds between the layers to prevent them from sliding past each other. In diamond each carbon atom is covalently bonded to four other carbon atoms in a tetrahedral shape, leading to an extremely stable three-dimensional array.

8. a) 3
   b) 2 (or 1 at each end of the chain)
   c) 0

9. a) sp^3 b) sp^2, sp^2 c) sp, sp

10. In BF_3 the B atom is sp^2 hybridized, and in BF_4^- it is sp^3 hybridized.

1. How does VSEPR theory help us to predict the likely shapes of molecules?

2. Explain why an ammonia molecule, NH_3, is trigonal pyramidal in shape while boron trichloride, BCl_3, is trigonal planar.

3. What are bond angles and how are they determined?

4. The bond angles in a water molecule are neither 90° nor 180°, as we might expect from the electron-dot formula. Why is this?

5. Explain, using VSEPR theory, why the bond angle in CO_2 is 180°.

6. How does VSEPR theory account for the fact that the bond angle in H_2O is less than that in NH_3?

7. Use VSEPR theory to explain the difference in shape between CO_2 and SO_2.

8. How do diamond and graphite differ, if at all, in the following properties:
   a) hardness
   b) electrical conductivity
   c) combustion in oxygen

9. Explain how the internal bonding patterns of graphite and diamond account for the difference in physical properties between these two allotropes.

10. On the basis of internal bonding and hence structure, explain why mica will flake and quartz will not.

11. Use hybridization theory to account for the bonding and shape of:
    a) CH_2Cl_2 b) H_2O

12. Show how hybridization theory can account for the shapes of BCl_3 and $BeCl_2$.

13. What is the difference between a sigma bond and a pi bond?

VSEPR Theory

14. Draw an electron-dot formula for each of the following and use VSEPR theory to predict the shape of these molecules:
    a) NBr_3 b) $SiCl_4$ c) H_2Se d) Br_2O

15. Use VSEPR theory to predict the shape of these molecules:
    a) BF_4^- b) AsH_3 c) OF_2 d) CH_2Cl_2

16. Deduce the shapes of the following molecules:
    a) BI_3 b) CO_2 c) AsF_5 d) O_3 e) $BeCl_2$ f) ClO_3^-

17. In which of the following compounds would you expect to find bond angles of 120°?
    a) NH_3 b) BF_3 c) PF_5 d) PCl_3

18. What would be the bond angles in the following compounds:
    a) HCN   b) CO_2 c) Cl_2O d) CCl_4

19. Which species has the greater bond angle, NO_2^+ or NO_2^-? Explain your answer by drawing an electron-dot formula for each species.

Hybridization Theory

20. What is the hybridization of the central atom in each of the following species:
a) PCl_3 b) BeI_2 c) CF_4

21. What type of hybrid orbitals would we construct on the central atoms to explain the bonding in a) H_3O^+ and b) C_2Cl_4?

---

22. In the following compounds label each bond as π or σ.

23. A solution of beryllium ions will react with sodium hydroxide solution to give a white precipitate of $Be(OH)_2$. If more sodium hydroxide solution is added, the precipitate will dissolve as the ion $[Be(OH)_4]^{2-}$ is formed. Draw an electron-dot formula for this ion and use VSEPR theory to deduce its shape.

24. Although we classify the element tin as a metal, the ionic character of the Sn—Cl bond is less than 35%. Draw the electron-dot formulas for $SnCl_4$ and $SnCl_3^-$ assuming that the bonds are mainly covalent. Use VSEPR theory to predict the shapes of these two species.

25. In xenon tetrafluoride, XeF_4, the four fluorine atoms surround the central xenon atom, forming a flat, square-shaped molecule. Draw an electron-dot formula for the compound, in which the valence level of xenon is expanded and the central atom is surrounded by six pairs of valence electrons. Show that the observed shape is consistent with VSEPR theory. What type of hybrid orbitals would have to be constructed to decribe the bonding, and account for the shape of XeF_4.

26. Carbon is the central atom in phosgene, $COCl_2$. Use VSEPR theory to predict the shape of the molecule.

27. Show how both VSEPR theory and hybridization theory can explain the shape of SCl_2.

28. Draw an electron-dot formula for CO_2. Label the bonds as σ or π. What would be the hybridization of the carbon atom in CO_2?

29. In the compound PCl_5, the phosphorus atom has an expanded valence level. Draw an electron-dot formula for PCl_5 and explain the shape of the molecule. The phosphorus atom must use five orbitals to make the five P—Cl bonds. Suggest a possible hybridization for phosphorus in this compound.

30. Peroxyacetyl nitrate, PAN, is one of the components of photochemical smog. A structural formula for PAN is given below.

a) How many pi and how many sigma bonds are there in this molecule?

b) Use VSEPR theory to determine the bond angles labelled i, ii, iii, and iv.

c) Deduce the hybridization of each carbon atom, each nitrogen atom, and each oxygen atom.

SUGGESTED PROJECTS

1. Using a model kit, build models of the following molecular shapes that we have studied in this chapter: tetrahedral, trigonal pyramidal, bent trigonal planar, linear, trigonal bipyramidal, and octahedral. (If you do not have access to a model kit, construct these models using gumdrops and toothpicks. Use different coloured gumdrops to represent different atoms. Use a toothpick to represent a pair of bonding electrons or a pair of non-bonding electrons.)

2. Using a model kit or the gumdrops/toothpicks method, construct a model of graphite and of diamond. Do not try to represent delocalized double bonds of graphite using bonds from the model kit bonds or toothpicks. Instead, use teased-out absorbant cotton balls spread between the layers. With your models demonstrate why graphite conducts electricity and diamond does not.

3. Elements other than carbon also display allotropy. Research and report on the structure and physical properties of the allotropes of phosphorus or sulfur.

Phases of Matter

Substances have a wide range of physical properties: some are solid at room temperature, and may have very high melting points; others are gaseous and have very low melting points. In addition, ionic compounds usually dissolve in water, while most covalent compounds do not. In this chapter we will see that it is the type of bonding, the type of crystal structure, or the shape of the molecules that determines the particular physical properties of a substance.

The Three Phases of Matter

4.1   Matter is found in three phases: solid, liquid, and gas. In a solid the particles are packed closely together. They vibrate slightly about fixed positions, but do not otherwise move. As a consequence, a solid has a definite shape and volume, and usually cannot be compressed to any large extent. In crystalline solids the particles are highly ordered. However, the particles in glasses and waxes are arranged in a random order.

Heat energy, when applied to a solid, is converted into kinetic energy causing the particles of the solid to vibrate more vigorously. If sufficient heat is added, the vibrations become so strong that the particles escape

Figure 4.1
Molten rock erupting from a volcano. Although we are used to rocks being solid, at high enough temperatures (about 2000°C) they melt.

from their fixed positions and the solid melts. In the resulting liquid phase the particles continue to **vibrate**, but also move slowly from one place to another, or **translate**. They also **rotate** slowly about their centre of gravity.

A liquid has a definite volume, but because the particles are able to move, its shape is determined by the shape of its container. Liquids, like solids, cannot be compressed to any significant extent because the particles are still closely packed together. However, in most cases the liquid form of a substance is slightly less dense than the solid form. As a result, if solid and liquid forms of the same substance are present in a container, the solid will sink to the bottom. Water is one of the few substances where this is not the case. Ice is less dense than water at 0 °C, and so will float.

If we heat a liquid, the kinetic energy of the particles will increase. Eventually a point is reached where the particles have sufficient energy to overcome the attractive forces between them. They will then escape from the liquid and move independently in the surrounding space. In this, the gas phase, the particles continue to vibrate and rotate. They translate much faster than in the liquid phase. A sample of gas will occupy all of the volume of a container, regardless of the container's size or shape. Gases have much lower densities than either solids or liquids, and are easily compressed.

TABLE 4.1   *Physical Properties of Solids, Liquids, and Gases*

Phase	Structure	Movement of Particles	Shape of Sample	Density	Compressibility
SOLID	particles closely packed in fixed positions	vibration only	definite shape and volume of its own	usually more dense than liquid or gas	cannot be compressed significantly
LIQUID	particles closely packed, not in fixed positions	vibration, rotation, and translation (slow)	takes on shape of container	usually less dense than solid	cannot be compressed significantly
GAS	particles widely spaced, not in fixed positions	vibration, rotation, and translation (fast)	occupies entire volume of container	much less dense than solid or liquid	can easily be compressed

Real Gases

In Chapter 1 we introduced the ideal gas equation, $PV = nRT$. An ideal gas can be defined as a gas in which the particles have zero volume and in which there are no forces between particles. For real gases at the normal range of pressures and temperatures that we use, the ideal gas equation seems to work quite well. However, if we compress a real gas under high pressure, the volume occupied by the particles is no longer negligible. We can show this graphically.

If we take a specific number of moles of gas and measure its temperature and pressure, we can use the ideal gas equation to calculate its theoretical volume, V_{ideal}. We can also measure the volume experimentally and record that value, $V_{observed}$. The ratio $V_{observed}/V_{ideal}$ will give us a measure of the deviation from ideal behaviour. A true ideal gas would give a constant value of unity (1) for this ratio.

When the values of $V_{observed}/V_{ideal}$ are plotted against pressure (Figure 4.2), we find that the values for real gases deviate considerably from unity. All the gases at very high pressures occupy a larger volume than the ideal gas model would predict. We conclude that at these high pressures, it is not valid to ignore the volume occupied by the molecules themselves.

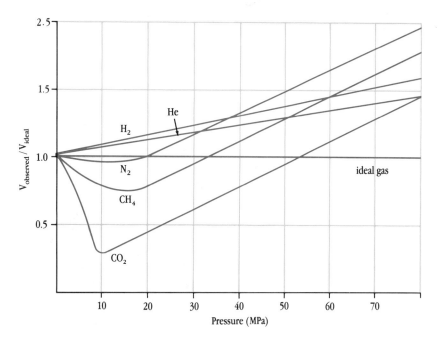

Figure 4.2

A graph of $V_{observed}/V_{ideal}$ plotted against pressure.

Some of the gases show a negative deviation at intermediate pressure values. We can explain this in terms of a second approximation of the ideal gas model. Namely, that molecules in the gas phase are not attracted to one another. The negative deviation is evidence that real molecules are attracted to each other at moderately high pressures. We will develop the concept of these forces between molecules later in the chapter.

QUESTIONS

1. How is the structure of a solid different from that of a liquid or gas?

Phase Changes   4.2

Most substances can exist in each of the solid, liquid, or gas phases; the particular phase at any moment depends upon the temperature and pressure conditions. Normally, if a gas is cooled at constant pressure, it will eventually become a liquid. This **change of phase** takes place at the **boiling point** of the substance. The boiling point depends upon the pressure that is being applied. If the temperature is reduced further, the liquid becomes a solid. This change of phase occurs at the **freezing point**. Once again, the precise value of the freezing point depends to a small extent upon the pressure.

If instead of reducing the temperature of a gas, we increase the pressure, we can also cause phase changes. Carbon dioxide, for example, will liquefy at room temperature if sufficient pressure is applied. However, many gases remain in the gas phase when the pressure is increased at room temperature, even when their volumes are reduced to the point where the molecules are just as close together as they are in the liquid phase.

Figure 4.3
Liquid hydrogen can be made by cooling hydrogen gas below -253°C.

Critical Temperatures and Pressures

Unless the temperature of the gas is below a specific value, a liquid will never be formed no matter how great the pressure. This temperature is known as the **critical temperature**. The minimum pressure necessary to liquefy a gas at the critical temperature is known as the **critical pressure**.

TABLE 4.2 Critical Temperatures and Pressures		
Substance	Critical Temperature (K)	Critical Pressure (MPa)
Helium	5	0.2
Hydrogen	33	1.3
Nitrogen	126	3.4
Oxygen	155	5.0
Carbon dioxide	304	7.4
Water	647	22.1

The critical temperatures and pressures of a number of substances are shown in Table 4.2. All of the substances listed, except for water, are gases at room temperature and pressure. Water becomes a gas at normal atmospheric pressure if the temperature rises above 100 °C (373 K). Helium can only be liquefied if the temperature is reduced to about 5 K. Putting this another way, we can say that helium cannot exist as a liquid at temperatures above 5 K, no matter how great the pressure. In contrast, water can exist as a liquid right up to 647 K (about 374 °C), as long as the pressure is high enough to prevent boiling.

Before we move on from the ideas of critical temperature and pressure, we must draw a distinction between a gas and a *vapour*. Both words refer to substances in the gaseous state, but the term **vapour** is usually used when a substance is below its critical temperature, and can be liquefied by the application of pressure alone. At room temperature, gaseous water and gaseous carbon dioxide would be vapours; gaseous helium, hydrogen, nitrogen, and oxygen would be gases.

Vapour Pressure

The temperature of a substance depends on the total amount of kinetic energy that the particles possess. In the case of a liquid, the molecules vibrate, rotate, and move from one place to another. As heat energy is added to a liquid, the total kinetic energy of the molecules increases; they move faster and the temperature rises. Not all of the molecules, however, will have exactly the same kinetic energy. At any moment some will be moving quickly and may possess a large amount of energy. Others may be moving more slowly and will possess less energy. From one moment to the next, collisions between the molecules will result in the transfer of energy from one molecule to another. The collisions do not cause energy to be lost from the liquid; rather, it is continually being redistributed among the molecules.

If a molecule at the surface of a liquid has a particularly large amount of energy, it may be able to escape from the surface and enter the gas phase. Such a process is known as **vaporization**. Since it is those molecules with the most energy that vaporize, it follows that the average energy, and thus the temperature, of the remaining liquid will fall. It also follows that the *rate* at which a liquid vaporizes must depend upon its temperature; at higher temperatures more molecules will possess enough energy to escape.

If we place a sample of liquid in a closed container, molecules of the liquid will gradually vaporize. After some time, many of the liquid molecules will have vaporized. Some of these molecules will collide with the surface of the liquid in the course of their random motion, and re-enter the liquid phase (Figure 4.4b).

The rate at which molecules return to the liquid phase will be determined by their concentration in the gas phase. If we leave the container for a sufficiently long time, the concentration of vapour molecules will rise to the point where they are returning to the liquid phase at exactly the same rate as they are leaving. A state of **dynamic equilibrium** will then exist within the container and the number of molecules in the gas phase will remain constant, although molecules of the liquid will continue to vaporize and molecules of the vapour will continue to condense. The volume above the surface of the liquid is said to be **saturated** with the vapour. Since the pressure of a gas depends upon the number of particles, the pressure due to the vapour, known as the **vapour pressure**, will also remain constant.

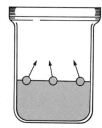

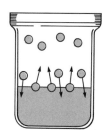

Figure 4.4

a) If we place a liquid in a closed container some of the molecules will vaporize.

b) At equilibrium, molecules condense at the same rate they evaporate.

Only if the temperature is altered will the equilibrium be affected. If we warm the container, the liquid will vaporize faster, molecules will enter the gas phase at a greater rate, and the concentration of vapour molecules will increase. Vapour molecules will return to the liquid at a faster rate, and a new equilibrium, with a higher vapour pressure, will eventually become established. If we cool the container, the opposite effect will occur and we will obtain a new equilibrium — at a lower temperature, with a lower vapour pressure. Each liquid has its own value of vapour pressure at a particular temperature. In Figure 4.5 we see how the vapour pressure for some common liquids rises with increasing temperature. The temperature at which vapour pressure equals atmospheric pressure is the normal boiling point of the liquid.

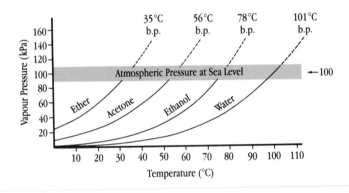

Figure 4.5

A graph of vapour pressure plotted against temperature. As the temperature increases, the vapour pressure of liquids increases.

Boiling Points of Liquids

What is the difference between evaporation and boiling? Both involve the vaporization of liquid molecules, but while evaporation occurs at any temperature, boiling takes place at a clearly-defined temperature that changes only if the pressure changes.

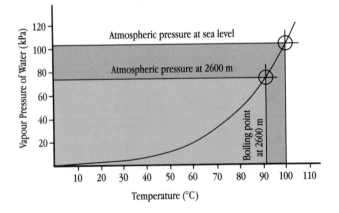

Figure 4.6

The vapour pressure curve for water. At sea level water boils at about 100°C (depending on the precise atmospheric pressure). At an altitude of 2600 m, water will boil at about 90°C.

Figure 4.7
Lake Louise, Alberta, is at an altitude of 1539 m, where the air pressure is about 84 kPa. At that pressure, water will boil at about 95°C.

Consider what happens when an open beaker of pure water is slowly heated. Initially, when the water is cold, the average energy of the molecules is relatively low and the rate of vaporization from the surface is slow. The escaping water molecules are free to leave the beaker. If the temperature were kept constant, the water would gradually **evaporate** at a constant rate until no liquid remained in the beaker. At no point would there be dynamic equilibrium between the liquid and vapour phases.

If we heat the beaker, the water molecules will evaporate more quickly. The vapour pressure of the water will continue to rise as the temperature rises until it becomes equal to the atmospheric pressure. When this occurs, water molecules are able to push apart from each other and to form bubbles of vapour *within the liquid.* The vapour pressure within the bubbles will be equal to atmospheric pressure and the bubbles will rise to the surface of the water because they are less dense than their surroundings. The water will now be *boiling.*

Freezing Points of Liquids

If we gradually warm a pure crystalline solid, we will reach a temperature at which it rapidly melts. This temperature is known as the **melting point**, and it has an exact value that depends very slightly on the outside pressure. If we cool the liquid again, it will solidify at the same temperature. The melting point and freezing point of a pure substance are identical.

We find that increasing the pressure favours the phase with higher density — that is, it will be the phase that occupies the smaller volume for a particular mass of substance. As mentioned earlier, most substances are denser in the solid form than the liquid. Applying high pressure to the liquid will convert it to the solid. Water is one of the few substances whose liquid form is denser than the solid. Subjecting ice just below 0 °C to very high pressures will cause it to melt.

Sublimation

The temperature of a solid, like that of a liquid and a gas, depends on the total amount of kinetic energy that the particles possess. In a solid, however, the particles are unable to move from their fixed positions. As a solid is warmed, the amount of vibration increases until the particles are freed from their fixed positions, and begin to move around. This happens at the melting point. Below the melting point, however, it is possible for particles at the surface of the solid to acquire sufficient energy to enter the vapour phase.

A phase change from solid to gas, without passing through the liquid phase, is known as **sublimation**. The reverse process, the change from gas phase directly to solid phase, is also known as sublimation. As a result of sublimation, solids often have low vapour pressures. The vapour pressure of ice at −5 °C, for example, is 0.87 kPa. If ice cubes are left uncovered in a frost-free fridge, they will slowly become smaller; water molecules will leave the surface of the ice cubes and enter directly into the vapour phase.

Figure 4.8
Skating on the Rideau Canal, Ottawa. The skates move on a thin layer of water caused by friction and pressure from the skate blade.

Figure 4.9
Hanging out the washing in Coral Harbour, Northwest Territories. The clothes will stay dry below 0°C because the water sublimes.

Figure 4.10
Possible phase changes.

Equilibrium between solid and vapour is never established because the vapour is removed from the freezer to ensure that it remains "frost-free."

Some solids have high vapour pressures even at room temperature and some household products make use of the phenomenon. Naphthalene crystals are used to kill moths in stored clothes. The vapour is toxic to moths. Para-dichlorobenzene is used as an air deodorizer. Both these compounds are useful because the air above the solid will contain a high enough concentration of vapour to be effective. You may have noticed how blocks of these compounds "disappear" with time. The element, iodine, also sublimes readily at room temperature. However, when heated, all three of these substances do change to a liquid before going into the gas phase.

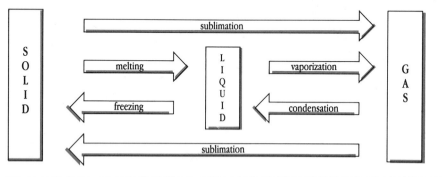

QUESTIONS

2. Use Figure 4.5 to estimate the boiling points of a) water, and b) ethanol in Canada's highest city: Kimberley, British Columbia (altitude 1120 m), where normal atmospheric pressure is about 90 kPa.

3. Explain what is meant by a dynamic equilibrium.

4. What is meant by a) vaporization, b) sublimation?

Phase Diagrams

4.3 There can be complex relationships between temperature, pressure, and phase changes for different substances. But no matter how complex these relations may be, we can gain a clearer understanding of them by representing phase changes in a **phase diagram**. Phase diagrams deal with closed systems.

The phase diagram for water, Figure 4.12, shows the phases for the substance over a range of temperatures and pressures. In addition, it shows how the melting and boiling points vary with pressure, and the conditions under which water will sublime.

Figure 4.11

Air freshener and moth flakes both have high vapour pressures. It is the vapour from these compounds that makes them effective.

The curve AB separates the solid phase from the vapour phase. The area above the curve and to the left of line BC represents the conditions under which ice exists. The curve AB indicates the equilibrium vapour pressure of ice at various temperatures. The diagram indicates that the equilibrium vapour pressure of ice at 0 °C is 0.6 kPa. Ice will sublime at 0 °C when the vapour pressure of water molecules in the gas phase is below this pressure.

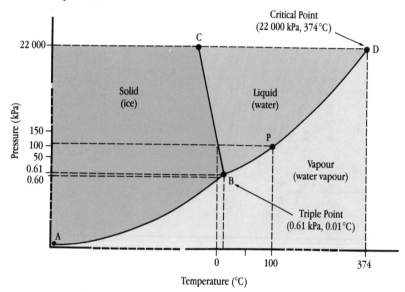

Figure 4.12

The phase diagram for water. The diagram is not to scale and the slope of line BC is exaggerated.

Figure 4.13

Saving water-damaged books by freeze-drying. This process is commonly used when a library has suffered flooding (often after a fire).

The line BC separates the solid phase from the liquid phase. It represents the variation in the melting point of ice as pressure increases from about 0.6 kPa to about 22 000 kPa. The backward slope of the line shows that water is a substance whose melting point decreases with increasing pressure.

The curve BD separates the liquid phase from the vapour phase. It shows the vapour pressures and temperatures at which liquid water is in equilibrium with its vapour. If the temperature and vapour pressure lie to the lower right of the curve, water will exist as a gas. If they lie to the upper left, it will exist as a liquid. The point P represents the boiling point of water at normal atmospheric pressure — at 100 °C and 101 kPa. From curve BD we can determine the boiling point of water at any other pressure.

Point B shows the only pressure and temperature at which all three phases exist together. This point is known as the **triple point**. The triple point for water is at 0.01 °C. The pressure at the triple point is 0.61 kPa. Point D is the critical temperature (374 °C) and the pressure (22 000 kPa). At temperatures above 374 °C, gaseous water cannot be liquefied by increasing the pressure. Liquid water cannot exist, under any pressure, above this temperature. The liquid-vapour equilibrium curve, BD, ends at D.

Making Diamonds

Diamonds were obtained from stream beds in India in prehistoric times, and have been discovered in many parts of the world including South America and the Soviet Union. Over 95 % of the world's current output of natural diamonds, however, comes from South Africa.

Figure 4.14
Industrially-synthesized diamonds produced at the General Electric research laboratory.

Diamonds occur naturally in rocks that have been pushed to the surface of the earth from depths of 150 km or more. At these depths the diamonds are formed from carbon dioxide gas that is dissolved in molten rock at extremely high pressures and at temperatures of over 1400 °C.

It has been recognized for a long time that diamonds are crystals of pure carbon, since they burn in oxygen to produce only carbon dioxide. It is also known that at normal pressures, graphite is the stable allotrope of carbon. Diamonds will in fact convert quite rapidly to graphite if they are heated at atmospheric pressure to around 1000 °C. At temperatures below 1000 °C, however, there is not enough energy available for the carbon atoms in a diamond crystal to rearrange into the graphite structure.

There were many attempts in the late 19th and early 20th centuries to make diamonds from graphite. Many of the methods were ingenious, but the researchers could only guess at the conditions necessary for the change. It was the careful and systematic construction of phase diagrams that enabled chemists and physicists to predict the conditions necessary for the formation of diamonds.

The phase diagram shows that graphite is the stable solid form of carbon at all temperatures up to the melting point, as long as the pressure is below 2 gigapascals (GPa). The line separating the graphite region from the diamond region tells us the pressure, at any particular temperature, that would have to be applied in order to convert graphite into diamond. At higher temperatures the pressure required for conversion becomes greater.

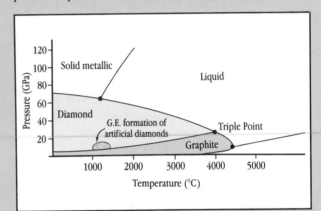

Figure 4.15
A simplified phase diagram for carbon. The pressure scale is in gigapascals (1 GPa = 10^9 Pa).

The principal difficulty that had to be overcome by those attempting to make diamonds was designing and making apparatus that would withstand the extremely high pressures required. As a result it was not until 1955 that anyone was successful. In that year General Electric announced that a team working in its research laboratory had managed to produce the world's first artificial diamonds by holding graphite at over 1200 °C under a pressure of about 5 GPa for a prolonged period. Molten metal was added to the graphite, and acted as a catalyst — that is, it caused the conversion to take place more quickly.

Since 1955 the techniques for making diamonds have improved as better high-pressure apparatus have been designed. A few large synthetic diamonds of gem quality have been obtained, but the cost of their manufacture exceeds their value in the marketplace. Most artificial diamonds are manufactured for industrial use, where the extreme hardness of the material makes it ideal for cutting, grinding, and in particular for shaping and sharpening tungsten carbide tools.

While large numbers of diamonds are made using high pressure techniques, researchers in the Soviet Union demonstrated about ten years ago that the diamonds can be made *without* the use of very high pressure. Thin films of diamond have been deposited on a variety of materials by passing microwaves through a mixture of hydrogen and methane gas. This technique, now being explored further by both Soviet and Japanese scientists, has the potential for producing very hard diamond coatings on any number of everyday items from cutting tools to lenses.

Figure 4.17
Diamond film is now being used to coat various items, such as speaker diaphragms, to enhance the quality and increase longevity.

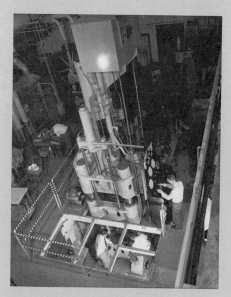

Figure 4.16
The very high-pressure, high-temperature apparatus used in the manufacture of diamonds.

The Phase Diagram for Carbon Dioxide

Each pure substance has a unique phase diagram. The phase diagram for carbon dioxide (Figure 4.18) shows one very significant difference from that of water. If we decrease the temperature of gaseous carbon dioxide at 100 kPa pressure, the gas changes phase at −78 °C. However, it changes directly from the gaseous to the solid phase without passing through the liquid phase. To obtain liquid carbon dioxide, a pressure greater than 516 kPa must be applied. Carbon dioxide is an important industrial chemical and it is usually supplied under pressure in the liquid form.

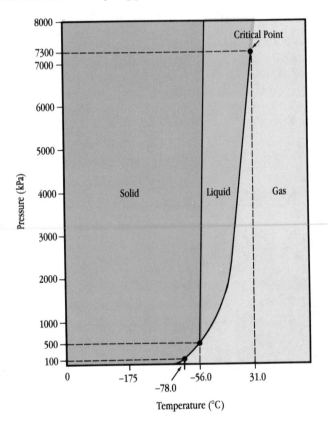

Figure 4.18
The phase diagram for carbon dioxide.

QUESTIONS

5. Using the phase diagram for carbon dioxide (Figure 4.18) determine the phase of carbon dioxide under these conditions.
   a) 40 °C and 120 kPa   c) −80 °C and 100 kPa
   b) −40 °C and 1500 kPa

6. Describe, using the phase diagram for water (Figure 4.12) the changes that take place if air at 100 °C containing water vapour at a pressure of 50.0 kPa is cooled.

Using Bond Types to Explain Physical Properties

<u>4.4</u> Why does hydrogen melt at $-259\,°C$ while tungsten melts at $3380\,°C$? Why is sodium soft while iron is hard? The differences in physical properties among elements and compounds relate to the different types of bonding and the strength of that bonding in each of the materials. To understand the principles involved, we first have to classify substances as either ionic, metallic, network covalent, or small-molecule covalent.

Explaining the Properties of Ionic Compounds

All ionic compounds are solids at room temperature, and they generally have high melting points and boiling points. These compounds usually have a wide temperature range within the liquid phase. For example, sodium chloride is a liquid between 800 and $1465\,°C$. Ionic compounds conduct electricity both in solution and in the liquid phase.

Ionic compounds consist of positive and negative ions. In the solid phase these ions are in alternating positions in the crystal lattice. It is electrostatic attraction between the positive and negative ions that we call the ionic bond. The stronger the bond, the more energy needed to break the bond, and hence, the higher the melting point of the compound. The bond is stronger for smaller ions because the charge is "spread over" a smaller volume of space. The bond is also stronger for ions with a high charge (such as Al^{3+} and O^{2-}).

Fact	Explanation
Ionic solids are hard, but also brittle. When hit with another object, they shatter.	The ions are held together by strong electrostatic forces. If a force is applied by one layer, and it moves, the two layers will repel each other because like charges repel.
When ionic solids dissolve in water, the solution conducts.	The ions in solution become free to move.

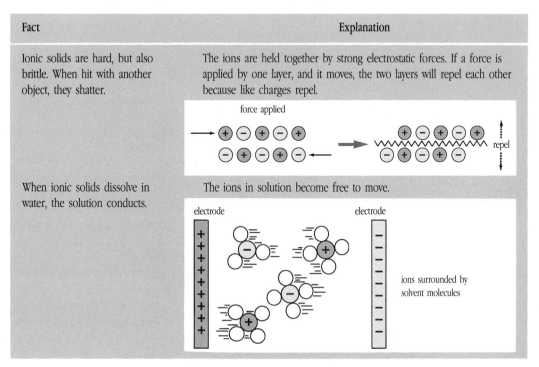

TABLE 4.3 *Ion Size and the Change in Melting Point (°C)*

Compound	NaF	NaCl	NaBr	NaI
Melting Point	993	801	747	661

—— increasing anion size ⟶

In the solid phase the ions are held rigidly in the lattice. However, when the compound is heated until it melts, the ions become free to carry an electric current. Similarly, if the compound can be dissolved in water, the ions can travel freely between electrodes placed in the solution.

Explaining the Properties of Metals

All metals, except for mercury, are solids at room temperature. The main group metals have low melting points, while the melting points of transition and lanthanon metals are almost all in the range of 1000 °C to 3000 °C. Irrespective of their melting points, all metals have wide temperature ranges in the liquid phase. Also, all metals conduct electricity in the solid and liquid phases.

TABLE 4.4 *The Melting and Boiling Points of Some Metals (°C)*

Metal	Hg	Na	Pb	Fe	W
Melting Point	−39	98	328	1535	3410
Boiling Point	357	883	1740	2750	5660
Range of Liquid Phase	396	785	1412	1215	2250

Solid metals consist of regular arrays of atoms forming a crystal lattice. The delocalized valence electrons form a sea of electrons that can move freely from one end of a piece of metal to the other, allowing for the conducting of an electric current. The "electron sea" is also present in the liquid phase. In the instant before vaporization, atoms reclaim their valence electrons. Thus in the gaseous phase no "electron sea" exists, and the gaseous metal atoms will not conduct electricity. The high energy necessary to completely break the metallic bonds accounts for the high boiling points of most metals.

We can explain patterns among the melting and boiling points of the main group metals in terms of the number of valence electrons. We find that the greater the number of valence electrons, the stronger will be the metallic bond and, hence, the higher will be the melting and boiling points. There are no simple correlations that we can find to relate the exact number of valence electrons to the melting and boiling points for both the transition and lanthanon metals.

Fact	Explanation
Metals are ductile and malleable; they can be bent and shaped.	Layers in the lattice slide over each other without breaking the metallic bond.
	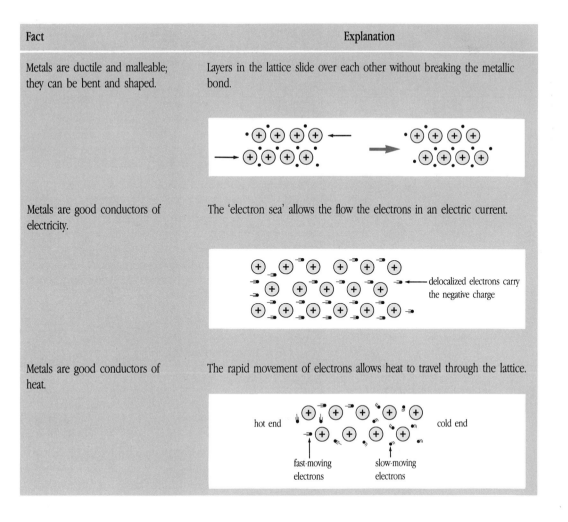
Metals are good conductors of electricity.	The 'electron sea' allows the flow the electrons in an electric current.
Metals are good conductors of heat.	The rapid movement of electrons allows heat to travel through the lattice.

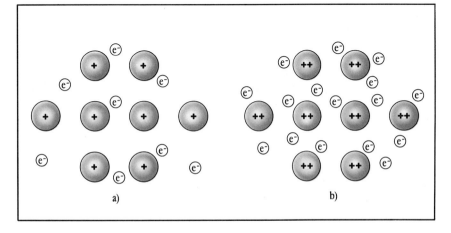

Figure 4.19

The 'electron sea' model of metallic bonding: a) Sodium has only one valence electron per atom, so it will have a lower melting point than b) magnesium, which has two.

TABLE 4.5	The Melting and Boiling Points of Third Period Metals (°C)		
Metal	Na	Mg	Al
Melting Point	98	649	660
Boiling Point	883	1107	2467

Explaining the Properties of Network Solids

Network solids contain atoms that are bound by covalent bonds to their neighbours. The most common examples of network solids — diamond and quartz (SiO_2) — form three-dimensional networks of atoms. In diamond each carbon atom is bonded to four other carbon atoms in a tetrahedral arrangement. In quartz each silicon atom is bonded in a tetrahedral arrangement to four oxygen atoms. Each of the oxygen atoms links to another silicon atom. These substances have very high melting and boiling points (Table 4.6).

TABLE 4.6	The Melting and Boiling Points of Some Network Covalent Substances (°C)	
Substance	C(diamond)	SiO_2
Melting Point	3550	1610
Boiling Point	4830	2230

The high melting points are a characteristic feature of three-dimensional network solids. To melt one of these substances, strong covalent bonds must be broken. This requires a large quantity of energy, or, in other words, a high temperature. Another property of these solids is their hardness. To break a crystal of a network solid, covalent bonds must also be broken, thus accounting for its strength.

Fact	Explanation
Network solids are very hard, have very high melting points, and very high boiling points.	Covalent bonds hold together the entire lattice, so a large amount of energy is needed to break up the lattice. 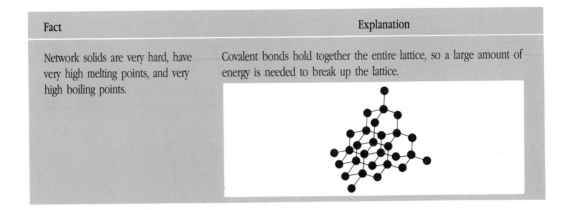

Figure 4.20

Layers of carbon atoms sliding over each other make graphite a good lubricant.

Graphite is the most common, two-dimensional network solid. The carbon atoms are covalently bonded in layers with only weak attractions between. The layers are free to slide over each other, accounting for the usefulness of graphite as a lubricant and as a writing material. Graphite is unique among network covalent substances in that it will conduct electricity within the layers.

Diversity of Small-Molecule Covalent Substances

In all of the substances that we have discussed so far the bonding is spread throughout the solid. An ionic solid consists of three-dimensional arrays of cations and anions attracted to each other by electrostatic forces. A metal consists of metal atoms held together by an "electron sea" of metallic bonds. A network solid consists of atoms held together by shared electron pairs, that is covalent bonds.

Small-molecule covalent substances, in constrast, consist of small units of atoms held together by covalent bonds within the unit. For example, water consists of independent sets of two hydrogen atoms and one oxygen atom. The three atoms are joined by shared electron pairs, covalent bonds. These covalent bonds *within the molecule* are referred to as **intramolecular forces**. There are no covalent bonds between different water molecules.

Small covalent molecules generally have low melting and boiling points, and are often gases at room temperature. They remain in the liquid phase over only a narrow temperature range. There are, however, a few exceptions (such as water) that have relatively high melting and boiling points.

If there were no forces of any kind *between* small covalent molecules, then there would be nothing to stop the molecules from flying apart. In other words, we would expect all small covalent substances to be gases at all temperatures. This is clearly not true. Water is a liquid, sucrose is a solid, and even gases such as carbon dioxide can be solidified if the temperature is reduced. In conclusion then, there have to be some attractive forces *between separate covalent molecules*. These forces are known as **intermolecular forces**.

Fact	Explanation
Small-molecule covalent substances have low melting points and low boiling points.	Each molecule is held together strongly. But the forces between molecules are weak, so the lattice is easily broken up. 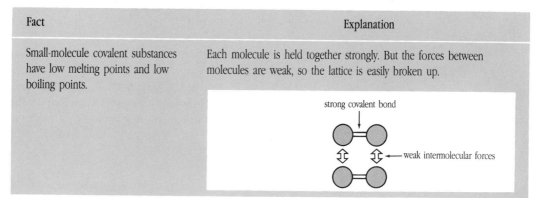

7. What are the principal differences in physical properties between ionic compounds and small-molecule covalent compounds?

8. Explain how, and under what conditions, ionic compounds conduct electricity.

9. Which of the following ionic compounds would have the higher melting point? Explain your answer.
   a) NaCl or LiF
   b) NaCl or AlN

Polarity of Molecules

4.5 As well as explaining the attraction between small covalent molecules, we must look at differences between them. For example, why is water a liquid while hydrogen sulfide is a gas at room temperature? Why does ethanol (C_2H_5OH) dissolve in water, but similarly-sized propane (C_3H_8) does not? Before we can examine these intermolecular forces, it is necessary to introduce the concept of molecular polarity.

Covalent compounds often have a degree of ionic character resulting from the unequal sharing of bonding electrons. This unequal sharing produces polar covalent bonds, or simply *polar bonds*. The presence of polar bonds in molecules of particular shapes can result in molecules which themselves are polar.

In order to determine whether a molecule is polar, we must first determine whether it contains polar bonds. Therefore, we examine the electronegativities of the atoms that form the bonds. The greater the difference in electronegativity, the more polar the bond. We consider a difference in electronegativity of less than 0.5 indicates a bond that is essentially nonpolar.

EXAMPLE

4.1 By referring to Figure 4.21, determine which of the following bonds is polar:
a) Cl—F   b) Cl—Cl

SOLUTION   To determine whether a bond is polar we must compare the electronegativities of the two atoms that form the bond.
a) From Figure 4.21 we can see that the electronegativity of chlorine is 3.0, while that of fluorine is 4.0. The electronegativity difference between the two atoms forming the bond is 1.0. We can conclude that fluorine will attract electrons more strongly than chlorine, and that the Cl—F bond will be polar.

$$\overset{\delta+}{Cl}\!\!-\!\!\overset{\delta-}{F}$$

b) From Figure 4.21 we can see that the electronegativity of chlorine is 3.0. Since both of the atoms forming the bond are chlorine atoms, there is no electronegativity difference between them. We can conclude that the Cl—Cl bond will not be polar.

EXAMPLE *4.2* By referring to Figure 4.21, place the following bonds in order of decreasing bond polarity: N—F, C—H, O—H, O—F, and F—F.

SOLUTION From Figure 4.21 we can see that the electronegativity differences between the atoms forming the bonds are as follows:

N—F	1.0
C—H	0.4
O—H	1.4
O—F	0.5
F—F	0.0

Clearly the O—H bond is the most polar, while the F—F bond is not polar at all. In order of decreasing polarity, the bonds are: O—H, N—F, O—F, C—H, and F—F.

A molecule that contains polar bonds will not necessarily be a polar molecule. If the shape of a molecule is such that the polar bonds are symmetrically arranged, their effects may cancel and there will be no positively-charged or negatively-charged side to the molecule.

Before we look at examples of such molecules, however, we shall examine briefly a very simple polar molecule so that we will be able to recognize characteristics that can be used to help us determine whether other, more complex molecules are polar.

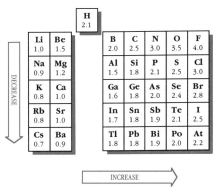

Figure 4.21
Electronegativity values for the main group elements.

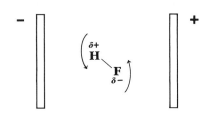

Figure 4.22
Polar hydrogen fluoride molecules will align themselves so that the partially-charged ends are near the plate of opposite charge.

Polarity of the Hydrogen Fluoride Molecule

The hydrogen fluoride molecule consists of a hydrogen atom bonded covalently to a fluorine atom. Since the electronegativity difference between hydrogen and fluorine (Figure 4.21) is 1.9, we can deduce that the bond is polar. The molecule therefore clearly possesses an end having a partial negative charge and an end having a partial positive charge. The molecule is said to possess a molecular **dipole**. The presence of a molecular dipole is indicated in a diagram by an arrow ($\longmapsto$) directed towards the negatively-charged end of the molecule.

$$\overset{\delta+}{H} - \overset{\delta-}{F} \qquad \overset{\longmapsto}{H-F}$$

Symmetrical Molecules

We have seen that the common basic geometries of molecules are linear, trigonal planar, tetrahedral, trigonal bipyamidal, and octahedral. If a molecule has one of these shapes, with identical atoms attached to a central atom, the molecule is said to be *symmetrical*. Let us consider three symmetrical molecules: carbon dioxide, boron trifluoride, and carbon tetrachloride. As we can determine from the electronegativity values, each of these molecules contains polar bonds.

Using VSEPR theory, we would predict that a carbon dioxide molecule is linear, with the oxygen atoms on opposite sides of the carbon atom. The partial negative charges on the oxygen atoms are directly opposing each other. The drift of electrons towards the more electronegative oxygen atoms will "cancel" each other. As a result, the molecule itself is nonpolar.

Figure 4.23
We can represent the electron drift in carbon dioxide by means of arrows pointing towards the negative ends. The two arrows cancel each other, so the molecule is nonpolar.

In the case of boron trifluoride, the three fluorine atoms are arranged 120° apart around the central boron atom. The electron drift towards the highly electronegative fluorine atoms will be of equal value at equal angles. Again, the net effect will be to "cancel out" the polarity of each bond.

Figure 4.24
Boron trifluoride also has polar bonds. In this case the equal electron drifts at 120° result in a nonpolar molecule.

The carbon tetrachloride molecule is tetrahedral. Each chlorine atom is arranged 109.5° from its neighbours, around the central carbon atom. In this tetrahedral arrangement, too, we find that the electron drift toward each of the more electronegative chlorine atoms is of equal value at equal angles. Therefore, carbon tetrachloride is another nonpolar molecule.

Figure 4.25
In carbon tetrachloride the four polar bonds cancel, resulting in a nonpolar molecule.

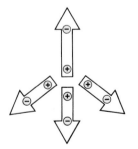

Molecules with Lone Pairs

If a molecule contains polar bonds that are not arranged so that polarities "cancel," then the molecule itself will be polar. The water molecule is the most important example of a polar molecule.

There is an electronegativity difference of 1.4 between hydrogen and oxygen, thus water contains very polar oxygen-hydrogen bonds. If we examine the shape of a water molecule (Figure 4.26), we see that the drift of the electrons is toward the more electronegative oxygen atom. In the water molecule, the oxygen atom will have a partial negative charge, and the direction of the two hydrogen atoms will have a partial positive charge. As a result the molecule is polar. We can say that the molecule has a **dipole moment**. The direction of the dipole would be with the negative end at the oxygen atom and the positive end at the midpoint between the two hydrogen atoms.

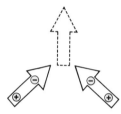

Figure 4.26

In water the individual polar bonds do not cancel, resulting in a net drift shown by the dotted arrow. The molecule is polar.

Another common polar molecule is ammonia. The three hydrogen atoms are in an unsymmetrical pyramidal arrangement around the central nitrogen atom. Thus there will be a net electron drift toward the nitrogen atom, giving it a partial negative charge and the hydrogen atoms a partial positive charge. The molecular dipole would be with the negative end at the nitrogen atom and the positive end at the midpoint between the three hydrogen atoms.

Figure 4.27

In ammonia the asymmetrical arrangement leads to an electron drift toward the nitrogen atom.

Other Symmetrical Molecules

Molecules that are linear, trigonal planar, or tetrahedral in shape may be polar if the atoms that surround the central atom are *not identical*. The molecule Cl—Be—F is an example. The fluorine atom, which is much more electronegative than beryllium, will carry a significant negative charge. The chlorine atom is also more electronegative than beryllium and thus will have a partial negative charge. However, the smaller electronegativity difference of the Cl—Be bond compared to the Be—F bond will result in a smaller partial charge on the chlorine atom. Since the partial charges on the two ends of this linear molecule are not identical, the molecule will be polar.

Figure 4.28

In BeClF the Be-F bond is more polar than the Cl-Be bond. There is more electron drift to the fluorine atom, and the molecule is polar.

Tetrahedral molecules will also be polar to a greater or lesser extent if the four atoms surrounding the central atom are *not all the same.* If we examine trichloromethane (CHCl$_3$), for example, we can see that there are clearly discernible positive and negative sides to the molecule, which result from one of the surrounding atoms — the hydrogen atom — being different from the rest. Therefore, trichloromethane molecules are polar.

Figure 4.29

In trichoromethane the C-Cl bonds are polar while the C-H bond is not. As a result, the molecule is polar.

Figure 4.30

Trichloromethane, commonly called chloroform, can be used as both an anesthetic and a solvent. Like most chlorine compounds, it is known to be toxic.

Evidence of Molecular Polarity

If a glass rod is rubbed with a piece of polythene, the rod will become positively charged with static electricity. As well, if an ebonite rod is rubbed with cat's fur, the rod will become negatively charged. When we hold the charged glass rod close to a stream of water, ethanol, or some other polar liquid, we find that the stream is deflected toward the rod. Repeating the experiment with the negatively-charged ebonite rod also causes the stream to be deflected toward the rod. If we repeat the test using a nonpolar liquid, such as carbon tetrachloride, CCl$_4$, we cannot detect any deflection.

We explain the deflection of water toward a charged rod in terms of molecular polarity. As the stream of liquid falls past the glass rod, the polar molecules tend to rotate and align themselves with the electric field surrounding the rod. The oxygen atoms, which possess a slight negative charge, are attracted by the positive charge on the rod. As a result, the stream of water will be pulled toward the rod. The same thing happens when a negatively-charged ebonite rod is used, but the water molecules become oriented in the opposite direction, and the positively-charged hydrogen atoms will pull the water molecules toward the rod.

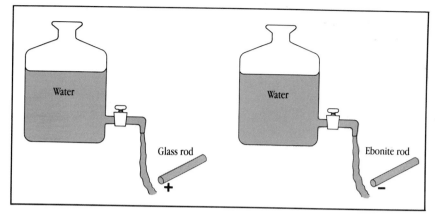

Figure 4.31

a) A stream of water is attracted to a positively-charged glass rod.

b) Water is also attracted to a negatively-charged ebonite rod.

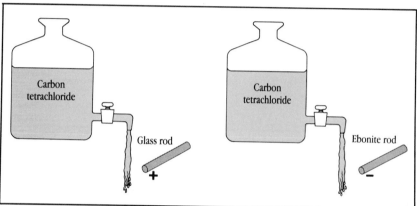

Figure 4.32

a) Carbon tetrachloride is not attracted toward a positively-charged glass rod.

b) Carbon tetrachloride is not attracted to a negatively-charged ebonite rod.

Figure 4.33

Polar water molecules align themselves to become attracted to negatively- and positively-charged rods.

We have seen that carbon tetrachloride molecules are nonpolar even though the individual carbon-chloride bonds are polar. The symmetry of the molecules is such that the individual bond dipoles cancel each other out, and there is no distinguishable positive and negative side to the molecule. As a result, carbon tetrachloride molecules are not attracted to the charged rod.

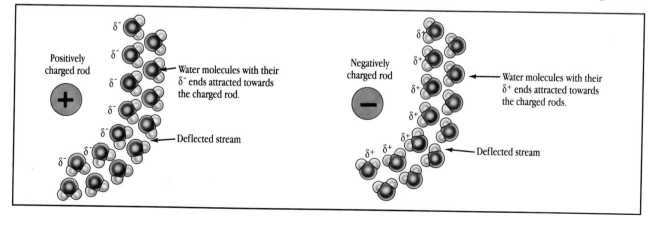

4.3 Indicate whether the following molecules would be polar or nonpolar:
a) CH_2Cl_2 b) NF_3

SOLUTION   a) For a molecule to be polar it is necessary for it to contain polar bonds. In the case of CH_2Cl_2 (dichloromethane) we can see in Figure 4.21 that the electronegativity of carbon is 2.5, that of hydrogen is 2.1, and that of chlorine is 3.0. Since chlorine is much more electronegative than carbon or hydrogen, there will be polar bonds in this molecule, and the chlorine atoms will carry a partial negative charge. The hydrogen atoms will carry a partial positive charge. For a molecule to be polar it is also necessary that the symmetry of the molecule should not be such that the effects of the polar bonds cancel. To determine whether or not this is the case, we must determine, using VSEPR theory, the shape of the molecule. By applying this theory we can determine that the CH_2Cl_2 molecule will be tetrahedral and that there are distinct positive and negative sides. Therefore the molecule CH_2Cl_2 is polar.

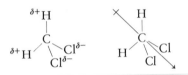

b) The electronegativity of nitrogen is 3.0, while that of fluorine is 4.0. The nitrogen trifluoride molecule therefore contains polar N—F bonds. By applying VSEPR theory we can determine that the molecule is trigonal pyramidal in shape. There is no centre of symmetry in the molecule, which possesses distinct positive and negative sides. Thus, the molecule NF_3 is a polar molecule.

QUESTIONS

10. For each of the following molecules determine whether polar bonds are present, use VSEPR theory to predict the molecular shape, and determine whether a molecular dipole is present.
a) H_2S b) CH_4 c) PF_3

11. Would you expect a stream of $CHCl_{3\,(\ell)}$ to move towards a charged rod? Explain briefly.

Intermolecular Forces

4.6 One of the earliest pieces of evidence that forces of attraction exist between molecules was the discovery that most gases get colder if they are allowed to expand suddenly into a large volume. This is referred to as the **Joule-Thomson effect** because it was first noted experimentally by physicists James Prescott Joule and William Thomson (later known as Lord Kelvin) in 1862.

If a carbon-dioxide fire extinguisher is discharged, the temperature of the gas leaving the extinguisher is much lower than that of the surroundings. In fact if the gas is discharged through a cotton gauze, the temperature can fall to below $-78\,°C$ — cold enough for solid carbon dioxide to be deposited on the gauze.

The carbon dioxide is stored in the extinguisher under very high pressure. When it is allowed to escape into the atmosphere, the pressure on the escaping gas is suddenly reduced, and its volume increases. The carbon dioxide molecules suddenly move much farther apart. The large drop in temperature is evidence that attractions exist between the carbon dioxide molecules. The temperature decreases because some of the kinetic energy possessed by the carbon dioxide molecules must be used up to overcome these attractions. It is not only carbon dioxide that exhibits this cooling effect; almost all gases get colder if they are allowed to expand suddenly into a large volume.

Figure 4.34

A refrigerator uses the Joule-Thomson cooling effect. Compressed gas is allowed to expand into a larger volume causing it to cool. The cold gas circulates through the cabinet.

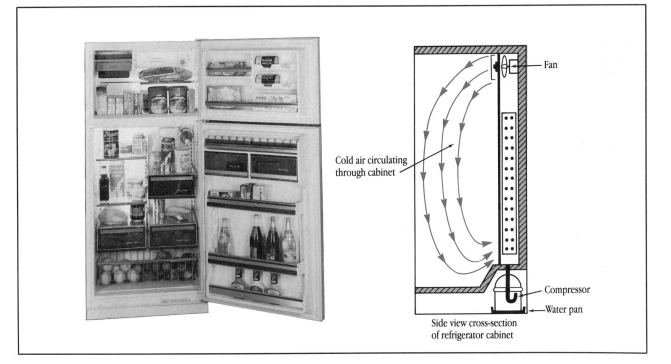

Fan

Cold air circulating through cabinet

Compressor

Water pan

Side view cross-section of refrigerator cabinet

Figure 4.35
Johannes van der Waals (1837-1923) was one of the first scientists to study intermolecular forces.

Figure 4.36
Fritz London (1900-1954) developed a theory to explain attracting forces between nonpolar molecules.

The forces of attraction between one molecule and another are known as intermolecular forces. One of the first experimenters to study intermolecular forces was the Dutch physicist Johannes van der Waals. For this reason these forces are often referred to as **van der Waals forces**.

Dispersion Forces

The discovery of the Joule-Thomson cooling effect prompted many scientists to attempt to understand the nature of intermolecular forces. But the task was not an easy one. Many of the gases that cool on expansion are, like carbon dioxide, nonpolar. This indicates that the effect is not a result of the interaction of the positive part of one molecule with the negative part of another. Many attempts were made to develop a satisfactory theory to account for the cooling effect, but without any great success until approximately eighty years after Joule and Thomson's original experiments.

During the late 1920s a German physicist, Fritz London, proposed a model to explain the presence of attractive forces between nonpolar molecules. He suggested that *all* molecules, including monatomic molecules like the noble gases, could possess very small temporary dipoles. London suggested that the electrons present in a molecule are continually vibrating back and forth, producing very short-lived positive and negative charges on different parts of the molecule. As soon as a slight positive charge is produced on one part of one molecule, it will immediately attract the electrons of the molecule next to it, and induce a small, temporary dipole in this molecule. This attraction lasts only for the very short period of time that the dipole exists. The force of attraction is weak, but since a large number of molecules are present in even a small quantity of material, some of the molecules will be attracting others all of the time. The overall result will be the presence of weak intermolecular forces.

Intermolecular forces of this type are known as **dispersion forces**, or sometimes as **London forces**. They are effective only over very short distances, and their strength is affected by both the size and the geometry of the molecules involved. Larger molecules possess greater numbers of electrons. If more electrons are able to shift temporarily away from one part of a molecule to another, the magnitude of the charge that is produced is greater.

The shape of the interacting molecules is important because it determines how closely they can come together. Shapes that allow for close contact result in greater dispersion forces.

Dipole-Dipole Forces

All covalent molecules, whether polar or not, are attracted by dispersion forces. Between polar molecules, however, there are additional forces of attraction resulting from the presence of permanent dipoles. These forces of attraction occur because the negatively-charged part of one molecule

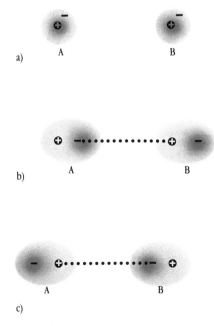

a)

b)

c)

Figure 4.37
Dispersion (London) forces.

a) Two nonpolar atoms. The concentration of negative charge is shown by the stippling density.

b) Electrons in A have moved to the right, and are then attracted to the nucleus in B.

c) At another instant, electrons in B move to the left, causing the electrons to be attracted to the nucleus of A.

is attracted to the oppositely-charged part of a neighbour. The forces are simply known as **dipole-dipole forces**; their strength depends on the magnitude of the charges on the molecules. This in turn will be determined by the difference in electronegativity between the atoms that are bonded together in the molecule.

Hydrogen Bonding — A Special Case of Dipole-Dipole Interactions

In most polar molecules the dipole-dipole forces account for no more than a fraction of the total intermolecular forces. Only when the difference in electronegativity is large, and the strength of the dipole is correspondingly high, is the dipole-dipole force much greater than the dispersion force.

The molecules that possess the largest dipoles are those in which the electronegative elements — particularly nitrogen, oxygen, and fluorine — are bonded to hydrogen. In these cases the hydrogen atoms forming the bonds carry a positive charge, and the more electronegative atoms carry a negative charge. Partly because the dipoles are so strong, and partly because hydrogen atoms have no other electrons to shield their positive nuclei from the electrons of neighbouring molecules, the resulting dipole-dipole forces are particularly strong.

These relatively strong intermolecular forces are distinguished from all of the other dipole-dipole forces, and are known as **"hydrogen bonds."** When we are considering the intermolecular forces that exist in ammonia, water, hydrogen fluoride, and other molecules that contain hydrogen atoms bonded to a highly electronegative element, we consequently talk of *hydrogen bonds* rather than of *dipole-dipole forces*.

TABLE 4.7 *Intermolecular Forces (van der Waals Forces)*		
Dispersion Forces	**Dipole-Dipole Forces**	
Forces that exist between *all* covalent molecules. They result from the presence of small temporary molecular dipoles caused by the momentary shifting of electrons away from parts of the molecule.	Forces that exist between molecules that possess permanent molecular dipoles, i.e. between polar molecules.	
	Regular Dipole-Dipole Forces	**Hydrogen Bonding**
	Weak forces that exist when there is only a small difference in electronegativity between the atoms that are bonded together. Molecular dipoles are not particularly large.	A special category of stronger dipole-dipole forces that exist between molecules containing hydrogen atoms bonded to particularly electronegative elements. Hydrogen bonds are not really "bonds" — they are simply attractions between highly polar molecules.

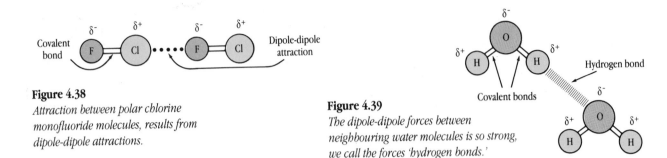

Figure 4.38
Attraction between polar chlorine monofluoride molecules, results from dipole-dipole attractions.

Figure 4.39
The dipole-dipole forces between neighbouring water molecules is so strong, we call the forces 'hydrogen bonds.'

EXAMPLE   *4.4*   Indicate what types of intermolecular forces exist between the following molecules:

a) CO_2 b) CH_2Cl_2

SOLUTION   The types of intermolecular forces that exist between small molecules will be dependent upon whether the molecules are polar or nonpolar.

a) Although the individual bonds in CO_2 are polar, the symmetry of the linear molecule cancels their effect and the molecule is nonpolar. Therefore only dispersion forces exist between molecules of CO_2.

b) Since chlorine is much more electronegative than either carbon or hydrogen, there will be polar bonds in the dichloromethane molecule. The shape of the molecule indicates that the positive and negative charges do not cancel each other out. Therefore, dipole-dipole attractions exist. Dispersion forces also exist.

QUESTIONS

12. For each of the following compounds indicate what types of intermolecular forces will be present between molecules of these compounds.

a) H_2O b) BF_3 c) PF_3

13. Explain how the discovery of the Joule-Thomson cooling effect provided evidence for the existence of intermolecular forces.

Standard Conditions

It should not be surprising that in chemistry, concepts and theories are refined from time to time as we gather more knowledge. Old theories and methods of gathering information are either discarded or modified. This applies to the quantitative as well as the qualitative aspects of the science. The traditional units of measurements need to be reassessed periodically to ensure consistency with other scientific data and to facilitate easy comparison.

For instance, the traditional unit of pressure was the *atmosphere*. One atmosphere is commonly defined as the pressure that would support a 760 mm high column of mercury. But actual atmospheric pressure varies widely, even at sea level. Thus the definition of the atmosphere is quite arbitrary. On the other hand the pascal, the SI unit of pressure, is defined in terms of SI base units as the pressure exerted by a force of one newton over an area of one square metre. One standard atmosphere is equivalent to 101.325 kPa.

In 1982 a commission of the International Union of Pure and Applied Chemistry (IUPAC) reported on its proposals for a new pressure standard. The commission produced a "wish list" of requirements — for example, that the standard value should be close to atmospheric pressure and the unit should be SI compatible. The commission chose the meteorological unit of one *bar*, which is exactly 100 kPa. IUPAC accepted this value and has embarked on re-calculating affected data.

Converting data from the old pressure standard to the new one involves changes of 1 % at the most. One such value that will change very little is the standard boiling point of water. It is often said that water boils at 100 °C at one atmosphere. In fact water boils at 99.975 °C at the traditional one atmosphere pressure! Using 100.0 kPa as standard pressure would give a boiling point of water of 99.610 °C.

For historical reasons the standard temperature for gas measurements was 0 °C. The commission recommended that 298.15 K (25 °C) be used as the standard temperature for all reported standard values. On this basis, one mole of an ideal gas would occupy 24.8 L at standard ambient temperature and pressure ("SATP"), that is, at 298.15 K and 100.0 kPa. New data tables are already being produced to these definitions of standard conditions.

Continual change is part of the excitement of science. We must be ready to jettison old outmoded units if in doing so we make the sciences into a more systematic and logical body of knowledge.

Figure 4.40
Blaise Pascal (1623-1662), the French physicist and mathematician after whom the SI unit of pressure was named.

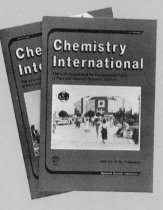

Figure 4.41
The International Union of Pure and Applied Chemistry publishes its own periodical, 'Chemistry International.'

Explaining the Phase Changes of Simple Covalent Molecules

<u>4.7</u> The process of vaporization requires that the forces attracting the particles to each other within the liquid must be completely overcome. It follows that more energy must be added to vaporize a substance with strong inter-molecular forces than one with weak forces. As we mentioned before, dispersion (London) forces are present between all molecules. Thus we will first examine what determines the strength of these basic forces.

Nonpolar Molecules

The primary factor determining the strength of dispersion forces is the number of electrons in the molecule. The more electrons, the bigger the induced dipole that can form. We can illustrate this by comparing the boiling points of the noble gases.

TABLE 4.8	The Boiling Points of the Noble Gases $(^{\circ}C)$				
Element	He	Ne	Ar	Kr	Xe
Boiling Point	-269	-246	-186	-152	-107
Number of Electrons	2	10	18	36	54

Although we will mainly be discussing boiling points, we usually find similar trends in melting points. This is because melting involves the partial overcoming of the same intermolecular forces.

The relationship between number of electrons and boiling point holds for any similar series in the Periodic Table. Figure 4.42 shows a graph of the boiling points for the diatomic halogen molecules. Note that there is almost a linear relationship between boiling point and the number of electrons.

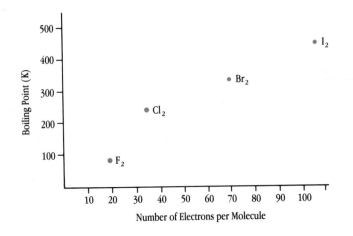

Figure 4.42

A graph of the boiling points of diatomic halogen elements plotted against the number of electrons per molecule.

Computers in Chemistry

Chemists use computers to analyze and calculate important data. The advent of microcomputers with both large memories and sophisticated graphics software has opened up new uses in chemistry and related fields of study.

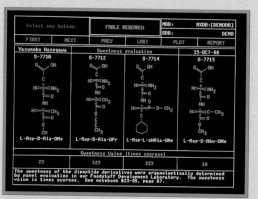

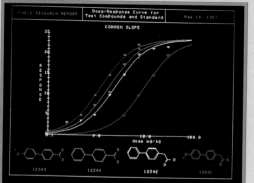

Chemical information can be easily retrieved using computer-based database systems. Four potential structures for an artificial sweetener are displayed above. The lower graph shows a dose response curve of four related compounds against a standard.

Scientific word processors and software allow researchers to write documents complete with data and chemical structures.

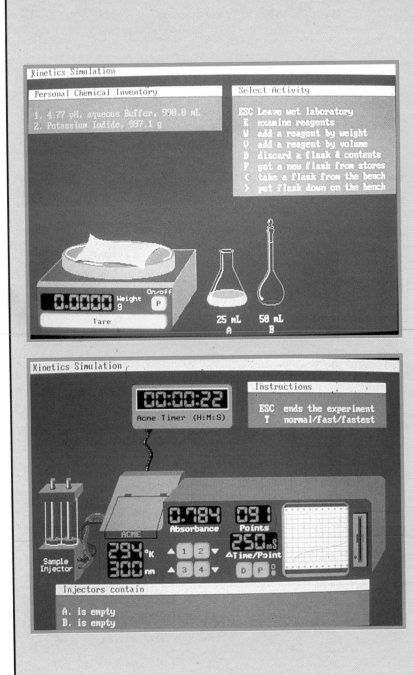

New chemistry software is being developed to simulate laboratory conditions. In the top computer screen, students are asked to select their apparatus and prepare reagents for a particular experiment. In the simulated spectrophotometer room, students follow the course of the reaction by observing the amount of light absorbed.

PLATE 2 — COMPUTERS IN CHEMISTRY

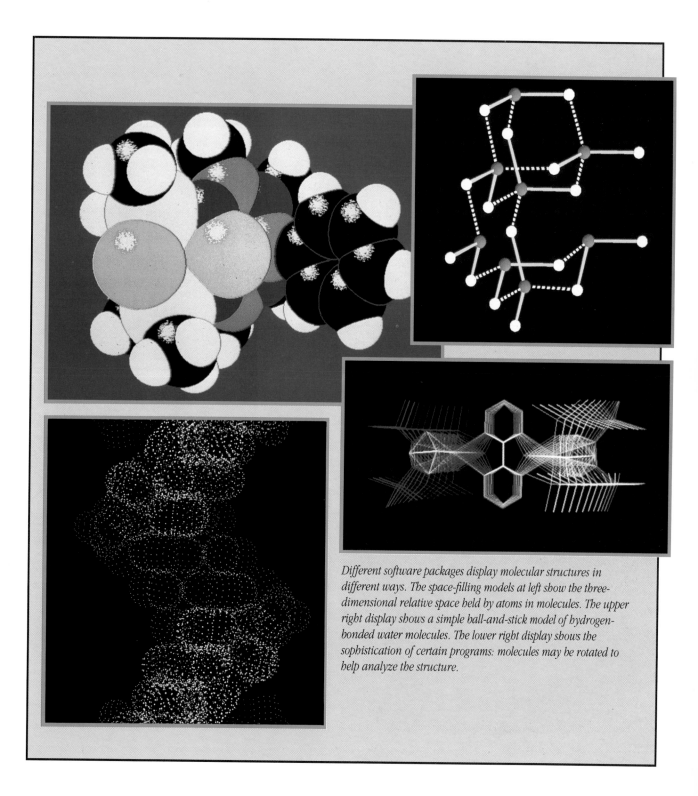

Different software packages display molecular structures in different ways. The space-filling models at left show the three-dimensional relative space held by atoms in molecules. The upper right display shows a simple ball-and-stick model of hydrogen-bonded water molecules. The lower right display shows the sophistication of certain programs: molecules may be rotated to help analyze the structure.

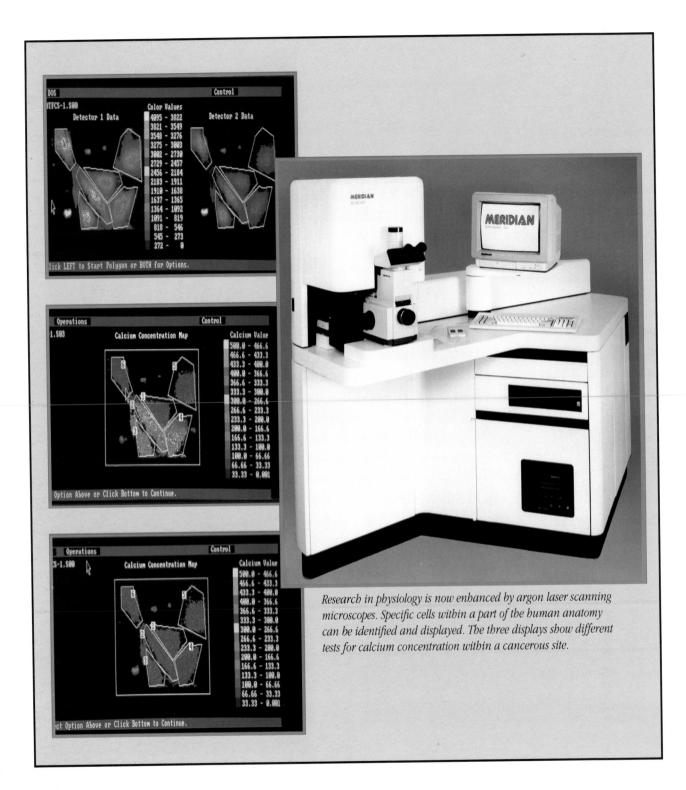

Research in physiology is now enhanced by argon laser scanning microscopes. Specific cells within a part of the human anatomy can be identified and displayed. The three displays show different tests for calcium concentration within a cancerous site.

PLATE 4 — COMPUTERS IN CHEMISTRY

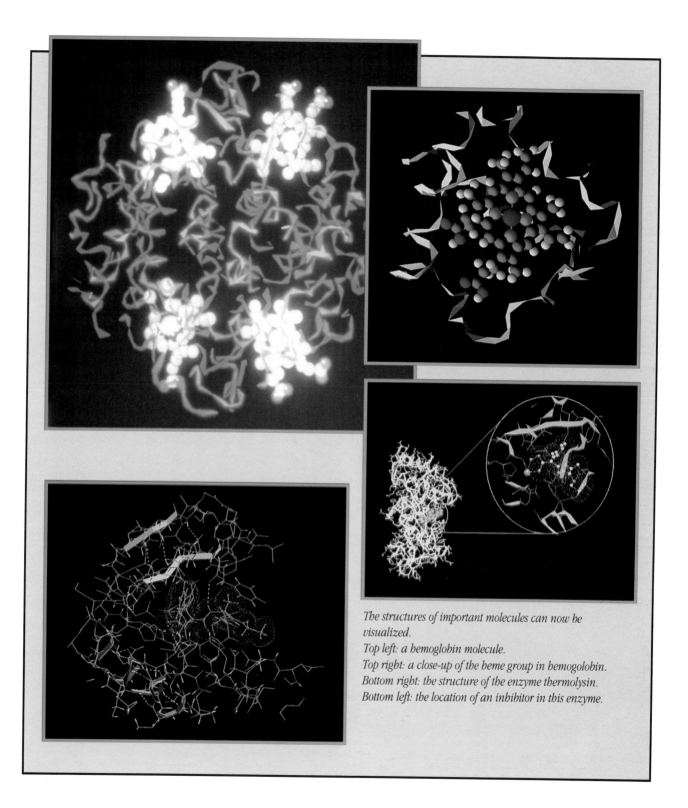

The structures of important molecules can now be visualized.

Top left: a hemoglobin molecule.

Top right: a close-up of the heme group in hemogolobin.

Bottom right: the structure of the enzyme thermolysin.

Bottom left: the location of an inhibitor in this enzyme.

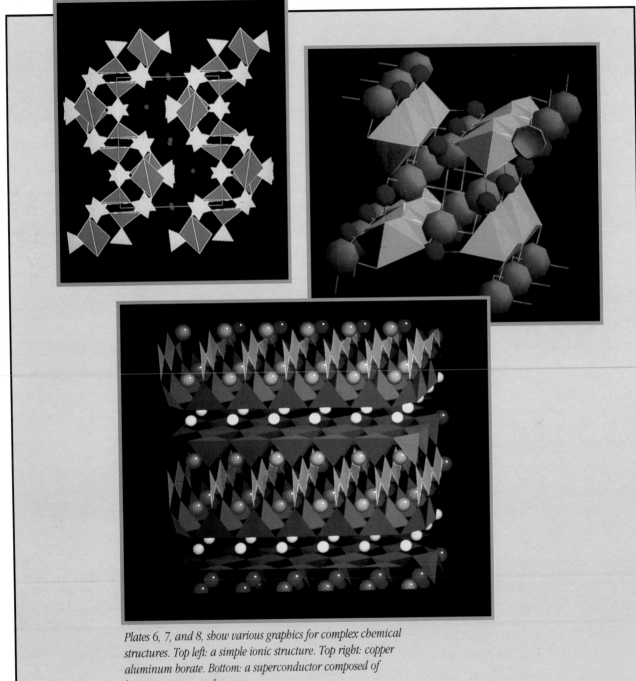

Plates 6, 7, and 8, show various graphics for complex chemical structures. Top left: a simple ionic structure. Top right: copper aluminum borate. Bottom: a superconductor composed of barium, copper, and oxygen.

PLATE 6 — COMPUTERS IN CHEMISTRY

A superconductor from the family called perovskites.

Three views of the compound zeolite, a hydrated silicate of aluminum, which is an important industrial catalyst.

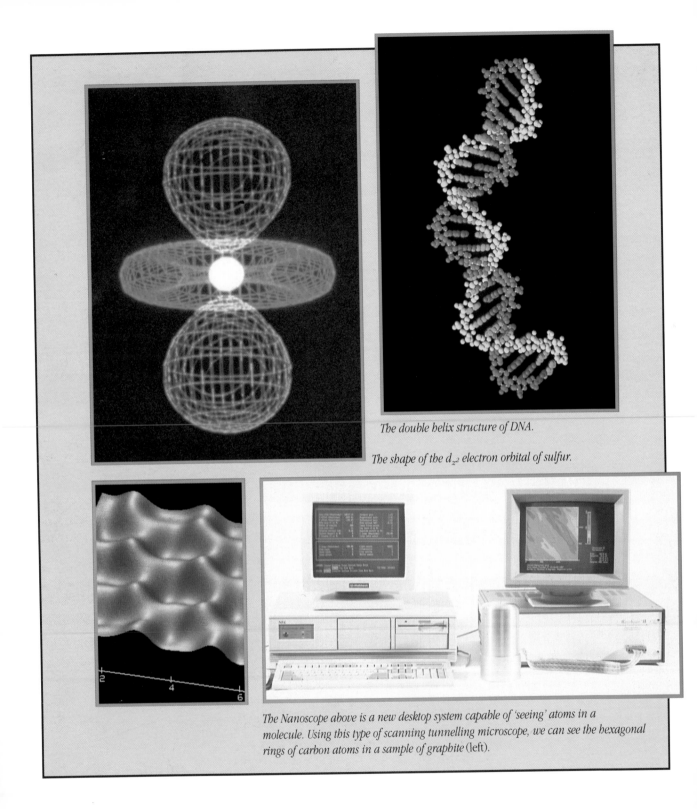

The double helix structure of DNA.

The shape of the d_{z^2} electron orbital of sulfur.

The Nanoscope above is a new desktop system capable of 'seeing' atoms in a molecule. Using this type of scanning tunnelling microscope, we can see the hexagonal rings of carbon atoms in a sample of graphite (left).

PLATE 8 — COMPUTERS IN CHEMISTRY

Figure 4.43

As the number of electrons increases, the boiling points and melting points increase. Thus at room temperature chlorine is a gas, bromine is a liquid, and iodine is a solid.

Figure 4.44

Both 2,2-dimethylpropane and pentane have the same formula, C_5H_{12}, but pentane has a higher boiling point.

We find that molecular shape has a secondary but important influence on boiling point. This is because dispersion forces decrease rapidly with molecular separation. Figure 4.44 shows two compounds with the molecular formula C_5H_{12}. These molecules contain the same numbers of the same types of atoms. The only difference is that the carbon atoms in pentane are arranged in a chain while in 2,2-dimethylpropane they are arranged in a compact group. Pentane has a boiling point 27 Celsius degrees higher than the compact form. The long, thin pentane molecules can get closer together by lying alongside each other, while the nearly spherical 2,2-dimethylpropane molecules can only touch each other at one point.

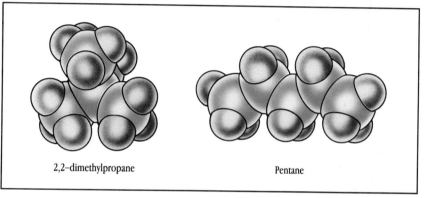

2,2–dimethylpropane   Pentane

Polar Molecules

While all molecules are attracted by dispersion forces, polar molecules also possess permanent dipoles. These permanent partial charges *enhance* the attraction between molecules; the permanent dipole has only a minor effect as compared to the effect of dispersion forces.

To conclusively demonstrate the existence of dipole-dipole forces, we compare molecules with the same number of electrons (isoelectronic) and with similar shapes. Only then can we be sure that differences in boiling points are due solely to the effects of the permanent dipole.

Elemental bromine, Br_2, and iodine monochloride, ICl, are one such pair. The difference of 38 Celsius degrees between the boiling points of the two substances (Table 4.9) can be attributed to the presence of dipole-dipole attractions between polar ICl molecules.

TABLE 4.9	The Effect of Polarity on Boiling Points	
Molecule	Br_2	ICl
Number of Electrons	70	70
Boiling Point (°C)	59	97

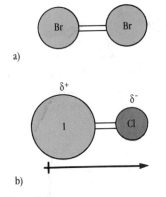

a)

b)

Figure 4.45

Both bromine and iodine monochloride have the same number of electrons, but the latter has a higher boiling point due to its permanent dipole.

We can also compare nitrogen gas, N_2, which is isoelectronic with carbon monoxide, CO. The polar nature of the carbon monoxide molecule results in a boiling point that is five Celsius degrees greater than the nitrogen molecule.

Hydrogen-bonded Molecules

Only when fluorine, oxygen, or nitrogen are attached to hydrogen is the bond so polar as to make a *significant* difference to the boiling and melting points of the resulting compounds. Figure 4.46 shows a graph of boiling point versus number of electrons for the series of hydrogen halides. Note that, apart from hydrogen fluoride, the values fall close to a straight line, matching the effect of the increasing numbers of electrons. The presence of very strong hydrogen bonds between hydrogen fluoride molecules results in a much higher boiling point.

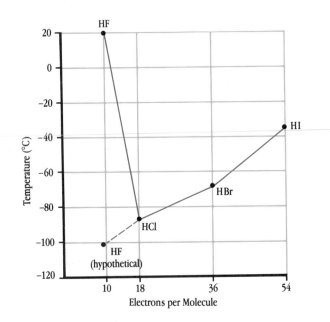

Figure 4.46

A graph of the boiling points of halogen halides plotted against number of electrons per molecule.

The strongest hydrogen bond is between hydrogen fluoride molecules. In the solid and liquid we find that the molecules line up in long zigzag chains.

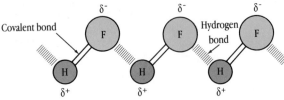

Figure 4.47

The hydrogen bonding between hydrogen fluoride molecules.

The greatest effect of hydrogen bonding, however, is illustrated by water. Although each hydrogen bond between water molecules is weaker than the hydrogen bonds between hydrogen fluoride molecules, the water molecules form a three-dimensional network of hydrogen bonds. Thus a hydrogen fluoride molecule is hydrogen bonded to two neighbours, whereas each water molecule is hydrogen bonded to four neighbours.

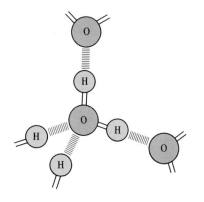

Figure 4.48
The hydrogen bonding between water molecules.

EXAMPLE   *4.5*   Which of the following substances would you expect to have a) the lowest and b) the highest boiling point: CO_2, He, CCl_4, or CH_4

SOLUTION   The boiling points of molecular substances are determined by the strength of their intermolecular forces. We must therefore determine whether or not each compound is polar, and then decide which type(s) of intermolecular forces exist between the molecules.

a) An examination of the bond polarities and shapes of the molecules indicates that all of these substances are nonpolar. The only forces of attraction between the molecules will therefore be dispersion forces. The strength of dispersion forces depends upon the number of electrons per molecule, and to some extent upon molecular shape. Helium molecules, which are monatomic, contain only two electrons, and so will have the weakest dispersion forces. We would therefore expect helium to have the lowest boiling point.

b) Carbon tetrachloride has the largest number of electrons per molecule, and so will probably have the strongest dispersion forces. We would expect carbon tetrachloride to have the highest boiling point.

EXAMPLE   *4.6*   Which of the following substances would you expect to have the highest boiling point?

$$NH_3 \qquad PH_3 \qquad AsH_3$$

SOLUTION There is a steady increase in the number of electrons in each molecule from NH_3 to AsH_3; and, because all of the molecules are the same shape and are of similar chemical composition, we would expect a corresponding increase in the magnitude of the dispersion forces. However, nitrogen is a particularly electronegative element and we would also expect hydrogen bonding to be present between ammonia molecules. For this reason it is likely that the total van der Waals forces in ammonia would be greater than in the other two compounds. We would therefore expect that ammonia (NH_3) would have the highest boiling point.

QUESTIONS

14. Place the following substances in order of increasing boiling point:

$$Cl_2 \qquad H_2 \qquad O_2$$

15. For each of the following substances indicate which intermolecular forces or bonds must be broken on vaporization:
a) Cu   b) BF_3 c) KBr   d) diamond

Hydrogen Bonding in Water

4.8 We have seen that the polar nature of water results in particularly strong hydrogen bonding attractions between its molecules. These forces cause the vapour pressure of water to be much lower at any given temperature

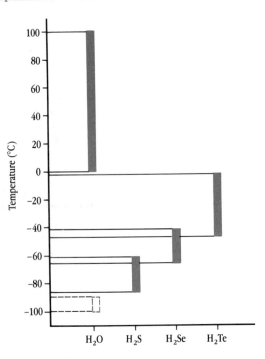

Figure 4.49
A graph showing the temperature range for the liquid phases of compounds of hydrogen and Group VIA elements. Hydrogen bonding is responsible for the high temperature ranges for water.

than would otherwise be the case. Water is a liquid at room temperature and pressure when, in the absence of hydrogen bonds, it would remain in the liquid phase only from about $-100\,^{\circ}C$ to $-90\,^{\circ}C$ (Figure 4.49).

Hydrogen bonding is also responsible for the unique structure of ice. As water cools from $4\,^{\circ}C$ to $0\,^{\circ}C$, the water molecules move into the positions that are adopted in ice crystals. In these crystals the water molecules are arranged to allow for the maximum degree of hydrogen bonding. Each water molecule is surrounded by four other close neighbours in such a way that there is a tetrahedral arrangement of four hydrogen atoms around every oxygen atom.

Figure 4.50

The structure of ice results from the tetrahedral arrangement of hydrogen atoms around each oxygen.

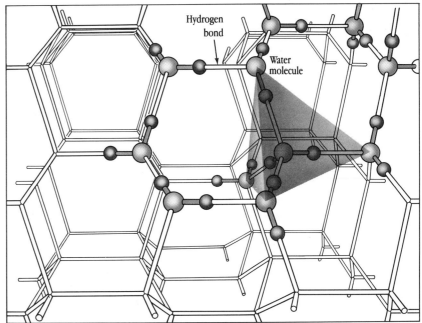

The result of this arrangement is that the crystals have a very open structure (Figure 4.50), and the volume of solid ice is greater than that of the same amount of liquid water at $0\,^{\circ}C$. This fact has very important biological consequences. If ice were denser than water, it would sink to the bottom of ponds and oceans during the winter. Ponds, rivers, and oceans would freeze from the bottom up, and fish and other aquatic life, that depend during the winter upon a layer of water at about $4\,^{\circ}C$ underneath the ice, would be unable to survive.

Surface Tension

Objects such as needles and old-fashioned razor blades would normally sink if dropped onto water. If we are careful, however, metal objects that are denser than water can be made to float on its surface. These objects do not float like ships do, by displacing their own mass of water. Instead

Figure 4.51

Molecules on surface of liquid only experience 'pulls' into the liquid. This imbalance of forces causes surface tension.

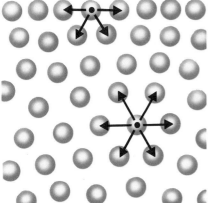

Figure 4.52
The high surface tension of water allows a water spider to skate across water.

they remain on the surface because the water molecules at the surface are hydrogen bonded only to molecules on both sides and below. This results in a strong force of attraction on these surface molecules called **surface tension**. The surface is thus like an elastic "skin." Some insects rely on surface tension to skate over the surface of water.

Hydrogen Bonding and Biochemistry

The study of biochemically important molecules is, to a large extent, a study of hydrogen bonding. Proteins are one of the more important biological compounds. They consist of long chain-like molecules. Along the chains are N—H groups and C=O groups. But for these groups, the protein chains would only form long inactive strands. It is hydrogen bonding from one part of the chain across to another that holds the molecules in compact units that can perform the required function.

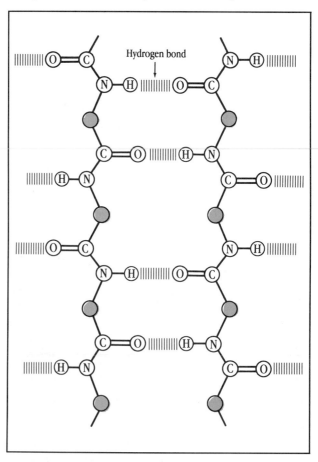

Figure 4.53
In silk and other insect fibres, chains of protein molecules are cross-linked by hydrogen bonds.

QUESTIONS

16. Why does ice float in water?

Gas Hydrates in the Arctic

We described how, in ice, the water molecules form open structures like cages. Other atoms and molecules can be trapped inside these structures. Only by melting the ice can the trapped substances, known as clathrates (from the Latin *clathratus*, meaning behind bars), be released. Until recently, clathrates were only laboratory curiosities.

However, the very high pressures and low temperatures that exist at the ocean floor have been found to produce ice with molecules of natural gas (methane) trapped inside. The methane is present at the ocean floor as a result of the decay of organic sediment deposited over millions of years. The substance is a solid natural-gas hydrate. The solid hydrate is very stable until either the pressure is reduced or the temperature is raised sufficiently for it to melt. When this happens, large quantities of natural gas are released.

Soviet scientists, who have studied the materials extensively, have hypothesized that deposits of gas hydrates extend over much of the world's ocean floor. In fact a number of discoveries have been made in northern Canada, at the bottom of the Beaufort Sea.

Recovery of the material for domestic and industrial use would involve warming the hydrate sufficiently for methane to be released. The gas would then rise to the ocean surface, where it could be collected and transported away. However, such a process would be more costly (particularly in the harsh Arctic environment) than extracting methane from existing land-based deposits in western Canada. It is therefore unlikely that the source will be tapped for some years.

Other substantial deposits of methane gas hydrate have been discovered at the bottom of the Pacific Ocean off the coast of California. Because of the more temperate climate, it could well be that gas will be recovered from this source in the near future. In this case warm surface water could be pumped to the ocean floor and used to melt the solid hydrate.

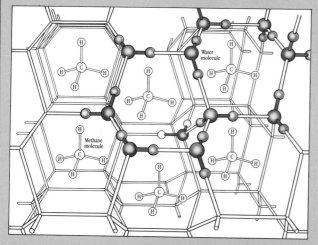

Figure 4.54
The structure of methane gas hydrate.

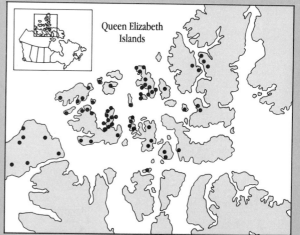

Figure 4.55
Methane gas hydrates have been found at a large number of sites in Canada's Arctic.

A Review of Bond Types and Physical Properties

4.9 In this chapter we have seen how the properties of elements and compounds can be explained in terms of bonding types. At this point it is useful to summarize these types and relate them to the forces within and between the units of substances. You will note from Table 4.10 that, in general, only small covalent molecules have forces between units.

TABLE 4.10 *Review of Bonding Types*		
Structural Units	Forces within Units	Forces between Units
Ionic crystal	ionic bond	
Metal crystal	metallic bond	
Network covalent molecule	covalent bond	
Small covalent molecule	covalent bond	dispersion dipole-dipole hydrogen bonding

For each bonding type, we must consider different factors when we try to explain trends in physical properties. As an example, Table 4.11 lists the factors that must be considered when we wish to explain trends in boiling points for substances containing a particular type of bond.

TABLE 4.11 *Factors Affecting Boiling Points*	
Bond Type	Factors
Ionic	Ion size Ion charge
Metallic	Atom size Number of valence electrons
Network Solid	Strength of covalent bond
Small covalent molecule	Number of electrons Molecular shape Polarity of molecule

Summary

- Matter can exist in three phases: solid, liquid, and gas.

- Phase changes result from the addition of energy to, or the removal of energy from, a substance. Phase changes take place at distinct temperatures and pressures.

- The relationship between pressure, temperature, and phase change can be represented in a phase diagram.

- The temperatures at which materials undergo phase changes, and the range of temperature over which they remain in the liquid phase, are closely related to their structures and types of bonding. Small covalent molecules are usually gases at both normal temperatures and pressures while ionic materials, metals, and network solids are almost always solids.

- Covalent bonds between atoms of similar or identical electronegativities will be nonpolar. Those between atoms of different electronegativities will be polar if the electronegativity difference is greater than or equal to 0.5.

- If the bonds within a molecule are polar, then the molecule may possess a net molecular dipole. If the molecule is symmetrical, however, the effects of the bond dipoles may cancel, in which case the molecule will be nonpolar.

- All molecules are attracted by weak dispersion forces that are effective only at very short distances. Additional dipole-dipole attractions exist between polar molecules. In compounds where hydrogen is bonded to one of the more electronegative elements, these dipole-dipole attractions are much stronger. They are then known as hydrogen bonds.

- Polar molecules melt and boil at higher temperatures than nonpolar molecules. The presence of hydrogen bonding results in even higher melting and boiling points.

- The unique nature of water results from the particularly strong hydrogen bonds that exist between water molecules.

KEY WORDS

boiling point	dynamic equilibrium
change of phase	evaporate
critical pressure	freezing point
critical temperature	hydrogen bonds
dipole	ideal gas
dipole-dipole forces	intermolecular forces
dipole moment	intramolecular forces
dispersion forces	ion-dipole attractions

Joule-Thomson effect   translate
London forces   triple point
melting point   van der Waals forces
phase diagram   vaporization
rotate   vapour
saturated   vapour pressure
sublimation   vibrate
surface tension

ANSWERS TO
SECTION QUESTIONS

1. Solid particles are closely packed in fixed positions. Liquid particles are closely packed, not in fixed positions. Gas particles are widely spaced, not in fixed positions.

2. a) approximately 96 °C   b) approximately 75 °C

3. A dynamic equilibrium exists when two opposing changes occur at the same rate.

4. a) Vaporization is the escape of a molecule into the gas phase from the surface of a liquid.
   b) Sublimation is a phase change from solid to gas, without passing through the liquid phase. It is also the reverse process.

5. a) gas   b) liquid   c) solid

6. Figure 4.12 shows that water can have a vapour pressure of 50.0 kPa at temperatures above 75 °C. As the warm air cools, we move horizontally from right to left across the phase diagram, at constant vapour pressure, until we meet the line BD. Further decrease in temperature causes water to condense and the vapour pressure to fall. We move down the curve as temperature and vapour pressure continue to drop while more water forms. At point B, ice forms. Ice, water, and water vapour are all present. Further cooling causes all of the liquid water to freeze, and some of the remaining water vapour to be deposited as ice.

7. Ionic compounds have high melting and boiling points. They remain in the liquid phase over a wide temperature range and conduct electricity when melted, as in aqueous solution. Small molecule covalent compounds have low melting and boiling points, remain in the liquid phase over a short temperature range, and do not conduct electricity.

8. Ionic compounds conduct electricity in the liquid phase, and when dissolved in water. In both cases the ions are free to move and to carry electrical charge.

9. a) LiF. Charges on smaller ions are concentrated over a smaller volume, leading to a stronger bond.
   b) AlN. Ions with $+3$ and -3 charges form stronger bonds than ions with $+1$ and -1 charges.

10. a) The molecule is bent. The difference in electronegativity between the two elements is 0.4, so the bonds will be essentially nonpolar. A molecular dipole is present.

   b) The molecule is tetrahedral. The electronegativity difference is 0.4, so the bonds will be essentially nonpolar. The molecule will be nonpolar.

   c) VSEPR theory tells us that phosphorus trifluoride will have a trigonal pyramidal shape with no centre of symmetry. The electronegativity difference between the two elements is 1.9, so there will be polar bonds. A molecular dipole exists.

11. Molecules of $CHCl_{3(\ell)}$ (trichloromethane) are polar. A stream of liquid would be attracted to a charged rod.

12. a) The molecule is polar. Both dispersion forces and hydrogen bonds are present.

   b) Although polar bonds are present, the molecule has no dipole. There are dispersion forces only.

   c) The molecule is polar. Both dispersion forces and dipole-dipole attractions are present.

13. A temperature drop upon the expansion of a gas indicates that energy is being used up to pull the molecules apart.

14. H_2, O_2, Cl_2

15. a) metallic bonds   c) ionic bonds
    b) dispersion forces   d) covalent bonds

16. Water molecules take up more volume in the highly-ordered crystal structure of ice than they do when disordered in the liquid phase. Ice is therefore less dense than water and floats at the surface.

COMPREHENSION QUESTIONS

1. Explain why gases may be compressed, while solids and liquids may not be compressed to any extent.

2. For an ideal gas, plotting $V_{observed}/V_{ideal}$ with increasing P on a graph produces a horizontal line. For H_2 gas we find that $V_{observed}/V_{ideal}$ increases with increasing P. Explain this phenomenon.

3. What is the critical temperature of a gas?

4. Describe and explain what will happen if warm, moist air suddenly cools.

5. Explain how a clothesline of washing will slowly dry on a day when the air temperature is below $0\,°C$.

6. What is the difference between evaporation and boiling?

7. Explain the difference between melting, vaporization, and sublimation.

8. How many phases exist at the triple point?

9. Explain, using Figure 4.12, what will happen if a sample of water, at a pressure of 150.0 kPa and a temperature of 45 °C, is cooled to −25 °C.

10. Explain, using Figure 4.18, what will happen if a sample of carbon dioxide, at a pressure of 100 kPa and a temperature of −100 °C, is warmed to 0 °C.

11. Why is it important to record the pressure when measuring the boiling point of a liquid, but not important when measuring the melting point of a solid?

12. What observations led to the conclusion that there are intermolecular forces between individual covalent molecules?

13. Explain the term "sea of electrons" as applied to metals in both the solid and liquid phases.

14. Under what conditions can a) ionic compounds, b) metals, and c) covalent small molecules conduct electricity?

15. Why is CH_2Cl_2 a polar molecule while CCl_4 is not?

16. Explain why a stream of water is attracted towards a charged glass rod.

17. What are intermolecular forces?

18. Explain the existence of dispersion forces between molecules of carbon dioxide.

19. Explain why pentane, C_5H_{12} (a straight-chain compound), has a higher boiling point, and remains in the liquid phase over a wider temperature range, than 2,2-dimethylpropane, C_5H_{12} (a branched, chain compound).

20. What is hydrogen bonding?

21. Why is liquid water more dense than ice?

22. What type of intermolecular forces exist between water molecules?

23. What would be the consequences if ice were denser than water?

PROBLEMS   *Phase Diagrams*

24. Use the phase diagram for carbon dioxide (Figure 4.18) to determine the phase of CO_2 at
    a) −60 °C and 100 kPa
    b) −10 °C and 7000 kPa
    c) 10 °C and 2000 kPa

25. Use Figure 4.12 to determine the phase of water at
    a) −5 °C and 0.1 kPa
    b) −10 °C and 5.0 kPa
    c) 20 °C and 5.0 kPa

Using Bond Types to Explain Physical Properties

26. Which of the following should have the higher boiling point:
  a) K or Ca?
  b) KF or KBr?

27. Arrange the following in order of increasing melting point: salt ($NaCl$), sand (SiO_2), sugar ($C_{12}H_{22}O_{11}$).

Polarity of Molecules

28. Determine which of the following bonds is polar:
  a) $O-H$ b) $N-Cl$ c) $F-F$ d) $B-Cl$

29. Place the following bonds in order of increasing polarity:
  $B-F$ $S-Cl$ $H-C$ $H-O$

30. For each of the following molecules draw an electron-dot formula and predict the molecular shape, determine whether polar bonds are present, and determine whether a molecular dipole is present:
  a) H_2O b) BCl_3 c) NCl_3 d) $BeCl_2$ e) $CHCl_3$

31. Indicate whether the following molecules will be polar or nonpolar:
  a) PF_3 b) CF_4 c) BF_2Cl d) SF_6 e) SCl_2

Intermolecular Forces

32. Indicate the type(s) of intermolecular forces that exist between molecules of these compounds:
  a) BCl_3 b) CF_4 c) NH_3 d) $CHCl_3$ e) CO_2

33. Indicate the type(s) of intermolecular forces that exist between molecules of
  a) PCl_5 b) SO_2 c) BF_2Cl d) SF_6 e) OF_2

Explaining Phase Changes of Simple Covalent Substances

34. Which of the following covalent molecules exhibit hydrogen bonding:
  a) CH_3OH b) CH_3Cl c) HF d) HI

35. Which of the following will have the higher boiling point? Explain briefly:
  a) Cl_2 or I_2
  b) SF_2 or SBr_2
  c) PH_3 or NH_3

36. Which of bromine, Br_2, or iodine monochloride, ICl, will remain in the liquid phase over the widest temperature range? Explain briefly.

37. Which of the following will have the higher boiling point? Explain briefly:
  a) $NaCl$ or PCl_3
  b) Cu or C_3H_8
  c) diamond, or $NaCl$

38. Using the following data, construct a phase diagram for iodine. Indicate the areas representing solid, liquid, and gas.

Triple point: 71.9 kPa, 110 °C
Normal boiling point of I_2 (100 kPa): 183 °C
Normal melting point of I_2 (100 kPa): 113 °C
At 44 °C 25 kPa, solid and gaseous I_2 are in equilibrium.

39. Using the phase diagram in Question 38, answer the following:
a) Under what conditions does I_2 sublime?
b) What phase is I_2 at 85 kPa and 160 °C?
c) How much pressure do you have to exert to get I_2 at 140 °C to liquefy?

40. Both CH_2F_2 (difluoromethane) and CF_4 (tetrafluoromethane) are tetrahedral compounds. Which would be polar? Explain your answer.

41. The following compounds all have a trigonal pyramidal shape. Which have a molecular dipole: PCl_3 (phosphorus trichloride), NCl_3 (nitrogen trichloride), PH_3 (phosphine), NH_3 (ammonia)?

42. All the bonds in Cl_2O (dichlorine oxide) and $BeCl_2$ (beryllium dichloride) are polar. Why is only Cl_2O a polar molecule?

43. For each of the following substances, indicate which bonds or intermolecular forces must be broken on vaporization:
a) Hg   b) H_2O c) KCl   d) N_2 e) SiO_2

44. What kind of chemical bonds or attractive forces must be broken or overcome in order to a) melt diamond, b) boil liquid ammonia, c) sublime solid iodine, d) melt solid neon?

45. Which of the following will have the lower melting point? Explain briefly.
a) $MgCl_2$ or SCl_2 b) Br_2 or I_2 c) NaCl or $AlCl_3$

46. DNA, the molecule that contains the genetic information for the cell, is composed of two separate polymer strands held together by hydrogen bonds between specific organic bases. One such base pair involves three hydrogen bonds between guanine and cytosine. On the diagram below, indicate the possible positioning of these hydrogen bonds.

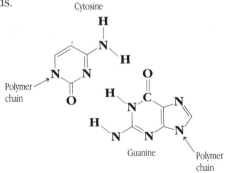

1. Build a model of an ice crystal. Use different coloured connectors to distinguish covalent bonds within the water molecule from hydrogen bonds between water molecules.

2. Prepare a report on the different uses of carbon dioxide in your area — both in the home and the workplace.

3. Obtain as many pure liquids as possible and investigate which liquids are deflected by charged rods. Make molecular models of substances and relate the deflections to the molecular polarity. Make sure you have checked the safety data on each liquid before using it.

4. Prepare a report on how it is believed diamond is formed by geological processes. In addition, investigate the different unsuccessful attempts to prepare diamonds in the past and explain why each failed. Report also on recent advances in the production of thin diamond films.

Thermochemistry

Thermochemistry is the study of heat changes associated with physical and chemical processes. Heat is a particular form of energy, and thermochemistry is part of a larger study of energy changes of all types, the study of thermodynamics. Thermodynamics is a subject that bridges chemistry and physics and that has important applications to biology and geology. We use thermodynamics to help us understand biochemical pathways and to explain the formation of different minerals. The subject involves not only the measurement of energy changes, but also theoretical calculations that enable us to predict whether or not a particular reaction is feasible under specific conditions.

Energy

5.1

We are all familiar with the term *energy*. In science, energy is often defined as "the ability to do work" or "the capacity to produce change." There are many forms of energy, but only some are relevant to chemistry.

Potential energy is the energy possessed by a body because of its position. In the atom an electron has electrical potential energy by virtue of its location relative to positively-charged protons and other electrons. **Kinetic energy** is the energy of motion. All bodies in motion, including atoms, molecules, and ions possess kinetic energy. **Radiant energy** is energy transmitted through space as electromagnetic waves. The most familiar form of radiant energy is light. **Chemical energy** is the energy necessary to keep atoms joined by chemical bonds. Different types of atoms and the various arrangements of atoms in chemical compounds result in the storage of different amounts of chemical energy. During a chemical reaction, chemical energy may be stored, released as heat, converted to other forms of energy such as radiant energy or kinetic energy, or converted to work.

Whatever changes take place, energy is always conserved. It is a fundamental law of nature — the **law of conservation of energy** — that energy can be neither created nor destroyed but may be converted from one form to another. As an alternative we can say that the *energy of the universe is constant*. This means if we add up all the energy components of a physical change or a chemical reaction, there will be no net loss or gain.

The Joule

Energy is defined as the ability to do work. Work, in turn, can be defined as the application of force through a distance. We can express this last statement by the word equation:

$$\textbf{Work = Force} \times \textbf{Distance}$$

The SI unit for measuring work and all forms of energy is the **joule (J)**. The joule is defined as the work done when a force of one newton $(1\,N = 1\,kg \cdot m \cdot s^{-2})$ acts over a distance of one metre. Substituting the appropriate units into the work equation, gives us the relationship between a joule and the SI base units:

$$
\begin{aligned}
1\,J &= 1\,N \times 1\,m \\
&= 1\,kg \cdot m \cdot s^{-2} \times 1\,m \\
&= 1\,kg \cdot m^2 \cdot s^{-2}
\end{aligned}
$$

QUESTIONS

1. A magazine advertisement claims that there is a brand new method of weight loss: no dieting and no exercising. Does this claim violate the law of conversion of energy?

2. In each of the following chemical reactions or physical processes, explain the main energy interconversions involved:
   a) the operation of a flashlight
   b) a stone dropping into a pool of water
   c) a cake baking in an oven.

Figure 5.1

'Waterfall' by M.C. Escher. Like all attempts at producing more energy than is used, this engraving of a water wheel driven by a circulating waterfall cannot exist.

Counting Calories

Although Canada is now a metric country it seems very unlikely that the term *calorie,* which is not an SI energy unit, will vanish. Most people probably associate the word calorie with food. Such expressions as "laden with calories," "low-cal," and "counting calories" are part of the language of our diet- and weight-conscious society. Would a "low-joule" soft drink have the same consumer appeal?

A calorie was originally defined as the amount of heat energy necessary to raise the temperature of one gram of water from 14.5 °C to 15.5 °C. It is now defined by its joule equivalent, which is 1 cal = 4.18 J. The nutritional calorie, however, is actually a kilocalorie and to avoid confusion is often written with a capital C. One Calorie (one kilocalorie) supplies the heat energy necessary to raise one thousand grams of water by one Celsius degree. Perhaps it is understandable that dieters would wish to retain the Calorie for food. Imagine the shock of finding that a 900-Calorie banana split resplendent with whipped cream, nuts, and cherries was nearly four million joules! Even a 50 Calorie raw carrot has over two hundred thousand joules.

The daily food energy input necessary to keep our bodies functioning at a minimum level is about 100 kJ for every kilogram of body weight. This value increases if we lead an active life, but exercise alone is rarely an effective way to lose weight. If we eat more food than necessary to fuel our body processes, the excess is stored in the body as fat. One kilogram of body fat corresponds to approximately 39 000 kJ (9330 Calories) of food energy and is the most efficient means of storing energy (Table 5.1). Thus hibernating animals build large supplies of fat during the summer months to last them through the long winter period.

TABLE 5.1   *Energy Values of Various Food Components*

Food	Energy Value in kilojoules per gram	Calories per gram
fats	39	9.3
carbohydrates	16	3.8
protein	17	4.1

Figure 5.2
A banana split contains nearly four million joules of energy.

Temperature and Heat

5.2   We often confuse the terms *temperature* and *heat.* Although they are related, they are not synonymous.

Temperature

The individual atoms and molecules of a substance are in constant motion. The kinetic energy associated with this random motion is the **thermal energy** of the substance. **Temperature**, on the other hand, is a measure of the *average* kinetic energy of the molecules. It does not reflect the *total* thermal energy of the system. For example, a cup of coffee at 80 °C has a higher temperature than a bathtub full of warm water at 50 °C. However, there is more thermal energy stored in the bathtub because there are many more water molecules in the bathtub than in the coffee cup.

In the physical sciences temperatures may be recorded in either metric units (Celsius scale) or SI units (Kelvin scale). The size of the degree is the same in each case, but remember that 0 K is −273.15 °C. (We use the rounded-off value of −273 °C for calculations.) Thus,

$$\text{Kelvin temperature} = \left(\text{Celsius temperature} \times \frac{1\,\text{K}}{1\,°\text{C}}\right) + 273\,\text{K}$$

In practice we ignore the conversion factor 1 K/1 °C and write

$$\text{Kelvin temperature} = \text{Celsius temperature} + 273\,\text{K}$$

Notice that the word *degree* is not used with the Kelvin scale.

EXAMPLE **5.1** A block of metal was heated from 47 °C to 122 °C. What is the temperature increase in degrees Celsius and in kelvins?

SOLUTION This calculation can be done in tabular form:

	°C		K
Final temperature	122	(+273)	395
Initial temperature	47	(+273)	320
Temperature change	75		75

The temperature increase is 75 °C, or 75 K. The change is the same on both scales because the size of a Celsius degree is the same as that of a kelvin.

Heat

Heat is thermal energy in transit. If you touch something hot, energy is transferred from the hot object to your hand. If you touch something cold, heat energy passes from your hand to the cold object. We should only use the term heat to describe energy that is flowing from one substance to another because of a temperature difference. Sometimes all the heat energy transferred causes the *molecules* of the substance to move more rapidly. This results in an immediate rise in temperature because most of the heat is converted to kinetic energy. In other cases, such as when ice melts, the energy transferred does not bring about an immediate rise in temperature. The added energy is used to remove the molecules from their ordered arrangement in the solid.

3. A quantity of gas was cooled from 323 K to 273 K. Express this temperature difference in degrees Celsius and kelvins.

4. Two beakers of water, one containing 50 mL and the other containing 250 mL, are heated to 75 °C. Using these beakers as your examples, explain the difference between heat and temperature.

Specific Heat and Heat Capacity   5.3

The **specific heat** of a substance is the amount of heat energy required to raise the temperature of one gram of a substance by one Celsius degree or one kelvin. More heat is required if the temperature is to be increased by more than one degree or if more than one gram is involved. The units for specific heat are joules per gram per degree Celsius ($J \cdot g^{-1} \cdot {}°C^{-1}$) or joules per gram per kelvin ($J \cdot g^{-1} \cdot K^{-1}$).

As we can see from Table 5.2, different substances have different specific heats. This is because substances vary in their ability to store energy. They also gain or lose heat at different rates. For example, let us compare water, which has a high specific heat, with a metal such as aluminum. It takes 4.18 J to raise the temperature of liquid water 1 °C; whereas for aluminum only 0.903 J are required. For the same increase in temperature, liquid water requires almost five times as much energy as the same mass of aluminum.

Water can absorb a large quantity of heat with only a slight rise in temperature. Conversely, it can give off a lot of heat with only a small decrease in temperature. The moderating effect that large bodies of water have on surrounding land is due to the ability of the water to absorb heat in the summer and give off heat in the winter.

Heat capacity is the heat energy required to raise the temperature of a given quantity of a substance by one Celsius degree or one kelvin. If we know the specific heat of the substance then we can determine the heat capacity through the following relationship:

$$\textbf{Heat capacity} = \textbf{Specific heat} \times \textbf{Mass}$$

Thus for 12.0 g of aluminum metal,

$$\textbf{Heat capacity} = \textbf{0.903} J \cdot g^{-1} \cdot {}°C^{-1} \times \textbf{12.0 g}$$
$$= \textbf{10.8} J \cdot {}°C^{-1}$$

The **molar heat capacity** of a substance is the amount of energy required to raise the temperature of one mole of a substance by one Celsius degree or one kelvin. This value is frequently used by chemists because they tend to work with molar quantities. Molar heat capacity can be calculated by substituting *molar mass* for *mass* in the relationship for heat capacity.

$$\textbf{Molar heat capacity} = \textbf{Specific heat} \times \textbf{Molar mass}$$

TABLE 5.2 *Representative Values of Specific Heat at 25 °C*

Substance	Specific heat ($J \cdot g^{-1} \cdot {}°C^{-1}$)
$Al_{(s)}$	0.903
$Fe_{(s)}$	0.449
$Hg_{(\ell)}$	0.139
$H_2O_{(\ell)}$	4.18
$N_{2\,(g)}$	1.04
$O_{2\,(g)}$	0.917
$He_{(g)}$	5.19
$CO_{2\,(g)}$	0.843

Figure 5.3
Brackley Beach, Prince Edward Island. Because of the high specific heat of water, lakes and seas are always cooler than the land in hot summers.

Units of molar heat capacity are $J \cdot mol^{-1} \cdot {}^{\circ}C^{-1}$ or $J \cdot mol^{-1} \cdot K^{-1}$. Experimental values obtained for the calculation of molar heat capacity are obtained under conditions of constant pressure. The symbol for molar heat capacity is $\boldsymbol{C_p}^{\circ}$, where C represents capacity, the subscript $_p$ denotes measurements taken at constant pressures, and the $^{\circ}$ denotes the substance is in its standard state. **Standard state** is now defined as the stable form of the element at a pressure of 100 kPa. Standard state does not usually imply a particular temperature; but, where applicable, we will use values measured at 25 °C.

EXAMPLE　　　　*5.2*　Calculate the molar heat capacity of water, given that the specific heat of water is $4.18 \, J \cdot g^{-1} \cdot {}^{\circ}C^{-1}$.

SOLUTION　The molar mass of H_2O is $18.02 \, g \cdot mol^{-1}$.
Thus for water,

$$C_p{}^{\circ} = \text{Specific heat} \times \text{Molar mass}$$
$$= 4.18 \, J \cdot g^{-1} \cdot {}^{\circ}C^{-1} \times 18.02 \, g \cdot mol^{-1}$$
$$= 75.3 \, J \cdot mol^{-1} \cdot {}^{\circ}C^{-1}$$

Each substance has its own heat capacity and molar heat capacity. The values depend on its composition and mass. On a volume basis, water has the greatest heat capacity of any liquid. This (and the fact that water is inexpensive) means that it is widely used as a coolant. It is the main coolant for most power plants (both conventional and nuclear) and for most internal combustion engines.

If we wish to raise the temperature of a substance by more than one degree, our heat calculations must account for the change in temperature (ΔT) as well as mass. Thus,

Heat required = Heat capacity × ΔT
= Specific heat × Mass × ΔT

If we know the specific heat of the substance, we can use this relationship to determine the quantity of heat necessary to raise the temperature of a given mass by a given amount. We can, of course, use the same equation to calculate specific heat.

EXAMPLE　　　　*5.3*　Determine the heat required to raise the temperature of 100 g of water from 298.0 K to 373.0 K.

SOLUTION　From Table 5.2, we know that the specific heat of water is $4.18 \, J \cdot g^{-1} \cdot {}^{\circ}C^{-1}$, or $4.18 \, J \cdot g^{-1} \cdot K^{-1}$. The change in temperature is given by the following:

$$\Delta T = 373.0 \, K - 298.0 \, K = 75.0 \, K$$

We can now use our equation for heat required:

$$\begin{aligned}
\text{Heat required} &= \text{Specific heat} \times \text{Mass} \times \Delta T \\
&= 4.18\,\text{J}\cdot\text{g}^{-1}\cdot\text{K}^{-1} \times 100\,\text{g} \times 75.0\,\text{K} \\
&= 3.14 \times 10^4\,\text{J} \\
&= 31.4\,\text{kJ}
\end{aligned}$$

Energy and Molecular Motion

The heat capacity of a substance is dependent on the way thermal energy is stored in the atoms, ions, or molecules. Three kinds of motion may be associated with the energy: translational, rotational, and vibrational. In **translational motion** the molecules are free to move along linear pathways from one place to another. A molecule has **rotational motion** if it rotates about an axis through its centre of mass. It has **vibrational motion** if atoms within the molecule oscillate along the direction of a bond. Gas molecules are, for example, widely separated from each other and are free to move in any of the three modes (Figure 5.4).

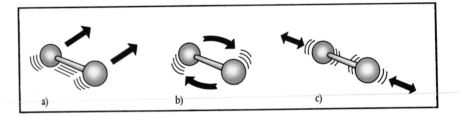

Figure 5.4
Different modes of molecular motion:
a) translational;
b) rotational;
c) vibrational.

Table 5.3 contains the molar heat capacities of several gases measured at 25 °C. The value for water was measured at 100 °C. (Because each mole contains the same number of molecules, we will use molar heat capacities to make comparisons.) As we would expect, the value for each gas is

TABLE 5.3	Molar Heat Capacitites of Various Gases
Gas	C_p° (J·mol^{-1}·°C^{-1})
$He_{(g)}$	20.8
$Ne_{(g)}$	20.8
$N_{2\,(g)}$	29.1
$O_{2\,(g)}$	29.4
$H_{2\,(g)}$	28.8
$H_2O_{(g)}$	33.6
$CO_{2\,(g)}$	37.1

Figure 5.5

A microwave oven. The microwave energy is absorbed as rotational energy, then becomes transformed into vibrational and translational energy resulting in a temperature increase.

unique. Notice, however, that the monatomic gases such as helium and neon have the lowest molar heat capacity. Monatomic gases have only translational motion since there is no bond about which to rotate or on which to vibrate. Adding heat to a monatomic system makes the atoms move faster, which in turn increases the temperature.

The diatomic gases such as hydrogen, nitrogen, and oxygen have higher (and similar) molar heat capacities. Some of the heat energy added to a diatomic gas is diverted into vibrational and rotational motion. Thus for the same temperature increase, a diatomic gas will require more heat energy than a monatomic gas. Triatomic gases such as water vapour and carbon dioxide can vibrate and rotate in more ways than diatomic gases. They have even higher heat capacities.

As shown in Table 5.4, molecules in the liquid and solid states are more restricted in their translational and rotational movements. As a result they tend to have lower heat capacities.

TABLE 5.4 *Molecular Motion in Different Phases*

	MODE OF MOLECULAR MOTION		
PHASE	Translational	Rotational	Vibrational
Gas	Free	Free	Free
Liquid	Restricted	Restricted	Free
Solid	Absent	Very restricted	Free

QUESTIONS

5. When 1.5×10^3 J of heat energy is absorbed by a beaker of water, its temperature rises by 3.1 °C. What is the heat capacity of the beaker of water?

6. If 10.5 g of iron, at 25 °C, absorbs 128 J of heat, what will be the final temperature of the metal? (The specific heat of iron is given in Table 5.2.)

7. Calculate the molar heat capacity of ethanol, $C_2H_5OH_{(\ell)}$. The specific heat of ethanol is $2.46 \, J \cdot g^{-1} \cdot °C^{-1}$.

8. Why is the molar heat capacity of gaseous ethene, C_2H_4 ($43.6 \, J \cdot mol^{-1} \cdot K^{-1}$), greater than the molar heat capacity of gaseous carbon dioxide, CO_2 ($37.1 \, J \cdot mol^{-1} \cdot K^{-1}$)?

9. Using the values for specific heat given in Appendix II, calculate the molar heat capacities of copper, gold, and silver. What do you observe about these molar heat capacities and how do they compare to the molar heat capacities of the polyatomic gases?

Firewalking

Firewalking is practised in numerous cultures around the world. It is usually associated with religious rites, and participants are considered to be protected from burning by the intensity of their beliefs or by a mystical spirit.

The idea of firewalking seems bizarre to most of us, but the application of a few simple scientific principles can give a fairly straightforward explanation of the way it works. The same scientific principles also help us to distinguish between temperature and heat.

If we bake cookies we never worry about putting our hands in the hot oven to remove them. We know not to touch the metal cookie tray without protective oven mitts, but we are not concerned about burning the rest of our hands or arms. Yet the air in the oven, the cookies, and the cookie tray are all at the same temperature.

Why will the cookie tray burn us but not the oven air? The answer has to do with the heat capacities of the substances involved. When we put our hands in a hot oven, energy flows from the hot air to our hands. But air has a low heat capacity; it cools down far more than our hands warm up. Air also has a very low thermal conductivity. This means that heat energy from other parts of the oven is transferred very slowly to the air in contact with our hands.

In contrast the metal cookie sheet has a high heat capacity. Even a quick touch of the hot sheet transfers a large amount of energy to our hands. The high thermal conductivity of the metal ensures that the heat lost from that part of the cookie sheet in contact with our hands is quickly replaced.

The same explanation can be used for firewalking. The ash layer surrounding the embers is light and fluffy. It has both low heat capacity and low thermal conductivity. The temperature of the embers, may be approximately 600 °C, but as long as we only tread on the embers very briefly, insufficient heat energy is transferred to our feet to cause a burn.

A word of caution: We strongly advise that you do not attempt firewalking yourselves! Although there is a scientific explanation, the preparation of an ideal bed of coals is an art. There is as much ritual associated with the lighting of the fire, the burning of the fire, and the raking over of hot coals as there is with the actual firewalking. This ensures that the embers are properly ashed and that no pieces of burning wood remain. It takes experience to prepare a safe bed of firewalking embers, and just understanding the scientific principles behind this phenomenon does not ensure that an amateur would not get burned.

Figure 5.6

Dr. Bernard J. Leikind, a research physicist at the University of California, has studied the physics involved in being able to walk on hot coals.

Introduction to Enthalpy

Figure 5.7

a) The instant cold pack utilizes an endothermic chemical reaction.

b) The instant hot pack utilizes an exothermic chemical reaction.

5.4 So far we have considered energy in terms of individual atoms, ions, and molecules. But in a chemical reaction these particles interact with each other. The interaction results in energy changes, which we can now begin to identify and to quantify.

Systems and Surroundings

In a chemical reaction, the chemical components involved in the process are known as the **system**. Everything outside the system then becomes the **surroundings**. If we carry out the reaction

$$HCl_{(aq)} + NaOH_{(aq)} \longrightarrow NaCl_{(aq)} + H_2O_{(\ell)}$$

in a beaker the system would include both the reactants (HCl and NaOH) and the products (NaCl and H_2O). Since solvents normally belong to the system, our system would also include the water of the reactant solutions. The beaker and everything else in the laboratory would be part of the surroundings. Exact definitions of system and surroundings depend, to some extent, on what we want to measure and how we want to measure it. In Section 5.8 we will see that sometimes the reaction vessel is part of the system.

Exothermic and Endothermic Reactions

Since energy is always conserved, energy lost by the system must be absorbed by the surroundings. Similarly, energy absorbed by the system must come from the surroundings. A reaction in which the system releases heat to the surroundings is known as an **exothermic** reaction. If the system absorbs heat from the surroundings, it is an **endothermic** reaction.

Constant-Pressure and Constant-Volume Reactions

Most chemical reactions in a laboratory occur under conditions of *constant pressure*. In other words experiments are carried out in reaction vessels that are open to the atmosphere. The reaction volume is allowed to expand or contract at will. *Constant-volume* reactions are more common in industrial operations such as the catalytic reforming and cracking processes of the petroleum industry. In this case specially reinforced reaction chambers are used to confine the components. If there is a change in the number of moles of gas in the chamber, the internal pressure of the system will vary but the volume is maintained.

Enthalpy

Every substance involved in a chemical reaction or a physical process has a particular heat content. This heat content is called **enthalpy** and is symbolized by **H**. We do not measure the absolute heat content of a substance directly. Instead, we measure the enthalpy difference between the initial and the final states of any process carried out at constant pressure. For the reaction

$$A \longrightarrow B$$

we would measure the amount of heat given off or absorbed during the process under conditions of constant pressure. This heat change is known as the **enthalpy of reaction** of the system, and is indicated by using the symbol ΔH. For an *exothermic* reaction ΔH is *negative*. The enthalpy of the system decreases because heat energy is given off to the surroundings. When the system absorbs energy in an *endothermic* reaction, the heat content, or enthalpy, increases and ΔH is *positive*.

When a thermochemical equation is written, it is often accompanied by the value of ΔH. For example, when one mole of copper(II) chloride is formed from solid copper and chlorine gas, we indicate that 220.1 kJ of heat energy is released by writing the equation

$$Cu_{(s)} + Cl_{2\,(g)} \longrightarrow CuCl_{2\,(s)} \qquad \Delta H = -220.1 \text{ kJ}$$

The value of ΔH is always based on the molar ratios given in the equation. If the molar ratios are changed, then the value of ΔH must be changed proportionally. Since the ΔH value often refers to the formation or reaction of one mole of a particular substance, fractional coefficients are permitted in balancing thermochemical equations. This is contrary to the usual practice.

EXAMPLE **5.4** The exothermic reaction of gaseous hydrogen and oxygen at constant pressure releases 241.8 kJ of heat energy for every mole of water vapour formed. Write the thermochemical equation for the production of one mole of water vapour.

SOLUTION The reaction is exothermic, therefore the sign of ΔH will be negative. The production of one mole of gaseous water requires one half mole of oxygen gas. The balanced thermochemical equation is as follows:

$$H_{2\,(g)} + \tfrac{1}{2}\,O_{2\,(g)} \longrightarrow H_2O_{(g)} \qquad \Delta H = -241.8 \text{ kJ} \cdot \text{mol}^{-1}$$

Enthalpy of Combustion

If the reaction is a combustion reaction, the enthalpy of reaction is often referred to as $\Delta H_{combustion}$, or ΔH_{comb}. Combustion, the burning of a substance in oxygen, is always accompanied by a loss of heat from the system. It is important to remember, however, that while nearly all combustion reactions are exothermic, not all exothermic reactions are classified as combustion reactions. In fact the term *combustion* is often used to mean the reaction that occurs when an organic compound, such as propane gas (C_3H_8), is burned. Propane gas is widely used as a fuel in gas barbecues, camping stoves, and even automobiles. The combustion of propane is a highly exothermic reaction.

$$C_3H_{8\,(g)} + 5\,O_{2\,(g)} \longrightarrow 3\,CO_{2\,(g)} + 4\,H_2O_{(\ell)}$$
$$\Delta H_{comb} = -2220 \text{ kJ} \cdot \text{mol}^{-1}$$

Although you might not associate the metabolism of glucose in the body with the term combustion, glucose undergoes a series of reaction steps that represent a slow, controlled, burning reaction.

$$C_6H_{12}O_{6\,(s)} + 6\,O_{2\,(g)} \longrightarrow 6\,CO_{2\,(g)} + 6\,H_2O_{(\ell)}$$
$$\Delta H_{comb} = -2802 \text{ kJ} \cdot \text{mol}^{-1}$$

QUESTIONS

10. In the following chemical reactions, identify the system and the surroundings.
   a) Addition of sodium to a beaker of water.
   b) The blast furnace production of iron from Fe_2O_3 and CO.

11. Are the following reactions exothermic or endothermic?
   a) The burning of methane:
   $$CH_{4\,(s)} + 2\,O_{2\,(g)} \longrightarrow CO_{2\,(g)} + 2\,H_2O_{(\ell)} \qquad \Delta H = -890 \text{ kJ}$$
   b) The decomposition of hydrogen chloride:
   $$2\,HCl_{(g)} \longrightarrow H_{2\,(g)} + Cl_{2\,(g)} \qquad \Delta H = +185 \text{ kJ}$$
   c) The combustion of ammonia:
   $$4\,NH_{3\,(g)} + 5\,O_{2\,(g)} \longrightarrow 4\,NO_{(g)} + 6\,H_2O_{(\ell)} \qquad \Delta H = -1169 \text{ kJ}$$

12. Which of the following exothermic reactions would you classify as combustion reactions?
   a) $CH_{4\,(g)} + 2\,O_{2\,(g)} \longrightarrow CO_{2\,(g)} + 2\,H_2O_{(\ell)}$
   b) $C_2H_{4\,(g)} + Br_{2\,(\ell)} \longrightarrow C_2H_4Br_{2\,(\ell)}$
   c) $C_2H_5OH_{(\ell)} + 3\,O_{2\,(g)} \longrightarrow 2\,CO_{2\,(g)} + 3\,H_2O_{(\ell)}$

13. When potassium nitrate dissolves in water, the beaker containing the solution gets cooler. Is dissolving this salt an exothermic or an endothermic process?

Count von Rumford — A Practical Scientist

Benjamin Thompson was born in Massachusetts in 1753. In his youth, Thompson found employment with a dry goods importer where he made his first investigation into the nature of heat, a topic that was to engross him for the rest of his life. The first experiment, preparing fireworks, blew up in his face causing him to lose his job but not his intense curiosity about how and why things worked.

When the Americans invaded Boston in the War of Independence, Thompson had already actively sided with the British and moved to England. By the age of 26 he had been elected to the Royal Society, an honour bestowed mainly for his investigations into the effectiveness of various mixtures of gun powders and other firearms used by the military.

A year later he was appointed Undersecretary of the Northern Department, and was able to use his scientific interest for personal gain. Investigation of properties of silk, used as the material for army redcoats, showed him that silk was able to absorb a large amount of water — eight times its dry weight. Thompson realized that by buying dry silk in London and selling it in New York, he would make a considerable profit. The dry silk absorbed much moisture on the long, humid journey by sailing ship.

Thompson moved to Munich as an advisor to the Elector of Bavaria and reorganized the Bavarian army. Until this time, few European armies fed or clothed their men. Soldiers scavenged for whatever food they could find and were required to buy their own uniforms. Thompson was determined to feed and clothe the army, thus improving its morale and military efficiency.

From the results of experiments he carried out on various fibres, he became convinced that cotton, linen, or flannel had better insulating properties than silk, the traditional fabric for uniforms. The silk manufacturers refused to make changes to accommodate Thompson, so he set up his own factories to weave and sew the new uniforms.

With large numbers of workers and soldiers to feed, Thompson turned his attention to increasing the efficiency of his kitchens. He designed new stoves, special double boilers, introduced the concept of mobile kitchens for the army, and investigated heats of combustion in order to find the most efficient fuel. From these experiments, Thompson realized that the prevailing ideas about heat were incorrect; the Caloric theory assumed heat to be a fluid substance. Thompson reasoned that heat could not be a form of matter, but was caused by the vibratory motion of particles. Thus temperature was measured as the average value of motion of the particles in touch with a thermometer. This concept of heat is essentially what we understand today.

In 1791 he was made count of the Holy Roman Empire. Thompson chose the title of Rumford — the name of the town his wife's family was from. In 1795 Count von Rumford (as he now insisted on being called) returned to London and was horrified at the crude methods used to heat houses. He designed an efficient fireplace, made to throw heat but not smoke into the room — a vast improvement on the dirty, smokey fireplaces then in use.

Thompson left a lasting legacy, not only from his practical inventions, monetary legacies, and social innovations, but also from his example of meticulous scientific experiments and carefully thought-out deductions on the nature of heat.

Figure 5.8

a) Benjamin Thompson (1753-1814).

b) The Rumford oven. Up until Rumford's work, food had been cooked over open fires. His 'New Contrivance for Roasting Meat' revolutionized cooking.

Enthalpy of Formation and Hess's Law

5.5

As we mentioned earlier, the heat content of a substance cannot be measured directly. Instead, we use the **standard enthalpy of formation** of a substance, which is the loss or gain in heat energy when one mole of the substance is formed from its elements in their standard states.

The symbol for standard enthalpy of formation is ΔH_f°, where the subscript $_f$ indicates formation. For example, the standard enthalpy of formation of liquid water, ΔH_f° of $H_2O_{(\ell)}$, is the change in heat energy when one mole of hydrogen gas reacts with a half mole of oxygen gas to produce one mole of water at 100 kPa.

$$H_{2\,(g)} + \tfrac{1}{2}O_{2\,(g)} \longrightarrow H_2O_{(\ell)}$$

The ΔH of this reaction is $-285.8\,\text{kJ}\cdot\text{mol}^{-1}$ under standard state conditions. Table 5.5 gives values of ΔH_f° for various substances. By convention the ΔH_f° *of the most stable form of an element in its standard state is defined as zero*. Hence, there is no loss or gain in heat energy in the formation of $O_{2\,(g)}$ from $O_{2\,(g)}$: by definition there is no reaction. Although it is possible to calculate enthalpy changes under non-standard conditions, we will always discuss chemical reactions and physical processes at standard conditions.

TABLE 5.5   *Examples of Enthalpy of Formation Equations*

Compound	Equation	$\Delta H_f^\circ(\text{kJ}\cdot\text{mol}^{-1})$
$CH_{4\,(g)}$	$C_{(s)} + 2\,H_{2\,(g)} \longrightarrow CH_{4\,(g)}$	-74.8
$CO_{2\,(g)}$	$C_{(s)} + O_{2\,(g)} \longrightarrow CO_{2\,(g)}$	-393.5
$CO_{(g)}$	$C_{(s)} + \tfrac{1}{2}O_{2\,(g)} \longrightarrow CO_{(g)}$	-110.5
$NO_{(g)}$	$\tfrac{1}{2}N_{2\,(g)} + \tfrac{1}{2}O_{2\,(g)} \longrightarrow NO_{(g)}$	$+90.3$
$Fe_2O_{3\,(s)}$	$2\,Fe_{(s)} + \tfrac{3}{2}O_{2\,(g)} \longrightarrow Fe_2O_{3\,(s)}$	-824.2

EXAMPLE　　**5.5**　Write the equation for the formation of solid ammonium chloride from its elements at standard state and, using the data table in Appendix III, determine whether the reaction is endothermic or exothermic.

SOLUTION　The formula of ammonium chloride is NH_4Cl. The elements from which this solid salt are formed are all diatomic gases at standard state. The balanced equation for the formation of one mole of NH_4Cl is therefore

$$\tfrac{1}{2}N_{2\,(g)} + 2\,H_{2\,(g)} + \tfrac{1}{2}Cl_{2\,(g)} \longrightarrow NH_4Cl_{(s)}$$

The value of ΔH_f° for $NH_4Cl_{(s)}$ given in Appendix III is $-314.4\,\text{kJ}\cdot\text{mol}^{-1}$. The reaction is therefore exothermic.

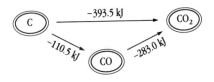

Figure 5.9

In the formation of carbon dioxide, the conversion of carbon to carbon monoxide and then to carbon dioxide releases the same total energy as the direct process.

Hess's Law

Many chemical reactions occur in steps. For example, when carbon is burned in the presence of excess oxygen, carbon dioxide is produced. In this reaction 393.5 kJ of heat energy is liberated for every mole of carbon (graphite) used. This means that the enthalpy change for the reaction is $-393.5 \, \text{kJ} \cdot \text{mol}^{-1}$.

$$C_{(s)} + O_{2\,(g)} \longrightarrow CO_{2\,(g)} \qquad \Delta H° = -393.5 \, \text{kJ}$$

However, if the carbon is burned in a *limited amount of oxygen*, the product is carbon monoxide and less heat energy is released.

$$C_{(s)} + \tfrac{1}{2} O_{2\,(g)} \longrightarrow CO_{(g)} \qquad \Delta H° = -110.5 \, \text{kJ}$$

The carbon monoxide produced in this reaction can undergo further combustion with the release of an extra 283 kJ of heat energy for every mole of carbon dioxide produced.

$$CO_{(g)} + \tfrac{1}{2} O_{2\,(g)} \longrightarrow CO_{2\,(g)} \qquad \Delta H° = -283.0 \, \text{kJ}$$

The overall enthalpy change in the production of one mole of CO_2 results from the combination of these two latter steps:

$$(-110.5 \, \text{kJ}) + (-283.0 \, \text{kJ}) = -393.5 \, \text{kJ}$$

The end result is the same whether it is formed in a one-step reaction or in a multi-step process. This is an illustration of *Hess's law of constant heat summation*. More commonly known as **Hess's law**, it can be stated as follows:

> **The enthalpy change for any reaction depends only on the products and reactants and is independent of the pathway or the number of steps between the reactant and product.**

This is really another way of stating the law of conservation of energy and allows us to calculate overall reaction enthalpies from intermediate-step enthalpies.

If we are given the intermediate steps (numbered 1 and 2) in the production of one mole of tetraphosphorus decaoxide, P_4O_{10}, we can determine the $\Delta H°$ for the overall reaction from its elements.

$$\textbf{(1)} \quad 4\,P_{(s)} + 3\,O_{2\,(g)} \longrightarrow P_4O_{6\,(s)} \qquad \Delta H° = -1640 \, \text{kJ}$$
$$\text{and}$$
$$\textbf{(2)} \quad P_4O_{6\,(s)} + 2\,O_{2\,(g)} \longrightarrow P_4O_{10\,(s)} \qquad \Delta H° = -1344 \, \text{kJ}$$

The overall reaction is the sum of (1) and (2):

$$\textbf{(1)} \quad 4\,P_{(s)} + 3\,O_{2\,(g)} \longrightarrow P_4O_{6\,(s)}$$
$$\textbf{(2)} \quad P_4O_{6\,(s)} + 2\,O_{2\,(g)} \longrightarrow P_4O_{10\,(s)}$$
$$\overline{4\,P_{(s)} + 3\,O_{2\,(g)} + P_4O_{6\,(s)} + 2\,O_{2\,(g)} \longrightarrow P_4O_{6\,(s)} + P_4O_{10\,(s)}}$$

Figure 5.10

Phosphorus burns in excess oxygen to give tetraphosphorus decaoxide.

Cancelling out species that appear on both sides of the reaction, we are left with the equation for the overall reaction:

$$4 P_{(s)} + 5 O_{2(g)} \longrightarrow P_4O_{10(s)}$$

The enthalpy of the overall reaction is the sum of the enthalpies of the intermediate steps.

$$\Delta H^\circ_{overall} = (-1640 \text{ kJ}) + (-1344 \text{ kJ}) = -2984 \text{ kJ}$$

Reaction steps and their enthalpies can be treated algebraically. If a reaction step is reversed the sign of its ΔH° value must be reversed. The decomposition of P_4O_{10} to its elements would be an endothermic process requiring the absorption of 2984 kJ of heat energy.

$$P_4O_{10(s)} \longrightarrow 4 P_{(s)} + 5 O_{2(g)} \qquad \Delta H^\circ = +2984 \text{ kJ} \cdot \text{mol}^{-1}$$

The decomposition of two moles of $P_4O_{10(s)}$ would require twice as much heat.

In summary the rules for using Hess's law to determine standard enthalpies of reaction are fairly simple.

1. Consider the intermediate steps of the overall reaction and the value of ΔH° for each.
2. Reverse intermediate reactions and change the sign of ΔH° values as necessary.
3. Multiply intermediate reactions as necessary to balance the overall equation and multiply ΔH° values of the steps as required.
4. Determine $\Delta H^\circ_{overall}$ from the algebraic sum of ΔH° values for the intermediate reactions.

EXAMPLE 5.6

The enthalpy changes for the following reactions are

(1) $\quad C_2H_{2(g)} + \frac{5}{2} O_{2(g)} \longrightarrow 2 CO_{2(g)} + H_2O_{(\ell)} \qquad \Delta H^\circ = -1299$ kJ
(2) $\quad C_6H_{6(\ell)} + \frac{15}{2} O_{2(g)} \longrightarrow 6 CO_{2(g)} + 3 H_2O_{(\ell)} \qquad \Delta H^\circ = -3267$ kJ

Using only the above data, find ΔH° for the following reaction:

(3) $\quad C_2H_{2(g)} \longrightarrow C_6H_{6(\ell)}$

Is the reaction endothermic or exothermic?

SOLUTION

Equations (1) and (2) are intermediate steps in the formation of C_6H_6 from C_2H_2. Equation (1) must be multiplied by three to balance the overall equation, (3); and, thus, ΔH° for this reaction must also be multiplied by three. Equation (2) must be reversed; ΔH° for this equation will now be positive. We add these rearranged equations, cancelling compounds appearing on both sides of the reaction to give equation (3).

$$(1) \quad 3\,C_2H_{2\,(g)} + \tfrac{15}{2}\,O_{2\,(g)} \longrightarrow 6\,CO_{2\,(g)} + 3\,H_2O_{(\ell)} \quad \Delta H° = 3(-1299\,kJ)$$

$$(2) \quad 6\,CO_{2\,(g)} + 3\,H_2O_{(\ell)} \longrightarrow C_6H_{6\,(\ell)} + \tfrac{15}{2}\,O_{2\,(g)} \quad \Delta H° = +3267\,kJ$$

$$(3) \quad 3\,C_2H_{2\,(g)} \longrightarrow C_6H_{6\,(\ell)}$$

Adding enthalpies, we get

$$\Delta H°_{overall} = 3(-1299\,kJ) + 3267\,kJ = -630\,kJ$$

Since $\Delta H°_{overall} < 0$, the reaction is exothermic.

It is also possible to calculate an enthalpy change for a reaction directly if we know the heats of formation values for *all* the reactants and products.

$\Delta H°_{reaction}$ = (Sum of $\Delta H_f°$ of products) – (Sum of $\Delta H_f°$ of reactants)

This is a mathematical statement of Hess's law and is often written as

$$\mathbf{\Delta H°_{reaction} = \sum \Delta H_f°{}_{products} - \sum \Delta H_f°{}_{reactants}}$$

where $\sum$ means "the sum of." However, we must be careful if we are given $\Delta H°$ values other than those of formation ($\Delta H_f°$). In this case we would have to set out all the thermochemical equations as we did in Example 5.6. We can apply this shorthand version of Hess's law in Example 5.7 because the necessary $\Delta H_f°$ values are available.

EXAMPLE   **5.7**   Using the $\Delta H_f°$ values from Appendix III, determine the enthalpy change for the combustion reaction of benzene, $C_6H_{6\,(\ell)}$.

$$C_6H_{6\,(\ell)} + \tfrac{15}{2}\,O_{2\,(g)} \longrightarrow 6\,CO_{2\,(g)} + 3\,H_2O_{(\ell)}$$

SOLUTION   Since we have $\Delta H_f°$ for all the reactants and products in this reaction, it is possible to use the relationship

$$\Delta H° = \sum \Delta H_f°{}_{products} - \sum \Delta H_f°{}_{reactants}$$

We substitute the appropriate values, remembering that the $\Delta H_f°$ value for an element is always zero.

$$\Delta H° = [6(-393.5) + 3(-285.8)] - [+49.0] = -3267\,kJ$$

This gives the same answer as if we had written out the thermochemical equations for the formation of the compounds involved and rearranged them.

We can use Hess's law to obtain values of enthalpies of formation for compounds that cannot be formed directly from their constituent elements. For example, the enthalpy of formation of ethanol, C_2H_5OH, is $-277.7\,kJ\cdot mol^{-1}$. However, the corresponding reaction does not occur.

$$\mathbf{2\,C_{(s)} + 3\,H_{2\,(g)} + \tfrac{1}{2}\,O_{2\,(g)} \longrightarrow C_2H_5OH_{(\ell)}}$$

The value has been obtained from enthalpy of combustion measurements. It is important to realize that although we can use enthalpy of formation data, very few of the formation reactions actually occur.

Finding Enthalpy Changes by Graphical Means

Up to now we have used algebraic methods to find enthalpy changes, but it is also possible to use graphical methods. First, let us see how enthalpies of formation can be displayed (Figure 5.11). The vertical axis will be used as an enthalpy scale. We will use two examples, nitrogen dioxide, for which ΔH_f° is $+33.2\,kJ\cdot mol^{-1}$, and silver chloride, for which ΔH_f° is $-127.1\,kJ\cdot mol^{-1}$. The initial step is to write the equations corresponding to the enthalpy of formation:

$$\tfrac{1}{2}\,N_{2\,(g)} + O_{2\,(g)} \longrightarrow NO_{2\,(g)} \qquad \Delta H_f^\circ = +33.2\,\mathbf{kJ\cdot mol^{-1}}$$
$$Ag_{(s)} + \tfrac{1}{2}\,Cl_{2\,(g)} \longrightarrow AgCl_{(s)} \qquad \Delta H_f^\circ = -127.1\,\mathbf{kJ\cdot mol^{-1}}$$

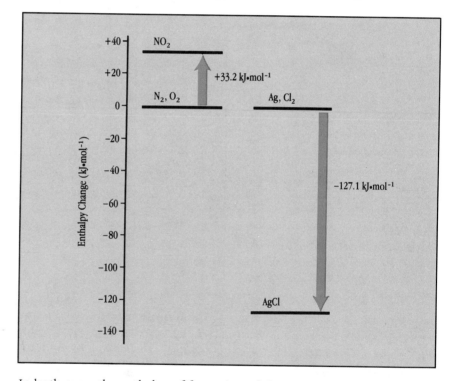

Figure 5.11

We can depict enthalpy of formation processes graphically.

In both cases the enthalpy of formation of elements is defined as zero, so we start at a zero enthalpy value. The formation of nitrogen dioxide is endothermic, causing an increase in enthalpy as shown on the graph. But for the exothermic formation of silver chloride there is a decrease in enthalpy, shown as a decrease into the negative portion of the graph. We can see graphically how the enthalpy of a compound compares with that of its constituent elements.

This process can be extended to include the use of Hess's law. For example, we may want to know the change in enthalpy for the following reaction:

$$SnCl_{2\,(s)} + Cl_{2\,(g)} \longrightarrow SnCl_{4\,(\ell)}$$

But we only know that the enthalpy of formation of tin(II) chloride is $-325.1\,kJ \cdot mol^{-1}$ and that of tin(IV) chloride is $-511.3\,kJ \cdot mol^{-1}$.

We first write out equations corresponding to the reactions for which we have enthalpy data:

$$Sn_{(s)} + Cl_{2\,(g)} \longrightarrow SnCl_{2\,(s)} \qquad \Delta H_f^\circ = -325.1\,kJ \cdot mol^{-1}$$
$$Sn_{(s)} + 2\,Cl_{2\,(g)} \longrightarrow SnCl_{4\,(\ell)} \qquad \Delta H_f^\circ = -511.3\,kJ \cdot mol^{-1}$$

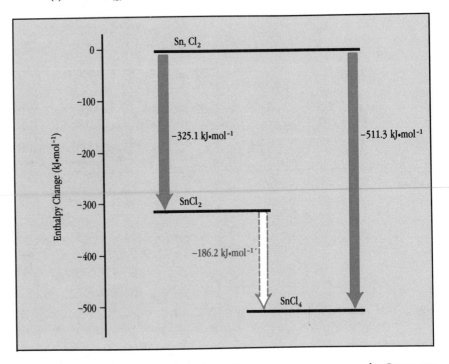

Figure 5.12

The enthalpy of reaction to form tin(IV) chloride from tin(II) chloride is given by the difference between the enthalpy of formation values.

The formations can be plotted starting at zero on our graph. Once we have reached the formation of $SnCl_{2\,(s)}$, the independent formation of $SnCl_{4\,(\ell)}$ can be reached by combining one mole of chlorine gas with one mole of tin(II) chloride.

$$SnCl_{2\,(s)} + Cl_{2\,(g)} \longrightarrow SnCl_{4\,(g)}$$

This allows us to reach the composite product tin(IV) chloride. The change in enthalpy is simply the algebraic difference between the two separate enthalpies of formation:

$$\Delta H^\circ = -511.3\,kJ \cdot mol^{-1} - (-325.1\,kJ \cdot mol^{-1})$$
$$= -186.2\,kJ \cdot mol^{-1}$$

Notice that the addition of chlorine gas to tin(II) chloride does not affect the overall change in enthalpy. That is because by definition ΔH_f° for an element is zero.

QUESTIONS

14. Write balanced equations for the formation of the following substances from their elements at standard state:
    a) copper sulfate pentahydrate, $CuSO_4 \cdot 5H_2O_{(s)}$
    b) ethanoic acid, $CH_3CO_2H_{(\ell)}$

15. Write balanced equations for
    a) the formation of pentane, $C_5H_{12\,(\ell)}$,
    b) the combustion of pentane

16. Using the values given in Appendix III, calculate the enthalpy of formation of
    a) 1.50 mol of sulfur dioxide gas, $SO_{2\,(g)}$
    b) 0.750 mol of enthanol, $C_2H_5OH_{(\ell)}$

17. From the following two thermochemical equations,

$$2\,Fe_{(s)} + \tfrac{3}{2}\,O_{2\,(g)} \longrightarrow Fe_2O_{3\,(s)} \qquad \Delta H^\circ = -824 \text{ kJ}$$
$$2\,Al_{(s)} + \tfrac{3}{2}\,O_{2\,(g)} \longrightarrow Al_2O_{3\,(s)} \qquad \Delta H^\circ = -1676 \text{ kJ}$$

calculate the enthalpy change for the reaction

$$2\,Al_{(s)} + Fe_2O_{3\,(s)} \longrightarrow 2\,Fe_{(s)} + Al_2O_{3\,(s)}$$

Enthalpy and Phase Change

5.6

When ice at $-10\,°C$ is heated at a constant rate, the temperature of the ice increases steadily until it reaches $0\,°C$. At this point, despite the continuing input of heat energy, there is no further temperature increase until all the ice has changed to water. Similarly, when the water is heated at a steady rate, the temperature increases steadily to $100\,°C$. Again, no further temperature increase occurs until all the water has turned to steam. At $0\,°C$ the heat energy supplied is used to overcome the attractive forces holding the H_2O molecules in the solid ice configuration. Once *melting* takes place, further heat input increases the temperature of the water. At $100\,°C$ the heat energy supplied is used to overcome the attractive forces holding the liquid molecules together. After *vaporization* has occurred, the added heat energy raises the temperature of the steam.

Both melting and vaporization are endothermic processes: heat is absorbed from the surroundings. The enthalpy changes involved are known as $\Delta H_{\text{melting}}$ and $\Delta H_{\text{vaporization}}$ (or ΔH_{melt} and ΔH_{vap}). During the reverse processes, in which steam condenses or water freezes, heat energy is

Perspiration—A Key to Survival

The normal human body temperature is close to 37 °C. Any change in this temperature, even by a degree or so, means a loss in efficiency of the biochemical reactions that drive the body mechanisms. However, it is possible to survive quite drastic reductions in body temperature under some circumstances. Patients whose body temperatures have dropped as low as 26 °C for a few minutes have been successfully revived. In fact the lowering of the body temperature to slow down metabolic processes is now an accepted medical technique in some forms of surgery. But an increase in body temperature by four or five degrees Celsius, for any extended period, is usually fatal.

Body temperature can be raised in a number of ways. Some illnesses cause an increase in body temperature. Although this may be the body's way of fighting the disease, high temperatures for a prolonged period can destroy the protein molecules, known as enzymes, that are essential to life. In a healthy body, temperature can be raised by generating heat through work and exercise, faster than it can be dissipated, or by absorbing heat faster than it can be dissipated.

At high temperatures and when our bodies are producing excess heat, an effective method of cooling is imperative. The process of perspiration involves the evaporation of water from the surface of the skin and a subsequent drop in body temperature. A large quantity of heat is needed to vaporize water ($\Delta H°_{vap} = 40.7 \, kJ \cdot mol^{-1}$). One litre of evaporated sweat removes over 2200 kilojoules of heat from the body.

As the external temperature rises or as the amount of work being done is increased, a higher rate of perspiration is required to maintain normal body temperature. High humidity reduces the effectiveness of sweating. If the surrounding air is already nearly saturated with water vapour, less sweat evaporates. Working under such conditions means that the sweat runs off as droplets, which does not have the same cooling effect as does evaporation. A fan can help because the air currents from the fan carry away the high humidity layer near the skin, allowing more effective evaporation.

In desert conditions the evaporative cooling from perspiration is very effective — so much, that it is possible to become dehydrated without realizing it. When the humidity is very low, sweat evaporates immediately. We are not aware we are perspiring: there are no beads of sweat forming on our foreheads; our clothes do not stick. This can be dangerous. Under these conditions, thirst is not a sufficient indication of how much water we need. If we drink only enough to satisfy our thirst, slow dehydration is still a possibility. To avoid desert dehydration, we should be aware of the problem and drink plenty of water throughout the day.

Figure 5.13
Perspiration is a means of dissipating heat from the body. We rely on the high value of the enthalpy of vaporization of water to provide us with this cooling mechanism.

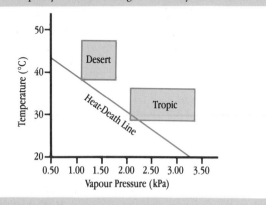

Figure 5.14
A graph of temperature plotted against humidity. We can tolerate higher temperatures if the humidity is low.

released to the surroundings. These are exothermic processes. The enthalpy of condensation, $\Delta H_{condensation}$ (ΔH_{cond}), and the enthalpy of freezing, $\Delta H_{freezing}$ (ΔH_{fre}), are negative.

Figure 5.15

Graph of temperature plotted against heat supplied to water. The slower warming rate of liquid water compared to ice and steam reflects the larger heat capacity of the liquid phase. The longer time for vaporization compared to melting reflects the larger value of the enthalpy of vaporization compared to the enthalpy of fusion.

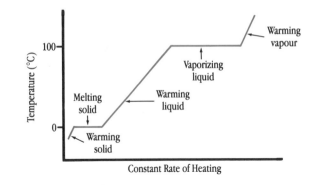

Table 5.6 gives enthalpies of phase change for various substances. These are generally quoted for a mole of the substance and are known as molar enthalpies of phase change. Note that for each substance, the values for condensation and vaporization have the same magnitude but opposite signs. This is also true for melting and freezing. Knowing the molar enthalpy of phase change for a substance allows us to determine the enthalpy changes involved for any mass of that substance.

TABLE 5.6	*Molar Enthalpies of Phase Change* ($kJ \cdot mol^{-1}$)			
Substance	ΔH_{vap}	ΔH_{cond}	ΔH_{melt}	ΔH_{fre}
Water	+40.7	−40.7	+6.02	−6.02
Methane	+10.4	−10.4	+0.94	−0.94
Mercury	+59.3	−59.3	+2.3	−2.3
Sodium chloride	+207	−207	+27.2	−27.2

EXAMPLE   *5.8*   Calculate the enthalpy change involved when 17.2 g of liquid mercury is vaporized. The molar enthalpy of vaporization is given in Table 5.6.

SOLUTION   First we must determine the number of moles of mercury in 17.2 g using the molar mass of mercury as a conversion factor:

$$\text{Number of moles of Hg} = 17.2\,\text{g Hg} \times \frac{1\,\text{mol Hg}}{200.6\,\text{g Hg}}$$

$$= 8.57 \times 10^{-2}\,\text{mol Hg}$$

The molar enthalpy of vaporization for mercury (Table 5.6) is $+59.3 \, kJ \cdot mol^{-1}$. We use this value as a conversion factor to find ΔH:

$$\Delta H = 8.57 \times 10^{-2} \, mol \times \frac{59.3 \, kJ}{1 \, mol}$$

$$= 5.08 \, kJ$$

The positive enthalpy value indicates that the process is endothermic. Heat must be applied to vaporize the liquid mercury.

QUESTIONS

18. Sublimation is the direct phase change from the solid to the gas phase. Would the enthalpy of sublimation be positive or negative? Explain your answer.

19. Why are burns from steam more severe than burns from boiling water?

20. How much heat is required to melt 45.0 g of ice? Molar enthalpies of phase change are given in Table 5.6.

Bond Energy 5.7

The combustion reaction to produce water vapour is extremely exothermic.

$$H_{2 \, (g)} + \tfrac{1}{2} O_{2 \, (g)} \longrightarrow H_2O_{(g)}$$

Figure 5.16

Sticks of dynamite. Explosives such as dynamite have much weaker bonds than the molecules to which they decompose. Such reactions are very exothermic.

This means that the product has stronger bonds than the reactants. When the reaction occurs, the hydrogen-hydrogen bond (H—H) is broken in one mole of hydrogen molecules and the oxygen-oxygen double bond (O=O) is broken in one half mole of oxygen molecules. At the same time two moles of oxygen-hydrogen bonds (O—H) are made. When chemical bonds are broken, energy (usually in the form of heat) must be supplied. When bonds are formed, heat energy is released. The correct name for the heat energy absorbed at constant pressure when a chemical bond is broken is **bond enthalpy**. However, chemists usually refer to this particular enthalpy term as **bond energy**. Table 5.7 gives average bond energies for a number of single, double, and triple bonds. Notice that as the number of bonds increases, the value of the bond energy increases.

We can use bond energies, such as those listed in Table 5.7, to estimate enthalpy changes for many chemical reactions. The values we obtain are theoretical values that are close, but not identical, to those values obtained experimentally. This is because the bond energies for specific bonding types vary slightly between molecules. Tabulated bond energy values therefore are usually the average values for breaking bonds between atoms in gaseous phase molecules. The exceptions are diatomic molecules. The values for these molecules are directly measurable and

TABLE 5.7 Average Bond Energies at 298 K

Bond	Bond Energy (kJ·mol^{-1})
H—H*	436.4
H—F*	568.2
H—Cl*	431.9
H—Br*	366.1
H—I*	298.3
C—H	414
C—O	327
C=O	804
N—F	275
N—N	393
N=N	418
N≡N*	941.4

The asterisk (*) indicates those bond energies for which actual values can be obtained from one molecule, rather than average values from the same bond in a number of different molecules.

thus reasonably accurate. This is reflected in Table 5.7, where the bond energies of diatomic molecules are given to four significant figures. For example, the bond energy required to break one mole of gaseous hydrogen into two moles of hydrogen atoms is 436.4 kJ.

$$H\text{---}H_{(g)} \longrightarrow 2\,H_{(g)} \qquad \Delta H° = +436.4\,kJ$$

But the energy required to break all four of the C—H bonds in the methane molecule is 1650 kJ·mol^{-1} of gaseous methane.

$$CH_{4\,(g)} \longrightarrow C_{(g)} + 4\,H_{(g)} \qquad \Delta H° = +1650\,kJ$$

The average bond energy of the C—H bond in methane is

$$\frac{\Delta H}{4} = \frac{1650\,kJ}{4}$$
$$= 412.5\,kJ$$

The bond energy for C—H given in Table 5.7 was obtained by averaging values from many of the polyatomic molecules that contain the carbon-hydrogen bond.

The energy required to break one particular bond in a polyatomic molecule is known as the **bond dissociation energy**. For example, 423 kJ are required to break the first C—H bond in one mole of methane.

$$CH_{4\,(g)} \longrightarrow CH_{3\,(g)} + H_{(g)} \qquad \Delta H° = +423\,kJ$$

Bond dissociation energies depend on the actual reaction under consideration and are not average values. In this chapter bond energy will always refer to average bond energy and not to bond dissociation energy. Example 5.9 shows how we can use bond energies to estimate reaction enthalpy changes.

EXAMPLE   5.9   Determine the enthalpy of formation of hydrogen chloride gas from the average bond energy data in Appendix IV.

$$\tfrac{1}{2}\,H_{2\,(g)} + \tfrac{1}{2}\,Cl_{2\,(g)} \longrightarrow HCl_{(g)}$$

SOLUTION   In the process, we break one half mole of hydrogen covalent bonds and one half mole of chlorine covalent bonds. This requires input of energy. One mole of hydrogen-chlorine bonds is then formed. Bond formation is an exothermic process.

Type of Bond Broken	Number of Bonds Broken	Bond Energy $(kJ \cdot mol^{-1})$	Energy Change (kJ)
H—H	$\frac{1}{2}$	436	+218
Cl—Cl	$\frac{1}{2}$	243	+122

Type of Bond Formed	Number of Bonds Formed	Bond Energy $(kJ \cdot mol^{-1})$	Energy Change (kJ)
H—Cl	1	432	−432

Total energy change: $218 + 122 - 432 = -92$ kJ
Calculated ΔH_f° hydrogen chloride $= -92\,kJ \cdot mol^{-1}$

The theoretical steps involved in the above reaction process can be displayed as an energy diagram, Figure 5.17. Reactants are shown at lower left. The bond-breaking steps require an input of energy (shown on the left-hand side). The bond-forming step is then shown descending on the right-hand side to the product. Thus, the enthalpy of reaction is the difference in energy between the reactant and product.

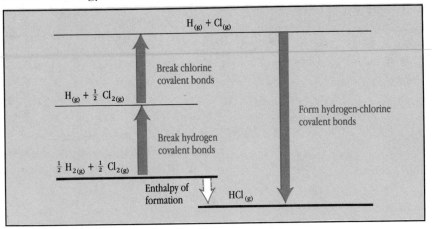

Figure 5.17

The theoretical steps involved in the formation of hydrogen chloride from its constituent elements.

If we analyze the bond making and breaking process, we find that

$$\Delta H = \sum \textbf{Bond energies of bonds broken} - \sum \textbf{Bond energies of bonds ma}$$

This a restatement of Hess's law as applied to bond energies. We can use experimentally-determined ΔH values and average bond energy values to estimate other bond energies.

Energy Changes in the Formation of Ionic Compounds

The formation of ionic compounds is usually accompanied by a release of energy, often quite substantial. Sodium, for example, reacts vigorously with chlorine to form sodium chloride, and intense amounts of heat and light are released when magnesium burns in oxygen. In an ionic reaction we have to account for more than the bond energies of gaseous diatomic molecules. We must account for phase changes as well as the loss or gain of electrons. For example, we can separate the reaction between one mole of solid magnesium and one mole of chlorine gas into five separate steps. The first three are endothermic, the remaining two are exothermic.

1. One mole of magnesium metal vaporizes so that indiviudal magnesium atoms are free to react.

$$Mg_{(s)} \longrightarrow Mg_{(g)} \qquad \Delta H_{vap} = +148 \, kJ$$

2. One mole of chlorine molecules dissociates into chlorine atoms.

$$Cl_{2\,(g)} \longrightarrow 2\,Cl_{(g)} \qquad \Delta H_{bond\ energy} = +243 \, kJ$$

The magnesium atoms can now react with the chlorine atoms. Each magnesium atom loses two electrons, while each chlorine atom gains one electron. Each magnesium atom must therefore react with two chlorine atoms.

3. Energy must be added to remove two electrons from each magnesium atom. This energy corresponds to the first and second ionization energies discussed in Section 2.2.

$$Mg_{(g)} \longrightarrow Mg^{2+}{}_{(g)} + 2\,e^- \qquad \Delta H = +2190 \, kJ$$

4. When chlorine atoms form negative ions the energy (electron affinity) is released. The value is $-348 \, kJ \cdot mol^{-1}$, but in this case we form two moles of chloride ions. Using this value for energy released as our conversion factor, we can find the overall enthalpy change:

$$\Delta H = 2 \text{ mol} \times \frac{(-348 \, kJ)}{1 \text{ mol}}$$
$$= -696 \, kJ$$

Therefore, our thermochemical equation is

$$2\,Cl_{(g)} + 2\,e^- \longrightarrow 2\,Cl^-{}_{(g)} \qquad \Delta H = -696 \, kJ$$

5. The positive and negative ions that have been formed will be attracted to each other. Energy is released as the isolated ions move together to form a crystal.

$$Mg^{2+}{}_{(g)} + 2\,Cl^-{}_{(g)} \longrightarrow MgCl_{2\,(s)} \qquad \Delta H = -2526 \, kJ$$

The enthalpy of formation of one mole magnesium chloride is the sum of the energy changes for each of the five steps. Thus,

$$\Delta H_f^\circ = 148 + 243 + 2190 + (-696) + (-2526)$$
$$= -641 \, kJ$$

This is the enthalpy change when one mole of solid magnesium chloride is formed from solid magnesium and gaseous chlorine. The overall reaction can be written as

$$Mg_{(s)} + Cl_{2(g)} \longrightarrow MgCl_{2(s)} \qquad \Delta H_f^\circ = -641 \text{ kJ} \cdot \text{mol}^{-1}$$

The energy changes for each of the five theoretical steps are illustrated in a graph known as a **Born-Haber cycle** (Figure 5.18). Notice that much of the energy released in this reaction is due to Step 5. This is true for the formation of most ionic solids from their elements. The energy absorbed in the reverse reaction, which would separate the crystal into gaseous ions, is called the **lattice energy**. The numerical value is the same as the enthalpy change of the forward reaction, but the sign is different. The lattice energy of $MgCl_2$ is therefore $+2526 \text{ kJ} \cdot \text{mol}^{-1}$. In general, the greater the lattice energy, the more stable the ionic compound.

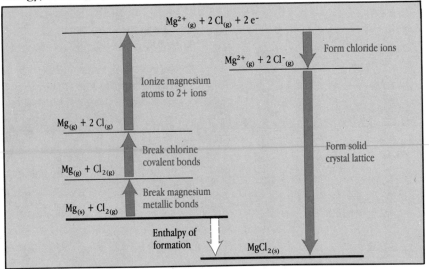

Figure 5.18

The Born-Haber cycle showing the energy changes in the formation of one mole of magnesium chloride from its elements.

Energy Changes in the Formation of Covalent Compounds

The formation of simple covalent compounds usually releases less energy than the formation of ionic compounds. In some cases the amount of energy is very small. If we analyze the steps involved in the formation of liquid sulfur dichloride from elemental sulfur and chlorine

$$\tfrac{1}{8} S_{8(s)} + Cl_{2(g)} \longrightarrow SCl_{2(\ell)}$$

we again have to account for more than just the bond enthalpies of gaseous diatomic molecules. There are four separate steps:

1. One mole of solid sulfur, consisting of S_8 molecules, must be vaporized and atomized so that individual sulfur atoms are free to react.

$$\tfrac{1}{8} S_{8(s)} \longrightarrow S_{(g)} \qquad \Delta H_{vap} = +276 \text{ kJ}$$

2. One mole of chlorine molecules must be broken into chlorine atoms.

$$Cl_{2\,(g)} \longrightarrow 2\,Cl_{(g)} \qquad \Delta H_{\text{bond energy}} = +243\,\text{kJ}$$

We have now broken sulfur-sulfur covalent bonds and chlorine-chlorine covalent bonds. The sulfur atoms can now react with the chlorine atoms, forming sulfur-chlorine bonds.

3. Energy is released when two moles of sulfur-chlorine bonds are formed.

$$S_{(g)} + 2\,Cl_{(g)} \longrightarrow SCl_{2\,(g)} \qquad \Delta H = -510\,\text{kJ}$$

4. Individual molecules of sulfur dichloride now condense to form a liquid, the normal state of the compound at room temperature.

$$SCl_{2\,(g)} \longrightarrow SCl_{2\,(\ell)} \qquad \Delta H_{\text{cond}} = -56\,\text{kJ}\cdot\text{mol}^{-1}$$

If we calculate the sum of the energy changes for the four steps, we find that the formation of one mole of sulfur dichloride from sulfur and chlorine is accompanied by the release of just 47 kJ. The overall reaction can be written as

$$\tfrac{1}{8}\,S_{8\,(s)} + Cl_{2\,(g)} \longrightarrow SCl_{2\,(\ell)} \qquad \Delta H_f^{\circ} = -47\,\text{kJ}\cdot\text{mol}^{-1}$$

The Born-Haber cycle diagram in Figure 5.19, shows that the formation of sulfur dichloride gas involves a net input of a small amount of energy. Condensation of the gas to a liquid results in the release of a very small amount of energy.

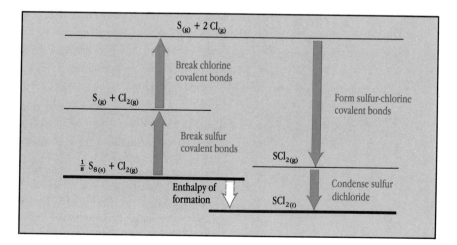

Figure 5.19

The Born-Haber cycle showing the energy changes in the formation of one mole of sulfur dichloride from its elements.

QUESTIONS

21. Estimate the $\Delta H°$ of the following reaction using the average bond energies from Appendix IV.

$$C_2H_4 + H_{2\,(g)} \longrightarrow C_2H_{6\,(g)}$$

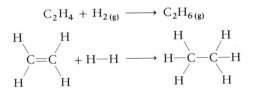

22. Using the data provided below, draw a Born-Haber cycle for the formation of lithium fluoride and calculate the enthalpy of formation of the compound.

$$Li_{(s)} + \tfrac{1}{2}F_{2\,(g)} \longrightarrow LiF_{(s)}$$

Enthalpy of vaporization of lithium metal $= 155\,kJ \cdot mol^{-1}$
Bond energy of molecular fluorine $= 150\,kJ \cdot mol^{-1}$
First ionization energy of lithium $= 520\,kJ \cdot mol^{-1}$
Electron affinity of fluorine atom $= -333\,kJ \cdot mol^{-1}$
Energy of lattice formation $= -1012\,kJ \cdot mol^{-1}$

Calorimetry   5.8

In previous sections of this chapter we used experimentally-determined values for heats of reactions, enthalpies of formation, and bond energies. The branch of thermochemistry concerned with measurement of such heat changes is known as **calorimetry**. Any device used for measuring a heat change is called a **calorimeter**. In high school labs, you will use constant-pressure calorimeters such as the simple, solution, or flame calorimeter. We will also describe the bomb (constant-volume) and human calorimeters.

A Simple Calorimeter

Figure 5.20 shows a very simple constant-pressure calorimeter made from a polystyrene cup. This type can be used for reactions involving aqueous solutions, and for this reason is sometimes known as a solution calorimeter. When we measure heat changes with this calorimeter, we assume that all the heat is absorbed by the water. We also assume that the polystyrene cup does not absorb heat and that no heat is lost to the surroundings. If the quantity of heat emitted during the reaction is not large, such a "coffee cup" calorimeter will give reasonably accurate results. If large quantities of heat are involved, then heat losses to the surroundings will lead to inaccuracies.

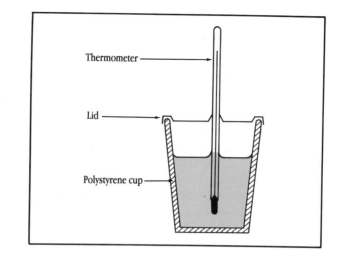

Figure 5.20
A cross-section of a simple 'coffee-cup' calorimeter.

EXAMPLE   **5.10**   A mass of 100 g of water is placed in a coffee cup calorimeter. The solution temperature is measured to be 14.4 °C. A mass of 0.412 g of calcium metal is placed in the calorimeter. When the reaction is complete the temperature is recorded as 24.6 °C. Calculate the standard molar enthalpy change for this reaction:

$$Ca_{(s)} + 2\,H_2O_{(\ell)} \longrightarrow Ca(OH)_{2\,(s)} + H_{2\,(g)}$$

Assume that the calcium is the limiting reagent. The specific heat of water is $4.18\,J{\cdot}g^{-1}{\cdot}°C^{-1}$.

SOLUTION   From the given data, we know the mass, specific heat, and temperature change ($24.6\,°C - 14.4\,°C = 10.2\,°C$) for this solution. Thus we can calculate the heat absorbed by the solution:

$$\text{Heat absorbed} = 4.18\,J{\cdot}g^{-1}{\cdot}°C^{-1} \times 100\,g \times 10.2\,°C$$
$$= 4.26 \times 10^3\,J$$

Using the correct conversion factor, we get

$$\text{Heat absorbed} = 4.26 \times 10^3\,J \times \frac{1\,kJ}{10^3\,J}$$
$$= 4.26\,kJ$$

The heat change in the reaction is therefore $-4.26\,kJ$. Since we require the molar enthalpy, the next step is to calculate the moles of calcium used:

$$\text{Number of moles of Ca} = 0.412\,g\,Ca \times \frac{1\,mol\,Ca}{40.08\,g\,Ca}$$
$$= 1.03 \times 10^{-2}\,mol\,Ca$$

To find the molar enthalpy, we simply divide the enthalpy by the number of moles:

$$\text{Molar enthalpy} = \frac{-4.26\,\text{kJ}}{1.03 \times 10^{-2}\,\text{mol}}$$
$$= -414\,\text{kJ}\cdot\text{mol}^{-1}$$

The simple coffee cup calorimeter can be used for many calorimetry measurements in aqueous solution. Provided the solutions that we use are dilute (i.e. mostly water), we can assume the solutions to have the same specific heat capacity as water.

For more precise measurements of molar enthalpies of reaction, a solution calorimeter is used (Figure 5.21). This consists of a metal can or beaker surrounded by an insulating jacket. Using such a calorimeter, some of the heat of reaction is absorbed by the metal can. Thus to calculate the heat absorbed, we would have two values: one for the heat absorbed by the water and one for the heat absorbed by the metal can.

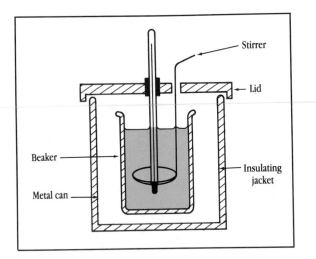

Figure 5.21
A common laboratory constant-pressure calorimeter.

The Flame Calorimeter

We are often interested in the molar enthalpy of combustion of fuels. The greater the heat produced upon combustion, the better the fuel will be as a heat source. Different fuels are usually compounds of carbon and hydrogen (and sometimes oxygen). When a fuel burns completely, carbon dioxide and water are formed. A commercial flame calorimeter is shown in Figure 5.22, though a homemade one can be constructed from a coffee can and some metal tubing. The fuel is placed in a burner and the wick is lit. The heated air rises through the tube inside the calorimeter and heats the water and the can. By measuring the temperature change of the calorimeter, and knowing the masses and specific heats involved, the molar enthalpy of combustion can be determined.

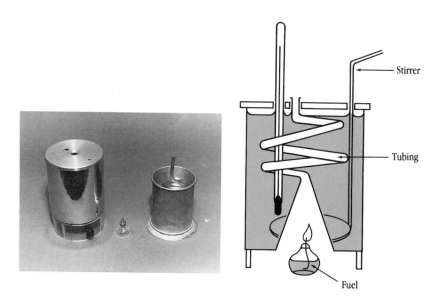

Figure 5.22
A flame (combustion) calorimeter.

EXAMPLE   *5.11*   A flame calorimeter composed of steel and with a mass of 322 g is filled with 225 g of water. The original temperature of the water and calorimeter is 10.6 °C. When 1.02 g of ethanol, C_2H_5OH, is burned, the temperature rises to 38.4 °C. Calculate the molar enthalpy of combustion of ethanol. Specific heat of steel = $0.44 \, J \cdot g^{-1} \cdot {}^{\circ}C^{-1}$
Specific heat of water = $4.18 \, J \cdot g^{-1} \cdot {}^{\circ}C^{-1}$

SOLUTION   The heat released by the combustion process will be absorbed (mainly) by the water and the calorimeter as the temperature rises by 27.8 °C (the change in temperature).

$$\text{Heat absorbed by water} = 4.18 \, J \cdot g^{-1} \cdot {}^{\circ}C^{-1} \times 225 \, g \times 27.8 \, {}^{\circ}C$$
$$= 2.61 \times 10^4 \, J$$

$$\text{Heat absorbed by steel} = 0.44 \, J \cdot g^{-1} \cdot {}^{\circ}C^{-1} \times 322 \, g \times 27.8 \, {}^{\circ}C$$
$$= 3.9 \times 10^3 \, J$$

$$\text{Total heat absorbed} = 2.61 \times 10^4 \, J + 3.9 \times 10^3 \, J$$
$$= 3.0 \times 10^4 \, J$$

Thus heat change by combustion = $-3.0 \times 10^4 \, J$
Using the correct conversion factor, we get

$$\text{Heat change by combustion} = -3.0 \times 10^4 \, J \times \frac{1 \, kJ}{10^3 \, J}$$
$$= -30 \, kJ$$

Again we need to find the molar enthalpy of combustion:

$$\text{Number of moles of } C_2H_5OH = 1.02 \text{ g } C_2H_5OH \times \frac{1 \text{ mol } C_2H_5OH}{46.07 \text{ g } C_2H_5OH}$$

$$= 2.21 \times 10^{-2} \text{ mol } C_2H_5OH$$

$$\text{Molar enthalpy of combustion} = \frac{-30 \text{ kJ}}{2.21 \times 10^{-2} \text{ mol}}$$

$$= -1.4 \times 10^3 \text{ kJ} \cdot \text{mol}^{-1}$$

Although most thermochemical measurements are reported in kilojoules, we can avoid using an exponent and a prefixed unit by expressing our answer in megajoules:

$$\text{Molar enthalpy of combustion} = -1.4 \times 10^3 \text{ kJ} \cdot \text{mol}^{-1} \times \frac{1 \text{ MJ}}{10^3 \text{ kJ}}$$

$$= -1.4 \text{ MJ} \cdot \text{mol}^{-1}$$

The Constant-Volume (Bomb) Calorimeter

To measure molar enthalpies of combustion more accurately, we need a device that will not release the heated combustion products (such as carbon dioxide and water vapour) into the surroundings. The most commonly used apparatus consists of a thick-walled steel container that is strong enough to contain the pressures produced during combustion reactions. This is called a bomb calorimeter (Figure 5.23).

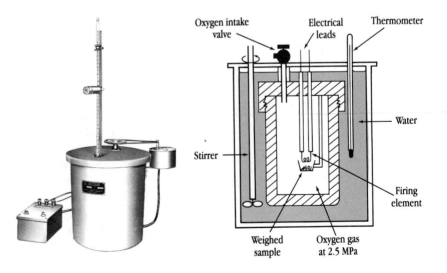

Figure 5.23
A constant-volume bomb calorimeter.

The sample to be burned is placed in the bomb, and oxygen is pumped in under pressure to ensure complete combustion. The bomb is then placed in an insulated water bath. Then the sample is ignited by means of an electrical heating wire. In general, measurements are the same as for the flame calorimeter; that is, we require the mass of sample, the specific heat and masses of water and of the bomb, and the temperature change of the water and bomb. Enthalpy of combustion of the sample can then be calculated. Because the reaction is performed at constant volume but enthalpies are defined at constant pressure, we must apply a small correction factor.

The Human Calorimeter

With the current concern about diets and excess body weight, you may have wondered how energy measurements are calculated for people. One way involves the use of a human calorimeter, which basically consists of a well-insulated room. Volunteers live in this room, performing different tasks, while the heat energy released is monitored continuously. By studying the results of such measurements, we can determine the energy consumptions for the same tasks among the different metabolic types in the population.

Figure 5.24

A human calorimeter. In a perfectly insulated room, the heat released from the body of a volunteer can be measured and related to activity over several days.

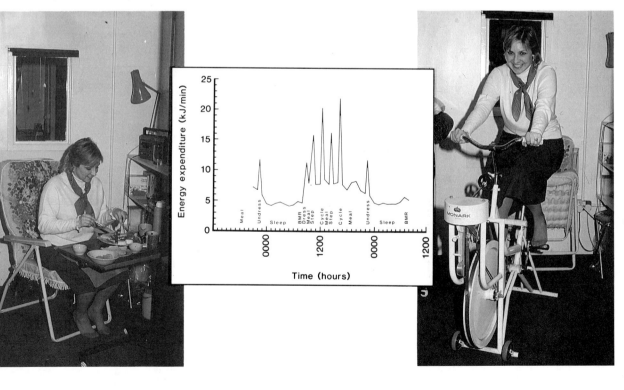

23. Why might constant-presssure calorimeters give inaccurate results?

24. A mass of 100 g of dilute hydrochloric acid is placed in a coffee cup calorimeter. The temperature of the solution is recorded to be 11.2 °C. A piece of magnesium ribbon of mass 0.18 g is placed in the acid and the lid is then replaced. The final temperature is recorded to be 20.0 °C. Calculate the molar enthalpy change for this reaction:

$$Mg_{(s)} + 2\,HCl_{(aq)} \longrightarrow MgCl_{2\,(aq)} + H_{2\,(g)}$$

Assume the hydrochloric acid to be in excess and assume the specific heat of the acid to be the same as that for water.

25. Explain why it is necessary for an experimenter to determine the heat capacity of his or her own calorimeter to use in calculations, rather than using the value obtained on another calorimeter.

26. A flame calorimeter made of copper has a mass of 587 g and is filled with 314 g of water. The original temperature of the water and calorimeter is 12.2 °C. When 0.920 g of 1-propanol, C_3H_7OH, is burned, the temperature rises to 32.3 °C. Calculate the molar enthalpy of combustion of 1-propanol, given the following additional information:
Specific heat of water = $4.18\,J \cdot g^{-1} \cdot °C^{-1}$
Specific heat of copper = $0.385\,J \cdot g^{-1} \cdot °C^{-1}$

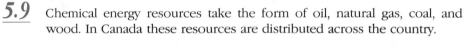

Chemical Energy Resources

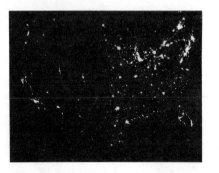

Figure 5.25
A night photograph of the United States and parts of Canada shows the extensive use of electrical energy.

5.9

Chemical energy resources take the form of oil, natural gas, coal, and wood. In Canada these resources are distributed across the country.

Conventional Crude Oil

Derivatives of crude oil, a complex mixture of organic hydrocarbon compounds, are used in the manufacture of a diverse range of products from plastics to weed killers. (A hydrocarbon is a particular type of organic compound.) But the main use of the hydrocarbons found in crude oil is as a source of energy. Combustion of hydrocarbons is an exothermic reaction in which chemical energy is converted to heat energy. At an oil refinery, crude oil is separated into a number of components by *fractional distillation*. Among the fractionation products are gasolines, cleaning solvents, kerosene, jet fuels, diesel fuels, lubricating oils, and paraffin wax. The tarry residues left after these fractions have been removed are the ashphalts used for roads and roofing materials.

Our lack of foresight in burning valuable hydrocarbons will surely be rued by our descendents. Energy alternatives exist, yet we continue to consume our limited and non-renewable supply of petrochemical based compounds as fuel. There are also pollution problems associated with the combustion of oil and oil-derived products. Most Canadian oil has a high sulfur content. When this oil is burned, sulfur dioxide gas is formed.

$$S_{(s)} + O_{2\,(s)} \longrightarrow SO_{2\,(g)}$$

Sulfur dioxide reacts with water to produce sulfurous acid, a major contributor to acid rain. Fortunately, sulfur can be recovered from oil. The process forms hydrogen sulfide, which is further treated to produce elemental sulfur. The sulfur is then used in fertilizers and in the pulp and paper industry.

Figure 5.26

The world's largest vertical-axis wind turbine at Cap Chat supplies power to Hydro-Quebec. Wind power is a promising source of supplementary energy. Canada has about 1200 installations producing electricity from wind.

Athabasca Tar Sands

Huge deposits of hydrocarbons occur in different forms in the Athabasca tar sands of northern Alberta. The deposits consist of quartz sand, SiO_2, in which each quartz grain is surrounded by a layer of water and then a layer of oil. The deposits are mined then processed through several stages to separate the oil from both the sand and associated water. The final product is a mixture of hydrocarbons called *bitumen*. Further treatment is necessary to produce synthetic oils, but once again the sulfur content is high and must be removed.

Other problems associated with development of tar sands include the impact of open-surface mining on the land, the disposal of a huge amount of spent sands, and the use and disposal of millions of litres of water. Such environmental problems can be solved or at least minimized. However, at present time they add to the final cost of the fuel and may make the tar sands uneconomical.

Figure 5.27

Mining the Athabasca tar sands.

Figure 5.28
A helium-filled balloon carrying sensors is used to measure wind and temperature profiles near a coal-fired electrical generating station. This enables the environmental scientists to predict the direction of the pollutant flow from the stacks.

Natural Gas

Natural gas is found in large quantities in Alberta, British Columbia, and on Sable Island, off the coast of Nova Scotia. Its constituents are similar to the gas fraction of crude oil. The main component is methane (50–90 %), but other gases are also present in small amounts. One advantage of natural gas is that its combustion is clean and efficient.

$$CH_{4(g)} + 2\ O_{2(g)} \longrightarrow CO_{2(g)} + 2\ H_2O_{(l)} \qquad \Delta H^{\circ} = -890\ kJ$$

Coal

Large coal deposits occcur in Alberta, British Columbia, and Nova Scotia. Coal, a complex mixture of hydrocarbons, is formed from the remains of plants that have been buried and subjected to pressure and heat for millions of years. The greatest pressures result in the formation of hard coal, or anthracite. It contains the smallest percentage of moisture of all coals and is a very efficient fuel. Soft coal, or bituminous coal, formed at lower pressures has a higher percentage of moisture and is the most plentiful coal. Lower grades of coal have a greater moisture content (above 25 %) and are less useful as fuels. Peat, one of the earliest stages of coal formation, contains about 90 % moisture. As a result, it is a much less efficient fuel. However, Canada has vast deposits of peat in the Atlantic provinces and the north that could eventually be used as a source of energy and petrochemicals. Like oil, coal contains varying amounts of sulfur, which can be removed by scrubbing methods. Scrubbing removes sulfur dioxide from waste gases after the burning of coal.

Wood

For millions of people around the world, wood is still the main energy source. Some areas have deteriorated to desert or semi-desert topography because the demand for wood led to forest destruction — to the detriment of the local ecology and climate.

Figure 5.29
Collecting wood for cooking fires is one of the most important daily tasks in many Third World countries.

Canada's forests contain vasts stores of chemical energy. But the use of this wood as a fuel is often impractical and too expensive. We have to expend too much energy to collect and transport wood to areas of high population. Where local supplies exist, wood burning is still a popular method of heating Canadian homes as it has been for hundreds of years.

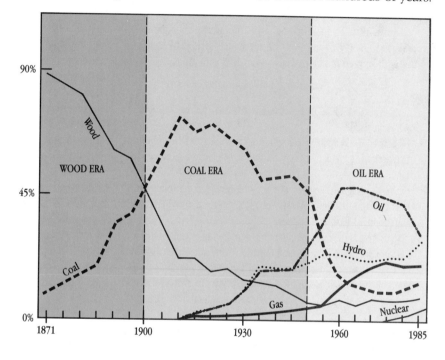

Figure 5.30
Canadian energy usage from 1871 to present day.

As we might expect, however, energy usage in Canada has changed over the years. The economics of different forms of energy has depended considerably on world prices. Skyrocketing oil prices in the 1970s focused attention on alternative energy sources. Several U.S. and European cities have now built plants that exploit urban garbage as a source of fuel. This requires sophisticated means of collection, sorting, and recycling and is economical only when traditional fuel prices increase. In Corner Brook, Newfoundland, the hospital has adapted part of its heating system to burning waste wood chips from the local paper mill in order to reduce the amount of oil consumed.

QUESTIONS

27. Briefly describe the differences among anthracite, bituminous coal, and peat.

28. What major environmental advantage does natural gas have over coal and oil?

Hydrogen as a Fuel

Hydrogen has been called the fuel of the future. Although this claim has not come to fruition, there are some distinct advantages to its use as a fuel.

On the basis of mass, hydrogen has the greatest ability to produce heat energy of any chemical fuel. The reaction of hydrogen gas with oxygen gas to produce water is exothermic.

$$H_{2(g)} + \tfrac{1}{2} O_{2(g)} \longrightarrow H_2O_{(\ell)}$$

At 25 °C, 285.8 kJ of heat energy is released for every mole of hydrogen used.

Because the reaction product is water or steam, the combustion of hydrogen is virtually non-polluting. It can be used in a variety of energy converters from fuel cells to the automobile internal-combustion engine. Engines designed to run on a combination of hydrogen and gasoline have substantially higher thermal efficiency than standard gasoline engines.

Hydrogen is the most abundant element in the universe. On Earth it is almost always found in combination with other elements and must be separated in elemental form for use as a fuel. The most common method of separation is *electrolysis*. In this process an electric current passing through an aqueous solution produces both hydrogen and oxygen gases.

But the present problem with hydrogen as a fuel lies not in producing or using it, but in storing the gas. Hydrogen stored as a compressed gas typically requires a pressure of thirteen or fourteen thousand kilopascals (about 130–140 atm). To withstand such pressures the containers are often more than thirty times the weight of the gasoline that would supply an equivalent amount of energy.

Nor is liquefaction the answer. Very cold temperatures (−240 °C) and a large amount of energy are required to liquefy hydrogen making it uneconomical. More energy is needed to maintain it as a liquid, and there are numerous safety hazards.

Current research on hydrogen storage focuses on the formation of solid interstitial metal hydrides. The interest in metal hydrides arises from the efficiency of hydrogen packing in the crystal. A metal hydride occupies less space than the same amount of hydrogen as liquid hydrogen.

Hydrogen gas in direct contact with a metal usually produces a metal hydride. Increasing the pressure of the gas increases the amount of metal hydride formed. The reaction is reversed by supplying heat. The hydrogen molecules apparently absorb onto the surface of the metal. Some molecules dissociate into hydrogen atoms and are able to enter the crystal lattice of the metal, occupying the spaces between the metal atoms without altering the overall volume.

Only some metal hydrides are acceptable for storing hydrogen. They must be safe and stable under the proposed operating conditions, and they must decompose and release hydrogen at fairly low temperatures (generally below 300 °C). A viable metal hydride should be abundant and relatively inexpensive, and should have the capacity to charge and discharge repeatedly. Magnesium hydride (MgH_2), a magnesium-nickel alloy hydride (Mg_2NiH_4), and various iron-titanium alloy hydrides ($FeTiH_x$) are all suitable.

Metal hydride storage units are still considerably heavier than conventional gasoline tanks and their contents. However, in city areas and mines, where pollution reduction is of prime importance, some hydrogen-fueled vehicles are already in use. As newer and better metal alloy hydrides are developed, and as fossil fuels become more expensive, hydrogen-driven cars will become more common.

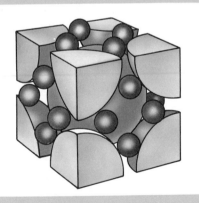

Figure 5.31

The arrangement of ions in the crystal of niobium hydride. Notice that the niobium atoms form a body-centred cube with the small hydrogen atoms fitting in between.

The Causes of Chemical Change

5.10   Why do chemical reactions proceed in the direction they do? Why does a new nail form a coating of brown rust whereas rusty nails never, if left to their own devices, return to the bright shiny state of the new nail? Why does gasoline burn? Why do salts dissolve in water?

Spontaneous Reactions

With a great deal of effort and expended energy, some spontaneous reactions can eventually be reversed. Carbon dioxide and water can combine to form gasoline through the energy-absorbing process of photosynthesis, subsequent oil formation, and eventual refining; but these actions are not spontaneous. Used in this context the word *spontaneous* acquires a special meaning. In everyday life when we say that something happened spontaneously, we not only mean that the event took place without outside intervention, but we often imply that the event occurred immediately.

In chemistry, **spontaneous** has a more limited meaning applicable to both chemical and physical changes. A reaction may be fast or slow, but if the reaction occurs at all, we say that it is spontaneous. The weathering of rocks is an example of a spontaneous physical process. It may take millions of years, but if the rocks are worn away, then the weathering process is spontaneous.

Shiny sodium will react with green chlorine gas to produce white sodium chloride. This is a spontaneous process. Fortunately for us, sodium chloride does not spontaneously break down to produce clouds of chlorine gas and leave behind a layer of reactive sodium metal on our food. It is possible to decompose sodium chloride into its constituent elements, but only by supplying external energy, usually in the form of an electric current. The fact that an external supply of energy is needed to "drive" the process, makes it a nonspontaneous reaction.

What makes a chemical reaction or a physical process spontaneous? Because many spontaneous reactions or processes are exothermic, you might think that it depends on whether or not heat is released. The reaction of zinc metal with acid solution is spontaneous. Enough heat is given off in this reaction, so that the reaction vessel becomes hot.

$$Zn_{(s)} + 2\ HCl_{(aq)} \longrightarrow ZnCl_{2\,(aq)} + H_{2\,(g)}$$

Once started, combustion reactions such as the burning of methane gas, are spontaneous.

$$CH_{4\,(g)} + 2\ O_{2\,(g)} \longrightarrow CO_{2\,(g)} + 2\ H_2O_{(\ell)}$$

If water is added to concentrated acid, the solution process is highly exothermic. Under these circumstances so much heat is given off that it is possible to crack the reaction vessel. This is the basis for the chemist's saying "Do as you oughta, add acid to water!" This expression helps us remember that it is much safer to add small portions of acid to water, thus allowing time for the dissipation of the heat generated.

There are many more examples of spontaneous exothermic reactions. However, being exothermic is not the sole criterion of spontaneity. There are also spontaneous endothermic processes such as the formation of gaseous bromine monochloride from its elements at $25\,°C$.

$$Br_{2\,(\ell)} + Cl_{2\,(g)} \longrightarrow 2\,BrCl_{(g)} \qquad \Delta H_f^° = +29.3\,kJ$$

Melting is an endothermic process

$$H_2O_{(s)} \xrightarrow{\Delta} H_2O_{(\ell)}$$

and some salts, such as potassium nitrate, absorb heat as they dissolve.

$$KNO_{3\,(s)} \xrightarrow[\text{in water}]{\text{dissolve}} KNO_{3\,(aq)}$$

Since these are spontaneous processes it follows that spontaneity depends on more than just the enthalpy change.

Entropy

The spontaneity of a reaction depends on two different thermodynamic factors: a decrease in the enthalpy of the reaction and an increase in the **entropy** of the reaction. The term entropy, indicated by the symbol S, means the degree of disorder or randomness. Each chemical reaction or physical process involves a change in the entropy of the system (ΔS).

The **law of disorder** states that a spontaneous reaction in an isolated system always proceeds in the direction of increasing entropy. Like the law of conservation of energy, it is a fundamental law of nature. Imagine yourself swimming off Kitsilano Beach in Vancouver. Suddenly, sodium ions and chloride ions in the sea precipitate out of solution and leave you marooned on a giant island of crystalline sodium chloride. Of course this is highly unlikely. The spontaneous direction of the reaction is for solid sodium chloride to dissolve in water. Randomly moving ions in solution do not arrange themselves spontaneously into a highly ordered crystal; they follow the law of disorder. Ions in solution have a higher entropy than ions in crystal lattice.

When a solid melts, the regular internal structure of the solid is lost and the more random arrangement of the particles in the liquid state appears. Melting, then, involves an increase in disorder; the entropy of the system increases.

$$\textbf{Solid phase} \longrightarrow \textbf{Liquid phase} \qquad \Delta S > 0$$

When a liquid becomes a gas, there is a further increase in the entropy of the system because the gas molecules are more randomly arranged. They have greater translational motion.

$$\textbf{Liquid phase} \longrightarrow \textbf{Gaseous phase} \qquad \Delta S > 0$$

If a chemical reaction results in a larger number of molecules in the same phase, there is a greater possibility for diverse arrangements; the entropy increases (Figure 5.32). It is often possible to predict whether the entropy will increase or decrease during a reaction. This is shown in the following example.

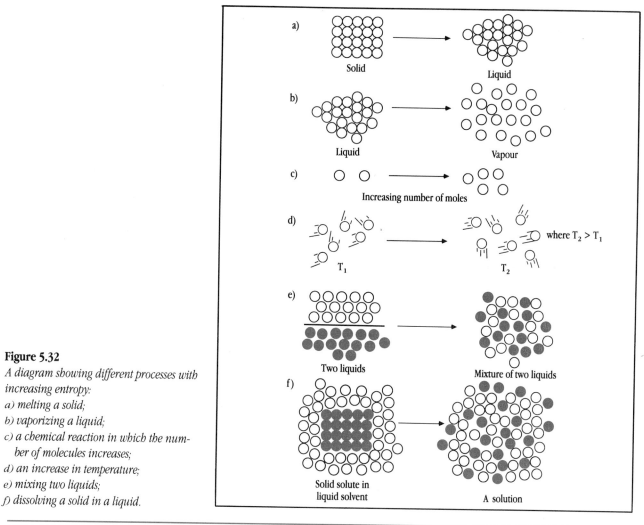

Figure 5.32

A diagram showing different processes with increasing entropy:

a) melting a solid;

b) vaporizing a liquid;

c) a chemical reaction in which the number of molecules increases;

d) an increase in temperature;

e) mixing two liquids;

f) dissolving a solid in a liquid.

EXAMPLE   *5.12*   Where possible, predict whether the entropy of each of the following reactions or processes increases (positive ΔS) or decreases (negative ΔS).

a) Steam condenses to water. ○

b) Solid carbon dioxide sublimes. |

c) $N_2O_{4(g)} \longrightarrow 2\,NO_{2(g)}$ |

d) $C_6H_{6(\ell)} + \frac{15}{2}\,O_{2(g)} \longrightarrow 6\,CO_{2(g)} + 3\,H_2O_{(\ell)}$ ○

e) Water is heated from 25 °C to 50 °C. |

SOLUTION We can predict that the entropy of a reaction or process increases if we can say that the disorder of the system increases.

a) Negative ΔS. Entropy decreases as the randomly moving gas molecules form a liquid in which the molecules have fewer possible arrangements.

b) Positive ΔS. Entropy increases as the ordered structure of solid CO_2 molecules becomes the random motion of CO_2 gas.

c) Positive ΔS. One mole of gas molecules becomes two moles of molecules; a greater number of arrangements is possible and randomness increases.

d) On the basis of phase change and number of moles alone, it is not really possible to predict how the entropy will change. Although the total number of moles increases ($8\frac{1}{2}$ moles becomes 9 moles), there are fewer gas molecules in the product.

e) Positive ΔS. Increased temperature increases molecular motion, leading to increased randomness.

A perfect crystal of a pure substance at absolute zero ($0\,K$) has zero entropy. The standard entropy is the entropy change between $0\,K$ and $298\,K$. Since entropy always increases with an increase in temperature, all standard entropy values are positive. The unit of standard entropy is the joule per kelvin per mole ($J \cdot K^{-1} \cdot mol^{-1}$). Table 5.8 gives the standard entropy (S°) for a number of substances at $298\,K$. Notice in the table that the standard entropy values of gases are generally greater than those of the liquids, which are, in turn, greater that those of the solids. Also note that whereas standard enthalpies of formation of elements are zero by definition, there are values of standard entropy for elements.

TABLE 5.8 *Standard Entropies of Various Substances**

Substance	$S\ (J \cdot K^{-1} \cdot mol^{-1})$
$Br_{2\,(\ell)}$	152.2
$C_{(s,\ graphite)}$	5.7
$C_6H_{6\,(\ell)}$	172.8
$CO_{2\,(g)}$	213.7
$H_2O_{(g)}$	188.8
$H_2O_{(\ell)}$	69.9
$NaCl_{(s)}$	72.1
$NH_4Cl_{(s)}$	94.6
$O_{2\,(g)}$	205.1

(* measured at $298\,K$ and $100\,kPa$)

We can calculate the standard entropy change ($\Delta S°$) for a chemical reaction from standard entropies in much the same manner that we calculated $\Delta H°_{reaction}$ from the values of $\Delta H°$.

$$\Delta S° = \sum S°_{products} - \sum S°_{reactants}$$

EXAMPLE   **5.13**   Calculate the $\Delta S°$ of the reaction

$$2\,NO_{(g)} + O_{2\,(g)} \longrightarrow N_2O_{4\,(g)}$$

using the values for $S°$ given in Appendix III.

SOLUTION   Qualitatively, we would predict a decrease in entropy because the number of moles is less than that of reactants. We will use the relationship between absolute entropies of products and reactants to determine the entropy change for this reaction.

$$\Delta S° = \sum S°_{products} - \sum S°_{reactants}$$

Substituting the values given in Appendix III.

$$\Delta S° = 304.3\,J \cdot K^{-1} - [(2 \times 210.8\,J \cdot K^{-1}) + 205.1\,J \cdot K^{-1}]$$
$$= -322.4\,J \cdot K^{-1}$$

QUESTIONS

29. Predict whether the entropy change (ΔS) for each of the following reactions is a negative or a positive quantity.
   a) $6\,CO_{2\,(g)} + 6\,H_2O_{(\ell)} \longrightarrow C_6H_{12}O_{6\,(s)} + 6\,O_{2\,(g)}$
   b) $PCl_{3\,(\ell)} + Cl_{2\,(g)} \longrightarrow PCl_{5\,(s)}$
   c) $H_2O_{(g)} \longrightarrow H_{2\,(g)} + \frac{1}{2}O_{2\,(g)}$

30. Using the values of $S°$ given in Appendix III, calculate $\Delta S°$ for the following reactions.
   a) $4\,Fe_{(s)} + 3\,O_{2\,(g)} \longrightarrow 2\,Fe_2O_{3\,(s)}$
   b) $C_2H_{4\,(g)} + 3\,O_{2\,(g)} \longrightarrow 2\,CO_{2\,(g)} + 2\,H_2O_{(\ell)}$
   c) $H_{2\,(g)} + Br_{2\,(\ell)} \longrightarrow 2\,HBr_{(g)}$

The Free Energy Concept   5.11

In the previous section we stated that the spontaneity of a reaction depended upon both enthalpy and entropy. We are now in a position to use our knowledge of enthalpy and entropy to develop this concept further.

Gibbs Free Energy

Any reaction in which ΔH is negative and ΔS is positive will always be spontaneous. Both thermodynamic factors are in its favour. Conversely, a reaction where ΔH is positive and entropy ΔS is negative will never be

Figure 5.33
Josiah Willard Gibbs (1839-1903), an American physicist, was one of the founders of the science of thermodynamics.

spontaneous. Both thermodynamic factors are working against it. An endothermic reaction will proceed only if it has increasing entropy. This relationship between enthalpy and entropy can be expressed as a new thermodynamic quantity known as **Gibbs free energy**, or simply **free energy**. Named after the American physicist Josiah Willard Gibbs, it is symbolized by the letter *G*. For a reaction at temperature T (Kelvin), the change in free energy (ΔG) is given by the equation:

$$\Delta G = \Delta H - T\Delta S°$$

For the standard state we substitute the values for standard enthalpy and entropy changes.

$$\Delta G° = \Delta H° - T\Delta S°$$

Using this relationship we find:

When $\Delta G° < 0$, Reaction is spontaneous.
When $\Delta G° > 0$, Reaction is nonspontaneous.
When $\Delta G° = 0$, Reaction is at equilibrium.
There is no net change.

Since the enthalpy contribution to ΔG is often much larger than the change due to entropy, most exothermic reactions are spontaneous. However, the entropy term, $T\Delta S$, can become significant at high temperatures. Table 5.9 shows the effect of $\Delta H°$ and $\Delta S°$ on $\Delta G°$ (whether $\Delta G°$ is negative or positive and hence the spontaneity of the reaction).

TABLE 5.9 *Factors Affecting the Sign of the Standard Free Energy Change, $\Delta G°$*

(Numbers correspond to examples discussed below.)

Example	$\Delta H°$	$\Delta S°$	$\Delta G°$	Spontaneity
1	negative	positive	always negative	spontaneous
2	negative	negative	negative at low temperatures	spontaneous
			positive at high temperatures	nonspontaneous
3	positive	positive	positive at low temperatures	nonspontaneous
			negative at high temperatures	spontaneous
4	positive	negative	always positive	spontaneous in reverse directions

We will illustrate these effects with some examples. The number of each example appears in Table 5.9 opposite the corresponding combination of $\Delta H°$ and $\Delta S°$.

1. The decomposition of hydrogen peroxide solution

$$2\,H_2O_{2\,(\ell)} \longrightarrow 2\,H_2O_{(\ell)} + O_{2\,(g)} \qquad \Delta H° = -197\,kJ$$

is an exothermic reaction (negative $\Delta H°$) in which the entropy is increasing as a mole of gas is produced (positive $\Delta S°$). In this reaction both entropy and enthalpy favour the progress of the reaction. The reaction will be spontaneous at all temperatures. You will recall that being spontaneous does not mean that the reaction is fast. At room temperatures hydrogen peroxide decomposes very slowly (except with the addition of a catalyst).

2. The combination reaction of ammonia and hydrogen chloride gases forming solid ammonium chloride is also exothermic.

$$NH_{3\,(g)} + HCl_{(g)} \longrightarrow NH_4Cl_{(s)} \qquad \Delta H° = -176\,kJ$$

However, in this case the entropy decreases as two moles of gas form one mole of solid (negative ΔS). At lower temperatures the negative enthalpy term is the larger contributor to $\Delta G°$, but as the temperature increases, the entropy term becomes increasingly significant. When the value of $T\Delta S°$ is greater than the $\Delta H°$ value, the reaction ceases to be spontaneous. The negative entropy is the controlling factor at higher temperatures, and solid ammonium chloride breaks down into ammonia and hydrogen chloride gases.

3. The decomposition reaction of water into hydrogen and oxygen is endothermic.

$$2\,H_2O_{(g)} \longrightarrow 2\,H_{2\,(g)} + O_{2\,(g)} \qquad \Delta H° = +484\,kJ$$

Heat must be supplied to break steam into hydrogen and oxygen gases. The $\Delta H°$ for this reaction is positive. The reaction is nonspontaneous at both room temperature and at the temperature of boiling water. When you boil water it turns to steam; it does not break up into hydrogen and oxygen. However, this reaction has an increasing entropy factor (positive ΔS). Once the value of the $T\Delta S°$ term exceeds the $\Delta H°$ value, the relationship $\Delta H° - T\Delta S°$ will yield a negative quantity and the reaction will be spontaneous. For the decomposition of steam, this occurs above a temperature of 5000 °C. When this happens we say the reaction is *entropy* driven.

4. The reaction to convert dioxygen gas into its allotrope commonly called ozone is endothermic (positive ΔH) and has decreasing entropy (negative ΔS).

$$3\,O_{2\,(g)} \longrightarrow 2\,O_{3\,(g)} \qquad \Delta H° = +285\,kJ$$

Thus, neither thermodynamic factor is working to make this reaction go, and therefore $\Delta G°$ is positive. The reaction is spontaneous in the reverse direction at all temperatures. This does not mean that ozone cannot be produced from oxygen gas. Ozone is formed from oxygen photochemically or by subjecting O_2 to an electrical discharge. Without this outside intervention, O_2 does not form O_3.

Calculating Standard Free Energy

The change in free energy of a reaction can be determined from the entropy and enthalpy changes of the reaction. The units of $\Delta G°$ are in kilojoules. We can calculate a value for the standard Gibbs free energy of the combination reaction of ammonia and hydrogen chloride gases by using the values in Appendix III to determine $\Delta H°$ and $\Delta S°$ for the following reaction:

$$NH_{3\,(g)} + HCl_{(g)} \longrightarrow NH_4Cl_{(s)} \quad \text{at } 25\,°C$$
$$\Delta H° = [-314.4] - [-46.1 + -92.3] = -176.0\,kJ$$
$$\Delta S° = 94.6 - [192.5 + 186.9] = -284.8\,J\cdot K^{-1}$$

We use the conversion factor to convert the units for our value of ΔS to $kJ\cdot K^{-1}$:

$$-284.8\,J\cdot K^{-1} \times \frac{1\,kJ}{1000\,J} = -0.2848\,kJ\cdot K^{-1}$$

Now using the Gibbs equation

$$\Delta G = \Delta H - T\Delta S$$
$$\Delta G° = -176.0\,kJ - (298\,K \times -0.2848\,kJ\cdot K^{-1})$$
$$= -176.0\,kJ - (-84.9\,kJ)$$
$$= -91.1\,kJ$$

Standard Free Energy of Formation

The standard free energy of formation, $\Delta G_f°$, is defined as the free energy change when one mole of a substance at its standard state is formed from its elements in their standard state. Values of $\Delta G_f°$ for various substances are given in Table 5.10. Notice that the standard free energy of formation of an element at its standard state is defined as zero. For the reaction

$$O_{2\,(g)} \longrightarrow O_{2\,(g)}$$

$\Delta G_f°$ is zero because, by definition, no reaction is occurring. We can use $\Delta G_f°$ values algebraically in much the same manner we use $\Delta H_f°$ in Hess's law:

$$\Delta G°_{reaction} = \sum \Delta G_f°_{\,\text{products}} - \sum \Delta G_f°_{\,reactants}$$

TABLE 5.10	Standard Free Energies of Formation of Various Compounds
Compound	ΔG_f° (kJ·mol^{-1})
$CH_3OH_{(\ell)}$	-166.3
$CO_{2\,(g)}$	-394.4
$Fe_3O_{4\,(s)}$	-1015.4
$H_2O_{(g)}$	-228.6
$H_2O_{(\ell)}$	-237.1
$NH_4Cl_{(s)}$	-202.9

EXAMPLE

5.14 Using the values given in Appendix III calculate ΔG° for the combination reaction of ammonia and hydrogen chloride gases at 25 °C.

$$NH_{3\,(g)} + HCl_{(g)} \longrightarrow NH_4Cl_{(s)}$$

SOLUTION We use the following relationship

$$\Delta G^{\circ}{}_{reaction} = \sum \Delta G_f^{\circ}{}_{products} - \sum \Delta G_f^{\circ}{}_{reactants}$$

Substituting the appropriate values, we get

$$\Delta G^{\circ}{}_{reaction} = -202.9\,\text{kJ·mol}^{-1} - (-16.5\,\text{kJ·mol}^{-1} + -95.3\,\text{kJ·mol}^{-1})$$
$$= -91.1\,\text{kJ·mol}^{-1}$$

Thus this reaction is spontaneous at 25 °C.

Predicting Changes in Spontaneity

We can also use the Gibbs equation to determine the temperature at which a reaction will become spontaneous or nonspontaneous at standard pressure. Since the reaction in Example 5.14 is spontaneous at 25 °C, the exothermic factor must be overcoming the decreasing entropy of the reaction. To determine the temperature at which this reaction ceases to be spontaneous, we need to find the temperature that the value of ΔG° changes sign from negative to positive. The "change-over" point is when

$$\Delta G^{\circ} = \Delta H^{\circ} - T\Delta S^{\circ} = 0$$

Rearranging the latter part of this equation, we get

$$T\Delta S^{\circ} = \Delta H^{\circ}$$

Therefore,

$$T = \frac{\Delta H^{\circ}}{\Delta S^{\circ}}$$

When we calculated ΔG° for this reaction, we found that $\Delta H^\circ = -176.0\,kJ$ and $\Delta S^\circ = -0.2848\,kJ \cdot K^{-1}$. Substituting these values into the expression for T above, we get

$$T = \frac{-176.0\,kJ}{-0.2848\,kJ \cdot K^{-1}}$$

$$= 618.0\,K$$

Thus at $618.0\,K$ ($345\,^\circ C$) the reaction is no longer spontaneous. At this temperature (and $100\,kPa$ pressure) the decreasing entropy term ($T\Delta S^\circ$) overcomes the exothermic factor. Above $345\,^\circ C$, solid ammonium chloride breaks down. Actually, the temperature of $345\,^\circ C$ is an estimation rather than an exact value. We are making the assumption that the values of ΔS° and ΔH° do not vary greatly with temperature. The ΔH° and ΔS° do vary with temperature, but the variation is small enough that we can ignore it.

QUESTIONS

Values for ΔH_f°, S°, and ΔG_f° can be found in Appendix III.

31. For the following reaction at $25\,^\circ C$ calculate ΔG°:

$$CH_3CO_2H_{(\ell)} + 2\,O_{2\,(g)} \longrightarrow 2\,CO_{2\,(g)} + 2\,H_2O_{(g)}$$

a) using values of ΔH and ΔS° for the reaction
b) using values of ΔG_f°

32. Using $\Delta G^\circ = \Delta H^\circ - T\Delta S^\circ$ calculate the temperature at which steam undergoes decomposition — that is, when the following reaction is spontaneous:

$$H_2O_{(g)} \longrightarrow H_{2\,(g)} + \tfrac{1}{2}O_{2\,(g)}$$

Summary

- Thermochemistry is the study of heat changes and transfers that accompany chemical reactions and physical changes.

- Energy is neither created nor destroyed but may be changed from one form to another.

- Temperature is a measure of thermal energy. When thermal energy is transferred we call it heat.

- Specific heat is the amount of heat necessary to raise the temperature of one gram of a substance by one Celsius degree (one kelvin).

- Heat capacity is the heat necessary to raise the temperature of an object by one Celsius degree (one kelvin) and molar heat capacity is the temperature necessary to raise the temperature of one mole of a substance by one Celsius degree (one kelvin).

- The change in enthalpy (ΔH) is a measure of the heat lost or gained during a chemical reaction or a physical process, occurring under constant-pressure conditions.

- An exothermic process produces heat; an endothermic process absorbs heat.

- The enthalpy change accompanying the formation of one mole of a substance from its elements in their standard states (at 100 kPa) is known as heat of formation (ΔH_f°).

- Hess's law can be used to determine the overall enthalpy of a reaction.

$$\Delta H^\circ_{reaction} = \sum \Delta H^\circ_f \text{ products} - \sum \Delta H^\circ_f \text{ reactants}$$

- For a given substance, ΔH°_{melt} and ΔH°_{fus} have the same magnitude but opposite sign, as have ΔH°_{vap} and ΔH°_{cond}

- Bond energy is the change in enthalpy required to break a chemical bond. Most bond energies are average values taken from measurements of the bond in a number of different compounds; however, exact values can be obtained for diatomic molecules.

- A spontaneous change, one that proceeds without any outside assistance, is favoured when the change is exothermic or when the change leads to an increase in randomness of the system.

- The randomness or disorder in the system is called entropy (S). Changes in standard entropy are indicated by the symbol ΔS°.

- The standard free energy change of a reaction, ΔG°, provides a means of determining the spontaneity of a reaction by using the equation

$$\Delta G^\circ = \Delta H^\circ - T\Delta S^\circ$$

KEY WORDS

bond energy	lattice energy
bond dissociation energy	law of conservation of energy
bond enthalpy	law of disorder
Born-Haber cycle	molar heat capacity
calorimeter	potential energy
calorimetry	radiant energy
chemical energy	rotational motion
endothermic	specific heat
enthalpy	spontaneous
enthalpy of reaction	standard enthalpy of formation
entropy	standard state
exothermic	surroundings
Gibbs free energy	system
heat	temperature
heat capacity	thermal energy
Hess's law	thermochemistry
joule	translational motion
kinetic energy	vibrational motion

1. Yes; unless energy input (diet) is decreased or energy output (exercise) is increased there will be no net weight loss.

2. a) Chemical energy stored in the battery is converted to electrical energy and then to radiant (light) energy.
   b) Potential energy is converted to kinetic energy.
   c) Electrical energy (if the oven is electrical) is converted to heat energy and then to chemical energy.

3. $50\,°C$; $50\,K$

4. Both beakers of water are at the same temperature; there is more thermal energy stored in the beaker containing $250\,mL$ of water, because more energy was required to raise the temperature of the larger volume of water.

5. $4.8 \times 10^2\,J \cdot °C^{-1}$

6. $52\,°C$

7. $113\,J \cdot mol^{-1} \cdot K^{-1}$

8. Carbon dioxide is a simpler molecule and has fewer vibrational modes of motion to absorb energy.

9. They are similar (around $25.1\,J \cdot C^{°-1} \cdot mol^{-1}$) and lower than the molar heat capacities of most polyatomic gases.

10. a) system: Na, H_2O and the reaction products (NaOH and H_2)
    surroundings: beaker, air
    b) system: Fe_2O_3, CO and the reaction products (Fe and CO_2)
    surroundings: blast furnace, air

11. a) Exothermic; ΔH is negative. In combustion reactions, heat is released.
    b) Endothermic: ΔH is positive. In decomposing, hydrogen chloride gas absorbs heat from the surroundings.
    c) Exothermic; ΔH is negative. Heat is produced in this reaction.

12. a) and c)

13. Endothermic. Because the beaker gets cooler, the reaction must have absorbed heat from its surroundings (i.e. the beaker).

14. a) $Cu_{(s)} + S_{(s)} + 5\,H_{2\,(g)} + \frac{9}{2}\,O_{2\,(g)} \longrightarrow CuSO_4 \cdot 5H_2O_{(s)}$
    b) $2\,C_{(s,\,graphite)} + 2\,H_{2\,(g)} + O_{2\,(g)} \longrightarrow CH_2CO_2H_{(\ell)}$

15. a) $5\,C_{(s,\,graphite)} + 6\,H_{2\,(g)} \longrightarrow C_5H_{12\,(\ell)}$
    b) $C_5H_{12\,(\ell)} + 8\,O_{2\,(\ell)} \longrightarrow 5\,CO_{2\,(g)} + 6\,H_2O_{(\ell)}$

16. a) $-445\,kJ$
    b) $-208\,kJ$

17. $-852\,kJ$

18. Positive; heat is absorbed during sublimation.

19. As steam at $100\,°C$ condenses it gives off heat (ΔH_{cond} is negative). A steam burn causes damage from heat of condensation as well as from a high temperature.

20. 15.0 kJ

21. −119 kJ

22. $\Delta H_f^\circ = -595\,\text{kJ}\cdot\text{mol}^{-1}$

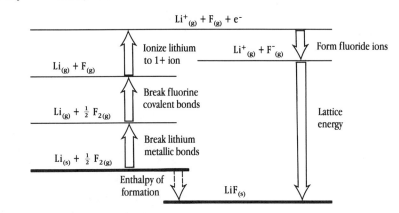

23. It may be possible for some of the heat liberated to escape to the surroundings. These calorimeters are usually not totally closed to the atmosphere since the reactions inside must be carried out at constant pressure.

24. $-0.50\,\text{MJ}\cdot\text{mol}^{-1}$

25. Each calorimeter has its own heat capacity. Data obtained from the calorimeter is directly related to that same heat capacity. Inaccurate results would thus occur by using the heat capacity of someone else's calorimeter.

26. $-2.02\,\text{MJ}\cdot\text{mol}^{-1}$

27. Anthracite, formed at greatest pressure, has less moisture than bituminous coal, formed at lower pressure. Peat, an initial form of coal, has an even higher moisture level.

28. The burning of natural gas does not release harmful sulfur dioxide into the atmosphere, which may be changed to sulfurous acid (i.e. acid rain).

29. a) negative   b) negative   c) positive

30. a) $-551.7\,\text{J}\cdot\text{K}^{-1}$ b) $-267.7\,\text{J}\cdot\text{K}^{-1}$ c) $+114.5\,\text{J}\cdot\text{K}^{-1}$

31. a) $\Delta G^\circ = -856.1\,\text{kJ}$ b) $\Delta G^\circ = -856.1\,\text{kJ}$

32. $5.16 \times 10^3\,^\circ\text{C}$

COMPREHENSION QUESTIONS

1. List five different forms of energy.

2. In each of the following chemical or physical reactions describe the main interconversions of energy involved:
a) hand-sewing a seam

b) sewing a seam on a treadle sewing machine
c) sewing a seam on an electric sewing macine

3. Using the example of the burning of methane gas in oxygen, explain how chemical reactions follow the law of conservation of energy.

4. List two units of energy.

5. What is the difference between specific heat and molar heat capacity?

6. Explain the three different modes of molecular motion.

7. Why do gases have greater molar heat capacities than solids?

8. Why does helium gas have a lower molar heat capacity than hydrogen gas?

9. The mining town of Flin Flon, Manitoba, is at approximately the same latitude $(54°)$ as the coastal community of Prince Rupert, B.C., and yet Prince Rupert has a far milder climate than Flin Flon. Explain this phenomenon using your knowledge of specific heat capacities.

10. Explain the difference between the system and the surroundings.

11. Are the following changes endothermic or exothermic?
    a) $C_2H_5OH_{(\ell)} + 3\,O_{2\,(g)} \longrightarrow 2\,CO_{2\,(g)} + 3\,H_2O_{(\ell)} + 1367\,kJ$
    b) $H_2O_{(\ell)} \longrightarrow H^+_{(aq)} + OH^-_{(aq)}\ \Delta H° = +56.2\,kJ$
    c) $H_2O_{(s)} + 6.01\,kJ \longrightarrow H_2O_{(\ell)}$
    d) $CS_{2\,(\ell)} + 3\,O_{2\,(g)} \longrightarrow CO_{2\,(g)} + 2\,SO_{2\,(g)}\ \Delta H° = -1105\,kJ$

12. What is meant by the term standard state?

13. Why is the standard enthalpy of formation of $O_{2\,(g)}$ zero when the enthalpy of formation of $O_{(g)}$ is $+249.2\,kJ \cdot mol^{-1}$?

14. Write the equation for the formation of the explosive TNT (trinitrotoluene), $C_7H_5O_6N_{3\,(\ell)}$, from its elements at standard state.

15. Is ΔH positive or negative for the chemical reaction occurring when oil burns? Explain briefly.

16. A common mistake made by students just starting thermochemistry is to use the heat of combustion as the reverse of the heat of formation. With methane gas as your example, explain why this is not so.

17. Explain why $\Delta H°_{freezing}$ is negative.

18. In part of the refrigerator cycle the liquid coolant (usually chlorofluorohydrocarbons, known commercially as freons) expands to form a gas. How does this cause a cooling of the inside of the refrigerator?

19. Explain the difference between the terms bond energy and bond dissociation energy.

20. Why is it possible to get an accurate measurement for the bond energy of the H—H bond but not for the C—O bond?

21. What is meant by the term lattice energy?

22. Explain the difference between a constant-pressure calorimeter and a constant-volume calorimeter.

23. Which of the following processes show increasing entropy?
    a) dissolving sugar in a cup of hot tea
    b) arranging a pack of playing cards into suits
    c) building a castle out of building blocks
    d) the normal state of a student's room

24. Describe how the entropy changes when ice melts and the water thus formed evaporates.

25. Without consulting the appendix values, arrange the following substances in order of increasing entropy at 25 °C. Give reasons for your arrangement.
    a) $He_{(g)}$ b) $Fe_{(s)}$ c) $Fe_2O_{3\,(s)}$ d) $NO_{2\,(g)}$

26. Predict whether of $\Delta S°$ is negative or positive for the following chemical reactions:
    a) $2\,HgO_{(s)} \longrightarrow 2\,Hg_{(\ell)} + O_{2\,(g)}$
    b) $H_{(g)} + H_{(g)} \longrightarrow H_{2\,(g)}$
    c) $2\,SO_{2\,(g)} + O_{2\,(g)} \longrightarrow 2\,SO_{3\,(g)}$
    d) $PCl_{3\,(\ell)} + Cl_{2\,(g)} \longrightarrow PCl_{5\,(s)}$

27. Explain how entropy and enthalpy contribute to the spontaneity of a chemical reaction.

28. The reaction of magnesium metal with oxygen gas

$$Mg_{(s)} + \tfrac{1}{2}O_{2\,(g)} \longrightarrow MgO_{(s)}$$

has both a negative $\Delta H°$ value and a negative $\Delta S°$ value. Explain how the free energy ($\Delta G°$) of this reaction varies with temperature.

PROBLEMS   *Thermochemical data for these problems can be found in Appendixes II, III, and IV.*

Specific Heat and Heat Capacity

29. The molar heat capacity of liquid sodium is $28.4\,J\cdot K^{-1}\cdot mol^{-1}$. How much heat is required to raise the temperature of 5.67 g of liquid sodium by 3.75 kelvins?

30. When 5.16 kJ of heat is added to 167 g of gaseous ammonia at 45.0 °C the temperature of the gas rises to 60.0 °C. From this data determine the following:
    a) the specific heat of $NH_{3\,(g)}$
    b) the molar heat capacity of $NH_{3\,(g)}$

31. If, at 25 °C, 15.7 g of carbon dioxide absorbs 1.2 kJ of heat, calculate the final temperature of the gas. The molar heat capacity of CO_2 is $37.11\,J\cdot K^{-1}\cdot mol^{-1}$.

Enthalpy of Formation and Hess's Law

32. From the following information calculate the $\Delta H_f°$ of nitrogen monoxide, $NO_{(g)}$:

$$4\,NH_{3\,(g)} + 5\,O_{2\,(g)} \longrightarrow 4\,NO_{(g)} + 6\,H_2O_{(\ell)} \qquad \Delta H° = -1170\,kJ$$
$$4\,NH_{3\,(g)} + 3\,O_{2\,(g)} \longrightarrow 2\,N_{2\,(g)} + 6\,H_2O_{(\ell)} \qquad \Delta H° = -1530\,kJ$$

33. Given that $\Delta H_f°$ of copper(II) chloride, $CuCl_{2\,(s)}$, is $-220.1\,kJ$ and of copper(I) chloride, $CuCl_{(s)}$, is $-137.2\,kJ$, calculate $\Delta H°$ for the following reaction:

$$CuCl_{2\,(s)} + Cu_{(s)} \longrightarrow 2\,CuCl_{(s)}$$

34. Using the values for $\Delta H_f°$, calculate $\Delta H°$ for each of the following reactions:

a) $2\,F_{2\,(g)} + 2\,H_2O_{(\ell)} \longrightarrow 4\,HF_{(g)} + O_{2\,(g)}$

b) $CS_{2\,(g)} + 2\,H_2O_{(\ell)} \longrightarrow CO_{2\,(g)} + 2\,H_2S_{(g)}$

c) $C_2H_{4\,(g)} + H_{2\,(g)} \longrightarrow C_2H_{6\,(g)}$

d) $10\,N_2O_{(g)} + C_3H_{8\,(g)} \longrightarrow 10\,N_{2\,(g)} + 3\,CO_{2\,(g)} + 4\,H_2O_{(g)}$

35. Using the values $\Delta H_f°$ calculate the amount of heat released if 200 g of brandy containing 40.0 % by weight ethanol, C_2H_5OH, is poured over a plum pudding and burned. (*Hint:* first write an equation for the combustion of ethanol.)

36. From the following three thermochemical equations:

a) $Fe_2O_{3\,(s)} + 3\,CO_{(g)} \longrightarrow 2\,Fe_{(s)} + 3\,CO_{2\,(g)} \qquad \Delta H° = -25\,kJ$

b) $3\,Fe_2O_{3\,(s)} + CO_{(g)} \longrightarrow 2\,Fe_3O_{4\,(s)} + CO_{2\,(g)} \qquad \Delta H° = -47\,kJ$

c) $Fe_3O_{4\,(s)} + CO_{(g)} \longrightarrow 3\,FeO_{(s)} + CO_{2\,(g)} \qquad \Delta H° = +38\,kJ$

calculate the enthalpy change for the reaction

$$FeO_{(s)} + CO_{(g)} \longrightarrow Fe_{(s)} + CO_{2\,(g)}$$

Enthalpy and Phase Change

37. Calculate the amount of heat released when 1.0 kg of water freezes.

38. Calculate the amount of heat necessary to vaporize 350 mL of diethyl ether, $C_4H_{10}O$. The density of diethyl ether is $0.713\,g\cdot mL^{-1}$. ΔH_{vap} for diethyl ether is $384\,J\cdot mol^{-1}$.

Bond Energy

39. Using the average bond energies, estimate the enthalpy of formation of hydrazine, N_2H_4.

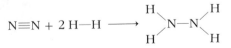

40. The $\Delta H°$ of the gaseous reaction

$$XeF_{2\,(g)} + H_{2\,(g)} \longrightarrow 2\,HF_{(g)} + Xe_{(g)}$$

is found to be $-430\,kJ$. Use this value and the average bond energies to determine the average bond energy of the Xe—F bond.

41. The lattice energy of calcium chloride, $CaCl_{2\,(s)}$, is $2197\,kJ \cdot mol^{-1}$. Given that ΔH_{vap} for solid calcium is $121\,kJ \cdot mol^{-1}$ and that it requires $1735\,kJ$ to remove two moles of electrons from a mole of calcium atoms, calculate the ΔH_f° of $CaCl_{2\,(s)}$. The average bond energy for $Cl_{2\,(g)}$ is $243\,kJ \cdot mol^{-1}$. When one mole of chloride ions forms from one mole of chlorine atoms, $348\,kJ$ of heat is released.

Calorimetry

42. A $24.6\,g$ sample of nickel is heated to $110.0\,°C$ and then placed in a coffee cup calorimeter containing $125\,g$ of water at a temperature of $23.00\,°C$. After the nickel cools, the final temperature of the metal and water is $24.83\,°C$. Assuming that no heat has escaped to the surroundings or has been absorbed by the calorimeter, calculate the specific heat of nickel.

43. When solutions of an acid and a base are mixed, heat is released. Using a coffee cup calorimeter, 100 mL of $1.00\,mol \cdot L^{-1}$ hydrochloric acid are mixed with 100 mL of $1.00\,mol \cdot L^{-1}$ sodium hydroxide solution. The initial temperature of the solutions was $22.6°C$, and the temperature after mixing was $29.5°C$. Calculate the molar enthalpy of neutralization for the reaction:

$$HCl_{(aq)} + NaOH_{(aq)} \longrightarrow NaCl_{(aq)} + H_2O_{(\ell)}$$

Assume that the density and specific heat of each solution is the same as that of water (Density of water $= 1.00\,g \cdot mL^{-1}$).

44. A $135\,g$ sample of dilute hydrochloric acid is placed in a copper calorimeter with a mass of $465\,g$. The temperature of the acid and calorimeter is $11.7\,°C$. A mass of $5.00\,g$ of aluminum metal is reacted with the acid. After reaction has ceased, the temperature is $22.3\,°C$. Calculate the molar enthalpy change for the reaction:

$$Al_{(s)} + 3\,HCl_{(aq)} \longrightarrow AlCl_{3\,(aq)} + \tfrac{3}{2}\,H_{2\,(g)}$$

Assume that dilute hydrochloric acid has the same specific heat as water.

45. A copper flame calorimeter has a mass of $305\,g$ and contains $255\,g$ of water. When $1.01\,g$ of propanol, C_3H_8O, is burned in the calorimeter, the calorimeter and contents increase in temperature by 28.8 Celsius degrees. Calculate the enthalpy of combustion of propanol.

The Causes of Chemical Change

46. Using the appropriate values for S°, calculate the entropy change (ΔS°) for the following reactions:
a) $Na_{(s)} + \tfrac{1}{2}\,Cl_{2\,(g)} \longrightarrow NaCl_{(s)}$
b) $C_2H_{6\,(g)} + \tfrac{7}{2}\,O_{2\,(g)} \longrightarrow 2\,CO_{2\,(g)} + 3\,H_2O_{(\ell)}$

47. Given that $\Delta S°$ for the combustion of glucose

$$C_6H_{12}O_{6(s)} + 6\,O_{2\,(g)} \longrightarrow 6\,CO_{2\,(g)} + 6\,H_2O_{(\ell)}$$

at $25\,°C$ is $+257.9\,J \cdot K^{-1}$, calculate the absolute entropy, $S°$, for glucose using other appendix values for $S°$.

The Free Energy Concept

48. For the following reaction calculate $\Delta S°$, $\Delta H°$, and $\Delta G°$ at $25\,°C$.

$$C_{(s,\ graphite)} + CO_{2\,(g)} \longrightarrow 2\,CO_{(g)}$$

Is the reaction spontaneous at this temperature?

49. Using the appendix values, calculate $\Delta G°$ for each of the following reactions at $25\,°C$:
a) $CH_3OH_{(\ell)} + \frac{3}{2}O_{2\,(g)} \longrightarrow CO_{2\,(g)} + 2\,H_2O_{(g)}$
b) $2\,NO_{2\,(g)} \longrightarrow N_2O_{4\,(g)}$
c) $3\,Fe_2O_{3\,(s)} \longrightarrow 2\,Fe_3O_{4\,(s)} + \frac{1}{2}O_{2\,(g)}$

50. For each of the reactions in Question 49, determine $\Delta G°$ using the appropriate values for $\Delta H_f°$ and $\Delta S°$.

51. For the following reaction $\Delta H°$ is $-366\,kJ$ and $\Delta S°$ is $+340\,J \cdot K^{-1}$.

$$2\,CHCl_{3\,(\ell)} + O_{2\,(g)} \longrightarrow 2\,COCl_{2\,(g)} + 2\,HCl_{(g)}$$

Over what temperature range is this reaction spontaneous?

52. Assuming that $\Delta H°$ and $\Delta S°$ do not change with temperature, determine (using the appropriate appendix values) the temperature above which the following reaction will no longer occur.

$$3\,C_2H_{2\,(g)} \longrightarrow C_6H_{6\,(\ell)}$$

53. Assuming that $\Delta H°$ and $\Delta S°$ do not change with temperature, determine the temperature above which you can theoretically prepare carbon disulfide $CS_{2\,(\ell)}$, directly from its elements ($\Delta S°$ for this reaction is $+81.5\,J \cdot K^{-1}$, $\Delta H_f°$ for $CS_{2\,(\ell)}$ is $87.9\,kJ \cdot mol^{-1}$):

$$C_{(s,\ graphite)} + 2\,S_{(s)} \longrightarrow CS_{2\,(\ell)}$$

MISCELLANEOUS PROBLEMS

54. A $50.0\,g$ piece of aluminum is heated to $100\,°C$ and then put into a beaker containing $150\,mL$ of water at $20.0\,°C$. Assuming no loss of heat to the surroundings, calculate the final temperature of the water. (The specific heat of aluminum is $0.903\,J \cdot g^{-1} \cdot °C^{-1}$)

55. A $4.05\,g$ sample of sulfur is burned in excess oxygen. The heat produced raises the temperature of $1.00\,L$ of water from $23.15\,°C$ to $32.03\,°C$. From this information calculate $\Delta H_f°$ of sulfur dioxide.

56. Calculate the amount of heat required to raise the temperature of $27.6\,g$ of water at $25\,°C$ to steam at $125.0\,°C$. Values for the molar heat capacities of $H_2O_{(g)}$ and $H_2O_{(\ell)}$ can be found in Appendix III.

57. Using the reaction for the combustion of ethane

$$2\,C_2H_{6\,(g)} + 7\,O_{2\,(g)} \longrightarrow 4\,CO_{2\,(g)} + 6\,H_2O_{(g)}$$

determine the following:

a) the molar heat of combustion of ethane using bond energies from Appendix IV

b) the molar heat of combustion of ethane using the standard enthalpy of formations given in Appendix III

Explain why the answers you get in a) and b) could be expected to slightly different.

58. The following combustion reaction takes place in the oxyacetylene torch:

$$C_2H_{2\,(g)} + \tfrac{5}{2}\,O_{2\,(g)} \longrightarrow 2\,CO_{2\,(g)} + H_2O_{(g)}$$

a) Calculate $\Delta H°$ for this reaction.

b) Construct a graph for this reaction showing the relative enthalpy of formations of reactants and products and overall $\Delta H°_{combustion}$.

59. Graphically determine $\Delta H°$ for the following reaction

$$2\,FeO_{(s)} + \tfrac{1}{2}\,O_{2\,(g)} \longrightarrow Fe_2O_{3\,(s)}$$

using $\Delta H_f°$ found in Appendix III for $FeO_{(s)}$ and $Fe_2O_{3(s)}$.

60. Given the following information,

$$2\,ClF_{3\,(g)} + 2\,NH_{3\,(g)} \longrightarrow N_{2\,(g)} + 6\,HF_{(g)} + Cl_{2\,(g)} \qquad \Delta H° = -1196\,kJ$$

$$N_2H_{4\,(\ell)} + O_{2\,(g)} \longrightarrow N_{2\,(g)} + 2\,H_2O_{(\ell)} \qquad\qquad \Delta H° = -622\,kJ$$

$$4\,NH_{3\,(g)} + 3\,O_{2\,(g)} \longrightarrow 2\,N_{2\,(g)} + 6\,H_2O_{(\ell)} \qquad\qquad \Delta H° = -1530\,kJ$$

determine the $\Delta H°$ for the following reaction:

$$3\,N_2H_{4\,(\ell)} + 4\,ClF_{3\,(g)} \longrightarrow 3\,N_{2\,(g)} + 12\,HF_{(g)} + 2\,Cl_{2\,(g)}$$

61. Calculate $\Delta H°$ for the reaction:

$$2\,H_3BO_{3\,(aq)} \longrightarrow B_2O_{3\,(s)} + 3\,H_2O_{(\ell)}$$

using the following data:

$$H_3BO_{3\,(aq)} \longrightarrow HBO_{2\,(aq)} + H_2O_{(\ell)} \qquad \Delta H° = -0.02\,kJ$$
$$2\,B_2O_{3\,(s)} + H_2O_{(\ell)} \longrightarrow H_2B_4O_{7\,(s)} \qquad \Delta H° = -17.5\,kJ$$
$$H_2B_4O_{7\,(aq)} + H_2O_{(\ell)} \longrightarrow 4\,HBO_{2\,(aq)} \qquad \Delta H° = -11.3\,kJ$$

62. The combination reaction of nitrogen and oxygen gases is an endothermic reaction with decreasing entropy.

$$N_{2\,(g)} + \tfrac{1}{2}\,O_{2\,(g)} \longrightarrow N_2O_{(g)}$$

According to the Gibbs equation this reaction is not spontaneous at any temperature. But laughing gas, N_2O, does exist. Explain how this is possible.

63. For solid sodium, $\Delta H°_{vap}$ is $+108\,kJ \cdot mol^{-1}$ and $\Delta H°_{ionization}$ is $+496\,kJ \cdot mol^{-1}$. The average bond energy of chlorine gas, $Cl_{2\,(g)}$, is $+243\,kJ \cdot mol^{-1}$, and $348\,kJ$ of heat is released when one mole of chloride ions forms from one mole of chlorine atoms. $\Delta H_f°$ of sodium chloride is $-411\,kJ \cdot mol^{-1}$. Draw a Born-Haber diagram for $NaCl_{(s)}$ and calculate the lattice energy of the salt.

64. The following data are the enthalpies of combustion for a series of hydrocarbons. Plot the values of ΔH_{comb} against the number of carbon atoms in the molecule. From the graph, predict the enthalpy of combustion of the compound $CH_3CH_2CH_2CH_2CH_2CH_3$.

Molecule	ΔH_{comb} $(MJ \cdot mol^{-1})$
CH_4	-0.89
CH_3CH_3	-1.56
$CH_3CH_2CH_3$	-2.22
$CH_3CH_2CH_2CH_3$	-2.88
$CH_3CH_2CH_2CH_2CH_3$	-3.51
$CH_3CH_2CH_2CH_2CH_2CH_2CH_3$	-4.85
$CH_3CH_2CH_2CH_2CH_2CH_2CH_2CH_3$	-5.51
$CH_3CH_2CH_2CH_2CH_2CH_2CH_2CH_2CH_3$	-6.12

SUGGESTED PROJECTS

1. Discuss whether we, as a society, should be allowing our non-renewable hydrocarbon reserves to be used as fuel or whether we should be saving them for their valuable petrochemical uses.

2. There are forms of pollution other than the problem of sulfur dioxide production associated with the combustion of oil. Research and report on these other forms of pollution. How are they affecting our planet?

3. In many areas of the world the use of wood as a primary fuel has meant the end of forests and the beginning of erosion and desert formation. Find out the location of some of these regions and report on possible alternative fuels or technologies that could provide energy for these populations.

4. Is every energy source also a source of pollution? Discover what alternative sources of energy, (e.g. tidal, wind, nuclear) if any, have been proposed for your community and investigate the advantages and disadvantages of each.

CHAPTER 6

Rates of Reactions

In the previous chapter we learned it was possible to predict whether or not a reaction would occur spontaneously. However, even if a reaction is spontaneous we cannot tell how long the reaction might take. The study of this latter factor, the rate of a reaction, is called kinetics. We will measure reaction rates and investigate the factors that influence them. We will also see how chemists use the information they obtain from studying kinetics to predict the possible steps involved in a chemical reaction. In addition, we will explore the function of catalysts, their influence on the rate of reactions, and their use in the Canadian chemical industry.

The Importance of Reaction Rates

6.1

Spontaneous chemical reactions do not necessarily occur very rapidly. Indeed we actually rely on the slow progress of some reactions, although we may not realize it. The reaction of nitrogen gas with water vapour and oxygen in the atmosphere is thermodynamically possible.

$$N_{2(g)} + \tfrac{5}{2} O_{2(g)} + H_2O_{(g)} \longrightarrow 2\, HNO_{3(aq)}$$

However, the reaction rate is far too slow for us to worry that all the nitrogen in our atmosphere will be converted into an ocean of nitric acid. Similarly, glucose burns in oxygen forming carbon dioxide and water,

$$C_6H_{12}O_{6\,(s)} + 6\,O_{2\,(g)} \longrightarrow 6\,CO_{2\,(g)} + 6\,H_2O_{(\ell)}$$

but under normal conditions glucose will remain as is for hundreds of years without undergoing this conversion. Only a series of biochemical reactions or the application of heat will make this combustion reaction occur at a rapid rate. Theoretically all organic material can be converted to carbon dioxide and water in the oxygen-rich atmosphere of our planet. But without a change in the conditions of the reaction, these conversions are too slow to detect.

Of course there are reactions that do proceed quickly. For example, a piece of potassium dropped in water reacts rapidly and often violently:

$$2\,K_{(s)} + 2\,H_2O_{(\ell)} \longrightarrow 2\,KOH_{(aq)} + H_{2\,(g)}$$

If white phosphorus is left exposed to the air, it will burn producing tetraphosphorus decaoxide smoke:

$$P_{4\,(s)} + 5\,O_{2\,(g)} \longrightarrow P_4O_{10\,(s)}$$

Some chemical reactions are virtually complete in only fractions of a second. The German chemist, Manfred Eigen, won the 1967 Nobel Prize in Chemistry for his work in measuring the rate of one of the fastest reactions known: the neutralization of an acid by a base. This reaction takes only 37 μs (0.000 037 s).

$$H^+_{(aq)} + OH^-_{(aq)} \longrightarrow H_2O_{(\ell)}$$

To those who suffer from acid indigestion it may not seem as if the "instant relief" promised by the antacid manufacturers works quite this fast. But remember that the antacid must first reach the stomach and then, depending on the substance used as the antacid, dissolve or react to produce the hydroxide ions necessary for neutralization.

A common task for chemists is to find ways to change the rates of chemical reactions. Think of the benefits of retarding metal corrosion and food spoilage. These problems alone result in world-wide losses of billions of dollars annually. On the other hand, increasing the rate of a reaction can also be an economic necessity. Without very fast reactions the cost of producing most industrial chemicals would be exorbitant. As a result, virtually every chemical reaction in any industrial process has been studied extensively for a means of altering its rate. Manufacturers of sulfuric and nitric acids, ammonia, alkalis, polymers, and pharmaceuticals are just a few examples of industries for which reaction rates are extremely important.

Average Rate of a Chemical Reaction

6.2

Reaction rate is a measure of how fast a reactant is used up or how fast a product is formed. Since these measurements are made over a period of time, we are actually dealing with an *average rate*. This is comparable to measuring the average speed of travel, in which we determine the distance covered and divide by time:

$$\text{Average speed (rate of travel)} = \frac{\text{Distance}}{\text{Time}}$$

Figure 6.1
We differentiate records by the rate at which they rotate: 33 ⅓ rpm or 45 rpm.

For chemical reactions we can determine the average reaction rate in a similar manner. Instead of using the distance covered within a specific period, we now use the amount of product formed in a specified period of time or the amount of reactant used up in that time. The amount of product formed, or reactant used, is determined by measuring their concentrations at various times during the reaction. In Table 6.1 we have recorded some sample data for the general reaction A ⟶ B. The table contains the initial reactants and product concentrations as well as additional measurements taken after the reaction has been running for three minutes and then for six minutes. Note that the concentration of the starting substance (A) *decreases over time* and that the concentration of the substance being formed (B) *increases*. The placing of square brackets around the species — either reactant or product — indicates *concentration*. Thus [A] means *the concentration of A*.

Figure 6.2
We cause a vehicle to accelerate by increasing the rate at which fuel is delivered to the engine.

TABLE 6.1	*Variation in Concentration of A and B with Time for the Reaction A ⟶ B*	
Time (min)	[A] (mol·L^{-1})	[B] (mol·L^{-1})
0.0	1.00	0.00
3.0	0.40	0.60
6.0	0.25	0.75

Measuring Rate by the Increase in Product Concentration

Using the data in Table 6.1, we can calculate the average rate of the reaction over the first three minutes from the increase in the concentration of the product formed:

$$\textbf{Average rate} = \frac{\textbf{Change in concentration of product}}{\textbf{Time elapsed}}$$

$$= \frac{(0.60 - 0.00) \text{ mol·L}^{-1}}{(3.0 - 0.0) \text{ min}}$$

$$= 0.20 \text{ mol·L}^{-1}\text{·min}^{-1}$$

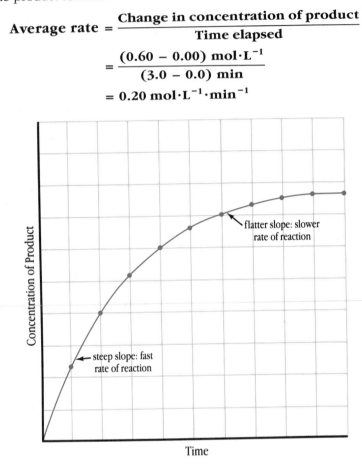

Figure 6.3

A graph showing concentration of product against time. As the reaction proceeds, the rate of product formation decreases.

We can also calculate the average rate for the next three minutes.

$$\textbf{Average rate} = \frac{\textbf{Change in concentration of product}}{\textbf{Time elapsed}}$$

$$= \frac{(0.75 - 0.60) \text{ mol·L}^{-1}}{(6.0 - 3.0) \text{ min}.}$$

$$= 0.05 \text{ mol·L}^{-1}\text{·min}^{-1}$$

The average rate for this second period is less than the average rate for the first three-minute period. We can therefore conclude, that the average rate actually depends on when you take the measurements.

Measuring Rate from a Decrease in Reactant Concentration

We can also calculate the average rate for any period by determining the change in the concentration of the reactant. In this case, when we subtract the initial concentration of the reactant from the concentration found after three minutes (Table 6.1), we get a negative value:

$$\textbf{Change in concentration of reactant} = \textbf{(0.40 − 1.00) mol·L}^{-1}$$
$$= \textbf{−0.60 mol·L}^{-1}$$

Since chemists, by convention, consider rate as a positive value, we show a *change in the concentration of a reactant as negative* so that the overall rate remains positive. Hence, the equation is written with a negative sign before the change in concentration of the reactant, which now appears in parentheses. For the first three minutes of this reaction, using values from Table 6.1, we find that

$$\textbf{Average rate} = \frac{\textbf{− (Change in concentration of reactant)}}{\textbf{Time elapsed}}$$

$$= \frac{\textbf{− (0.40 − 1.00) mol·L}^{-1}}{\textbf{(3.0 − 0.0) min}}$$

$$= \textbf{0.20 mol·L}^{-1}\textbf{·min}^{-1}$$

This is the same result as we obtained by following the increase in the concentration of the product.

In fact for any reaction where we have the *same number of moles of product and reactant*, we can use the specific statements that follows:

$$\textbf{Average rate} = \frac{\textbf{− (Change in conc. of reactant)}}{\textbf{Time elapsed}}$$

or

$$\textbf{Average rate} = \frac{\textbf{(Change in conc. of product)}}{\textbf{Time elapsed}}$$

For example, in the reaction

$$\textbf{SO}_{2(g)} + \textbf{NO}_{2(g)} \longrightarrow \textbf{SO}_{3(g)} + \textbf{NO}_{(g)}$$

the average rate of production of sulfur trioxide or nitrogen monoxide is the same as the average rate of loss of sulfur dioxide or nitrogen dioxide. When we compare these average rates of gain or loss, however, we must always compare the average rate over the *same* time period.

In the decomposition of hydrogen peroxide, the rate of loss of the reactant will not be the same as the rate of formation of oxygen gas. This is because only one mole of oxygen gas is formed for every two moles of hydrogen peroxide that decompose.

$$\textbf{2 H}_2\textbf{O}_{2(\ell)} \longrightarrow \textbf{2 H}_2\textbf{O}_{(\ell)} + \textbf{O}_{2(g)}$$

Conversely, we can say that oxygen is produced at half the rate that hydrogen peroxide decomposes. The average rate of decomposition of hydrogen peroxide is therefore

$$\frac{-(\textbf{Change in conc. of H}_2\textbf{O}_2)}{\textbf{Time elapsed}} = \frac{2(\textbf{Change in conc. of O}_2)}{\textbf{Time elapsed}}$$

and the average rate of production of oxygen in this reaction is

$$\frac{(\textbf{Change in con. of O}_2)}{\textbf{Time elapsed}} = \frac{-\frac{1}{2}(\textbf{Change in conc. of H}_2\textbf{O}_2)}{\textbf{Time elapsed}}$$

When we specify the rate of a reaction, we should always indicate whether we are following the *loss of a reactant* or *the gain of a product*. We should also specify which reactant or product we are following. Again, to be valid, comparisons of average rates must always be made over the same time period.

EXAMPLE   **6.1**   In the following decomposition reaction,

$$2\,N_2O_5 \longrightarrow 4\,NO_2 + O_2$$

which takes place in carbon tetrachloride solution at $45\,°C$, oxygen gas is produced at the average rate of $9.1 \times 10^{-4}\ mol \cdot L^{-1} \cdot s^{-1}$. Over the same period, what is the average rate of the following:
a) the production of nitrogen dioxide
b) the loss of nitrogen pentoxide

SOLUTION   a) From the equation we see that for every mole of oxygen formed, four moles of nitrogen dioxide are produced. Thus, the rate of production of nitrogen dioxide is four times that of oxygen.

$$\text{Rate of production of } NO_2 = 4 \times (9.1 \times 10^{-4}\ mol \cdot L^{-1} \cdot s^{-1})$$
$$= 3.6 \times 10^{-3}\ mol \cdot L^{-1} \cdot s^{-1}$$

b) Nitrogen pentoxide is consumed at twice the rate that oxygen is produced.

$$\text{Rate of loss of } N_2O_5 = 2 \times (9.1 \times 10^{-4}\ mol \cdot L^{-1} \cdot s^{-1})$$
$$= 1.8 \times 10^{-3}\ mol \cdot L^{-1} \cdot s^{-1}$$

QUESTIONS

1. When can we equate the rate of formation of a product with the rate of decomposition of a reactant?
2. Using the values given in Table 6.1, calculate the average rate of loss of reactant A during the first six minutes of the reaction.

3. Measurements taken during the reaction

$$CO_{(g)} + NO_{2\,(g)} \longrightarrow CO_{2\,(g)} + NO_{(g)}$$

showed a concentration of carbon monoxide of 0.019 mol·L^{-1} at 27 min and of 0.013 mol·L^{-1} at 45 min. Calculate the average rate, over this 18 min period, of each of the following:
   a) the loss of carbon monoxide
   b) the gain of carbon dioxide

4. In the following reaction the average rate of loss of carbon monoxide, over a set period, is 0.15 mol·L^{-1}·s^{-1}.

$$2\,CO_{(g)} \longrightarrow CO_{2\,(g)} + C_{(s)}$$

What is the average rate of production of carbon dioxide during the same period?

5. At high temperatures, ammonia reacts with oxygen to produce nitrogen monoxide and steam:

$$4\,NH_{3\,(g)} + 5\,O_{2\,(g)} \longrightarrow 4\,NO_{(g)} + 6\,H_2O_{(g)}$$

In one experiment the average rate of decomposition of ammonia was found to be 4.5×10^{-2} mol·L^{-1}·s^{-1}. For this same time interval calculate the following:
   a) the rate of the production of water
   b) the rate of production of nitrogen monoxide
   c) the rate at which oxygen is consumed

How Rates are Measured

6.3

In a reaction, it is not always clear how to measure the amount of reactant used up or the amount of product formed within. To measure the change in concentration with time, we need to be able to measure a change in a physical property. For example, gas production can be followed by monitoring the change in volume at constant pressure. An example is the reaction between dilute hydrochloric acid and marble chips (calcium carbonate).

$$\mathbf{CaCO_{3\,(s)} + 2\,HCl_{(aq)} \longrightarrow CaCl_{2\,(aq)} + H_2O_{(\ell)} + CO_{2\,(g)}}$$

We can perform this reaction in a flask connected to a gas burette. The acid is placed in the flask in a small container. When the flask is tipped the reaction will start. As carbon dioxide is produced, it will bubble into the gas burette. Readings of the burette scale are taken at equal time intervals. In this way we can obtain a measure of the rate of reaction.

If the reaction is accompanied by a colour change, the increase or decrease in colour intensity can be monitored on an instrument called a *spectrometer*. The oxidation of oxalic acid, $H_2C_2O_4$, by permanganate ion, MnO_4^-, in acid solution is a reaction of this kind.

$$5\,H_2C_2O_{4\,(aq)} + 2\,MnO_4{}^-{}_{(aq)} + 6\,H^+{}_{(aq)} \longrightarrow$$
$$10\,CO_{2\,(g)} + 2\,Mn^{2+}{}_{(aq)} + 8\,H_2O_{(\ell)}$$

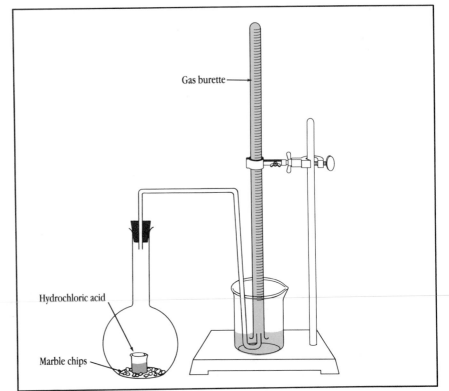

Figure 6.4

We can follow the rate of reaction between marble chips and dilute hydrochloric acid using a gas burette.

Figure 6.5

We can measure changes in light absorbance using a student colorimeter, a simple type of spectrometer.

Permanganate, which is a deep purple colour, strongly absorbs green light. As the reaction progresses, the intensity of the purple in the reaction vessel decreases as the colourless manganese(II) ion is formed and the spectrometer readings show a decrease in the absorption of green light. This decrease corresponds to the gradual disappearance of the permanganate ion.

If the reaction involves a change in acidity, as in the hydrolysis of *t*-butyl bromide,

$$C_4H_9Br_{(aq)} + H_2O_{(\ell)} \longrightarrow C_4H_9OH_{(aq)} + H^+{}_{(aq)} + Br^-{}_{(aq)}$$

the easiest and most accurate way to follow the course of the reaction is to use a pH meter. This instrument gives a direct reading of the acidity of the reaction mixture. An alternative is to remove small samples from the reaction vessel at set intervals and titrate them to determine the concentration of hydrogen ions.

In reactions that take place in solution, there is often a change in the total number of ions as the reaction proceeds. The reaction between bromine and formic acid is a good example:

$$Br_{2(aq)} + HCO_2H_{(aq)} \longrightarrow 2\,Br^-_{(aq)} + 2\,H^+_{(aq)} + CO_{2(g)}$$

Such changes in ionic concentrations can be followed by measuring the electrical conductivity of the solution at predetermined intervals.

QUESTIONS

6. The reaction (in aqueous solution) between bromine and formic acid can be followed by methods other than measuring conductivity. Suggest at least two other physical properties that could be used to measure the rate of this reaction.

7. What physical property could you measure in order to follow the rate of the following chemical reactions?
   a) $C_2H_6N_{2(g)} \longrightarrow N_{2(g)} + C_2H_{6(g)}$
   b) $H_{2(g)} + I_{2(g)} \longrightarrow 2\,HI_{(g)}$
   c) $5\,Br^-_{(aq)} + BrO_3^-_{(aq)} + 6\,H^+_{(aq)} \longrightarrow 3\,Br_{2(aq)} + 3\,H_2O_{(\ell)}$
   d) $2\,MnO_4^-_{(aq)} + 10\,Cl^-_{(aq)} + 16\,H^+_{(aq)} \longrightarrow$
   $$2\,Mn^{2+}_{(aq)} + 5\,Cl_{2(aq)} + 8\,H_2O_{(\ell)}$$

A Simple Kinetics Experiment

6.4

In Section 6.2 we made two separate rate calculations using experimental data and concluded that the average rate depends on when we take the measurements. But rate measurements taken at the same point in the reaction may still show variations due to other factors.

Consider the reaction of calcium carbonate, a white solid, with hydrochloric acid:

$$CaCO_{3(s)} + 2\,HCl_{(aq)} \longrightarrow CaCl_{2(aq)} + CO_{2(g)} + H_2O_{(\ell)}$$

If we run this experiment in an open beaker, the carbon dioxide will bubble off and we can measure the time it takes for the effervescence (bubbling) to subside. The less time the reaction takes, the faster the rate. We will run this simple kinetics experiment under different experimental conditions, tabulate the results, and make some comparisons (Table 6.2).

Trial One: When 100 mL of 0.50 mol·L⁻¹ hydrochloric acid is added to 2.00 g of *powdered* calcium carbonate, there is a fairly vigorous reaction as the carbon dioxide is released. After 45 s the reaction is virtually over.

Trial Two: If we change the concentration of the acid to 1.00 mol·L⁻¹ we find it takes about 23 s for the effervescence to subside to the same level as in the first trial. An increase in reactant concentration has increased the rate of the reaction.

a)

b)

Figure 6.6

a) *The reaction of powdered calcium carbonate with dilute hydrochloric acid is rapid.*

b) *Using lumps of calcium carbonate (marble chips), the reaction with dilute hydrochloric acid is much slower.*

Trial Three: In the third trial we use a solid 2.00 g of solid calcium carbonate (marble) chips instead of the powdered form. The concentration of the acid remains at 0.50 mol·L^{-1}. The reaction is considerably slower. There is effervescence on the outside of the marble as it gradually dissolves in the acid. But even after four hours the reaction is not complete. The reaction rate is not as fast as when the reactants are in a finely-divided form.

Trial Four: This time we use the same concentration, volume, form, and mass as in our first trial, but now we increase the temperature of the reactants. The other trials were carried out at a room temperature of 22 °C. In this trial we heat the 100 mL of 0.50 mol·L^{-1} hydrochloric acid solution to 40 °C before adding it to the calcium carbonate. The reaction is very vigorous. At this higher temperature the completion point is reached in about 14 s.

TABLE 6.2 *Summary of Experimental Data*

Trial	Form of CaCO$_3$	Conc. of HCl (mol·L^{-1})	Temp. (°C)	Approximate time taken	Conclusion
1	powdered	0.50	22	45 s	
2	powdered	1.00	22	23 s	rate dependent on reactant concentration
3	solid chips	0.50	22	>4 h	rate dependent on form of reactant
4	powdered	0.50	40	14 s	rate dependent on reaction temperature

Our experimental results show that there are at least three factors that affect the rate of a chemical reaction:

1. **The temperature at which the reaction takes place;**
2. **The form of the reactants;**
3. **The concentration of the reactants.**

QUESTIONS

8. In one experiment involving calcium carbonate and hydrochloric acid the reaction is complete in 51 s. A later experiment under different conditions takes 17 s. What can you say about the average rate of the second reaction compared to the first reaction?

9. Would the rate of the calcium carbonate and hydrochloric acid reaction in Question 8 increase or decrease if we made the following changes to the experimental conditions:

a) The acid solution was cooled in an ice bath before it was added to the powdered calcium carbonate.
b) We used a block of marble instead of powdered calcium carbonate.
c) We further increased the concentration of the hydrochloric acid.

Dependence of Reaction Rate on Temperature and Other Factors

6.5

As we discovered in Section 6.4, there are several factors that affect reaction rates. In this section we will consider a few that are especially important to industry and biochemistry.

Temperature

The rate of virtually all chemical reactions increases if the temperature is increased. This is particularly important in the chemical industry. For example, the first step of the Ostwald nitric acid process involves the reaction of ammonia with oxygen. This is carried out at temperatures near 800 °C.

$$4 \, NH_{3\,(g)} + 5 \, O_{2\,(g)} \longrightarrow 4 \, NO_{(g)} + 6 \, H_2O_{(g)} \quad .$$

The nitrogen monoxide from this reaction is oxidized to nitrogen dioxide then dissolved in water to produce nitric acid. Commercially, nitric acid is sold as a concentrated aqueous solution of 68 % by mass of the acid. Nitric acid is corrosive and should always be handled with caution. It reacts with proteins, such as those in the skin, producing a yellow compound. This explains the yellow stain that appears on your skin if you come in contact with the acid. In Canada over half a million tonnes of nitric acid is produced annually for use in explosives, fertilizers, and the plastics, and pharmaceuticals industries.

Other industrial processes use low temperatures to slow down reaction rates. Food is stored at low temperatures, or frozen, to retard bacterial growth and the resulting decay. The pharmaceutical industry provides us with a number of products that can slow our biochemical reactions by lowering body temperature.

Other Factors

Finely-divided reactants have been responsible for some serious industrial accidents in Canada. In 1975 dust in a grain elevator in North Vancouver was considered to be the cause of a massive explosion that killed five people. It is thought that the reaction rate in such explosions is so rapid that the heat generated cannot be dissipated. This, in turn, causes the reaction to proceed at an even faster rate. Although much work has been done on the kinetics of explosions, they are very difficult to investigate and are still not well understood.

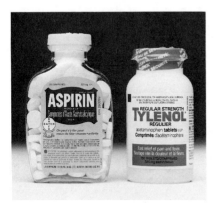

Figure 6.7
Products that contain acetylsalicylic acid or acetominophen are taken to reduce a fever. But the lowering of body temperature may slow the body's responses to fight an infection.

Rates and Reptiles

The body temperature of reptiles, fish, and amphibians varies with that of the environment. We sometimes call these groups of animals "cold-blooded" although it is not an accurate description. Cold-blooded animals do not necessarily have cooler body temperatures than the so-called "warm-blooded" mammals and birds, who maintain a relatively short body-temperature range through insulation and internal regulation of metabolic rate. Reptiles have relatively little insulation. Their means of controlling body temperature depends on an ability to absorb or lose heat mostly as a result of behaviour patterns. For example, some lizards and turtles will pant heavily when their skin temperature or core temperature exceeds a certain level.

Many reptiles thermoregulate by moving to a hotter or cooler place. This strategy is particularly well developed in desert lizards and marine iguanas of the Galapagos Islands off the coast of Ecuador. Like all chemical reactions, the physiological processes of any animal's body are temperature dependent. At higher temperatures these biochemical reactions increase and more energy is produced. But there is an upper limit to the body temperature and before this point is reached the animal must make efforts to dissipate body heat.

In the early morning, the Galapagos iguanas spread out on the lava rocks above the ocean, facing the sun to expose the maximum body surface. As the sun rises, body temperature increases, forcing them to prevent a further increase in body temperature. By turning directly into the sun they are able to minimize exposure to its rays. But the temperature increase continues and so they crawl into cracks in the rocks or under boulders. They also stand up to take advantage of the cooling sea breezes.

For most of the year, the cool Humbolt Current keeps the ocean too cold in the Galapagos region for ectotherms like iguanas to stay in the ocean for long periods. Ten or fifteen minutes of feeding on green algae lowers body temperatures enough that they must retreat to the land. As the temperature drops, metabolic reaction rates decrease, energy output decreases, and body movements slow down. If the body temperature were to drop more than ten degrees, they would no longer have the strength to fight the strong currents, and the surf would smash them against the rocks.

The cooled-down iguanas cling to the rocks, climbing sluggishly to bask in the sun again. Digestive reactions begin only when metabolic rates increase with rising body temperature. As night falls the danger of overcooling returns and the iguanas huddle together in hollows and cervices to conserve as much body heat as possible until the rays of the morning sun signal a start to another day of effort at heat conservation and loss.

Figure 6.8

A marine iguana at the Galapagos Islands. As the temperature rises, so does the rate of all the iguana bodily reactions.

Figure 6.9
The explosion of a grain elevator in North Vancouver, British Columbia. The finely-divided grain dust can act to greatly accelerate such a violent reaction.

Reaction rate is also increased by stirring. A cook attempting to thicken a sauce or gravy by dumping all the flour into the pot at once ends up with thin liquid and lots of lumps. Thickening agents such as flour, cornstarch, and tapioca come in a finely-divided form so that there will be a large ratio of surface-area to mass. The intent is that the chemical reaction involved in the thickening process will occur rapidly and evenly throughout the solution. Adding the flour a small amount at a time while stirring ensures that the reactants come into contact with each other.

The phase of the reactants also determines the rate of a chemical reaction. For example, if solid sodium chloride is mixed with solid silver nitrate, the reaction rate is so slow that we do not detect it. However, in aqueous solution the ions react almost instantaneously:

$$NaCl_{(aq)} + AgNO_{3\,(aq)} \longrightarrow NaNO_{3\,(aq)} + AgCl_{(s)}$$

Experimental results show that such reactions take about one millionth of a second. In general, reactions in solution, reactions of liquids, and reactions between gases occur much faster than solid-phase reactions. We have already seen that the rate of reaction increases greatly when the compound is finely divided. Compounds in solution, or in liquid, or gaseous phases can be considered finely divided at the molecular (or ionic) level. Thus we should expect these reactions to be extremely rapid.

Figure 6.10
An Alka-Seltzer® tablet contains a carbonate and a solid acid. In the solid phase, no measurable reaction occurs. When dissolved in water, reaction is rapid.

The rate of a particular reaction can also be affected by gas pressures, electrical sparks, reactant and solvent substitutions, ultraviolet light (in photochemistry), and visible light (in photography). Recent experiments have shown that very high frequency sound waves (ultrasound) dramatically increase reaction rates and often increase the yield of the desired product. While the reasons for this are not yet fully understood, it is

Figure 6.11

An ultrasonic bath. The ultrasound waves greatly speed up the reaction happening within a flask placed in the bath.

Figure 6.12

Different geological strata. Layers of rock have been in contact for millions of years without reacting together. The rate of reaction of solids is usually very slow.

thought that the very energetic ultrasound waves rapidly compress and decompress fluids through which they pass. The energy released in this process may more finely divide and further mix the reactants. The net result is greatly increased surface area and a dramatically increased reaction rate. This technique shows promise in speeding up many commercially important reactions, especially in the pharmaceutical industry.

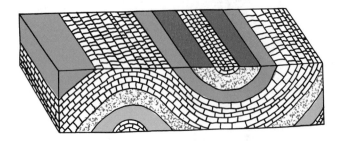

QUESTIONS

10. Which one of the following reactions would you expect to be faster at room temperature?
    a) $Pb^{2+}_{(aq)} + 2 Cl^-_{(aq)} \longrightarrow PbCl_{2 (s)}$
    b) $Pb_{(s)} + Cl_{2 (g)} \longrightarrow PbCl_{2 (s)}$

11. Suggest at least two ways of increasing the rate of dissolving sugar in water when making candy.

Theories of Reaction Rates

6.6 In the early part of this century, a theory explaining reaction rates was developed from the kinetic-molecular theory of gases. The theory, known as **collision theory**, holds that for a chemical reaction to occur the reacting molecules must collide with each other. If the molecules do not collide, there will be no reaction. The theory also states that the rate of the reaction will depend on the *number* of collisions between reacting molecules. This explains the dependence of reaction rate on the concentration of the reactants. The more concentrated the reactants, the closer together they are, and the more likely they are to collide and react.

Collision theory also explains why a reaction rate decreases with time. As soon as the reaction begins, some reactant molecules are consumed and thus their concentration decreases. As the concentrations of reactants are reduced, the reaction slows down because collisions occur less frequently.

Fact	Explanation
As the size of a solid particle decreases, the reaction rate increases.	With greater surface area, collisions of gas molecules with the surface are more frequent. More collisions result in a faster reaction.

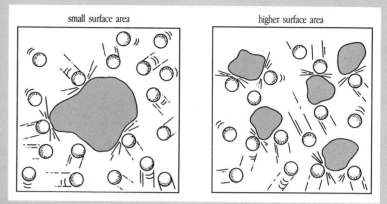

Fact	Explanation
As the concentration of a solution increases, so does the rate of reaction.	At higher concentrations, there is a greater probability of collision. More collisions result in a faster reaction.

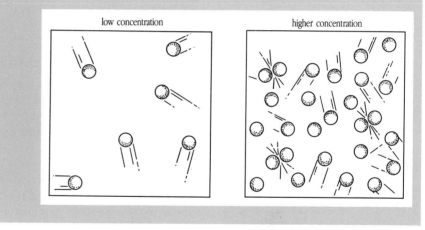

Why Every Collision Does Not Lead to a Reaction

Simple collision theory implies that every collision leads to a reaction. But calculations indicate that in a one-litre volume of gas at 25 °C and atmospheric pressure there are approximately 1×10^{30} collisions every second. If every one of these collisions were to result in a reaction, then almost all gas-phase reactions would occur instantaneously. A similar situation would exist for liquids. Because not all gas and liquid phase reactions are instantaneous at room temperature, we can conclude that not all molecular collisions lead to a reaction.

Two factors that are not acknowledged by simple collision theory are the orientation and the energy of the colliding molecules. For many simple reactions, the way the molecules are facing does not affect the possibility of a reaction. For other reactions, usually those involving more complex molecules, the way the collisions occur is very important.

But even if the molecules collide with the correct orientation, a reaction will only occur if the molecules involved have sufficient energy. When two molecules collide, the energy of the collision has to be sufficient to cause bonds to break. Clearly, collision theory must be modified to include these two factors.

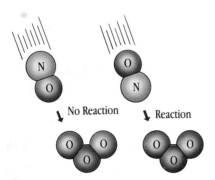

Figure 6.13
For nitrogen monoxide to react with ozone (trioxygen) the nitrogen atom of the nitrogen monoxide must collide with one of the oxygen atoms of the ozone molecule.

Figure 6.14
For reaction to occur, the colliding molecules must have sufficient energy.

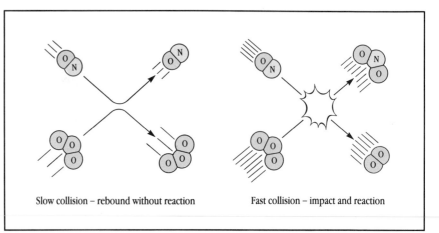

Slow collision – rebound without reaction   Fast collision – impact and reaction

Activation Energies and Transition States

Transition state theory looks specifically at the moments at which the molecules begin to collide and then break apart. First proposed by the American chemist Henry Eyring, this theory explains a reaction in terms of the formation of an **activated complex**. This is an unstable grouping of reactant molecules that is considered to have bonds that are in the process of being formed and bonds that are in the process of being broken. Chemists have sufficient evidence to suggest a possible structure for the activated complex in some reactions, but in many other cases the shape of the activated complex is a matter of sheer speculation.

Figure 6.16 is an **energy diagram**. It shows how the energy of the reacting system changes as the reaction proceeds. The energy of each chemical (reactants and products) is indicated along the vertical axis. The progress of the reaction is plotted along the horizontal axis or **reaction pathway**. All energy diagrams have a similar profile. The reaction passes through an energy maximum, known as the **transition state**. At this highest energy point, the temporary intermediate product, referred to as the activated complex, is formed.

The difference between the inital energy of the reactants and the transition state is known as the **activation energy**, E_a. The activation energy

Figure 6.15
Henry Eyring (1901–   ) was the founder of the transition state concept.

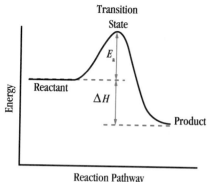

Figure 6.16

An energy diagram showing the energy barrier between reactants and products.

is the minimum energy required for the reaction to occur and corresponds to the energy necessary to reach the transition state. For the reaction between nitrogen monoxide and trioxygen (ozone), the activation energy is only $10 \, kJ \cdot mol^{-1}$. This is an unusually low activation energy value. Most reactions have activation energies in the range of 100 to $200 \, kJ \cdot mol^{-1}$. For example, the gas-phase decomposition of nitrogen dioxide to nitrogen monoxide and oxygen has an activation energy of about $120 \, kJ \cdot mol^{-1}$.

$$2 \, NO_{2 \, (g)} \longrightarrow 2 \, NO_{(g)} + O_{2 \, (g)}$$

Figure 6.17a shows that if the products of the reaction are at a lower energy level than the reactants, the reaction is exothermic. This type of reaction gives out energy, usually in the form of heat and the change in enthalpy for such a reaction is negative. (Recall that in Section 5.4, we defined the change in enthalpy (ΔH) as the heat energy released or absorbed under conditions of constant pressure.) If the products are of a higher energy than the reactants (Figure 6.17b), we are dealing with an endothermic reaction. In either case the activation energy is always the energy difference between the reactants and the highest energy point on the reaction pathway.

Figure 6.17

Energy diagrams for a) an exothermic reaction, b) an endothermic reaction.

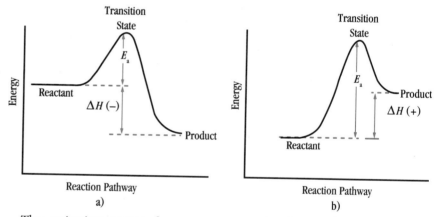

The activation energy for a reverse reaction is not the same as the activation energy for its forward reaction. As we have discussed, nitrogen monoxide will react with ozone to produce nitrogen dioxide and oxygen.

$$NO_{(g)} + O_{3 \, (g)} \longrightarrow NO_{2 \, (g)} + O_{2 \, (g)}$$

For this reaction, the activation energy, E_a, is $+10 \, kJ \cdot mol^{-1}$ while the enthalpy change is $-200 \, kJ \cdot mol^{-1}$. We find that collisions between nitrogen dioxide and oxygen will sometimes lead to the formation of nitrogen monoxide and ozone. This reverse reaction will have an enthalpy change of $+200 \, kJ \cdot mol^{-1}$. As a result, the activation energy of the reverse reaction

(E'_a) will be $210\,\text{kJ}\cdot\text{mol}^{-1}$ ($10\,\text{kJ}\cdot\text{mol}^{-1}$ + $200\,\text{kJ}\cdot\text{mol}^{-1}$). The activation energy of this reverse reaction is very high, therefore this reaction will be very slow.

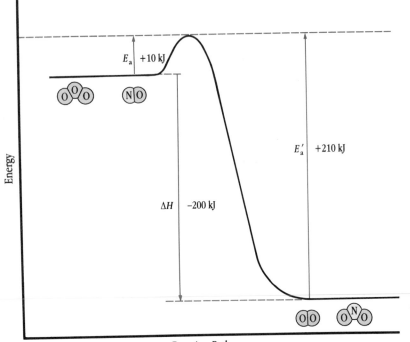

Figure 6.18
Comparison of the activation energies for the forward and reverse reaction between ozone and nitrogen monoxide.

Why Increased Temperature Increases the Reaction Rate

The concept of a reaction pathway that passes through a transition state gives us an explanation for the relationship between increasing temperature and increasing reaction rate. At higher temperatures the average kinetic energy of the reactant molecules increases. This affects the reaction rate in two ways:

At higher molecular speeds there are more molecular collisions and hence a greater chance of a reaction.

If the average molecular kinetic energy increases, more of the collisions will have enough energy to overcome the activation energy barrier.

At any given temperature, not all molecules have the same energy. Some molecules will have more energy than others. As collisions occur, individual molecules lose or gain energy, but the overall average energy remains constant and proportional to the temperature. It is important to note that an increase in temperature does *not* change the pathway by which the reaction occurs. Also note that the activation energy is constant for a particular reaction at any given temperature.

If we graph the number of molecules along a horizontal axis against molecular kinetic energy of the vertical axis, we will obtain a curve showing the distribution of molecular energy. Distributions of this kind are known as **Maxwell-Boltzmann distributions** or simply, Boltzmann distribution diagrams (Figure 6.19). The proportion of molecules with enough energy to undergo reaction is indicated by the shaded portion.

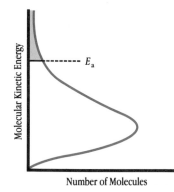

Figure 6.19

A Boltzmann distribution of molecular kinetic energies. The curve tapers off at high energies.

For a reaction with a low activation energy, many of the molecules will have enough energy to overcome the activation energy barrier. Where the activation energy is greater, fewer molecules have the necessary kinetic energy and the reaction rate is slower.

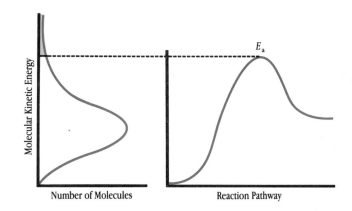

Figure 6.20

We can compare a distribution of molecular energies with a reaction pathway curve. Only a few molecules (shaded) have an energy greater than that of the activation energy, E_a.

As the temperature of a particular reaction increases, the average kinetic energy increases as well, and the curve stretches upward (Figure 6.23a). The value for the activation energy remains the same, but there are now more molecules that have enough energy to react when they collide and the rate of the reaction increases.

Matches — A Striking Example of Activation Energy

The head of a match stores energy in the form of chemical energy. When the match is struck, the heat generated by the friction supplies the activation energy for the match head to burst into flame. The heat of this exothermic reaction then supplies the continuing activation energy needed for burning.

Phosphorus has been used in match heads along with other chemicals since about 1833. Originally, white phosphorus was used, but white phosphorus can be unstable; these matches often ignited spontaneously. But there was also another problem. The girls and young women, who were usually employed in match factories, showed signs of bone deterioration, especially in the lower jaw. This condition known as "phossy jaw" was traced to the exposure to white phosphorus. By 1848 another allotrope of phosphorus, red phosphorus, had been used as a substitute. The ignition process in modern matches is still based on the chemical reactivity of red phosphorus or its compounds with oxygen.

Figure 6.21
Phosphorus exists as two common allotropes: white phosphorus, which must be stored under water, and red phosphorus, which is stable in air.

Two types of matches are produced today: strike anywhere matches and safety matches. Strike anywhere matches have a yellow tip of tetraphosphorus trisulfide over a layer composed of lead(IV) oxide and diantimony trisulfide (Figure 6.22a). Friction ignites the tetraphosphorus trisulfide in air and the heat of this reaction starts another reaction between lead(IV) oxide and diantimony trisulfide, which produces a flame.

The head of a safety match is composed of a mixture of diantimony trisulfide and potassium chlorate. This type of match is struck on a special rough surface containing a mixture of red phosphorus, glue, and abrasive (Figure 6.22b). The red phosphorus ignites momentarily, igniting the diantimony trisulfide and potassium chlorate mixture on the match tip.

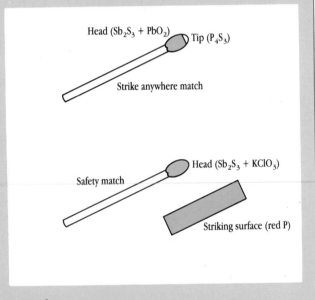

Figure 6.22
a) Strike-anywhere matches have a tetraphosphorus trisulfide ignition agent as part of the match tip.
b) Safety matches have a red phosphorus ignition agent in the special striking surface.

The sticks of both types of matches are commonly dipped in various salt solutions such as ammonium sulfate, ammonium phosphate, or sodium phosphate. This controlled fireproofing process prevents the match from smouldering and glowing after it is extinguished. It also keeps the used match in one piece; otherwise it would crumble into ashes.

Figure 6.23

Raising the temperature increases molecular energies. As a result, many more molecules have an energy greater than the activation energy, E_a.

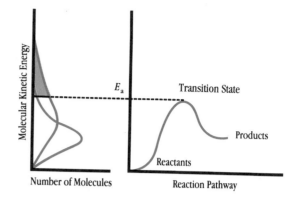

QUESTIONS

12. Give two reasons why most molecular collisions do not lead to a molecule reaction.

13. What is meant by the term activation energy?

14. In the following reaction the enthalpy of the forward reaction is $\Delta H = -36\,kJ\cdot mol^{-1}$:

$$A + B \longrightarrow C$$

The activation energy for the forward reaction is $73\,kJ\cdot mol^{-1}$
a) Draw an energy diagram for this reaction.
b) What is the activation energy for the reverse reaction?

Catalysis

6.7

It is possible to increase the rate of a chemical reaction, without increasing the temperature, by introducing a catalyst. A **catalyst** is a substance that increases the reaction rate without being consumed itself. A catalyst works by providing an alternate pathway with a lower activation energy. Thus at the same temperature, more molecules will have sufficient energy to overcome the new, smaller activation energy barrier, and the reaction will be faster.

When the reagents and the catalyst are in the same phase, usually the gas phase or in aqueous solution, we classify the reaction as a **homogeneous catalysis**. One example of this form of catalysis is the reaction of sulfur dioxide and oxygen in the presence of gaseous nitrogen dioxide to produce sulfur trioxide.

$$2\,SO_{2\,(g)} + O_{2\,(g)} \xrightarrow{\;NO_2\;} 2\,SO_{3\,(g)}$$

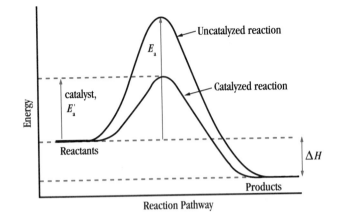

Figure 6.24

In the presence of a catalyst, the reaction proceeds on a pathway with a lower activation energy, E_a'.

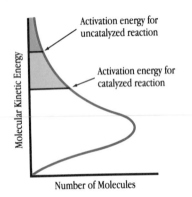

Figure 6.25

As a Boltzmann distribution diagram shows, more molecules will have enough energy for the catalyzed pathway compared to the uncatalyzed route.

As a catalyst, nitrogen dioxide is shown over the arrow of the reaction equation. Without the nitrogen dioxide this reaction is extremely slow. The use of nitrogen dioxide as a catalyst for this reaction is part of the traditional lead chamber process of commercial sulfuric acid production.

When catalysis occurs at the point between two phases, it is classified as **heterogeneous catalysis**, such as the decomposition of hydrogen peroxide solution to water and oxygen. This is a slow reaction at room temperature, but in the presence of finely-divided manganese(IV) oxide, the reaction is vigorous.

$$2\ H_2O_{2\,(aq)} \xrightarrow{\ MnO_2\ } 2\ H_2O_{(\ell)} + O_{2\,(g)}$$

Figure 6.26

a) *Hydrogen peroxide normally decomposes very slowly.*

b) *Some manganese(IV) oxide is added.*

c) *Very rapid decomposition of the hydrogen peroxide occurs.*

Figure 6.27
Butylated hydroxytoluene (BHT) is added to some foodstuffs, such as potato chips, to inhibit the oxidation reaction leading to spoilage.

Substances that slow down a chemical reaction are known as **inhibitors**. They usually work by tying up the catalyst or the reactant. We do not want an inhibitor stopping, or "poisoning," the catalyst if we are trying to increase the rate of a reaction, but there are times when an inhibitor is deliberately added to slow down a particular reaction.

Catalytic Converters

Heterogeneous catalysis is the basis of the catalytic converters attached to the exhaust systems of many late-model cars. Exhaust gases are mixed with additional air and passed over beds of mixed metal oxides within the converter. In internal combustion engines, hydrocarbon fuel, such as octane (C_8H_{18}) burns in oxygen to produce carbon dioxide and water.

$$2\ C_8H_{18\,(\ell)} + 25\ O_{2\,(g)} \longrightarrow 16\ CO_{2\,(g)} + 18\ H_2O_{(\ell)}$$

If carbon dioxide and water vapour were the sole products of combustion, we would not have a pollution problem. Unfortunately, because of the inefficiency of internal combustion engines, some gasoline is released unburned, while an additional proportion is partially combusted to carbon monoxide.

$$2\ C_8H_{18\,(\ell)} + 17\ O_{2\,(g)} \longrightarrow 16\ CO_{(g)} + 18\ H_2O_{(\ell)}$$

As well, in the high temperature of the explosion some oxygen gas and nitrogen gas within the cylinder combine to form nitrogen monoxide gas.

$$N_{2\,(g)} + O_{2\,(g)} \longrightarrow 2\ NO_{(g)}$$

When released to the atmosphere, the nitrogen monoxide rapidly reacts with oxygen in the air to produce toxic reddish-brown nitrogen dioxide gas. It is the nitrogen dioxide that gives the brown colour to the photochemical smog that we see over major cities.

Figure 6.28
A police officer checking the exhaust emission of a truck in Hungary. The pollution caused by the internal combustion engine is an international problem.

Figure 6.29
A catalytic converter is located between the engine and the muffler.

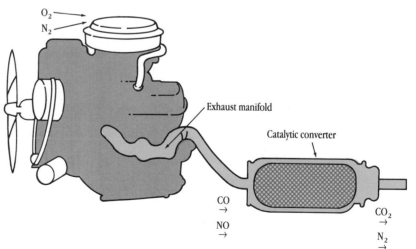

Figure 6.30
A catalytic converter.

The role of the catalytic converter is twofold. In one chamber additional air is added and a transition metal catalyst is used to cause an efficient conversion of unburned hydrocarbons and carbon monoxide to carbon dioxide and water. In the other chamber a different transition metal catalyst is used to dissociate the nitrogen monoxide back to nitrogen gas and oxygen gas. Because the reactions in the first chamber are quite exothermic, the converter becomes very hot. Several fires have been started by converter-equipped cars when they park over long, dry grass.

Catalysts in Industry

Both homogeneous and heterogeneous catalysis are extremely important in industry. The presence of a catalyst usually allows the reaction to be carried out at a lower temperature. For chemical companies this can mean thousands of dollars in annual savings on fuel bills. At the Cominco Ltd. smelter in Trail, British Columbia, zinc metal is produced from zinc sulfide ore. The first step in this new process involves the reaction of the zinc sulfide with sulfuric acid and oxygen gas (from the atmosphere):

$$ZnS_{(s)} + H_2SO_{4(aq)} + \tfrac{1}{2}O_{2(g)} \longrightarrow ZnSO_{4(aq)} + S_{(s)} + H_2O_{(\ell)}$$

With pure zinc sulfide this reaction is exceedingly slow. Fortunately, the ore contains some iron(II) sulfide. This reacts in a similar way to the zinc sulfide to produce iron(II) sulfate:

$$FeS_{(s)} + H_2SO_{4(aq)} + \tfrac{1}{2}O_{2(g)} \longrightarrow FeSO_{4(aq)} + S_{(s)} + H_2O_{(\ell)}$$

The iron(II) sulfate is a catalyst for the reaction of the zinc sulfide. First the iron(II) sulfate reacts with more sulfuric acid and oxygen to produce iron(III) sulfate. Then, the iron(III) sulfate reacts with zinc sulfide to produce zinc sulfate and return the iron to the iron(II) ion.

$$2\,FeSO_{4(aq)} + H_2SO_{4(aq)} + \tfrac{1}{2}O_{2(g)} \longrightarrow Fe_2(SO_4)_{3(aq)} + H_2O_{(\ell)}$$
$$Fe_e(SO_4)_{3(aq)} + ZnS_{(s)} \longrightarrow ZnSO_{4(aq)} + 2\,FeSO_{4(aq)} + S_{(s)}$$

Notice that the iron(II) sulfate *did* take part in the reaction sequence: it is changed to iron(III) sulfate, but then it is returned to iron(II) sulfate. This is true for almost all homogeneous catalysts; they change during the reaction sequence, but at the end they revert to their initial state.

One of the most important industrial chemicals is sulfuric acid. This was once produced by the complex lead chamber process. It was long known that a simpler route would involve the reaction of sulfur dioxide (a common by-product of smelting) with oxygen from the air to produce sulfur trioxide. Sulfuric acid could be easily obtained from the sulfur trioxide. But the problem with this method was the slowness of the reaction between sulfur dioxide and oxygen gas. As early as 1841, it was realized that platinum was an effective catalyst. However, the cost of this catalyst was so high that few companies tried to use it for large-scale industrial use. Also, the platinum reacted with many impurities in the reactants, stopping

Figure 6.31
A sulfuric acid plant.

its catalytic activity. A laboratory discovery in 1929 showed that a comparatively cheap compound, vanadium(V) oxide (V_2O_5) also increased the rate of the reaction substantially. Almost all commercial sulfuric acid production now uses this **contact process** involving the vanadium(V) oxide catalyst.

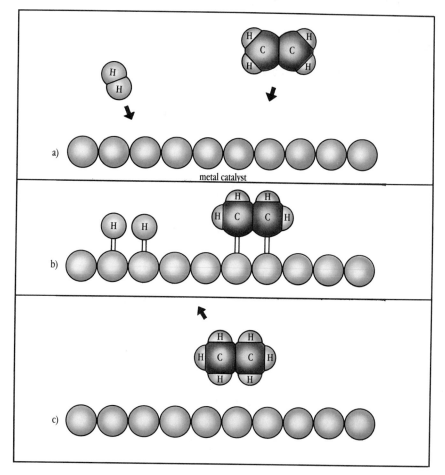

Figure 6.32

The reaction between ethene and hydrogen on a metal catalyst.

a) The two reactants approach the metal surface.

b) The hydrogen molecule splits into atoms as it bonds to the metal surface; the ethene changes shape as bonding occurs with the metal surface.

c) The hydrogen atoms attach themselves to the ethene molecule to give ethane, C_2H_6; and the molecule leaves the metal surface.

It is important that, for a specific slow reaction, we must find a specific catalyst. In the past, trial-and-error was the most common method of finding a catalyst. Most work centred on the transition metals and their compounds because this part of the Periodic Table seemed to produce most of the known heterogeneous catalysts. Now we are able to study the surfaces of these catalysts and determine exactly how the catalysis is occurring. With this knowledge, we should be able to design better and cheaper catalysts.

Hydrogenation is another important industrial reaction requiring the use of a catalyst. This is a reaction involving addition of hydrogen to some of the carbon-carbon double bonds (C=C) as found in unsaturated fats.

The process converts these liquid oils into higher-melting solid fats, such as those found in margarine and solid shortenings.

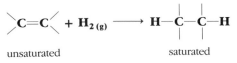

Uncatalyzed hydrogenation is slow, mainly because of the very large activation energy necessary to break the strong bond in the hydrogen molecule. The overall rate is greatly increased by the use of a metal catalyst such as platinum, palladium, or nickel. The metal provides an absorption surface for both reactants (Figure 6.32). The attractive forces between the metal and hydrogen weaken the hydrogen-hydrogen bonds as a result, and the activation energy for the reaction is lowered. Almost all heterogeneous catalysis occurs in a similar manner, at the catalytic surface, and for this reason catalysts are generally used in a finely-divided state. This increases the surface area and, thus, the efficiency of the catalyst.

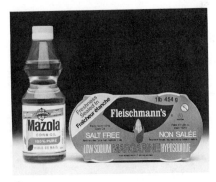

Figure 6.33

a) a vegetable oil (liquid fat)

b) liquid fat after hydrogenation

Figure 6.34

These metals and their compounds are the most effective homogeneous and heterogeneous catalysts.

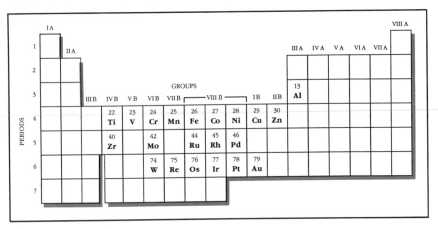

QUESTIONS

15. What effect does a catalyst have on the following:
    a) enthalpy change of the reaction
    b) energy of the reactants
    c) pathway of the reaction

16. The reaction of ethyl acetate (a component of nail polish) with acid can be written as follows:

$$CH_3CO_2C_2H_{5\,(aq)} + H^+_{(aq)} + H_2O_{(\ell)} \longrightarrow$$

ethyl acetate

$$CH_3CO_2H_{(aq)} + C_2H_5OH_{(aq)} + H^+_{(aq)}$$

acetic acid   ethanol

a) What is the catalyst in this series of reactions?
b) Is this a homogeneous or a heterogeneous catalyst?

A Quantitative Approach to Reaction Rates

6.8

When reaction rates are followed, we find that the rate decreases as the reaction continues. This is because the concentration of the reactants decreases during the course of the reaction. Table 6.3 shows the changes in concentrations of carbon monoxide and carbon dioxide during the gaseous reaction between carbon monoxide and nitrogen dioxide.

$$CO_{(g)} + NO_{2\,(g)} \longrightarrow CO_{2\,(g)} + NO_{(g)}$$

If we examine the data carefully, we will find that both the rate of loss of carbon monoxide and the rate of formation of carbon dioxide, decrease as the reaction proceeds.

TABLE 6.3   *Data From a Kinetics Experiment for the Reaction between Carbon Monoxide and Nitrogen Dioxide*

Time (seconds)	Concentration of CO $(mol \cdot L^{-1})$	Concentration of CO_2 $(mol \cdot L^{-1})$
0	0.100	0.000
20	0.050	0.050
40	0.033	0.067
60	0.026	0.074
80	0.020	0.080
100	0.017	0.083

During the first time interval, the concentration of carbon monoxide changes from $0.100 \; mol \cdot L^{-1}$ to $0.050 \; mol \cdot L^{-1}$. The average reaction rate for this period is therefore

$$\frac{-(0.050 - 0.100) \; mol \cdot L^{-1}}{(20 - 0) \; s} = 2.5 \times 10^{-3} \; mol \cdot L^{-1} \cdot s^{-1}$$

However, the average reaction rate between 80 and 100 seconds has dropped to

$$\frac{-(0.017 - 0.020) \; mol \cdot L^{-1}}{(100 - 80) \; s} = 1.5 \times 10^{-4} \; mol \cdot L^{-1} \cdot s^{-1}$$

The average rate of formation of the product, carbon dioxide, would show the same decrease, provided that measurements were taken over identical time intervals.

Initial Rate

If we wish to compare rates for the same reaction but starting with different concentrations we must make sure that we compare rates taken over the same time interval. This is usually done by determining the initial rate. The **initial rate** is measured over a very short time interval at the beginning of the reaction.

Once initial rates have been determined for a series of separate experiments of the same reaction, it is possible to compare initial concentrations with initial rates. Table 6.4 shows kinetic data for the decomposition of dinitrogen pentoxide in carbon tetrachloride solution:

$$N_2O_5 \longrightarrow 2 NO_2 + \tfrac{1}{2} O_2$$

TABLE 6.4 *Experimental Data Showing the Effect of Changing the Initial Concentration on Reaction Rate*

Trial	Initial $[N_2O_5]$ $(mol \cdot L^{-1})$	Initial Rate of Formation of O_2 $(mol \cdot L^{-1} \cdot s^{-1})$
1	0.45	2.7×10^{-4}
2	0.90	5.4×10^{-4}
3	1.35	8.2×10^{-4}

The data in Table 6.4 shows that if we double the concentration of the reactant, the rate doubles. If we increase the concentration of the reactant by a factor of three, the rate increases by a factor of three. We can say, therefore, that the rate is proportional to the concentration of the dinitrogen pentoxide. We can express the relationship between rate and reactant concentration as a rate proportionality statement. For the decomposition of dinitrogen pentoxide, the proportionality statement is written as

$$\text{Rate } \alpha \, [N_2O_5]$$

The rate depends on the reactant concentration raised to a power. The exponent may be 1, 2, or even 0. If the exponent is zero, the rate is independent of the concentration of that specific reactant. The values of the exponents cannot be predicted but must be obtained from experimental measurements.

EXAMPLE   *6.2*   The following data are for the reaction between carbon monoxide and nitrogen dioxide at 400 °C:

$$CO_{(g)} + NO_{2\,(g)} \longrightarrow CO_{2\,(g)} + NO_{(g)}$$

Trial	Initial [CO] $(mol \cdot L^{-1})$	Initial [NO$_2$] $(mol \cdot L^{-1})$	Initial Rate of Formation of CO$_2$ $(mol \cdot L^{-1} \cdot s^{-1})$
1	0.10	0.10	5.0×10^{-3}
2	0.10	0.20	20.0×10^{-3}
3	0.20	0.10	5.0×10^{-3}

From these experiments write the rate proportionality statement for each of the reactants.

SOLUTION We start by comparing Trial 1 with each of the other trials in turn. In Trial 2 the initial concentration of the carbon monoxide has remained the same while the nitrogen dioxide concentration has been doubled. In column 4 we see that the rate of the reaction has quadrupled. This means that the rate is proportional to the square of the concentration of the nitrogen dioxide.

When we compare Trial 3 to Trial 1, we see that the concentration of the nitrogen dioxide has remained at $0.10 \ mol \cdot L^{-1}$ and the carbon monoxide concentration has been doubled. This time the rate of the reaction has not changed, indicating that the rate does not depend on the concentration of carbon monoxide. Therefore, our proportionality statement is written as follows:

$$\text{Rate} \propto [NO_2]^2$$

You may find it surprising that the rate of reaction does not depend upon the concentration of carbon monoxide. Obviously, some carbon monoxide has to be present otherwise the reaction cannot take place. However, more carbon monoxide will not make the reaction any faster. This finding is a clue that the reaction is not as simple as it appears.

Reaction Order

A proportionality statement can be written as an equality provided we use a proportionality constant. When written this way, the expression is known as a **rate law**. For the general reaction

$$A \longrightarrow \textbf{products}$$

the rate law takes the form

$$\textbf{Rate} = \textbf{\textit{k}[A]}^{\textbf{\textit{x}}}$$

The proportionality constant, k, is the **rate constant**. The value of x, the exponent in the rate law equation, is known as the **order** of the reaction.

Throughout the course of the reaction, the rate constant remains the same. This makes it a very useful measurement. For example, given that two reactions are run at the same temperature, a chemist in Halifax should get the same rate constant for a particular reaction as a chemist in Montreal. It would not matter if their reactions were run at different concentrations. The *rates* would vary with the different concentrations but the *rate constant* would not. The value of x can only be determined by experiment. *It cannot be determined from the coefficients in the balanced reaction equation.*

First-Order Reactions

If the value of x is 1 in the rate law equation, the reaction is known as a **first-order reaction**. Its reaction rate depends on the concentration of only one species irrespective of the number of reactants present. (The term *species* refers to a molecule, a formula unit, an atom, or an ion.)

$$\text{Rate} = k[\text{reactant}]^1 \quad \text{or} \quad \text{Rate} = k[\text{reactant}]$$

To calculate the rate constant, we need to know the rate law and the order for the reaction. For example, we can now calculate the rate constant for the decomposition of dinitrogen pentoxide:

$$N_2O_5 \longrightarrow 2\,NO_2 + \tfrac{1}{2}O_2$$

The rate law for this reaction is Rate $= k[N_2O_5]$ and the reaction is of first order. If we use the data from Table 6.4, the equation becomes

$$\text{Initial rate} = k[N_2O_5]$$

To determine the rate constant, we rearrange this equation to

$$k = \frac{\text{Initial rate}}{[N_2O_5]}$$

Now, substituting the data from Table 6.4, we find that for Trial 1

$$k = \frac{2.7 \times 10^{-4}\ \text{mol·L}^{-1}\text{·s}^{-1}}{0.45\ \text{mol·L}^{-1}}$$
$$= 6.0 \times 10^{-4}\ \text{s}^{-1}$$

We can show that the rate constant does not vary by repeating the calculation with data from Trial 2:

$$k = \frac{\text{Initial rate}}{[N_2O_5]}$$
$$= \frac{5.4 \times 10^{-4}\ \text{mol·L}^{-1}\text{·s}^{-1}}{0.90\ \text{mol·L}^{-1}}$$
$$= 6.0 \times 10^{-4}\ \text{s}^{-1}$$

The value of k is the same in both cases.

EXAMPLE **6.3** The following data were collected from the reaction between the hydroxide ion and *t*-butyl bromide, an organic halogen compound. All the experiments were carried out at the same temperature.

$$(CH_3)_3CBr + OH^- \longrightarrow (CH_3)_3COH + Br^-$$

Trial	Initial $[(CH_3)_3CBr]$ $(mol \cdot L^{-1})$	Initial $[OH^{-1}]$ $(mol \cdot L^{-1})$	Initial Rate of Formation of $(CH_3)_3COH$ $(mol \cdot L^{-1} \cdot s^{-1})$
1	0.10	0.10	4.0×10^{-3}
2	0.20	0.10	8.0×10^{-3}
3	0.10	0.20	4.0×10^{-3}

Use the data to calculate the rate law for the reaction and calculate the rate constant, *k*.

SOLUTION We start by comparing Trial 1 with each of the others. In Trial 2 the concentration of the organic compound has been doubled and the rate of the reaction has doubled. This means that the rate is proportional to the concentration of the organic compound.

In Trial 3 the concentration of the hydroxide ion has been doubled but there has been no change in the initial reaction rate. This tells us that the rate does not depend on the concentration of the hydroxide ion. The reaction is therefore first order and the rate law can be written as follows:

$$Rate = k[(CH_3)_3CBr]$$

We can use any of the three trials to calculate the value of *k*. For example, using data from Trial 1,

$$Initial\ Rate = k[(CH_3)_3CBr]$$

Once again we rearrange this equation to give

$$k = \frac{Initial\ Rate}{[(CH_3)_3CBr]}$$

$$= \frac{4.0 \times 10^{-3}\ mol \cdot L^{-1} \cdot s^{-1}}{0.10\ mol \cdot L^{-1}}$$

$$= 0.040\ s^{-1}$$

Second-Order Reactions

We return to our general reaction

$$A \longrightarrow products$$

and the corresponding rate equation

$$Rate = k[A]^x$$

If $x = 2$ then this is a **second-order reaction** and the rate depends on the concentration of one species raised to a power of two:

$$\text{Rate} = k[A]^2$$

Doubling the concentration of the reactant in this type of reaction will increase the rate by a factor of four.

Once we know the form of the rate law for a given second-order reaction, we can calculate the rate constant. The procedure is similar to the one used to determine first-order rate constants.

EXAMPLE **6.4** The following table provides experimental data for the decomposition of acetaldehyde under certain conditions:

$$CH_3CHO_{(g)} \longrightarrow CH_{4(g)} + CO_{(g)}$$

Trial	Initial $[CH_3CHO]$ $(mol \cdot L^{-1})$	Initial Rate of Formation of CO $(mol \cdot L^{-1} \cdot s^{-1})$
1	0.10	8.6×10^{-4}
2	0.20	3.44×10^{-3}

Use this data to determine the following:
a) the rate law for this reaction
b) the rate constant for the reaction

SOLUTION a) In Trial 2 the rate quadruples as the concentration of the reactant doubles. Thus, the rate law for this reaction is

$$\text{Rate} = k[CH_3CHO]^2$$

b) Using the data from Trial 1 in the rearranged rate law gives

$$k = \frac{\text{Initial rate}}{[CH_3CHO]^2}$$

$$k = \frac{8.6 \times 10^{-4} \, mol \cdot L^{-1} \cdot s^{-1}}{(0.10 \, mol \cdot L^{-1})^2}$$

$$= \frac{8.6 \times 10^{-4} \, mol \cdot L^{-1} \cdot s^{-1}}{0.01 \, mol^2 \cdot L^{-2}}$$

$$= 8.6 \times 10^{-2} \, L \cdot mol^{-1} \cdot s^{-1}$$

Overall Reaction Order

The overall order of a reaction is the *sum of the exponents* of the concentrations given in the rate law. For the general rate law

$$\text{Rate} = k[A]^x[B]^y$$

the order of the reaction is $(x + y)$.

If the reaction rate does not depend on the concentration of one of the reactants, we say that the reaction is **zero order** with respect to that reactant. Although zero-order, higher-order, and even fractional-order reactions are possible, we will limit our discussion to first- and second-order reactions. For example, when the reaction has the general form

$$A + B \longrightarrow products$$

and the rate depends on the concentration of two reactant species (A and B), the reaction is second order if it has been determined that

$$Rate = k[A]^1[B]^1 \quad or \quad Rate = k[A][B]$$

This reaction is considered to be first order in A and first order in B, but the overall order is two.

EXAMPLE   **6.5**   For the reaction, in solution, between bromoethane and hydroxide ion,

$$C_2H_5Br_{(aq)} + OH^-_{(aq)} \longrightarrow C_2H_5OH_{(aq)} + Br^-_{(aq)}$$

it was found that doubling the concentration of the hydroxide ion caused the rate to double. When the concentration of both reactants was doubled, the rate of the reaction increased by a factor of four. What is the order of the reaction with respect to
a) hydroxide ions?
b) bromoethane?
c) the overall reaction order?

SOLUTION   a) Since the rate doubles when the concentration of the hydroxide ion doubles, the reaction is first order with respect to hydroxide ion.
b) Since the rate doubles again when the bromoethane concentration is doubled, the rate must also be first order with respect to bromoethane.
c) The overall order of the reaction is the sum of the orders. Therefore, the overall rate is second order.

QUESTIONS

17. For the following reaction in aqueous solution,

$$I^-_{(aq)} + OCl^-_{(aq)} \longrightarrow IO^-_{(aq)} + Cl^-_{(aq)}$$

which statement represents the relationship between reaction rate and reactant concentration?
a) Rate $= k[I^-]^2$
b) Rate $= k[I^-][OCl^-]$
c) This relationship cannot be determined from the reaction equation.

John Polanyi and the Nature of Chemical Reactions

John Polanyi was born in Berlin, Germany in 1929, and he received his Ph. D. in chemistry at the University of Manchester, in England. He worked at the National Research Laboratories in Ottawa and then at Princeton University, New Jersey, where he studied visible and ultraviolet light emissions during certain chemical reactions.

He obtained a post at the University of Toronto in 1956 and he decided to look for infrared light emission from reactions, the field of *infrared chemiluminescence*. Polanyi chose to examine the reaction between hydrogen atoms and chlorine molecules (shown below) because a text on his bookshelf had a complete set of theoretical data on the hydrogen chloride molecule.

$$H + Cl_2 \longrightarrow HCl + Cl$$

Since this reaction was known to be highly exothermic, Polanyi reasoned that a newly-created hydrogen chloride molecule would come out of the reaction vigorously vibrating and rotating. The molecule would be expected to release this energy as a cascade of infrared photons. He persuaded the university's Dean of Science and Arts to help him obtain funds for an expensive infrared spectrometer to investigate his proposal. The Dean retorted that for the cost, "Polanyi had better win a Nobel Prize!"

With the assistance of his first graduate student, Ken Cashion, he found that about half the energy produced in the reaction was released in the form of infrared radiation. The wavelengths of this radiation could be used to obtain important information about the molecular collisions. He suggested that such reactions might form the basis of what he called a "chemical laser." In fact they had occasionally produced very intense bursts of infrared light by

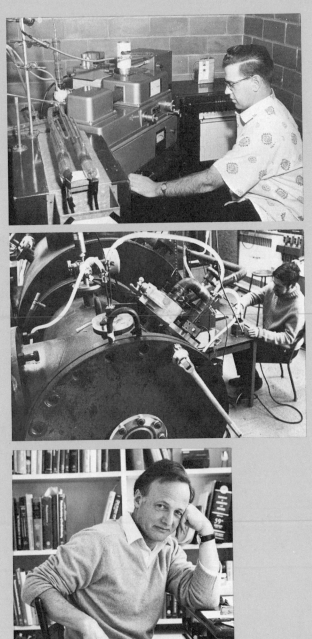

Figure 6.35

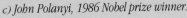

a) *Graduate student Ken Cashion working in lab.*

b) *A reaction chamber similar to those used in Polanyi's experiments.*

c) *John Polanyi, 1986 Nobel prize winner.*

accident. At the time (1960), Polanyi regarded these occurrences as a nuisance because they interfered with his measurements. It was this work, and his lifetime achievement in chemistry, that led to his Nobel Prize in 1986.

Polanyi has also had a strong social conscience. In particular, he has been an outspoken critic of the superpower arms race, and has written many articles on arms control and the dangers of nuclear war. Thus it is a disappointment that the greatest interest in these powerful infrared lasers has been for the "Star Wars" strategic defense system.

About 1980, Polanyi decided that the study of infrared emissions was essentially completed, and he looked for a new challenge. One of his current fields of work involves the study of chemistry on solid surfaces. In the gas phase, molecules strike each other at an infinite number of different angles. It would make chemical synthesis much more predictable and understandable if molecules could be held somehow at a particular orientation.

Over the past two years, Polanyi's research group has devised a novel way for doing this by aligning molecules on the surface of a crystal. The group has christened this the SAP technique officially standing for Surface Aligned Photoreaction. However, as Polanyi has said, they chose the name SAP because they had been turned down for funding so often and been laughed at so thoroughly. In fact it was the Venture Research Unit of the British Petroleum company that has been a major funding source for this new research.

Polanyi believes that life itself may have started as molecules building up on mineral surfaces in a similar way to SAP. He bemoans the lack of financial support in this country for basic research. In his case, he has studied the reactions of molecules to obtain a better understanding of the physical world. Polanyi remarks: "To the people who asked 'What is it for?' I had to say 'I haven't any idea but if we are lucky enough to gain some understanding, I can't imagine that it will not be useful to somebody.'"

18. The reaction between the iodide and peroxydisulfate ion in aqueous solution

$$2\,I^-_{(aq)} + S_2O_8^{2-}{}_{(aq)} \longrightarrow I_{2\,(aq)} + 2\,SO_4^{2-}{}_{(aq)}$$

was studied by following the rate of production of iodine for different initial concentrations of the reactants.

Trial	$[I^-]$ (mol·L^{-1})	$[S_2O_8^{2-}]$ (mol·L^{-1})	Initial Rate of Formation of I_2 (mol·L^{-1}·s^{-1})
1	0.04	0.04	6.25×10^{-6}
2	0.08	0.04	12.5×10^{-6}
3	0.04	0.08	12.5×10^{-6}

What is the relationship between the rate of production of iodine and the concentrations of the reactants?

19. For the general reaction

$$A + B \longrightarrow \text{products}$$

the following data were obtained:

Trial	[A] $(\text{mol}\cdot\text{L}^{-1})$	[B] $(\text{mol}\cdot\text{L}^{-1})$	Initial Rate of Formation of Products $(\text{mol}\cdot\text{L}^{-1}\cdot\text{s}^{-1})$
1	0.10	0.20	3.0×10^{-2}
2	0.20	0.20	6.0×10^{-2}
3	0.20	0.30	6.0×10^{-2}

a) Determine the order of the reaction with respect to both A and B.
b) Write the rate law for the reaction.
c) Calculate k, the rate constant, for the reaction.

20. For the general reaction

$$A + B \longrightarrow \text{products}$$

the following data were obtained:

Trial	[A] $(\text{mol}\cdot\text{L}^{-1})$	[B] $(\text{mol}\cdot\text{L}^{-1})$	Initial Rate of Formation of Products $(\text{mol}\cdot\text{L}^{-1}\cdot\text{s}^{-1})$
1	0.10	0.10	4.0×10^{-2}
2	0.20	0.20	1.6×10^{-1}
3	0.20	0.10	8.0×10^{-2}

a) Write the rate law for the reaction.
b) What is the order of the reaction?
c) Calculate k, the rate constant, for the reaction.

Reaction Mechanisms

6.9

We can classify reactions as being either simple or complex. A **complex reaction** consists of a number of steps. Each of these steps involves one collision and is known as an **elementary step**. A **simple reaction**, on the other hand, consists of one elementary step. The step or series of steps that make up a reaction is known as the **mechanism** of that reaction. The mechanism can be considered to be the pathway that the reaction takes.

Figure 6.36

A space-filling model of dinitrogen dioxide, a molecule that is believed to be an intermediate in the reaction between nitrogen monoxide and oxygen. This molecule is known to exist at low temperatures.

Nitrogen monoxide is a pollutant in automobile exhaust. The mechanism whereby nitrogen monoxide reacts with oxygen to form nitrogen dioxide (another pollutant) is believed to consist of the following elementary steps,

$$\text{Step (1)} \quad 2\ NO \longrightarrow N_2O_2$$
$$\text{Step (2)} \quad N_2O_2 + O_2 \longrightarrow 2\ NO_2$$

If we add these two steps we get

$$2\ NO + N_2O_2 + O_2 \longrightarrow N_2O_2 + 2\ NO_2$$

leading to the overall reaction equation:

$$2\ NO_{(g)} + O_{2\,(g)} \longrightarrow 2\ NO_{2\,(g)}$$

The dinitrogen dioxide (N_2O_2) cancels out and does not appear as part of the overall equation. It is produced in the first elementary step and used up in the second. Species such as dinitrogen dioxide are known as **reaction intermediates**. They can be atoms, molecules, or ions. They are very short-lived and are usually difficult, although not impossible, to isolate (Figure 6.36).

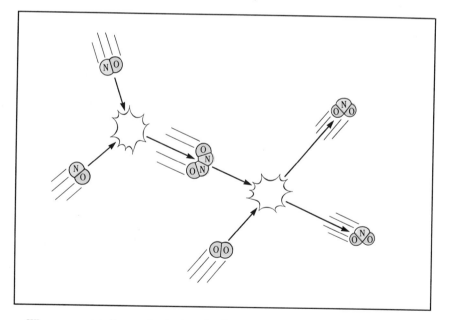

Figure 6.37

A molecular schematic of the reaction between nitrogen monoxide and oxygen.

We can not tell conclusively whether a reaction is simple or complex just by looking at the overall reaction equation. Nor can we determine a mechanism from the relative mole ratios of the balanced equation. Experimentally-determined relationships between rate and reactant concentration must be used to predict possible reaction mechanisms.

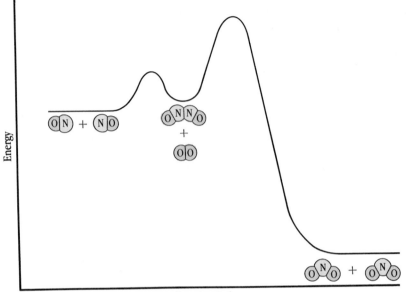

Figure 6.38

An energy-level diagram for the reaction of nitrogen monoxide with oxygen.

Molecularity

We use the term **molecularity** to indicate the number of reactant molecules (or ions or atoms) involved in an *elementary step*. This also indicates the number of species forming the activated complex.

The reaction by which ozone gas (trioxygen) is converted to oxygen gas (dioxygen) has the following overall reaction equation,

$$2\ O_{3\,(g)} \longrightarrow 3\ O_{2(g)}$$

but kinetic studies indicate that this reaction probably occurs in two different elementary steps:

Step (1) $\quad O_3 \longrightarrow O_2 + O$

Step (2) $\quad O_3 + O \longrightarrow 2\ O_2$

In the first step, a trioxygen molecule with sufficient energy breaks up into a dioxygen molecule and an oxygen atom. Since only one reactant molecule (O_3) is involved, the molecularity of this step is one. In the second step there are two reactant species, an oxygen atom and a trioxygen molecule. The molecularity therefore is two. Another way of saying this is that Step 1 is unimolecular and Step 2 is bimolecular.

Originally the reaction of hydrogen and iodine was thought to be a bimolecular reaction involving a collision of one hydrogen molecule and one iodine molecule.

$$H_{2\,(g)} + I_{2\,(g)} \longrightarrow 2\ HI_{(g)}$$

In the early 1960s a two-step mechanism was proposed by both Henry Eyring and the Soviet chemist Nikolai Semenov. The first step of this mechanism was considered to be the dissociation of the iodine molecule into iodine atoms, the reaction intermediate. The second step was originally thought to involve a three-body collision — two iodine atoms colliding with a hydrogen molecule. More recent research on this reaction favours a three-step mechanism:

$$\text{Step (1)} \quad I_2 \xrightarrow[\text{light}]{\text{ultraviolet}} I + I$$

$$\text{Step (2)} \quad I + H_2 \longrightarrow H_2I$$

$$\text{Step (3)} \quad H_2I + I \longrightarrow 2\,HI$$

Ultraviolet light is known to increase the dissociation of iodine molecules (Step 1) and, in turn, to increase the concentration of the reaction intermediate, the iodine atom. Although both mechanisms account for the effect of irradiation, the three-step mechanism does not require a three-body collision.

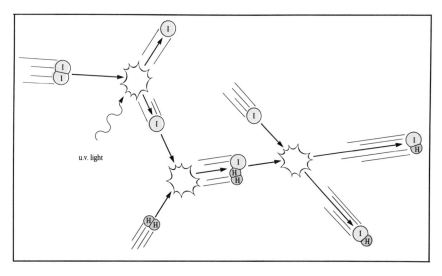

Figure 6.39

A molecular schematic for the currently-accepted mechanism for the reaction between hydrogen and iodine.

EXAMPLE　　6.6　Nitrogen monoxide reacts with hydrogen gas to produce nitrogen gas and water vapour. The mechanism is believed to be:

$$\text{Step (1)} \quad 2\,NO \longrightarrow N_2O_2$$

$$\text{Step (2)} \quad N_2O_2 + H_2 \longrightarrow N_2O + H_2O$$

$$\text{Step (3)} \quad N_2O + H_2 \longrightarrow N_2 + H_2O$$

For this reaction find the following:
a) the overall balanced equation
b) any reaction intermediates
c) the molecularity of each elementary step

SOLUTION   a) The overall equation is obtained by adding the three elementary reaction steps

$$2\,NO + N_2O_2 + N_2O + 2\,H_2 \longrightarrow N_2O_2 + N_2O + N_2 + 2\,H_2O$$

and cancelling the species appearing on both sides.

$$2\,NO + 2\,H_2 \longrightarrow N_2 + 2\,H_2O$$

b) Both N_2O_2 and N_2O are reaction intermediates.

c) Each step is bimolecular.

The Rate-determining Step

Every reaction mechanism has a **rate-determining step**. This is the slowest step in the reaction. If the first elementary step of the mechanism is the rate-determining step, then we can say that the overall reaction rate depends on this initial step and thus on the concentrations of the species involved in this step. Any subsequent step is faster and does not affect the overall rate.

We can use the analogy of washing the dishes to help explain how the rate-determining step governs the whole reaction. Assume that doing the dishes is a two-step process:

Step (1)   (washing) dirty dishes $\longrightarrow$ clean wet dishes
Step (2)   (drying) clean wet dishes $\longrightarrow$ clean dry dishes

The dirty dishes represent the reactants; the clean wet dishes are analogous to a reaction intermediate; and, the clean dry dishes are the product. If the person washing the dishes is very slow, then the drier will have no trouble keeping up and in fact will probably be waiting for clean wet dishes. In this case the reaction intermediate will be short-lived and the overall speed of doing the dishes will depend on just how slowly the washer performs the first task (Figure 6.40a). But if the person washing the dishes is speedy and the drier is slow, the clean wet dishes accumulate and the drying step is the rate-determining one (Figure 6.40b).

Figure 6.40
Energy level diagrams for doing the dishes.
a) The slow (rate-determining) step is the washing.
b) The slow (rate-determining) step is the drying.

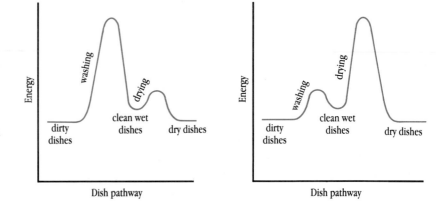

Kinetics experiments on the reaction of nitrogen dioxide with carbon monoxide show that the rate of this reaction depends on the concentration of the nitrogen dioxide to the power of two. Further experimental evidence indicates the existence of nitrogen trioxide as a reaction intermediate. A proposed mechanism for this reaction would then be the following:

Step (1) $\quad NO_2 + NO_2 \longrightarrow NO_3 + NO \qquad$ slow

Step (2) $\quad NO_3 + CO \longrightarrow NO_2 + CO_2 \qquad$ fast

Since two molecules of nitrogen dioxide are involved in the rate-determining step the rate law is

$$Rate = k[NO_2]^2$$

Addition of the two steps, with appropriate cancellations, gives the overall equation:

$$NO_{2\,(g)} + CO_{(g)} \longrightarrow NO_{(g)} + CO_{2\,(g)}$$

Chain Reactions

A mechanism that involves a step (or steps) in which a reaction intermediate is continually regenerated is known as a **chain reaction**. When hydrogen and chlorine gases are mixed at room temperature, the reaction is very slow. However, if the reaction mixture is exposed to high-energy light (such as ultraviolet light), there is a very rapid reaction. The light supplies the energy necessary to break the chlorine molecule into chlorine atoms.

$$Cl_2 \xrightarrow[\text{light}]{\text{ultraviolet}} Cl + Cl \qquad \text{chain initiation}$$

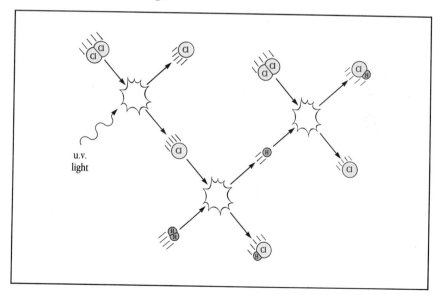

Figure 6.41

The initiation and chain propogation steps in the reaction between hydrogen and chlorine.

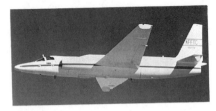

Figure 6.42
An ER-2 plane (the former U-2 'spy' plane) is now used to fly to an altitude of 21 km to probe the chemistry of the ozone layer.

This is referred to as the **chain initiation** step; the chlorine atoms produced are extremely reactive intermediates and attack the hydrogen molecule, splitting off a hydrogen atom. Each hydrogen atom can, in turn, attack another chlorine molecule generating another chlorine atom. The latter two steps are known as **chain propagation** steps.

$$\left.\begin{array}{l} Cl + H_2 \longrightarrow HCl + H \\ H + Cl_2 \longrightarrow HCl + Cl \end{array}\right\} \text{chain propagation}$$

Chain propagation continues until all the reactant is used up or until the intermediates combine with themselves in **chain termination** steps. With the reaction intermediates being consumed the chain reaction cannot continue.

$$\left.\begin{array}{l} Cl + Cl \longrightarrow Cl_2 \\ H + H \longrightarrow H_2 \\ H + Cl \longrightarrow HCl \end{array}\right\} \text{chain termination}$$

Mechanisms of Catalyzed Reactions

One of the best studied examples of catalyzed mechanism is that involving the destruction of the ozone layer.

In the upper atmosphere, much of the ultraviolet light from the sun is absorbed by molecules of ozone (trioxygen). The molecules dissociate to produce dioxygen molecules and oxygen atoms. (At the high altitudes the pressure is very low and atomic oxygen can exist for measurable lengths of time.)

$$O_3 \xrightarrow[\text{light}]{\text{ultraviolet}} O_2 + O$$

The oxygen atoms will then recombine with the dioxygen molecules to produce trioxygen.

$$O_2 + O \longrightarrow O_3$$

A catalyst is provided by chlorine-containing aerosol propellants, which rise slowly into the upper atmosphere. There, the propellants dissociate to produce free chlorine atoms. These chlorine atoms undergo the following two-step reaction with trioxygen.

$$\begin{array}{l} Cl + O_3 \longrightarrow ClO + O_2 \\ ClO + O_3 \longrightarrow Cl + 2\,O_2 \end{array}$$

The overall equation is

$$2\,O_{3\,(g)} \longrightarrow 3\,O_{2\,(g)}$$

In this reaction chlorine atoms are acting as a catalyst and chlorine monoxide, ClO, is an intermediate. This pathway, which has a low activation energy, results in a rapid decomposition of the trioxygen. As a result, the concentration of the trioxygen (ozone) is continually diminished.

Figure 6.43
The Nimbus 7 satellite monitors the stratospheric ozone concentrations.

The Chlorofluorocarbon Problem

When they were first prepared and studied, the chlorofluorocarbons (CFCs) appeared to be the answer to concerns about chemical toxicity. This family of compounds, having a carbon chain bonded to chlorine and fluorine atoms, were stable, non-toxic, and nonflammable. Since 1946 the compounds have been used in refrigeration and air conditioning systems, as aerosol propellants, as the gas in plastic foam materials (such as egg and hamburger containers), as degreasing agents of computer circuit boards, and in fire extinguishers for electrical systems.

It was not until June 1974 that it was realized that the very stability of these compounds was a problem. The chlorofluorocarbons (and bromofluorocarbons) drifted intact into the upper layers of the atmosphere where the chlorine and bromine atoms were severed from the molecules by ultraviolet radiation. The chlorine and bromine atoms would then react with the ozone.

The destruction of a proportion of the ozone layer by CFCs would lead to an increase in ultraviolet light reaching the earth's surface and consequently an increase in skin cancer from this high-energy radiation. Once the danger was recognized, steps were taken to deal with the crisis. In 1978 both Canada and the U.S. banned the use of CFCs in aerosols. However, CFCs are an international problem, and it was not until 1985 that the Vienna Convention for the Protection of the Ozone Layer was set up as part of the United Nations Environment Program. So far 28 nations have signed the convention, including Canada, the United States, and the Soviet Union. Future meetings of the signatories will propose cutbacks in production of CFCs. The Canadian proposal is that production of CFCs should be limited in each country according to a formula including gross national product and total population.

There is a chemical as well as a political aspect to the crisis. The crucial problem for chemists is to design chemical compounds that can be used as substitutes. CFC 134a is a recently developed chlorofluorocarbon that decomposes before it reaches the upper atmosphere. It could replace CFC 12 in automobile air conditioning systems. (Leaky air conditioners are a major source of released CFCs).

TABLE 6.5 *The Most Important Chlorofluorocarbons*

Trade Name	Formula	Uses
CFC 11	$CFCl_3$	aerosols, foams, air conditioning
CFC 12	CF_2Cl_2	aerosols, foams, air conditioning
CFC 113	$C_2F_3Cl_3$	cleaning electronic components
Halon 1211	CF_2ClBr	fire extinguisher
Halon 1301	CF_3Br	fire extinguisher
Halon 2402	$C_2F_4Br_2$	fire extinguisher
Halothan	C_2HF_3ClBr	inhalation anesthetic

But finding replacements for other CFCs is not so easy. All current possible substitutes for the cleaning of electronic circuits are known or suspected carcinogens. Thus workers would be exposed to much greater health risks. Traditional aerosol propellants have included dinitrogen oxide, which was sometimes used as an illegal intoxicant, and propane and butane, both of which are highly flammable. Several deaths and many serious burns have resulted from the accidental ignition of the vapour from spray cans containing propane or butane. A tremendous amount of preparative and reaction chemistry will need to be done to find safe substitutes for each of the chlorofluorocarbons.

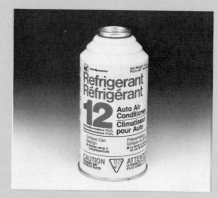

Figure 6.44
The chlorofluorocarbon Freon-12 is used in automobile air conditioners.

QUESTIONS

21. The following mechanism has been proposed for the reaction between iodobutane and chloride ion:

    Step (1) $C_4H_9I \longrightarrow C_4H_9^+ + I^-$

    Step (2) $C_4H_9^+ + Cl^- \longrightarrow C_4H_9Cl$

    a) Give the overall equation for the reaction.
    b) Identify any reaction intermediates.
    c) Determine the molecularity of each of the elementary steps.

22. The following mechanism has been proposed for the reaction between nitrogen dioxide and methane (CH_4):

    Step (1) $NO_2 + NO_2 \longrightarrow NO_3 + NO$

    Step (2) $NO_3 + CH_4 \longrightarrow HNO_3 + CH_3$

    Step (3) $CH_3 + NO_2 \longrightarrow CH_3NO_2$

    Answer parts a), b), and c) of Question 21 using this data.

23. The following mechanism has been proposed for the reaction between bromine and methane. Identify each step as chain initiation, chain propagation, or chain termination.

    Step (1) $Br_2 \longrightarrow Br + Br$

    Step (2) $Br + CH_4 \longrightarrow CH_3 + HBr$

    Step (3) $CH_3 + Br_2 \longrightarrow CH_3Br + Br$

    Step (4) $Br + Br \longrightarrow Br_2$

24. The following mechanism has been proposed for the decomposition of hydrogen peroxide, H_2O_2, in the presence of iodide ions:

    Step (1) $H_2O_2 + I^- \longrightarrow H_2O + IO^-$

    Step (2) $IO^- + H_2O_2 \longrightarrow H_2O + O_2 + I^-$

    Overall reaction $2\,H_2O_{2\,(aq)} \longrightarrow 2\,H_2O_{(\ell)} + O_{2\,(g)}$

    a) What is the catalyst in this mechanism?
    b) What is the reaction intermediate in this mechanism?

Enzymes: Biological Catalysis

6.10 The many chemical reactions that take place in living cells are catalyzed by large molecules known as **enzymes**. Enzymes are extremely efficient catalysts, increasing the rate of a reaction by factors varying from 10^6 to 10^{12}. For example, the reaction of carbon dioxide with water is necessary for the transfer of carbon dioxide from the tissues into the blood:

$$CO_{2\,(g)} + H_2O_{(\ell)} \longrightarrow H_2CO_{3\,(aq)}$$

One molecule of the enzyme carbonic anhydrase, that catalyzes this reaction, can convert 10^5 molecules of carbon dioxide to carbonic acid in one second. The rate of the uncatalyzed reaction is 10^7 times slower. Enzymes are protein molecules: very long chains of amino acids, coiled and folded

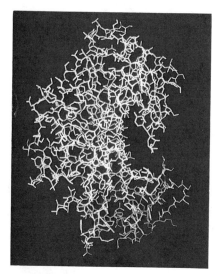

Figure 6.45
A computer-generated image of the molecular structure of the enzyme pepsin. The chains of atoms are arranged in a specific configuration.

Figure 6.46
a) Papaya, kiwi fruit, and pineapple contain the enzyme papain.

b) Meat tenderizer contains the enzyme papain, which catalyzes the breakdown of the fibrous protein in meat, making it less tough.

into specific configurations. More than 1500 enzymes are known today and many of these have been isolated and purified Their structures have been determined by a combination of chemical and instrumental analysis. X-ray crystallography, for example, has been used extensively in this process.

The catalytic ability of an enzyme is dependent on a well-defined region of the enzyme molecule known as the **active site**. For catalysis to occur, a reactant molecule must fit into the active site, which is usually a groove or fold in the surface structure of the enzyme. This explains why each enzyme is specific for catalyzing one specific reaction or group of reactions. Only the particular reactant molecule for the enzyme matches the shape of the active site, rather like a lock and its corresponding key (Figure 6.47). Unlike locks and keys, however, neither active sites nor reactants are rigid structures. It is believed that the active site adjusts its shape as the two fit together.

Many enzymes require the presence of another species, known as a **coenzyme**, to function effectively. Vitamins are a well-known class of coenzymes. A balanced diet with sufficient vitamin content is therefore necessary to keep the body's enzymes working efficiently.

Figure 6.47
a) The reactant molecule fits the active site of the enzyme in the same way a key fits a lock.

b) Bonds are both made and broken while the reactant is held at the active site.

c) A product molecule breaks away from the enzyme.

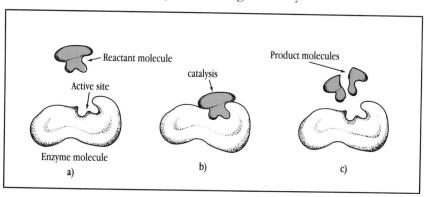

Enzyme Kinetics and Alcohol

The mathematical treatment of reactions catalyzed by enzymes is complex. We can show a simplified version of these enzyme kinetics by graphing the rate of the enzyme-catalyzed reaction against the concentration of the reactant molecule, known as the substrate (Figure 6.48). Initially, an enzyme-catalyzed reaction has a rate proportional to the concentration of the reactant. In other words the reaction is first order. As the concentration of the reactant increases, the rate increases. However, once all the active sites of the enzyme are filled, an increase in the concentration of the substrate does not increase the rate of the reaction. The rate is now independent of concentration and the reaction is said to display zero-order kinetics. We could, of course, increase the reaction rate if we had a means of increasing the amount of enzyme in the reaction, but because as we are discussing reactions occurring in living cells, this is not a possible option.

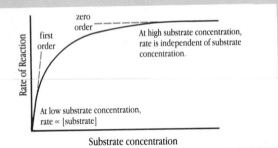

Figure 6.48

The effect of changing substrate concentration on the reaction rate of an enzyme-catalyzed reaction.

We can apply the above facts to one of Canada's serious social problems. The enzyme involved in the first step of the series of reactions necessary to metabolize alcohol (ethanol) is *alcohol dehydrogenase*. At first, with increasing concentration of alcohol, the rate of alcohol metabolism increases. However, the active sites in the alcohol dehydrogenase are soon fully occupied. At this point the rate of metabolism remains constant and further alcohol consumption leads only to increased blood alcohol content. Nothing can increase the rate of alcohol metabolism — not hot coffee, not cold showers, not fresh air, not walking or running. We are dealing with zero-order kinetics. There is also no way to increase the amount of the enzyme alcohol dehydrogenase in our cells.

Larger people often have a greater overall amount of alcohol dehydrogenase in their bodies, and are thus able to consume more alcohol before they reach the active-site saturation point. It is also thought that there is some genetic variation in the concentration of this enzyme in cells of different individuals. Consequently, the same level of alcohol consumption in two people of the same size may give very different readings for blood alcohol content.

Figure 6.49

'Gin Lane' by William Hogarth depicts alcoholism in 18th-century England. Alcoholism has been a serious problem throughout history.

The effect of a poison is often due to a reaction with an enzyme. The molecules of the poison bond with the enzyme and prevent it from carrying out its normal catalytic role. When the enzyme is tied up in this way, it is said to be **inhibited**. Cyanide inhibits one of the enzymes in the series of reactions that allows the cell to utilize oxygen. We could think of cyanide poisoning therefore as a form of chemical suffocation. Malathion is an organophosphate insecticide that acts as a poison in the central nervous system. It inhibits acetylcholine esterase, an enzyme necessary for the transmission of nerve impulses.

Enzyme inhibition is sometimes the basis for medical treatment, especially in chemotherapy. As a twelve-year-old cancer victim, Steve Fonyo, was treated with the drug methotrexate. This compound inhibits dihydrofolate reductase, an enzyme that is involved in many biochemical pathways including the synthesis of DNA (deoxyribonucleic acid). Because cancer cells grow faster than normal, the methotrexate affects the cancer cells more severely and thus prevents the spread of cancer to other organs. The success of this drug helped stop the cancer of spread in Fonyo, who was then able to complete an 8000 km run across Canada on an artificial leg.

A number of inherited diseases are due to the lack of a particular enzyme. Such inborn errors of metabolism are called metabolic deficiency diseases. *Phenylketonuria* (PKU) is a common disorder of this type, affecting about one in every ten thousand newborn. The disease is caused by a deficiency in one of the enzymes necessary to breakdown phenylalanine, an amino acid found in numerous proteins. The baby is normal at birth, but once feeding is started, the unmetabolized phenylalanine builds up in all the body fluids. The net result of untreated PKU is severe mental retardation. Treatment for PKU victims consists of a diet low in phenylalanine, started within a few weeks after birth. In most parts of Canada, newborn babies are tested for PKU by testing the level of phenylalanine the blood.

Summary

- The rate of a chemical reaction can be followed by measuring changes in the physical properties of the species involved.

- Reaction rate depends on a number of factors including concentration and form of the reactants, phase and temperature of the reaction, agitation of the reaction solution, and presence of visible or ultraviolet light.

- Collision theory explains reaction rates in terms of molecular collisions.

- Transition state theory explains a reaction in terms of an intermediate product called the activated complex.

- Increased temperature increases the reaction rate. At higher temperatures more molecules are involved in collisions which have enough energy to overcome the activation energy barrier.

- Although the reaction rate is normally dependent in some way on the concentration of the reactants, the actual relationship must be determined by experiment; it cannot be deduced from the balanced reaction equation.

- A reaction mechanism is the series of elementary steps making up the reaction, with the slowest step being the rate-determining step.

- A catalyst speeds up the reaction by providing an alternate pathway having a lower activation energy.

KEY WORDS

activated complex	hydrogenation
activation energy	inhibitor
active site	initial rate
catalyst	kinetics
chain initiation	Maxwell-Boltzmann distribution
chain propagation	mechanism
chain reaction	molecularity
chain termination	order
coenzyme	rate constant
collision theory	rate-determining step
complex reaction	rate law
contact process	reaction pathway
elementary step	reaction intermediate
energy diagram	reaction rate
enzyme	second-order reaction
first-order reaction	simple reaction
heterogeneous catalysis	transition state
homogeneous catalysis	zero-order reaction

ANSWERS TO SECTION QUESTIONS

1. Only when the product and reactant are of equal molar quantities and when the rate is measured over the same time period.

2. $0.13 \ mol \cdot L^{-1} \cdot min^{-1}$

3. a) $3.3 \times 10^{-4} \ mol \cdot L^{-1} \cdot min^{-1}$
   b) $3.3 \times 10^{-4} \ mol \cdot L^{-1} \cdot min^{-1}$

4. $0.075 \ mol \cdot L^{-1} \cdot s^{-1}$

5. a) $6.8 \times 10^{-2} \ mol \cdot L^{-1} \cdot s^{-1}$
   b) $4.5 \times 10^{-2} \ mol \cdot L^{-1} \cdot s^{-1}$
   c) $5.6 \times 10^{-2} \ mol \cdot L^{-1} \cdot s^{-1}$

6. The loss of colour of the bromine solution; increase in solution acidity; increase in the pressure or volume of the carbon dioxide gas.

7. a) increase in gas volume or pressure

   b) loss of the purple colour of gaseous iodine

   c) decrease in acidity of the solution; increase in the brown-red colour of the solution due to increasing bromine concentration; decrease in conductivity of the solution

   d) decrease in the acidity of the solution; decrease in the conductivity of the solution; loss of the pink colour as the permanganate ion is consumed

8. The second reaction is three times faster than the first.

9. a) decrease

   b) decrease

   c) increase

10. a); ions in aqueous solutions react almost instantaneously.

11. heating the toffee mixture; stirring continuously; using very finely-ground sugar

12. The collision may not have the correct orientation or the necessary energy.

13. The difference in a reaction between the initial energy of the reactants and energy maximum, called the transition state.

14. a)

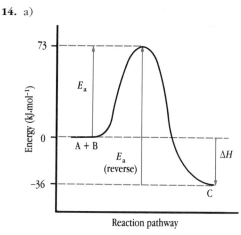

   b) $109 \, \text{kJ} \cdot \text{mol}^{-1}$

15. a) No effect.

   b) No effect.

   c) A new activated complex of lower energy is formed.

16. a) $H^+_{(aq)}$

   b) homogeneous

17. c) You cannot determine the relationship between rate and reactant concentration from the reaction equation alone. You need experimental data.

18. The rate depends on both I^- and $S_2O_8^-$. Rate $= k[I^-][S_2O_8^{2-}]$

19. a) The reaction is first order with respect to A and zero order with respect to B.
  b) Rate = $k[A]$
  c) $k = 3.0 \times 10^{-1}\text{s}^{-1}$

20. a) The reaction is first order with respect to both A and B.
  b) second order
  c) $k = 4.0\,\text{L·mol}^{-1}\text{·s}^{-1}$

21. a) $C_4H_9I + Cl^- \longrightarrow C_4H_9Cl + I^-$
  b) $C_4H_9^+$
  c) The first step is unimolecular; the second is bimolecular.

22. a) $3\,NO_2 + CH_4 \longrightarrow NO + CH_3NO_2 + HNO_3$
  b) NO_3 and CH_3 are reaction intermediates.
  c) All three elementary steps are bimolecular.

23. Step (1) chain initiation
  Step (2) chain propagation
  Step (3) chain propagation
  Step (4) chain termination

24. a) I^-
  b) IO^-

COMPREHENSION QUESTIONS

1. What is the meant by the term rate of reaction?

2. For the following reaction, would the rate of loss of oxygen be the same as the rate of loss of propane (C_3H_8)? Explain your answer.

$$C_3H_{8\,(g)} + 5\,O_{2\,(g)} \longrightarrow 3\,CO_{2\,(g)} + 4\,H_2O_{(\ell)}$$

3. What physical property could be measured to follow the rate of each of the following reactions?
  a) $Cu_{(s)} + 2\,AgNO_{3\,(aq)} \longrightarrow 2\,Ag_{(s)} + Cu(NO_3)_{2\,(aq)}$
  b) $PCl_{3\,(g)} + Cl_{2\,(g)} \longrightarrow PCl_{5\,(g)}$
  c) $2\,H_2O_{2\,(aq)} \longrightarrow 2\,H_2O_{(\ell)} + O_{2\,(g)}$
  d) $CH_3Br_{(aq)} + H_2O_{(\ell)} \longrightarrow CH_3OH_{(aq)} + H^+_{(aq)} + Br^-_{(aq)}$

4. What are three factors affecting the rate of a chemical reaction?

5. Which of the following are likely to be very rapid reactions? Why?
  a) $Zn^{2+}_{(aq)} + S^{2-}_{(aq)} \longrightarrow ZnS_{(aq)}$
  b) $H_2SO_{4\,(aq)} + 2\,NaOH_{(aq)} \longrightarrow Na_2SO_{4\,(aq)} + 2\,H_2O_{(\ell)}$
  c) $Zn_{(s)} + S_{(s)} \longrightarrow ZnS_{(s)}$

6. Explain the term activated complex.

7. Why does an increase in temperature increase the rate of a reaction?

8. The following reaction is extremely slow at room temperatures, but with even a very small spark proceeds with explosive violence.

$$2 H_{2(g)} + O_{2(g)} \longrightarrow 2 H_2O_{(g)}$$

Explain this observation.

9. Although methane, the main component of natural gas, burns readily in oxygen

$$CH_{4(g)} + 2 O_{2(g)} \longrightarrow CO_{2(g)} + 2 H_2O_{(\ell)}$$

this reaction is so slow at room temperature that it is not detectable. Explain this observation.

10. Briefly describe the collision theory of reaction rates.

11. Using collision theory explain why aqueous reactions involving simple ions are usually much faster than those involving complex molecules.

12. What does the highest point in an energy diagram of a reaction represent?

13. Distinguish between the activation energy of a reaction and the activated complex in a reaction.

14. Distinguish between homogeneous catalysis and heterogeneous catalysis.

15. Why is the rate of a reaction fastest at the beginning of the reaction?

16. The following is the reaction representing the thermal decomposition of acetaldehyde:

$$CH_3CHO_{(g)} \longrightarrow CH_{4(g)} + CO_{(g)}$$

Which of these statements are true?
a) The rate of the reaction is proportional to $[CH_3CHO]$.
b) The rate of the reaction is proportional to $[CH_3CHO]^2$.
c) The rate of the reaction cannot be determined from the equation.

17. What is the order of a chemical reaction?

18. How can the order of a reaction be determined?

19. Distinguish between reaction rate and reaction rate constant.

20. Would the reaction rate constant change if
a) the concentration of the reactant increased?
b) the pressure of a gaseous reactant increased?
c) the temperature increased?
Explain your answers.

21. What is the order of the reactions with the following rate laws?
a) Rate = $k[A][B]$
b) Rate = $k[B]^2$
c) Rate = $k[A][B]^2$

22. What is an elementary reaction?

23. Distinguish between an elementary reaction and a reaction mechanism.

24. What is a unimolecular reaction step?

25. Which of the following elementary reactions are bimolecular?
   a) $A + A \longrightarrow A{-}A$
   b) $A + 2\,B \longrightarrow AB$
   c) $A + B \longrightarrow AB$
   d) $A \longrightarrow A$

26. Why are trimolecular reactions rare?

27. Which step in a mechanism controls the rate of the reaction?

28. What is a chain reaction?

29. Explain one difference between a catalyst and a reaction intermediate.

PROBLEMS *Average Rate of a Chemical Reaction*

30. At high temperatures ($250\,°C$) butadiene gas is converted to cyclobutene gas.

$$CH_2{=}CH{-}CH{=}CH_{2\,(g)} \longrightarrow \begin{array}{c} CH = CH \\ | \qquad | \\ CH_2{-}CH_2 \end{array}^{(g)}$$

In one kinetics experiment the following data were obtained.

Time (s)	Concentration of butadiene ($mol \cdot L^{-1}$)
190	0.0162
600	0.0148
1245	0.0129
2180	0.0110

Calculate the average rate of loss of butadiene during these time periods:
   a) between 190 and 600 seconds
   b) between 190 and 2180 seconds

31. The rate of appearance of I_2 in aqueous solution, in the reaction of I^- ion with hydrogen peroxide, was found to be 3.7×10^{-5} $mol \cdot L^{-1} \cdot s^{-1}$ over a time interval.

$$2\,H^+{}_{(aq)} + 2\,I^-{}_{(aq)} + H_2O_{2\,(aq)} \longrightarrow I_{2\,(aq)} + 2\,H_2O_{(\ell)}$$

During the same interval, what was the rate of disappearance of each of the following:
   a) H_2O_2
   b) I^-
   (*Hint*: consider the balanced equation.)

32. Nitrogen dioxide treated with flourine gas produces an explosive compound, nitryl fluoride.

$$2\,NO_{2\,(g)} + F_{2\,(g)} \longrightarrow 2\,NO_2F_{(g)}$$

The rate of loss of nitrogen dioxide in one experiment was found to be $5.40 \times 10^{-4}\,mol \cdot L^{-1} \cdot s^{-1}$. In the same experiment, what would be
a) the rate of loss of F_2
b) the rate of production of NO_2F

Theories of Reaction Rates

33. For the following reactions, activation energies were determined as follows

$$C_2H_{4\,(g)} + H_{2\,(g)} \longrightarrow C_2H_{6\,(g)} \qquad E_a = 180\,kJ \cdot mol^{-1}$$
$$C_2H_{6\,(g)} \longrightarrow C_2H_{4\,(g)} + H_{2\,(g)} \qquad E_a = 317\,kJ \cdot mol^{-1}$$

a) Draw an energy level diagram for this reversible reaction.
b) Calculate ΔH for each reaction.

34. For the following reaction, activation energy is $254\,kJ$

$$C_2H_5Cl_{(\ell)} \longrightarrow C_2H_{4\,(g)} + HCl_{(g)}$$

and for this next reaction, activation energy is $219\,kJ$

$$C_2H_5Br_{(\ell)} \longrightarrow C_2H_{4\,(g)} + HBr_{(g)}$$

Which substance would decompose more rapidly under the reaction conditions and temperature, $C_2H_5Cl_{(\ell)}$ or $C_2H_5Br_{(\ell)}$?

A Quantitative Approach to Reaction Rates

35. In an experiment, the decomposition of phosphine, PH_3, is followed by measuring the change in gas volume.

$$4\,PH_{3\,(g)} \longrightarrow P_{4\,(g)} + 6\,H_{2\,(g)}$$

The results are summarized below.

Initial $[PH_3]$ (mol·L^{-1})	Initial Rate of Decomposition of PH_3 (mol·L^{-1}·s^{-1})
0.0010	2.0×10^{-4}
0.0020	4.0×10^{-4}
0.0030	6.0×10^{-4}

a) Using these data determine the relationship between the rate of decomposition of phosphine and its initial concentration.
b) Calculate the initial rate of decomposition if the initial concentration of phosphine is $0.0050\,mol \cdot L^{-1}$.

36. The initial rate of thermal decomposition of gaseous acetaldehyde

$$CH_3CHO_{(g)} \longrightarrow CH_{4\,(g)} + CO_{(g)}$$

was measured using different initial concentrations of the reactant. The results are summarized below.

Initial $[CH_3CHO]$ $(mol \cdot L^{-1})$	Initial Rate of Decomposition of $CH_3CHO(mol \cdot L^{-1} \cdot s^{-1})$
0.050	0.005
0.10	0.020
0.20	0.081
0.30	0.181

From these data determine the relationship between rate of decomposition and the concentration of acetaldehyde.

37. The initial rate of production of bromine in the gaseous reaction

$$4\,HBr_{(g)} + O_{2\,(g)} \longrightarrow 2\,Br_{2\,(g)} + 2\,H_2O_{(g)}$$

was measured using different initial concentrations of each reactant. The results are summarized below.

Initial $[HBr]$ $(mol \cdot L^{-1})$	Initial $[O_2]$ $(mol \cdot L^{-1})$	Initial Rate of Reaction $(mol \cdot L^{-1} \cdot s^{-1})$
0.010	0.010	0.0042
0.010	0.020	0.0083
0.020	0.020	0.0168
0.030	0.010	0.0126

Determine the relationship between rate of decomposition and the concentration of each reactant.

38. From the data in Question 36, determine the following:
  a) the rate law for the reaction
  b) the order of the reaction
  c) k, the rate constant

39. From the data in Question 37 determine the following:
  a) the rate law for the reaction
  b) the order of the reaction
  c) k, the rate constant

40. Some proportion of photochemical smog, now found in a number of Canadian cities, is thought to be due to the light-initiated breakdown of nitrogen dioxide producing nitrogen monoxide and atomic oxygen. A scientist decides to study the subsequent reaction of nitrogen monoxide with molecular oxygen.

$$2\,NO_{(g)} + O_{2\,(g)} \longrightarrow 2\,NO_{2\,(g)}$$

She finds that when the initial concentration of the oxygen is doubled and that of nitrogen monoxide is held constant, the initial reaction rate doubles. On the basis of this information only, which of the following statements is/are true?

a) The reaction is first order in nitrogen monoxide.
b) The reaction is first order in oxygen.
c) The reaction is first order overall.
d) The reaction is second order overall.
e) More kinetic experiments have to be conducted before the overall order of the reaction can be determined.

Reaction Mechanisms

41. Draw an energy diagram for the reaction A $\longrightarrow$ B using the following information. Label all parts of the curve.

a) The mechanism for the reaction consists of one elementary step.
b) The reaction is endothermic.
c) The activation energy of the reaction has a value of three times the enthalpy value of the reaction.

42. For the following reaction between dinitrogen pentoxide and nitrogen monoxide

$$N_2O_{5\,(g)} + NO_{(g)} \longrightarrow 3\,NO_{2\,(g)}$$

one suggested reaction mechanism is

$$\text{Step (1)} \quad N_2O_5 \longrightarrow NO_2 + NO_3$$
$$\text{Step (2)} \quad NO + NO_3 \longrightarrow 2\,NO_2$$

a) What is the molecularity of each elementary step?
b) Identify the reaction intermediate.
c) If the first step is the slower step, does the overall reaction rate depend on the concentration of N_2O_5 or NO?

43. Propose a mechanism for the gas phase reaction of hydrogen and bromine

$$H_{2\,(g)} + Br_{2\,(g)} \longrightarrow 2\,HBr_{(g)}$$

knowing that this is a chain reaction and that Br, the bromine atom, is a reaction intermediate. Label the steps as initiation, propagation, or termination.

44. Phosgene, $COCl_2$, one of the poison gases used during World War I, is formed from chlorine and carbon monoxide. The mechanism is thought to proceed by:

$$\text{Step (1)} \quad Cl + CO \longrightarrow COCl$$
$$\text{Step (2)} \quad COCl + Cl_2 \longrightarrow COCl_{2(g)} + Cl$$

a) Write the overall reaction equation.
b) Identify any reaction intermediates.
c) Identify any catalysts.
d) What is the molecularity of each of the elementary steps?

MISCELLANEOUS PROBLEMS

45. For the general reaction $A + B \longrightarrow$ products, the following data is obtained

[A] $(mol \cdot L^{-1})$	[B] $(mol \cdot L^{-1})$	Initial Rate $(mol \cdot L^{-1} \cdot s^{-1})$
0.10	0.20	0.030
0.20	0.20	0.120
0.10	0.30	0.031

a) Estimate the order of the reaction with respect to both A and B.
b) Give the rate law for the reaction.
c) Calculate k, the rate constant for the reaction.
d) Calculate the initial rate of the reaction if $[A] = 0.50 \, mol \cdot L^{-1}$, $[B] = 0.050 \, mol \cdot L^{-1}$.

46. Determine the rate constant for the reaction

$$CHCl_{3(g)} + Cl_{2(g)} \longrightarrow CCl_{4(g)} + HCl_{(g)}$$

given the following information:
a) The reaction is first order for both trichloromethane, $CHCl_3$, and chlorine gas.
b) The rate of production of carbon tetrachloride, CCl_4, is $1.25 \times 10^{-2} \, mol \cdot L^{-1} \cdot s^{-1}$ when the concentration of $CHCl_3$ is $0.050 \, mol \cdot L^{-1}$ and of Cl_2 is $0.035 \, mol \cdot L^{-1}$.

47. This first-order gas phase reaction has a rate constant of $5.50 \times 10^{-3} \, s^{-1}$ at $65 \, °C$.

$$2 \, N_2O_{5(g)} \longrightarrow 4 \, NO_{2(g)} + O_{2(g)}$$

Calculate the rate of this reaction at $65 \, °C$ if the concentration of N_2O_5 is $0.67 \, mol \cdot L^{-1}$ at this temperature.

48. Under certain specific conditions, data for the reaction

$$2 H_{2(g)} + O_{2(g)} \longrightarrow 2 H_2O_{(g)}$$

is obtained by measuring the rate of production of water.

$[H_2]$ $(mol \cdot L^{-1})$	$[O_2]$ $(mol \cdot L^{-1})$	Initial Rate of Production of H_2O $(mol \cdot L^{-1} \cdot min^{-1})$
0.020	0.020	0.0036
0.040	0.020	0.0144
0.020	0.040	0.0073

Determine the rate law for the reaction and calculate the value of k, the rate constant.

49. The decomposition of the peroxydisulfate ion, $S_2O_8^{2-}$, in an aqueous solution results in the following data.

Time (min)	$[S_2O_8^{2-}]$ $(mol \cdot L^{-1})$
0	0.100
17	0.050
34	0.025
51	0.012

Draw a graph, plotting time against $[S_2O_8^{2-}]$ and use this graph for the following:
a) Determine the concentration of $S_2O_8^{2-}$ at 46 min.
b) Determine how long it takes for the concentration of $S_2O_8^{2-}$ to drop to 0.035 $mol \cdot L^{-1}$.
c) By measuring the slope of a tangent to the curve at a particular point, it is possible to determine the rate of the reaction at that point. Using this method, determine
   i) the rate of the reaction after 20 min
   ii) the initial rate of the reaction

50. The hydrolysis of a tosylate derivative of a naturally-occurring organic terpene compound, has an initial reaction rate of 6.15×10^{-7} $mol \cdot L^{-1} \cdot s^{-1}$ at 25.0 °C. Assuming that a 10 °C increase in temperature doubles the reaction rate, calculate the initial rate of this same reaction at a temperature of
a) 15.0 °C
b) 55.0 °C

51. Which one of the following sets can be correctly identified with the forward reaction in the energy diagram below.

Set	Reactant	Activated complex	Reaction intermediates	Catalyst(s)	Product(s)
1	A	X	Z	Y	B
2	B	X, Z	Y	—	A
3	A	X, Z	Y	—	B
4	A	X	Y	Z	B
5	A	Z	—	X, Y	A

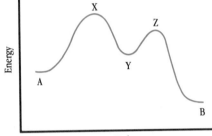

Reaction Pathway

52. Redraw the energy diagram for the reaction in Question 51, labelling the activation energy for both forward and reverse reactions, and indicating the enthalpy change for the forward reaction.

53. Draw an energy level diagram for the reaction

$$X + Y \longrightarrow Z$$

using the following information.
a) The mechanism consists of two elementary steps.
b) The second elementary step is the rate-determining step.
c) The reaction is exothermic.

54. Ozone in the upper atmosphere protects the earth from harmful ultraviolet radiation by absorbing it and re-emitting the energy as radiation of a different wavelength. One threat to the ozone layer is thought to involve nitrogen monoxide from supersonic transport (SST) exhaust. The proposed mechanism involves three steps:

$$\text{Step (1)} \quad O_3 \longrightarrow O_2 + O$$
$$\text{Step (2)} \quad NO + O_3 \longrightarrow NO_2 + O_2$$
$$\text{Step (3)} \quad NO_2 + O \longrightarrow NO + O_2$$

a) What is role of NO_2 in this catalyzed mechanism?
b) By comparing this mechanism with that for the uncatalyzed ozone decomposition mechanism in Section 6.9, explain how nitrogen monoxide acts as a catalyst in this reaction.

SUGGESTED PROJECTS

1. A number of recent publications have reported so-called "holes" in the ozone layer of the atmosphere. Although there is not complete agreement among scientists on whether this is a natural or man-made phenomenon, there seems little doubt that substances such as chlorine atoms and nitrogen monoxide can greatly increase the rate of ozone decomposition. Discuss whether we should be passing laws to restrict the possibility of these catalysts reaching the upper atmosphere.

2. Report on what catalysts are used in the chemical industries in your community or province. Do any of these catalysts have detrimental effects on the environment?

3. Various techniques, such as the addition of preservatives, the lowering of the temperature, and irradiation are used to prevent food from spoiling. What are the advantages and disadvantages of each of these methods? Discover what other methods are available and list their advantages and disadvantages.

4. Do some research on diseases that are considered to be inborn errors of metabolism due to lack of a particular enzyme (a biological catalyst). What are the effects of such missing enzymes? Are there any cures or treatments available?

C H A P T E R **7**

Chemical Equilibrium

So far we have discussed the energy and entropy conditions necessary for spontaneous reactions and the rate at which such reactions proceed. But we have not considered how much or to what extent the reactants are transformed into products. In this chapter we will examine this issue by looking at systems in which no further net reaction is possible. In so doing we will introduce the concept of equilibrium.

Reversible Reactions

7.1   Many chemical reactions proceed in only one direction. They cannot be reversed. For example, if we boil an egg, irreversible chemical changes occur. Also, when solid lead(II) nitrate is heated the white crystals decompose, and nitrogen dioxide and oxygen are given off leaving a different solid, lead(II) oxide. This too is a one-way reaction.

$$2\,Pb(NO_3)_{2\,(s)} \xrightarrow{\Delta} 2\,PbO_{(s)} + 4\,NO_{2\,(g)} + O_{2\,(g)}$$

Figure 7.1

Eggs can be cooked but not uncooked. This is an example of an irreversible change.

We cannot recombine lead(II) oxide, nitrogen dioxide, and oxygen to get the lead(II) nitrate back.

However, there are many chemical reactions that *can* be reversed. Two moles of nitrogen dioxide (a reddish-brown gas) combine to form one mole of dinitrogen tetroxide (a colourless gas).

$$2\ NO_{2\,(g)} \longrightarrow N_2O_{4\,(g)}$$

Dinitrogen tetroxide, in turn, breaks down to form nitrogen dioxide.

$$N_2O_{4\,(g)} \longrightarrow 2\ NO_{2\,(g)}$$

We can write these two equations as one, using a double arrow ($\rightleftharpoons$) to indicate that the reaction is reversible:

$$2\ NO_{2\,(g)} \rightleftharpoons N_2O_{4\,(g)}$$

The reaction caused by the gentle heating of copper(II) sulfate is also reversible. Copper(II) sulfate pentahydrate, $CuSO_4 \cdot 5H_2O$, is a blue solid containing five molecules of water, which are removed by heating. The white anhydrous copper(II) sulfate formed in this way can reabsorb the lost water and revert to the hydrated form.

$$\underset{\text{blue}}{CuSO_4 \cdot 5H_2O_{(s)}} \rightleftharpoons \underset{\text{white}}{CuSO_{4\,(s)}} + 5H_2O_{(\ell)}$$

Most physical changes are reversible. As we warm ice it turns to water. Lowering the temperature turns it to ice again.

$$H_2O_{(s)} \rightleftharpoons H_2O_{(\ell)}$$

Figure 7.2

The conversion of liquid water to ice or steam is a reversible process.

Under certain conditions the forward step in such a process *may proceed at the same rate as the reverse step.* When this happens the process reaches a balanced state and there is no *net* reaction. In this balanced state the system is said to be at **equilibrium**.

QUESTIONS

1. Which of the following processes are reversible?
   a) the evaporation of water
   b) the combustion of coal
   c) the magnetization of an iron bar
2. For each of the following reversible chemical changes, write a balanced equation indicating the two-way nature of the reaction.
   a) Hydrogen gas passed over a heated iron oxide, Fe_3O_4, forms iron and steam.
   b) Hydrogen iodide gas decomposes into its gaseous elements.
   c) Hydrogen and nitrogen gases combine to form ammonia gas, NH_3.

A Simple Equilibrium Experiment

7.2

We will begin our study of equilibrium with an experiment that introduces us to some basic principles. Suppose that we place 1.00 mol of hydrogen gas and 1.00 mol of iodine vapour in a 10 L tank at a temperature of 448 °C. The purple colour of the iodine vapour slowly fades to about one fifth of its original intensity as colourless hydrogen iodide forms.

$$H_{2\,(g)} + I_{2\,(g)} \longrightarrow 2\,HI_{(g)}$$

colourless   purple   colourless

No matter how long we observe the system, the colour never completely disappears. If we analyze the mixture quanitatively, we find 0.22 mol of hydrogen, 0.22 mol of iodine, and 1.56 mol of hydrogen iodide. On the other hand, if we start with 2.00 mol of colourless hydrogen iodide under the same conditions, eventually a pale purple colour develops. Analysis shows that, once again, we have 0.22 mol of hydrogen, 0.22 mol of iodine, and 1.56 mol of hydrogen iodide in the 10 L volume.

Results from the above and similar experiments show that there are two important characteristics of a system at equilibrium:

1. **An equilibrium can be approached from either side of the reaction equation.**
2. **At equilibrium the concentrations of the reactants and products do not change.**

The Concept of Equilibrium

7.3

For every reversible reaction, a point is eventually reached in which the rate of the forward reaction is equal to the rate of the reverse reaction. At this point the system is said to be in **dynamic equilibrium**.

Consider a saturated sugar solution in contact with sugar crystals. All that we see are the sugar crystals in a clear solution. Initially no changes are apparent. But, over time, the shape of the crystals can be observed to change. This is evidence that sugar molecules are dissolving from the crystals into the solution, and, at the same time, that dissolved sugar molecules are settling out onto the crystals. When equilibrium is reached, the rates of these two processes are equal.

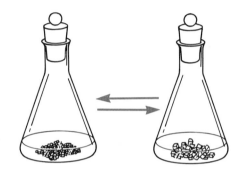

Figure 7.3

If we leave some solid in a saturated solution for a long period of time in a sealed container, we find that the mass of solid is unchanged but the crystals have changed in size. This observation can be explained in terms of a dynamic equilibrium.

For a physical process or a chemical reaction to be at equilibrium it must be part of a **closed system**. In a closed system neither products nor reactants can enter or leave the system. This is in contrast to an **open system**, in which products or reactants are able to enter or leave.

For example, water in an open beaker represents an open system. As the water evaporates, it is free to escape from the beaker. As a result, all the water will evaporate. This system will not reach a state of equilibrium. However, if the beaker is covered, the water vapour molecules are no longer free to escape. Being trapped in the beaker, some of the water vapour molecules will condense, thus returning to the liquid phase. Eventually, the condensation rate and the evaporation rate will be equal and the system will be at equilibrium.

$$H_2O_{(\ell)} \rightleftharpoons H_2O_{(g)}$$

The reaction shown in the following equation will reach an equilibrium, as long as it is carried out in a closed container.

$$NH_4Cl_{(s)} \rightleftharpoons NH_{3\,(g)} + HCl_{(g)}$$

If we remove the top from the container, the ammonia and hydrogen chloride gases will escape. This allows further decomposition of the solid ammonium chloride until eventually it disappears.

Figure 7.4

a) *If ammonium chloride is placed in a closed container, an equilibrium with ammonia gas and hydrogen chloride gas is established.*

b) *In an open container, the solid will eventually disappear.*

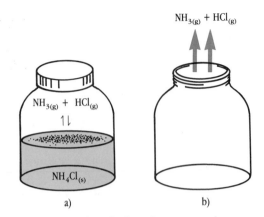

a)   b)

Thus far, we have considered closed systems that are relatively small. Consider now a much larger closed system — that of the earth and its atmosphere. In this larger system, calcium carbonate is in equilibrium with calcium oxide and carbon dioxide.

$$CaCO_{3\,(s)} \rightleftharpoons CaO_{(s)} + CO_{2\,(g)}$$

Fortunately, there is a high enough concentration of carbon dioxide in the atmosphere that marble does not decompose to any measurable extent. If this were not the case, our marble buildings would crumble into calcium oxide powder.

Figure 7.5

The Taj Mahal, in India, is constructed from marble (calcium carbonate). It is the partial pressure of carbon dioxide in the atmosphere that prevents any significant decomposition of the marble.

QUESTIONS

3. A very tiny proportion of water molecules are radioactive due to the presence of the hydrogen isotope, tritium. We can concentrate (enrich) the water containing this isotope. Ice, containing a high proportion of these radioactive molecules, is added to a sample of pure water at 0 °C. After a period of time, a sample of the water is tested for radioactivity. What result would you expect from the following observations?
   a) There was no exchange between the ice and water in the system.
   b) The water-ice system was in dynamic equilibrium.

4. If the system represented by the following equation is found to be at equilibrium at a specific temperature, which of the following statements is true? Explain your answer.

$$H_2O_{(g)} + CO_{(g)} \rightleftharpoons H_{2\,(g)} + CO_{2\,(g)}$$

   a) All species must be present in the same concentration.
   b) The rate of the forward reaction equals the rate of the reverse reaction.
   c) We can measure continual changes in the reactant concentrations.

The Equilibrium Constant

7.4 If we repeat the experiment in Section 7.2 involving hydrogen and iodine gases several times, each time using different initial concentrations of the gases, we obtain the following sets of equilibrium values.

TABLE 7.1	*Equilibrium Concentrations for Several Trials of the Reaction Between Hydrogen and Iodine Gas at 448°C*		
Trial	**[HI]**	**[H₂]**	**[I₂]**

Trial	[HI]	[H$_2$]	[I$_2$]
1	0.156	0.0220	0.0220
2	0.750	0.106	0.106
3	1.00	0.820	0.0242
4	1.00	0.0242	0.820
5	1.56	0.220	0.220

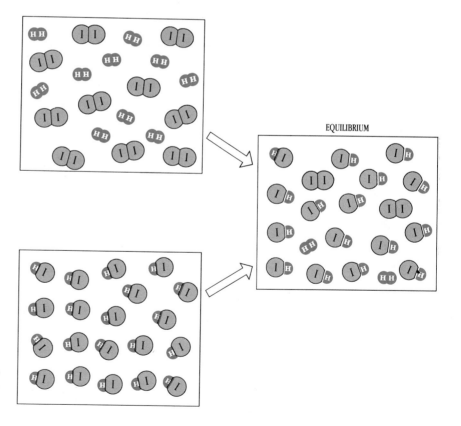

Figure 7.6
Equilibrium between molecules of hydrogen, iodine, and hydrogen iodide. We obtain the same equilibrium proportions if we start with a mixture of hydrogen and iodine, a), or with hydrogen iodide, b).

Is there a pattern that can be found in this data? Similar experimental observations made in 1864 led two Norwegian chemists, Cato Guldberg and Peter Waage, to ask themselves the same question. The outcome of their work was the development of a relationship between the equilibrium concentrations of reactants and products. For our particular reaction

$$H_{2(g)} + I_{2(g)} \rightleftharpoons 2\ HI_{(g)}$$

the relationship is given by the following:

$$\frac{[HI]^2}{[H_2][I_2]}$$

which we can now include in a revised table.

TABLE 7.2	Equilibrium Concentrations and the Relationship Between Them			
Trial	[HI]	[H$_2$]	[I$_2$]	Equilibrium ratio [HI]^2/[H$_2$][I$_2$]
1	0.156	0.0220	0.0220	50.3
2	0.750	0.106	0.106	50.1
3	1.00	0.820	0.0242	50.4
4	1.00	0.0242	0.820	50.4
5	1.56	0.220	0.220	50.3

This constant ratio is called the **equilibrium constant**, K_{eq}. It is dimensionless and its value changes with the temperature of the system. If, for example, we perform the above reaction at 800 °C, instead of at 448 °C, the value of K_{eq} becomes 433.

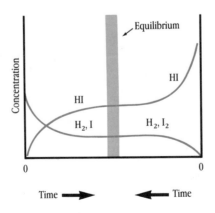

Figure 7.7

A graph of concentration against time shows that the equilibrium concentrations are the same whether we start with the reactants or products.

The General Form of the Equilibrium Expression

For the general reaction

$$a\,A + b\,B \longrightarrow c\,C + d\,D$$

the value for K_{eq} is given by

$$K_{eq} = \frac{[C]^c[D]^d}{[A]^a[B]^b}$$

This is known as the **equilibrium constant expression**, or simply the **equilibrium expression**. Guldberg and Waage proposed the expression from numerous experimental observations. Later, derivations from both thermodynamics and kinetics gave a rigorous theoretical basis for it. By convention, the equilibrium expression is *always* written with the products as the numerator and the reactants as the denominator. Notice also that the exponents in the expression *are the same as the coefficients in the balanced chemical equation*. This is different from the rate equation (Section 6.8), in which the exponents do not necessarily have the same values as the coefficients of the balanced equation.

QUESTIONS

5. Write equilibrium expressions for the following reversible reactions:

a) $2\,NO_{2\,(g)} \rightleftharpoons N_2O_{4\,(g)}$

b) $N_{2\,(g)} + 3\,H_{2\,(g)} \rightleftharpoons 2\,NH_{3\,(g)}$

6. For the reaction,

$$2\,SO_{2\,(g)} + O_{2\,(g)} \rightleftharpoons 2\,SO_{3\,(g)}$$

which of the following is the correct equilibrium expression:

a) $\dfrac{[SO_3]}{[SO_2][O_2]}$ b) $\dfrac{[SO_3]^2}{[SO_2]^2[O_2]}$ c) $\dfrac{[SO_2]^2[O_2]}{[SO_3]^2}$

7. The following table gives some values for reactant and product equilibrium concentrations at 700 K for the Shift reaction, an important method for the commercial production of hydrogen gas:

$$CO_{(g)} + H_2O_{(g)} \rightleftharpoons CO_{2\,(g)} + H_{2\,(g)}$$

All concentrations are in moles per litre.

Trial	$[CO_2]$	$[H_2]$	$[CO]$	$[H_2O]$
1	0.600	0.600	0.266	0.266
2	0.600	0.800	0.330	0.286
3	2.00	2.00	0.887	0.887
4	1.00	1.50	0.450	0.655
5	1.80	2.00	0.590	1.20

Using the data show that the ratio of the concentration of the products to that of the reactants,

$$\frac{[CO_2][H_2]}{[CO][H_2O]}$$

is a constant value at equilibrium.

Equilibrium and Reaction Rates

7.5 Consider the general reversible reaction

$$A \rightleftharpoons B$$

If we assume that this reaction is an elementary reaction, then it occurs by the simple one-step reaction: a molecule of A changes to a molecule of B. From our study of kinetics in the previous chapter, we know that the forward reaction rate is given by

$$\textbf{Rate}_f = k_f[A]$$

and the reverse rate is given by

$$\textbf{Rate}_r = k_r[B]$$

where k_f and k_r are the forward and reverse rate constants. Since at equilibrium the rate of the forward reaction is equal to the rate of the reverse reaction, we have

$$k_f[A] = k_r[B]$$

On rearranging this becomes

$$\frac{k_f}{k_r} = \frac{[B]}{[A]} = K_{eq}$$

Since both k_f and k_r are constants, the ratio k_f/k_r is also a constant. It is, in fact, the equilibrium constant, K_{eq}. It can also be shown that this ratio is valid even if the reaction is not an elementary one.

We should realize that although the forward and reverse rates of reaction are the same at equilibrium, this does *not* mean that the rate constants are equal. If, for example, k_f is very much larger than k_r, then at equilibrium the concentration of A must be much less than the concentration of B.

As we saw in Chapter 6, reaction rates change with temperature. When, for example, the temperature of a reaction is increased, both the forward and the reverse reaction rate constants increase. But, because the activation energies for these forward and reverse reactions are not the same, the rate constants increase differently. At some point the forward reaction rate will again equal the reverse reaction rate and equilibrium

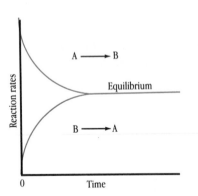

Figure 7.8
As a reaction proceeds, the rate of the forward reaction decreases and the rate of the reverse reaction increases. When the values are equal, equilibrium has been reached.

will be re-established. At this new equilibrium point, the concentrations of reactants and of products will be different from their values at the lower temperature. Hence the equilibrium constant, K_{eq}, will have a different value.

QUESTIONS

8. Consider the physical equilibrium in which ice is in contact with water at $0\,°C$. What is the relationship between the rate that the ice melts and the rate the water freezes?

9. The following reaction is thought to occur in two steps:

$$NO_{2\,(g)} + CO_{(g)} \rightleftharpoons NO_{(g)} + CO_{2\,(g)}$$

   a) What is the relationship between the overall forward and reverse reaction rates at equilibrium?
   b) What is the relationship between the overall forward and reverse reaction rate constants and the equilibrium constant for this reaction?

The Magnitude of the Equilibrium Constant

7.6

What does the equilibrium constant tell us about a particular chemical reaction? When K_{eq} is very large, the concentration of the products must be much greater than the concentration of the reactants. In other words, the equilibrium lies very much to the right. This is an example of a reaction that essentially "goes to completion." If K_{eq} is very small, then the concentration of the products is much less than the concentration of the reactants and we say that the equilibrium lies very much to the left. This is an example of a reaction that "does not occur to any great extent." When K_{eq} is neither very large nor very small, neither reactants nor products are favoured at equilibrium.

It is the magnitude of K_{eq} that is of interest to chemists. To get a better idea of how to interpret different values of K_{eq}, we will consider some examples of reversible reactions in which the value of K_{eq} is typical of the three different categories mentioned above.

Reactions with Large K_{eq}

First, we will consider a reaction we have encountered before: the decomposition of ozone.

$$2\,O_{3\,(g)} \rightleftharpoons 3\,O_{2\,(g)}$$

At $298\,K$ the value of K_{eq} is 2.0×10^{57}. This means that the ratio of product concentration, $[O_2]$, to reactant concentration, $[O_3]$, is very large. The equilibrium lies very much to the right, favouring product formation.

$$2\,O_3 \rightleftharpoons 3\,O_2$$

The enlarged symbols represent the proportions of reactants and products at equilibrium. This reaction has a large K_{eq}, hence few reactant molecules exist.

At this temperature, if we start the reaction with one mole per litre of ozone, we are left with one molecule per litre when equilibrium is reached. Fortunately, in our atmosphere dioxygen is the favoured species: ozone is a poisonous gas.

The following reaction has a K_{eq} of 1.5×10^{90}, indicating that the formation of carbon dioxide is favoured.

$$2\ CO_{(g)} + O_{2(g)} \rightleftharpoons 2\ CO_{2(g)}$$

If the equilibrium lay to the left, we would all be killed by the carbon monoxide, which is poisonous even at low concentrations. (Our atmosphere contains about 0.04 % carbon dioxide.)

Reactions with Small K_{eq}

For the following combination reaction, the value of the equilibrium constant is 1.0×10^{-25} at 298 K:

$$N_{2(g)} + O_{2(g)} \rightleftharpoons 2\ NO_{(g)}$$

The equilibrium lies to the left, which explains why oxygen does not combine appreciably with nitrogen in the atmosphere.

Reactions with Intermediate Values of K_{eq}

When the value for K_{eq} in an equilibrium reaction is neither very small nor very large, we can say that there are measurable concentrations of both reactants and products. In general, if the value of K_{eq} is greater than 1 there will be a higher concentration of products. If the value of K_{eq} is less than 1 there will be a higher concentration of reactants. The Shift reaction for the production of hydrogen gas, is a reaction of the former type:

$$CO_{(g)} + H_2O_{(g)} \rightleftharpoons CO_{2(g)} + H_{2(g)}$$

At 700 K, the K_{eq} for this reaction is 5.09. If we start with 1.00 mol·L^{-1} CO and 1.00 mol·L^{-1} H$_2$O, the concentrations of these two reactions at equilibrium will each be 0.307 mol·L^{-1}. Each of the products will have a concentration of 0.693 mol·L^{-1}.

QUESTIONS

10. For each of the following reactions, state whether the value of the equilibrium constant favours the formation of reactants or products.
    a) $I_{2(g)} + Cl_{2(g)} \rightleftharpoons 2\ ICl_{(g)}$ $\qquad K_{eq} = 2 \times 10^6$
    b) $H_{2(g)} + Cl_{2(g)} \rightleftharpoons 2\ HCl_{(g)}$ $\qquad K_{eq} = 1.08$
    c) $I_{2(g)} \rightleftharpoons I_{(g)} + I_{(g)}$ $\qquad K_{eq} = 3.8 \times 10^{-7}$

11. The equilibrium constant for the decomposition of molecular chlorine at 298 K is 1.4×10^{-38}. Would many chlorine atoms result from the dissociation of the chlorine molecules at this temperature?

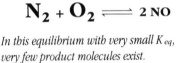

$$N_2 + O_2 \rightleftharpoons 2\ NO$$

In this equilibrium with very small K_{eq}, very few product molecules exist.

Figure 7.9
An artist's impression of the Carboniferous period. The lush forests that gave rise to our coal deposits grew at a time when the concentration of atmospheric carbon dioxide was significantly higher than today.

The Equilibrium Constant Expression

7.7 It is important to remember that when we write an equilibrium expression it applies only to a particular reaction equation. For the reaction

$$H_{2\,(g)} + I_{2\,(g)} \rightleftharpoons 2\,HI_{(g)}$$

the equilibrium expression is

$$K_{eq} = \frac{[HI]^2}{[H_2][I_2]}$$

However, if we are interested in the production of only one mole of hydrogen iodide, we write the reaction equation as follows:

$$\tfrac{1}{2}\,H_{2(g)} + \tfrac{1}{2}\,I_{2(g)} \rightleftharpoons HI_{(g)}$$

The equilibrium expression corresponding to this equation would be

$$K'_{eq} = \frac{[HI]}{[H_2]^{\frac{1}{2}}[I_2]^{\frac{1}{2}}}$$

In other words, if we *halve* the equation coefficients, the corresponding equilibrium constant is the *square root* of the original. Likewise, when we double the equation coefficients, the equilibrium constant is raised to the power of two. If the coefficients in the equation are tripled, the equilibrium constant is raised to a power of three. In general, when the original equation coefficients have changed by a particular factor, the corresponding equilibrium expression is raised to the same power.

Since a reversible equation can be written in either direction, the combination reaction of hydrogen and iodine can be written as a decomposition of hydrogen iodide.

$$2\,HI_{(g)} \rightleftharpoons H_{2\,(g)} + I_{2\,(g)}$$

The equilibrium expression for this reaction would be

$$K''_{eq} = \frac{[H_2][I_2]}{[HI]^2} = \frac{1}{K_{eq}}$$

This shows that for the reverse reaction the equilibrium constant is the reciprocal of the value for the forward reaction.

EXAMPLE

7.1 a) Write the equilibrium expression for the following reaction:

$$2\,O_{3\,(g)} \rightleftharpoons 3\,O_{2\,(g)}$$

b) If the equilibrium constant for the above reaction is 1.0×10^{12} at $2300\,°C$, what will be the value of the equilibrium constant at the same temperature, for the following reaction?

$$3\,O_{2\,(g)} \rightleftharpoons 2\,O_{3\,(g)}$$

SOLUTION   a) The equilibrium expression is

$$K_{eq} = \frac{[O_2]^3}{[O_3]^2}$$

b) Since this is the reverse reaction, the equilibrium constant here will be the inverse of 1.0×10^{12}:

$$\frac{1}{1.0 \times 10^{12}} \quad \text{or} \quad 1.0 \times 10^{-12}$$

The equilibrium expression that we have used so far, involves a ratio of concentrations (in $mol \cdot L^{-1}$) of the equilibrium product and reactant species. The equilibrium constant for this is usually written as K_c, where the subscript denotes an equilibrium constant based on concentrations. For gaseous equilibria, a further equilibrium expression involving the partial pressures of the gases involved is sometimes used. This leads to a different equilibrium constant known as K_p.

Homogeneous and Heterogeneous Equilibria

A **homogeneous equilibrium** is one in which the products and reactants are all in the same phase. Although most of the equilibria that we have discussed so far have been in the gas phase, not all homogeneous equilibria are in the gas phase. Reversible reactions in aqueous solution are also homogeneous equilibria. The partial ionization of the weak organic acid, acetic acid, in aqueous solution is one example.

$$CH_3CO_2H_{(aq)} \rightleftharpoons CH_3CO_2^-{}_{(aq)} + H^+{}_{(aq)}$$

In a **heterogeneous equilibrium** the reactants and products are not all in the same phase. For example, in the reaction

$$CaCO_{3(s)} \rightleftharpoons CaO_{(s)} + CO_{2(g)}$$

both solid and gaseous components are present. Before writing equilibrium expressions for this reaction, we should note that the densities of both liquids and solids remain constant irrespective of the amount of the liquid or solid in the sample. Since concentration is a measure of the amount of mass per unit volume, the concentration of liquids and solids can also be considered to be constants. Therefore, in the equilibrium expression for the decomposition of calcium carbonate

$$K_c = \frac{[CaO][CO_2]}{[CaCO_3]}$$

we can transfer all the constant terms to the left side as

$$K_c \times \frac{[CaCO_3]}{[CaO]} = [CO_2]$$

Since the product of a constant times another constant is a constant, the terms on the left can be replaced by an overall constant, K'_c.

$$K'_c = [CO_2]$$

Thus, when we write the equilibrium expression for a heterogeneous equilibrium, *we do not include the pure solid or pure liquid terms.* They are accounted for in the equilibrium constant. The overall constant K'_c is written simply as K_c.

EXAMPLE **7.2** Write the equilibrium expressions for each of the following reactions:
a) $Fe_3O_{4(s)} + H_{2(g)} \rightleftharpoons 3\,FeO_{(s)} + H_2O_{(g)}$
b) $Ag_2S_{(s)} \rightleftharpoons 2\,Ag^+_{(aq)} + S^{2-}_{(aq)}$

SOLUTION The concentrations of the solids do not appear in the equilibrium expression.

a) $K_c = \dfrac{[H_2O]}{[H_2]}$

b) $K_c = [Ag^+]^2[S^{2-}]$

QUESTIONS

12. Write the equilibrium expression, K_c, for each of the following reactions:
a) $2\,NO_{(g)} + O_{2(g)} \rightleftharpoons 2\,NO_{2(g)}$
b) $4\,HCl_{(g)} + O_{2(g)} \rightleftharpoons 2\,H_2O_{(g)} + 2\,Cl_{2(g)}$
c) $NOCl_{(g)} \rightleftharpoons NO_{(g)} + \frac{1}{2}Cl_{2(g)}$

13. The equilibrium constant for the equilibrium

$$CO_{(g)} + H_2O_{(g)} \rightleftharpoons CO_{2(g)} + H_{2(g)}$$

is 302 at 600 K. What is the value of the equilibrium constant for the reverse reaction at the same temperature?

14. Classify the following equilibria as heterogeneous or homogeneous, and write an equilibrium expression for each.
a) $NH_4NO_{2(s)} \rightleftharpoons N_{2(g)} + 2\,H_2O_{(g)}$
b) $H_2O_{(\ell)} \rightleftharpoons H_2O_{(g)}$
c) $SO_{2(g)} + \frac{1}{2}O_{2(g)} \rightleftharpoons SO_{3(g)}$
d) $S_{8(s)} + 8\,O_{2(g)} \rightleftharpoons 8\,SO_{2(g)}$

How Equilibrium Constants are Determined

Values for equilibrium constants are determined from the concentrations of products and reactants at equilibrium. There are various methods of making these measurements, depending on the physical properties of the components involved.

For example, when ammonium chloride decomposes, the starting compound is a solid, but the products are gases:

$$NH_4Cl_{(s)} \rightleftharpoons NH_{3\,(g)} + HCl_{(g)}$$

We could measure the pressure of the gases formed using a manometer. For a gaseous reaction, such as the decomposition of colourless dinitrogen tetroxide, we could find the amount of the product formed at equilibrium

$$N_2O_{4\,(g)} \rightleftharpoons 2\,NO_{2\,(g)}$$

by measuring the intensity of the brown nitrogen dioxide. In an aqueous equilibrium, such as the partial dissociation of acetic acid,

$$CH_3CO_2H_{(aq)} \rightleftharpoons CH_3CO_2^{-}{}_{(aq)} + H^{+}{}_{(aq)}$$

it would be possible to determine the concentration of ions present at equilibrium by measuring the electrical conductivity of the solution.

Problem Types

Different equilibrium reactions will require different methods to determine concentrations, leading to the equilibrium constant. We make use of equilibrium constants in many ways, but we find that problem types requiring their use can be listed as follows:

1. those in which we are given equilibrium concentrations and asked to calculate the equilibrium constant;
2. those in which we are given the equilibrium constant and asked to calculate equilibrium concentrations.

In this section we will examine the first type; problems requiring the second type will be covered in the next section.

The very first thing to do in solving an equilibrium problem is to write the reaction equation (if it is not already given) and the appropriate equilibrium expression. In the solved examples we start every equilibrium calculation in this manner. If we are then given the concentration of the reactants and products at equilibrium, all we have to do is substitute these values in the equilibrium expression.

Figure 7.10
We can study equilibria under high pressures using this Micro Reactor. Reactions can be studied up to a total pressure of 20 MPa.

EXAMPLE   **7.3**   At 990 °C the following system is at equilibrium:

$$H_{2\,(g)} + CO_{2\,(g)} \rightleftharpoons H_2O_{(g)} + CO_{(g)}$$

The equilibrium concentrations of reactants and products are: 0.24 mol·L^{-1} H$_2$, 1.80 mol·L^{-1} CO$_2$, 0.88 mol·L^{-1} H$_2$O, and 0.88 mol·L^{-1} CO.

Calculate the equilibrium constant, K_c, for this reaction.

SOLUTION   First, we write the equilibrium expression for the given reaction:

$$K_c = \frac{[H_2O][CO]}{[H_2][CO_2]}$$

Next, we substitute the equilibrium concentrations in the above expression:

$$K_c = \frac{(0.88)(0.88)}{(0.24)(1.80)}$$

$$= 1.8$$

EXAMPLE   **7.4**   At 460 °C the concentrations of the reactants and products of a reaction at equilibrium are measured. The results are as follows: 0.100 mol·L^{-1} NO, 0.0140 mol·L^{-1} O$_2$, 0.100 mol·L^{-1} NO$_2$.

From these data determine the equilibrium constant, K_c, for each of the following equations.

a) $2\,NO_{(g)} + O_{2\,(g)} \rightleftharpoons 2\,NO_{2\,(g)}$

b) $NO_{(g)} + \frac{1}{2}O_{2\,(g)} \rightleftharpoons NO_{2\,(g)}$

SOLUTION   a) The equilibrium expression for this equation is

$$K_c = \frac{[NO_2]^2}{[NO]^2[O_2]}$$

Substituting the given equilibrium concentrations, we get

$$K_c = \frac{(0.100)^2}{(0.100)^2(0.0140)}$$

$$= 71.4$$

b) The equilibrium expression for this equation is

$$K_c = \frac{[NO_2]}{[NO][O_2]^{\frac{1}{2}}}$$

Substituting the given equilibrium concentrations, we get

$$K_c = \frac{(0.100)}{(0.100)(0.0140)^{\frac{1}{2}}}$$

$$= 8.45$$

This value is, of course, the square root of that in part a).

7.5 Solid ammonium carbamate, $NH_4CO_2NH_2$, decomposes as shown below:

$$NH_4CO_2NH_{2\,(s)} \rightleftharpoons 2\,NH_{3\,(g)} + CO_{2\,(g)}$$

At $40\,°C$ the total gas concentration (of ammonia and carbon dioxide) is $1.41 \times 10^{-2}\ mol \cdot L^{-1}$. Calculate the equilibrium constant, K_c, at this temperature.

SOLUTION

Recall that the concentration of a pure solid, in this case the ammonium carbamate, does not appear in the equilibrium expression. Thus, the equilibrium expression for this reaction is

$$K_c = [NH_3]^2[CO_2]$$

We now determine the equilibrium concentrations of the NH_3 and the CO_2. From the balanced equation, we see that at equilibrium there are twice as many moles of NH_3 as there are of CO_2. Given this, we let x represent the concentration of CO_2 in moles per litre,

$$[CO_2] = x$$

and let $2x$ represent the concentration of NH_3 in moles per litre.

$$[NH_3] = 2x$$

The total concentration of the gases is then found by adding these two concentrations.

$$x + 2x = 1.41 \times 10^{-2}\ mol \cdot L^{-1}$$

After solving for x

$$3x = 1.41 \times 10^{-2}\ mol \cdot L^{-1}$$

$$x = \frac{1.41 \times 10^{-2}\ mol \cdot L^{-1}}{3}$$

$$= 4.70 \times 10^{-3}\ mol \cdot L^{-1}$$

we find that

$$[CO_2] = 4.70 \times 10^{-3}\ mol \cdot L^{-1}$$
$$[NH_3] = 2(4.70 \times 10^{-3})\ mol \cdot L^{-1}$$
$$= 9.40 \times 10^{-3}\ mol \cdot L^{-1}$$

Substituting these values into the equilibrium expression, we get

$$K_c = (9.40 \times 10^{-3})^2(4.70 \times 10^{-3})$$
$$= 4.15 \times 10^{-7}$$

15. At the equilibrium point in the decomposition of phosphorus pentachloride

$$PCl_{5\,(g)} \rightleftharpoons PCl_{3\,(g)} + Cl_{2\,(g)}$$

the following concentrations are obtained:
0.010 mol·L^{-1} PCl$_5$, 0.15 mol·L^{-1} PCl$_3$, 0.37 mol·L^{-1} Cl$_2$.
Determine the equilibrium constant, K_c, for the reaction.

16. The colourless gas dinitrogen tetroxide and the brown-coloured air pollutant nitrogen dioxide exist in equilibrium as

$$N_2O_{4\,(g)} \rightleftharpoons 2\,NO_{2\,(g)}$$

Assume that 0.125 mol of dinitrogen tetroxide gas is introduced into a 1.00 L container and allowed to decompose. When equilibrium with nitrogen dioxide is reached, the concentration of the dinitrogen tetroxide is 0.0750 mol·L^{-1}. What is the value of K_c for this reaction?

Determining Equilibrium Concentrations

7.9

Once values of equilibrium constants have been determined they are usually published, along with the appropriate equation, in chemical journals. Those who wish to calculate reactant or product concentrations in a particular equilibrium can refer to the established tabulated value for the equilibrium constant. Since these calculations can be somewhat complicated, we classify them according to the type of arithmetical method required for the solution.

Problems Involving Simple Algebraic Relationships

In determining equilibrium concentrations for a heterogeneous equilibrium, we first write the equilibrium expression that corresponds to the reaction equation. The next step involves substitution in this expression using the known value for K_c and unknown values denoting the equilibrium concentrations. One of these unknown values is usually represented by x. The other unknown values are related to x by the coefficients in the balanced equation.

EXAMPLE

7.6

The white solid salt, ammonium chloride (NH$_4$Cl), decomposes on heating to form gaseous hydrogen chloride and ammonia.

$$NH_4Cl_{(s)} \rightleftharpoons NH_{3\,(g)} + HCl_{(g)}$$

At 400 K the equilibrium constant, K_c, for this reaction is 6.0×10^{-9}. Calculate the equilibrium concentration of each gas at this temperature.

The first step is to write the equilibrium expression. Remember that the concentration of a pure solid does not appear in this expression.

$$K_c = [NH_3][HCl] = 6.0 \times 10^{-9}$$

From the reaction equation we can see that an equal number of moles of ammonia and hydrogen chloride are formed. So, we let x represent the concentrations of both NH_3 and HCl in moles per litre.

$$[NH_3] = x = [HCl]$$

Next we substitute these values in the equilibrium expression:

$$K_c = (x)(x) = 6.0 \times 10^{-9}$$
$$x^2 = 6.0 \times 10^{-9}$$
$$x = 7.7 \times 10^{-5}$$

Thus the equilibrium concentrations are:

$$[NH_3] = [HCl] = 7.7 \times 10^{-5} \ mol \cdot L^{-1}$$

Calculations Involving a Perfect Square

We are often required to calculate the change in the concentration of one or more reactants or products during the course of a reaction. In this case we let x represent the *change* in concentration between the starting point and the point of equilibrium.

In the following problem, the end result is a perfect square, and it is possible to determine the equilibrium concentrations by taking the square root of each side of the algebraic equation obtained.

EXAMPLE   **7.7** At 430 °C the equilibrium constant, K_c, for the following reaction is 1.84×10^{-2}.

$$2 \ HI_{(g)} \ \rightleftharpoons \ H_{2\,(g)} + I_{2\,(g)}$$

If 0.100 mol of hydrogen iodide is placed in a 1.00 L container and allowed to reach equilibrium at this temperature, find the concentrations of all the species at equilibrium.

SOLUTION Again, the first step is writing the equilibrium expression:

$$K_c = \frac{[H_2][I_2]}{[HI]^2}$$

Knowing the equilibrium constant, we rewrite the above as

$$\frac{[H_2][I_2]}{[HI]^2} = 1.84 \times 10^{-2}$$

Now we make a table showing the changes in concentrations. We can see from the reaction equation that for every two moles of hydrogen iodide that dissociate, one mole of hydrogen gas and one mole of iodine gas are formed. So if we let the change in concentration of hydrogen and iodine be x, the change in concentration of hydrogen iodide would be $-2x$.

	[HI]	[H$_2$]	[I$_2$]
Initial	0.100		
Change	$-2x$	$+x$	$+x$
Equilibrium	$(0.100 - 2x)$	x	x

Adding the "Initial" and "Change" entries for each species, gives the corresponding equilibrium concentration:

Equilibrium concentration = Initial concentration + Change in concentration

So for this data table, the appropriate equilibrium concentrations are

$$[HI] = (0.100) + (-2x) = (0.100 - 2x)$$
$$[H_2] = 0 + (+x) = x$$
$$[I_2] = 0 + (+x) = x$$

Now we substitute the above equilibrium concentrations into the equilibrium expression:

$$\frac{(x)(x)}{(0.100 - 2x)^2} = 1.84 \times 10^{-2}$$

In solving for x, we start by taking the square root of both sides of the equation.

$$\sqrt{\frac{x^2}{(0.100 - 2x)^2}} = \sqrt{1.84 \times 10^{-2}}$$

$$\frac{x}{(0.100 - 2x)} = 0.136$$

$$x = 0.0136 - 0.272x$$

$$1.272x = 0.0136$$

$$x = \frac{0.0136}{1.272}$$

$$x = 1.07 \times 10^{-2}$$

Thus at equilibrium the concentrations of hydrogen and iodine gases are as follows:

$$[H_2] = [I_2] = 1.07 \times 10^{-2} \text{ mol·L}^{-1}$$

For hydrogen iodide gas, the equilibrium concentration is given by

$$[HI] = 0.100 - 2(1.07 \times 10^{-2}) \, \text{mol} \cdot \text{L}^{-1}$$
$$= 7.86 \times 10^{-2} \, \text{mol} \cdot \text{L}^{-1}.$$

CHECK

We can check our work by substituting the calculated concentration values into the equilibrium expression.

$$K_c = \frac{(1.07 \times 10^{-2})(1.07 \times 10^{-2})}{(7.86 \times 10^{-2})^2}$$
$$= 1.85 \times 10^{-2}$$

This K_c value is very close (within rounding-off error) to the original.

Calculations using Approximations

If the value of the equilibrium constant is extremely small, it is often possible to use an approximation that will reduce the amount of arithmetic necessary to solve the problem.

| EXAMPLE | 7.8 | At 727 °C the equilibrium constant, K_c, for the dissociation of molecular iodine into iodine atoms is 3.80×10^{-5}. |

$$I_{2\,(g)} \rightleftharpoons 2 \, I_{(g)}$$

If the original concentration of molecular iodine is 0.200 mol·L⁻¹, calculate the concentration of atomic iodine at equilibrium.

SOLUTION First, we write the equilibrium expression for this reaction:

$$K_c = \frac{[I]^2}{[I_2]} = 3.80 \times 10^{-5}$$

Next, we establish a table representing the changes in concentration. For every mole of molecular iodine that dissociates, two moles of atomic iodine are formed. Therefore, we can represent the change in the concentration of the atomic iodine as $+2x$ and the change in the concentration of the molecular iodine as $-x$.

	$[I_2]$	$[I]$
Initial	0.200	
Change	$-x$	$+2x$
Equilibrium	$(0.200 - x)$	$2x$

We can now substitute the above equilibrium concentrations into the equilibrium expression:

$$\frac{(2x)^2}{(0.200 - x)} = 3.80 \times 10^{-5}$$

This is *not* a perfect square. However, in this case the equilibrium constant, K_c, is very small. Thus the equilibrium lies very much to the left. This indicates that very little molecular iodine dissociates at this temperature, so the initial concentration of molecular iodine is approximately the same as the equilibrium concentration. Therefore, we can say that within the precision of our values, $(0.200 - x)$ can be approximated to 0.200.

$$\frac{(2x)^2}{(0.200)} = 3.80 \times 10^{-5}$$

After rearranging we get

$$4x^2 = (3.80 \times 10^{-5}) \times 0.200$$
$$x^2 = 1.90 \times 10^{-6}$$
$$x = 1.38 \times 10^{-3}$$

We use this value of x to find the concentration of atomic iodine at equilibrium,

$$[I] = 2x$$
$$= 2 \times (1.38 \times 10^{-3}) \, \text{mol} \cdot \text{L}^{-1}$$
$$= 2.76 \times 10^{-3} \, \text{mol} \cdot \text{L}^{-1}$$

When is it reasonable to use an approximation? If the value of the equilibrium constant is very small, we can safely use an approximation method. But this leads to the question: "What is very small?" The following is the approximation rule we will use:

An approximation can be made if the concentration from which x is subtracted, or to which x is added, is at least 1000 times the value of the equilibrium constant.

In the previous example, the ratio of concentration to K_c is

$$\frac{0.200}{3.80 \times 10^{-5}} = 5.26 \times 10^3$$

This verifies that our approximation was valid. If this value was less than 1000 the approximation was not valid, and we should use the quadratic formula to solve the problem.

QUESTIONS

17. Gaseous dinitrogen tetroxide, N_2O_4, is placed in a flask and allowed to reach equilibrium at 100 °C.

$$N_2O_{4(g)} \rightleftharpoons 2\,NO_{2(g)}$$

At the temperature of the reaction, the value of the equilibrium constant, K_c, is 0.212. The concentration of dinitrogen tetroxide at equilibrium is 0.155 mol·L⁻¹. Calculate the concentration of nitrogen dioxide at equilibrium.

18. For the following reaction the equilibrium constant, K_c, has a value of 85.0 at 460 °C:

$$SO_{2(g)} + NO_{2(g)} \rightleftharpoons NO_{(g)} + SO_{3(g)}$$

If a mixture of sulfur dioxide and nitrogen dioxide is prepared, each with an initial concentration of 0.100 mol·L⁻¹, calculate the equilibrium concentrations of nitrogen dioxide and nitrogen monoxide at this temperature.

19. At 100 °C the following reaction has an equilibrium constant, K_c, value of 2.2×10^{-10}.

$$COCl_{2(g)} \rightleftharpoons CO_{(g)} + Cl_{2(g)}$$

If 1.00 mol of phosgene, $COCl_2$, is placed in a 10.0 L flask, calculate the concentration of carbon monoxide at equilibrium.

Le Châtelier's Principle

7.10

Any system at equilibrium represents a delicate balance between the forward and reverse reactions. Even small changes in the external conditions can cause a shift in the position of the equilibrium. We can think of the equilibrium as adjusting itself to accommodate the changes forced upon it. During this adjustment, the concentrations of the reactants and the products may increase or decrease.

This response of an equilibrium to change was first described by the French chemist, Henri Louis Le Châtelier. **Le Châtelier's principle** states:

> **If a system at equilibrium is subjected to an external stress, the equilibrium will shift so as to minimize the stress.**

By external stress, we generally mean a change in concentration of a reactant or product, a change in pressure or volume, or a change in temperature. The addition of a catalyst does *not* change the position of an equilibrium. A catalyst speeds up the reverse reaction to the same degree as the forward reaction. Generally then, a catalyst allows the reaction to reach the equilibrium point sooner.

Figure 7.11
Henri Le Châtelier (1850-1936) devised the principles of equilibrium while researching the chemical nature of cements.

Changes in Concentration of Reactant or Product

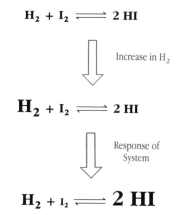

If we add more hydrogen gas to our representative system at equilibrium,

$$H_{2\,(g)} + I_{2\,(g)} \rightleftharpoons 2\,HI_{(g)}$$

we will upset the balance. The system will respond by trying to use up the additional hydrogen. The only way this can happen is for some of the iodine gas to combine with some of the extra hydrogen, forming more hydrogen iodide. Eventually equilibrium will be re-established. There will be more hydrogen iodide and less iodine present; there will also be more hydrogen, although not as much as when the excess hydrogen is first added.

This situation is shown graphically in Figure 7.12. The equilibrium expression for this reaction is

$$K_c = \frac{[HI]^2}{[H_2][I_2]}$$

If K_c is to remain the same, an increase in $[H_2]$ must be accompanied by a decrease in $[I_2]$ *or* by an increase in $[HI]$ *or* by both.

We now have a means of predicting the direction that an equilibrium will move if we increase or decrease the concentration of one of the components. If we increase the concentration of one of the reactants, the equilibrium will shift in the forward direction, to use up the excess reactant. If we decrease the concentration of one of the components, the equilibrium will shift in the direction that tends to replace that component.

Le Châtelier's principle tells us that a system at equilibrium adjusts to maintain the same value for the equilibrium constant. But why does the addition of more of a reactant or a product change the position of an equilibrium? To answer this, consider what happens when we add more hydrogen iodide to the system below:

$$H_{2\,(g)} + I_{2\,(g)} \rightleftharpoons 2\,HI_{(g)}$$

If more hydrogen iodide molecules are added to the system, there is a greater possibility that these molecules will collide. Hence, increasing the concentration of hydrogen iodide molecules increases the reverse reaction rate, and this in turn, produces an increase in reactant concentrations. Both product and reactant concentrations increase, but at equilibrium the ratio of their concentrations does not change.

Similarly, the addition of one of the reactants, hydrogen for example, increases its concentration and the likelihood for collisions between hydrogen and iodine molecules. Thus, the rate of the forward reaction increases. Equilibrium is re-established at a point where both hydrogen iodide and hydrogen concentrations have increased and that of iodine has decreased. A general summary of the effects that changes in concentration have on equilibrium is given in Table 7.3.

Figure 7.12
Adding hydrogen to this equilibrium results in an increase in hydrogen iodide and a decrease in iodine while the concentration of hydrogen remains up slightly.

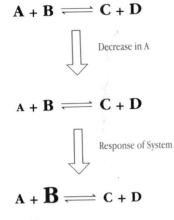

$$A + B \rightleftharpoons C + D$$

Decrease in A

$$A + B \rightleftharpoons C + D$$

Response of System

$$A + \mathbf{B} \rightleftharpoons C + D$$

Figure 7.13
Effect on an equilibrium of decreasing the concentration of reagent A.

TABLE 7.3	*Summary of the Effects of Concentration Changes in the General Equilibrium Reaction* $A + B \rightleftharpoons C + D$	
Disturbance	**Response of the Reaction**	**Result**
Concentration of A increased.	Shifts to the right. Some of the excess A is used up by reaction with B.	More C and D formed.
Concentration of A decreased.	Shifts to the left. Some of C and D used up by this reaction.	More A and B formed.
Concentration of C increased.	Shifts to the left. Some of the excess C is used up by reaction with D.	More A and B formed.
Concentration of C decreased.	Shifts to the right. Some of A and B used up by this reaction.	More C and D formed.

EXAMPLE   **7.9**   For the reaction below, predict the direction the equilibrium will shift

$$2\,NO_{2\,(g)} + 7\,H_{2\,(g)} \rightleftharpoons 2\,NH_{3\,(g)} + 4\,H_2O_{(g)}$$

given the following changes (assuming constant temperature and volume):
a) addition of ammonia
b) removal of nitrogen dioxide
c) removal of water vapour
d) addition of hydrogen

SOLUTION   a) To use up the extra ammonia the system will shift to the left.
b) To replace some of the nitrogen dioxide the system will shift to the left.
c) To replace some of the water vapour the system will shift to the right.
d) To use up some of the extra hydrogen the system will shift to the right.

If we know the value of the equilibrium constant, we can use the equilibrium expression to determine which way a system will shift to establish equilibrium. This is done by substituting the initial, or non-equilibrium, concentrations into the equilibrium expression, and comparing the resulting value with the known value of the equilibrium constant.

EXAMPLE   **7.10**   At a particular temperature, the following reaction has an equilibrium constant value, K_c, of 0.18.

$$PCl_{3\,(g)} + Cl_{2\,(g)} \rightleftharpoons PCl_{5\,(g)}$$

Predict the direction in which the reaction shifts to establish equilibrium, in an experiment for which the starting concentration of each gas is $0.10\ mol \cdot L^{-1}$.

The equilibrium expression for the reaction is

$$K_c = \frac{[PCl_5]}{[PCl_3][Cl_2]}$$

If we substitute the initial (non-equilibrium) concentrations into the right side of this expression we get

$$\frac{(0.10)}{(0.10)(0.10)} = 10$$

This value is greater than the value of the equilibrium constant of 0.18. Thus to attain equilibrium, the concentration of the phosphorus pentachloride must decrease and the concentrations of phosphorus trichloride and chlorine must increase. The reaction would shift to the left.

Changes in Volume or Pressure

Since liquids, solids, and solutions are generally incompressible, pressure changes do not affect their concentrations. However, gaseous equilibria are sensitive to changes in pressure and volume. A decrease in volume or an increase in pressure favours the side of the equation with *fewer* numbers of moles of gas. These occupy a smaller volume, thus relieving the stress of the added pressure on the system. Conversely, an increase in volume or a decrease in pressure favours the side of the reaction with the *greater* number of moles of gas.

If there are equal numbers of gas molecules on each side of the equation, there will be no change in the position of the equilibrium, since changes in pressure or volume affect each side equally. Also, the addition of an inert gas or gases to a constant-volume system at equilibrium does not change the position of the equilibrium. Although the total pressure in the system will increase, the partial pressure of each gas, and hence the concentration of each gas, does not change.

We can explain the effects by relating pressure changes to concentration. If the pressure is increased, gas concentration increases. Molecules are now closer together, and molecular collisions are more likely. As pressure is increased for both sides of the reaction, both the forward and reverse reaction rates are increased. But only if there are equal numbers of molecules on each side of the equation are the forward and reverse reaction rates increased by the same factor. In this case, of course, there are no overall changes in equilibrium concentrations.

We can also show mathematically that changes in volume shift the position of some equilibria. Consider the gaseous equilibrium

$$N_2O_{4(g)} \rightleftharpoons 2\,NO_{2(g)}$$

for which the equilibrium expression is

$$K_c = \frac{[NO_2]^2}{[N_2O_4]}$$

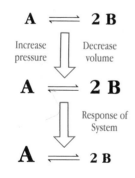

A $\rightleftharpoons$ **2 B**

Increase pressure | Decrease volume

A $\rightleftharpoons$ **2 B**

Response of System

A $\rightleftharpoons$ **2 B**

Figure 7.14

If the volume is decreased, the equilibrium shifts to the side with the fewer number of molecules.

Let us suppose that the volume of this system is reduced by one half; this means that the concentrations of both dinitrogen tetroxide and nitrogen dioxide are doubled and the system is no longer at equilibrium. The concentration of nitrogen dioxide is squared in the equilibrium expression; the concentration of dinitrogen tetroxide is not. To keep the value of K_c constant, the reaction shifts to the left, reducing the concentration of nitrogen dioxide and increasing the concentration of dinitrogen tetroxide, until equilibrium is re-established.

EXAMPLE   **7.11**   The pressure on each of the following systems is increased by decreasing the volume of the container. Explain whether each system would shift in the forward direction, the reverse direction, or stay the same.

a) $2\,SO_{2\,(g)} + O_{2\,(g)} \rightleftharpoons 2\,SO_{3\,(g)}$
b) $H_{2\,(g)} + I_{2\,(g)} \rightleftharpoons 2\,HI_{(g)}$
c) $CaCO_{3\,(s)} \rightleftharpoons CaO_{(s)} + CO_{2\,(g)}$
d) $AgCl_{(s)} \rightleftharpoons Ag^+_{\,(aq)} + Cl^-_{\,(aq)}$

SOLUTION   Increased pressure favours the side of the reaction with fewer moles of gas.

a) The right side of the equation has fewer moles of gas. Thus a shift in the forward direction reduces the pressure and minimizes the effect of the disturbance.
b) Both sides have two moles of gas; therefore, an increase in pressure does not change the position of the equilibrium.
c) A shift in the reverse direction is favoured because the left side of the equation has fewer moles of gas.
d) The equilibrium is unchanged; pressure does not affect the position of aqueous equilibria.

QUESTIONS

20. List three ways that the following equilibrium reaction could be forced to shift to the right:

$$2\,NO_{2\,(g)} \rightleftharpoons 2\,NO_{(g)} + O_{2\,(g)}$$

21. Given the following equilibrium reaction

$$2\,C_{(s)} + O_{2\,(g)} \rightleftharpoons 2\,CO_{(g)}$$

what will be the effect of the following disturbances to the system?

a) addition of carbon monoxide (at constant volume and temperature)
b) addition of oxygen (at constant volume and temperature)
c) addition of solid carbon (at constant volume and temperature)
d) decreasing the container volume (at constant temperature)
e) addition of helium gas to the container (at constant volume)

Changing Currents in Our Waters

For hundreds of years, Canada has been renowned for its fishing industry. Today, commercial fishing lands about $1.5 billion of fish each year worth about $3.0 billion after processing. But the industry is now changing, both in its catching methods and in its usage of the by-products of processing. Its continued success is now dependent on chemical research to enhance product quality.

Heavy loads from deep sea trawlers provide the bulk of the catch processed in small communities such as Ramea, Newfoundland.

The efficiency of standard trawling gear can now be studied in a 'flume tank', which simulates the effects of ocean currents.

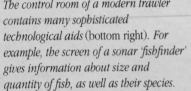

The control room of a modern trawler contains many sophisticated technological aids (bottom right). For example, the screen of a sonar 'fishfinder' gives information about size and quantity of fish, as well as their species.

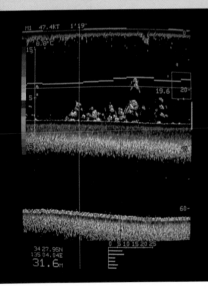

PLATE 10 — CHANGING CURRENTS IN OUR WATERS

Fresh fish is filleted, trimmed, and packaged for rapid freezing. Quality control is important at all stages of processing.

The shells of some species of shrimp contain a protein–carotene complex. When boiled, the carotene is released as a bright red pigment.

Like shrimp, lobster shells contain a carotene complex which also results in a bright red pigment after boiling.

PLATE 12 — CHANGING CURRENTS IN OUR WATERS

FMC
PHOSPHATES

IMPROVE
YOUR FISH
AND
SHELLFISH
NATURALLY.

IMPROVE QUALITY
FMC food-grade phos-
phates lock in seafood's natural flavor, protein, and
moisture to give you the
quality product your custom-
ers demand. That means a
cooked product that is more
juicy and tender with more of
its natural nutrients.

IMPROVE YIELDS
By retaining more of a
product's natural moisture
and reducing product de-
hydration during cold storage,
FMC phosphates increase
your product yields, retain
nutritional value, and improve
your operating efficiency.

FMC phosphates also in-
crease product yields during
secondary processing applications such as seafood smoking.
If you use surimi or minced
fish, FMC phosphates help
retain more natural protein
and color, and improve textural
qualities. And if you bread or
form, they improve binding.
FMC phosphates soften
shellfish underskins so the
meat separates easily from
the shell. Yield stays first class
because shape is preserved.
Processing costs are less,
even in automated processing.

IMPROVE PROFITS
All these benefits pay off in

more profit. So does FMC's
convenient, prompt distribution. And when there's a problem you can't solve, FMC's
technical specialists are ready
to help. They also have new
ideas for you.
To find out more about
what FMC phosphates can do
for you, write: FMC Corporation, Phosphorus Division,
2000 Market Street,
Philadelphia, PA 19103. Or call
our marketing department
collect at (215) 299-6863.

FMC.

The decomposition of fish, a result of protein breakdown, starts almost immediately after they are caught. Above: a fresh fish fillet. Below: a deteriorated fish fillet. Phosphates are used to combat this decomposition. They prevent oxidation, stop moisture loss, and help retain the natural protein.

Surimi (minced fish) is used to simulate more expensive products like crab and lobster. Surimi research is concentrating on linking proteins and avoiding their breakdown.

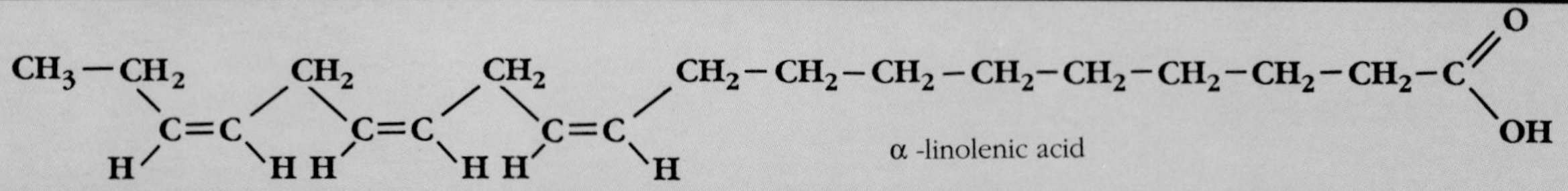

$$CH_3-CH_2 \qquad CH_2 \qquad CH_2$$
$$C=C \qquad C=C \qquad C=C \qquad CH_2-CH_2-CH_2-CH_2-CH_2-CH_2-CH_2-CH_2-C$$

α -linolenic acid

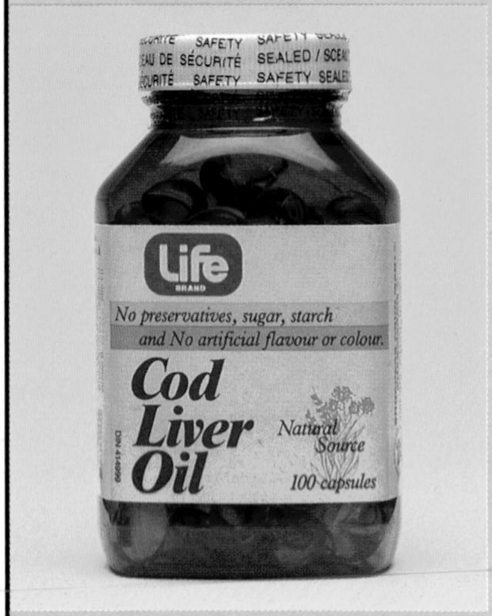

Recent research has shown that certain polyunsaturated fats, called omega-3's, reduce blood cholesterol levels. α-linolenic acid is a typical omega-3. Interest in traditional health aids is rising, resulting in new products such as omega capsules.

Many marine organisms are now being used in medicine. Here, horseshoe crabs are milked for their blue blood—required in a test for bacterial contamination of drugs.

PLATE 14 — CHANGING CURRENTS IN OUR WATERS

Marine pharmacologists have been examining colonies of various marine life-forms such as the algae contained in these petri dishes. Extracts from such colonies may provide drugs that are active against viruses, including AIDS.

Mussels produce a strong glue that has been extracted and synthesized for use in medicine. Ophthalmologists are testing the glue to repair corneas and dentists are using it as a bonding and sealing compound.

The Pacific coral Telesto riisei *contains organic acids called prostaglandins that are active against leukemia.*

An anti-cancer test drug called Didemnin B is derived from the sea organism Trididemnum solidum, *a colonial tunicate.*

PLATE 16 — CHANGING CURRENTS IN OUR WATERS

High Living

The combination of oxygen gas with hemoglobin (Hb) in the blood is one of the most sensitive equilibria in nature. This equilibrium reaction can be written as

$$Hb_{(aq)} + O_{2\,(g)} \rightleftharpoons HbO_{2\,(aq)}$$

where HbO_2 represents oxyhemoglobin, an oxygen hemoglobin compound. The corresponding equilibrium expression is

$$K_c = \frac{[HbO_2]}{[Hb][O_2]}$$

The concentration of a gas is proportional to its partial pressure, which means we can use partial pressures of oxygen to describe the application of Le Châtelier's principle to this equilibrium. Any increase in the partial pressure of oxygen will force the equilibrium to the right; any decrease in the partial pressure of oxygen causes a shift favouring the reverse reaction. At the partial pressures of oxygen normally found in the lungs, 90–95 % of the hemoglobin is in the oxyhemoglobin form.

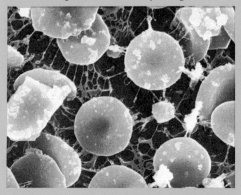

Figure 7.15
Human blood cells. Each is about 7.5 μm in diameter. In our bodies, we have about 1×10^{12} red blood cells, each of which contains about 2.5×10^5 molecules of hemoglobin.

At the sea level the partial pressure of oxygen is about 20.3 kPa. In Calgary, Alberta (elevation: 1050 m), the partial pressure of oxygen is about 18.2 kPa. Canada's highest peak is Mount Logan, in the Yukon Territory; at this elevation (5951 m) the partial pressure of oxygen is around 9.42 kPa. These figures show us that the partial pressure of oxygen declines as altitude increases, a situation that leads inevitably to a reduced concentration of oxyhemoglobin in the blood.

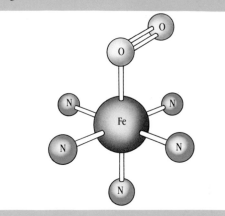

Figure 7.16
In hemoglobin, the oxygen molecule bonds to the iron atoms. Each iron atom is surrounded by five nitrogen atoms. The hemoglobin molecule contains about 1×10^4 atoms, mainly carbon and hydrogen, together with some nitrogen and sulfur, and four iron atoms.

The effect of a sudden introduction to this high living is known as *hypoxia*, commonly referred to as altitude sickness. The reduced amount of oxygen reaching the body tissues under these conditions brings on symptoms that include headaches, fatigue, and nausea. In extreme cases the victim can fall into a coma and die.

Yet people *can* live comfortably at altitudes as high as 5000 m. The problem is not with the high living but with the sudden change in altitude. Given enough time the body will produce more hemoglobin, so that the equilibrium will eventually shift to the right again, increasing the concentration of oxyhemoglobin and supplying the tissues with sufficient oxygen. The production of hemoglobin is fairly slow; it may take weeks, months, or even years to develop full capacity, depending on the altitude. Studies have shown that the blood of people who have lived at these high altitudes for many years carries hemoglobin concentrations up to 50% greater than people at sea level

The Effect of Temperature on Equilibrium

7.11

When energy in the form of heat is added to a system at equilibrium the temperature increases. There are two consequences of this temperature change. First, according to Le Châtelier's principle, the equilibrium will shift in the direction that *absorbs* heat. Second, the value of the equilibrium constant changes, since an equilibrium constant is only constant at a specific temperature. The direction of the shift in equilibrium and the increase or decrease in the equilibrium constant depends on whether the reaction is exothermic or endothermic.

Let us consider first the shift in equilibrium. In this context it helps to think of heat as a reactant or product in the equation. The following reaction is endothermic.

$$N_2O_{4\,(g)} \rightleftharpoons 2\,NO_{2\,(g)} \qquad \Delta H° = +58.0\,kJ$$

This means that heat is absorbed when the reaction moves in the *forward* direction. We can write the reaction equation by including heat as one of the reactants:

$$N_2O_{4\,(g)} + heat \rightleftharpoons 2\,NO_{2\,(g)}$$

To increase the temperature, more heat must be added to the system. The forward reaction is then favoured, partially compensating for the increased temperature. To decrease the temperature, heat must be removed from the system. A reverse, or heat-producing reaction, is then favoured, partially compensating for the lowered temperature.

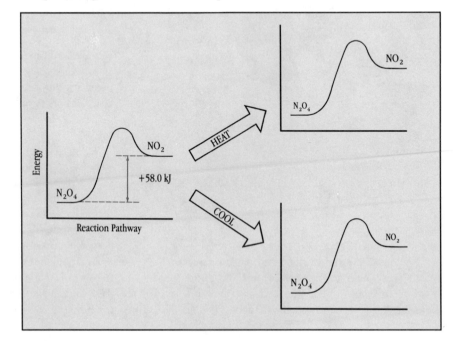

Figure 7.17

As the temperature is increased, the endothermic direction is favoured. A decrease in temperature favours the reverse reaction.

EXAMPLE	7.12

For each of the following equilibria, predict whether the system will shift in the forward or reverse direction. Note the energy changes involved and assume that the volume remains constant.

a) heat removed from system: $A \rightleftharpoons B$ $\Delta H° = +40.0\,kJ$
b) heat removed from system: $A + B \rightleftharpoons 2\,C$ $\Delta H° = -25.5\,kJ$
c) heat added to system: $A + 2\,B \rightleftharpoons 3\,C$ $\Delta H° = -32.0\,kJ$

SOLUTION

We rewrite each of the equations including heat as a component.

a) $A + heat \rightleftharpoons B$
The removal of heat favours the reverse reaction.

b) $A + B \rightleftharpoons 2\,C + heat$
In this equilibrium, the removal of heat favours the forward reaction.

c) $A + 2\,B \rightleftharpoons 3\,C + heat$
In this equilibrium the addition of heat favours the reverse reaction.

Now we consider changes to the equilibrium constant. If the reaction is *exothermic*, the equilibrium constant decreases when the temperature is raised. When the temperature is increased during the reaction

$$2\,NO_{(g)} + O_{2(g)} \rightleftharpoons 2\,NO_{2(g)} + heat \qquad \textbf{(negative } \Delta H°\textbf{)}$$

the equilibrium moves in the reverse direction. This absorbs heat and offsets the applied stress. It also increases the concentrations of nitrogen monoxide and oxygen, and decreases the concentration of nitrogen dioxide. Hence, the value for K_c in the equilibrium expression will decrease.

$$K_c = \frac{[NO_2]^2}{[NO]^2[O_2]}$$

If the reaction is *endothermic*, the value of K_c increases with increasing temperature. This is exemplified in the equilibrium between aqueous and gaseous carbon dioxide that occurs in carbonated beverages.

$$CO_{2\,(aq)} + heat \rightleftharpoons CO_{2\,(g)} \qquad \textbf{(positive } \Delta H°\textbf{)}$$

This reaction is endothermic in the forward direction. At higher temperatures production of gaseous carbon dioxide is favoured. Probably all of us have removed the cap from a warm bottle of pop and watched the rapid bubbling as more gas is produced. When carbonated beverages are cooled before they are opened, gas is not released quite as vigorously.

QUESTIONS

22. In each of the following equilibria, would you increase or decrease the temperature to force the reaction in the forward direction?
a) $H_{2\,(g)} + CO_{2\,(g)} \rightleftharpoons H_2O_{(g)} + CO_{(g)}$ $\Delta H° = +41\,kJ$
b) $2\,SO_{2\,(g)} + O_{2\,(g)} \rightleftharpoons 2\,SO_{3\,(g)}$ $\Delta H° = -198\,kJ$

23. For each of the equilibria in Question 22 will the value for K_c increase or decrease if the temperature is raised?

Figure 7.18
Silica gel is often used as a drying agent in chemistry. It absorbs water exothermically to form a hydrate. As can be predicted from Le Châtelier's principle, heating the gel releases the water. The substance can then be re-used.

The Synthesis of Ammonia

7.12

Ammonia is one of the most important chemicals manufactured today. More than 2.5 million tonnes are produced annually in Canada, a significant part of which is used to make nitrogen-containing fertilizers. Ammonia is also used in the production of nitric acid, synthetic fibres (e.g. nylon and rayon), dyestuffs, polymers (e.g. polyurethanes), explosives, and pharmaceuticals. It is used as a refrigerant, as a household cleaning agent, in the metallurgical industry, and in the plastics and petroleum industries.

The Nitrogen Cycle

Nitrogen compounds are essential for growth of both plants and animals. Whether we obtain dietary nitrogen directly from plants, such as legumes and nuts, or indirectly from animal sources such as meat, milk, and eggs, the initial source is plants. Since only a few micro-organisms can assimilate atmospheric nitrogen directly, significant amounts of soluble nitrogen, phosphorus, and potassium must be available in the soil, from natural sources or in fertilizers. For this reason, we can expect an ever-increasing demand for nitrogenous fertilizers as the problem of feeding the world's population escalates.

The circulation of nitrogen atoms between the atmosphere, soil, water, and living organisms is known as the **nitrogen cycle**. Soil bacteria act on dead plants and animals, as well as their waste products, and release nitrogen in the form of ammonia. Another group of bacteria converts the ammonia to nitrites (NO_2^-), and yet another group changes the nitrites to nitrates (NO_3^-). Most green plants assimilate nitrogen as nitrates, and use it to synthesize protein. Some plants in the legume family, such as clover and alfalfa, have root nodules containing "nitrogen-fixing" bacteria. These micro-organisms convert atmospheric nitrogen into a form of nitrate that can be directly used by the plant. It has been estimated that the annual production of nitrates by these bacteria is 222 kg per hectare. Another, although minor, source of nitrogen compounds is from atmospheric nitrogen through the action of lightning.

TABLE 7.4 *Estimated World Nitrogen Fixation*	
Atmospheric lightning	25 million tonnes
Combustion (mainly from internal combustion engines)	20
Fixation through land plants	80
Fixation through water plants	20
Chemical fixation (Haber process)	60

Figure 7.19

The nitrogen cycle.

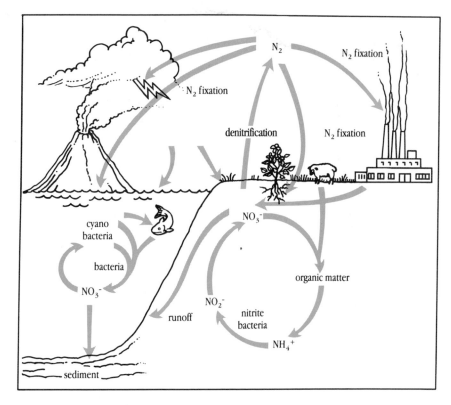

Unfortunately, nitrates are very soluble in water. As a result, rain washes much of the nitrate ions into rivers or lakes, where they cause pollution problems. More nitrate ion must then be applied to the fields.

The Haber Process

Most areas under intensive agriculture require more nitrogen than can be supplied from natural processes. Nitrogen must be returned to the soil as fertilizer in the form of nitrates or ammonium salts. During the 19th century, two thirds of the fertilizer needs of the world were being supplied from saltpeter (sodium nitrate) deposits in Chile. As the deposits became depleted, it became apparent that an industrial synthetic route was needed. The industrial process for manufacturing ammonia from elemental hydrogen and nitrogen was developed by the German chemist Fritz Haber. For this reason, it is called the **Haber process**. The reaction can be written as follows:

$$N_{2(g)} + 3 H_{2(g)} \rightleftharpoons 2 NH_{3(g)} \qquad \Delta H° = -92.6 \, kJ$$

The reaction is exothermic. It is also reversible, which means that we can apply Le Châtelier's principle and predict the best conditions for the industrial preparation of ammonia. Remember that in an industrial process we want to produce the highest yield at the lowest possible cost. There

Figure 7.20

The port of Tocopilla, Chile, in 1920. Nitrate fertilizer was once exported from here. During that year, shipments amounted to 2.5 million tonnes. But the Haber process enabled each country to produce its own fertilizers (and explosives). As a result, the Chilean economy was devastated by the loss of one of its major exports.

are four moles of gas on the left side and only two moles of gas on the right side of the equation as written above. We would predict that this process should be carried out at high pressures because increased pressure favours the side with the smaller number of moles of gas.

Another way of forcing the reaction to the right is to increase the concentrations of nitrogen and hydrogen, and decrease the concentration of ammonia. This can be achieved by the continuous addition of nitrogen and hydrogen and the continuous removal of ammonia. Because the forward reaction is favoured by removal of heat, the process should be run at low temperatures.

In practice, the predictions for pressure and concentration are followed, but not the temperature prediction. Typical operating pressures in this process are between 20 000 and 60 000 kPa. Nitrogen and hydrogen are continuously pumped into the system; ammonia is condensed as it is formed. Although lower temperatures favour the forward reaction, the *rate* at which equilibrium is attained, and thus the rate at which ammonia is produced, is very slow (even at 200 °C). The synthesis is usually carried out at temperatures of 400–500 °C. Although this temperature favours the reverse reaction, ammonia is immediately removed, which makes the concentration factor favour the forward reaction to replace the lost ammonia.

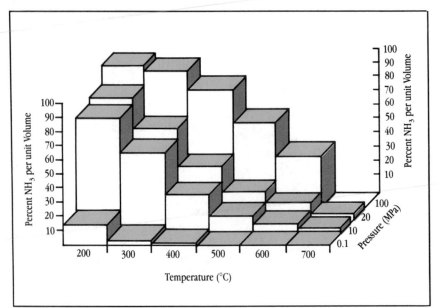

Figure 7.21

The equilibrium for the Haber process depends upon the temperature and pressure. Increased equilibrium yield of ammonia is favoured by high pressure and low temperature.

Much of Haber's initial work on the process was devoted to finding a catalyst that would speed up the rate at which equilibrium was reached. In present day plants, the catalyst is usually a specially prepared mixture of iron, potassium oxide, and aluminum oxide. The presence of a catalyst does not change the position of the equilibrium; it increases the rate of the forward reaction by the same factor that it increases the rate of the reverse reaction. All the catalyst does is allow equilibrium to be reached more rapidly. A schematic representation of the Haber process is shown in Figure 7.22.

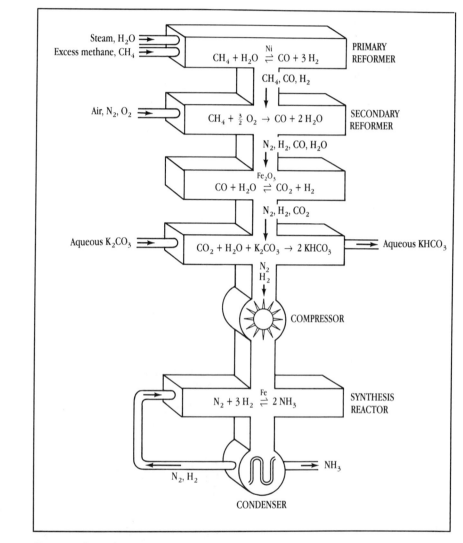

Figure 7.22

A schematic representation of the Haber process.

Economics of Ammonia Production

Haber process plants are usually established where there is an abundant supply of the raw materials. Because nitrogen can be obtained from the atmosphere, the deciding factor is the availability of hydrogen. The source of hydrogen is most often natural gas; a reforming process is used, which releases hydrogen. The development of other newer catalysts now allow ammonia synthesis using naptha from coal or oil.

In addition to raw materials, ammonia plants also require low energy costs, abundant water supply, and transport for the finished product. All of these combined factors will influence the decision to build in a particular area. The larger the chemical plant, the cheaper it becomes to manufacture the product. Although the initial capital costs are high, ammonia plants are usually designed for the maximum capacity of the marketplace. Application of Le Châtelier's principle to ammonia production must be balanced against other economic factors. Higher operating pressures would increase ammonia yields, but high pressure equipment becomes increasingly expensive as the desired pressure increases. Higher temperatures increase the rate of the reaction, but the life of the catalyst is prolonged at lower temperatures. Other operating costs must also be considered: catalysts must be replaced every few years and plants have to be shut down regularly for periodic overhauls and safety checks.

QUESTIONS

24. Why is the Haber process carried out under high pressures?

25. During the Haber process, the ammonia produced is cooled and removed as a liquid. Why does this not also remove the hydrogen and nitrogen from the system? (*Hint*: ammonia condenses to a liquid at $-33\,°C$.)

26. Why would it not be economical to build a Haber process plant in the Canadian Arctic, despite abundant natural gas for energy, and for the production of hydrogen, from the nearby gas fields?

Figure 7.23

The C-I-L Inc. world scale fertilizer plant at Courtright, Ontario. The complex in the foreground with the two tall towers is a new unit for the synthesis of ammonia employing the latest energy-saving technology. At the far right are the two ammonia storage tanks, holding a total of 60 000 tonnes of ammonia.

Haber and the Morality of Science

The 1919 Nobel Prize for Chemistry is the only Nobel Prize in science that was ever openly contested. Why did the awarding of this prize to the German chemist, Fritz Haber, create such an uproar? Haber's process for the production of synthetic ammonia definitely increased fertilizer production and hence the ability of agriculture to feed the world's population. Surely this was enough of a scientific and humanitarian achievement to deserve a Nobel Prize. The protest was not that Haber was undeserving of the prize for his scientific accomplishments, but that other research had, both unintentionally and intentionally, led to a mass destruction of people. The double irony here is that Alfred Nobel, the Swedish millionaire who endowed these prestigious prizes, made his fortune from the development of dynamite, an explosive that is also used in other than beneficial ways.

The world's first synthetic ammonia plant was established in Germany in 1913. In 1914 World War I broke out. Germany's supply of nitrates from Chile were cut off by a British naval blockade. However, the synthetic ammonia plants were able to supply raw material not only for fertilizers but also for production of ammunition and explosives. Nitrogen fixation quickly became a vital factor in the waging of war.

But it was not really this use for Haber's process that caused his scientific colleagues to protest his Nobel Prize. At the outbreak of the war, Haber, now the director of the Kaiser Wilhem Institute for Physical Chemistry and Electrochemistry, worked on a variety of military problems. Foremost in his research was the development of gas warfare. By the end of January 1915, preliminary studies were complete and in April 1915, 5000 cylinders of the yellowish-green chlorine gas were released over a six-kilometre front near Ypres, Belgium. Five thousand men were killed and another ten thousand suffered devastating effects from chlorine exposure. A new era in the horror of war had begun. This initial attempt at gas warfare was, in Haber's opinion, too conservative. If the military had taken his advice they would have conducted a large scale attack rather than the experimental attack at Ypres.

Under Haber's leadership a number of new substances including mustard gas, $(ClCH_2CH_2)_2S$, and phosgene, $COCl_2$, were also tested and used. Ultimately, gas warfare was not the deciding factor in the outcome of World War I. Of the 20 million casualties only 5 % are attributed to gas. But even 50 years later, survivors of gas warfare still had the appalling symptoms of exposure to these chemicals. In the eyes of many scientists, Haber's part in the development of these early chemical weapons could not be cancelled by his earlier great innovation that had done so much to advance world agriculture. They considered a Nobel Prize under these circumstances as a travesty and the resulting outcry deeply affected Haber, who saw little difference between conventional and gas warfare.

After the war, Haber devoted himself to the extraction of gold from sea water, a project based on the assumption that each tonne of sea water contained 10 mg of gold. The assumption was erroneous. There is less than one tenth of that amount of gold in seawater, and Haber's process proved uneconomic.

In 1933 Haber was told by the Nazi government to dismiss all Jewish workers on his staff at the Kaiser Wilhelm Institute. With little regard to his own personal safety, Haber left the institute, writing in his letter of resignation that "... for more than forty years I have selected my collaborators on the basis of their intelligence and their character and not on the basis of their grandmothers, and I am not willing for the rest of my life to to change this method which I have found so good."

Figure 7.24
Fritz Haber (1868-1934), left, with Albert Einstein.

Equilibrium and Spontaneity

7.13

In Chapter 5 we saw that reactions for which the value of Gibbs free energy is positive do not occur spontaneously. Those reactions in which ΔG is negative do occur spontaneously. Remember that the word "spontaneous" used in this sense means only that the reaction is thermodynamically possible. How slow or fast the reaction occurs depends on the kinetic factors discussed in Chapter 6. When ΔG is zero the reaction is spontaneous in both directions and is at equilibrium. In this chapter we have seen that a reaction with a very small value for K_c does not occur to any appreciable extent. On the other hand, when the value of K_c is very large, the reaction goes virtually to completion. There is a relationship between the equilibrium constant, K_c, and the Gibbs free energy, ΔG, of a reaction.

In Chapter 5 we made the distinction between ΔG and $\Delta G°$. We recall that ΔG is the free energy change under a variety of conditions; $\Delta G°$ is the free energy change under standard conditions. The value of ΔG for a given reaction constantly changes as the concentrations of the reactants and products change. However, one particular combination of concentrations gives ΔG a value of zero (the equilibrium point). The relationship between ΔG and $\Delta G°$ for a reaction can be calculated from non-equilibrium concentration values. Then we can use $\Delta G°$, as in the equation given below, to find the equilibrium constant K_c. Conversely, we may also determine $\Delta G°$ if we know the value of K_c. The relationship for a reaction in solution is

$$\Delta G° = -RT \ln K_c$$

where $\Delta G°$ is the free energy of the reaction under standard conditions,
   R is the universal gas constant $(8.314\,\mathrm{J \cdot mol^{-1} \cdot K^{-1}})$,
   T is the absolute temperature of the reaction, in kelvins,
   $\ln$ is the natural logarithm,
   K_c is the equilibrium constant.
Notice that our units for R are in joules per mole per kelvin $(\mathrm{J \cdot mol^{-1} \cdot K^{-1}})$, although in previous chapters the units were kilopascal litres per mole per kelvin $(\mathrm{kPa \cdot L \cdot mol^{-1} \cdot K^{-1}})$. This is because it can be shown that $1\,\mathrm{J} = 1\,\mathrm{kPa \cdot L}$. For a gas phase reaction we would use a similar relationship involving K_p. the equilibrium constant in terms of partial pressures.

EXAMPLE

7.13

At 298 K the equilibrium constant, K_c, for the following reaction is 3.5×10^{-8}.

$$HClO_{(aq)} \rightleftharpoons H^+_{(aq)} + ClO^-_{(aq)}$$

Calculate $\Delta G°$ for this reaction at this temperature.

Using $\Delta G° = -RT \ln K_c$

We get, $\Delta G° = -8.314 \, \text{J} \cdot \text{mol}^{-1} \cdot \text{K}^{-1} \times 298 \, \text{K} \times \ln(3.5 \times 10^{-8})$

$\qquad\qquad = -8.314 \, \text{J} \cdot \text{mol}^{-1} \cdot \text{K}^{-1} \times 298 \, \text{K} \times (-17.17)$

$\qquad\qquad = +4.25 \times 10^4 \, \text{J} \cdot \text{mol}^{-1}$

Applying the necessary conversion factor, we get

$$\Delta G° = 42.5 \, \text{kJ} \cdot \text{mol}^{-1}$$

+ve

This value for $\Delta G°$ is large and negative, as expected from a reaction where K_c is very small. If the value of K_c is greater than 1, the natural log of K_c is a positive quantity, and $\Delta G°$ is then negative.

QUESTIONS

27. What is the thermodynamic definition of equilibrium?

28. For the following reactions would the value of the equilibrium constant be less than or greater than 1?
    a) $CO_{(g)} + 2\,H_{2\,(g)} \rightleftharpoons CH_3OH_{(\ell)}$ $\qquad \Delta G° = -29 \, \text{kJ}$
    b) $2\,SO_{3\,(g)} \rightleftharpoons 2\,SO_{2\,(g)} + O_{2\,(g)}$ $\qquad \Delta G° = +142 \, \text{kJ}$

29. For the dissolving of solid silver chloride in water at 25 °C

$$AgCl_{(s)} \underset{\text{water}}{\overset{\text{dissolve in}}{\rightleftharpoons}} Ag^+_{(aq)} + Cl^-_{(aq)}$$

$\Delta G°$ is +55.6 kJ. Calculate the equilibrium constant, K_c, for the reaction at this temperature.

Summary

- In chemical and physical systems, a reaction or process that is reversible to a measurable extent can reach equilibrium under the appropriate conditions. At equilibrium the rate of the forward reaction is equal to the rate of the reverse reaction.

- An equilibrium in which all the reactants and products are in the same phase is known as a homogeneous equilibrium. If they are not all in the same phase it is a heterogeneous equilibrium.

- Although the rates of forward and reverse reactions are the same at equilibrium, their rate constants are different. The equilibrium concentrations of reactants and products are also different.

- The equilibrium constant, K_c, is the ratio of product concentrations to reactant concentrations. Each concentration is raised to a power which is given by the coefficient in the balanced chemical equation.

- The magnitude of K_c indicates the extent of the forward and reverse reactions. In general, if the value of K_c is greater than 1, the forward reaction is favoured; if K_c is less than 1, the reverse reaction is favoured.

- Le Châtelier's principle states that an equilibrium will shift in response to an external stress. An increase in concentration of any product or reactant will favour a move in the direction that uses up that component. Increased pressure favours a shift towards the side of the equilibrium with fewer moles of gas. Increased temperature favours a shift in the direction that absorbs heat. The Haber process is an example of the application of Le Châtelier's principle in industry.

- The relationship between the spontaneity of a reaction in solution and its equilibrium constant is given by the following equation.

$$\Delta G^\circ = -RT \ln K_c$$

An equilibrium constant greater than 1 corresponds to a negative value for ΔG° (a spontaneous reaction in the forward direction). An equilibrium constant of less than 1 has a positive value for ΔG° (the forward reaction is nonspontaneous).

KEY WORDS

closed system
dynamic equilibrium
equilibrium
equilibrium constant
equilibrium constant expression
Haber Process

heterogeneous equilibrium
homogeneous equilibrium
Le Châtelier's principle
nitrogen cycle
open system

ANSWERS TO
SECTION QUESTIONS

1. a) and c)

2. a) $4\,H_{2\,(g)} + Fe_3O_{4\,(s)} \rightleftharpoons 3\,Fe_{(s)} + 4\,H_2O_{(g)}$

   b) $2\,HI_{(g)} \rightleftharpoons H_{2\,(g)} + I_{2\,(g)}$

   c) $3\,H_{2\,(g)} + N_{2\,(g)} \rightleftharpoons 2\,NH_{3\,(g)}$

3. a) The radioactivity would remain confined to the ice cubes.

   b) As some radioactive ice molecules melted into the water and some water molecules froze onto the ice, there would eventually be a distribution of the radioactivity through the liquid as well as the solid.

4. b); this is the definition of equilibrium

5. a) $\dfrac{[N_2O_4]}{[NO_2]^2}$ b) $\dfrac{[NH_3]^2}{[N_2][H_2]^3}$

6. b)

7. Any set of equilibrium concentrations produces the same value (5.09) if substituted in the given equilibrium expression.

8. The rate ice melts equals the rate water freezes.

9. a) The rate of the forward reaction equals the rate of the reverse reaction.

b) $K_{eq} = \dfrac{k_f}{k_r}$

10. a) products   b) neither   c) reactants

11. No; very few chlorine atoms would be present at this temperature. The extremely small value for the equilibrium constant indicates that the formation of chlorine atoms is not favoured.

12. a) $K_c = \dfrac{[NO_2]^2}{[NO]^2[O_2]}$

b) $K_c = \dfrac{[H_2O]^2[Cl_2]^2}{[HCl]^4[O_2]}$

c) $K_c = \dfrac{[NO][Cl_2]^{\frac{1}{2}}}{[NOCl]}$

13. $K_c = 3.31 \times 10^{-3}$

14. a) heterogeneous: $K_c = [N_2][H_2O]^2$

b) heterogeneous: $K_c = [H_2O]$

c) homogeneous: $K_c = \dfrac{[SO_3]}{[SO_2][O_2]^{\frac{1}{2}}}$

d) heterogeneous: $K_c = \dfrac{[SO_2]^8}{[O_2]^8}$

15. $K_c = 5.6$

16. $K_c = 1.33 \times 10^{-1}$

17. 0.181 mol·L^{-1}

18. $[NO] = 0.0902$ mol·L^{-1}; $[NO_2] = 0.010$ mol·L^{-1}

19. $[CO] = 4.7 \times 10^{-6}$ mol·L^{-1}

20. Any three of the following: add more NO_2, remove NO, remove O_2, or decrease the pressure by increasing the volume of the reaction vessel.

21. a) Equilibrium shifts to the left.
b) Equilibrium shifts to the right.
c) No change to position of the equilibrium.
d) Equilibrium moves to left. Decreased volume (increased pressure) favours the side with fewer moles of gas.
e) No change to position of the equilibrium.

22. a) Increase the temperature.
b) Decrease the temperature.

23. a) K_c increases.
b) K_c decreases.

24. Increased pressure favours the side with the fewer number of moles of gas — that is, the formation of ammonia.

25. The liquefaction temperature of ammonia is far above the liquefaction temperature of hydrogen or nitrogen.

26. Very high transportation costs would be incurred in transporting the ammonia to markets; there would be very high operating costs in the Arctic; climate and the available water required for the process would be frozen for most of the year.

27. A reaction is at equilibrium when $\Delta G = 0$.

28. a) $K_c > 1$ b) $K_c < 1$

29. $K_c = 1.8 \times 10^{-10}$

COMPREHENSION QUESTIONS

1. What is meant by a reversible reaction?

2. Would you consider the combustion of methane, CH_4, with oxygen to form carbon dioxide and water, to be a reversible reaction?

3. What is the difference between a physical and a chemical equilibrium?

4. Which of the following equilibria are chemical and which are physical?
   a) the sublimation of dry ice (solid carbon dioxide)
   b) a saturated sodium chloride solution in contact with excess solid sodium chloride
   c) the partial dissociation of two moles of hydrogen bromide into one mole of hydrogen and one mole of bromine

5. Which of the following remains constant at equilibrium?
   a) the concentration of the products
   b) the concentration of the reactants
   c) the ratio of product concentration to reactant concentration

6. What is the relationship between the forward and reverse reaction rates at equilibrium?

7. What does the magnitude of the equilibrium constant indicate about the extent of the reaction?

8. At $25\,°C$ the equilibrium constant, K_c, for the following reaction is known to be 7.1×10^{27}.

$$Cd^{2+}_{(aq)} + S^{2-}_{(aq)} \rightleftharpoons CdS_{(s)}$$

   Would it be possible to use this reaction to accurately determine the sulfide ion concentration in a solution?

9. What is the relationship between the equilibrium constant and the forward and reverse reaction rates?

10. If an equilibrium reaction is written as reversed, what happens to its equilibrium constant?

11. Why is this statement incomplete?
    "The equilibrium constant for the reaction of sulfur dioxide with oxygen is $K_c = 2.2 \times 10^{10}$."

12. Distinguish between a homogeneous and a heterogeneous equilibrium.

13. Which of the following is a homogeneous and which is a heterogeneous equilibrium?
    a) $2\,H_{2\,(g)} + O_{2\,(g)} \rightleftharpoons 2\,H_2O_{(g)}$
    b) $2\,H_{2\,(g)} + O_{2\,(g)} \rightleftharpoons 2\,H_2O_{(\ell)}$
    c) $C_{(s)} + CO_{2\,(g)} + 2\,Cl_{2\,(g)} \rightleftharpoons 2\,COCl_{2\,(g)}$

14. Why does the concentration of carbon not appear in the equilibrium expression for the reaction

$$C_{(s)} + O_{2\,(g)} \rightleftharpoons CO_{2\,(g)}$$

15. When can we use an approximation in a calculation of equilibrium concentrations?

16. What is Le Châtelier's principle?

17. What are three outside stresses that can affect the position of an equilibrium?

18. Water molecules are taken up by cobalt(II) chloride molecules as shown by the following equilibrium equation;

$$[Co(H_2O)_6]Cl_{2\,(s)} \rightleftharpoons [Co(H_2O)_4]Cl_{2\,(s)} + 2\,H_2O_{(g)}$$
$$\text{pink} \qquad\qquad\qquad \text{blue}$$

A weather indicator can be made using this reaction as the basis for the colour change. Does a blue colour indicate "dry" or "moist" air?

19. Describe the Haber process for the industrial production of ammonia.

20. Explain why the value of K_c for an exothermic reaction increases as the temperature decreases.

21. Why is ammonia such an important industrial chemical?

22. Why is the production of ammonia of such importance to agriculture?

23. Why is a catalyst used in the Haber process?

24. What is the relationship between spontaneity and the equilibrium constant?

25. Explain why a K_c value of less than 1 always gives a positive $\Delta G°$ value.

PROBLEMS   *The Equilibrium Constant Expression*

26. Write the equilibrium expression for each of the following processes:
    a) $Br_{2\,(g)} + 5\,F_{2\,(g)} \rightleftharpoons 2\,BrF_{5\,(g)}$
    b) $Ca_3(PO_4)_{2\,(s)} \rightleftharpoons 3\,Ca^{2+}_{\;(aq)} + 2\,PO_4^{\;3-}_{\;(aq)}$
    c) $5\,Fe^{2+}_{\;(aq)} + MnO_4^{\;-}_{\;(aq)} + 8\,H^+_{\;(aq)} \rightleftharpoons$
    $$5\,Fe^{3+}_{\;(aq)} + Mn^{2+}_{\;(aq)} + 4\,H_2O_{(\ell)}$$

27. Write the reaction equation and the equilibrium expression for each of the following physical changes:
   a) the condensation of steam
   b) the dissolving of silver bromide in water
   c) the sublimation of solid carbon dioxide

28. At 1200 °C, hydrogen sulfide decomposes according to the following reaction:

$$2 H_2S_{(g)} \rightleftharpoons 2 H_{2\,(g)} + S_{2\,(g)}$$

The equilibrium constant, K_c, for this reaction is 4.22×10^{-4}. If the temperature remains constant, what is the equilibrium constant for the following reaction?

$$3 S_{2\,(g)} + 6 H_{2\,(g)} \rightleftharpoons 6 H_2S_{(g)}$$

29. Write the equilibrium expression for each of the following equilibria:
   a) $P_{4\,(g)} + 5 O_{2\,(g)} \rightleftharpoons P_4O_{10\,(g)}$
   b) $ZnO_{(s)} + CO_{(g)} \rightleftharpoons Zn_{(s)} + CO_{2\,(g)}$
   c) $2 N_2O_{5\,(g)} \rightleftharpoons 4 NO_{2\,(g)} + O_{2\,(g)}$
   Which of these equilibria are homogeneous?

How Equilibrium Constants are Determined

30. At 1000 °C, methane reacts with water as follows:

$$CH_{4\,(g)} + H_2O_{(g)} \rightleftharpoons CO_{(g)} + 3 H_{2\,(g)}$$

In one experiment the equilibrium concentrations of the gases were $[CH_4] = 2.97 \times 10^{-3}$, $[H_2O] = 7.94 \times 10^{-3}$, $[CO] = 5.45 \times 10^{-3}$, and $[H_2] = 2.1 \times 10^{-3}$ (all in mol·L^{-1}). Calculate K_c at this temperature.

31. Phosphorus pentachloride decomposes via the reaction

$$PCl_{5\,(g)} \rightleftharpoons PCl_{3\,(g)} + Cl_{2\,(g)}$$

A sample of phosphorus pentachloride of concentration 1.10 mol·L^{-1} was placed in a container. Once equilibrium was attained, it was found that the concentration of chlorine in the vessel was 0.33 mol·L^{-1}. Calculate K_c for the reaction at this temperature.

32. For the following process, the equilibrium constant, K_c, is 0.98.

$$2 FeBr_{3\,(s)} \rightleftharpoons 2 FeBr_{2\,(s)} + Br_{2\,(g)}$$

A 3.0 litre reaction vessel contains 3.6 moles of iron(II) bromide, 1.2 moles of iron(III) bromide, and 2.1 moles of bromine gas at this temperature. Is the system at equilibrium?

33. A 0.921 mol sample of dinitrogen tetroxide is placed in a 1.00 litre reaction vessel and heated to 100 °C. At equilibrium at this temperature it is found that 20.7 % of the dinitrogen tetroxide has decomposed to nitrogen dioxide according to the reaction

$$N_2O_{4\,(g)} \rightleftharpoons 2\,NO_{2\,(g)}$$

Calculate K_c for the reaction at this temperature.

34. At a certain temperature the equilibrium concentration of dinitrogen tetroxide gas is 6.38×10^{-3} mol·L^{-1}. The gas concentration of the system is 1.23×10^{-2} mol·L^{-1}. Determine K_c at this temperature, for the following equilibrium between dinitrogen tetroxide and nitrogen dioxide gas:

$$N_2O_{4\,(g)} \rightleftharpoons 2\,NO_{2\,(g)}$$

Determining Equilibrium Concentrations

35. At a high temperature the equilibrium constant for the reaction

$$CaCO_{3\,(s)} \rightleftharpoons CaO_{(s)} + CO_{2\,(g)}$$

was found to be 0.15.
a) What is equilibrium concentration of carbon dioxide at this temperature?
b) If 100.0 g of solid calcium carbonate was placed in a 10.0 L vessel and heated to the above temperature, could equilibrium be reached?

36. The equilibrium constant for the following reaction is 0.11.

$$2\,ICl_{(g)} \rightleftharpoons I_{2\,(g)} + Cl_{2\,(g)}$$

Calculate all the equilibrium concentrations if 0.33 mol of iodine chloride gas is placed in a 1.00 L vessel and the reaction is allowed to reach equilibrium.

37. At 1200 °C, the value of K_c for the reaction below is 2.51×10^4.

$$H_{2\,(g)} + Cl_{2\,(g)} \rightleftharpoons 2\,HCl_{(g)}$$

If 0.250 mol of chlorine gas and 0.250 mol of hydrogen gas are introduced into a 1.00 L vessel, determine the concentration of hydrogen chloride gas once equilibrium is reached.

38. At 1530°C, K_c for the reaction

$$N_{2\,(g)} + O_{2\,(g)} \rightleftharpoons 2\,NO_{(g)}$$

is 1.20×10^{-4}. The reaction, with nitrogen and oxygen initially at a concentration of 1.00 mol·L^{-1} each, is allowed to reach equilibrium. Determine the equilibrium concentration of nitrogen monoxide under these conditions.

39. At 2000 °C, the following reaction has an equilibrium constant, K_c, of 6.40×10^{-7}:

$$2\, CO_{2\,(g)} \rightleftharpoons 2\, CO_{(g)} + O_{2\,(g)}$$

If 1.00 mol of carbon dioxide is placed in a 1.00 L vessel, what will be the concentration of oxygen gas when equilibrium is established?

40. The dissociation of ammonia at 27 °C, has a K_c value of 2.63×10^{-9}.

$$2\, NH_{3\,(g)} \rightleftharpoons N_{2\,(g)} + 3\, H_{2\,(g)}$$

If 1.00 mol of ammonia is placed in a 1.00 L vessel, calculate the equilibrium concentration of nitrogen and hydrogen.

Le Châtelier's Principle

41. In which direction will the equilibrium

$$N_{2\,(g)} + O_{2\,(g)} \rightleftharpoons 2\, NO_{(g)} \qquad \Delta H = +179\,kJ$$

shift, with the following changes:
a) addition of nitrogen gas
b) removal of oxygen gas
c) addition of a catalyst
d) halving of the volume of the system

42. For the following gaseous equilibrium

$$2\, SO_{2\,(g)} + O_{2\,(g)} \rightleftharpoons 2\, SO_{3\,(g)} \qquad \Delta H = -198\,kJ$$

predict the effect on the equilibrium of the following changes:
a) sulfur trioxide is added
b) the volume of the system is doubled
c) sulfur dioxide is removed
d) an inert gas such as helium is added

43. The following reaction occurs readily at 425 °C:

$$2\, NO_{(g)} + Cl_{2\,(g)} \rightleftharpoons 2\, NOCl_{(g)}$$

The equilibrium constant, K_c, is 14.9 at this temperature. Predict the shift that the reaction would take to establish equilibrium for each of the following starting conditions:
a) all gases are at a concentration of 0.100 mol·L^{-1}
b) all gases are at a concentration of 1.00 mol·L^{-1}
c) [NOCl] = 0.100, [NO] = 0.0500, [Cl$_2$] = 0.100 mol·L^{-1}

44. The dissociation of acetic acid in water

$$CH_3CO_2H_{(aq)} \rightleftharpoons CH_3CO_2{}^-{}_{(aq)} + H^+{}_{(aq)}$$

has a K_c value of 1.8×10^{-5} at 25°C.
a) Calculate the equilibrium concentration of $H^+{}_{(aq)}$ in a solution that was originally 0.010 mol·L^{-1} acetic acid.
b) In which direction will this equilibrium move if H^+ ions from concentrated hydrochloric acid are added?

The Effect of Temperature on Equilibrium

45. For the equilibrium in Question 41, in which direction will the equilibrium move if the temperature is decreased?

46. For the equilibrium in Question 42, predict the change in the equilibrium constant under the following changes.
   a) the temperature is increased
   b) the temperature is decreased

Equilibrium and Spontaneity

47. For the reaction in which barium sulfate dissolves in water

$$BaSO_{4\,(s)} \underset{\text{water}}{\overset{\text{dissolve in}}{\rightleftharpoons}} Ba^{2+}_{(aq)} + SO_4^{2-}_{(aq)}$$

K_c at 298 K is 1.20×10^{-10}. Calculate $\Delta G°$ for this reaction.

48. For the reaction of methylamine, CH_3NH_2, with water, $\Delta G°$ is 18.8 kJ at 298 K.

$$CH_3NH_{2\,(aq)} + H_2O_{(\ell)} \rightleftharpoons CH_3NH_3^+{}_{(aq)} + OH^-_{(aq)}$$

Determine K_c for this reaction.

MISCELLANEOUS PROBLEMS

49. Fe^{2+} reacts with SCN^- forming a complex ion:

$$Fe^{2+}_{(aq)} + x\,SCN^-_{(aq)} \rightleftharpoons [Fe(SCN)_x^{2-x}]_{(aq)}$$

Determine the value of x from the following equilibrium concentrations, measured from three different experiments at the same temperature.

	$[Fe^{2+}]$	$[SCN^-]$	$[Fe(SCN)_x^{2-x}]$
Expt 1	0.048	0.061	0.019
Expt 2	0.027	0.027	0.0046
Expt 3	0.17	0.0085	0.0092

50. The following reaction takes place in a 1.00 L vessel at 500 °C.

$$2\,HI_{(g)} \rightleftharpoons H_{2\,(g)} + I_{2\,(g)}$$

Equilibrium concentrations were found to be 1.76 mol·L^{-1} HI, 0.20 mol·L^{-1} H_2, and 0.20 mol·L^{-1} I_2. If an additional 0.500 mol of hydrogen iodide gas is introduced, what are the concentrations of all gases once equilibrium has again been reached?

Problems 51 through 54 require the use of the quadratic formula (shown below) to find the value of the unknown:

$$\frac{-b \pm \sqrt{b^2 - 4ac}}{2a}$$

51. The dissociation of ammonia at $400\,°C$ has a K_c value of 1.92.

$$2\,NH_{3\,(g)} \rightleftharpoons N_{2\,(g)} + 3\,H_{2\,(g)}$$

If 0.500 mol of ammonia is placed in a 500.0 mL container, determine the equilibrium concentrations of all the gases.

52. The equilibrium constant, K_c, for the following reaction is 85.0 at $460\,°C$.

$$SO_{2\,(g)} + NO_{2\,(g)} \rightleftharpoons NO_{(g)} + SO_{3\,(g)}$$

If a mixture is prepared where the initial concentration of sulfur dioxide is $1.00\,mol \cdot L^{-1}$ and that of nitrogen dioxide is $2.00\,mol \cdot L^{-1}$, calculate the equilibrium concentration of nitrogen monoxide and of nitrogen dioxide at this temperature.

53. The equilibrium constant for the reaction is $K_c = 9.09$.

$$I_{2\,(g)} + Cl_{2\,(g)} \rightleftharpoons 2\,ICl_{(g)}$$

Calculate all equilibrium concentrations if 0.100 mol of iodine and 0.0500 mol of chlorine are placed in a 1.00 L vessel and allowed to reach equilibrium.

54. In an experiment at $240\,°C$, it was found that for the reaction

$$PCl_{3\,(g)} + Cl_{2\,(g)} \rightleftharpoons PCl_{5\,(g)}$$

equilibrium concentrations were $0.100\,mol \cdot L^{-1}\,PCl_3$, $0.100\,mol \cdot L^{-1}\,Cl_2$, and $0.200\,mol \cdot L^{-1}\,PCl_5$.
a) Calculate K_c for the reaction at this temperature.
b) If the volume of the reaction vessel is halved, calculate the new concentrations once equilibrium is re-established.

SUGGESTED PROJECTS
1. Smokers absorb carbon monoxide through inhalation. The equilibrium reaction

$$HbO_{2\,(aq)} + CO_{(g)} \rightleftharpoons HbCO_{(aq)} + O_{2\,(g)}$$

between oxyhemoglobin, HbO_2, and carboxyhemoglobin, $HbCO$, has a K_{eq} value of around 200 at body temperature. Suggest what effect this has on the oxygen carrying capacity of the smoker's blood. Why is this of importance to smokers?

2. Breakthroughs in science do not always benefit humanity. Investigate several areas of current research and comment on the potential for misuse of the resulting knowledge. Suggest, as well, whether guidelines can be drawn up that might restrict the potential for abuse of new discoveries and techniques.

CHAPTER 8

Solutions and Solubility

The rate of a chemical reaction depends on the concentration of the reactants and on the reaction temperature. Both of these factors can be readily controlled in liquid solutions. For this reason most chemical reactions in the laboratory and in industry are carried out in solution.

This chapter deals with solutions and factors that determine solubility. Since water is the most important solvent in chemistry, and it is also the medium in which all biochemical reactions occur, we will restrict our study to aqueous solutions. We will see how equilibrium principles can be applied to saturated solutions of ionic compounds as well as carry out some calculations involving solutions.

Types of Solutions

8.1 A *solution* is a homogeneous mixture of two or more substances. The substance that is present in the largest amount, and which therefore usually determines the phase of the solution, is called the *solvent*. The substance that is dissolved in the solvent is called the *solute*. When sugar is dissolved in water, sugar is the solute and water is the solvent. However, solutions are not restricted to a single solute; some solutions contain several.

The substances that make up a solution may be in any one of the three phases: gas, liquid, or solid. The terms solvent and solute are most commonly applied to liquid solutions, such as those we encounter in the laboratory. The solvent is usually water or one of the many other common liquids such as acetone, ether, or ethanol. The solute may be a gas, liquid, or solid. If the solute dissolves well in the solvent, we say it is **soluble**. If it does not dissolve or dissolves only slightly we say it is **insoluble**. On the other hand, if we are discussing the **solubility** of one liquid in another, we use the terms **miscible** and **immiscible** to describe the solubility.

Air is a solution in which all the components are gases. The main constituents are nitrogen (78 %), oxygen (21 %), argon (0.9 %), and carbon dioxide (0.03 %). Varying trace amounts of other gases are also present.

The most common types of solid-in-solid solutions are mixtures of metals, called alloys. Brass, for instance, is a solution of zinc (15–30 % by mass) in copper, and sterling silver is a solution of copper (7.5 % by mass) in silver.

Amalgams are liquid-in-solid solutions. An example of this is the metal mercury dissolved in a metallic solid or in a mixture of metals, such as silver, tin and copper.

QUESTIONS

1. Cola drinks contain water, sugar, flavouring and colouring agents, and carbon dioxide gas under pressure. Identify the solutes and solvent in this solution.

2. Which of the following could be classified as solutions: milk, salad dressing, apple juice, bronze.

The Solution Process of Covalent Compounds

8.2 Why does alcohol mix with water, but gasoline does not? We can investigate this by looking for common patterns in the miscibility of liquids. Let us take four liquids — ethanol, acetone, carbon tetrachloride, and hexane — and try to mix each with water. The results are shown in Table 8.1. The structure of each liquid is given in Figure 8.1.

TABLE 8.1	*The Miscibility of Liquids with Water*	
Miscible	Immiscible	
ethanol	carbon tetrachloride	
acetone	hexane	

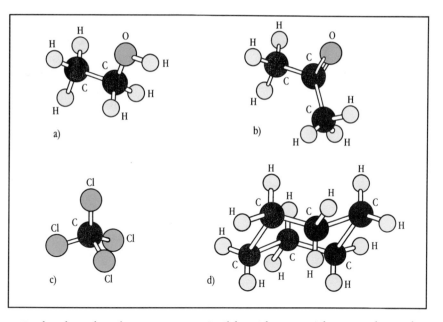

Figure 8.1
The chemical structures of a) ethanol, b) acetone, c) carbon tetrachloride, and d) cyclohexane.

Both ethanol and acetone are miscible with water. They are also polar molecules. Hexane and carbon tetrachloride are nonpolar molecules. Neither one is miscible with water. Studies with a wide range of substances indicate that the miscibility of two liquids or the solubility of a solid in a liquid depends on the attractive forces that operate between the substances. These intermolecular forces can be of various types.

A Review of Intermolecular Forces

Dispersion Forces These are attractions that exist between all covalent molecules. The strength of these forces increases with molecular size because the forces are related to the number of electrons. Dispersion forces also depend on the shape of the molecules because the shape determines how well molecules can approach and interact with each other.

Dipole-Dipole Forces In addition to dispersion forces, polar molecules are also attracted to one another by permanent charges on neighbouring molecules. The strength of these dipole-dipole forces depends on the magnitude of the dipole, which is mainly affected by the difference in electronegativity of atoms in the molecule and the molecular shape of the molecule.

Hydrogen Bonds We encounter an exceptionally strong dipole-dipole attraction in substances that contain a hydrogen atom bonded to a highly-electronegative fluorine, oxygen, or nitrogen atom. For this reason we give it the special name of *hydrogen bond*, even though it is only an intermolecular force.

Miscibility of Liquids

Because hexane and carbon tetrachloride are nonpolar molecules, their only intermolecular attractions are dispersion forces. Acetone is a polar molecule; it has dipole-dipole forces between its molecules. Water and ethanol are also polar, both possessing hydrogen bonds. It is the similarity of intermolecular forces that indicates whether or not two liquids will mix. Water will only mix with other polar liquids with which it can share the same type of intermolecular forces (Figure 8.2).

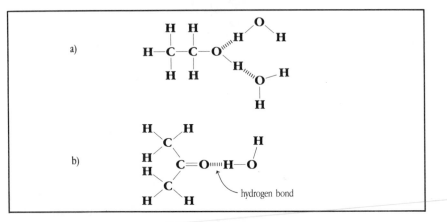

Figure 8.2

a) *Hydrogen bonds formed between ethanol and water.*

b) *A hydrogen bond formed between acetone and water*

The frequently quoted guideline "like dissolves like" should be used with caution. Many organic liquids mix even when one is polar and the other is not. For example, ethanol will mix with gasoline and many other nonpolar liquids. If a long molecule has a small polar "end," we find the nonpolar chain dominates its properties. For example, octanol has an —OH group and thus should be able to hydrogen bond with water. In fact, it only mixes with water to the extent of $0.5 \, \text{g} \cdot \text{L}^{-1}$ because of the long nonpolar chain.

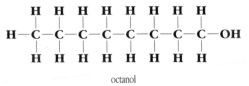

octanol

Dry Cleaning Solvents

Clothing made of natural fibers such as wool, silk, or cotton tend to lose their shape when cleaned with hot water and soap. These items will often be brought to the dry cleaner for cleaning. Here, the dirt, usually oil or grease, is removed with solvents that are immiscible with water. A good **dry cleaning solvent** has the following features:

1. low polarity in order to dissolve the nonpolar grease but not the more polar dyes;

2. liquid at room temperature but sufficiently volatile so that clothes "dry" quickly;

3. nonflammable and nontoxic.

Hydrocarbons in which all the hydrogen atoms are replaced by chlorine or fluorine atoms have proved to be most useful.

Figure 8.3

a) tetrachloroethene and b) 1,1,2-trichlorotrifluoroethane are used as dry cleaning solvents.

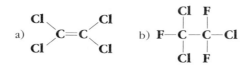

Dry cleaning may seem to be the answer for removing the soup stains from a pleated wool skirt, but the process also raises concerns. Some of the solvent vapour rises to the upper atmosphere where ultraviolet light can remove some of the chlorine atoms. Eventually, these chlorine atoms may seriously deplete the ozone layer. This would allow more dangerous ultraviolet radiation to reach the surface of the earth.

Solubility of Solids

Nonpolar solids generally dissolve well in nonpolar solvents, but solubility in a polar solvent such as ethanol will be low. A nonpolar solid will always be insoluble in water. However, the caution against "like dissolves like" applies here as well. An experienced chemist is often unable to predict the solubility of one substance in another and has to rely on experiment.

This is also the case with polar substances. The solubility in water often must be determined by experiment. Molecular substances that dissolve in water usually do so by forming hydrogen bonds with the water molecules. Sugar molecules, although quite large, dissolve easily in water because each sugar molecule can form several hydrogen bonds.

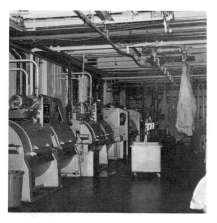

Figure 8.4

The inside of a dry cleaning plant. Non-polar stains of oil or grease can be removed from clothing using nonpolar solvents in the dry cleaning process.

Figure 8.5

a) The structure of vitamin C. With the large number of polar -OH groups, vitamin C is highly water soluble. As a result, it is readily excreted from the body.

b) The structure of vitamin A. This largely nonpolar molecule tends to dissolve in the body's fatty tissues.

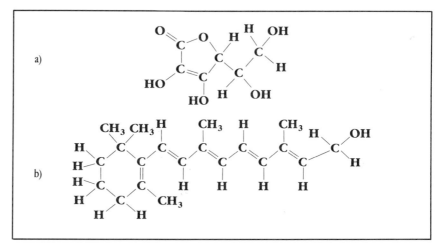

Figure 8.6

The common vitamins. Vitamins A,D,E, and K are essentially nonpolar. These fat-soluble vitamins accumulate in our fatty tissues. Large doses can be harmful. Vitamins B and C are water soluble. Large doses of these polar vitamins can be taken without great harm since they are readily excreted.

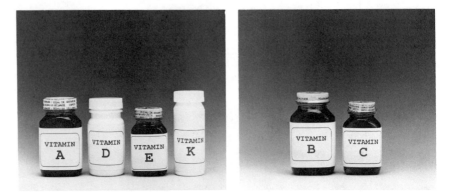

Effect of Temperature on Solubility

The solubility of a solid in a liquid will always be limited. The solid will dissolve until the concentration of the dissolved solid, or solute, reaches a maximum. At that point the solution is said to be **saturated**. The same situation applies to a solution of a gas in a liquid or to a solution of a partially miscible liquid in another liquid (e.g. ethyl ether in water).

The maximum solubility will vary with the temperature of the solution. Consider the situation in which we increase the temperature of a saturated solution.

$$\textbf{solute}_{(s,\ell,g)} \rightleftharpoons \textbf{solute}_{(sol'n)}$$

We are adding heat to an equilibrium system which will result in a shift in the equilibrium position. The direction of this shift can be predicted by Le Châtelier's principle. The equilibrium will shift in the direction in which the added heat, or at least part of it, is used up. If the solution process is exothermic, some solute will crystallize from the solution. If the solution process is endothermic, more solute will dissolve into the solution.

We can, therefore, state a few general trends for the effect of temperature on solubility. For most gases, the dissolving process in liquids is exothermic and thus the solubility decreases upon heating. For example, a lake is generally saturated with oxygen gas, which is necessary for the survival of fish and other aquatic life. A small temperature increase can prove beneficial, but a major increase in temperature would cause a decrease in the amount of dissolved oxygen and threaten the survival of life in the lake. Heat pollution of this type can occur when industries use small lakes and rivers for cooling water.

For molecular substances other than gases, the dissolving process is endothermic. As a result, these substances have a higher solubility as the temperature increases. More sugar will dissolve in hot water than in cold.

In the process of **recrystallization** (Figure 8.7), used in the purification of solid substances, we take advantage of the difference in solubility at different temperatures. If we wish to purify a solid substance, a solvent is needed in which the substance has a low solubility at 0 °C but an increased solubility at the boiling point of the solvent. The impure solid is dissolved in the minimum amount of boiling solvent. Any insoluble impurities are removed by filtration. The solution is next cooled in ice, which causes the dissolved solid to crystallize in a very pure form.

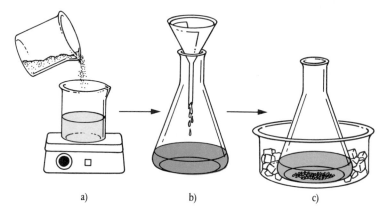

Figure 8.7
We can purify a solid by a) dissolving it in a hot solvent, b) filtering off any insoluble impurities, and c) then cooling the solution in ice to give us a crop of pure crystals.

a)   b)   c)

Effect of Pressure on Solubility of Gases

The solubility of a gas in a liquid increases when the pressure of the gas above the liquid is increased. Carbonated beverages contain carbon dioxide which is dissolved under pressure. When the cap of the bottle is removed, the carbon dioxide pressure is reduced and the gas starts to escape from the liquid.

The effect of pressure on the solubility of a gas in a liquid is another example of Le Châtelier's principle. The gas above the liquid is in equilibrium with the gas dissolved in the liquid.

$$CO_{2\,(g)} \rightleftharpoons CO_{2\,(aq)}$$

When the pressure of the gas above the solution is increased, the equilibrium shifts to the right. When the pressure of the gas above the solution is decreased by removing the cap of a soft drink bottle, the equilibrium shifts to the left and gas escapes from the solution. There is, of course, a double effect on this equilibrium when the soft drink bottle is warmed. Increased temperature also shifts the equilibrium to the left, hence the excessive bubbling when the cap is removed.

Divers who breathe compressed air at depths where the pressure is high, must be very careful when they return to the surface. More air dissolves in the bloodstream under the greater pressure, and small bubbles of nitrogen gas can form inside blood vessels if the pressure is reduced too suddenly. The bubbles of nitrogen produce a painful and potentially fatal condition called "the bends." For this reason most divers now breathe an oxygen-helium mixture rather than compressed air, since helium is much less soluble under pressure in water than nitrogen.

Figure 8.8
Deep-sea divers breathe a mixture of oxygen and helium.

Colloids and Beauty Products

Many substances do not dissolve readily in any of the commonly used solvents. However, it is often possible to suspend these substances in a suitable medium, provided that the particles are small enough. Such suspensions are called *colloids*. Colloids play a major role in our lives, and as such should be studied in greater detail.

Each combination of phases that makes up a colloid is given a separate name. For example, a liquid dispersed in another liquid is called an *emulsion*. Some emulsions, such as milk, are suspensions of a nonpolar substance (fat) in a polar substance (water). Butter, another emulsion, is a suspension of a polar substance (water) in a nonpolar substance (fat). Many beauty products are also emulsions. In fact the skin care and cosmetic industry involves an enormous amount of chemical research and is a major purchaser of chemicals.

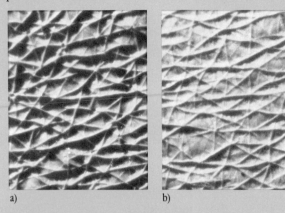

Figure 8.9

a) Dry skin before application of moisturizer.
b) After twenty days of moisturizer application, the skin is smoother and healthier.

To remain healthy, the moisture content of skin must stay near 10 %. If it is higher, micro-organisms will grow more easily. If it is lower, the outer layer will flake off. Washing the skin removes the surface fats that retain the moisture. If dry skin is treated with a fat after washing, it will be protected until enough natural fats have been regenerated. Most skin moisturizers then consist of an emulsion of a fat in water. Many contain lanolin as the fat component. Although the compounds in lanolin are predominately nonpolar, they have some hydroxyl (—OH) groups. As the

nonpolar side of the molecules in lanolin "stick" to the skin proteins, the hydroxyl groups hydrogen-bond to water molecules, holding them close to the skin surface and holding in the skin moisture content.

The skin on our lips is covered by a thin layer that is free of fat and consequently dries out easily. Lipstick is used not only as a beauty aid, but also to control drying. Lipsticks consist of a suspension of solid organic dyes in a fat or hydrocarbon base. The colloid is mixed with a wax to raise its melting point. A colloid consisting of a solid suspended in a liquid is called a *sol*.

Eye colourings (eye shadow, mascara, etc.) are also sols. The liquid is often a mixture of long-chain hydrocarbons with formulas in the range of $C_{16}H_{34}$ to $C_{32}H_{66}$. The suspended solids used for colouring are often inorganic. For example, carbon powder is used for black, iron(III) oxide for brown, and chromium(III) oxide for dark green. Both lipstick and eye colourings are composed of nonpolar molecules: a polar liquid would wash off with water.

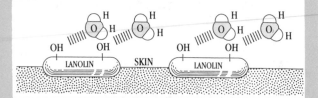

Figure 8.10

The fat parts of the lanolin molecule are 'soluble' in the protein and fat layers of the skin. The -OH groups of lanolin form hydrogen bonds with water molecules and keep the skin moist.

Figure 8.11

A statuette of Queen Nefertiti of Egypt, who lived in the 14th century B.C., showing the early use of cosmetics. The ancient Egyptians of both sexes used eye colourings and other make-up.

QUESTIONS

3. Which intermolecular forces act between the molecules of the following pure substances? Which substances would you expect to be soluble in water?

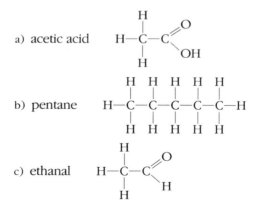

a) acetic acid

b) pentane

c) ethanal

4. Match the solutes on the left with the solvent that affords greater solubility.

Solute	Solvent
phenol (C_6H_5OH)	gasoline
naphthalene $(C_{10}H_8)$	methanol

The Solution Process of Ionic Compounds

8.3

Ionic compounds are rarely soluble in low-polarity solvents. They are often soluble in water, but even in this very polar solvent many ionic compounds are insoluble. Consider what happens when an ionic compound dissolves in water.

Sodium chloride crystals consist of a regular array of equal numbers of positive sodium ions and negative chloride ions. When these crystals are placed in water, the water molecules surround the ions on the surface of the crystals (Figure 8.12). The slightly positive hydrogen atoms of the water molecules are attracted to the negative chloride ions. The slightly negative oxygen atoms of water molecules are attracted to the positive sodium ions. Layer by layer the ions are pulled into the solution as a result of this attraction. We call this kind of attraction an **ion-dipole attraction**. The small size and highly-polar nature of the water molecules allow each ion to be closely surrounded by many water molecules. This phenomenon is referred to as **hydration**.

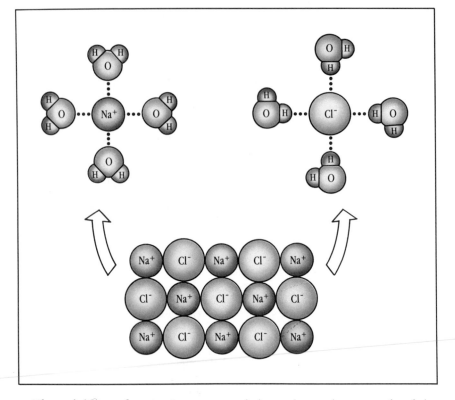

Figure 8.12

In the crystal of sodium chloride (below) the ions are packed together in the crystal lattice. In the solution process, the ions are hydrated (above).

The solubility of an ionic compound depends on the strength of the ionic bond when compared with the strength of the ion-dipole forces that would be present in the solution. Few solvents produce ion-dipole forces as strong as those found in water. When an ionic compound dissolves in water, the ion-dipole attractions between the ions and water molecules exceed the ionic attractions in the solid. When the attraction between the oppositely-charged ions is very strong and exceeds the ion-dipole attractions, the compound is only slightly soluble.

We can represent the solution process of an ionic compound in water by a chemical equation. For example, when calcium chloride goes into solution, the reaction is written as follows:

$$CaCl_{2\,(s)} \longrightarrow Ca^{2+}_{\,(aq)} + 2\,Cl^{-}_{\,(aq)}$$

The symbols $Ca^{2+}_{\,(aq)}$ and $Cl^{-}_{\,(aq)}$ indicate that the separated calcium ions and chloride ions are hydrated.

Solid Hydrates

The hydration of ions does not take place only in solution. It can also occur in the solid phase when an ionic compound incorporates water molecules in its crystal structure. We call such compounds **hydrates**. Most substances that form hydrates are very soluble in water. The mole ratio between the water and the hydration compound is characteristic for a given hydrate and is shown in the formula of the compound. For example, the formula, $CuSO_4 \cdot 5H_2O$, indicates that five molecules of water are associated with every formula unit of copper(II) sulfate. When the hydrate is heated, the water is driven off and the anhydrous compound is obtained.

$$CuSO_4 \cdot 5H_2O_{(s)} \longrightarrow CuSO_{4(s)} + 5\,H_2O_{(g)} \quad \Delta H^\circ = +78.8\,kJ \cdot mol^{-1.}$$

hydrate   anhydrous

(blue)   (white)

By examining the crystal structure of the compound, we find that four of the water molecules are clustered around the copper(II) ion, while the fifth is hydrogen-bonded to the sulfate ion.

Figure 8.13

In the solid crystal of copper(II) sulfate pentahydrate, the copper(II) ions are surrounded by four water molecules while the sulfate ion is hydrogen-bonded to one water molecule.

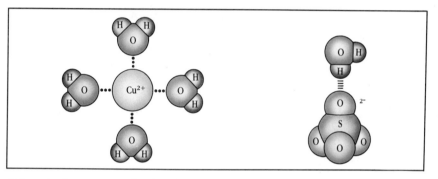

Dissociation versus Ionization

Hydrated ions can be produced in solution by two different processes:

1. by dissociation of ionic bonds;
2. by ionization of specific covalent bonds.

The term **dissociation** means separation and is used when a solvent such as water separates the ions that are present in *ionic compounds*. If we add sodium carbonate to water, the strength of the ion-dipole attractions with the water molecules causes the sodium ions and carbonate ions to dissociate from each other.

$$Na_2CO_{3(s)} \longrightarrow 2\,Na^+_{(aq)} + CO_3^{2-}_{(aq)}$$

The term **ionization** should be used when the ions are produced from *covalent compounds* by the action of a solvent. Many pure acids and bases are covalent compounds that undergo ionization in aqueous solution. A strong acid such as hydrogen chloride is completely ionized when dissolved in water. The hydrated ions are produced when covalent bonds are broken by the action of water molecules.

$$HCl_{(g)} \longrightarrow H^+_{(aq)} + Cl^-_{(aq)}$$

Ionization reactions between acids and bases will be dealt with in more detail in Chapter 10.

Soaps and Detergents — Nonpolar and Ionic Groups Join Forces

Soaps and detergents are compounds whose molecules contain two characteristic features: a long nonpolar chain of carbon and hydrogen atoms attached to a very polar end-group, which is usually ionic. Both features play an important role in the cleansing action of these substances.

Soaps are the sodium or potassium salts of carboxylic acids that have a linear chain of 12 to 18 carbon atoms. For more than 2000 years they have been prepared from animal fats and vegetable oils. Detergents are synthetic soaps that are synthesized mainly from petroleum products. The hydrocarbon chain, which also contains 12 to 18 carbon atoms, is attached to either a nonionic but polar group or to an ionic group such as a sulfate ion.

Figure 8.14
Common detergents such as these contain molecules with polar 'heads' and long nonpolar 'tails.'

Calcium ions and magnesium ions, which are present in relatively large amounts in hard water, form a precipitate with soaps in water. This precipitate is the cause of the "ring" in the bathtub for example. Soap is therefore often ineffective and inefficient for washing laundry. Because calcium and magnesium salts of sulfates are soluble in water, detergents are more effective in hard water.

Although soaps and detergents are water-soluble, they do not form true solutions. The nonpolar hydrocarbon chains are hydrophobic ("water-fearing") and are attracted to each other. The polar ends however, are hydrophilic ("water-loving") and tend to dissolve in the water. The result is that as many as a hundred molecules form a water-soluble spherical particle known as a micelle (Figure 8.15). The hydrocarbon chains form the inside of the micelle; the negative ions form the outside. The large amount of negative charge, which is compensated by the sodium ions in solution, keeps the micelles away from each other and in solution.

Water by itself will not remove oil and grease containing dirt from the surface of clothing or skin. But a solution of soap or detergent will. The hydrocarbon chains that form micelles will dissolve in the nonpolar oil or grease and the polar end groups then pull the dirt particles apart, away from the fabric or skin, and into the water solution.

The detergent industry is a major consumer of chemicals. In fact, about half a million tonnes of detergent is used in this country every year. A commercial detergent contains much more than a single type of detergent molecule. It contains builders that make the washing solution basic (and hence more effective), anti-redeposition agents to prevent the dirt from sticking back onto the clothes, and optical brighteners to make whites appear whiter. Small quantities of other substances, such as anticorrosion agents and perfumes, are also added.

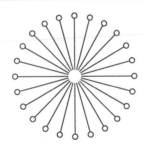

Figure 8.15
A detergent micelle in water. Each detergent molecule is shown as a 'matchstick.'

Figure 8.16
Detergent molecules 'attack' an oil droplet on a fabric and pull the oil away, into the water solution.

QUESTIONS

5. Write balanced reaction equations that show which ions are produced when the following substances are dissolved in water.
   a) lithium hydroxide
   b) potassium phosphate
   c) strontium chloride
   d) chromium(III) sulfate

6. The ionic solid silver chloride is very slightly water soluble. Explain this in terms of ionic attractions and ion-dipole attractions.

Determination of Solution Concentrations

8.4

There are several ways to indicate the strength or concentration of a solution. Generally, it is expressed as *the number of moles of solute dissolved in one litre of solution*. When expressed in this way it is sometimes called **molarity**. Since the term molarity is not part of the SI system, we will use the term **concentration**, *c*.

For calculations dealing with concentration we make use of the following relationship for concentration:

$$c = \frac{n}{V}$$

where *n* is the number of moles of solute,
   V is the volume of the solution in litres,
   c is the concentration in moles per litre.

EXAMPLE

8.1

Antifreeze is a solution of ethylene glycol, $C_2H_6O_2$, in water. If 4.50 L of antifreeze contains 2.00 kg of ethylene glycol, what is the concentration of the solution?

SOLUTION

First we convert the units for our volume of solute $(C_2H_6O_2)$ from kilograms to grams. Then we use the molar mass of ethylene glycol as a conversion factor to find the number of moles of this solute:

$$\text{Moles of } C_2H_6O_2 = 2.00 \times 10^3 \text{ g } C_2H_6O_2 \times \frac{1 \text{ mol } C_2H_6O_2}{62.07 \text{ g } C_2H_6O_2}$$

$$= 32.2 \text{ mol } C_2H_6O_2$$

Using the equation for concentration,

$$c = \frac{n}{V}$$

$$c = \frac{32.2 \text{ mol}}{4.50 \text{ L}}$$

$$= 7.16 \text{ mol} \cdot L^{-1}$$

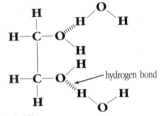

Figure 8.17
Automobile antifreeze is a solution of ethylene glycol, which can hydrogen bond with water. As a result, the compound is completely miscible with water.

If we are using a solution of known concentration and wish to calculate the mass or the number of moles of solute in a certain volume of solution, we can rearrange the formula for concentration to

$$n = Vc$$

If we wish to know the volume of solvent required for a specific concentration of solution, we can rearrange the relationship to

$$V = \frac{n}{c}$$

EXAMPLE　　　**8.2**　What mass of sodium carbonate, Na_2CO_3, is present in 50.00 mL of a 0.750 mol·L^{-1} aqueous solution?

SOLUTION　First we convert the units for volume of solution to litres. Then we rearrange the formula for concentration to find the number of moles of Na_2CO_3:

$$n = Vc$$
$$n = 0.0500 \, L \times 0.750 \, mol·L^{-1}$$
$$= 0.0375 \, mol$$

We use the molar mass of sodium carbonate to calculate the mass in solution:

$$Mass \ of \ Na_2CO_3 = 0.0375 \ mol \ Na_2CO_3 \times \frac{106.0 \, g \ Na_2CO_3}{1 \ mol \ Na_2CO_3}$$

$$= 3.98 \, g \ Na_2CO_3$$

EXAMPLE　　　**8.3**　What volume of a 1.50 mol·L^{-1} hydrochloric acid solution contains 10.0 g of hydrogen chloride?

SOLUTION　Using the molar mass of hydrochloric acid, we find the corresponding number of moles:

$$Moles \ of \ HCl = 10.0 \, g \ HCl \times \frac{1 \ mol \ HCl}{36.46 \, g \ HCl}$$

$$= 0.274 \ mol \ HCl$$

We can now substitute the known values into the equation for volume:

$$V = \frac{n}{c}$$

$$V = \frac{0.274 \ mol}{1.50 \ mol·L^{-1}}$$

$$= 0.183 \, L$$
$$= 183 \ mL$$

The Dilution of a Solution

Suppose we start with a solution of volume V_1 and concentration c_1 and we wish to dilute it to a volume V_2 and concentration c_2. If a solution is diluted with solvent the number of moles of solute remains unchanged. Thus for our initial solution, we can write:

$$c_1 = \frac{n}{V_1} \quad \text{or} \quad n = V_1 c_1$$

and for our diluted solution:

$$c_2 = \frac{n}{V_2} \quad \text{or} \quad n = V_2 c_2$$

The initial and diluted solutions are related as follows:

$$V_1 c_1 = V_2 c_2$$

before   after
dilution   dilution

EXAMPLE   **8.4**   What volume of concentrated sulfuric acid (containing $18.0\ \text{mol·L}^{-1}$ H_2SO_4) is required to prepare $5.00\ \text{L}$ of $0.150\ \text{mol·L}^{-1}$ aqueous sulfuric acid solution by dilution with water?

SOLUTION   Since this is a dilution problem, it is advisable to list the information, including the unknown value, in tabular format:

$$V_1 = ? \qquad\qquad V_2 = 5.00\ \text{L}$$
$$c_1 = 18.0\ \text{mol·L}^{-1} \qquad c_2 = 0.150\ \text{mol·L}^{-1}$$

Then we rearrange the formula $V_1 c_1 = V_2 c_2$ and solve for V_1:

$$V_1 = \frac{V_2 c_2}{c_1}$$

Substituting the known values in the above expression, we get

$$V_1 = \frac{5.00\ \text{L} \times 0.150\ \text{mol·L}^{-1}}{18.0\ \text{mol·L}^{-1}}$$
$$= 0.0417\ \text{L}$$
$$= 41.7\ \text{mL}$$

Thus, we would measure out a volume of $41.7\ \text{mL}$ of the concentrated sulfuric acid, add it slowly and carefully to about $4\ \text{L}$ of water with stirring, then increase the volume to a total of $5.00\ \text{L}$ with additional water.

Standard Solutions

Solutions containing a precise mass of solute in a precise volume of solution are called **standard solutions**. They are often required in experimental work in which the concentration of one or more components must

Figure 8.18
Concentrated sulfuric acid is a dense oily liquid that dissolves in water very exothermically.

be known accurately and precisely. The preparation of a standard solution requires a special container called a **volumetric flask**. These flasks vary in size from 10 mL to 2000 mL. The required mass of solute is placed in the volumetric flask and a solvent, usually water, is added until the level of the solution reaches the calibration mark on the narrow stem of the flask. The tolerance (margin of error) in the better quality volumetric flasks ("class A" flasks) is very small and varies from 0.02 mL for the 10 mL flask to 0.50 mL for the 2000 mL flask.

EXAMPLE   **8.5**   Describe the preparation of 2.000 L of a standard aqueous solution containing 0.1000 $mol \cdot L^{-1}$ potassium nitrate, KNO_3.

SOLUTION   We substitute the known values into the equation for moles of the solute, KNO_3:

$$n = Vc$$
$$n = 2.000 \, L \times 0.1000 \, mol \cdot L^{-1}$$
$$= 0.2000 \, mol$$

We now use the molar mass of solute, KNO_3 to find the equivalent mass:

$$\text{Mass of } KNO_3 = 0.2000 \text{ mol } KNO_3 \times \frac{101.1 \text{ g } KNO_3}{1 \text{ mol } KNO_3}$$

$$= 20.22 \text{ g } KNO_3$$

To prepare the solution we place 20.22 g of potassium nitrate in a 2000 mL volumetric flask. About half the required amount of water is added. When all the potassium nitrate is dissolved, the solution is diluted with the remaining water.

Ion Concentration

In dilute aqueous solutions, all ionic compounds and strong acids are present as ions. As we discovered in Section 8.3, these ions are the result of either dissociation or ionization. If we know the formula for the compound and the concentration of the solution, we can determine the concentration of these ions.

Consider a 0.20 $mol \cdot L^{-1}$ aqueous solution of sodium carbonate. The sodium carbonate will be completely dissociated into ions:

$$Na_2CO_{3(s)} \longrightarrow 2\,Na^+_{(aq)} + CO_3^{2-}_{(aq)}$$

The concentration of the sodium ions and carbonate ions can be calculated using the equation factors from the balanced equation.

$$[Na^+] = 0.20 \text{ mol} \cdot L^{-1} \, Na_2CO_3 \times \frac{2 \text{ mol } Na^+}{1 \text{ mol } Na_2CO_3}$$

$$= 0.40 \text{ mol} \cdot L^{-1} \, Na^+$$

$$[CO_3^{2-}] = 0.20 \text{ mol} \cdot L^{-1} \text{ Na}_2CO_3 \times \frac{1 \text{ mol } CO_3^{2-}}{1 \text{ mol } Na_2CO_3}$$
$$= 0.20 \text{ mol} \cdot L^{-1} CO_3^{2-}$$

EXAMPLE   **8.6**   What are the concentrations of the ions in an aqueous solution containing 0.15 mol·L^{-1} iron(III) nitrate?

SOLUTION   The balanced equation for the dissociation of the ionic compound iron(III) nitrate is as follows:

$$Fe(NO_3)_{3\,(s)} \longrightarrow Fe^{3+}_{(aq)} + 3\,NO_3^{-}_{(aq)}$$

Using the appropriate equation factors, we can calculate the concentrations of the iron(III) ions and nitrate ions:

$$[Fe^{3+}] = 0.15 \text{ mol} \cdot L^{-1} \text{ Fe(NO}_3)_3 \times \frac{1 \text{ mol } Fe^{3+}}{1 \text{ mol Fe(NO}_3)_3}$$
$$= 0.15 \text{ mol} \cdot L^{-1} Fe^{3+}$$

$$[NO_3^{-}] = 0.15 \text{ mol} \cdot L^{-1} \text{ Fe(NO}_3)_3 \times \frac{3 \text{ mol } NO_3^{-}}{1 \text{ mol Fe(NO}_3)_3}$$
$$= 0.45 \text{ mol} \cdot L^{-1} NO_3^{-}$$

QUESTIONS

7. What happens to the concentration of a solution when
   a) more solute is added?
   b) the solution is heated and the solvent evaporates?
   c) part of the solution is poured off?

8. Calculate the concentrations of the following solutions:
   a) a 0.750 L aqueous solution containing 90.0 g ethanol, C_2H_5OH
   b) a 25.00 mL solution of 0.1250 mol·L^{-1} iron(II) sulfate, $FeSO_4$, diluted with water to a volume of 500.0 mL

9. Determine the mass of solute present in the following solutions:
   a) a 2.00 L solution of 2.00 mol·L^{-1} sodium hydroxide
   b) a 50.00 mL aqueous solution containing 4.550×10^{-3} mol·L^{-1} copper(II) nitrate, $Cu(NO_3)_2$

10. What volume of concentrated hydrochloric acid, containing 11.9 mol·L^{-1} hydrogen chloride, is needed to make 2.00 L of 0.200 mol·L^{-1} solution by dilution with water?

11. Calculate the concentrations of ions in the following solutions:
    a) a 0.015 mol·L^{-1} solution of sodium sulfate, Na_2SO_4
    b) a 2.00 L aqueous solution containing 17.1 g aluminum sulfate, $Al_2(SO_4)_3$

The Solubility of Ionic Compounds

8.5

The terms *soluble* and *insoluble*, when used to describe the solubility of ionic compounds in water, should not be interpreted literally. No ionic compound has unlimited solubility in water. Neither is an ionic compound ever completely insoluble. The term insoluble indicates that the solubility of the substance in water is less than $1.0 \, g \cdot L^{-1}$. This translates into a concentration of less than $0.01 \, mol \cdot L^{-1}$. Two other frequently encountered terms are *slightly soluble* and *very soluble*. Each term represents a range of solubility, as shown in Table 8.2.

Figure 8.19

Each ionic salt has a characteristic solubility curve. These graphs show solubility as mass of solute in grams per 100 g of water.

a) Potassium nitrate has low solubility at 0° C, but extremely high solubility at 100° C.

b) The moderate solubility of sodium chloride increases only slightly with increasing temperature.

c) The low solubility of lithium carbonate decreases with temperature.

TABLE 8.2	*Terms Used to Describe Solubility*
Solubility term	**Solubility in water (approx. concentrations)**
insoluble	$< 1.0 \, g \cdot L^{-1}$
slightly soluble	$1.0 - 10 \, g \cdot L^{-1}$
soluble	$10 - 100 \, g \cdot L^{-1}$
very soluble	$> 100 \, g \cdot L^{-1}$

Temperature has the same effect on the solubility of most ionic compounds in water as it has on molecular compounds: the solubility increases when the temperature of the solution is increased. A few ionic compounds however, show a decreased solubility in water at higher temperatures (Figure 8.19).

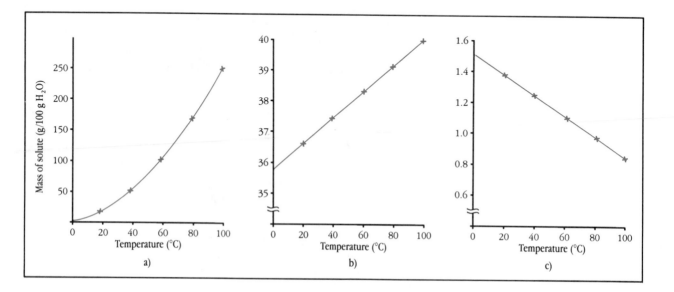

In a saturated solution of an ionic compound, there exists a dynamic equilibrium between the undissolved solid and the hydrated ions in solution. For example, in a saturated solution of slightly soluble silver sulfate, the following equilibrium exists:

$$Ag_2SO_{4\,(s)} \rightleftharpoons 2\,Ag^+_{\,(aq)} + SO_4^{2-}_{\,(aq)}$$

Silver ions and sulfate ions continue to pass from the solid to the hydrated, dissolved state, and vice versa. The rate of dissociation equals the rate of crystallization.

Solubility Rules

Table 8.3 provides us with some general rules about the solubilities of ionic compounds in water. These solubility rules should be treated with caution since they do not apply to all ionic compounds. As a first approximation, however, they are useful.

Using this information, we can predict that the solubilities of aluminum nitrate, $Al(NO_3)_3$, and copper(II) sulfate, $CuSO_4$, would be quite high; but the solubilities of aluminum hydroxide, $Al(OH)_3$, and copper(II) carbonate, $CuCO_3$, would be low.

TABLE 8.3   *Solubility Rules for Ionic Compounds in Water*

Soluble Compounds	Exceptions
Nitrates	None
Na^+, K^+, NH_4^+ compounds	None
Halides (Cl^-, Br^-, I^-)	Except Ag^+, Hg_2^{2+}, Cu^+, Pb^{2+}
Sulfates (SO_4^{2-})	Except Ca^{2+}, Sr^{2+}, Ba^{2+}, Pb^{2+}, Hg_2^{2+}, Ag^+

Insoluble Compounds	Exceptions
Sulfides (S^{2-})	Except NH_4^+, Group IA, and IIA ions
Carbonates (CO_3^{2-})	Except NH_4^+ and Group IA ions
Phosphates (PO_4^{3-})	Except NH_4^+ and Group IA ions
Hydroxides (OH^-)	Except NH_4^+ and Group IA ions, and Ba^{2+}

NO_3^-

Water-insoluble ionic compounds make up the major portion of our earth. The composition of many of these substances is highly complex. This is especially true of the silicates. What we commonly refer to as minerals or ores are actually ionic compounds of extremely low solubility. Some ores, however, have relatively simple formulas; those mined in Canada are listed in Table 8.4. Most ores are metal sulfides, but oxides, carbonates, and silicates are also common.

Figure 8.20
An aerial view of the open pit copper mine, Craigmont Merit, British Columbia. The ores that we obtain from the earth's surface are very insoluble compounds.

TABLE 8.4	*Common Canadian Ores*
Ore	Formula
Calcite, limestone	$CaCO_3$
Galena	PbS
Magnetite	Fe_3O_4
Chalcopyrite	$CuFeS_2$
Argentite	Ag_2S
Cobaltite	$CoAsS$
Malachite	$CuCO_3 \cdot Cu(OH)_2$
Molybdenite	MoS_2
Spheralite	ZnS

The Oceans, our Planet's Largest Ionic Solution

The oceans comprise 71 % of the surface of the earth. At an average depth of 3.8 km, the oceans represent about 5 % of the mass of the earth. Almost 98 % of the water on earth is found in its oceans.

More than 70 different elements are present in sea water as ions. Many of these ionic constituents are dissolved from the earth's crust by the action of streams and rivers. But a major portion of the ions reach the ocean in hot, mineral-rich water that originates deep within the earth and is discharged into the oceans through holes in the ocean floor.

Figure 8.21
Evaporating sea water at a tank farm near Tripoli, in Libya. Sodium chloride crystallizes first and is separated off. Much of the world's supply of sodium chloride is still obtained this way.

The ionic composition of the oceans in different parts of the world varies only slightly and this composition has not changed much in more than a billion years. Four cations and four anions comprise well over 99 %

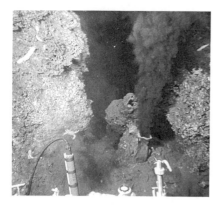

Figure 8.22
Vents in the ocean floor, through which hot mineral-rich water enters the ocean.

of the mass of the ions present in sea water. One litre of sea water upon evaporation leaves approximately 35 g of solid residues, about 80 % of which is sodium chloride. It is not surprising, considering their relatively high solubility, that the halides and sulfates of the alkali metals (Group IA) and the alkaline earth metals (Group IIA) are most prevalent. Table 8.5 lists the eight ions and their relative abundance in sea water.

TABLE 8.5	Major Ions Present in Sea Water	
Ion	Concentration $(g \cdot L^{-1})$	Percent of sea salt
Cl^-	18.8	53.7
Na^+	10.8	30.8
$SO_4{}^{2-}$	2.65	7.6
Mg^{2+}	1.29	3.7
Ca^{2+}	0.412	1.2
K^+	0.38	1.1
$HCO_3{}^-$	0.14	0.4
Br^-	0.067	0.2

Many valuable metals are present in sea water in extremely small concentrations. However, considering the extent of the oceans, the total amounts present are quite staggering. The German chemist Fritz Haber spent eight unsuccessful years after World War I trying to develop an economically feasible process to recover gold from sea water. The process was supposed to help Germany pay its war debt. A quick calculation shows that his dreams were not so unrealistic.

EXAMPLE　　　*8.7*　Given that the concentration of gold in sea water is $4 \, ng \cdot L^{-1}$ (nanograms per litre) and that the volume of the oceans is 1.3×10^{24} L, calculate the total mass of gold present in sea water.

SOLUTION　First we convert the units of concentration to grams per litre:

$$\text{Concentration of Au} = 4 \, ng \cdot L^{-1} \, Au \times \frac{1 \, g \, Au}{10^9 \, ng \, Au}$$
$$= 4 \times 10^{-9} \, g \cdot L^{-1} \, Au$$

Then we multiply the above figure by the number of litres:

$$\text{Mass of Au} = 4 \times 10^{-9} \, g \cdot L^{-1} \, Au \times (1.3 \times 10^{24}) \, L$$
$$= 5.2 \times 10^{15} \, g \, Au \quad \text{(5.2 billion tonnes!)}$$

Although an economical process for extracting gold from sea water may never come to fruition, the prospects are much better for extracting uranium which is present in an amount of $3.2 \times 10^{-6}\, g \cdot L^{-1}$ of sea water.

The sea has been the source of many chemicals for hundreds of years. Those substances that are currently obtained from sea water on a very large scale are sodium chloride, magnesium metal, magnesium oxide, bromine, and pure water. The total value of these products amounts to almost two billion dollars per year.

TABLE 8.6 *Estimated Annual World Production of Chemicals from Sea Water*

Product	Production from Sea Water (tonnes)	Percent of Total World Production
Sodium chloride	65 215 000	38 %
Magnesium	159 000	70 %
Magnesium compounds	1 814 000	33 %
Bromine	42 000	13 %
Water	2 382 000 000	64 %

QUESTIONS

12. Write formulas for the following ionic compounds and, using Table 8.3, predict the solubility of each in water.
    a) potassium carbonate
    b) gold(III) chloride
    c) iron(II) phosphate
    d) magnesium hydroxide
    e) ammonium nitrate
    f) lead(II) sulfate

13. What would be the total mass of uranium in all the oceans if one litre of sea water contains $3.2\, \mu g$ of uranium? The approximate total volume of the oceans is $1.3 \times 10^{24}\, L$.

The Potash Industry

8.6 A discussion of the substances that are obtained from the sea would not be complete without a reference to one of Canada's major resources — potash. A few hundred million years ago most of the area that now comprises our prairie provinces formed part of a large inland sea. In the course of millions of years this sea dried up and the ionic compounds that were dissolved in it gradually crystallized. But they did not all crystallize at the same time and at the same place. As the water evaporated in this huge basin the least soluble, calcium sulfate ($CaSO_4$), crystallized first, as the mineral *anhydrite*. This was followed by sodium chloride as the mineral *halite*. The last ones to crystallize, near the southeasterly portion of the basin,

Figure 8.23
An aerial view of the potash mine at Rocanville, Saskatchewan. This mine can produce more than 1.4 million tonnes of potassium chloride per year.

were the more soluble salts of potassium and magnesium. These settled out as the minerals *sylvite* (KCl) and *carnallite* ($KCl \cdot MgCl_2 \cdot 6H_2O$). Over time these mineral beds, which are over two hundred metres thick in places, became covered with several hundred metres of sediment and erosion products. The potassium-containing minerals, collectively known as **potash**, lie in beds up to seven metres thick.

The term potash is somewhat misleading. It used to refer solely to potassium carbonate, but now it usually indicates potassium chloride. The importance of potassium carbonate can be traced back to Roman times. It was used for making glass and soap, and later for making gunpowder. In 1840 it was discovered that potassium is essential for plant growth. Since then, potassium compounds have become increasingly important as fertilizers. The name potash is derived from an early production method whereby the extracts of ashes were boiled down in iron pots until the potassium carbonate crystallized. In 1790 the very first patent in the United States was issued for a process for making potassium carbonate from wood. To produce one tonne of potash, approximately four hundred tonnes of wood were required. When wood supplies dwindled in the 19th century, seaweed became an important source of potash, but for most of its uses, potassium carbonate has now been replaced by sodium carbonate, which can be produced much more cheaply by the Solvay process from calcium carbonate and sodium chloride.

Figure 8.24
The large, continuous mining machine used to excavate 300 tonnes of potash ore per hour at depths of over 1000 m below the prairie surface.

Currently, 98 % of the potassium we get from ore or brine (salt water) is recovered as potassium chloride. As Table 8.7 shows, Canada is one of the world's major potash producers and has more than half of the world's total reserves. In fact the world's largest deposits occur in Saskatchewan. At present, these deposits account for nearly all Canadian potash production. However, it is projected that in a few years New Brunswick will produce at least 10 % of Canada's potash. Studies are also underway to investigate the feasibility of mining Manitoba's large deposits.

The New Brunswick deposits are geologically more complex than those in Saskatchewan. The Saskatchewan deposits resemble a layer cake, while the deposits in New Brunswick are like a marble cake.

TABLE 8.7   *World Potash Reserves and Production*

Country or Region	Estimated Reserves KCl (10^6 tonnes)	Production KCl (10^6 tonnes)
Canada	7210	12.2
USSR and East Germany	5016	19.6
Western Europe	529	8.7
Israel and Jordan (The Dead Sea)	344	2.1
United States	295	2.5

More than half of the potash produced in Canada is exported to the United States. Only 5 % is used in the domestic market. Approximately 95 % of all the potash produced is used in agriculture, the remainder is used by industry for making other potassium compounds such as potassium hydroxide and potassium nitrate.

TABLE 8.8   *Annual Potash Capacity in Canada*

Province	Number of Mines	Projected Capacity KCl (10^6 tonnes)
Saskatchewan	11	16.4
New Brunswick	2	1.6

The Solubility Product Constant

8.7   In the previous chapter we were shown how to calculate the equilibrium constant for gaseous equilibria. A similar equilibrium constant can be derived for saturated solutions of ionic compounds. For example, the equilibrium between silver ions, sulfate ions, and solid silver sulfate in a saturated aqueous solution can be represented by the equation:

$$Ag_2SO_{4(s)} \rightleftharpoons 2\ Ag^+_{(aq)} + SO_4^{2-}_{(aq)}$$

Figure 8.25
When a solution of potassium iodide is added to a solution of lead(II) nitrate, a bright yellow precipitate of lead(II) iodide is formed because the concentrations of the two ions exceed the value of the solubility product.

From this balanced equation, the expression for the equilibrium constant is the ratio of the concentrations of products to the concentrations of reactants, *when excess solid is present.* The coefficients in the balanced equation become the exponents. For the dissociation of silver sulfate, the equilibrium constant expression can be written as follows:

$$K = \frac{[Ag^+_{(aq)}]^2[SO_4^{2-}_{(aq)}]}{[Ag_2SO_{4\,(s)}]}$$

Expressions of this kind can be simplified because the concentration of a solid is a constant. Thus, the concentration of solid silver sulfate can be incorporated in the equilibrium constant to give us a new constant. This new equilibrium constant is called the **solubility product constant**, K_{sp}:

$$K_{sp} = K[Ag_2SO_{4\,(s)}] = [Ag^+_{(aq)}]^2[SO_4^{2-}_{(aq)}]$$

This is usually written in the simplified form, without indicating the phases of the particular ions.

$$K_{sp} = [Ag^+]^2[SO_4^{2-}]$$

EXAMPLE   *8.8*   Write an expression for the solubility product constant, K_{sp}, of calcium phosphate, $Ca_3(PO_4)_2$.

SOLUTION   First we write a balanced reaction equation for the equilibrium between the ions in saturated aqueous solution and excess solid:

$$Ca_3(PO_4)_{2\,(s)} \rightleftharpoons 3\,Ca^{2+}_{(aq)} + 2\,PO_4^{2-}_{(aq)}$$

The expression for K_{sp} can now be derived from the above equation:

$$K_{sp} = [Ca^{2+}]^3[PO_4^{3-}]^2$$

Values for the solubility product constants are only determined for ionic compounds that are classified as insoluble or slightly soluble in water. One could also determine K_{sp} values for soluble compounds, but in practice this is not done. It is important to remember that the expression for K_{sp} only holds when excess solid is present.

The solubility product constant, K_{sp}, like all equilibrium constants, is temperature specific and its value is independent of the source of the ions. Table 8.9 lists some representative K_{sp} values and also shows the wide range in magnitude. Notice that the K_{sp} values of the highly insoluble sulfides are among the lowest. A more comprehensive list of solubility product constants can be found in Appendix V.

Figure 8.26
These kidney stones consist of calcium oxalate and are produced when the product of the concentrations of the ions exceeds the solubility product of calcium oxalate.

TABLE 8.9 *Representative Solubility Product Constants, K_{sp}, at 25°C*

Compound	K_{sp}
Li_2CO_3	1.7×10^{-3}
Ag_2SO_4	1.2×10^{-5}
$BaSO_4$	1.1×10^{-10}
$Fe(OH)_2$	1.8×10^{-15}
ZnS	1.6×10^{-24}
Ag_2S	1.8×10^{-50}

Determining Individual Ion Concentrations from K_{sp}

Concentrations of individual ions in water can be calculated from the K_{sp} values of compounds. These calculations will vary depending on the number of moles of each ion produced in the reaction.

EXAMPLE   *8.9*   Calculate the concentrations of barium ions and sulfate ions in a saturated aqueous solution of barium sulfate, $BaSO_4$, in which the value for K_{sp} is 1.1×10^{-10}.

SOLUTION   The first step is to write the balanced equation for the dissociation of the compound barium sulfate. This shows that equal molar amounts of the two ions are produced from the same source. Assume that the concentration of each of these ions is x mol·L^{-1}.

$$BaSO_{4\,(s)} \rightleftharpoons Ba^{2+}_{\,(aq)} + SO_4^{\,2-}_{\,(aq)}$$
$$x \text{ mol·L}^{-1} \qquad x \text{ mol·L}^{-1}$$

Next we substitute the concentrations into the expression for K_{sp} and solve for x:

$$K_{sp} = [Ba^{2+}][SO_4^{\,2-}] = x^2 = 1.1 \times 10^{-10}$$
$$x = 1.0 \times 10^{-5}$$

Since x represents the concentration of both the barium ion and the sulfate ion

$$[SO_4^{\,2-}] = [Ba^{2+}] = 1.0 \times 10^{-5} \text{ mol·L}^{-1}$$

EXAMPLE   *8.10*   Calculate the concentrations of silver ions and sulfate ions in a saturated aqueous solution of silver sulfate Ag_2SO_4, in which the K_{sp} is 1.2×10^{-5}.

SOLUTION   From the balanced equation we see that a saturated solution of silver sulfate has two moles of silver ions for every mole of sulfate ions. If we assume

Figure 8.27
A colony of coral growing on a giant clam shell. Both clams and coral polyps construct their shells from insoluble calcium carbonate.

the sulfate ion concentration is x mol·L^{-1}, then the silver ion concentration will be $2x$ mol·L^{-1}.

$$Ag_2SO_{4\,(s)} \rightleftharpoons 2\,Ag^+_{\,(aq)} + SO_4^{\,2-}_{\,(aq)}$$
$$\phantom{Ag_2SO_{4\,(s)} \rightleftharpoons} 2x\,\text{mol·L}^{-1} \quad x\,\text{mol·L}^{-1}$$

We substitute the above concentrations into the expression for K_{sp} and solve for x:

$$K_{sp} = [Ag^+]^2[SO_4^{\,2-}] = (2x)^2(x) = 1.2 \times 10^{-5}$$
$$4x^3 = 1.2 \times 10^{-5}$$
$$x^3 = 3.0 \times 10^{-6}$$
$$x = 1.4 \times 10^{-2}$$

The required concentrations are

$$[SO_4^{\,2-}] = 1.4 \times 10^{-2} \text{ mol·L}^{-1}$$
$$[Ag^+] = 2(1.4 \times 10^{-2}) \text{ mol·L}^{-1}$$
$$= 2.8 \times 10^{-2} \text{ mol·L}^{-1}$$

Determining K_{sp} Values From Measured Solubilities of Ions

In the high school laboratory, we can estimate solubility product constants for various substances. This is done by measuring the solubilities of the ionic compounds in water. When we do this, we are making the assumption that all of the solid that dissolves is present in the solution as independent hydrated ions, which do not interfere with each other. This means that the value for K_{sp} calculated by this method is usually somewhat larger than the real value.

EXAMPLE **8.11** Calcium carbonate, $CaCO_3$, has a solubility in water of 7.1×10^{-5} mol·L^{-1} at 20 °C. Calculate the K_{sp} value of calcium carbonate.

SOLUTION We first write the balanced equation:

$$CaCO_{3\,(s)} \rightleftharpoons Ca^{2+}_{\,(aq)} + CO_3^{\,2-}_{\,(aq)}$$

If we assume complete dissociation, then 7.1×10^{-5} moles of calcium carbonate will produce an equal number of moles of the two ions. Therefore the concentrations of the two ions are

$$[Ca^{2+}] = [CO_3^{\,2-}] = 7.1 \times 10^{-5} \text{ mol·L}^{-1}$$

The value for K_{sp} at 20 °C is found by substituting these values into the following expression.

$$K_{sp} = [Ca^{2+}][CO_3^{\,2-}]$$
$$= (7.1 \times 10^{-5})(7.1 \times 10^{-5})$$
$$= 5.0 \times 10^{-9} \quad \text{at 20 °C}$$

EXAMPLE   *8.12* When 10.0 L of a saturated solution of magnesium carbonate, $MgCO_3$, at 22 °C is evaporated to dryness, 0.12 g of solid magnesium carbonate is obtained. Calculate the K_{sp} of magnesium carbonate.

SOLUTION The expression for K_{sp} follows from the balanced equation

$$MgCO_{3\,(s)} \rightleftharpoons Mg^{2+}_{(aq)} + CO_3^{2-}_{(aq)}$$

Thus,

$$K_{sp} = [Mg^{2+}][CO_3^{2-}]$$

Next we use the molar mass of magnesium carbonate to calculate the number of moles of magnesium carbonate dissolved in one litre of saturated solution.

$$\text{Moles of } MgCO_3 = 0.12\,\text{g } MgCO_3 \times \frac{1 \text{ mol } MgCO_3}{84.32 \text{ g } MgCO_3}$$

$$= 1.4 \times 10^{-3} \text{ mol } MgCO_3$$

We can now substitute the known values into the equation

$$c = \frac{n}{V}$$

to find the concentration of magnesium carbonate:

$$[MgCO_3] = \frac{1.4 \times 10^{-3} \text{ mol}}{10.0 \text{ L}}$$

$$= 1.4 \times 10^{-4} \text{ mol} \cdot L^{-1}$$

The ion concentrations are therefore

$$[CO_3^{2-}] = [Mg^{2+}] = 1.4 \times 10^{-4} \text{ mol} \cdot L^{-1}$$

When these values are substituted into the expression for K_{sp}, the value obtained is as follows:

$$K_{sp} = (1.4 \times 10^{-4})(1.4 \times 10^{-4})$$

$$= 2.0 \times 10^{-8}$$

EXAMPLE   *8.13* A saturated solution of ionic calcium hydroxide, $Ca(OH)_2$, has an hydroxide ion concentration of 3.0×10^{-3} mol·L^{-1}. Calculate the solubility product of calcium hydroxide at the same temperature.

SOLUTION First, we write the balanced equation

$$Ca(OH)_{2\,(s)} \rightleftharpoons Ca^{2+}_{(aq)} + 2\,OH^-_{(aq)}$$

The concentration of the calcium ion is found by multiplying the hydroxide ion concentration by the appropriate equation factor:

$$[Ca^{2+}] = 3.0 \times 10^{-3} \text{ mol} \cdot L^{-1} \text{ OH}^- \times \frac{1 \text{ mol Ca}^{2+}}{2 \text{ mol OH}^-}$$

$$= 1.5 \times 10^{-3} \text{ mol} \cdot L^{-1}$$

We can now substitute the known values into the expression for K_{sp}:

$$K_{sp} = [Ca^{2+}][OH^-]^2$$
$$= (1.5 \times 10^{-3})(3.0 \times 10^{-3})^2$$
$$= 1.4 \times 10^{-8}$$

QUESTIONS

14. What are the concentrations of the resulting ions in saturated aqueous solutions of the following compounds?
    a) lead(II) sulfate, $PbSO_4$ $K_{sp} = 1.3 \times 10^{-8}$
    b) silver carbonate, Ag_2CO_3 $K_{sp} = 6.2 \times 10^{-12}$
    c) magnesium hydroxide, $Mg(OH)_2$ $K_{sp} = 1.2 \times 10^{-11}$
15. Calculate the K_{sp} values of the following substances from their solubilities in water.
    a) silver chloride, AgCl, with a solubility of $1.6 \times 10^{-3} g \cdot L^{-1}$ at 20 °C
    b) lithium carbonate, Li_2CO_3, with a solubility of $13 g \cdot L^{-1}$ at 20 °C

Reactions Involving Precipitates

8.8

When aqueous solutions of silver nitrate and sodium chloride are mixed, solid silver chloride separates out as a white precipitate. This precipitation is an example of a double displacement reaction and can be represented by the following equation:

$$AgNO_{3\,(aq)} + NaCl_{(aq)} \longrightarrow AgCl_{(s)} + NaNO_{3\,(aq)}$$

We can rewrite this equation to show the ions that are actually present in solution:

$$Ag^+_{(aq)} + NO_3^-_{(aq)} + Na^+_{(aq)} + Cl^-_{(aq)} \longrightarrow$$
$$AgCl_{(s)} + Na^+_{(aq)} + NO_3^-_{(aq)}$$

Sodium ions and nitrate ions appear on both the reactant side and the product side of the reaction equation. They are called **spectator ions** because they do not undergo reaction. If we omit them from the reaction equation, we are left with a **net ionic equation**:

$$Ag^+_{(aq)} + Cl^-_{(aq)} \longrightarrow AgCl_{(s)}$$

The following example illustrates how we can use the solubility rules of Table 8.3 to predict whether or not a precipitation reaction may be expected when aqueous solutions of ionic compounds are mixed.

Calcium and Your Health

What do sardines, aerobic dancing, ice cream, spinach, and suntanning have in common? They all contribute to the formation of a healthy bone structure and therefore help to prevent the condition called *osteoporosis* ("porous bones"). This disease is caused by the excessive loss of calcium from the bones, which leaves them porous and brittle. It can result in loss of height, deformity of the spine, and fractures of the wrist and thigh bone. The effects of the disease usually do not appear until well after the age of 50, but at that stage the condition cannot be reversed. Women are much more prone to it than men, and as our population ages it is becoming a more common problem. From an early age, however, much can be done to prevent osteoporosis.

Calcium is the fifth most abundant element on earth. It is found in many rock formations in the form of ionic compounds, (e.g. silicates, carbonates, and phosphates). In our body it is a major component in teeth and bone. Bone consists mainly of calcium phosphate and the protein collagen. Of the calcium in the body, 99 % is stored in the bones. Most of the remaining 1 % serves important functions in muscle contraction and vision. If the appropriate concentration of calcium in the blood is lowered, the balance can be restored by the bones losing calcium:

$$Ca_3(PO_4)_{2\,(s)} \rightleftharpoons 3\ Ca^{2+}_{\ (aq)} + 2\ PO_4^{\ 3-}_{\ (aq)}$$
$$\text{(in bone)}$$

However, the process is not nearly as simple as the above equilibrium equation would lead us to believe. The biochemistry of bone formation and destruction is immensely complex.

Bone breakdown and rebuilding processes occur continuously during our lifetime. By about age 35 our bones reach their maximum mass and strength. From then on we can expect to experience a slow deterioration. Much of what will happen to the bones in later life will depend on the quality of the bones developed up to age 35, especially from ages 10 to 20, when bone growth is most rapid. The consequences of inevitable bone loss in later years will be less severe if we can start out with a dense bone structure that has a high calcium content.

Figure 8.29
A low-radiation densitometer machine is used to measure the calcium content of the wrist and radius bone. Routine testing with such machines may play a major role in preventive medicine.

Exercise and diet are the two important ingredients for building strong bones. A minimum of three hours each week of weight-bearing exercise, such as running and walking, increases the mass and quality of the bones. The recommended daily dietary intake of calcium is 1000 mg, the best sources of which are dairy products such as milk, cheese, and yogurt. Canned salmon and sardines, because of the bones present, are also good sources. Other nutrients that are required by the bones are vitamin C (from fruits and vegetables), vitamin D (produced by sunlight), fluoride, magnesium, copper, and manganese. Manganese seems to play an especially crucial role. A daily dose of 4 mg has been shown to reverse the condition of osteoporosis in manganese-deficient athletes. Manganese is readily absorbed by the body from such sources as milk, eggs, and red meat.

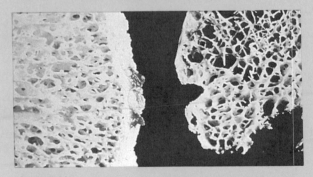

Figure 8.28
Normal healthy bone (left), which reaches its peak mass and strength at about age 35. Osteoporotic bone (right), which has lost calcium, is porous and brittle.

The male hormone testosterone and the female hormone estrogen play a key role in the absorption of calcium in bones and, thereby, in the prevention of bone loss. The extent of bone loss after age 50 is directly linked to the drop in hormone levels. This also explains why women are much more affected by osteoporosis than men. Whereas in men the testosterone level decreases very gradually with increasing age, in women there is a sudden sharp decrease in the estrogen level when they reach menopause. Within 10 to 15 years women lose about one third of their skeletal mass, at which point fractures can start to occur. When estrogen is kept at a "natural" level by a daily tablet, the incidence of osteoporosis is drastically reduced. This type of hormone replacement therapy is considered the only effective means of preventing osteoporosis in the elderly.

The intake of calcium supplements to prevent osteoporosis has become a recent fad. However, all indications are that this does nothing to prevent bone disease. In fact too much calcium may be detrimental as it decreases the absorption of manganese and can cause a reduction of vitamin D. Large amounts of calcium may also give rise to the formation of kidney stones, a very painful condition whereby one or more large crystals of a calcium salt are produced in the kidneys.

Smoking has been blamed for contributing to many illnesses, osteoporosis being one of them. In both men and women smoking seems to double the chances of developing the disease.

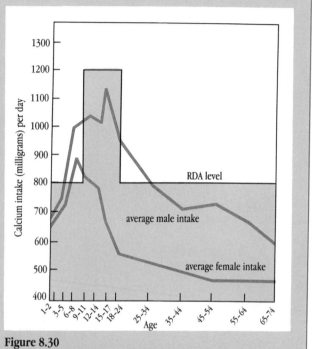

Figure 8.30

This graph of actual calcium intake compared against age groups shows that at most ages our calcium intake is well below the recommended daily allowance (RDA).

EXAMPLE 8.14   Is a precipitation reaction likely to occur when aqueous solutions of copper(II) sulfate and sodium hydroxide are mixed? If yes, what is the balanced net ionic equation?

SOLUTION   If these two compounds react, it will be a double displacement reaction.

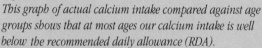

$$CuSO_{4\,(aq)} + 2\,NaOH_{(aq)} \longrightarrow Cu(OH)_{2\,(?)} + Na_2SO_{4\,(?)}$$

Table 8.3 tells us that sodium sulfate is soluble in water, but copper(II) hydroxide is insoluble. We can now write the above equation showing the ions present in solution.

$$Cu^{2+}_{(aq)} + SO_4^{2-}_{(aq)} + 2\,Na^+_{(aq)} + 2\,OH^-_{(aq)} \longrightarrow$$
$$Cu(OH)_{2\,(s)} + 2\,Na^+_{(aq)} + SO_4^{2-}_{(aq)}$$

Cancelling the spectator ions gives the net ionic equation for the reaction:

$$Cu^{2+}_{(aq)} + 2\,OH^-_{(aq)} \longrightarrow Cu(OH)_{2\,(s)}$$

Qualitative Analysis

Ions in solutions can be analyzed by selective precipitation with an appropriate reagent. Suppose we have a solution that we suspect contains any or all of the following ions: silver ions, copper(II) ions, magnesium ions. To find out which ions are present, we can test the unknown solution with aqueous solutions of the following reagents: sodium sulfide, sodium chloride, and sodium hydroxide. But first we must determine the order in which the above reagents should be used and the balanced net ionic reactions in each case.

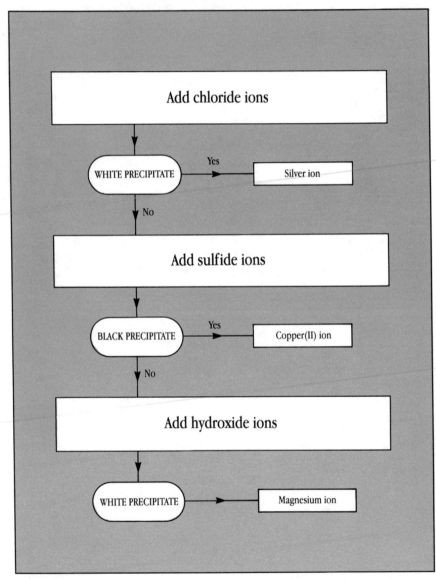

Figure 8.31

A flow chart for distinguishing silver ion, copper(II) ion, and magnesium ion. Similar flow charts can be devised for identifying other ions.

The correct order can be determined by consulting Table 8.3. We see that silver forms an insoluble chloride, sulfide, and hydroxide. Copper forms an insoluble sulfide and hydroxide, whereas magnesium only forms an insoluble hydroxide. If we added hydroxide ions first, a precipitate could indicate any or all of the three cations. However, if chloride ions are added first, a precipitate would indicate the presence of silver ions, since copper(II) chloride and magnesium chloride are both soluble.

$$Ag^+_{(aq)} + Cl^-_{(aq)} \longrightarrow AgCl_{(s)}$$

We then remove any precipitate produced and add the sodium sulfide solution. Only copper ions, if present, will form a precipitate.

$$Cu^{2+}_{(aq)} + S^{2-}_{(aq)} \longrightarrow CuS_{(s)}$$

We filter the solution to remove any solid and add the sodium hydroxide solution to the clear filtrate. If magnesium ions are present, a precipitate of magnesium hydroxide will form.

$$Mg^{2+}_{(aq)} + 2\,OH^-_{(aq)} \longrightarrow Mg(OH)_{2\,(s)}$$

Using K_{sp} Values to Predict Precipitate Formation

The value of the solubility product constant can be used to predict the formation of a precipitate when solutions of ions are mixed. The method is useful when the concentration of at least one of the ions of a potential precipitate is very low. If the product of the ion concentrations (with the appropriate exponents) exceeds the value of K_{sp}, the formation of a precipitate becomes likely. The following two examples show how K_{sp} values can be used in our predictions.

EXAMPLE **8.15** A 0.050 mL drop of 6.0 mol·L^{-1} hydrochloric acid is added to 1.0 L of a 0.10 mol·L^{-1} aqueous silver nitrate solution. Can we expect a precipitate of silver chloride to form? The K_{sp} value for silver chloride is 1.6×10^{-10}.

SOLUTION If we disregard the volume change by the addition of the one drop of hydrochloric acid, the concentration of the silver ions is 0.10 mol·L^{-1}. The number of moles of chloride ions in 5.0×10^{-5} L (0.050 mL) of 6.0 mol·L^{-1} hydrochloric acid is

$$n = Vc$$
$$n = 5.0 \times 10^{-5}\,L \times 6.0\ mol\cdot L^{-1}$$
$$= 3.0 \times 10^{-4}\ mol$$
$$[Cl^-] = 3.0 \times 10^{-4}\,mol/1.0\,L$$
$$= 3.0 \times 10^{-4}\,mol$$

We use the above two concentration values to calculate the ion-concentration product,

$$[Ag^+][Cl^-] = (0.10)(3.0 \times 10^{-4}) = 3.0 \times 10^{-5}$$

This value is much larger than the K_{sp} value for silver chloride, indicating that silver chloride ions will form a precipitate.

EXAMPLE	8.16	Can we expect a precipitate of lead(II) iodide, PbI_2, to form when 20.00 mL of 0.0050 mol·L^{-1} aqueous calcium iodide, CaI_2, solution is added to 80.0 mL of 0.0010 mol·L^{-1} aqueous solution of lead(II) nitrate, $Pb(NO_3)_2$? The K_{sp} for lead(II) iodide is 1.4×10^{-8}.

SOLUTION   The calcium iodide and lead(II) nitrate in the solutions are completely dissociated:

$$CaI_{2\,(s)} \longrightarrow Ca^{2+}{}_{(aq)} + 2\,I^-{}_{(aq)}$$
$$Pb(NO_3)_{2\,(s)} \longrightarrow Pb^{2+}{}_{(aq)} + 2\,NO_3^-{}_{(aq)}$$

First we use the appropriate equation factors to calculate the initial ion concentrations.

$$[I^-] = 0.0050 \text{ mol·L}^{-1}\,CaI_2 \times \frac{2 \text{ mol } I^-}{1 \text{ mol } CaI_2}$$
$$= 1.0 \times 10^{-2} \text{ mol·L}^{-1}\,I^-$$

$$[Pb^{2+}] = 0.0010 \text{ mol·L}^{-1}\,Pb(NO_3)_3 \times \frac{1 \text{ mol } Pb^{2+}}{1 \text{ mol } Pb(NO_3)_3}$$
$$= 1.0 \times 10^{-3} \text{ mol·L}^{-1}\,Pb^{2+}$$

After mixing the total volume is 100.0 mL and the new ion concentrations can be calculated as follows:

$$[Pb^{2+}] = \frac{80.0 \text{ mL}}{100.0 \text{ mL}} \times 1.0 \times 10^{-3} \text{ mol·L}^{-1}$$
$$= 0.800 \times 1.0 \times 10^{-3} \text{ mol·L}^{-1}$$
$$= 8.0 \times 10^{-4} \text{ mol·L}^{-1}$$

$$[I^-] = \frac{20.00 \text{ mL}}{100.0 \text{ mL}} \times 1.0 \times 10^{-2} \text{ mol·L}^{-1}$$
$$= 0.2000 \times 1.0 \times 10^{-2} \text{ mol·L}^{-1}$$
$$= 2.0 \times 10^{-3} \text{ mol·L}^{-1}$$

After mixing the two solutions the ion-concentration product is

$$[Pb^{2+}][I^-]^2 = (8.0 \times 10^{-4})(2.0 \times 10^{-3})^2$$
$$= 3.2 \times 10^{-9}$$

This value is smaller than the K_{sp} value, which means that at these concentrations the lead ions and iodide ions can co-exist in aqueous solution and will *not* combine to form a precipitate of lead(II) iodide.

Dissolving a Precipitate

If you have ever tried to remove iron(III) oxide (rust) from a bicycle, calcium carbonate (scale) from a kettle, or silver sulfide from a tarnished

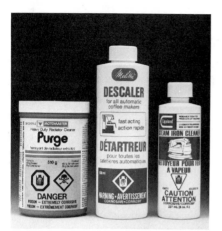

Figure 8.32

Common cleaners that work by complex ion formation.

silver spoon, you know that dissolving an ionic precipitate can be a demanding task. Precipitates can be brought into solution by several methods:

1. dilution with large amounts of water
2. addition of acid
3. addition of base
4. conversion of the metal ion to a soluble complex ion

Many of the ionic compounds present in the oceans, lakes, and streams were dissolved by the first method. In the laboratory, however, this is an impractical procedure, unless the substance is at least slightly soluble.

The addition of an acid will dissolve many insoluble oxides, sulfides, hydroxides, carbonates, and phosphates by chemical reaction. Rust (Fe_2O_3) and scale ($CaCO_3$) for instance will dissolve in concentrated hydrochloric acid.

$$Fe_2O_{3(s)} + 6\ HCl_{(aq)} \longrightarrow 2\ FeCl_{3(aq)} + 3\ H_2O_{(l)}$$
$$CaCO_{3(s)} + 2\ HCl_{(aq)} \longrightarrow CaCl_{2(aq)} + H_2O_{(l)} + CO_{2(g)}$$

Certain insoluble metal hydroxides and metal oxides can be brought into solution by the addition of either an acid or a base. Aluminum hydroxide is an example. The addition of an acid results in an aqueous solution of aluminum ions. A base leads to the formation of an aqueous solution of the aluminate ion (AlO_2^-).

$$Al(OH)_{3(s)} + 3\ HCl_{(aq)} \longrightarrow AlCl_{3(aq)} + 3\ H_2O_{(l)}$$
$$Al(OH)_{3(s)} + NaOH_{(aq)} \longrightarrow NaAlO_{2(aq)} + 2\ H_2O_{(l)}$$

The addition of a reagent that converts the metal ion into a water-soluble complex ion is a very important method for dissolving ionic precipitates. A **complex ion** is a metal ion that is bonded to a number of neutral molecules (e.g. water or ammonia molecules), or negative ions (e.g. chloride, hydroxide, or cyanide ions). Many commercial rust removers work by forming a soluble complex ion with the iron(III) oxide.

We are not always interested in dissolving ionic substances. Sometimes the low solubility of some of these substances has practical applications. Barium sulfate, for example, is used for digestive tract X-rays. The patient is given an aqueous suspension of this insoluble ionic compound to drink; the barium sulfate does not allow the X-rays to pass through, thus making it possible to photograph the stomach and intestine.

Lead(II) chromate is put to practical use as yellow lines on the roads and titanium(IV) oxide is used in white paint pigments. Many animals use insoluble calcium carbonate as a protective coating. It is the main component of egg shells and the shells of marine organisms such as oysters, clams, and crabs.

Figure 8.33

A selection of artist's paints. Many of the paint pigments are very insoluble inorganic compounds. For example, titanium white contains titanium dioxide while cadmium yellow contains cadmium sulfide.

QUESTIONS

16. Consult Table 8.3 to predict whether or not a precipitate will form when aqueous solutions of the following ionic compounds are mixed. Write the balanced net ionic equation for the formation of each precipitate.
    a) barium hydroxide, $Ba(OH)_2$, and iron(II) sulfate, $FeSO_4$
    b) copper(II) nitrate, $Cu(NO_3)_2$, and magnesium chloride, $MgCl_2$
    c) sodium sulfide, Na_2S, and aluminum sulfate, $Al_2(SO_4)_3$

17. An aqueous solution may contain any or all of the cations Sr^{2+}, Zn^{2+}, and Hg_2^{2+}. Aqueous solutions of sodium sulfide, Na_2S, sodium chloride and sodium carbonate, Na_2CO_3, may be added to determine which cations are present. Write the balanced net ionic equations, and provide a flow chart to illustrate the order in which the test solutions should be used.

18. Would we expect a precipitate of silver bromate, $AgBrO_3$ ($K_{sp} = 5.9 \times 10^{-5}$), to form when 50.00 mL of 0.0020 mol·L^{-1} aqueous solution of silver nitrate, $AgNO_3$, is added to 250.0 mL of 0.020 mol·L^{-1} aqueous solution of potassium bromate, $KBrO_3$?

19. Will a precipitate of magnesium hydroxide, $Mg(OH)_2$ ($K_{sp} = 1.2 \times 10^{-11}$) form when 1.00 mL of 0.010 mol·L^{-1} aqueous solution of calcium hydroxide, $Ca(OH)_2$, is added to 1.0 L of 0.20 mol·L^{-1} aqueous solution of magnesium nitrate, $Mg(NO_3)_2$? The change in volume caused by the addition of 1.00 mL can be ignored.

The Common Ion Effect

8.9

The solubility of an ionic substance in water is decreased when another substance is added that contains one of the ions involved in the solution equilibrium. If, for instance, a small volume of concentrated hydrochloric acid is added to a saturated aqueous solution of sodium chloride, some solid sodium chloride will precipitate. Le Châtelier's principle helps us explain these results.

The concentration of chloride ions in the equilibrium is increased by the addition of concentrated hydrochloric acid. This constitutes a stress and the equilibrium shifts to the left (Figure 8.34). Some of the chloride ions will combine with the sodium ions and solid sodium chloride separates from the solution. The chloride ion, in this example, is a common ion. When the concentration of the chloride ions is increased, the solubility of sodium chloride and hence the concentration of the sodium ions, will decrease. This effect is referred to as the **common ion effect**.

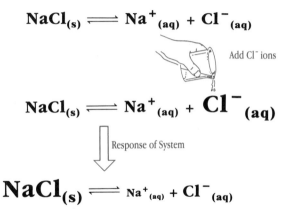

$$NaCl_{(s)} \rightleftharpoons Na^+_{(aq)} + Cl^-_{(aq)}$$

Add Cl⁻ ions

$$NaCl_{(s)} \rightleftharpoons Na^+_{(aq)} + Cl^-_{(aq)}$$

Response of System

$$NaCl_{(s)} \rightleftharpoons Na^+_{(aq)} + Cl^-_{(aq)}$$

Figure 8.34
The common ion effect for addition of concentrated hydrochloric acid to an aqueous solution of sodium chloride.

The presence of a common ion dramatically affects the solubility of an ionic compound that is only slightly soluble in water. For example, the solubility of silver bromide is decreased several fold by the addition of a small amount of a water-soluble substance, such as silver nitrate or sodium bromide, that can supply a common ion. The equilibrium

$$AgBr_{(s)} \rightleftharpoons Ag^+_{(aq)} + Br^-_{(aq)}$$

will shift almost completely to the left upon addition of either silver ions or bromide ions. The effect of common ions can be predicted from the value of the solubility product constant. Remember that the K_{sp} value is independent of the source of the ions. For silver bromide in equilibrium with an aqueous solution of the ions, K_{sp}, the product of the silver and bromide ion concentrations, is 6.5×10^{-13} at 25 °C regardless of whether the ions originate from the silver bromide or from other sources.

EXAMPLE   *8.17*   Silver bromide in a gelatin emulsion is the light-sensitive material in most photographic film and paper. A developing solution often contains a small amount of potassium bromide to minimize the solubility of silver bromide. Calculate the maximum silver ion concentration in water at 25 °C in the absence of a common ion and in the presence of 0.020 mol·L⁻¹ potassium bromide, KBr. The K_{sp} of silver bromide at 25 °C is 6.5×10^{-13}.

SOLUTION   In the absence of a common ion, the concentrations of silver ions and bromide ions are the same. We let this concentration be x mol·L⁻¹. The equilibrium equation is

$$AgBr_{(s)} \rightleftharpoons Ag^+_{(aq)} + Br^-_{(aq)}$$
$$x \text{ mol·L}^{-1} \qquad x \text{ mol·L}^{-1}$$

Knowing the value for K_{sp}, we can calculate the ion concentrations

$$K_{sp} = [Ag^+][Br^-] = x^2$$
$$6.5 \times 10^{-13} = x^2$$

Solving for x, we find the concentration of silver ions

$$x = 8.1 \times 10^{-7} \text{ mol} \cdot \text{L}^{-1}$$

Thus

$$[\text{Ag}^+] = 8.1 \times 10^{-7} \text{ mol} \cdot \text{L}^{-1}$$

In a solution that already contains 0.020 mol·L^{-1} of bromide ions from potassium bromide, the small number of bromide ions resulting from silver bromide can be ignored in the calculation. Hence, we can assume that the K_{sp} is unchanged.

$$K_{sp} = [\text{Ag}^+][\text{Br}^-] = 6.5 \times 10^{-13}$$
$$[\text{Ag}^+] \times 0.020 = 6.5 \times 10^{-13}$$
$$[\text{Ag}^+] = 3.3 \times 10^{-11} \text{ mol} \cdot \text{L}^{-1}$$

Thus, the maximum concentration of silver ions is reduced almost 25 000 times by the addition of a relatively small amount of potassium bromide.

EXAMPLE   **8.18**   Some solid sodium flouride is added to a 0.10 mol·L^{-1} aqueous solution of calcium chloride. What will be the maximum concentration of flouride ions in this solution? The K_{sp} for calcium flouride at 25°C is 3.9 $\times$ 10^{-11}.

SOLUTION   The equilibrium reaction for the dissociation of calcium fluoride is

$$\text{CaF}_{2\,(s)} \rightleftharpoons \text{Ca}^{2+}_{(aq)} + 2\,\text{F}^-_{(aq)}$$

Since the calcium ion concentration in the solution is 0.10 mol·L^{-1}, we can substitute this value in the solubility product expression and solve for [F$^-$].

$$K_{sp} = [\text{Ca}^{2+}][\text{F}^-]^2 = 3.9 \times 10^{-11}$$
$$K_{sp} = 0.10 \times [\text{F}^-]^2 = 3.9 \times 10^{-11}$$
$$[\text{F}^-]^2 = 3.9 \times 10^{-10}$$
$$[\text{F}^-] = 2.0 \times 10^{-5} \text{ mol} \cdot \text{L}^{-1}$$

When the fluoride concentration exceeds 2.0 $\times$ 10^{-5} mol·L^{-1} we can expect the calcium ions to combine with the fluoride ions to form a precipitate of calcium fluoride.

QUESTIONS

20. Explain why sodium chloride will precipitate from a saturated aqueous solution when sodium nitrate is dissolved in this solution.
21. Calculate the maximum barium ion concentration in an aqueous solution of 0.010 mol·L^{-1} sodium sulfate, Na$_2$SO$_4$. The K_{sp} of barium sulfate, BaSO$_4$, is 1.1 $\times$ 10^{-10} at 25 °C.
22. Calculate the maximum magnesium ion concentration in an aqueous solution of 0.020 mol·L^{-1} barium hydroxide, Ba(OH)$_2$. The K_{sp} of magnesium hydroxide, Mg(OH)$_2$, is 1.2 $\times$ 10^{-11} at 25 °C.

Riches on the Sea Floor

We do not normally associate the mining of minerals with the ocean. However the large-scale mining of mineral deposits on the ocean floor, four to five kilometres under the surface of the water, may soon be a reality. For many years special cameras have scanned the ocean floors and, as a result, large deposits of minerals have been discovered, mainly in the form of nodules about five centimetres in diameter. The United States is particularly interested in mining these ore deposits because it currently must import almost all its manganese and cobalt, and most of its nickel.

These nodules were discovered as long ago as 1873 by the Challenger expedition to the Pacific ocean. On average, manganese and iron each make up 15–20 % of the content of these nodules, and valuable elements such as titanium, nickel, copper and cobalt each contribute a further 0.2–1 %. However, the composition does vary widely with the location. (Nodules containing up to 35 % manganese have been found.) The question of how these nodules formed puzzled scientists for sometime.

In the 1960s the Swedish chemist L. G. Sillén proposed that the oceans be treated as a giant chemical reaction vessel. As the metal ions accumulate in the seas due to run-off from the land and from undersea volcanic vents, the product of their concentrations and those of anions in the sea water exceed the solubility product. The compounds then start to crystallize out in the form of nodules. The rate of crystallization is not a rapid process; it can be as slow as a few millimetres per million years.

New mining techniques are being developed to deal with the difficult problem of mineral recovery. One technique that has been successfully tested uses up to six kilometres of pipe, at the end of which is a nodule collection scoop equipped with television cameras. A commercial version could bring more than 200 tonnes of nodules to the surface each hour by using either compressed air or submersible pumps.

The question of ownership of the minerals on the sea floor has not yet been settled. Should the countries whose companies have spent large sums of money in developing the technical know-how have the sole ownership of the minerals? Or do all the countries of the world, through the United Nations, own the wealth on the ocean floor collectively. This issue has been debated in several Law of the Sea conferences held by the United Nations. Whatever the outcome of the political discussions, we can expect that in the near future much of the manganese used in steel will originate from the ocean floor.

Figure 8.35

The JOIDIES Resolution. A number of specially-designed ships are exploring the sea floor for mineral resources.

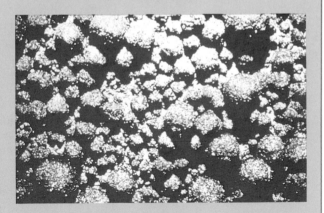

Figure 8.36

These nodules are found on the ocean floor. They contain compounds of manganese, iron, cobalt, nickel, copper, zinc, chromium, vanadium, tungsten, and lead.

Colligative Properties of Solutions

8.10

Up to this point we have been discussing solution properties that vary with the nature of the solute. However, there is a group of physical properties whose values are independent of the identity of the solute. These physical properties depend strictly on the number of solute particles in solution.

Properties of solutions that depend upon the number of dissolved solute particles are known as **colligative properties**. These properties are as follows:

1. the effect of solute on vapour pressure
2. the effect of solute on the boiling point
3. the effect of solute on the freezing point
4. osmosis

The Lowering of Vapour Pressure

The vapour pressure of a liquid results from the escape of molecules of the liquid into the vapour phase. The rate at which a liquid vaporizes will be reduced if a solute is dissolved in the liquid, because some solute particles will displace solvent molecules at the surface of the liquid. There will be fewer solvent molecules escaping from the surface and, as a result, the vapour pressure of the liquid will be reduced. The size of this effect does not depend upon the nature of the solute, only upon the concentration of solute particles.

The effect of vapour pressure lowering can be seen in the experiment illustrated in Figure 8.38. If a beaker of pure water and a beaker of sugar solution are left in a closed container for some time, all of the water in the liquid phase will be transferred to the beaker containing the solution. This occurs because the vapour pressure of the pure water is greater than that of the sugar solution. The pure water therefore evaporates more quickly than the sugar solution, but the rate of condensation of vapour molecules into each of the two beakers will be the same. Water vapour will thus continue to condense into the solution faster than water molecules are evaporating from it, until all of the pure water has been transferred. Eventually, an equilibrium will become established between water in the solution and water vapour. The vapour pressure will be lower than it is for pure water at the same temperature.

The lowering of the vapour pressure of a liquid by the solute particles can be expressed by the following equation:

$$\text{Vapour pressure of solution} = \text{Vapour pressure of solvent} \times \text{Mole fraction of solvent}$$

The expression for **mole fraction** is given by the following:

$$\text{Mole fraction} = \frac{\text{Moles of solvent}}{\text{Moles of solute} + \text{Moles of solvent}}$$

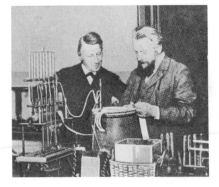

Figure 8.37
Jacobus van't Hoff (1852-1911) and Wilhelm Ostwald (1853-1932) in the laboratory. These chemists provided the basis of our present knowledge of the nature of solutions. Van't Hoff received the Nobel Prize in 1901 and Ostwald in 1909.

The same mole fraction of any solute will produce the same lowering of the vapour pressure, provided that the solute does not itself evaporate.

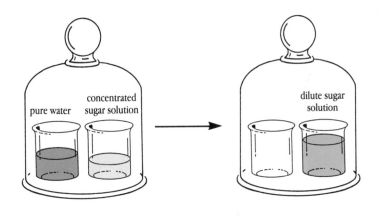

Figure 8.38
If a beaker containing pure water and a beaker containing a sugar solution are placed in a closed container and left for some time, the water will transfer to the beaker containing the sugar solution.

EXAMPLE   *8.19*   At 99.61 °C water has a vapour pressure of 100.0 kPa. Under these conditions, what would be the vapour pressure of a solution of 50.0 g of table sugar (surcose, $C_{12}H_{22}O_{11}$) in 100.0 g of water?

SOLUTION   First we calculate the number of moles of solute (sucrose) and the number of moles of solvent (water).

$$\text{Moles of } C_{12}H_{22}O_{11} = 50.0\,g\ C_{12}H_{22}O_{11} \times \frac{1\ mol\ C_{12}H_{22}O_{11}}{342.3\,g\ C_{12}H_{22}O_{11}}$$

$$= 0.146\ mol\ C_{12}H_{22}O_{11}$$

$$\text{Moles of } H_2O = 100.0\,g\ H_2O \times \frac{1\ mol\ H_2O}{18.02\,g\ H_2O}$$

$$= 5.549\ mol\ H_2O$$

We can now calculate the mole fraction of water:

$$\frac{\text{Moles of } H_2O}{\text{Total number of moles}} = \frac{5.549}{5.549 + 0.146}$$

$$= 0.9744$$

The vapour pressure of the solution can now be calculated:

$$\text{Vapour pressure of solution} = 100.0\,kPa \times 0.9744$$

$$= 97.44\,kPa$$

Soluble ionic compounds will also cause a reduction in vapour pressure proportional to the mole fraction of solute particles, but only if the solution is dilute. If the solute is a salt, however, we must write a balanced equation to determine the number of moles of particles present in the

Figure 8.39

The common additive for automobile radiators. As a summer 'coolant,' it does not cool. Instead it raises the boiling point of the solution. As a winter antifreeze, it depresses the freezing point of the solution.

solution. For example, one mole of sodium chloride will dissolve in water to produce two moles of ions.

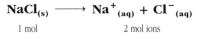

$$NaCl_{(s)} \longrightarrow Na^+{}_{(aq)} + Cl^-{}_{(aq)}$$

1 mol   2 mol ions

One mole of magnesium bromide will produce three moles of ions.

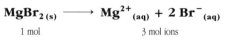

$$MgBr_{2\,(s)} \longrightarrow Mg^{2+}{}_{(aq)} + 2\,Br^-{}_{(aq)}$$

1 mol   3 mol ions

We must use the total number of ions when calculating the effect of the solute on the vapour pressure of the water, or on any of the other colligative properties.

Boiling-point Elevation

We define the boiling point of a liquid as *the temperature at which its vapour pressure becomes equal to the external pressure.* When a solute is added to a pure solvent, the vapour pressure of the resulting solution will be decreased, as compared to the original pure solvent.

For any particular solvent, the same conentration of any solute will elevate the boiling point by the same value. We must remember that atmospheric pressure, and hence boiling point, vary slightly from day to day. Even at sea level, it is a rare occasion that the atmospheric pressure is 101.325 kPa. Thus in all our calculations and measurements, we must note the atmospheric pressure and check data tables for the corresponding boiling point of pure water.

When we raise the boiling point of a pure solvent by adding a small quantity of solute, it is normally the pure solvent that boils first. This method of obtaining pure liquids from solutions containing solid solutes is called *distillation*.

For calculations involving boiling point elevation, we work with concentrations in *moles of solute per kilogram of solvent.* These units ($mol \cdot kg^{-1}$) of concentration are commonly called **molality**, **m**. Therefore,

$$m = \frac{\textbf{Moles of solute}}{\textbf{Mass of solvent}}$$

The relationship between boiling-point elevation and concentration is given by the equation:

$$\Delta T_b = k_b m$$

where ΔT_b is the boiling-point elevation,
       k_b is the boiling-point elevation constant,
       m is the concentration of the solution in moles per kilogram.

For example, the boiling-point elevation constant, k_b, of water has a value of $0.512\,°C \cdot mol^{-1} \cdot kg$. (This applies mainly to dilute solutions.)

EXAMPLE   8.20   The atmospheric pressure is measured and found to be 99.15 kPa, at which water boils at 99.40 °C. Under these conditions, what would be the boiling point of a solution of 50.0 g of table sugar (sucrose, $C_{12}H_{22}O_{11}$) in 100.0 mL of water, given that the boiling-point elevation constant for water is 0.512 °C·mol⁻¹·kg?

SOLUTION   If we refer back to Example 8.19 we can see that there are 0.146 moles of sucrose in this solution. To determine the boiling-point elevation, we first calculate molality.

$$m = \frac{0.146 \text{ mol}}{0.1000 \text{ kg}}$$
$$= 1.46 \text{ mol·kg}^{-1}$$

Substituting the known values into the formula $\Delta T_b = k_b m$, gives us

$$\Delta T_b = (0.512 \text{ °C·mol}^{-1}\text{·kg})(1.46 \text{ mol·kg}^{-1})$$
$$= 0.748 \text{ °C}$$

The boiling point of the solution is therefore

$$(99.40 + 0.748) \text{ °C} = 100.15 \text{ °C} \quad \text{at 99.15 kPa}$$

Freezing-point Depression

We can also show that the addition of a solute to a liquid lowers the freezing point. For any particular solvent, the same concentration of any solute will depress the freezing point by the same amount.

Most of us have observed that sprinkling salt on snow and ice causes a change from solid to liquid phase of water. This is a result of lowering the melting point of the ice. As observed for the boiling point effect, the change in freezing point is comparatively small. Thus, in conditions below −15 °C, salt will be ineffective in melting ice. Other examples of this principle are all around us. One, for example, is that fresh water freezes before sea water because river water contains much lower concentrations of dissolved solutes.

Ice-salt mixtures are often used to lower temperature, as in the making of ice cream. Here both the phenomena of freezing-point depression and the enthalpy of fusion come into play. For example, the making of ice cream requires two buckets: an outer containing bucket and a smaller one that fits inside. In preparing the ice cream, we must first reduce the temperature of the inner bucket below 0 °C. This is done by preparing an ice-salt mixture in the larger bucket, which melts some ice because the freezing point of water has been lowered. In supplying the necessary heat of fusion involved in melting the ice, energy is absorbed from the surroundings: that is, the temperature of the ice cream mixture in the inner bucket gets colder.

Figure 8.40
The ice fishes around Antarctica produce their own antifreeze to stop their plasma from freezing. These fishes belong to the family Chaenichthydia and they grow to a length of about 0.7 m.

Several organisms produce their own antifreezes. Plants produce molecules in the fall that will lower the freezing point of the sap. In the late spring, the plants cease to produce the compounds, thus an abnormally late spring or early fall frost will do more damage than winter temperatures. The temperature of the salt water around Antarctica is $0\,°C$. Under these conditions the plasma of fishes living in the region would be expected to freeze. A family of fishes, known as ice fishes, produces a natural antifreeze in which the chemical structure closely resembles radiator antifreeze. This compound therefore enables the fish to survive in waters that would be below the freezing point of the plasma of other groups.

When we depress the freezing point of a pure solvent by adding a small quantity of solute, it is normally the pure solvent that crystallizes first. This is another method of obtaining a pure substance from an impure sample and is the method used to obtain ultra-pure silicon for solid-state circuits. The technique is called *zone-refining*.

The relationship between the freezing-point depression and concentration can be expressed as

$$\Delta T_f = k_f m$$

where ΔT_f is the freezing-point depression,
    k_f is the freezing-point depression constant,
    m is the concentration of the solution in moles per kilogram.

The freezing-point depression constant of water is $1.86\,°C \cdot mol^{-1} \cdot kg$.

EXAMPLE   *8.21*   What would be the freezing point of a solution containing $1.46\ mol \cdot kg^{-1}$ of the ionic compound calcium chloride? Assume that the calcium chloride is completely dissociated in solution.

SOLUTION   We first write the equation for the dissociation:

$$CaCl_{2\,(s)} \longrightarrow Ca^{2+}_{(aq)} + 2\,Cl^-_{(aq)}$$

         1 mol   3 mol ions

As we can see, one mole of calcium chloride dissociates into three moles of ions. Thus, we use the given molality of calcium chloride and a modified equation factor to find molality of the solution.

$$m = 1.46\ mol \cdot kg^{-1}\ CaCl_2 \times \frac{3\ mol\ ions}{1\ mol\ CaCl_2}$$

$$= 4.38\ mol \cdot kg^{-1}$$

Substituting the known values into the formula $\Delta T_f = k_f m$, gives

$$\Delta T_f = (1.86\,°C \cdot mol^{-1} \cdot kg)(4.38\ mol \cdot kg^{-1})$$

$$= 8.15\,°C$$

The actual freezing point of the solution is

$$(0.00 - 8.15)\,°C = -8.15\,°C$$

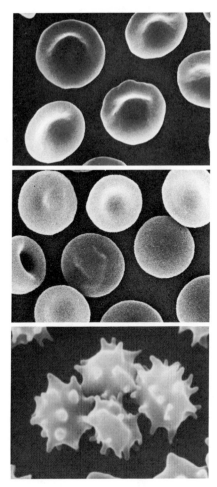

Figure 8.41

a) Red Blood cells in a solution of similar osmotic pressure.

b) In pure water, the cells swell and ultimately burst.

c) In a concentrated sugar or salt solution, the cells shrivel up.

Osmotic Pressure

This colligative property is of crucial importance in biology and biochemistry. **Osmosis** occurs when a solution is separated by a semipermeable membrane from the pure solvent. We can think of a membrane as a thin film of material with small holes in it. If the holes are relatively large, as in a filter paper, the membrane will be permeable. Solutions may pass through, but precipitates will not. On the other hand, the holes may be so small that nothing may pass through. In this case the membrane would be impermeable. **Semipermeable membranes** will allow small solute molecules to pass through, but will block the passage of larger ones.

Different semipermeable membranes will allow different materials to pass through. Cell membranes, for example, are semipermeable. They will allow nutrients and waste materials to pass through by osmosis, while retaining larger molecules such as proteins. Red blood cells placed into pure water will swell and burst as water molecules pass through the cell walls to dilute the contents of the cells. If the cells are placed into fairly concentrated sugar solution, they will shrivel as water passes out of the cell. Care must therefore be taken when hospital patients are given intravenous transfusions of nutrients, like glucose, to ensure that the osmotic pressure of the administered solution is the same as that inside the cells.

The skins of fruits and vegetables are also semipermeable. A cucumber placed into a fairly concentrated solution of salt will shrivel to a pickle as water leaves the more dilute solution inside the vegetable. The reverse process occurs when a dried prune or raisin, both of which contain sugar, is soaked in a bowl of water. In this case, water passes through the skin of the fruit causing it to swell.

If we try to prevent the flow of solvent molecules into the solution, a pressure will be exerted. This pressure is called the **osmotic pressure**. The magnitude of the osmotic pressure of a solution will be determined by the number of solute particles present. The type of particle, or its size, makes no difference. We can calculate osmotic pressures from concentration data in much the same way as we calculate freezing-point depression and boiling-point elevation. The osmotic pressure of a solution is very temperature dependent, however, and this factor must be considered in any calculations.

When both concentration and temperature are taken into account, experiments show that the osmotic pressure of a solution, Π, is given by the equation

$$\Pi = cRT$$

where c is the concentration of the solution in moles per litre,

R is the universal gas constant ($8.314 \ kPa \cdot L \cdot mol^{-1} \cdot K^{-1}$),

T is the tempeature in kelvins.

EXAMPLE 8.22

What would be the osmotic pressure at 23 °C of a solution containing 2.50 g of table sugar (sucrose) in 100.0 mL of solution?

SOLUTION   We use the molar mass of sucrose, 342.3 g·mol^{-1}, to determine the number of moles in 2.50 g:

$$\text{Moles of } C_{12}H_{22}O_{11} = 2.50 \text{ g } C_{12}H_{22}O_{11} \times \frac{1 \text{ mol } C_{12}H_{22}O_{11}}{342.3 \text{ g } C_{12}H_{22}O_{11}}$$
$$= 7.30 \times 10^{-3} \text{ mol } C_{12}H_{22}O_{11}$$

Next we calculate the concentration of the solution.

$$c = \frac{n}{V}$$
$$= \frac{7.30 \times 10^{-3} \text{ mol}}{0.1000 \text{ L}}$$
$$= 7.30 \times 10^{-2} \text{ mol·L}^{-1}$$

We then substitute the known values into the formula for osmotic pressure:

$$\Pi = cRT$$
$$= (7.30 \times 10^{-2} \text{ mol·L}^{-1})(8.314 \text{ kPa·L·mol}^{-1} \cdot \text{K}^{-1})(296 \text{ K})$$
$$= 180 \text{ kPa}$$

If we have a solution separated from a solvent by a semipermeable membrane and we apply a pressure to the solution that is greater than the osmotic pressure, pure liquid will be "forced" out of the solution. This *reverse osmosis* is often used to purify water, a process called *desalination*. In terms of energy, reverse osmosis is cheaper than distillation for obtaining pure water.

Calculating Molar Mass

We have seen that we can calculate boiling-point elevations and freezing-point or vapour-pressure depressions from a knowledge of the concentrations of the solutions. Conversely, we can use colligative properties to determine the molar mass of a substance.

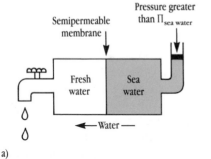

a)

b)

Figure 8.42

a) *The schematic of an apparatus used for desalinating (purifying) sea water by reverse osmosis.*

b) *A portable desalinator has been developed for life rafts. Thus survivors of marine accidents will no longer face the prospect of death by dehydration.*

EXAMPLE 8.23

When 12.0 g of a non-ionic solute is dissolved in 300.0 g of water, a solution that freezes at −1.62 °C is obtained. Calculate the molar mass of the solute. (The freezing-point depression constant for water is 1.86 °C·mol^{-1}·kg.)

SOLUTION   Substituting the known values into the formula $\Delta T_f = k_f m$, we find that

$$1.62 \text{ °C} = (1.86 \text{ °C·mol}^{-1} \cdot \text{kg}) \times m$$

Figure 8.43
This apparatus measures changes in vapour pressure of a solvent to determine the molar mass of a solute.

Therefore,

$$m = \frac{1.62\,^\circ\text{C}}{1.86\,^\circ\text{C}\cdot\text{mol}^{-1}\cdot\text{kg}}$$
$$= 0.871\ \text{mol}\cdot\text{kg}^{-1}$$

We can also calculate the solution concentration in grams of solute per kilogram of solvent

$$\text{Concentration} = \frac{12.0\,\text{g}}{0.3000\,\text{kg}}$$
$$= 40.0\,\text{g}\cdot\text{kg}^{-1}$$

The molar mass found by using the above two values for concentration:

$$\text{Molar mass} = \frac{40.0\,\text{g}\cdot\text{kg}^{-1}}{0.871\ \text{mol}\cdot\text{kg}^{-1}}$$
$$= 45.9\,\text{g}\cdot\text{mol}^{-1}$$

EXAMPLE   **8.24**   The osmotic pressure of 0.100 g of hemoglobin in 10.00 mL of solution is 0.383 kPa at 25 °C. Calculate the molar mass of hemoglobin.

SOLUTION   We rearrange the formula for osmotic pressure to get

$$c = \frac{\Pi}{RT}$$

The molar concentration of the solution is therefore

$$c = \frac{0.383\,\text{kPa}}{8.314\,\text{kPa}\cdot\text{L}\cdot\text{mol}^{-1}\cdot\text{K}^{-1} \times 298\,\text{K}}$$
$$= 1.55 \times 10^{-4}\ \text{mol}\cdot\text{L}^{-1}$$

The concentration of hemoglobin in grams per litre is

$$\text{Concentration} = \frac{0.100\,\text{g}}{0.010\,00\,\text{L}}$$
$$= 10.0\,\text{g}\cdot\text{L}^{-1}$$

We can now find the molar mass of hemoglobin

$$\text{Molar mass} = \frac{10.0\,\text{g}\cdot\text{L}^{-1}}{1.55 \times 10^{-4}\ \text{mol}\cdot\text{L}^{-1}}$$
$$= 6.45 \times 10^{4}\,\text{g}\cdot\text{mol}^{-1}$$

QUESTIONS

23. Which will be more effective in de-icing a stretch of sidewalk: 1.0 kg of calcium chloride or 1.0 kg of sodium chloride?

24. Fish and meat can be preserved with salt. What will happen to any contaminating bacteria in a concentrated solution of sodium chloride?

25. At 100.0 °C water has a vapour pressure of 101.3 kPa. Under these conditions, calculate the vapour pressure of a solution of 21.00 g of potassium sulfate in 1000 g of water.

26. Calculate the freezing point of a solution of 6.00 g of ethanol, C_2H_5OH, in 150 g of water.

27. A 60.0 g sample of a non-ionic compound elevates the boiling point of 500 g of water by 0.564 °C. Calculate the molar mass of the solute.

28. Calculate the osmotic pressure at 20 °C of a solution of 5.00 g of sucrose in 100.00 mL of solution. The molar mass of the sucrose is $342 \, g \cdot mol^{-1}$.

Summary

- The miscibility of liquids and the solubility of solids and gases in liquids depend on the intermolecular attractive forces.

- The solubility of solids in liquids increases with increasing temperature, except in the case of some ionic compounds.

- The solubility of a gas in a liquid increases as the pressure of the gas above the liquid increases.

- Concentrations of solutions are commonly expressed in terms of moles of solute per litre of solution or in terms of moles per kilogram of solvent (molality).

- Ionic substances dissociate into ions when they are dissolved in water; these ions are hydrated as a result of ion-dipole attractions. Some molecular substances ionize in water.

- The solubility of ionic substances in water varies widely and can be qualitatively predicted by the solubility rules.

- Most of the earth's mineral deposits are highly insoluble ionic compounds; however, the oceans contain a large variety of dissolved ions.

- Potash has its origin in the ocean and is one of Canada's largest mineral resources.

- The solubility product constant, K_{sp}, gives the mathematical relationship between ion concentrations in saturated aqueous solutions of ionic compounds with low solubility.

- Precipitation reactions can occur when ionic solutions are mixed. Precipitate formation can be represented by net ionic equations and predicted from the ion concentrations and K_{sp} values.

- The solubility of ionic compounds is affected by the presence of common ions contributed by other substances in the solution. The effect of a common ion can be calculated using the solubility product constant, K_{sp}.

- Non-volatile solute particles lower the vapour pressure of liquid solutions. This results in an increase in the boiling point and a decrease in the freezing point of the solution.

- The magnitude of the boiling-point elevation, the freezing-point depression, and the osmotic pressure of a solution is directly proportional to the number of solute particles. The molar mass of a solute can be calculated from the colligative properties of a solution.

KEY WORDS

amalgam	molarity
colligative properties	mole fraction
common ion effect	net ionic equation
complex ion	osmosis
concentration	osmotic pressure
dissociation	potash
dry cleaning solvent	recrystallization
hydration	saturated
hydrate	semipermeable membrane
insoluble	soluble
immiscible	solubility
ion-dipole attraction	solubility product constant
ionization	spectator ion
miscible	standard solutions
molality	volumetric flask

ANSWERS TO SECTION QUESTIONS

1. solutes: sugar, flavouring and colouring agents, carbon dioxide
   solvent: water

2. apple juice, bronze

3. a) dispersion forces, hydrogen bonds
   b) dispersion forces
   c) dispersion forces, dipole-dipole forces.
      Both acetic acid and ethanal are water soluble.

4. phenol with methanol, naphthalene with gasoline

5. a) $LiOH_{(s)} \longrightarrow Li^+_{(aq)} + OH^-_{(aq)}$
   b) $K_3PO_{4(s)} \longrightarrow 3 K^+_{(aq)} + PO_4^{3-}_{(aq)}$
   c) $SrCl_{2(s)} \longrightarrow Sr^{2+}_{(aq)} + 2 Cl^-_{(aq)}$
   d) $Cr_2(SO_4)_{3(s)} \longrightarrow 2 Cr^{3+}_{(aq)} + 3 SO_4^{2-}_{(aq)}$

6. The attractions between silver ions and chloride ions are greater than the ion-dipole attractions between these ions and the dipoles in water molecules.

7. a) concentration increases
   b) concentration increases
   c) concentration remains the same.

8. a) $2.61 \ mol \cdot L^{-1}$ b) $6.250 \times 10^{-3} \ mol \cdot L^{-1}$

9. a) $160 \ g$ b) $4.267 \times 10^{-2} \ g$

10. a) $33.6 \ mL$

11. a) $[Na^+] = 0.030 \ mol \cdot L^{-1}$; $[SO_4{}^{2-}] = 0.015 \ mol \cdot L^{-1}$
    b) $[Al^{3+}] = 0.0500 \ mol \cdot L^{-1}$; $[SO_4{}^{2-}] = 0.0750 \ mol \cdot L^{-1}$

12. a) K_2CO_3, soluble
    b) $AuCl_3$, soluble
    c) $Fe_3(PO_4)_2$, insoluble
    d) $Mg(OH)_2$, insoluble
    e) NH_4NO_3, soluble
    f) $PbSO_4$, insoluble

13. $4.2 \times 10^{18} \ g$

14. a) $[Pb^{2+}] = 1.1 \times 10^{-4} \ mol \cdot L^{-1}$; $[SO_4{}^{2-}] = 1.1 \times 10^{-4} \ mol \cdot L^{-1}$
    b) $[Ag^+] = 2.3 \times 10^{-4} \ mol \cdot L^{-1}$; $[CO_3{}^{2-}] = 1.2 \times 10^{-4} \ mol \cdot L^{-1}$
    c) $[Mg^{2+}] = 1.4 \times 10^{-4} \ mol \cdot L^{-1}$; $[OH^-] = 2.9 \times 10^{-4} \ mol \cdot L^{-1}$

15. a) 1.2×10^{-10}
    b) 4.5×10^{-2}

16. a) $Ba^{2+}{}_{(aq)} + SO_4{}^{2-}{}_{(aq)} \longrightarrow BaSO_{4 (s)}$
       $Fe^{2+}{}_{(aq)} + 2 \ OH^-{}_{(aq)} \longrightarrow Fe(OH)_{2 (s)}$
    b) no precipitate
    c) $2 \ Al^{3+}{}_{(aq)} + 3 \ S^{2-}{}_{(aq)} \longrightarrow Al_2S_{3 (s)}$

17. first add NaCl: $Hg_2{}^{2+}{}_{(aq)} + 2 \ Cl^-{}_{(aq)} \longrightarrow Hg_2Cl_{2 (s)}$
    next add Na_2S: $Zn^{2+}{}_{(aq)} + S^{2-}{}_{(aq)} \longrightarrow ZnS_{(s)}$
    then Na_2CO_3: $Sr^{2+}{}_{(aq)} + CO_3{}^{2-}{}_{(aq)} \longrightarrow SrCO_{3 (s)}$

18. $[Ag^+][BrO_3{}^-] = 5.5 \times 10^{-6}$: this is less than the K_{sp} value, therefore no precipitate would be expected.

19. $[Mg^{2+}][OH^-]^2 = 8.0 \times 10^{-11}$: this is slightly more than the K_{sp} value, therefore some precipitate would be expected.

20. Additional sodium ions from the sodium nitrate will increase the concentration of these ions in the resulting solution, thus shifting the equilibrium to the left and producing solid sodium chloride.

21. $1.1 \times 10^{-8} \ mol \cdot L^{-1}$

22. $7.5 \times 10^{-9} \ mol \cdot L^{-1}$

23. $1.0 \ kg$ of NaCl because it contains more ions

24. The bacteria will shrivel due to loss of water.

25. 99.36 kPa
26. −1.62 °C
27. 109 g mol^{-1}
28. 356 kPa

COMPREHENSION QUESTIONS

1. Classify the following in terms of the types of solutions they represent:
   a) air
   b) sea water
   c) an alloy
   d) an amalgam

2. What are the differences between the following intermolecular forces: dispersion forces, dipole-dipole attractions, hydrogen bonding.

3. Ethanol, C_2H_5OH, and decanol, $C_{10}H_{21}OH$, are both alcohols, but only ethanol dissolves in water. Why does decanol not dissolve in water?

4. Explain why acetone, CH_3COCH_3, is miscible with water but butane, C_4H_{10}, which has about the same molecular mass, is insoluble.

5. What are the requirements for a good dry cleaning solvent?

6. Explain why sugar does not dissolve in gasoline but dissolves very well in water.

7. Describe how a solid can be purified by the process of recrystallization.

8. a) What is a hydrate?
   b) What is meant by the hydration of ions?

9. Aqueous solutions of ions can be produced by a dissociation or an ionization process. Explain the difference between these processes.

10. What is a standard solution?

11. Why are many metals found in nature in the form of sulfides?

12. What are the two most common cations and anions in sea water?

13. List four substances that are obtained from sea water on a commercial scale.

14. To what substance does the name potash usually refer?

15. Discuss the origin of the potash deposits in Saskatchewan.

16. What is the major use of potassium compounds? How does this relate to the fact that major sources of potassium carbonate in the past were wood and seaweed.

17. Give a definition of the solubility product constant, K_{sp}.

18. What are spectator ions?

19. Give four general methods by which insoluble ionic compounds can be made to dissolve in water.

20. Explain with a reaction equation why egg shells dissolve in hydrochloric acid.

21. Explain why less sodium chloride will dissolve in one litre of sea water than in one litre of pure water.

22. What does the term colligative properties of solution refer to?

23. Why does the presence of a solute cause the vapour pressure of a solvent to be reduced?

24. Which of the two buckets described in the making of ice cream (Section 8.10) should be insulated? Explain your answer.

25. Explain why spinach is substantially reduced in volume when sprinkled and rubbed with sodium chloride.

26. Is there any general rule that links increased solubility, temperature, and the enthalpy of the solution process? If so, what might that rule be?

PROBLEMS *The Solution Process of Ionic Compounds*

27. Write balanced equations that show which ions are produced when the following ionic substances are dissolved in water:
    a) sodium sulfide
    b) calcium iodide
    c) lithium carbonate
    d) iron(III) sulfate
    e) cobalt(II) nitrate

28. Write balanced equations showing the ions produced when the following covalent substances dissociate.
    a) $HI_{(g)}$ (in water)
    b) $CH_3CO_2H_{(aq)}$ (in water)

The Determination of Solution Concentrations

29. Calculate the concentrations (in moles per litre) of the following solutions:
    a) a 250.0 mL aqueous solution containing 25.50 g of sodium phosphate, Na_3PO_4
    b) a 75.00 mL solution of concentrated aqueous ammonia, NH_3 ($14.8 \ mol \cdot L^{-1}$), diluted with water to a volume of 2.000 L

30. What mass of lead(II) nitrate is present in 25.00 mL of a $0.1000 \ mol \cdot L^{-1}$ aqueous solution?

31. What are the concentrations of the ions in the following solutions:
    a) an aqueous solution containing $0.075 \ mol \cdot L^{-1}$ strontium nitrate, $Sr(NO_3)_2$

b) a 200 mL aqueous solution containing 4.26 g sodium sulfate, Na_2SO_4

c) a 2.000 L aqueous solution containing 107.0 g ammonium chloride, NH_4Cl

The Solubility of Ionic Compounds

32. Write formulas for the following compounds, and using Table 8.3 predict their solubilities in water.

a) potassium phosphate

b) calcium carbonate

c) copper(II) bromide

d) aluminum sulfide

e) nickel(II) sulfate

33. Calculate the concentrations (in moles per litre) of the eight most common ions in sea water from the information in Table 8.5.

The Solubility Product Constant

34. Calculate the concentrations of ions in a saturated aqueous solution of the following:

a) silver iodide, AgI; $K_{sp} = 1.5 \times 10^{-16}$

b) strontium carbonate, $SrCO_3$; $K_{sp} = 1.6 \times 10^{-9}$

35. What are the concentrations of the ions in saturated aqueous solutions of the following:

a) lead(II) iodide, PbI_2; $K_{sp} = 1.4 \times 10^{-8}$

b) silver sulfate, Ag_2SO_4; $K_{sp} = 1.5 \times 10^{-4}$

c) iron(III) hydroxide, $Fe(OH)_3$; $K_{sp} = 6.3 \times 10^{-38}$

36. Calculate the K_{sp} values of the substances from their solubilities in water:

a) thallium(I) chloride, TlCl; $3.4 \, g \cdot L^{-1}$ at 25 °C

b) silver bromide, AgBr; $1.3 \times 10^{-4} \, g \cdot L^{-1}$ at 20 °C

c) calcium fluoride, CaF_2; $1.6 \times 10^{-2} \, g \cdot L^{-1}$ at 20 °C

Reactions Involving Precipitates

37. Use Table 8.3 to predict whether a precipitate will form when aqueous solutions of the following substances are mixed. If a precipitate is expected, give the balanced net ionic equation.

a) sodium sulfide, Na_2S, and chromium(III) sulfate, $Cr_2(SO_4)_3$

b) sodium sulfate, Na_2SO_4, and iron(III) nitrate, $Fe(NO_3)_3$

c) potassium hydroxide, KOH, and cobalt(II) chloride, $CoCl_2$

d) aluminum sulfate, $Al_2(SO_4)_3$, and sodium carbonate, Na_2CO_3

38. To an aqueous solution containing the cations Ca^{2+}, Ag^+, Cu^{2+}, and K^+ is added a sodium bromide solution. The precipitate A is filtered off and a sodium sulfide solution is added to the filtrate. The black precipitate B that forms is removed by filtration. A solution of sodium carbonate is added next, again resulting in a precipitate C. Identify A, B, and C, and give the balanced net ionic reactions for their formation.

39. Will a precipitate of calcium fluoride, CaF_2, form when 0.084 g of sodium fluoride, NaF, is dissolved in 1.00 L of a 0.010 mol·L^{-1} aqueous solution of calcium chloride, $CaCl_2$? The K_{sp} for calcium fluoride is 3.9×10^{-11}.

40. A 0.10 mol·L^{-1} aqueous solution of sodium sulfate, Na_2SO_4, is added one drop at a time to 1.00 L of a 0.0010 mol·L^{-1} aqueous solution of lead(II) nitrate, $Pb(NO_3)_2$. What is the minimum volume that has to be added before a precipitate of lead(II) sulfate, $PbSO_4$, starts to form? The K_{sp} for lead(II) sulfate is 1.3×10^{-8}, and the change in volume can be ignored.

The Common Ion Effect

41. Calculate the maximum iodide ion concentration possible in an aqueous solution that is already 0.010 mol·L^{-1} in lead(II) nitrate, $Pb(NO_3)_2$. The K_{sp} for lead(II) iodide, PbI_2, is 1.4×10^{-8}.

42. Upon addition of hydroxide ions to sea water, magnesium hydroxide, $Mg(OH)_2$, will precipitate. If the magnesium ion concentration in sea water is 5.3×10^{-2} mol·L^{-1}, calculate the maximum hydroxide ion concentration, in moles per litre, in sea water. The K_{sp} for magnesium hydroxide is 1.2×10^{-11}.

43. A sample of sea water contains 5.3×10^{-1} mol·L^{-1} chloride ion and 8.4×10^{-4} mol·L^{-1} bromide ion. What concentration of added silver ion would cause precipitation of silver chloride, AgCl, and silver bromide, AgBr? Which of these two silver halides would precipitate first? The K_{sp} for silver chloride is 1.6×10^{-10}; the K_{sp} for silver bromide is 6.5×10^{-13}.

Colligative Properties of Solutions

44. A 17.00 g sample of ethanol, C_2H_5OH, is dissolved in 100.0 mL of water. Calculate the mole fraction of ethanol and the mole fraction of water. (The density of water is 1.000 g·mol^{-1}.)

45. The vapour pressure of water is 101.3 kPa at 100.0 °C. Under these conditions, calculate the vapour pressure of the following solutions:
a) 49.0 g of glycerol, $C_3H_8O_3$, in 100.0 g of water
b) 4.90 g of lead(II) nitrate, $Pb(NO_3)_2$, in 100.0 g of water

For Questions 46–50, k_b for water is 0.512 °C·mol^{-1}·kg, k_f for water is 1.86 °C·mol^{-1}·kg.

46. The atmospheric pressure is measured and found to be 104.2 kPa. At this pressure, water boils at 100.80 °C and freezes at 0.00 °C. Under these conditions a solution contains 38.00 g of glucose, $C_6H_{12}O_6$, in 50.00 g of water. Determine the following:
a) the solution boiling point
b) the solution freezing point

47. The atmospheric pressure is measured and found to be 99.86 kPa. At this pressure, water boils at 99.60 °C and freezes at 0.00 °C. Under these conditions, a solution contains 4.86 g of sodium chloride in 100.0 g of water. Determine the following:
    a) the solution boiling point
    b) the solution freezing point

48. A solution of 18.0 g of urea in 250 g of water has a freezing point of −2.24 °C. Calculate the molar mass of urea.

49. A solution of 36.00 g of a non-ionic compound in 200 g of water has a boiling point of 101.3 °C. Calculate the molar mass of the compound.

50. What mass of ethylene glycol, $C_2H_4(OH)_2$, would need to be added to 2.500 kg of water to reduce the freezing point to −40 °C?

51. An aqueous solution containing 10.0 g of a protein in 500.0 mL of solution has an osmotic pressure of 1.92 kPa at 27 °C. Calculate the molar mass of the protein.

52. Calculate the osmotic pressures of the following aqueous solutions at 15 °C.
    a) 15.0 g of glucose, $C_6H_{12}O_6$, in 250.0 mL of solution
    b) 26.0 g of magnesium iodide, MgI_2, in 150.0 mL of solution

53. The blood of many marine animals has the same osmotic pressure as sea water. If sea water freezes at −2.50 °C, calculate the osmotic pressure of this blood at 5.0 °C. We can assume that the value for molality of sea water $(mol \cdot kg^{-1})$ has the same value as concentration $(mol \cdot L^{-1})$.

MISCELLANEOUS PROBLEMS 54. Water-insoluble calcium carbonate reacts with hydrochloric acid according to the following equation:

$$CaCO_{3(s)} + 2\, HCl_{(aq)} \longrightarrow CaCl_{2(aq)} + CO_{2(g)} + H_2O_{(\ell)}$$

How much of 10.0 g of calcium carbonate remains undissolved when it is heated with 100.0 mL of 1.05 mol·L^{-1} hydrochloric acid until no more carbon dioxide is produced?

55. What volume of 0.10 mol·L^{-1} aqueous calcium bromide, $CaBr_2$, must be added to 100.0 mL of 0.100 mol·L^{-1} aqueous lead(II) nitrate, $Pb(NO_3)_2$, before a precipitate of lead(II) bromide, $PbBr_2$, starts to form? Assume in your calculation that the total volume remains 100.0 mL. The K_{sp} for lead(II) bromide is 1.4×10^{-8}.

56. How many litres of water at 25 °C have to be added to mercury(II) sulfide, HgS, in order for one mercury atom to be present in solution? (There are 6.02×10^{23} ions in one mole of ions. K_{sp} for mercury(II) sulfide is 3.0×10^{-54}.)

57. A 100.0 mL solution of 1.00 mol·L^{-1} aqueous sodium sulfate, Na_2SO_4, is added to a 200.0 mL solution of 1.00 mol·L^{-1} aqueous barium chloride, $BaCl_2$. Barium sulfate, $BaSO_4$, precipitates from the mixture. (K_{sp} for barium sulfate is 1.1×10^{-10}.) Calculate the following:
   a) mass of barium sulfate that precipitates
   b) concentrations of all ions that remain in solution

58. A 1.50 L solution of 0.250 mol·L^{-1} aqueous sodium hydroxide is added to a 1.00 L solution of 0.150 mol·L^{-1} magnesium nitrate, $Mg(NO_3)_2$. Magnesium hydroxide, $Mg(OH)_2$, precipitates from the mixture. K_{sp} for magnesium hydroxide is 1.2×10^{-11}. Calculate the following:
   a) mass of magnesium hydroxide that precipitates
   b) concentrations of all ions that remain in solution

59. A 0.100 mol·L^{-1} aqueous solution of silver nitrate is slowly added to 25.00 mL of 0.100 mol·L^{-1} aqueous sodium chloride to which 1.0×10^{-4} mol sodium chromate, Na_2CrO_4, has been added. Initially only silver chloride, $AgCl$ ($K_{sp} = 1.6 \times 10^{-10}$) precipitates but the reddish silver chromate, Ag_2CrO_4 ($K_{sp} = 1.9 \times 10^{-12}$) starts to form when slightly more than 25.00 mL of the silver nitrate solution has been added.
   a) What are the silver ion and the chloride ion concentrations when exactly 25.00 mL of the silver nitrate solution has been added?
   b) At what silver ion concentration does silver chromate start to precipitate? What is the chloride ion concentration at this point?
   c) What is the exact volume of the silver nitrate solution added when the silver chromate precipitate just starts to form? Assume that the final volume is 50.0 mL.

60. A solution containing 180.0 g of sodium hydroxide in 2.250 kg of water has a density of 1.22 g·mL^{-1}. For this solution calculate the following:
   a) the solution freezing point
   b) the solution osmotic pressure at 10 °C

61. The antimalarial agent quinine is a natural product extracted from the bark of the South American cinchona tree. When 1.52 g of quinine is dissolved in 10.0 g of cyclohexane the solution has a freezing point of −2.97 °C. The freezing point of pure cyclohexane is 6.50 °C. (k_f for cyclohexane is 20.2 °C·mol^{-1}·kg) Using this information calculate the molar mass of quinine.

62. From the following data construct a graph showing the variation of solubility (grams per 100 g of solution) as a function of temperature, for each of the salts given.

	Temperature (°C)				
	10	**30**	**50**	**70**	**90**
Solubility (g/100g)					
$NaNO_3$	44.2	48.3	53.0	57.5	62.0
Li_2SO_4	26.0	25.2	24.3	24.0	23.0
NaCl	27.0	27.2	27.4	27.7	28.0
$HgCl_2$	4.5	6.9	12.0	17.5	30.1

a) For which of these salts is the dissolving process exothermic and for which is it endothermic?

b) At what temperature do lithium sulfate and mercury(II) chloride have the same solubility?

c) Estimate the solubility of each of these salts at 100 °C.

SUGGESTED PROJECTS

1. Investigate the changing supply and demand for Canadian potash. Consider as well, why Canada continues to export the raw material instead of developing its own secondary level industry.

2. "Reverse osmosis" is used commercially to prepare pure water. Research this method and draw an explanatory diagram of the process. In what regions is reverse osmosis used and why?

3. Stain removal from clothes can pose many problems. Obtain a chart of suggested methods of stain removal and determine the chemistry behind the method for as many stains as possible.

4. Sea water is often considered as a source of many elements or salts. Choose one or two of these and discuss the economics of extraction.

Acids and Bases

Acids and bases are common substances. Dilute acids are present in most of our favourite drinks. Bases form the active ingredient in many strong cleaners. They also bring us relief in the form of antacid tablets.

The characteristic properties of acids and bases have long been recognized. Acids are sour-tasting substances that react with certain active metals to produce hydrogen gas. Bases usually have a bitter taste and feel "soapy." At one time, taste was an important property of a substance. Fortunately, the dangerous practice of tasting an unknown substance has been discontinued.

Many natural and synthetic substances show different colours in the presence of acids or bases. The natural dye litmus, extracted from lichens, turns red in acids and blue in bases. We call these substances acid-base indicators. As we proceed through this chapter we will study how indicators work, and as well, look at several different ways of distinguishing acids from bases. In the process, we will use the knowledge acquired in the two previous chapters.

A Simple Theory of Acids and Bases

9.1

Our present knowledge of acids and bases has its origin in 19th century studies on the electrical properties of solutions. These studies showed that some solutions are excellent conductors of electricity, some conduct an electric current only slightly, and others do not conduct at all. Those substances that conduct an electric current when dissolved in water are called **electrolytes**. The terms *strong* or *weak electrolyte* indicate whether the solution is a good or poor conductor. Both acids and bases are electrolytes.

It was a young graduate student, Svante Arrhenius, at the University of Uppsala in Sweden, who offered an explanation for these electrical phenomena. A little more than a century ago he came up with the idea that aqueous solutions of electrolytes contain positive and negative particles, which he called ions. He also offered an explanation for the difference in behaviour between acids and bases.

The **Arrhenius theory** can be stated as follows:

> **All acids produce hydrogen ions when they are dissolved in water. The hydrogen ions are responsible for the acidic properties of these solutions.**

> **All bases produce hydroxide ions when they are dissolved in water. The hydroxide ions are responsible for the basic properties of these solutions.**

Hydrochloric acid is a solution of hydrogen chloride gas in water. It is an excellent conductor of electricity which, by the Arrhenius theory, must mean that the solution contains many ions. When hydrogen chloride is dissolved in water, molecules ionize into hydrogen ions and chloride ions:

$$HCl_{(g)} \xrightarrow[\text{in water}]{\text{dissolve}} H^+_{(aq)} + Cl^-_{(aq)}$$

Nitric acid, HNO_3, which in pure form is a liquid, is also a very good conductor in aqueous solution. This can be explained by assuming that the nitric acid molecules ionize into hydrogen ions and nitrate ions:

$$HNO_{3\,(\ell)} \xrightarrow[\text{in water}]{\text{dissolve}} H^+_{(aq)} + NO_3^-_{(aq)}$$

The acidic properties of these aqueous solutions must be due to the hydrogen ions since they are the only ions common to both solutions.

The Arrhenius Model of Neutralization

When equal molar quantities of an acid and a base are mixed in water, a solution is obtained that does not act as an acid or a base; it is *neutral* in terms of its acid-base properties. This kind of chemical reaction is

Figure 9.1
Some common household acids.

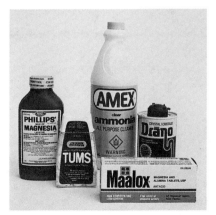

Figure 9.2
Some common household bases.

referred to as a **neutralization** reaction. The solution is still an excellent conductor of electricity, which indicates that ions are present.

According to the Arrhenius theory, neutralization reactions produce a salt and water:

$$\textbf{ACID + BASE} \longrightarrow \textbf{SALT + WATER}$$

A **salt** is composed of cations (positive ions) and anions (negative ions). The cations originate from the base and the anions come from the acid. Consider, for example, the reaction between hydrochloric acid and sodium hydroxide.

$$\textbf{HCl}_{(aq)} + \textbf{NaOH}_{(aq)} \longrightarrow \textbf{NaCl}_{(aq)} + \textbf{H}_2\textbf{O}_{(\ell)}$$

This equation can be rewritten to show the ions that are present before and after the solutions are mixed:

$$\textbf{H}^+_{(aq)} + \underbrace{\textbf{Cl}^-_{(aq)} + \textbf{Na}^+_{(aq)}}_{\text{spectator ions}} + \textbf{OH}^-_{(aq)} \longrightarrow \underbrace{\textbf{Na}^+_{(aq)} + \textbf{Cl}^-_{(aq)}}_{\text{spectator ions}} + \textbf{H}_2\textbf{O}_{(\ell)}$$

Sodium ions and chloride ions appear on both sides of the reaction equation and are called spectator ions. If we omit them we are left with the following net ionic equation, which represents only the key reactants and products:

$$\textbf{H}^+_{(aq)} + \textbf{OH}^-_{(aq)} \longrightarrow \textbf{H}_2\textbf{O}_{(\ell)}$$

Thus, when a salt is dissolved in water, the resulting solution should be neutral and should not exhibit any acidic or basic properties.

The main advantage of this traditional subdivision of electrolytes into acids, bases, and salts is its simplicity. As we shall see, this classification has some serious shortcomings.

What the Arrhenius Theory Cannot Explain

9.2

There are two cases involving acids, bases, and salts that cannot be explained by the Arrhenius theory.

The Solvent Problem

According to the Arrhenius theory, an acid produces hydrogen ions. However, when we dissolve hydrogen chloride in toluene, a nonpolar solvent, we find that the solution does not conduct electricity. This is in contrast to an aqueous solution of hydrogen chloride, which is a very good conductor. As another example, let's examine the reaction of an acid with a metal such as magnesium. We find that an aqueous solution of hydrogen chloride reacts rapidly with magnesium to produce hydrogen gas; a toluene solution does not.

Arrhenius and the Skepticism of the Times

Every major new theory in science has encountered a great deal of initial opposition. This was true of Lavoisier's combustion theory, Dalton's atomic theory, and Avogadro's idea of the existence of molecules in gases. Arrhenius's ionic theory was no exception.

Svante Arrhenius had completed two years of laboratory work on the electrical properties of solutions before he developed his ionic theory in 1883. Although this theory formed part of his doctoral thesis, he was granted a doctorate mainly on the basis of his course work. His thesis was considered only barely acceptable.

Over the next few years Arrhenius worked in the laboratories of two well-known chemists, Ostwald and van't Hoff. With their backing he was able to gather more experimental data to support his theory. In 1887 his classical paper "On the Dissociation of Substances in Aqueous Solutions" was published.

Although Arrhenius had now reached an international audience, his fight for the acceptance of his theory was far from over. Many "authorities" in science still rejected his theory. When the University of Stockholm was established in 1894, Arrhenius was not, at first, considered a suitable candidate for the position of professor of chemistry.

Slowly the scientific community began to recognize his contribution and in 1903 he was awarded the Nobel Prize for Chemistry. We now consider Ostwald, van't Hoff, and Arrhenius as the three scientists who founded the major branch of chemistry referred to as physical chemistry. Van't Hoff received the first Nobel Prize for Chemistry, in 1901. Interestingly enough, it was Ostwald, the strong supporter of the ionic theory, who was one of the last scientists to remain opposed to the atomic theory developed a hundred years earlier by Dalton.

Figure 9.3
Svante August Arrhenius (1859-1927)

From this evidence it should be clear that the nature of the solvent is very important in determining the acidic behaviour of a substance such as hydrogen chloride. The Arrhenius theory does not explain the important role of the solvent.

The Salt Problem

If we take a series of salts, dissolve them in water, and insert strips of red and blue litmus paper, the colour of the litmus should remain unchanged. An acidic solution should turn the blue litmus red, and a basic solution should turn red litmus blue. But the following findings do not confirm this.

TABLE 9.1 *Effect of Aqueous Salt Solutions on Litmus*

Salt	Effect on Litmus	Conclusion
Sodium chloride	none	neutral
Sodium phosphate	red turns blue	basic
Sodium carbonate	red turns blue	basic
Sodium nitrate	none	neutral
Ammonium chloride	blue turns red	acidic
Aluminum nitrate	blue turns red	acidic

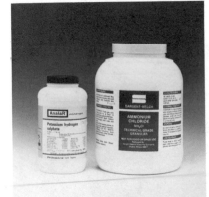

a)

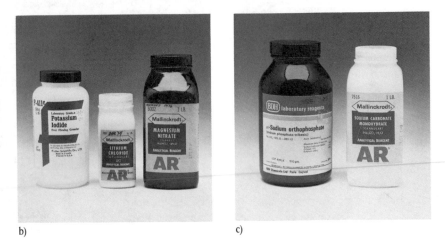

b)   c)

Figure 9.4

Salts can be categorized into these categories:

a) those that give an acidic solution;

b) those that are neutral;

c) those that give a basic solution.

The results show that solutions of salts are not necessarily neutral. Apparently, salts can be neutral, acidic, or basic. How can a salt such as aluminum nitrate that contains no hydrogen atoms still produce hydrogen ions in water? How can salts such as sodium phosphate and sodium carbonate produce hydroxide ions in water? We need an explanation for these observations. The Arrhenius theory merely states that acids produce hydrogen ions in water and bases produce hydroxide ions in water. It does not explain how salts can have acidic or basic properties.

The Brønsted-Lowry Theory

9.3   In 1923 a Danish chemist, Johannes Brønsted, and an English chemist, Thomas Lowry, independently developed a more general theory of acids and bases. This theory was able to explain the role of the solvent as well as the existence of acidic and basic salt solutions. In addition, it was not restricted to one solvent and could be applied equally well to the gaseous, liquid, and solid states. The **Brønsted-Lowry theory** can be stated as follows:

**An acid is a molecule or ion that can give up a hydrogen ion.
A base is any molecule or ion that can react with a hydrogen ion.**

Thus, an acid is a **hydrogen-ion donor**, and a base is a **hydrogen-ion acceptor**. Any molecule or ion that contains hydrogen atoms is a potential acid and any molecule or ion that has a pair of valence electrons available for bonding with a hydrogen ion is a potential base. In other words, acid-base reactions are **hydrogen-ion exchange reactions**. As well, an acid can only behave as an acid in the presence of a base willing and able to accept the hydrogen ion. This applies to all solvents and to all physical states.

Because water is the most important solvent used in chemistry, we will first apply the Brønsted-Lowry theory to aqueous solutions.

Brønsted-Lowry Acids

When hydrogen chloride gas is added to water, an acid-base reaction takes place between the molecules of hydrogen chloride and those of water. The covalent bond in a hydrogen chloride molecule is broken and the hydrogen ion bonds to the oxygen of a water molecule.

$$H:\overset{..}{\underset{..}{Cl}}: + :\overset{..}{\underset{H}{O}}:H \longrightarrow \left[H:\overset{..}{\underset{H}{O}}:H \right]^+ + \left[:\overset{..}{\underset{..}{Cl}}: \right]^-$$

or

$$HCl_{(g)} + H_2O_{(l)} \longrightarrow H_3O^+{}_{(aq)} + Cl^-{}_{(aq)}$$

Water functions as a hydrogen-ion acceptor, or base, in this reaction. The resulting positive ion is called a **hydronium ion, H_3O^+**. (A free hydrogen ion, a proton, cannot exist in water; it will always be bonded to a water molecule in the form of a hydronium ion.) The hydronium ion in turn is surrounded by other water molecules. However, you will still see the symbol $H^+{}_{(aq)}$ being used as a convenience, even though it is really referring to the hydronium ion.

The hydronium ion is itself an acid and if it comes in contact with the right base it can pass on a hydrogen ion. It can do this, for instance, with a water molecule, the result being that a hydrogen ion is rapidly transferred from one water molecule to another.

$$H_3O^+{}_{(aq)} + H_2O_{(l)} \longrightarrow H_2O_{(l)} + H_3O^+{}_{(aq)}$$

Evidence for the Hydronium Ion

How do we know that the hydronium ion exists? The first evidence was found in 1924, when it was shown that perchloric acid, $HClO_4$, crystallizes as a monohydrate, $HClO_4 \cdot H_2O$. The crystals of this monohydrate have an identical appearance to ammonium perchlorate, $NH_4^+ ClO_4^-$. Hence, the monohydrate form of perchloric acid was assigned the analogous formula $OH_3^+ \cdot ClO_4^-$ (or more conventionally, $H_3O^+ \cdot ClO_4^-$).

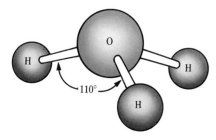

Figure 9.5
The structure of hydronium ions in crystals.

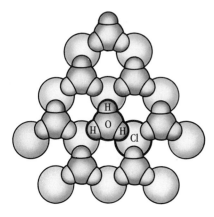

Figure 9.6
The ions in hydrogen chloride monohydrate show conclusive evidence of the existence of the hydronium ion.

Figure 9.7

Dr. Paul Giguère of the Université Laval proved that hydronium ions exist in solution.

More recently the structure of a similar solid hydrate of hydrochloric acid, $HCl \cdot H_2O$, was shown to consist of alternating layers of hydronium ions and chloride ions (Figure 9.6). Thus it was in fact $H_3O^+Cl^-$.

The existence of hydronium ions in solution has been conclusively proven by Professor Paul Giguère at the Université Laval, Quebec. Giguère passed infrared light through solutions of acids. He found that the wavelengths of light absorbed corresponded to the predicted vibrations of the atoms in the H_3O^+ ion.

Brønsted-Lowry Bases

Soluble metal hydroxides, such as sodium hydroxide or barium hydroxide, are ionic compounds that dissociate in water to produce hydroxide ions directly:

$$NaOH_{(s)} \xrightarrow[\text{in water}]{\text{dissolve}} Na^+_{(aq)} + OH^-_{(aq)}$$

$$Ba(OH)_{2\,(s)} \xrightarrow[\text{in water}]{\text{dissolve}} Ba^{2+}_{(aq)} + 2\,OH^-_{(aq)}$$

Ammonia is an example of a compound that is not considered as a base by the Arrhenius theory. Yet when the gas is dissolved in water, a basic solution is produced. The formation of this solution can be explained in terms of Brønsted-Lowry theory. The lone electron pair on the ammonia molecule can act as a hydrogen-ion acceptor, removing a hydrogen ion from a water molecule. The resulting solution will contain a free hydroxide ion.

$$NH_{3\,(g)} + H_2O_{(\ell)} \longrightarrow NH_4^+_{(aq)} + OH^-_{(aq)}$$

EXAMPLE **9.1** Liquid hydrogen perchlorate, $HClO_4$, dissolves in water to form a solution of perchloric acid. Identify the hydrogen ion donor and acceptor, and write an equation for the solution process.

SOLUTION To act as an acid, the hydrogen perchlorate must be a hydrogen-ion donor. Hydronium ions will be produced in the reaction. Thus the water molecule must be the hydrogen-ion acceptor.

$$HClO_{4\,(\ell)} + H_2O_{(\ell)} \longrightarrow H_3O^+_{(aq)} + ClO_4^-_{(aq)}$$

EXAMPLE **9.2** A solution of gaseous methylamine, CH_3NH_2, turns red litmus blue. Write the balanced equation and explain this observation.

SOLUTION Methylamine must be acting as a base. Looking at its formula, we can see a similarity to that of ammonia. Once again, there will be a lone pair of electrons. We can write an equation for the reaction with water that is analogous to the one for ammonia.

$$CH_3NH_{2\,(g)} + H_2O_{(\ell)} \longrightarrow CH_3NH_3^+_{(aq)} + OH^-_{(aq)}$$

The methylamine will act as a hydrogen ion acceptor and the water will be a hydrogen ion donor. Hydroxide ions will be produced in the reaction and the solution will turn red litmus blue.

QUESTIONS

1. Identify the hydrogen-ion donor and acceptor in each of the following reactions:
   a) $HNO_{3(\ell)} + H_2O_{(\ell)} \longrightarrow H_3O^+_{(aq)} + NO_3^-_{(aq)}$
   b) $C_2H_5NH_{2(\ell)} + H_2O_{(\ell)} \longrightarrow C_2H_5NH_3^+_{(aq)} + OH^-_{(aq)}$
   c) $CH_3CO_2H_{(\ell)} + H_2O_{(\ell)} \longrightarrow CH_3CO_2^-_{(aq)} + H_3O^+_{(aq)}$

2. Which of the following would you expect to act as Brønsted-Lowry bases:
   a) Br^- c) H_3PO_4 e) H_2O
   b) Li^+ d) NH_4^+ f) NH_2^-

Weak and Strong Acids and Bases

9.4   Up to now we have assumed that all acids and bases *react completely* with water to give hydronium ions or hydroxide ions respectively. A simple experiment indicates that this claim is not always valid.

Compare $1.0 \ mol \cdot L^{-1}$ solutions of hydrochloric acid and acetic acid, CH_3CO_2H. To neutralize 25 mL samples of each acid with $1.0 \ mol \cdot L^{-1}$ sodium hydroxide solution, the same volume of sodium hydroxide solution is required in each case (25 mL). This confirms, as expected, that each acid has the same concentration.

If we insert a conductivity tester in each acid, we find that the bulb glows brightly in the hydrochloric acid but weakly in the acetic acid. This suggests that the acetic acid solution contains fewer ions.

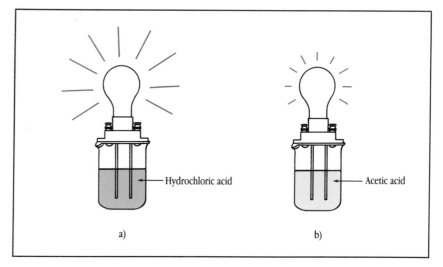

Figure 9.8

We can distinguish weak and strong acids by their conductivity.

a) Strong acids cause a light bulb to shine brightly.

b) Weak acids only give a weak glow.

To reinforce this conclusion we can test the two acids with some magnesium ribbon and marble chips. When the magnesium ribbon is put in the hydrochloric acid it bubbles rapidly, whereas the magnesium in the acetic acid bubbles only slowly. The *rate* of the latter reaction is apparently much slower. Similarly, the marble chips bubble rapidly in the hydrochloric acid, but only slowly in the acetic acid. In both cases it is the hydronium ions that react with the magnesium and the marble chips.

$$Mg_{(s)} + 2\,H_3O^+_{(aq)} \longrightarrow Mg^{2+}_{(aq)} + H_{2\,(g)} + 2\,H_2O_{(\ell)}$$
$$CaCO_{3\,(s)} + 2\,H_3O^+_{(aq)} \longrightarrow Ca^{2+}_{(aq)} + CO_{2\,(g)} + 3\,H_2O_{(\ell)}$$

It would appear then that the acetic acid has a lower concentration of hydronium ions than the hydrochloric acid. In the solution process, the reaction between acetic acid and water does not go to completion but establishes an equilibrium, as shown below:

$$CH_3CO_2H_{(aq)} + H_2O_{(\ell)} \rightleftharpoons H_3O^+_{(aq)} + CH_3CO_2^-_{(aq)}$$

We can account for the fact that the same amount of sodium hydroxide is required to neutralize each solution by applying Le Châtelier's principle. As the hydronium ions are used up in the neutralization of acetic acid, more molecular acetic acid reacts with water to replace the lost hydronium ions until neutralization is complete.

To differentiate acids that ionize completely from those that do not, we use the terms strong and weak. A **strong acid** is completely ionized in solution. A **weak acid** is only partially ionized in solution. Be careful to distinguish these two terms from concentrated and dilute. Hydrochloric acid is a strong acid even when it is dilute. Acetic acid is a weak acid even when it is concentrated.

Figure 9.9

Acids can be categorized into a) strong acids and b) weak acids.

a)

b)

TABLE 9.2   *Common Strong and Weak Acids*

Strong	Weak
HCl, hydrochloric acid	H_2SO_3, sulfurous acid
HNO_3, nitric acid	HF, hydrofluoric acid
$HClO_4$, perchloric acid	CH_3CO_2H, acetic acid
H_2SO_4, sulfuric acid	H_2CO_3, carbonic acid

Bases can also be weak or strong. Sodium hydroxide is an example of a **strong base**. It completely dissociates in water. Ammonia, however, is a **weak base**. It is mostly present in solution as aqueous ammonia molecules. The proportions of ammonium ions and hydroxide ions are much lower. Even though a container may be labelled "ammonium hydroxide," it is more accurate to call the contents "aqueous ammonia."

$$NH_{3\,(aq)} + H_2O_{(\ell)} \rightleftharpoons NH_4^+{}_{(aq)} + OH^-{}_{(aq)}$$

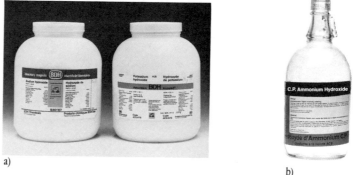

Figure 9.10

Bases can be categorized into a) strong bases and b) weak bases.

a)

b)

QUESTIONS

3. A light bulb conductivity test was carried out on 1.0 mol·L^{-1} solutions of various bases. The bulb glowed brightly for potassium hydroxide, barium hydroxide, and lithium hydroxide solutions, but gave only weak flickers for methylamine and caffeine solutions. From this information determine which of these bases are strong and which are weak.

4. Write equations for the reaction of water with the following Brønsted-Lowry acids. Assume that only one hydrogen ion is transferred in each case.
   a) hydrogen bromide, HBr, a strong acid
   b) perchloric acid, $HClO_4$, a strong acid
   c) hydrogen cyanide, HCN, a weak acid
   d) hydrogen sulfide, H_2S, a weak acid
   e) formic acid, HCO_2H, a weak acid

What Makes a Substance an Acid or a Base?

9.5

Why do some substances release hydrogen ions and others release hydroxide ions when dissolved in water? An examination of electronegativities and bond strengths will help us to answer this question. For example, compare the two compounds, sodium hydroxide (NaOH) and hypochlorous acid (HClO). When the ionic compound sodium hydroxide dissolves, the existing sodium and hydroxide ions are dissociated by the polar water molecules into hydrated ions. When covalent hypochlorous acid dissolves, the bond between oxygen and hydrogen is broken. In this case, chlorine has a higher electronegativity than hydrogen and the bond between hydrogen and oxygen will be weakened, allowing the hydrogen to be released as a hydrogen ion. This becomes a hydronium ion in water.

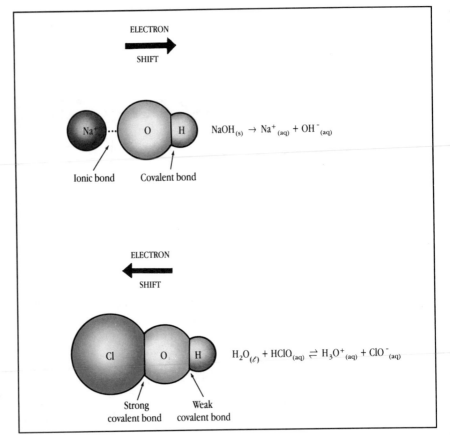

ELECTRON
SHIFT

$$NaOH_{(s)} \rightarrow Na^+_{(aq)} + OH^-_{(aq)}$$

Ionic bond   Covalent bond

ELECTRON
SHIFT

$$H_2O_{(\ell)} + HClO_{(aq)} \rightleftharpoons H_3O^+_{(aq)} + ClO^-_{(aq)}$$

Strong   Weak
covalent bond   covalent bond

Figure 9.11
Electron pairs are pulled towards the element of higher electronegativity. We can use this concept to explain why sodium hydroxide produces hydroxide ions, a), but hypochlorous acid produces hydrogen ions, b).

The Acidity of Oxyacids

The acidic hydrogens of most of the common acids are covalently bonded to an oxygen atom which, in turn, is bonded to another atom such as carbon, nitrogen, sulfur, or a halogen. These acids are called **oxyacids**.

TABLE 9.3	*Oxyacids of Chlorine*	
Common Formula	Name	Strength
HClO	hypochlorous acid	very weak
HClO$_2$	chlorous acid	weak
HClO$_3$	chloric acid	strong
HClO$_4$	perchloric acid	very strong

The strength of an oxyacid increases with the number of oxygen atoms that are *not bonded to hydrogen atoms*. We will use the above series of chlorine oxyacids and the concept of electronegativity to help us understand this trend in acid strength. As the number of oxygen atoms increases (each oxygen atom being very electronegative), the pull of electrons away from the O—H bond increases (Figure 9.12). The O—H bond will break more easily, hence the substance will ionize more readily and be a stronger acid.

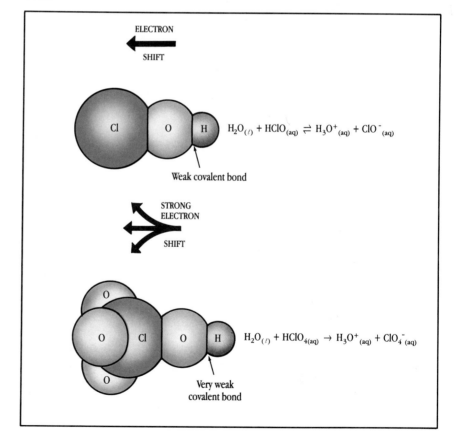

Figure 9.12
The more oxygen atoms attached to the chlorine atom, the more the electrons will be pulled away from the O-H bond. The weaker this bond, the more easily the acid will ionize.

Litmus, a Dye with a History

Litmus blue and the related violet-red dye orseille (also called orchil) were introduced into Europe around the year 1300 from Asia Minor. These dyes were, and still are, produced by the fermentation of certain lichens. For many centuries they had great commercial importance as dyes for silk and wool.

Many lichens can be used to produce litmus and orseille, most of them species of *Roccella* and *Leconora*. The name Roccella refers to the Roccella family, 14th century Florentine merchants who became very rich from their monopoly on dye production from lichens. In the 16th century, however, Amsterdam became the principal manufacturing centre. Most of the world's litmus is still produced in Holland from lichens found around the Mediterranean.

Figure 9.13
Certain lichens provide the source of litmus. Lichens can differ greatly in appearance; from left to right: genera Lobaria, Parmelia, Cladonia, and Usnea.

The details of the extraction process have always been a manufacturer's secret, but it appears that the method for making litmus from lichens has changed little over the centuries. The lichen material is fermented for several weeks in open vessels with ammonia, potash, and lime. After fermentation, litmus blue is precipitated from the mixture. It changes colour when acid is added, first to violet, then to red. The orseille dyes, which do not change colour with acid, are obtained when the potash and the lime are omitted in the fermentation.

Both orseille and litmus originate from a simple chemical compound, orcinol (Figure 9.14b) which is formed from the lecanoric acid (Figure 9.14a) present in the lichens. The overall composition of orseille and litmus is very complex. At least fourteen different dyes have been isolated from orseille.

Litmus is also a mixture of dyes. The main component in litmus is a substance with a molecular mass of about 3300, in which the colour-producing group (the chromophore, Figure 9.14c) appears five to six times in a molecule. As the litmus changes colour from blue to violet to red, hydrogen ions are successively added to the chromophore. The colour of litmus therefore depends on the acidity of the solution.

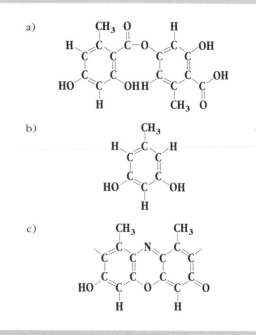

Figure 9.14
The constituent compounds of litmus:
a) lecanoric acid, b) orcinol, c) litmus chromophore.

Litmus and orseille, like most natural dyes, fade when exposed to light. For dyeing silk and wool they have now been replaced by synthetic dyes. Currently, the main use for litmus is as an acid-base indicator (red and blue litmus paper), but it is also used as a colouring agent in food, alcoholic beverages, cosmetics, and medicines.

| EXAMPLE | **9.3** | Manganese(II) hydroxide, $Mn(OH)_2$, behaves as a typical base, but permanganic acid, $HMnO_4$, is a strong acid. Account for this difference. (Permanganic acid can be written as $(HO)MnO_3$.) |

SOLUTION The central, and least electronegative, atom in manganese(II) hydroxide is manganese. Thus, the structure of $Mn(OH)_2$ is

$$H—O—Mn—O—H$$

The bonding electrons are pulled towards the O—H bond and away from the manganese. The result is an Mn^{2+} ion and two OH^- ions. Permanganic acid is similar in structure to perchloric acid.

$$H—O—\overset{\displaystyle O}{\underset{\displaystyle O}{\overset{\|}{\underset{\|}{Mn}}}}=O$$

The oxygens not bonded to the hydrogen pull the electrons away from the O—H bond. The result is that a hydrogen ion is released and it combines with a water molecule to form a hydronium ion.

QUESTIONS

5. For each of the following, which one is the stronger acid:
 a) HNO_2 or HNO_3
 b) HIO_2 or HIO
 c) H_3AsO_4 or H_3AsO_3

6. Arrange the following in order of increasing acid strength:

$$HNO_2 \qquad H_2SO_4 \qquad HClO$$

7. Arrange the following in order of increasing base strength:

$$CH_3OH \qquad ClOH \qquad LiOH$$

Polyprotic Acids

9.6 Acids that can give up more than one hydrogen ion per molecule are called **polyprotic acids**. Diprotic acids, which can release two hydrogen ions, are much more common than triprotic acids, which can release three hydrogen ions. For example, the hydronium ions present in an aqueous solution of sulfuric acid have originated from two sources: sulfuric acid molecules and hydrogen sulfate ions. Sulfuric acid is a strong acid because the first hydrogen is completely transferred to water molecules.

$$H_2SO_{4\,(aq)} + H_2O_{(l)} \longrightarrow H_3O^+_{\,(aq)} + HSO_4^-{}_{(aq)}$$

The transfer of the second hydrogen ion is not complete and can be written as an equilibrium equation.

$$HSO_4^-{}_{(aq)} + H_2O_{(\ell)} \rightleftharpoons H_3O^+{}_{(aq)} + SO_4^{2-}{}_{(aq)}$$

For a triprotic acid such as phosphoric acid, there are three ionization steps:

$$H_3PO_4{}_{(aq)} + H_2O_{(\ell)} \rightleftharpoons H_3O^+{}_{(aq)} + H_2PO_4^-{}_{(aq)}$$
$$H_2PO_4^-{}_{(aq)} + H_2O_{(\ell)} \rightleftharpoons H_3O^+{}_{(aq)} + HPO_4^{2-}{}_{(aq)}$$
$$HPO_4^{2-}{}_{(aq)} + H_2O_{(\ell)} \rightleftharpoons H_3O^+{}_{(aq)} + PO_4^{3-}{}_{(aq)}$$

These equilibria lie progressively further to the left. In other words, the acid strength decreases from H_3PO_4 to HPO_4^{2-}. This is not surprising. The positive hydrogen ion in the second and third equation has to break away from a negative ion. As the charge on the anion increases it becomes progressively more difficult for the hydrogen ion to escape.

TABLE 9.4   *Common Polyprotic Acids*

Diprotic Acids	Triprotic Acids
H_2SO_4, sulfuric acid	H_3BO_3, boric acid
H_2SO_3, sulfurous acid	H_3PO_4, phosphoric acid
H_2CO_3, carbonic acid	
H_2S, hydrogen sulfide	

EXAMPLE   *9.4*   Write equations for the ionization of sulfurous acid, H_2SO_3, in water.

SOLUTION   Since sulfurous acid is a weak acid, the first ionization step is incomplete and should therefore be represented by an equilibrium equation. The second ionization step will be even less complete.

$$H_2SO_3{}_{(aq)} + H_2O_{(\ell)} \rightleftharpoons H_3O^+{}_{(aq)} + HSO_3^-{}_{(aq)}$$
$$HSO_3^-{}_{(aq)} + H_2O_{(\ell)} \rightleftharpoons H_3O^+{}_{(aq)} + SO_3^{2-}{}_{(aq)}$$

The molecular formula of an acid does not always indicate how many of the hydrogen atoms in the molecule are acidic. The acidic hydrogens are the ones that can be released to form hydronium ions in water. Acetic acid, for instance, has the formula CH_3CO_2H, but only one of the four hydrogen atoms in the molecule is released. Acetic acid is a monoprotic acid. Similarly, citric acid has the formula $C_6H_8O_7$, but only three of the eight hydrogen atoms can be released. It is therefore a triprotic acid.

8. Write the equations for the ionization of the weak diprotic acid, carbonic acid, H_2CO_3.

9. Hydrazine, N_2H_4, is a diprotic base. Write the equations for the ionization steps.

Conjugate Acid-Base Pairs

9.7

Acid-base reactions involve the exchange of hydrogen ions. When an acid loses a hydrogen ion it becomes a base, and when a base accepts a hydrogen ion it becomes an acid.

$$H_2O_{(\ell)} + NH_{3\,(g)} \longrightarrow NH_4^{+}{}_{(aq)} + OH^{-}{}_{(aq)}$$
$$\text{acid}_1 \qquad \text{base}_2 \qquad\qquad \text{acid}_2 \qquad \text{base}_1$$

$$HNO_{3\,(aq)} + H_2O_{(\ell)} \longrightarrow H_3O^{+}{}_{(aq)} + NO_3^{-}{}_{(aq)}$$
$$\text{acid}_1 \qquad \text{base}_2 \qquad\qquad \text{acid}_2 \qquad \text{base}_1$$

In these reactions, not only the reactants but also the products are acids and bases. Notice that water is acting as an acid in the first reaction, but as a base in the second one.

Structures that differ in only one hydrogen ion are called **conjugate acid-base pairs**. Acid$_1$ is the conjugate acid of base$_1$, and base$_2$ is the conjugate base of acid$_2$. Notice, as well, that the formula for the conjugate base always has one more negative charge (or one fewer positive charge) than the formula for the corresponding acid.

TABLE 9.5 *Some Common Acids and Their Conjugate Bases*

Acid		Conjugate Base	
Hydrochloric acid	HCl	Chloride ion	Cl^-
Nitric acid	HNO_3	Nitrate ion	NO_3^-
Sulfuric acid	H_2SO_4	Hydrogen sulfate ion	HSO_4^-
Hydrogen sulfate ion	HSO_4^-	Sulfate ion	SO_4^{2-}
Hydronium ion	H_3O^+	Water	H_2O
Water	H_2O	Hydroxide ion	OH^-
Ammonium ion	NH_4^+	Ammonia	NH_3

The *stronger* the acid, the *weaker* will be its conjugate base, and vice versa. Consider the reaction between hydrogen chloride and water:

$$HCl_{(g)} + H_2O_{(\ell)} \rightleftharpoons H_3O^{+}{}_{(aq)} + Cl^{-}{}_{(aq)}$$
$$\text{acid}_1 \qquad \text{base}_2 \qquad\qquad \text{acid}_2 \qquad \text{base}_1$$

Hydrogen chloride is a strong acid in aqueous solution. The chloride ions produced are surrounded by water molecules. These hydrated chloride ions are highly stabilized and show little tendency to join with a hydrogen ion again. Because of this, the chloride ions are poor hydrogen-ion acceptors and hence are extremely weak bases.

There are many examples of ions and molecules that can function both as acids and as bases. The particular role or function depends on the hydrogen-ion releasing or hydrogen-ion accepting capabilities of their reaction partners. We can use the hydrogen carbonate ion as an example:

$$HCO_3^-{}_{(aq)} + OH^-{}_{(aq)} \rightleftharpoons H_2O_{(l)} + CO_3^{2-}{}_{(aq)}$$
$$\text{acid}_1 \qquad \text{base}_2 \qquad \text{acid}_2 \qquad \text{base}_1$$

$$H_3O^+{}_{(aq)} + HCO_3^-{}_{(aq)} \rightleftharpoons H_2CO_3{}_{(aq)} + H_2O_{(l)}$$
$$\text{acid}_1 \qquad \text{base}_2 \qquad \text{acid}_2 \qquad \text{base}_1$$

QUESTIONS

10. What is the conjugate base for each of the following acids?
    a) NH_3 c) HSO_3^- e) $H_2PO_4^-$
    b) H_3O^+ d) NH_4^+

11. What is the conjugate acid for each of the following bases?
    a) PO_4^{3-} b) NH_3 c) HCO_3^- d) CH_3OH

12. Complete the following acid-base reactions, assuming that only one hydrogen ion is exchanged. Identify the conjugate acid-base pairs by writing them below the equations.
    a) $H_3PO_4{}_{(aq)} + NH_3{}_{(aq)} \longrightarrow$
    b) $CO_3^{2-}{}_{(aq)} + H_2SO_4{}_{(aq)} \longrightarrow$
    c) $OH^-{}_{(aq)} + NH_4^+{}_{(aq)} \longrightarrow$
    d) $H_3O^+{}_{(aq)} + OH^-{}_{(aq)} \longrightarrow$

Self-Ionization   9.8

If we prepare ultrapure water, we find that the liquid conducts electricity to a very small extent. To explain this, it is proposed that water can act as its own acid and conjugate base. Thus one molecule of water donates a hydrogen ion to another molecule of water. As equal numbers of hydronium ions and hydroxide ions are produced, the solution will remain neutral.

$$H_2O_{(l)} + H_2O_{(l)} \rightleftharpoons H_3O^+{}_{(aq)} + OH^-{}_{(aq)}$$

We have already mentioned the important role of water in acid-base behaviour. The concept of self-ionization leads us to two further statements:

Figure 9.15
The planet Jupiter. It is believed that such outer planets in our solar system have oceans of liquid ammonia.

The strongest acid that can exist in water is the hydronium ion. The strongest base that can exist in water is the hydroxide ion.

If we dissolve a stronger base (hydrogen-ion acceptor) in water, such as the oxide ion in sodium oxide, we find that hydroxide ions are rapidly produced.

$$Na_2O_{(s)} + H_2O_{(\ell)} \longrightarrow 2\,Na^+_{(aq)} + 2\,OH^-_{(aq)}$$

Similarly, if we dissolve a stronger acid (hydrogen-ion donor) in water, such as hydrogen chloride, hydronium ions are produced.

$$HCl_{(g)} + H_2O_{(\ell)} \longrightarrow H_3O^+_{(aq)} + Cl^-_{(aq)}$$

Solvents other than Water

We are used to water as a solvent because it is the most common liquid on earth. However, other liquids can be solvents and undergo similar self-ionization. Some science fiction writers have proposed life based on solvents other than water, ammonia being one example. To work with this substance as a liquid, it must be cooled below its boiling point of $-33\,°C$. Liquid ammonia self-ionizes slightly to give ammonium ions and amide ions, NH_2^-. It acts as its own acid-base conjugate.

$$NH_{3\,(\ell)} + NH_{3\,(\ell)} \rightleftharpoons NH_4^+_{(am)} + NH_2^-_{(am)}$$

("am" refers to the solvent ammonia)

In liquid ammonia, the ammonium ion is the strongest acid and the amide ion is the strongest base. We can now generalize the concept of self-ionization to include solvents other than water.

The strongest acid is always the solvent molecule that has accepted a hydrogen ion. The strongest base is always the solvent molecule that has donated a hydrogen ion.

EXAMPLE **9.5** Pure liquid hydrogen fluoride can act as a solvent system. Write an equation to represent the self-ionization, and identify the strongest acid and strongest base in this system.

SOLUTION We write an equation that is similar to the equation for the self-ionization of water or ammonia. One molecule of hydrogen fluoride will gain a hydrogen ion at the expense of another hydrogen fluoride molecule.

$$HF_{(\ell)} + HF_{(\ell)} \longrightarrow H_2F^+_{(hf)} + F^-_{(hf)}$$

The strongest acid will be the H_2F^+ ion and the strongest base will be the F^- ion.

QUESTIONS

13. What is the strongest acid that can exist in ethanol, C_2H_5OH? What is the strongest base that can exist in this solvent?

14. Write the self-ionization equation for liquid hydrazine, N_2H_4.

pH Scale and Indicators

9.9   As we have just described, water will self-ionize to a small extent.

$$H_2O_{(l)} + H_2O_{(l)} \rightleftharpoons H_3O^+_{(aq)} + OH^-_{(aq)}$$

The equilibrium expression for the self-ionization of water can be written as follows:

$$K = \frac{[H_3O^+][OH^-]}{[H_2O]^2}$$

In pure water and in dilute aqueous solutions the concentration of water, $[H_2O]^2$, has a constant value. By incorporating this value into the equilibrium constant, we can simplify the equilibrium expression. The new equilibrium constant is denoted by a subscript and is called the **ion product constant of water**, K_w.

$$K_w = [H_3O^+][OH^-]$$

The ion product constant, K_w, relates the concentrations of hydronium ions and hydroxide ions in pure water and in all dilute aqueous solutions, regardless of the source of these ions. The self-ionization of water is an endothermic process, and the value of K_w therefore increases with increasing temperature. Hence, the concentrations of the individual ions will vary with temperature.

TABLE 9.6   *Values of Ion-Product Constant of Water, K_w*

Temperature (°C)	K_w	$[H_3O^+]$	$[OH^-]$
0	1.1×10^{-15}	3.3×10^{-8}	3.3×10^{-8}
25	1.0×10^{-14}	1.0×10^{-7}	1.0×10^{-7}
50	5.5×10^{-14}	2.3×10^{-7}	2.3×10^{-7}

The ion product constant is valid for all aqueous solutions. If an acid is added to pure water, the hydronium ion concentration will increase. Since the value of K_w is constant, the concentration of the hydroxide ion will decrease.

9.6 What are the hydronium ion and hydroxide ion concentrations in a 0.050 $mol \cdot L^{-1}$ aqueous solution of hydrogen chloride at 25 °C?

SOLUTION   Hydrogen chloride is a strong acid and ionizes completely in water. Therefore 0.050 mol of hydronium ions per litre are produced by the following reaction:

$$HCl_{(g)} + H_2O_{(\ell)} \longrightarrow H_3O^+_{(aq)} + Cl^-_{(aq)}$$

By substituting the hydronium ion concentration into the ion product constant equation, we can determine the hydroxide ion concentration:

$$K_w = [H_3O^+][OH^-] = 1.0 \times 10^{-14} \quad \text{at } 25\,^\circ\text{C}$$

$$[OH^-] = \frac{1.0 \times 10^{-14}}{0.050}$$

$$= 2.0 \times 10^{-13} \ mol \cdot L^{-1}$$

Addition of the acid has decreased the hydroxide ion concentration from $1.0 \times 10^{-7} \ mol \cdot L^{-1}$ to $2.0 \times 10^{-13} \ mol \cdot L^{-1}$. This represents a decrease by a factor of almost 10^6! Similarly, in a solution of a strong base there are still some hydronium ions present, as the calculation in Example 9.7 indicates.

EXAMPLE

9.7 What are the hydroxide ion and hydronium ion concentrations in an aqueous solution containing 0.010 $mol \cdot L^{-1}$ barium hydroxide, $Ba(OH)_2$?

SOLUTION   Barium hydroxide is a strong base and will dissociate completely.

$$Ba(OH)_{2\,(s)} \longrightarrow Ba^{2+}_{(aq)} + 2\,OH^-_{(aq)}$$

According to the above equation, the hydroxide ion concentration is twice the concentration of the barium hydroxide.

$$K_w = [H_3O^+][OH^-] = 1.0 \times 10^{-14} \quad \text{at } 25\,^\circ\text{C}$$

$$[H_3O^+] = \frac{1.0 \times 10^{-14}}{0.020}$$

$$= 5.0 \times 10^{-13} \ mol \cdot L^{-1}$$

The pH Scale

In 1909 the Danish biochemist, Søren P. Sørenson, introduced the pH scale as a way to express the acidity and basicity of an aqueous solution. The **pH** of a solution is defined as *the negative logarithm, to the base ten, of the hydronium ion concentration.*

$$\mathbf{pH = -log_{10}\,[H_3O^+]}$$

TABLE 9.7 *Relationship between [H₃O⁺] and pH*

$[H_3O^+]$	pH
1	0
10^{-1}	1
10^{-2}	2
10^{-3}	3
10^{-4}	4
10^{-5}	5
10^{-6}	6
10^{-7}	7
10^{-8}	8
10^{-9}	9
10^{-10}	10
10^{-11}	11
10^{-12}	12
10^{-13}	13
10^{-14}	14

Figure 9.16

a) *The result of an earthquake. Like the pH scale, we use a logarithmic unit to measure the power of an earthquake—the Richter scale. An earthquake of 8 on the Richter scale is ten times as strong as one of 7.*

b) *A rock concert. The intensity of sound is measured by the logarithmic unit of bels. A sound of 90 decibels is ten times the intensity of a sound of 80 decibels.*

In a neutral solution at 25 °C, the hydronium ion and the hydroxide ion concentrations are both 1.0×10^{-7} mol·L⁻¹. Thus, the pH of a neutral solution is 7.

$$pH = -\log_{10}(1.0 \times 10^{-7}) = 7.00$$

A solution with a pH less than 7 is acidic and a solution with a pH greater than 7 is basic. Almost all aqueous solutions have a pH in the range 0–14.

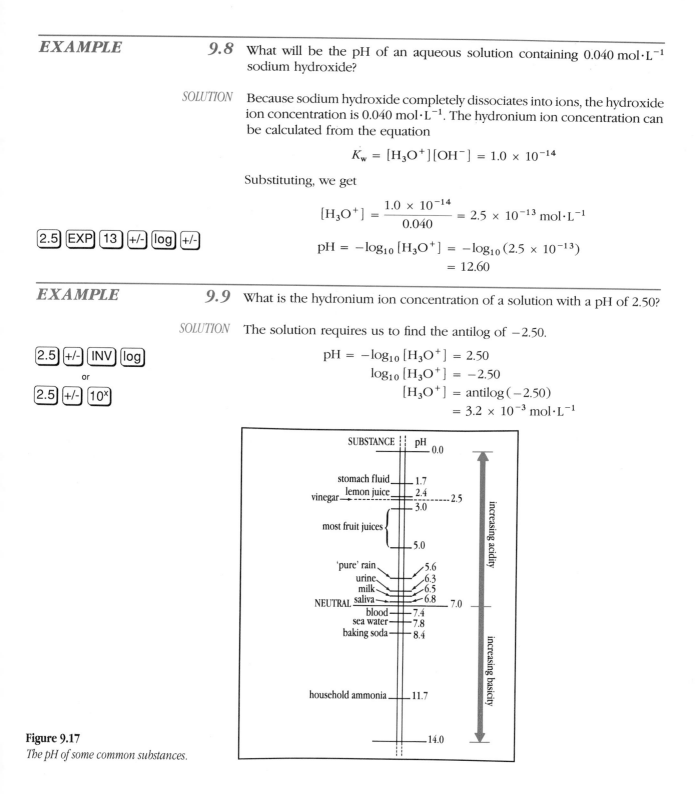

EXAMPLE   **9.8**   What will be the pH of an aqueous solution containing 0.040 mol·L⁻¹ sodium hydroxide?

SOLUTION   Because sodium hydroxide completely dissociates into ions, the hydroxide ion concentration is 0.040 mol·L⁻¹. The hydronium ion concentration can be calculated from the equation

$$K_w = [H_3O^+][OH^-] = 1.0 \times 10^{-14}$$

Substituting, we get

$$[H_3O^+] = \frac{1.0 \times 10^{-14}}{0.040} = 2.5 \times 10^{-13} \text{ mol·L}^{-1}$$

$$pH = -\log_{10}[H_3O^+] = -\log_{10}(2.5 \times 10^{-13})$$
$$= 12.60$$

2.5 EXP 13 +/- log +/-

EXAMPLE   **9.9**   What is the hydronium ion concentration of a solution with a pH of 2.50?

SOLUTION   The solution requires us to find the antilog of −2.50.

$$pH = -\log_{10}[H_3O^+] = 2.50$$
$$\log_{10}[H_3O^+] = -2.50$$
$$[H_3O^+] = \text{antilog}(-2.50)$$
$$= 3.2 \times 10^{-3} \text{ mol·L}^{-1}$$

2.5 +/- INV log
or
2.5 +/- 10ˣ

SUBSTANCE   pH
                  0.0

stomach fluid   1.7
lemon juice   2.4
vinegar →   -------- 2.5
                 3.0

most fruit juices {
                 5.0

'pure' rain   5.6
urine   6.3
milk   6.5
NEUTRAL saliva   6.8   7.0
blood   7.4
sea water   7.8
baking soda   8.4

household ammonia   11.7

                 14.0

increasing acidity

increasing basicity

Figure 9.17
The pH of some common substances.

Determining pOH

If we use the term **pOH** for the negative logarithm of the hydroxide ion concentration, we can write a simple relationship between pOH and pH.

$$pH + pOH = 14.00$$

The use of pOH will simplify some pH calculations. If either the pH or pOH concentration is known, the other can easily be found. For example, an aqueous solution containing $0.040 \ mol \cdot L^{-1}$ sodium hydroxide has the following pOH:

$$pOH = -\log_{10}(0.040) = 1.40$$

Because pH + pOH = 14.00, this solution will have a pH = 12.60.

Acid-Base Indicators

Many natural and synthetic organic dyes change colour when treated with an acid or base. Examples of natural substances whose colours are pH dependent are tea, beet juice, many fruit juices, and litmus. Because these dyes exhibit different colours in acidic and basic solutions, these dyes are called **acid-base indicators**.

All acid-base indicators are either weak acids or weak bases. In aqueous solution, the acid form of the indicator is in equilibrium with its conjugate base. These two forms will exhibit different colours. The colour of the solution is determined by the form that predominates. If we assign the formula HIn to the acid form of the indicator and In^- to the base form, we can write the general acid-base equilibrium reaction for the indicator:

$$\underset{\text{colour x}}{HIn_{(aq)}} + H_2O_{(\ell)} \rightleftharpoons H_3O^+_{(aq)} + \underset{\text{colour y}}{In^-_{(aq)}}$$

In a strongly acidic solution, the high concentration of hydronium ions will force the equilibrium point of the indicator to the left, and the colour of the solution will be that of the acid form HIn. In a strongly basic solution, the extremely low hydronium ion concentration will cause the equilibrium to shift to the right and In^- will determine the colour of the solution. Thus the colour of the indicator will depend on the pH of the solution.

The colour will also depend on the acidic behaviour of the HIn form of the indicator. If HIn is an extremely weak acid, the In^- form will only predominate in a very basic solution. If, on the other hand, the HIn form is quite a strong acid, the equilibrium is shifted to the right.

A solution that contains a few drops of an indicator will change colour when a strong acid or base is added. This colour change will be completed in a pH range of 1–2 units. Table 9.8 lists some representative indicators and gives the pH range in which the colour change takes place.

Figure 9.18
A precise method of measuring pH is to use a pH meter.

TABLE 9.8	*Some Acid-Base Indicators*		
Indicator	Acid Colour (HIn)	pH interval of Colour Change	Base Colour (In⁻)
Thymol blue	red	1.2–2.8	yellow
Methyl orange	red	3.1–4.4	orange yellow
Methyl red	red	4.2–6.3	yellow
Bromthymol blue	yellow	6.0–7.6	blue
Phenolphthalein	colourless	8.2–10.0	red
Alizarin yellow	yellow	10.0–12.0	violet

Figure 9.19
Arnold Beckman devised the first pH meter in 1935. Initially its main use was for quality control in the citrus industry of Southern California.

Measurement of pH

The most accurate way to determine the pH of a solution is by using a pH meter. A pH meter measures the electrical potential of a solution; this potential is related to the hydronium ion concentration. Rather than indicating the voltage, the instrument is calibrated in pH units.

A simpler but somewhat less accurate method to quickly determine the pH of a solution is to use pH paper. All pH paper is absorbent paper that has been soaked in a mixture of acid-base indicators and then dried. Various kinds of pH paper are available. Some papers cover the whole pH range and are accurate within one pH unit. Other kinds of paper cover a range of only a few pH units. The colour that the paper acquires in a solution will depend on the mixture of indicators used and the pH of the solution.

Figure 9.20
We can obtain approximate values of pH using test papers.

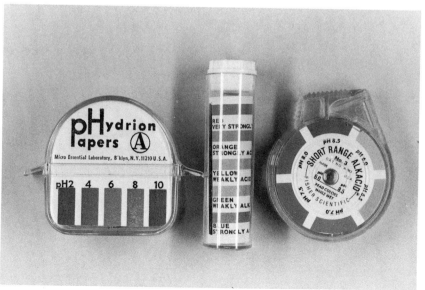

Swimming Pool Chemistry

The two main problems associated with swimming pools are algae growth and the presence of disease-causing bacteria. A small amount of chlorine takes care of both these problems and for that reason chlorine and swimming pools are inseparable. Actually, the active ingredient is usually not free chlorine but the weak acid hypochlorous acid, HClO. This acid is produced from any of the many "chlorines" added to swimming pools. Commonly used chlorinating agents are free chlorine gas, "liquid chlorine," and "dry chlorine." Liquid chlorine is an aqueous solution of sodium hypochlorite, NaClO, whereas dry chlorine consists of about 70% calcium hypochlorite, $Ca(ClO)_2$.

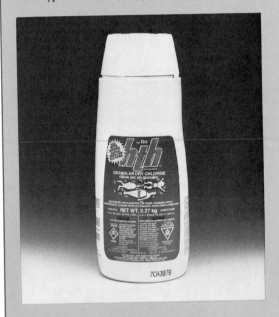

Figure 9.21
Large swimming pools generally use chlorine gas to control algae and bacteria. But calcium hypochlorite, 'dry chlorine,' is more convenient for small pools.

When chlorine gas is bubbled into water, it reacts to form hydrochloric acid and hypochlorous acid.

$$Cl_{2(g)} + 2\,H_2O_{(l)} \longrightarrow H_3O^+_{(aq)} + Cl^-_{(aq)} + HClO_{(aq)}$$

At the normal pH range of swimming pools, this reaction essentially goes to completion.

If we use a salt, such as sodium hypochlorite, we similarly produce hypochlorous acid:

$$NaClO_{(aq)} + H_2O_{(l)} \longrightarrow Na^+_{(aq)} + HClO_{(aq)} + OH^-_{(aq)}$$

Hypochlorous acid is a weak acid, which undergoes the following dissociation:

$$HClO_{(aq)} + H_2O_{(l)} \rightleftharpoons H_3O^+_{(aq)} + ClO^-_{(aq)}$$

It is the undissociated hypochlorous acid that is most effective in killing bacteria. To maximize the proportion of undissociated acid in this equilibrium, we would predict from Le Châtelier's principle that the hydrogen ion concentration should be as high as possible (lowest possible pH). You might think that we should try and use the lowest pH we can tolerate. Unfortunately, there are other reactions we have to consider.

Bathers excrete ammonia and ammonia-like compounds into the water. These compounds react to produce chloramines. For example:

$$NH_{3(aq)} + HClO_{(aq)} \longrightarrow NH_2Cl_{(aq)} + H_2O_{(l)}$$

It is the chloramines that cause the eye irritation, and it is the nitrogen trichloride, another chloramine, that gives rise to the so-called "smell of chlorine." To destroy these eye-burning chloramines, extra chlorine must be added to the pool, a process known as superchlorination. The lower the pH, the more readily chloramines form. Above a pH of 7, the levels are tolerable.

Too low a pH will cause the conversion of hypochlorous acid into free chlorine. Too high a pH will cause the hypochlorous acid to ionize.

For freshwater pools, a pH of between 7.2 and 7.6 is preferred. At this pH range about half of the hypochlorite is in the form of undissociated hypochlorous acid. We adjust the pH of a pool by adding sodium hydrogen sulfate to lower pH or sodium hydrogen carbonate to raise it.

QUESTIONS

15. Calculate the pH of each of the following:
  a) an aqueous solution that has a hydronium ion concentration of 3.0×10^{-3} mol·L^{-1}
  b) an aqueous solution that has a hydroxide ion concentration of 6.0×10^{-4} mol·L^{-1}
  c) an aqueous solution containing 0.0020 mol·L^{-1} barium hydroxide, $Ba(OH)_2$
  d) 250.0 mL of an aqueous solution containing 1.26 g of nitric acid, HNO_3
  e) pure water at 0 °C

16. Calculate the hydronium ion concentration of
  a) 100.0 mL of an aqueous solution containing 0.60 g of sodium hydroxide, NaOH
  b) a blood sample with a pH of 7.40
  c) orange juice with a pH of 3.20

17. Which of the indicators in Table 9.8 is the strongest acid?

<table>
<tr><td>

Salts of Weak Acids and Bases

</td><td>

9.10

</td><td>

As we mentioned earlier not all solutions of salts are neutral; some are acidic and some are basic. But we cannot explain this observation using the Arrhenius theory. We will now see how to account for the facts using Brønsted-Lowry theory.

</td></tr>
</table>

Salts of Weak Acids

Hydrochloric acid is a strong acid. When hydrogen chloride molecules dissolve in water, virtually all of them react with the water to give hydronium ions and chloride ions.

$$HCl_{(aq)} + H_2O_{(\ell)} \longrightarrow H_3O^+_{(aq)} + Cl^-_{(aq)}$$

The chloride ion is an extremely weak base and is unlikely to remove a hydrogen ion from either a hydronium ion or water.

Unlike hydrochloric acid, hydrofluoric acid is a weak acid. Thus a solution of this acid contains a high proportion of non-ionized hydrogen fluoride molecules:

$$HF_{(aq)} + H_2O_{(\ell)} \rightleftharpoons H_3O^+_{(aq)} + F^-_{(aq)}$$

The fluoride ion is a much stronger base than the chloride ion. It will readily remove a hydrogen ion from a hydronium ion or even from water:

$$F^-_{(aq)} + H_2O_{(\ell)} \rightleftharpoons HF_{(aq)} + OH^-_{(aq)}$$

This equilibrium reaction, sometimes referred to as a hydrolysis reaction, will occur whenever a simple fluoride salt, such as sodium fluoride, is

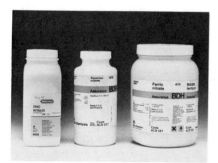

Figure 9.22

The salts of zinc, aluminum, and iron(III) are particularly acidic.

dissolved in water. A solution of a fluoride will always produce some molecular hydrofluoric acid and some hydroxide ions. In other words a solution of sodium fluoride will be basic.

For simple anions, we can generalize by saying that *anions from weak acids will give basic solutions. Anions from strong acids will give neutral solutions.*

TABLE 9.9 *Acid-Base Properties of Some Common Anions*		TABLE 9.10 *Acid-Base Properties of Some 'Acid' Anions*	
Neutral	Basic	Basic	Acidic
NO_3^-	F^-	HCO_3^-	HSO_4^-
ClO_4^-	NO_2^-	HS^-	HSO_3^-
Cl^-	CN^-	HPO_4^{2-}	$H_2PO_4^-$
Br^-	$CH_3CO_2^-$		
I^-	S^{2-}		
SO_4^{2-}	SO_3^{2-}		
	CO_3^{2-}		
	PO_4^{3-}		

EXAMPLE   **9.10** Using an equation, show why a sodium nitritie solution is basic.

SOLUTION When sodium nitrite is dissolved in water, sodium and nitrite ions will be formed:

$$NaNO_{2(s)} \xrightarrow[\text{in water}]{\text{dissolve}} Na^+_{(aq)} + NO_2^-_{(aq)}$$

The sodium ions will remain as is, but the basic nitrite ions (Table 9.9) will react with water:

$$NO_2^-_{(aq)} + H_2O_{(\ell)} \rightleftharpoons HNO_{2(aq)} + OH^-_{(aq)}$$

The formation of some hydroxide ions will render the solution basic.

Polyprotic acids are more complex. With these acids we can have salts that also contain a hydrogen atom. Whether these "acid" salts will act as acids or bases depends upon the strength of the particular acid.

EXAMPLE   **9.11** Account for the fact that sodium hydrogen carbonate produces a basic solution when it is dissolved in water.

SOLUTION   When sodium hydrogen carbonate is dissolved in water, aqueous sodium ions and hydrogen carbonate ions will be formed:

$$NaHCO_{3\,(s)} \xrightarrow[\text{in water}]{\text{dissolve}} Na^+_{(aq)} + HCO_3^-_{(aq)}$$

The sodium ions will remain as is, but the hydrogen carbonate ions, being basic (Table 9.10), will react with water:

$$HCO_3^-_{(aq)} + H_2O_{(\ell)} \rightleftharpoons H_2CO_{3\,(aq)} + OH^-_{(aq)}$$

The formation of hydroxide ions will render the solution basic.

EXAMPLE   **9.12**   Account for the fact that sodium hydrogen sulfite produces an acidic solution when it is dissolved in water.

SOLUTION   When sodium hydrogen sulfite is dissolved in water, aqueous sodium ions and hydrogen sulfate ions will be formed:

$$NaHSO_{3\,(s)} \xrightarrow[\text{in water}]{\text{dissolve}} Na^+_{(aq)} + HSO_3^-_{(aq)}$$

The sodium ions will remain as is, but the hydrogen sulfite ions, being acidic (Table 9.10), will react with water:

$$HSO_3^-_{(aq)} + H_2O_{(\ell)} \rightleftharpoons SO_3^{2-}_{(aq)} + H_3O^+_{(aq)}$$

The formation of some hydronium ions will render the solution acidic.

Salts of Weak Bases

The only common example of a weak base is ammonia. This reacts with water to produce the ammonium ion and the hydroxide ion.

$$NH_{3\,(g)} + H_2O_{(\ell)} \rightleftharpoons NH_4^+_{(aq)} + OH^-_{(aq)}$$

A solution of the ammonium ion, then, will be acidic:

$$NH_4^+_{(aq)} + H_2O_{(\ell)} \rightleftharpoons NH_{3\,(aq)} + H_3O^+_{(aq)}$$

This accounts for the fact that salts such as ammonium chloride and ammonium nitrate produce acidic solutions when they are dissolved in water.

Salts of Acidic Metal Ions

Although we usually think of solutions of metal ions as being neutral, most of them are acidic. It is only the ions of the alkali metals (Group IA) and the ions of the alkaline earth metals (Group IIA) that give neutral solutions. As you have probably realized, these are the most commonly used ions in an introductory chemistry course.

To understand how metal ions could form acid solutions, we must remember that as a salt dissolves in water, the ions are surrounded by a shell of water molecules. A precise number of water molecules, usually four or six, surrounds each metal ion. This cluster, consisting of the ion and the water molecules, is called a **hydrated ion**. Table 9.11 shows the number of water molecules associated with some common metal ions. The water molecules are written as "OH_2" to indicate that the oxygen atom of the water molecule is closest to the metal ion.

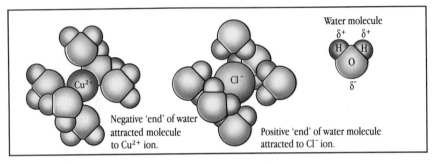

Figure 9.23

The hydrated Cu^{2+} ions and Cl^- ions in a copper(II) chloride solution.

TABLE 9.11	*Formulas of Some Common Hydrated Metal Ions*	
Metal Ion	Number of Water Molecules	Formula
Al^{3+}	6	$Al(OH_2)_6^{3+}$
Fe^{3+}	6	$Fe(OH_2)_6^{3+}$
Cu^{2+}	6	$Cu(OH_2)_6^{2+}$
Zn^{2+}	4	$Zn(OH_2)_4^{2+}$

These ions can reduce their positive charge by transferring a hydrogen ion to another water molecule. Thus the resulting solution will be acidic. For the $3+$ ions the equilibrium lies further to the right and hence it is these ions that produce the most noticeably acid solutions.

QUESTIONS

18. Predict whether aqueous solutions of the following salts are neutral, acidic, or basic:
   a) potassium iodide, KI
   b) sodium cynide, NaCN
   c) ammonium dihydrogen phosphate, $NH_4H_2PO_4$
   d) sodium hydrogen sulfite, $NaHSO_3$
   e) potassium hydrogen sulfide, KHS
   f) copper(II) nitrate, $Cu(NO_3)_2$

19. Show, using equations, why sodium acetate produces a basic solution in water.

Summary

- Acids and bases are substances that, according to the Arrhenius theory, produce hydrogen ions and hydroxide ions in water. The more general Brønsted-Lowry theory defines an acid as a hydrogen-ion donor and a base as a hydrogen-ion acceptor. It also relates strength of an acid or a base to the ability to donate and accept hydrogen ions.

- Conjugate acid-base pairs differ in one hydrogen atom and their strength is related: the stronger the acid, the weaker its conjugate base, and vice versa.

- The strength of oxyacids increases with the number of oxygen atoms not bonded to hydrogen atoms.

- The product of hydronium ion and hydroxide ion concentrations of water is known as the ion product constant of water, K_w. This has a value of 1.0×10^{-14} at $25\,°C$.

- A convenient way to express the acidity, or basicity, of aqueous solutions is by the use of pH.

- Acid-base indicators are either weak acids or weak bases. The acid and base forms have different colours. The colours in aqueous solution will depend on the pH of the solution.

KEY WORDS

acid	ion product constant of water
acid-base indicator	neutralization
Arrhenius theory	pH
base	pOH
Brønsted-Lowry theory	polyprotic acid
conjugate acid-base pair	oxyacid
electrolyte	salt
hydrated ion	strong acid
hydrogen-ion acceptor	strong base
hydrogen-ion donor	weak acid
hydrogen-ion exchange reaction	weak base
hydronium ion	

ANSWERS TO SECTION QUESTIONS

1. a) donor: HNO_3, acceptor: H_2O
   b) donor: H_2O, acceptor: $C_2H_5NH_2$
   c) donor: CH_3CO_2H, acceptor: H_2O

2. a), e), f)

3. strong bases: potassium hydroxide, barium hydroxide, lithium hydroxide
   weak bases: methylamine, caffeine

16. Which compound in each of the following pairs is the stronger acid:
   a) H_2O or H_2S
   b) H_2O or NH_3
   c) HCl or HI

Conjugate Acid-Base Pairs

17. Which of the following do not represent a conjugate acid-base pair:
   a) SO_3^{2-} and SO_2
   b) CO_3^{2-} and CO
   c) H_3O^+ and H_2
   d) NH_4^+ and NH_3

18. For each of the following reactions identify, where possible, the acid-base conjugate pairs:
   a) $CH_3CO_2^-{}_{(aq)} + H_2O_{(\ell)} \rightleftharpoons CH_3CO_2H_{(aq)} + OH^-{}_{(aq)}$
   b) $HClO_{(aq)} + CH_3NH_2{}_{(aq)} \rightleftharpoons CH_3NH_3^+{}_{(aq)} + ClO^-{}_{(aq)}$
   c) $H_2CO_3{}_{(aq)} \rightleftharpoons CO_2{}_{(g)} + H_2O_{(\ell)}$
   d) $H_2{}_{(g)} + I_2{}_{(g)} \rightleftharpoons 2\,HI_{(g)}$
   e) $NaH_{(s)} + H_2O_{(\ell)} \rightleftharpoons NaOH_{(aq)} + H_2{}_{(g)}$
   f) $ClCH_2CO_2H_{(aq)} + H_2O_{(\ell)} \rightleftharpoons ClCH_2CO_2^-{}_{(aq)} + H_3O^+{}_{(aq)}$

Polyprotic Acids

19. Write the reaction equations for the ionization in water of the weak triprotic acid, citric acid ($C_6H_5O_7H_3$).

20. Arrange the following in order of increasing acid strength:

$$NaH_2PO_4 \qquad H_3PO_4 \qquad Na_2HPO_4$$

pH Scale and Indicators

21. Calculate the pH of the following aqueous solutions:
   a) an aqueous solution containing 3.0×10^{-5} mol·L^{-1} hydronium ions
   b) an aqueous solution containing 6.5×10^{-4} mol·L^{-1} hydroxide ions
   c) the solution obtained when 7.2 g hydrogen chloride is dissolved in 5.0 L of water
   d) a 500.0 mL aqueous solution containing 1.0 g sodium hydroxide

22. What are the hydronium ion and the hydroxide ion concentrations of the following:
   a) a solution with pH = 5.00
   b) a solution with pH = 9.55

23. Fill in the blanks in the following table. For each solution indicate whether the solution is acidic or basic.

	pH	pOH	$[H_3O^+]$	$[OH^-]$
a)	4.0	—	—	—
b)	—	11.6	—	—
c)	—	—	1.8×10^{-9}	—
d)	—	—	—	3.5×10^{-2}

24. Calculate the pH of an aqueous solution of strong acid prepared by adding 50.00 mL of 1.50 mol·L^{-1} hydrochloric acid to 100.0 mL of 0.500 mol·L^{-1} nitric acid, HNO_3.

MISCELLANEOUS PROBLEMS

25. Complete the following acid-base reactions, assuming that only one hydrogen ion is exchanged. Identify the conjugate acid-base pairs in each reaction.

a) $HSO_4^- + OH^- \longrightarrow$

b) $CH_3OH + NH_2^- \longrightarrow$

c) $H_3O^+ + S^{2-} \longrightarrow$

d) $CH_3^- + H_2O \longrightarrow$

e) $H_2NOH + H_2SO_4 \longrightarrow$

f) $CH_3OH + HCl \longrightarrow$

26. The K_w of water varies with temperature. For example, at 10 °C $K_w = 2.92 \times 10^{-15}$; at 45 °C, $K_w = 4.02 \times 10^{-14}$.

a) What is the pH of water at 10 °C? at 45 °C?

b) Is pure water acidic, basic, or neutral at these temperatures?

27. Compare aqueous solutions of the following compounds, all having the same concentrations. Which one in each pair is the most acidic (or the least basic)?

a) H_3PO_4 and HNO_3

b) HCl and HF

c) NH_4Cl and HCl

d) $NaHSO_4$ and $NaHCO_3$

e) H_3BO_3 and H_3PO_4

f) $ZnCl_2$ and $CaCl_2$

28. Compare aqueous solutions of the following compounds, all having the same concentrations. Which one in each pair is the most basic (or the least acidic)?

a) NaOH and NaSH

b) K_2S and K_2O

c) Na_2CO_3 and $NaHCO_3$

d) $NaNO_3$ and $NaCN$

e) NH_4Cl and $NaCl$

f) Na_2SO_3 and Na_2SO_4

29. In liquid ammonia, sulfuric acid (H_2SO_4) and the hydrogen sulfate ion (HSO_4^-) both behave as strong acids. But in 100% acetic acid (glacial acetic acid), sulfuric acid behaves as a weak acid. Write the reaction equations for the following:

a) the reaction between sulfuric acid and ammonia

b) the reaction between sulfuric acid and acetic acid, CH_3CO_2H

30. Calculate the volume of sea water with a pH of 7.80 that contains 1.0 mol of hydroxide ions.

31. The following reactions occur in aqueous solution:

a) $H_2O_{(\ell)} + H_2O_{(\ell)} \rightleftharpoons H_3O^+_{(aq)} + OH^-_{(aq)}$

b) $OH^-_{(aq)} + HCO_3^-_{(aq)} \longrightarrow H_2O_{(\ell)} + CO_3^{2-}_{(aq)}$

c) $H_3O^+_{(aq)} + HCO_3^-_{(aq)} \longrightarrow 2\,H_2O_{(\ell)} + CO_{2\,(g)}$

Rewrite these reaction equations for the liquid ammonia system, by replacing water and its conjugate acid and base by ammonia and its conjugate acid and base.

SUGGESTED PROJECTS

1. If you have access to a pH meter, collect a number of different solutions (fruit juices, colas and other pop drinks, lake water, stream water, household cleaning solutions, etc.). Measure and record their respective pHs. Can you draw any conclusions from your observations?

2. Some lakes that have had their pH lowered by acid rain have been treated by the addition of bases such as calcium hydroxide. Have any of the lakes in your area been treated this way? Research and report on the cost, effectiveness, and possible problems in such a large-scale neutralization.

3. Many indicators are naturally-occurring weak acids. Choose one or two of these indicators and report on where they come from, how they are extracted, and how they are used.

C H A P T E R 10

Neutralization and Titration

When an acid is combined with a base in the right quantity, we are performing an important type of reaction, called a neutralization reaction. The process of neutralization can be followed experimentally by a titration. And, the study of these reactions enables us to understand pH changes in terms of Le Châtelier's principle.

Analysis of acids and bases shows that the Brønsted-Lowry theory has some shortcomings. The Lewis theory on acids and bases is an extension of traditional models, and is explained at the end of this chapter.

Neutralization Reactions

10.1 When hydrochloric acid is added to a sodium hydroxide solution, an aqueous solution of sodium chloride is produced.

$$HCl_{(aq)} + NaOH_{(aq)} \longrightarrow NaCl_{(aq)} + H_2O_{(\ell)}$$

Double displacement reactions of this type, in which an acid and a base combine to form a salt and water, are called neutralization reactions. The hydrochloric acid solution contains hydronium ions and chloride ions; the sodium hydroxide solution contains sodium ions and hydroxide ions.

$$HCl_{(aq)} + H_2O_{(\ell)} \longrightarrow H_3O^+_{(aq)} + Cl^-_{(aq)}$$
$$NaOH_{(aq)} \longrightarrow Na^+_{(aq)} + OH^-_{(aq)}$$

The following equation represents the total ionic equation for the reaction.

$$H_3O^+_{(aq)} + Cl^-_{(aq)} + Na^+_{(aq)} + OH^-_{(aq)} \longrightarrow$$
$$2\,H_2O_{(\ell)} + Na^+_{(aq)} + Cl^-_{(aq)}$$

Omitting the sodium ions and the chloride ions, which are spectator ions, we can represent this neutralization reaction between a strong acid and a strong base by the net ionic equation:

$$H_3O^+_{(aq)} + OH^-_{(aq)} \longrightarrow 2\,H_2O_{(\ell)}$$

Neutralization of a Weak Base

If we use a weak base, such as ammonia, the reaction with hydrochloric acid will be slightly different. As before, the hydrochloric acid solution contains only hydronium ions and chloride ions. The ammonia solution, being a weak base, contains mainly ammonia molecules, and relatively few ammonium and hydroxide ions, in equilibrium with each other.

$$HCl_{(aq)} + H_2O_{(\ell)} \longrightarrow H_3O^+_{(aq)} + Cl^-_{(aq)}$$
$$NH_{3\,(aq)} + H_2O_{(\ell)} \rightleftharpoons NH_4^+_{(aq)} + OH^-_{(aq)}$$

Upon mixing these solutions, the hydronium ions will react with the hydroxide ions to produce water. As the hydroxide ions are removed, more of them will be produced, for according to Le Châtelier's principle, the equilibrium will shift to the right. If sufficient hydrochloric acid is added, this shift will be complete. The overall reaction is represented by the two equations

$$H_3O^+_{(aq)} + OH^-_{(aq)} \longrightarrow 2\,H_2O_{(\ell)}$$
$$NH_{3\,(aq)} + H_2O_{(\ell)} - \qquad NH_4^+_{(aq)} + OH^-_{(aq)}$$

Here again, the actual neutralization involves the reaction between hydronium ions and hydroxide ions. The net reaction equation can be written as follows. (The chloride ions are spectator ions.)

$$H_3O^+_{(aq)} + NH_{3\,(aq)} \longrightarrow NH_4^+_{(aq)} + H_2O_{(\ell)}$$

Neutralization of a Weak Acid

We can also neutralize a strong base, such as sodium hydroxide, with the weak acid, acetic acid, to produce a solution of sodium acetate:

$$CH_3CO_2H_{(aq)} + NaOH_{(aq)} \longrightarrow CH_3CO_2Na_{(aq)} + H_2O_{(\ell)}$$

The solution of sodium hydroxide is completely dissociated into ions, whereas the solution of acetic acid consists mainly of acetic acid molecules in equilibrium with relatively few hydronium and acetate ions.

$$NaOH_{(aq)} \longrightarrow Na^+_{(aq)} + OH^-_{(aq)}$$
$$CH_3CO_2H_{(aq)} + H_2O_{(\ell)} \rightleftharpoons H_3O^+_{(aq)} + CH_3CO_2^-_{(aq)}$$

Figure 10.1

Nitric acid pours out of a railroad car in Denver, Colorado, in 1985. To neutralize the pools of acid, huge piles of sodium carbonate were blown onto the acid using an airport snowblower.

Upon mixing the two solutions, a reaction takes place between the hydroxide ions and the hydronium ions:

$$OH^-_{(aq)} + H_3O^+_{(aq)} \longrightarrow 2\, H_2O_{(\ell)}$$

When sodium hydroxide is added to the acetic acid solution, enough hydroxide ions are available to combine with the hydronium ions that resulted from the ionization of the weak acetic acid. The removal of the hydronium ions in the formation of water molecules shifts the equilibrium to the right. With sufficient sodium hydroxide, this shift will be complete. Sodium ions act as spectator ions and the net overall reaction is as follows:

$$CH_3CO_2H_{(aq)} + OH^-_{(aq)} \longrightarrow CH_3CO_2^-_{(aq)} + H_2O_{(\ell)}$$

Neutralization reactions between acids and bases are only successful when both are strong or at least one of the two is strong. *A weak acid will not react completely with a weak base.*

Figure 10.2

a) Aqueous acetic acid dissolved in water is ionized only slightly. A light bulb glows only dimly in the solution.

b) Aqueous ammonia dissolved in water is ionized only slightly. A light bulb in this solution glows only dimly.

c) When these two solutions are mixed, the equilibrium lies to the right; hence, the light bulb glows brightly.

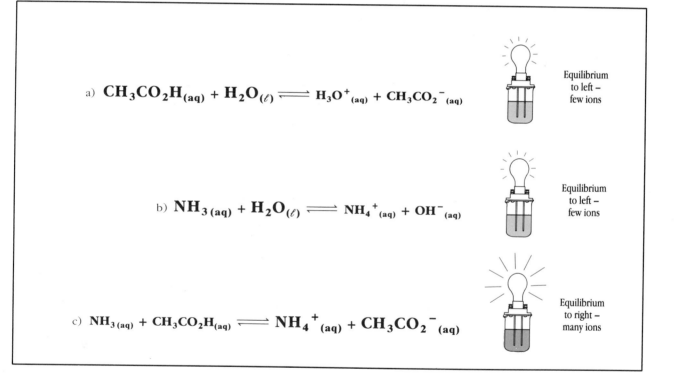

a) $CH_3CO_2H_{(aq)} + H_2O_{(\ell)} \rightleftharpoons H_3O^+_{(aq)} + CH_3CO_2^-_{(aq)}$

Equilibrium to left – few ions

b) $NH_{3\,(aq)} + H_2O_{(\ell)} \rightleftharpoons NH_4^+_{(aq)} + OH^-_{(aq)}$

Equilibrium to left – few ions

c) $NH_{3\,(aq)} + CH_3CO_2H_{(aq)} \rightleftharpoons NH_4^+_{(aq)} + CH_3CO_2^-_{(aq)}$

Equilibrium to right – many ions

The pH of a Neutralized Solution

The term neutralization infers that we end up with a neutral solution; that is, a solution with pH of 7. This, however, is only the case when both the acid and the base are strong. For example, when sodium hydroxide solution is neutralized with hydrochloric acid, a sodium chloride solution is

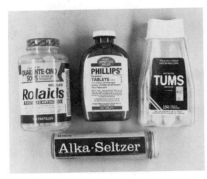

Figure 10.3
A selection of antacids. These are used to neutralize excess stomach acid.

produced. Since neither of these ions hydrolyze, the solution is neutral.

In the neutralization of ammonia (a weak base) with hydrochloric acid (a strong acid) a solution of ammonium chloride will be produced.

$$NH_{3(aq)} + HCl_{(aq)} \longrightarrow NH_4Cl_{(aq)}$$

Ammonium chloride is completely ionized in water into ammonium ions and chloride ions:

$$NH_4Cl_{(aq)} \longrightarrow NH_4^+{}_{(aq)} + Cl^-{}_{(aq)}$$

The chloride ions will remain unchanged but the ammonium ions, being a weak acid, will hydrolyze slightly and some hydronium ions will be produced. The solution of ammonium chloride will be acidic.

$$NH_4^+{}_{(aq)} + H_2O_{(\ell)} \rightleftharpoons NH_{3(aq)} + H_3O^+{}_{(aq)}$$

In the neutralization of acetic acid (a weak acid) with sodium hydroxide solution (a strong base) a solution of sodium acetate is formed. The sodium ions will remain unchanged, but the acetate ions, being a weak base (Table 9.9), will hydrolyze slightly to give some hydroxide ions.

$$CH_3CO_2^-{}_{(aq)} + H_2O_{(\ell)} \rightleftharpoons CH_3CO_2H_{(aq)} + OH^-{}_{(aq)}$$

TABLE 10.1   *Types of Neutralization Reactions*

Acid	Base	pH of Neutralized Solution
strong	strong	7 (neutral)
strong	weak	<7 (acidic)
weak	strong	>7 (basic)

The Neutralization of Polyprotic Acids

Polyprotic acids can contribute more than one hydrogen ion per molecule. In a neutralization reaction an acid will donate all its acidic hydrogen ions, and the base will accept the maximum number of hydrogen ions that it can. For example, sulfuric acid will give up its two hydrogen ions when it is neutralized with an aqueous solution of sodium hydroxide:

$$H_2SO_{4(aq)} + 2\,NaOH_{(aq)} \longrightarrow Na_2SO_{4(aq)} + 2\,H_2O_{(\ell)}$$

EXAMPLE   *10.1*   Write the equation for the reaction in aqueous solution between phosphoric acid, a weak acid, and sodium hydroxide. What is the net ionic equation? Will the neutralized solution be acidic, neutral, or basic?

SOLUTION   The overall neutralization equation is

$$H_3PO_{4(aq)} + 3\,NaOH_{(aq)} \longrightarrow Na_3PO_{4(aq)} + 3\,H_2O_{(\ell)}$$

Since phosphoric acid is a weak acid, it must remain written in molecular form. The sodium ions are left out because they are spectator ions. This leaves the net ionic equation:

$$H_3PO_{4\,(aq)} + 3\,OH^-_{\ (aq)} \longrightarrow PO_4^{\ 3-}_{\ (aq)} + 3\,H_2O_{(\ell)}$$

The neutralized solution will consist of sodium phosphate. The sodium ions will remain unchanged, but the phosphate ions, being a strong base, will hydrolyze (Table 9.9).

$$PO_4^{\ 3-}_{\ (aq)} + H_2O_{(\ell)} \rightleftharpoons HPO_4^{\ 2-}_{\ (aq)} + OH^-_{\ (aq)}$$

QUESTIONS

1. Write the overall neutralization reaction equation and the net ionic equation for the reaction in aqueous solution between the following acids and bases:
    a) sulfuric acid and sodium hydroxide
    b) hydrochloric acid and calcium hydroxide
    c) potassium hydrogen sulfate, $KHSO_4$, and sodium hydroxide
2. For the reaction in aqueous solution between the diprotic weak acid, sulfurous acid, H_2SO_3, and sodium hydroxide write the following:
    a) the overall neutralization equation
    b) the net ionic equation

Acid-Base Titrations

10.2 An acid-base titration is one of the most accurate methods of quantitative analysis. This process involves the gradual addition of either an acid to a base or a base to an acid. One of the solutions is placed in a burette, while the other is placed in an Erlenmeyer flask along with a small amount of indicator. The solution in the burette, called the **titrant**, is added slowly. When the indicator changes colour, the acid or base in the Erlenmeyer flask has been neutralized and we stop the addition of titrant. The goal of the titration is to stop adding the titrant when the stoichiometrically equal amounts of the two solutions have been combined. This point is called the **equivalence point**. The change in colour "tells" the experimenter to stop adding the titrant. This is the **end point**. If the titration is performed well, the end point coincides with the equivalence point.

If we know the volumes of acid and base used in the titration, and the concentration of one of the solutions, we can calculate the unknown concentration of the other solution. Example 10.2 shows how this calculation is carried out.

Successful acid-base titrations can be carried out when both the acid and the base are strong, or when one of the two is strong. Inaccurate results are obtained when both the acid and the base are weak. The choice of indicator is also important. As we have discussed, the resulting salt

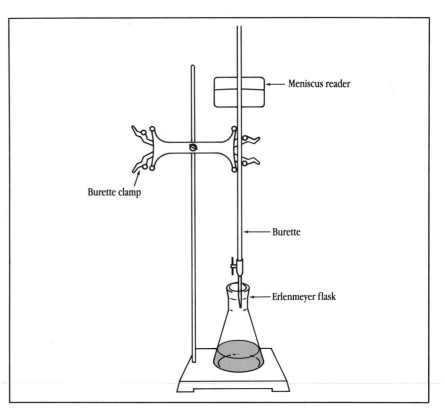

Figure 10.4
A titration apparatus.

Meniscus reader

Burette clamp

Burette

Erlenmeyer flask

solution for a titration involving a strong acid and a strong base, will be neutral. An indicator should be used that changes colour near the pH value of 7, such as bromothymol blue. If the acid is weak, the salt solution produced will be slightly basic. In this case an indicator that changes in the pH range 7–11 should be used; for example, phenolphthalein. When the base is weak, a slightly acidic solution is obtained. The indicator should change colour in the pH range 3–7; for example, methyl red.

EXAMPLE   *10.2*   In a titration, 16.80 mL of an aqueous sodium hydroxide solution of unknown concentration is neutralized by 25.00 mL of a 0.190 mol·L^{-1} solution of sulfuric acid. What is the concentration of the sodium hydroxide solution?

SOLUTION   We must first write the balanced overall neutralization reaction equation:

$$H_2SO_{4\,(aq)} + 2\,NaOH_{(aq)} \longrightarrow Na_2SO_{4\,(aq)} + 2\,H_2O_{(\ell)}$$

We convert the units for volume of acid to litres and then use the relationship $n = Vc$ to determine the number of moles of sulfuric acid.

$$\text{Moles of } H_2SO_4 = 2.500 \times 10^{-2}\,L \times 0.190\,\text{mol·L}^{-1}$$
$$= 4.75 \times 10^{-3}\,\text{mol}$$

Using the appropriate equation factor, we calculate the number of moles of base:

$$\text{Moles of NaOH} = 4.75 \times 10^{-3} \text{ mol H}_2\text{SO}_4 \times \frac{2 \text{ mol NaOH}}{1 \text{ mol H}_2\text{SO}_4}$$

$$= 9.50 \times 10^{-3} \text{ mol NaOH}$$

Knowing both the number of moles and the volume of NaOH, we can find the concentration

$$c = \frac{n}{V}$$

$$[\text{NaOH}] = \frac{9.50 \times 10^{-3} \text{ mol}}{0.0168 \text{ L}} = 0.565 \text{ mol} \cdot \text{L}^{-1}$$

EXAMPLE   **10.3**   An impure sample of oxalic acid, $C_2O_4H_2$, with a mass of 0.465 g, is dissolved in water. A few drops of phenolphthalein indicator solution are added, and the solution is titrated with 0.190 mol·L^{-1} aqueous sodium hydroxide held in a burette. The solution turns red when 49.50 mL of sodium hydroxide has been added. What is the percent purity of the oxalic acid sample?

SOLUTION   The balanced overall neutralization reaction equation is

$$C_2O_4H_{2\,(aq)} + 2\,\text{NaOH}_{(aq)} \longrightarrow Na_2C_2O_{4\,(aq)} + 2\,H_2O_{(\ell)}$$

Using the expression $n = Vc$,

$$\text{Moles of NaOH} = 0.0495 \text{ L} \times 0.190 \text{ mol} \cdot \text{L}^{-1}$$

$$= 9.41 \times 10^{-3} \text{ mol}$$

To determine the number of moles of pure oxalic acid in the sample, we use the appropriate equation factor:

$$\text{Moles of } C_2O_4H_2 = 9.41 \times 10^{-3} \text{ mol NaOH} \times \frac{1 \text{ mol } C_2O_4H_2}{2 \text{ mol NaOH}}$$

$$= 4.71 \times 10^{-3} \text{ mol } C_2O_4H_2$$

We can now convert moles of pure $C_2O_4H_2$ to mass

$$\text{Mass } C_2O_4H_2 = 4.71 \times 10^{-3} \text{ mol } C_2O_4H_2 \times \frac{90.04 \text{ g } C_2O_4H_2}{1 \text{ mol } C_2O_4H_2}$$

$$= 0.424 \text{ g } C_2O_4H_2$$

$$\text{Percent oxalic acid in sample} = \frac{0.424 \text{ g}}{0.465 \text{ g}} \times 100\% = 91.2\%$$

Back Titrations

The technique of back titrating is used to neutralize a base or an acid that is only slightly soluble in water. Suppose we wish to neutralize a slightly soluble base. A precise mass of the base is measured out and placed in an Erlenmeyer flask. An excess of a strong acid of known concentration is added to react quickly and completely with the base. An indicator is added to the solution, and a strong base solution of known concentration is then titrated from a burette into the excess acid until it is neutralized. Then we calculate the moles of acid used and the moles of strong base added. The difference between the two values must represent the moles of slightly soluble base. This technique is used in Example 10.4 to determine the mass of active ingredient in an antacid tablet.

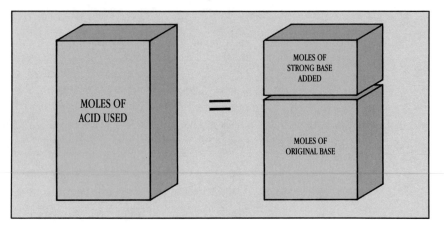

Figure 10.5
In a back titration the moles of acid equals the moles of original base plus the moles of strong base added.

EXAMPLE   *10.4*   A 0.600 g antacid tablet of "Phillips Milk of Magnesia" is crushed into a powder and treated with 100.0 mL of 0.160 $mol \cdot L^{-1}$ hydrochloric acid. The excess of hydrochloric acid is back titrated with 0.200 $mol \cdot L^{-1}$ aqueous sodium hydroxide. A total of 24.90 mL of the base solution is needed to neutralize the excess acid. The active ingredient of the antacid tablet is magnesium hydroxide, $Mg(OH)_2$. What mass of magnesium hydroxide is present in the tablet?

SOLUTION   We begin by writing the balanced overall equations for both reactions:

$$Mg(OH)_{2\,(s)} + 2\,HCl_{(aq)} \longrightarrow MgCl_{2\,(aq)} + 2\,H_2O_{(\ell)}$$

$$\underset{(excess)}{HCl_{(aq)}} + NaOH_{(aq)} \longrightarrow NaCl_{(aq)} + H_2O_{(\ell)}$$

The number of moles of sodium hydroxide used is determined from the expression $n = Vc$

$$\text{Moles of NaOH} = 0.024\,90\,L \times 0.200\,mol \cdot L^{-1}$$
$$= 4.98 \times 10^{-3}\,mol$$

Using the appropriate equation factor we can now determine the number of moles of excess HCl:

$$\text{Moles of excess HCl} = 4.98 \times 10^{-3} \text{ mol NaOH} \times \frac{1 \text{ mol HCl}}{1 \text{ mol NaOH}}$$

$$= 4.98 \times 10^{-3} \text{ mol HCl}$$

Next, we determine the original number of moles of HCl:

$$\text{Original moles of HCl} = 0.1000 \text{ L} \times 0.160 \text{ mol} \cdot \text{L}^{-1}$$

$$= 1.60 \times 10^{-2} \text{ mol}$$

Then we subtract the excess moles of HCl from the original number to find the amount of HCl that was required to neutralize the $Mg(OH)_2$:

$$1.60 \times 10^{-2} - 4.98 \times 10^{-3} = 1.10 \times 10^{-2} \text{ mol}$$

Now we can calculate the number of moles of $Mg(OH)_2$ in the tablet:

$$\text{Moles of } Mg(OH)_2 = 1.10 \times 10^{-2} \text{ mol HCl} \times \frac{1 \text{ mol } Mg(OH)_2}{2 \text{ mol HCl}}$$

$$= 5.50 \times 10^{-3} \text{ mol } Mg(OH)_2$$

Converting moles of $Mg(OH)_2$ to mass we get

$$\text{Mass of } Mg(OH)_2 = 5.50 \times 10^{-3} \text{ mol } Mg(OH)_2 \times \frac{58.33 \text{ g } Mg(OH)_2}{1 \text{ mol } Mg(OH)_2}$$

$$= 0.321 \text{ g } Mg(OH)_2$$

Primary Standards

To perform a titration, the concentration of one of the solutions must be precisely and accurately known. The most commonly used solutions in acid-base titrations are solutions of hydrochloric acid and sodium hydroxide. Expensive sealed ampoules containing precise concentrations of these substances are available, but once an ampoule is opened, the concentration of its contents changes over time. This is mainly due to evaporation. Sodium hydroxide will also react with the carbon dioxide in the air as well as with glass containers. Therefore, we need substances against which the concentrations of solutions can be checked. These substances are called **primary standards**. A primary standard must meet the following criteria:

1. It should be obtainable as a very pure solid at reasonable cost.
2. The substance should be air stable. That is, it should not react with any component in the air, such as oxygen, carbon dioxide, or water vapour.
3. The substance should be stable in solution for a reasonable length of time.
4. A substance with a high molar mass is preferred. This minimizes weighing errors.

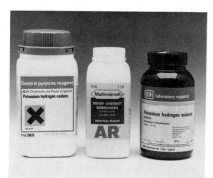

Figure 10.6

Some primary standards for acid-base titration.

Titration Curves

So far, we have used indicators to determine the equivalence point of a titration. The choice of indicator depended upon the strengths of acid and base solutions. If a pH meter is used instead of an indicator, the pH of the solution can be monitored throughout the titration and the equivalence point can be identified more precisely. To carry out this procedure, one of the solutions is placed in a beaker and a pH electrode is inserted. The other solution is placed in a burette and small measured volumes are run into the beaker. The pH and total volume added are noted with each addition. A graph of pH against volume of titrant is then plotted. This graph is called a **titration curve**. Figure 10.8 shows a typical titration curve for a strong acid with a strong base. Notice how there is an extremely rapid change in pH over a very small volume addition. The equivalence point is to be found at the midpoint of this steep part of the curve.

Figure 10.7

An automated titration apparatus.

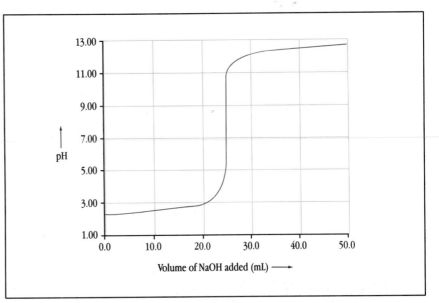

Figure 10.8

Titration curve for 25.0 mL of 0.100 mol·L⁻¹ hydrochloric acid with 0.100 mol·L⁻¹ sodium hydroxide solution.

Titration curves for weak acids or weak bases differ from those obtained when both the acid and the base are strong. Notice that the titration of hydrochloric acid with ammonia results in a curve displaced towards a lower pH (Figure 10.9). The equivalence point is in the acidic region. The titration curve of acetic acid with sodium hydroxide results in a curve displaced towards a higher pH. The equivalence point is in the basic region (Figure 10.10).

Acetic acid is about as weak an acid as ammonia is a base. When the two are titrated together, the pH around the equivalence point is close to 7. However, the shallow curve makes it very difficult to find the precise location of the equivalence point (Figure 10.11). For this reason, weak acids and weak bases should not be titrated against each other.

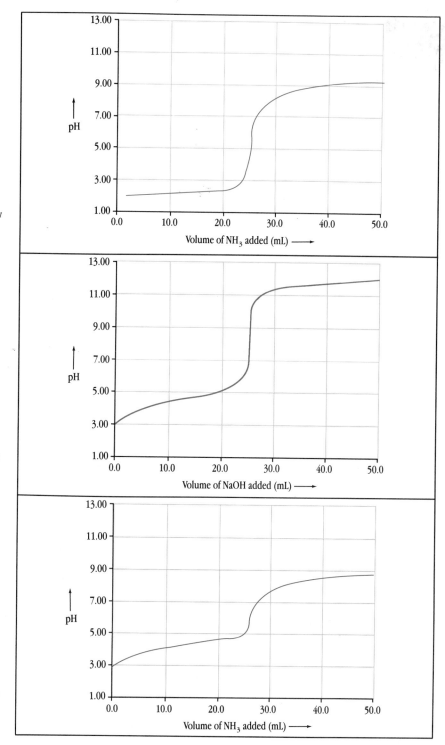

Figure 10.9

Titration curve for 25.0 mL of 0.100 mol·L⁻¹ hydrochloric acid with 0.100 mol·L⁻¹ ammonia solution.

Figure 10.10

Titration curve for 25.0 mL of 0.100 mol·L⁻¹ acetic acid with 0.100 mol·L⁻¹ sodium hydroxide solution.

Figure 10.11

Titration curve for 25.0 mL of 0.100 mol·L⁻¹ acetic acid with 0.100 mol·L⁻¹ ammonia solution.

Titration Curves and Indicators

The indicator method is still very useful when we have a large number of titrations to perform. It is inexpensive and quick (with practice). However, it is important to first identify which indicator should be used because, as we have seen, the equivalence point is not always around pH 7. When the titration involves a weak base or acid, it is advisable to do a titration curve first to identify the pH range of the steep portion of the curve. An indicator table can then be used to find an appropriate indicator which changes colour over that particular pH range.

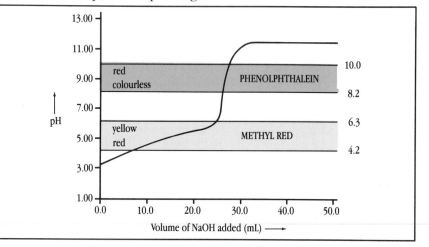

Figure 10.12

The indicator should change colour over the steep part of the curve. In the titration of acetic acid with sodium hydroxide solution, methyl red should not be used. Phenolphthalein would be a good choice.

QUESTIONS

3. The following aqueous acid solutions were titrated with a $0.150 \ mol \cdot L^{-1}$ aqueous sodium hydroxide solution. Write the overall reaction equations and calculate the concentrations of the acid solutions.
   a) 25.00 mL of hydrochloric acid requiring 16.50 mL of base solution
   b) 25.00 mL of sulfuric acid solution requiring 42.00 mL of the base solution
   c) 10.00 mL of vinegar, containing acetic acid, CH_3CO_2H, requiring 55.0 mL of the base solution

4. A sample of powdered vitamin C (ascorbic acid) tablet was suspended in water and titrated with a $0.150 \ mol \cdot L^{-1}$ aqueous solution of sodium hydroxide. A total of 21.50 mL of the base solution was required to change the colour of the indicator. How many grams of ascorbic acid, $C_6H_8O_6$, did the tablet contain assuming the presence of one acidic hydrogen atom per molecule?

5. Calcium carbonate, $CaCO_3$, is the active ingredient in "Tums." A powdered sample of the antacid, weighing 1.30 g, was treated with 100.0 mL of $0.200 \ mol \cdot L^{-1}$ hydrochloric acid. A back titration to

neutralize the excess hydrochloric acid required 52.0 mL of 0.180 mol·L^{-1} aqueous sodium hydroxide. Write the overall reaction between calcium carbonate and hydrochloric acid, and calculate the number of grams of calcium carbonate the sample contains.

6. Choose appropriate indicators from Table 9.8 for titrations involving the following acids and bases:
   a) phosphoric acid and sodium hydroxide
   b) sulfuric acid and sodium hydroxide
   c) hydrochloric acid and sodium carbonate

Ionization Constants for Acids and Bases

10.3

When we refer to acids and bases as weak or strong, we are only considering them in qualitative terms. But since we can write equilibrium reaction equations for their ionization or dissociation, we can also write the corresponding quantitative equilibrium expressions. For example, hydrofluoric acid ionizes in water as follows:

$$HF_{(aq)} + H_2O_{(\ell)} \rightleftharpoons H_3O^+_{(aq)} + F^-_{(aq)}$$

The equilibrium expression is

$$K = \frac{[H_3O^+][F^-]}{[HF][H_2O]}$$

For dilute solutions, the water will be at an almost constant concentration of 1000 g·L^{-1} (55.49 mol·L^{-1}). This value can be incorporated into the above equilibrium constant, K, to give us the **acid ionization constant**, K_a. This means that for hydrofluoric acid

$$K_a = \frac{[H_3O^+][F^-]}{[HF]}$$

Some examples of values for acid ionization constants are given in Table 10.2. The stronger the acid, the larger will be its acid ionization constant.

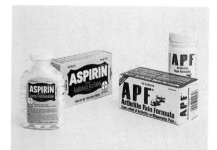

Figure 10.13
Acetylsalicylic acid (commonly called aspirin) is a weak monoprotic acid.

TABLE 10.2	Acid Ionization Constants of Some Common Monoprotic Acids at 25°C
Acid	K_a
HNO$_2$, nitrous acid	4.6×10^{-4}
HF, hydrofluoric acid	3.5×10^{-4}
CH$_3$CO$_2$H, acetic acid	1.8×10^{-5}
HClO, hypochlorous acid	3.0×10^{-8}
HCN, hydrocyanic acid	4.9×10^{-10}
NH$_4^+$, ammonium ion	5.6×10^{-10}

We can calculate the value of an acid ionization constant if we know the acid concentration and the pH of the solution. Conversely, if we know the concentration and acid ionization constant, we can calculate the expected pH of the solution.

EXAMPLE   *10.5*   Acetylsalicylic acid (aspirin) is a weak monoprotic acid, which we can abbreviate to HAsp. A 0.100 mol·L^{-1} solution of the acid has a pH of 2.24. Calculate the acid ionization constant of the acid.

SOLUTION   First we write an equilibrium equation:

$$HAsp_{(aq)} + H_2O_{(\ell)} \rightleftharpoons H_3O^+{}_{(aq)} + Asp^-{}_{(aq)}$$

This gives us the equilibrium expression

$$K_a = \frac{[H_3O^+][Asp^-]}{[HAsp]}$$

The initial acid concentration is 0.100 mol·L^{-1} and some of this must have ionized to give hydronium ion.

$$\text{Since } [H_3O^+] = \text{antilog}(-pH)$$
$$[H_3O^+] = \text{antilog}(-2.24)$$
$$= 0.0058 \text{ mol·L}^{-1}$$

We can now set up a table as we have done for other equilibrium calculations, remembering the following rule:

Equilibrium concentration = Initial concentration + Change in concentration

	[HAsp]	[H₃O⁺]	[Asp⁻]
Initial	0.100		
Change	−0.0058	+0.0058	+0.0058
Equilibrium	0.094	0.0058	0.0058

Entering these values into the equilibrium expression we get

$$K_a = \frac{(0.0058)(0.0058)}{(0.094)}$$
$$= 3.6 \times 10^{-4}$$

EXAMPLE   *10.6*   Ascorbic acid (vitamin C) is a weak monoprotic acid, which we can abbreviate to HAsc. It has an acid ionization constant of 8.0×10^{-5}. Calculate the pH of a 0.100 mol·L^{-1} solution.

SOLUTION   First we write the equilibrium equation:

$$HAsc_{(aq)} + H_2O_{(\ell)} \rightleftharpoons H_3O^+{}_{(aq)} + Asc^-{}_{(aq)}$$

The corresponding equilibrium expression is

$$K_a = \frac{[H_3O^+][Asc^-]}{[HAsc]}$$

If we let x be the hydronium ion concentration, we can set up the following table.

	[HAsc]	[H_3O^+]	[Asc^-]
Initial	0.100		
Change	$-x$	$+x$	$+x$
Equilibrium	$0.100 - x$	x	x

Entering these values into the equilibrium expression gives us

$$8.0 \times 10^{-5} = \frac{(x)(x)}{(0.100 - x)}$$

We calculate the following ratio to determine whether we can use an approximation:

$$\frac{0.100}{8.0 \times 10^{-5}} = 1.3 \times 10^3$$

Since this value is greater than 1000 (approximation rule, Chapter 7) the expression $(0.100 - x)$ can be approximated to 0.100. We can now solve for x.

$$8.0 \times 10^{-5} = \frac{(x)(x)}{0.100}$$
$$x^2 = (8.0 \times 10^{-5})(0.100) = 8.0 \times 10^{-6}$$
$$x = 2.8 \times 10^{-3}$$

Substituting the value for x into the expression $pH = \log_{10}[H_3O^+]$, we get

$$pH = -\log_{10}(2.8 \times 10^{-3}) = 2.55$$

Percent Ionization

It is difficult to determine the proportion of ionized acid simply from inspecting the value of the acid ionization constant. Instead, we use **percent ionization**, which is defined as follows:

$$\textbf{Percent ionization} = \frac{\textbf{[H}_3\textbf{O}^+\textbf{] at equilibrium}}{\textbf{Initial acid concentration}} \times \textbf{100\%}$$

The percent ionization depends upon the concentration of the solution. For example, hydrofluoric acid is only 3.5 % ionized at a concentration of 0.60 mol·L⁻¹, but 65 % ionized at a concentration of 6.0×10^{-4} mol·L⁻¹.

Polyprotic Acids

Polyprotic acids undergo stepwise ionization in water; they lose one hydrogen ion at a time. Each ionization step has its own K_a value. At each step the value of K_a decreases by several factors of 10 as shown below for phosphoric acid:

$$H_3PO_{4\,(aq)} + H_2O_{(\ell)} \rightleftharpoons H_3O^+_{\,(aq)} + H_2PO_4^-_{\,(aq)} \quad K_a = 7.5 \times 10^{-3}$$
$$H_2PO_4^-_{\,(aq)} + H_2O_{(\ell)} \rightleftharpoons H_3O^+_{\,(aq)} + HPO_4^{2-}_{\,(aq)} \quad K_a = 6.2 \times 10^{-8}$$
$$HPO_4^{2-}_{\,(aq)} + H_2O_{(\ell)} \rightleftharpoons H_3O^+_{\,(aq)} + PO_4^{3-}_{\,(aq)} \quad K_a = 2.2 \times 10^{-13}$$

Base Ionization Constants

Equilibrium expressions can also be written for bases. The constant is referred to as the **base ionization constant**, K_b. For example, ammonia dissolves in water in the reaction

$$NH_{3\,(aq)} + H_2O_{(\ell)} \rightleftharpoons NH_4^+_{\,(aq)} + OH^-_{\,(aq)}$$

and the expression for the base ionization constant, K_b, is written as

$$K_b = \frac{[NH_4^+][OH^-]}{[NH_3]}$$

TABLE 10.3	Ionization Constants of Some Common Weak Bases at 25°C	
Formula	Name	K_b
PO_4^{3-}	phosphate ion	4.5×10^{-2}
CO_3^{2-}	carbonate ion	1.8×10^{-4}
NH_3	ammonia	1.8×10^{-5}
CN^-	cyanide ion	2.0×10^{-5}
$CH_3CO_2^-$	acetate ion	5.6×10^{-10}
SO_4^{2-}	sulfate ion	8.3×10^{-13}

The larger the base ionization constant, the stronger the base. By applying the procedure used for weak acids, we can calculate the pH of a base solution.

EXAMPLE   **10.7**   Caffeine is a weak base that is related to ammonia. For the purposes of this example we can abbreviate its formula to cafN. It has a base ionization constant of 4.1×10^{-4}. Calculate the pH of a 0.70 mol·L⁻¹ solution.

SOLUTION First we write the equilibrium equation:

$$cafN_{(aq)} + H_2O_{(\ell)} \rightleftharpoons cafNH^+_{(aq)} + OH^-_{(aq)}$$

The equilibrium expression is therefore

$$K_b = \frac{[cafNH^+][OH^-]}{[cafN]}$$

The initial concentration of caffeine is $0.70 \ mol \cdot L^{-1}$ and some of this must have ionized to produce hydroxide ions. If we let the hydroxide ion concentration be x, we can set up a table as follows:

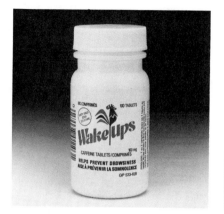

	[cafN]	[cafNH$^+$]	[OH$^-$]
Initial	0.70		
Change	$-x$	$+x$	$+x$
Equilibrium	$0.70 - x$	x	x

Figure 10.14
Caffeine is a weak base and can be found in many consumable forms.

Entering these values into the equilibrium expression gives us

$$4.1 \times 10^{-4} = \frac{(x)(x)}{(0.70 - x)}$$

We calculate the following ratio to determine if an approximation is appropriate:

$$\frac{0.70}{4.1 \times 10^{-4}} = 1.7 \times 10^3$$

Since this value is greater than 1000, the value $(0.70 - x)$ becomes 0.70, and the equilibrium expression becomes

$$4.1 \times 10^{-4} = \frac{(x)(x)}{0.70}$$

We can now solve for x.

$$x^2 = (4.1 \times 10^{-4})(0.70) = 2.9 \times 10^{-4}$$
$$x = 1.7 \times 10^{-2}$$

We can use this value of x to calculate pOH, and then find pH.

$$[OH^-] = 1.7 \times 10^{-2} \ mol \cdot L^{-1}$$
$$pOH = -\log_{10}(1.7 \times 10^{-2}) = 1.77$$
$$pH = 14.00 - 1.77 = 12.23$$

Figure 10.15

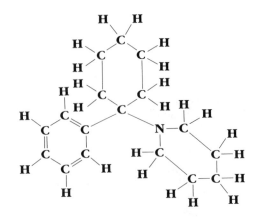

The structure of phencyclidine, a street drug commonly called 'angel dust.' Its low polarity results in it being stored in fatty tissues, where it is released slowly giving 'flashbacks.' Treatment of overdose victims with intravenous ammonium ion gives the following equilibrium which lies to the right:

$$C_{17}H_{25}N + NH_4^+ \rightleftharpoons C_{17}H_{25}NH^+ + NH_3$$

Ionization Constants of Conjugate Acid-Base Pairs

There is a simple mathematical relationship between the ionization constants of conjugate acid-base pairs. As we discussed in Section 9.7, such a pair consists of an acid and a base that differ by one hydrogen ion. Hydrofluoric acid and its conjugate base, the fluoride ion, provide a good example. For each of them, we can write an equilibrium equation and a corresponding equilibrium expression.

$$HF_{(aq)} + H_2O_{(\ell)} \rightleftharpoons H_3O^+_{(aq)} + F^-_{(aq)} \qquad K_a = \frac{[H_3O^+][F^-]}{[HF]}$$

$$F^-_{(aq)} + H_2O_{(\ell)} \rightleftharpoons HF_{(aq)} + OH^-_{(aq)} \qquad K_b = \frac{[HF][OH^-]}{[F^-]}$$

When we multiply these two expressions, we obtain a much simpler one: the ion product constant of water, K_w.

$$K_a \times K_b = \frac{[H_3O^+][F^-]}{[HF]} \times \frac{[HF][OH^-]}{[F^-]} = [H_3O^+][OH^-] = K_w$$

We can repeat this calculation with any combination of acid and conjugate base. The result is the same. Thus, for any conjugate acid-base pair

$$K_a \times K_b = K_w = 1.0 \times 10^{-14} \quad \text{at } 25\,°C$$

If we know one of the equilibrium expressions, we can determine the other. For example, the acid ionization constant of hydrofluoric acid is 3.5×10^{-4}. The base ionization constant of the fluoride ion will be given by

$$K_b = \frac{K_w}{K_a} = \frac{1.0 \times 10^{-14}}{3.5 \times 10^{-4}} = 2.9 \times 10^{-11}$$

Determining K_a and K_b from the pH of Aqueous Solutions

If we know the acid or base concentration and the pH of the solution, the corresponding ionization constant can be found by substituting the known values into the equilibrium expression. Once again, we can then make use of the relationship

$$K_w = K_a \times K_b$$

to determine the ionization constant of the conjugate acid or base.

EXAMPLE   **10.8**   A 0.100 mol · L^{-1} aqueous solution of sodium cyanide, NaCN, is found to have a pH of 11.15. From this information, calculate the K_b of the cyanide ion and the K_a of the conjugate acid, hydrocyanic acid.

SOLUTION   The sodium cyanide is completely dissociated into ions in water:

$$NaCN_{(aq)} \longrightarrow Na^+_{(aq)} + CN^-_{(aq)}$$

The cyanide ions, in turn, undergo an equilibrium reaction with water:

$$CN^-_{(aq)} + H_2O_{(\ell)} \rightleftharpoons HCN_{(aq)} + OH^-_{(aq)}$$

Since pH = 11.15

$$pOH = 14.00 - 11.15 = 2.85$$

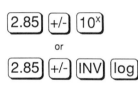

By taking the antilog of this value we can find the concentration of hydroxide ions and then arrange the data in a table.

$$[OH^-] = antilog\,(-2.85)$$
$$[OH^-] = 1.4 \times 10^{-3}$$

	$[CN^-]$	$[HCN]$	$[OH^-]$
Initial	0.100		
Change	-1.4×10^{-3}	$+1.4 \times 10^{-3}$	1.4×10^{-3}
Equilibrium	0.099	1.4×10^{-3}	1.4×10^{-3}

Substituting these values into the corresponding equilibrium expression gives

$$K_b = \frac{[HCN][OH^-]}{[CN^-]} = \frac{(1.4 \times 10^{-3})(1.4 \times 10^{-3})}{0.099}$$
$$= 2.0 \times 10^{-5}$$

We rearrange the relationship $K_a \times K_b = K_w$ to find K_a:

$$K_a = \frac{1.0 \times 10^{-14}}{2.0 \times 10^{-5}}$$
$$= 5.0 \times 10^{-10}$$

Determining K_a and K_b from pH at Half-Neutralization Point

An alternative method requires the use of a pH titration curve. For example, consider the titration of hydrofluoric acid (a weak acid) with sodium hydroxide solution.

$$HF_{(aq)} + NaOH_{(aq)} \longrightarrow NaF_{(aq)} + H_2O_{(\ell)}$$

As we discussed in Section 10.2, the equivalence point can be found by locating the total volume of base added. This is shown by the midpoint of the steep portion of the titration curve. If we divide the volume by two, this will give us the half-neutralization value. This is the point at which the concentration of fluoride ions formed equals the concentration of unreacted hydrofluoric acid. The equilibrium expression for the hydrofluoric acid is

$$K_a = \frac{[H_3O^+][F^-]}{[HF]}$$

When $[F^-] = [HF]$, the expression simplifies to

$$K_a = [H_3O^+]$$

Thus, the K_a value of the acid is equal to the hydronium ion concentration at the half-neutralization point.

Similarily the ionization constant of a weak base can be determined from the pH at the point where exactly half of the base in an aqueous solution is neutralized with a strong acid.

QUESTIONS

7. The reaction of oxalate ions, $C_2O_4{}^{2-}$, with water is an equilibrium reaction. Write the equation for the reaction and the equilibrium expression for the ionization constant. Given that the K_b of oxalate ions is 1.6×10^{-10}, calculate the value of K_a for hydrogen oxalate ions.

8. An aqueous solution containing 1.00 mol·L^{-1} boric acid (H_3BO_3) is found to have a pH of 4.57. From this information, calculate the K_a value of boric acid and the percent ionization. Consider only the first ionization step of boric acid.

9. Calculate the pH of an aqueous solution containing 0.20 mol·L^{-1} ammonia from the K_b value of 1.8×10^{-5} for ammonia. What will be the percent ionization of the ammonia in this solution?

10. At what concentration will hydrofluoric acid, HF ($K_a = 3.5 \times 10^{-4}$) be ionized in water to an extent of 50 %?

11. Using the K_a value for nitrous acid from Table 10.2, determine K_b for the basic anion, $NO_2{}^-$. Use this value to calculate the pH of a 0.15 mol·L^{-1} solution of sodium nitrite, $NaNO_2$.

12. A solution of a weak acid requires 25.40 mL of base for neutralization. After 12.70 mL of this base had been added during the titration, the pH of the solution was 4.82. Determine the K_a for the weak acid.

The Common Ion Effect

10.4

In Section 8.9 we saw that the addition of a common ion to a salt reduced the solubility of the salt. This is a specific case of Le Châtelier's principle. Let us examine the following case to see how the common ion effect applies to acid-base equilibria.

If we measure the pH of $0.10 \ mol \cdot L^{-1}$ solution of acetic acid, we will find that it is about 2.9. If we then dissolve 0.10 mol of sodium acetate in 1.0 L of this solution, the pH increases to about 4.8. The addition of the sodium acetate has reduced the concentration of hydronium ions to almost one hundredth of its former value! (Remember that the pH scale is a log scale.)

Our next step is to explain these results. The equilibrium for acetic acid in water is

$$CH_3CO_2H_{(aq)} + H_2O_{(\ell)} \rightleftharpoons H_3O^+_{(aq)} + CH_3CO_2^-_{(aq)}$$

When the sodium acetate is added, it produces sodium ions and acetate ions, which greatly increase the concentration of acetate ions.

$$NaCH_3CO_{2(s)} \xrightarrow[\text{in water}]{\text{dissolve}} Na^+_{(aq)} + CH_3CO_2^-_{(aq)}$$

According to Le Châtelier's principle, the acetic acid equilibrium will shift to the left and the concentration of hydronium ion will decrease. Thus, some of the added acetate ions have reacted with a substantial proportion of the hydronium ions to increase the concentration of undissociated acetic acid.

$$CH_3CO_2H_{(aq)} + H_2O_{(\ell)} \rightleftharpoons H_3O^+_{(aq)} + CH_3CO_2^-_{(aq)}$$

Increase in $CH_3CO_2^-$

$$CH_3CO_2H_{(aq)} + H_2O_{(\ell)} \rightleftharpoons H_3O^+_{(aq)} + CH_3CO_2^-_{(aq)}$$

Response of System

$$CH_3CO_2H_{(aq)} + H_2O_{(\ell)} \rightleftharpoons H_3O^+_{(aq)} + CH_3CO_2^-_{(aq)}$$

Figure 10.16
Addition of acetate ion causes a reduction in hydronium ion concentration.

EXAMPLE   **10.9** What will be the resulting acetate ion concentration when 0.10 mol of hydrogen chloride gas is added to 1.0 L of 0.10 mol·L⁻¹ aqueous acetic acid solution? K_a for acetic acid is 1.8×10^{-5}.

SOLUTION First, we write the balanced equation and the equilibrium expression:

$$CH_3CO_2H_{(aq)} + H_2O_{(\ell)} \rightleftharpoons H_3O^+_{(aq)} + CH_3CO_2^-_{(aq)}$$

$$K_a = \frac{[H_3O^+][CH_3CO_2^-]}{[CH_3CO_2H]}$$

Since hydrochloric acid is a strong acid, we can assume that it completely ionizes to give 0.10 mol·L⁻¹ of hydronium ions. Initially, we consider the acetic acid to be present only in molecular form because it is a weak acid. We will let the acetate ion concentration be x, and arrange the data in a table.

	$[CH_3CO_2H]$	$[H_3O^+]$	$[CH_3CO_2^-]$
Initial	0.10	0.10	
Change	$-x$	$+x$	$+x$
Equilibrium	$0.10 - x$	$0.10 + x$	x

These values can now be substituted into the equilibrium expression:

$$1.8 \times 10^{-5} = \frac{(0.10 + x)(x)}{(0.10 - x)}$$

In this common ion problem, we can use the approximation method. Hence the above equilibrium expression reduces to:

$$1.8 \times 10^{-5} = \frac{(0.10)(x)}{(0.10)}$$

$$x = 1.8 \times 10^{-5}$$

Thus $[CH_3CO_2^-] = 1.8 \times 10^{-5} \ mol·L^{-1}$

EXAMPLE   **10.10** Calculate the hydroxide ion concentration, the pH, and the percent ionization of a 1.0 mol·L⁻¹ aqueous solution of ammonia that also contains 0.10 mol·L⁻¹ of ammonium chloride. K_b of ammonia is 1.8×10^{-5}.

SOLUTION The ammonium chloride is completely dissociated producing 0.10 mol·L⁻¹ of ammonium ions:

$$NH_4Cl_{(s)} \longrightarrow NH_4^+_{(aq)} + Cl^-_{(aq)}$$

Now we can write the balanced equation and the equilibrium expression for ammonia:

$$NH_{3\,(aq)} + H_2O_{(\ell)} \rightleftharpoons NH_4^+{}_{(aq)} + OH^-{}_{(aq)}$$

$$K_b = \frac{[NH_4^+][OH^-]}{[NH_3]}$$

We let the hydroxide ion concentration be x and arrange the data in a table:

	$[NH_3]$	$[NH_4^+]$	$[OH^-]$
Initial	1.0	0.10	
Change	$-x$	$+x$	$+x$
Equilibrium	$1.0 - x$	$0.10 + x$	x

These values can now be substituted into the equilibrium expression:

$$1.8 \times 10^{-5} = \frac{(0.10 + x)(x)}{(1.0 - x)}$$

We can use the approximation method again:

$$1.8 \times 10^{-5} = \frac{(0.10)(x)}{(1.0)}$$

$$x = 1.8 \times 10^{-4}$$

Therefore $[OH^-] = 1.8 \times 10^{-4}$ mol·L^{-1}
Using this value we can calculate pH:

$$pOH = -\log_{10}[OH^-] = -\log_{10}(1.8 \times 10^{-4}) = 3.74$$
$$pH = 14.00 - 3.74 = 10.26$$

$$\text{Percent ionization of ammonia} = \frac{[OH^-] \text{ at equilibrium}}{\text{Initial base concentration}} \times 100\,\%$$

$$= \frac{1.8 \times 10^{-4} \text{ mol·L}^{-1}}{1.0 \times \text{ mol·L}^{-1}} \times 100\,\%$$

$$= 0.018\,\%$$

The presence of the ammonium ions has reduced the pH from 11.63 to 10.26, and the percent ionization of the ammonia from 0.42 % to 0.018 %.

QUESTIONS

13. Calculate the nitrite ion concentration in a 0.50 mol·L^{-1} aqueous solution of nitrous acid, HNO$_2$, if the K_a for nitrous acid is 4.6×10^{-4}. What will be the nitrite ion concentration if the solution also contains 1.0 mol·L^{-1} nitric acid?

14. Calculate the change in pH when one pellet (0.10 g) of sodium hydroxide is dissolved in 1.0 L of pure water.

15. Calculate the ammonium ion concentration in 500.0 mL of a 0.050 mol·L^{-1} aqueous solution of ammonia to which 4.0 g of sodium hydroxide has been added. K_b for ammonia is 1.8×10^{-5}.

Buffers

10.5

Many chemical reactions are only successful if the pH of the solution is carefully controlled. Biochemical reactions are especially sensitive to pH changes. Chemical substances that minimize pH changes when small amounts of acids or bases are added are called **buffers**. The word "buffer" is an adaptation of the German word "puffer" meaning pad or cushion. A buffer solution then is one that *acts as a cushion against the effect of the addition of acids or bases.* Without the presence of buffers, the pH of blood would never remain stable at 7.4 because, at near neutral pH, even a small change in the hydronium ion concentration would result in a dramatic change in pH.

We can compare the behaviour of a simple buffer with that of water. A sample of water will usually have a pH of about 5.6 due to the dissolved carbon dioxide from the atmosphere. A buffer of about the same pH can be prepared from 0.10 mol·L^{-1} acetic acid and 0.63 mol·L^{-1} of sodium acetate. The acetate ion suppresses the ionization of the acetic acid.

If we add drops of hydrochloric acid to water, the pH decreases dramatically. If the hydrochloric acid is added one drop at a time to the buffer solution, the pH decreases very slightly. However, if we continue to add acid to the buffer, a point is reached when the pH undergoes a substantial decrease. At this point, we have exceeded the buffer capacity of the solution.

How can these observations be related to the equilibrium equation for the acetic acid-acetate ion system? Since acetic acid is a weak acid, the equilibrium in the buffer solution lies to the left.

$$CH_3CO_2H_{(aq)} + H_2O_{(\ell)} \rightleftharpoons H_3O^+{}_{(aq)} + CH_3CO_2{}^-{}_{(aq)}$$

The presence of additional acetate ions from the sodium acetate will reduce the concentration of hydronium ion even more. Because hydrochloric acid is a strong acid, it will be completely ionized into hydronium ions and chloride ions. As we add the hydrochloric acid, the hydronium ions will react with some of the acetate ions to form molecular acetic acid. The reservoir of acetate ions has "soaked up" the added hydronium ions. As a consequence of this, the pH will remain fairly constant.

$$\underset{\substack{\text{acetate} \\ \text{from buffer}}}{CH_3CO_2{}^-{}_{(aq)}} + \underset{\substack{\text{added} \\ \text{acid}}}{H_3O^+{}_{(aq)}} \longrightarrow CH_3CO_2H_{(aq)} + H_2O_{(\ell)}$$

If we add sodium hydroxide to the buffer instead of acid, the hydroxide ion will react with the hydronium ion in the buffer solution to produce water.

$$OH^-_{(aq)} + H_3O^+_{(aq)} \longrightarrow 2\,H_2O_{(\ell)}$$

added base   from buffer

As the hydronium ion is used up, more of the acetic acid ionizes to replace the lost hydronium ion. Again, the pH remains almost unchanged.

$$CH_3CO_2H_{(aq)} + H_2O_{(\ell)} \rightleftharpoons H_3O^+_{(aq)} + CH_3CO_2^-_{(aq)}$$

Increase in H_3O^+

$$CH_3CO_2H_{(aq)} + H_2O_{(\ell)} \rightleftharpoons H_3O^+_{(aq)} + CH_3CO_2^-_{(aq)}$$

Response of System

$$CH_3CO_2H_{(aq)} + H_2O_{(\ell)} \rightleftharpoons H_3O^+_{(aq)} + CH_3CO_2^-_{(aq)}$$

Figure 10.17

Addition of hydronium ion to an acetic acid/acetate ion mixture causes a reaction of most of the excess hydronium ion with acetate ion. As a result there is a minimal change in pH.

The Bicarbonate Buffer

The most important buffer in the blood is the hydrogen carbonate (bicarbonate) ion. This single ion is the conjugate base of carbonic acid and the conjugate acid of the carbonate ion. It can therefore act as an acid or a base. The reaction in the presence of added acid is

$$HCO_3^-_{(aq)} + H_3O^+_{(aq)} \longrightarrow H_2CO_{3(aq)} + H_2O_{(\ell)}$$

The reaction in the presence of added base is

$$HCO_3^-_{(aq)} + OH^-_{(aq)} \longrightarrow CO_3^{2-}_{(aq)} + H_2O_{(\ell)}$$

The mole ratio of hydrogen carbonate to carbonic acid is kept close to 20:1 in blood. The pH is lowered to a value between 7.35 and 7.45 by the presence of other buffers, notably the conjugate acid-base pair, dihydrogen phosphate ($H_2PO_4^-$) and hydrogen phosphate (HPO_4^{2-}). The carbonic acid also takes part in a second equilibrium:

$$H_2CO_{3(aq)} \rightleftharpoons H_2O_{(\ell)} + CO_{2(aq)}$$

When the blood reaches the lungs, the aqueous carbon dioxide escapes into the gas phase:

$$CO_{2(aq)} \longrightarrow CO_{2(g)}$$

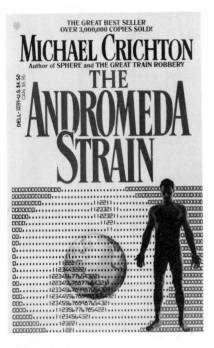

THE GREAT BEST SELLER
OVER 3,000,000 COPIES SOLD!

MICHAEL CRICHTON
Author of SPHERE and THE GREAT TRAIN ROBBERY

THE
ANDROMEDA
STRAIN

DELL · 10199 · U.S. $4.50
CAN $5.95

Figure 10.18

The plot of the science fiction book 'The Andromeda Strain' deals with abnormal blood pH.

Irregularities in breathing can cause the pH of blood to increase or decrease. For example, shallow breathing can result in a carbon dioxide level which is too high, thereby reducing the pH. When a person breathes more deeply and more rapidly than necessary (hyperventilation), he expels more carbon dioxide than usual. To restore the concentration of carbon dioxide in the blood, more carbonic acid dissociates. In turn, more hydrogen carbonate ion reacts with available hydronium ion to attempt to restore the concentration of carbonic acid. This uses up hydronium ion, and the blood pH increases. One response of the body is to constrict the blood vessels in the brain. As blood flow to the brain is reduced, the individual becomes dizzy and then unconscious. The body's reflex mechanisms then usually restore normal breathing. Hyperventilation can be stopped by re-breathing exhaled air, and a common, effective remedy is to cover the victim's face with a paper bag. The higher level of carbon dioxide in the re-inhaled air allows less to escape from the blood, and facilitates a return to normal levels of pH.

Buffer Calculations

We can predict the quantitative effect of the addition of acid or base on a buffer solution from the equilibrium constant expression for the weak acid. We could continue to use the conventional equilibrium expression for problem solving; however, there is a simpler relationship we can use when dealing with moles of solute mixtures. For example, for an acetic acid-sodium acetate buffer mixture, the acid ionization constant is given by

$$K_a = \frac{[H_3O^+][CH_3CO_2^-]}{[CH_3CO_2H]}$$

Rearranging we get:

$$[H_3O^+] = K_a \times \frac{[CH_3CO_2H]}{[CH_3CO_2^-]}$$

We must keep in mind that concentration is defined as moles of solute divided by volume of solution. Because the acetic acid and sodium acetate are present in the same solution, the concentration ratio in this expression can be replaced by a mole ratio.

$$[H_3O^+] = K_a \times \frac{\text{moles of } CH_3CO_2H}{\text{moles of } CH_3CO_2^-}$$

For buffer mixtures in general, the expression for the hydronium ion concentration becomes

$$[H_3O^+] = K_a \times \frac{n_a}{n_b}$$

where n_a is the number of moles of buffer acid,
n_b is the number of moles of buffer base.

When the number of moles of acid and base in the buffer mixture is the same, the terms cancel. Under these conditions, the hydronium ion concentration equals the acid ionization constant

$$[H_3O^+] = K_a \quad \text{when } n_a = n_b$$

EXAMPLE   *10.11*   A 1.00 L sample of an aqueous solution contains 0.200 mol acetic acid and 0.100 mol sodium acetate. Given that the K_a of acetic acid is 1.8×10^{-5}, calculate the following:
a) the pH of the solution
b) the pH of the solution after the addition of 1.00 mL of concentrated hydrochloric acid ($12.0 \text{ mol} \cdot L^{-1}$)

SOLUTION   a) We start by writing the reaction equation:

$$CH_3CO_2H_{(aq)} + H_2O_{(\ell)} \rightleftharpoons H_3O^+_{(aq)} + CH_3CO_2^-_{(aq)}$$

Since we know the initial amounts of acid and conjugate base in the buffer solution we can substitute the values in the expression

$$[H_3O^+] = K_a \times \frac{n_a}{n_b} = 1.8 \times 10^{-5} \times \frac{0.200 \text{ mol}}{0.100 \text{ mol}}$$
$$= 3.6 \times 10^{-5} \text{ mol} \cdot L^{-1}$$

We can now calculate the pH of the initial buffer solution.

$$pH = -\log_{10}[H_3O^+] = -\log_{10}(3.6 \times 10^{-5})$$
$$= 4.44$$

b) We can assume that the hydrochloric acid is completely ionized to hydronium ions and chloride ions. Therefore,

$$\text{Moles of } H_3O^+ = 0.001\,00 \text{ L} \times 12.0 \text{ mol} \cdot L^{-1}$$
$$= 0.012 \text{ mol}$$

The hydronium ions will completely react with the acetate ions to produce more acetic acid according to the following reaction:

$$H_3O^+_{(aq)} + CH_3CO_2^-_{(aq)} \longrightarrow H_2O_{(\ell)} + CH_3CO_2H_{(aq)}$$

We arrange the data in a table, only this time using moles instead of concentrations:

	n_a	n_b
Initial	0.200	0.100
Change	+0.012	−0.012
Equilibrium	0.212	0.088

We substitute the equilibrium values into the expression

$$[H_3O^+] = K_a \times \frac{n_a}{n_b}$$

$$[H_3O^+] = 1.8 \times 10^{-5} \times \frac{0.212 \text{ mol}}{0.088 \text{ mol}}$$

$$= 4.3 \times 10^{-5} \text{ mol} \cdot L^{-1}$$

We can now calculate the pH of the buffer after the HCl has been added:

$$pH = -\log_{10}[H_3O^+]$$
$$= -\log_{10}(4.3 \times 10^{-5}) = 4.37$$

The addition of this relatively large amount of hydrochloric acid decreases the pH of the buffered solution by approximately 0.07 pH units.

A large amount of strong acid added to a buffered solution will eventually use up all the base component of the buffer and the pH will rapidly decrease. Similarly, a large amount of strong base added to a buffered solution will eventually react with all the acid component of the buffer and the pH will rise sharply. *The buffer capacity of a solution is directly dependent upon the number of moles of the acid and conjugate base in the solution.*

QUESTIONS

16. Calculate the pH of the buffer solution in Example 10.11 after the addition of 0.010 mol of sodium hydroxide.

17. How many grams of sodium acetate, $NaCH_3CO_2$, must be dissolved in a 0.500 L solution of 0.50 mol·L^{-1} aqueous acetic acid, CH_3CO_2H, to obtain a buffer solution with a pH value of 5.00? K_a for acetic acid is 1.8×10^{-5}.

Lewis Acids   10.6

As the field of organic chemistry developed, it became apparent that substances could act as acids or bases even if they did not accept or donate hydrogen ions. Gilbert N. Lewis, who developed the concepts of valence electrons and covalent bonds, introduced a theory of acids and bases in 1923 that is even more general than the theory of Brønsted and Lowry. Whereas the Brønsted-Lowry theory interprets acid-base reactions as the exchange of hydrogen ions, Lewis went one step further, and interpreted these reactions in terms of whether electron pairs were given away or received. He defined an acid and a base as follows:

An acid is a molecule or ion that can accept an electron pair. A base is a molecule or ion that can donate an electron pair.

The Lewis definition of a base conforms with the Brønsted-Lowry definition. It is because of the availability of an electron pair that a base can accept a hydrogen ion. The Lewis definition of an acid as an electron-pair acceptor broadens considerably the concept of what an acid is. According to the Brønsted-Lowry theory, an acid contains hydrogen atoms. In the Lewis theory, substances that do not contain hydrogen can be considered acids as long as they have the ability to form a covalent bond by accepting an electron pair.

Normally when we use the term acid, we are referring to an acid in the Arrhenius or Brønsted-Lowry sense. The term **Lewis acid** is reserved for substances that are good electron-pair acceptors. Lewis acids are substances such as boron trifluoride, BF_3, and aluminum chloride, $AlCl_3$, in which the central boron and aluminum atoms do not have an octet of valence electrons. These atoms can accept an additional electron pair which results in the formation of a coordinate covalent bond. Boron and aluminum acquire a negative charge in these reactions. The electron pair can, for instance, be donated by ammonia or a chloride ion:

$$AlCl_3 + Cl^- \longrightarrow AlCl_4^-$$

Transition metal cations can also function as Lewis acids. We have seen that these cations form complex ions with water molecules. The formation of these and other complex ions is an example of a Lewis acid-base reaction. The cations accept electron pairs from water molecules, or other donors.

$$Cu^{2+}_{(aq)} + 6\,H_2O_{(\ell)} \longrightarrow Cu(OH_2)_6^{2+}_{(aq)}$$
$$Ag^+_{(aq)} + 2\,NH_{3\,(aq)} \longrightarrow Ag(NH_3)_2^+_{(aq)}$$

It is their ability to accept electron pairs that allow substances containing the transition metals, aluminum, antimony, and boron to perform the role of catalysts in many chemical reactions.

Carbon monoxide is a strong Lewis base. Because it is a much stronger Lewis base than the oxygen molecule, carbon monoxide bonds more strongly to the iron ions in hemoglobin than oxygen, preventing the hemoglobin from carrying oxygen around the body. Consequently, only very small concentrations of carbon monoxide are needed to bind most of our hemoglobin. Using the symbol Hb to represent the Lewis acid hemoglobin, we can write

$$Hb_{(aq)} + CO_{(g)} \longrightarrow HbCO_{(aq)}$$

Carbon monoxide reacts with nickel metal more readily than it does with other metals. In the industrial purification of nickel metal (the Mond process), carbon monoxide gas is passed over impure nickel metal. In this case, elemental nickel is acting as a Lewis acid. The product of the reaction is tetracarbonylnickel, $Ni(CO)_4$. At the temperature of the reaction (between 50 °C and 150 °C) the compound is swept off as a gas. By heating the gas to 230 °C, the compound decomposes and 99 % pure solid nickel is deposited. The carbon monoxide is then recycled.

$$Ni(CO)_{4\,(g)} \rightleftharpoons Ni_{(s)} + 4\,CO_{(g)}$$

Figure 10.19
The Inco plant in Copper Cliff, Ontario where carbon monoxide is used as a Lewis base in the purification of nickel.

QUESTIONS

18. Classify the following reactions as Lewis acid-base reactions or Brønsted-Lowry acid-base reactions. Identify the Lewis acids.

a) $H^- + H_2O \longrightarrow H_2 + OH^-$

b) $H^- + H^+ \longrightarrow H_2$

c) $HNO_2 + NH_3 \longrightarrow NH_4^+ + NO_2^-$

d) $Fe^{3+} + 6\,CN^- \longrightarrow Fe(CN)_6^{3-}$

e) $H_2O + NO_2^+ \longrightarrow H_2NO_3^+$

f) $SbF_5 + HF \longrightarrow H^+ + SbF_6^-$

Superacids

In 1927 James Conant realized that stronger acids could exist than the traditional mineral acids, such as sulfuric and hydrochloric acids. He named such acids *superacids*. However, it was not until about 1965 that detailed studies began on the chemistry of such acids. Two names have dominated the work in this field: Ronald Gillespie of McMaster University in Hamilton (also known for his work on VSEPR theory) and George Olah, at Dow Chemical Company in Sarnia, Ontario (currently at the University of Southern California). We still use Gillespie's definition of a superacid: an acid that is a stronger acid than 100 % sulfuric acid. Acids are now known that range from 10^7 to 10^{19} times stronger than pure sulfuric acid.

Figure 10.20

a) George Olah, one of the pioneers of superacids.

b) A bottle of magic acid.

There are four categories of superacid: Brønsted, Lewis, conjugate Brønsted-Lewis, and solid superacids. The only common superacid is perchloric acid, $HClO_4$. If sulfuric acid is dissolved in perchloric acid, the perchloric acid acts as a hydrogen-ion donor (Brønsted acid) and the sulfuric acid as a hydrogen-ion acceptor (Brønsted base).

$$HClO_4 + H_2SO_4 \rightleftharpoons H_3SO_4^+ + ClO_4^-$$

A Brønsted-Lewis superacid is a mixture of a powerful Lewis acid and a strong Brønsted-Lowry acid. The most potent combination is a 10 % solution of antimony pentafluoride, SbF_5, in fluorosulfonic acid, HSO_3F. Fluorosulfonic acid by itself is the strongest

Brønsted-Lowry acid that exists. It is more than one thousand times stronger than sulfuric acid. It is ideally suited as a solvent because it is a liquid over a wide temperature range (from $-89\,^\circ C$ to $+164\,^\circ C$). The addition of antimony pentafluoride increases the acidity of fluorosulfonic acid several thousand fold. The reaction between the two acids is very complex, but the super hydrogen-ion donor present in the mixture is the protonated fluorosulfonic acid ion, $H_2SO_3F^+$. The overall reaction can be represented by the following equation:

$$SbF_5 + 2\,HSO_3F \longrightarrow (H_2SO_3F)^+ + (SbF_5SO_3F)^-$$

This acid mixture will react with many substances that do not react with normal acids. It is given the name of "Magic Acid" for its ability to act as a hydrogen-ion donor to hydrocarbons (simple compounds of carbon and hydrogen). For example, propene, C_3H_6, will react to give the propyl cation:

$$C_3H_6 + H_2SO_3F^+ \longrightarrow C_3H_7^+ + HSO_3F$$

The name "Magic Acid" originated in Olah's laboratory at Case Western Reserve University in 1966. A researcher working with Olah put a small piece of Christmas candle left over from a lab party into the acid and found that it dissolved readily. He studied the solution formed and, to the amazement of the research group, found that the long-chain hydrocarbon molecules of the paraffin wax had added hydrogen ions, and that the resulting cations had rearranged themselves to form more stable branched molecules. It impressed them so much that they started to nickname the acid "Magic Acid." The name stuck, and soon others started to use it too. It is now a registered trade name and is used by all workers in the field.

Superacids have already found important applications in the synthesis of new organic compounds. In the petroleum industry, superacids similar to Magic Acid are being used to convert straight-chain hydrocarbons into more highly-branched molecules. The latter ones are more effective as fuel in the internal combustion engine and eliminate the need for lead-containing additives.

A Review of the Equilibrium Constant

10.7 In this and the three previous chapters we have introduced you to equilibrium constant and to several of its variant forms. The following are some rules to consider when working with these constants.

1. We can only consider systems that have reached equilibrium.

2. An equilibrium constant relates to a specific equation written in a particular form. Thus the equilibrium constant for

$$H_{2(g)} + Cl_{2(g)} \rightleftharpoons 2\ HCl_{(g)} \qquad K_{eq} = \frac{[HCl]^2}{[H_2][Cl_2]}$$

will be different to that for

$$\tfrac{1}{2}\ H_{2\,(g)} + \tfrac{1}{2}\ Cl_{2\,(g)} \rightleftharpoons HCl_{(g)} \qquad K_{eq} = \frac{[HCl]}{[H_2]^{\frac{1}{2}}[Cl_2]^{\frac{1}{2}}}$$

(in fact, it will be the square of the second one).

3. An equilibrium constant will change with temperature. By altering the temperature, we can increase the yield of economically important reactions.

4. When we write an equilibrium expression, we do not include any pure solid or liquid phases. For example, the equilibrium expression for the reaction:

$$2\ C_{(s)} + O_{2\,(g)} \rightleftharpoons 2\ CO_{(g)}$$

will be $\qquad K_{eq} = \dfrac{[CO]^2}{[O_2]}$

However, for an equilibrium to exist, some of the solid phase (in this case carbon) must be present.

Forms of the Equilibrium Constant

All types of the equilibrium constant work by the principles described above. However, for convenience we use specific terms for particular situations.

The solubility product constant (K_{sp}) is the equilibrium constant for the specific case of the equilibrium between an ionic solid and its ions in solution. We can use lead(II) chloride as an example:

$$PbCl_{2\,(s)} \rightleftharpoons Pb^{2+}_{(aq)} + 2\ Cl^-_{(aq)} \qquad K_{sp} = [Pb^{2+}][Cl^-]^2$$

The ion product constant for water is one of the most important relationships. It enables us to relate the concentration of hydronium ion to the concentration of hydroxide ion in a solution:

$$2\ H_2O_{(\ell)} \rightleftharpoons H_3O^+_{(aq)} + OH^-_{(aq)} \qquad K_w = [H_3O^+][OH^-]$$

At 25 °C the value of K_w is 1.0×10^{-14}. Since this is such a convenient figure, we generally do our measurements as close to this temperature as possible. We can convert the ion-product constant relationship to logarithmic form, and at 25 °C we can say that

$$\textbf{pH} + \textbf{pOH} = \textbf{14}$$

The acid ionization constant, K_a, refers to the ionization of a weak acid in solution. As an example, we can use hydrofluoric acid.

$$HF_{(aq)} + H_2O_{(\ell)} \rightleftharpoons H_3O^+{}_{(aq)} + F^-{}_{(aq)} \qquad K_a = \frac{[H_3O^+][F^-]}{[HF]}$$

If the acid can lose more than one hydrogen, we write separate ionization expressions. Aqueous hydrogen sulfide (hydrosulfurous acid) is an example:

$$H_2S_{(aq)} + H_2O_{(\ell)} \rightleftharpoons H_3O^+{}_{(aq)} + HS^-{}_{(aq)} \qquad K_a = \frac{[H_3O^+][HS^-]}{[H_2S]}$$

$$HS^-{}_{(aq)} + H_2O_{(\ell)} \rightleftharpoons H_3O^+{}_{(aq)} + S^{2-}{}_{(aq)} \qquad K_a = \frac{[H_3O^+][S^{2-}]}{[HS^-]}$$

The base ionization constant, K_b, refers to the equilibrium expression for a base. Ammonia is the only common weak base that you will encounter:

$$NH_{3\,(aq)} + H_2O_{(\ell)} \rightleftharpoons NH_4^+{}_{(aq)} + OH^-{}_{(aq)} \qquad K_b = \frac{[NH_4^+][OH^-]}{[NH_3]}$$

As you can see, all of these relationships obey the standard rules for equilibrium expressions.

Summary

- Titration is an accurate analytical technique for determining the concentration of acid or base solutions. It makes use of neutralization reactions.

- The strength of weak acids and weak bases is quantitatively expressed by the acid and base ionization constants K_a and K_b. From the value of the constants, the pH, the percent ionization in water, and the quantitative effects of common ions can be calculated.

- Aqueous solutions of salts can be acidic, basic, or neutral depending on the acidity and basicity of the cations and the anions.

- Titration curves are graphical representations of the change in pH during a titration. They clearly show the sharp change in pH at the equivalence point, the range of which determines the proper choice of indicator.

- Buffers maintain a relatively constant pH of aqueous solutions. They generally consist of a mixture of a weak acid and its conjugate base. The pH of buffers and the effect of the addition of strong acids or bases can be calculated from the K_a value of the buffer acid.

- In the Lewis theory, an acid is defined as an electron-pair acceptor and a base as an electron-pair donor. The term Lewis acid is reserved for substances that are good electron-pair acceptors, but which do not qualify as Brønsted-Lowry acids.

KEY WORDS

acid ionization constant
acid-base titration
base ionization constant
buffer
end point
equivalence point

Lewis acid
percent ionization
primary standard
titrant
titration curve

ANSWERS TO
SECTION QUESTIONS

1. a) $H_2SO_{4\,(aq)} + 2\,NaOH_{(aq)} \longrightarrow Na_2SO_{4\,(aq)} + 2\,H_2O_{(\ell)}$
   b) $2\,HCl_{(aq)} + Ca(OH)_{2\,(aq)} \longrightarrow CaCl_{2\,(aq)} + 2\,H_2O_{(\ell)}$
   c) $KHSO_{4\,(aq)} + NaOH_{(aq)} \longrightarrow KNaSO_{4\,(aq)} + H_2O_{(\ell)}$

2. a) $H_2SO_{3\,(aq)} + 2\,NaOH_{(aq)} \longrightarrow Na_2SO_{3\,(aq)} + 2\,H_2O_{(\ell)}$
   b) $H_2SO_{3\,(aq)} + 2\,OH^-_{(aq)} \longrightarrow SO_3^{2-}_{(aq)} + 2\,H_2O_{(\ell)}$

3. a) $HCl_{(aq)} + NaOH_{(aq)} \longrightarrow NaCl_{(aq)} + H_2O_{(\ell)}$, $0.0990\ mol \cdot L^{-1}$
   b) $H_2SO_{4\,(aq)} + 2\,NaOH_{(aq)} \longrightarrow Na_2SO_{4\,(aq)} + 2\,H_2O_{(\ell)}$, $0.126\ mol \cdot L^{-1}$
   c) $CH_3CO_2H_{(aq)} + NaOH_{(aq)} \longrightarrow$
   $NaCH_3CO_{2\,(aq)} + H_2O_{(\ell)}$, $0.825\ mol \cdot L^{-1}$

4. $0.568\,g$

5. $CaCO_{3\,(aq)} + 2\,HCl_{(aq)} \longrightarrow CaCl_{2\,(aq)} + CO_{2\,(g)} + H_2O_{(\ell)}$,
   $0.53\,g$ calcium carbonate per tablet

6. a) phenolphthalein
   b) phenolphthalein, bromthymol blue
   c) methyl orange, methyl red

7. $C_2O_4^{2-}_{(aq)} + H_2O_{(\ell)} \longrightarrow HC_2O_4^-_{(aq)} + OH^-_{(aq)}$,
   $$K_b = \frac{[HC_2O_4^-][OH^-]}{[C_2O_4^{2-}]},\ K_a \text{ for } HC_2O_4^- = 6.3 \times 10^{-5}$$

8. $K_a = 7.3 \times 10^{-10}$, $0.0027\,\%$ ionization

9. pH = 11.28; $0.95\,\%$ ionization

10. $7.0 \times 10^{-4}\ mol \cdot L^{-1}$

11. 2.2×10^{-11}, 8.26

12. 1.5×10^{-5}

13. 1.5×10^{-2} mol·L^{-1}; 2.3×10^{-4} mol·L^{-1}

14. pH changes from 7.00 to 11.40

15. 4.5×10^{-6} mol·L^{-1}

16. pH = 4.51

17. 37 g

18. a) and c) are Brønsted-Lowry acid-base reactions
Lewis acids: b) H$^+$ d) Fe^{3+} e) NO$_2$$^+$ f) SbF$_5$

COMPREHENSION QUESTIONS

1. Why does a neutralization reaction not result in a neutral solution when either the acid or the base is weak? How does this affect the choice of the indicator in a titration?

2. What do we mean by a primary standard in an acid-base titration?

3. Choose a suitable indicator from the ones listed in Table 9.8 for titrations between the following acids and bases:
   a) formic acid, HCO$_2$H, and sodium hydroxide
   b) hydrochloric acid and methylamine, CH$_3$NH$_2$
   c) sulfurous acid, H$_2$SO$_3$, and sodium hydroxide

4. What do the ionization constants K_a and K_b indicate? Derive expressions for K_a and K_b for the hypothetical acid and base with formulas HA and A$^-$.

5. Outline two methods for determining K_a and K_b values.

6. Use Le Châtelier's principle to explain why the ionization of nitrous acid, HNO$_2$, in aqueous solution is greatly suppressed by the addition of some nitric acid, HNO$_3$.

7. Use Le Châtelier's principle to explain how an aqueous solution containing a buffer maintains a fairly constant pH in the following situations:
   a) some strong acid is added
   b) some strong base is added

8. Discuss how the pH of blood is maintained at a value close to 7.4. How does the rate of breathing affect the pH?

9. What is a Lewis acid?

PROBLEMS *Acid-Base Titrations*

10. Calculate the pH of the solution obtained when
   a) 50.00 mL of 0.150 mol·L^{-1} hydrochloric acid is added to 75.0 mL of a 0.111 mol·L^{-1} aqueous sodium hydroxide solution
   b) 25.00 mL of a 0.200 mol·L^{-1} aqueous sodium hydroxide solution is added to 20.00 mL of 0.300 mol·L^{-1} hydrochloric acid

11. The following aqueous acid solutions were all titrated with a $0.180 \text{ mol} \cdot \text{L}^{-1}$ sodium hydroxide solution. In each case write the overall reaction equation for the neutralization reaction and calculate the concentration of the acid solution.
    a) 25.00 mL of formic acid, HCO_2H (with one acidic hydrogen per molecule) requiring 37.50 mL of the base solution
    b) 10.00 mL of a sodium dihydrogen phosphate, NaH_2PO_4, solution requiring 25.00 mL of the base solution
    c) 25.00 mL of a phosphoric acid solution requiring 62.00 mL of the base solution

12. The following aqueous base solutions were all titrated with a $0.126 \text{ mol} \cdot \text{L}^{-1}$ hydrochloric acid solution. Write the overall reaction equation for the neutralization reactions and calculate the concentration of the base solutions.
    a) 10.00 mL of an ammonia solution requiring 22.50 mL of the acid solution
    b) 10.00 mL of a diaminoethane, $H_2NCH_2CH_2NH_2$ requiring 36.00 mL of the acid solution
    c) 25.00 mL of a sodium carbonate, Na_2CO_3, solution requiring 45.50 mL of the acid solution

13. An acetylsalicylic acid (ASA, or "aspirin") tablet with a mass of 0.36 g was powdered, suspended in water, and titrated with 10.80 mL of $0.150 \text{ mol} \cdot \text{L}^{-1}$ aqueous sodium hydroxide. How much ASA does the tablet contain? Acetylsalicylic acid has the formula $C_9H_8O_4$ and contains one acidic hydrogen per molecule.

14. An aqueous solution containing 0.840 g of impure sodium hydrogen carbonate, $NaHCO_3$ (baking power), requires 47.00 mL of $0.200 \text{ mol} \cdot \text{L}^{-1}$ hydrochloric acid for neutralization. Write the overall reaction equation and calculate the percent purity of the sodium hydrogen carbonate.

15. An aqueous solution containing 1.06 g of soda, Na_2CO_3, requires 92.0 mL of $0.200 \text{ mol} \cdot \text{L}^{-1}$ hydrochloric acid for neutralization. Write the overall reaction equation and calculate the percent purity of the soda.

Ionization Constants for Acids and Bases

16. A $0.200 \text{ mol} \cdot \text{L}^{-1}$ aqueous solution of the base pyridine, C_5H_5N, has a pH of 9.25. Write the reaction equation between pyridine and water, and calculate the following:
    a) hydroxide ion concentration of the solution
    b) K_b of pyridine
    c) percent ionization of pyridine
    d) K_a of pyridinium ions, $C_5H_6N^+$

17. The hydronium ion concentration of a 0.100 mol·L^{-1} aqueous solution of butanoic acid is 1.24×10^{-3}. Calculate the K_a of butanoic acid.

18. The pH of a 0.16 mol·L^{-1} aqueous solution of benzoic acid is 2.50. Calculate the K_a of benzoic acid.

19. The pH of a 0.10 mol·L^{-1} bromoacetic solution in water is 1.96. Calculate the K_a value of bromoacetic acid and the percent ionization of this solution.

20. The pH of the solution obtained by reacting 50.00 mL of 0.200 mol·L^{-1} aqueous iodoacetic acid with 25.00 mL of 0.200 mol·L^{-1} aqueous sodium hydroxide is 2.10. Calculate the K_a of iodoacetic acid.

21. What will be the pH of the following aqueous acid solutions?
    a) 100.0 mL of solution containing 0.146 g HCl
    b) 500.0 mL of solution containing 1.20 g of acetic acid, CH_3CO_2H; $K_a = 1.8 \times 10^{-5}$
    c) 500.0 mL of solution containing 0.063 g nitric acid, HNO_3
    d) 100.0 mL of solution containing 1.76 g ascorbic acid (vitamin C: $C_6H_8O_6$); $K_a = 7.9 \times 10^{-5}$

22. Write equations for the reaction with water, and calculate the pH and percent ionization of the following solutions of weak acids. For the acids with more than one acidic hydrogen, consider only the first ionization step.
    a) 0.10 mol·L^{-1} carbonic acid, H_2CO_3; $K_a = 4.3 \times 10^{-7}$
    b) 0.10 mol·L^{-1} hydrogen sulfide, H_2S; $K_a = 9.1 \times 10^{-8}$
    c) 0.40 mol·L^{-1} sodium dihydrogen phosphate NaH_2PO_4; $K_a = 6.2 \times 10^{-8}$
    d) 1.5 mol·L^{-1} chloroacetic acid, $ClCH_2CO_2H$; $K_a = 1.4 \times 10^{-3}$

23. Write the equation for the reaction with water, and calculate the pH and the percent ionization for each of the following solutions of weak bases:
    a) 0.50 mol·L^{-1} sodium acetate, $NaCH_3CO_2$; $K_b = 5.6 \times 10^{-10}$
    b) 0.020 mol·L^{-1} calcium hypochlorite, $Ca(ClO)_2$; $K_b = 3.3 \times 10^{-7}$
    c) 100.0 mL of solution containing 1.68 g sodium hydrogen carbonate, $NaHCO_3$; $K_b = 2.3 \times 10^{-8}$
    d) 200.0 mL of solution containing 6.30 g sodium sulfite, Na_2SO_3; $K_b = 1.0 \times 10^{-7}$

The Common Ion Effect

24. Calculate the percent ionization of a 0.20 mol·L^{-1} aqueous solution of formic acid, HCO_2H ($K_a = 1.8 \times 10^{-4}$) under the following conditions:
    a) in the absence of a common ion
    b) in the presence of 1.0 mol·L^{-1} sodium formate, HCO_2Na

25. Calculate the ammonium ion concentration in an aqueous solution that is $0.50 \text{ mol} \cdot \text{L}^{-1}$ in ammonia ($K_b = 1.8 \times 10^{-5}$) and $0.20 \text{ mol} \cdot \text{L}^{-1}$ in potassium hydroxide, KOH.

Buffers

26. A 500.0 mL solution of an aqueous buffer solution contains 0.20 mol formic acid, HCO_2H, and 0.30 mol sodium formate, HCO_2Na. Calculate the following:
    a) pH of this solution
    b) pH of the solution after 10 drops (0.50 mL) of $12 \text{ mol} \cdot \text{L}^{-1}$ hydrochloric acid are added
    c) pH of the solution after 0.50 g sodium hydroxide is added

27. Calculate the pH of the following aqueous buffer solutions:
    a) a solution containing $0.10 \text{ mol} \cdot \text{L}^{-1}$ ammonium chloride, NH_4Cl, and $0.050 \text{ mol} \cdot \text{L}^{-1}$ ammonia, NH_3 (K_b for ammonia is 1.8×10^{-5})
    b) a solution containing $0.10 \text{ mol} \cdot \text{L}^{-1}$ carbonic acid and $0.020 \text{ mol} \cdot \text{L}^{-1}$ sodium hydrogen carbonate, $NaHCO_3$ (K_a for carbonic acid is 4.3×10^{-7})
    c) a solution containing $0.50 \text{ mol} \cdot \text{L}^{-1}$ of ascorbic acid, $C_6H_8O_6$, and $0.20 \text{ mol} \cdot \text{L}^{-1}$ sodium ascorbate, $C_6H_7O_6Na$ (K_a for ascorbic acid is 7.9×10^{-5})

28. Calculate the pH of the buffer solutions made by mixing the following solutions:
    a) 200.0 mL of $0.10 \text{ mol} \cdot \text{L}^{-1}$ acetic acid, CH_3CO_2H and 400.0 mL of $0.10 \text{ mol} \cdot \text{L}^{-1}$ sodium acetate, $NaCH_3CO_2$ (K_a for acetic acid is 1.8×10^{-5})
    b) 200.0 mL of $0.10 \text{ mol} \cdot \text{L}^{-1}$ ammonia and 200.0 mL of $0.25 \text{ mol} \cdot \text{L}^{-1}$ ammonium chloride, NH_4Cl. (K_b for ammonia is 1.8×10^{-5})
    c) 200.0 mL of $0.10 \text{ mol} \cdot \text{L}^{-1}$ acetic acid and 300.0 mL of $0.20 \text{ mol} \cdot \text{L}^{-1}$ sodium acetate

29. How much sodium hydrogen phosphate, Na_2HPO_4, does one have to dissolve in 1.0 L of an aqueous solution containing 100 g of sodium dihydrogen phosphate, NaH_2PO_4 ($K_a = 6.2 \times 10^{-8}$), to obtain a concentrated buffer solution with a pH of 7.00?

30. Calculate the pH of a solution obtained when 30.00 mL of a $0.100 \text{ mol} \cdot \text{L}^{-1}$ hydrochloric acid solution is added to 50.00 mL of a $0.100 \text{ mol} \cdot \text{L}^{-1}$ aqueous ammonia solution, $NH_{3(aq)}$ (K_b for ammonia is 1.8×10^{-5}).

Lewis Acids

31. Classify the reactions as either Brønsted-Lowry acid-base reactions or Lewis acid-base reactions. Identify the Lewis acids.
    a) $Cr^{3+} + 6 H_2O \longrightarrow Cr(H_2O)_6^{3+}$
    b) $CH_2O + HCl \longrightarrow CH_3O^+ + Cl^-$

c) $BF_3 + HF \longrightarrow H^+ + BF_4^-$

d) $Br_2 + FeBr_3 \longrightarrow Br^+ + FeBr_4^-$

e) $NH_3 + H^- \longrightarrow NH_2^- + H_2$

f) $HNO_3 + H_2SO_4 \longrightarrow H_2NO_3^+ + HSO_4^-$

32. Eyewash solution often contains boric acid, H_3BO_3, whose structure might better be written as $B(OH)_3$. The reaction with water is

$$B(OH)_{3\,(aq)} + H_2O_{(\ell)} \rightleftharpoons B(OH)_4^-{}_{(aq)} + H^+{}_{(aq)}$$

Is boric acid a Brønsted acid or a Lewis acid?

MISCELLANEOUS PROBLEMS

33. An aqueous buffer solution contains 0.20 mol sodium dihydrogen phosphate, NaH_2PO_4, and 0.20 mol sodium hydrogen phosphate, Na_2HPO_4. The K_a for dihydrogen phospate ion is 6.2×10^{-8}. Calculate the following:

a) pH of the buffered solution

b) pH of the solution after 2.0 g hydrogen chloride has been added

c) pH of the solution after 2.0 g sodium hydroxide has been added

34. An aqueous solution containing 0.302 g of an acid with three acidic hydrogens per molecule requires 39.30 mL of a 0.120 mol·L⁻¹ sodium hydroxide solution for neutralization. Calculate the molecular mass of the acid.

35. Calculate the hydroxide ion concentration and the pH of a 0.10 mol·L⁻¹ aqueous solution of sodium phosphate, Na_3PO_4. The K_b of phosphate ion is 4.5×10^{-2}. (To obtain the answer you will have to use the quadratic formula.)

36. Calculate the pH of the following salt solutions:

a) 1.0 mol·L⁻¹ sodium hydrogen carbonate in water
   (*Hint:* use K_b since $K_b > K_a$)

b) 1.0 mol·L⁻¹ potassium hydrogen sulfate in water
   (*Hint:* use K_a since $K_a > K_b$)
   K_a values: H_2CO_3, 4.3×10^{-7}
   $\qquad\qquad\quad HCO_3^-$, 5.6×10^{-11}
   $\qquad\qquad\quad HSO_4^-$, 1.2×10^{-2}

(To obtain answers you may have to use the quadratic formula.)

37. The pH of water is lowered by carbon dioxide and as a result most natural waters are slightly acidic. What will be the pH of an aqueous solution of carbon dioxide containing 10 ppm carbon dioxide (e.g. 10^6 g water contains 10 g carbon dioxide)? Assume that all carbon dioxide is converted to carbonic acid. (K_b for carbonic acid is 4.3×10^{-7})

38. The following data (in the following table) was obtained using a pH meter during the titration of 25.00 mL of 0.100 mol·L⁻¹ acetic acid with a sodium hydroxide solution of approximately 0.1 mol·L⁻¹.

Volume of NaOH added (mL)	pH of solution
0.00	3.10
2.00	3.71
4.00	4.01
6.00	4.24
8.00	4.42
10.00	4.59
12.00	4.75
14.00	4.89
16.00	5.08
18.00	5.28
20.0	5.60
21.0	5.89
22.0	6.40
22.2	6.71
22.4	7.41
22.5	9.50
22.6	9.85
22.8	10.30
23.0	10.59
23.5	10.90
24.0	11.03
26.0	11.38
28.0	11.51

Construct a graph of pH against added volume of the sodium hydroxide solution and determine the following:

a) the precise volume of base necessary to neutralize the acid, and calculate the exact concentration of the sodium hydroxide solution

b) determine the pH at the half-neutralization point and hence K_a for acetic acid

39. A 100.0 mL solution of 0.100 mol·L^{-1} hypochlorous acid, $HClO_{(aq)}$, was titrated against 0.100 mol·L^{-1} sodium hydroxide solution. Calculate the pH of the solution after each of the following additions of the base:

a) zero base added

b) a total of 5.00 mL of base added

c) a total of 25.00 mL of base added

d) a total of 50.00 mL of base added

e) a total of 75.00 mL of base added

f) a total of 95.00 mL of base added

g) a total of 100.00 mL of base added

h) a total of 105.00 mL of base added

Using this calculated data, sketch a titration curve of pH against added NaOH solution for this neutralization. (K_a for HClO is 3.0×10^{-8})

40. A 100.0 mL solution of 0.100 $mol \cdot L^{-1}$ aqueous ammonia, NH_3, was titrated against 0.100 $mol \cdot L^{-1}$ hydrochloric acid. Calculate the pH of the solution after each of the following additions of the acid.

a) zero acid added

b) a total of 5.00 mL of acid added

c) a total of 25.00 mL of acid added

d) a total of 50.00 mL of acid added

e) a total of 75.00 mL of acid added

f) a total of 95.00 mL of acid added

g) a total of 100.00 mL of acid added

h) a total of 105.00 mL of acid added

Using this calculated data, sketch a titration curve of pH against added HCl solution for this neutralization. (K_b for NH_3 is 1.8×10^{-5})

SUGGESTED PROJECTS

1. Research and find the chemical structures of common indicators. How do the structures differ in their acid and base forms?

2. Write a report on the types of biochemically important buffer systems.

3. As well as acid-base titrations, we can perform precipitation titrations. The most common of these is the silver ion-chloride ion titration, using chromate ion as an indicator. Read more on this method and explain how it works. If possible arrange with your instructor to perform such a titration.

CHAPTER 11

Oxidation and Reduction

Few chemical processes affect us more than those involving the transfer of electrons from one substance to another. These reactions are called oxidation-reduction, or redox reactions. Most forms of life can only be sustained through the energy produced by the oxidation of carbohydrates to water and carbon dioxide. All combustion and corrosion processes are examples of redox reactions. The chemical industry utilizes redox processes to produce metals and nonmetals, and in the home we benefit from redox reactions whenever we use oxidizers such as bleaches.

A Simple Redox Experiment

11.1

Many reactions that we carry out in the laboratory are redox reactions. To find out what actually happens to the reactants, let us look at the following experiment.

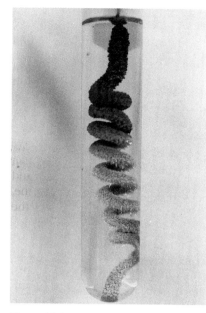

Figure 11.1

A copper wire reacts with an aqueous solution of silver nitrate. Metallic silver and blue copper(II) nitrate are formed.

When a copper wire is placed in an aqueous solution of silver nitrate, a spectacular reaction results. Within minutes a large number of shiny metallic crystals forms on the wire, and the solution turns pale blue. When we shake off the crystals, we observe that much of the copper wire has disappeared. The crystals are silver crystals and the blue colour of the solution indicates the presence of hydrated copper ions. Copper metal has displaced silver from its salt.

$$Cu_{(s)} + 2\,AgNO_{3\,(aq)} \longrightarrow Cu(NO_3)_{2\,(aq)} + 2\,Ag_{(s)}$$

When we omit the nitrate spectator ions from this equation, we obtain the following net ionic equation:

$$Cu_{(s)} + 2\,Ag^+_{(aq)} \longrightarrow Cu^{2+}_{(aq)} + 2\,Ag_{(s)}$$

Copper atoms in the wire each lose two electrons and go into solution as hydrated copper ions. The electrons are transferred to hydrated silver ions, which crystallize as metallic silver.

Any reaction in which electrons are lost is called an **oxidation** reaction. A reaction that involves the gain of electrons is called a **reduction** reaction. In the copper-silver nitrate reaction, the copper metal is oxidized to copper ions and the silver ions are reduced to silver metal. Because oxidation and reduction reactions always take place concurrently, we refer to these reactions as **redox reactions**.

Electronegativity and Oxidation Numbers *11.2*

Figure 11.2

Our energy, which is most evident in sport activities, comes from the oxidation of carbohydrates to carbon dioxide and water.

Electronegativity was introduced in Section 2.2 as a measure of the ability of bonded atoms to attract electrons that are shared with other atoms. Electronegativity varies with position in the Periodic Table. The values increase from left to right across a period and decrease from top to bottom in a group.

Metals have relatively low electronegativities and tend to lose electrons to other atoms. The lowest electronegativity values are found among the alkali metals (Group IA). Atoms of these elements lose electrons easily and thus can be said to oxidize readily. Gold, on the other hand, has the highest electronegativity of any metal. It is the least reactive metal and is very difficult to oxidize.

Nonmetals have high electronegativities. Atoms of these elements accept electrons readily. Elements such as chlorine, oxygen, and fluorine are therefore easily reduced.

The transfer of electrons in a redox reaction can be complete or nearly complete. This is the case in the formation of ionic compounds. In the formation of molecular compounds, however, the transfer of electrons is incomplete.

We can keep track of the electrons being transferred by assigning oxidation numbers to the various atoms. The **oxidation number** tells us how many electrons an atom in a compound would gain or lose. In assigning oxidation numbers we assume that the electrons of each bond are transferred to the more electronegative atom in the bond. A positive oxidation number indicates a loss of electrons and a negative number indicates a gain of electrons.

Oxidation Numbers of Elements

The oxidation number of an atom in its pure form, as an element, *is zero*. This is not very surprising since electrons in an element have neither been lost or gained by the atoms. Electrons may be shared in both metals and nonmetals, but all the atoms receive an equal share. The element fluorine, for example, consists of diatomic molecules that can be represented by the following electron-dot formula:

$$\ddot{:}\!F\!\!:\!\!\ddot{F}\!\!:$$

The bonding electron pair is attracted equally by the two fluorine atoms. The result is that each of the fluorine atoms has exactly the same net number of valence electrons as a single fluorine atom. Therefore the oxidation number of each atom is zero.

Diamond is an allotrope of carbon. Each carbon atom in diamond is covalently bonded to four other carbon atoms. But the bonding electron pairs are shared equally, and we can assign an oxidation number of zero to each carbon atom.

Oxidation Numbers of Ions

The oxidation number of a monatomic ion *is equal to the charge on the ion*, since the charge indicates the number of electrons lost or gained. In a positive ion, electrons have been lost and the positive charge tells us how many electrons have been lost. Similarly, the charge on a negative ion indicates how many electrons have been gained.

The alkali metals (Group IA) always have an oxidation number of $+1$ in compounds and the alkaline earth metals (Group IIA) always have a value of $+2$. Aluminum and most of the other metals in Group IIIA have an oxidation number of $+3$ in their compounds.

The oxidation number of the nonmetal in a binary ionic compound (consisting of one metal and one nonmetal) follows from its position in the Periodic Table. The Group VIIA elements all have values of -1 and the Group VIA elements have values of -2.

EXAMPLE   *11.1*   What are the oxidation numbers of each element in calcium chloride, $CaCl_2$?

   SOLUTION   Calcium chloride consists of Ca^{2+} and Cl^- ions. The oxidation number of the calcium is therefore $+2$, and for each of the chlorine ions the value is -1.

Because the total charge in ionic compounds is zero, the sum of the oxidation numbers of the atoms that make up the compound will also be zero. The following example illustrates how we can make use of this rule.

EXAMPLE   *11.2*   What are the oxidation numbers of iron in the two iron oxides, FeO and Fe_2O_3? Assume that oxygen has an oxidation number of -2 in each case.

SOLUTION   The sum of the oxidation numbers in each compound will be zero. Therefore, in FeO, the oxidation number of iron will be $+2$ because $(+2) + (-2) = 0$. In Fe_2O_3, the iron has an oxidation number of $+3$ because $2 \times (+3) + 3 \times (-2) = 0$.

Oxidation Numbers of Atoms with Covalent Bonds

Usually the electrons in a covalent bond between *two different atoms* are not shared equally. The unequal sharing gives rise to a polar covalent bond. To assign oxidation numbers to covalently-bonded atoms, we draw the electron-dot formula of the molecule and refer to the electronegativity values of the elements involved. Although the transfer of electrons is by no means complete, for the purpose of assigning oxidation numbers we assume that it is complete and *unequally shared electrons are counted with the more electronegative atom.*

The hydrogen chloride molecule will serve as an example. This molecule has the following electron-dot formula

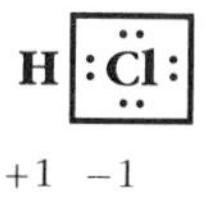

$$+1 \quad -1$$

The electronegativity values of hydrogen and chlorine are 2.1 and 3.0 respectively. As shown by the position of the box in the electron-dot formula, the difference in electronegativity means that the chlorine atom attracts the shared electron pair more strongly than the hydrogen atom. For the purpose of assigning oxidation numbers, we count the shared electron pair with the chlorine. Thus in hydrogen chloride the oxidation number of chlorine is -1 and the oxidation number of hydrogen is $+1$. The chlorine atom "gains" one electron, giving it an oxidation number of -1. The hydrogen atom "loses" one electron giving it an oxidation number of $+1$ in hydrogen chloride.

In the water molecule, oxygen shares two electron pairs unequally with two hydrogen atoms. The electronegativity value of oxygen is 3.5, which means it attracts electrons more strongly than hydrogen does. Therefore, the electrons are counted with the oxygen atom.

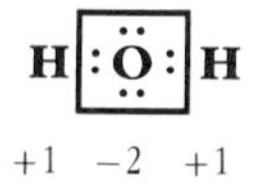

$$+1 \quad -2 \quad +1$$

Figure 11.3

Electronegativities for the main group elements and two of the noble gases.

The oxygen in water has an oxidation number of -2 and each of the two hydrogens has an oxidation number of $+1$.

EXAMPLE   *11.3*   What are the oxidation numbers of oxygen and fluorine in oxygen difluoride, OF_2?

SOLUTION   We obtain the electronegativity values of oxygen and fluorine from Figure 11.4. The values, which are 3.5 and 4.0 respectively, indicate that fluorine atoms attract a shared electron pair more strongly than oxygen. The electron-dot formula for oxygen difluoride can then be written as

The shared electron pairs are counted with the fluorine atoms. Each of the fluorine atoms has an oxidation number of -1 and the oxygen atom has an oxidation number of $+2$.

Oxygen difluoride is the only substance in which oxygen has an oxidation number of $+2$. In all other compounds, oxygen is the more electronegative atom and its oxidation number is usually -2. In molecules that contain an oxygen-oxygen bond, such as the peroxides, an electron pair is shared equally between the two oxygen atoms and, for the purpose of assigning oxidation numbers, we divide this pair between the two oxygens. For example, in hydrogen peroxide the oxidation number of each hydrogen atom is $+1$ and that of each oxygen atom is -1.

Figure 11.4

In water, the oxygen atoms have an oxidation number of -2, but in hydrogen peroxide they have an oxidation number of -1.

In most of its compounds, hydrogen has the lowest electronegativity value and an oxidation number of $+1$. But in metal hydrides, such as sodium hydride, NaH, the hydrogen is bonded to a less electronegative metal and has an oxidation number of -1.

Carbon dioxide represents a situation in which carbon shares two pairs of electrons with each of the two oxygens. The molecule contains two covalent double bonds. Since oxygen is more electronegative than carbon (3.5 versus 2.5) the electron pairs are counted with the oxygen atoms. Because each oxygen gains two electrons, oxygen is assigned an oxidation number of -2. The carbon atom has partially lost all its four valence electrons and therefore has an oxidation number of $+4$.

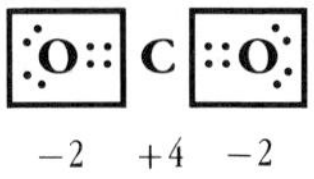

$$\boxed{:\ddot{O}::}\ C\ \boxed{::\ddot{O}:}$$
$$\quad -2 \qquad +4 \quad -2$$

Some chemists prefer the term **oxidation state** to oxidation number. The words may be used interchangeably. We could say that the oxidation states of carbon and oxygen in carbon dioxide are $+4$ and -2 respectively.

EXAMPLE   *11.4*   What is the oxidation number of carbon in each of the following compounds:
a) ethane, C_2H_6 b) ethyne, C_2H_2

SOLUTION   Since the electronegativity values for carbon and hydrogen are 2.5 and 2.1 respectively, the shared electrons between these elements will be more attracted to the carbon atoms. Electron pairs between carbon atoms will be shared equally. We can now draw the following diagrams and assign oxidation numbers.

a) ethane

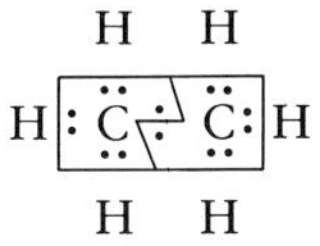

$$\begin{array}{cc} H & H \\ H:\ddot{C} \overset{\cdot}{\cdot} \ddot{C}:H \\ H & H \end{array}$$

Since the electrons from the hydrogen atoms are counted with carbon, each carbon atom gains 3 electrons. Carbon, therefore, has an oxidation number of -3 and hydrogen has an oxidation number of $+1$.

b) ethyne

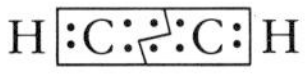

$$H:C:\overset{\cdot}{\cdot}:C:H$$

The electrons from the hydrogen atoms are counted with the carbon atoms. For the purpose of assigning oxidation numbers, each carbon has gained an electron and hence has an oxidation number of -1. Hydrogen has an oxidation number of $+1$. We can check the above answers by seeing if the sum of the oxidation numbers in each compound is zero.

$$\text{ethane:} \quad 6(+1) + 2(-3) = 0$$
$$\text{ethyne:} \quad 2(+1) + 2(-1) = 0$$

Oxidation Numbers of Atoms in Polyatomic Ions or Molecules

We can use the above method to assign oxidation numbers to molecules and ions that contain three or more different elements.

After constructing the electron-dot diagram for hydrogen cyanide, HCN, we simply assign the shared electrons in each bond to the more electronegative atom.

$$+1 \quad +2 \quad -3$$

Thus the hydrogen atom will have an oxidation number of +1 because it loses its electron to the more electronegative carbon atom. The nitrogen atom has an oxidation number of −3 because it gains three electrons from carbon. Since the carbon atom gains one electron but loses three, it is assigned an oxidation number of +2. Note that the sum of the oxidation numbers is zero.

When an ion or molecule contains two or more atoms of the same element, the oxidation numbers of these atoms are not necessarily the same. The two sulfur atoms in the thiosulfate ion, $S_2O_3^{2-}$, provide such an example. We know from the chemical reactions involving this ion that the two sulfur atoms behave very differently. The ion itself has an electron-dot structure related to that of the sulfate ion:

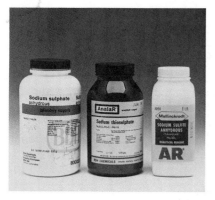

Figure 11.5

The sulfate, thiosulfate, and sulfite ions contain sulfur atoms in different oxidation states. In sulfate, it is +6, in sulfite it is +4, and in thiosulfate the central sulfur has an oxidation number of +5 and the other one an oxidation number of -1.

Since oxygen is more electronegative than sulfur, the shared electrons are counted with the oxygens. As a consequence, each oxygen gains two electrons and has an oxidation number of −2. Splitting the bonding electron pair equally between the two sulfur atoms gives the central sulfur an oxidation number of +5, and the other an oxidation number of −1. These very different values are consistent with the known chemistry of the ion.

EXAMPLE **11.5** What are the oxidation numbers of the elements in the fluorosulfate ion, FSO_3^-?

SOLUTION Because sulfur has the lowest electronegativity, it is the central atom and the bonding electrons are counted with the fluorine and the oxygen.

The oxidation numbers of fluorine, sulfur, and oxygen are −1, +6, and −2 respectively.

QUESTIONS

1. What are the oxidation numbers for each element in the following ionic compounds:
   a) $SnCl_4$ b) Ca_3P_2 c) SnO d) Ag_2S

2. Draw an electron-dot formula for each of the following compounds or ions. Then assign oxidation numbers to the atoms involved.
   a) hydrogen iodide, HI
   b) hydrazine, N_2H_4
   c) propane, C_3H_8
   d) chlorate ion, ClO_3^-
   e) sulfate ion, SO_4^{2-}

Oxidation Numbers and the Periodic Table

11.3

Many elements, especially the nonmetals, can have several different oxidation numbers (Figure 11.6). However, the oxidation number of an element never exceeds the group number of the element. This observation has a very logical explanation. The oxidation number indicates how many electrons are given up, either completely or partially. The number of valence electrons of an element is the same as the group number, and this is also the maximum number of electrons that an atom of the element can give up.

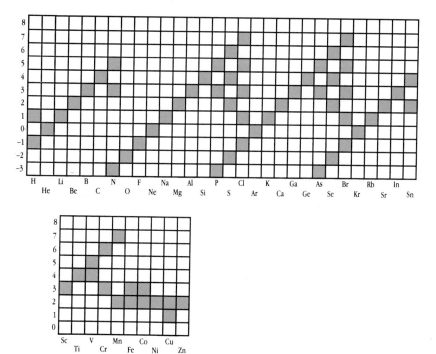

Figure 11.6

The common oxidation numbers of the first thirty main group elements.

Figure 11.7

There are also patterns in the oxidation numbers for the first row of the transition metals.

The table below shows a series of chlorine-containing molecules having oxidation numbers ranging from -1 to $+7$. As more oxygen atoms are combined with the chlorine atom, more of the chlorine's outer electrons are assigned to the oxygen atoms and the oxidation number of chlorine increases.

TABLE 11.1   *Oxidation Numbers of Chlorine*

Substance	Electron-dot Formula	Oxidation Number of Chlorine
Chloride ion		-1
Chlorine		0
Hypochlorite ion		$+1$
Chlorite ion		$+3$
Chlorate ion		$+5$
Perchlorate ion		$+7$

QUESTIONS

3. What are the formulas of the oxides of nitrogen in which nitrogen has oxidation numbers of $+1$, $+2$, $+3$, $+4$, and $+5$?

4. Which of the following fluorine compounds are unlikely to exist: BaF_2, AlF, NaF, $NaFO_2$, OF_2?

Finding a New Route to Ammonia

Plants require compounds containing nitrogen to grow and reproduce. Bacteria on the roots of plants in the legume family convert nitrogen gas to ammonia. In the process the oxidation number of the element nitrogen changes from zero in gaseous nitrogen to -3 in ammonia. The bacteria accomplish this at a normal range of temperature and pressure. The industrial synthesis of ammonia, on the other hand, requires expensive equipment and high temperatures and pressures. One of the goals of inorganic chemistry has been to find a simple aqueous synthesis of ammonia that can be performed in the laboratory.

One of the first steps toward the above-mentioned goal was to prepare a compound that contained the dinitrogen, N_2, unit. The bonding of nitrogen would result in a change in oxidation number of the element and hopefully make the resulting atoms easier to reduce to ammonia. The key discovery was made at the Lash Miller Laboratories of the University of Toronto. In the early spring of 1965, C.V. Senoff was trying to finish his Ph.D. thesis. He had been working on compounds of ruthenium, and a particular pale yellow compound defied all attempts at identification. Finally, Senoff became convinced that the only way to explain the data was to assume that the dinitrogen unit was bonded to the ruthenium. His supervisor, A.D. Allen, slowly convinced himself of the same conclusion.

With much apprehension, they submitted a report to *Chemical Communications*, a journal for the rapid publication of important findings. The report was rejected outright by the two referees. Allen was teaching a course in advanced inorganic chemistry at the time. He presented the data to the class and offered a grade of 100 % to any student who could come up with an alternative explanation of the data. None was forthcoming. They similarly challenged the referees of the journal to propose another explanation. The editor consulted several internationally known inorganic chemists for their opinion. At least one of these chemists is believed to have prepared the compound and analyzed it himself. Finally, the editor published the article.

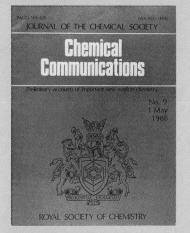

Figure 11.9
'Chemical Communications' is a weekly journal for the publication of the most exciting discoveries in chemistry.

The correctness of the proposal was established by the end of 1966, when the crystal structure of the compound was determined. The nitrogen molecule was indeed attached to the ruthenium ion. By the summer of 1966 the same compound was produced by bubbling atmospheric nitrogen through a solution of a ruthenium compound. The "inertness" of nitrogen was no more!

Since then, dozens of compounds of dinitrogen have been produced, opening a whole new field of chemistry. There is still much research to be done before we can find a simple, aqueous method of producing ammonia from nitrogen gas. However, the first step of the simple reduction of the oxidation number of nitrogen has been taken.

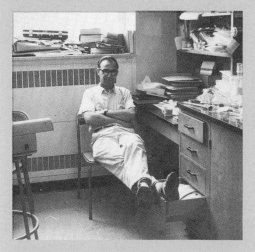

Figure 11.8
Dr. C.V. Senoff of the University of Toronto prepared the first compound containing molecular nitrogen.

Oxidation Number Rules

11.4 Using electron-dot formulas to determine oxidation numbers can be rather complicated, especially when the ions or molecules consist of three or more different elements. However, in most situations we can determine the oxidation numbers directly from the formula by applying the following simple rules:

1. The oxidation number of an atom in its pure form, as an element, is zero.

2. The oxidation number of a monatomic ion is equal to the charge on the ion.

3. The algebraic sum of the oxidation numbers in a neutral polyatomic compound is zero.

4. The algebraic sum of the oxidation numbers in a polyatomic ion is equal to the charge on the ion.

5. The most common oxidation number for hydrogen is $+1$; in metal hydrides it is -1.

6. The most common oxidation number for oxygen is -2; in peroxides it is -1, and in combination with fluorine it is $+2$.

7. In combinations of nonmetals, the oxidation number of the more electronegative atom is negative. The oxidation number of the less electronegative atom is positive.

Consider, for example, the molecular compound sulfuric acid, H_2SO_4. According to the rules just given, each of the two hydrogen atoms has an oxidation number of $+1$ and each of the four oxygen atoms has an oxidation number of -2. Since the molecule is neutral, the sum of the oxidation numbers must equal zero. Therefore, the oxidation number for sulfur must be $+6$.

$$\overbrace{2 \times (+1)}^{H_2} + \overbrace{(+6)}^{S} + \overbrace{4 \times (-2)}^{O_4} = 0$$

In the dihydrogen phosphate ion, $H_2PO_4^-$, the phosphorus atom has an oxidation number of $+5$. In this case the sum of the oxidation numbers of two hydrogen atoms, one phosphorus atom, and four oxygen atoms must equal the charge of the ion, or -1.

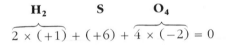

$$\overbrace{2 \times (+1)}^{H_2} + \overbrace{(+5)}^{P} + \overbrace{4 \times (-2)}^{O_4} = -1$$

| EXAMPLE | 11.6 | What are the oxidation numbers of each of the elements in sodium perxenate, Na_4XeO_6? |

SOLUTION Write the known oxidation numbers for each element. Sodium is a Group IA metal and always has an oxidation number of +1 in its compounds (Rule 2). In this case we can assign a value of −2 to oxygen (Rule 6). For the element xenon, we use its symbol:

$$\begin{array}{ccc} Na & Xe & O \\ +1 & Xe & -2 \end{array}$$

Next, we multiply these oxidation numbers by the number of atoms in the formula for sodium perxenate.

$$\underset{4 \times (+1)}{Na_4} \quad \underset{Xe}{Xe} \quad \underset{6 \times (-2)}{O_6}$$

Since the sum of oxidation numbers in a neutral compound is zero (Rule 3), we set up an equation and solve for xenon:

$$\underset{4 \times (+1)}{Na_4} + \underset{Xe}{Xe} + \underset{6 \times (-2)}{O_6} = 0$$
$$Xe = 8$$

The oxidation numbers of sodium, oxygen, and xenon are +1, −2, and +8 respectively.

| EXAMPLE | 11.7 | What are the oxidation numbers of each element in ammonium carbonate, $(NH_4)_2CO_3$? |

SOLUTION Write the known oxidation numbers for each element. We assign values of +1 and −2 to hydrogen and oxygen respectively (Rules 5 and 6).

$$\begin{array}{cccc} N & H & C & O \\ N & +1 & C & -2 \end{array}$$

Next, we multiply the oxidation numbers by the number of atoms in the formula for ammonium carbonate:

$$2\left[\underset{N}{N} + \underset{4 \times (+1)}{H_4} \right] + \underset{C}{C} + \underset{3 \times (-2)}{O_3} = 0$$

Because we have two unknowns, we cannot use Rule 3 directly. But because ammonium carbonate is an ionic substance, we can apply Rule 4 to each of the ions, NH_4^+ and CO_3^{2-} separately. The ammonium ion has an overall charge of $+1$, so we can set up an equation to solve for nitrogen:

$$\overset{N}{N} + \overset{\overbrace{}^{H_4}}{4 \times (+1)} = +1$$
$$N = -3$$

Similarly we can solve for carbon in the carbonate ion

$$\overset{C}{C} + \overset{\overbrace{}^{O_3}}{3 \times (-2)} = -2$$
$$C = +4$$

The oxidation numbers of hydrogen, oxygen, nitrogen, and carbon are $+1$, -2, -3, and $+4$ respectively.

Determining oxidation numbers by the rule method, although applicable for most simple compounds, has its drawbacks. It does not distinguish between atoms of the same elements that have different values. In the case of the thiosulfate ion, covered earlier, the rule method would assign an average value of $+2$ for each sulfur atom. But according to the electron-dot formula, one sulfur atom has a value of $+5$ and the other one has a value of -1.

QUESTIONS

5. Using the rules given in this section, assign oxidation numbers to all elements in the following compounds:
   a) nitrous acid, HNO_2
   b) potassium permanganate, $KMnO_4$
   c) ammonium sulfate, $(NH_4)_2SO_4$
   d) sodium aluminate, $NaAlO_2$
   e) hydronium ion, H_3O^+

6. What is the oxidation number of carbon in each of the following compounds:
   a) methane, CH_4
   b) formaldehyde, CH_2O
   c) carbon monoxide, CO

Redox Reactions

11.5 An increase in the oxidation number of an atom indicates that it has lost electrons and has undergone oxidation. A decrease in the oxidation number of an atom means an increase in the number of electrons and indicates reduction. Since electrons are neither created nor destroyed in chemical reactions, the total number of electrons will always remain unchanged.

This means that the loss of electrons must always be accompanied by the opposite process — the gain of electrons. In other words, oxidation and reduction are processes that always take place together.

EXAMPLE　　　　　*11.8*　Which of the following reactions is a redox reaction?

a) $2\ NaBr_{(aq)} + Cl_{2\,(aq)} \longrightarrow 2\ NaCl_{(aq)} + Br_{2\,(aq)}$

b) $2\ HCl_{(aq)} + Na_2S_{(aq)} \longrightarrow 2\ NaCl_{(aq)} + H_2S_{(g)}$

SOLUTION　　First we determine the oxidation number of each atom in the various substances by using the rule method.

a) $2\ NaBr_{(aq)} + Cl_{2\,(aq)} \longrightarrow 2\ NaCl_{(aq)} + Br_{2\,(aq)}$
　　　+1 −1　　　　0　　　　　　　+1 −1　　　　0

b) $2\ HCl_{(aq)} + Na_2S_{(aq)} \longrightarrow 2\ NaCl_{(aq)} + H_2S_{(g)}$
　　　+1 −1　　+1 −2　　　　　　　+1 −1　　+1 −2

The next step is to look for changes in oxidation numbers. In equation a) the bromine atom increases in oxidation number from −1 to 0 (oxidation) and the chlorine atoms decrease from 0 to −1 (reduction). This change in oxidation numbers indicates that this is a redox reaction. In equation b) none of the atoms undergo a change in oxidation number. This reaction is therefore not a redox reaction.

Reactions Between Elements

Elements react with each other to form compounds. These compounds are either ionic or molecular depending on the difference in electronegativity between the elements. All of these reactions are redox reactions.

Consider the reaction between magnesium and oxygen. The product from this rather spectacular reaction is the ionic compound magnesium oxide.

$$2\ Mg_{(s)} + O_{2\,(g)} \longrightarrow 2\ MgO_{(s)}$$

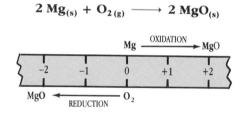

The oxidation number for magnesium increases from 0 to +2. Because it donates electrons to oxygen, we call magnesium the **reducing agent**. Since the oxygen accepts these electrons from the magnesium, we can call it the **oxidizing agent**. In a reaction between a metal and a nonmetal, the metal is always oxidized and is the reducing agent; the nonmetal is always reduced and is the oxidizing agent.

Figure 11.10
Alchemists experienced the explosive nature of many redox reactions.

The Chemistry of Fireworks

The chemical reactions occurring in a fireworks display are highly exothermic redox processes that have their origin in the development of gunpowder, or "black powder," several centuries ago.

It is believed that black powder was discovered in China well before A.D. 1000 and introduced into western Europe in the 14th century. It consists of a strong oxidizing agent, potassium nitrate, and two reducing agents, charcoal and sulfur. The composition of the mixture has remained essentially unchanged for the last 400 years. However, the action of black powder is greatly affected by the way in which the ingredients are mixed, and proper milling techniques are all-important. The aerial shells used in fireworks displays are propelled into the air by the large amounts of gases produced by ignition of black powder.

Fireworks formulations, from simple firecrackers to complex shells producing multicolour displays and loud explosions, all consist of mixtures of oxidizing agents and reducing agents (fuels) in addition to specific metal ions for the colour effects.

Figure 11.12 illustrates an aerial shell with three special effects, each contained in a separate compartment. The shell can be fired from a small steel canon. A fast-burning fuse ignites the slow-burning fuse A before igniting the black powder propellant. By the time fuse A has ignited the charge in the first compartment, the shell is high up in the air. The first compartment explodes in a burst of red colour which ignites the slow-burning fuse B in the second compartment. This results, a few seconds later, in a burst of blue colour which ignites the slow-burning fuse C. After a short while, the third compartment explodes with a bright flash and a loud bang.

The manufacture of fireworks is a hazardous operation in which safety precautions and experience are all-important. The People's Republic of China has become the world's largest fireworks producer. The Chinese factories are also actively experimenting with new formulations and new effects. It is only fitting that the art of fireworks, or pyrotechnics, has returned to the country where it originated more than a thousand years ago.

Figure 11.11
Black powder was first produced in ancient China.

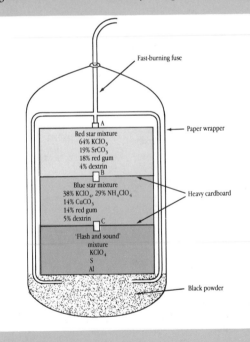

Figure 11.12
The three-stage aerial fireworks shell.

The Production and Uses of Copper

Copper metal (above) forms several ores including chalco-pyrite, $CuFeS_2$ (below).

Cuprite (below) has the formula Cu_2O.

Azurite (above), $Cu_3(OH)_2(CO_3)_2$

Malachite (left), $Cu_2(OH)_2CO_3$

Becium homblei *(left and below left)*, Ascolepis metallorum *(above), and* Haumaniastrum katangese *(below) are plants that accumulate the copper ion. Prospectors can locate underground copper ore deposits by finding where these plants flourish. Archeologists in Africa have used the plants to find sites of ancient copper smelters.*

PLATE 18 — THE PRODUCTION AND USES OF COPPER

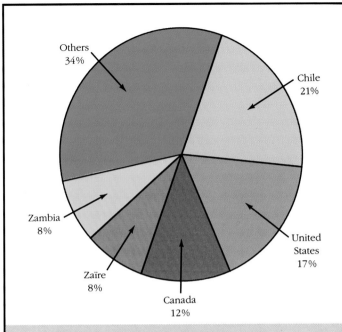

Pie chart of copper mined in Western countries.

The Lornex Copper Mine tailings in British Columbia.

The HBMS Company Copper Mine complex in Flin Flon.

Wheel for producing copper anodes.

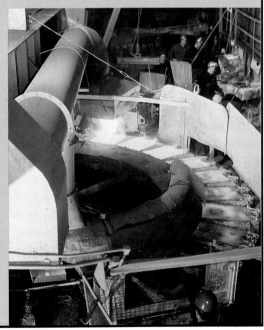

Strapped copper bars ready for shipment.

The tank house at the Copper Cliff refinery near Sudbury.

Inside the Copper Cliff smelter complex.

The Inco copper refinery, located west of Sudbury.

PLATE 20 — THE PRODUCTION AND USES OF COPPER

Inside a copper mine in Whitehorse.

Drilling operations inside the mine.

A crusher inside the copper mill.

Flotation equipment at the mill.

Copper roofs, such as those of the Parliament Buildings, form a green layer of hydrated basic carbonate.

Copper kettles and utensils are sometimes plated with other metals.

Copper has traditionally been used in the construction of ships' hulls and propellors.

PLATE 22 — THE PRODUCTION AND USES OF COPPER

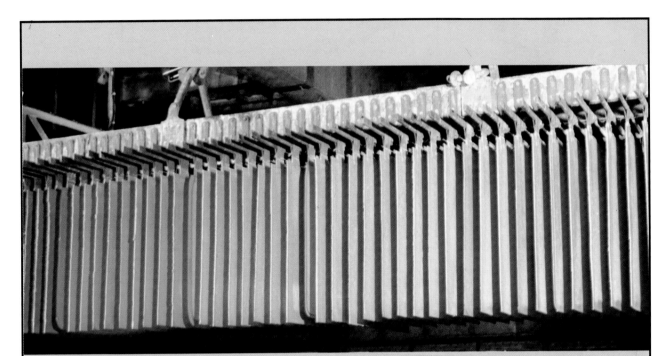

An electrolytic process is used to plate these cathodes with copper.

Copper is used for electrical cables
because of its high conductivity.

Copper is used by sculptors because it is malleable, ductile, and by
oxidation produces a wide variety of colours.

Copper(II) sulfate has the typical colour of most copper(II) compounds.

The colour of copper compounds depends largely on the oxidation state of copper.

PLATE 24 — THE PRODUCTION AND USES OF COPPER

When two nonmetals react, the element with the lower electronegativity loses electrons and is therefore the reducing agent. The element that has the greater electronegativity gains electrons and is reduced. The reaction between nitrogen and hydrogen is a good example.

$$N_{2(g)} + 3\,H_{2(g)} \longrightarrow 2\,NH_{3(g)}$$

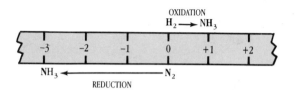

The nitrogen is reduced and the hydrogen is oxidized. Nitrogen is an oxidizing agent and hydrogen is a reducing agent in this reaction. In general then,

**The element that undergoes oxidation is the reducing agent.
The element that undergoes reduction is the oxidizing agent.**

Activity Series of Metals

As we saw in Section 11.1, copper metal will react with an aqueous solution of silver nitrate according to the following net ionic equation:

$$Cu_{(s)} + 2\,Ag^{+}_{(aq)} \longrightarrow Cu^{2+}_{(aq)} + 2\,Ag_{(s)}$$

When we place a piece of silver metal in an aqueous solution of copper(II) nitrate, no reaction results.

$$Ag_{(s)} + Cu(NO_3)_{2(aq)} \longrightarrow \text{NO REACTION}$$

Apparently copper metal will transfer electrons to silver ions, but silver metal will not give up its electrons to copper ions.

By adding a metal to dilute sulfuric acid or hydrochloric acid, we can test whether the metal is capable of transferring electrons to hydrogen ions. Hydrogen gas is produced when hydrogen ions gain electrons. We find that most metals react but a few — such as copper, silver, and gold — do not react with either hydrochloric acid or sulfuric acid.

The results of these and other experiments allow us to arrange the metals in an **activity series**. A metal in the series will displace another metal from its salt in aqueous solution as long as the second metal is located further down in the series. This means that a metal will *donate electrons* to the positive ions of another metal placed below it in the series.

Figure 11.13

Welding rails using the redox Thermite reaction. Aluminum metal is reacted with iron(III) oxide. The reaction is so exothermic that the iron metal produced is liquid. The liquid metal flows down over the joints and welds them.

TABLE 11.2	*The Activity Series*

Lithium Potassium Barium Calcium Sodium	These metals displace hydrogen from water.
Magnesium Aluminium Zinc Chromium Iron Cadmium Nickel Tin Lead	These metals displace hydrogen from acids.
Hydrogen	
Copper Mercury Silver Gold	These metals do not displace hydrogen from acids or water.

Hydrogen, although not a metal, is included in the series. Any metal placed above hydrogen will react with acids such as hydrochloric acid and sulfuric acid. The first five metals are so reactive that they will even transfer electrons directly to water:

$$Ca_{(s)} + 2\,H_2O_{(\ell)} \longrightarrow Ca(OH)_{2\,(aq)} + H_{2\,(g)}$$

EXAMPLE   *11.9*   Use the activity series to predict whether a reaction takes place when the following substances are mixed. If there is a reaction, complete and balance the equation, and then write the net ionic equation.

a) $Fe_{(s)} + ZnSO_{4\,(aq)} \longrightarrow$

b) $Al_{(s)} + H_2SO_{4\,(aq)} \longrightarrow$

c) $Sn_{(s)} + CuSO_{4\,(aq)} \longrightarrow$

SOLUTION   From the relative positions of the elements in the activity series, we can conclude the following:

a) Because iron will not transfer electrons to zinc ions no reaction will occur.

b) Aluminum will transfer electrons to hydrogen ions according to the following balanced equation:

$$2\,Al_{(s)} + 3\,H_2SO_{4\,(aq)} \longrightarrow Al_2(SO_4)_{3\,(aq)} + 3\,H_{2\,(g)}$$

Figure 11.14
Household bleaches are oxidizing agents. Most of them contain a solution of sodium hypochlorite.

When the spectator ions are deleted, the net ionic equation becomes

$$2\,Al_{(s)} + 6\,H^+_{(aq)} \longrightarrow 2\,Al^{3+}_{(aq)} + 3\,H_{2\,(g)}$$

c) Tin will transfer electrons to copper(II) ions.

$$Sn_{(s)} + CuSO_{4\,(aq)} \longrightarrow SnSO_{4\,(aq)} + Cu_{(s)}$$

With the spectator ions deleted, the net ionic equation becomes

$$Sn_{(s)} + Cu^{2+}_{(aq)} \longrightarrow Sn^{2+}_{(aq)} + Cu_{(s)}$$

As we will see, the activity series can be expanded to include many non-metals. The position of these substances is determined by their ability to donate or accept electrons.

Oxidizing and Reducing Agents

Many substances in the laboratory and in the chemical industry are classified as either oxidizing agents or reducing agents. A good *oxidizing agent* must be a good electron acceptor and a good *reducing agent* must be a good electron donor.

The cheapest and most widely-used oxidizing agent is atmospheric oxygen. Most of the oxidizing agents used in the laboratory are compounds that are rich in oxygen. These substances all accept electrons readily and lose oxygen in the process. Elemental chlorine is also a good oxidizing agent since it will readily accept electrons to produce chloride ions.

The most commonly-used reducing agent is hydrogen gas. Compounds such as lithium aluminum hydride, $LiAlH_4$, that can release hydrogen in the form of hydride ions, H^-, are powerful reducing agents in the laboratory. Reactive metals such as magnesium and aluminum are also good reducing agents because they readily release electrons to form positive metal ions.

Disastrous explosions have often resulted when a powerful oxidizing agent such as a perchlorate has been inadvertently brought into contact with a strong reducing agent. Gunpowder and fireworks formulations are examples of potentially explosive redox mixtures.

Many redox reactions, especially in organic chemistry, involve increases and decreases in the amount of oxygen contained in the reactants. The terms oxidation and reduction actually originated from these kinds of reactions. Thus, an element or compound is oxidized when it combines with oxygen and a compound is reduced when oxygen is removed from it. During the reaction

$$\mathbf{PbO_{(s)} + C_{(s)} \longrightarrow Pb_{(s)} + CO_{(g)}}$$

Figure 11.15
Ascorbic acid (vitamin C) is a reducing agent. We can stop the surface oxidation of fruit and vegetables with this compound.

the lead(II) oxide loses its oxygen to the carbon and is therefore reduced. The carbon is oxidized to carbon monoxide. A look at the change in oxidation numbers leads us to the same conclusion but allows us to be more specific. It is the lead in lead(II) oxide that is reduced.

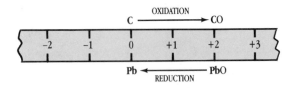

In all combustion reactions the substance burned is oxidized and oxygen is reduced. In the combustion of methane, it is the methane — actually the carbon in methane — that is oxidized, and elemental oxygen that is reduced. The oxidation number of the hydrogen atoms is unchanged in the reaction.

$$CH_{4\,(g)} + 2\,O_{2\,(g)} \longrightarrow CO_{2\,(g)} + 2\,H_2O_{(\ell)}$$

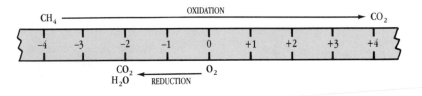

The combustion of glucose can be accomplished in two different ways: by lighting it with a match and by metabolic reactions in the body. In both instances, the overall reaction is the same:

$$C_6H_{12}O_{6\,(s)} + 6\,O_{2\,(g)} \longrightarrow 6\,CO_{2\,(g)} + 6\,H_2O_{(\ell)}$$

In our bodies, and in those of most other animals, the glucose is oxidized to carbon dioxide and water by a very complex sequence of events. The energy released is stored in other chemical substances from which it can be readily released upon demand.

Figure 11.16
Life around a deep-sea vent. Marine organisms obtain their energy from the oxidation of sulfide ion spewed out of the vent.

EXAMPLE   *11.10*   Consider the addition or removal of oxygen atoms, as well as the change in oxidation numbers, to determine which substance is oxidized and which one is reduced in the following reaction:

$$\underset{\text{methanol}}{CH_3OH_{(aq)}} + \underset{\substack{\text{hypochlorous}\\\text{acid}}}{2\,HClO_{(aq)}} \longrightarrow \underset{\substack{\text{formic}\\\text{acid}}}{HCO_2H_{(aq)}} + 2\,HCl_{(aq)} + H_2O_{(\ell)}$$

SOLUTION   The oxygen content of methanol increases in its conversion to formic acid. The methanol is oxidized and the hypochlorous acid is reduced. Oxidation numbers shed more light on the reaction.

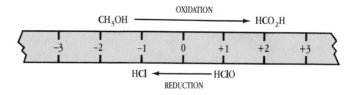

The oxidation number of the carbon atoms increases from -2 to $+2$. Carbon is therefore oxidized. The oxidation number of the chlorine atoms decreases from $+1$ to -1. Chlorine is reduced. The oxidation numbers of the oxygen and hydrogen atoms remain unchanged.

QUESTIONS

7. Using the activity series (Table 11.2), predict whether a reaction takes place, and if so, give a balanced reaction equation.
   a) $Ag_{(s)} + HCl_{(aq)} \longrightarrow$
   b) $Mg_{(s)} + FeSO_{4\,(aq)} \longrightarrow$
   c) $Cu_{(s)} + AuCl_{3\,(aq)} \longrightarrow$
   d) $Sn_{(s)} + Al_2(SO_4)_{3\,(aq)} \longrightarrow$

8. Which of the following reactions are redox reactions?
   a) $Na_2S_{(aq)} + FeCl_{2\,(aq)} \longrightarrow 2\,NaCl_{(aq)} + FeS_{(s)}$
   b) $2\,Na_{(s)} + 2\,H_2O_{(\ell)} \longrightarrow 2\,NaOH_{(aq)} + H_{2\,(g)}$
   c) $2\,KClO_{3\,(s)} \longrightarrow 2\,KCl_{(s)} + 3\,O_{2\,(g)}$

9. Which reactant in each of the following is oxidized? Which reactant is the oxidizing agent?
   a) $H_{2\,(g)} + I_{2\,(g)} \longrightarrow 2\,HI_{(g)}$
   b) $O_{2\,(g)} + 2\,F_{2\,(g)} \longrightarrow 2\,F_2O_{(g)}$
   c) $3\,Mg_{(s)} + N_{2\,(g)} \longrightarrow Mg_3N_{2\,(s)}$

10. Identify the reducing agents in the following reactions. Which of the reactants are reduced?
    a) $CO_{(g)} + PbO_{(s)} \longrightarrow CO_{2\,(g)} + Pb_{(s)}$
    b) $Br_{2\,(aq)} + SO_{2\,(g)} + 2\,H_2O_{(\ell)} \longrightarrow 2\,HBr_{(aq)} + H_2SO_{4\,(aq)}$
    c) $2\,NaBr_{(aq)} + Cl_{2\,(aq)} \longrightarrow 2\,NaCl_{(aq)} + Br_{2\,(aq)}$

Nickel and Zinc Production

11.6

The production of metals from their ores involves many redox reactions. Two of the most important metals mined and processed in Canada are nickel and zinc. In this section, we will examine the chemistry associated with the production of these two metals.

Natural Sources

Nickel is found in the crust of the earth in the form of sulfides, oxides, and silicates. The sulfides have been produced by the reaction of nickel with sulfur in rock several kilometres under the surface of the earth. In northern regions, much of the surface rock has been removed by glacial action. As a result large nickel sulfide deposits are found near the surface in Canada and the Soviet Union. The most common ore is pentlandite, $(Ni, Fe)_9S_{16}$ which is usually found together with chalcopyrite, $CuFeS_2$, and pyrrhotite, Fe_7S_8.

The total, world nickel reserve is estimated at 6×10^7 tonnes. The largest reserves are in New Caledonia and Canada. If the present rate of consumption continues, these reserves will be depleted within a century. However, this period can be extended considerably if sea-bed nodules are mined on a large scale. The nodules contain an estimated 7.8×10^8 tonnes of nickel.

Although zinc-containing ores are widely distributed around the world, Canada has the most extensive deposits of zinc sulfide. These zinc sulfide deposits usually contain large amounts of iron sulfides and galena, PbS, along with smaller amounts of copper and silver ores.

Canadian Production

Canada produces 25 % of the world's nickel. The major mines are near Sudbury, Ontario, and Thompson, Manitoba.

TABLE 11.3 *Nickel Production in Canada*

Province	Number of Mines	Annual Production (tonnes)
Ontario	18	155 700
Manitoba	2	39 300

TABLE 11.4 *Zinc Production in Canada*

Province	Number of Mines	Annual Production (tonnes)
Ontario	5	303 000
Northwest Territories	2	226 700
New Brunswick	2	171 600
Yukon	2	98 400
Quebec	4	78 800
British Columbia	5	71 100
Manitoba & Saskatchewan	4	57 400
Newfoundland	2	47 100
Nova Scotia	1	4 800

Canadian zinc production represents about 25 % of the production of the western world. Approximately half of the recovered zinc ore concentrate is exported. The rest is processed in four domestic metallurgical plants. The largest plant is operated by Cominco Ltd., in Trail, B.C., and has an annual production capacity of 245 000 tonnes.

Zinc ranks fourth (after iron, copper, and aluminum) in annual metal consumption. About half of the world's zinc production is used in galvanized steel.

Roasting, Smelting, and Leaching

The traditional methods of processing sulfide ores involve roasting and smelting, which take place in a plant called a smelter. During the roasting procedure, the metal sulfides are converted into metal oxides by heating with air. The sulfide is oxidized to sulfur dioxide. For nickel sulfide, the reaction is

$$2\,NiS_{(s)} + 3\,O_{2\,(g)} \longrightarrow 2\,NiO_{(s)} + 2\,SO_{2\,(g)}$$

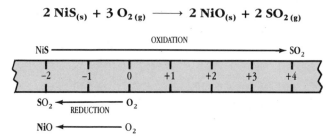

The smelting process takes place in large furnaces. Here, some of the metal oxide is reduced in a reaction with coke (solid carbon).

$$NiO_{(s)} + C_{(s)} \longrightarrow Ni_{(\ell)} + CO_{(g)}$$

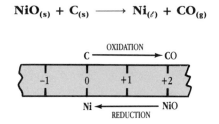

Then the remaining nickel(II) oxide is reduced by one of the products of the first reaction, carbon monoxide:

$$NiO_{(s)} + CO_{(g)} \longrightarrow Ni_{(\ell)} + CO_{2\,(g)}$$

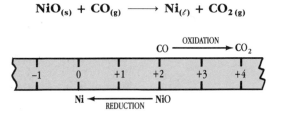

The resulting liquid metal must then be separated from the solids and further purified. Much of this purified nickel is eventually used to make stainless steel.

Figure 11.17
The Inco nickel smelter is one of the largest in the world. The 381 m high superstack releases gaseous emissions into the upper atmosphere.

While the roasting and smelting operations described above supply most of our nickel, over 75 % of the world's zinc is recovered from zinc sulfide by a three-stage process. In the first stage the sulfide ore is roasted to produce zinc oxide.

$$2\ ZnS_{(s)} + 3\ O_{2\,(g)} \longrightarrow 2\ ZnO_{(s)} + 2\ SO_{2\,(g)}$$

The second stage is a leaching procedure in which the zinc oxide is extracted with dilute sulfuric acid.

$$ZnO_{(s)} + H_2SO_{4\,(aq)} \longrightarrow ZnSO_{4\,(aq)} + H_2O_{(\ell)}$$

After removal of insoluble materials, the resulting solution contains only zinc sulfate and a small amount of cadmiun sulfate. Zinc powder is then added to this solution. Since cadmium is below zinc in the activity series (Table 11.2), the cadmium is reduced in the reaction.

$$CdSO_{4\,(aq)} + Zn_{(s)} \longrightarrow Cd_{(s)} + ZnSO_{4\,(aq)}$$

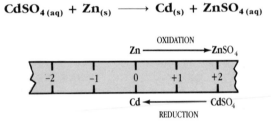

In the third stage, pure zinc is removed from solution by electrolysis (electrowinning). The overall reaction equation for the electrolysis procedure is

$$2\ ZnSO_{4\,(aq)} + 2\ H_2O_{(\ell)} \longrightarrow 2\ Zn_{(s)} + 2\ H_2SO_{4\,(aq)} + O_{2\,(g)}$$

We will discuss the purification of metals by electrolysis further in Chapter 12.

Metal Extraction Using Hydrometallurgy

The formation of gaseous sulfur dioxide is the main drawback to roasting. Not only is sulfur dioxide highly toxic, it is also a major source of acid rain. Because of this, most smelting operations now convert sulfur dioxide to sulfuric acid, which can be sold or used in the leaching process. Since large quantities of sulfuric acid are needed for making fertilizers, many smelters have associated fertilizer plants. However, in spite of drastic reductions in sulfur dioxide emissions from smelters over the past twenty years, a substantial amount still ends up in the atmosphere.

New recovery methods eliminate roasting altogether. The metals are extracted under pressure in solution directly from sulfide ores in a process called **hydrometallurgy**. The sulfides are oxidized to sulfates instead of sulfur dioxide. About 17 000 tonnes of nickel are produced annually by this process at Fort Saskatchewan, Alberta.

Concentrated nickel ore is suspended in an aqueous ammonium sulfate solution and treated under pressure at 100 °C with ammonia and air.

$$NiS_{(s)} + 2\,NH_{3\,(aq)} + 2\,O_{2\,(g)} \longrightarrow Ni(NH_3)_2^{2+}{}_{(aq)} + SO_4^{2-}{}_{(aq)}$$

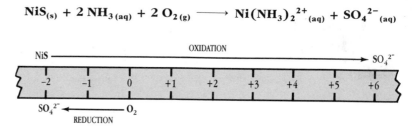

The sulfide ions are oxidized to sulfate ions and the nickel ions form a water soluble complex with ammonia. This purified nickel diammine sulfate solution is then reduced with hydrogen gas under pressure. One of the products of the reaction is very pure nickel.

$$Ni(NH_3)_2^{2+}{}_{(aq)} + SO_4^{2-}{}_{(aq)} + H_{2\,(g)} \longrightarrow$$
$$Ni_{(s)} + 2\,NH_4^+{}_{(aq)} + SO_4^{2-}{}_{(aq)}$$

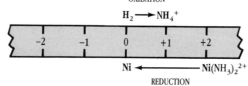

Another product, ammonium sulfate, is a useful fertilizer. It is recovered from the solution by evaporation and crystallization.

The process for zinc is somewhat different. Powdered zinc sulfide ore in aqueous sulfuric acid is treated with pure oxygen under 1 MPa pressure at 150 °C. The sulfide ions are oxidized to elemental sulfur and the zinc dissolves as zinc sulfate.

$$2\,ZnS_{(s)} + 2\,H_2SO_{4\,(aq)} + O_{2\,(g)} \longrightarrow 2\,ZnSO_{4\,(aq)} + 2\,S_{(s)} + 2\,H_2O_{(\ell)}$$

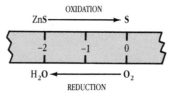

Figure 11.18
The smelters in Trail, British Columbia. About 6% of the world's lead and zinc are produced here. The zinc is now being produced by a pressure-leach system.

Zinc metal is obtained from the zinc sulfate in the conventional manner by electrolysis. The sulfur can be easily stored and converted into sulfuric acid when the demand is sufficient.

Balancing Redox Equations Using Oxidation Numbers

Thus far, we have balanced reaction equations by the inspection method. We might also call it the trial-and-error method. The coefficients in the equation are manipulated until the atoms and the charges are balanced. Many redox reactions, however, are difficult to balance because of the number of reactants and products and because the coefficients can be quite large. It would take us a long time, for instance, to balance the following reaction:

$$ClO_3^-{}_{(aq)} + I_{2\,(aq)} + H_2O_{(\ell)} \longrightarrow IO_3^-{}_{(aq)} + Cl^-{}_{(aq)} + H^+{}_{(aq)}$$

We would need the following coefficients:

$$5\,ClO_3^-{}_{(aq)} + 3\,I_{2\,(aq)} + 3\,H_2O_{(\ell)} \longrightarrow$$
$$6\,IO_3^-{}_{(aq)} + 5\,Cl^-{}_{(aq)} + 6\,H^+{}_{(aq)}$$

One of the virtues of oxidation numbers is that they offer us a systematic method for balancing redox reactions. The method is based on the fact that the number of electrons released by the oxidized substance is equal to the number of electrons gained by the reduced substance. Thus, *in a balanced redox equation, the total increase in oxidation number of the element that is oxidized must equal the total decrease in oxidation number of the element that is reduced.*

The procedure for balancing equations can be broken down into the following steps. We must keep in mind that not all the reactants or products contain elements that undergo a change in oxidation number.

1. Assign oxidation numbers to all the atoms in the equation.
2. Identify which atoms undergo a change in oxidation number.
3. Determine the ratio in which these atoms must react so that the total increase in oxidation numbers equals the decrease.
4. Balance the redox participants in the equation.
5. Balance the other atoms by the inspection method.

We will use this method to balance the following reaction:

$$HNO_3 + H_2S \longrightarrow NO + S + H_2O$$

First we determine all the oxidation numbers.

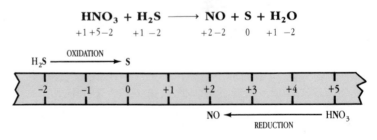

$$\underset{+1\ +5\ -2}{HNO_3} + \underset{+1\ -2}{H_2S} \longrightarrow \underset{+2\ -2}{NO} + \underset{0}{S} + \underset{+1\ -2}{H_2O}$$

Figure 11.19

A Chinese religious sculpture made of the mineral realgar, As_2S_2. The mineral oxidizes in light to diarsenic trisulfide and diarsenic trioxide. These sculptures were believed to promote good health. By briefly handling the statues, the arsenic intake could be enough to kill intestinal parasites. Excessive handling of the statues would not have been so beneficial!

Only nitrogen and sulfur undergo a change. The oxidation number of each nitrogen atom decreases by three and the oxidation number of each sulfur atom increases by two.

For the increase to be the same as the decrease, we need three sulfur atoms for every two nitrogen atoms in the balanced equation. Since these atoms are part of molecules, we need three hydrogen sulfide molecules for every two nitric acid molecules. The partially-balanced reaction equation is

$$2\ HNO_3 + 3\ H_2S \longrightarrow 2\ NO + 3\ S + H_2O$$

The coefficient for water can now be determined by inspection, and the balanced equation is as follows:

$$2\ HNO_3 + 3\ H_2S \longrightarrow 2\ NO + 3\ S + 4\ H_2O$$

We can also use oxidation numbers to balance equations involving ions. The following reaction between the permanganate ion and sulfurous acid will serve as an example. We follow the same steps as we did in the previous solution.

$$MnO_4^-{}_{(aq)} + H_2SO_3{}_{(aq)} + H^+{}_{(aq)} \longrightarrow Mn^{2+}{}_{(aq)} + HSO_4^- + H_2O_{(\ell)}$$

Only manganese and sulfur undergo a change in oxidation number. Each manganese atom decreases in oxidation number by five and each sulfur atom increases by two.

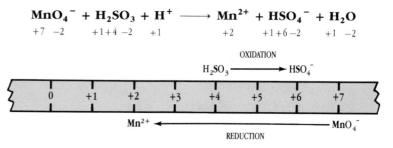

The lowest common multiple of five and two is ten. Thus, in the balanced reaction we need five sulfur atoms for every two manganese atoms. The increase and the decrease will then both be ten. The partially balanced reaction equation is:

$$2\ MnO_4^- + 5\ H_2SO_3 + H^+ \longrightarrow 2\ Mn^{2+} + 5\ HSO_4^- + H_2O$$

The remaining coefficients can be determined by inspection and the balanced equation is

$$2\ MnO_4^- + 5\ H_2SO_3 + H^+ \longrightarrow 2\ Mn^{2+} + 5\ HSO_4^- + 3\ H_2O$$

In balancing equations that include ions, we should always do a final check to determine whether the total charge on the reactant side is actually the same as the total charge on the product side. The reactants in our equation have a total charge of $2 \times (-1) + (+1) = -1$. This is indeed the same as the total charge of the products: $2 \times (+2) + 5 \times (-1) = -1$.

QUESTIONS

11. Show that in the following balanced redox reactions the increase in oxidation numbers equals the decrease:
    a) $N_2 + 3 H_2 \longrightarrow 2 NH_3$
    b) $2 Fe^{3+} + 2 I^- \longrightarrow 2 Fe^{2+} + I_2$
    c) $2 KClO_3 \longrightarrow 2 KCl + 3 O_2$

12. Balance the following reactions by the oxidation number method.
    a) $I_2 + HNO_3 \longrightarrow HIO_3 + NO_2 + H_2O$
    b) $HBr + HBrO_3 \longrightarrow Br_2 + H_2O$
    c) $MnO_4^- + H^+ + Cl^- \longrightarrow Mn^{2+} + Cl_2 + H_2O$
    d) $CrO_2^- + ClO^- + OH^- \longrightarrow CrO_4^{2-} + Cl^- + H_2O$

The Breathalyzer Test — Green Means Trouble

The breathalyzer test is used to determine whether a person has consumed more than the legally-acceptable amount of alcohol for driving a vehicle. The test is based on the assumption that alcohol in the blood, which is absorbed into the blood via the small intestine, is in equilibrium with alcohol vapour in the lungs:

$$C_2H_5OH_{(blood)} \rightleftharpoons C_2H_5OH_{(lungs)}$$

The alcohol vapour in breath is analyzed by its reaction with potassium dichromate, $K_2Cr_2O_7$, in the presence of sulfuric acid. The dichromate ions, which are yellowish-orange in colour, are reduced to chromium(III) ions, which are green. The alcohol is oxidized to acetic acid.

$$\underset{\text{yellowish-orange}}{2 Cr_2O_7^{2-}{}_{(aq)}} + 3 C_2H_5OH_{(aq)} + 16 H^+{}_{(aq)} \longrightarrow$$

$$4 Cr^{3+}{}_{(aq)} + \underset{\text{green}}{3 CH_3CO_2H_{(aq)}} + 11 H_2O_{(\ell)}$$

In the breathalyzer machine, a known volume of breath is passed through an acidic solution of potassium dichromate of known concentration. The decrease in the intensity of the yellowish-orange colour is measured. Since this decrease is directly proportional to the decrease in the concentration of the dichromate concentration, the amount of alcohol in the breath sample can be calculated. The machine then converts breath alcohol to blood alcohol content.

In Canada a person is generally considered to be legally intoxicated when the blood alcohol content is 0.08 % or higher. For a person weighing 65 kg this condition will be reached immediately after consuming about 1 L of beer or 0.5 L of wine. The blood alcohol level decreases by 0.015 % for every hour elapsed after the alcohol is consumed.

Figure 11.20
A breathalyzer in use.

Half-Reactions

Oxidation numbers provide us with a good bookkeeping method for following redox reactions. However, we should also be concerned with obtaining a better understanding of how redox reactions take place. We can do this by separating a redox reaction into two **half-reactions**. In one half reaction, oxidation occurs and electrons are produced; in the other half-reaction, reduction occurs and electrons are consumed. We will use the reaction between magnesium and chlorine as an example:

$$Mg_{(s)} + Cl_{2(g)} \longrightarrow MgCl_{2(s)}$$

Magnesium chloride is an ionic compound containing magnesium ions, Mg^{2+}, and chloride ions, Cl^-. In this reaction neutral magnesium atoms lose two electrons to form magnesium ions. The oxidation half-reaction is

$$Mg_{(s)} \longrightarrow Mg^{2+}_{(s)} + 2\ e^-$$

The chlorine molecule contains neutral chlorine atoms. These gain electrons to form chloride ions.

$$Cl_{2(g)} + 2\ e^- \longrightarrow 2\ Cl^-_{(s)}$$

Deriving half-reactions is an especially useful exercise for ionic reactions in solution. It gives us insight as to which species are actually involved in the redox process. In addition, when we study electrochemical processes in Chapter 12, we will find that the half-reactions represent chemical changes that occur at electrodes.

To make sense of ionic reactions in solution, we should always remove the spectator ions. For example, the reaction between copper metal and silver nitrate solution produces copper(II) nitrate solution and silver metal.

$$Cu_{(s)} + 2\ AgNO_{3(aq)} \longrightarrow Cu(NO_3)_{2(aq)} + 2\ Ag_{(s)}$$

We write the total ionic equation then remove the spectator ions, in this case the nitrate ions:

$$Cu_{(s)} + 2\ Ag^+_{(aq)} + 2\ NO_3^-_{(aq)} \longrightarrow Cu^{2+}_{(aq)} + 2\ NO_3^-_{(aq)} + 2\ Ag_{(s)}$$
$$Cu_{(s)} + 2\ Ag^+_{(aq)} \longrightarrow Cu^{2+}_{(aq)} + 2\ Ag_{(s)}$$

Now it is more evident that copper is oxidized to the copper(II) ion while the silver ion is reduced to silver metal. The two half-reactions are:

$$Cu_{(s)} \longrightarrow Cu^{2+}_{(aq)} + 2\ e^-$$
$$2\ Ag^+_{(aq)} + 2\ e^- \longrightarrow 2\ Ag_{(s)}$$

EXAMPLE **11.11** Write the half-reactions for the reaction

$$2\ Al_{(s)} + 6\ HCl_{(aq)} \longrightarrow 2\ AlCl_{3(aq)} + 3\ H_{2(g)}$$

SOLUTION First we write the net ionic equation. The chloride ions are spectator ions and can be omitted:

$$2 \, Al_{(s)} + 6 \, H^+_{(aq)} \longrightarrow 2 \, Al^{3+}_{(aq)} + 3 \, H_{2\,(g)}$$

The aluminum loses three electrons per atom and these electrons are gained by the hydrogen ions. The half-reactions are as follows:

Oxidation: $2 \, Al_{(s)} \longrightarrow 2 \, Al^{3+}_{(aq)} + 6 \, e^-$

Reduction: $6 \, H^+_{(aq)} + 6 \, e^- \longrightarrow 3 \, H_{2\,(g)}$

QUESTIONS

13. Write the oxidation and reduction half-reactions for the preparation of the following ionic compounds:

a) $2 \, Na_{(s)} + Br_{2\,(\ell)} \longrightarrow 2 \, NaBr_{(s)}$

b) $Zn_{(s)} + S_{(s)} \longrightarrow ZnS_{(s)}$

c) $4 \, Al_{(s)} + 3 \, O_{2\,(g)} \longrightarrow 2 \, Al_2O_{3\,(s)}$

14. Write net ionic equations and half-reactions for each of the following reactions:

a) $2 \, CrSO_{4(aq)} + Ag_2SO_{4(aq)} \longrightarrow Cr_2(SO_4)_{3\,(aq)} + 2 \, Ag$

b) $Ca_{(s)} + 2 \, H_2O_{(\ell)} \longrightarrow Ca(OH)_{2\,(aq)} + H_{2\,(g)}$

c) $Cl_{2\,(aq)} + 2 \, NaI_{(aq)} \longrightarrow 2 \, NaCl_{(aq)} + I_{2\,(aq)}$

Ion-Electron Method of Balancing Redox Equations

11.9 We can use half-reactions to balance redox equations. When we do so, we are using the **ion-electron method**. This method can be broken down into the following steps:

1. Write balanced oxidation and reduction half-reactions.

2. Change the coefficients in the balanced half-reactions so that the number of electrons produced in the oxidation half-reaction equals the number of electrons consumed in the reduction half-reaction.

3. Add the two half-reactions to obtain a balanced net ionic equation for the redox reaction.

Balancing Half-Reactions

As mentioned previously, half-reactions are especially useful for balancing ionic reactions. Although the method for balancing these half-reactions can be outlined as a general case, it is better to outline the process with respect to acidic and basic solutions separately.

In Acidic Solution To write a balanced half-reaction for the oxidation of ethanol, C_2H_5OH to acetic acid, CH_3CO_2H, in acidic solution, we would follow the steps outlined below.

1. Write the skeletal equation:

$$C_2H_5OH \longrightarrow CH_3CO_2H$$

2. Balance for species other than oxygen and hydrogen:

$$C_2H_5OH \longrightarrow CH_3CO_2H \quad \text{(no change)}$$

3. Balance for oxygen using one water molecule for each oxygen you require:

$$C_2H_5OH + H_2O \longrightarrow CH_3CO_2H$$

4. Balance for hydrogen using a hydrogen ion for each hydrogen you require:

$$C_2H_5OH + H_2O \longrightarrow CH_3CO_2H + 4\,H^+$$

5. Balance for charge by adding electrons to either the product or reactant side:

$$C_2H_5OH + H_2O \longrightarrow CH_3CO_2H + 4\,H^+ + 4\,e^-$$

In Basic Solution We will use the reduction of the permanganate ion to manganese(IV) oxide in basic solution as an example.

1. Write the skeletal half-reaction:

$$MnO_4^- \longrightarrow MnO_2$$

2. Balance for species other than oxygen or hydrogen:

$$MnO_4^- \longrightarrow MnO_2 \quad \text{(no change)}$$

3. Balance for oxygen atoms by adding two hydroxide ions for each oxygen that you require. We need two more oxygen atoms on the right, so we add four hydroxide ions. This will temporarily unbalance the oxygen atoms again:

$$MnO_4^- \longrightarrow MnO_2 + 4\,OH^-$$

4. Balance for hydrogen atoms with water molecules. This rebalances the oxygen atoms:

$$MnO_4^- + 2\,H_2O \longrightarrow MnO_2 + 4\,OH^-$$

5. Finally, balance for charge by adding electrons to either the reactant or product side of the equation:

$$MnO_4^- + 2\,H_2O + 3\,e^- \longrightarrow MnO_2 + 4\,OH^-$$

11.12 Write a balanced half-reaction for the oxidation of aluminum metal to the aluminate ion (AlO_2^-) in basic solution.

SOLUTION Write the skeletal equation:

$$Al \longrightarrow AlO_2^-$$

Balance for species other than oxygen and hydrogen; in this case, aluminum:

$$Al \longrightarrow AlO_2^- \quad \text{(no change)}$$

Balance for hydrogen with water molecules:

$$Al + 4\,OH^- \longrightarrow AlO_2^- + 2\,H_2O$$

Balance for charge by adding electrons to the product side of the equation:

$$Al + 4\,OH^- \longrightarrow AlO_2^- + 2\,H_2O + 3\,e^-$$

EXAMPLE

11.13 Write a balanced half-reaction for the oxidation of ammonia, NH_3, to dinitrogen oxide, N_2O, in basic solution.

SOLUTION Write the skeletal equation:

$$NH_3 \longrightarrow N_2O$$

Balance for species other than oxygen and hydrogen; in this case, nitrogen:

$$2\,NH_3 \longrightarrow N_2O$$

Balance for oxygen by adding two hydroxide ions for each oxygen you require:

$$2\,NH_3 + 2\,OH^- \longrightarrow N_2O$$

Balance the hydrogen with water molecules. In this example we must account for the fact that hydrogen appears in both NH_3 and OH^-. We add seven water molecules to the right side of the equation. By doing so we must add an additional six hydroxide ions to the left side.

$$2\,NH_3 + 8\,OH^- \longrightarrow N_2O + 7\,H_2O$$

Balance for charge by adding electrons to the product side of the equation.

$$2\,NH_3 + 8\,OH^- \longrightarrow N_2O + 7\,H_2O + 8\,e^-$$

Combining Half-Reactions

The combining of half-reactions to give balanced redox equations is a simple procedure. We just need to realize that the total number of electrons produced in the oxidation half-reaction must balance the number of electrons consumed in the reduction half-reaction. As a simple example, we can combine the half-reactions for the reduction of iron(III) to iron(II) with the oxidation of hydrogen gas to hydrogen ion.

$$Fe^{3+}_{(aq)} + e^- \longrightarrow Fe^{2+}_{(aq)}$$
$$H_{2(g)} \longrightarrow 2\,H^+_{(aq)} + 2\,e^-$$

To balance the number of electrons, the first equation must be multiplied by 2. We can then add the two half-reactions and "cancel" the electrons.

$$2\,Fe^{3+}_{(aq)} + 2\,e^- \longrightarrow 2\,Fe^{2+}_{(aq)}$$
$$\underline{H_{2(g)} \longrightarrow 2\,H^+_{(aq)} + 2\,e^-}$$
$$2\,Fe^{3+}_{(aq)} + H_{2(g)} \longrightarrow 2\,Fe^{2+}_{(aq)} + 2\,H^+_{(aq)}$$

The Full Ion-Electron Method

We can now work through a complete problem using this method. We will use the reaction between the purple permanganate ion and iron(II) ion *in acid solution* to produce the colourless manganese(II) ion and the iron(III) ion.

First, we will develop the equation for the permanganate-manganese(II) ion half-reaction.

1. Write the skeletal equation:

$$MnO_4^- \longrightarrow Mn^{2+}$$

2. Balance for manganese:

$$MnO_4^- \longrightarrow Mn^{2+} \quad \text{(no change)}$$

3. Balance for oxygen. We add four water molecules to the right side to balance the four oxygen atoms on the left:

$$MnO_4^- \longrightarrow Mn^{2+} + 4\,H_2O$$

4. Balance for hydrogen. We add eight hydrogen ions to the left side of the equation to balance those on the right:

$$MnO_4^- + 8\,H^+ \longrightarrow Mn^{2+} + 4\,H_2O$$

5. Balance for charge by adding five electrons on the left:

$$MnO_4^- + 8\,H^+ + 5\,e^- \longrightarrow Mn^{2+} + 4\,H_2O$$

Now we will develop the equation for the iron(II)-iron(III) half-reaction. In this case we can go straight from the skeletal equation to the full half-equation by simply balancing electrons.

1. Write the skeletal equation:

$$Fe^{2+} \longrightarrow Fe^{3+}$$

2. Balance for charge by adding one electron on the right:

$$Fe^{2+} \longrightarrow Fe^{3+} + e^-$$

We can now add the sum of the two half-reactions. To cancel the electrons, the iron half-reaction must be multiplied by 5.

$$MnO_4^- + 8\,H^+ + 5\,e^- \longrightarrow Mn^{2+} + 4\,H_2O$$
$$\underline{5\,Fe^{2+} \longrightarrow 5\,Fe^{3+} + 5\,e^-}$$
$$MnO_4^- + 5\,Fe^{2+} + 8\,H^+ \longrightarrow Mn^{2+} + 5\,Fe^{3+} + 4\,H_2O$$

Finally, we insert the phases:

$$MnO_4{}^-{}_{(aq)} + 5\,Fe^{2+}{}_{(aq)} + 8\,H^+{}_{(aq)} \longrightarrow$$
$$Mn^{2+}{}_{(aq)} + 5\,Fe^{3+}{}_{(aq)} + 4\,H_2O_{(\ell)}$$

EXAMPLE   **11.14**   Use the ion-electron method to write a balanced equation for the reaction between copper metal and concentrated nitric acid to produce copper(II) ions and nitrogen dioxide gas.

SOLUTION   We will start with the nitric acid-nitrogen dioxide half-reaction. Write the skeletal equation:

$$HNO_3 \longrightarrow NO_2$$

Balance for nitrogen:

$$HNO_3 \longrightarrow NO_2 \quad \text{(no change)}$$

Balance for oxygen. We add one water molecule to the right side of the equation:

$$HNO_3 \longrightarrow NO_2 + H_2O$$

Balance for hydrogen. We add one hydrogen ion to the left side of the equation:

$$HNO_3 + H^+ \longrightarrow NO_2 + H_2O$$

Balance for electrons by adding one electron to the right side:

$$HNO_3 + H^+ + e^- \longrightarrow NO_2 + H_2O$$

Now we will write the copper-copper(II) ion half-reaction. Once again, we can go straight to the half-equation by adding electrons to the skeletal equation.

Write the skeletal equation:

$$Cu \longrightarrow Cu^{2+}$$

Balance for charge by adding two electrons to the right side.

$$Cu \longrightarrow Cu^{2+} + 2\,e^-$$

Now the two half-reactions can be added, with the first being multiplied by two:

$$2\,HNO_3 + 2\,H^+ + 2\,e^- \longrightarrow 2\,NO_2 + 2\,H_2O$$
$$\underline{Cu \longrightarrow Cu^{2+} + 2\,e^-}$$
$$2\,HNO_3 + Cu + 2\,H^+ \longrightarrow 2\,NO_2 + Cu^{2+} + 2\,H_2O$$

Finally, we insert the phases:

$$2\,HNO_{3\,(aq)} + Cu_{(s)} + 2\,H^+_{\,(aq)} \longrightarrow 2\,NO_{2\,(g)} + Cu^{2+}_{\,(aq)} + 2\,H_2O_{(\ell)}$$

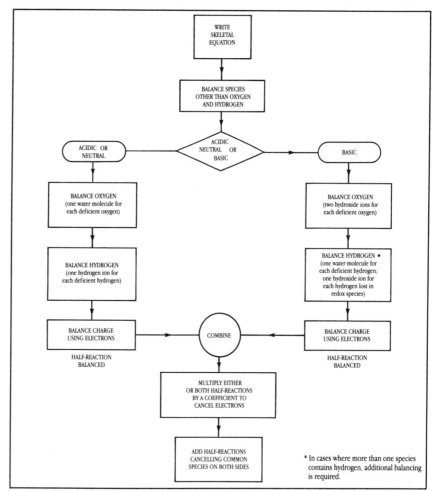

Figure 11.21

A summary of the ion-electron method of balancing redox reactions.

The Chemistry of Photography

Of the many everyday applications of redox reactions, photography is one of the most common. Black and white film consists of a coating of light-sensitive silver bromide crystals suspended in gelatin. (Colour film is more complex.) The gelatin is spread in a thin layer on clear plastic.

The film is placed in a camera, which allows light to enter through the aperture. Light strikes the film and "activates" the silver bromide crystals. Electrons are transferred from the bromide ions to the silver ions. The number of crystals affected on the film is directly proportional to the amount of light received during the exposure: that is, the more light, the more "activated" crystals.

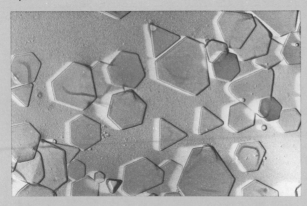

Figure 11.22
The microcrystals of silver bromide on photographic film.

Once the photographs are taken, the next step is to develop the film. In this process, performed in darkness, the film is placed in an organic reducing agent (the developer). All the silver ions in the activated crystals are reduced to metallic silver, which appears as a dark area on the film. The unaffected silver bromide crystals remain unchanged if the developing process is performed well.

The film is then placed in a solution of aqueous sodium thiosulfate (the fixer), which dissolves away the remaining, unaffected silver bromide crystals. This leaves the film with transparent areas, which *were not* exposed to light, and dark areas, which *were* exposed to light. For this reason, the developed film is called a *negative*.

$$AgBr_{(s)} + 2\,S_2O_3^{2-}{}_{(aq)} \longrightarrow Ag(S_2O_3)_2^{3-}{}_{(aq)} + Br^-{}_{(aq)}$$

With our roll of negatives we can now obtain a positive image, usually in a size larger than the negative image. This is done by using an enlarger. The negative is placed in the enlarger, which passes light through the negative onto photographic paper. The paper also has a coating of silver bromide crystals, making it light sensitive, too.

Since the negative acts as a screen through which light passes, the dark areas on the negative block the light from the surface of the paper, making these areas the least exposed to the enlarger light. The light passes through the transparent areas on the negative and activates the silver bromide crystals. When the paper is developed, the activated silver ions in silver bromide are once again reduced to silver, appearing black on the print. Those areas least exposed to the enlarger light appear as white areas on the print.

Although the conversion of silver bromide to silver metal can be explained in terms of a redox reaction, the process by which these crystals are activated is not fully understood. These chemical reactions are part of a study called photochemistry.

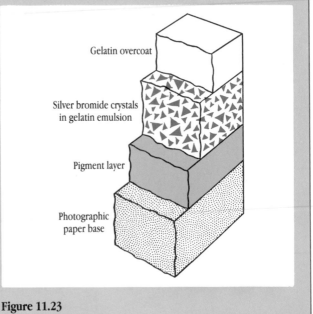

Figure 11.23
Conventional photographic paper.

QUESTIONS

15. What steps are different when balancing half-reactions in acidic solution compared to the procedure for basic solutions?

16. Balance the following half-reactions:
    a) $Au^+_{(aq)} \longrightarrow Au^{3+}_{(aq)}$
    b) $S^{2-}_{(aq)} \longrightarrow S_{(s)}$
    c) $Ag_2O_{(s)} + H_2O_{(\ell)} \longrightarrow Ag_{(s)} + OH^-_{(aq)}$
    d) $Br_{2(\ell)} + H_2O_{(\ell)} \longrightarrow BrO_3^-_{(aq)} + H^+_{(aq)}$

17. Write balanced equations for the following half-reactions in acidic aqueous solution:
    a) the reduction of sulfurous acid, H_2SO_3, to elemental sulfur
    b) the oxidation of formic acid, HCO_2H, to carbon dioxide, CO_2
    c) the conversion of lead(IV) oxide, PbO_2, into lead(II) ions, Pb^{2+}

18. The following half-reactions proceed in basic aqueous solution. Write a balanced reaction equation for each.
    a) the reduction of sulfur dioxide, SO_2, to elemental sulfur
    b) the conversion of methane, CH_4, into carbon dioxide
    c) the oxidation of nickel into nickel(II) oxide, NiO

19. Complete and balance the following redox reactions by the ion-electron method.
    a) $Ag_{(s)} + Cr_2O_7^{2-}_{(aq)} \longrightarrow Ag^+_{(aq)} + Cr^{3+}_{(aq)}$; acidic solution
    b) $MnO_4^-_{(aq)} + NO_2^-_{(aq)} \longrightarrow MnO_{2(s)} + NO_3^-_{(aq)}$; basic solution
    c) $CH_3OH_{(aq)} + MnO_4^-_{(aq)} \longrightarrow CO_{2(g)} + Mn^{2+}_{(aq)}$; acidic solution
    d) $Ce^{4+}_{(aq)} + I^-_{(aq)} \longrightarrow Ce^{3+}_{(aq)} + IO_3^-_{(aq)}$; basic solution
    e) $H_2O_{2(aq)} + ClO_3^-_{(aq)} \longrightarrow O_{2(g)} + Cl_{2(g)}$; acidic solution
    f) $NiO_{2(s)} + S_2O_3^{2-}_{(aq)} \longrightarrow Ni(OH)_{2(s)} + SO_3^{2-}_{(aq)}$; basic solution

---

A Comparison of Balancing Methods

11.10

Which is the "best" method for balancing redox equations? There is no one answer to this question. In part it is the method that you find the easiest. Let us first review the methods.

The Oxidation Number Method

1. Assign oxidation numbers to all the atoms in the equation.
2. Identify which atoms undergo a change in oxidation number.
3. Determine the ratio in which these atoms must react so that the total increase in oxidation numbers equals the decrease.
4. Balance the redox participants in the equation.
5. Balance the other atoms by the inspection method.

The Ion-Electron Method

1. Write balanced oxidation and reduction half-reactions.
2. Change the coefficients in the balanced half-reactions so that the number of electrons produced in the oxidation half-reaction equals the number of electrons consumed in the reduction half-reaction.
3. Add the two half-reactions to obtain a balanced net ionic equation for the redox reaction.

The ion-electron method is most appropriate for dealing with ionic reactions in solution. As we shall see in the next chapter, it is the only way that we can relate redox reactions to electrical processes. The oxidation number method is most advantageous when working with covalent compounds. From several studies on educational methods, it has been shown that people generally prefer whichever method they are taught first.

Summary

- Redox reactions are reactions that involve the complete or partial transfer of electrons, for example, during the formation of ionic and covalent bonds.

- A process in which electrons are lost or oxygen is added is called an oxidation, whereas one in which electrons are gained or oxygen is removed is called a reduction. The two processes take place simultaneously, since electrons are conserved in chemical reactions.

- Oxidation numbers can be used to keep track of electron loss and gain in a reaction, and to identify the oxidizing agent and the reducing agent. Oxidation numbers increase in an oxidation and decrease in a reduction.

- A metal can exchange electrons with the positive ions of another metal if the first metal is placed above the other in the activity series of metals.

- Metals such a nickel and zinc can be produced from their ores by a series of redox reactions.

- Balanced redox reactions can be obtained by equalizing the increase and decrease of oxidation numbers.

- Redox reactions can be broken down into two half-reactions: an oxidation half-reaction, in which electrons are released, and a reduction half-reaction, in which electrons are consumed.

- In the ion-electron method, redox reactions are balanced by the addition of half-reactions.

KEY WORDS

activity series	oxidation state
half-reactions	oxidizing agent
hydrometallurgy	redox reaction
ion-electron method	reducing agent
oxidation	reduction
oxidation number	

ANSWERS TO SECTION QUESTIONS

1. a) Sn, +4: Cl, −1
b) Ca, +2; P, −3
c) Sn, +2; O, −2
d) Ag, +1; S, −2

2. a) H, +1; I, −1
b) H, +1; N, −2
c) H, +1, C, −3, and −2
d) Cl, +5; O, −2
e) S, +6; O, −2

3. N_2O, NO, N_2O_3, NO_2 and N_2O_4, N_2O_5

4. AlF, $NaFO_2$

5. a) H, +1; O, −2; N, +3
b) K, +1; O, −2; Mn, +7
c) H, +1; O, −2; N, −3; S, +6
d) Na, +1; O, −2; Al, +3
e) H, +1; O, −2

6. a) −4 b) 0 c) +2

7. b) $Mg_{(s)} + FeSO_{4\,(aq)} \longrightarrow MgSO_{4\,(aq)} + Fe_{(s)}$
c) $3\,Cu_{(s)} + 2\,AuCl_{3\,(aq)} \longrightarrow 3\,CuCl_{2\,(aq)} + 2\,Au_{(s)}$

8. b) and c)

9.

	Oxidized	Oxidizing agent
a)	H_2	I_2
b)	O_2	F_2
c)	Mg	N_2

10.

	Reduced	Reducing agent
a)	PbO	CO
b)	Br_2	SO_2
c)	Cl_2	NaBr

11. a) N 0 to −3, H 0 to +1; 3 H per 1 N
b) I −1 to 0, Fe +3 to +2; 1 Fe per 1 I
c) O −2 to 0, Cl +5 to −1; 3 O per 1 Cl

12. a) $I_2 + 10\,HNO_3 \longrightarrow 2\,HIO_3 + 10\,NO_2 + 4\,H_2O$
b) $5\,HBr + HBrO_3 \longrightarrow 3\,Br_2 + 3\,H_2O$
c) $2\,MnO_4^- + 16\,H^+ + 10\,Cl^- \longrightarrow 2\,Mn^{2+} + 5\,Cl_2 + 8\,H_2O$
d) $2\,CrO_2^- + 3\,ClO^- + 2\,OH^- \longrightarrow 2\,CrO_4^{2-} + 3\,Cl^- + H_2O$

13. a) Oxidation: $2\,Na \longrightarrow 2\,Na^+ + 2\,e^-$
Reduction: $Br_2 + 2\,e^- \longrightarrow 2\,Br^-$

b) Oxidation: $Zn \longrightarrow Zn^{2+} + 2\,e^-$
Reduction: $S + 2\,e^- \longrightarrow S^{2-}$

c) Oxidation: $4\,Al \longrightarrow 4\,Al^{3+} + 12\,e^-$
Reduction: $3\,O_2 + 12\,e^- \longrightarrow 6\,O^{2-}$

14. a) $Cr^{2+} + Ag^+ \longrightarrow Cr^{3+} + Ag$
Oxidation: $Cr^{2+} \longrightarrow Cr^{3+} + e^-$
Reduction: $Ag^+ + e^- \longrightarrow Ag$

b) $Ca + 2\,H_2O \longrightarrow Ca^{2+} + 2\,OH^- + H_2$
Oxidation: $Ca \longrightarrow Ca^{2+} + 2\,e^-$
Reduction: $2\,H_2O + 2\,e^- \longrightarrow 2\,OH^- + H_2$

c) $Cl_2 + 2\,I^- \longrightarrow 2\,Cl^- + I_2$
Oxidation: $2\,I^- \longrightarrow I_2 + 2\,e^-$
Reduction: $Cl_2 + 2\,e^- \longrightarrow 2\,Cl^-$

15. In acidic solution we add one water molecule for each deficient oxygen; in basic solution we use two moles of hydroxide ions. In acidic solution we balance for hydrogen using hydrogen ions; in basic solution we use water molecules.

16. a) $Au^+_{(aq)} \longrightarrow Au^{3+}_{(aq)} + 2\,e^-$

b) $S^{2-}_{(aq)} \longrightarrow S_{(s)} + 2\,e^-$

c) $Ag_2O_{(s)} + H_2O_{(\ell)} + 2\,e^- \longrightarrow 2\,Ag_{(s)} + 2\,OH^-_{(aq)}$

d) $Br_{2(aq)} + 6\,H_2O_{(\ell)} \longrightarrow 2\,BrO_3^-{}_{(aq)} + 12\,H^+_{(aq)} + 10\,e^-$

17. a) $H_2SO_3 + 4\,H^+ + 4\,e^- \longrightarrow S + 3\,H_2O$

b) $CH_2O_2 \longrightarrow CO_2 + 2\,H^+ + 2\,e^-$

c) $PbO_2 + 4\,H^+ + 2\,e^- \longrightarrow Pb^{2+} + 2\,H_2O$

18. a) $SO_2 + 2\,H_2O + 4\,e^- \longrightarrow S + 4\,OH^-$

b) $CH_4 + 8\,OH^- \longrightarrow CO_2 + 6\,H_2O + 8\,e^-$

c) $Ni + 2\,OH^- \longrightarrow NiO + H_2O + 2\,e^-$

19. a) $6\,Ag_{(s)} + Cr_2O_7^{2-}{}_{(aq)} + 14\,H^+_{(aq)} \longrightarrow$
$$6\,Ag^+_{(aq)} + 2\,Cr^{3+}_{(aq)} + 7\,H_2O_{(\ell)}$$

b) $2\,MnO_4^-{}_{(aq)} + 3\,NO_2^-{}_{(aq)} + H_2O_{(\ell)} \longrightarrow$
$$2\,MnO_{2\,(s)} + 3\,NO_3^-{}_{(aq)} + 2\,OH^-_{(aq)}$$

c) $5\,CH_3OH_{(aq)} + 6\,MnO_4^-{}_{(aq)} + 18\,H^+_{(aq)} \longrightarrow$
$$5\,CO_{2\,(g)} + 6\,Mn^{2+}_{(aq)} + 19\,H_2O_{(\ell)}$$

d) $6\,Ce^{4+}_{(aq)} + I^-_{(aq)} + 6\,OH^-_{(aq)} \longrightarrow 6\,Ce^{3+}_{(aq)} + IO_3^-{}_{(aq)} + 3\,H_2O_{(\ell)}$

e) $5\,H_2O_{2\,(aq)} + 2\,ClO_3^-{}_{(aq)} + 2\,H^+_{(aq)} \longrightarrow 5\,O_{2\,(g)} + Cl_{2\,(g)} + 6\,H_2O_{(\ell)}$

f) $2\,NiO_{2\,(s)} + S_2O_3^{2-}{}_{(aq)} + 2\,OH^-_{(aq)} + H_2O_{(\ell)} \longrightarrow$
$$2\,Ni(OH)_{2\,(s)} + 2\,SO_3^{2-}{}_{(aq)}$$

1. Define the term electronegativity.

2. Why do all atoms in their elemental form have an oxidation number of zero?

3. Explain why the oxidation number of oxygen is -1 in peroxides.

4. What is the relationship between the group number of an element and its oxidation number?

5. Explain why the sum of all the oxidation numbers in a molecule must be zero.

6. Explain what is meant by the following terms:
   a) oxidation
   b) reduction
   c) redox reaction
   d) oxidizing agent
   e) reducing agent

7. Why is zinc a better reducing agent than iron?

8. Explain why silver salts, such as silver nitrate and silver sulfate, behave as strong oxidizing agents.

9. Why should a mixture of aluminum metal and potassium chlorate never be ground up with a mortar and pestle?

10. In what forms, and where, is nickel mainly found on earth?

11. Name two other ores that are usually found together with zinc sulfide.

12. In metal production, what is meant by the following terms:
   a) roasting
   b) smelting
   c) leaching

13. Why is a smelter often associated with fertilizer production?

14. Explain why the increase in oxidation number equals the decrease in a balanced redox reaction.

15. Outline the steps involved in balancing an oxidation half-reaction in basic aqueous solution.

16. Outline the steps involved in the ion-electron method of balancing.

Electronegativity and Oxidation Numbers

17. What are the oxidation numbers of the following:
   a) copper in Cu_2SO_4 and in $CuSO_4$
   b) lead in $PbBr_2$ and in $PbBr_4$

18. Use an electron-dot formula and assign oxidation numbers to each element in the following:
   a) bromine, Br_2
   b) sulfur dioxide, SO_2
   c) hydroxide ion, OH^-
   d) ammonium ion, NH_4^+
   e) chloramine, $ClNH_2$
   f) acetone, CH_3COCH_3

Oxidation Number and the Periodic Table

19. Write the formula of compounds that display the different oxidation numbers of phosphorus.

20. Which of the following iodine compounds are unlikely to exist: CaI_2, K_2I, IF_5, HIO_5, HIO?

Oxidation Number Rules

21. Determine the oxidation numbers for each element in the following substances by the standard rules (Section 11.4):
    a) lithium iodide, LiI
    b) aluminum sulfide, Al_2S_3
    c) phosphorus, P_4
    d) sodium oxide, Na_2O
    e) sodium peroxide, Na_2O_2
    f) calcium nitrate, $Ca(NO_3)_2$

22. Determine the oxidation numbers for each element in the following substances or ions:
    a) copper(I) sulfide, Cu_2S
    b) sulfur, S_8
    c) lithium aluminum hydride, $LiAlH_4$
    d) manganate ion, MnO_4^{2-}
    e) chromate ion, CrO_4^{2-}
    f) ammonium chloride, NH_4Cl

Redox Reactions

23. Which of the following reactions are redox reactions?
    a) $H_2S + Na_2O \longrightarrow Na_2S + H_2O$
    b) $Ca + H_2O \longrightarrow CaO + H_2$
    c) $CO + 2 H_2 \longrightarrow CH_3OH$
    d) $SO_3 + H_2O \longrightarrow H_2SO_4$
    e) $CaCO_3 + SO_2 \longrightarrow CaSO_3 + CO_2$

24. Identify the reactant that is oxidized and the reactant that is reduced in each reaction. Which reactants are the oxidizing agents?
    a) $H_2 + Br_2 \longrightarrow 2 HBr$
    b) $Cl_2 + 2 NaI \longrightarrow I_2 + 2 NaCl$
    c) $H_2C_2O_4 + H_2O_2 \longrightarrow 2 CO_2 + 2 H_2O$
    d) $MnO_2 + 4 HCl \longrightarrow Cl_2 + MnCl_2 + 2 H_2O$
    e) $2 Fe + O_2 + 2 H_2O \longrightarrow 2 Fe(OH)_2$

25. Use the activity series to predict whether a reaction takes place between the following substances. Write a balanced equation when a reaction is predicted.
    a) $Ni_{(s)} + Ba(NO_3)_{2\,(aq)}$
    b) $Hg_{(\ell)} + H_2SO_{4\,(aq)}$
    c) $Mg_{(s)} + Al_2(SO_4)_{3\,(aq)}$
    d) $Fe_{(s)} + Pb(NO_3)_{2\,(aq)}$
    e) $Sn_{(s)} + HCl_{(aq)}$

Balancing Redox Equations Using Oxidation Numbers

26. Show that in the following balanced redox reactions the increase in oxidation number of one element is equal to the decrease in oxidation number of another element.
    a) $Zn_{(s)} + CuCl_{2\,(aq)} \longrightarrow Cu_{(s)} + ZnCl_{2\,(aq)}$
    b) $2 HCl_{(aq)} + 2 HNO_{3\,(aq)} \longrightarrow 2 NO_{2\,(g)} + Cl_{2\,(g)} + 2 H_2O_{(\ell)}$
    c) $MnO_4^-{}_{(aq)} + 5 Fe^{2+}{}_{(aq)} + 8 H^+{}_{(aq)} \longrightarrow$
    $Mn^{2+}{}_{(aq)} + 5 Fe^{3+}{}_{(aq)} + 4 H_2O_{(\ell)}$

27. Balance the following reactions by the oxidation number method:

a) $As_2O_{3(s)} + Cl_{2(g)} + H_2O_{(\ell)} \longrightarrow H_3AsO_{4(aq)} + HCl_{(aq)}$

b) $CO_{(g)} + K_2Cr_2O_{7(aq)} + H_2SO_{4(aq)} \longrightarrow$
$$CO_{2(g)} + Cr_2(SO_4)_{3(aq)} + K_2SO_{4(aq)} + H_2O_{(\ell)}$$

c) $Se_{(s)} + HNO_{3(aq)} \longrightarrow SeO_{2(s)} + NO_{(g)} + H_2O_{(\ell)}$

d) $PH_{3(g)} + O_{2(g)} \longrightarrow P_4O_{10(s)} + H_2O_{(\ell)}$

28. Balance each of the following ionic equations by the oxidation number method.

a) $IO_3{}^-_{(aq)} + H_2O_{(\ell)} + SO_{2(g)} \longrightarrow I_{2(aq)} + SO_4{}^{2-}_{(aq)} + H^+_{(aq)}$

b) $NO_2{}^-_{(aq)} + MnO_4{}^-_{(aq)} + H_2O_{(\ell)} \longrightarrow$
$$NO_3{}^-_{(aq)} + MnO_{2(s)} + OH^-_{(aq)}$$

c) $Ce^{4+}_{(aq)} + Sn^{2+}_{(aq)} \longrightarrow Ce^{3+}_{(aq)} + Sn^{4+}_{(aq)}$

d) $CH_3OH_{(aq)} + Cr_2O_7{}^{2-}_{(aq)} + H^+_{(aq)} \longrightarrow$
$$CH_2O_{(aq)} + Cr^{3+}_{(aq)} + H_2O_{(\ell)}$$

Half-Reactions

29. Write oxidation and reduction half-reactions for each reaction.

a) $2\,Al + 3\,S \longrightarrow Al_2S_3$

b) $2\,K + I_2 \longrightarrow 2\,KI$

c) $2\,Fe + 3\,Cl_2 \longrightarrow 2\,FeCl_3$

d) $4\,Na + O_2 \longrightarrow 2\,Na_2O$

e) $2\,Rb + 2\,H_2O \longrightarrow 2\,RbOH + H_2$

30. Write net ionic equations and half-reactions for each reaction.

a) $Mg_{(s)} + 2\,HCl_{(aq)} \longrightarrow MgCl_{2(aq)} + H_{2(g)}$

b) $Zn_{(s)} + 2\,AgNO_{3(aq)} \longrightarrow Zn(NO_3)_{2(aq)} + 2\,Ag_{(s)}$

c) $2\,FeCl_{3(aq)} + 2\,KI_{(aq)} \longrightarrow 2\,FeCl_{2(aq)} + 2\,KCl_{(aq)} + I_{2(aq)}$

d) $2\,CrSO_{4(aq)} + 2\,Ce(SO_4)_{2(aq)} \longrightarrow Cr_2(SO_4)_{3(aq)} + Ce_2(SO_4)_{3(aq)}$

31. Balance the following half-reactions:

a) $Br_2 \longrightarrow Br^-$

b) $Fe^{2+} \longrightarrow Fe^{3+}$

c) $ClO_2{}^- + H^+ \longrightarrow Cl^- + H_2O$

d) $S_2O_4{}^{2-} + OH^- \longrightarrow SO_4{}^{2-} + H_2O$

32. Write balanced half-reactions in acidic aqueous solutions.

a) $H_2MoO_4 \longrightarrow Mo^{3+}$ 　　c) $NH_4{}^+ \longrightarrow NO_3{}^-$

b) $BrO_3{}^- \longrightarrow Br^-$

33. Write balanced half-reactions in basic aqueous solutions.

a) $OCl^- \longrightarrow Cl^-$

b) $AsO_3{}^{3-} \longrightarrow As$

c) $S^{2-} \longrightarrow SO_4{}^{2-}$

d) $N_2H_4 \longrightarrow N_2$

Ion-Electron Method

34. Balance the reactions by the ion-electron method. All reactions take place in acidic aqueous solutions.
    a) $H_2C_2O_4 + IO_3^- \longrightarrow CO_2 + I^-$
    b) $NO + Cr_2O_7^{2-} \longrightarrow NO_3^- + Cr^{3+}$
    c) $Cl_2 + S_2O_8^{2-} \longrightarrow ClO_3^- + SO_4^{2-}$
    d) $Cu + NO_3^- \longrightarrow Cu^{2+} + NO_2$
    e) $H_2O_2 + Cr_2O_7^{2-} \longrightarrow O_2 + Cr^{3+}$
    f) $MnO_4^- + SO_2 \longrightarrow Mn^{2+} + SO_4^{2-}$
    g) $CO(NH_2)_2 + HNO_2 \longrightarrow CO_2 + N_2$

35. Balance the reactions by the ion-electron method. All reactions take place in basic aqueous solutions.
    a) $S_2O_4^{2-} + O_2 \longrightarrow SO_4^{2-}$
    b) $Cr(OH)_3 + IO_3^- \longrightarrow CrO_4^{2-} + I^-$
    c) $Ag_2O + CH_2O \longrightarrow Ag + CHO_2^-$
    d) $MnO_4^- + N_2H_4 \longrightarrow MnO_2 + N_2$
    e) $S_2O_3^{2-} + OCl^- \longrightarrow SO_4^{2-} + Cl^-$
    f) $MnO_4^- + I^- \longrightarrow MnO_4^{2-} + IO_4^-$

MISCELLANEOUS PROBLEMS

36. What is the oxidation state of xenon in each of the following compounds:
    a) XeF_2 b) $XeOF_2$ c) $CsXeF_6$ d) Ba_2XeO_6

37. One of the reasons that gold has always been so highly prized is that it is so inactive. Gold does not dissolve with acids, gold does not tarnish, gold is at the bottom of the activity series. However gold does dissolve in aqua regia, a mixture of hydrochloric and nitric acids. The products of the reaction are gaseous nitrogen dioxide, NO_2, and the soluble gold tetrachloride ion, $AuCl_4^-$. Write a balanced redox equation to represent this reaction.

38. In some redox reactions, a given element is both oxidized and reduced. Such reactions are known as *disproportionation reactions*. Balance the following disproportionation reactions.
    a) $H_2O_{2(aq)} \longrightarrow H_2O_{(\ell)} + O_{2(g)}$
    b) $HNO_{2(aq)} \longrightarrow HNO_{3(aq)} + NO_{(g)} + H_2O_{(\ell)}$
    c) $Cl_{2(g)} + OH^-_{(aq)} \longrightarrow ClO_4^-_{(aq)} + Cl^-_{(aq)} + H_2O_{(\ell)}$
    d) $P_{4(s)} + H_2O_{(\ell)} \longrightarrow H_2PO_4^-_{(aq)} + PH_{3(g)} + H^+_{(aq)}$

39. Balance the following redox equations by either the oxidation number method or the ion-electron method. Notice that in this reaction both chromium and iodine are being oxidized.

    $CrI_{3(aq)} + KOH_{(aq)} + Cl_{2(g)} \longrightarrow$
    $$K_2CrO_{4(aq)} + KIO_{4(aq)} + KCl_{(aq)} + H_2O_{(\ell)}$$

40. Balance the following equations using either the oxidation number method or the ion-electron method.

a) $H_2O_{2(aq)} + Cr_2O_7^{2-}{}_{(aq)} \xrightarrow{\text{(in acid solution)}} Cr^{3+}{}_{(aq)} + O_{2(g)} + H_2O_{(\ell)}$

b) $Na_2HAsO_{3(aq)} + KBrO_{3(aq)} + HCl_{(aq)} \longrightarrow$
$$NaCl_{(aq)} + KBr_{(aq)} + H_3AsO_{4(aq)}$$

c) $Al_{(s)} + MnO_4^-{}_{(aq)} \xrightarrow{\text{(in base solution)}} MnO_{2(s)} + Al(OH)_4^-{}_{(aq)}$

d) $V_{(s)} + ClO_3^-{}_{(aq)} \xrightarrow{\text{(in base solution)}} HV_2O_7^{3-}{}_{(aq)} + Cl^-_{(aq)}$

e) $Hg_{(\ell)} + NO_3^-{}_{(aq)} + Cl^-{}_{(aq)} \xrightarrow{\text{(in acid solution)}} HgCl_4^{2-}{}_{(aq)} + NO_{2(g)}$

f) $Pb_{(s)} + PbO_{2(s)} + SO_4^{2-}{}_{(aq)} \xrightarrow{\text{(in acid solution)}} PbSO_{4(s)}$

g) $Ag_{(s)} + KCN_{(aq)} + O_{2(g)} + H_2O_{(\ell)} \longrightarrow KAg(CN)_{2(aq)} + KOH_{(aq)}$

h) $Sb_2O_{3(s)} + KIO_{3(aq)} + HCl_{(aq)} + H_2O_{(\ell)} \longrightarrow$
$$HSb(OH)_{6(aq)} + KCl_{(aq)} + ICl_{(aq)}$$

41. As with acid-base titrations, we can determine the concentration of an oxidizing agent or reducing agent using a redox titration. For example, iodine reacts with arsenious acid, H_3AsO_3, to produce iodide ion and arsenic acid, H_3AsO_4. Write a balanced equation for the reaction. If 0.514 g of arsenious acid are needed to reduce 20.60 mL of aqueous iodine to iodide, what is the concentration of the aqueous iodine?

42. We can determine the concentration of an iodide solution by titrating it with an acidic aqueous dichromate ion solution. The products are the chromium(III) ion and aqueous iodine. Write a balanced equation for the reaction. If 28.70 mL of 0.100 mol·L^{-1} dichromate ion are needed to oxidize 20.00 mL of iodide ion, what is the concentration of the iodide ion solution?

SUGGESTED PROJECTS
1. Identify common oxidizing and reducing agents in your home. What are they being used for? In each case, try to find out why they are effective.

2. As well as zinc and nickel, many other metals occurring in an oxidized form are mined and processed in Canada. Research and report on the methods involved in producing a metal such as copper, lead, or iron from its ores.

3. For over one hundred years gold has been separated from ores using a process developed in 1887 by a Scottish metallurgist, J.S. MacArthur. Prepare a report on this cyanidation process, giving the redox reactions involved and explaining any environmental hazards involved.

Electrochemistry

In Chapter 11, we introduced the concept of half-reactions. In this chapter, we will see that splitting a redox reaction into two components is more than a convenient tool for balancing equations, it is also the basis of electrochemistry — the branch of chemistry that deals with the interconversion of chemical energy and electrical energy. Spontaneous redox reactions may be used to generate electricity or, conversely, electricity may be used to drive nonspontaneous redox reactions. Without the former, we would have no battery-operated flashlights, calculators, hearing aids, or watches, and possibly no space flight. Without the latter, many of our most important industrial processes would not be possible. These processes will be examined later in the chapter.

Electrochemical Cells

12.1 An electrochemical cell uses energy released from a spontaneous redox reaction to generate an electric current. The current is derived from the flow of electrons through metal, called **metallic conduction**, and the

Figure 12.1
Allessandro Volta (1745-1827) demonstrating his voltaic pile to Napoleon Bonaparte in Paris in 1802. A painting by Nicola Cianfanelli, 1841.

Figure 12.2
If we place two different metals in a potato (or other fruits or vegetables) a voltage is produced.

movements of ions in solution, called **electrolytic conduction**. A **battery** consists of a single electrochemical cell or a number of cells connected in series.

The story of the modern electrochemical cell begins with the 18th century experiments of two Italians, anatomist Luigi Galvani and physicist Allessandro Volta. Electrochemical cells are still often called galvanic cells or voltaic cells. In the 1780s Galvani conducted a series of experiments on frog muscle at the University of Bologna. He found that the muscle of a frog's leg contracted when both the main nerve to the leg and a smaller nerve in the leg were connected by a bridge made of two different metals. Galvani believed that he had discovered a new type of electricity. According to him, this "animal electricity" originated in the nerves and passed to the muscles, causing a contraction.

Allessandro Volta disagreed with Galvani's theory. He believed that the electricity originated in the two connecting metals rather than the nerve. His experiments showed that an electric current was produced when an electrical connection was made between two different metals separated by a conducting solution, such as sulfuric acid or aqueous sodium chloride.

By 1799 Volta had constructed the world's first battery. One of his early designs consisted of a large stack of electrical units on a wooden base. Each element contained a zinc disk and a copper disk separated by cloth that was moistened with sodium chloride solution. The voltage of this "voltaic pile" was directly proportional to the number of electrical units.

The voltaic pile and other early batteries were not very practical. They were bulky, short-lived, and incapable of generating more that a weak electric current. But by 1836 John F. Daniell had developed a system called the **Daniell cell**, which could supply a steady current for several hours. This cell, in its modern form, consists of a copper rod in an aqueous copper(II) sulfate solution. An unglazed earthenware pot containing a zinc rod in zinc sulfate solution is placed in this solution.

Figure 12.3
A Daniell cell. In this zinc-copper electrochemical cell, the zinc electrode/zinc ion solution is contained in a porous pot.

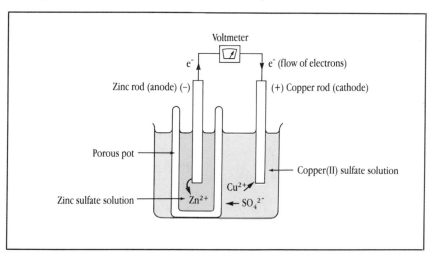

How Electrochemical Cells Work

When a piece of zinc metal is placed in an aqueous solution of copper(II) sulfate, a rapid redox reaction takes place. Electrons are transferred from the zinc metal to the copper ions. The reaction is spontaneous since zinc oxidizes more readily than copper. It appears above copper in the activity series (Table 11.2).

$$Zn_{(s)} + Cu^{2+}_{(aq)} \longrightarrow Zn^{2+}_{(aq)} + Cu_{(s)}$$

The reaction can also be written as two half-reactions.

Oxidation: $Zn_{(s)} \longrightarrow Zn^{2+}_{(aq)} + 2\,e^-$

Reduction: $Cu^{2+}_{(aq)} + 2\,e^- \longrightarrow Cu_{(s)}$

This same reaction occurs in the Daniell cell (Figure 12.3). There is, however, one important difference. In the Daniell cell, each half-reaction takes place in a separate compartment, or **half-cell**. Because the zinc metal is not in contact with the copper sulfate solution, electrons cannot pass directly from the zinc to the copper ions. But when the zinc rod and the copper container are connected by a metal wire, the zinc oxidizes and zinc ions go into solution. Electrons are transferred through the wire to the copper in the reduction reaction.

The electrical circuit of an electrochemical cell consists of two parts, an external circuit and an internal circuit. In the external circuit, electrons leave the cell and re-enter it through another electrical conductor called an **electrode**. The zinc rod and the copper container are the electrodes of the Daniell cell. The zinc is the **anode**. The copper is the **cathode**. For any electrochemical cell, *the anode is the site of oxidation and electron release; the cathode is the site of reduction and electron consumption.* The electrons move through the external circuit from the anode to the cathode. The force that pushes them along is the **potential difference**, or **electromotive force (emf)**, that exists between the electrodes. Since the potential difference is measured in **volts**, it is commonly referred to as the **voltage** of the cell.

Suppose we construct the half-cells in separate containers (Figure 12.4). In the anode container, we put a solution containing zinc sulfate. Similarly, in the cathode container, we place a solution of copper(II) sulfate. Both solutions are electrically neutral.

When the electrodes are connected by a wire, a current will flow for a very short period of time and then stop. The current lasts for only a short duration because electrons that leave the zinc metal are carried by the wire to the copper rod. As the zinc electrode loses electrons, zinc ions are released from the zinc rod into solution. This creates an imbalance in the number of zinc ions over sulfate ions in the anode container. A similar imbalance develops in the cathode container. Copper ions in solution gain electrons that are released at the copper electrode and copper atoms are deposited on the copper rod. It is this imbalance in charge in each container that prevents any further reaction and stops any further current from flowing.

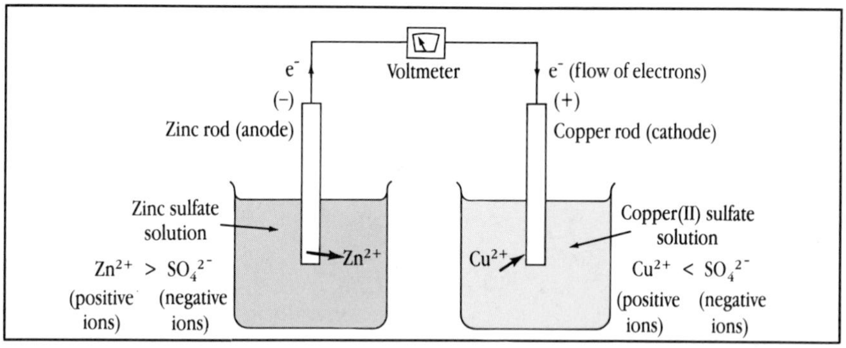

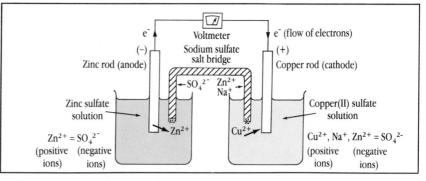

Figure 12.4

An incomplete zinc-copper electrochemical cell. The flow of electrons will cease in microseconds as soon as there is an imbalance of ions in each cell.

For the reaction to proceed, the half-cells must be connected *internally* as well as externally. We can do this in a number of ways, one of which is to use an inverted U-tube filled with a salt solution to link the half-cells. This is called a **salt bridge**. The salt bridge allows negative or positive ions to move to the other container and hence to maintain the electrical neutrality of the two solutions. As Figure 12.5 shows, the sulfate anions will move towards the anode half-cell while the zinc cations will move towards the cathode half-cell.

Figure 12.5

A zinc-copper electrochemical cell in which the half-cells are linked by a salt bridge. Note that electrons flow through the external circuit while ions move through the salt bridge.

We must be careful to choose an inert electrolyte for the salt bridge. If the salt reacts with other ions in the half-cells, or with either electrode, it will interfere with the redox reaction of the cell. In our example the salts in each half-cell are sulfates, thus a sulfate is the obvious choice for a salt bridge. As we shall see, the sodium ions do not participate in any aqueous electrochemical cell reaction.

How do we know that ions migrate from one half-cell to the other? If we analyze the solution in the cathode half-cell after the reaction has run for some time, we find that there is a significant concentration of *zinc* ions. In fact if we use zinc nitrate solution in the anion half-cell, after some time we can detect sulfate ions that have crossed over the salt bridge from the cathode container.

Once the internal and external circuits are complete, the reaction takes place, producing zinc ions in solution and additional copper metal on the cathode. As the reaction continues, the voltage decreases and finally becomes zero when the reaction reaches equilibrium. The cell will then be "dead."

$$Zn_{(s)} + Cu^{2+}_{(aq)} \rightleftharpoons Zn^{2+}_{(aq)} + Cu_{(s)}$$

Notation for an Electrochemical Cell

In chemist's shorthand, the standard cell in Figure 12.5 is written as

$$Zn_{(s)}|Zn^{2+}_{(aq)}(1.0 \text{ mol·L}^{-1})||Cu^{2+}_{(aq)}(1.0 \text{ mol·L}^{-1})|Cu_{(s)}$$

By convention the anode appears on the left, the cathode on the right. The single vertical lines indicate the contact boundaries between phases in each half-cell. The double vertical lines represent the salt bridge or separator. An electrochemical cell is referred to as a **standard cell** *when the reactant and product ions or molecules are present in concentrations of 1.0 mol·L⁻¹.*

EXAMPLE   **12.1**   When the metal electrodes of the electrochemical cell shown below are connected by a voltmeter, the meter indicates a potential difference of 0.46 V.

a) Using the activity series in Table 11.2, identify the half-reaction taking place at each electrode.

b) Write the shorthand notation for the cell, identifying the anode and cathode, and indicate the direction of movement of electrons and ions.

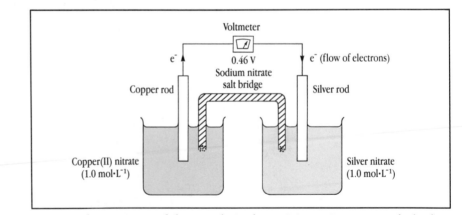

SOLUTION   a) From the position of the metals in the activity series we conclude that copper oxidizes more readily than silver and that silver ions reduce more readily than copper ions. The half-reactions are therefore:

$$\text{Anode (oxidation):} \quad Cu_{(s)} \longrightarrow Cu^{2+}_{(aq)} + 2 \, e^-$$
$$\text{Cathode (reduction):} \quad Ag^+_{(aq)} + e^- \longrightarrow Ag_{(s)}$$

b) The copper electrode is the anode; the silver electrode is the cathode. The correct notation for this standard cell is

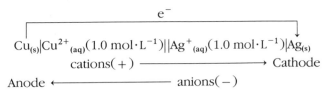

$$Cu_{(s)}|Cu^{2+}{}_{(aq)}(1.0 \text{ mol} \cdot L^{-1})||Ag^{+}{}_{(aq)}(1.0 \text{ mol} \cdot L^{-1})|Ag_{(s)}$$

cations(+) ⟶ Cathode

Anode ⟵ anions(−)

The arrows indicate the direction of electron and ion movement.

Electrochemical cells can also be made from half-cells in which either the reactant or the product of the half-reaction is a gas. In standard cells, the gases have a pressure of 100 kPa. Figure 12.6 shows a standard hydrogen half-cell linked by a salt bridge to a standard zinc half-cell. The hydrogen gas is bubbled into a solution of 1.0 mol·L⁻¹ hydrochloric acid over a platinum electrode. The platinum itself does not react but serves as an inert surface where exchange of electrons can take place. From the activity series we can conclude that zinc will be oxidized and hydrogen ions will be reduced:

Anode (oxidation): $Zn_{(s)} \longrightarrow Zn^{2+}{}_{(aq)} + 2\,e^-$

Cathode (reduction): $2\,H^+{}_{(aq)} + 2\,e^- \longrightarrow H_{2\,(g)}$

The overall reaction is the same as the reaction observed when zinc is directly exposed to hydrochloric acid:

$$Zn_{(s)} + 2\,H^+{}_{(aq)} \longrightarrow Zn^{2+}{}_{(aq)} + H_{2\,(g)}$$

The shorthand representation for this cell is:

$$Zn_{(s)}|Zn^{2+}(1.0 \text{ mol} \cdot L^{-1})||H^+{}_{(aq)}(1.0 \text{ mol} \cdot L^{-1})|H_{2\,(g)}(100 \text{ kPa}),\ Pt_{(s)}$$

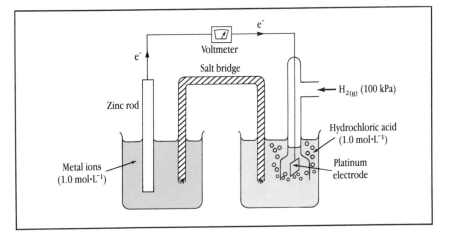

Figure 12.6
We can determine the relative potential of another half-cell by combining it with a standard hydrogen half-cell.

QUESTIONS

1. An electrochemical cell consists of two half-cells connected by a salt bridge. One half consists of an aluminum electrode placed in a $1.0 \text{ mol} \cdot \text{L}^{-1}$ aluminum ion solution. The other half-cell contains a nickel electrode in a $1.0 \text{ mol} \cdot \text{L}^{-1}$ nickel ion solution. The salt bridge contains sodium sulfate.
   a) From the activity series (Table 11.2) determine the reaction taking place in each half-cell.
   b) Write a shorthand notation of the cell.
   c) Make a sketch of the cell marking in the anode and cathode, and indicate the direction of electron and ion movement.

2. Write the anode and cathode half-reactions for the following standard cell.

$$Fe_{(s)}\big|Fe^{2+}_{(aq)}(1.0 \text{ mol} \cdot \text{L}^{-1})\big|\big|Cl^{-}_{(aq)}(1.0 \text{ mol} \cdot \text{L}^{-1})\big|Cl_{2\,(g)}(100 \text{ kPa}), Pt_{(s)}$$

Standard Electrode Potentials

12.2

An almost unlimited number of half-cells can be constructed and combined into electrochemical cells. However, the **reduction potential** of each half-cell, the tendency of its ions and molecules to *gain electrons*, will be different. As a result, the electrodes will all have different electrical potentials. Unfortunately we cannot measure the electrical potential of one half-cell. We can only measure the voltage difference, or emf, between two half-cells by combining them into an electrochemical cell. For example, a cell voltage of 1.10 V in the standard zinc-copper ion cell tells us that the reduction potential of the metal ions is 1.10 V greater for copper ions than for zinc ions, since copper is below zinc in the activity series. It also means that the oxidation potential (the tendency to lose electrons) is 1.10 V greater for zinc than for copper.

Standard Half-Cell Potentials

Because half-cell potentials can only be determined from the emf ($\mathscr{E}$) of a complete electrochemical cell, the **standard hydrogen electrode** has been assigned a **standard potential** ($\mathscr{E}°$) of 0.00 V.

$$2 H^{+}_{(aq)} + 2 e^{-} \rightleftharpoons H_{2\,(g)} \qquad \mathscr{E}° = 0.00 \text{ V}$$
$$1 \text{ mol} \cdot \text{L}^{-1} \qquad\qquad 100 \text{ kPa} \qquad T = 25°C$$

This electrode is then used as a reference to assign potentials to other half-cells. *The measured electromotive force of a standard electrochemical cell containing a hydrogen half-cell is the standard potential ($\mathscr{E}°$) of the second half-cell.* The superscript ° indicates that the measurements are made at standard conditions (aqueous solutions, $1 \ mol \cdot L^{-1}$; gas pressures, $100 \ kPa$; temperature, $25 \ °C$, or $298 \ K$). The **standard reduction potential** of a half-cell is a measure of the tendency to gain electrons from the hydrogen half-cell. The **standard oxidation potential** is a measure of the tendency to lose electrons to the standard hydrogen electrode. Standard reduction and oxidation potentials for a given half-cell are thus numerically identical but opposite in sign. For example,

$$Zn^{2+}_{(aq)} + 2 \ e^- \longrightarrow Zn_{(s)} \qquad \mathscr{E}°_{reduction} = -0.76 \ V$$

$$Zn_{(s)} \longrightarrow Zn^{2+}_{(aq)} + 2 \ e^- \qquad \mathscr{E}°_{oxidation} = +0.76 \ V$$

By convention, however, half-cells are compared on the basis of their reduction potentials and the symbol $\mathscr{E}°$ refers to a *standard reduction potential* unless otherwise indicated.

The $\mathscr{E}°$ values of some representative standard half-cells are given in Table 12.1. A more complete list appears in Appendix VII. Ions or molecules with negative reduction potentials gain electrons less easily than hydrogen ions. Those with positive values gain electrons more easily than hydrogen ions. Lithium ions in aqueous solution have the weakest tendency to gain electrons ($\mathscr{E}° = -3.00 \ V$); molecular fluorine has the greatest tendency to gain electrons ($\mathscr{E}° = +2.86 \ V$).

TABLE 12.1 *Standard Reduction Potentials for Common Half-Reactions*

Half-Reaction	$\mathscr{E}°$ (volts)
$Li^+_{(aq)} + e^- \rightleftharpoons Li_{(s)}$	-3.00
$Al^{3+}_{(aq)} + 3 \ e^- \rightleftharpoons Al_{(s)}$	-1.67
$2 \ H_2O_{(\ell)} + 2 \ e^- \rightleftharpoons 2 \ OH^-_{(aq)} + H_{2 \ (g)}$	-0.83
$Zn^{2+}_{(aq)} + 2 \ e^- \rightleftharpoons Zn_{(s)}$	-0.76
$Cr^{3+}_{(aq)} + 3 \ e^- \rightleftharpoons Cr_{(s)}$	-0.74
$Fe^{2+}_{(aq)} + 2 \ e^- \rightleftharpoons Fe_{(s)}$	-0.44
$2 \ H^+_{(aq)} + 2 \ e^- \rightleftharpoons H_{2 \ (g)}$	0.00
$Cu^{2+}_{(aq)} + 2 \ e^- \rightleftharpoons Cu_{(s)}$	$+0.34$
$O_{2 \ (g)} + 2 \ H_2O_{(\ell)} + 4 \ e^- \rightleftharpoons 4 \ OH^-_{(aq)}$	$+0.40$
$Ag^+_{(aq)} + e^- \rightleftharpoons Ag_{(s)}$	$+0.80$
$Br_{2 \ (aq)} + 2 \ e^- \rightleftharpoons 2 \ Br^-_{(aq)}$	$+1.06$
$Cl_{2 \ (g)} + 2 \ e^- \rightleftharpoons 2 \ Cl^-_{(aq)}$	$+1.36$
$MnO_4^-_{(aq)} + 8 \ H^+_{(aq)} + 5 \ e^- \rightleftharpoons Mn^{2+}_{(aq)} + 4 \ H_2O_{(\ell)}$	$+1.50$
$F_{2 \ (g)} + 2 \ e^- \rightleftharpoons 2 \ F^-_{(aq)}$	$+2.86$

Increasing strength as oxidizing agent for species to left of double arrow

Increasing strength as reducing agent for species to right of double arrow

Calculating Standard Cell Potentials

In an electrochemical cell, one half-cell undergoes reduction while the other undergoes oxidation. Thus when we are combining half-reactions and calculating the cell potential, one of the tabulated reduction equations will have to be reversed and the sign of the potential changed. Let us find the potential for the following standard cell

$$Fe_{(s)}|Fe^{2+}_{(aq)}(1.0 \text{ mol}\cdot L^{-1})||Cu^{2+}_{(aq)}(1.0 \text{ mol}\cdot L^{-1})|Cu_{(s)}$$

From Table 12.1 we find that

$$Fe^{2+}_{(aq)} + 2\,e^- \longrightarrow Fe_{(s)} \qquad \mathscr{E}° = -0.44\,V$$
$$Cu^{2+}_{(aq)} + 2\,e^- \longrightarrow Cu_{(s)} \qquad \mathscr{E}° = +0.34\,V$$

The description of this cell, as it appears here, follows accepted shorthand notation (Section 12.1). The $Fe^{2+}|Fe$ half-cell is the anode. Thus we reverse the $Fe^{2+}|Fe$ standard half-cell reduction reaction and the sign of $\mathscr{E}°$ to give:

Anode (oxidation): $Fe_{(s)} \longrightarrow Fe^{2+}_{(aq)} + 2\,e^- \qquad \mathscr{E}°_{ox} = +0.44\,V$
Cathode (reduction): $Cu^{2+}_{(aq)} + 2\,e^- \longrightarrow Cu_{(s)} \qquad \mathscr{E}° = +0.34\,V$

The sum of these half-cell potentials provides the potential of the cell.

$$\mathscr{E}°_{cell} = 0.44\,V + 0.34\,V = 0.78\,V$$

EXAMPLE   **12.2** Calculate the potential of the standard cell

$$Zn_{(s)}|Zn^{2+}_{(aq)}(1.0 \text{ mol}\cdot L^{-1})||Cl^-_{(aq)}(1.0 \text{ mol}\cdot L^{-1})|Cl_{2\,(g)}(100\,kPa), Pt_{(s)}$$

SOLUTION First we determine the half-reactions from the shorthand notation of the cell. We reverse the $Zn|Zn^{2+}$ standard half-cell reduction and the sign of $\mathscr{E}°$ given in Table 12.1. Thus,

Anode (oxidation): $Zn_{(s)} \longrightarrow Zn^{2+}_{(aq)} + 2\,e^- \qquad \mathscr{E}°_{ox} = +0.76\,V$
Cathode (reduction): $Cl_{2\,(g)} + 2\,e^- \longrightarrow 2\,Cl^-_{(aq)} \qquad \mathscr{E}° = +1.36\,V$

The cell potential is the sum of these standard half-cell potentials.

$$\mathscr{E}°_{cell} = 0.76\,V + 1.36\,V = 2.12\,V$$

Because the reduction potentials only depend on the concentrations, the standard values do not change when we change the coefficients in the half-reactions as shown by the following reactions:

$$Ag^+_{(aq)} + e^- \longrightarrow Ag_{(s)} \qquad \mathscr{E}° = +0.80\,V$$
$$2\,Ag^+_{(aq)} + 2\,e^- \longrightarrow 2\,Ag_{(s)} \qquad \mathscr{E}° = +0.80\,V$$

Predicting Spontaneity of Redox Reactions

Reduction potentials can also be used to predict whether a redox reaction is spontaneous or nonspontaneous. A redox reaction is spontaneous when the sum of the potentials of the half-reactions is positive. The reaction is nonspontaneous when the sum is negative. For example, if we wish to know whether bromine will spontaneously exchange electrons with chloride ions, we first reverse the sign of the standard reduction potential for chlorine and then add the standard potentials of the half-reactions:

Oxidation: $2\,Cl^-_{(aq)} \longrightarrow Cl_{2\,(g)} + 2\,e^-$ $\quad \mathscr{E}^\circ_{ox} = -1.36\,V$

Reduction: $Br_{2\,(aq)} + 2\,e^- \longrightarrow 2\,Br^-_{(aq)}$ $\quad \mathscr{E}^\circ = +1.06\,V$

$$\mathscr{E}^\circ_{cell} = -1.36\,V + 1.06\,V = -0.30\,V$$

From the negative value of the hypothetical cell voltage we can conclude that, at least under standard conditions, the reaction will not be spontaneous. The reverse reaction, however, has a positive value and will be spontaneous.

EXAMPLE   **12.3**   Predict whether sulfur dioxide and bromine will react in aqueous solution given the equation:

$$SO_{2\,(g)} + Br_{2\,(aq)} + 2\,H_2O_{(\ell)} \longrightarrow SO_4^{2-}{}_{(aq)} + 2\,Br^-_{(aq)} + 4\,H^+_{(aq)}$$

SOLUTION   By consulting Appendix VII on standard reduction potentials, we can break down the reaction into two half-reactions:

Oxidation: $SO_{2\,(g)} + 2\,H_2O_{(\ell)} \longrightarrow SO_4^{2-}{}_{(aq)} + 4\,H^+_{(aq)} + 2\,e^-$

$$\mathscr{E}^\circ_{ox} = -0.18\,V$$

Reduction: $Br_{2\,(g)} + 2\,e^- \longrightarrow 2\,Br^-_{(aq)}$ $\qquad \mathscr{E}^\circ = +1.06\,V$

$$\mathscr{E}^\circ_{cell} = -0.18\,V + 1.06\,V = +0.88\,V$$

Since the hypothetical cell voltage is positive, we can expect the reaction to be spontaneous.

We must be careful in using this method for predicting spontaneity. When the concentrations and temperatures drastically differ from the standard conditions of 1.0 mol·L^{-1} in aqueous solutions at 25 °C, our prediction may be wrong. For example, the reaction

$$2\,H_2O_{(\ell)} + 2\,e^- \longrightarrow H_{2\,(g)} + 2\,OH^-_{(aq)}$$

has a standard reduction potential of $-0.83\,V$ when the hydroxide concentration is 1.0 mol·L^{-1}. In neutral aqueous solution, when the hydroxide concentration is 1.0×10^{-7} mol·L^{-1}, the reduction potential is $-0.41\,V$.

QUESTIONS

Values for standard reduction potentials can be found in Appendix VII.

3. Write the anode and cathode reactions for each of the following electrochemical cells and calculate the cell potential ($\mathscr{E}°$) for each cell. In b) and c) the electrodes are platinum.

   a) $Cr_{(s)}|Cr^{3+}_{(aq)}(1.0\ mol\cdot L^{-1})||Ag^{+}_{(aq)}(1.0\ mol\cdot L^{-1})|Ag_{(s)}$

   b) $Pb_{(s)}|Pb^{2+}_{(aq)}(1.0\ mol\cdot L^{-1})||Cl^{-}_{(aq)}(1.0\ mol\cdot L^{-1})|Cl_{2\,(g)}, Pt_{(s)}$

   c) $Pt_{(s)}, H_{2\,(g)}|OH^{-}_{(aq)}(1.0\ mol\cdot L^{-1})||OH^{-}_{(aq)}(1.0\ mol\cdot L^{-1})|O_{2\,(g)}, Pt_{(s)}$

4. Use half-reaction potentials to predict whether the following reactions are spontaneous or nonspontaneous in aqueous solutions.

   a) $H_2O_{2\,(aq)} + Sn^{2+}_{(aq)} \longrightarrow Sn_{(s)} + O_{2\,(g)} + 2\,H^{+}_{(aq)}$

   b) $I_{2\,(aq)} + 2\,Cl^{-}_{(aq)} \longrightarrow 2\,I^{-}_{(aq)} + Cl_{2\,(g)}$

   c) $MnO_4^{-}_{(aq)} + 5\,Br^{-}_{(aq)} + 8\,H^{+}_{(aq)} \longrightarrow$
   $$Mn^{2+}_{(aq)} + \tfrac{5}{2}\,Br_{2\,(g)} + 4\,H_2O_{(\ell)}$$

   d) $H_{2\,(g)} + S_2O_8^{2-}_{(aq)} \longrightarrow 2\,H^{+}_{(aq)} + 2\,SO_4^{2-}_{(aq)}$

5. Using the half-cell reduction potentials, determine which one of the following substances is the best oxidizing agent in acidic aqueous solution: $KMnO_4$, $K_2Cr_2O_7$, or $K_2S_2O_8$.

6. Using the half-cell reduction potentials, determine which of the following is the best reducing agent in acidic aqueous solution: H_2, H_2O, or H_2S.

Batteries   12.3

As we discussed earlier, when we place a zinc rod in a solution of copper(II) sulfate, zinc sulfate and copper metal are formed. If we measure the temperature of the solution, we find it increases as the reaction proceeds. That is, the reaction is exothermic, producing heat energy. If we perform the reaction in a cell, the energy is released in a much more useful form, as electrical energy. Electrochemical cells used for power generation are called batteries.

Batteries come in all shapes and sizes. The very small ones are used when the current requirements are low — in cameras, calculators, watches and hearing aids. The largest batteries, consisting of many cells, are built for industrial usage where the current requirements are high — in lift trucks, mining vehicles, diesel engine starters, and rapid transit systems.

Primary Batteries

Primary batteries, also called dry cells, are non-rechargeable. The electrolytes are present as a paste rather than a liquid. The oldest, least expensive, and still most common type is the Leclanché, or manganese(IV)

Figure 12.7

The first battery is thought to be about 2000 years old. This is a replica of a device found in archeological excavations near Baghdad. The original was dated at about 250 B.C.

Figure 12.8

General-purpose and alkaline batteries such as these can only be used once, while nickel-cadmium batteries can be recharged.

oxide-zinc cell (Figure 12.9). It is a general-purpose battery used for flashlights, transistor radios, toys, etc. The zinc case of the cell acts as the anode. The cathode is a graphite rod surrounded by a moist paste of manganese(IV) oxide, MnO_2, ammonium chloride, NH_4Cl, and zinc chloride, $ZnCl_2$. Although the half-reaction at the cathode is complex and not fully understood, the reactions taking place in the Leclanché cell may be summarized as follows:

Anode (Oxidation): $\quad Zn_{(s)} \longrightarrow Zn^{2+}_{(aq)} + 2\,e^-$

Cathode (Reduction): $\quad 2\,MnO_{2(s)} + 2\,NH_4^+_{(aq)} + 2\,e^- \longrightarrow$

$$Mn_2O_{3(s)} + H_2O_{(\ell)} + 2\,NH_{3(aq)}$$

The maximum voltage of the cell is 1.5 V; however, as zinc ions accumulate, the voltage will steadily decrease. By connecting several of these cells in series, we can make a battery with a potential difference as high as 90 V.

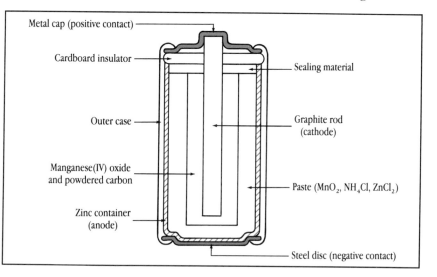

Figure 12.9

The construction of the general-purpose cell.

The 1.5 V alkaline manganese(IV) oxide-zinc cell, also called simply the alkaline battery, has now replaced the Leclanché cell in many of its applications. The electrolyte is potassium hydroxide, and the anode consists of a gel of zinc dust and potassium hydroxide. The redox reaction is similar to that in the Leclanché cell, and the voltage is also 1.5 V. Advantages of the alkaline battery are its consistent voltage, increased capacity, longer shelf-life, and reliable operation at temperatures as low as −40 °C. The main disadvantage is its higher cost.

Tiny "button" dry cells are especially useful for small instruments such as watches and hearing aids. The three button dry cells in common use all have zinc anodes but different cathodes. In addition to size, the great advantage of this type is that the voltage remains virtually constant throughout the life of the cell. Provided that the air intake is sealed, the zinc-air button cell also has an unlimited shelf-life.

TABLE 12.2 *Features of Common Button Dry Cell Batteries*

COMPONENT	TYPE OF DRY CELL BATTERY		
	Mercury Oxide Cell	**Silver Oxide Cell**	**Zinc-air Cell**
Anode	Zn	Zn	Zn
Anode Half-reaction	$Zn_{(s)} + 2\,OH^-_{(aq)} \longrightarrow$ $ZnO_{(s)} + H_2O_{(\ell)} + 2\,e^-$	$Zn_{(s)} + 2\,OH^-_{(aq)} \longrightarrow$ $ZnO_{(s)} + H_2O_{(\ell)} + 2\,e^-$	$Zn_{(s)} + 2\,OH^-_{(aq)} \longrightarrow$ $ZnO_{(s)} + H_2O_{(\ell)} + 2\,e^-$
Cathode	Graphite-HgO	Ag_2O	O_2
Cathode Half-reaction	$HgO_{(s)} + H_2O_{(\ell)} + 2\,e^- \longrightarrow$ $Hg_{(\ell)} + 2\,OH^-_{(aq)}$	$Ag_2O_{(s)} + H_2O_{(\ell)} + 2\,e^- \longrightarrow$ $2\,Ag_{(s)} + 2\,OH^-_{(aq)}$	$\frac{1}{2}O_{2\,(g)} + H_2O_{(\ell)} + 2\,e^- \longrightarrow$ $2\,OH^-_{(aq)}$
Electrolyte	KOH	KOH	KOH
Voltage	1.35 V	1.5 V	1.5 V

Secondary Batteries

Unlike primary batteries, secondary batteries (also called storage batteries) are rechargeable. They vary in size from calculator button cells and flashlight "D" cells to large, heavy-duty, industrial batteries. By far the most important, however, is the lead-acid battery used in automobiles. These batteries account for more than 70 % of the world's secondary battery sales.

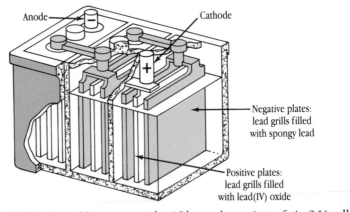

Figure 12.10
The lead-acid battery.

Anode—— Cathode

Negative plates: lead grills filled with spongy lead

Positive plates: lead grills filled with lead(IV) oxide

A typical, 12-V, lead-acid battery weighs 15 kg and consists of six 2-V cells connected in series (Figure 12.10). The anode of each cell is a grid of lead-antimony or lead-calcium alloy packed with spongy lead. The cathode is a similar grid packed with lead(IV) oxide and the electrolyte is aqueous sulfuric acid (approximately $4.5\ mol\cdot L^{-1}$). The use of grids as electrodes means that each cell is actually a number of smaller cells connected in parallel (anode to anode and cathode to cathode), thereby effectively increasing the current output. The following expression summarizes the spontaneous redox reaction that takes place when each cell discharges.

		$\mathscr{E}^\circ_{ox} = +0.36\,V$
Anode: $Pb_{(s)} + SO_4^{2-}{}_{(aq)} \longrightarrow PbSO_{4\,(s)} + 2\,e^-$		
Cathode: $PbO_{2\,(s)} + 4\,H^+{}_{(aq)} + SO_4^{2-}{}_{(aq)} + 2\,e^- \longrightarrow PbSO_{4\,(s)} + 2\,H_2O_{(\ell)}$		$\mathscr{E}^\circ = +1.68\,V$

Redox reaction: $Pb_{(s)} + PbO_{2\,(s)} + 2\,SO_4^{2-}{}_{(aq)} + 4\,H^+{}_{(aq)} \longrightarrow 2\,PbSO_{4\,(s)} + 2\,H_2O_{(\ell)}$ $\mathscr{E}^\circ = +2.04\,V$

The cells can be recharged by passing a current through the battery in the opposite direction, thus providing the energy for the nonspontaneous reverse reaction. In an automobile battery, this reaction occurs when the engine is running.

$$2\,PbSO_{4\,(s)} + 2\,H_2O_{(\ell)} \longrightarrow Pb_{(s)} + PbO_{2\,(s)} + 4\,H^+{}_{(aq)} + 2\,SO_4^{2-}{}_{(aq)}$$

The extent to which a lead-acid battery is charged is indicated by the density of the electrolyte. A fully charged battery has a density of $1.25-1.28\,g \cdot mL^{-1}$, but as discharge continues, sulfuric acid is used up and the density decreases. If the density drops below $1.08\,g \cdot mL^{-1}$, the battery cannot generally be recharged. Cold weather battery problems are usually the result of increased electrolyte viscosity. Under these conditions, ion migration slows and the power output of the battery declines.

As we can see from Table 12.3, there are alternatives to the lead-acid storage battery. The Edison, or nickel-iron alkaline battery, introduced in 1908, was developed by Thomas A. Edison. It powered an early electric car and may still be useful for this purpose, although the nickel-zinc battery shows more promise. Sealed nickel-cadmium alkaline batteries are popular in Europe for industrial machinery and electric delivery vans. They are also available in button and "D" forms. Silver-zinc and silver-cadmium batteries are used in military and aerospace programs where the emphasis is on high performance rather than cost.

TABLE 12.3   *Features of the Edison, Nickel-Cadmium, and Nickel-Zinc Storage Batteries*

	TYPE OF STORAGE BATTERY		
COMPONENT	**Edison**	**Nickel-Cadmium**	**Nickel-Zinc**
Anode	Fe	Cd	Zn
Anode Half-reaction	$Fe_{(s)} + 2\,OH^-{}_{(aq)} \longrightarrow$ $FeO_{(s)} + H_2O_{(\ell)} + 2\,e^-$	$Cd_{(s)} + 2\,OH^-{}_{(aq)} \longrightarrow$ $CdO_{(s)} + H_2O_{(\ell)} + 2\,e^-$	$Zn_{(s)} + 2\,OH^-{}_{(aq)} \longrightarrow$ $ZnO_{(s)} + H_2O_{(\ell)} + 2\,e^-$
Cathode	NiO_2	NiO_2	NiO_2
Cathode Half-reaction	$NiO_{2\,(s)} + H_2O_{(\ell)} + 2\,e^- \longrightarrow$ $NiO_{(s)} + 2\,OH^-{}_{(aq)}$	$NiO_{2\,(s)} + H_2O_{(\ell)} + 2\,e^- \longrightarrow$ $NiO_{(s)} + 2\,OH^-{}_{(aq)}$	$NiO_{2\,(s)} + H_2O_{(\ell)} + 2\,e^- \longrightarrow$ $NiO_{(s)} + 2\,OH^-{}_{(aq)}$
Electrolyte	KOH	KOH	KOH
Voltage	1.4 V	1.3 V	1.7 V

Fuel Cells

Fuel cells are electrochemical cells that convert the energy of a redox combustion reaction directly into electrical energy. Operation requires a continuous supply of reactants and constant removal of products. The cathode reactant is usually air or pure oxygen, and the anode fuel is a gas, such as hydrogen, methane, or propane.

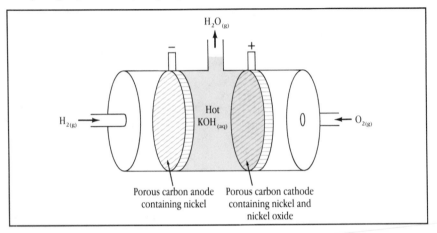

Figure 12.11
A schematic of a fuel cell.

In the hydrogen-oxygen fuel cell, hydrogen and oxygen gas are passed through catalyst-containing carbon electrodes into a hot, concentrated potassium hydroxide electrolyte solution. The electrode reactions are as follows:

Anode (oxidation):	$2\,H_2 + 4\,OH^- \longrightarrow 4\,H_2O + 4\,e^-$
Cathode (reduction):	$O_2 + 2\,H_2O + 4\,e^- \longrightarrow 4\,OH^-$
Redox reaction:	$2\,H_2 + O_2 \longrightarrow 2\,H_2O$

One hydrogen-oxygen fuel cell has a potential of about 1.2 V. Notice that there are no toxic wastes produced.

Both the Gemini and Apollo spacecraft used hydrogen-oxygen fuel cells. On the Apollo flights, each fuel cell operated continuously for 440 hours, producing 292 kilowatt-hours of electrical energy and 100 L of water.

Although fuel cells represent a very efficient energy conversion (70–80 % efficiency), the cost is still prohibitive for large-scale use. However, phosphoric acid fuel cells have been used to generate power for large urban centres. New York City, for example, installed a 4.8 megawatt unit in the early 1980s.

Figure 12.12
Electrical power for the Space Shuttle is provided by these hydrogen-oxygen fuel cells. The shuttle carries three cells, each capable of providing up to twelve kilowatts of energy.

New Developments in Storage Batteries

The present high demand for batteries is expected to continue. In addition to the usual domestic applications, storage batteries will be required to power electric cars and trucks, and to store excess energy from electrical power plants, a process called electrical load levelling.

Figure 12.13

A battery-powered vehicle used in Britain, where electric propulsion for urban delivery trucks has been popular for many decades.

Although the lead-acid battery has been used in all kinds of electric vehicles, from wheelchairs to delivery vans, its weight and short periods between recharging are serious disadvantages. It is also too expensive to be used for commercial electrical load levelling. As a result, two new types of systems are now being investigated: aqueous systems, operating at ordinary temperatures; and non-aqueous systems, requiring temperatures of 200–400 °C. The sodium-sulfur cell, for example, is a non-aqueous system. It uses a ceramic electrolyte and operates at temperatures of 300–350 °C. This cell has a number of positive features: neither sodium nor sulfur is costly, the cell is light, and the system has a long life. It is possible that these cells could be combined into very large batteries for load levelling at electrical power plants. A zinc-chlorine aqueous system also shows promise for load levelling installations.

Figure 12.14

A model plane powered by an aluminum battery. This new type of cell has been devised at Alcan's research laboratories in Kingston, Ontario. The cell has tremendous possibilities because it is inexpensive and of low density. A 2 kg aluminum battery has the same power output as a 10 kg lead-acid battery.

QUESTIONS

7. List both the advantages and disadvantages that fuel cells have in relation to storage batteries.
8. Given that the electrolyte in each case is potassium hydroxide, write discharge electrode reactions for each of the following cells:
   a) aluminum-air (oxygen) cell
   b) methane (CH_4)-oxygen fuel cell (The methane is oxidized to carbon dioxide.)

Corrosion   *12.4*

Corrosion is a spontaneous electrochemical process that leads to the deterioration of metals. It occurs as a direct result of the tendencies of most

Figure 12.15
Rusted automobiles. The corrosion of iron is a major problem.

metals to lose electrons and to exist in nature as oxides and sulfides. Evidence of corrosion is everywhere — from tarnished silver and green copper roofs to rusty cars and garden tools.

Corrosion of Iron

A corroding metal is an electrochemical cell with a distinct anode and cathode. The reactions usually begin on an exposed surface where the crystalline structure of the metal has been stressed (e.g. the heads and sharpened tips of nails). When iron corrodes, it loses electrons at an anodic site. The electrons migrate through the metal to a separate cathodic site where water and oxygen are reduced. In the presence of oxygen, the iron(II) ions are further oxidized to iron(III) ions. It is the reaction of these iron(III) ions with hydroxide ions that produces the flaky brown solid we call rust. The process is illustrated in Figure 12.16.

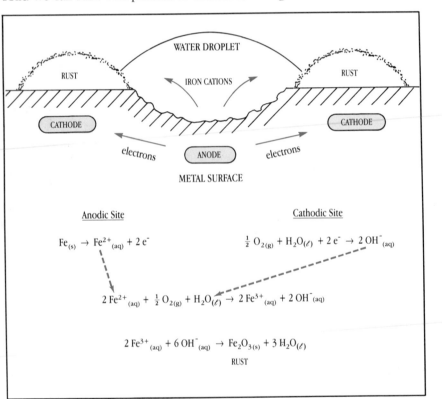

Figure 12.16
The process of iron corrosion.

The separation of anodic and cathodic sites can be shown experimentally by the arrangement illustrated in Figure 12.17. The reaction between the potassium iron(III) cyanide indicator and iron(II) ions turns the anodic sites deep blue. The reaction between the phenolphthalein indicator and hydroxide ions turns the cathodic site red. Usually the head and tip of the nail turn blue, and the shaft turns red.

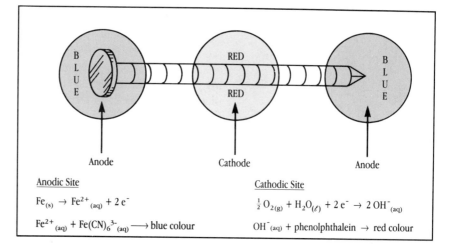

Anodic Site	Cathodic Site
$Fe_{(s)} \rightarrow Fe^{2+}_{(aq)} + 2\,e^-$	$\frac{1}{2}\,O_{2(g)} + H_2O_{(\ell)} + 2\,e^- \rightarrow 2\,OH^-_{(aq)}$
$Fe^{2+}_{(aq)} + Fe(CN)_6^{3-}_{(aq)} \longrightarrow$ blue colour	$OH^-_{(aq)} +$ phenolphthalein $\rightarrow$ red colour

Figure 12.17

Corrosion of an iron nail in agar gel. The production of iron(II) ions and hydroxide ions at different sites can be seen using indicators.

Figure 12.18

The Statue of Liberty, New York. When the copper statue was strengthened early this century, iron bolts were used. At the contact points, extensive corrosion occurred. In 1987 the statue had to undergo major reconstruction to enable it to last into the 21st century.

A nail in a piece of wood has only the head fully exposed to moisture and oxygen. The head therefore, becomes the cathodic site; the anodic sites are inside the wood. Although most of the rust appears around the head, it is mainly the iron inside the wood that corrodes.

The rate at which corrosion occurs may be affected by several factors. As anyone living in an area where the roads are salted in winter knows, metal corrodes much faster in salt water than fresh water. This is because the ions in salt water form a salt bridge between the anodic and cathodic sites. A metal also corrodes faster when it is in contact with another metal that has a higher reduction potential. A potential difference is generated between the metals and the two function as an electrochemical cell. For example, the corrosion of an iron pipe in a plumbing system will be enhanced if it is attached to a copper pipe. Iron also rusts faster in acidic solutions, and is one of the problems associated with acid rain.

Corrosion Protection

There are a number of ways to slow down corrosion, if not prevent it. Once again we examine iron to demonstrate how this protection can be achieved.

Alloys

To provide a corrosion-free metal, we can use an alloy such as stainless steel. The addition of about 5 % chromium to steel reduces the rate of rusting by about 80 %. If the chromium content is raised to 16 %, the problem of rusting is almost completely eliminated.

This would appear to be an ideal solution to the problem of rusting, but chromium is a very expensive metal. For smaller items, such as kitchen utensils, the convenience outweighs the added cost. For larger items, cost is usually the most important factor. For example, it is only on higher priced cars that stainless steel mufflers are now being introduced.

Metal Coatings

To prevent contact with oxygen and moisture, iron can be coated with paint, grease, plastic, or another metal. The metals used for this purpose are mainly tin and chromium. The coatings must completely cover the iron to be effective. Any scratch will expose the iron to attack. With metal-plated iron, a break in the coating will result in the formation of an electrochemical cell. The rate of corrosion will be faster than with pure iron.

When iron corrodes, it produces the characteristic crumbly brown rust that accelerates corrosion by absorbing moisture. By dipping iron briefly in concentrated nitric acid or in molten potassium nitrate, a more corrosion-resistant layer of iron oxide can be formed.

For the inside of water-containing systems, such as automobile radiators, chromate ion is added. The chromate ion will react with surface layers of rust to produce a surface layer of very insoluble iron(II) chromate. This will prevent any attack by air and water on the underlying metal.

Active Metal Contact

Previously we indicated that some metals, by being in contact with iron, might cause the iron to rust. These metals are *less* reactive than iron. Hence any exposed iron would be oxidized. An alternative approach is to use a *more* reactive metal, which will be oxidized away, leaving the iron cathode intact.

The most commonly used metal for this purpose is zinc. An iron object coated with zinc is said to have been **galvanized**. Corregated iron sheets, buckets, and many other objects have this zinc coating. Even when the iron is exposed, it is the zinc that is attacked. Rusting will only occur when all the zinc has been oxidized away.

Blocks of zinc can be bolted to the hulls of ships used in salt water to protect the metal hull. New blocks last for about a year. Steel pipelines can be protected by burying a zinc cable alongside or by connecting blocks of magnesium to them every few hundred metres. The more expensive domestic water heaters contain a rod of magnesium metal to minimize tank corrosion.

Metal objects and installations can also be protected against corrosion by connecting them to a source of direct electric current. The metal becomes cathodic in relation to its environment, which inhibits the loss of electrons.

Figure 12.19
Zinc blocks on a ship's rudder. The zinc is oxidized, leaving the metal intact.

QUESTIONS

9. A metal submerged in water is slowly corroding. What are the most likely reduction half-reactions under the following conditions? Which of these half-reactions is the least spontaneous?
   a) The water solution is acidic.
   b) The water solution is neutral or basic and saturated with oxygen.
   c) The water solution is neutral or basic and contains no oxygen.

10. In the 18th century the British Navy experimented with the use of copper sheathing to protect the bottoms of their vessels against fouling by marine organisms. Explain why this had a disastrous effect on the iron rudder and the iron nails used to fasten the keel.

11. Generally, impure metals corrode much faster than pure metals. Explain why 99.97 % pure aluminum corrodes a thousand times faster than 99.998 % pure aluminum.

12. Calcium metal can inhibit the corrosion of engines in cars and trucks. When calcium disks are connected to the drain plugs of the oilpans the oil stays clean up to ten times longer. Explain the effect of the calcium disks.

13. You are the proud owner of a large iron sculpture on your front lawn and you would hate to see it become a heap of rust in a few years. Give at least three practical ways of slowing down the corrosion process.

14. Write the oxidation and reduction half-reactions of a corroding galvanized nail exposed to rain.

⅄ Electrolysis   12.5

Electrochemical cells use spontaneous redox reactions to convert chemical energy to electrical energy. **Electrolysis** is the process by which electrical energy is passed through a solution containing ions or through a molten ionic compound to cause a nonspontaneous reaction to occur. The cell in which such a process is carried out is called an **electrolytic cell**.

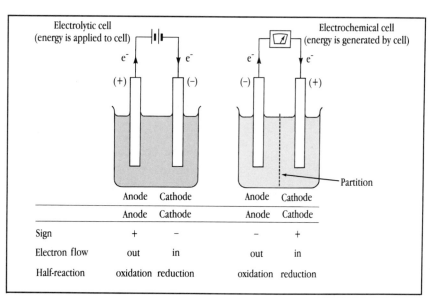

Figure 12.20

A comparison of an electrolytic cell and an electrochemical cell.

Electrolysis is one of the most important industrial processes. Metals are purified, and both metals and nonmetals are isolated from compounds by electrolytic methods. Because of very large power requirements, electrochemical plants are generally located in areas with an abundance of inexpensive hydro power.

Electrolysis of Aqueous Solutions

Pure water and ionic solids are very poor electrical conductors; the former because it contains very few ions, the latter because the ions are not mobile. Solutions of ionic compounds in water are good conductors, but for an electric current to flow through these solutions electrons must be transported through the solution by ions or molecules. In electrolytic cells as well as electrochemical cells, *positive ions (cations) move toward the cathode and negative ions (anions) move toward the anode.*

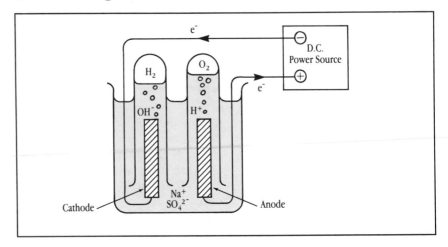

Figure 12.21

Electrolysis of water.

Figure 12.21 illustrates an electrolytic cell in which an electric current is passed through an aqueous solution of sodium sulfate. The power source is actually an electron pump, circulating electrons in a nonspontaneous direction. Electrons are forced into the solution at the cathode and removed from the solution at the anode. The redox half-reactions in this cell are

Anode (oxidation): $\quad H_2O_{(\ell)} \longrightarrow \frac{1}{2} O_{2\,(g)} + 2\,H^+_{\,(aq)} + 2\,e^-$

Cathode (reduction): $\quad 2\,H_2O_{(\ell)} + 2\,e^- \longrightarrow H_{2\,(g)} + 2\,OH^-_{\,(aq)}$

Adding the two half-reactions gives the overall reaction:

$$3\,H_2O_{(\ell)} \longrightarrow H_{2\,(g)} + \frac{1}{2}\,O_{2\,(g)} + 2\,OH^-_{\,(aq)} + 2\,H^+_{\,(aq)}$$

Since the hydroxide ion and hydrogen ions neutralize each other, the overall reaction involves the decomposition of water:

$$H_2O_{(\ell)} \longrightarrow H_{2\,(g)} + \frac{1}{2}\,O_{2\,(g)}$$

The electrolysis of water will not take place in the absence of an electrolyte. Like a salt bridge in an electrochemical cell, the electrolyte ensures that electrical neutrality is maintained throughout the solution by the migration of ions.

Predicting of Electrode Reactions

Depending on the species present, there may be a few potential half-reactions for the electrodes of an electrolytic cell. The problem is to predict which of these reactions will actually take place. In theory these reactions will be the half-cell reactions requiring the lowest voltage. In practice, however, electrode reactions are often difficult to predict. Let us return to the electrolytic cell containing aqueous sodium sulfate (Figure 12.21). The species present are sodium ions, sulfate ions, and water. From the table of half-cell potentials (Appendix VII), we see that two of our species can be reduced at the cathode — the sodium ions to sodium metal and water to hydrogen gas.

$$Na^+_{(aq)} + e^- \longrightarrow Na_{(s)} \qquad \mathscr{E}° = -2.71\,V$$
$$2\,H_2O_{(\ell)} + 2\,e^- \longrightarrow H_{2\,(g)} + 2\,OH^-_{(aq)} \qquad \mathscr{E}° = -0.83\,V$$

Of the two, the water has the more positive reduction potential $(-0.83 > -2.71)$ and is therefore more likely to be reduced, thus producing hydrogen gas.

There are two species that can be oxidized at the anode. Water can be oxidized to oxygen gas and the sulfate ion can be oxidized to peroxodisulfate ion $S_2O_8^{2-}$.

$$H_2O_{(\ell)} \longrightarrow \tfrac{1}{2}O_{2\,(g)} + 2\,H^+_{(aq)} + 2\,e^- \qquad \mathscr{E}°_{ox} = -1.23\,V$$
$$2\,SO_4^{2-}_{(aq)} \longrightarrow S_2O_8^{2-}_{(aq)} + 2\,e^- \qquad \mathscr{E}°_{ox} = -2.01\,V$$

In this case, we would expect the production of oxygen. We would also predict that for every two volumes of hydrogen gas, one volume of oxygen gas should be produced. Instead, we often find a slightly smaller volume of oxygen. This can be explained if we assume that some sulfate ion reacts instead of water.

Predictions based on standard electrode potentials should be made with caution. For example, the standard oxidation potential of the half-cell reaction

$$2\,H_2O_{(\ell)} \longrightarrow O_{2\,(g)} + 4\,H^+_{(aq)} + 4\,e^- \qquad \mathscr{E}° = -1.23\,V$$

is only true provided the half-cell contains $1.0\ mol \cdot L^{-1}$ of hydrogen ion and oxygen gas at a pressure of $100\,kPa$. In the neutral sodium sulfate solution (pH 7) we used, the concentration of hydrogen ion would have been $1.0 \times 10^{-7}\ mol \cdot L^{-1}$, and the pressure of oxygen gas from the atmosphere would have been about $20\,kPa$ (air is about 20% O_2). Under these conditions, the half-cell potential would be $-0.41\,V$. Thus the choice of electrode reactions is strongly affected by deviations from standard conditions.

The actual voltage required for an electrode reaction to take place may also exceed the calculated value by an amount referred to as the **overvoltage**. The overvoltages are low for the formation of metals from their positive ions, but high for the formation of gases such as hydrogen and oxygen. The overvoltage depends strongly on the electrode material used and is lowest for platinum electrodes.

We should keep in mind, however, that when the differences in standard potentials of the possible half-reactions are very large we can make reasonable predictions about electrode reactions.

EXAMPLE 12.4 Predict the half-reactions occurring at the anode and cathode of an electrolytic cell containing aqueous potassium iodide.

SOLUTION Only potassium ions and water molecules need to be considered in the reduction half-reaction at the cathode. The negative iodide ion will not gain another electron.

$$K^+_{(aq)} + e^- \longrightarrow K_{(s)} \qquad \mathscr{E}^\circ = -2.92\,V$$
$$2\,H_2O_{(\ell)} + 2\,e^- \longrightarrow H_{2\,(g)} + 2\,OH^- \qquad \mathscr{E}^\circ = -0.83\,V$$

Looking at the difference in the standard reduction potentials, it is safe to conclude that water will be reduced, not potassium ions. The already positive potassium ions will not lose an additional electron. This leaves iodide ions and water molecules as possible electron donors in the oxidation half-reaction at the anode.

$$2\,I^-_{(aq)} \longrightarrow I_{2\,(aq)} + 2\,e^- \qquad \mathscr{E}^\circ_{ox} = -0.54\,V$$
$$H_2O_{(\ell)} \longrightarrow \tfrac{1}{2}O_{2\,(g)} + 2\,H^+_{(aq)} + 2\,e^- \qquad \mathscr{E}^\circ_{ox} = -1.23\,V$$

The much higher (more positive), standard potential of iodide ions leaves little doubt that the iodide ions will be oxidized. The predicted electrode reactions are therefore:

Anode (oxidation): $\quad 2\,I^-_{(aq)} \longrightarrow I_{2\,(aq)} + 2\,e^-$
Cathode (reduction): $\quad 2\,H_2O_{(\ell)} + 2\,e^- \longrightarrow H_{2\,(g)} + 2\,OH^-_{(aq)}$

QUESTIONS

15. What are the cathode and anode reactions for the electrolytic cells in which the following nonspontaneous overall reactions occur:
    a) $MgCl_{2\,(\ell)} \longrightarrow Mg_{(\ell)} + Cl_{2\,(g)}$
    b) $Al_2O_{3\,(\ell)} \longrightarrow 2\,Al_{(\ell)} + \tfrac{3}{2}O_{2\,(g)}$
    c) $ZnSO_{4\,(aq)} + H_2O_{(\ell)} \longrightarrow Zn_{(s)} + \tfrac{1}{2}O_{2\,(g)} + H_2SO_{4\,(aq)}$

16. Using standard reduction potentials, predict the cathode and anode half-reactions in the electrolysis of the following solutions. (Assume the electrolytic cells contain inert platinum electrodes.)
    a) $HBr_{(aq)}$ c) $AgNO_{3\,(aq)}$
    b) $LiI_{(aq)}$ d) $CuSO_{4\,(aq)}$

Consumer Beware

A knowledge of chemistry can help you make informed decisions in your life. An example of the importance of chemistry was described by Joseph Hesse, a high school teacher, in the magazine *Chem Matters*. He recounted how a salesperson representing a company that sold water distillers visited his parents house. The salesperson described how the drinking water was contaminated with minerals. The salesperson produced a "precipitator," a box connected to two electrodes. When the box was connected to the electrical supply and the electrodes were inserted into a glass of drinking water, a yellowish colour started to develop. In a few minutes, a brownish scum covered the surface of the water. The explanation was given that "electricity caused the minerals and heavy metals to precipitate," and that this showed the true content of the water.

Hesse became suspicious. The longer the current ran, the thicker the precipitate. He determined that one electrode was iron while the other was aluminum. Indeed, on chemical analysis the precipitate was shown to be almost entirely iron(III) hydroxide. The electrodes were weighed before and after a run, and it was shown that the iron electrode decreased in mass. No scum was produced if the metal electrodes were replaced by carbon ones. Opening the box revealed a rectifier, a device that converts the alternating current to direct current. Finally, a friend of his at a nearby junior college analyzed the original tap water and showed it to have only a trace metal content.

He came to the conclusion that the device was acting as an electrolytic cell. At the anode iron was oxidized, and at the cathode water was reduced. The hydroxide ions then combined with the iron(III) ions to produce iron(III) hydroxide.

$$Fe_{(s)} \longrightarrow Fe^{3+}_{(aq)} + 3\,e^-$$
$$2\,H_2O_{(\ell)} + 2\,e^- \longrightarrow H_{2\,(g)} + 2\,OH^-_{(aq)}$$
$$Fe^{3+}_{(aq)} + 3\,OH^-_{(aq)} \longrightarrow Fe(OH)_{3\,(s)}$$

This "precipitator" was obviously a device that was used by the unscrupulous to prey upon people's fears of water pollution and to convince them to purchase an expensive home water purification unit. How many others have been pursuaded by such a startling "demonstration?"

Figure 12.22
The 'precipitator' that was supposed to indicate ions in solution. In fact, it was an electrolytic cell.

Electroplating 12.6

Electroplating is an electrolytic process that deposits a thin, uniform layer of metal on a conducting surface. All kinds of articles are routinely electroplated with gold, silver, copper, nickel, chromium, zinc, or tin to enhance their aesthetic appeal or to provide corrosion protection. Even nonconducting materials such as wood, plastic, or leather can be electroplated if they are first treated with wax or a lacquer containing graphite.

When an object is to be electroplated, it is used as the cathode of an electrolytic cell. The anode is usually the electroplating metal. The composition of the electrolyte varies with different plating processes. Cyanide, for example, forms a water-soluble complex with gold and silver ions; hence, cyanide ions are added in gold and silver plating to keep the gold and silver ions in alkaline solution.

$$Ag^+_{(aq)} + 2\,CN^-_{(aq)} \longrightarrow Ag(CN)_2{}^-_{(aq)}$$

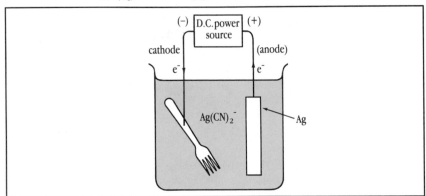

Figure 12.23
An electroplating cell for silver.

A simple electrolytic cell for silver plating is illustrated in Figure 12.23. Silver cyanide, potassium cyanide, and potassium carbonate each constitute about 4 % of the electroplating solution. The electrode half-reactions are

Anode (oxidation): $Ag_{(s)} + 2\,CN^-_{(aq)} \longrightarrow Ag(CN)_2{}^-_{(aq)} + e^-$
Cathode (reduction): $Ag(CN)_2{}^-_{(aq)} + e^- \longrightarrow Ag_{(s)} + 2\,CN^-_{(aq)}$

The end result is the transfer of silver from the anode to the cathode.

$$\underset{\text{(anode)}}{Ag_{(s)}} \longrightarrow \underset{\text{(cathode)}}{Ag_{(s)}}$$

How to Make Money

Millions of bank notes are produced annually by the Bank of Canada. The engraved metal plates of the printing presses are produced by a series of electroplating processes.

The starting point is a hand-engraved steel plate. Since several artists contribute in the engraving of this plate, it is impossible to reproduce it by hand. Plastic molds are made from this original. These molds are next used as cathodes in an electrolytic cell, which has a nickel anode and an electrolyte solution containing nickel ions. A total of 40 nickel copies of the original plate are produced. They are soldered together, provided with a graphite coating, and nickel plated. The graphite facilitates the metal-plating process and makes it easier for the image to be separated from the master. From the obtained 40-subject reverse image, any number of printing masters can be "grown" electrolytically.

The printing plates have a nickel thickness of about 0.075 cm. For improved wear resistance, they are electrolytically coated with a very thin layer of chromium (about 0.001 cm). Such a printing plate is good for up to half a million impressions before it has to be rechromed.

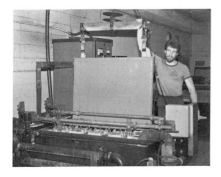

Figure 12.24
Removing a banknote printing plate that has been coated with a layer of nickel from an electrolytic cell.

Figure 12.25
Separating the printing plate from the master plate after removal from the electrolytic cell.

Electrolytic Purification of Metals

Electroplating is also used on a very large scale for the **electrolytic purification** of metals such as copper and lead. The electrolytic cells designed for this purpose consist of many closely-packed anodes and cathodes. The anodes contain the impure metal and the cathodes are thin sheets of very pure metal. When the cell is in operation, the anodes slowly dissolve as pure metal is deposited on the cathodes. The impurities form a sludge on the bottom.

In the purification of lead, the impure metal is obtained by reduction of lead(II) oxide with coke, and further reduced by carbon monoxide.

$$PbO_{(s)} + C_{(s)} \longrightarrow Pb_{(l)} + CO_{(g)}$$
$$PbO_{(s)} + CO_{(g)} \longrightarrow Pb_{(l)} + CO_{2(g)}$$

The liquid lead thus obtained is poured into anodes that are approximately 98% pure and weigh about 200 kg each. The cathodes are thin sheets of pure lead placed between the anodes. A common arrangement is to have 25 anodes and 24 cathodes per cell. The electrolyte solution consists of lead hexafluorosilicate, $PbSiF_6$, and hydrofluoric acid, HF.

During the electrolysis, lead from the anodes transfers to the cathodes. The electrode half-reactions are thus

$$\textbf{Anode (oxidation):} \quad Pb_{(s)} \longrightarrow Pb^{2+}{}_{(aq)} + 2\ e^-$$
$$\textbf{Cathode (reduction):} \quad Pb^{2+}{}_{(aq)} + 2\ e^- \longrightarrow Pb_{(s)}$$

In about seven days the process is complete and the anodes and cathodes are replaced. The lead on the cathodes is now over 99.99 % pure. The sludge at the bottom of the cells contains recoverable amounts of several metals, including silver and gold, and is removed periodically for further processing.

QUESTIONS

17. Write the anode and cathode half-reactions and identify the electrodes for each of the following electrolytic processes:
   a) nickel plating an object using an electrolyte solution containing nickel(II) chloride and nickel(II) sulfate
   b) the electrolytic purification of copper using an electrolyte solution containing copper(II) sulfate.

Electrolysis of Sodium Chloride 12.7

Sodium chloride (table salt) is one of the world's most abundant ionic compounds. As the raw material for making chlorine, sodium hydroxide, sodium sulfate, sodium carbonates, and metallic sodium, it is also one of the most important.

Salt can be obtained by direct solar evaporation of sea water (Section 8.5) or recovered from subterranean deposits left behind by ancient oceans. The annual world sodium production is approximately two hundred million tonnes, of which Canada contributes about nine million tonnes. Since there are large deposits in most provinces, Canada is self-sufficient in salt (Table 12.4). Almost half of the country's salt production is used for snow and ice removal; much of the rest is used by the chemical industry.

Figure 12.26
A salt mine.

TABLE 12.4   *Sodium Chloride Producers in Canada*

Province	Number of Mines	Annual Salt Production (Tonnes)
Nova Scotia & New Brunswick	4	1 114 000
Quebec	1	1 250 000
Ontario	6	4 967 000
Saskatchewan & Alberta	6	1 273 000

Sodium and Chlorine from Sodium Chloride

The electrolytic process that converts molten sodium chloride into its constituent elements takes place in a **Downs cell** (Figure 12.27). The overall reaction is as follows:

$$2\,NaCl_{(l)} \longrightarrow 2\,Na_{(l)} + Cl_{2\,(g)}$$

Although sodium chloride melts at 800 °C, the cell can operate at a temperature of 600 °C by using an electrolyte mixture of sodium chloride (40 %) and calcium chloride (60 %). Sodium is produced at the cathode, chlorine gas is produced at the anode. The half-reactions for the Downs cell are

Anode (oxidation): $\quad 2\,Cl^-_{(l)} \longrightarrow Cl_{2\,(g)} + 2\,e^-$

Cathode (reduction): $\quad Na^+_{(l)} + e^- \longrightarrow Na_{(l)}$

The design of the Downs cell eliminates the possibility that the sodium and the chlorine will recombine. Sodium has a lower density than the electrolyte. It rises to the surface where it can be transferred to a reservoir.

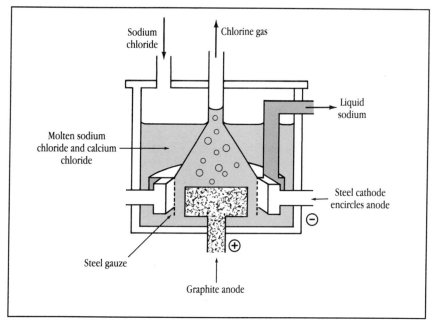

Figure 12.27

A Downs cell, used for the production of sodium metal.

Sodium Hydroxide and Chlorine from Sodium Chloride

The chlor-alkali industry produces sodium hydroxide and chlorine by the electrolysis of aqueous sodium chloride. The two electrolytic cells commonly used for this purpose are the diaphragm cell and the mercury cell. The overall reaction is the same in each cell.

$$2\,NaCl_{(aq)} + 2\,H_2O_{(l)} \longrightarrow 2\,NaOH_{(aq)} + H_{2\,(g)} + Cl_{2\,(g)}$$

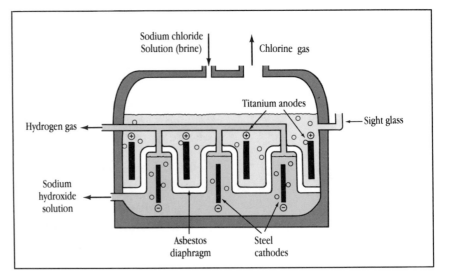

Figure 12.28

A diaphragm cell, used for the production of sodium hydroxide and chlorine.

Like other industrial electrolytic cells, the diaphragm cell has many anodes and cathodes, in this case separated by asbestos diaphragms, which prevent the chlorine from reacting with either the hydrogen gas or the sodium hydroxide. The electrode half-reactions are

Anode (oxidation): $2\,Cl^-_{(aq)} \longrightarrow Cl_{2\,(g)} + 2\,e^-$

Cathode (reduction): $2\,H_2O_{(l)} + 2\,e^- \longrightarrow H_{2\,(g)} + 2\,OH^-_{(aq)}$

The initial concentration of the sodium chloride is about 25 %. When the concentration of sodium hydroxide in the cell reaches 11–12 %, the solution is concentrated by evaporation. Most of the sodium chloride crystallizes from the concentrated sodium hydroxide solution and is recycled. Thus, 50 % sodium hydroxide solution, which is sufficient for most purposes, only contains about 1 % sodium chloride. The hydrogen produced can be used as a heat source for the evaporators or it can be "burned" in a chlorine atmosphere to give hydrogen chloride.

QUESTIONS

18. Give the anode and cathode half-reactions of the Downs cell, and for the diaphragm chlor-alkali cell.

19. What reactions would take place between chlorine, hydrogen, and sodium hydroxide in the diaphragm cell if the electrodes were not separated by a diaphragm?

Quantitative Electrolysis

12.8 Between 1831 and 1834 the English chemist Michael Faraday conducted a series of experiments with electrolytic cells. These investigations led him to conclude that the amount of substance produced or consumed at an electrode is related to the quantity of electricity applied to the cell. His findings, now known as **Faraday's laws**, are the basis of quantitative electrochemistry. Faraday also gave us such familiar terms as electrode, electrolysis, electrolyte, anode, and cathode. We will examine Faraday's laws, but first we must define some common electrical units.

Electrical Units

So far, we have been concerned with the measurements of potential difference (voltage). In quantitative electrolysis it is the **current**, or amount of electrical charge passing through the cell per unit time, that becomes important. This overall relationship can be expressed in a word equation.

Electrical charge = Electric current × Seconds

Current is measured in **amperes**, **A**. The **coulomb**, **C**, is the unit of electrical charge. By definition, one coulomb is the quantity of charge transported in one second by a current of one ampere.

1 C = 1 A × 1 s

EXAMPLE **12.5** How much electric charge is transported when a constant electric current of 5.0 A is passed through a circuit for 30 minutes?

SOLUTION

$$\text{Electric charge} = \text{Electric Current} \times \text{Seconds}$$
$$= 5.0\,\text{A} \times 30\,\text{min} \times \frac{60\,\text{s}}{1\,\text{min}}$$
$$= 5.0\,\text{A} \times 1.8 \times 10^3\,\text{s}$$
$$= 9.0 \times 10^3\,\text{C} \ (\text{or } 9000\,\text{C})$$

In the following half-reaction one electron must be gained by each silver ion to form one atom of silver:

$$\mathbf{Ag^+_{(aq)} + e^- \longrightarrow Ag_{(s)}}$$

This means that every mole of silver produced uses one mole of electrons. The amount of charge equivalent to one mole of electrons is called the **faraday**, **F**. One faraday is $9.65 \times 10^4\,\text{C}$.

How Much is Consumed and Produced in Electrolysis

Now that we have defined the essential terms, we are in a position to examine Faraday's laws. They are as follows:

1. In an electrolysis, the amount of product produced or reactant consumed is directly proportional to the length of time that a constant current is passed through the circuit.

2. To produce one mole of product or consume one mole of reactant requires $9.65 \times 10^4 \times n$ coulombs of charge, where n is the number of moles of electrons gained or lost per mole of reactant.

This means that if a constant current is passed through an aqueous solution of silver nitrate, for example, the amount of silver deposited at the cathode in twenty minutes will be twice the amount produced in ten minutes because twice as many electrons have been supplied to the cathode during the reaction.

But to produce one mole of copper by the electrolysis of an aqueous copper(II) sulfate solution requires twice as much charge as the production of one mole of silver because twice as many electrons have to be delivered to the cathode for the reaction

$$Ag^+_{(aq)} + e^- \longrightarrow Ag_{(s)}$$
$$Cu^{2+}_{(aq)} + 2\,e^- \longrightarrow Cu_{(s)}$$

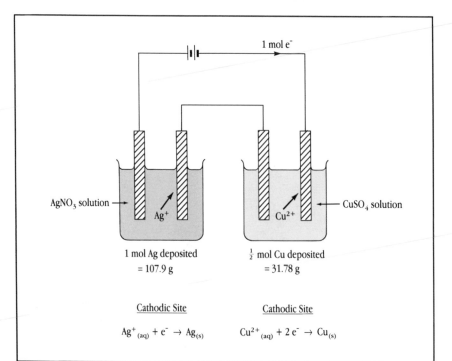

Figure 12.29

A series of electrochemical cells. According to Faraday's Laws, 9.65×10^4 coulombs of electricity (1 mol of electrons) will produce one mole of silver and one half mole of copper.

Example 12.6 illustrates how the amounts of products in an electrolysis can be calculated from the applied electric current.

EXAMPLE   *12.6*   The electrolysis of an aqueous copper(II) sulfate solution results in the formation of copper at the cathode. Calculate the mass of copper produced if a constant current of 1.00 A is passed through the cell for 1.00 hour.

SOLUTION First we calculate the amount of electric charge circulated.

$$\text{Electric charge} = \text{Electric current} \times \text{Seconds}$$

$$= 1.00\,\text{A} \times \left(1.00\,\text{h} \times \frac{3600\,\text{s}}{1\,\text{h}} \right)$$

$$= 3.60 \times 10^3\,\text{A} \cdot \text{s}$$

$$= 3.60 \times 10^3\,\text{C}$$

We can then calculate how many electrons were delivered to the cathode and removed at the anode using the faraday as a conversion factor:

$$\text{Number of electrons} = 3.60 \times 10^3\,\text{C} \times \frac{1\,\text{mol e}^-}{9.65 \times 10^4\,\text{C}}$$

$$= 3.73 \times 10^{-2}\,\text{mol e}^-$$

The next step is to calculate the moles of copper metal produced from the half-reactions, using the appropriate equation factor:

Anode (oxidation): $\quad H_2O_{(l)} \longrightarrow 2\,H^+_{(aq)} + \frac{1}{2}O_{2\,(g)} + 2\,e^-$

Cathode (reduction): $\quad Cu^{2+}_{(aq)} + 2\,e^- \longrightarrow Cu_{(s)}$

$$\text{Moles of copper produced} = 3.73 \times 10^{-2}\,\text{mol e}^- \times \frac{1\,\text{mol Cu}}{2\,\text{mol e}^-}$$

$$= 1.87 \times 10^{-2}\,\text{mol Cu}$$

Converting moles to mass gives us

$$\text{Mass of copper produced} = 1.87 \times 10^{-2}\,\text{mol Cu} \times \frac{63.55\,\text{g Cu}}{1\,\text{mol Cu}}$$

$$= 1.19\,\text{g Cu}$$

If we are given the amount of product produced within a specified time at one of the electrodes during an electrolysis, we can determine the electric current strength.

EXAMPLE   **12.7**   What is the strength of a constant electric current that deposits 0.155 g of silver from an aqueous silver nitrate solution in 11.0 minutes?

SOLUTION The half-reaction for the deposition of silver is

$$Ag^+_{(aq)} + e^- \longrightarrow Ag_{(s)}$$

and the number of moles of silver produced is

$$\text{Moles of silver} = 0.155\,\text{g Ag} \times \frac{1\,\text{mol Ag}}{107.9\,\text{g Ag}} = 1.44 \times 10^{-3}\,\text{mol Ag}$$

Since one mole of electrons is used for each mole of silver formed,

$$\text{Number of electrons} = 1.44 \times 10^{-3}\,\text{mol Ag} \times \frac{1\,\text{mol e}^-}{1\,\text{mol Ag}}$$

$$= 1.44 \times 10^{-3}\,\text{mol e}^-$$

We must now calculate the total charge passed through the circuit in 11.0 minutes (660 s). We start by using the faraday as a conversion factor to find the total number of coulombs, or electric charge.

$$\text{Electric charge} = 1.44 \times 10^{-3} \text{ mol e}^- \times \frac{9.65 \times 10^4 \text{ C}}{1 \text{ mol e}^-}$$

$$= 139 \text{ C}$$

We rearrange our expression for electric charge to find the value for electric current. Then we substitute our known values into this expression.

$$\text{Electric current} = \frac{\text{Electric charge}}{\text{Seconds}} = \frac{139 \text{ C}}{660 \text{ s}}$$

$$= 0.211 \text{ A}$$

Michael Faraday

Few scientists have influenced modern life as much as Michael Faraday. To him we owe, not only the fundamental laws of electrolysis, but also the electric motor and the electric generator.

Born in 1791, the son of a British blacksmith, he had little formal education. At thirteen, he was apprenticed to a bookbinder, a job he did not like but used to good advantage. He educated himself by reading virtually every book that entered the bindery including *Conversations in Chemistry* by Jane Marcet. She was a great fan of England's leading chemist Humphry Davy, Director of the Royal Institute in London and a very popular lecturer. Faraday began to attend Davy's lectures and prepared a carefully bound set of lecture notes, which he sent to Davy with a job application. In 1812, he was hired as Davy's assistant.

In the following years Faraday travelled extensively in Europe with his mentor and met most of the leading scientists of the day.

The personalities of Davy and Faraday were quite different. Davy was an outgoing person who had many other interests besides chemistry, such as poetry and fishing. He was a very practical chemist and the only use he saw in theories was that they might suggest new experiments. Faraday had no real interests besides science. Scientific research was a passion for him and rarely did he take a day off from his laboratory work. His search for a theory of electricity and magnetism occupied him throughout his life. He discovered benzene as a component of lighting oil in 1825, the same year in which he succeeded Davy as Directory of the Royal Institute. Neither Davy nor Faraday had much use for the new atomic theory suggested by Dalton in 1806.

In 1831 Faraday started his work on electrolysis. He set out to prove that electricities from different sources, such as electrostatic generators and voltaic piles, were identical and concluded by establishing the basis of quantitative electrochemistry. He showed that the mass of a substance produced in electrolysis is directly proportional to the quantity of electricity that passed into the solution. He also showed that the masses of different substances deposited or consumed by the same quantity of electricity are proportional to their equivalent weights.

As a result of overwork, Faraday suffered a nervous breakdown in 1839 from which he never totally recovered. He continued to work and lecture, however, and did not resign his post at the Royal Institute until 1862. His groundwork for the field theory of electricity and magnetism, and the electromagnetic nature of light, was fully developed by James Clerk Maxwell in the 1850s and 1860s.

Figure 12.30
Faraday lecturing at the Royal Institute.

QUESTIONS

20. A constant current of 2.00 A is passed through an aqueous solution of sulfuric acid for 2.00 hours. Calculate the number of litres of hydrogen and oxygen gas produced at the electrodes at Standard Ambient Temperature and Pressure, given that the molar volume of a gas at SATP is 24.8 L.

21. A current of 2.00×10^4 A for each cell is used for the electrolysis of a concentrated aqueous solution of sodium chloride. Calculate the number of kilograms of hydrogen, chlorine, and sodium hydroxide produced by one cell in a single day, assuming that the only reaction is

$$2\,NaCl_{(aq)} + 2\,H_2O_{(\ell)} \longrightarrow 2\,NaOH_{(aq)} + Cl_{2(g)} + H_{2\,(g)}$$

22. An electroplating technician wishes to apply an even layer of silver, 0.100 mm thick, on a spoon with a total surface area of $50.0\,cm^2$. How long should the electrolysis cell be left in operation if the technician applies a constant current of 0.500 A? The density of silver is $11.5\,g \cdot cm^{-3}$ and the electrolyte of the cell is aqueous silver nitrate.

23. A constant current was passed through an aqueous solution of copper(II) sulfate for 40.0 minutes. During this time the cathode gained 1.50 g in mass. Calculate the electric current, assuming that the formation of copper was the only cathode reaction.

Free Energy and Electrochemistry

12.9

In Section 7.13, we encountered the relationship between the standard free energy $\Delta G°$ of a reaction and the equilibrium constant, K:

$$\Delta G° = -RT \ln K_c$$

A similar relationship exists between the free energy and the cell potential of a redox reaction. In this case,

$$\Delta G° = -nF\mathscr{E}°_{cell}$$

where n is the number of moles of electrons transferred in the reaction,
F is the charge of one mole of electrons (9.65×10^4 C),
$\mathscr{E}°_{cell}$ is the standard cell potential.

Thus, if we know the $\mathscr{E}°_{cell}$, we can calculate not only the standard free energy $\Delta G°$ of the redox reaction but also the equilibrium constant.

$$\Delta G° = -RT \ln K_c = -nF\mathscr{E}°_{cell}$$

$$\ln K_c = \frac{nF\mathscr{E}°_{cell}}{RT}$$

12.8 Using the standard potential, calculate the standard free energy ($\Delta G°$) and the equilibrium constant values of the reaction

$$Zn_{(s)} + Cu^{2+}_{(aq)} \longrightarrow Zn^{2+}_{(aq)} + Cu_{(s)}$$

SOLUTION The standard cell potential can be calculated from the standard potentials of the half-reactions.

Anode (oxidation):	$Zn_{(s)} \longrightarrow Zn^{2+}_{(aq)} + 2\,e^-$	$\mathscr{E}° = +0.76\,V$
Cathode (reduction):	$Cu^{2+}_{(aq)} + 2\,e^- \longrightarrow Cu_{(s)}$	$\mathscr{E}° = +0.34\,V$

For the overall reaction the standard cell electrical potential is

$$\mathscr{E}°_{cell} = 0.76\,V + 0.34\,V = 1.10\,V$$

Since two moles of electrons are transferred in the reaction, $n = 2$, we can substitute our known values to find $\Delta G°$:

$$\Delta G° = -nF\mathscr{E}° = -2 \times 9.65 \times 10^4\,C \times 1.10\,V$$
$$= -2.12 \times 10^5\,C \cdot V$$

We can convert the units of this quantity into joules by using the following relationship:

$$1\,J = 1\,C \times 1\,V$$

or

$$1\,J = 1\,C \cdot V$$

Therefore, $\Delta G° = -2.12 \times 10^5\,J$ (per mole of reactants)

The equilibrium constant at 25 °C can be calculated from the standard cell potential.

$$\ln K_c = \frac{nF\mathscr{E}°}{RT}$$
$$= \frac{2.12 \times 10^5\,J \cdot mol^{-1}}{8.314\,J \cdot mol^{-1} \cdot K^{-1} \times 298\,K}$$
$$= 85.6$$
$$K_c = 1.50 \times 10^{37}$$

This very large value of K_c indicates that the reaction will go virtually to completion.

QUESTIONS

24. Using the standard half-reaction potentials, calculate the standard free energy $\Delta G°$ and the equilibrium constant K_c of the reaction:

$$Fe_{(s)} + Ni^{2+}_{(aq)} \longrightarrow Fe^{2+}_{(aq)} + Ni_{(s)}$$

Summary

■ Electricity-producing electrochemical cells are based on spontaneous redox reactions. Two half-cells are separate, but connected by a salt bridge. Electrons are exchanged via an external circuit.

■ Standard reduction potentials have been determined for many reduction half-reactions by arbitrarily assigning a value of 0.00 volts to the standard hydrogen electrode. Cell potentials can be calculated from the half-reaction potentials.

■ The corrosion of metals is a redox process involving cathodic and anodic sites. Several corrosion protection methods are available, all of them based on electrochemical principles.

■ In an electrolytic cell, a continuous supply of electrical energy causes a normally nonspontaneous redox reaction to take place. Due to over-voltage it is often difficult to predict the electrode reactions in aqueous solutions.

■ In both the electrochemical cell and the electrolytic cell, oxidation takes place at the anode and reduction at the cathode. Positive ions (cations) migrate towards the cathode and negative ions (anions) migrate towards the anode.

■ Electroplating and electrolytic purification of metals are examples of applied electrolysis, in which pure metal is deposited at the cathode.

■ Electrolysis of molten sodium chloride produces sodium and chlorine, whereas the electrolysis of a concentrated aqueous solution of sodium chloride gives rise to sodium hydroxide, chlorine, and hydrogen.

■ Quantitative electrochemistry is based on the laws developed by Faraday. The amount of products produced and reactants consumed in an electrolysis can be calculated from both the strength of the electric current and the time over which the current is applied.

■ The standard free energy and the equilibrium constant of a reaction can be determined from the standard cell potential.

KEY WORDS

ampere	electrochemical cell
anode	electrode
battery	electrolysis
cathode	electrolytic cell
corrosion	electrolytic conduction
coulomb	electrolytic purification
current	electromotive force
Daniell cell	electroplating
Downs cell	faraday

16. a) Anode: $2\,Br^-_{(aq)} \longrightarrow Br_{2\,(aq)} + 2\,e^-$

Cathode: $2\,H^+_{(aq)} + 2\,e^- \longrightarrow H_{2\,(g)}$

b) Anode: $2\,I^-_{(aq)} \longrightarrow I_{2\,(aq)} + 2\,e^-$

Cathode: $2\,H_2O_{(\ell)} + 2\,e^- \longrightarrow H_{2\,(g)} + 2\,OH^-_{(aq)}$

c) Anode: $H_2O_{(\ell)} \longrightarrow \frac{1}{2}O_{2\,(g)} + 2\,H^+_{(aq)} + 2\,e^-$

Cathode: $Ag^+_{(aq)} + e^- \longrightarrow Ag_{(s)}$

d) Anode: $H_2O_{(\ell)} \longrightarrow \frac{1}{2}O_{2\,(g)} + 2\,H^+_{(aq)} + 2\,e^-$

Cathode: $Cu^{2+}_{(aq)} + 2\,e^- \longrightarrow Cu_{(s)}$

17. a) Anode (Ni): $Ni_{(s)} \longrightarrow Ni^{2+}_{(aq)} + 2\,e^-$

Cathode (object): $Ni^{2+}_{(aq)} + 2\,e^- \longrightarrow Ni_{(s)}$

b) Anode (impure Cu): $Cu_{(s)} \longrightarrow Cu^{2+}_{(aq)} + 2\,e^-$

Cathode (pure Cu): $Cu^{2+}_{(aq)} + 2\,e^- \longrightarrow Cu_{(s)}$

18.

	Downs cell	Diaphragm cell
Anode:	$2\,Cl^-_{(\ell)} \longrightarrow Cl_{2\,(g)} + 2\,e^-$	$2\,Cl^-_{(aq)} \longrightarrow Cl_{2\,(g)} + 2\,e^-$
Cathode:	$Na^+_{(\ell)} + e^- \longrightarrow Na_{(\ell)}$	$2\,H_2O_{(\ell)} + 2\,e^- \longrightarrow H_{2\,(g)} + 2\,OH^-_{(aq)}$

19. $H_{2\,(g)} + Cl_{2\,(g)} \longrightarrow 2\,HCl_{(aq)}$

$2\,NaOH_{(aq)} + Cl_{2\,(g)} \longrightarrow NaCl_{(aq)} + NaOCl_{(aq)} + H_2O_{(\ell)}$

20. $1.85\,L\,H_2$, $0.925\,L\,O_2$

21. $18.0\,kg\,H_2$, $635\,kg\,Cl_2$, $716\,kg\,NaOH$

22. 2 h 51 min

23. 1.90 A

24. $\Delta G^\circ = -41\,kJ$; $K_c = 8.9 \times 10^6$

COMPREHENSION QUESTIONS

1. Describe the experiments of Galvani and Volta that led to the development of electrochemical cells.

2. Explain the function of each of the following components of an electrochemical cell:

a) electrodes   b) anode   c) cathode   d) separator

3. Explain the function of a salt bridge in an electrochemical cell.

4. Distinguish between metallic conduction and electrolytic conduction.

5. When the voltage of an electrochemical cell has dropped to zero, what can you say about the reaction on which the cell is based?

6. What are the limitations of using standard cell potentials for predicting the spontaneity of a reaction?

7. Distinguish between the following:

a) primary batteries

b) secondary batteries

c) fuel cells

8. Describe the components and the electrode reactions of the following:
   a) a mercury oxide cell
   b) a lead-acid cell
   c) a nickel-cadmium cell

9. What are some of the disadvantages of using lead-acid batteries in electric cars?

10. Because copper is much more corrosion resistant than iron or zinc, an engineer has specified copper eavestroughs and drains, supported by steel brackets, for a large building. Explain the mistake this engineer has made, on a chemical basis.

11. Why should sharp bends be avoided in metal structures?

12. Explain why magnesium rods, when inserted into hot water tanks, prevent formation of rusty water.

13. Why is sea water so much more corrosive to metals than fresh water?

14. The Titanic sank to a depth of 4 km and lay on the ocean floor for 73 years before it was discovered, its main features still discernible. Explain why metal objects deeply submerged in the ocean corrode only very slowly.

15. Aluminum, although a very reactive metal, is highly corrosion resistant. Explain the effect that chloride ions and other impurities have on the properties of aluminum.

16. Compare the processes occurring in an electrolytic cell with those of an electrochemical cell.

17. Why is an electrolyte required for the electrolysis of water?

18. Why are all the aluminum smelters in Canada located in Quebec and British Columbia?

19. Explain why standard half-reaction potentials cannot always be used to predict the electrode reactions in an electrolysis.

20. Describe the procedure by which you could copper plate a leather shoe.

21. How can a metal be purified by a metal plating process?

22. Sodium chloride is very soluble in water, but only 1 % sodium chloride can be present in 50 % aqueous sodium hydroxide. Explain this decrease in solubility.

23. Sodium chloride melts at 800 °C. Why can a Downs cell, in which liquid sodium chloride is electrolyzed, be operated at 600 °C?

24. Define the following electrical units and give the relationship between them:
    a) ampere   b) coulomb   c) volt

25. State the relationship between the standard cell potential, standard free energy, and the equilibrium constant of a redox reaction.

Values for standard reduction potentials can be found in Appendix VII.

Electrochemical Cells

26. An electrochemical cell consists of an iron electrode in a 1.0 $mol \cdot L^{-1}$ aqueous iron(II) sulfate solution and an inert platinum electrode in a solution of 1.0 $mol \cdot L^{-1}$ hydrochloric acid. Oxygen gas is bubbled into the hydrochloric acid over the platinum electrode. The two half-cells are connected with a salt bridge containing aqueous sodium chloride.
    a) Make a diagram of the cell indicating the anode and cathode, the sign (electrical charge) of each, the direction of electron flow, and the direction of ion movement.
    b) Write the electrode reactions and calculate the cell voltage.
    c) Write a shorthand notation for the cell.

Standard Electrode Potentials

27. Write the half-reactions and calculate the potentials of the following cells:
    a) $Ti_{(s)}|Ti^{2+}_{(aq)}(1.0 \ mol \cdot L^{-1})| |Co^{2+}_{(aq)}(1.0 \ mol \cdot L^{-1})|Co_{(s)}$
    b) $Pt, H_{2(g)}(100 \ kPa)|H^{+}_{(aq)}(1.0 \ mol \cdot L^{-1})| |Au^{+}_{(aq)}(1.0 \ mol \cdot L^{-1})|Au_{(s)}$
    c) $Ni_{(s)}|Ni^{2+}_{(aq)}(1.0 \ mol \cdot L^{-1})| |Ag^{+}_{(aq)}(1.0 \ mol \cdot L^{-1})|Ag_{(s)}$

28. Which of the following is the best oxidizing agent in aqueous solution: Cl_2, Cu^{2+}, or Ag^+?

29. Which of the following is the best reducing agent in aqueous solution: Sn, Zn, or I^-?

30. Use half-reaction potentials to predict whether the following reactions are spontaneous or nonspontaneous in aqueous solutions.
    a) $Ca^{2+}_{(aq)} + 2 I^{-}_{(aq)} \longrightarrow Ca_{(s)} + I_{2(aq)}$
    b) $2 H_2S_{(g)} + O_{2(g)} \longrightarrow 2 H_2O_{(\ell)} + 2 S_{(s)}$
    c) $SO_{2(g)} + MnO_{2(s)} \longrightarrow Mn^{2+}_{(aq)} + SO_4^{2-}_{(aq)}$
    d) $2 H^{+}_{(aq)} + 2 Br^{-}_{(aq)} \longrightarrow H_{2(g)} + Br_{2(aq)}$
    e) $Ce^{4+}_{(aq)} + Fe^{2+}_{(aq)} \longrightarrow Ce^{3+}_{(aq)} + Fe^{3+}_{(aq)}$
    f) $Cr^{2+}_{(aq)} + Cu^{2+}_{(aq)} \longrightarrow Cr^{3+}_{(aq)} + Cu^{+}_{(aq)}$

Batteries

31. Write the electrode reactions for the following:
    a) a zinc-chlorine battery
    b) a sodium-sulfur battery

32. Write the electrode reactions and determine the standard cell voltage of a hydrogen-oxygen fuel cell in which the electrolyte is an aqueous acid solution.

33. What are the electrode reactions of an Edison battery when it is being recharged?

Corrosion

34. Bronze sculptures and copper roofs slowly turn green because of the formation of basic copper(II) carbonate, $Cu_2(OH)_2CO_3$. Write a reaction equation that shows how this substance can be formed from copper, water, oxygen and carbon dioxide.

35. A buried steel pipeline is connected to blocks of magnesium. What corrosion reactions occur at the surfaces of the magnesium and the steel pipe?

36. Hydrogen gas is slowly produced when an iron nail is added to an aqueous solution of a strong acid. When half the nail is coated with tin, hydrogen is produced much more quickly. Explain the difference in reaction rate and write the equations for the half-reactions. Where on the tin-coated nail is the hydrogen produced?

Electrolysis

37. An electrolytic cell consists of a power source and inert platinum electrodes in an aqueous solution of potassium bromide, KBr.
   a) Make a diagram of the cell indicating the cathode, the anode, the sign of each, the direction of electron flow, and the direction of ion movement.
   b) Predict the cathode and anode reactions.

Quantitative Electrolysis

38. An aqueous solution of silver nitrate is subjected to electrolysis for 30.0 min using a constant current of 1.50 A. Calculate the amount of silver deposited at the cathode.

39. Calculate the constant electric current required to deposit 0.256 g of silver from an aqueous solution of silver nitrate in 20.0 min.

40. A current of 0.200 A is passed through an aqueous solution of iridium bromide for 1.00 h, resulting in the deposition of 0.478 g of iridium at the cathode. What is the charge on the iridium ion?

Free Energy and Electrochemistry

41. Using the standard half-reaction potentials, calculate the standard cell potential, the standard free energy, and the equilibrium constant at 25 °C of the reaction:

$$Fe^{2+}_{(aq)} + Ag^+_{(aq)} \rightleftharpoons Fe^{3+}_{(aq)} + Ag_{(s)}$$

42. Using the standard potentials of the half-reactions

$$2\,H_2O + 2\,e^- \longrightarrow H_2 + 2\,OH^-$$
$$\text{and}$$
$$2\,H^+ + 2\,e^- \longrightarrow H_2$$

Calculate the standard cell potential and the value of K_w at 25 °C for the reaction:

$$H_2O_{(\ell)} \rightleftharpoons H^+_{(aq)} + OH^-_{(aq)}$$

43. A commercial cell used for the electrolytic purification of lead contains 24 anodes and 25 cathodes. Initially the cathodes are thin sheets of pure lead, and each anode consists of 200 kg of lead with a purity of 98%. The electrolyte solution contains a high concentration of lead(II) ions. How long will it take to transfer all the lead from the anodes to the cathodes if the applied current is 7.0×10^3 A per cell?

44. Aluminum metal is produced by the electrolysis of molten aluminum oxide, Al_2O_3. Consider one such cell with a potential difference between the anode and cathode of 5.00 V. Electrons are supplied at a rate of 1.00×10^5 $C \cdot s^{-1}$ (A). How much time will it take for one cell to produce 1100 kg of aluminum?

45. If acid hydrogen peroxide is added to an aqueous solution of iron(II) ions, which of the following reactions will occur?
a) Fe^{2+} is oxidized to Fe^{3+} while H_2O_2 is reduced to H_2O.
b) Fe^{2+} is reduced to Fe, while H_2O_2 is oxidized to O_2 gas.

46. The ampere was initially defined as the strength of the electric current that will deposit 0.001 118 g of silver per second at the cathode in the electrolysis of an aqueous solution of silver nitrate. Use this definition to calculate the charge on one mole of electrons.

47. a) Select two half-reactions from Appendix VII that (by addition) combine to form the following reaction:

$$2 H_2O_{2\,(aq)} \longrightarrow 2 H_2O_{(\ell)} + O_{2\,(g)}$$

b) Calculate the equilibrium constant at 25 °C for the above decomposition of hydrogen peroxide.
c) Explain why an aqueous solution of hydrogen peroxide can safely be stored in a refrigerator, even though the decomposition is a spontaneous process.

48. A commercial electrolytic cell used for the purification of copper contains 20 anodes of copper, with a purity of 98% each weighing 100 kg. The cathodes consist of thin sheets of pure copper. If the total amount of current per cell is 1.00×10^4 A, how much time will be required to transfer all the copper from the anodes to the cathodes?

49. Anodized aluminum is aluminum that has been coated electrolytically with a thin layer of aluminum oxide, Al_2O_3. This coating not only makes the aluminum more corrosion resistant but also provides a surface to which dyes better adhere. In the electrolysis, the aluminum to be anodized is the anode; dilute sulfuric acid is the electrolyte. Hydrogen escapes at the cathode but the oxygen produced at the anode reacts virtually completely with the aluminum to produce the aluminum oxide coating. A lab technician wants to coat a thin piece of aluminum, 10.0 cm × 5.00 cm × 0.100 cm, evenly with a

0.002 00 cm coating of aluminum oxide using a current of 5.00 A. How long should the cell be kept in operation? The density of aluminum oxide is 3.00 g·cm^{-3}.

50. Write equations for the reactions occurring at the anode and cathode in each of the following electrochemical cells. Calculate the standard cell potentials. All solutions have concentrations of 1.0 mol·L^{-1}.
    a) one half-cell consisting of platinum wire dipped into a solution of iron(II) chloride and iron(III) chloride, the other half-cell containing a nickel wire dipped into a solution of nickel(II) sulfate
    b) one half-cell consisting of a platinum wire dipped in a solution of sodium iodide and iodine, the other half-cell consisting of hydrogen gas bubbling over a platinum wire dipped in a sodium hydroxide solution.

SUGGESTED PROJECTS

1. Make a list of the various types of small dry cells available in retail outlets near you. Make a sketch of the insides of these cells and find out on which chemical reactions the cells are based.

2. Battery-powered cars will become more common in the near future, and most automobile manufacturers are developing electric cars. Discuss the advantages and disadvantages of electric cars as compared with gasoline powered ones in relation to automobile batteries.

3. Electric wheelchairs have been in use for quite some time. Investigate which batteries are used for this purpose and how many for each wheelchair. What maximum distance can be covered before the batteries must be recharged?

4. Find out which electrochemical processes are being used on a commerical scale in your province. List all the chemical reactions involved and obtain annual production figures for each process.

13

Nuclear Chemistry

In our discussion of atomic structure in Chapter 2, we emphasized the arrangement of electrons around the nucleus. We saw that this electron arrangement determined each element's chemical properties. Nuclear chemistry is concerned with changes that occur *within* the nucleus. These changes result in the transformation of one element to another and are always accompanied by the emission of radiation.

After a brief review of the atomic nucleus we will examine the different types of radiation that can be emitted and then proceed to a study of both nuclear fission and fusion and the potential that these processes provide in the harnessing of energy. We will also discuss the potential dangers involved in using this technology.

A Review of the Nucleus

13.1 When studying nuclear chemistry, we are interested in only three subatomic particles: the proton, the neutron, and the electron. The properties of these particles are shown below.

TABLE 13.1	*A Summary of the Three Main Subatomic Particles*	
Particle	Mass(u)	Relative Charge
proton	1.00728	+1
neutron	1.00867	0
electron	0.00055	−1

The protons and neutrons in an atom are collectively known as the **nucleons**. The number of protons in an atom is known as the **atomic number**, while the total number of nucleons is called the **mass number**, or nucleon number. It is the atomic number that determines the identity of the element. For example, all atoms with six protons have the properties of the element carbon.

Atoms of an element that have the same number of protons but a different number of neutrons are called **isotopes**. One way of representing an isotope is to place the mass number of the isotope after the name of the element. Thus, the two common isotopes of chlorine are represented as chlorine-35 and chlorine-37. An alternative method is to represent the element by its symbol, with the mass number as a superscript and the atomic number as a subscript. Using this method, the two common isotopes of chlorine are written as follows:

$$^{35}_{17}\text{Cl} \quad \text{and} \quad ^{37}_{17}\text{Cl}$$

The percentage by mass of a particular isotope in a sample of an element is called the **abundance** of that isotope. For example, naturally-occurring chlorine, chlorine-35, has an abundance of 76.5 %. Since there are only two isotopes of chlorine, the abundance of chlorine-37 is 23.5 %.

The Common Types of Nuclear Radiation

13.2

In 1896 the French scientist Antoine-Henri Becquerel placed uranium salts on several glass plates coated with light-sensitive material. Even though the plates had previously been wrapped in black paper, the light-sensitive material darkened. Since no light could have penetrated the paper, Bequerel deduced that the uranium must have emitted rays capable of penetrating the paper and darkening the light-sensitive surface of the plates. Becquerel called the production of these kinds of rays **radioactivity**.

In later experiments, Ernest Rutherford showed that two different types of rays were produced by radioactive materials. One type was easily stopped by any solid material, such as paper. Rutherford called these *alpha* (α) *rays*. The other rays, which were one hundred times more penetrating than alpha rays, he called *beta* (β) *rays*. Subsequently a third type of ray called a *gamma* (γ) *ray*, was identified by Paul Villard. Gamma rays proved to be even more penetrating that beta rays.

Figure 13.1

The MacDonald Physics Laboratory at McGill University, Montreal. Many of Ernest Rutherford's discoveries were made here.

Alpha Rays

An alpha ray is a beam of helium nuclei. Particles of this type consist of two protons and two neutrons, and therefore have a charge of $+2$. We can represent these alpha particles using the format introduced in Section 13.1. The atomic number is shown as a subscript to the lower left of the chemical symbol and the mass number as a superscript to the upper left.

$$^{4}_{2}\text{He}$$

When discussing nuclear chemistry we are usually only concerned with nuclei. Thus the overall charge on an ion is usually ignored, and for an alpha particle the sumbol $^{4}_{2}\text{He}$ is preferred to the alternative $^{4}_{2}\text{He}^{2+}$.

Beta Rays

A beta ray is a beam of electrons. These electrons result from a transformation within the nucleus during which a neutron changes into a proton and an electron. In earlier chapters, we represented an electron as e^-. Although this is a useful way of depicting an electron in conventional chemistry, a slightly different format is preferred for nuclear chemistry:

$$^{0}_{-1}\text{e}$$

The zero in this representation indicates that the electron has a negligible mass when compared to a proton or neutron. The subscript represents the charge, which is negative for an electron.

Figure 13.2

The penetrating ability of alpha (α), beta (β), and gamma (γ) rays. Skin will stop alpha rays, but not beta or gamma rays.

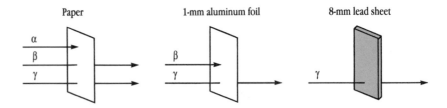

Gamma Rays

A gamma ray is a high-energy form of electromagnetic radiation. Like other types of electromagnetic radiation, gamma rays are transmitted in the form of waves. Energy emitted or absorbed as gamma rays can be represented as

$$^{0}_{0}\gamma$$

The zero subscript and superscript show that a gamma ray has neither mass nor charge.

In addition to alpha, beta, and gamma rays, other types of radiation have also been identified as being emitted by certain nuclei. This radiation includes streams of protons (symbol $^{1}_{1}\text{p}$ or $^{1}_{1}\text{H}$), and streams of neutrons (symbol $^{1}_{0}\text{n}$). One rather unusual type of radiation consists of a stream of positive electrons ($^{0}_{+1}\text{e}$), usually called **positrons**.

TABLE 13.2	*Common Forms of Radiation and Their Symbols*
Name	**Symbol**
Alpha particle (helium nucleus)	^4_2He
Beta particle (electron)	$^{\ 0}_{-1}\text{e}$
Gamma ray	$^0_0\gamma$
Proton	^1_1p or ^1_1H
Neutron	^1_0n
Positron (positive electron)	$^{\ 0}_{+1}\text{e}$

Nuclear Equations

13.3

When we balance a conventional chemical equation, we must ensure that each type of atom occurs the same number of times on each side of the equation. During a nuclear reaction, nuclei change their identity, so we cannot balance an equation for these reactions in the usual way. Instead we balance mass number and the total nuclear charge.

The simplest nuclear reactions involve the **radioactive decay** (or decomposition) of radioactive isotopes. When such a decay occurs, radiation is emitted by the nucleus. If alpha or beta particles are given off, new elements are formed. On the other hand, neutrons and gamma rays have no charge, and their loss from the nucleus does not change the atomic number of the nucleus or its identity. Thus a radioactive element is only transformed into another element when a *charged particle* is emitted during the decay process.

As an example, let us consider the decomposition of tritium, a rare isotope of hydrogen that has one proton and two neutrons in its nucleus. In the decay process, tritium releases a beta particle and changes into an isotope of helium containing one neutron and two protons. Tritium can be represented as ^3_1H and the helium isotope as ^3_2He. We represent a beta particle (i.e. an electron) as $^{\ 0}_{-1}\text{e}$. The nuclear equation is therefore

$$^3_1\text{H} \longrightarrow \ ^3_2\text{He} + \ ^{\ 0}_{-1}\text{e}$$

In order for the equation to be balanced, the sum of the mass numbers on each side of the equation must be the same. We can see that this is the case. Similarly, the total nuclear charge on each side of the equation must also be the same. When we add the charges we see that $1 = 2 + (-1)$.

Although we may think of neutrons and protons as being unchangeable, this is not true. For example, the above decay process involves the conversion of one of the neutrons within the tritium nucleus to a proton and an electron. During the conversion, the electron is expelled from the nucleus.

Harriet Brooks — Pioneer Canadian Nuclear Scientist

When we mention famous scientists, we usually overlook the fact that much of the work was probably performed by students of the scientist. When Ernest Rutherford moved to Canada, he began acquiring a group of research students. One of the first to join his researches was Harriet Brooks.

Harriet Brooks was born in Exeter, Ontario, in 1876. She went to school at the Seaforth Collegiate Institute and from there entered McGill University. She was an outstanding student in mathematics and the physical sciences, winning awards every year. Immediately upon graduation, she started work with Rutherford. During three years of research work at McGill, she obtained an M.A. and also taught at the Royal Victoria College, the newly-founded branch of McGill for women students.

She subsequently spent a year doing research with J.J. Thomson at Cambridge University, England, and then obtained a teaching position at Barnard College, New York. When she became engaged to be married, the Dean at Barnard insisted on her resignation, for the Dean considered it impossible for her to continue a physics career and be married. The engagement was terminated but Brooks left Barnard anyway and resumed her research career, this time with Marie Curie in Paris.

During 1907 Brooks was offered a renewal of the position at Paris and was almost guaranteed a position at Manchester University in England. Instead, she decided to marry a former lab instructor from McGill. She returned to Montreal and gave up any further aspirations in physics, though she continued to lead an active life including the raising of three children. After her death in 1933, Rutherford wrote a lengthy obituary in the journal *Nature*, remarking on her outstanding abilities in nuclear science.

Her main contribution was her work on radon, a topic which has gained in interest today. Although not credited with its discovery, she was one of the first to identify it, and she was the first to attempt to determine its atomic mass. Her main studies were on the product of decay of radon which she did in her typical thorough manner. A Canadian pioneer in the study of radioactivity, her story has been forgotten until now.

Figure 13.3
Harriet Brooks (1876-1933). A Canadian pioneer researcher who worked with Ernest Rutherford.

When we write a nuclear equation we usually show only particles that have mass and/or charge. Thus such equations often give no indication as to whether or not a gamma ray is emitted during the reaction.

If we know the type of radiation produced during the simple radioactive decay of a radioactive isotope, we should be able to predict the identity and mass number of the element that will be produced.

| EXAMPLE | 13.1 | One of the radioactive isotopes of radon, radon-222, releases one alpha particle per nucleus as it decays into another element. What element is formed and what is its mass number? |

SOLUTION   Initially, we can write the equation as

$$^{222}_{86}\text{Rn} \longrightarrow {}^{4}_{2}\text{He} + ?$$

The sum of the mass numbers and the sum of the atomic numbers on each side of the equation must be the same. Therefore the element that is produced must have a mass number of 218 and an atomic number of 84. From the Periodic Table we see that the element with atomic number 84 is polonium, Po. Thus the symbolic representation of the isotope that is produced is $^{218}_{84}\text{Po}$. The completed nuclear equation for the process that occurs is therefore

$$^{222}_{86}\text{Rn} \longrightarrow {}^{4}_{2}\text{He} + {}^{218}_{84}\text{Po}$$

Similarly, if we know the atomic number and the mass number of the isotope produced during the simple radioactive decay of a given nucleus, we can deduce the type of radiation released during the decay process.

| EXAMPLE | 13.2 | A radioactive isotope of oxygen, oxygen-15, undergoes radioactive decay to form nitrogen-15. What type of radiation is released during this process? |

SOLUTION   We can represent this process as follows:

$$^{15}_{8}\text{O} \longrightarrow {}^{15}_{7}\text{N} + ?$$

The particles that are produced must have a mass number of zero and an atomic number, or nuclear charge, of +1. By referring to Table 13.2 we see that the positron ($^{0}_{+1}\text{e}$) is the only particle that fits this description. The complete equation is therefore

$$^{15}_{8}\text{O} \longrightarrow {}^{15}_{7}\text{N} + {}^{0}_{+1}\text{e}$$

Radioactive Series

Although most radioactive isotopes change directly into a stable isotope during a decay process, certain isotopes with high atomic numbers go through a series of decay steps before a stable isotope is reached. The product of each intermediate step is itself radioactive, and the series of isotopes produced during a given sequence of decay processes is called a **radioactive series**. The radioactive series for uranium is a good example.

Uranium exists in nature as two isotopes, uranium-235 (percent abundance, 0.7%) and uranium-238 (percent abundance, 99.3%). Uranium-238 undergoes radioactive decay by releasing an alpha particle to form thorium-234:

$$^{238}_{92}\text{U} \longrightarrow {}^{234}_{90}\text{Th} + {}^{4}_{2}\text{He}$$

However, thorium-234 is also radioactive and releases a beta particle to form protactinium-234:

$$^{234}_{90}\text{Th} \longrightarrow {}^{234}_{91}\text{Pa} + {}^{0}_{-1}\text{e}$$

Protactinium is radioactive, as is the product of its decay, uranium-234. These decays continue in a series of steps, each step involving the release of an alpha particle or a beta particle. After a total of fourteen steps a stable isotope, lead-206, is finally obtained. Similar radioactive series exist for other actinon isotopes.

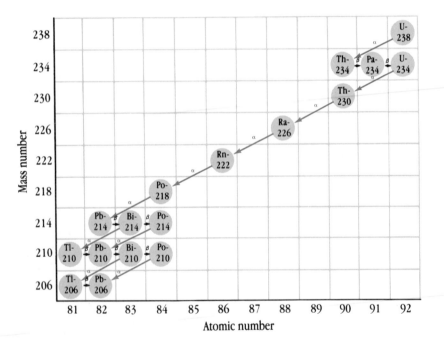

Figure 13.4

The uranium-238 radioactive decay series. As can be seen, at certain points in the series, two alternative routes are available. Ultimately, however, the final product is always lead-206.

Nuclear versus Chemical Reactions

It is important for us to recognize that there are fundamental differences between nuclear and chemical reactions. These differences can be easily demonstrated by a few representative reactions. Let us consider two isotopes of carbon. Carbon-12 is the common, stable isotope of carbon whereas carbon-14 is a rare, radioactive isotope which releases one electron per atom and decays to nitrogen-14. Carbon-14 can be oxidized to carbon monoxide or carbon dioxide in exactly the same chemical reactions as carbon-12. It will decay at the same rate to give the same product whether it is bonded to one oxygen atom (CO) or two (CO_2). By contrast, carbon monoxide and carbon dioxide behave quite differently in chemical reactions. Only carbon monoxide burns in air for example. When one mole of carbon-14 decays to nitrogen-14, 1.5×10^{10} J of energy is released. This is considerably more than the 4×10^5 J of energy released in the chemical oxidation of one mole of carbon to carbon dioxide. Such observations lead us to the general comparative statements about nuclear and chemical reactions which appear in Table 13.3

TABLE 13.3	*A Comparison of Nuclear and Chemical Reactions*	
Nuclear Reactions	**Chemical Reactions**
Different isotopes of an element behave differently.	Different isotopes of an element behave the same.
Reactions are not affected by chemical state.	Reactions depend on chemical state.
Energy changes are very large.	Energy changes are comparatively small.

QUESTIONS

1. Complete the following nuclear equations:

   a) $^{190}_{75}Re \longrightarrow \, ^{190}_{76}Os \, + \, ?$ d) $^{162}_{69}Tm \longrightarrow \, ^{0}_{+1}e \, + \, ?$

   b) $^{214}_{83}Bi \longrightarrow \, ^{4}_{2}He \, + \, ?$ e) $^{9}_{3}Li \longrightarrow \, ^{8}_{3}Li \, + \, ?$

   c) $^{120}_{49}In \longrightarrow \, ^{0}_{-1}e \, + \, ?$

The Shell Model of the Nucleus

13.4   The chemical properties of an element can be related to the electron shells which envelop the nucleus of the atom. Similarly, in nuclear chemistry we can interpret the behaviour of the nucleus in terms of proton and neutron shells. This concept was developed in 1948 by Maria Goeppert Mayer, a German physicist. She showed that although the neutrons and protons were both contained in the nucleus, they fill separate sets of shells. The number of protons or neutrons necessary to fill each shell appears to be 2, 8, 20, 28, 50, 82, and 126. Filling a shell with protons or neutrons confers a special stability to the nucleus, just as a filled electron shell gives stability to the noble gases.

The helium-4 nucleus, or alpha particle, provides a good illustration of the shell model. Since this nucleus contains a combination of two protons and two neutrons, it possesses a full shell of each nuclear particle. Hence it is an exceptionally stable nucleus. This explains why alpha particles are so commonly released by radioactive isotopes.

For all the actinons, elements with atomic numbers 90–103, the final product of decay is an isotope of lead. Again the concept of nuclear shells will help to explain this observation. Lead has an atomic number of 82, which means it has a full shell of protons. We should therefore expect this element to be particularly stable.

QUESTIONS

2. Only one isotope of bismuth is stable, bismuth-209. Suggest a reason for the extra stability of this particular isotope.

Figure 13.5
Maria Goeppert Mayer (1906-1972) and German physicist Max Born. Mayer devised the shell model of the nucleus.

The Rate of Nuclear Change   *13.5*

In 1899 Rutherford and one of his co-workers, Frederick Soddy, noted that the amount of radiation emitted by a radioactive substance decreased over time, and that the rate of decrease depended on the identity of the substance.

In order to understand why this is so, let us analyze what happens when a radioactive isotope decays in a single step to a non-radioactive isotope.

If we begin by measuring the initial level of radiation being produced by our hypothetical sample, we can then determine the time that it takes for this level of radiation to decrease by half, i.e. to 50 % of the original level. Let us say that it takes twenty seconds for this to happen. What we would then observe is that during the next twenty seconds the radiation level would again decrease by half; that is, to one fourth the original level. Similarly, over the next twenty-second period the radiation level would again decrease by half so that after a total elapsed time of sixty seconds the radiation level would have decreased to one-eighth of the initial value.

Since the level of radiation being emitted from a sample must be directly proportional to the number of radioactive nuclei present, this simple experiment tells us that, for this particular isotope, the number of radioactive nuclei present is halved every twenty seconds. In other words, after twenty seconds only 50 % of our original nuclei remains, while after forty seconds only 25 % remains, and so on. The time required for half of the nuclei in a given sample of a radioactive isotope to decay is called the **half-life** of the isotope. Isotopic half-lives range from fractions of a second to billions of years (Table 13.4).

TABLE 13.4   *Half-Life of Selected Isotopes*

Isotope	Half-life ($t_{\frac{1}{2}}$)	Isotope	Half-life ($t_{\frac{1}{2}}$)
$^{238}_{92}U$	4.51×10^9 a	$^{251}_{100}Fm$	7 h
$^{14}_{6}C$	5730 a	$^{11}_{6}C$	20.5 min
$^{60}_{27}Co$	5.27 a	$^{15}_{6}C$	2.5 s
$^{131}_{53}I$	8.05 d	$^{212}_{84}Po$	3×10^{-7} s

a = year, d = day, h = hour, min = minute, s = second

As a more concrete example of half-life, let us again consider the case of tritium, ^3_1H, which has a half-life of 12.3 years and decays according to the equation

$$^3_1\text{H} \longrightarrow \ ^3_2\text{He} + \ ^0_{-1}\text{e}$$

If we started out with 8×10^{23} tritium nuclei, half of these would have decayed into helium-3 after 12.3 years. We would then be left with 4×10^{23} tritium nuclei. After a further 12.3 years the number of tritium nuclei would again be halved, this time to 2×10^{23}. By this time, a total of 6×10^{23} helium-3 nuclei would have been produced. At the end of the third 12.3-year period, 1×10^{23} tritium nuclei would remain, and so the process would continue.

In order to introduce the concept of half-life, we used an example of a radioactive element that decayed directly into a stable isotope in a single step. If we had studied an isotope that goes through a series of decay steps, we would have recorded the *total* radiation emitted by *each* of the radioactive isotopes involved in the decay sequence. In such situations it is much more difficult to determine the half-life of a particular isotope in the decay series.

The following example shows how we can use the half-life of a radioactive isotope to determine how much of a given sample of that isotope will remain after a certain time has elapsed.

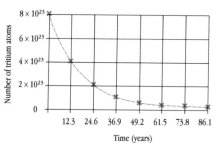

Figure 13.6

The decay of a sample of tritium. With the passage of each 12.3-year period, the number of tritium nuclei remaining is halved.

EXAMPLE　　*13.3*　Iodine-131 has a half-life of eight days. It decays to xenon-131 and produces beta particles. If we started with 2.000 g of iodine-131, what mass of iodine-131 would remain after 32 days?

SOLUTION　The number of elapsed half-lives is determined as follows:

$$32 \text{ days} \times \frac{1 \text{ half-life}}{8 \text{ days}} = 4 \text{ half-lives}$$

For each half-life, the mass of iodine-131 will decrease by one-half. Therefore the mass remaining after four half-lives will be

$$2.00 \text{ g} \times (\tfrac{1}{2})^4 = 0.1 \text{ g}$$

QUESTIONS

3. Oxygen-20 has a half-life of 14 s. If we start with a 64 g sample, what mass of oxygen-20 will remain after 56 seconds?

4. Cobalt-60 is used in cancer treatment. If three-quarters of a sample of cobalt-60 decays in 10.5 years, what is the half-life of the isotope?

Radiation Dosage

13.6

The effect of radiation on living organisms is a major concern. As we mentioned in Section 13.2, each type of radiation differs in its ability to penetrate materials. Thus the various types of radiation can cause different degrees of damage to living tissue. In general, alpha rays are blocked by the outer layers, beta rays are more penetrating, and gamma rays are extremely penetrating.

The half-life of an isotope is also an important factor when we consider the effect that the isotope might have on a living organism. Isotopes with short half-lives decompose rapidly and release radiation at a *faster rate* than isotopes with longer half-lives. An isotope with a short half-life is thus more dangerous to handle than an isotope with a very long half-life.

We measure the rate at which a sample is emitting radiation in **becquerels (Bq)**. A sample that releases one particle per second is said to have an activity of one becquerel. Because a radioactive sample releases an enormous number of particles per second, it is common to work with prefixed units, such as gigabecquerel (GBq). One gigabecquerel represents 10^9 becquerel. There is also a traditional unit still in use, the **curie (Ci)**; one curie is equal to 37 GBq.

Figure 13.7
A portable radiation detector.

TABLE 13.5	*Radiation Units*	
Unit	Symbol	Definition
Radiation		
becquerel (SI)	Bq	1 particle·s^{-1}
gigabecquerel	GBq	10^9 Bq
curie	Ci	37 GBq
Absorbed Dose		
gray (SI)	Gy	1 J·kg^{-1}
radiation absorbed dose	rad	10^{-2} Gy

When we consider the biological effects of radiation, we must be concerned with the energy of radiation. This energy is measured in **grays (Gy)**. A gray is defined as the dose of radiation received when one joule of energy is absorbed by one kilogram of matter. Again, there is a traditional unit still in use, the **rad (rad)**; one rad is equal to 10^{-2} Gy.

Artificial Changes to the Nucleus

13.7

When most nuclei are bombarded with a stream of high-energy particles, a nuclear reaction takes place and different nuclei are produced. One method of initiating such a reaction is to use a **particle accelerator**. When an accelerated particle such as a neutron strikes one of the target nuclei, the nucleus can split into two or more smaller nuclei. Splitting a nucleus in this manner is called **nuclear fission**. Alternatively, an accelerated particle can be captured by a target nucleus to produce a larger nucleus. This process is known as **nuclear fusion**. Nuclear fission and fusion are both examples of **artificial transmutation**; that is, they are artificial processes by which one element is changed into another.

Nuclear Fission

In 1934 Enrico Fermi, an Italian physicist, bombarded certain elements with beams of neutrons. He found that different elements were produced. Some of the isotopes formed had atomic numbers higher than those of the target elements. When Fermi tried this experiment with uranium-238 he was hoping to create a new element with atomic number 93. Fermi expected a neutron to be absorbed by the uranium-238 nucleus to give uranium-239, which he thought would then be rapidly transformed into the new element, X, with the release of an electron:

$$^{238}_{92}\text{U} + {}^{1}_{0}\text{n} \longrightarrow {}^{239}_{92}\text{U}$$
$$^{239}_{92}\text{U} \longrightarrow {}^{239}_{93}\text{X} + {}^{0}_{-1}\text{e}$$

Figure 13.8
Lise Meitner (1878-1968) and German chemist Otto Hahn.

However, the expected reaction did not occur. Over the next three years, Fermi and his co-workers had no success in identifying the products of the reaction. It was not until 1939 that two German physicists, Lise Meitner and her nephew Otto Frisch, reported that instead of forming an element with a higher atomic number, the neutrons were splitting the uranium-238 nuclei to produce nuclei of lower atomic number. They also reported that considerable quantities of energy were released in this nuclear fission process.

Another important observation was that the fission of uranium-238 did not always yield the same two products. From a single sheet of uranium that had been bombarded with neutrons it was possible to identify a wide range of products, including bromine, krypton, rubidium, strontium, molybdenum, antimony, tellurium, iodine, xenon, cesium, and barium.

Natural Radiation

We are exposed to radiation throughout our lives. Some of this radiation comes from outer space as cosmic rays. A high proportion of these fast-moving sub-atomic particles penetrates the atmosphere and, in turn, our bodies.

In addition, we are exposed to radiation from some short-lived isotopes that occur naturally (Table 13.6). Two of these, hydrogen-3 (tritium) and carbon-14 are formed in the upper atmosphere. Approximately one in every 10^{18} atoms of hydrogen is tritium, while about one in every 10^{12} atoms of carbon is radioactive carbon-14. All living matter contains high proportions of carbon and hydrogen, and as a result all living matter will be slightly radioactive.

TABLE 13.6	Some Short-lived Radioactive Isotopes in Nature	
Isotope	Radiation	Half-life
Hydrogen-3	β-rays	12.3 a
Carbon-14	β-rays	5720 a
Radon-222	γ-rays	3.82 d

A third naturally-occurring short-lived isotope, radon-222, is produced by the radioactive decay of "heavy" elements. These elements exist around us in very small quantities. The radon produced amounts to about 30% of the natural radiation. With modern, well-insulated houses, radon concentrations can build up to hazardous levels. In fact in North America it is believed that a substantial number of lung cancers are caused by excessive radon levels in poorly ventilated homes. The lung cancer is caused not so much by the gaseous radon, as by its solid decay product, polonium-218. It is the decay of the polonium on the surface of the lungs that is believed to promote cancer formation.

$$\ce{^{218}_{84}Po} \longrightarrow \ce{^{214}_{82}Pb} + \ce{^{4}_{2}He}$$

It is therefore important to ensure that the air in our homes is being exchanged with the outside. If this is done with a heat exchanger, little heat loss will occur.

Another source of short half-life isotopes are the radioactive isotopes produced during surface nuclear weapons tests. One isotope of special concern is strontium-90. Strontium is a Group IIA element with physical and chemical properties similar to calcium. Strontium ions are readily absorbed by the body in place of calcium ions to form part of the bone structure. Since strontium decays by beta emission, the rays can penetrate the bone marrow and cause cell damage. The United States and the Soviet Union have agreed to ban surface nuclear testing, but some other countries continue to test their nuclear weapons in the atmosphere.

There are seven naturally-occurring elements that have common radioactive isotopes. Some of these elements, such as uranium, exist only as radioactive isotopes. Others, such as rubidium, can be handled in the laboratory without realizing that a high proportion of the atoms are radioactive (Table 13.7). The half-lives of these elements are so long that they provide very low radiation levels.

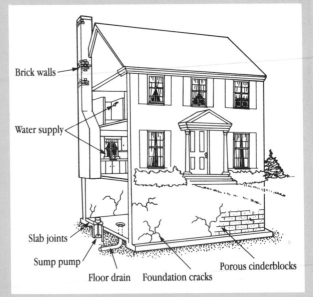

Figure 13.9
Some of the ways in which radon enters a house.

Many other elements have much lower proportions of naturally-occurring radioactive isotopes. One of particular importance is potassium-40 ($t_{\frac{1}{2}} = 1 \times 10^9$ a), an element that is necessary for both plant and animal life. This isotope has an abundance of only 0.012 %.

TABLE 13.7 *Some Common Long-lived Radioactive Isotopes in Nature*

Isotope	Abundance	Radiation	Half-life
Rubidium-87	27 %	β-rays	6×10^{10} a
Indium-115	95 %	β-rays	5×10^{14} a
Neodymium-144	23 %	α-rays	2×10^{15} a
Samarium-147	14 %	α-rays	1×10^{11} a
Rhenium-187	63 %	β-rays	6×10^{10} a
Thorium-232	100 %	α-rays	1×10^{10} a
Uranium-238	99 %	α-rays	4×10^{9} a

Figure 13.10
The major contributors to naturally-occurring radiation. The value for radon exposure varies drastically with the type of rocks underlying a community.

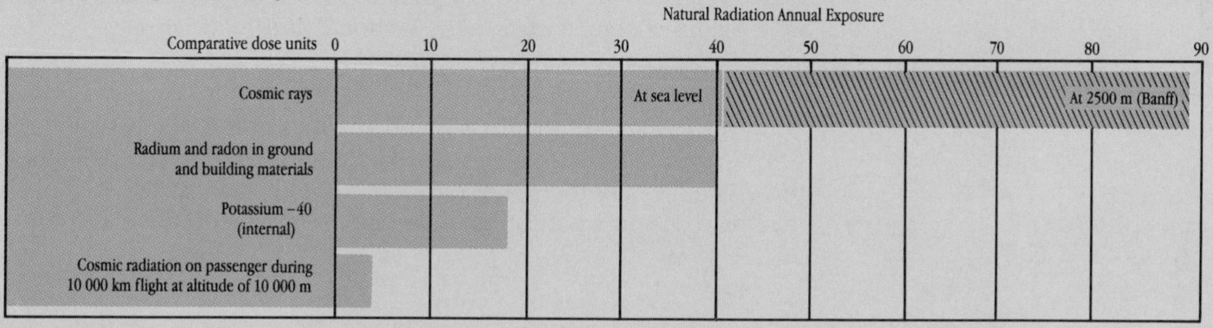

Natural Radiation Annual Exposure

To explain these results we have to use a different model of the nucleus. First proposed by Niels Bohr, the **liquid-drop model** considers a nucleus to be similar to a drop of liquid. When a neutron collides with the nucleus, the drop will break into two halves (Figure 13.11). In addition to the new pair of nuclei formed, neutrons are also released. We can picture these neutrons as being formed at the point where the product nuclei separate to become new droplets. We assume that the wide range of product nuclei is the result of size variations in the two droplets.

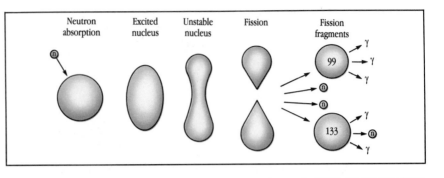

Figure 13.11
The fission process according to the liquid-drop model of the nucleus.

EXAMPLE **13.4** Uranium-235 undergoes fission much more readily than the uranium-238 isotope. If a uranium-235 nucleus is split by a neutron to give a barium-141 nucleus and a krypton-92 nucleus, how many neutrons are released?

SOLUTION We first refer to the Periodic Table for atomic numbers before we write the following nuclear equation:

$$^{235}_{92}U + ^{1}_{0}n \longrightarrow ^{141}_{56}Ba + ^{92}_{36}Kr + ? \, ^{1}_{0}n$$

Next, we check the atomic numbers to make sure they balance. (A neutron has no charge, therefore these should already balance.)

$$92 + 0 = 56 + 36 + 0$$

However, the sum of the mass numbers on the left of the equation is 236 (235 + 1), while that on the right is 233 (141 + 92). The difference of three in mass number, and zero in charge, means that to balance the nuclear equation we must add three neutrons to the right-hand side.

$$^{235}_{92}U + ^{1}_{0}n \longrightarrow ^{141}_{56}Ba + ^{92}_{36}Kr + 3 \, ^{1}_{0}n$$

As we can see from the equation above, when a single neutron collides with a uranium-235 nucleus, two nuclei with lower atomic numbers are formed, together with three neutrons. If these neutrons then collide with other nearby uranium nuclei, these nuclei will also subdivide and release still more neutrons (Figure 13.12).

A self-sustaining sequence of nuclear fission reactions is called a **nuclear chain reaction**. Under controlled conditions, a chain reaction can be used to produce a steady quantity of heat in a nuclear fission reactor. However, if these controls are removed, an explosion or meltdown may result.

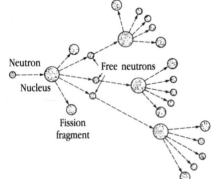

Figure 13.12
The start of a nuclear chain reaction.

QUESTIONS

5. Complete the following nuclear equations involving fission reactions:

a) $^{235}_{92}U + ^{1}_{0}n \longrightarrow ^{87}_{35}Br + ? + 3 \, ^{1}_{0}n$

b) $^{235}_{92}U + ^{1}_{0}n \longrightarrow ^{103}_{42}Mo + ? + 2 \, ^{1}_{0}n$

c) $^{235}_{92}U + ^{1}_{0}n \longrightarrow ^{90}_{37}Rb + ^{144}_{55}Cs + ?$

The Energy Changes that Accompany Nuclear Reactions

13.8

In the preceding section we mentioned that Meitner and Frisch reported that considerable quantities of energy were released by nuclear fission reactions. We also mentioned that, under controlled conditions, fission reactions could be used to produce a steady quantity of heat in a nuclear reactor. Now we shall see why nuclear reactions are capable of producing far greater quantities of energy than the conventional chemical reactions that we have studied in previous chapters.

Very precise measurements show that the mass of a helium nucleus is 4.0015 u. However, if we take the sum of the masses of each of the four particles in a helium nucleus, 2 protons (2×1.0073 u) and 2 neutrons (2×1.0087 u), we obtain a value of 4.0320 u. This difference (here 0.0305 u) between the total mass of the separate particles within a nucleus and the mass of the nucleus itself is called the **mass defect**. We can explain the origin of mass defect by using Einstein's proposition that energy and matter are equivalent. According to Einstein, energy (E) and mass (m) are related by the simple formula

$$E = mc^2$$

where c is the speed of light (3.00×10^8 m·s^{-1}).

Using this relationship, we could say that the mass "missing" from a helium nucleus is accounted for by the energy released when two protons and two neutrons come together to form such a nucleus. Conversely, we could argue that, if we want to break up a helium nucleus into its component particles, i.e. two protons and two neutrons, we would require energy equivalent to 0.0305 u.

EXAMPLE 13.5

The mass lost when a mole of helium nuclei is formed from two moles of protons and two moles of neutrons is 0.0305 g. Calculate how much energy would be required to break up a mole of helium nuclei into its constituent particles.

SOLUTION

Before starting the calculation, we must identify the units that we will use. The SI unit of energy is the joule, defined in the base units kg·m^2·s^{-2}. The speed of light (c) is measured in m·s^{-1}. The change in mass will have to be expressed in kilograms. Therefore

$$0.0305\,\text{g} = 0.0305\,\text{g} \times \frac{1\,\text{kg}}{1000\,\text{g}} = 3.05 \times 10^{-5}\,\text{kg}$$

Substituting values for mass and the speed of light into Einstein's equation gives

$$E = 3.05 \times 10^{-5}\,\text{kg} \times (3.00 \times 10^8\,\text{m}\cdot\text{s}^{-1})^2$$
$$= 2.75 \times 10^{12}\,\text{kg}\cdot\text{m}^2\cdot\text{s}^{-2} \times \frac{1\,\text{J}}{1\,\text{kg}\cdot\text{m}^2\cdot\text{s}^{-2}}$$
$$= 2.75 \times 10^{12}\,\text{J}$$

There is an increase in mass as the reaction takes place:

$${}^{4}_{2}\text{He} \longrightarrow 2\,{}^{1}_{1}\text{p} + 2\,{}^{1}_{0}\text{n}$$

This means that energy must be added in order for the reaction to occur. This added energy results in the increase in mass.

As we have just seen, a very large amount of energy ($2.75 \times 10^{12}\,\text{J}$) is required in order to break down one mole of helium nuclei into two moles of protons and two moles of neutrons. The energy required to break any nucleus into its constituent protons and neutrons is called the **binding energy** of that nucleus. Since energy and mass are related by Einstein's equation $E = mc^2$, the greater the mass defect of a nucleus, the greater will be its binding energy.

Mass Defect and Binding Energy

The size of the mass defect of a nucleus depends upon the number of particles present in the nucleus, although the two quantities are not directly proportional. The nuclear mass of ${}^{16}_{8}\text{O}$ (sixteen particles, $15.9905\,\text{u}$) is less than double that of ${}^{8}_{4}\text{Be}$ (eight particles, $8.0031\,\text{u}$). These figures tell us that, if we were to combine two beryllium-8 nuclei to form one oxygen-16 nucleus, there would be an overall decrease in mass, and energy would be released:

$$2\,{}^{8}_{4}\text{Be} \longrightarrow {}^{16}_{8}\text{O} + \text{energy}$$
$$16.0062\,\text{u} \longrightarrow 15.9905\,\text{u} + \text{energy}$$
$$(2 \times 8.0031\,\text{u})$$

Let us see if the outcome is similar when we are dealing with nuclei with much higher atomic numbers. Suppose we combine two strontium-92 nuclei in order to produce one osmium-184 nucleus. Here we find that the mass of the product ($183.9112\,\text{u}$) is greater than the mass of the reactants ($2 \times 91.8898\,\text{u} = 183.7796\,\text{u}$). In other words, mass must be created by the absorption of a large amount of energy in order for this transformation to occur:

$$2\,{}^{92}_{38}\text{Sr} + \text{energy} \longrightarrow {}^{184}_{76}\text{Os}$$
$$183.7796\,\text{u} + \text{energy} \longrightarrow 183.9112\,\text{u}$$
$$(2 \times 91.8898\,\text{u})$$

Since different nuclei have different numbers of nucleons, accurate comparisons of binding energies can only be made on the basis of the binding energy per nucleon. This quantity is obtained by dividing the binding energy of the nucleus by the total number of nuclear particles.

If we plot binding energy per nucleon against atomic number, we will see that the graph reaches a maximum at atomic number 26 (iron) and then declines (Figure 13.13). This means that energy is released (and mass lost) when we combine nuclei of lower atomic number than iron. If we combine nuclei with atomic numbers greater than iron, energy will be absorbed (and mass gained) in the process.

Notice also that the helium-4 nucleus does not fit on the curve of Figure 13.13. The abnormally high binding energy is a reflection of the stability of the helium nucleus. According to the shell model of the nucleus, the stability of the helium-4 nucleus is due to the fact that it has full shells of protons and neutrons. On fusing of the nuclei to form helium-4 there is a great increase in binding energy per nucleon. This makes the process of using helium as a source of energy very promising.

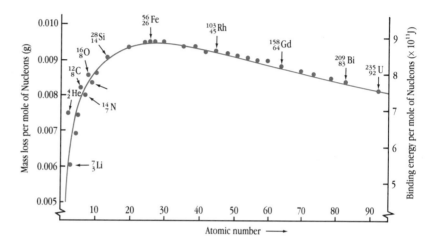

Figure 13.13
A graph of loss of mass per mole of nucleons, and of binding energy per mole of nucleons, against atomic number.

QUESTIONS

6. Calculate how much energy would be released when two moles of ^8_4Be nuclei combine to form one mole of $^{16}_8O$ nuclei. The mass decrease is 0.0157 g.

7. To heat 100 g of water from 10 °C to 100 °C, about 38 kJ of heat energy is required. If this energy is supplied by a nuclear reaction, what mass would have to be converted into energy?

Fusion Reactions

13.9

When two nuclei combine in a nuclear reaction, a fusion reaction occurs. In some cases, one or more subatomic particles are released in the process. Fusion reactions take place in the extremely hot interiors of stars, and are the source of the heat and light energy provided by our sun.

Although scientists believe that several reactions take place in our sun, the most important involves the transformation of hydrogen-1 to helium-4:

$$\begin{aligned} {}^{1}_{1}\text{H} + {}^{1}_{1}\text{H} &\longrightarrow {}^{2}_{1}\text{H} + {}^{0}_{+1}\text{e} \\ {}^{2}_{1}\text{H} + {}^{1}_{1}\text{H} &\longrightarrow {}^{3}_{2}\text{He} \\ {}^{3}_{2}\text{He} + {}^{3}_{2}\text{He} &\longrightarrow {}^{4}_{2}\text{He} + 2\,{}^{1}_{1}\text{H} \end{aligned}$$

Every second, about 6×10^8 t (600 million t) of our sun's hydrogen is converted to helium. The sun has enough hydrogen to last for several billion years. However, when the hydrogen is almost all used up, the core of the sun will shrink. The sun's temperature will then rise from its present level of 1.5×10^7 K to about 10^8 K. At this point, the helium-4 nuclei will start combining to form carbon-12 and oxygen-16 according to the following equations:

$$\begin{aligned} {}^{4}_{2}\text{He} + {}^{4}_{2}\text{He} &\longrightarrow {}^{8}_{4}\text{Be} \\ {}^{8}_{4}\text{Be} + {}^{4}_{2}\text{He} &\longrightarrow {}^{12}_{6}\text{C} \\ {}^{12}_{6}\text{C} + {}^{4}_{2}\text{He} &\longrightarrow {}^{16}_{8}\text{O} \end{aligned}$$

Our sun is not likely to reach the temperature 8×10^8 K required to initiate the fusion reactions that would produce nuclei with atomic numbers greater than eight. It is more likely that the sun will become a white-dwarf star consisting of a carbon-oxygen core surrounded by a shell of helium. Eventually its temperature will begin to decline. As it does so, the sun will slowly die in much the same way that a dying ember fades in a fireplace once the fire has gone out.

The Origin of the Elements

We have just examined a future scenario for our sun. Not all stars meet their end in this way. Stars much more massive than our sun are able to sustain the high temperatures required to initiate the fusion reactions that result in the formation of all the elements up to and including iron (atomic number 26).

You will recall that the formation of nuclei above atomic number 26 requires vast amounts of energy. Since a dying star cannot supply this energy, fusion ceases at this point and the star begins to collapse. As it does so, the star's density increases as its nuclei are pulled closer together. Eventually the repulsive forces acting between the nuclei cause a gigantic explosion called a *supernova*. During such a supernova great amounts of energy are released. Nuclei capture free neutrons and all of the natural elements above iron are formed. The elements present in our solar system are thought to have been formed by the death of such stars. (All the non-hydrogen atoms in your body were formed in the death of stars.)

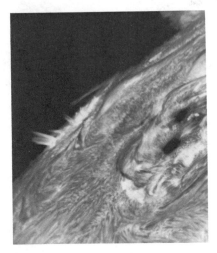

Figure 13.14
The sun is a gigantic fusion reactor.

Figure 13.15
An exploding star (near centre). Vast quantities of high-mass atoms were formed in this massive nuclear explosion, discovered in 1987 by University of Toronto astronomer Ian Shelton.

Formation of New Elements

Although we cannot reproduce the conditions at the centres of stars, we can still combine nuclei in small-scale reactions. The major reason for doing so is to create isotopes and even new elements that do not exist naturally.

Many synthetic elements have been produced by using deuterium or helium nuclei as "bullets." For example, neptunium-239 is synthesized by "firing" deuterium nuclei at uranium-238 nuclei.

$$^{238}_{92}U + {}^{2}_{1}H \longrightarrow {}^{239}_{93}Np + {}^{1}_{0}n$$

For elements of atomic number greater than 102, more massive bullets such as oxygen, calcium, argon, or iron nuclei are required.

The Transuranium Elements

Elements that occur after uranium in the Periodic Table, i.e. elements with atomic numbers greater than 92, do not occur in nature. These elements, usually referred to as the synthetic or **transuranium elements**, are produced by nuclear reactions in which a target nucleus is bombarded with suitable particles such as neutrons. The first two transuranium elements to be produced in this manner were neptunium (atomic number 93) and plutonium (atomic number 94). These elements were named after the planets Neptune and Pluto, which lie beyond Uranus in our solar system. Uranium, as you may have deduced, was named after Uranus.

Neptunium-239 was obtained in 1940 by bombarding uranium-238 nuclei with neutrons. The uranium-239 initially produced in this reaction rapidly decays to produce neptunium-239, as follows:

$$^{238}_{92}U + {}^{1}_{0}n \longrightarrow {}^{239}_{92}U$$
$$^{239}_{92}U \longrightarrow {}^{239}_{93}Np + {}^{0}_{-1}e$$

Similarly, plutonium-238 was first obtained in 1942 according to the following process:

$$^{238}_{92}U + {}^{2}_{1}H \longrightarrow {}^{238}_{93}Np + 2{}^{1}_{0}n$$
$$^{238}_{93}Np \longrightarrow {}^{238}_{94}Pu + {}^{0}_{-1}e$$

You will notice that the latter process involves the use of deuterium nuclei (deuterons, ${}^{2}_{1}H$) as bombarding particles. Other particles used to bring about similar transmutations include α-particles, carbon nuclei, and oxygen nuclei:

$$^{242}_{96}Cm + {}^{4}_{2}He \longrightarrow {}^{245}_{98}Cf + {}^{1}_{0}n$$
$$^{246}_{96}Cm + {}^{12}_{6}C \longrightarrow {}^{254}_{102}No + 4{}^{1}_{0}n$$
$$^{249}_{98}Cf + {}^{18}_{8}O \longrightarrow {}^{263}_{106}Unh + 4{}^{1}_{0}n$$

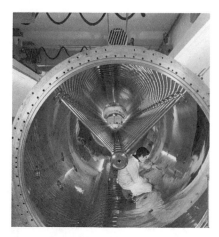

Figure 13.16
Inside the giant particle accelerator at the Institute for Heavy Ion Research in Darmstadt, West Germany. It was in this apparatus that elements 107, 108, and 109 were first synthesized.

Figure 13.17

The inside of a smoke detector. Almost all smoke detectors use tiny quantities of radioactive americium-241, a synthetic transuranium element.

In 1982 it was reported that a single atom of element 109 (unnilennium, symbol Une) had been prepared through the fusion of an iron projectile nucleus and a bismuth target.

The transuranium elements were originally prepared in very small amounts. However, neptunium, plutonium, americium, and curium have now been produced in large enough quantities that their properties can be studied. This is possible because some isotopes of these elements have half-lives measured in years.

These metals are silvery in appearance with very high densities, neptunium being the densest at $20 \text{ g} \cdot \text{cm}^{-3}$. They tarnish rapidly in air, forming a surface coating of oxide. Compounds with oxidation numbers from $+2$ to $+7$ have been formed, but the most common oxidation numbers are $+3$ and $+4$. Most of the compounds are brightly coloured.

Nuclear Fusion and Technology

For thirty years, scientists have been working to find a way of harnessing the energy from fusion reactions. The major problem is that temperatures of about $5.8 \times 10^6 \text{ K}$, close to those found in the centre of the sun, are necessary for large-scale fusion reactions to occur. At such high temperatures, any solid container would vaporize instantly. Thus, such reactions must be confined in very intense magnetic fields. To have any practical value, the fusion reaction must also be maintained for a measurable length of time.

The most promising fusion reaction involves the fusion of deuterium (^2_1H) and tritium (^3_1H):

$$^2_1\text{H} + ^3_1\text{H} \longrightarrow ^4_2\text{He} + ^1_0\text{n}$$

Figure 13.18

The Tokamak fusion Test Reactor. This device is designed to develop sufficiently high temperatures to produce a fusion reaction. A temperature of $3 \times 10^8 \text{ K}$ (twenty times hotter than the centre of the sun) has been attained inside this apparatus.

However, another problem with fusion power is controlling the level of radioactivity. Tritium is highly radioactive but, more importantly, its reaction with deuterium produces neutrons. Many of these neutrons will collide with the nuclei of surrounding materials, including the giant magnets used to produce the magnetic container. As the collisions continue, more radioactive isotopes will be created and the container will become increasingly radioactive, presenting a safety hazard to on-site personnel. Consequently, scientists are continuing to search for materials that are less likely to produce radioactive isotopes upon neutron bombardment.

QUESTIONS

8. Complete the following nuclear equations:
   a) $^{27}_{13}Al + ^{4}_{2}He \longrightarrow ^{1}_{1}H + ?$
   b) $4\,^{1}_{1}H \longrightarrow 2\,^{0}_{+1}e + ?$
   c) $^{118}_{50}Sn + ^{1}_{0}n \longrightarrow ?$
   d) $^{116}_{48}Cd + ^{4}_{2}He \longrightarrow ^{1}_{0}n + ?$
   e) $^{249}_{98}Cf + ^{11}_{5}B \longrightarrow 6\,^{1}_{0}n + ?$

Fission Reactors

13.10 When elements of high atomic number are formed from less massive nuclei, energy is absorbed. In the reverse process, when massive nuclei undergo fission to form nuclei with low atomic numbers, energy is released in the form of heat. In general it is the heat that interests us because it can be used to generate electrical power.

Nuclear Reactors

In a nuclear power plant, controlled nuclear reactions take place in a **nuclear reactor**. The heat released during the nuclear reaction is absorbed by a liquid or gas **coolant**. This hot liquid or gas is then passed through a heat exchanger where steam is generated. The steam in turn drives a turbine which is connected to an electrical generator.

The Advantages and Disadvantages of Fission Power

In Canada the four major sources of fuel for the large-scale production of electricity are water, oil, coal, and uranium. Only the water-rich provinces of British Columbia, Manitoba, Quebec, and Newfoundland can use water to any great extent as an energy source. Where power plants use oil or coal, the fuel cost constitutes a large and often unpredictable portion of the electricity price. Burning coal and oil also produces large quantities of sulfur dioxide and carbon dioxide, and therefore contributes to acid rain. By contrast, nuclear power plants have comparatively low running costs although the initial construction costs are very high. This is because a nuclear reactor is far more complex than an oil- or coal-burning boiler. Nuclear power is an attractive option in Canada because we have very large deposits of uranium. However, for this option to be exercised we need to solve the problem of how and where to store the spent fuel rods from the nuclear reactors. As well, our politicians will continue to have a tough time convincing their electorate that the present nuclear technology is safe enough.

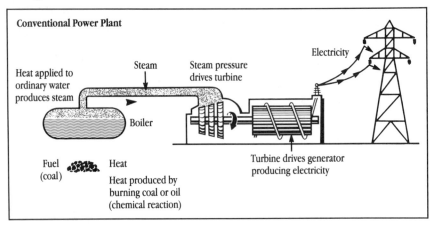

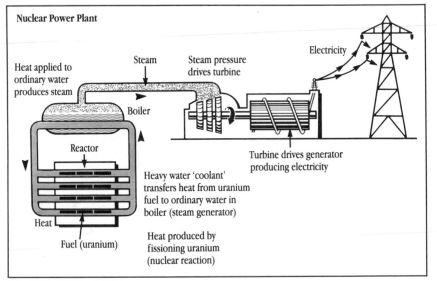

Figure 13.19

Comparison of the workings of a coal-powered plant and a uranium fission plant.

The Basic Requirements of a Fission Reactor

Only one isotope of uranium, uranium-235, readily undergoes fission. But natural uranium is 0.7 % uranium-235 and 99.3 % uranium-238. For most reactors this means that the proportion of uranium-235 in the fuel must be increased, or **enriched** (usually to 3–4 %), to sustain the chain reaction. The procedure requires an extremely expensive processing plant.

Nuclear Chemistry

As conventional sources of energy become depleted, nuclear energy offers almost limitless potential. This diagram provides a comparison, drawn to scale, of the coal required and the ashes produced in the 2000 megawatt Lakeview generating station and the uranium needed for the 2000 megawatt generating station at Pickering. Most of the nuclear waste is retained within the uranium fuel.

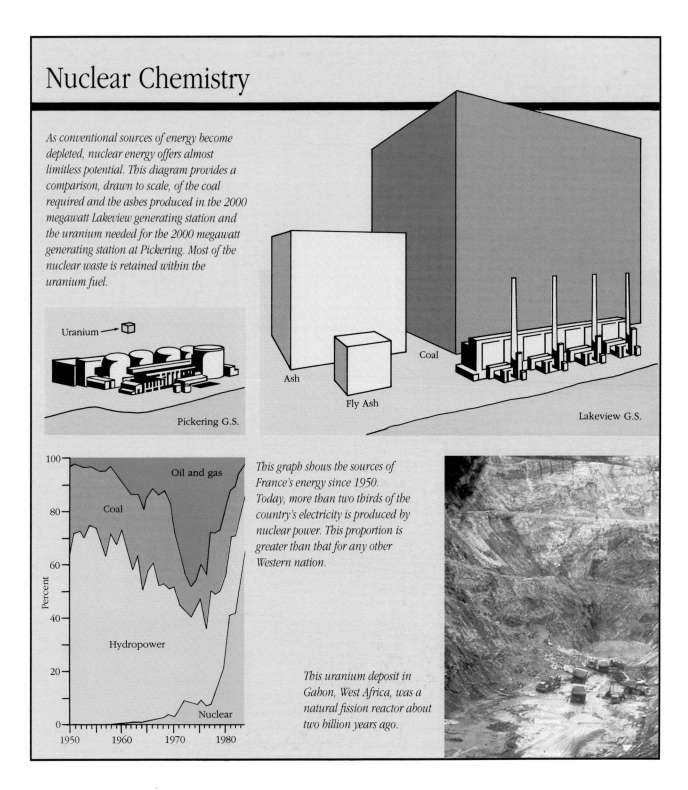

Uranium

Pickering G.S.

Ash

Fly Ash

Coal

Lakeview G.S.

Oil and gas

Coal

Hydropower

Nuclear

Percent

100

80

60

40

20

0

1950   1960   1970   1980

This graph shows the sources of France's energy since 1950. Today, more than two thirds of the country's electricity is produced by nuclear power. This proportion is greater than that for any other Western nation.

This uranium deposit in Gabon, West Africa, was a natural fission reactor about two billion years ago.

A heavy water plant.

The Top Ten

Lifetime World Power Reactor Performance to March 31, 1988*
from among 260 reactors over 500 MW

Country	Ranking	Unit	Type	Capacity † Factor %
🇨🇦	1.	Pickering 7	CANDU	90.3
🇨🇦	2.	Bruce 7	CANDU	89.0
🇨🇦	3.	Pickering 8	CANDU	88.2
🇨🇦	4.	Point Lepreau	CANDU	87.9
🇩🇪	5.	Philippsburg 2	PWR	87.8
🇨🇦	6.	Bruce 3	CANDU	86.8
🇩🇪	7.	Grohnde A-1	PWR	85.7
🇨🇦	8.	Bruce 5	CANDU	85.1
🇨🇦	9.	Bruce 6	CANDU	84.9
🇧🇪	10.	Tihange 3	PWR	84.8

*Source: *Nuclear Engineering International*

† Capacity Factor = actual electricity generation / perfect electricity generation

CANDU reactors are among the most reliable in the world.

An aerial view of the Pickering generating station.

PLATE 26 — NUCLEAR CHEMISTRY

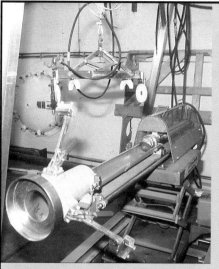

Loading fuel at the Bruce generating station.

Distribution of energy from fission

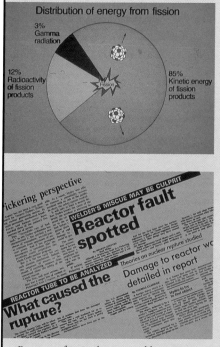

3%
Gamma
radiation

12%
Radioactivity
of fission
products

Fission

85%
Kinetic energy
of fission
products

Reactor safety is always a public concern.

Refuelling a Bruce reactor.

This apparatus in West Germany uses nuclear fusion to produce element 109.

Researchers seek to improve methods of separating radioactive chemicals from solution.

This chemist is testing various catalysts for use in the production of deuterium oxide.

PLATE 28 — NUCLEAR CHEMISTRY

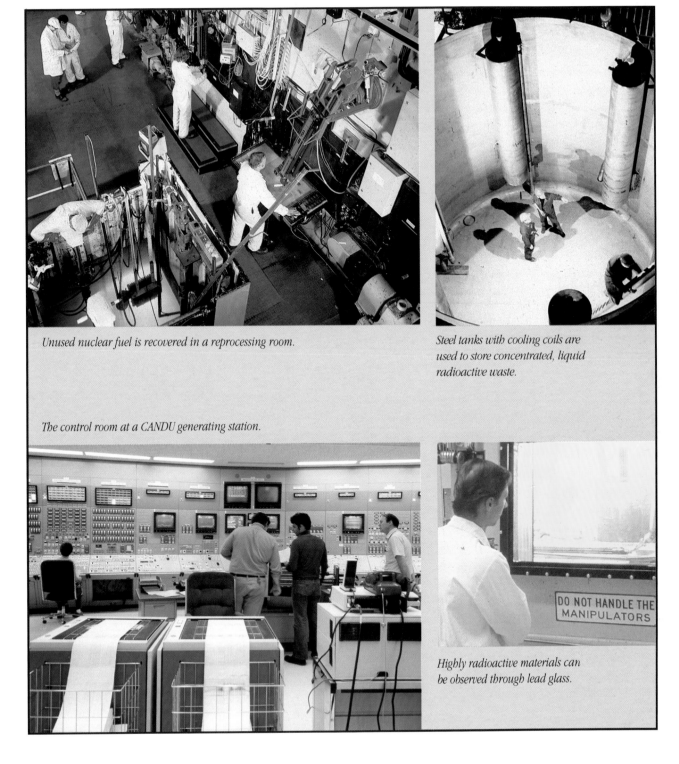

Unused nuclear fuel is recovered in a reprocessing room.

Steel tanks with cooling coils are used to store concentrated, liquid radioactive waste.

The control room at a CANDU generating station.

DO NOT HANDLE THE MANIPULATORS

Highly radioactive materials can be observed through lead glass.

A canister for spent fuel at the Pickering generating station.

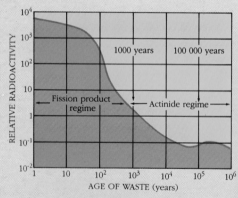

Highly radioactive isotopes decay within 100 years. Plutonium and the other actinons produce significant levels of radiation for 10 000 years.

Spent fuel storage bay at the Pickering generating station.

PLATE 30 — NUCLEAR CHEMISTRY

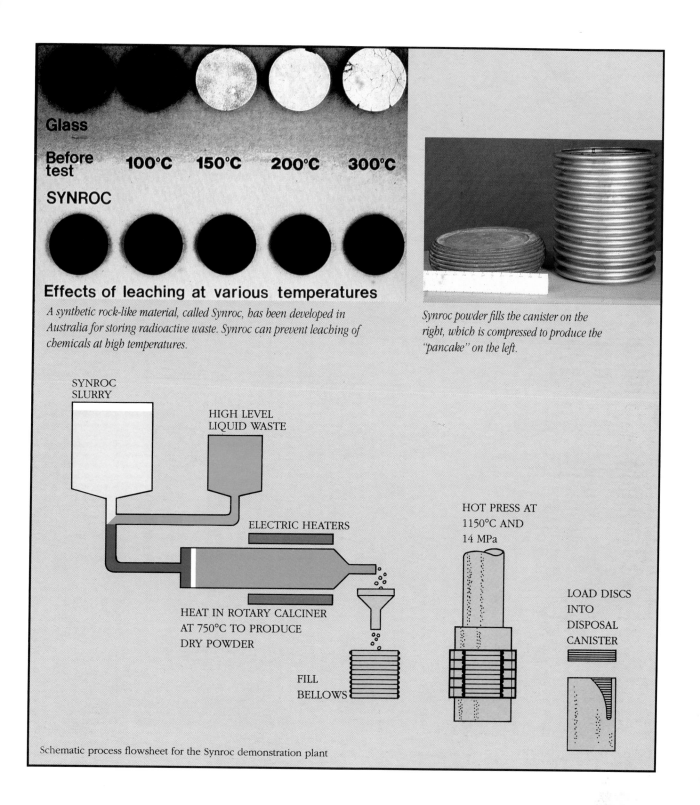

Glass

Before test | 100°C | 150°C | 200°C | 300°C

SYNROC

Effects of leaching at various temperatures

A synthetic rock-like material, called Synroc, has been developed in Australia for storing radioactive waste. Synroc can prevent leaching of chemicals at high temperatures.

Synroc powder fills the canister on the right, which is compressed to produce the "pancake" on the left.

SYNROC SLURRY

HIGH LEVEL LIQUID WASTE

ELECTRIC HEATERS

HOT PRESS AT 1150°C AND 14 MPa

HEAT IN ROTARY CALCINER AT 750°C TO PRODUCE DRY POWDER

FILL BELLOWS

LOAD DISCS INTO DISPOSAL CANISTER

Schematic process flowsheet for the Synroc demonstration plant

The United States has had experience in decommissioning an old nuclear reactor. The pictures above show the Elk River reactor before and during the dismantling.

During the decommissioning operations at Elk River, special underwater cutting tools were required to dismantle certain radioactive metal components.

PLATE 32 — NUCLEAR CHEMISTRY

Figure 13.20

The Soviet Union's nuclear ice-breaker, Artika. This huge, extremely powerful vessel can cruise through ice three metres thick.

When uranium-235 is bombarded by neutrons, the resulting fission reaction releases more neutrons. However, these neutrons are moving too fast to be absorbed by surrounding uranium-235 nuclei. They must be slowed down by a **moderator** such as water or graphite so that the controlled chain reaction will continue. Most large reactors use water as a moderator.

Most nuclear-powered ships also use enriched uranium fuel and water as a moderator. Like other reactors, the construction costs of nuclear-powered ships are very high. The advantage is that these ships only need refuelling once every two to five years. Thus the use of nuclear power is generally restricted to naval vessels where initial cost is of little concern but where long endurance is of paramount importance. The U.S. Navy for example, has several nuclear-powered vessels. Ice-breakers built by the Soviet Union are among the few non-military uses for nuclear ships.

The CANDU Reactor

In the Canadian-designed **CANDU** (*Can*adian *D*euterium-*U*ranium) **reactor**, natural uranium is used as the fuel. Although this fuel is cheaper than enriched uranium, its use means that ordinary water cannot be used as a moderator. Ordinary water absorbs too many neutrons to allow the chain reaction to continue. Instead, CANDU reactors use **heavy water**. Heavy water consists of water molecules in which the hydrogen-1 atoms (^1_1H) have been replaced by deuterium atom (^2_1H). The process used to separate the water molecules containing deuterium atoms from those containing normal hydrogen atoms is very expensive. Thus savings in cost obtained by using natural uranium is balanced by the extra cost of producing heavy water.

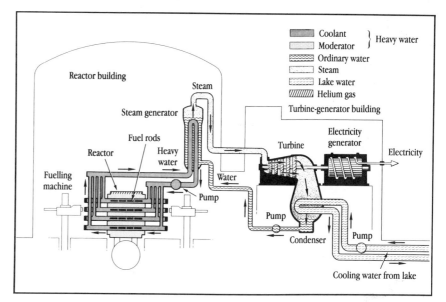

Figure 13.21

A schematic of the CANDU system.

A Natural Fission Reactor

Nature beat us to the fission reactor. About two billion years ago, a deposit of uranium ore at Oklo in Gabon, West Africa began operating as a nuclear reactor.

The first evidence of this occurrence came from an assay of uranium-235 in the ore. At other locations around the world, the abundance of this uranium isotope is 0.720%. Yet at the Oklo mine, French scientists were amazed to find that the ore contained as little as 0.296% uranium-235. Somehow, a large proportion of the uranium-235 had disappeared. As a test of the natural nuclear fission hypothesis, the ore was analyzed for other elements. Fifteen common fission products not found normally in such ores were identified.

How did this natural nuclear fission reaction occur? There are several contributing factors to be considered. Because uranium-235 has a much shorter half-life than uranium-238, the abundance of uranium-235 has been steadily decreasing. The rocks at Oklo were laid down about two billion years ago. At that time the abundance of uranium-235 was about three percent. Rain water is believed to have leached the uranium compounds into pockets in the rock where almost pure uranium(IV) oxide precipitated. This concentration of uranium and the availability of rainwater as a moderator was enough to start the fission chain reaction. It is believed that the chain reaction continued for two hundred thousand to one million years.

With the present abundance of uranium-235, such a natural reactor could not happen. However, there might have been other "Oklos" even earlier in the earth's history, since the abundance of uranium-235 when the earth was formed is believed to have been about 25%.

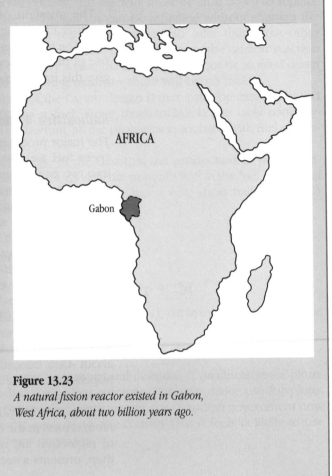

Figure 13.23
A natural fission reactor existed in Gabon, West Africa, about two billion years ago.

Applications of Nuclear Chemistry

13.11 Nuclear chemistry has been applied to a number of fields, including medicine, biology and biochemistry, geology, and archaeology. Several typical applications in these fields are described below.

Medicine In medicine, radioactive isotopes are used to diagnose and treat disease. In the treatment of certain types of cancer, gamma radiation is used to kill cancerous cells. Cobalt-60 is often used as the source of the γ-radiation. This isotope is prepared by placing the only natural isotope of

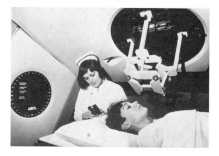

Figure 13.24
A technician adjusts the controls of a linear accelerator. The high-energy X-ray machine, which delivers radiation faster and to a greater depth, is an alternative to cobalt treatment of cancer.

cobalt, cobalt-59, in a nuclear reactor. Here cobalt-59 absorbs a neutron to produce cobalt-60:

$$^{59}_{27}\text{Co} + ^{1}_{0}\text{n} \longrightarrow ^{60}_{27}\text{Co}$$

About 90 % of the cobalt-60 used throughout the world is produced in Canada. Cobalt-60 has a half-life of about five years and releases both beta and gamma rays:

$$^{60}_{27}\text{Co} \longrightarrow ^{60}_{28}\text{Ni} + ^{0}_{-1}\text{e} + ^{0}_{0}\gamma$$

Radioactive tracers are equally important. Their use is based on the fact that certain tissues and organs accumulate specific elements. Giving a patient a minute quantity of radioactive tracer enables medical staff to monitor the uptake and location of that element (Table 13.8). The path of the tracer can then be followed by tracking the radiation emitted as some of the atoms decay. The chemical activity of the radioactive isotope will be the same as the normal, non-radioactive one. Because of the high sensitivity of modern detectors, the radiation hazard is negligible.

TABLE 13.8	*Some Isotopes Used as Radioactive Tracers*		
Isotope	Form	Application	Half-life
Chromium-51	Na_2CrO_4	red blood cell lifetime	28 d
Iron-59	$FeCl_2$	iron turnover	45 d
Strontium-85	$Sr(NO_3)_2$	bone scan	65 d
Technetium-99	NH_4TcO_4	brain scan	6 h
Iodine-131	NaI	thyroid function	8 d
Gold-198	Au	liver scan	3 d

Medicine also has other uses for radioactive materials. Some heart pacemakers contain nuclear batteries that use the heat generated by a radioactive element (such as plutonium) to generate electricity. Batteries such as these can last up to twenty years.

Biology and Biochemistry Biologists and biochemists also use radioactive tracers extensively to investigate biological processes in plants and animals. The use of carbon-14 in studies on photosynthesis in plants is a good example. The plants are placed in a container filled with radioactive carbon dioxide, in which normal carbon-12 has been replaced by carbon-14. The plant will absorb the radioactive carbon dioxide as it would normal carbon dioxide. We can then follow the location of the radioactive carbon atoms as they are incorporated into the plant carbohydrates. This is easy to do since the radioactive carbon emits beta-rays, which can be detected with a Geiger counter. The decay reaction is as follows:

$$^{14}_{6}\text{C} \longrightarrow {}^{14}_{7}\text{N} + {}^{0}_{-1}\text{e}$$

Chemistry As we described in Section 13.9, new elements can be synthesized using fusion reactions. Chemists still use Mendeléev's Periodic Table to predict the properties of these new elements. Once the elements are synthesized, these predictions can be checked.

Nuclear reactions can also be used in qualitative and quantitative analysis. A very sensitive technique, known as **neutron activation analysis**, is used to determine concentrations as low as one part per billion. In neutron activation analysis, the sample is placed in a small nuclear reactor where it is bombarded by neutrons. The reactions between the sample nuclei and the neutrons produce radioactive isotopes. The sample, which is now radioactive, is removed from the reactor and the gamma rays emitted from it are studied. Each radioactive isotope produces characteristic gamma rays of very precise wavelengths. For example, natural gold consists of one isotope: gold-197. When it is exposed to neutrons, gold-198 is produced:

$$^{197}_{79}\text{Au} + {}^{1}_{0}\text{n} \longrightarrow {}^{198}_{79}\text{Au}$$

Gold-198 is radioactive. As it decays it releases both beta and gamma rays:

$$^{198}_{79}\text{Au} \longrightarrow {}^{198}_{80}\text{Hg} + {}^{0}_{-1}\text{e} + {}^{0}_{0}\gamma$$

The gamma rays have a wavelength of 3.01×10^{-12} m (3.01 pm). If we measure the intensity of the gamma-rays at this wavelength, we can calculate the concentration of gold in the sample.

Geology and Archaeology We can determine the age of rocks, fossils, and ancient artifacts from the half-lives of the radioactive isotopes they contain. Rocks are usually dated from isotopes with very long half-lives. One very useful isotope for this purpose is potassium-40. It decays to argon-40 by an unusual nuclear reaction, in which the potassium nucleus captures an electron:

$$^{40}_{19}\text{K} + {}^{0}_{-1}\text{e} \longrightarrow {}^{40}_{18}\text{Ar} \qquad t_{\frac{1}{2}} = 1.3 \times 10^{9}\,\text{a}$$

Dating of rocks containing potassium is based on the ratio of potassium-40 to argon-40 in the rock. Argon is a gas, and as long as the rock is in molten form inside the earth, the argon can escape. Once the rock has solidified near the surface of the earth, any subsequent argon produced will be trapped in the solid rock. If we melt a sample of the rock in the laboratory, we can measure the volume of argon released. We can then compare the amount of gas released with the amount of potassium-40 remaining in the rock. This will give us a good estimate of the time elapsed since the rock solidified.

TABLE 13.9	Some of the Isotopes used for Geological Dating	
Isotope	Half-life	Decay product
Potassium-40	1.4×10^9 a	Argon-40
Rubidium-87	4.9×10^{10} a	Strontium-87
Samarium-147	1.1×10^{11} a	Neodymium-143
Rhenium-187	4.6×10^{10} a	Osmium-183

Potassium-argon dating can be used for objects that are millions of years old, but comparatively young materials have not produced sufficient argon to date them by this method. For these we use carbon-14 or tritium dating. Both of these isotopes are being continuously produced in the upper atmosphere by the collision of neutrons from outer space with nitrogen-14 nuclei:

$$^{14}_{7}\text{N} + {}^1_0\text{n} \longrightarrow {}^{14}_{6}\text{C} + {}^1_1\text{H}$$
$$^{14}_{7}\text{N} + {}^1_0\text{n} \longrightarrow {}^{12}_{6}\text{C} + {}^3_1\text{H}$$

Let us consider carbon-14 first. This isotope decays to nitrogen-14:

$$^{14}_{6}\text{C} \longrightarrow {}^{14}_{7}\text{N} + {}^0_{-1}\text{e} \qquad t_{\frac{1}{2}} = 5720 \text{ a}$$

The radioactive carbon atoms will react with the oxygen in the atmosphere to form carbon dioxide molecules. These molecules will be distributed throughout the atmosphere. Plants will absorb some of this carbon dioxide through photosynthesis and the radioactive carbon will become part of the plant tissue. While the plant is still alive, the level of radioactive carbon will remain relatively constant; as some decays, more will be absorbed from the atmosphere. However, once the plant dies, no more carbon-14 will be absorbed and the level of β radiation will decrease. Thus, the lower the radiation level, the older the object. This method has been used to estimate the age of carbon-containing objects which are hundreds to tens of thousands of years old.

The tritium produced in the upper atmosphere reacts with oxygen to produce water. This radioactive water joins the natural precipitation to give us a fairly constant level of radiation in the seas, lakes, and rivers. The reaction equation for tritium decay is

$$^3_1\text{H} \longrightarrow {}^3_2\text{He} + {}^0_{-1}\text{e} \qquad t_{\frac{1}{2}} = 12.3 \text{ a}$$

Once the sample of water is removed from contact with the air, no more tritium will enter the sample and the level of emitted β radiation will decrease with time. Thus the lower the radiation level, the longer it is since the sample was removed from contact with the atmosphere. The method has been used to find how long surface water takes to enter underground supplies. It has also been used to verify the age of expensive wines.

Geologists and archaeologists now use radioactive dating techniques routinely in their work.

Food Irradiation

Food irradiation involves exposing food to ionizing radiation, such as gamma rays. When the radiation passes through food, covalent bonds are broken and new products form. This chemical change stops normal cell division, thus sterilizing or killing insects and destroying parasites and micro-organisms. It also inhibits sprouting and ripening in vegetables and fruit. The radiation passes through the product causing no radioactivity in the food itself.

Food irradiation was first proposed in 1921, and was used to kill trichina worms in pork. Today one of the major arguments is for the use of radiation to kill harmful organisms. In underdeveloped countries, diseases from contaminated foods are a major cause of sickness and disability. Even in the economically developed nations, salmonella poisoning is a major problem. One area of concern, however, is the misuse of irradiation to compensate for poor hygiene in meat processing plants.

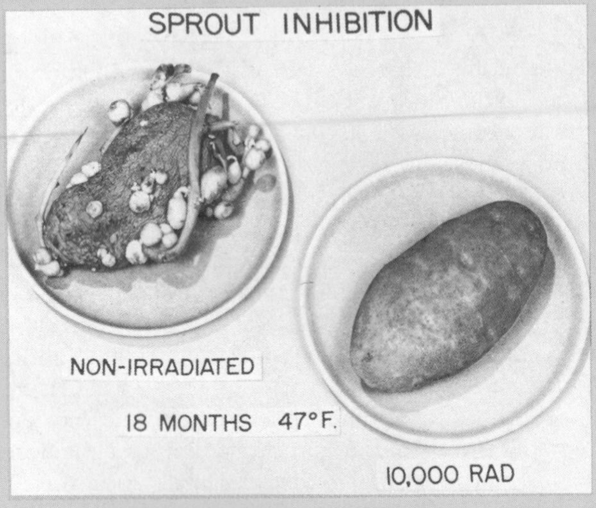

Figure 13.25
These potatoes were stored at 8°C for 18 months. The non-irradiated one (left) sprouted while the irradiated one remained edible.

Killing insects in stored grain, fruit, and spices has also become a possible use for irradiation now that many of the pesticides and fumigants used on fruit and spices are banned for safety reasons. Another major use is to extend the shelf life of fruit and vegetables, reducing spoilage — a particular problem in hot climates.

There are three levels of irradiation. Doses of less than one kilogray will inhibit sprouting and kill infesting insects and parasites (Low-Dose Applications). Destroying spoilage and pathogenic (dangerous) bacteria requires between one and ten kilograys (Intermediate-Dose Applications). Reducing or eliminating virus contamination requires 10–100 kilograys (High-Dose Applications). In other words, the simpler the organism, the higher the level of radiation needed to destroy it.

Many articles have been written about food irradiation, some of which play on people's fears or report poorly-controlled studies. The food itself does not become radioactive — the radiation is not of high enough energy to cause any nuclear changes — just as the treatment of cancer patients with the same radiation does not cause them to become radioactive. The food undergoes a slight decrease in vitamin content. And, the disruption of covalent bonds can cause changes in flavour, odour, texture, and colour when the dose is too high for the particular food. Dairy products in particular are poor candidates for irradiation. The one justifiable area of concern is that of formation of hazardous compounds during the molecular changes.

Food irradiation is carried out in Japan, the Soviet Union, South Africa, Holland, Hungary, and Israel. For example, the Soviet Union irradiates about 200 000 tonnes of stored grain each year to kill insects. Holland irradiates some seafood to kill bacteria.

One of the best methods of irradiation is to use a cobalt-60 source. Canada has been in the forefront of the worldwide sale of cancer radiation-therapy units using this isotope. Thus a natural extension of our technological expertise would be to similarly market food irradiation units. But there are political as well as health and economic reasons for introducing food irradiation in Canada.

Many countries are planning irradiation facilities. They are already under construction in Taiwan, the United States, Italy, Korea, Pakistan, and Thailand. The tropical countries are eager to start using irradiation as a replacement for the banned fumigants and pesticides. In return, these countries need to know whether we, the consumers in the developed world, will accept the irradiated products.

14. A sample of well water contained only one-sixteenth of the tritium of surface water. How long had the well water been out of contact with the atmosphere?

15. Write balanced nuclear equations for the following decays used in medicine:

a) $^{198}_{79}\text{Au} \longrightarrow {}^{0}_{-1}\text{e} + ?$

b) $^{59}_{26}\text{Fe} \longrightarrow {}^{0}_{-1}\text{e} + ?$

16. Write balanced nuclear equations for the following decays used in geology:

a) $^{147}_{62}\text{Sm} \longrightarrow {}^{143}_{60}\text{Nd} + ?$

b) $^{87}_{37}\text{Rb} \longrightarrow {}^{87}_{38}\text{Sr} + ?$

The Destructive Side of Nuclear Energy

13.12

The transformation of matter into energy by nuclear reactions can be used for destructive as well as constructive purposes. A fission bomb (popularly called an atomic bomb) consists of uranium-235 or plutonium-239 surrounded by a layer of ordinary explosive. When the explosive is detonated, the uranium or plutonium is compressed into a small single lump in which a chain reaction can take place. Unlike the chain reactions that are used in nuclear reactors, this reaction is not controlled, and an enormous explosion results.

A temperature of millions of kelvins is required to detonate a fusion bomb (a hydrogen bomb). The only "easy" way to achieve this temperature level is to set off a fission reaction first. Thus every fusion bomb also contains a small fission bomb. The fusion reaction, once begun, releases much more energy than a fission reaction, and the resulting explosion is greater than that of a fission bomb.

The effects of nuclear warfare would be disastrous. The total explosive power of existing nuclear weapons is great enough to destroy the world several times over. Studies indicate that hundreds of millions of people would die as a result of even a limited nuclear war. In addition, scientists now believe that the dust and smoke from the explosions and fires would result in darkness over most of the earth's surface. This darkness could last for months or even years, preventing heat and light from the sun from reaching the earth. Without this light and heat, temperatures would drop to well below freezing even at the equator, and plants would not be able to survive. Without plants for food, any surviving animals or humans would not live very long in this aptly named "nuclear winter."

A nuclear war would also destroy the ozone layer in the upper atmosphere that protects us from the sun's ultraviolet rays. Thus, the "nuclear winter" would be followed by an equally inhospitable "ultraviolet spring."

Figure 13.26
The hands on the Doomsday clock, kept at three minutes to midnight by the Bulletin of Atomic Scientists, was moved back three more minutes in 1987 following signs of easing East-West tensions.

Summary

- Nuclear chemistry is concerned with changes that occur in the nucleus of an atom.

- The nucleus of a radioactive isotope can emit several types of radiation. Common types include alpha, beta, and gamma rays.

- In a balanced nuclear equation the sum of the mass numbers and the total nuclear charge on each side of the equation must balance.

- Radioactive isotopes may decay through a series of steps before a stable isotope is produced.

- The time required for half the atoms of a radioactive isotope to decay is called the half-life of the isotope.

- The effects of radiation are measured in terms of the energy released when the rays are stopped by a sample of matter. The harmful effects of radiation depend upon the type of radiation and the half-life of the isotope.

- Most nuclei can be changed by bombarding them with particles. The nuclei can either split into smaller nuclei (fission), or capture the bombarding particles to form larger nuclei (fusion).

- The energy released by the sun and other stars is due to a series of nuclear reactions that take place within them.

- Nuclear reactions involve the transformation of a small amount of matter into a large amount of energy.

- The energy produced by nuclear reactions may be converted into electrical energy through the use of nuclear reactor.

- The CANDU reactor is a Canadian-designed nuclear reactor.

- Nuclear chemistry has been applied to many fields including medicine, biology, chemistry, geology, and archaeology.

- Nuclear weapons have been designed that utilize both nuclear fission and nuclear fusion.

KEY WORDS

abundance	coolant
alpha ray	curie
artificial transmutation	enriched uranium
atomic number	gamma ray
becquerel	gray
beta ray	half-life
binding energy	heavy water
CANDU reactor	isotope

liquid-drop model
mass defect
mass number
moderator
neutron activation analysis
nuclear chain reaction
nuclear fission
nuclear fusion
nuclear reactor

nucleons
particle accelerator
positron
rad
radioactive decay
radioactive series
radioactive tracer
radioactivity
transuranium elements

1. a) $^{190}_{75}\text{Re} \longrightarrow {}^{190}_{76}\text{Os} + {}^{0}_{-1}\text{e}$ d) $^{162}_{69}\text{Tm} \longrightarrow {}^{0}_{+1}\text{e} + {}^{162}_{68}\text{Er}$

   b) $^{214}_{83}\text{Bi} \longrightarrow {}^{4}_{2}\text{He} + {}^{210}_{81}\text{Tl}$ e) $^{9}_{3}\text{Li} \longrightarrow {}^{8}_{3}\text{Li} + {}^{1}_{0}\text{n}$

   c) $^{120}_{49}\text{In} \longrightarrow {}^{0}_{-1}\text{e} + {}^{120}_{50}\text{Sn}$

2. This isotope of bismuth has a full shell of neutrons (126). Hence it has a particular stability.

3. 4.0 g

4. As $\frac{3}{4}$ of the cobalt-60 decays in 10.5 years, $\frac{1}{4}$ must remain after this time. Two half-lives must have elapsed; therefore the half-life is 5.25 years.

5. a) $^{235}_{92}\text{U} + {}^{1}_{0}\text{n} \longrightarrow {}^{87}_{35}\text{Br} + {}^{146}_{57}\text{La} + 3{}^{1}_{0}\text{n}$

   b) $^{235}_{92}\text{U} + {}^{1}_{0}\text{n} \longrightarrow {}^{103}_{42}\text{Mo} + {}^{131}_{50}\text{Sn} + 2{}^{1}_{0}\text{n}$

   c) $^{235}_{92}\text{U} + {}^{1}_{0}\text{n} \longrightarrow {}^{90}_{37}\text{Rb} + {}^{144}_{55}\text{Cs} + 2{}^{1}_{0}\text{n}$

6. 1.411×10^{12} J

7. 4.2×10^{-10} g

8. a) $^{27}_{13}\text{Al} + {}^{4}_{2}\text{He} \longrightarrow {}^{1}_{1}\text{H} + {}^{30}_{14}\text{Si}$ d) $^{116}_{48}\text{Cd} + {}^{4}_{2}\text{He} \longrightarrow {}^{1}_{0}\text{n} + {}^{119}_{50}\text{Sn}$

   b) $4{}^{1}_{1}\text{H} \longrightarrow 2{}^{0}_{+1}\text{e} + {}^{4}_{2}\text{He}$ e) $^{249}_{98}\text{Cf} + {}^{11}_{5}\text{B} \longrightarrow 6{}^{1}_{0}\text{n} + {}^{254}_{103}\text{Lr}$

   c) $^{118}_{50}\text{Sn} + {}^{1}_{0}\text{n} \longrightarrow {}^{119}_{50}\text{Sn}$

9. The CANDU reactor uses natural uranium as a fuel and heavy water as a moderator. Conventional reactors use enriched uranium as fuel and "ordinary" water as the moderator.

10. Ontario has a shortage of other energy sources (e.g. coal and oil) and a convenient source of uranium.

11. New Brunswick and Quebec also have nuclear power plants.

12. $^{239}_{94}\text{Pu} \longrightarrow {}^{4}_{2}\text{He} + {}^{235}_{92}\text{U}$

13. $^{131}_{53}\text{I} \longrightarrow {}^{0}_{-1}\text{e} + {}^{131}_{54}\text{Xe}$

14. 49.2 years

15. a) $^{198}_{79}\text{Au} \longrightarrow {}^{0}_{-1}\text{e} + {}^{198}_{80}\text{Hg}$

    b) $^{59}_{26}\text{Fe} \longrightarrow {}^{0}_{-1}\text{e} + {}^{59}_{27}\text{Co}$

16. a) $^{147}_{62}\text{Sn} \longrightarrow {}^{143}_{60}\text{Nd} + {}^{4}_{2}\text{He}$

    b) $^{87}_{37}\text{Rb} \longrightarrow {}^{87}_{38}\text{Sr} + {}^{0}_{-1}\text{e}$

1. Describe the nature of each of the three common types of radiation: alpha, beta, and gamma.
2. What happens to the number of protons and neutrons in a nucleus when it undergoes decay by releasing beta particles?
3. How does balancing a nuclear equation differ from balancing a conventional chemical equation?
4. Explain the term radioactive series.
5. Define the term half-life.
6. What is the difference between a rad and a gray?
7. What two factors determine the effect of radiation on body tissue?
8. Explain the difference between a fission reaction and a fusion reaction. Give an example of each.
9. Briefly describe how a nuclear reactor converts nuclear fuel into electrical energy.
10. What are the advantages and disadvantages of the use of nuclear power compared to the use of water or fossil fuels to produce electricity?
11. What are the advantages and disadvantages of a CANDU reactor compared to a conventional nuclear reactor?
12. Explain the role of a moderator in a nuclear reactor.
13. List four applications of nuclear chemistry to areas other than the production of energy in nuclear reactors and the manufacture of nuclear weapons.
14. Describe two of the difficulties involved in the development of a commercial fusion reactor.
15. Why is the disposal of nuclear waste containing plutonium-239 considered to be a particular problem?
16. Why is it more dangerous to handle a radioactive isotope with a short half-life than one with a long half-life?
17. Why are radioactive isotopes with short half-lives unlikely to occur naturally?
18. Why can we combine only nuclei with low atomic numbers in a fusion reactor?
19. Why is there no such thing as a pure radioactive isotope?
20. Why would you expect the chemical properties of carbon-14 to be the same as those of carbon-12?

PROBLEMS   *Nuclear Equations*

21. Complete each of the following equations:

   a) $^{18}_{10}\text{Ne} \longrightarrow {}^{0}_{+1}e + ?$

b) $^{212}_{86}Rn \longrightarrow ^{208}_{84}Po + ?$

c) $^{6}_{2}He \longrightarrow ^{6}_{3}Li + ?$

d) $^{214}_{83}Bi \longrightarrow ^{4}_{2}He + ?$

e) $^{207}_{84}Po \longrightarrow ^{207}_{83}Bi + ?$

22. Identify the missing particle in each of the following equations:

a) $^{226}_{88}Ra \longrightarrow ^{222}_{86}Rn + ?$

b) $^{12}_{6}C + ? \longrightarrow ^{13}_{7}N + ^{0}_{0}\gamma$

c) $^{31}_{15}P + ^{4}_{2}He \longrightarrow ^{34}_{17}Cl + ?$

d) $^{120}_{49}In \longrightarrow ^{0}_{-1}e + ?$

e) $^{31}_{15}P + ^{4}_{2}He \longrightarrow ? + ^{1}_{1}H + ^{1}_{0}n$

23. Write a balanced nuclear equation for each step in the radioactive decay series from uranium-238 to lead-214 (Figure 13.4).

24. Write a balanced nuclear equation for each step in the uranium-238 decay series from lead-214 to lead-206 (Figure 13.4).

The Rate of Nuclear Change

25. Iodine-132 is used in the treatment of thyroid conditions. It has a half-life of 2.33 hours. How much of an 8.0 mg sample of this isotope would remain after 9.32 hours?

26. The half-life of fermium-253 is 4.5 days. If you start with 1.00 g of this isotope, how much would remain after 45 days?

Nuclear Reactions and Energy Changes

27. Uranium-233 undergoes alpha decay to form thorium-229. The mass loss during this reaction is 0.0055 g for each mole of uranium used. What is the total energy released when 1.00 mol of uranium-233 decays in this manner?

28. When 1.00 mol of plutonium-239 is bombarded with neutrons there is a decrease in mass of 0.188 g. How much energy is released in the reaction?

$$^{239}_{94}Pu + ^{1}_{0}n \longrightarrow ^{90}_{38}Sr + ^{144}_{58}Ce + 2\,^{0}_{-1}e + 6\,^{1}_{0}n$$

29. In order to convert 1.00 kg of water at 25 °C into steam at 100 °C we would require a heat input of 2.57 MJ. What mass would have to be converted to energy if the required 2.57 MJ is to be provided by a nuclear reaction?

30. The sun is estimated to produce 3.6×10^{23} kJ of energy every second. What mass must be converted to energy each second in order to sustain this output?

Fusion Reactions

31. The following equations each represent a fusion reaction that can occur in the sun and other stars. Identify the missing particle in each equation.

a) $^{12}_{6}C + ^{12}_{6}C \longrightarrow ^{23}_{12}Mg + ?$

b) $^{18}_{8}O + ? \longrightarrow ^{15}_{7}N + ^{4}_{2}He$

c) $^{3}_{2}He + ^{4}_{2}He \longrightarrow ? + ^{0}_{0}\gamma$

32. Artificial transmutation can be brought about by bombarding target nuclei with a variety of particles. Identify the isotope produced in each of the equations below:

a) $^{253}_{99}Es + ^{4}_{2}He \longrightarrow ^{1}_{1}H + ?$

b) $^{98}_{42}Mo + ^{1}_{0}n \longrightarrow ^{0}_{-1}e + ?$

c) $^{244}_{96}Cm + ^{4}_{2}He \longrightarrow ? + ^{1}_{1}p + 2\,^{1}_{0}n$

Applications of Nuclear Chemistry

33. Technetium-99 is used in medicine as a radioactive tracer because it concentrates in abnormal heart tissue. The presence of this isotope is detected by measuring the beta radiation that is produced as it decays. Write a balanced nuclear equation for this decay process.

34. Gold-188 decays by positron emission. Write a balanced nuclear equation to describe this process.

MISCELLANEOUS PROBLEMS

35. Determine whether each of the following equations represents a natural decay process or an artificial transmutation. In the case of a natural decay, identify the type of particle that is emitted (e.g. alpha particle, positron, etc.). If the process is a transmutation, determine whether a fission or fusion reaction is involved.

a) $^{234}_{90}Th \longrightarrow ^{234}_{91}Pa + ^{0}_{-1}e$

b) $^{54}_{26}Fe + ^{1}_{1}H \longrightarrow ^{54}_{27}Co + ^{1}_{0}n$

c) $^{101}_{46}Pd \longrightarrow ^{101}_{45}Rh + ^{0}_{+1}e$

d) $^{238}_{92}U + ^{14}_{7}N \longrightarrow ^{247}_{99}Es + 5\,^{1}_{0}n$

e) $^{10}_{5}B + ^{1}_{0}n \longrightarrow ^{3}_{1}H + 2\,^{4}_{2}He$

36. State which of the following equations represent natural decay processes and which represent artificial transmutations. Identify the type of particle emitted in each of the natural decay processes.

a) $^{216}_{85}At \longrightarrow ^{212}_{83}Bi + ^{4}_{2}He$

b) $^{89}_{36}Kr \longrightarrow ^{88}_{36}Kr + ^{1}_{0}n$

c) $^{59}_{27}Co + ^{1}_{0}n \longrightarrow ^{60}_{27}Co$

d) $^{235}_{92}U + ^{1}_{0}n \longrightarrow ^{90}_{38}Sr + ^{143}_{54}Xe + 3\,^{1}_{0}n$

e) $^{24}_{11}Na \longrightarrow ^{24}_{12}Mg + ^{0}_{-1}e$

37. Carbon-11 is produced by bombarding boron-10 with hydrogen-2 nuclei. Write a balanced nuclear equation and identify the other product.

38. Given the following atomic masses, how much energy has been released by the 7.00×10^5 atoms of carbon-11 that has decayed? (carbon-11 = 11.011 431 u, boron-11 = 11.009 305, positron = 0.000 549 u)

39. The decay of uranium-235 involves the emission of alpha and beta particles. The following is the order in which they are released: α, β, α, β, α, α, α, α, β, α, β. Write a balanced nuclear equation for each step, and plot a decay series for uranium-235 similar to that of uranium-238 in Figure 13.4.

SUGGESTED PROJECTS

1. Nuclear radiation is a cause of cancer, yet it is also used in the treatment of certain types of cancer. Write a report on this apparent contradiction.

2. "Nuclear winter" and the "greenhouse effect" are two gloomy prospects for the future of our planet. Find out what each of these terms means and what events could bring on these phenomena. Be prepared to take part in a group discussion on the consequences of nuclear winter and the greenhouse effect, and on our ability to survive them.

3. Is nuclear power a viable means of meeting Canada's future energy requirements? Is it a viable means for providing energy for the rest of the world? If so, what should be Canada's role? What are some of the alternative energy sources that should be considered? Write a report or hold a class discussion on these issues.

4. In order to synthesize new elements by bombarding target nuclei with positively charged particles such as protons or helium nuclei, the bombarding particle must be accelerated to a very high velocity. Write a report on the different types of particle accelerators and their use in this and other fields.

5. Nuclear waste disposal is one of the most fundamental problems for us to solve. Debates over "burial" locations are raised almost monthly in our major newspapers. Investigate this issue and prepare a formal report on both the short-term and long-term solutions that are being proposed.

6. Collect current information on food irradiation. Prepare a report on the status of our knowledge of this technology. Discuss the possible uses of technology in industrialized and economically underdeveloped countries.

Organic Chemistry I: Hydrocarbons

It is a reflection of the historical development of chemistry that we introduce this subject by a study of inorganic compounds and only later develop the study of organic chemistry. Yet over 96 % of known chemicals are classified as organic compounds. By introducing organic chemistry towards the end of the text, we can apply the principles discussed in earlier chapters to explain some of the observed physical and chemical properties of these abundant compounds.

This chapter will focus on organic compounds containing only the elements carbon and hydrogen. We will look at a classification scheme for these compounds and at their structures and reactions. We will also introduce you to the rules for naming organic compounds. As you will see, these rules are quite different from those used when naming inorganic compounds.

Historical Background

14.1

Figure 14.1
Friedrich Wöhler (1800-1882). His synthesis of urea was a major factor in the rejection of the vitalism theory of organic chemistry.

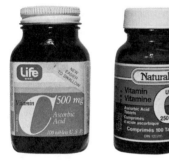

Figure 14.2
A molecule of vitamin C has the same structure and properties whether it is synthesized by a living plant or in a chemical laboratory.

Before 1828, any substance that was isolated from animal or plant material was thought to contain some kind of "vital force." This theory of vitalism suggested that compounds found in living organisms could not be prepared in a laboratory. The study of these compounds came to be called organic chemistry. Textbooks of the day discussed "animal chemistry" and "vegetable chemistry," and compounds were described from the standpoint of their biological sources and medicinal uses rather than their chemical structures.

In 1828, through the work of Friedrich Wöhler, the vitalism theory was shown to be incorrect. Wöhler was trying to prepare ammonium cyanate (the cyanate ion is OCN^-) by the double displacement reaction of silver cyanate with ammonium chloride:

$$AgOCN_{(aq)} + NH_4Cl_{(aq)} \longrightarrow AgCl_{(s)} + NH_4OCN_{(aq)}$$

After the insoluble silver chloride was filtered off, Wöhler evaporated the water from the remaining solution and obtained some white crystals. He found that the crystals possessed none of the properties of a typical inorganic compound. Instead, the crystals were shown to be identical to crystals of urea, an organic compound that had previously been isolated from urine. Wöhler had achieved the "impossible" and had prepared an organic compound from inorganic sources!

Wöhler did not isolate ammonium cyanate as he had hoped because, during evaporation of the filtrate, the atoms in the ammonium cyanate had rearranged to form urea:

$$NH_4OCN_{(aq)} \xrightarrow{60\,°C} (NH_2)_2CO_{(aq)}$$

Although the results of Wöhler's experiment marked the beginning of the end of the vitalism theory, the theory was not renounced immediately by the scientific community. Over the next ten years the synthesis of additional organic compounds from inorganic sources gradually convinced chemists that the vitalism theory was incorrect.

The Characteristics of Organic Compounds

14.2

Organic chemistry can be defined as the chemistry of compounds that contain carbon. However, some carbon-containing compounds (such as carbon monoxide, carbon dioxide, and hydrogen cyanide) and carbon-containing salts (such as carbonates and cyanides) are not generally considered to be organic.

Let us examine the characteristic features of organic compounds.

1. **Organic compounds contain covalent bonds.**

In our discussion of inorganic compounds, we emphasized those compounds containing ionic bonds. Organic chemistry, on the other hand, is dominated by covalent bonding.

2. **Organic compounds contain carbon atoms joined together in chains or rings.**

The ability of carbon atoms to bond together and form long chains or rings of atoms is called **catenation**. Carbon, more than any other element, can form these extended chains and rings.

3. **Dispersion (London) forces are the principal intermolecular forces acting between organic molecules.**

Since carbon and hydrogen have similar electronegativities, the carbon-hydrogen bond is almost purely covalent. Besides contributing to the stability of the many compounds of carbon and hydrogen, this also means that dispersion forces are the principal intermolecular force acting between organic molecules. As a result, because melting and boiling points usually correlate with the number of electrons in the molecule, the smaller organic molecules have relatively low melting and boiling points.

4. **One molecular formula can often represent a large number of different organic compounds.**

The many different ways in which it is possible to arrange atoms can result in a number of organic compounds having the same molecular formula. To take an extreme example, the formula $C_{20}H_{42}$ represents 366 319 different chemical compounds! Different compounds with the same molecular formula are called **isomers**.

5. **The properties of organic compounds are determined by the presence of certain groups of atoms within the compound.**

A carbon-carbon double bond in any organic molecule will undergo the same general reactions regardless of the nature and complexity of the rest of the molecule. Groups of atoms such as these that impart specific properties to an organic compound, are referred to as **functional groups**.

QUESTIONS

1. Compare a simple organic compound, such as CH_4, with an inorganic compound, such as NaCl, in terms of the following:
   a) bonding   b) melting point   c) solubility in water
2. Why do compounds of carbon and hydrogen generally have low melting points and boiling points?

Hydrocarbons _14.3_

Organic compounds containing only carbon and hydrogen are called **hydrocarbons**. The simplest hydrocarbon has the formula, CH_4.

$$\begin{matrix} & H & \\ & \cdot\cdot & \\ H & \!\!:\!\!C\!\!:\!\! & H \\ & \cdot\cdot & \\ & H & \end{matrix}$$

We can construct three electron-dot formulas for hydrocarbon molecules that contain two carbon atoms. If the carbon atoms are joined by a carbon-carbon single bond, we need six hydrogen atoms to provide enough electrons to complete the valence shell of each carbon atom. The resulting compound, ethane, has the molecular formula, C_2H_6. If the two carbon atoms are joined by a carbon-carbon double bond, only four hydrogen atoms are needed. This compound, ethene, has the formula C_2H_4. Finally, if the carbon atoms are joined by a carbon-carbon triple bond, only two hydrogen atoms are required and we have the compound ethyne, with the formula C_2H_2. The corresponding electron-dot formulas are shown below:

As mentioned in the previous section, the presence of a functional group has a major influence on the properties of an organic compound. The carbon-carbon double bond and carbon-carbon triple bond represent two examples of functional groups. The carbon-carbon single bond and the carbon-hydrogen bond are not considered to be functional groups.

Hydrocarbons can be subdivided into two main categories, **aliphatic** and **aromatic**. The term aliphatic comes from the Greek _aleiphatos_, meaning fat. Early chemists used this term because these compounds were insoluble in water and less dense than water, like fats. Aliphatic compounds are subdivided into **alkanes**, **alkenes**, and **alkynes**. Alkanes, such as ethane, contain only carbon-carbon single bonds. Alkenes, such as ethene, contain one or more carbon-carbon double bonds, while alkynes, such as ethyne, contain one or more carbon-carbon triple bonds. The word _aromatic_ was originally used to classify hydrocarbons with fragrant odours. Since aromatic compounds contain a more complex type of carbon-carbon bond, we will leave discussion of these until later.

QUESTIONS

3. Draw the electron-dot structure for the compound C_3H_8. Is it an alkane, an alkene, or an alkyne?

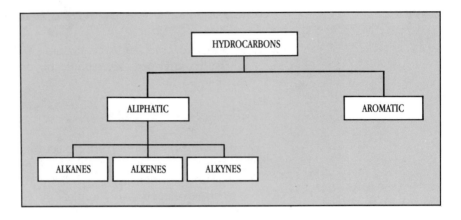

Figure 14.3

Classification scheme for hydrocarbons.

The Shapes of Alkanes

14.4   As we saw in Chapter 3, a molecule in which the central atom is surrounded by four electron pairs adopts a **tetrahedral** arrangement. The tetrahedral shape, with the bond angles of 109.5°, is common among organic compounds. The simplest hydrocarbon molecule, methane, will serve to illustrate this shape.

Using the ball-and-stick model (Figure 14.5), we can build the next simplest member of the alkanes — that is, ethane. This can be formed by first removing a hydrogen atom from two methane molecules, then combining the two methyl fragments, CH_3, to restore the octet around each carbon atom. Each of the carbon atoms is now surrounded by three hydrogen atoms and one other carbon atom.

The electron-dot formula of this sequence is shown below. The arrangement of the four electron pairs around each carbon in the ethane molecule will still be tetrahedral.

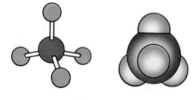

Figure 14.4

The shape of the methane molecule, CH_4:
a) as a ball-and-stick model;
b) as a space-filling model.

$$\begin{matrix} & H & & & H \\ & \overset{\cdot\cdot}{H\!:\!C\!:\!H} & \longrightarrow & & H\!:\!\overset{\cdot\cdot}{C}\!\cdot & + & \cdot H \\ & H & & & H \end{matrix}$$

$$\begin{matrix} & H & & H & & & H & H \\ & H\!:\!\overset{\cdot\cdot}{C}\!\cdot & + & \cdot\overset{\cdot\cdot}{C}\!:\!H & \longrightarrow & & H\!:\!\overset{\cdot\cdot}{C}\!:\!\overset{\cdot\cdot}{C}\!:\!H \\ & H & & H & & & H & H \end{matrix}$$

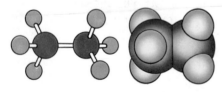

Figure 14.5

The shape of the ethane molecule, C_2H_6:
a) as a ball-and-stick model;
b) as a space-filling model.

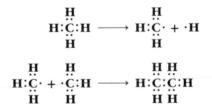

Similarly, we could remove a hydrogen atom from ethane and replace it with another CH_3 fragment to form propane, C_3H_8. This procedure can be repeated again and again to produce C_4H_{10}, C_5H_{12}, C_6H_{14}, etc. What shapes will these larger molecules have? Because the angle between one carbon bonded to two others is always the tetrahedral angle of 109.5°, a chain of carbon atoms will not form a straight line, but will be arranged in a zigzag manner. This is illustrated for the molecule C_5H_{12} (Figure 14.7).

The more carbon atoms there are in a molecule, the more difficult it becomes to draw the actual shape of that molecule. To overcome this drawback, the ball-and-stick model is projected onto a two-dimensional surface. Figure 14.6 shows how this is done for methane. Note that the two-dimensional representation makes the H—C—H angles appear to be 90°, although in their real three-dimensional state, the bond angles have the tetrahedral values of 109.5°.

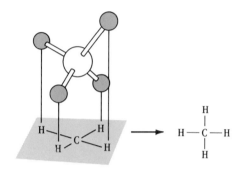

Figure 14.6

The projection of the ball-and-stick model of CH_4 onto a flat (two-dimensional) surface.

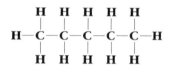

The two-dimensional representations described above are called *structural formulas.* The structural formula of pentane would be drawn as follows:

$$\text{H}-\overset{\displaystyle\text{H}}{\underset{\displaystyle\text{H}}{\text{C}}}-\overset{\displaystyle\text{H}}{\underset{\displaystyle\text{H}}{\text{C}}}-\overset{\displaystyle\text{H}}{\underset{\displaystyle\text{H}}{\text{C}}}-\overset{\displaystyle\text{H}}{\underset{\displaystyle\text{H}}{\text{C}}}-\overset{\displaystyle\text{H}}{\underset{\displaystyle\text{H}}{\text{C}}}-\text{H}$$

Although structural formulas are useful for showing the arrangement of atoms in a molecule, they are cumbersome to draw when the molecule is complex. Therefore, an even more compact form, called a **condensed formula**, is used. In a condensed formula, the hydrogen atoms are written beside the carbon atom to which they are attached. When dealing with condensed formulas, it is important to remember that it is the carbon atoms that are bonded together even though this is not apparent from the formulas. The condensed formula of pentane is

$$\text{CH}_3-\text{CH}_2-\text{CH}_2-\text{CH}_2-\text{CH}_3$$

As a further simplification, the lines representing bonds may be omitted and similar units summed together. Thus the condensed formula of pentane can also be written as $\text{CH}_3(\text{CH}_2)_3\text{CH}_3$. This representation is particularly useful when a long chain of CH_2 units is present in a molecule.

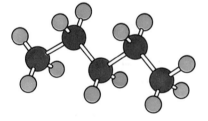

Figure 14.7

The shape of the pentane molecule, C_5H_{12}:
a) as a ball-and-stick model;
b) as a space-filling model.

Cyclic Hydrocarbons

A large number of organic compounds contain carbon atoms joined to form rings. When hydrogen and carbon are the only elements involved, such ring compounds are called **cyclic hydrocarbons**. The simplest

Figure 14.8
One of the most important research journals of organic chemistry is called 'Tetrahedron.' It reflects the importance of shape in organic chemistry.

example can be constructed from the molecule CH_3—CH_2—CH_3 by removing a hydrogen atom from each end. The end carbon atoms can then be joined to form a three-membered ring:

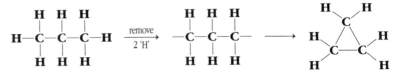

Similarly we can take C_4H_{10}, remove two end hydrogen atoms and create a four-membered ring. Likewise, a five-membered ring can be created from C_5H_{12}, a six-membered ring from C_6H_{14}, and so on.

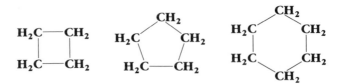

There is an even simpler way of depicting ring structures. The lines of the carbon-carbon bonds are retained, but the CH_2 symbols are removed. In the geometric representations obtained, each corner marks the location of a CH_2 unit. Using this system, the structures of the three-, four-, five-, and six-membered rings would be represented as follows:

QUESTIONS

4. Draw the structural formula for each of the following compounds:
   a) C_2H_6 b) C_3H_8 c) C_4H_{10}
5. Write the condensed formula for each of the compounds listed in Question 4.

Structural Isomers

14.5

Up to now, we have only considered compounds in which the methylene (CH_2) units join to form a single chain or ring. Many more structures are possible, however, because each carbon atom in an organic compound may bond with up to four other carbon atoms. Alkanes in which one or more carbon atoms is bonded to three or four other carbon atoms are known as **branched-chain alkanes**. As an example, there are two ways of arranging the four carbon atoms in a molecule that has the formula C_4H_{10}:

$$C—C—C—C \quad \text{or} \quad C—C—C$$
$$\phantom{C—C—C—C \quad \text{or} \quad C—} | $$
$$\phantom{C—C—C—C \quad \text{or} \quad C—} C$$

When these structures are completed by including the hydrogen atoms, the following condensed formulas are obtained:

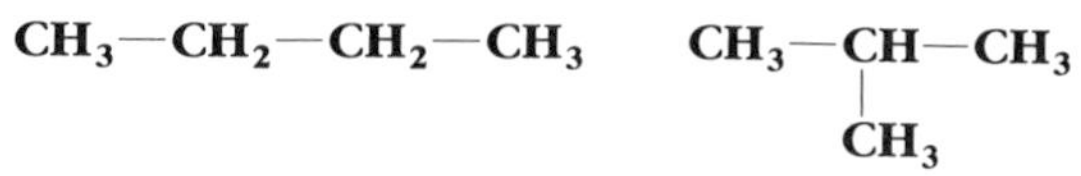

$$CH_3-CH_2-CH_2-CH_3 \qquad CH_3-\underset{\underset{CH_3}{|}}{CH}-CH_3$$

Each of these structures corresponds to a molecular formula of C_4H_{10}, but the arrangements of the atoms are different. Compounds that have the same molecular formula, but different structures, are called **structural isomers**. Such compounds always have different physical properties and often have very different chemical properties.

Let us see how many different condensed formulas can be drawn to correspond with a molecular formula of C_5H_{12}. We start by constructing the carbon "backbone" of the molecule. The three possibilities are shown below:

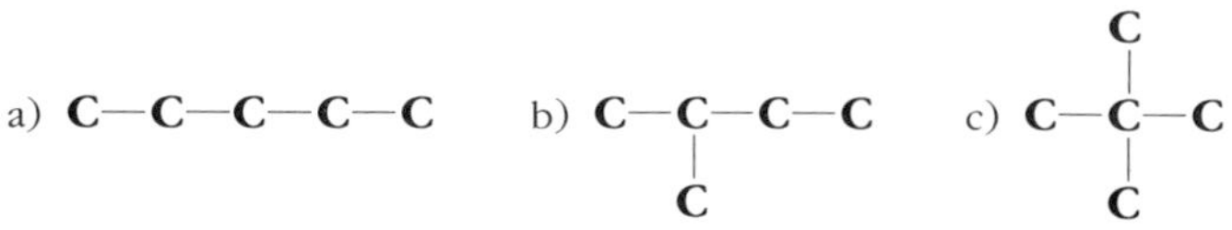

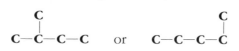

You might think there are other possibilities, such as:

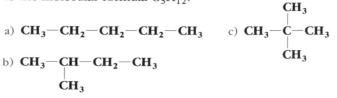

However, you must keep in mind that these two-dimensional structures represent three-dimensional molecules with equal bond angles of 109.5° around each carbon atom. Taking this into consideration, you should see that these two "isomers" are really identical to structures b) and a) respectively. By filling in the hydrogen atoms so that there are four bonds to each carbon atom, we arrive at the three condensed formulas that correspond to the molecular formula C_5H_{12}.

a) $CH_3-CH_2-CH_2-CH_2-CH_3$

c) $CH_3-\underset{\underset{CH_3}{|}}{\overset{\overset{CH_3}{|}}{C}}-CH_3$

b) $CH_3-\underset{\underset{CH_3}{|}}{CH}-CH_2-CH_3$

One of the crucial skills that you need to develop in organic chemistry is that of being able to relate a two-dimensional condensed formula to a three-dimensional molecular shape. Example 14.1 tests your skill at this.

EXAMPLE   ***14.1***   How many different isomers of C_6H_{14} are shown below?

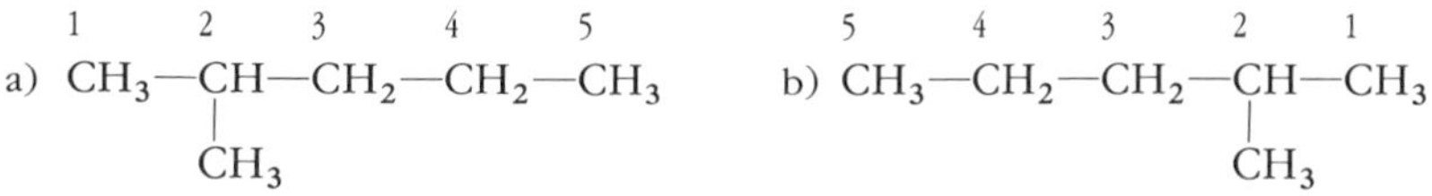

a) $\overset{1}{CH_3}-\underset{\underset{CH_3}{|}}{\overset{2}{CH}}-\overset{3}{CH_2}-\overset{4}{CH_2}-\overset{5}{CH_3}$

b) $\overset{5}{CH_3}-\overset{4}{CH_2}-\overset{3}{CH_2}-\underset{\underset{CH_3}{|}}{\overset{2}{CH}}-\overset{1}{CH_3}$

c) $\overset{1}{C}H_3$
    $|$
   $2\overset{}{C}H-CH_2-CH_2-CH_3$ (with labels 3, 4, 5)
    $|$
    CH_3

d) $\overset{1}{C}H_3-\overset{2}{C}H-\overset{3}{C}H_2-\overset{4}{C}H_2$
         $|$ $|$
        CH_3 CH_3 (5)

SOLUTION Only one isomer is shown! All the structures represent the same isomer. If you look carefully, you will see that each structure has a main chain of five carbons with a one-carbon side chain attached to the second carbon of the main chain.

You may wonder how many isomers are possible for a particular alkane formula. There is, in fact, a very complex set of mathematical expressions for calculating this, and the results are shown in Table 14.1. As you can see, the number of possible isomers increases very rapidly as the number of carbon atoms increases.

TABLE 14.1 *The Possible Number of Structural Isomers of Different Alkanes*

Number of Carbon atoms	Number of Isomers	Number of Carbon atoms	Number of Isomers
1	1	11	159
2	1	12	355
3	1	13	802
4	2	14	1 858
5	3	15	4 347
6	5	20	366 319
7	9	25	36 797 588
8	18	30	4 111 846 763
9	35	40	62 491 178 805 831
10	75		

Isomerism also occurs in cyclic systems. For example, the formula C_5H_{10} corresponds to five different cycloalkanes.

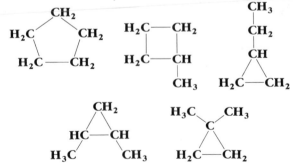

Optical Isomerism

Suppose we construct a model of the molecule bromochlorofluoromethane, CHFClBr. We find that we can arrange the four atoms around the central carbon atom in two different ways. These two arrangements are related: one is the mirror image of the other. That is, if we hold one of the models up to a mirror, the image that we see is identical to our second model.

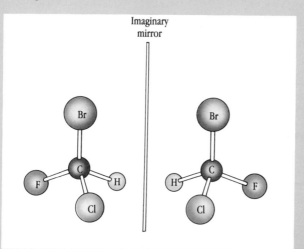

Imaginary mirror

One common example of a mirror image with which we are perhaps familiar is the sign on the front of an ambulance. When viewed normally the writing appears to be back-to-front, but when the sign is viewed through the rear-view mirror of a motor vehicle it can be read normally:

AMBULANCE | **AMBULANCE**

mirror

Two molecules that are mirror images of one another are referred to as *optical isomers*. The simplest examples of optical isomerism occur when four different groups are attached to a carbon atom. Such carbon atoms are said to be *chiral*. Although optical isomers have almost identical chemical behaviour, they have considerable and important differences in biological systems.

When a compound that can exist as two optical isomers is synthesized in the laboratory, for example, the resulting mixture usually contains 50 % of each isomer. Inside a living organism, however, only one form is produced. To realize the importance of this, consider that many compounds of biological importance contain a number of chiral carbon atoms. For n chiral carbon atoms in a compound, there are 2^n possible optical isomers. Cholesterol, a compound found in practically all animal tissue, has eight chiral carbon atoms and, therefore, 2^8 (or 256) possible optical isomers. Yet only one isomer occurs in nature!

The taste and smell of optical isomers are often different. Spearmint, for example, gets its smell from a chemical that is an optical isomer of the chemical that flavours caraway seeds. These two plants are very different in odour and taste because caraway plants produce only one isomer, and spearmint produces the other.

The differences in properties between two optical isomers can be of great significance in the field of medicine. For example, one optical isomer of the anti-malarial drug, chloroquine, is much more effective and, also much less toxic than the other isomer.

You may have heard of the drug thalidomide that was marketed in the 1960s as a sedative. This drug was a mixture of two optical isomers. Many pregnant women who took the drug gave birth to deformed children, but we now know that only one of the two optical isomers actually causes birth defects. Even today, when thalidomide must be used in medical treatments, it is still the mixture of isomers that is used.

The common sugar, sucrose, that we eat to provide food energy consists of only one optical isomer. Fortunately, it is the isomer that our systems can metabolize to provide energy. If you ate the other isomer, you would starve! In our discussion of rates of reaction in Chapter 6 we mentioned that enzymes (biological catalysts) speed up reactions in our bodies by enormous factors. The enzymes work by having "active sites" in which the reacting molecules can fit. The site is often shaped so that only the naturally-occuring isomer can fit in.

The uniqueness of one set of optical isomers in most known biological systems raises questions about the origin of life. If we were to travel to another planet where carbon-based life exists, would there be the same set of naturally-occurring optical isomers? When we embark on interstellar journeys it might be wise to take our own food supply!

QUESTIONS

6. Which, if any, of the structures shown below represents a compound that is different from the others?

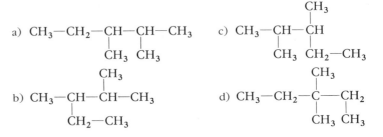

a) $CH_3-CH_2-CH-CH-CH_3$
                     CH_3 CH_3

b) $CH_3-CH-CH-CH_3$
               CH_3
               CH_2-CH_3

c) $CH_3-CH-CH$
                     CH_3
               CH_3 CH_2-CH_3

d) $CH_3-CH_2-C-CH_2$
                     CH_3
               CH_3 CH_3

7. Draw the condensed formula for each of the five isomers of C_6H_{14}.

8. Draw the five structural isomers of the cycloalkane, C_6H_{12}, that involve, six-, five-, or four-membered rings.

The Naming of Alkanes

14.6

The system used to name organic compounds is very different from the system used to name inorganic compounds. Over the centuries, many organic compounds have been given **common** (or **trivial**) **names** that indicate little or nothing about their structures.

As in inorganic chemistry, however, a more systematic method of naming organic compounds has been established by the International Union of Pure and Applied Chemistry (IUPAC). The **IUPAC system** is based on a series of rules that enables us to deduce the structure of a compound from its name. Conversely, we can write an IUPAC (or **systematic**) name for every organic compound. The name indicates both the number and arrangement of the carbon atoms, and the type(s) of functional group(s) in the compound.

Nevertheless, many organic compounds are still known by their common names rather than by their IUPAC names. Sometimes the common name is used because it is so well established. For example, CH_3CO_2H is often called acetic acid rather than by its IUPAC name of ethanoic acid. In other cases, the systematic name is very complex and the trivial name is much easier to remember. An example of this is the pain-relieving drug, ibuprofen, which has the IUPAC name of 2-(4-isobutylphenyl)-propanoic acid. However, it would be impossible for a chemist to identify the structure of the drug from its common name.

Straight-Chain Alkanes

In systematic naming, we rely on the use of prefixes (derived from Greek words) to indicate the number of carbon atoms in a structure. The prefixes for the numbers one to ten are listed in Table 14.2.

TABLE 14.2 Prefixes Used to Indicate the Number of Carbon Atoms

Number of Atoms	Prefix	Number of Atoms	Prefix
1	*meth-*	6	*hex-*
2	*eth-*	7	*hept-*
3	*prop-*	8	*oct-*
4	*but-*	9	*non-*
5	*pent-*	10	*dec-*

To indicate that we have an alkane, the suffix *-ane* is used. We will show how to name a straight-chain alkane in the following example:

$$CH_3-CH_2-CH_2-CH_2-CH_2-CH_3$$

1. Count the number of carbon atoms in the chain and choose the appropriate prefix.

$$CH_3-CH_2-CH_2-CH_2-CH_2-CH_3$$ There are 6 carbons, so the prefix is *hex-*.

2. Since there are only single carbon-carbon bonds, the ending *-ane* is added. Hence, the compound's name is hexane.

The formulas and names of the six simplest straight-chain alkanes are shown in Table 14.3.

TABLE 14.3 The Six Simplest Straight-Chain Alkanes

Number of Carbon Atoms	Formula	Name
1	CH_4	methane
2	CH_3CH_3	ethane
3	$CH_3CH_2CH_3$	propane
4	$CH_3(CH_2)_2CH_3$	butane
5	$CH_3(CH_2)_3CH_3$	pentane
6	$CH_3(CH_2)_4CH_3$	hexane

Branched-Chain Alkanes

To name these alkanes, we first identify the longest *continuous chain* of carbon atoms in the molecule. We name this chain according to the method for a straight-chain alkane, and refer to this as the base name.

TABLE 14.4 *Common Alkyl Groups*	
CH_3-	methyl
CH_3CH_2-	ethyl
$CH_3CH_2CH_2-$	propyl
$(CH_3)_2CH-$	isopropyl
$CH_3CH_2CH_2CH_2-$	butyl

Then we name any side-chains or **substituents**. The names of the substituents are written in front of the base name. A system of numbers is used to identify where the substituents are located along the main chain.

The prefixes for the side chains are the same as those of the alkane from which they are derived. For example, the substituent CH_3 comes from the alkane, methane. As it is a substituent, the ending *-ane* is replaced by *-yl*. Hence it is called a methyl group. The common **alkyl groups** and their names are shown in Table 14.4. We can see that the removal of an "end" hydrogen from propane gives us a propyl group, whereas the removal of a "middle" hydrogen gives us an isopropyl group.

We will now illustrate this method for the following compound:

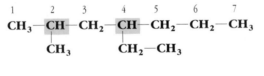

1. Identify the longest continuous chain of carbon atoms and assign the base name.

$$CH_3—CH—CH_2—CH—CH_2—CH_2—CH_3$$
$$\quad\;\;|\qquad\qquad\;\;\;|$$
$$\quad\;\;CH_3\qquad\quad CH_2—CH_3$$

The longest chain has 7 carbons, so the base name is heptane.

2. Number the carbon atoms along the main chain, beginning at the end which will result in the lowest possible numbers for the substituents.

$$\overset{1}{CH_3}—\overset{2}{CH}—\overset{3}{CH_2}—\overset{4}{CH}—\overset{5}{CH_2}—\overset{6}{CH_2}—\overset{7}{CH_3}$$
$$\qquad\;\;|\qquad\qquad\;\;\;|$$
$$\qquad\;\;CH_3\qquad\quad CH_2—CH_3$$

Alkyl groups are located at carbon 2 and 4 (4 and 6 if numbered from other end).

3. Name each substituent, and indicate its location on the main chain.

$$CH_3—\overset{2}{CH}—CH_2—\overset{4}{CH}—CH_2—CH_2—CH_3$$
$$\qquad\;\;|\qquad\qquad\;\;\;|$$
$$\qquad\;\;CH_3\qquad\quad CH_2—CH_3$$

Methyl at carbon 2, ethyl at carbon 4.

4. List the substituents in alphabetical order. Separate the numbers and substituents by hyphens. This gives us the name 4-ethyl-2-methylheptane.

If the same substituent occurs more than once in a compound, the quantity of identical groups is indicated by the prefixes, di- (two), tri- (three), tetra- (four), penta- (five), hexa- (six), hepta- (seven). A numerical location must still be given for each substituent, and the numbers are separated by commas.

Thus the name for:

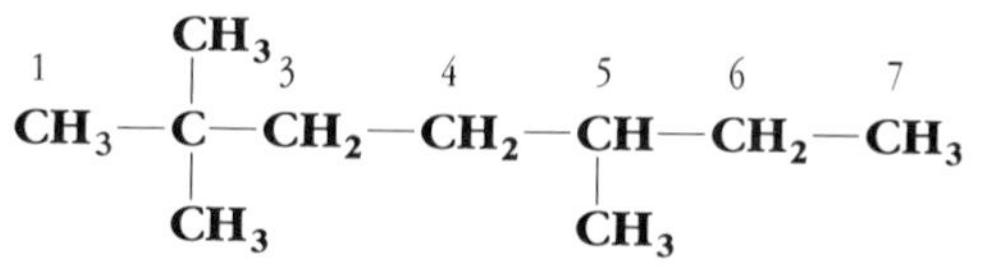

$$\overset{1}{CH_3}-\overset{\overset{\displaystyle \overset{3}{CH_3}}{|}}{\underset{\underset{\displaystyle CH_3}{|}}{C}}-\overset{4}{CH_2}-\overset{5}{CH_2}-\overset{\overset{6}{CH}}{\underset{\underset{\displaystyle CH_3}{|}}{}}-\overset{7}{CH_2}-CH_3$$

Three methyl groups, two at carbon 2, one at carbon 5.

would be 2,2,5-trimethylheptane.

EXAMPLE   *14.2* Use the IUPAC system to name the following compound:

$$CH_3-CH_2-CH_2-\underset{\underset{\displaystyle CH_2-CH_3}{|}}{CH}-CH_2-CH_3$$

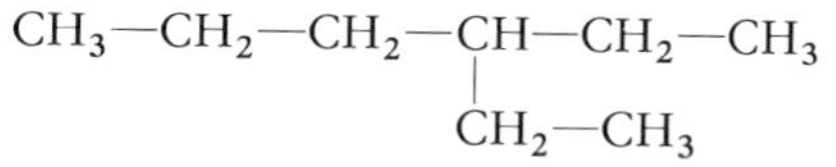

SOLUTION   a) The longer continuous carbon chain contains six carbon atoms; therefore the base name is **hexane**.
b) An ethyl substituent is present. We combine this with the base name to obtain the name **ethylhexane**.
c) Counting in from the end of the compound that is closest to the carbon atom carrying the substituent, we find that the substituent is on the third carbon atom. Hence the name of the compound is **3-ethylhexane**.

EXAMPLE   *14.3* Use the IUPAC system to name the following compound:

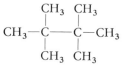

SOLUTION   a) The longest continuous carbon chain contains four carbon atoms, therefore the base name is **butane**.
b) There are four methyl substituents. We use the prefix *tetra-* to indicate four identical substituents and obtain the name **tetramethylbutane**.
c) Two methyl groups are on carbon atom two. The other two are on carbon atom three. Therefore **2,2,3,3,-tetramethylbutane** is the complete name.

EXAMPLE   *14.4*   Draw the condensed formula for 3-ethylheptane.

SOLUTION   Since the name of the compound ends with the suffix *heptane*, we know that the longest carbon chain contains seven carbon atoms:

$$C-C-C-C-C-C-C$$

The name also tells us that we have an ethyl substituent attached at the third carbon in the chain as shown in the following formula:

$$
\begin{array}{c}
CH_2-CH_3 \\
| \\
C-C-C-C-C-C-C
\end{array}
$$

Thus the complete (condensed) formula is

$$
\begin{array}{c}
CH_2-CH_3 \\
| \\
CH_3-CH_2-CH-CH_2-CH_2-CH_2-CH_3
\end{array}
$$

Cycloalkanes

Cycloalkanes are named in much the same way as straight-chain alkanes. We identify the presence of a ring by the prefix *cyclo-*. If there are substituents attached to any of the carbons in the ring, the name(s) of the substituent(s) precedes the name of the ring itself. Once again we use numbers to indicate the position of any substituent. The ring is numbered so that we have the lowest possible numbers. We will illustrate this with the following example:

1. Identify the ring of carbon atoms and assign the base name.

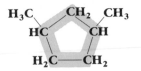

Since the ring has 5 carbons, the base name is cyclopentane.

2. Number the ring beginning with the location which will result in the lowest possible numbers for the substituents.

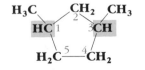

Alkyl groups at carbon 1 and carbon 3.

3. Name each substituent and indicate its position by the number of the carbon atoms on the ring to which it is attached.

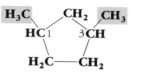

Methyl at carbon 1, methyl at carbon 3.

4. Separate the numbers from each other by commas and the numbers from the substituents by hyphens. This gives us the name 1,3-dimethylcyclopentane.

QUESTIONS

9. Give the IUPAC name of each of the following compounds. The carbon atoms that form the longest chain are not necessarily shown in a straight chain.

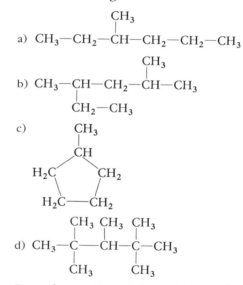

a) $CH_3-CH_2-\underset{\underset{CH_3}{|}}{CH}-CH_2-CH_2-CH_3$

b) $CH_3-\underset{\underset{CH_2-CH_3}{|}}{CH}-CH_2-\underset{\overset{CH_3}{|}}{CH}-CH_3$

c)

d) $CH_3-\underset{\underset{CH_3}{|}}{\overset{\overset{CH_3}{|}}{C}}-CH-\underset{\underset{CH_3}{|}}{\overset{\overset{CH_3}{|}}{C}}-CH_3$

10. Draw the condensed formula for each of the following:
   a) 5-isopropylnonane
   b) 3,4-diethylhexane
   c) 2,2,3-trimethylpentane
   d) 1,4-diethylcyclohexane

The Properties of Alkanes

14.7 *Physical Properties*

Because carbon and hydrogen have very similar electronegativities, alkane molecules are essentially nonpolar. Thus the only attraction between neighbouring molecules is by dispersion forces (Section 4.6). For straight-chain alkanes, the dispersion forces increase with increasing number of carbon atoms in the molecule. If we compare the molecular shapes of the straight-chain alkanes, we find that all the molecules are basically cylindrical, but that the length of the cylinder increases as the number of carbon atoms increases.

The straight-chain alkane molecules can be arranged in an orderly sequence, in which each molecule differs from the one preceding it by a single additional CH_2 unit. Thus ethane, CH_3—CH_3, with the addition of one CH_2, becomes propane, CH_3—CH_2—CH_3. A series of compounds that differ in structure by the addition of the same structural unit is called a **homologous series**. Because an increase in chain length increases the intermolecular forces, and this in turn produces differences in molecular properties, we would expect that the properties of alkanes will vary in a predictable way according to their position in the sequence.

We can test this idea by looking at boiling points. The stronger the intermolecular force, the higher the boiling point, since more energy is needed to separate the molecules into the gaseous state. When we examine the boiling points of the straight-chain alkanes (Figure 14.9), we find there is a steady increase in boiling point with the length of the carbon chain. Since the molecular shapes of the alkanes are similar, the increase in boiling point can be related to the increase in the number of electrons caused by addition of CH_2 units to the chain.

We can examine the effect of different molecular shapes on boiling point by considering two isomers of C_5H_{12}. Whereas pentane has a cylindrical shape, the isomer 2,2-dimethylpropane has a much more compact, almost spherical shape. The more compact shape leads to weaker dispersion forces and, therefore, a lower boiling point. In fact we find that 2,2-dimethylpropane has a boiling point of 9.5 °C compared to 36 °C for pentane. In general it is true to say that branched-chain alkanes have lower boiling points than straight-chain molecules with the same number of carbon atoms.

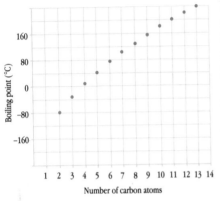

Figure 14.9

A graph of boiling point versus the number of carbon atoms for the straight-chain alkanes.

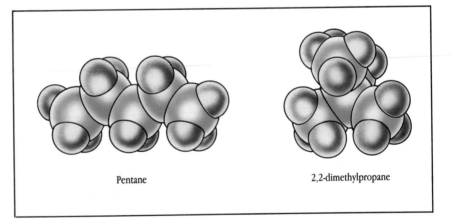

Pentane   2,2-dimethylpropane

Figure 14.10

Pentane and its structural isomer 2,2-dimethylpropane differ considerably in shape.

Figure 14.11
Saturn's moon, Titan. From data sent back by the space probe Voyager I, it is thought that Titan is covered by an ocean consisting mainly of ethane.

A second physical property, density, is also related to the intermolecular forces. The stronger the intermolecular forces, the more closely neighbouring molecules are attracted to one another, and the higher the density. With their weak dispersion forces, we would expect alkanes to have low densities. In fact alkanes are less dense than water. For example, pentane has a density of $0.63 \, \text{g} \cdot \text{mL}^{-1}$. As the number of carbon atoms in the alkane chain increases, the density slowly increases. The nonpolar nature of alkanes also accounts for their immiscibility with water and other polar solvents.

Chemical Properties

In general, alkanes have low chemical reactivity. Yet, from thermodynamic calculations, we would expect these compounds to be highly reactive. The explanation lies with kinetic factors. That is, there must be a high activation energy acting as a barrier to their reaction.

Why is there such an energy barrier? It appears to be a result of the way in which organic reactions occur. Many simple inorganic reactions involve charged ions, and these reactions are fast. For nonpolar molecules, however, ion formation is difficult or impossible, and a different reaction mechanism has to operate. This mechanism involves breaking the strong covalent bonds, and thus requires a high activation energy.

Reaction with Oxygen

The combustion of alkanes is by far their most important reaction. Because of their high activation energy, alkanes do not burn spontaneously upon coming into contact with oxygen. A spark or other high energy source is required to initiate the reaction. These combustion reactions are highly exothermic and, provided there is enough oxygen, the products are carbon dioxide and water. Alkanes are therefore important as fuels.

$$CH_{4\,(g)} + 2\,O_{2\,(g)} \longrightarrow CO_{2\,(g)} + 2\,H_2O_{(\ell)} \qquad \Delta H = -890 \, \text{kJ} \cdot \text{mol}^{-1}$$

Reaction with Chlorine

The reaction of an alkane with chlorine, as in the reaction with oxygen, involves a high activation energy. In this case, ultraviolet light can be used to initiate the reaction between chlorine and an alkane such as methane. The reaction proceeds stepwise, with one hydrogen after another being replaced by chlorine. A reaction in which one atom is replaced by another is called a **substitution reaction**.

$$CH_{4\,(g)} + Cl_{2\,(g)} \xrightarrow[\text{light}]{\text{heat or}} CH_3Cl_{(g)} + HCl_{(g)}$$

$$CH_3Cl_{(g)} + Cl_{2\,(g)} \longrightarrow CH_2Cl_{2\,(\ell)} + HCl_{(g)}$$

$$CH_2Cl_{2\,(\ell)} + Cl_{2\,(g)} \longrightarrow CHCl_{3\,(\ell)} + HCl_{(g)}$$

$$CHCl_{3\,(\ell)} + Cl_{2\,(g)} \longrightarrow CCl_{4\,(\ell)} + HCl_{(g)}$$

Other alkanes, such as ethane, propane, etc., react in a similar manner, but an even more complex series of steps is involved. Alkanes also undergo a parallel series of reactions with the other halogens, such as bromine.

Tetrachloromethane, CCl_4, and other toxic chlorinated hydrocarbons are produced whenever chlorine reacts with organic materials. Because we use chlorine to kill organisms in municipal water supplies, it is important that such water sources be free of any significant quantities of organic compounds.

Cracking Reactions

When alkanes are heated in the absence of air, some of the carbon-carbon bonds will break. This process, known as **cracking**, is accelerated by the use of aluminum oxide as catalyst. Any carbon-carbon bond along the chain can break, leading to a large variety of products of shorter chain length. We will give the example of one possible cracking reaction for butane to produce ethane and an alkene of formula C_2H_4:

$$CH_3CH_2CH_2CH_{3\,(g)} \xrightarrow{500\,°C} CH_3CH_{3\,(g)} + CH_2{=}CH_{2\,(g)}$$

The breaking of longer alkanes is of major importance in the petroleum industry, as we will discuss later.

The Preparation of Alkanes

In industry the alkanes of lower molar mass, from methane through pentane, are obtained by separating the components of crude oil. In the laboratory, methane can be prepared by strongly heating a mixture of calcium acetate and calcium hydroxide.

$$Ca(CH_3CO_2)_{2\,(s)} + Ca(OH)_{2\,(s)} \xrightarrow{\Delta} 2\,CaCO_{3\,(s)} + 2\,CH_{4(g)}$$

The other alkanes can be prepared by reaction of the appropriate alkene with hydrogen gas in the presence of a platinum or palladium catalyst. We can use the preparation of ethane as an example:

$$C_2H_{4\,(g)} + H_{2\,(g)} \xrightarrow{Pt} C_2H_{6\,(g)}$$

QUESTIONS

11. Which compound would you expect to have the higher boiling point, hexane or 2,2-dimethylbutane? Give reasons for your answer.

12. Write a series of equations for the reaction of methane with bromine.

13. Write an equation to describe the combustion of pentane in air.

Organometallic Chemistry

Organic and inorganic chemistry are not completely independent fields of study. They are linked by organometallic chemistry, which is the study of compounds containing metal-carbon bonds.

The study of organometallic compounds originated with the discovery in 1849 of diethylzinc, $Zn(C_2H_5)_2$, by Edward Frankland. Since then, the number of known organometallic compounds has grown rapidly, and by 1937, a 1000 page book was needed to summarize the chemistry of these compounds. Until 1951 the main interest was in compounds that contained a bond between carbon and one of the other main group elements. Work by E.O. Fischer in Germany and Geoffrey Wilkinson in England, however, opened the floodgates to studies of transition-metal organometallic chemistry. Not only did they make new types of compounds, but they also recognized that novel types of bonds were formed.

Organometallic compounds are not just of academic interest. Many industrial processes use them as intermediates or catalysts. Two of the most widely used compounds are tetraethyllead, $Pb(C_2H_5)_4$, and tetramethyllead, $Pb(CH_3)_4$. Over half a million tonnes of these lead compounds are produced every year as gasoline additives.

Figure 14.12

Sir Geoffrey Wilkinson (1921-   ) was awarded the Nobel Prize in 1973 for his work in organometallic chemistry.

One of the most useful and versatile families of reagents in organic chemistry contains the organometallic compounds called the Grignard reagents. Grignard reagents are named after Victor Grignard, who received a Nobel Prize in 1912 for their discovery. The reagents contain a carbon-magnesium bond, and are used in many organic syntheses, such as in the preparation of alcohols.

Another organometallic compound is being used by the U.S. Library of Congress to preserve books. Most inexpensive paper, such as newspaper, discolours and rots from reactions which produce acid within the fibres of paper. As you can imagine, it would be difficult to treat each page of every book with an acid-neutralizing solution. Chemists have devised a method involving an organometallic compound diethylzinc (DEZ), which can be used to treat up to 9000 books at a time. In the DEZ process the books are loaded into a chamber and the air is pumped out of the chamber and replaced by pure nitrogen under low pressure. (DEZ catches fire in oxygen.) DEZ vapour is introduced into the chamber and the gas permeates through the pages of the books. The DEZ neutralizes the hydrogen ions and also reacts with water in the paper to produce zinc oxide, ZnO. The white zinc oxide is a basic oxide and it acts as a "reserve" of alkalinity:

$$Zn(C_2H_5)_{2\,(g)} + 2\,H^+_{(aq)} \longrightarrow Zn^{2+}_{(aq)} + 2\,C_2H_{6\,(g)}$$

$$Zn(C_2H_5)_{2\,(g)} + H_2O_{(\ell)} \longrightarrow ZnO_{(s)} + 2\,C_2H_{6\,(g)}$$

The excess DEZ and the ethane that is formed during the process are then pumped out of the chamber. The whole procedure takes between three to five days for each batch of books. This might seem to be time consuming, but it will ensure that the important books in the library's collection will survive into the twenty-first century.

Organometallic compounds play an important role in nature. The coenzyme of vitamin B_{12}, methylcobalamin, is an organometallic that contains a methyl group bonded to a cobalt atom. Various micro-organisms can synthesize the organometallic methyl mercury from inorganic mercury salts. This covalently-bonded compound is absorbed by the fatty tissues (lipids) and concentrated up the food chain, creating a greater health hazard than inorganic mercury.

As another example, many marine shellfish synthesize the organometallic arsenic ion, $(CH_3)_4As^+$. This ion is one of the few arsenic species with a low toxicity, so it is safe to eat large quantities of shellfish that have been exposed to arsenic. Much of the research on the arsenic compounds in marine organisms is being performed by chemists at the University of British Columbia.

From the study of toxic elements in the environment to the synthesis of new organic compounds, organometallic chemistry is of great and growing importance in today's world.

Hydrocarbon Fuels

14.8 The earth's abundant supplies of hydrocarbon deposits originated from processes that began millions of years ago. They started with the decomposition of plant material in tropical forests and of marine organisms on the bottom of the oceans. As the decomposed organic materials became buried in the earth's crust, the heat and pressure converted them to complex mixtures of hydrocarbons. Movements of the earth's crust then brought many of these hydrocarbon deposits back closer to the surface of the earth. We can classify these deposits according to their major components.

TABLE 14.5 *Typical Compositions of Hydrocarbon Deposits*

Deposit	Principal Constituents	Other Constituents
Natural Gas	up to 99 % methane, CH_4	up to 10 % ethane, C_2H_6 up to 20 % propane, C_3H_8 other hydrocarbons: up to 95 % CO_2, up to 30 % H_2S
Crude oil	straight-chain alkanes 0–75 % cycloalkanes 20–70 % aromatic hydrocarbons 5–40 %	organic compounds of nitrogen and/or sulfur, 0–5 %
Tar sands	complex hydrocarbon mixture (bitumen)	clays, sands and/or sandstone, water
Oil shale	hydrocarbon polymer called 'kerogen'	various minerals
Coal	complex aromatic structure with high C:H ratio	some sulfur and nitrogen combined in structure

---

Natural Gas

Earlier we stated that natural gas is formed by the decay of organic materials. However, there is a controversial theory that some natural gas deposits are in fact the result of outgassing from the interior of the earth. These sources would be of inorganic (i.e. non-living) origin. To investigate this possibility, geologists are drilling deep into the earth's crust. Needless to say it will be several years before this debate is settled.

Natural gas is an important source of heat energy, particularly in western Canada. Unfortunately, at many oil wells and refineries, methane is "flared off" into the atmosphere, giving a bright glow to the sky, but wasting a non-renewable energy resource.

Figure 14.13

Propane is a less expensive fuel for motor vehicles than gasoline. Maintenance costs are also lower.

Two of the minor components of natural gas, propane and butane, are also used as fuels. Propane, commonly known as bottled gas, has been used for some time in campers and "gas" barbecues. It is now becoming an inexpensive fuel for modified gasoline engines. Compared to gasoline, the use of propane results in less engine wear, thus propane is a particularly attractive fuel for the operators of commercial vehicles such as taxis. Butane is used in pocket cigarette lighters.

Crude Petroleum

Crude petroleum is perhaps the world's most important source of organic chemicals. It is also an important source of energy. The world's major oil-producing areas include the Middle East, Mexico, Texas, Venezuela, Alberta, Nigeria, and the North Sea.

In general, petroleum is a homogeneous mixture of hydrocarbons. The exact composition depends on the source. Because petroleum is derived from living material, small quantities of sulfur and inorganic salts may also be present. The hydrocarbons present include alkanes and cycloalkanes (also called paraffins and naphthenes) and aromatics (benzene and its homologues, also known as the asphalts). Many different compounds of each class may be present in a deposit of crude petroleum. Crude petroleum is often classified by its main components: oil from Iran tends to be paraffinic and that from California is mainly asphaltic. Mexican crude contains about equal amounts of paraffins and asphalts and has a high sulfur content. To effect a partial separation of the components of crude petroleum, a process known as **fractionation** is used (Figure 14.15).

The crude petroleum is pumped through pipes into a furnace where it is heated to about 350 °C. The resulting mixture of gases and liquids is passed to a distillation tower. The gases are cooled as they rise and condense on trays at different levels in the tower. The layers, or fractions of

Figure 14.14

The complex industrial towers used in the fractionation of petroleum.

liquid on the trays, are then drawn off. The separate fractions contain a variety of different compounds with boiling points in the same range as the temperature of the distillation tower at the particular level.

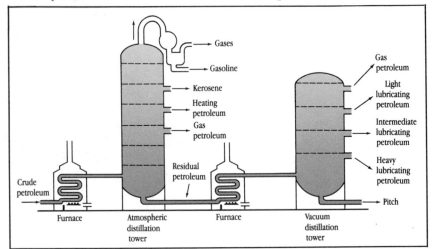

Figure 14.15
The fractionation of crude petroleum.

Any material that does not vaporize in the first tower is passed to a second tower, which is operated at a reduced pressure and is called a vacuum distillation tower. Here, because of the reduced pressure, the material boils at a lower temperature. Thus, many of the compounds that remain as liquids in the first tower are vaporized and separated into additional fractions. The remaining material that does not vaporize in the second tower is called pitch, and is used in asphalt.

The fractions obtained from the distillation process consist of mixtures of compounds rather than pure compounds, but isolation of the individual compounds is not necessary for most commercial uses.

Gasoline

The internal-combustion engine is one of the best known devices used to convert the chemical energy of petroleum to kinetic energy. We can briefly describe how a gasoline engine works. Air and a fine spray of gasoline are injected into a cylinder. A piston compresses the mixture and a spark (from the spark plug) ignites the mixture. The gas pressure generated by the explosion forces the piston back. The motion of the piston is then conveyed through gears and a driveshaft to the wheels, which propel the vehicle.

Some hydrocarbons ignite under the influence of pressure alone. This phenomenon, called premature ignition, results in a knocking sound. It is possible to correlate premature ignition (knocking) with molecular shape. Straight-chain molecules burn more readily under pressure, because there are many sites along the chain where a molecule of oxygen could impact and react. The more compact shape of a branch-chain molecule offers fewer sites of reaction, and subsequently there is less engine knock.

TABLE 14.6 Some Common Petroleum Products

Product	Main alkane component	Boiling range	Phase at room temperature
Natural gas	CH_4	Below 0°	gas
Propane	C_3H_8	Below 0°	gas
Butane	C_4H_{10}	Below 0°	gas
Gasoline	C_5H_{12} to $C_{10}H_{22}$	35° to 175°	liquid
Kerosene, jet fuel	$C_{10}H_{22}$ to $C_{18}H_{38}$	175° to 275°	liquid
Diesel fuel	$C_{12}H_{26}$ to $C_{20}H_{42}$	190° to 330°	liquid
Fuel oil	$C_{14}H_{30}$ to $C_{22}H_{46}$	230° to 360°	liquid
Lubricating oil	$C_{20}H_{42}$ to $C_{30}H_{62}$	Above 350°	liquid
Petroleum jelly	$C_{22}H_{46}$ to $C_{40}H_{82}$	m.p.* 40–60°	semi-solid
Paraffin wax	$C_{25}H_{52}$ to $C_{50}H_{102}$	m.p.* 50–65°	solid

*melting point

Gasoline is graded according to its **octane rating**, a system that was developed in 1928. The branched-chain alkane, isooctane (IUPAC name, 2,2,4-trimethylpentane) was found to be the best alkane for use in internal-combustion engines of that time, and was given an octane rating of 100. On the other hand, heptane, a straight-chain alkane, gave severe pre-ignition problems and was given a rating of zero. Other gasoline mixtures were then tested and given a comparative rating on this scale.

Because there is a greater demand for the gasoline fractions of petroleum than for the higher-boiling components, a proportion of the higher-boiling fractions is subjected to cracking to produce more short-chain molecules.

The gasoline fraction normally obtained from the fractionation process tends to be high in straight-chain molecules and consequently has a low octane rating. Until recently, tetraethyllead, $Pb(C_2H_5)_4$, was added to gasoline to raise its octane number. However, concern about lead pollution in the environment has led chemists and chemical engineers to devise an alternative process called **reforming**. The reforming reactions convert straight-chain alkanes to branched-chain isomers using beds of inorganic catalysts, such as aluminum chloride and antimony(III) chloride. Thus using this process, pentane can be isomerized to 2-methylbutane.

$$CH_3{-}CH_2{-}CH_2{-}CH_2{-}CH_3 \xrightarrow{\text{catalyst}} CH_3{-}\underset{\underset{\displaystyle CH_3}{|}}{CH}{-}CH_2{-}CH_3$$

Diesel Fuel

The diesel engine operates by simply compressing a fuel/air mixture and causing the mixture to spontaneously ignite. No sparking device is employed. From what we remarked about the gasoline engine, it should be apparent that a good diesel fuel must have the opposite characteristics of a gasoline fuel. That is, a diesel fuel should have a high proportion of straight-chain alkanes. The ignition quality of a diesel fuel is rated as its **cetane number**. Hexadecane, $C_{16}H_{34}$, is rated as 100 on this scale. Diesel fuels also come from a higher boiling range than gasoline.

Tar Sands

Tar sands, also known as oil sands, are a mixture of about 85 % sand and mineral-rich clays, 4 % water, and 10 % bitumen. Bitumen is a dense, sticky, semi-solid mixture of hydrocarbons that contains about 83% carbon.

Canada has the largest confirmed deposits of tar sands in the world, the equivalent of about 900 billion barrels of oil. There are also enormous deposits along the north bank of the Orinoco river, in Venezuela. The Canadian tar sands can be divided into three categories, depending upon their viscosity. The deposits near Lloydminster are free-flowing enough that they can be pumped directly from the ground. At Peace River and Cold Lake, the mixture is about 1000 times more viscous, while the surface deposits in the Athabasca and Wabasca regions are ten times more viscous again and are mined in open pits.

Mining tar sand is a difficult task. Its high sand content makes it extremely abrasive and mining equipment wears out at a rapid rate. In addition, the sticky particles cling to everything, including moving parts of the machinery, clogging conveyor belts and other moving parts. Finally, bitumen in the tar sands acts as a solvent for rubber, thus conventional vehicle tires slowly dissolve.

Processing tar sand is relatively simple. The mixture is first treated with hot water. The sands and clays sink to the bottom, while the bitumen floats to the top. The bitumen is separated and then heated strongly in the absence of air, a process known industrially as "coking," although the correct chemical term is **pyrolysis**. During the process, the large carbon-rich molecules break down to produce coke, an impure form of carbon, and short-chain hydrogen-rich molecules that can be used commercially instead of the hydrocarbons produced from the fractionation of crude oil.

Oil Shale

Oil shale differs markedly from tar sand. Oil shale looks like rock, but provided the organic content is high enough, the oil shale will burn. The United States has enormous reserves of oil shale, approaching the equivalent of 172 trillion barrels of oil. However, with the difficulties of extracting the oil from the shale, the obtainable quantity of oil would be much lower than this figure.

Figure 14.16
The locations of the major tar sands deposits, in Alberta and Saskatchewan.

Figure 14.17
Pitch Lake, Trinidad. On this Caribbean island, there is a large lake of almost pure bitumen.

Chromatography

In 1897 D. T. Day described how he could purify natural petroleum by passing it down a column of powdered limestone. Nineteen years later, the Russian botanist, M. Tswett, reported how plant pigments could be separated using the same procedure. These discoveries marked the founding of the branch of separation science known as *chromatography*.

Chromatography is used to separate mixtures of compounds into their components. An interesting chromatography experiment is to separate the different coloured components in a food dye. For this, we can use the technique known as paper chromatography. A small sample of the dye is placed near the end of a piece of chromatography (or filter) paper. The paper is then dipped into a liquid. As the liquid level rises up the paper, the dye spot moves along with the liquid front. However, each of the compounds present in the dye is carried along by the liquid at a slightly different rate. Thus the original spot of dye becomes a series of spots, with each spot corresponding to a different compound. By comparing the positions of these spots with samples made from known compounds, the identities of the components of the dye can be deduced.

have a different chemical structure. Those molecules with polar groups will tend to stick briefly to the paper molecules, while the lower-polarity molecules will be carried past them in the solvent. As a result, the dye components will become separated.

Gas-phase chromatography, which was developed in 1952, is a technique that is used for separating mixtures of gases or low-boiling liquids. One of the many interesting applications of gas chromatography is the analysis of exhaled breath. Using this technique, over 100 different organic chemicals have been identified in normal breath. Eventually, it is hoped that we will be able to diagnose certain illnesses by analyzing a person's breath and comparing the results with those obtained from healthy individuals.

Figure 14.19
A 'bomb-sniffer.' This gas chromatograph is used at many airports to detect bombs.

A more recent advance in the field of chromatography is the development of high-performance liquid chromatography (HPLC). The application of pressure can force a liquid through a long, tightly-packed column in a reasonable length of time, making the separation of very similar non-volatile compounds possible. HPLC is used in the detection and identification of illegal drugs in blood and urine samples, and in separating the mixtures of products that are obtained in many organic reactions.

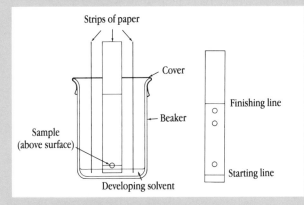

Figure 14.18
The progress of a paper chromatography experiment

How does paper chromatography work? A simplified explanation is as follows. The dye dissolves in the chosen solvent and the solution starts moving between the solid paper fibres. The molecules in the paper fibres contain —OH groups capable of hydrogen-bonding with any passing molecule that contains a polar oxygen or nitrogen atom. Each compound in the dye mixture will

Figure 14.20
This two-person analytical company uses liquid chromatography to provide analyses for 500 Californian wineries.

The nature of the organic material in all oil shale deposits is fairly constant and is called "kerogen." The average molar mass of the molecules in this material is about 3000 g·mol^{-1}. The extraction of the organic component from the shale involves crushing the rock and then employing a coking process similar to that used for processing tar sands. With the oil crisis in the 1970s, there was an upsurge of interest in oil shale, but as gasoline shortages receded, the high cost of processing oil shale delayed the exploitation of these energy reserves.

Alkenes

14.9

Hydrocarbons containing one or more carbon-carbon double bonds are called alkenes. These compounds and compounds containing carbon-carbon triple bonds are classified as **unsaturated hydrocarbons**. Alkanes, on the other hand, in which all the bonds are single bonds, are referred to as being **saturated hydrocarbons**.

Alkenes, like alkanes, are nonpolar. As we would expect, the boiling points of the alkenes increase with chain length. The boiling point of a particular alkene is slightly less than that of the alkane having the same chain length. Thus the lower members of the alkene series are gases at room temperature.

The presence of a double bond, the first functional group that we have studied, provides a centre for reaction. Thus alkenes are chemically more reactive than alkanes and they undergo different types of reactions.

For alkanes, all the bond angles have the tetrahedral value of 109.5°. In alkenes however, the double bond results in only three bonding directions around each carbon atom, and hence the bond angle is 120°. The geometry of the simplest alkene, ethene, is shown in Figure 14.21.

Figure 14.21

The shape of the ethene molecule, C_2H_4:
a) the geometry;
b) as a ball-and-stick model;
c) as a space-filling model.

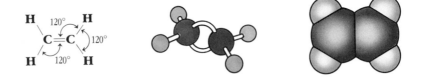

The Naming of Alkenes

The rules for naming alkenes by the IUPAC system are very similar to those used to name alkanes. One important difference is that the carbon chain chosen as the main chain *must contain* the double bond, even if it is not the longest chain. The presence of a double bond is indicated by the ending *-ene*. If structural isomers are possible, a number is used to indicate at which carbon atom the double bond starts. This number should be as low as possible. If two double bonds are present, the ending *-diene* is used and two numbers are required to specify the positions of the double bonds. Three double bonds in a molecule are indicated by the ending *-triene*. In this case three numbers are required to specify the location of the double bonds.

TABLE 14.7 *Names and Formulas of the Simplest Alkenes*

Formula	Name	Structure
CH_2=CH_2	ethene	2 carbon atoms
CH_2=$CHCH_3$	propene	3 carbon atoms
CH_2=$CHCH_2CH_3$	1-butene	double bond carbon 1
CH_3CH=$CHCH_3$	2-butene	double bond at carbon 2
CH_2=$CHCH$=CH_2	1,3-butadiene	double bonds at carbon 1 and 3

Let us work through the naming of a more complex example:

$$CH_3-\underset{\underset{CH_3}{|}}{C}=CH-CH_2-\underset{\underset{CH_3}{|}}{CH}-CH_3$$

1. Identify the longest continuous chain of carbon atoms containing the double bond and assign the base name.

$$CH_3-\underset{\underset{CH_3}{|}}{C}=CH-CH_2-\underset{\underset{CH_3}{|}}{CH}-CH_3$$

The longest chain containing C=C is six carbons, so the base name is hexene.

2. Number the main chain beginning at the end which will result in the lowest possible number for the double bond.

$$\overset{1}{CH_3}-\overset{2}{\underset{\underset{CH_3}{|}}{C}}=\overset{3}{CH}-\overset{4}{CH_2}-\overset{5}{\underset{\underset{CH_3}{|}}{CH}}-\overset{6}{CH_3}$$

The double bond starts at carbon 2, hence 2-hexene.

3. Identify each substituent and indicate its position by the number of the carbon atom on the main chain to which it is attached.

$$CH_3-\overset{2}{\underset{\underset{CH_3}{|}}{C}}=CH-CH_2-\overset{5}{\underset{\underset{CH_3}{|}}{CH}}-CH_3$$

A methyl group is at carbon 2 and at carbon 5.

This gives us the name 2,5-dimethyl-2-hexene.

Geometric Isomerism

In alkanes, there is free rotation of the molecule about the single bonds. In alkenes however, the carbon-carbon double bond is quite rigid, preventing any rotation. If each carbon in the double bond has two different groups attached to it, it is possible to have **geometric** isomers. The simplest alkene in which this type of isomerism can occur is 2-butene. The molecule with both methyl groups on the same side of the double bond is named *cis*-2-butene, while the isomer with the methyl groups diagonally across the double bond is called *trans*-2-butene. This type of isomerism is sometimes given the name ***cis-trans* isomerism**.

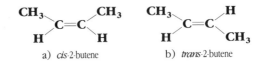

a) *cis*-2-butene   b) *trans*-2-butene

In total there are six different compounds with the formula C_4H_8. There are five structural isomers, one of which exists as two geometric isomers.

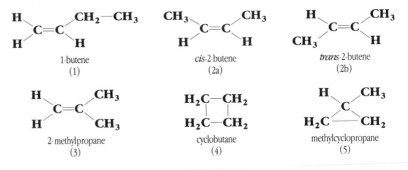

Reactions of Alkenes

As we saw in Section 14.7, among the most important reactions for alkanes are substitution reactions, where one atom is replaced by another. Alkenes generally undergo reactions in which atoms or groups of atoms add across the double bond. Such reactions are called **addition reactions**. The tendency for alkenes to undergo addition reactions can be readily understood if we consider the energies of the bonds involved.

The energy of a carbon-carbon single bond is $347 \, kJ \cdot mol^{-1}$, while that of a carbon-carbon double bond is $620 \, kJ \cdot mol^{-1}$. In the double bond, the two bonds are not equivalent. One is a sigma bond, identical to that of the carbon-carbon bond in an alkane. Thus it has an energy of $347 \, kJ \cdot mol^{-1}$. The second bond is classified as a pi bond. This must have an energy of $273 \, kJ \cdot mol^{-1}$ $(620 - 347)$. It is the pi bond that is broken in addition reactions. Its weakness, in comparison to the sigma bond, accounts for the greater reactivity of alkenes.

Common Addition Reactions

Reaction with Halogens Alkenes react rapidly with halogens, such as chlorine and bromine. If a gaseous alkene, such as ethene, is bubbled into a solution of bromine, the reddish-brown colour of bromine disappears. The bromine reacts with the alkene to produce a colourless dibromoalkane. We can use this reaction to test for the presence of an unsaturated carbon-carbon bond.

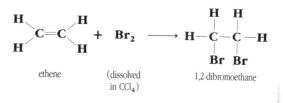

Reaction with Hydrogen A similar reaction occurs between an alkene and hydrogen gas. This process, called **hydrogenation**, proceeds under quite mild conditions to produce the corresponding alkane.

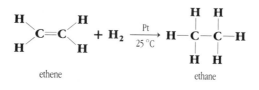

Hydrogenation is used during the preparation of margarine. The molecules in liquid cooking oils contain long hydrocarbon chains with several double bonds. The hydrogenation of some of these double bonds produces a less unsaturated compound with a slightly higher melting point. This is desirable because it gives us a solid product at room temperature which can be spread on bread or toast.

Figure 14.22
Oils are hydrogenated to margarine in these large pressure vessels.

Reaction with Hydrogen Halides Alkenes also react with hydrogen halides. For example, hydrogen chloride reacts with ethene to produce chloroethane, C_2H_5Cl.

$$CH_2{=}CH_{2\,(g)} + HCl_{(g)} \longrightarrow CH_3{-}CH_2Cl_{(g)}$$

If we perform the reaction with propene, a similar reaction occurs.

$$CH_2-CH=CH_{2\,(g)} + HCl_{(g)} \longrightarrow CH_3-CHCl-CH_{3\,(g)}$$

You might expect the formation of some of the structural isomer, $CH_3-CH_2-CH_2Cl$, as well. In fact, when we perform this reaction in the laboratory only the one isomer is formed. To predict which isomer will be formed, we use **Markovnikov's Rule**. One way of expressing this rule is to say that the hydrogen of a hydrogen halide adds to the carbon that is already bonded to the most hydrogen atoms, as seen in the above example.

Reaction with Water In acidic solution, alkenes undergo an addition reaction with water to produce an alcohol. Most industrial ethanol is made by this reaction.

$$CH_2=CH_{2\,(g)} + H_2O_{(\ell)} \xrightarrow[100\,°C]{H_2SO_4} CH_3-CH_2OH_{(aq)}$$

Oxidation Reactions

Alkenes, like alkanes, can be oxidized by burning them in air. For example,

$$CH_2=CH_{2\,(g)} + 3\,O_{2\,(g)} \longrightarrow 2\,CO_{2\,(g)} + 2\,H_2O_{(\ell)}$$

However, by using an aqueous oxidizing agent, such as potassium permanganate, we can obtain a more interesting reaction. If an alkene is bubbled through a dilute aqueous solution of potassium permanganate, the purple colour of the permanganate ion disappears and a brown precipitate of manganese(IV) oxide is formed. In this reaction the oxidation number of manganese is reduced from +7 to +4, while each carbon is oxidized from −2 to +1. This is a common test for the presence of an unsaturated carbon-carbon bond.

$$3\,CH_2=CH_{2\,(g)} + 2\,KMnO_{4\,(aq)} + 4\,H_2O_{(\ell)} \longrightarrow 3\,\underset{OH\quad OH}{CH_2-CH_{2\,(aq)}} + 2\,MnO_{2\,(s)} + 2\,KOH_{(aq)}$$

Polymerization Reactions

From the perspective of the chemical industry, the single most important reaction of alkenes is **polymerization**. A polymer is a large organic molecule that consists of many small, identical units. An example of a polymerization reaction is the formation of polyethene (commonly called polyethylene) from ethene. In this reaction the carbon-carbon double bond is broken and new single bonds are formed between neighbouring ethene molecules. In a typical polymerization reaction, between 2000 and 50 000 alkene units may become bonded together. To represent this large and variable number of units, we place the symbol n outside the parenthesis that contains the repeating unit. This is shown below by the equation representing the formation of polyethene.

$$n\ CH_2\!\!=\!\!CH_{2\,(g)} \xrightarrow[\text{high pressure}]{\text{high temperature}} (-CH_2\!\!-\!\!CH_2\!\!-)_{n\,(s)}$$

$$\text{ethene} \hspace{6cm} \text{polyethene}$$

The Biochemistry of Ethene

Ethene gas plays an important role in the ripening of fruit. At the onset of the ripening phase, enzymes in the fruit start producing ethene. The gas causes the colour change, softening, and sweetening that we associate with ripening fruit. Understanding the ripening process has enabled farmers to produce more marketable produce for the grocery store. Bananas and other fruit are now picked when they are unripe. During shipping the fruit is kept at low temperature and, if necessary, in an atmosphere of carbon dioxide. The combination of a low temperature and an inert atmosphere supresses the action of any ethene produced. At the destination, ethene gas is pumped into the container to produce a concentration of about 1–2 ppm and the fruit then ripens rapidly. It is the production of ethene that leads to the saying "one rotten apple will spoil the barrel," for once one apple starts producing ethene early in the packing process, it will start ripening all the other apples in the same container.

Preparation of Alkenes

Alkenes can be prepared in the laboratory from the **dehydration** of an alcohol. A dehydration reaction is one in which the elements of water (hydrogen and oxygen) are removed from a compound in a 2:1 mole ratio. Hot concentrated sulfuric acid is a commonly used (but very dangerous!) reagent for this purpose. In the laboratory preparation of ethene, we can alternatively pass ethanol vapour over heated aluminum oxide.

$$CH_3\!\!-\!\!CH_2\!\!-\!\!OH_{(g)} \xrightarrow[300\,°C]{Al_2O_3} CH_2\!\!=\!\!CH_{2\,(g)} + H_2O_{(g)}$$

QUESTIONS

14. Draw the condensed formula of each of the following alkenes:
   a) 2,4-dimethyl-3-heptene   b) 2,3-dimethyl-2-pentene

15. Does geometric isomerism occur in 2,4-dimethyl-3-heptene and 2,3-dimethyl-2-pentene?

16. Write the equation for the following:
   a) the reaction of propene with hydrogen at 25 °C in the presence of a platinum catalyst
   b) the reaction of propene with bromine in carbon tetrachloride
   c) the reaction of propene with potassium permanganate

Carrots, Vision, and Geometric Isomers

For several generations, parents have encouraged their children to eat their carrots by using the argument that it will help them "see in the dark." This example of modern folklore dates back to World War II when radar was first used by the Royal Air Force. To account for the sudden rise in success of night fighter operations without revealing the existence of this new device to the enemy, it was said that the pilots were improving their night vision by eating lots of carrots.

In fact there is a link between night blindness and the orange pigment in carrots, β-carotene. In the liver, this 40-carbon hydrocarbon that contains 11 double bonds is broken down to give 11-*cis*-retinol, (vitamin A). Some of the vitamin A is conveyed through the blood to the eye where it is converted to 11-*cis*-retinal.

impulse is generated and transmitted through the optic nerve to the brain. The structure of *all-trans*-retinal is shown below:

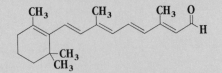

The *all-trans*-retinal travels through the blood stream to the liver where it is isomerized back to the *cis* form. The *cis* form is then conveyed back to the eye by the bloodstream, where it reinserts itself in the pocket in the opsin. An amazing journey!

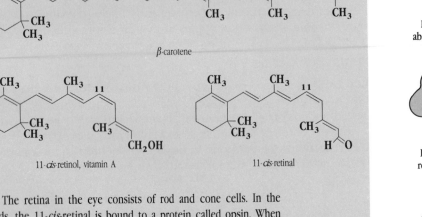

β-carotene

11-*cis*-retinol, vitamin A

11-*cis*-retinal

The retina in the eye consists of rod and cone cells. In the rods, the 11-*cis*-retinal is bound to a protein called opsin. When visible light falls on the rods, it causes the carbon-carbon double bond between carbon atoms 11 and 12 to break. The chain can then rotate and the double bond reforms in the more stable trans arrangement, called *all-trans*-retinal. The *all-trans* isomer, with its very different shape, can no longer bond to the opsin molecule. When the opsin and the *all-trans*-retinal separate, an electrical

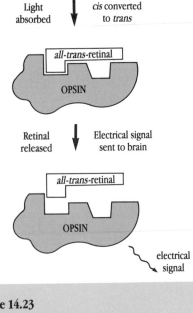

Figure 14.23
A diagram showing the process of geometric isomers involved in sight.

Alkynes

14.10

Hydrocarbons containing one or more triple bonds are called alkynes. Being unsaturated compounds, alkynes undergo basically the same types of reactions as alkenes. Since each carbon of the triple carbon-carbon bond can only bond to one other atom, alkynes do not exhibit geometrical isomerism, only structural isomerism. The linear arrangement of atoms about the carbon-carbon triple bond can be seen in the simplest alkyne, ethyne.

Figure 14.24

The shape of the ethyne molecule, C_2H_2:
a) the geometry;
b) as a ball-and-stick model;
c) as a space-filling model.

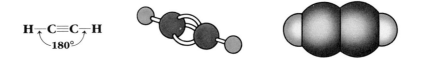

$$H \overset{}{-} C \equiv C \overset{}{-} H$$
$$180°$$

The Naming of Alkynes

The rules for naming alkynes are the same as those for alkenes, except that the ending *-yne* is used to denote the presence of the triple bond.

TABLE 14.8	*Names and Formulas of the Simplest Alkynes*	
Formula	**Name**	**Structure**
$CH \equiv CH$	ethyne	2 carbon atoms
$CH \equiv CCH_3$	propyne	3 carbon atoms
$CH \equiv CCH_2CH_3$	1-butyne	triple bond at carbon 1
$CH_3C \equiv CCH_3$	2-butyne	triple bond at carbon 2

Let us work through naming a more complex alkyne, with the formula

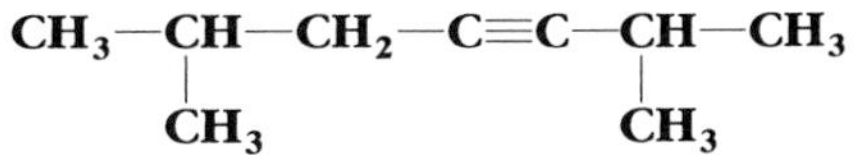

$$CH_3 - CH - CH_2 - C \equiv C - CH - CH_3$$
$$CH_3 CH_3$$

1. Identify the longest continuous chain of carbon atoms containing the triple bond and assign the base name.

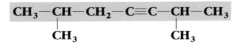

The longest chain containing C≡C is seven carbons, so the base name is heptyne.

2. Number the main chain beginning at the end that will result in the lowest possible number for the triple bond.

$$\overset{7}{CH_3}-\overset{6}{CH}-\overset{5}{CH_2}-\overset{4}{C}\equiv\overset{3}{C}-\overset{2}{CH}-\overset{1}{CH_3}$$
with CH_3 branches on carbon 6 and carbon 2.

The triple bond starts at carbon 3, hence 3-heptyne.

3. Name each substituent and indicate its position by the number of the carbon atom on the main chain to which it is attached.

$$\overset{6}{CH_3}-CH-CH_2-C\equiv C-\overset{2}{CH}-CH_3$$
with CH_3 groups below carbon 6 and carbon 2.

Methyl groups are located at carbon 2 and 6.

This gives us the name 2,6-dimethyl-3-heptyne.

Reactions of Alkynes

Alkynes behave like alkenes in that they undergo addition reactions. However, one major difference is that it is possible for two moles of reagent to add to one mole of an alkyne. For example, two moles of hydrogen react with one mole of ethyne to produce the corresponding alkane:

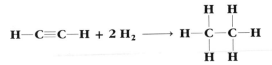

Similarly, in the common test for an unsaturated carbon-carbon bond, two moles of bromine add to one mole of an ethyne.

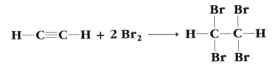

In another reaction parallel to that of alkenes, a hydrogen halide will add to a triple bond. In this case we write the reaction in two steps:

$$H-C\equiv C-H + HCl \longrightarrow \underset{H}{\overset{H}{>}}C=C\underset{Cl}{\overset{H}{<}}$$

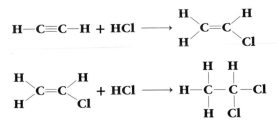

When the second mole of hydrogen chloride adds across the double bond, you might expect the formation of some of the structural isomer, CH_2ClCH_2Cl as well. However, if we apply Markovnikov's Rule, which we described when discussing alkenes, then only one isomer is predicted.

Figure 14.25

A cave-explorer's lamp uses the reaction between calcium carbide and water to produce ethyne gas.

Ethyne, the simplest alkyne, is commonly called acetylene. Ethyne burns in oxygen with a very hot flame and is used in welding.

$$CH\equiv CH_{(g)} + \tfrac{5}{2}O_{2\,(g)} \longrightarrow 2\,CO_{2\,(g)} + H_2O_{(g)} \qquad \Delta H = -1300\;kJ\cdot mol^{-1}$$

The Acidity of Alkynes

Although the carbon-hydrogen bond is normally of very low polarity, we find that the carbon-hydrogen bond next to a carbon-carbon triple bond is quite polar. As a result, 1-alkynes can behave as very weak acids. For example, ethyne reacts with sodium metal to form an ionic compound, sodium ethanide.

$$2\,CH\equiv CH_{(g)} + 2\,Na_{(s)} \longrightarrow 2\,CH\equiv C^-Na^+{}_{(s)} + H_2$$

Bubbling a 1-alkyne into a solution of silver nitrate produces a silver salt.

$$CH_3CH_2C\equiv CH_{(g)} + AgNO_{3\,(aq)} \longrightarrow CH_3CH_2C\equiv C^-Ag^+{}_{(s)} + HNO_{3\,(aq)}$$

Heavy metal ethanides such as this are dangerously (and often unpredictably) explosive when dry.

Preparation of Ethyne

Large quantities of ethyne are produced annually by a process that uses two abundant and inexpensive materials: limestone and coal. The limestone (calcium carbonate) is first converted to calcium oxide, and the coal is converted to coke (impure carbon). These two products are then reacted together to produce calcium carbide, CaC_2.

$$CaO_{(s)} + 3\,C_{(s)} \longrightarrow CaC_{2\,(s)} + CO_{(g)}$$

Treatment of the calcium carbide with water produces ethyne gas.

$$CaC_{2\,(s)} + 2\,H_2O_{(\ell)} \longrightarrow CH\equiv CH_{(g)} + Ca(OH)_{2\,(s)}$$

At one time, the reaction between calcium carbide and water was used in automobile headlamps. In more recent times, it has been used in the lamps of cave explorers and miners. The lamp contains two compartments. Calcium carbide is placed in the lower compartment and water in the upper compartment. A tap is used to allow the water to drip onto the calcium carbide. The ethyne produced escapes through a tube which exits from the centre of a reflector. A lighter mechanism is used to ignite the gas.

QUESTIONS

17. Name the following alkynes according to the IUPAC system:

a) $CH_3-CH_2-C\equiv C-CH_3$

b) $CH_3-\overset{\displaystyle CH_3}{\underset{\displaystyle CH_3}{\overset{|}{\underset{|}{C}}}}-C\equiv C-\overset{\displaystyle CH_3}{\underset{\displaystyle CH_3}{\overset{|}{\underset{|}{C}}}}-CH_3$

18. Draw the structure of each of the following compounds:
 a) 2-butyne   b) 3,3,-dimethyl-1-pentyne

19. Write an equation for the reaction of 1-butyne under the following conditions:
 a) excess hydrogen in the presence of a nickel catalyst at 25 °C
 b) excess bromine in carbon tetrachloride

20. Write the equation for the reaction of hydrogen bromide with
 a) ethyne and b) propyne.

Aromatic Compounds

14.11 The word "aromatic" means fragrant. However, in organic chemistry the term has come to refer to a class of hydrocarbons that are, for the most part, substituted derivatives of benzene. The compounds have significantly different properties from those of the alkanes, alkenes, and alkynes that we have studied so far.

The simplest aromatic hydrocarbon is benzene, C_6H_6. This colourless, sweetish-smelling liquid was first isolated in 1825 by Michael Faraday from the oily residue that had collected in the gas lines in London, England. However, over 100 years elapsed before a totally satisfactory explanation of the bonding in benzene was developed. We will briefly examine the facts known about benzene and we will see why the bonding in this compound presented such a challenge to chemists.

1. Benzene has the molecular formula C_6H_6.

This formula has so few hydrogen atoms for the number of carbon atoms that an unsaturated molecule would seem likely. In 1864 (some texts say 1858), August Kekulé proposed a ring structure involving alternating single and double bonds. A few years later, two other chemists, Dewar (1867) and Ladenburg (1868) proposed very different structures for the benzene molecule.

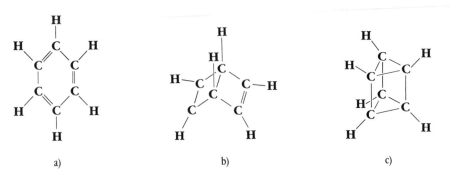

Figure 14.26
The structure of benzene according to a) Kekulé, b) Dewar, and c) Ladenburg.

a)   b)   c)

Figure 14.27
Kathleen Lonsdale (1903-1971) used X-ray crystallography to show that the benzene molecule was planar.

2. Benzene is a planar molecule.

The planar nature of the benzene molecule was established in the 1920s, supporting the Kekulé model.

3. Benzene undergoes substitution rather than addition reactions.

The Kekulé representation suggests that benzene should behave as if it were cyclohexatriene, an alkene. If so it should react with bromine to give an addition product and with potassium permanganate to give an oxidation product. In fact when bromine and benzene react together a substitution product is formed. Benzene and potassium permanganate do not react at all. From enthalpy measurements, we find that benzene is about $150\,kJ\cdot mol^{-1}$ more stable than a compound having the Kekulé structure should be.

4. Benzene yields only one monosubstitution product.

If we replace one of the hydrogen atoms of a benzene molecule by an atom of chlorine, we find that only one compound of the formula C_6H_5Cl is formed. This indicates that all the carbon atoms in the benzene molecule must be equivalent (that is, have identical environments).

5. The carbon-carbon bonds in benzene are all of equal length.

The carbon-carbon bonds in benzene all have the same length of 139 pm. This value is intermediate between the length of a carbon-carbon single bond (148 pm) and the length of a carbon-carbon double bond (134 pm).

The explanation of the structure of benzene that was developed in the 1930s relates to the orbital model of atomic structure. We assume that each carbon has a **p** orbital at right angles to the plane of the benzene ring. Each of the **p** orbitals contains one electron. In Section 3.4, we saw that overlap can occur between two **p** orbitals to give a pi bond. In the case of benzene we believe that the **p** orbitals overlap all around the benzene ring to give a continuous pi bond around the molecule. We indicate this arrangement by placing a circle in the centre of the structural formula for the **benzene ring**. Alternatively, we can use the geometric representation of a hexagon with a circle inside.

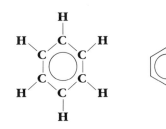

Figure 14.28

A comparison of the geometric representations of a) cyclohexane, b) cyclohexene, c) benzene.

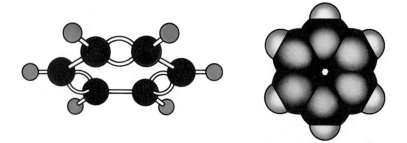

Figure 14.29

The shape of the benzene molecule, C_6H_6: a) as a Kekulé ball-and-stick model; b) as a space-filling model.

Until recently, the Dewar and Ladenburg representations of benzene were rejected as fanciful inventions that could not possibly exist. However, compounds with these forms have now been prepared. They are structural isomers of benzene that are not aromatic. Dewar benzene (synthesized in 1962) behaves as an unsaturated compound, whereas Ladenburg benzene (prismane, synthesized in 1973) behaves as a cycloalkane.

Reactions of Benzene

Substitution reactions dominate the chemistry of benzene. A typical example is the reaction of bromine with benzene in the presence of an iron catalyst to produce bromobenzene.

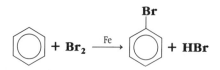

Despite its preference for substitution, under extreme conditions benzene can be made to undergo addition reactions. For example, at pressures of 20 to 30 MPa, benzene can be hydrogenated to cyclohexane.

Other Common Aromatic Compounds

Benzene is a good solvent. Unfortunately it is extremely carcinogenic and for this reason, it is banned from general use. However, the next simplest aromatic hydrocarbon, toluene (methylbenzene), is almost as good a solvent as benzene and is comparatively less harmful.

It is possible to have compounds containing connected benzene rings. Naphthalene, a compound in which two benzene rings share a common side, is used as a moth repellent. The carcinogenic compound 3,4-benzopyrene is produced in significant quantities in any burning or charring process. Thus both cigarette smoke and char-broiled foods contain significant quantities of this hazardous compound.

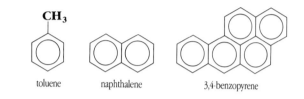

Figure 14.30
The structures of toluene, naphthalene, 3,4-benzopyrene.

CH₃

toluene   naphthalene   3,4-benzopyrene

QUESTIONS

21. Draw the structures of the four isomeric aromatic compounds with the formula C_8H_{10}.

22. How would Dewar benzene react with bromine? Write an equation for the reaction using Figure 14.26b as the structure for Dewar benzene.

Summary

- Organic chemistry is the study of compounds of carbon.

- The large number of known carbon compounds is due to the tendency of carbon to catenate.

- Hydrocarbons can be classified into two broad categories: aliphatic and aromatic hydrocarbons.

- There are three important families in the aliphatic hydrocarbons: alkanes, alkenes, and alkynes.

- The tetrahedral arrangement of four atoms or groups around a central carbon atom determines the shape of many organic compounds.

- Structural isomers have the same molecular formula but different structural formulas.

- The IUPAC system provides a systematic way of naming organic compounds.

- Alkanes are comparatively unreactive. However, when they do react, alkanes generally undergo substitution reactions.

- Crude petroleum is a source of many petrochemicals as well as a source of energy.

- Alkenes and alkynes are more reactive than alkanes. They generally undergo addition reactions.

- Geometric (*cis-trans*) isomerism can occur in certain alkenes.

- Aromatic hydrocarbons contain a benzene ring. They undergo substitution reactions rather than addition reactions.

KEY WORDS

addition reaction	hydrocarbon
aliphatic	isomers
alkane	IUPAC system
alkene	Markovnikov's Rule
alkyl group	octane rating
alkyne	organic chemistry
aromatic	polymerization
benzene ring	pyrolysis
branched-chain	reforming
catenation	saturated hydrocarbons
cetane number	side chain
combustion reaction	straight-chain
common name	structural formula
condensed formula	structural isomer
cracking	substituent
cyclic hydrocarbon	substitution reaction
dehydration	systematic name
fractionation	tetrahedral
functional group	trivial name
geometric (*cis-trans*) isomerism	unsaturated hydrocarbon
homologous series	

ANSWERS TO
SECTION QUESTIONS

1. CH_4 possesses covalent bonds and dispersion forces between molecules; it has a low melting point and is not very soluble in water. NaCl possesses ionic bonds; it has a high melting point and is very soluble in water.

2. The compounds are nonpolar. As a result, they have only the weakest intermolecular forces, dispersion forces. Thus the compounds will melt and boil with very little input of energy.

3. 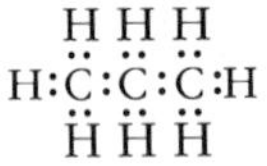 H:C:C:C:H   an alkane

4. a) 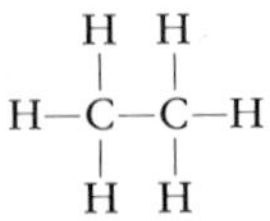 H—C—C—H   b) H—C—C—C—H   c) H—C—C—C—C—H

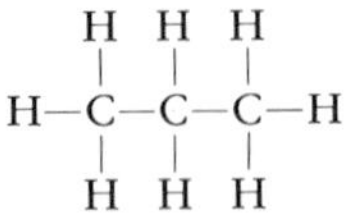

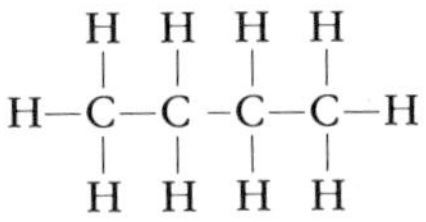

5. a) CH_3-CH_3 b) $CH_3-CH_2-CH_3$ c) $CH_3-CH_2-CH_2-CH_3$

6. d)

7. 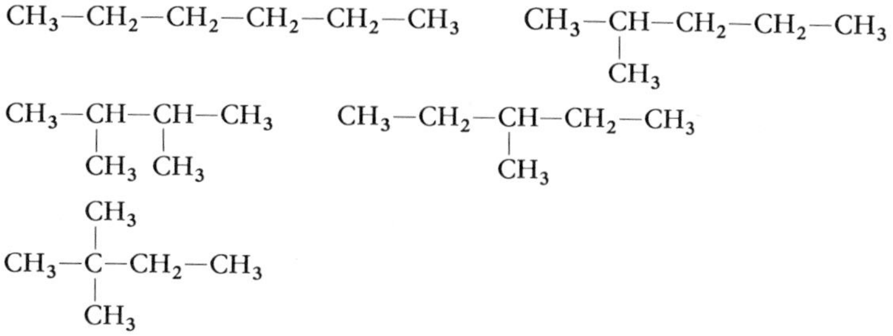 $CH_3-CH_2-CH_2-CH_2-CH_2-CH_3$ $\underset{\underset{\displaystyle CH_3}{|}}{CH_3-CH-CH_2-CH_2-CH_3}$

$\underset{\underset{\displaystyle CH_3\ \ CH_3}{|\quad\ |}}{CH_3-CH-CH-CH_3}$ $\underset{\underset{\displaystyle CH_3}{|}}{CH_3-CH_2-CH-CH_2-CH_3}$

$CH_3-\overset{\overset{\displaystyle CH_3}{|}}{\underset{\underset{\displaystyle CH_3}{|}}{C}}-CH_2-CH_3$

8.

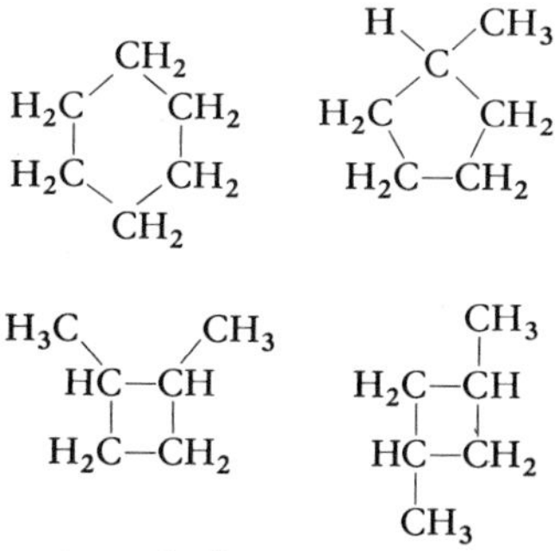

9. a) 3-methylhexane
b) 2,4-dimethylhexane
c) methylcyclopropane
d) 2,2,3,4,4-pentamethylpentane

10. a) 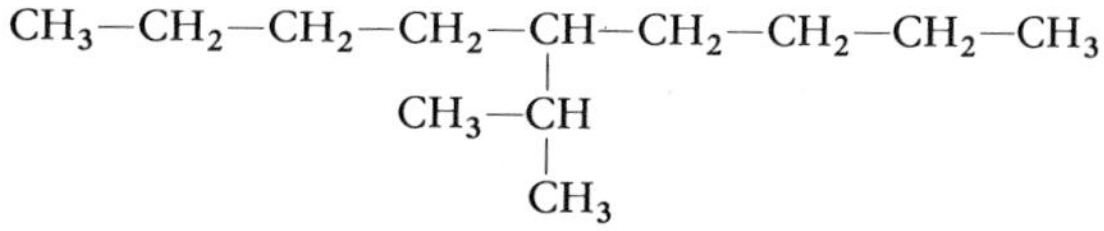 $CH_3-CH_2-CH_2-CH_2-\overset{\overset{\displaystyle CH_3-CH}{|}}{\underset{\underset{\displaystyle CH_3}{}}{CH}}-CH_2-CH_2-CH_2-CH_3$

b) 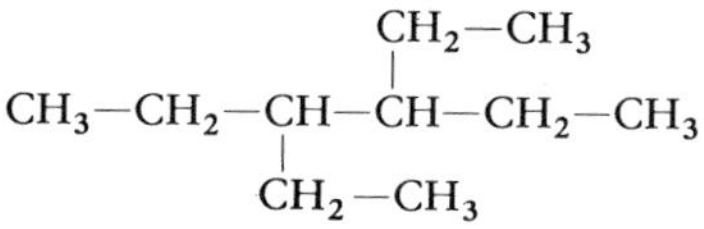 $CH_3-CH_2-\overset{\overset{\displaystyle CH_2-CH_3}{|}}{\underset{\underset{\displaystyle CH_2-CH_3}{|}}{CH-CH}}-CH_2-CH_3$

c) 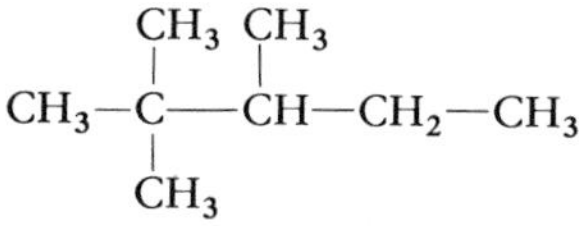 $CH_3-\overset{\overset{\displaystyle CH_3}{|}}{\underset{\underset{\displaystyle CH_3}{|}}{C}}-\overset{\overset{\displaystyle CH_3}{|}}{CH}-CH_2-CH_3$

d)

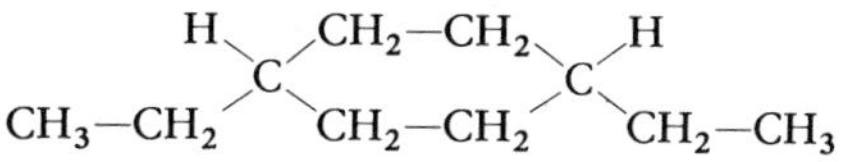

11. Hexane (2,2-dimethylbutane) is a more compact molecule. Hence it will have weaker dispersion forces between molecules and a lower boiling point.

12. $CH_4 + Br_2 \longrightarrow CH_3Br + HBr$
$CH_3Br + Br_2 \longrightarrow CH_2Br_2 + HBr$
$CH_2Br_2 + Br_2 \longrightarrow CHBr_3 + HBr$
$CHBr_3 + Br_2 \longrightarrow CBr_4 + HBr$

13. $C_5H_{12(\ell)} + 8\,O_{2\,(g)} \longrightarrow 5\,CO_{2\,(g)} + 6\,H_2O_{(g)}$

14. 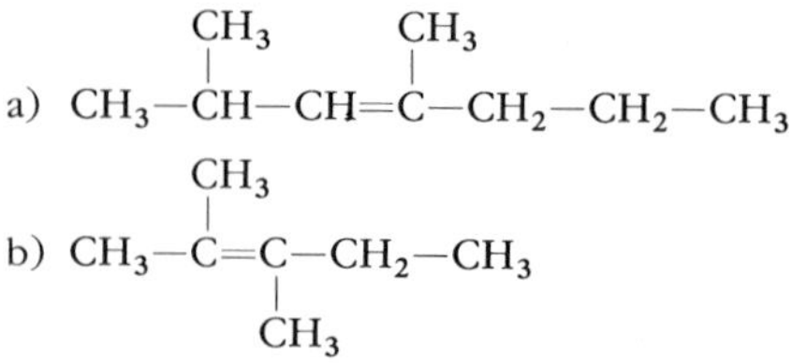 a)
$$\underset{\substack{|\\CH_3}}{CH_3-CH}-CH=\underset{\substack{|\\CH_3}}{C}-CH_2-CH_2-CH_3$$

b)
$$CH_3-\underset{\substack{|\\CH_3}}{\overset{\substack{CH_3\\|}}{C}}=C-CH_2-CH_3$$

15. Geometrical isomerism occurs in 2,4-dimethyl-3-heptane, but not in 2,3-dimethyl-2-pentene.

16. 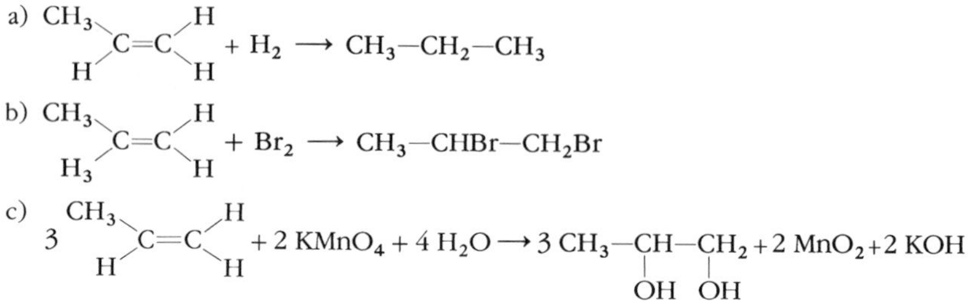 a)
$$\underset{H}{\overset{CH_3}{>}}C=C\underset{H}{\overset{H}{<}} + H_2 \longrightarrow CH_3-CH_2-CH_3$$

b)
$$\underset{H_3}{\overset{CH_3}{>}}C=C\underset{H}{\overset{H}{<}} + Br_2 \longrightarrow CH_3-CHBr-CH_2Br$$

c)
$$3\,\underset{H}{\overset{CH_3}{>}}C=C\underset{H}{\overset{H}{<}} + 2\,KMnO_4 + 4\,H_2O \longrightarrow 3\,CH_3-\underset{\substack{|\\OH}}{CH}-\underset{\substack{|\\OH}}{CH_2} + 2\,MnO_2 + 2\,KOH$$

17. a) 2-pentyne   b) 2,2,5,5-tetramethyl-3-hexyne

18. a) $CH_3-C\equiv C-CH_3$ b) 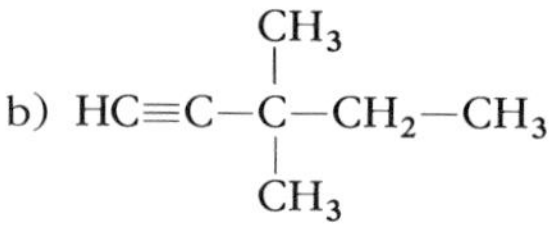
$$HC\equiv C-\underset{\substack{|\\CH_3}}{\overset{\substack{CH_3\\|}}{C}}-CH_2-CH_3$$

19. a) $HC\equiv C-CH_2-CH_3 + 2\,H_2 \longrightarrow CH_3-CH_2-CH_2-CH_3$

b) $HC\equiv C-CH_2-CH_3 + 2\,Br_2 \longrightarrow CHBr_2-CBr_2-CH_2-CH_3$

20. a) $HC\equiv CH + 2\,HBr \longrightarrow CH_3-CHBr_2$

b) $HC\equiv C-CH_3 + 2\,HBr \longrightarrow CH_3-CBr_2-CH_3$

21.

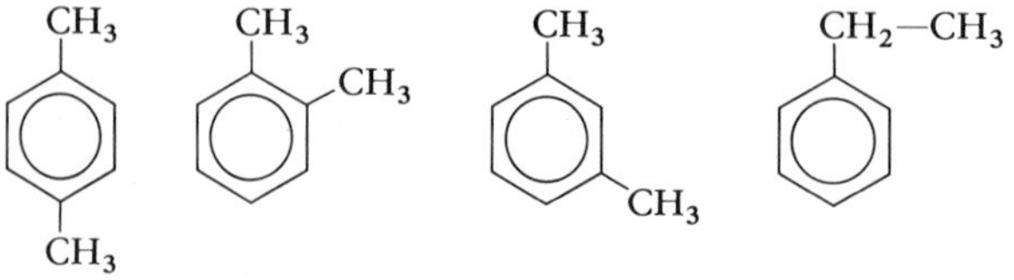

22.

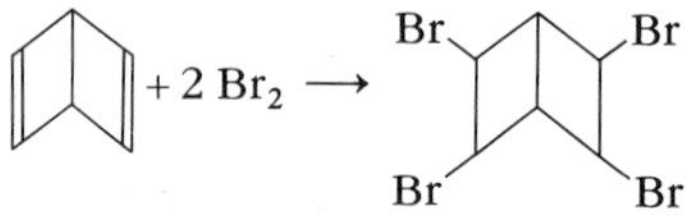

---

1. If organic and inorganic compounds were known from the time of the alchemists, why is Wöhler often referred to as the father of organic chemistry?

2. What carbon-containing compounds are not generally considered to be organic compounds?

3. How do the properties of organic compounds differ from those of inorganic compounds?

4. What are the unique features of organic compounds?

5. Explain briefly the difference between alkanes, alkenes, and alkynes.

6. Why do we draw tetrahedral bonds on paper as 90° when they are really 109.5°?

7. Explain the difference between a structural formula and a condensed formula.

8. Why is there a difference in structural formula between a straight-chain alkane and the cycloalkane having the same number of carbon atoms?

9. Explain briefly how we construct the name of a branched-chain alkane.

10. Why should municipal water sources be free of any significant quantities of organic compounds?

11. Briefly describe the difference between tar sands and oil shale.

12. Explain what is meant by the following terms:
    a) fractionation   c) cracking
    b) pyrolysis   d) reforming

13. Explain the difference between each of the following:
    a) structural isomers and geometric isomers
    b) addition reactions and substitution reactions

14. How do the addition reactions of alkynes differ from the addition reactions of alkenes?

15. a) What is our current bonding model for the benzene molecule?
    b) What is the evidence for the accuracy of this model.

16. What does the discovery of Dewar and Ladenburg forms of C_6H_6 teach us?

PROBLEMS   *The Characteristics of Organic Compounds*

17. Compound A melts at 801 °C and is very soluble in water, whereas compound B melts at 24 °C and is insoluble in water. Which of these two compounds is more likely to be organic?

Hydrocarbons

18. Draw the electron-dot structure of C_3H_6, a molecule with one carbon-carbon single bond and one carbon-carbon double bond.

Structural Isomers

19. Pair up those formulas below which represent the same compound:
    a) $CH_3-CH_2-CH_2-CH_2-CH_3$ c) $CH_2-CH_2-CH_2-CH_3$
                                              |
                                             CH_3

    b) $CH_3-CH_2-CH-CH_3$ CH_3
                   | |
                  CH_3 d) $CH_3-CH-CH_2-CH_3$

e) 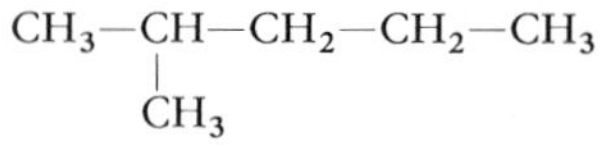 $CH_3-CH-CH_2-CH_2-CH_3$
    $|$
    CH_3

g) 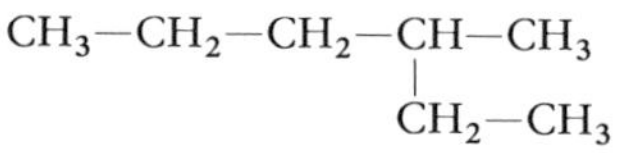 $CH_3-CH_2-CH_2-CH-CH_3$
    $|$
    CH_2-CH_3

f) 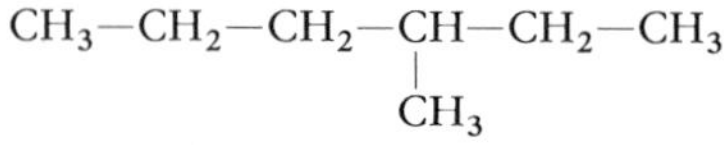 $CH_3-CH_2-CH_2-CH-CH_2-CH_3$
    $|$
    CH_3

20. Write the condensed formula for each possible structural isomer of
   a) C_4H_{10} b) C_6H_{14} c) C_7H_{16}
   Hint: there are two isomers of a), five of b), and nine of c).

21. Write the condensed formula for each possible structural isomer of
   C_8H_{16}, which is a cyclo-alkane having a six-membered ring.

The Naming of Alkanes

22. Give the IUPAC name for each of the following alkanes:

a) 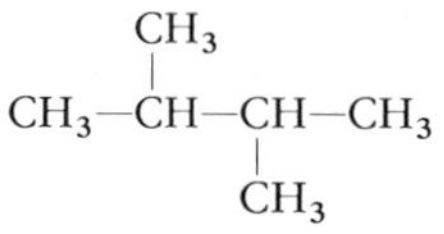
$$CH_3$$
$$|$$
$$CH_3-CH-CH-CH_3$$
$$|$$
$$CH_3$$

b) 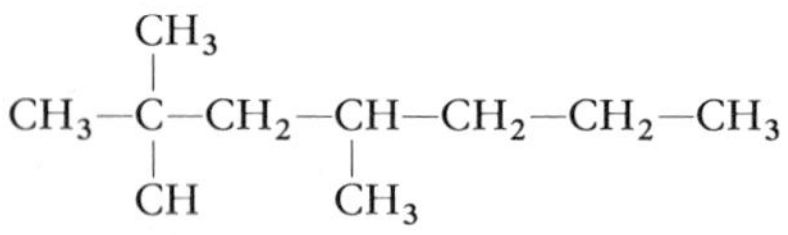
$$CH_3$$
$$|$$
$$CH_3-C-CH_2-CH-CH_2-CH_2-CH_3$$
$$|\qquad\qquad|$$
$$CH\qquad CH_3$$

c) $H_2C-CH-CH_3$
   $\ \ \ |\ \ \ \ |$
   $\ H_2C-CH_2$

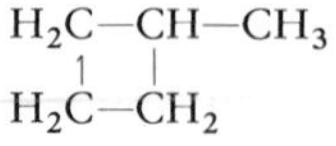

d) 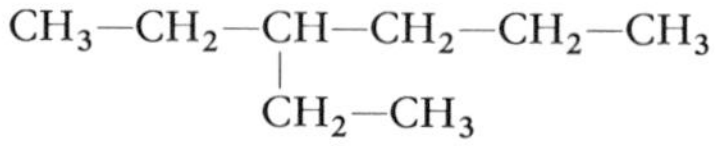 $CH_3-CH_2-CH-CH_2-CH_2-CH_3$
   $\qquad\qquad\ |$
   $\qquad\qquad CH_2-CH_3$

e) 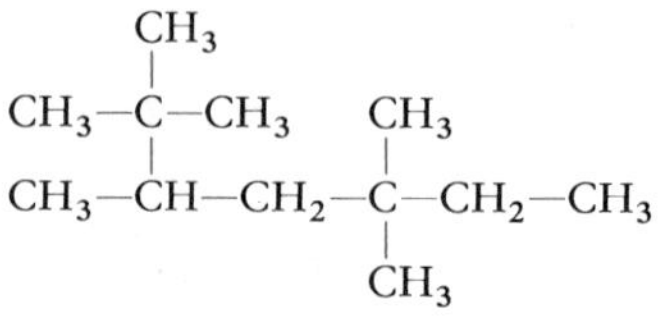
$$CH_3$$
$$|$$
$$CH_3-C-CH_3\qquad CH_3$$
$$|\qquad\qquad\ \ |$$
$$CH_3-CH-CH_2-C-CH_2-CH_3$$
$$|$$
$$CH_3$$

23. Determine the IUPAC name corresponding to each of the following
   alkanes:

a) 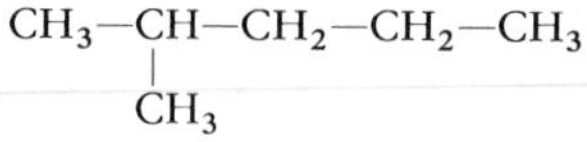 $CH_3-CH-CH_2-CH_2-CH_3$
   $\qquad\ |$
   $\qquad CH_3$

b) 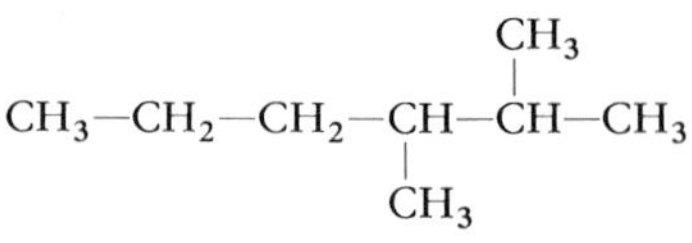
$$CH_3$$
$$|$$
$$CH_3-CH_2-CH_2-CH-CH-CH_3$$
$$|$$
$$CH_3$$

c) 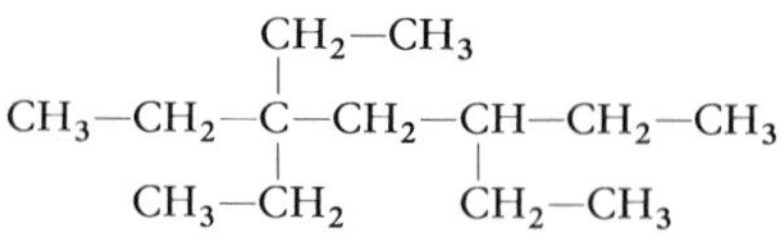
$$CH_2-CH_3$$
$$|$$
$$CH_3-CH_2-C-CH_2-CH-CH_2-CH_3$$
$$|\qquad\qquad\ |$$
$$CH_3-CH_2\qquad CH_2-CH_3$$

d)

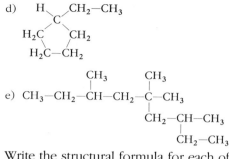

e)

$$CH_3-CH_2-\underset{\underset{CH_2-\underset{\underset{CH_2-CH_3}{|}}{CH-CH_3}}{|}}{\overset{\overset{CH_3}{|}}{CH}}-CH_2-\underset{\underset{CH_2-\underset{\underset{CH_2-CH_3}{|}}{CH-CH_3}}{|}}{\overset{\overset{CH_3}{|}}{C}}-CH_3$$

24. Write the structural formula for each of the following alkanes:

a) 3,4-dimethylnonane   c) ethylcyclopentane

b) 3-ethylpentane   d) 2,2,3,3-tetramethylbutane

25. Write the condensed formula for each of the following alkanes:

a) 2-methylhexane   c) cyclobutane

b) 3,5-dimethylheptane   d) 1,3,5-trimethylcyclohexane

The Properties of Alkanes

26. You have a bottle of hexane and a bottle of octane. However, the labels have fallen off. Suggest two physical properties that you could use to distinguish between them.

27. When one mole of a particular alkane is combusted, 10 mol of carbon dioxide and 11 mol of water are produced. What was the molecular formula of the alkane?

28. Write the condensed formulas for all the possible products of reaction between ethane and chlorine gas in the presence of ultraviolet light.

Alkenes

29. Give the IUPAC name for each of the following alkenes:

a) $CH_3-CH=CH-CH_3$

b) 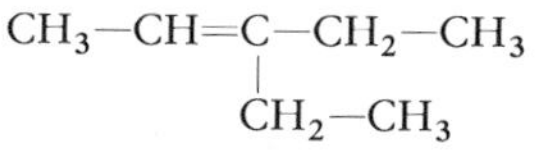 $CH_3-CH=\underset{\underset{CH_2-CH_3}{|}}{C}-CH_2-CH_3$

c) $CH_3-\underset{\underset{CH_3}{|}}{C}=CH-CH_2-CH_3$

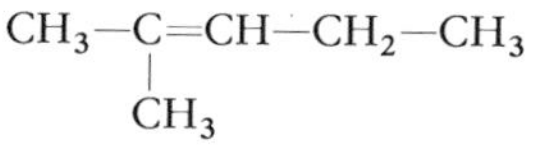

d) 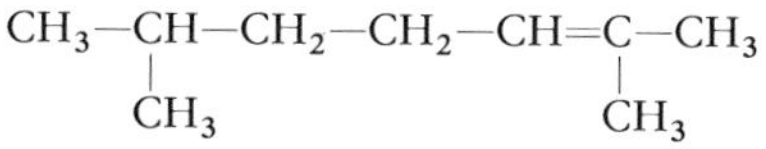 $CH_3-\underset{\underset{CH_3}{|}}{CH}-CH_2-CH_2-CH=\underset{\underset{CH_3}{|}}{C}-CH_3$

e) 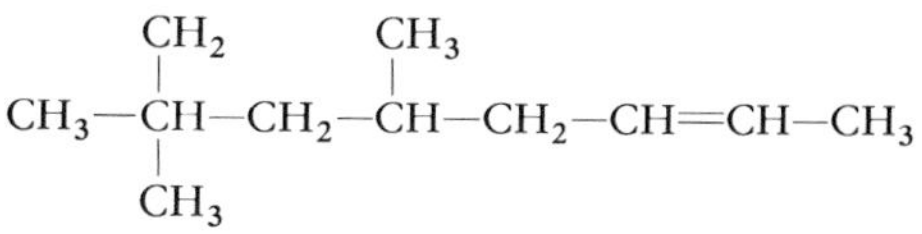 $CH_3-\underset{\underset{CH_3}{|}}{\overset{\overset{CH_2}{|}}{CH}}-CH_2-\underset{\overset{\overset{CH_3}{|}}{}}{CH}-CH_2-CH=CH-CH_3$

30. What is the IUPAC name for each of the alkenes shown below:

a) $CH_3-CH=CH_2$

b) 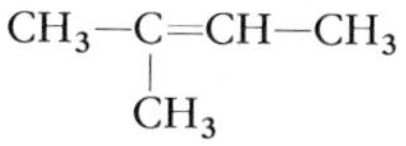 $CH_3-\underset{\underset{CH_3}{|}}{C}=CH-CH_3$

c) $CH_3-CH_2-CH_2-CH_2-CH=CH-CH_3$

d)
$$CH_3 \underset{CH_3}{\overset{}{\diagdown}} C=C \underset{CH_3}{\overset{CH_3}{\diagup}}$$

e)
$$CH_3-CH_2-\underset{\underset{CH_2-CH_3}{|}}{\overset{\overset{CH_2-CH_3}{|}}{C}}=C-CH_2-CH_2-CH_3$$

31. Two of the compounds shown in Question 29 exhibit geometric isomerism. For each one draw the structures of the two isomers and name them accordingly.

32. Which one of the alkenes listed in Question 30 exhibits *cis-trans* isomerism? Draw the structures of the isomers and give the appropriate IUPAC names.

33. a) Draw the condensed formula for each of the alkenes having the formula C_4H_8. Which of these alkenes can exist as *cis-trans* isomers?

   b) What other structures can you draw that correspond to the formula C_4H_8? Give the IUPAC name for each structure that you draw.

34. Write the condensed formula of each of the alkenes having the molecular formula C_5H_{10}. Which of these alkenes exhibit geometrical isomerism?

35. Write the condensed formula for each of the following alkenes:
   a) 1-hexene
   b) cyclohexene
   c) *cis*-2-butene
   d) 4,4-dimethyl-2-pentene
   e) 4-ethyl-3-octene

36. Write the condensed formula for each of the alkenes listed below:
   a) 1-butene
   b) *trans*-2-butene
   c) 5,6-dimethyl-3-octene
   d) 3-ethyl-1-pentene
   e) 2,3-dimethyl-2-butene

37. Write a balanced equation for the reaction between the following compounds:
   a) 1,3-butadiene and bromine
   b) 1-butene and potassium permanganate

Alkynes

38. Give the IUPAC name for each of the following alkynes:
   a) $HC{\equiv}C-CH_2-CH_2-CH_3$
   b) $CH_3-C{\equiv}C-\underset{\underset{CH_3}{|}}{CH}-CH_3$

   c) $CH_3-C{\equiv}C-\underset{\underset{CH_3}{|}}{\overset{\overset{CH_3}{|}}{C}}-CH_2-CH_3$

$$\text{d) } CH_3-CH_2-C\equiv C-\underset{\underset{CH_3}{|}}{CH}-CH_2-\underset{\overset{|}{CH_3}}{\overset{\overset{CH_3}{|}}{CH}}-CH_3$$

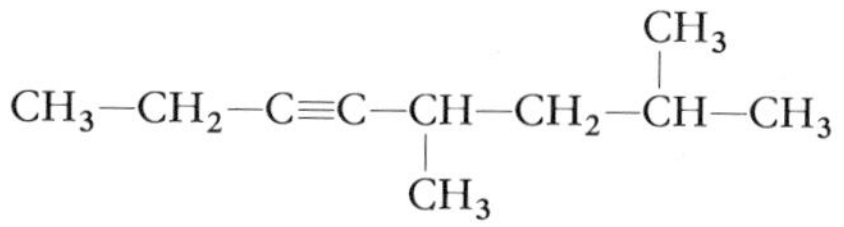

$$\text{e) } CH_3-C\equiv C-(CH_2)_3-\underset{\underset{CH_3}{|}}{CH}-CH_3$$

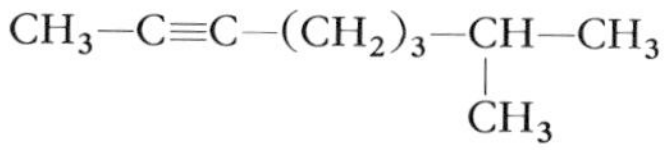

39. What is the IUPAC name of each alkyne shown below:

a) $CH_3-C\equiv C-CH_3$

b) 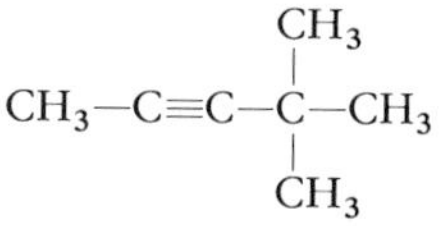 $CH_3-C\equiv C-\underset{\underset{CH_3}{|}}{\overset{\overset{CH_3}{|}}{C}}-CH_3$

c) $CH_3-CH_2-\underset{\underset{CH_3}{|}}{CH}-C\equiv CH$

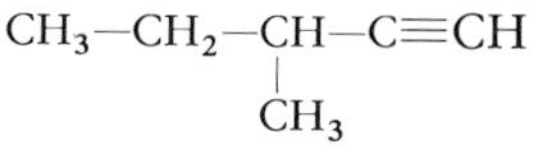

d) 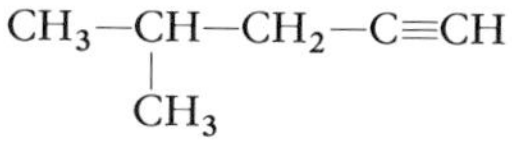 $CH_3-\underset{\underset{CH_3}{|}}{CH}-CH_2-C\equiv CH$

e) 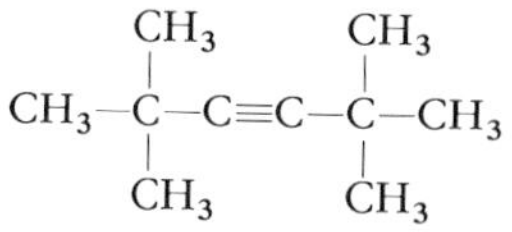 $CH_3-\underset{\underset{CH_3}{|}}{\overset{\overset{CH_3}{|}}{C}}-C\equiv C-\underset{\underset{CH_3}{|}}{\overset{\overset{CH_3}{|}}{C}}-CH_3$

40. Write the condensed formula for each of the following alkynes:

a) 1-heptyne   d) 2,3-dimethyl-4-octyne
b) 3-hexyne   e) 2,2,5,5-tetramethyl-3-hexyne
c) 3,4-dimethyl-1-pentyne

41. Write the condensed formula for each of the alkynes below:

a) 2-pentyne   d) 3,3-diethyl-1-octyne
b) 5-methyl-1-hexyne   e) 3,3-dimethyl-1-butyne
c) 4,4-dimethyl-2-pentyne

42. a) Write the condensed formula for each possible alkyne having the molecular formula C_4H_6.

b) What other condensed formulas can you draw that correspond to a molecular formula of C_4H_6?

43. Write the condensed formula for each alkyne having the molecular formula C_5H_8.

44. Write a balanced equation for the reaction of $CH_3-C\equiv C-C\equiv C-CH_3$ with the following:

a) hydrogen gas
b) bromine

Aromatic Compounds

45. Write a balanced equation for the reaction of the following:

a) benzene with chlorine plus an iron catalyst
b) toluene with hydrogen under high pressure with a platinum catalyst

46. A second atom of bromine can be substituted into the benzene ring to give $C_6H_4Br_2$. How many structural isomers of this compound will exist?

47. Draw all the possible structural isomers of C_4H_6. Classify the compounds as alkynes or alkenes. Identify which compound(s) can exist as geometric isomers.

48. We can express the formula of an alkane as C_nH_{2n+2} where n is any integer. Use this form to express the formula of the following:
   a) a cyclic alkane   c) an alkyne
   b) an alkene   d) an alkadiene

49. Assuming that the average composition of gasoline can be represented by the formula C_8H_{18}, determine the following:
   a) Write a balanced equation for the reaction of gasoline with oxygen.
   b) Calculate the volume of carbon dioxide gas produced at $20\,°C$ and $100\,kPa$ pressure from the combustion of $1.00\,L$ of gasoline (density $0.69\,g \cdot mL^{-1}$).

50. If $1.0 \times 10^2\,g$ of calcium carbide is to be used to generate acetylene in the laboratory by its reaction with water determine the following:
   a) What volume of water (density $1.00\,g \cdot mL^{-1}$) will be needed to completely react with calcium carbide?
   b) What volume of ethyne (acetylene gas) measured at $100\,kPa$ and $25\,°C$, will be produced when the two reactants are mixed?

1. What is the International Union of Pure and Applied Chemistry (IUPAC)? Find out where it is located, what its functions are and who supports it.

2. Molecular models enable us to obtain a much better understanding of the three-dimensional nature of organic compounds. Obtain a set of molecular models and construct examples of each of the four classes of hydrocarbons that we have studied in this chapter. Prepare a display of these models, giving information about the names, properties and uses of each of the compounds exhibited.

3. In addition to gasoline and other fuels, petroleum can be converted into a wide variety of useful products ranging from edible oil products, such as powdered coffee whiteners or whipped cream substitutes, to plastics and synthesized fibres. The production of chemicals from petroleum (i.e. the petrochemical industry) is very important to the Canadian economy. Prepare a report on this industry, giving details of the range of petrochemical products that are made in Canada.

4. As our hydrocarbon resources are used up, we must start using tar sands, as well as Arctic and off-shore oil reserves. Prepare a report that discusses the problems with each of these sources.

The Canadian Petroleum Industry

Petroleum deposits are formed over millions of years by the action of heat and pressure on decomposed marine organisms. Such deposits are most often found in sedimentary basins.

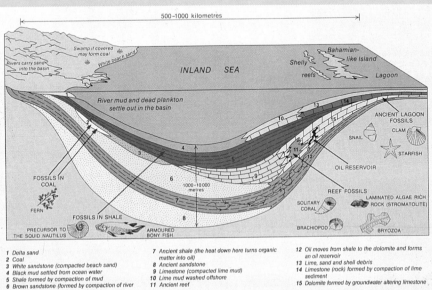

1 Delta sand
2 Coal
3 White sandstone (compacted beach sand)
4 Black mud settled from ocean water
5 Shale formed by compaction of mud
6 Brown sandstone (formed by compaction of river and delta sand)

7 Ancient shale (the heat down here turns organic matter into oil)
8 Ancient sandstone
9 Limestone (compacted lime mud)
10 Lime mud washed offshore
11 Ancient reef

12 Oil moves from shale to the dolomite and forms an oil reservoir
13 Lime, sand and shell debris
14 Limestone (rock) formed by compaction of lime sediment
15 Dolomite formed by groundwater altering limestone

In 1858, James Miller Williams purchased land in southwestern Ontario and obtained oil from a well dug to a depth of about 15 m. Williams drilled wells on the assumption that where there was oil on the surface, there would be oil underground. Today, deciding where to drill for oil is much more sophisticated and expensive.

Modern drilling operations continue around the clock. As many as 190 people can be involved in drilling a single onshore well.

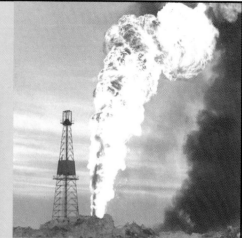

Oil seepages were discovered in western Canada as early as 1874, but it was not until the 1914 discovery of wet gas and oil at Turner Valley, southwest of Calgary, that oil fever swept Alberta. Today, several major oil companies have their Canadian headquarters in Calgary.

An extensive network of pipelines is used to distribute oil and gas to major North American markets.

One of the most spectacular discoveries of oil in western Canada occurred at Leduc, just south of Edmonton. About 100 onlookers were present when the well, Leduc 1, was 'brought in' at 4:00 p.m. on February 12, 1947.

Major oil and gas pipe line systems in Canada

There are about 200,000 km (125,000 miles) of oil and gas pipe lines in Canada, including gathering systems and main trunk lines.

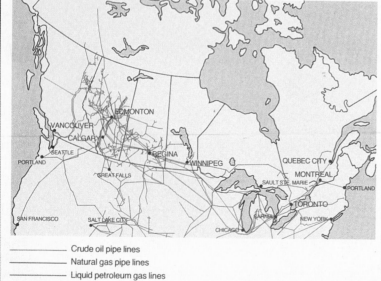

————— Crude oil pipe lines
————— Natural gas pipe lines
————— Liquid petroleum gas lines

In western Canada, the agricultural industry and the oil industry both use the same land.

PLATE 34 — THE CANADIAN PETROLEUM INDUSTRY

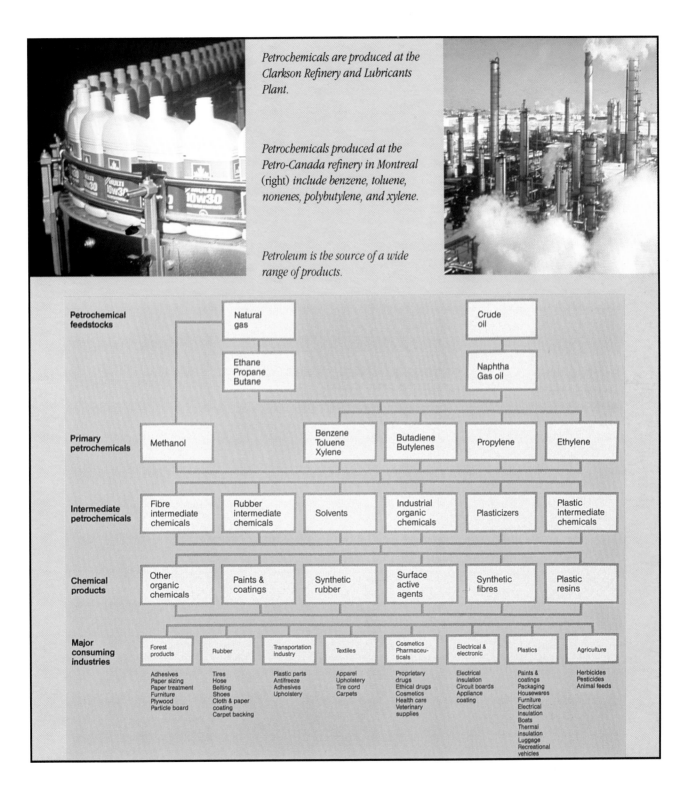

Petrochemicals are produced at the Clarkson Refinery and Lubricants Plant.

Petrochemicals produced at the Petro-Canada refinery in Montreal (right) include benzene, toluene, nonenes, polybutylene, and xylene.

Petroleum is the source of a wide range of products.

Petrochemical feedstocks

Natural gas

Crude oil

Ethane Propane Butane

Naphtha Gas oil

Primary petrochemicals

Methanol

Benzene Toluene Xylene

Butadiene Butylenes

Propylene

Ethylene

Intermediate petrochemicals

Fibre intermediate chemicals

Rubber intermediate chemicals

Solvents

Industrial organic chemicals

Plasticizers

Plastic intermediate chemicals

Chemical products

Other organic chemicals

Paints & coatings

Synthetic rubber

Surface active agents

Synthetic fibres

Plastic resins

Major consuming industries

Forest products

Rubber

Transportation industry

Textiles

Cosmetics Pharmaceuticals

Electrical & electronic

Plastics

Agriculture

Adhesives
Paper sizing
Paper treatment
Furniture
Plywood
Particle board

Tires
Hose
Belting
Shoes
Cloth & paper coating
Carpet backing

Plastic parts
Antifreeze
Adhesives
Upholstery

Apparel
Upholstery
Tire cord
Carpets

Proprietary drugs
Ethical drugs
Cosmetics
Health care
Veterinary supplies

Electrical insulation
Circuit boards
Appliance coating

Paints & coatings
Packaging
Housewares
Furniture
Electrical insulation
Boats
Thermal insulation
Luggage
Recreational vehicles

Herbicides
Pesticides
Animal feeds

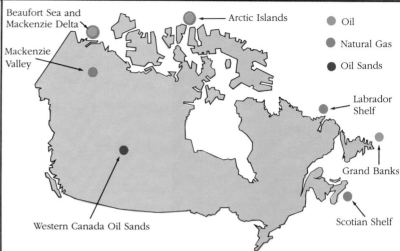

Beaufort Sea and
Mackenzie Delta

Arctic Islands

Oil

Natural Gas

Oil Sands

Mackenzie
Valley

Labrador
Shelf

Grand Banks

Western Canada Oil Sands

Scotian Shelf

As conventional supplies of oil and gas are depleted, oil companies must develop new sources to meet Canada's future requirements. The three main areas of activity are in the Arctic, off the coast of Newfoundland, and the oil sand deposits in Alberta and Saskatchewan.

Enormous excavators, such as the one pictured below, are used in the open-pit mining of oil sands.

Offshore oil rigs must operate for much of the year under severe ocean conditions. In 1982, 84 men drowned when the Ocean Ranger capsized off the coast of Newfoundland.

The Franklin Mountains provide an impressive back-drop to the man-made island upon which this Artic oil rig is located.

PLATE 36 — THE CANADIAN PETROLEUM INDUSTRY

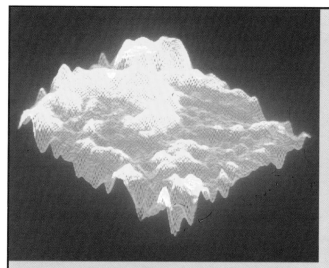

Research and high technology play an important role in the development of new petroleum sources. Above we see a computer-generated 3-D seismic image of an underground sand channel. Such images are of great assistance in the search for new sources of oil.

Chemists continue to play a role in the development of new petroleum products.

Far from Petro-Canada's headquarters, studies carried out in the Arctic help to increase the safety of off-shore drilling.

The Unlimited Potential of Plastics

One of the earliest forms of plastic was shellac. When mixed with wood flour and other fillers, it formed a useful moulding material. The photograph cases above were made in the 1850s.

Cellulose acetate has been used in eyeglass frames for over 50 years.

One major advantage of plastics is that they can be made to resemble other materials. Below, the plastic products in the 'tortoise shell look' are displayed next to a genuine tortoise shell.

Cellulose plastics have made the film industry possible. The cellulose nitrate originally used for film was highly flammable and has been replaced by the less flammable cellulose acetate.

PLATE 38 — THE UNLIMITED POTENTIAL OF PLASTICS

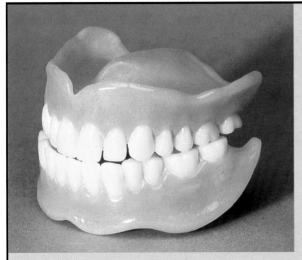

Acrylic resins, developed in the 1950s, are used in the production of dentures.

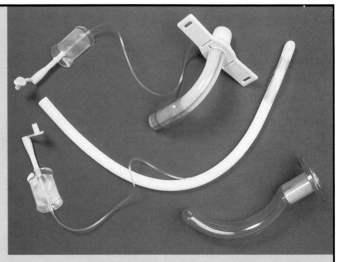

Plastics used in disposable surgical instruments allow for high standards of hygiene and safety.

Replacement body parts containing plastics, such as the artificial legs of the man holding the basketball, provide hope for amputees.

Polyvinylchloride is used in bandages, in waterproof clothing, and imitation leather.

This plastic-based, bullet-proof vest and raincoat combination sells for about $2000.00.

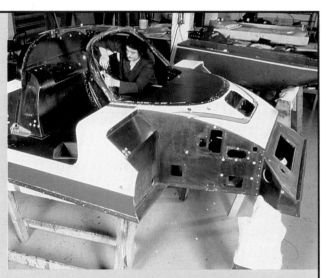

The body and chassis of this Le Mans racing car are being made from a combination of carbon fibres and epoxy resin.

The recording industry uses various plastics, including polyvinylchloride for long-play records, polycarbonate for compact discs, and polyester for tapes.

PLATE 40 — THE UNLIMITED POTENTIAL OF PLASTICS

Organic Chemistry II:
Common Functional Groups

In the previous chapter we discussed organic compounds that contained only carbon and hydrogen. Most organic compounds also contain at least one other element. In this chapter we will mainly be discussing compounds that contain carbon, hydrogen, and oxygen. We will see that this combination of elements gives rise to a number of functional groups, each of which undergoes unique types of reaction. We will also examine the chemistry of some organic compounds containing halogens and nitrogen.

Alcohols

15.1

Members of the alcohol family all contain a **hydroxyl group** (—OH). The presence of this group has a major effect on the physical properties of these compounds. Unlike hydrocarbons, in which the only intermolecular forces are dispersion forces, alcohols can form hydrogen bonds with one another. As we discussed in Section 4.6, the hydrogen bond is a very strong intermolecular force. As a result, the melting points and boiling points of alcohols are far higher than those of alkanes having a similar molar mass. Even methanol, CH_3OH, the first of the alcohol series, is a liquid at room temperature.

Another major difference between alcohols and hydrocarbons is their solubility in water. Hydrocarbons are immiscible with water while many alcohols are miscible. In fact the first three members of the alcohol series methanol, ethanol, and 1-propanol are miscible with water in any proportion. As the length of the carbon chain increases however, the miscibility is reduced. The higher members of the series are only partially soluble in water. We can explain this behaviour in terms of the intermolecular forces. As the carbon chain becomes longer, there is an increasingly large nonpolar component to the molecule. The hydrogen-bonding —OH group becomes an increasingly small portion of the molecule. Thus the dispersion forces of the nonpolar carbon chains come to dominate the physical properties of the molecule.

Figure 15.1

A graph showing the solubility of alcohol in water versus number of carbon atoms in the alcohol chain.

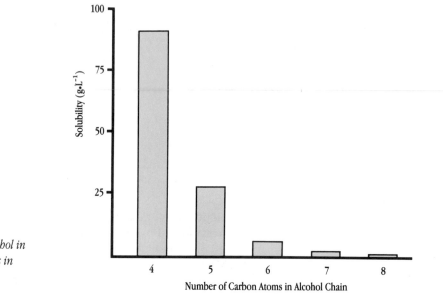

The Naming of Alcohols

The IUPAC name for an alcohol is obtained by taking the name of the alkane containing the same number of carbon atoms as the longest carbon chain, deleting the ending -*e*, and adding the ending -*ol*. We have listed the IUPAC and common names of the simplest alcohols in Table 15.1. If there is more than one possible isomer, the location of the hydroxyl group is indicated by the number of the carbon to which the hydroxyl group is attached.

TABLE 15.1 IUPAC and Common Names of Some Simple Alcohols

Formula	IUPAC name	Common Names
CH_3OH	methanol	methyl alcohol, wood alcohol, methyl hydrate
CH_3CH_2OH	ethanol	ethyl alcohol, grain alcohol
$CH_3CH_2CH_2OH$	1-propanol	n-propyl alcohol
$CH_3CH(OH)CH_3$	2-propanol	isopropyl alcohol, rubbing alcohol
$(CH_3)_3COH$	2-methyl-2-propanol	t-butyl alcohol
$(CH_3)_2CHCH_2OH$	3-methyl-1-propanol	isobutyl alcohol
$CH_3(CH_2)_3OH$	1-butanol	n-butyl alcohol
$CH_3(CH_2)_4OH$	1-pentanol	amyl alcohol

The following example illustrates the method of naming alcohols:

$$CH_3-CH-CH_2-CH-CH_3$$
$$CH_3 OH$$

1. Identify the longest carbon chain and name the alkane from which it is derived.

$$CH_3-CH-CH_2-CH-CH_3$$
$$CH_3 OH$$

There are five carbons in the longest chain. The base name is pentane.

2. Locate the hydroxyl functional group. Replace the alkane ending of $-e$ by the alcohol ending $-ol$.

$$CH_3-CH-CH_2-CH-CH_3$$
$$CH_3 OH$$

Remove the ending -e, add the ending -ol, hence pentanol.

3. Identify the location of the hydroxyl group, counting from the lowest end:

$$\overset{5}{CH_3}-\overset{4}{CH}-\overset{3}{CH_2}-\overset{2}{CH}-\overset{1}{CH_3}$$
$$CH_3 OH$$

A hydroxyl group is on carbon atom 2, hence 2-pentanol.

4. Identify and number any alkyl substituents as in the rules for naming branched-chain hydrocarbons.

$$CH_3-\overset{4}{CH}-CH_2-\overset{2}{CH}-CH_3$$
$$CH_3 OH$$

The methyl group is on carbon 4, hence 4-methyl-2-pentanol.

It is possible to have compounds containing two or three hydroxyl groups. When naming such compounds, the endings -*diol* and -*triol* are used. The location of each hydroxyl group must be identified with the numerical prefix. For example, HO—CH$_2$—CH$_2$—CH$_2$—OH will have the name 1,3-propanediol. Notice that we leave the "*e*" in the name.

Isomers of Alcohols

When we look at some of the reactions of alcohols, it is necessary to look not just at the functional group, but also at the carbon atom to which the functional group is attached. There are three distinct types of alcohols, and we can see an example of each type if we consider the three isomers of C$_4$H$_9$OH.

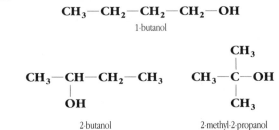

CH$_3$—CH$_2$—CH$_2$—CH$_2$—OH
1-butanol

2-butanol   2-methyl-2-propanol

In 1-butanol, only one alkyl group is attached to the carbon atom bearing the hydroxyl group. Alcohols in which such an arrangement occurs are called **primary alcohols**. In 2-butanol, two alkyl groups are attached to the carbon bearing the hydroxyl group. Such alcohols are called **secondary alcohols**. In 2-methyl-2-propanol, the hydroxyl group is attached to a carbon atom that is also bonded to three alkyl groups. This is a **tertiary alcohol**. We can summarize the differences between the three classes of alcohol using the symbol "R" to denote an alkyl group.

$$
\begin{array}{ccc}
\text{H} & \text{R} & \text{R} \\
| & | & | \\
\text{R—C—OH} & \text{R'—C—OH} & \text{R'—C—OH} \\
| & | & | \\
\text{H} & \text{H} & \text{R''}
\end{array}
$$

primary   secondary   tertiary
alcohol   alcohol   alcohol

Acid-Base Reactions of Alcohols

Alcohols, like water, can act as Brønsted-Lowry acids or bases. The reaction of an alcohol with sodium metal is an example of the acidic nature of alcohols.

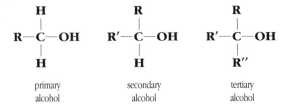

2 CH$_3$—CH$_2$—OH + 2 Na $\longrightarrow$ 2 CH$_3$—CH$_2$—O$^-$ + 2 Na$^+$ + H$_2$
ethanol   ethoxide
ion

2 HOH + 2 Na $\longrightarrow$ 2 Na$^+$ + 2 OH$^-$ + H$_2$
hydroxide
ion

With a concentrated acid, such as sulfuric acid, an alcohol will react as a base by accepting a proton and forming an oxonium ion, or protonated alcohol:

$$CH_3-CH_2-OH + H_2SO_4 \rightleftharpoons CH_3-CH_2-OH_2^+ + HSO_4^-$$
ethyloxonium
ion

$$HOH + HCl \longrightarrow H_3O^+ + Cl^-$$
hydronium
ion

The ethoxide ion is the equivalent of the hydroxide ion, while the ethyloxonium ion parallels the hydronium ion.

The transfer of a proton from an acid to an alcohol to form the protonated alcohol is the first step in a number of important organic reactions. With concentrated sulfuric acid, there are two possible products, depending upon the choice of reaction conditions. With an excess of acid and heating, the protonated alcohol eliminates a molecule of water to form an alkene. The dehydration of alcohol is an illustration of a common organic reaction called an **elimination reaction**. Ethanol, for example, forms ethene as the product:

$$CH_3-CH_2-OH_2^+ \longrightarrow CH_2{=}CH_2 + H_2O + H^+$$
ethene

On the other hand, with an excess of the alcohol the protonated alcohol molecule will react with another molecule of alcohol to form a new class of compounds called an ether, by again eliminating a molecule of water. Such joining of molecules is known as a **condensation reaction**. Ethanol, for example, produces ethoxyethane as the major product:

$$CH_3-CH_2-OH_2^+ + HO-CH_2-CH_3 \xrightarrow{140\,°C} CH_3-CH_2-O-CH_2-CH_3 + H_2O + H^+$$
ethoxyethane

If the acid used is concentrated hydrochloric, hydrobromic, or hydroiodic, the halide ion displaces H_2O from the oxonium ion. Thus the overall result of this substitution reaction is the replacement of the hydroxyl group by a halogen.

$$CH_3-CH_2-OH + HCl \longrightarrow CH_3-CH_2-OH_2^+ + Cl^-$$
$$CH_3-CH_2-OH_2^+ + Cl^- \longrightarrow CH_3-CH_2-Cl + H_2O$$

This reaction can be used as a means of distinguishing among primary, secondary, and tertiary alcohols. If we add concentrated hydrochloric acid containing zinc chloride (known as Lucas Reagent) as a catalyst to an alcohol, the rate of reaction is found to be different for each class. Tertiary alcohols rapidly give a cloudiness to the solution, due to the immiscibility of the alkyl chloride produced. A secondary alcohol requires up to five minutes for the cloudiness to develop, while primary alcohols take much longer still.

Oxidation Reactions of Alcohols

Alcohols, like most organic compounds, burn in air to produce carbon dioxide. Thus alcohols are good fuels.

$$2 \, CH_3OH_{(l)} + 3 \, O_{2 \, (g)} \longrightarrow 2 \, CO_{2 \, (g)} + 4 \, H_2O_{(l)}$$

Combustion represents a drastic way of oxidizing an alcohol. The reagents most frequently used for a milder oxidation are dichromate ion or permanganate ion in acid solution. The half-reactions for these oxidizing agents are as follows:

$$Cr_2O_7{}^{2-}{}_{(aq)} + 14 \, H^+{}_{(aq)} + 6 \, e^- \longrightarrow 2 \, Cr^{3+}{}_{(aq)} + 7 \, H_2O_{(l)}$$
$$MnO_4{}^-{}_{(aq)} + 4 \, H^+{}_{(aq)} + 3 \, e^- \longrightarrow MnO_{2 \, (s)} + 2 \, H_2O_{(l)}$$

Both of these reactions are accompanied by colour changes. When acidic dichromate is used, the orange colour of dichromate is replaced by the deep green colour of the chromium(III) ion. Alternatively, if permanganate is used as the oxidizing agent, the deep purple of the permanganate ion disappears and a brown sludge of the insoluble manganese(IV) oxide is formed. Unlike most inorganic reactions with permanganate, reduction to the colourless manganese(II) ion does not normally occur in the reaction with an alcohol.

Each type of alcohol undergoes a different oxidation reaction. With a primary alcohol, two hydrogen atoms are initially lost to give a product containing the $-C{\overset{O}{\underset{H}{\diagdown}}}$ functional group, and called *aldehyde*.

$$CH_3-CH_2-OH \longrightarrow CH_3-C{\overset{O}{\underset{H}{\diagdown}}} + 2 \, H^+ + 2 \, e^-$$

If oxidation is continued, the hydrogen on the aldehyde functional group can be oxidized to a hydroxyl group. The $-C{\overset{O}{\underset{OH}{\diagdown}}}$ functional group is called a *carboxylic acid* group. The permanganate ion is such a strong oxidizing agent that the carboxylic acid is usually produced directly from the alcohol:

$$CH_3-C{\overset{O}{\underset{H}{\diagdown}}} + H_2O \longrightarrow CH_3-C{\overset{O}{\underset{OH}{\diagdown}}} + 2 \, H^+ + 2 \, e^-$$

For a secondary alcohol, the same first step occurs. That is, oxidation occurs by the removal of two hydrogen atoms, one of which is from the hydroxyl group. Since the secondary alcohol does not have another hydrogen atom to form a hydroxyl group, a second step in the oxidation is not possible. The product of this reaction is called a *ketone*.

$$\underset{\underset{\displaystyle H}{|}}{\overset{\overset{\displaystyle OH}{|}}{CH_3-\overset{}{C}-CH_3}} \longrightarrow CH_3-\overset{\overset{\displaystyle O}{\|}}{C}-CH_3 + 2\,H^- + 2\,e^-$$

The oxidation of both primary and secondary alcohols involves the removal of a hydrogen from the carbon to which the hydroxyl is attached. A tertiary alcohol cannot be oxidized under normal conditions because it has no such hydrogen atom.

EXAMPLE   **15.1**   Write a balanced equation for the reaction of ethanol with permanganate ion to give acetic acid and manganese(IV) oxide.

SOLUTION   We will use the half-reaction method to derive this redox equation. The half-reaction for the reduction of permanganate was given above. That is,

$$MnO_4^- + 4\,H^+ + 3\,e^- \longrightarrow MnO_2 + 2\,H_2O$$

(Alternatively, we could have derived it using the ion-electron or oxidation number method).
To obtain a half-reaction equation for the oxidation, we write the species:

$$CH_3CH_2OH \longrightarrow CH_3CO_2H$$

Balance for species other than hydrogen or oxygen. In this case, carbon:

$$CH_3CH_2OH \longrightarrow CH_3CO_2H \qquad \text{(no change)}$$

Balance for oxygen using one water molecule for each oxygen you require:

$$CH_3CH_2OH + H_2O \longrightarrow CH_3CO_2H$$

Balance for hydrogen using a hydrogen ion for each hydrogen you require:

$$CH_3CH_2OH + H_2O \longrightarrow CH_3CO_2H + 4\,H^+$$

Balance for charge with electrons:

$$CH_3CH_2OH + H_2O \longrightarrow CH_3CO_2H + 4\,H^+ + 4\,e^-$$

To combine the half-reaction equations, the electrons must "cancel out." Thus the permanganate half-reaction must be multiplied by four and the ethanol half-reaction must be multiplied by three.

$$4\,MnO_4^- + 16\,H^+ + 12\,e^- \longrightarrow 4\,MnO_2 + 8\,H_2O$$
$$3\,CH_3CH_2OH + 3\,H_2O \longrightarrow 3\,CH_3CO_2H + 12\,H^+ + 12\,e^-$$

Adding the half-reactions gives:

$$3\,CH_3CH_2OH + 4\,MnO_4^- + 4\,H^+ \longrightarrow 3\,CH_3CO_2H + 4\,MnO_2 + 5\,H_2O$$

Figure 15.2

Methanol is often referred to as methyl hydrate.

Common Alcohols

Methanol is commercially obtained from methane, the major component in natural gas. The methane undergoes partial combustion to carbon monoxide and hydrogen gas, and the products are then passed over a catalyst to produce methanol.

$$2 \, CH_{4(g)} + O_{2(g)} \longrightarrow 2 \, CO_{(g)} + 4 \, H_{2(g)}$$

$$CO_{(g)} + 2 \, H_{2(g)} \xrightarrow[ZnO/Cr_2O_3]{350 \, ^\circ C/20 \, MPa} CH_3OH_{(g)}$$

Methanol is used as an ingredient in some brands of paint stripper, as windshield wiper fluid, and is used in some types of printing processes. It is also an important starting material from which many organic compounds can be synthesized.

Pure methanol can be used in modified internal combustion engines and as an octane-booster of normal gasoline. Because methanol is only slightly soluble in alkanes, an equal volume of 2-methyl-2-propanol is mixed with it for this latter use. This three-component mixture forms a single, liquid phase.

Methanol, also known as wood alcohol or methyl hydrate, is poisonous. Ingestion of only 15 mL of methanol by an adult (less for children) will cause blindness, and 30 mL can be fatal. Many deaths and permanent disabilities have resulted from the consumption of homemade distilled beverages that contained methanol. Methanol is readily absorbed through the skin and lungs, and the danger from inhaled or skin-absorbed methanol is much higher than that caused by drinking. The use of methanol should be avoided wherever possible.

Ethanol has been produced by the fermentation of sugar or starch solutions using yeast enzymes for at least the last nine thousand years:

$$C_6H_{12}O_{6(aq)} \longrightarrow 2 \, CH_3-CH_2-OH_{(g)} + 2 \, CO_{2(g)}$$

Figure 15.3

The shape of the ethanol molecule,
C_2H_5OH:
a) as a ball-and-stick model;
b) as a space-filling model.

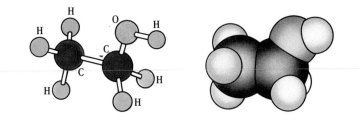

The yeast cells die when the ethanol content of the fermentation mixture reaches between 12–18 % ethanol (depending upon the yeast strain). The proportion of ethanol in this mixture can only be increased further by distillation. However, the product from the distillation of a water-ethanol mixture contains a maximum of 95 % ethanol. To remove the final 5 % of water, calcium oxide is added. The anhydrous ethanol can then be distilled off.

$$CaO_{(s)} + H_2O_{(\ell)} \longrightarrow Ca(OH)_{2\,(s)}$$

The fermentation process described above also produces trace amounts of other organic compounds. These compounds, which give each alcoholic beverage its unique flavour and odour, are produced from the non-starch components of the raw materials or from the yeast. Although alcohol consumption causes dehydration, it is these other organic compounds that are usually responsible for the headaches associated with drinking excessive quantities of ethanolic beverages. If large amounts of alcohol are consumed rapidly, death can result; a regular intake of smaller quantities causes liver and brain damage.

Industrially, ethanol is obtained by the catalyzed reaction of ethene with water:

$$CH_2{=}CH_{2\,(g)} + H_2O_{(\ell)} \xrightarrow[100\,°C]{H_2SO_4} CH_3{-}CH_2{-}OH_{(aq)}$$

To render commercial ethanol undrinkable, benzene or methanol is added. Alcohol that has been so treated is called denatured alcohol.

Ethanol is alkane-miscible and is added to gasoline to raise the octane rating. In parts of Canada and the United States, a number of oil companies sell "gasohol," an alcohol-gasoline mixture. These companies provide evidence that gasohol gives a better-combusting, lower-polluting reaction than gasoline alone. Also, the production of alcohol from farm crops provides rural employment, absorbs any grain surplus, and reduces the consumption of non-renewable oil resources.

The alcohol, 2-propanol, is commonly known as rubbing alcohol. Though it is toxic to drink, it is not skin-absorbed. One medical use is to reduce a person's skin temperature. It readily vaporizes and absorbs $42 \text{ kJ} \cdot \text{mol}^{-1}$ of heat energy in the process.

The simplest *diol*, 1,2-ethanediol, commonly called ethylene glycol, is used as an anti-freeze agent in automobile radiators. In 1986, television, radio, and newspapers reported that in some European countries, this compound had been added to wine as a sweetener. In the outcry that followed, bottles of wine from those countries were removed from the shelves of retail outlets. This is a good example of the saying "a little knowledge is a dangerous thing," for the compound actually used was diethylene glycol (IUPAC name, 3-oxa-1,5-pentanediol). Presumably, the reporters did not realize that ethylene glycol and diethylene glycol are two completely different compounds. Although it is illegal to add diethylene glycol to wine, it is comparatively harmless. Ethylene glycol, however, is

Figure 15.4
Gasohol is a good motor vehicle fuel. In the United States over 3×10^9 L of ethanol is used each year for this purpose.

exceedingly toxic. Notice how the minor difference in common names can reflect a major difference in chemical formula:

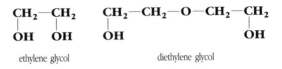

ethylene glycol   diethylene glycol

Glycerol, the simplest *triol*, has the IUPAC name of 1,2,3-propanetriol. This compound is used in the manufacture of plastics and synthetic fibres, as a sweetening agent, as a solvent for medicines, and is a component of many cosmetic preparations:

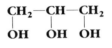

1,2,3-propanetriol (glycerol)

If glycerol (or glycerin, as it is sometimes called) is treated with a mixture of sulfuric acid and nitric acid, a yellow liquid called nitroglycerin is produced. Nitroglycerin can explode without warning, but when it is absorbed by diatomaceous earth and packed in tubes, it may be handled safely until detonated. The material in the tube, known as dynamite, is used extensively in the construction industry. The reaction to prepare this powerful explosive is as follows:

Figure 15.5

The blasting of Ripple Rock in a coastal channel off British Columbia represents the largest peaceful use of an explosive. About 1.3 × 10³ tonnes of dynamite was used to demolish this navigation hazard, which had caused the sinking of over 100 ships.

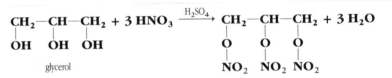

glycerol   glycerol trinitrate (nitroglycerin)

QUESTIONS

1. Which would you expect to be miscible with water, 1-propanol or 1-decanol? Give reasons for your answer.

2. Draw the structure for each of the eight alcohols with the formula $C_5H_{12}O$. Give the IUPAC name for each.

3. Draw the structure of each of the following alcohols:
   a) 3-hexanol   b) 2-methyl-3-hexanol   c) 2, 3-dimethyl-2-hexanol

4. Identify whether each structure drawn for your answer to Question 2 represents a primary, a secondary, or a tertiary alcohol.

5. Write a balanced chemical equation for each of the following reactions:
   a) methanol with sodium metal
   b) methanol with concentrated hydrobromic acid
   c) 1-propanol with an excess of concentrated sulfuric acid (two equations)
   d) the burning of ethanol in air
   e) 1-butanol with acidified dichromate ion (two equations)
   f) 2-butanol with acidified dichromate ion

Ethers

15.2

Ethers are compounds in which an oxygen atom is bonded to two alkyl groups. They contain the C—O—C functional group. The oxygen atom possesses two bonding pairs (one to each carbon atom) and two lone pairs. Thus we would expect the bond angles to be close to those found in a tetrahedron. In fact the C—O—C bond angle is slightly larger, about 116°.

The presence of the oxygen atom in this V-shaped compound gives the molecule a permanent dipole. However, as an ether does not have a hydrogen atom bonded to the oxygen atom, it cannot hydrogen bond to other ether molecules. The comparative weakness of the dipole-dipole forces in an ether are apparent if we compare them to the hydrogen bond in the alcohol of the same formula (a structural isomer). For example, CH_3—CH_2—OH has a boiling point of 78 °C while CH_3—O—CH_3 has a boiling point of −25 °C. As the length of the carbon chain is increased, the solubility of an ether in water decreases. Thus CH_3—O—CH_3 is miscible with water but CH_3—CH_2—O—CH_2—CH_3 (common ether) is only slightly soluble in water. Ethers tend to be soluble in low polarity or nonpolar solvents such as alkanes.

The Naming of Ethers

To name an ether using the IUPAC system, the longer of the two alkyl groups is selected as the parent hydrocarbon. The other alkyl group and the oxygen atom are regarded as forming a substituent, called an **alkoxy group**. This substituent is named by deleting the -yl ending of the alkyl group and replacing it with the ending *-oxy*. The position of the alkoxy group along the main chain is indicated by the lowest possible number. We will use the naming of the following compound as an example:

$$CH_3-CH_2-O-CH_2-CH_2-CH_3$$

1. Identify the longest chain, and make it the base name.

$$CH_3-CH_2-O-CH_2-CH_2-CH_3$$ Three carbons represent the longest chain. Propane is selected as the parent hydrocarbon.

2. Name the alkyl group on the other side of the oxygen atom, delete the *-yl*, and add the ending *-oxy*.

$$CH_3-CH_2-O-CH_2-CH_2-CH_3$$ There are two carbons in the alkyl group. Ethyl becomes ethoxy.

3. Identify where the substituent group is attached to the parent chain.

$$CH_3-CH_2-O-\overset{1}{CH_2}-\overset{2}{CH_2}-\overset{3}{CH_3}$$ The ethoxy is attached to carbon 1, resulting in the name 1-ethoxypropane.

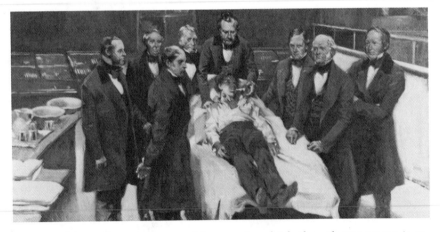

Figure 15.6

Ethoxyethane (diethyl ether) being used in the first public demonstration of surgical anesthesia at the Massachusetts General Hospital in Boston, in 1846.

It is possible to have a structural isomer in which the ethoxy group is attached to the middle of the propane chain. This compound would have the name 2-ethoxypropane.

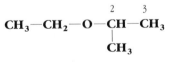

2-ethoxypropane

Reactions of Ethers

Ethers are comparatively unreactive compounds. The ether linkage, C—O—C, is unreactive to bases, oxidizing agents, or reducing agents. The only common reaction that ethers undergo is with a concentrated acid, such as hydroiodic acid. At high temperatures, this acid splits the ether linkage to give the alkyl iodides. Thus ethoxyethane will give two moles of iodoethane, while methoxyethane gives one mole of iodomethane and one mole of iodoethane:

$$CH_3—CH_2—O—CH_2—CH_3 + 2\ HI \xrightarrow{\Delta} 2\ CH_3—CH_2—I + H_2O$$

$$CH_3—O—CH_2—CH_3 + 2\ HI \xrightarrow{\Delta} CH_3—I + CH_3—CH_2—I + H_2O$$

There is one other reaction of ethers that is very important to anyone working in a chemical laboratory. On standing in contact with air, ethers are slowly converted to unstable peroxides. Although present in only low concentrations, these peroxides are very dangerous, since they can cause a violent explosion. A stored, opened container of ether should be checked periodically for peroxide formation. Old opened bottles of ethers should be handled with extreme caution. The formation of an organic peroxide from the reaction of ethoxyethane with oxygen can be represented by the following equation:

$$\underset{\text{ethoxyethane}}{2\ CH_3—CH_2—O—CH_2—CH_3} + O_2 \longrightarrow \underset{\text{diethyl peroxide}}{2\ CH_3—CH_2—O—O—CH_2—CH_3}$$

Common Ethers

Ethoxyethane (diethyl ether) is the only ether that is commonly used. Automobile starting fluids and lock de-icers contain high proportions of this compound. Care should be taken when using these consumer items because mixtures of ethoxyethane and air can readily explode. At one time, ethoxyethane was widely used as an anesthetic. However, because of its side effects (nausea and irritation of the lungs) and the dangers of operating room fires and explosions, it has been replaced by less hazardous substitutes.

As we mentioned in the reactions of alcohols, ethoxyethane can be prepared by the reaction of concentrated sulfuric acid with an excess of ethanol:

$$2\ CH_3CH_2—OH \xrightarrow[140\ °C]{H_2SO_4} CH_3CH_2—O—CH_2CH_3 + H_2O$$

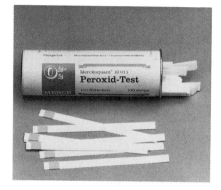

Figure 15.7
Peroxide test strips enable a chemist to determine the peroxide concentration in an ether.

Figure 15.8
Ethoxyethane is used in engine starting fluids.

Polyethers

One of the most exciting events in chemistry is the discovery of a completely new and unexpected type of compound. In 1964 Charles Pedersen was performing some organic syntheses in a laboratory in Wilmington, Delaware. In one of his reactions, he accidentally used some contaminated starting material. Besides the main compound he was making, a small quantity of another product was formed.

Being a careful chemist, he did not throw the by-product away, but instead, he decided to examine it. He found that it had an unusual structure consisting of a ring in which six $—CH_2—CH_2—$ units were joined by ether-type oxygen atoms between each unit. That is, the compound was a *polyether*. This type of compound was completely new, but the real excitement was in its behaviour as a solvent.

Figure 15.9
Charles Pedersen was awarded the Nobel Prize for Chemistry in 1987 for his discovery of polyethers.

Inorganic salts require very polar solvents to dissolve them. This makes life difficult for a chemist who wants to perform a reaction using an inorganic compound in a low-polarity organic solvent, such as ethoxyethane or benzene. Pedersen found that a mixture of a polyether and a low-polarity solvent would "dissolve" ionic compounds, such as sodium hydroxide. In this process, the polyether adopts a crown-like shape and wraps itself around the sodium cation, with the partially-negative oxygen atoms clustered around the positively-charged metal ion. The ionic metal ion is now buried within the polyether and the combination can now move into the low-polarity solvent. The polyether is commonly called a crown ether because of the shape it adopts. Du Pont, for whom Pedersen worked, held up publication of his results for four years until patents on this new family of compounds had been approved.

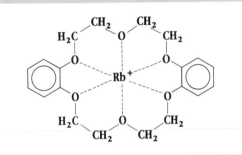

Figure 15.10
The structure of a crown ether compound with the rubidium ion.

Chemists have since constructed crown ethers with different ring sizes that will preferentially take up metal cations of a specific size. This provides a useful separation technique that is used in inorganic chemistry. Organic chemists also benefit from these compounds because they can now use reagents that were previously regarded as too insoluble in organic solvents. With this use has come the discovery that the free anion in these solutions is much more reactive than it would be in an aqueous solution, where it is surrounded by water molecules. Chemists are still reporting easier routes to known compounds and the synthesis of new compounds using the crown ether method. Finally, biochemists have found that the holes in crown ethers can be altered so that one optical isomer of an organic compound will fit in while the other will not. This mimics the behaviour of enzymes, and provides a simple method for the separation of mixtures of certain optical isomers.

QUESTIONS

6. Give the IUPAC name for each of the following compounds:

a) $CH_3-O-CH_2-CH_3$

b) $CH_3-O-\underset{\underset{\displaystyle CH_3}{|}}{CH}-CH_2-CH_3$

7. Write an equation for the reaction between the ether in Question 6a) and concentrated hydrobromic acid.

Aldehydes and Ketones

15.3

As we discussed in Section 15.1, the mild oxidation of a primary alcohol gives an aldehyde and the oxidation of a secondary alcohol produces a ketone. Both aldehydes and ketones contain a carbon atom that is joined by a double bond to an oxygen atom. The C=O unit is referred to as a **carbonyl group**. In the case of an **aldehyde**, the carbon atom of the carbonyl group is bonded to a hydrogen atom. In a **ketone**, the carbon atom of the carbonyl group is "sandwiched" between two other carbon atoms. This difference can be seen by comparing two structural isomers of C_3H_6O.

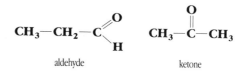

aldehyde   ketone

So far, all the oxygen-containing functional groups we have studied have involved single bonds. Thus the molecular geometry has been based on the tetrahedron. In the aldehydes and ketones, there are only three directions for the electron pairs around the carbon atom of the carbonyl group. Using VSEPR theory (Section 3.1), we would conclude that the carbonyl group must be planar with bond angles of about 120°.

The carbonyl group is quite polar. As a result of this polarity, both aldehydes and ketones have melting points and boiling points that are much higher than the ether having the same number of carbon atoms. However, the boiling and melting points are lower than those of the alcohol having the same number of carbon atoms. This is because there is no hydrogen bonding between the molecules of an aldehyde or ketone.

The strong polarity of the carbonyl group does mean that the lower members of the aldehyde and ketone series are miscible with water. As we saw with alcohols and ethers, the longer the carbon chain, the lower the solubility. This is due to the nonpolar character of the alkyl groups becoming dominant.

The Naming of Aldehydes and Ketones

When naming an aldehyde or ketone by the IUPAC system, we begin by choosing the longest chain containing the carbonyl carbon atom to obtain the base name. The ending -*e* is removed from the base name and replaced by -*al* in the case of an aldehyde. In the case of a ketone the -*e* is replaced by -*one*. Since the carbonyl group of an aldehyde is always at one end of the main chain, its position does not require a number. However, for ketones we attach a prefix to the name to show the location of the carbonyl carbon.

TABLE 15.2	IUPAC and Common Names of Some Common Aldehydes and Ketones	
Formula	IUPAC Name	Common Names
HCHO	methanal	formaldehyde
CH_3CHO	ethanal	acetaldehyde
$(CH_3)_2CO$	propanone	acetone, dimethyl ketone

As an example, we will name of following aldehyde:

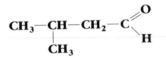

1. Identify the longest carbon chain containing the carbonyl group and assign the base name. Replace the -*e* with the aldehyde ending -*al*.

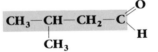 The longest chain containing the carbonyl group has four carbons, hence butanal.

2. Number the chain beginning at the end that will result in the lowest possible number for the carbonyl group. As the carbonyl group in an aldehyde is always at the end of the chain, we do not need to identify its position by the number.

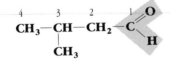

3. Name each substituent and indicate its position by the number of the carbon atom on the base chain to which it is attached.

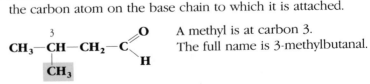

A methyl is at carbon 3.
The full name is 3-methylbutanal.

As an example, of naming a ketone, we will use the following compound:

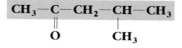

$$CH_3-C-CH_2-CH-CH_3$$
$$\quad\quad \underset{O}{\|} \quad\quad\quad \underset{CH_3}{|}$$

1. Identify the longest carbon chain containing the carbonyl group and assign the base name. Replace the -e with the ketone ending -one.

$$CH_3-C-CH_2-CH-CH_3$$ The longest chain containing
the carbonyl group has five
carbons, hence pentanone.

2. Number the chain beginning at the end which will result in the lowest possible number for the carbonyl group and indicate its location on the carbon chain.

$$\overset{1}{CH_3}-\overset{2}{C}-\overset{3}{CH_3}-\overset{4}{CH}-\overset{5}{CH_3}$$ The carbonyl group is on
carbon 2, hence 2-pentanone.

3. Name each substituent and indicate its position by the number of the carbon atom on the base chain to which it is attached.

$$\overset{2}{CH_3}-C-CH_2-\overset{4}{CH}-CH_3$$ A methyl is at carbon 4,
hence the full name is
4-methyl-2-pentanone.

Reactions of Aldehydes and Ketones

The carbon-oxygen double bond is more than twice as strong as the carbon-oxygen single bond. This is quite different from the situation that we found when comparing carbon-carbon double and single bonds. As a result, carbonyl groups are less reactive than alkenes. However, because carbonyl groups are very polar, they can undergo a wide variety of reactions that are quite different from those that alkenes undergo.

TABLE 15.3	*Comparative Carbon-Oxygen and Carbon-Carbon Bond Strengths* $(kJ \cdot mol^{-1})$			
C—C	347		C—O	327
C=C	620		C=O	804

Both aldehydes and ketones can be reduced to alcohols. This reaction can be performed using a wide variety of reducing agents. One method is to use hydrogen gas and a platinum catalyst.

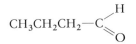

EXAMPLE   15.2   Write the equation for the reaction of butanal with hydrogen gas over a platinum catalyst.

SOLUTION   All aldehydes are reduced to alcohols by hydrogen gas in the presence of platinum. To identify which alcohol is produced, we need to write the formula for butanal:

$$CH_3CH_2CH_2-C\overset{H}{\underset{O}{}}$$

In the reaction, one atom of hydrogen will bond to the oxygen atom and another atom hydrogen will bond to the neighbouring carbon atom to give

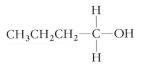

We can now write the equation as:

$$CH_3CH_2CH_2CHO + H_2 \xrightarrow{\text{Pt}} CH_3CH_2CH_2CH_2OH$$

A major difference between aldehydes and ketones is the resistance of ketones to oxidation. We first mentioned this point about resistance to oxidation in our discussion of the oxidation of the different types of alcohols. Aldehydes can easily be oxidized by a variety of oxidizing agents to carboxylic acids. One inexpensive method is to use an acidic solution of sodium or potassium dichromate. However, as dichromates are known carcinogens they should be handled with particular care. The two half-reactions for the oxidation of ethanal by dichromate ion are as follows:

$$CH_3CHO_{(aq)} + H_2O_{(\ell)} \longrightarrow CH_3CO_2H_{(aq)} + 2\,H^+_{(aq)} + 2\,e^-$$
$$Cr_2O_7{}^{2-}{}_{(aq)} + 14\,H^+{}_{(aq)} + 6\,e^- \longrightarrow 2\,Cr^{3+}{}_{(aq)} + 7\,H_2O_{(\ell)}$$

There are two common tests used to distinguish between aldehydes and ketones. Both of these tests rely on the reducing properties of the aldehyde. The first uses Fehling's solution, which is essentially a basic solution of copper(II) ion. The aldehyde reduces the blue copper(II) ion to solid copper(I) oxide. Traces of the copper(I) oxide give a green tinge to the

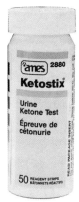

Figure 15.11

Test sticks are now used to check for the presence of ketones or aldehyde groups.

solution. As more of the oxide is formed, a yellow cloudiness develops, followed by a thick red precipitate as the particles grow in size.

$$2\,Cu^{2+}_{(aq)} + 2\,OH^-_{(aq)} + 2\,e^- \longrightarrow Cu_2O_{(s)} + H_2O_{(l)}$$

$$CH_3CHO_{(aq)} + 3\,OH^-_{(aq)} \longrightarrow CH_3CO_2^-_{(aq)} + 2\,H_2O_{(l)} + 2\,e^-$$

The second test to distinguish aldehydes and ketones uses Tollen's reagent, a solution of silver ion in aqueous ammonia. In this solution, the silver is part of the polyatomic cation, $Ag(NH_3)_2^+$. An aldehyde reduces the colourless solution of silver ion to silver metal. The metal may form as a black precipitate, but with gentle warming and a clean glass container, a thin uniform deposit of shiny silver metal can be produced over the inside of the container walls. This "silver mirror" is produced on a commercial scale for some mirror coatings.

$$Ag(NH_3)_2^+_{(aq)} + e^- \longrightarrow Ag_{(s)} + 2\,NH_3{}_{(aq)}$$

$$CH_3CHO_{(aq)} + 3\,OH^-_{(aq)} \longrightarrow CH_3CO_2^-_{(aq)} + 2\,H_2O_{(l)} + 2\,e^-$$

Unused Tollen's reagent should be decomposed immediately with dilute acid. If the reagent is not destroyed, a precipitate of explosive silver azide, AgN_3, is formed. Ketones do not react with either Fehling's solution or Tollen's reagent.

EXAMPLE 15.3   A compound of molecular formula C_3H_6O gives a red precipitate with Fehling's solution. Write the structural formula of the compound.

SOLUTION   This question is a simple example of the deductive questions that are common in organic chemistry. The positive test with Fehling's solution indicates that the aldehyde functional group, —CHO, is present. If we "subtract" these atoms from the molecular formula, we are left with C_2H_5, the ethyl group. Thus the structural formula would have to be:

$$CH_3CH_2CHO \qquad \text{(propanal)}$$

Note that the only structural isomer, CH_3COCH_3, is a ketone. This would not react with Fehling's solution.

Common Aldehydes and Ketones

Methanal, commonly called formaldehyde, is a gas at room temperature. A 40 % aqueous solution of methanal is known as formalin and is used as a preservative of biological specimens. The methanal reacts with the protein of the specimen, inhibiting decomposition and maintaining a firmer tissue structure. Since methanal is now regarded as hazardous to health, once the specimen has been preserved by reaction with the formalin, it is removed and placed in a holding solution for storage and subsequent handling. These proprietary solutions contain about 95 % water together with anti-fungal agents and methanal "scavengers" to remove traces of formalin from the specimen.

For a period of time, homeowners were encouraged to use urea-formaldehyde foams (called UFFI) to improve their house insulation. However, it became apparent that some of the gaseous methanal in the insulation was leaking into houses and causing a number of health problems. As a result, government grants were made available to enable homeowners to remove the foam.

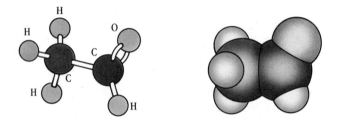

Figure 15.12

The shape of the ethanal molecule,
CH₃CHO:
a) as a ball-and-stick model;
b) as a space-filling model.

Ethanal (acetaldehyde) boils at 20 °C. However, it can form a cyclic ether involving four ethanal units. This solid compound is commonly called metaldehyde. It is used as a solid fuel in camp stoves and in slug pellets, because its highly toxic vapour kills slugs and snails.

The aromatic aldehyde, vanillin, is responsible for the aroma of vanilla. However, the major ingredient in artificial vanilla extract is the synthetic compound ethovan, since its aroma is about five times stronger than that of vanillin. Note that the only structural difference between the two compounds is the extra CH_2 unit in ethovan.

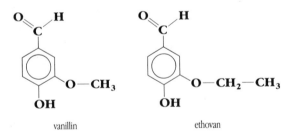

vanillin   ethovan

Propanone (acetone) is prepared on an industrial scale by the fermentation of corn and molasses. Fermentation of these substances would normally produce ethanol, but by using a different strain of yeast, acetone is produced. An alternative route uses propene, a common petroleum product, as a starting material. The propene is **hydrated** (by the addition of two hydrogen atoms and one oxygen atom) to 2-propanol. The 2-propanol is then oxidized by air in the presence of a catalyst to produce propanone.

Propanone is widely used as a solvent because it is miscible with water as well as with most low-polarity organic liquids. Its vapour is somewhat toxic and very flammable, thus the solvent should always be handled in a ventilated room without any flames being used. Propanone is also formed in the human body as a metabolic product. However, its concentration in the blood rarely rises above 10 ppm, since it is oxidized to carbon dioxide and water. Some forms of diabetes affect this oxidation process, and acetone can then be detected in the urine and on the breath of people with this condition.

QUESTIONS

8. Draw the structure of each of the following:
   a) 3-pentanone
   c) butanal
   b) 2,4-dimethyl-3-hexanone
   d) 2-methylpentanal

9. Name the following compounds by the IUPAC system:

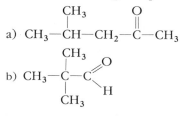

10. Write an equation for each of the following reactions:
   a) methanal with acidified dichromate ion (give the two half-reactions and then the combined reaction)
   b) propanone with hydrogen gas over a platinum catalyst

Carboxylic Acids 15.4

Common organic acids contain the **carboxyl group**. The carboxyl group is a combination of a hydroxyl group and a carbonyl functional group. Thus the carbon of the carboxyl group has one single-bonded oxygen and one double-bonded oxygen attached to it.

the carboxyl functional group

Carboxylic acids are capable of hydrogen bonding because they contain a hydroxyl group. Extensive intermolecular hydrogen bonding between carboxylic acid molecules accounts for the high melting points and boiling points in these compounds. For example, acetic acid (CH_3CO_2H) melts at 17 °C. On cold days, before the use of central heating, chemists would find their acetic acid had solidified. For this reason, pure acetic acid used to be called glacial acetic acid.

Since hydrogen bonding is the major intermolecular force, we would expect the acids with short carbon chains to be miscible with water. This is what we find. Once again, though, as the nonpolar carbon chains become longer, the hydrogen bonding component becomes less significant in determining the physical properties of the compound.

The Naming of Carboxylic Acids

The IUPAC names of carboxylic acids are obtained by selecting the longest carbon chain containing the carboxylic carbon and replacing the final -e of the alkane name with the ending -oic acid. If a substitutent is present, the numbering starts from the carbon of the carboxyl group. For the simpler acids, traditional names are still widely used.

TABLE 15.4 *IUPAC and Common Names of Some Carboxylic Acids*

Formula	IUPAC name	Common Names
HCO_2H	methanoic acid	formic acid
CH_3CO_2H	ethanoic acid	acetic acid
$CH_3CH_2CO_2H$	propanoic acid	propionic acid
$CH_3CH_2CH_2CO_2H$	butanoic acid	butyric acid

We will show the general naming procedure using the following example:

$$CH_3-CH_2-CH-CH_2-CH_2-C{\overset{O}{\underset{OH}{}}}$$
$$\underset{CH_2-CH_3}{|}$$

1. Identify the longest carbon chain containing the carboxyl group and assign the base name. Replace the -e with the carboxyl ending -oic acid.

$$CH_3-CH_2-CH-CH_2-CH_2-C{\overset{O}{\underset{OH}{}}}$$
$$\underset{CH_2-CH_3}{|}$$

The longest chain containing the carboxyl group has six carbons, hence hexanoic acid.

2. Number the chain from the end that will give the lowest possible number for the carboxyl group. Since the carboxyl group is always at the end of the chain, we do not need to identify its position by the number.

$$\overset{6}{C}H_3-\overset{5}{C}H_2-\overset{4}{C}H-\overset{3}{C}H_2-\overset{2}{C}H_2-\overset{1}{C}{\overset{O}{\underset{OH}{}}}$$
$$\underset{CH_2-CH_3}{|}$$

3. Name each substituent and indicate its position by the number of the carbon atom on the base chain to which it is attached.

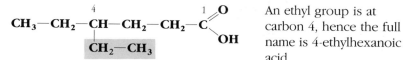

An ethyl group is at carbon 4, hence the full name is 4-ethylhexanoic acid.

Reactions of Carboxylic Acids

Carboxylic acids are weak acids that will dissociate slightly in water to form carboxylate ions:

$$CH_3CO_2H_{(aq)} + H_2O_{(\ell)} \rightleftharpoons CH_3CO_2^-{}_{(aq)} + H_3O^+{}_{(aq)}$$

carboxylate ion

One might think that the carboxylate anion would have one double-bonded oxygen atom and one single-bonded oxygen atom with a negative charge. In fact, both carbon-oxygen bonds are of equal length and the bond order is about one and one half. Thus, it is best to represent a carboxylate ion as follows:

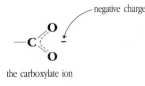

the carboxylate ion

Carboxylic acids, like inorganic acids, can be neutralized using an inorganic base. For example, ethanoic acid reacts with sodium hydroxide solution to produce sodium ethanoate (sodium acetate) and water:

ethanoic acid (acetic acid) — sodium ethanoate (sodium acetate)

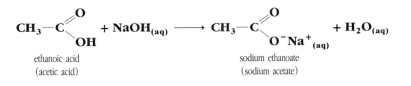

Another reaction that is common to both carboxylic and inorganic acids is the reaction with a carbonate. This is a useful test for the presence of a carboxylic acid.

$$2\,CH_3CO_2H_{(aq)} + Na_2CO_{3(aq)} \longrightarrow 2\,CH_3CO_2^-{}_{(aq)} + 2\,Na^+{}_{(aq)} + CO_{2\,(g)} + H_2O_{(\ell)}$$

In the presence of a strong, concentrated acid, such as sulfuric acid, a carboxylic acid will react with an alcohol to produce an ester. We will look at this reaction in more depth in the next section.

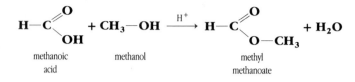

methanoic acid + methanol → methyl methanoate + H₂O

Carboxyl groups are among the most difficult functional groups to reduce. Even conditions that will reduce aldehydes and ketones to alcohols will leave carboxylic acids untouched. Thus if we have a compound that contains a ketone and a carboxylic acid functional group, the carbonyl of the ketone can be reduced to a secondary alcohol without affecting the carbonyl of the carboxyl group:

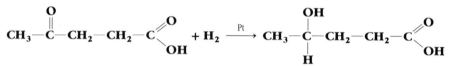

It is this kind of understanding of the properties of functional groups that enables organic chemists to selectively synthesize a given complex chemical compound.

Common Carboxylic Acids

Methanoic acid (formic acid) is produced by ants (Latin name, *Formica*) which inject the acid into their victims, killing other insects and producing a stinging sensation in humans. A large number of ant bites can be fatal to humans as well.

Ethanoic acid (acetic acid) provides the characteristic sharp taste and odour of vinegar. Wine and malt vinegars are produced by the oxidation of grape and grain alcohol solutions using bacteria (*Acetobacter*) in the presence of air. A similar but unintentional reaction occurs when wine or beer is left open to the air, and results in an unpleasant taste. Commercial white vinegar is usually a 5% solution of industrially produced ethanoic acid.

Carboxylic acids have characteristic odours that depend upon the length of the carbon chain. Butanoic acid (butyric acid) is found in rancid butter and is also partially responsible for perspiration odour. Hexanoic, octanoic, and decanoic acids, were commonly called caproic, caprylic, and capric acid, respectively. *Caper* is Latin for goat, and all of these acids are found in butter made from goat's milk. The characteristic odour of meat from sheep is due in large part to a number of carboxylic acids containing an odd number of carbon atoms.

Figure 15.13
The classic science-fiction movie 'Them' featured giant ants. The human victims were found to contain massive quantities of formic acid, which alerted the hero to the identity of the mysterious killers.

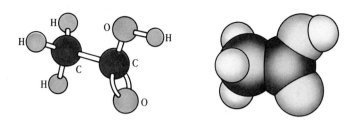

Figure 15.14

The shape of the ethanoic acid molecule, CH_3CO_2H:
a) as a ball-and-stick model;
b) as a space-filling model.

Ethanedioic acid, commonly called oxalic acid, contains two carboxyl groups. This acid is diprotic, that is, one mole of acid requires two moles of hydroxide ions for complete neutralization.

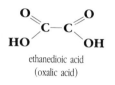

ethanedioic acid
(oxalic acid)

$$(CO_2H)_{2\,(aq)} + 2\,NaOH_{(aq)} \longrightarrow (CO_2)_2^{\,2-}{}_{(aq)} + 2\,Na^+{}_{(aq)} + 2\,H_2O_{(\ell)}$$

Oxalic acid is very toxic. It occurs in high concentrations in rhubarb leaves and is present in low concentrations in spinach. The quantity in spinach is not hazardous unless one has a Popeye-like craving for the vegetable.

Oxalic acid reacts with calcium ions to form insoluble calcium oxalate. Some sufferers with kidney stones have stones that consist of this salt. These people must avoid any foods containing the oxalate ion so that the product of the concentrations of calcium and oxalate ions in their bodies do not exceed the solubility product of the salt.

$$(CO_2H)_{2\,(aq)} + Ca^{2+}{}_{(aq)} \longrightarrow (CO_2)_2Ca_{(s)} + 2\,H^+{}_{(aq)}$$

Lactic acid, 2-hydroxypropanoic acid, contains two different functional groups, a hydroxyl group and a carboxyl group. This biologically important acid is produced when milk goes sour. Lactic acid is also a product of carbohydrate metabolism in the body during periods of strenous activity. Muscular soreness is a result of lactic acid build-up.

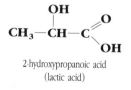

2-hydroxypropanoic acid
(lactic acid)

Figure 15.15

A whip scorpion spraying a defensive jet of acid. The droplets can be seen on the acid-sensitive paper. The jet consists of 84% ethanoic acid, 5% octanoic acid, and 11% water.

Tartaric acid possesses two carboxyl and two hydroxyl groups. It is combined with sodium hydrogen carbonate to produce tartrate baking powder. When a cake is being baked, the tartaric acid in the baking powder dissolves and reacts with the sodium hydrogen carbonate, releasing bubbles of carbon dioxide gas inside the cake mix.

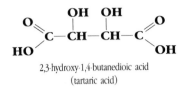

2,3-hydroxy-1,4-butanedioic acid
(tartaric acid)

Citric acid has three carboxyl groups and one hydroxyl group. This acid is found in fruits, particularly in lemons, oranges, and other citrus fruits. Citric acid plays an important role in the metabolic pathway known as the TCA, or Krebs cycle. It is used to give a mild acidity to soft drinks, preventing mold formation and giving the drinks a pleasant taste. It is also commonly used in effervescent tablets, and as a rust remover. Most of the citric acid we use today is produced by growing the fungus, *Aspergillus niger*, in a glucose solution. Citric acid is produced metabolically by the fungus as it consumes the glucose. The mat of fungus is filtered off from the mixture and citric acid is crystallized from the remaining solution.

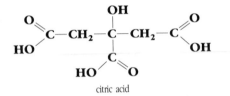

citric acid

QUESTIONS

11. Name the following compounds according to the IUPAC system:

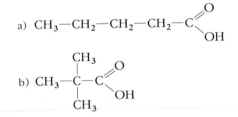

12. Draw the condensed formula for each of the following carboxylic acids:

a) heptanoic acid
b) 3-methylpentanoic acid

13. Write an equation for each of the following reactions:
a) methanoic acid with potassium hydroxide solution
b) propanoic acid with solid calcium carbonate
c) ethanoic acid with 2-propanol

Phenols

As we have seen, the ending -*ol* in the IUPAC name of an organic compound indicates the presence of a hydroxyl group (Section 15.1). In the case of phenols, the hydroxyl group is directly attached to an aromatic ring. The simplest phenol, C_6H_5OH, has the hydroxyl group attached to a benzene ring. The IUPAC name of this compound is hydroxybenzene, but we generally use the common name, phenol.

We have deferred discussion of phenols until now because the bonding of a hydroxyl group to an aromatic ring causes the hydroxyl group to behave like the hydroxyl part of a carboxyl group, rather than like the hydroxyl group of an alcohol. One illustration of this is in the acidity of phenolic compounds. For example, phenol reacts with sodium hydroxide solution to produce water and a solution of sodium phenoxide.

$$C_6H_5OH_{(aq)} + NaOH_{(aq)} \longrightarrow C_6H_5O^-{}_{(aq)} + Na^+{}_{(aq)} + H_2O_{(\ell)}$$

However, phenols are very weak acids and will not react with weak bases such as ammonia. Phenols have a number of applications. An aqueous solution of phenol was once used by physicians as a disinfectant under the name of carbolic acid. Various substituted phenols, such as butylated hydroxytoluenes (BHT), are added to potato chips and similar foods to prevent oxidation of the fat components. There is some evidence that such anti-oxidant compounds inhibit cancer formation.

Esters

These compounds contain two hydrocarbon units separated by the ester functional group. In the ester functional group, one of the oxygen atoms is doubly bonded to the carbon atom, while the other oxygen is singly bonded between the same carbon atom and a hydrocarbon chain or alkyl group.

Since esters cannot form hydrogen bonds, they have lower boiling points than the isomeric carboxylic acids. For example, the ester $CH_3CO_2CH_3$ boils at 57 °C while the carboxylic acid $CH_3CH_2CO_2H$ boils

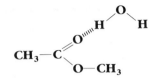

Figure 15.16
Hydrogen bonds can form between water and an ester.

at 141 °C. Esters have characteristic odours, usually pleasant ones. The simpler esters are miscible with water, because the hydrogen atoms of the water molecules can hydrogen bond to the carboxyl oxygens of the ester.

The Naming of Esters

When naming an ester, we consider the molecule to be a carboxylic acid in which the hydrogen of the carboxyl group has been replaced by an alkyl group. Thus we start by identifying the parent carboxylic acid. The chain joined to the carbon to which the two oxygen atoms are attached provides the base name. This is given the ending *-oate* (the equivalent carboxylic acid would have the ending *-oic acid*). The hydrocarbon chain attached to the single-bonded oxygen is written as an alkyl group. The following example should make this clear:

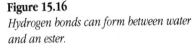

1. Identify the chain that provides the base name. Replace the *-e* with the ester ending *-oate*.

There are three carbons in the longest chain of the parent carboxylic acid, hence propanoate.

2. Name the substituent alkyl group.

The alkyl group is an ethyl. The name is ethyl propanoate.

If either of the parts of the molecule is branched, we use numbers to locate the position of the substituents. The numbering always starts from the ester functional group. Two examples are shown below:

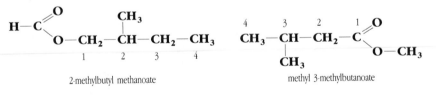

2-methylbutyl methanoate

methyl 3-methylbutanoate

Flavours and Aromas

Esters are responsible for many of the characteristic tastes and odours of our foods. A small change in structure can produce a very large change in smell or taste. Table 15.5 shows the structure of a number of esters and lists the aromas associated with them.

The basic structure of the esters in Table 15.5.

TABLE 15.5 *Structure and Aroma of Some Esters*

R	R'	Aroma	IUPAC Name
CH_3-	$-CH_2CH_2CHCH_3$ (with CH_3 branch)	banana	3-methylbutyl ethanote
CH_3-	$-CH_2(CH_2)_6CH_3$	orange	octyl ethanoate
CH_3-	$-CH_2CH_2CH_3$	pear	propyl ethanoate
CH_3CH_2-	$-CH_2CHCH_3$ (with CH_3 branch)	rum	2-methylpropyl propanoate
$CH_3(CH_2)_2-$	$-CH_2CH_3$	pineapple	ethyl butanoate
$CH_3(CH_2)_2-$	$-CH_3$	apple	methyl butanoate

The Preparation of Esters

The simplest method of preparing an ester involves the reaction of a carboxylic acid with an alcohol in the presence of an acid catalyst. For example, we can make methyl ethanoate by reacting ethanoic acid with methanol in the presence of sulfuric acid.

$$CH_3-C\underset{OH}{\overset{O}{<}} + HO-CH_3 \xrightarrow{H_2SO_4} CH_3-C\underset{O-CH_3}{\overset{O}{<}} + H_2O$$

Such reactions are equilibrium reactions in which the value of the equilibrium constant is close to unity. To extend this idea, if one mole of ethanoic acid is mixed with one mole of 1-propanol in the presence of a few drops of concentrated sulfuric acid, at equilibrium we find that only 0.67 mol of propyl ethanoate has been formed.

$$CH_3-C\underset{OH}{\overset{O}{<}} + HO-CH_2CH_2CH_3 \xrightarrow{H_2SO_4} CH_3-C\underset{O-CH_2CH_2CH_3}{\overset{O}{<}} + H_2O$$

How can we increase the yield of the ester? As we mentioned, simple esters have relatively low boiling points. Thus, as it is formed, the ester can be gently distilled off from the reaction mixture. By Le Châtelier's principle, as the concentration of ester in the mixture drops, more ester will be produced. Alternatively if the acid, alcohol, and ester all boil well above 100 °C, distillation will remove the water as fast as it is formed, again increasing the yield of ester. A third method of increasing the yield is to use a large excess of whichever reagent is least expensive.

You might wonder whether the ether-like oxygen in an ester prepared in this way comes from the hydroxyl of the alcohol or the hydroxyl of the carboxylic acid. We can find out by a technique called **isotopic labelling**. It is possible to buy alcohols, such as methanol, in which the oxygen atom is the oxygen-18 isotope instead of the normal oxygen-16 isotope. When methanol that contains oxygen-18 is reacted with ethanoic acid, we find that the oxygen-18 atoms all finish up in the ester. Thus the oxygen present in the water must have originated from the carboxylic acid. Many organic, inorganic, and biochemical reactions are now being studied by using isotopic labelling.

$$CH_3-C\!\!\diagup\!\!^O_{OH} + H^{18}O-CH_3 \overset{H_2SO_4}{\rightleftharpoons} CH_3-C\!\!\diagup\!\!^O_{^{18}O-CH_3} + H_2O$$

EXAMPLE   *15.4*   Write the equation for the reaction between butanol and propanoic acid in the presence of sulfuric acid.

SOLUTION   First, we write out the formulas of the two reactants:

$$CH_3CH_2CH_2CH_2-OH \quad \text{and} \quad CH_3CH_2-C\!\!\diagup\!\!^O_{OH}$$

When the ester is formed, water is eliminated. By convention, the part of the ester derived from the acid is written on the left.

$$CH_3CH_2-C\!\!\diagup\!\!^O_{OH} + HO-CH_2CH_2CH_2CH_3 \overset{H_2SO_4}{\rightleftharpoons} CH_3CH_2-C\!\!\diagup\!\!^O_{O-CH_2CH_2CH_2CH_3} + H_2O$$

Reactions of Esters

Because the preparation of an ester from an alcohol and a carboxylic acid is an equilibrium reaction, it follows that we can adjust the conditions so that we can **hydrolyze** an ester. The term *hydrolyze* means the breakdown of a compound by reacting it with water. Using an excess of water is a convenient way to ensure that the equilibrium lies well to the right.

$$CH_3-C\!\!\diagup\!\!^O_{O-CH_3} + H_2O \overset{H_2SO_4}{\rightleftharpoons} CH_3-C\!\!\diagup\!\!^O_{OH} + HO-CH_3$$

In basic solution, esters are irreversibly hydrolyzed. This is because the stable carboxylate anion is formed, which has no tendency to re-combine with the alcohol.

$$CH_3-C\!\!\diagup\!\!^O_{O-CH_3} + OH^- \longrightarrow CH_3-C\!\!\diagup\!\!^O_{O}{}^- + HO-CH_3$$

carboxylate ion

Waxes

Waxes make up the protective water-repellant coating found on the fruit and leaves of plants. Waxes are also secreted by insects and birds. These waxes consist mainly of a mixture of esters having carbon chains of between 16 and 34 atoms on each side of the ester group. In the waxes produced by plants and insects, the carbon chains are unbranched. For example, the major components in beeswax and in carnauba palm wax are shown below:

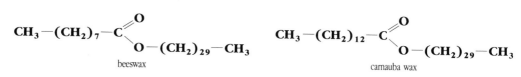

The waxes produced in the preen glands of birds contain branched-chain esters. Since these molecules are more compact than their straight-chain isomers, they have lower melting points. Thus the mixture is an oil rather than a solid wax. Each genus of bird produces a unique mixture of esters. When birds have become coated with toxic fuel oil from oil spills, washing with detergent removes the natural waxes as well as the fuel oil. Until the birds can replace the lost preen oils, their feathers will absorb water, making them "waterlogged" and resulting in rapid heat loss. A synthetic preen wax, octadecyl 2-methylhexanoate, has been produced which can be coated over the stricken birds until they can produce sufficient natural oils.

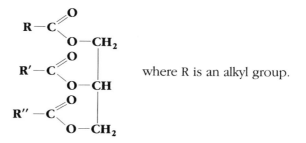

Fats

Fats are all tri-esters of 1,2,3-propanetriol (glycerol),

where R is an alkyl group.

The alkyl groups in these esters contain between 14 and 18 carbon atoms. In most animal fats, these alkyl groups consist of completely saturated carbon chains while in most vegetable fats the alkyl groups contain one, two, or three double bonds. The presence of double bonds reduces the melting point. Thus most vegetable fats are liquids at room temperature, while most animal fats are solids. We can explain this behaviour in terms of molecular shape. The presence of the rigid double bonds produces "kinks" in the molecules. As a result, they are unable to pack together as closely as those molecules in which the alkyl groups are completely saturated. With the molecules being farther apart, the dispersion forces will be less effective.

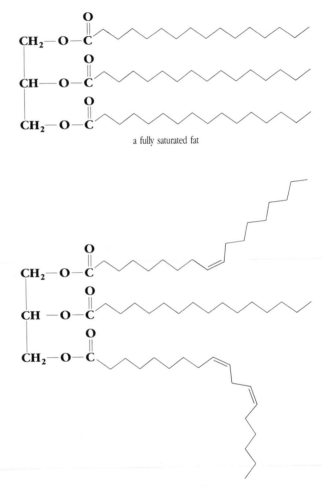

a fully saturated fat

a partially unsaturated fat

A more important consequence of the presence of double bonds in vegetable oils is that the double bonds provide sites at which reactions can occur. Our bodies can break down unsaturated fats much more effectively than saturated ones. Diets containing large amounts of saturated fats may result in the build-up of blood cholesterol, which can eventually cause high blood pressure and heart disease. For this reason, it is important to use unsaturated fats in our diet. There is a very wide range of unsaturation among vegetable sources (Table 15.6), while fish have the lowest proportion of saturated fats among animal sources.

TABLE 15.6	A Comparison of the Composition of Vegetable Oils	
Source	Saturated Fats (%)	Unsaturated Fats (%)
Coconut oil	76.2	23.8
Corn oil	14.6	85.4
Peanut oil	13.8	86.2
Olive oil	9.3	90.7

Oils that contain a large number of double bonds are very susceptible to air oxidation. In edible fats this oxidation leads to a rancid taste. However, this property is made use of in oil-based paints and varnishes. When highly unsaturated oils, such as linseed oil, are spread over a surface in a thin layer they react with the oxygen in air. The oxygen atoms form cross-links between the oil molecules, providing a tough flexible film on the surface.

Salicylates

Salicylic acid was known by the practitioners of folk medicine to have soothing, pain-relieving, and antiseptic properties. It is still used in ointments for skin diseases. By reacting the carboxylic functional group with methanol, we obtain methyl salicylate, commonly called oil of wintergreen. Oil of wintergreen is used as a flavouring and in ointments for sore muscles.

Esters can also be produced by reaction with the hydroxyl functional group of salicylic acid. The most important of these is acetylsalicylic acid (ASA). Acetylsalicylic acid is the most widely used synthetic drug. It is an inexpensive pain-reliever and fever-reducer. However, heavy use of acetylsalicylic acid can cause internal bleeding due to the action of the acid on the stomach lining.

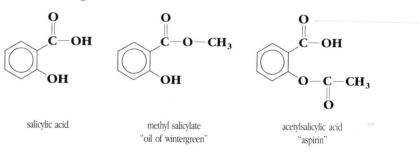

salicylic acid   methyl salicylate   acetylsalicylic acid
                        "oil of wintergreen"   "aspirin"

14. Give the IUPAC name of the following esters:

a)
$$H-C\overset{\displaystyle O}{\underset{\displaystyle O-CH_2-CH_2-CH_3}{<}}$$

b)
$$CH_3-CH_2-CH_2-C\overset{\displaystyle O}{\underset{\displaystyle O-CH_3}{<}}$$

15. There are two esters with the formula $C_3H_6O_2$.
    a) Draw their condensed structural formulas.
    b) Give their IUPAC names.
    c) Identify the alcohol and carboxylic acid used in their preparation.

16. Olive oil contains a variety of triglycerides, the majority of which have been formed (at least in part) from oleic acid. Oleic acid has the formula $C_{18}H_{34}O_2$ and contains a double bond between carbon atoms 9 and 10. Draw the structure of oleic acid (In this compound, the groups around the double bond have a *cis* arrangement.)

17. Write a balanced equation for the hydrolysis of each of the esters shown in Question 14.

Halogen-Containing Hydrocarbons

15.7

Most of our discussions on the oxygen-containing functional groups have related to compounds containing only one of that functional group. Hydrocarbons containing halogens are referred to as **haloalkanes** (or **halogenated hydrocarbons**). In these compounds it is quite common to have many halogen atoms attached to the hydrocarbon chain. In our discussion we will be looking mainly at compounds containing chlorine atoms, as these are the most important.

Chloroalkanes are mostly dense low-boiling liquids with characteristic odours. As the number of chlorine atoms increases, the boiling point and density also increases.

The liquid chloroalkanes are immiscible with water, but are good solvents for low-polarity fats, oils, and greases. As the number of chlorine atoms in the chloroalkanes increases, the flammability of the compounds decreases. At one time this combination of properties resulted in these compounds being used as dry-cleaning and de-greasing agents. Chloroalkanes are no longer used in this way however, since it has become apparent that they cause a number of health problems, including liver damage and cancer.

The carbon-fluorine bond in fluoroalkanes is extremely strong. Compounds containing such bonds are very unreactive and have very low toxicity. For these reasons, compounds containing both fluorine and chlorine, the **chlorofluorocarbons**, or **CFCs**, have been used widely as pressurizing gases in aerosol cans, as foaming agents in plastics, and in air conditioning systems. Their use in aerosol cans has probably saved many

TABLE 15.7 *Some Chloromethanes and Their Properties*

Formula	Boiling Point (°C)	Density (g·mL^{-1})
CH_3Cl	−24	—
CH_2Cl_2	40	1.3
$CHCl_3$	61	1.5
CCl_4	77	1.6

lives; they are much safer than previously-used, highly flammable hydro-carbons. However, it is now realized that the very stability of the CFCs presents a danger to the ozone layer in the upper levels of the atmosphere. A tremendous research effort is currently underway trying to find substitutes for CFCs that are non-toxic and non-flammable and have a high rate of decomposition in the environment.

Perfluorocarbons are hydrocarbons in which all the hydrogen atoms have been replaced by fluorine atoms. Some of these compounds show potential as artificial blood substitutes. These would be of great value in emergency situations.

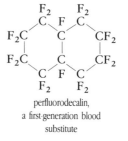

perfluorodecalin,
a first-generation blood
substitute

The Naming of Halogenated Hydrocarbons

The naming of these compounds is very straightforward. We construct the name of the parent hydrocarbon and use the prefixes fluoro-, chloro-, bromo-, and iodo- for the appropriate substituent halogen. As with alkyl groups, *mono-*, *di-*, *tri-*, *tetra-*, etc., are used to indicate the number of each halogen. If there is the possibility of isomers, numbers are used to identify the carbon to which the halogen atoms are attached.

TABLE 15.8	Common Halogenated Hydrocarbons	
Formula	IUPAC name	Common Names
CH_2Cl_2	dichloromethane	methylene chloride
$CHCl_3$	trichloromethane	chloroform
CCl_4	tetrachloromethane	carbon tetrachloride

We will illustrate the naming of these compounds in the following example:

1. Name the parent hydrocarbon.

   A two carbon chain with one double bond. The parent hydrocarbon is ethene.

2. Number the chain so that the carbon atom with the most substituents has the lowest number. Prefix the base name.

 Two chlorine atoms at carbon 1.
One chlorine at carbon 2.
The name is 1,1,2-trichloroethene.

Preparation of Chloroalkanes

There are a number of ways that we can make chloroalkanes in the laboratory. One method is to react an alcohol (usually a tertiary alcohol) with concentrated hydrochloric acid using zinc chloride as a catalyst (Lucas reagent). The chloroalkane formed is immiscible with the alcohol, and separates as an oily layer.

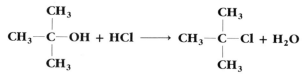

Alkenes can be used as starting materials. Reaction of alkenes with hydrogen chloride will produce the monochloro compound, while reaction with chlorine gas will produce the dichloro compound:

$$CH_2{=}CH_{2\,(g)} + HCl_{(g)} \longrightarrow CH_3{-}CH_2Cl_{(g)}$$
$$CH_2{=}CH_{2\,(g)} + Cl_{2\,(g)} \longrightarrow CH_2Cl{-}CH_2Cl_{(g)}$$

Reactions of Monochloroalkanes

The predominant reaction of chloroalkanes is the replacement of the halogen. For example, using a strong base, such as sodium hydroxide, a monochloroalkane (also called an alkyl chloride) can be converted by a substitution reaction to an alcohol:

$$CH_3{-}CH_2Cl + OH^- \longrightarrow CH_3{-}CH_2{-}OH + Cl^-$$

There is also the alternative of an elimination reaction to give an alkene:

$$(CH_3)_2CH{-}CH_2Cl + OH^- \longrightarrow (CH_3)_2C{=}CH_2 + H_2O + Cl^-$$

Elimination reactions are particularly favoured when there are alkyl substituents on the carbon to which the halogen is attached. It is important to realize that many organic reactions give mixtures of products and that the nature of the preferred product depends upon a number of factors, including temperature, solvent, and structure of the reactant.

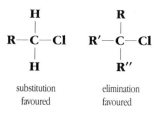

Some Common Chloroalkanes

Trichloromethane (chloroform) was once used as an inhalation anesthetic in surgery. Now we are aware of its toxicity, the compound has been replaced by safer compounds such as halothane, $CHClBr—CF_3$ and methoxyfluorane, $CHCl_2—CF_2—O—CH_3$.

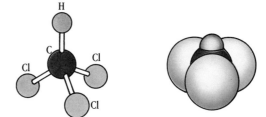

Figure 15.17

The shape of the trichloromethane molecule, CHCl₃:
a) as a ball-and-stick model;
b) as a space-filling model.

Tetrachloromethane (carbon tetrachloride) was used widely as a grease-spot remover. As we discussed earlier, the nonpolar tetrachloromethane is a good solvent for low-polarity stains. It was also used as a fire-extinguishing liquid because the high density of the vapour would smother the flames. We now realize that not only is the compound toxic, but the vapour reacts with water vapour at high temperatures (such as found near fires) to produce the poisonous gas phosgene.

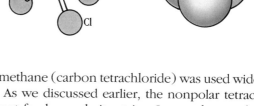

Figure 15.18

An early carbon tetrachloride automatic fire extinguisher. A high temperature would release a pin, breaking the glass bulb, and the tetrachloromethane would drop onto the fire.

Many chlorine-containing compounds are extremely toxic. This property has been used in many insecticides, such as DDT (dichlorodiphenyltrichloroethane), lindane, and chlordane. Many of these compounds are also harmful to other forms of life (such as humans). The herbicide 2,4-D (2,4-dichlorophenoxyacetic acid) mimics a plant growth hormone and causes broadleaf weeds, such as dandelions, to literally grow themselves to death. The compound is commonly added to lawn fertilizers for "weed-free" lawns.

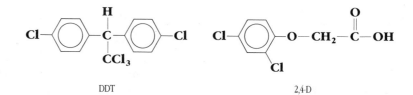

DDT   2,4-D

Another chlorine-containing herbicide, 2,4,5-T (2,4,5-trichlorophenoxy-acetic acid) is especially effective against woody plants. It acts as a defoliant, causing the leaves to fall off. In North America 2,4,5-T has been used extensively for keeping trees from growing near power lines. Combined with 2,4-D it was given the name Agent Orange. In the Vietnam War, Agent Orange was used by the U.S. to remove the tree cover from the North Vietnamese forces and to destroy their food crops. When pure, 2,4-D and 2,4,5-T are comparatively harmless. However, problems arise from the method of synthesis which produces, as by-products, a family of contaminants called dioxins. Dioxins are hazardous at the parts per billion level, causing among other things, birth defects. Chemicals that cause birth defects are known as **teratogens**. As a result of the dioxin impurity in 2,4,5-T, this compound is not generally acceptable for use as a herbicide.

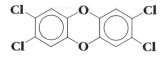

2,4,5-trichlorophenoxyacetic acid
(2,4,5-T)

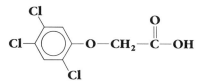

2,3,7,8-tetrachlorodibenza-para-dioxin
(a "dioxin")

Figure 15.19

The effects of spraying a forest in Vietnam over a five-year period with 2,4,5-T.

Polychlorinated Biphenyls

Polychlorinated biphenyls, or PCBs, as they are commonly called, are a group of compounds prepared by reacting chlorine gas with biphenyl, $C_{12}H_{10}$.

This reaction produces a complex mixture of chlorinated biphenyls, with the chlorine atoms substituted at different locations around the rings. A total of 209 different compounds could theoretically exist, but the commercial PCB mixtures usually contain 50 to 70 components.

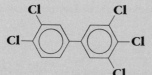

3,4,3′,4′,5′-pentachlorobiphenyl
(a typical polychlorinated biphenyl—PCB)

Figure 15.20
Drums filled with PCBs at Alberta's waste management corporation facilities, await the development of a safe disposal method.

PCBS were manufactured in North America from about 1930 until 1977, and about 700 000 tonnes were produced in the United States alone during this period. PCBS were particularly useful as coolants in transformers, since they conducted heat well, did not break down at high voltages, and had high boiling points. They were also used in hydraulic fluids, specialized lubricants, and in special inks.

Only in the 1960s was it realized that polychlorinated biphenyls were harmful to mammals. Occupational exposure resulted in skin disorders, liver damage, and reproductive (teratogenic) effects.

Apart from their toxicity, there are three major factors that contribute to the PCB problem. First, these chemicals are very stable and persist for decades in the environment. Second, they are water-insoluble and fat-soluble. Because of this, they remain in animal bodies and accumulate in the food chain. Finally, they have high vapour pressures, which means that they readily disperse through the atmosphere. In the northern hemisphere the concentrations of PCBs in the air is about $1 \, ng \cdot m^{-3}$. In organisms this concentration is increased to about $1 \, mg \cdot kg^{-1}$ of body mass. The current range of concentrations of PCBs in our food is from $0.1 \, \mu g \cdot g^{-1}$ in eggs to $2 \, \mu g \cdot g^{-1}$ in fish.

Figure 15.21
Professor Thomas Barton at the Royal Military College demonstrates his high temperature method of destroying PCBs.

We can do nothing about the PCBs already in the environment. However, we must destroy the enormous quantities of stored PCBs. Manitoba Hydro has been one of the leaders in the treatment of its wastes. For oils containing small concentrations of PCBs, Ontario Hydro research scientists have devised a method that uses metallic sodium to remove the chlorine from the PCBs to give useful hydrocarbons and sodium chloride. Another route for destroying PCB-contaminated wastes is the use of special strains of bacteria that seem to thrive on chlorine-rich aromatic compounds. For wastes containing high concentrations of PCBs, an engineer at the Royal Military College, Kingston, has devised a disposal method which uses high-voltage electrical discharges to break the molecules apart. The fragments can then be burned to give carbon dioxide, water and hydrogen chloride. More research is needed, but techniques for disposing of large quantities of these hazardous compounds should soon be available.

QUESTIONS

18. Give the IUPAC name for each of the following compounds:

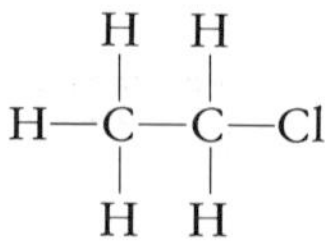

a)

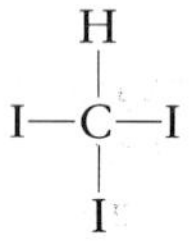

$$I-\underset{\underset{I}{|}}{\overset{\overset{H}{|}}{C}}-I$$

b)

$$H-\underset{\underset{H}{|}}{\overset{\overset{H}{|}}{C}}-\underset{\underset{H}{|}}{\overset{\overset{H}{|}}{C}}-Cl$$

c)

$$Cl-\underset{\underset{H}{|}}{\overset{\overset{H}{|}}{C}}-\underset{\underset{H}{|}}{\overset{\overset{Cl}{|}}{C}}-\underset{\underset{Cl}{|}}{\overset{\overset{H}{|}}{C}}-\underset{\underset{Cl}{|}}{\overset{\overset{H}{|}}{C}}-H$$

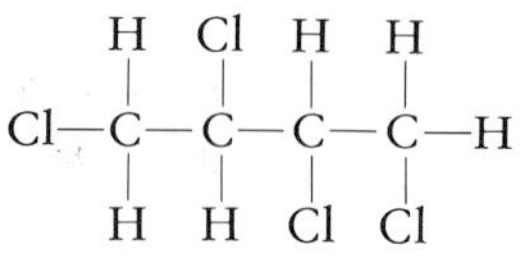

19. Draw the structure of each of the following compounds:
a) 1,1,1-trichloropropane
c) 3-bromopentane
b) 1,2,3,4,5,6-hexachlorocyclohexane

20. Write a balanced equation for each of the following reactions:
a) bromine with propene
b) hydrogen iodide with 2-butene

Amines And Amino Acids

15.8

Nitrogen is found in a wide variety of organic compounds, many of which are important in biological systems. Although nitrogen can also form a double bond and a triple bond with carbon, we will only discuss the compounds that contain nitrogen-carbon single bonds. Even then, there are a large number of compounds to consider. If we regard ammonia as the parent compound, it is possible to have three series of amines, depending upon whether we replace one, two, or three hydrogen atoms with alkyl groups. These series are named **primary**, **secondary**, and **tertiary amines**. We can illustrate this progression by using methyl groups:

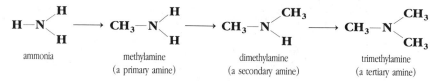

In the discussion of alcohols, the terms primary, secondary, and tertiary are used to describe the number of alkyl groups attached to the *carbon* atom bearing the hydroxyl group. With amines, these same terms refer to the number of alkyl groups attached to the *nitrogen* atom.

TABLE 15.9 *Classification of Amines*		
Number of Alkyl Groups	Number of Hydrogen Atoms	Classification
1	2	primary amine
2	1	secondary amine
3	0	tertiary amine

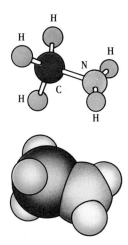

Figure 15.22

The shape of the methylamine molecule, CH_3NH_2:

a) as a ball-and-stick model;

b) as a space-filling model.

Since a nitrogen-hydrogen bond is less polar than an oxygen-hydrogen bond, the hydrogen bonding in primary amines is weaker than in alcohols of related formula. As a result, the boiling points of amines are lower.

TABLE 15.10	*A Comparison of Boiling Points*	
Compound	Number of electrons	Boiling Point (°C)
$CH_3—CH_3$	18	−88
$CH_3—NH_2$	18	−6
$CH_3—OH$	18	65

All simple amines are miscible with water. This can be explained in terms of the formation of networks of hydrogen bonds between the amine molecules and the water molecules.

Most amines have unpleasant odours that range from fishy to putrid. In fact the odour of decaying fish is caused by amine-producing bacteria. The common names of these compounds often reflect their origin and/or odour:

$$NH_2—CH_2—CH_2—CH_2—CH_2—CH_2—NH_2$$
1,5-diaminopentane
(cadaverine)

$$NH_2—CH_2—CH_2—CH_2—CH_2—NH_2$$
1,4-diaminobutane
(putrescine)

The Naming of Amines

There are three commonly-used systems of naming amines. In this book we will only attempt to name simple primary amines. To construct the IUPAC name for these compounds we follow the same rules that we have used before. The base name is taken from the longest chain that contains the **amino group**, $—NH_2$. The prefix *amino-* is used to indicate the presence of the amine functional group. As usual, numbers are used to indicate the carbon to which the amine substituent is attached.

We will use the following example to illustrate this method:

$$CH_3—CH—CH_2—CH—CH_2—CH_3$$
$$\quad\quad\ |\quad\quad\quad\quad\quad |$$
$$\quad\quad NH_2\quad\quad\quad\ CH_3$$

1. Name the longest carbon chain to which the $—NH_2$ group is attached.

$$CH_3—CH—CH_2—CH—CH_2—CH_3$$
$$\quad\quad\ |\quad\quad\quad\quad\quad |$$
$$\quad\quad NH_2\quad\quad\quad\ CH_3$$

The longest chain has six carbon atoms. The base name is hexane.

2. Number the chain so that the numerical prefixes for the substituents are the lowest possible. Name the substituents as prefixes.

$$\overset{1}{CH_3}-\overset{2}{CH}-\overset{3}{CH_2}-\overset{4}{CH}-\overset{5}{CH_2}-\overset{6}{CH_3}$$

with NH_2 at carbon 2 and CH_3 at carbon 4.

An amino substituent is at carbon 2. A methyl substituent is at carbon 4. The name is 2-amino-4-methylhexane.

Reactions of Amines

Amines, like ammonia, are weak bases. For example, aminomethane reacts slightly with water to produce a solution of methylammonium hydroxide:

$$CH_3-NH_{2\,(g)} + H_2O_{(\ell)} \rightleftharpoons CH_3-NH_3^+{}_{(aq)} + OH^-{}_{(aq)}$$

The amines are generally stronger bases than the parent compound. For example, a 1.0 mol·L^{-1} solution of aminomethane has a pH of 12.3 compared to a pH of 11.6 for the same concentration of an ammonia solution.

All amines react with acids to form ionic salts. Thus aminomethane will react with hydrochloric acid to produce a solution of methylammonium chloride:

$$CH_3-NH_2 + HCl \rightleftharpoons CH_3-NH_3^+ + Cl^-$$

Common Amines

One amine is a particularly widespread addictive drug — nicotine. It is produced naturally in plants of the tobacco family. In small doses nicotine is a stimulant. In large doses it causes depression, nausea, and vomiting. In even larger doses it causes death. Solutions of nicotine in water can be used as an insecticide. Nicotinic acid, an oxidation product of nicotine, is vitamin B_3. Unfortunately for smokers, our bodies do not possess an enzyme capable of catalyzing this oxidation. Thus we must rely on food intake for all our supply of this vitamin.

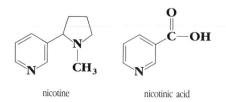

nicotine   nicotinic acid

Histamine is an amine released in the body during allergic reactions, such as to bites or pollen. To counteract the body's immune responses such as sneezing, inflamed eyes, etc., antihistamine compounds such as Benadryl have been developed. These, too, are amines.

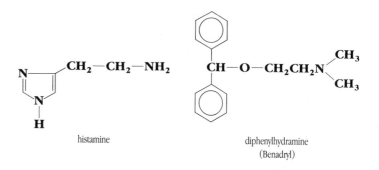

histamine

diphenylhydramine
(Benadryl)

Amino Acids

Most of the organic compounds we have discussed up to this point contain only one functional group. A large proportion of all organic molecules are **bifunctional**, containing two functional groups. The **α-amino acids**, which contain both an amino (NH_2) group and a carboxyl (CO_2H) group, are an example. The α in the name α-amino acid indicates that the amino group and the carboxyl group are both attached to the same carbon atom.

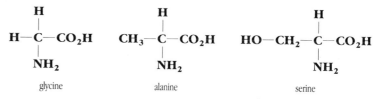

glycine   alanine   serine

The α-amino acids have an important biological role. They are intermediates in metabolic pathways and are used as building blocks for larger molecules such as peptides and proteins.

Peptides and Proteins

A simple amine will react with a carboxylic acid to form an **amide**:

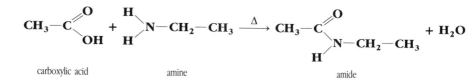

carboxylic acid   amine   amide

Similarly, the amino group of one amino acid can react with the carboxyl group of another amino acid to produce a **dipeptide**:

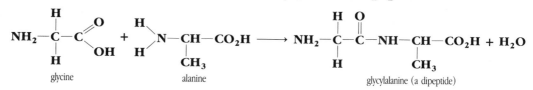

glycine   alanine   glycylalanine (a dipeptide)

Smell, Taste, Toxicity, and Molecular Shape

Molecular shape is as important a property of organic compounds as their molecular structures. Shape is often significant in the biological activity of a molecule, and is fundamental to the detection of smell and taste.

The sense of smell is a fascinating phenomenon. We know that the odour-detecting system in humans consists of about 5×10^6 receptor sites located in the nose, and that "smelly" molecules attach themselves to these sites. The attachment process generates an electric nerve signal that the brain identifies as a smell.

For some time, it was realized that the chemical structures of similarly-smelling compounds were often quite different. In 1949 John Amoore started investigating the relationship between smell and molecular structure. With the help of many volunteers, he first identified a set of primary odours and the chemical compounds that produced them. These odours were categorized as floral, pepperminty, musky, camphoraceous, ethereal, pungent, and putrid. Other odours seemed to be combinations of these primary ones. Amoore then made space-filling molecular models of each compound studied, and constructed cavities into which the models of one type of odour would fit. The cavity had to be designed so that molecules of compounds with other odours would not fit. This proved a most successful exercise. Compounds that had odours that were mixtures of two of his primary odours were found to fit both types of cavity. The only exceptions were the odours of putrid and pungent. Molecules in those two categories had a variety of shapes, were usually polar, and often contained nitrogen or sulfur. Although other theories of odour have since been developed, Amoore's concept of molecular shape controlling odour is widely accepted.

Taste can also be explained in terms of molecular shape, but it appears that intermolecular forces play an important role as well. A sweet-tasting molecule, for example, must have two hydrogen-bonding sites. One site must be slightly positive, such as the hydrogen of a hydroxyl group, and the other must be slightly negative, such as the oxygen of a carbonyl group. To generate a sweet taste, the molecule must also have a bulky nonpolar group.

Molecular shape can be used as a guide to toxicity. In our bodies, we have two families of enzymes: cytochromes P450 and cytochromes P448. Cytochromes P450 metabolize organic compounds into innocuous forms, which the body can eliminate. Cytochromes P448 activate certain substances into forms which can interact with DNA and cause cancerous growth. Using computer-generated space-filling models, it has been found that only flat, thin molecules fit into the cytochromes P448, whereas molecules that are globular tend to fit in the cytochromes P450. As a result the possible hazard of a newly discovered compound can be anticipated on the basis of its molecular shape. One drug that was used in the treatment of arthritis, benoxaprofen (Opren), was later found to be carcinogenic. By examining its molecular shape (Figure 15.23), we can see that benoxaprofen would be a prime suspect as a carcinogen.

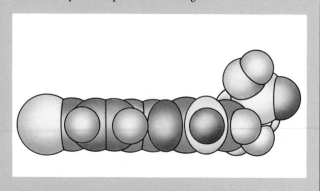

Figure 15.23
A space-filling model of benoxaprofen: flat, thin, and dangerous.

Almost every drug works by this lock-and-key model, in which a natural or synthetic chemical molecule can fit only into certain receptor sites in the body. As we gain a knowledge of the shapes and polarity of the receptor sites, we can start designing molecules that will fit into a specific site, combatting pain or disease. Ideally, such chemical drugs would only affect the problem area, have no side effects, and be non-addictive. This represents a great leap forward from the trial-and-error method that has often been used in the past.

A dipeptide still contains a free amino group and a free carboxyl group. Each of these can react with additional amino acids to produce a **polypeptide**. Polypeptides, with well-defined sequences of amino acids, are found in all living organisms and are called **proteins**.

Every cell in an organism contains many different peptides and proteins, each with a specific function. Large amounts of protein are found in eggs, meat, and milk. When these foods are consumed, their proteins are broken down by digestive enzymes (usually proteins also) into individual amino acids. These acids are then absorbed into the bloodstream and transferred to the various regions of the body. There they combine to form new proteins that are used to build new cells and larger structures such as hair and muscle.

QUESTIONS

21. Give the IUPAC name for:

a) $CH_3—CH_2—CH_2—NH_2$ b) $NH_2—CH_2—CH_2—CH_2—NH_2$

22. Draw the structure of four amines that have the formula C_3H_9N. Two should be primary amines, one a secondary amine, and one a tertiary amine. Attach the appropriate labels to each.

23. Write a balanced equation for the reaction between 1-aminopropane and hydrochloric acid.

Carbohydrates   <u>*15.9*</u>

Simple carbohydrates or **monosaccharides** (also called sugars) have the general formula $(CH_2O)_n$. They are polyhydroxyl compounds, glucose and fructose being typical examples:.

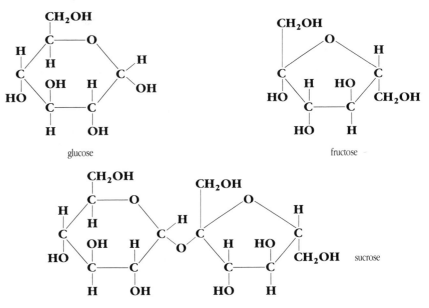

glucose

fructose

sucrose

Ray Lemieux — Carbohydrate Chemist

A major problem in society has been the separation of academic scientific research, performed in universities, and the application of science carried out in industry. Sometimes it may take years for the commercial applications of academic research to be realized. Furthermore, the industrial scientists in another country may see the potential applications sooner and be first to produce the money-making commercial products. Thus it is of major importance that our universities and our technological industries develop links that allow the rapid development of any new discoveries in basic science and to ensure that university researchers are aware of the needs of industry. One of the foremost believers in such university-industry liaison is Ray Lemieux.

Lemieux was born at Lac la Biche, Alberta, in 1920. It was in 1953, at the National Research Council Laboratories in Saskatoon, that he commenced his work on carbohydrates by synthesizing sucrose. For more than 100 years, organic chemists had been attempting this feat, but without success.

In 1961 Lemieux moved to the University of Alberta, where he worked on identifying the structures of some carbohydrates. In 1977 Lemieux started work on a class of complex carbohydrates, called Biosynsorb, that would absorb antibodies from blood. By absorbing antibodies from the blood of patients undergoing transplant surgery, a transplanted organ would be less likely to be rejected.

Lemieux wanted to see the University of Alberta participate in the development of this compound, and with the strong support of then-President, Harry Gunning, he set up Chembiomed, a company wholly-owned by the university. Since then, the company

has flourished and currently employs 65 people, more than half of whom are working in the research and development of new and better products. This symbiotic partnership between the company and the university has provided a source of high-tech employment, a new research group, and a good financial return on investment to the university.

Figure 15.24
Raymond Lemieux (1920-   ) of the University of Alberta.

Table sugar, or sucrose, is also a carbohydrate; however, sucrose is classed as a **disaccharide** since it can be broken down into two simpler monosaccharides. Some organisms, most notably yeast and bees, can convert sucrose into a mixture of glucose and fructose. This mixture, called invert sugar, is sweeter than sucrose alone because of the presence of the free fructose (the sweetest sugar). Honey consists mainly of invert sugar.

Glucose, which is found in blood, is the repeating unit in starch and cellulose, both of which are examples of **polysaccharides**. The only difference between starch and cellulose is the way in which the glucose units are linked together.

Cellulose is an architectural polysaccharide that gives strength to the stems and branches of plants. Dry leaves contain about 20 % cellulose;

wood, 50% cellulose; and cotton, 90% cellulose. Starch is a nutritional polysaccharide that is found in many of our foodstuffs (e.g. potatoes and wheat). Human beings can digest starch but not cellulose. Grazing animals such as cattle and sheep cannot digest cellulose directly, but their digestive tracts contain colonies of bacteria that break down cellulose into smaller molecules. These molecules can then be used by the animals for food. Eating would be much simpler if the human digestive system contained the same bacteria as that of grazing animals — a bowl of grass and bag of sawdust would then make a meal that was both inexpensive and tasty!

QUESTIONS

24. What is the simplest formula for a carbohydrate?

25. Explain the difference between glucose, sucrose, starch, and cellulose.

An Introduction To Polymers

15.10

No branch of chemistry affects our daily lives as much as **polymer chemistry**. Our bodies' proteins and nucleic acids are polymers, as are many of our clothing materials. Synthetic polymers have become such an important part of our technological society that it would be no exaggeration to divide human history into the Stone Age, the Bronze Age, the Iron Age, and the Polymer Age.

The term polymer comes from the Greek words *polus* and *mer*, meaning many parts. Polymers are giant molecules made up of repeating units called monomers. The number of monomer units depends upon the identity of the polymer. For example, nylon contains about 90 monomer units per molecule while natural rubber has between 20 000 and 100 000 monomer units per molecule. Within a sample of a polymer there is always a variation in the actual number of monomer units per molecule, so we can only note the average number. The only exceptions are the nucleic acids and many of the proteins, in which the number of monomer units is precisely defined.

There are several ways to categorize polymers. For example, we can sort them as to whether they are synthetic or naturally-occurring. In the brief space available in this book, we will only look at some of the simpler synthetic polymers.

There are a number of ways of subdividing synthetic polymers. One method is to differentiate them by their response to heat. **Thermoplastics** soften and melt when heated. The melting occurs when the intermolecular forces between neighbouring polymer chains are partially overcome. Hydrocarbon polymers, such as polyethylene, are bonded by dispersion forces, and polyethylene melts in the range of 110 °C to 130 °C. In Section 4.6 we remarked that dispersion forces are the weakest intermolecular forces. With the enormous chain lengths in polymers, however, the combined dispersion forces are so strong that polymers are solid at room temperature. Nylon molecules are attracted to one another by hydrogen bonds as well as dispersion forces. Hence, as we might expect, its melting point of 265 °C is significantly higher than that of polyethylene.

By contrast, **thermoset polymers** do not soften or melt when heated. In these polymers, the chains are cross-linked by covalent bonds. To break the covalent bonds usually requires temperatures in excess of the decomposition temperature of the compound. Because all the molecules are cross-linked, an item made of a thermoset polymer can be considered as one giant molecule.

A Very Brief History of Synthetic Polymers

The beginning of polymer science was concerned with modifying the properties of natural materials. In 1839 Charles Goodyear began experiments to harden natural rubber by heating it with sulfur. Goodyear called this process "vulcanization" after Vulcan, the Roman god of fire. The rising demand for this improved rubber eventually led to shortages and higher prices. This, in turn, prompted chemists to develop a completely synthetic rubber.

Because Britain had access to the rubber plantations of Malaya, while the United States developed a massive rubber reclamation program, neither country had an urgent need for synthetics. It was Germany and the Soviet Union that came to dominate the development and production of synthetic rubber during the early part of this century. When the Japanese forces invaded Malaya in World War II, however, Britain and the United States had to develop a massive synthetic rubber industry almost overnight to replace their lost source of natural rubber. As part of this development, a major expansion in polymer science research was initiated. This led to U.S. dominance in the field of polymers.

Probably the most important single breakthrough in early polymer research was the discovery of Bakelite by Leo Baekeland in 1907. This first completely synthetic polymer was produced by the reaction of phenol with methanal in the presence of a base. Bakelite was the first plastic material to become a household name. It was used for everything from billiard balls (where it replaced ivory) to electric plugs to radio cabinets. Baekeland received the ultimate reward of fame — the cover photo of *Time* magazine — in September 1924.

Polymer science developed from the guesswork of mixing organic reagents and seeing what happened to a science in which a molecular structure could be designed to have desired properties. Also, the work is no longer done by individual chemists. Instead, the work requires teams of polymer, organic, inorganic, physical, and analytical chemists working in large industrial or academic laboratories. A recent example of the team approach is the synthesis of the high-strength fibre, Kevlar, by Paul Morgan, Stephanie Kwolek and many others at the Du Pont research laboratories in 1965.

Two of the simplest types of thermoplastics are formed by addition and condensation reactions. We will look at these two types of polymers next.

Figure 15.25

Three of the team of scientists that developed Kevlar for Du Pont. From left to right: Stephanie Kwolek, Herbert Blades, and Paul Morgan.

Figure 15.26

The Gossamer Albatross, a human-powered plane, is covered by a thin skin of the polyester called Mylar. Its frame is composed of Kevlar, Teflon, and polystyrene.

Addition Polymers

The simple linking of a large number of identical monomer units results in an **addition polymer**. If we use the letter "A" to represent a molecule of a monomer, the polymer would appear as:

$$\cdots-A-A-A-A-A-A-A-A-A-A-A-A-A-A-\cdots$$

The most elementary example is that of ethene which polymerizes to produce polyethene, commonly called polyethylene. Much of the world's supply of polyethylene is produced using the Zeigler catalyst, a mixture of titanium tetrachloride and triethylaluminum. A major area of research has been the development of new and better catalysts for polymerization.

$$n\,CH_2{=}CH_2 \xrightarrow[\text{Al}(C_2H_5)_3]{\text{TiCl}_4} (-CH_2-CH_2-)_n$$

By using alkenes with different substituents, we can produce addition polymers with different properties. Table 15.11 lists some of these:

TABLE 15.11 *Some Addition Polymers and their Uses*

Alkene (monomer) used	Polymer (repeating unit)	Uses
ethene (ethylene)	polyethylene	plastic containers
chloroethene (vinyl chloride)	polyvinyl chloride (PVC)	phonograph records, garden hose, electrical insulation
propene (propylene)	polypropylene	fishing nets
tetrafluoroethene (tetrafluoroethylene)	polytetrafluoroethylene PTFE (Teflon)	nonstick cooking utensils
cyanoethene (acrylonitrile)	polyacrylonitrile (orlon)	fibre for clothes
methyl 2-propenoate (methyl methacrylate)	polymethyl methacrylate (lucite, plexiglas)	transparent plastic, glass substitute
vinylbenzene (styrene)	polystyrene (styrofoam)	packaging, insulation, buoyancy materials

Condensation Polymers

A **condensation polymer** is formed by reacting two components together and, in the process, splitting off small molecules, usually water, from the functional groups. If we use the letter "A" to represent one component and "B" to represent the other, then a condensation polymer can be represented as:

$$\cdots\text{—A—B—A—B—A—B—A—B—A—B—A—B—A—B—A—}\cdots$$

The two components are linked by means of a chemical reaction between functional groups. For example, we saw in Section 15.6 that an alcohol will react with a carboxylic acid to form an ester. If we react a dialcohol with a dicarboxylic acid, then we can form a polymer chain with ester linkages. An example of this is given below:

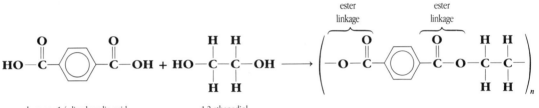

benzene-1,4-dicarboxylic acid   1,2-ethanediol   a polyester

An alternative condensation reaction is that between an amine and a carboxylic acid. This gives rise to the nylon family of polymers.

Figure 15.27
The public first saw nylon stockings when they were worn by these models at the New York World's Fair in 1939.

TABLE 15.12 *Some Condensation Polymers and their Uses*

Repeating Unit	Name	Uses
$\left(-\overset{\underset{\mid}{H}}{N}-(CH_2)_6-\overset{\underset{\mid}{H}}{N}-\overset{\underset{\parallel}{O}}{C}-(CH_2)_4-\overset{\underset{\parallel}{O}}{C}-\right)_n$	Polyhexamethylene adipamide (Nylon-66)	clothing fibre
$\left(-O-\overset{\underset{\parallel}{O}}{C}-⬡-\overset{\underset{\parallel}{O}}{C}-O-CH_2-CH_2-\right)_n$	Polyethylene teraphthalate (Dacron, Mylar)	permanent crease fabric audio/video tape
$\left(-\overset{\underset{\mid}{H}}{N}-⬡-\overset{\underset{\mid}{H}}{N}-\overset{\underset{\parallel}{O}}{C}-⬡-\overset{\underset{\parallel}{O}}{C}-\right)_n$	Polyparaphenyleneterephthalamide (Kevlar)	high-strength fibre

Inorganic Polymers

Most organic polymers have the disadvantages of high flammability and low melting points. To overcome these problems, we can incorporate elements other than carbon and oxygen into the polymer chain. The resulting compounds are called **inorganic polymers** even though various carbon containing substituents are involved.

The most widely-used inorganic polymers are the **silicones**. The structure of most silicones can be represented by the general formula:

where "X" represents an organic side-chain. If X is short, a methyl group for example, the polymer will be a liquid oil that is stable to very high temperatures. With longer side groups on the polymer chains we can produce waterproof coatings. If the chains are cross-linked, a heat resistant polymer is produced.

Among the most promising new families of polymers is the **phosphazenes**. These compounds have alternating phosphorus and nitrogen atoms. We can represent them by the general formula:

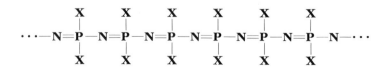

Like the silicones, the properties of the phosphazenes depend upon the nature of the organic substituent. For example, when X is $-O-CH_2-CF_3$, the polymer is more water-repellant than the silicones. In addition, these polymers are highly compatible with living tissue, making them excellent materials for replacement of human anatomical parts.

QUESTIONS

26. What monomer units would be used to prepare the following:
   a) Teflon   b) PVC

27. What would be the repeating unit of a condensation polymer formed from $HO_2C-(CH_2)_4-CO_2H$ and $HO-(CH_2)_{10}-OH$?

Summary

- The family or class to which a given organic compound belongs is determined by the functional group(s) present in that compound.

- Alcohols contain a hydroxyl group and can be classified as primary, secondary, or tertiary, depending on the number of alkyl groups attached to the carbon atom that is bonded to the hydroxyl group. The IUPAC name of an alcohol always ends with -ol.

- Ethers contain an oxygen atom bonded to two alkyl groups. The chemical and physical properties of ethers are similar to those of the alkanes.

- Aldehydes and ketones both contain a carbonyl group, which consists of an oxygen atom joined to a carbon atom by a double bond. An aldehyde has at least one hydrogen attached to the carbonyl carbon atom.

- A ketone has only other carbon atoms directly attached to the carbonyl carbon atom. The IUPAC name of an aldehyde always ends with -al whereas the ending of the IUPAC name of a ketone is -one.

- Carboxylic acids contain a carboxyl group. Like mineral acids, carboxylic acids undergo neutralization reactions with bases to form water plus the corresponding salts. The IUPAC name of a carboxylic acid always ends with -oic acid.

- Phenols contain a hydroxyl group linked to an aromatic ring. The phenols are more acidic than the alcohols.

- Esters can be considered to be formed by replacing the hydrogen of a carboxyl group with an alkyl group. The name of this alkyl group gives us the first part of the ester's name. The second part of the name is derived from the name of the carboxylic acid from which the ester is considered to be formed.

- Fats are triesters derived from three units of carboxylic acid and one unit of glycerol. Unsaturated fats contain one or more carbon-carbon double bonds. Saturated fats contain no carbon-carbon double bonds.

- Halogenated hydrocarbons can be considered to be alkanes in which one of the hydrogen atoms has been replaced by a halogen atom.

- Amines consist of one or more alkyl groups bonded to a nitrogen atom. They are classified as primary, secondary, or tertiary according to the number of alkyl groups attached to the nitrogen atom.

- Amino acids are bifunctional. They contain two functional groups, an amino group and a carboxyl group. The α-amino acids are biologically important because they are building blocks from which proteins are made.

- Simple carbohydrates (or monosaccharides) have the general formula $(CH_2O)_n$. Examples are glucose and fructose, both having the formula $C_6H_{12}O_6$.

- Polymers consist of a large number of repeating monomer units. There are two main classes of synthetic polymers; thermoplastics and thermosetting polymers. We can also categorize them as addition or condensation polymers, depending upon the method of synthesis.

KEY WORDS

addition polymer
alcohol
alkoxy group
aldehyde
amide
amine
α-amino acid
amino group
bifunctional
carbohydrate
carbonyl group
carboxyl group
carboxylic acid
chlorofluorocarbon
condensation polymer
condensation reaction
dipeptide
disaccharide
elimination reaction
ester
ether
haloalkane
halogenated hydrocarbons
hydrated
hydration reaction

hydrolyze
hydroxyl group
inorganic polymer
isotopic labelling
ketone
monosaccharide
peptide
phenol
phosphazenes
polyether
polymer
polymer chemistry
polypeptide
polysaccharide
primary alcohol
primary amine
protein
secondary alcohol
secondary amine
silicones
teratogens
tertiary alcohol
tertiary amine
thermoplastic
thermoset polymer

1. The miscible alcohol is 1-propanol. As the dispersion forces dominate for long-chain alcohols, we would expect 1-decanol to have very low solubility in water.

2. $CH_3-CH_2-CH_2-CH_2-CH_2$, 1-pentanol
$\quad\quad\quad\quad\quad\quad\quad\quad\quad\quad\quad |$
$\quad\quad\quad\quad\quad\quad\quad\quad\quad\quad\quad OH$

$\quad CH_3-CH_2-CH_2-CH-CH_3$, 2-pentanol
$\quad\quad\quad\quad\quad\quad\quad\quad\quad\quad |$
$\quad\quad\quad\quad\quad\quad\quad\quad\quad\quad OH$

$\quad CH_3-CH_2-CH-CH_2-CH_3$, 3-pentanol
$\quad\quad\quad\quad\quad\quad\quad |$
$\quad\quad\quad\quad\quad\quad\quad OH$

$\quad\quad\quad\quad\quad CH_3$
$\quad\quad\quad\quad\quad\quad |$
$\quad CH_3-C-CH_2-CH_3$, 2-methyl-2-butanol
$\quad\quad\quad\quad\quad\quad |$
$\quad\quad\quad\quad\quad OH$

$\quad\quad\quad\quad\quad CH_3$
$\quad\quad\quad\quad\quad\quad |$
$\quad CH_2-CH-CH_2-CH_3$, 2-methyl-1-butanol
$\quad\quad |$
$\quad OH$

$\quad\quad\quad\quad\quad CH_3$
$\quad\quad\quad\quad\quad\quad |$
$\quad CH_3-CH-CH-CH_3$, 3-methyl-2-butanol
$\quad\quad\quad\quad\quad\quad\quad |$
$\quad\quad\quad\quad\quad\quad\quad OH$

$\quad\quad\quad\quad\quad CH_3$
$\quad\quad\quad\quad\quad\quad |$
$\quad CH_3-CH-CH_2-CH_2-OH$, 3-methyl-1-butanol

$\quad\quad\quad\quad\quad CH_3$
$\quad\quad\quad\quad\quad\quad |$
$\quad CH_3-C-CH_2-OH$, 2,2-dimethyl-1-propanol
$\quad\quad\quad\quad\quad\quad |$
$\quad\quad\quad\quad\quad CH_3$

3. a) $CH_3-CH_2-CH-CH_2-CH_2-CH_3$
$\quad\quad\quad\quad\quad\quad\quad\quad |$
$\quad\quad\quad\quad\quad\quad\quad\quad OH$

$\quad\quad\quad\quad\quad CH_3$
$\quad\quad\quad\quad\quad\quad |$
b) $CH_3-CH-CH-CH_2-CH_2-CH_3$
$\quad\quad\quad\quad\quad\quad\quad\quad |$
$\quad\quad\quad\quad\quad\quad\quad\quad OH$

$\quad\quad\quad\quad\quad CH_3\ CH_3$
$\quad\quad\quad\quad\quad\quad |\quad\ |$
c) $CH_3-C-CH-CH_2-CH_2-CH_3$
$\quad\quad\quad\quad\quad\quad |$
$\quad\quad\quad\quad\quad OH$

4. Primary: 1-pentanol, 2-methyl-1-butanol, 3-methyl-1-butanol, and 2,2-dimethyl-1-propanol
Secondary: 2-pentanol, 3-pentanol, and 3-methyl-2-butanol
Tertiary: 2-methyl-2-butanol

5. a) $2\ CH_3OH + 2\ Na \longrightarrow 2\ CH_3O^- + 2\ Na^+ + H_2$

b) $CH_3OH + HBr \longrightarrow CH_3Br + H_2O$

c) $CH_3CH_2CH_2OH + H_2SO_4 \longrightarrow CH_3CH_2CH_2OH_2^+ + HSO_4^-$
$CH_3CH_2CH_2OH_2^+ \longrightarrow CH_3CH{=}CH_2 + H_3O^+$

d) $CH_3CH_2OH + 3\ O_2 \longrightarrow 2\ CO_2 + 3\ H_2O$

e) $3\ CH_3CH_2CH_2CH_2OH + Cr_2O_7^{2-} + 8\ H^+ \longrightarrow$
$$3\ CH_3CH_2CH_2CHO + 2\ Cr^{3+} + 7\ H_2O$$
$3\ CH_3CH_2CH_2COH + Cr_2O_7^{2-} + 8\ H^+ \longrightarrow$
$$3\ CH_3CH_2CH_2CO_2H + 2\ Cr^{3+} + 4\ H_2O$$

f) $3\ CH_3CH(OH)CH_2CH_3 + Cr_2O_7^{2-} + 8\ H^+ \longrightarrow$
$$3\ CH_3COCH_2CH_3 + 2\ Cr^{3+} + 7\ H_2O$$

6. a) methoxyethane   b) 2-methoxybutane

7. $CH_3OCH_2CH_3 + 2\ HBr \longrightarrow CH_3Br + CH_3CH_2Br + H_2O$

8. a)
$$CH_3-CH_2-\overset{\overset{\displaystyle O}{\|}}{C}-CH_2-CH_3$$

b)
$$CH_3-\overset{\overset{\displaystyle CH_3}{|}}{CH}-\overset{\overset{\displaystyle O}{\|}}{C}-\overset{\overset{\displaystyle CH_3}{|}}{CH}-CH_2-CH_3$$

c)
$$CH_3-CH_2-CH_2-\overset{\overset{\displaystyle O}{\diagup}}{\underset{\diagdown H}{C}}$$

d)
$$CH_3-CH_2-CH_2-\overset{\overset{\displaystyle CH_3}{|}}{CH}-\overset{\overset{\displaystyle O}{\diagup}}{\underset{\diagdown H}{C}}$$

9. a) 4-methyl-2-pentanone   b) 2,2-dimethylpropanal

10. a) $HCHO + H_2O \longrightarrow HCO_2H + 2\ H^+ + 2\ e^-$
$Cr_2O_7^{2-} + 14\ H^+ + 6\ e^- \longrightarrow 2\ Cr^{3+} + 7\ H_2O$
$3\ HCHO + Cr_2O_7^{2-} + 8\ H^+ \longrightarrow 3\ HCO_2H + 2\ Cr^{3+} + 4\ H_2O$

b) $CH_3COCH_3 + H_2 \longrightarrow CH_3CH(OH)CH_3$

11. a) pentanoic acid   b) 2,2-dimethylpropanoic acid

12. a)
$$CH_3-CH_2-CH_2-CH_2-CH_2-CH_2-\overset{\overset{\displaystyle O}{\diagup}}{\underset{\diagdown OH}{C}}$$

b)
$$CH_3-CH_2-\overset{\overset{\displaystyle CH_3}{|}}{CH}-CH_2-\overset{\overset{\displaystyle O}{\diagup}}{\underset{\diagdown OH}{C}}$$

13. a) $HCO_2H + KOH \longrightarrow HCO_2^- + K^+ + H_2O$

b) $2\ CH_3CH_2CO_2H + CaCO_3 \longrightarrow Ca(CH_3CH_2CO_2)_2 + H_2O + CO_2$

c) $CH_3CO_2H + CH_3CH(OH)CH_3 \longrightarrow CH_3-\overset{\overset{\displaystyle O}{\diagup}}{\underset{\diagdown O-\overset{\overset{\displaystyle CH_3}{|}}{\underset{\underset{\displaystyle CH_3}{|}}{CH}}}{C}} + H_2O$

14. a) propyl methanoate   b) methyl butanoate

15. a)

$$CH_3-C{\overset{O}{\underset{O-CH_3}{\lessgtr}}} \qquad H-C{\overset{O}{\underset{O-CH_2-CH_3}{\lessgtr}}}$$

b) methyl ethanoate, ethyl methanoate

c) methanol, ethanoic acid; ethanol, methanoic acid

16.

$$CH_3(CH_2)_7{\underset{H}{\overset{}{\diagdown}}}C=C{\underset{H}{\overset{(CH_2)_7CO_2H}{\diagup}}}$$

17. $HCO_2CH_2CH_2CH_3 + H_2O \rightleftharpoons HCO_2H + CH_3CH_2CH_2OH$

$CH_3CH_2CH_2CO_2CH_3 + H_2O \rightleftharpoons CH_3CH_2CH_2CO_2H + CH_3OH$

18. a) triiodomethane   b) chloroethane   c) 1,2,3,4-tetrachlorobutane

19. a)

$$Cl-\underset{\underset{Cl}{|}}{\overset{\overset{Cl}{|}}{C}}-\underset{\underset{H}{|}}{\overset{\overset{H}{|}}{C}}-\underset{\underset{H}{|}}{\overset{\overset{H}{|}}{C}}-H$$

b)

$$\text{(cyclohexane ring with Cl, H, Cl, H, Cl, H, Cl, H substituents)}$$

c)

$$H-\underset{\underset{H}{|}}{\overset{\overset{H}{|}}{C}}-\underset{\underset{H}{|}}{\overset{\overset{H}{|}}{C}}-\underset{\underset{H}{|}}{\overset{\overset{Br}{|}}{C}}-\underset{\underset{H}{|}}{\overset{\overset{H}{|}}{C}}-\underset{\underset{H}{|}}{\overset{\overset{H}{|}}{C}}-H$$

20. a) $CH_2{=}CHCH_3 + Br_2 \longrightarrow CH_2BrCHBrCH_3$

b) $CH_3CH{=}CHCH_3 + HI \longrightarrow CH_3CHICH_2CH_3$

21. a) 1-aminopropane

b) 1,3-diaminopropane

22. $CH_3-CH_2-CH_2-NH_2$

primary amine

$$CH_3-\overset{\overset{NH_2}{|}}{CH}-CH_3$$

primary amine

$$CH_3-\overset{\overset{CH_3}{|}}{N}-CH_3$$

tertiary amine

$$CH_3-CH_2-\overset{\overset{H}{|}}{N}-CH_3$$

secondary amine

23. $CH_3CH_2CH_2NH_2 + HCl \rightarrow CH_3CH_2CH_2NH_3{}^+ + Cl^-$

24. $C_6H_{12}O_6$

25. Glucose is the building block for other sugars that contain a six-membered ring. It is a monosaccharide. Starch and cellulose are polysaccharides made up of glucose polymers and differ only in the manner in which the glucose units are linked together. Sucrose is a disaccharide made up of a glucose and a fructose molecule linked together.

26. a)

$$\underset{F}{\overset{F}{\diagdown}}C=C\underset{F}{\overset{F}{\diagup}}$$

b)

$$\underset{H}{\overset{Cl}{\diagdown}}C=C\underset{H}{\overset{H}{\diagup}}$$

27.

$$-O-\overset{\overset{O}{||}}{C}-(CH_2)_4-\overset{\overset{O}{||}}{C}-O-(CH_2)_{10}-$$

1. What is the difference between primary, secondary, and tertiary alcohols? Given an example of each.

2. What is the difference between wood alcohol, grain alcohol, and rubbing alcohol?

3. What is denatured alcohol?

4. What is the approximate carbon-oxygen-carbon bond angle in an ether?

5. Why do ethers have a lower boiling point than the alcohol with the same number of carbon atoms?

6. What is the difference between an aldehyde and an ester?

7. Why is propanone a useful solvent?

8. How does the bonding in the carboxylate ion differ from that in a carboxylic acid?

9. What is a phenol?

10. What two classes of compounds react together to produce an ester?

11. What are two ways of improving the yield during ester synthesis?

12. a) What is the difference between a saturated and an unsaturated triglyceride (fat)?
    b) Why can eating large amounts of saturated animal fats be harmful?
    c) Why are unsaturated fats generally liquid while saturated fats are solids?

13. Why would you expect PCBs to be water-insoluble and fat-soluble?

14. What is the difference between primary, secondary, and tertiary amines?

15. Of what repeating chemical units are the following composed:
    a) proteins   b) cellulose and starch

16. What is the main difference between a thermoplastic and a thermoset polymer?

17. What is the difference between an addition polymer and a condensation polymer?

18. Draw the functional group(s) present in each of the following classes of organic compounds:
    a) aldehydes   d) carboxylic acids   g) alcohols
    b) primary amines e) ketones   h) amino acids
    c) ethers   f) esters

Alcohols

19. What is the minimum number of carbon atoms that must be present in each of the following:
    a) a secondary alcohol   b) a tertiary alcohol

20. Draw the structure and give the IUPAC name for all the possible alcohols with the formula C_4H_9OH. Identify each as a primary, secondary, or tertiary alcohol.

21. Write a balanced equation for the reaction between the following:
    a) an excess of methanol and sulfuric acid
    b) methanol and permanganate ion
    c) 2,2-dimethyl-1-butanol with hydrochloric acid
    d) 1,4-butanediol and an excess of sulfuric acid

Ethers

22. Draw the structure and give both the common and IUPAC names of each of the three ethers with the formula $C_4H_{10}O$.

23. a) Draw the structure and provide the IUPAC name of the ether with the formula C_2H_6O.
    b) Which common organic compound, belonging to a different family or class, has the same formula as the ether in part a)? Draw the structure of this compound and give its IUPAC name.

24. Why would it be difficult to prepare methoxyethane by reacting a mixture of methanol and ethanol with sulfuric acid? What physical method might enable you to obtain the required product?

Aldehydes and Ketones

25. Draw the structure and give the IUPAC name of both an aldehyde and a ketone with the formula C_3H_6O.

26. Two aldehydes and one ketone have the formula C_4H_8O. Draw the structures of these compounds and name each one according to the IUPAC system.

27. Which alcohol would you oxidize to prepare:
    a) pentanal   b) 3-pentanone

28. Write a balanced equation for the oxidation of 2-methylpropanal with dichromate ion.

Carboxylic Acids

29. Give the IUPAC names of the following acids:

a) $CH_3-CH-CH_2-CH_2-CH_2-C\overset{\displaystyle O}{\underset{\displaystyle OH}{\diagup}}$
   $\qquad\quad |$
   $\qquad\ CH_3$

b) $CH_3-\overset{\displaystyle CH_3}{\underset{\displaystyle CH_3}{\overset{|}{\underset{|}{C}}}}-C\overset{\displaystyle O}{\underset{\displaystyle OH}{\diagup}}$

30. Write a balanced chemical equation for the following:
    a) the ionization of methanoic acid in water
    b) the reaction between propanoic acid and barium hydroxide
    c) the reaction between 1 mol of 1,2-ethanediol and 2 mol of ethanoic acid

Esters

31. Give the IUPAC names of the following esters:

a) CH$_3$—CH$_2$—C(=O)—O—CH$_2$—CH$_3$

b) CH$_3$—CH$_2$—C(=O)—O—CH$_2$—CH$_2$—CH$_3$

32. Draw the condensed formula of each carboxylic acid and ester that has the molecular formula $C_4H_8O_2$.

33. Draw the condensed formula of each carboxylic acid and ester with the molecular formula $C_5H_{10}O_2$. (*Hint:* there are four carboxylic acids and nine esters.)

34. Write a balanced equation to show how each of the following esters could be prepared in the laboratory:

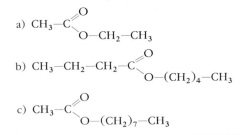

a) CH$_3$—C(=O)—O—CH$_2$—CH$_3$

b) CH$_3$—CH$_2$—CH$_2$—C(=O)—O—(CH$_2$)$_4$—CH$_3$

c) CH$_3$—C(=O)—O—(CH$_2$)$_7$—CH$_3$

Halogen-Containing Compounds

35. Give the IUPAC name of each of the following:
a) CHBr$_2$CH$_2$CHBr$_2$ c) CH$_2$FCHCl$_2$
b) CCl$_3$CH$_2$CH$_2$CH$_3$ d) CH$_3$CCl(CH$_3$)CH$_3$

36. Deduce the formula of the alkene that you would react with bromine to give (CH$_3$)$_2$CBrCH$_2$Br.

Amines and Amino Acids

37. Give the IUPAC name of each of the following:
a) CH$_2$—CH$_2$—CH—CH$_2$—CH$_2$—CH$_2$
    | | |
    NH$_2$ NH$_2$ NH$_2$

b) CH$_3$—CH—CH—CH$_2$—CH$_2$—CH$_3$
        | |
        NH$_2$ CH$_2$—CH$_3$

38. Write a balanced equation for the reaction between the following:
a) aminobutane and water
b) 1,2-diaminoethane and hydrochloric acid

39. Draw the structures of the eight amines that have the formula $C_4H_{11}N$. Identify which are primary, secondary and tertiary amines.

Carbohydrates

40. Distinguish between mono-, di-, and polysaccharides.

41. Use structural formulas to show how sucrose may be formed from its basic sugar units of glucose and fructose.

42. Classify each of the following structures into mono-, di-, or polysaccharides.

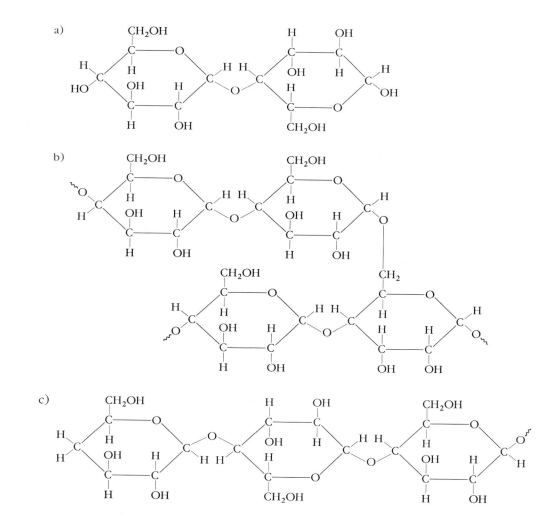

a)

b)

c)

An Introduction to Polymers

43. Draw the structure of the repeating unit of the addition polymer formed by 2-methylpropene.

44. Identify, by formula, the diamine and the dicarboxylic acid that are used to make the polymer, Nomex.

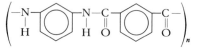

45. Because of the high density of its vapour, carbon tetrachloride was at one time used in fire extinguishers. Calculate the density of carbon tetrachloride, $CCl_{4\,(g)}$, at 200 °C and 100.0 kPa.

46. The balanced equation for the explosive reaction of nitroglycerin is

$$4\,C_3H_5(ONO_2)_{3\,(\ell)} \longrightarrow 12\,CO_{2\,(g)} + O_{2\,(g)} + 6\,N_{2\,(g)} + 10\,H_2O_{(g)}$$

If 5.0 g of nitroglycerin explodes in a 1.0 L container, calculate the resulting pressure inside the container if the final temperature is 45 °C.

47. Suggest chemical and physical tests to distinguish between
a) ethanol and methoxylmethane   c) propanol and propanone
b) butanoic acid and ethylethanoate

48. Compound A, of formula C_2H_6O, is oxidized to compound B of formula C_2H_4O. B is further oxidized to compound C of formula $C_2H_4O_2$. C reacts with A to produce a compound D of formula $C_4H_8O_2$. Give the IUPAC names and draw the structures of the four compounds.

49. A compound of formula C_3H_8O exists as two isomers, A and B. With a strong oxidizing agent, A forms a compound C of formula C_3H_6O. While B forms compound D of formula $C_3H_6O_2$. D turns blue litmus paper to red. Give the IUPAC names and draw the structures of the four compounds.

50. A compound has the chemical composition of 40.0 % carbon, 53.3 % oxygen and 6.7 % hydrogen. A mass of 1.00 g of the compound occupies a volume of 0.645 L at 80 kPa and 100 °C. Determine the molecular formula. Draw two possible molecular structures corresponding to this formula. Suggest a test that you could use to determine which was the correct structure of the compound.

51. The compounds butanone, 1-butanol, ethoxyethane, and butane have boiling points of 272 K, 307 K, 352 K and 390 K, though not in that order. Match the compound to its boiling point.

1. The pharmaceutical industry produces a wide variety of chemicals for medicinal purposes. Using reference books, write an essay on some of the chemicals produced by this industry and their use in medicine.

2. Steroids are a group of naturally-occurring organic compounds. Find out all you can about the structures of these compounds and the roles they play in the human body.

3. Prepare and purify a number of organic esters that have distinctive aromas. Organize a display of these compounds, including information on their structures and method of preparation. Be sure you are aware of the necessary safety precautions before preparing these compounds. This will require checking with your instructor.

4. Identify the different synthetic polymers used as fibres in clothing. Use reference books to determine the repeating unit in each one. Prepare a report on the advantages and disadvantages of each polymer as a clothing material.

Appendix I

Atomic Masses and Electronegativity Values of the Elements

Name	Symbol	Atomic Number	Atomic Mass(u)*	Electronegativity Value**	Name	Symbol	Atomic Number	Atomic Mass(u)*	Electronegativity Value**
Actinium	Ac	89	227.0	1.1	Hafnium	Hf	72	178.5	1.3
Aluminum	Al	13	26.98	1.5	Helium	He	2	4.003	
Americium	Am	95	(243)	1.3	Holmium	Ho	67	164.9	1.2
Antinomy	Sb	51	121.8	1.9	Hydrogen	H	1	1.008	2.1
Argon	Ar	18	39.95		Indium	In	49	114.8	1.7
Arsenic	As	33	74.92	2.0	Iodine	I	53	126.9	2.5
Astatine	At	85	(210)	2.2	Iridium	Ir	77	192.2	2.2
Barium	Ba	56	137.3	0.9	Iron	Fe	26	55.85	1.8
Berkelium	Bk	97	(247)	1.3	Krypton	Kr	36	83.80	3.0
Beryllium	Be	4	9.012	1.5	Lanthanum	La	57	138.9	1.1
Bismuth	Bi	83	209.0	1.9	Lawrencium	Lr	103	(257)	
Boron	B	5	10.81	2.0	Lead	Pb	82	207.2	1.8
Bromine	Br	35	79.90	2.8	Lithium	Li	3	6.941	1.0
Cadmium	Cd	48	112.4	1.7	Lutetium	Lu	71	175.0	1.3
Calcium	Ca	20	40.08	1.0	Magnesium	Mg	12	24.31	1.2
Californium	Cf	98	(249)	1.3	Manganese	Mn	25	54.94	1.6
Carbon	C	6	12.01	2.5	Mendelevium	Md	101	(256)	1.3
Cerium	Ce	58	140.1	1.1	Mercury	Hg	80	200.6	2.0
Cesium	Cs	55	132.9	0.7	Molybdenum	Mo	42	95.94	2.3
Chlorine	Cl	17	35.45	3.0	Neodymium	Nd	60	144.2	1.1
Chromium	Cr	24	52.00	1.7	Neon	Ne	10	20.18	
Cobalt	Co	27	58.93	1.9	Neptunium	Np	93	237.0	1.3
Copper	Cu	29	63.55	2.0	Nickel	Ni	28	58.69	1.9
Curium	Cm	96	(247)	1.3	Niobium	Nb	41	92.91	1.6
Dysprosium	Dy	66	162.5	1.2	Nitrogen	N	7	14.01	3.0
Einsteinium	Es	99	(254)	1.3	Nobelium	No	102	(254)	1.3
Erbium	Er	68	167.3	1.2	Osmium	Os	76	190.2	2.2
Europium	Eu	63	152.0		Oxygen	O	8	16.00	3.5
Fermium	Fm	100	(253)	1.3	Palladium	Pd	46	106.4	2.2
Fluorine	F	9	19.00	4.0	Phosphorus	P	15	30.97	2.1
Francium	Fr	87	(223)	0.7	Platinum	Pt	78	195.1	2.3
Gadolinium	Gd	64	157.3	1.2	Plutonium	Pu	94	(242)	1.3
Gallium	Ga	31	69.72	1.6	Polonium	Po	84	(210)	2.0
Germanium	Ge	32	72.59	1.8	Potassium	K	19	39.10	0.8
Gold	Au	79	197.0	2.5	Praseodymium	Pr	59	140.9	1.1

Name	Symbol	Atomic Number	Atomic Mass(u)*	Electronegativity Value**	Name	Symbol	Atomic Number	Atomic Mass(u)*	Electronegativity Value**
Promethium	Pm	61	(147)		Thulium	Tm	69	168.9	1.3
Protactinium	Pa	91	231.0	1.5	Tin	Sn	50	118.7	1.8
Radium	Ra	88	226.0	0.9	Titanium	Ti	22	47.88	1.5
Radon	Rn	86	(222)		Tungsten	W	74	183.9	2.4
Rhenium	Re	75	186.2	1.9	Unnilennium	Une	109	(266)	
Rhodium	Rh	45	102.9	2.3	Unnilhexium	Unh	106	(263)	
Rubidium	Rb	37	85.47	0.8	Unniloctium	Uno	108	(265)	
Ruthenium	Ru	44	101.1	2.2	Unnilpentium	Unp	105	(260)	
Samarium	Sm	62	150.4	1.2	Unnilquadium	Unq	104	(257)	
Scandium	Sc	21	44.96	1.4	Unnilseptium	Uns	107	(262)	
Selenium	Se	34	78.96	2.4	Uranium	U	92	238.0	1.7
Silicon	Si	14	28.09	1.8	Vanadium	V	23	50.94	1.6
Silver	Ag	47	107.9	1.9	Xenon	Xe	54	131.3	2.6
Sodium	Na	11	22.99	0.9	Ytterbium	Yb	70	173.0	
Strontium	Sr	38	87.62	1.0	Yttrium	Y	39	88.91	1.2
Sulfur	S	16	32.07	2.5	Zinc	Zn	30	65.39	1.7
Tantalum	Ta	73	180.9	1.5	Zirconium	Zr	40	91.22	1.3
Technetium	Tc	43	98.91	1.9					
Tellurium	Te	52	127.6	2.1					
Terbium	Tb	65	158.9						
Thallium	Tl	81	204.4	1.8					
Thorium	Th	90	232.0	1.3					

* Values have been rounded to four significant figures. Approximate values for the atomic masses of non-naturally occurring elements are given in parentheses.
** Pauling's values rounded to two significant figures. An element without an entry does not have a measured electronegativity value.

Appendix II

Specific Heat Capacities of Various Substances (at 100 kPa and 25°C)

Substance	Specific Heat Capacity* $(J \cdot g^{-1} \cdot °C^{-1})$	Substance	Specific Heat Capacity* $(J \cdot g^{-1} \cdot °C^{-1})$	Substance	Specific Heat Capacity* $(J \cdot g^{-1} \cdot °C^{-1})$
$Na_{(s)}$	1.24	$Hg_{(\ell)}$	0.139	$He_{(g)}$	5.19
$Al_{(s)}$	0.903	$H_2O_{(\ell)}$	4.18	$CO_{2\,(g)}$	0.843
$Fe_{(s)}$	0.449	$C_2H_5OH_{(l)}$	2.46	$C_2H_{4\,(g)}$	1.56
$Cu_{(s)}$	0.385	$H_{2\,(g)}$	14.4	$H_2O_{(g)}$	1.86
$Ag_{(s)}$	0.235	$N_{2\,(g)}$	1.04		
$Au_{(s)}$	0.129	$O_{2\,(g)}$	0.917	* Values rounded to three significant figures.	

Appendix III

Thermochemical Data of Selected Elements and Compounds*

Substance	ΔH_f° $(\text{kJ}\cdot\text{mol}^{-1})$	S° $(\text{J}\cdot\text{K}^{-1}\cdot\text{mol}^{-1})$	ΔG_f° $(\text{kJ}\cdot\text{mol}^{-1})$	C_p° $(\text{J}\cdot\text{K}^{-1}\cdot\text{mol}^{-1})$
$Al_{(s)}$	0	28.3	0	24.4
$Al_2O_{3\,(s)}$	−1675.7	50.9	−1582.3	79.0
$Br_{2\,(\ell)}$	0	151.6	0	75.7
$HBr_{(g)}$	−36.4	198.7	−53.5	29.1
$Ca_{(s)}$	0	41.4	0	26.3
$CaCO_{3\,(s)}$ (calcite)	−1206.9	92.9	−1128.8	81.9
$CaCl_{2\,(s)}$	−795.8	104.6	−748.1	72.6
$C_{(s)}$ (graphite)	0	5.7	0	8.5
$C_{(s)}$ (diamond)	1.90	2.38	2.90	6.1
$CCl_{4\,(\ell)}$	−135.4	216.4	−65.2	131.8
$CCl_{4\,(g)}$	−96.0	309.9	−60.6	83.4
$CHCl_{3\,(\ell)}$	−134.5	201.7	−73.7	124.3
$CH_{4\,(g)}$	−74.8	186.3	−50.7	35.3
$C_2H_{2\,(g)}$	226.7	200.9	209.2	43.9
$C_2H_{4\,(g)}$	52.3	219.6	68.2	43.6
$C_2H_{6\,(g)}$	−84.7	229.6	−32.8	52.6
$C_3H_{8\,(g)}$	−103.8	269.9	−23.5	73.5
$C_6H_{6\,(\ell)}$	49.0	172.8	124.5	81.7
$CH_3OH_{(\ell)}$	−238.7	126.8	−166.3	81.6
$C_2H_5OH_{(\ell)}$	−277.7	160.7	−174.8	113.2
$CH_3CO_2H_{(\ell)}$	−484.5	159.8	−389.9	124.3
$CO_{(g)}$	−110.5	197.7	−137.2	29.1
$CO_{2\,(g)}$	−393.5	213.7	−394.4	37.1
$COCl_{2\,(g)}$	−218.8	283.5	−204.6	57.7
$CS_{2\,(g)}$	+117.4	237.8	67.1	45.7
$Cl_{2\,(g)}$	0	223.1	0	33.9
$HCl_{(g)}$	−92.3	186.9	−95.3	29.1
$Cr_{(s)}$	0	23.8	0	23.3
$CrCl_{3\,(s)}$	−556.5	123.0	−486.1	91.8
$Cu_{(s)}$	0	33.2	0	24.5
$CuO_{(s)}$	−157.3	42.6	−129.7	42.3
$CuCl_{(s)}$	−137.2	86.2	−119.9	48.5
$CuCl_{2\,(s)}$	−220.1	108.1	−175.7	71.9
$F_{2\,(g)}$	0	202.8	0	31.3
$HF_{(g)}$	−271.1	173.8	−273.2	29.1

* measured at 100 kPa and 25 °C

Substance	ΔH_f° (kJ·mol^{-1})	S° (J·K^{-1}·mol^{-1})	ΔG_f° (kJ·mol^{-1})	C_p° (J·K^{-1}·mol^{-1})
He$_{(g)}$	0	126.0	0	20.8
H$_{2\,(g)}$	0	130.7	0	28.8
H$_2$O$_{(\ell)}$	−285.8	69.9	−237.1	75.3
H$_2$O$_{(g)}$	−241.8	188.8	−228.6	33.6
H$_2$O$_{2\,(\ell)}$	−187.8	109.6	−120.4	89.1
Fe$_{(s)}$	0	27.8	0	25.1
FeO$_{(s)}$	−272.0	57.6	245.1	48.1
Fe$_2$O$_{3\,(s)}$	−824.2	87.4	−742.2	103.8
Fe$_3$O$_{4\,(s)}$	−1118.4	146.4	−1015.4	143.4
FeCl$_{2\,(s)}$	−341.8	118.0	−302.3	76.7
FeCl$_{3\,(s)}$	−399.5	142.3	−344.0	96.7
FeS$_{2\,(s)}$ (pyrite)	−178.2	52.9	−166.9	62.2
Pb$_{(s)}$	0	64.8	0	26.4
PbCl$_{2\,(s)}$	−359.4	136.0	−314.1	77.1
Mg$_{(s)}$	0	32.7	0	23.9
MgCl$_{2\,(s)}$	−641.3	89.6	−591.8	71.4
MgO$_{(s)}$	−601.7	26.9	−569.4	37.8
Hg$_{(\ell)}$	0	76.0	0	27.9
HgS$_{(s)}$	−58.2	82.4	−50.6	48.4
Ne$_{(g)}$	0	146.2	0	20.8
N$_{2\,(g)}$	0	191.6	0	29.1
NH$_{3\,(g)}$	−46.1	192.5	−16.5	35.1
N$_2$H$_{4\,(\ell)}$	50.6	121.2	149.3	98.9
NH$_4$Cl$_{(s)}$	−314.4	94.6	−202.9	84.1
NH$_4$NO$_{3\,(s)}$	−365.6	151.1	−183.9	139.3
NO$_{(g)}$	90.3	210.8	86.6	29.8
NO$_{2\,(g)}$	33.2	240.1	51.3	37.2
N$_2$O$_{(g)}$	82.1	219.9	104.2	38.5
N$_2$O$_{4\,(g)}$	9.2	304.3	97.9	77.3
HNO$_{3\,(\ell)}$	−174.1	155.6	−80.7	109.9
O$_{(g)}$	249.2	161.1	231.7	21.9
O$_{2\,(g)}$	0	205.1	0	29.4
O$_{3\,(g)}$	142.7	238.9	163.2	39.2
P$_{4\,(s)}$ (white)	0	164.4	0	23.8
P$_{4\,(s)}$ (red)	−70.4	91.2	−48.4	21.2
PH$_{3\,(g)}$	5.4	310.2	13.4	37.1
PCl$_{3\,(g)}$	−287.0	311.8	−267.8	71.8

(continued on page 716)

Substance	ΔH_f° $(\text{kJ} \cdot \text{mol}^{-1})$	S° $(\text{J} \cdot \text{K}^{-1} \cdot \text{mol}^{-1})$	ΔG_f° $(\text{kJ} \cdot \text{mol}^{-1})$	C_p° $(\text{J} \cdot \text{K}^{-1} \cdot \text{mol}^{-1})$
$P_4O_{6\,(s)}$	−2144.3	345.6	−2247.4	142.2
$P_4O_{10\,(s)}$	−2984.0	228.9	−2697.7	211.7
$H_3PO_{4\,(s)}$	−1279.0	110.5	−1119.1	106.1
$K_{(s)}$	0	64.2	0	29.2
$KCl_{(s)}$	−436.7	82.6	−409.1	51.5
$KClO_{3\,(s)}$	−397.7	143.1	−296.3	100.2
$KOH_{(s)}$	−424.8	78.9	−379.1	64.9
$Ag_{(s)}$	0	42.6	0	25.4
$AgCl_{(s)}$	−127.1	96.2	−109.8	50.8
$AgNO_{3\,(s)}$	−124.4	140.9	−33.4	93.1
$Na_{(s)}$	0	51.2	0	28.5
$NaCl_{(s)}$	−411.2	72.1	−384.1	49.7
$NaOH_{(s)}$	−425.6	64.5	−379.5	59.5
$Na_2CO_{3\,(s)}$	−1130.7	135.0	−1044.0	112.3
$S_{(s)}$ (rhombic)	0	31.8	0	22.6
$S_{(g)}$	278.8	167.8	238.3	23.7
$SF_{6\,(g)}$	−1209.0	291.8	−1105.3	97.0
$H_2S_{(g)}$	−20.6	205.8	−33.6	34.2
$SO_{2\,(g)}$	−296.8	248.2	−300.2	39.9
$SO_{3\,(g)}$	−395.7	256.8	−371.1	50.7
$H_2SO_{4\,(\ell)}$	−814.0	156.9	−690.0	138.9
$Sn_{(s)}$ (white)	0	51.6	0	27.0
$Sn_{(s)}$ (gray)	−2.1	44.1	0.1	25.8
$SnCl_{2\,(s)}$	−325.1	122.6	−302.1	79.3
$SnCl_{4\,(\ell)}$	−511.3	258.6	−440.1	165.3

Appendix IV

Average Bond Energies at 298 K					
Bond	Bond Energy $(\text{kJ} \cdot \text{mol}^{-1})$	Bond	Bond Energy $(\text{kJ} \cdot \text{mol}^{-1})$	Bond	Bond Energy $(\text{kJ} \cdot \text{mol}^{-1})$
H—N	393	H—F*	568.2	C—C	347
H—O	460	H—Cl*	431.9	C=C	620
H—S	368	H—Br*	366.1	C≡C	812
H—P	326	H—I*	298.3	C—N	276
H—H*	436.4	C—H	414	C=N	615

Bond	Bond Energy $(kJ \cdot mol^{-1})$	Bond	Bond Energy $(kJ \cdot mol^{-1})$	Bond	Bond Energy $(kJ \cdot mol^{-1})$
C≡N	891	N—O	176	S=S	352
C—O	327	N—P	209	F—F*	150.4
C=O	804	O—O	142	Cl—Cl*	242.7
C—P	263	O=O	498.7	Br—Br*	192.5
C—S	255	O—P	502	I—I*	151.0
C=S	477	O=S	469	C—Cl	326
N—N	393	P—P	197	N—F	275
N=N	418	P=P	489		
N≡N*	941.4	S—S	268		

* Bond energies for which actual values can be obtained.

Appendix V

Solubility Product Constants for Various Compounds at 25°C

Compound	K_{sp}	Compound	K_{sp}
Aluminum hydroxide, $Al(OH)_3$	3.7×10^{-15}	Silver chloride, AgCl	1.6×10^{-10}
Barium carbonate, $BaCO_3$	8.1×10^{-9}	Silver chromate, Ag_2CrO_4	1.9×10^{-12}
Barium fluoride, BaF_2	1.7×10^{-6}	Silver iodide, AgI	1.5×10^{-16}
Barium sulfate, $BaSO_4$	1.1×10^{-10}	Silver sulfate, Ag_2SO_4	1.2×10^{-5}
Calcium carbonate, $CaCO_3$	8.7×10^{-9}	Silver sulfide, Ag_2S	1.8×10^{-50}
Calcium fluoride, CaF_2	3.9×10^{-11}	Strontium carbonate, $SrCO_3$	1.6×10^{-9}
Calcium sulfate, $CaSO_4$	2.0×10^{-4}	Strontium fluoride, SrF_2	7.9×10^{-10}
Copper(II) oxalate, CuC_2O_4	2.9×10^{-9}	Strontium sulfate, $SrSO_4$	7.6×10^{-7}
Copper(II) sulfide, CuS	1.0×10^{-44}	Thallium(I) bromide, TlBr	3.8×10^{-6}
Iron(II) hydroxide, $Fe(OH)_2$	1.8×10^{-15}	Thallium(I) chloride, TlCl	2.2×10^{-4}
Iron(III) hydroxide, $Fe(OH)_3$	$1.1 \times 10^{-36}*$	Thallium(I) iodide, TlI	3.1×10^{-8}
Iron(II) sulfide, FeS	$3.7 \times 10^{-19}*$	Zinc sulfide, ZnS	1.6×10^{-24}
Lead(II) bromide, $PbBr_2$	1.4×10^{-8}	* at 18°C	
Lead(II) iodide, PbI_2	1.4×10^{-8}	** at 27°C	
Lead(II) sulfate, $PbSO_4$	1.3×10^{-8}		
Lithium carbonate, Li_2CO_3	1.7×10^{-3}		
Magnesium fluoride, MgF_2	$6.4 \times 10^{-9}**$		
Magnesium hydroxide, $Mg(OH)_2$	$1.2 \times 10^{-11}*$		
Mercury(II) sulfide, HgS	3.0×10^{-54}		
Silver bromate, $AgBrO_3$	5.8×10^{-5}		
Silver bromide, AgBr	6.5×10^{-13}		
Silver carbonate, Ag_2CO_3	6.2×10^{-12}		

Appendix VI

Acid and Base Ionization Constants of Conjugate Acid-Base Pairs

Acid		K_a	K_b		Base
perchloric acid	$HClO_4$	2.0×10^7	5.0×10^{-22}	ClO_4^-	perchlorate
sulfuric acid	H_2SO_4	1.0×10^3	1.0×10^{-17}	HSO_4^-	hydrogen sulfate
nitric acid	HNO_3	2.2×10^1	4.5×10^{-16}	NO_3^-	nitrate
hydrochloric acid	HCl	1.0×10^6	1.0×10^{-20}	Cl^-	chloride
hydrogen sulfate	HSO_4^-	1.2×10^{-2}	8.3×10^{-13}	SO_4^{2-}	sulfate
phosphoric acid	H_3PO_4	7.5×10^{-3}	1.3×10^{-12}	$H_2PO_4^-$	dihydrogen phosphate
dihydrogen phosphate	$H_2PO_4^-$	6.2×10^{-8}	1.6×10^{-7}	HPO_4^{2-}	hydrogen phosphate
hydrogen phosphate	HPO_4^{2-}	2.2×10^{-13}	4.5×10^{-2}	PO_4^{3-}	phosphate
carbonic acid	H_2CO_3	4.3×10^{-7}	2.3×10^{-8}	HCO_3^-	hydrogen carbonate
hydrogen carbonate	HCO_3^-	5.6×10^{-11}	1.8×10^{-4}	CO_3^{2-}	carbonate
ammonium	NH_4^+	5.6×10^{-10}	1.8×10^{-5}	NH_3	ammonia
nitrous acid	HNO_2	4.6×10^{-4}	2.2×10^{-11}	NO_2^-	nitrate
hydrogen cyanide	HCN	4.9×10^{-10}	2.0×10^{-5}	CN^-	cyanide
hydrogen sulfide	H_2S	9.1×10^{-8}	1.1×10^{-7}	HS^-	hydrogen sulfide
hydrogen sulfide	HS^-	1.1×10^{-12}	9.1×10^{-3}	S^{2-}	sulfide
hypochlorous acid	$HClO$	3.0×10^{-8}	3.3×10^{-7}	ClO^-	hypochlorite
sulfurous acid	H_2SO_3	1.5×10^{-2}	6.7×10^{-13}	HSO_3^-	hydrogen sulfite
hydrogen sulfite	HSO_3^-	1.0×10^{-7}	1.0×10^{-7}	SO_3^{2-}	sulfite
hydrofluoric acid	HF	3.5×10^{-4}	2.9×10^{-11}	F^-	fluoride
boric acid	H_3BO_3	7.3×10^{-10}	1.4×10^{-5}	$H_2BO_3^-$	dihydrogen borate
formic acid	HCO_2H	1.8×10^{-4}	5.6×10^{-11}	HCO_2^-	formate
acetic acid	CH_3CO_2H	1.8×10^{-5}	5.6×10^{-10}	$CH_3CO_2^-$	acetate
oxalic acid	HO_2CCO_2H	5.9×10^{-2}	1.7×10^{-13}	$O_2CCO_2H^-$	hydrogen oxalate
hydrogen oxalate	$O_2CCO_2H^-$	6.4×10^{-5}	1.6×10^{-10}	$O_2CCO_2^{2-}$	oxalate
chloroacetic acid	$ClCH_2CO_2H$	1.4×10^{-3}	7.1×10^{-12}	$ClCH_2CO_2^-$	chloroacetate
lactic acid	$CH_3CH(OH)CO_2H$	8.4×10^{-4}	1.2×10^{-11}	$CH_3CH(OH)CO_2^-$	lactate
ascorbic acid	$C_6H_8O_6$	7.9×10^{-5}	1.3×10^{-10}	$C_6H_7O_6^-$	ascorbate
phenol	C_6H_5OH	1.3×10^{-10}	7.7×10^{-5}	$C_6H_5O^-$	phenoxide

* Values for ionization constants are rounded off to two significant figures.

Appendix VII

Standard Reduction Potentials for Half-Reactions*

Half-reaction	$\mathscr{E}°$ (volts)
$Li^+ + e^- \rightleftharpoons Li$	-3.00
$K^+ + e^- \rightleftharpoons K$	-2.92
$Ca^{2+} + 2\,e^- \rightleftharpoons Ca$	-2.81
$Na^+ + e^- \rightleftharpoons Na$	-2.71
$Mg^{2+} + 2\,e^- \rightleftharpoons Mg$	-2.37
$Ti^{2+} + 2\,e^- \rightleftharpoons Ti$	-1.75
$Al^{3+} + 3\,e^- \rightleftharpoons Al$	-1.67
$V^{2+} + 2\,e^- \rightleftharpoons V$	-1.19
$Mn^{2+} + 2\,e^- \rightleftharpoons Mn$	-1.18
$2\,H_2O + 2\,e^- \rightleftharpoons 2\,OH^- + H_2$	-0.83
$Zn^{2+} + 2\,e^- \rightleftharpoons Zn$	-0.76
$Cr^{3+} + 3\,e^- \rightleftharpoons Cr$	-0.74
$Ag_2S + 2\,e^- \rightleftharpoons 2\,Ag + S^{2-}$	-0.69
$Au(CN)_2^- + e^- \rightleftharpoons Au + 2\,CN^-$	-0.60
$Fe^{2+} + 2\,e^- \rightleftharpoons Fe$	-0.44
$Cr^{3+} + e^- \rightleftharpoons Cr^{2+}$	-0.41
$Cd^{2+} + 2\,e^- \rightleftharpoons Cd$	-0.40
$PbSO_4 + 2\,e^- \rightleftharpoons Pb + SO_4^{2-}$	-0.36
$Co^{2+} + 2\,e^- \rightleftharpoons Co$	-0.28
$V^{3+} + e^- \rightleftharpoons V^{2+}$	-0.26
$Ni^{2+} + 2\,e^- \rightleftharpoons Ni$	-0.23
$Sn^{2+} + 2\,e^- \rightleftharpoons Sn$	-0.14
$Pb^{2+} + 2\,e^- \rightleftharpoons Pb$	-0.13
$Fe^{3+} + 3\,e^- \rightleftharpoons Fe$	-0.04
$2\,H^+ + 2\,e^- \rightleftharpoons H_2$	0.00
$S + 2\,H^+ + 2\,e^- \rightleftharpoons H_2S$	$+0.14$
$Sn^{4+} + 2\,e^- \rightleftharpoons Sn^{2+}$	$+0.15$
$Cu^{2+} + e^- \rightleftharpoons Cu^+$	$+0.15$
$SO_4^{2-} + 4\,H^+ + 2\,e^- \rightleftharpoons SO_2 + 2\,H_2O$	$+0.18$
$Cu^{2+} + 2\,e^- \rightleftharpoons Cu$	$+0.34$
$O_2 + 2\,H_2O + 4\,e^- \rightleftharpoons 4\,OH^-$	$+0.40$
$Cu^+ + e^- \rightleftharpoons Cu$	$+0.52$
$I_2 + 2\,e^- \rightleftharpoons 2\,I^-$	$+0.54$
$O_2 + 2\,H^+ + 2\,e^- \rightleftharpoons H_2O_2$	$+0.68$
$Fe^{3+} + e^- \rightleftharpoons Fe^{2+}$	$+0.77$
$NO_3^- + 2\,H^+ + e^- \rightleftharpoons NO_2 + H_2O$	$+0.78$

Increasing strength as oxidizing agent for species to left of double arrow

Increasing strength as reducing agent for species to right of double arrow

* Ionic concentrations of 1.0 mol·L^{-1} in water at 25 °C.

(continued on page 720)

Half-reaction	$\mathcal{E}°$ (volts)
$Hg_2^{2+} + 2e^- \rightleftharpoons 2Hg$	+0.79
$Ag^+ + e^- \rightleftharpoons Ag$	+0.80
$Hg^{2+} + 2e^- \rightleftharpoons Hg$	+0.85
$NO_3^- + 4H^+ + 3e^- \rightleftharpoons NO + 2H_2O$	+0.96
$AuCl_4^- + 3e^- \rightleftharpoons Au + 4Cl^-$	+1.00
$Br_2 + 2e^- \rightleftharpoons 2Br^-$	+1.06
$O_2 + 4H^+ + 4e^- \rightleftharpoons 2H_2O$	+1.23
$MnO_2 + 4H^+ + 2e^- \rightleftharpoons Mn^{2+} + 2H_2O$	+1.23
$Cr_2O_7^{2-} + 14H^+ + 6e^- \rightleftharpoons 2Cr^{3+} + 7H_2O$	+1.33
$Cl_2 + 2e^- \rightleftharpoons 2Cl^-$	+1.36
$Au^{3+} + 3e^- \rightleftharpoons Au$	+1.46
$ClO_3^- + 6H^+ + 5e^- \rightleftharpoons \frac{1}{2}Cl_2 + 3H_2O$	+1.47
$MnO_4^- + 8H^+ + 5e^- \rightleftharpoons Mn^{2+} + 4H_2O$	+1.50
$Ce^{4+} + e^- \rightleftharpoons Ce^{3+}$	+1.61
$PbO_2 + SO_4^{2-} + 4H^+ + 2e^- \rightleftharpoons PbSO_4 + 2H_2O$	+1.68
$Au^+ + e^- \rightleftharpoons Au$	+1.69
$H_2O_2 + 2H^+ + 2e^- \rightleftharpoons 2H_2O$	+1.77
$Co^{3+} + e^- \rightleftharpoons Co^{2+}$	+1.81
$S_2O_8^{2-} + 2e^- \rightleftharpoons 2SO_4^{2-}$	+2.01
$F_2 + 2e^- \rightleftharpoons 2F^-$	+2.86

Increasing strength as oxidizing agent for species to left of double arrow

Increasing strength as reducing agent for species to right of double arrow

Appendix VIII

Alternative Rules for Rounding Off

As you have seen throughout this text, we have employed the following rules for rounding off:

1. If the first nonsignificant digit is less than 5, it is dropped and the last significant digit remains the same.
2. If the first nonsignificant digit is 5 or greater, it is dropped and the last significant digit is increased by one.

It should be noted, however, that there is another set of rules for rounding off, which may be used:

1. If the first nonsignificant digit is less than 5, it is dropped and the last significant digit remains the same.
2. If the first nonsignificant digit is greater than 5 or 5 is followed by numbers other than zero, it is dropped and the last significant digit is increased by one.
3. If the first nonsignificant digit is 5 or 5 followed by zeros, the 5 is dropped and the significant digit in increased by one only if it is odd, not if it is even.

For instance, if we round off 0.2645 to three significant figures using this latter set of rules, the answer is 0.264. The final significant figure is even and thus is not rounded up.

Glossary of Terms

A

abundance   the percentage of a particular isotope in a sample of an element.

acid   a substance that produces hydrogen ions in solution (Arrhenius theory); a proton donor (Brønsted-Lowry theory).

acid-base indicator   a dye that exhibits different colours in acidic and basic solutions.

acid-base titration   an accurate method of quantitative analysis involving the gradual addition of either an acid to a base or a base to an acid.

acid ionization constant   (symbol K_a); an equilibrium constant relating to the ionization of a weak acid in solution.

activated complex   the grouping of reactant molecules (found at the top of the potential energy diagram) with bonds in the processes both of being formed and being broken.

activation energy   (symbol E_a); the difference between the initial energy of the reactants and the energy of the activated complex at the transition state.

active site   the region of an enzyme molecule onto which reactant molecules must fit for a catalytic reaction to occur.

activity series   a list of metals, plus hydrogen, arranged in order of their reactivity, such that any element in the series will displace ions of the elements below it from aqueous solutions of their salts.

actual yield   the actual mass of a product formed in a given chemical reaction, usually less than the theoretical yield.

addition reaction   a reaction in which atoms or groups of atoms add across a multiple bond; common among alkenes and alkynes.

aliphatic hydrocarbons   a group of organic compounds that contain only hydrogen and carbon atoms within the molecular structure, subdivided into alkanes, alkenes, and alkynes.

alkane   aliphatic hydrocarbons with only carbon-carbon single bonds; for example, ethane.

alkene   aliphatic hydrocarbons with one or more carbon-carbon double bonds; for example, ethene.

alkyl group   the general name given to any side chain of a branch-chain alkane; for example, methyl, ethyl, and propyl.

alkyne   aliphatic hydrocarbons with one or more carbon-carbon triple bonds; for example, ethyne.

allotropes   elements that can exist in two or more different physical forms; diamond and graphite, for example, are allotropes of carbon.

alloy   a homogeneous mixture of a pure metal with another metal (or sometimes with carbon or other nonmetals); the alloy has properties different from those of its component metals.

alpha ray   a stream of helium nuclei produced by the decay of certain radioactive isotopes.

amalgam   the solution of a liquid in a solid; for example, mercury dissolved in gold.

amide   an organic compound containing the —CO—NH— group.

amine   an organic compound derived from ammonia by replacing one or more hydrogen atoms with alkyl groups.

α-amino acid   a bifunctional organic compound containing both an amino group and a carboxyl group attached to the same carbon atom.

amino group   a name for the —NH$_2$ unit in an organic compound.

ampere   (symbol A); the SI unit of electrical current.

anode   the site of oxidation and electron release in an electrochemical cell.

aqueous solution   a solution in which water is the solvent.

aromatic   a group of hydrocarbons characterized by a benzenoid structure in the molecule; for example, toluene.

Arrhenius theory   all acids produce hydrogen ions when they are dissolved in water, and all bases produce hydroxide ions; the hydrogen ions are responsible for the acidic properties of a solution and the hydroxide ions are responsible for the basic properties.

artificial transmutation   artificial processes of changing one element into another; for example, neutron capture by Th-232 followed by radioactive decay results in an isotope of uranium, U-233.

atomic number   the number of protons in the nucleus of an atom.

Aufbau principle   a statement that each additional electron added to an atom will occupy the lowest available energy level.

B

base   a substance that produces hydroxide ions in solution (Arrhenius theory); a proton acceptor (Brønsted-Lowry theory).

base ionization constant   (symbol K_b); an equilibrium constant relating to the ionization of a weak base in solution.

battery   a practical electrochemical cell, or a number of cells connected in series.

becquerel (symbol Bq); a measure of the rate at which an isotope emits radiation; an activity of one becquerel is equal to one disintegration per second.

bent molecule also called V-shaped, describes the shape of molecules such as water in which three atoms are bonded in the shape of a V.

benzene ring the molecular arrangement of six carbon atoms and in a planar hexagonal ring structure in which all carbon-carbon bonds are of the same length.

beta ray a stream of electrons produced by the decay of radioactive isotopes.

bifunctional organic molecules containing two functional groups.

binding energy the energy released when an atomic nucleus is formed from its constituent nuclear particles.

body-centred cubic an arrangement of unit cells in which the second layer of atoms is placed over the spaces in the first layer, and the third layer is placed over spaces in the second layer so that it lies directly above the first layer.

boiling point the temperature (at a certain pressure) at which the vapour pressure of a liquid is equal to the pressure of the atmosphere above it.

bond angle the angle between bonds in a molecule; the degree of the angle determines the shape of the molecule.

bond dissociation energy the energy required to break one particular bond in a molecule; the value depends on the actual reaction and is not an average value.

bond energy the common term for bond enthalpy.

bond enthalpy the correct name for the heat energy absorbed at constant pressure when a chemical bond is broken; commonly called bond energy.

bonding pair a pair of electrons that is involved in the covalent bonding of one atom with another; the arrangement of bonding pairs helps determine the shape of a molecule.

Born-Haber cycle a graphic method of considering the formation of an ionic compound to occur in a series of simple, hypothetical steps.

branched-chain alkane an alkane in which one or more carbon atoms are bonded to three or four other carbon atoms; for example,

Brønsted-Lowry theory an acid is a molecule or ion that can give up a hydrogen ion, and a base is any molecule or ion that can accept a hydrogen ion.

buffer a substance that minimizes large pH changes in a solution when small amounts of acids or bases are added.

C

calorimeter a device used for measuring a heat change.

calorimetry the branch of thermochemistry concerned with the measurement of heat changes during reactions, using a calorimeter.

CANDU reactor CANadian Deuterium-Uranium reactor; a Canadian-designed nuclear reactor that uses natural uranium as fuel.

carbohydrates organic compounds with the general formula $(CH_2O)_n$; commonly known as sugars.

carbonyl group name for the C=O unit; found in aldehydes and ketones.

carboxyl group found in the molecule of an organic acid, these groups are a combination of a carbonyl and a hydroxyl group:

carboxylic acid a class of organic compounds containing the carboxyl group.

catalyst a substance that changes the reaction rate, but which is generated at the conclusion of the reaction.

catenation the ability of carbon compounds to bond together to form long chains.

cathode the site of reduction and electron consumption in an electrochemical cell.

cetane number a rating for the ignition quality of diesel fuels against a standard value of 100 for hexadecane.

chain initiation a step that begins a chain reaction.

chain propagation intermediate steps in a chain reaction.

chain reaction a mechanism involving steps in which a reaction intermediate is continually regenerated and consumed.

chain termination a step or steps in a chain reaction in which intermediate products are consumed so the chain reaction cannot continue.

change of phase the change of a substance from one phase (i.e. liquid, solid, or gas) to another, brought about by a change in pressure and temperature.

chemical energy the energy released by the formation of chemical bonds between atoms; often used to mean the energy change in a chemical reaction.

chlorofluorocarbons very stable and unreactive compounds containing carbon bonded with fluorine and chlorine atoms.

closed system a system in which neither reactants nor products can enter or leave the system.

coenzyme a species that must be present for an enzyme to function effectively; for example, vitamins.

colligative properties properties of solutions that depend only upon the number of dissolved particles present, and not on their type; for example, osmosis.

collision theory for a chemical reaction to occur, the reacting molecules must collide with one another.

combination reaction a reaction in which two or more simple substances combine to form a more complex substance:

$$A + B \longrightarrow C$$

combustion a chemical reaction in which substances react with oxygen to produce heat and light.

combustion reaction the burning of an organic substance containing carbon and hydrogen; these react with oxygen from the air to produce carbon dioxide and water vapour (assuming an excess of oxygen).

common ion effect the solubility of an ionic substance in water is decreased when another substance containing one of the ions in the solution is added.

common name alternative term for trivial name.

complex ion a metal ion that is bonded to a number of neutral molecules or negative ions.

complex reaction a reaction involving several steps.

concentration (symbol c); the strength of a solution expressed as the number of moles of solute per litre of solution.

condensation polymer a polymer formed by a reaction in which a small molecule, usually water, is produced as the monomers form the polymer.

condensed formula a compact way of writing the formula of complex organic molecules; the hydrogen atoms are written beside the carbon atom to which they are attached; for example:
$$CH_3 - CH_2 - CH_3.$$

conjugate acid-base pair structures that differ in only one hydrogen ion.

contact process the commercial production of sulfuric acid using heated vanadium(V) oxide or platinum as a catalyst.

conversion factor a ratio that relates two quantities, which are expressed in different units.

coolant a liquid or gas used to absorb heat, produced in a nuclear reactor.

coordinate covalent bond a covalent bond between two atoms in which one atom contributes both of the electrons in the bond.

corrosion the oxidation of metals by spontaneous electrochemical reaction.

covalent bond a type of bonding in which the bonded atoms share a pair of electrons.

coulomb (symbol C) the SI unit of electrical charge:

$$1 \, C = 1 \, A \times 1 \, s$$

cracking a process in which the carbon-carbon bonds of an alkane are broken by heating the compound in the absence of air and in the presence of a catalyst such as aluminum oxide.

critical pressure the minimum pressure needed to liquefy a gas at the critical temperature.

critical temperature the temperature above which a gas will never change into a liquid, no matter how much pressure is applied.

crystal lattice the arrangement of atoms in a repeated, closely-packed order in a solid.

curie (symbol Ci); a traditional unit used to measure the rate of radioactive decay; one curie is equal to 37 GBq, or 3.7×10^{10} disintegrations per second.

current the amount of electrical charge passing through a point per unit time. Current is measured in units of amperes.

cyclic hydrocarbon compound in which the carbon atoms are joined to one another in the form of a ring.

D

Daniell cell an early battery, developed in 1836, that could supply a steady current for several hours.

decomposition reaction a chemical reaction in which a complex substance breaks down to produce two or more simpler substances:

$$AB \longrightarrow A + B$$

dehydration a reaction in which the elements of water (hydrogen and oxygen) are removed from a compound in a 2:1 mole ratio.

delocalized a description of the valence electrons in a molecular or metallic structure when the electrons are no longer held to a particular atom, but are mobile and able to move throughout the structure.

diffraction pattern a pattern produced by the interference of reflected and diffracted waves of energy as they interfere with one another; used, for example, to determine the structure of crystals by X-ray crystallography.

dipeptide two amino acids joined by an amide bond.

dipole an alternative name for a polar molecule with an asymmetrical distribution of charge.

dipole-dipole forces   the attraction between the negatively-charged part of one dipole and the positively-charged part of another dipole; the strength of the force depends on the magnitude of the partial charge on the molecules.

dipole moment   the measurement of the extent of polarity in a polar molecule; it is the product of the electric charge and the distance between the positive and negative centres in the dipole.

disaccharide   a carbohydrate that can be broken down into two simpler monosaccharides; for example, sucrose or table sugar.

dissociation   the separation of ions in an ionic compound by ion-dipole attraction to the molecules of a solvent.

dispersion forces   weak forces of attraction between molecules as a result of short-lived charges on different parts of a molecule caused by the oscillations of its electrons; theory proposed by Fritz London.

double bond   the covalent bonding between a pair of atoms by which four elections are shared.

double displacement reaction   a reaction between two ionic compounds in which the cation of one compound changes place with the cation of the second compound; the net result is that the positive ions exchange their negative partners:

$$AB + CD \longrightarrow BC + AD$$

Downs cell   a cell used for the electrolytic conversion of molten sodium chloride into sodium and chlorine.

dry cleaning solvent   a solvent, immiscible with water, used to dissolve dirt from clothes; it usually has low polarity and is liquid at room temperature.

dynamic equilibrium   the point in a reversible reaction at which the rate of the forward process is equal to the rate of the reverse process, and the concentrations no longer change.

E

electrochemical cell   a cell that uses a spontaneous redox reaction to generate an electric current.

electrode   an electrically-conducting medium, usually a solid, that is used to make electrical contact.

electrolysis   the production of a chemical reaction by means of an electric current.

electrolyte   a substance that conducts an electric current when in solution or when melted.

electrolytic cell   the cell in which electrolysis takes place.

electrolytic purification   the use of electroplating to purify metals such as copper and nickel.

electromotive force   (symbol $\mathcal{E}°$); an alternative term for the potential difference between electrodes in a circuit; commonly referred to as the voltage of a cell.

electron   a negatively-charged particle found outside the nucleus of the atom; it has a much smaller mass than a proton or neutron.

electron affinity   the energy released when an electron is gained by a neutral gaseous atom to form a negative ion.

electron configuration   the arrangement of electrons in each occupied energy level of an atom; for example a neon atom has the electron configuration: $1s^2 2s^2 2p^6$.

electron deficient   molecules in which one of the bonded atoms is surrounded by fewer than eight electrons.

electron-dot formula   an alternative name for the Lewis formula.

electronegativity   a measure of the tendency of an atom to attract shared electron pairs when forming a covalent bond.

electroplating   the deposition of pure metal on a conducting surface used as a cathode during electrolysis.

elementary step   a single step in a complex reaction, involving one collision between molecules.

elimination reaction   an organic reaction in which a small molecule, such as water, is removed from a larger molecule.

end point   the point in a titration at which the change in indicator colour occurs.

endothermic   a chemical reaction in which the system absorbs heat from the surroundings.

energy diagram   an illustration showing how the energy of a reacting system changes as the reaction proceeds.

energy level   the energy state into which an electron is permitted. Each of these states has a definte energy associated with it.

enriched uranium   natural uranium in which the proportion of the isotope uranium-235 has been increased from the normal level of 0.7% to between 3 and 4%.

enthalpy   (symbol H); the heat content of a system.

enthalpy of reaction   (symbol ΔH); the difference between the enthalpies of the initial and final state of a process; ΔH is negative for an exothermic reaction, and positive for an endothermic reaction.

entropy   (symbol S); a measure of the degree of disorder or randomness of a system.

enzymes   large protein molecules that catalyze specific biochemical reactions in living cells.

equation factor   a type of conversion factor derived from the balanced chemical equation, which compares the number of moles of the different chemicals in the reaction: for example, in the reaction

$$2 \, Na + 2 \, H_2O \longrightarrow H_2 + 2 \, (NaOH)$$

the equation factors relating water and hydrogen are:

$$\frac{2 \text{ mol } H_2O}{1 \text{ mol } H_2} \text{ and } \frac{1 \text{ mol } H_2}{2 \text{ mol } H_2O}$$

equilibrium   the balanced state of a reversible reaction in which there is no net observable change. The rate of the forward reaction equals that of the reverse reaction.

equilibrium constant   (symbol K_{eq}); a dimensionless number that relates the concentrations in an equilibrium system; the value of the constant changes with the temperature of the system.

equilibrium constant expression   for the general reaction

$$a\,A + b\,B \longrightarrow c\,C + d\,D$$

the value for the equilibrium constant, K_{eq}, is given by the equilibrium constant expression

$$K_{eq} = \frac{[C]^c[D]^d}{[A]^a[B]^b}$$

equivalence point   the point in a titration at which the stoichiometric amount of titrant has been added.

ester   a class of organic compounds having the following grouping in the molecule.

$$-\overset{\displaystyle O}{\underset{\displaystyle \|}{C}}-O-$$

ether   a class of organic compounds having the C−O−C grouping in the molecule.

evaporate   the change of matter from a liquid to a gas phase at a temperature below the boiling point of the liquid.

excited state   the state of an electron that has absorbed energy and moved from the ground state to a higher energy level.

exothermic   a chemical reaction in which the system releases heat to the surroundings.

F

face-centred cubic   an arrangement of unit cells consisting of a cube containing eight spheres; there is a sphere at the centre of each face of the cube.

faraday   (symbol F); the amount of charge equivalent to one mole of electrons; one faraday is 9.65×10^4 C.

Faraday's laws of electrolysis   there are two laws; the first one states that the amount of substance produced or consumed at an electrode is proportional to the quantity of electricity applied to the cell; the second law states that the amounts of elements liberated by the same quantity of electricity are proportional to their molar masses.

first ionization energy   the minimum amount of energy required to convert an atom into an ion by removing its most weakly bound electron; the noble gases have the highest ionization energies and the alkali metals have the lowest.

first order reaction   a reaction whose rate depends on the concentration of only one species, irrespective of the number of reactants present; the exponent of the concentration term in the rate equation equals one.

fractionation   a distillation method used to partially separate the components of a liquid mixture into a number of fractions according to the desired boiling range.

freezing point   the conditions of temperature and pressure at which a liquid changes to a solid; it is identical to the melting point for the same pure substance.

fuel cell   an electrochemical cell that converts the energy of a redox combustion reaction directly into electrical energy.

functional group   a group of atoms in an organic molecule that undergo characteristic general reactions, regardless of the nature of the rest of the molecule.

G

galvanized   the process by which an iron has been coated with zinc.

gamma ray   high-energy electromagnetic radiation, with a high frequency and very short wavelength.

geometric (*cis-trans*) isomerism   isomers that owe their existence to hindered rotation about a double bond; the isomer that has two similar groups joined to the carbons on the same side of the double bond is called the *cis*- isomer; the isomer that has two similar groups joined to the opposite side of the double bond is called the *trans*-isomer.

Gibbs free energy   also simply known as free energy (symbol G); a thermodynamic quantity relating enthalpy and entropy. For a reaction at constant pressure and temperature T (Kelvin), the change in free energy (ΔG) is

$$\Delta G = \Delta H - T\Delta S$$

gray   a measure of the energy of radiation; one gray is the dose of radiation received when one joule of energy is absorbed by one kilogram of matter.

ground state   the state of lowest energy for the electrons in an atom.

H

Haber process   the industrial process for manufacturing ammonia from hydrogen and nitrogen:

$$N_{2(g)} + 3\,H_{2(g)} \rightleftharpoons 2\,NH_{3(g)}$$

half cell a separate compartment in an electrochemical cell, in which a redox half-reaction takes place.

half-life the time required for half of the nuclei in a sample of a radioactive isotope to decay; ranges from fractions of a second to millions of years.

half-reactions the two parts of a redox reaction; electrons are produced in one half-reaction and consumed in the other half-reaction.

haloalkane an organic compound that contains carbon, hydrogen, and one or more halogen.

halogenated hydrocarbons alternative name for haloalkanes.

heat thermal energy transferred from one substance to another substance with a lower temperature.

heat capacity the heat energy required to raise the temperature of a given quantity of substance by one Celsius degree or one kelvin; it is related to specific heat as follows:

$$\text{Heat capacity} = \text{Specific heat} \times \text{Mass}$$

heavy water water molecules in which the hydrogen-1 atoms ($_1^1H$) have been replaced by deuterium atoms ($_1^2H$); used in CANDU reactors as a moderator.

Heisenberg uncertainty principle a statement that we cannot know both the position and energy of an electron at the same moment because the measurement of one of these properties would inevitably disturb the value of the other.

Hess's law (or the law of constant heat summation); the enthalpy change for any reaction is the sum of all enthalpy changes regardless of the pathways taken by the reactants to become products.

heterogeneous catalysis a catalytic reaction that occurs at the point between two phases; for example, the decomposition of hydrogen peroxide solution with manganese(IV) oxide as a catalyst:

$$2\ H_2O_{2\,(aq)} \xrightarrow{\ MnO_{2\,(s)}\ } 2\ H_2O_{(\ell)} + O_{2\,(g)}$$

heterogeneous equilibrium an equilibrium in which the reactants and the products are not all in the same phase.

homogeneous catalysis a reaction in which the reactants and catalyst are in the same phase (usually gas or aqueous solution).

homogeneous equilibrium an equilibrium in which the reactants and the products are all in the same phase.

homologous series a series of compounds in which each member differs in structure from the next by the addition of the same structural unit; for example, the straight-chain alkanes differ from each other by the addition of a CH_2 unit.

Hund's rule a rule that states that electrons must be distributed among orbitals of equal energy in such a way that as many electrons as possible remain unpaired.

hybrid orbital a new set of orbitals, which possess different directional properties, produced by mixing atomic orbitals together mathematically.

hybridization theory an explanation for the bonding angles found in molecules; it proposes that orbitals in bonding atoms combine to form hybrid orbitals that then overlap with the orbitals of other atoms to form covalent bonds.

hydrated ion a metal ion surrounded by a shell of water molecules.

hydration the process in which ionic species are closely surrounded by many water molecules.

hydrates compounds that incorporate water molecules into their crystal structure.

hydrocarbon an organic compound containing only carbon and hydrogen.

hydrogenation a reaction involving the addition of hydrogen to carbon-carbon multiple bonds; commercially used in the conversion of unsaturated fats in liquid oils to produce margarine and shortenings.

hydrogen bonds a strong intermolecular interaction occurring when the hydrogen atom in an O–H, N–H, or F–H bond is attracted to a partially-negative atom.

hydrogen-ion acceptor a base, in the Brønsted-Lowry theory.

hydrogen-ion donor an acid, in the Brønsted-Lowry theory.

hydrogen-ion exchange reaction a reaction between an acid and a base, in the Brønsted-Lowry theory.

hydrometallurgy a method for extracting metals from sulfide ores under pressure in solution; the sulfides are oxidized to sulfates.

hydronium ion (H_3O^+) a hydrated hydrogen ion.

I

ideal gas a theoretical gas in which the particles have zero volume and exert no force on each other.

ideal gas equation an equation that relates the number of moles (n) of a gas to its volume, pressure and temperature, using the universal gas constant (R):

$$PV = nRT$$

immiscible a liquid that cannot be mixed with another liquid to form a homogeneous solution.

inhibitor substance that slows down a reaction.

initial rate the reaction rate measured for a very short period of time at the beginning of a reaction.

inorganic polymers   polymers that incorporate elements other than carbon and oxygen into structures; for example, silicones.

insoluble   a substance that does not dissolve, or dissolves only slightly, in a solvent.

intermolecular forces   attractive forces between separate molecules.

interstitial alloy   a type of alloy in which the atoms of the added substance are much smaller than those of the pure metal, and fit into spaces between the atoms in the pure metal crystal structure.

intramolecular forces   the forces of attraction within a molecule that hold the atoms together.

ion-dipole attraction   an attraction between the ions of an ionic compound and the oppositely-charged ends of a solvent molecule; for example, the attraction between sodium ions and the oxygen ends of water molecules.

ion-electron method   a method of balancing redox equations by matching the number of electrons in each half-reaction.

ionic bond   a type of bonding between two atoms when there is a substantial (or near complete) transfer of bonding electrons to only one of the two-bonding atoms.

ionic character   the degree of the separation of charges on the atoms of a polar covalent bond; the degree of ionic character depends on the difference in electronegativity between the two atoms that form the bond.

ionization   the production of ions from a neutral substance; one method involves the action of a solvent on a covalent compound.

ion product constant of water   (symbol K_w); an equilibrium constant that relates the concentrations of hydronium and hydroxide ions in pure water and in all dilute aqueous solutions:

$$K_w = [H_3O^+]\,[OH^-]$$

isoelectronic   atoms or ions that have the same electron configuration as one another; the sodium ion, for example, has the electron configuration $1s^2\,2s^2\,2p^6$, which is the same as that of the neon atom.

isomers   different compounds which have the same molecular formula.

isotopes   atoms of the same element that have the same number of protons but a different number of neutrons.

IUPAC system   a systematic method of naming organic compounds in a way that indicates the compound's structure; established by the International Union of Pure and Applied Chemistry.

J

joule   (symbol J); the SI unit for measuring energy; one joule is the amount of energy used when a force of one newton acts over a distance of one metre.

Joule-Thompson effect   the observation that most gases get colder if they are allowed to expand suddenly into a large volume; this was an early piece of evidence that there are forces of attraction between molecules.

K

ketones   organic compounds which contain the carbonyl group between two other carbon atoms.

kinetic energy   the energy possessed by a moving object; for any object in motion, the kinetic energy

$$E_K = \tfrac{1}{2}\,mv^2$$

kinetics   a study of the rate of a chemical reaction.

L

lattice energy   the energy released during the formation of a mole of crystalline substance from the gaseous ions that are separated from each other by infinite distances.

law of conservation of energy   a universal law which states that energy can be neither created nor destroyed, but may be converted from one form to another.

law of disorder   a universal law which states that spontaneous reaction in an isolated system always proceeds in the direction of increasing entropy.

Le Châtelier's principle   if a system at equilibrium is subjected to an external stress, the equilibrium will shift so as to minimize the stress.

Lewis acid   a substance that is a good electron-pair acceptor; for example, boron trifluoride.

Lewis formula   (or the electron-dot formula); a shorthand system for showing electron configurations; it uses dots arranged around the symbol for the element to show the number and distribution of the valence electrons.

limiting reagent   the substance in a balanced equation that determines the maximum amount of product(s) that can be formed; this depends on the stoichiometry of the reactants used, and is not necessarily the reactant present in the least amount.

linear   a molecular shape consisting of three atoms bonded together in a straight line; for example, carbon dioxide.

liquid drop model   a model that compares the behaviour of the atomic nucleus to a drop of water; proposed by Niels Bohr.

London forces   an alternative name for dispersion forces.

M

magnetic quantum number   a number used to identify the direction of orientation of an orbital with respect to an external magnetic field.

Markovnikov's rule   predicts which isomer will be formed in an addition reaction between an alkene and hydrogen halides; the hydrogen of a hydrogen halide adds to the carbon that is already bonded to the most hydrogen atoms.

mass defect   the difference between the total mass of the separate particles within a nucleus and the mass of the nucleus itself; accounted for by the energy released when particles combine to form the nucleus.

mass number   the sum of the number of protons and neutrons present in the nucleus of an atom.

Maxwell-Boltzmann distribution   a curve showing the distribution of molecular energy among a number of molecules in a system.

mechanism   the pathway of a reaction considered in terms of the elementary step(s).

melting point   the temperature at which a solid changes to a liquid under a given pressure; it is identical to the freezing point for the same pure substance.

metallic bond   a type of bonding between atoms that occurs when both atoms have low ionization energies and low electronegativity.

metallic conduction   current derived from the flow of electrons through metal.

miscible   the ability of two (or more) liquids to mix.

moderator   material such as water or graphite, used in a nuclear reactor to slow down neutrons so that a controlled chain reaction will take place.

molality   (symbol m); a unit of concentration defined as number of moles of solute in one kilogram of solvent.

molarity   (symbol M); a non-SI term for the concentration of a solution, expressed as the number of moles of solute dissolved in one litre of solution; the SI symbol is c; the symbol M is still commonly used as an abbreviation for moles per litre.

molar concentration   the number of moles of solute dissolved in one litre of solution.

molar heat capacity   (symbol C_p°) the heat energy required to raise the temperature of one mole of a substance by one Celsius degree or one kelvin; it is related to specific heat as follows:

$$\text{Molar heat capacity} = \text{Specific heat} \times \text{Molar mass}$$

molar mass   (symbol M); the mass of one mole of an element or compound, measured in $g \cdot mol^{-1}$; it can be used as a conversion factor when converting from moles to mass and vice versa.

mole   a standard unit for measuring the amount of a substance; one mole is equal to 6.02×10^{23} atoms, molecules, or formula units of a substance.

mole fraction   a unit of concentration equal to the number of moles of solute in a mole of solution.

mole method   a systematic approach to solving chemical problems concerned with the quantities of chemicals produced or consumed in a given chemical reaction.

molecular model   a structure built from balls (representing atoms) and sticks or springs (representing bonds) that helps to envisage the three-dimensional structures of molecules.

molecularity   the number of reactant molecules, ions, or atoms involved in an elementary step.

monosaccharide   a simple carbohydrate; for example, glucose.

N

net ionic equation   an equation that records the reacting ions only, and omits the spectator ions.

network solid   a giant arrangement of matter in which atoms are covalently bonded together in continuous two- or three-dimensional arrays; for example, graphite and diamond.

neutralization   a double displacement reaction between an acid and a base to produce a salt plus water.

neutron   an electrically-neutral particle found in the nucleus of an atom; its mass is about equal to that of a proton.

neutron activation analysis   a technique used in quantitative analysis to measure concentrations as low as one part per thousand million; samples are made radioactive by neutron bombardment, and characteristic gamma ray wavelengths are measured.

nitrogen cycle   the circulation of nitrogen atoms between the atmosphere, soil, water, and living organisms.

non-bonding pair   also known as a lone pair, is a set of two electrons in the valency orbital of an atom that is not involved in bonding the atom in a particular molecule.

nuclear chain reaction   a self-sustaining sequence of nuclear reactions.

nuclear fission   the splitting of a heavy nuclear atom into fragments of lighter nuclei.

nuclear fusion   the combining of light nuclear particles to produce a larger nucleus.

nuclear reactor   the part of a nuclear power plant in which controlled nuclear reactions take place to produce heat.

nucleons   the collective name for the protons and neutrons in an atom.

nucleus   the region at the centre of an atom in which nuclear particles such as the protons and neutrons are located; it is electrically positive and contains practically all the mass of the atom.

O

octahedral   a molecular shape in which the central atom is joined to six other atoms, and there are no lone pairs of electrons.

octane rating   a system of grading gasoline on a scale against a standard rating of 100 for isooctane.

octet rule   atoms other than hydrogen tend to form bonds until they are surrounded by eight valence electrons; there are exceptions to this rule among elements in the third and subsequent rows of the Periodic Table whose valence energy levels contain more than eight electrons.

open system   a system in which products and/or reactants can enter or leave.

orbital   a volume of space in which there is a high probability of finding an electron; each orbital of an atom can contain a maximum of two electrons.

order of reaction   the sum of the exponents of all the concentration terms in a rate equation.

organic chemistry   the chemistry of compounds containing carbon; some common carbon-containing compounds, such as carbon monoxide and carbon dioxide, however, are not generally considered organic.

osmosis   the diffusion of solute particles through a semi-permeable membrane from a region of high concentration to a region of low concentration.

osmotic pressure   the pressure developed across a semi-permeable membrane by the difference in concentration of solute particles.

overvoltage   the amount by which the actual voltage required for an electrode reaction to take place exceeds the calculated value.

oxidation   any reaction in which electrons are lost.

oxidation number   an integer that is assigned to each atom in a compound when considering redox reactions; an increase in oxidation number in a reaction indicates oxidation, while a decrease indicates reduction.

oxidizing agent   the substance that accepts electrons and undergoes reduction. Usually a nonmetal.

oxyacid   an acid in which the hydrogen is covalently bonded to an oxygen atom of an oxyanion.

P

paramagnetism   attraction of a substance by a magnetic field due to atoms, ions, and molecules that have orbitals containing unpaired electrons; the strength of the attraction is directly proportional to the number of unpaired electrons.

particle accelerator   a device used to speed up a particle such as a neutron and use it to strike and split a target nucleus.

Pauli exclusion principle   states that no two electrons within an atom can have the same set of four quantum numbers.

percent ionization   for an acid in solution:

$$\text{Percent ionization} = \frac{[H_3O^+] \text{ at equilibrium}}{\text{Initial acid concentration}} \times 100\%$$

percent yield   an expression of the efficiency with which a reaction converts the reactants(s) into a product:

$$\text{Percent yield} = \frac{\text{Actual yield}}{\text{Theoretical yield}} \times 100\%$$

pH   a scale of acidity and basicity:

$$pH = -\log_{10}[H_3O^+]$$

phase diagram   a diagram that shows the relationships between temperature, pressure, and changes of phase for a given substance in a closed system.

phosphazenes   a family of polymers having alternating phosphorus and nitrogen atoms.

pi (π) bond   one of the bonds, together with a sigma (σ) bond, used in hybridization theory to explain the formation of multiple bonds; double bonds contain two sigma electrons and two pi electrons, while triple bonds contain two sigma electrons and four pi electrons.

pOH   a term for the negative logarithm of the hydroxide ion concentration, used to simplify some pH calculations

$$pOH = -\log_{10}[OH^-]$$

polar covalent bond   a covalent bond formed between atoms with different electronegativities; such that there is a slight separation of charge between the bonded atoms.

polyether   an organic compound with an unusual structure consisting of a ring in which six $-CH_2-CH_2-$ units are joined by ether-type oxygen atoms between each unit; first discovered in 1964.

polymer   a very large molecule made from simple units repeated many times; for example, proteins, plastics, and nucleic acids.

polymer chemistry   the study of polymers, synthesis, and properties of polymers.

polymerization   a reaction in which many small identical units join together to form large molecules.

polypeptides   organic polymers with well-defined sequences of amino acids.

polyprotic acid   an acid that can give up more than one hydrogen ion per molecule (Arrhenius theory).

polysaccharide   complex carbohydrate made from several monosaccharide units; for example, starch and cellulose, which are both made from glucose.

positron   positive electron.

potash   potassium carbonate, which is a major component of wood ashes; now the term is also used to mean potassium-containing minerals, found in deep beds in the prairie provinces.

potential energy   the energy possessed by a body because of its relative position in space.

primary alcohol   alcohol in which only the hydroxyl group is attached to a primary carbon atom (which is linked to only one other carbon atom).

primary amine   an organic compound derived from ammonia by replacing one hydrogen atom with an alkyl group; for example, methylamine.

primary battery   a non-rechargable battery.

primary standard   a stable substance against which the concentrations of solutions can be checked.

principal quantum number   an integer used to identify each principle energy level in the quantum model of the atom.

protein   the common name for polypeptides found in living organisms.

proton   a positively-charged particle found in the nucleus of an atom.

pyrolysis   known industrially as "coking," the treatment of bitumen by heating it strongly in the absence of air; the large molecules break down to produce coke and a variety of short-chain molecules.

Q

quantum model   a description of the behaviour of electrons in an atom in terms of their specific quantities of energy.

R

rad   a traditional measure of the energy of radiation; one rad is equal to 10^{-2} J of energy per kilogram of absorbing materials.

radiant energy   the energy transmittted through space as electromagnetic waves; for example, light, heat, and gamma rays.

radioactive decay   the spontaneous decomposition of a radioactive nuclei.

radioactive series   a series of nuclear decays by which a radioactive isotope of the actinon elements becomes a stable isotope; for example, uranium-238 decays to thorium-234, which decays to form protactinium-234, which decays to form uranium-234, and so on for a total of 14 steps.

radioactive tracer   a radioactive isotope used in medicine to track biochemical processes; the path of the tracer in the body can be followed by tracking the radiation.

radioactivity   same as radioactive decay; the name first given by Becquerel to his discovery that uranium produces rays that can penetrate paper; caused by the spontaneous disintegration of atomic nuclei into high energy particles.

rate constant   the proportionality constant (k) used in the rate law.

rate-determining step   the slowest elementary step in a reaction; it determines the overall reaction rate.

rate law   a mathematical expression that governs the rate of a given reaction; for the general reaction

$$A \longrightarrow products$$

the rate law takes the form

$$Rate = k\,[A]^x$$

where k is the rate constant, and x is the order of the reaction.

reaction intermediate   a species produced during a step of a reaction, but which is consumed to form the product. Its existence is marked as a minimum on the potential energy curve.

reaction pathway   the horizontal axis of a potential energy diagram, showing the progress of a reaction.

reaction rate   a measure of how fast a reactant is used up or how fast a product is formed.

recrystallization   a process used to purify solid substances by cooling a saturated solution until pure crystals are formed.

redox reaction   a reaction in which oxidation and reduction occur together.

reducing agent   a substance that donates electrons and undergoes oxidation.

reduction   any reaction that involves a gain of electrons.

reduction potential   the tendency of the reactants in a half-cell to gain electrons.

reflected   the throwing back of energy waves (light, heat, sound, X-rays, etc.) in the same direction from which they arrive at the reflecting surface.

reforming   a process for converting straight-chain alkanes in gasoline fractions to branched-chain isomers, using beds of inorganic catalysts.

resonance structures   electron-dot diagrams representing the bonding pattern in certain molecules when two or more structures, that differ only in the arrangement of electrons, can be drawn.

rotational motion   the rotation of a molecule about an axis through its centre of mass; the movement is associated with the thermal energy of the molecule.

S

salt   a compound composed of a positive ion and a negative ion.

salt bridge   a device filled with a salt solution that connects the half cells to allow the passage of ions and to maintain the electrical neutrality of the two solutions.

saturated   the state of a solvent in which no more solute will dissolve.

saturated hydrocarbons   organic compounds of carbon and hydrogen that do not contain any double or triple bonds; for example, alkanes.

second ionization energy   the energy required to remove a second electron from an atom; this amount of energy is greater than the first ionization energy.

secondary alcohol   alcohol in which two alkyl groups are attached to the carbon atom bearing the hydroxyl (—OH) group.

secondary amine   an organic compound derived from ammonia by replacing two hydrogen atoms with alkyl groups.

secondary battery   a rechargable battery; also called storage battery.

secondary quantum number   a number used to identify sublevels; indicated in order of increasing energy by the letters s, p, d, and f.

second-order reaction   a reaction whose rate depends on the concentration of one species raised to a power of two; the value of x in the rate equation equals two.

semimetal   an element that has some of the properties of a metal and some of the properties of a nonmetal; its bonding may be considered metallic or covalent.

semipermeable membrane   a membrane that allows small solute molecules to pass through it but blocks the passage of larger ones.

shielding effect   as the number of electrons between the nucleus and the valence electrons increases, the ionization energy decreases.

side-chain   a short chain of carbon atoms attached to the main carbon chain in a branched organic compound.

sigma (σ) bond   a covalent bond formed by sigma electrons; in ethyne, for example, a sigma bond is formed between the two carbon atoms by the overlapping of an sp orbital from each; sigma bonds always occur on a direct line between the nucleii of the bonding atoms.

simple cubic packing   the simplest type of unit cell structure, made by placing a second layer of atoms directly over the first.

simple reaction   a reaction consisting of one elementary step.

single displacement reaction   a reaction in which one element replaces another element in an ionic compound:

$$A + CD \longrightarrow C + AD$$

specific heat   the amount of heat energy required to raise the temperature of one gram of a substance by one Celsius degree or one kelvin.

soluble   a solute that dissolves to a significant extent in a solvent.

solubility   the degree to which a substance can dissolve.

solubility product constant   (symbol K_{sp}); an equilibrium constant that relates the ion concentrations in saturated solutions of ionic compounds.

solute   a substance, either solid, liquid or gas, that dissolves in a solvent to produce a solution.

solution   a mixture of uniform composition, prepared by dissolving a solute in a solvent.

solvent   the substance in which a solute is dissolved to produce a solution; it is commonly but not always a liquid.

spectator ion   an ion in solution that appears on both sides of an equation but does not take part in a reaction.

spin quantum number   a number used to distinguish between electrons with opposite spins; usually expressed as $+\frac{1}{2}$ or $-\frac{1}{2}$.

spontaneous   a physical or chemical change that takes place without outside intervention; the reaction may be fast or slow.

standard cell   an electrochemical cell, used as the accepted standard reference for measuring voltages.

standard cell potential   the potential of a cell containing gases at 100 kPa pressure and solutions at 1.0 mol.L^{-1} concentration.

standard enthalpy of formation   the enthalpy changes when one mole of a substance is formed from its elements in their standard states.

standard hydrogen electrode   a reference electrode involving hydrogen gas (100 kPa) and hydrogen ion (1.0 mol.L^{-1}) which is assigned a standard potential of 0.00 V.

standard oxidation potential   the potential of a half-cell under standard conditions, expressed as an oxidation.

standard reduction potential   the potential of a half-cell under standard conditions expressed as a reduction.

standard solution   a solution prepared by dissolving a precise mass of solute in a precise volume of solution, so that its concentration is known accurately.

standard state   a chosen set of conditions for comparison purposes; for gases, it is taken as a pressure of 100 kPa at 25°C; for ions it is taken as a 1.0 mol.L⁻¹ solution; for other substances, the standard state is taken as the state in which the pure substance exists at 25°C and 100 kPa presure.

stoichiometric calculations   calculations that use the mole relationships in a balanced equation to calculate the quantities of reactants and products involved in a reaction.

straight-chain alkane   a saturated hydrocarbon in which there are no alkyl side-chains.

strong acid   an acid that is completely ionized in solution (Arrhenius theory).

strong base   a base that completely dissociates in water (Arrhenius theory).

structural formula   a two-dimensional diagram showing the way in which atoms are arranged in a molecule; lines represent covalent bonds:

$$H-\overset{\displaystyle H}{\underset{\displaystyle H}{C}}-H$$

structural isomers   compounds that have the same molecular formula but different structures; they have different physical and chemical properties.

sublevel   an energy level within the principal energy level; all except the first principal energy level can be subdivided.

sublimation   a change in matter from the solid to the gas phase without passing through a liquid phase; the reverse process — from gas to solid — is also called sublimation.

substituent   an atom or a side chain along the parent chain in an organic molecule.

substitution reaction   an organic reaction in which one atom is replaced by another.

substitutional alloy   a type of alloy in which the atoms of the added metal are similar in size to those of the original pure metal; when the molten mixture solidifies, the added metal atoms are dispersed throughout the metal crystal structure in place of some of the original metal atoms.

surface tension   the attraction between molecules on the surface of a liquid that tends to pull them towards the centre of the liquid, since there is no attractive force from molecules above them; this creates the properties of a fine elastic "skin" on the liquid surface.

surroundings   those parts outside of a system; for example, the beaker holding the reacting chemicals is usually part of the surroundings.

system   all the chemical components involved in a reaction — both reactants and products — comprise a system

systematic name   another term for IUPAC name.

T

temperature   a measure of the average thermal energy of a substance.

teratogens   chemicals that cause birth defects.

tertiary alcohol   alcohol in which three alkyl groups are attached to the carbon atom bearing the hydroxyl (—OH) group.

tertiary amine   an organic compound derived from ammonia by replacing the three hydrogen atoms with alkyl groups.

tetrahedral   a symmetrical shape with four equal faces; in tetrahedral molecules, a central atom is joined to four other atoms and the bond angles between each are all equal to 109.5°.

theoretical yield   the maximum possible mass of a product that could be produced in a given reaction.

thermal decomposition   a decomposition reaction brought about by heating the reactant.

thermal energy   the sum of the kinetic energy and potential energy associated with the random motion of the individual atoms and molecules in a substance.

thermochemistry   a study of chemical reactions involving heat changes.

thermoplastic   synthetic polymer that softens and melts when heated.

thermoset polymer   synthetic polymer that does not soften or melt when heated; its long chains are cross-linked by covalent bonds.

third ionization energy   the amount of energy needed to remove a third electron from an atom of an element.

titrant   the solution held in the burette during a titration.

titration curve   a graph of pH against volume of titrant used during a titration.

transition state   the highest energy point on a reaction pathway; the point at which the activated complex is formed.

translational motion   is the movement of particles along linear pathways; it occurs in liquids and gases but not in solids.

transuranium elements   synthetic elements (i.e. not found in nature) with an atomic number greater than that of uranium (92).

trigonal planar   describes the shape of a molecule with one central atom and three other atoms joined to it so that all four atoms are in the same plane.

trigonal bipyramidal   a molecular shape consisting of two pyramids sharing the same triangular base.

trigonal pyramidal   the shape of a pyramid with a triangular base.

triple bond   the bonding between a pair of atoms by three covalent bonds; the pair shares six electrons.

triple point   the condition of temperature and pressure at which all three phases (solid, liquid, gas) of a substance can co-exist.

trivial names   also known as common names; older terms used to name some organic compounds, now largely replaced by the IUPAC system.

U

unit cell   the smallest repeating unit of atoms or ions in a crystal lattice structure.

universal gas constant   (symbol R); the constant in the ideal gas equation: $PV = nRT$; the value of R depends on the units used, but is usually given as 8.314 kPa·L·mol^{-1}·K^{-1}.

unsaturated hydrocarbon   a hydrocarbon containing one or more double or triple carbon-carbon bonds.

V

V-shaped   another name for a bent molecule.

valence electrons   the electrons that are contained in the outermost principal energy level of an atom; valence electrons determine the bonding and chemical behaviour of an atom.

van der Waals forces   very short-range, weak attractive forces by which atoms or molecules attract one another; the only intermolecular force for nonpolar molecules.

vaporization   the process in which molecules near the surface of a liquid have enough energy to escape from the liquid and enter the gas phase.

vapour   a substance in the gaseous state that is below its critical temperature and can be liquefied by an increase in pressure alone.

vapour pressure   the pressure exerted by the molecules of a vapour; in a saturated state when the vapour and the liquid are in a state of equilibrium.

vibrational motion   the rapid oscillation of atoms within a molecule along the direction of a bond.

voltage   a measure of the potential difference in an electrochemical cell.

volt   a unit used to measure potential difference.

volumetric flask   a special container with a calibration mark on a narrow stem, used for preparing standard solutions.

VSEPR theory   the valence-shell electron pair repulsion theory, used to predict the shapes of molecules from their electron-dot formulas: the pairs of electrons that surround the core of the central atom in a molecule repel each other and arrange themselves in space in such a way that they are as far apart as possible.

W

weak acid   an acid that is partially ionized in solution (Arrhenius theory).

weak base   a base that is partially ionized in solution (Arrhenius theory).

X

X-ray crystallography   a technique for studying crystal structure by passing a beam of X-rays through a sample of crystalline compound; the pattern of bending of the X-rays by the crystal reveals the arrangement of ions in the crystal.

Z

zero-order reaction   a reaction in which the reaction rate does not depend on the concentration of any one of the reactants; the exponent of the concentration term in the rate equation equals zero.

Answers to Odd-Numbered Problems

Because of variation in the rounding-off procedure, you may observe slight differences between answers given here and those that you obtain.

Chapter 1

17. b) and d)

19. a) $Ca_{(s)} + 2\,HCl_{(aq)} \longrightarrow CaCl_{2\,(aq)} + H_{2\,(g)}$
b) $Mg_{(s)} + Pb(NO_3)_{2\,(aq)} \longrightarrow Mg(NO_3)_{2\,(aq)} + Pb_{(s)}$
c) no reaction

21. a) $554\ g \cdot L^{-1}$ b) $0.554\ kg \cdot L^{-1}$ c) $554\ kg \cdot m^{-3}$

23. 30.1 g

25. a) 8.40×10^{-3} g (3 significant figures)
b) 3.650×10^{2} s (4 significant figures)
c) 2.000×10^{1} mL (4 significant figures)
d) 2.37×10^{-1} g (3 significant figures)

27. 141.75 g

29. a) 78.5 g b) 39.6 g c) 42.5 g

31. a) 199 g b) 213 g c) 209 g

33. 0.864 g

35. a) 0.31 L b) 1.35 L

37. $6.25 \times 10^{-2}\ mol \cdot L^{-1}$

39. 25.1 g

41. 3.702 L

43. a) 2.02 g b) 1.79×10^{-2} L c) 4.23 L

45. 20.1 L

47. 2.01 L

49. a) $Al_{(s)} + 3\,AgNO_{3\,(aq)} \longrightarrow 3\,Ag_{(s)} + Al(NO_3)_{3\,(aq)}$
b) aluminum c) 3.24 g d) 9.20 %

51. a) 9.12 g b) 3.70 g

53. $1.125\ mol \cdot L^{-1}$

55. $2\,NO_{(g)} + 5\,H_{2\,(g)} \longrightarrow 2\,NH_{3\,(g)} + 2\,H_2O_{(l)}$;
37.5 mL; 15.0 mL

57. a) $FeCl_{3\,(aq)} + 3\,NaOH_{(aq)} \longrightarrow Fe(OH)_{3\,(s)} + 3\,NaCl_{(aq)}$
b) $NaOH_{(aq)}$ c) 0.712 g d) 84.3 %

59. a) 5.534 g b) 0.228 L c) 85.5 %

Chapter 2

23.

	Neutrons	Protons	Electrons
a)	10	9	9
b)	10	8	8
c)	22	19	19
d)	146	92	92
e)	41	33	33
f)	78	55	55

25. atomic number: 29, mass number: 63

27. $^{17}_{9}F$ and $^{18}_{9}F$; $^{18}_{7}N$ and $^{14}_{7}N$

29. 36

31. a) $1s^2\,2s^2\,2p^1$
b) $1s^2\,2s^2\,2p^6\,3s^1$
c) $1s^2\,2s^2\,2p^6\,3s^2\,3p^5$
d) $1s^2\,2s^2\,2p^6\,3s^2\,3p^6\,4s^2$
e) $1s^2\,2s^2\,2p^6\,3s^2\,3p^6\,4s^2\,3d^{10}\,4p^6\,5s^2$

33. a) carbon b) beryllium c) argon

35. a) chlorine b) titanium c) nickel

37. a) potassium: ionization energy decreases going down a group
b) lithium: ionization energy increases going left to right across a period

39. a) $1s^2\,2s^2\,2p^6\,3s^2\,3p^6$ c) $1s^2\,2s^2\,2p^6$
b) $1s^2\,2s^2\,2p^6$ d) $1s^2\,2s^2\,2p^6$

41. Three of the following ions: P^{3-}, S^{2-}, Cl^-, K^+, Ca^{2+}

43. a) $\left[Mg\right]^{2+}$ b) $\left[:\overset{..}{\underset{..}{Cl}}:\right]^-$ c) $\left[:\overset{..}{\underset{..}{P}}:\right]^{3-}$

45. a) $\dot{Al}\cdot + 3\ :\overset{..}{F}: \longrightarrow \left[Al\right]^{3+}\left[:\overset{..}{\underset{..}{F}}:\right]\left[:\overset{..}{\underset{..}{F}}:\right]\left[:\overset{..}{\underset{..}{F}}:\right]^-$
b) $2\,Na\cdot + :\overset{..}{S}\cdot \longrightarrow \left[Na\right]^+\left[Na\right]^+\left[:\overset{..}{\underset{..}{S}}:\right]^{2-}$

47. a) $H^{\delta+}$, $Cl^{\delta+}$ d) $O^{\delta+}$, $F^{\delta+}$
b) $P^{\delta+}$, $Cl^{\delta+}$ e) neither has partial charge
c) $C^{\delta+}$, $F^{\delta+}$

49. a) metal   d) semimetal
b) metal   e) metal
c) nonmetal   f) metal

51. c), a), b) = d)

53. a) oxygen, nitrogen, phosphorus
b) oxygen, nitrogen, phosphorus
c) phosphorus, nitrogen, oxygen
d) phosphorus, oxygen, nitrogen
e) phosphorus, nitrogen, oxygen

55. c)

57. a) and d)

59. 40 %

Chapter 3

15. a) tetrahedral
b) trigonal pyramidal
c) bent
d) tetrahedral

17. b) and c)

19. NO_2^+; $\left[\ddot{O}=N=\ddot{O}\right]^+$ linear, $\left[\begin{array}{c} \text{trigonal} \\ \text{planar} \end{array}\right]^-$ trigonal planar

21. a) sp^3 b) sp^2

23.

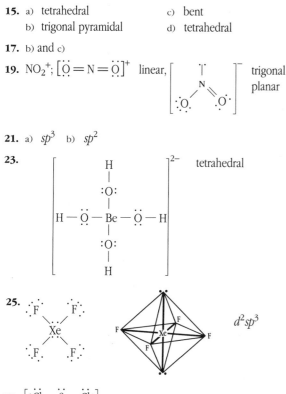 tetrahedral

25.

d^2sp^3

27. $\left[:\ddot{\underset{..}{C}l}-\ddot{S}-\ddot{\underset{..}{C}l}:\right]$

The sulfur atom, which is the central atom, has two bonded pairs of electrons and two lone pairs; therefore, VSEPR says the shape will be tetrahedral. Hybridization theory says these four electrons in the valence level will hybridize to form four sp^3 orbitals. Two of these orbitals are filled, the other two each overlap the $3p$ orbitals of the chlorine atoms to form covalent bands.

29.

 trigonal bipyramidal; dsp^3

Chapter 4

25. a) gas b) solid c) liquid

27. sugar, salt, sand

29. H — C, S — Cl, H — O, B — F

31. a) polar
b) nonpolar
c) polar
d) nonpolar
e) polar

33. a) dispersion
b) dispersion and dipole-dipole
c) dispersion and dipole-dipole
d) dispersion
e) dispersion and dipole-dipole

35. a) I_2; dispersion forces only present, which are greater in I_2 since the larger molecule contains more electrons.
b) SF_2; dipole-dipole forces greater in this more polar molecule.
c) NH_3; hydrogen bonding present in NH_3, not in PH_3.

37. a) NaCl; an ionic compound has a higher boiling point than a covalent compound.
b) Cu; a metal has higher boiling point than a covalent compound.
c) diamond; more energy is required to break bonds in a covalent network than is required to overcome inter-ionic forces in NaCl.

39. a) at temperature and pressure conditions indicated by the line drawn from the triple point through the point (44 °C, 25 kPa)
b) gas c) > 85 kPa

41. PCl_3 and NH_3

43. a) metallic bonds
b) intermolecular forces: dispersion forces and hydrogen bonds
c) ionic bonds
d) intermolecular forces: dispersion forces
e) covalent bonds

45. a) SCl_2; dispersion forces plus dipole-dipole forces in SCl_2 are weaker than ionic bonds in $MgCl_2$.

   b) Br_2; intermolecular forces in Br_2 are weaker than those in I_2, since Br_2 has fewer electrons.

   c) $AlCl_3$; more covalent character than strongly-ionic NaCl.

Chapter 5

29. 26.3 J

31. 116 °C

33. −54.3 kJ

35. $C_2H_5OH_{(\ell)} + 3\,O_{2\,(g)} \longrightarrow 2\,CO_{2\,(g)} + 3\,H_2O_{(\ell)}$; 2.38×10^3 kJ released

37. 3.3×10^2 kJ released

39. -1.51×10^2 kJ·mol^{-1}

41. −794 kJ·mol^{-1}

43. −58 kJ·mol^{-1}

45. -2.03×10^3 kJ·mol^{-1}

47. 213.1 J·K^{-1}

49. a) −685.3 kJ   b) −4.7 kJ   c) 195.8 kJ

51. At all temperatures; (ΔH is negative, ΔS is positive)

53. 805°C

55. −295 kJ·mol^{-1}

57. a) -1.400×10^3 kJ·mol^{-1} b) −1427.7 kJ·mol^{-1};
   Bond energy values are not necessarily specific to these molecules.

59. −280.2 kJ;

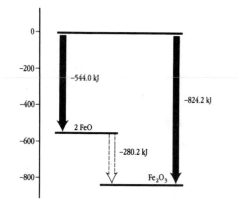

61. 14.4 kJ

63. 789 kJ·mol^{-1};

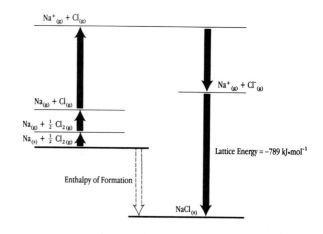

Chapter 6

31. a) 3.7×10^{-5} mol·L^{-1}·s^{-1}

   b) 7.4×10^{-5} mol·L^{-1}·s^{-1}

33. a)

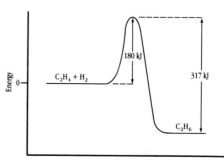

   b) $\Delta H = -137$ kJ·mol^{-1} for first reaction
      $\Delta H = +137$ kJ·mol^{-1} for second reaction

35. a) Rate $\propto$ [PH_3]

   b) 1.0×10^{-3} mol·L^{-1}·s^{-1}

37. Rate $\propto$ [O_2], Rate $\propto$ [HBr]

39. a) Rate = k[O_2][HBr]

   b) second order

   c) 4.2×10^1 L·mol^{-1}·s^{-1}

41.

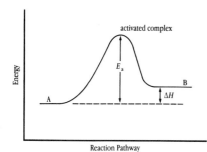

43. $Br_2 \longrightarrow 2\,Br$ (chain initiation)

$H_2 + Br \longrightarrow HBr + H$ (chain propagation)

$H + Br_2 \longrightarrow HBr + Br$ (chain propagation)

$H + Br \longrightarrow HBr$ (chain termination)

$H + H \longrightarrow H_2$ (chain termination)

$Br + Br \longrightarrow Br_2$ (chain termination)

45. a) second order in A, zero order in B

    b) Rate $= k[A]^2$

    c) $3.0\ L\cdot mol^{-1}\cdot s^{-1}$

    d) $7.5 \times 10^{-1}\ mol\cdot L^{-1}\cdot s^{-1}$

47. $3.7 \times 10^{-3}\ mol\cdot L^{-1}\cdot s^{-1}$

49. a) $0.015\ mol\cdot L^{-1}$

    b) 26 min

    c) i) $1.9 \times 10^{-3}\ mol\cdot L^{-1}\cdot min^{-1}$

        ii) $4.8 \times 10^{-3}\ mol\cdot L^{-1}min^{-1}$

51. Set 3

53.

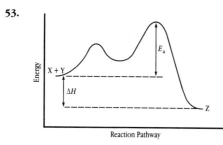

Chapter 7

27. a) $H_2O_{(g)} \rightleftharpoons H_2O_{(l)}$ $K_c = \dfrac{1}{[H_2O_{(g)}]}$

    b) $AgBr_{(s)} + H_2O_{(l)} \rightleftharpoons Ag^+_{(aq)} + Br^-_{(aq)}$ $K_c = [Ag^+][Br^-]$

    c) $CO_{2(s)} \rightleftharpoons CO_{2(g)}$ $K_c = [CO_{2(g)}]$

29. a) $K_c = \dfrac{[P_4O_{10}]}{[P_4][O_2]^5}$

    b) $K_c = \dfrac{[CO_2]}{[CO]}$

    c) $K_c = \dfrac{[NO_2]^4[O_2]}{[N_2O_5]^2}$

    a) and c) are homogeneous

31. 0.14

33. 0.199

35. a) $0.15\ mol\cdot L^{-1}$ b) no

37. $0.494\ mol\cdot L^{-1}$

39. $5.43 \times 10^{-3}\ mol\cdot L^{-1}$

41. a) forward   b) reverse   c) no change   d) no change

43. a) forward   b) forward   c) reverse

45. reverse

47. +56.6 kJ

49. 1

51. $[N_2] = 0.315\ mol\cdot L^{-1}$; $[H_2] = 0.945\ mol\cdot L^{-1}$; $[NH_3] = 0.37\ mol\cdot L^{-1}$

53. $[ICl] = 0.0782\ mol\cdot L^{-1}$; $[Cl_2] = 0.0109\ mol\cdot L^{-1}$; $[I_2] = 0.0609\ mol\cdot L^{-1}$

Chapter 8

27. a) $Na_2S_{(s)} \longrightarrow 2\,Na^+_{(aq)} + S^{2-}_{(aq)}$

    b) $CaI_{2(s)} \longrightarrow Ca^{2+}_{(aq)} + 2\,I^-_{(aq)}$

    c) $Li_2CO_{3(s)} \longrightarrow 2\,Li^+_{(aq)} + CO_3^{2-}_{(aq)}$

    d) $Fe_2(SO_4)_{3(s)} \longrightarrow 2\,Fe^{3+}_{(aq)} + 3\,SO_4^{2-}_{(aq)}$

    e) $Co(NO_3)_{2(s)} \longrightarrow Co^{2+}_{(aq)} + 2\,NO_3^-_{(aq)}$

29. a) $0.6220\ mol\cdot L^{-1}$

    b) $0.555\ mol\cdot L^{-1}$

31. a) $[Sr^{2+}] = 0.075\ mol\cdot L^{-1}$; $[NO_3^-] = 0.15\ mol\cdot L^{-1}$

    b) $[Na^+] = 0.300\ mol\cdot L^{-1}$; $[SO_4^{2-}] = 0.150\ mol\cdot L^{-1}$

    c) $[NH_4^+] = [Cl^-] = 1.000\ mol\cdot L^{-1}$

33. $[Cl^-] = 5.30 \times 10^{-1}\ mol\cdot L^{-1}$; $[Na^+] = 4.70 \times 10^{-1}\ mol\cdot L^{-1}$;

    $[SO_4^{2-}] = 2.76 \times 10^{-2}\ mol\cdot L^{-1}$

    $[Mg^{2+}] = 5.31 \times 10^{-2}\ mol\cdot L^{-1}$; $[Ca^{2+}] = 1.03 \times 10^{-2}\ mol\cdot L^{-1}$;

    $[K^+] = 9.7 \times 10^{-3}\ mol\cdot L^{-1}$

    $[HCO_3^-] = 2.3 \times 10^{-3}\ mol\cdot L^{-1}$; $[Br^-] = 8.4 \times 10^{-4}\ mol\cdot L^{-1}$

35. a) $[Pb^{2+}] = 1.5 \times 10^{-3}\ mol\cdot L^{-1}$; $[I^-] = 3.0 \times 10^{-3}\ mol\cdot L^{-1}$

    b) $[Ag^+] = 6.6 \times 10^{-2}\ mol\cdot L^{-1}$; $[SO_4^{2-}] = 3.3 \times 10^{-2}\ mol\cdot L^{-1}$

    c) $[Fe^{3+}] = 2.2 \times 10^{-10}\ mol\cdot L^{-1}$; $[OH^-] = 6.6 \times 10^{-10}\ mol\cdot L^{-1}$

37. a) $2\,Cr^{3+}_{(aq)} + 3\,S^{2-}_{(aq)} \longrightarrow Cr_2S_{3(s)}$
  b) no precipitate
  c) $Co^{2+}_{(aq)} + 2\,OH^-_{(aq)} \longrightarrow Co(OH)_{2(s)}$
  d) $2\,Al^{3+}_{(aq)} + 3\,CO_3^{2-}_{(aq)} \longrightarrow Al_2(CO_3)_{3(s)}$

39. $[Ca^{2+}][F^-]^2 = 4.0 \times 10^{-8}$; this is greater than the K_{sp} value and a precipitate is expected.

41. 1.2×10^{-3} mol·L^{-1}

43. Silver chloride will start to precipitate when $[Ag^+] = 3.0 \times 10^{-10}$ mol·L^{-1}, silver bromide when $[Ag^+] = 7.7 \times 10^{-10}$ mol·L^{-1}. Silver chloride is the first one to precipitate.

45. a) 91.25 kPa
  b) 100.5 kPa

47. a) 100.45 °C
  b) −3.09 °C

49. 72 g·mol^{-1}

51. 2.60×10^4 g·mol^{-1}

53. 3.10×10^3 kPa

55. 0.19 mL

57. a) 23.34 g
  b) $[SO_4^{2-}] = 3.30 \times 10^{-10}$ mol·L^{-1}; $[Na^+] = 0.667$ mol·L^{-1}; $[Cl^-] = 1.33$ mol·L^{-1}; $[Ba^{2+}] = 0.333$ mol·L^{-1}

59. a) $[Ag^+] = [Cl^-] = 1.3 \times 10^{-5}$ mol·L^{-1}
  b) $[Ag^+] = 3.1 \times 10^{-5}$ mol·L^{-1}; $[Cl^-] = 5.2 \times 10^{-6}$ mol·L^{-1}
  c) 25.013 mL

61. 324 g·mol^{-1}

Chapter 9

13. a) $FSO_3H_{(\ell)} + H_2O_{(\ell)} \longrightarrow H_3O^+_{(aq)} + FSO_3^-_{(aq)}$
  b) $CaO_{(s)} \xrightarrow{\text{dissolve in water}} Ca^{2+}_{(aq)} + O^{2-}_{(aq)}$
   $O^{2-}_{(aq)} + H_2O_{(\ell)} \longrightarrow 2\,OH^-_{(aq)}$
  c) $H_2SO_{3(aq)} + H_2O_{(\ell)} \rightleftharpoons H_3O^+_{(aq)} + HSO_3^-_{(aq)}$
  d) $NaH_2PO_{4(s)} \xrightarrow{\text{dissolve in water}} Na^+_{(aq)} + H_2PO_4^-_{(aq)}$
   $H_2PO_4^-_{(aq)} + H_2O_{(\ell)} \rightleftharpoons H_3O^+_{(aq)} + HPO_4^{2-}_{(aq)}$
  e) $NaHCO_{3(s)} \xrightarrow{\text{dissolve in water}} Na^+_{(aq)} + HCO_3^-_{(aq)}$
   $HCO_3^-_{(aq)} + H_2O_{(\ell)} \rightleftharpoons H_2CO_{3(aq)} + OH^-_{(aq)}$
  f) $ClNH_{2(aq)} + H_2O_{(\ell)} \rightleftharpoons ClNH_3^+_{(aq)} + OH^-_{(aq)}$

15. a) H_2SO_4 b) $HBrO_3$ c) H_3PO_4

17. a), b), and c)

19. $C_6H_5O_7H_{3(aq)} + H_2O_{(\ell)} \rightleftharpoons H_3O^+_{(aq)} + C_6H_5O_7H_2^-_{(aq)}$
  $C_6H_5O_7H_2^-_{(aq)} + H_2O_{(\ell)} \rightleftharpoons H_3O^+_{(aq)} + C_6H_5O_7H^{2-}_{(aq)}$
  $C_6H_5O_7H^{2-}_{(aq)} + H_2O_{(\ell)} \rightleftharpoons H_3O^+_{(aq)} + C_6H_5O_7^{3-}_{(aq)}$

21. a) 4.52 b) 10.81 c) 1.40 d) 12.70

23.

	pH	pOH	$[H_3O^+]$	$[OH^-]$
a)	4.0	10.0	1×10^{-4}	1×10^{-10}
b)	2.4	11.6	4×10^{-3}	3×10^{-12}
c)	8.74	5.26	1.8×10^{-9}	5.6×10^{-6}
d)	12.54	1.46	2.9×10^{-13}	3.5×10^{-2}

25. a) $HSO_4^- + OH^- \rightleftharpoons H_2O + SO_4^{2-}$
   acid$_1$ HSO_4^-, base$_1$ SO_4^{2-}; acid$_2$ H_2O, base$_2$ OH^-
  b) $CH_3OH + NH_2^- \rightleftharpoons CH_3O^- + NH_3$
   acid$_1$ CH_3OH, base$_1$ CH_3O^-; acid$_2$ NH_3, base$_2$ NH_2^-
  c) $H_3O^+ + S^{2-} \rightleftharpoons H_2O + HS^-$
   acid$_1$ H_3O^+, base$_1$ H_2O; acid$_2$ HS^-, base$_2$ S^{2-}
  d) $CH_3^- + H_2O \rightleftharpoons CH_4 + OH^-$
   acid$_1$ CH_4, base$_1$ CH_3^-; acid$_2$ H_2O, base$_2$ OH^-
  e) $H_2NOH + H_2SO_4 \rightleftharpoons H_3N^+OH + HSO_4^-$
   acid$_1$ H_3N^+OH, base$_1$ H_2NOH; acid$_2$ H_2SO_4, base$_2$ HSO_4^-
  f) $CH_3OH + HCl \rightleftharpoons CH_3OH_2^+ + Cl^-$
   acid$_1$ $CH_3OH_2^+$, base$_1$ CH_3OH; acid$_2$ HCl, base$_2$ Cl^-

27. a) HNO_3 d) $NaHSO_4$
  b) HCl e) H_3PO_4
  c) HCl f) $ZnCl_2$

29. a) $H_2SO_{4(\ell)} + NH_{3(\ell)} \longrightarrow NH_4^+_{(am)} + HSO_4^-_{(am)}$
   $HSO_4^-_{(am)} + NH_{3(\ell)} \longrightarrow NH_4^+_{(am)} + SO_4^{2-}_{(am)}$
  b) $H_2SO_{4(\ell)} + CH_3CO_2H_{(\ell)} \rightleftharpoons CH_3CO_2H_2^+_{(ac)} + HSO_4^-_{(ac)}$

31. a) $NH_{3(\ell)} + NH_{3(\ell)} \rightleftharpoons NH_4^+_{(am)} + NH_2^-_{(am)}$
  b) $NH_2^-_{(am)} + HCO_3^-_{(am)} \longrightarrow NH_{3(\ell)} + CO_3^{2-}_{(am)}$
  c) $NH_4^+_{(am)} + HCO_3^-_{(am)} \longrightarrow 2\,NH_{3(\ell)} + CO_{2(g)}$

Chapter 10

11. a) $HCO_2H_{(aq)} + NaOH_{(aq)} \longrightarrow NaHCO_{2(aq)} + H_2O_{(\ell)}$
   $[HCO_2H] = 0.270$ mol·L^{-1}
  b) $NaH_2PO_{4(aq)} + 2\,NaOH_{(aq)} \longrightarrow Na_3PO_{4(aq)} + 2\,H_2O_{(\ell)}$
   $[NaH_2PO_4] = 0.225$ mol·L^{-1}
  c) $H_3PO_{4(aq)} + 3\,NaOH_{(aq)} \longrightarrow Na_3PO_{4(aq)} + 3\,H_2O_{(\ell)}$
   $[H_3PO_4] = 0.149$ mol·L^{-1}

13. 0.29 g

15. $Na_2CO_{3(aq)} + 2\,HCl_{(aq)} \longrightarrow H_2CO_{3(aq)} + 2\,NaCl_{(aq)}$; 92 %

17. 1.6×10^{-5}

19. 1×10^{-3}; 11 %

21. a) 1.40 b) 3.07 c) 2.70 d) 2.55

23. a) $NaCH_3CO_{2(aq)} \longrightarrow Na^+_{(aq)} + CH_3CO_2^-_{(aq)}$
  $CHCO_2^-_{(aq)} + H_2O_{(\ell)} \rightleftharpoons CH_3CO_2H_{(aq)} + OH^-_{(aq)}$
  pH = 9.23; 0.0034 %
  b) $Ca(ClO)_{2(aq)} \longrightarrow Ca^{2+}_{(aq)} + 2\,ClO^-_{(aq)}$
  $ClO^-_{(aq)} + H_2O_{(\ell)} \rightleftharpoons HClO_{(aq)} + OH^-_{(aq)}$
  pH = 10.04; 0.28 %
  c) $NaHCO_{3(aq)} \longrightarrow Na^+_{(aq)} + HCO_3^-_{(aq)}$
  $HCO_3^-_{(aq)} + H_2O_{(\ell)} \rightleftharpoons H_2CO_{3(aq)} + OH^-_{(aq)}$
  pH = 9.83; 0.034 %
  d) $Na_2SO_{3(aq)} \longrightarrow 2\,Na^+_{(aq)} + SO_3^{2-}_{(aq)}$
  $SO_3^{2-}_{(aq)} + H_2O_{(\ell)} \rightleftharpoons HSO_3^-_{(aq)} + OH^-_{(aq)}$
  pH = 10.20; 0.064 %

25. 4.5×10^{-5} mol·L^{-1}

27. a) 8.96 b) 5.66 c) 3.70

29. 73.3 g

31. b), e), and f) are Brønsted-Lowry acid-base reactions;
  a), c), and d) are Lewis acid-base reactions; Cr^{3+}, BF_3, and $FeBr_3$
  are Lewis acids.

33. a) 7.21 b) 6.92 c) 7.43

35. $[OH^-] = 5 \times 10^{-2}$ mol·L^{-1}; pH = 12.7

37. 5.00

39. a) 4.26   e) 8.00
  b) 6.24   f) 8.80
  c) 7.05   g) 9.59
  d) 7.52   h) 11.38

Chapter 11

17. a) +1 in Cu_2SO_4, +2 in $CuSO_4$
  b) +2 in $PbBr_2$, +4 in $PbBr_4$

19. PF_3 (P = +3), PF_5 (P = +5), Na_3P (P = −3), P_4 (P = 0),
  P_4O_6 (P = +3), etc.

21. a) Li = +1, I = −1
  b) Al = +3, S = −2
  c) P = 0
  d) Na = +1, O = −2
  e) Na = +1, O = −1
  f) Ca = +2, N = +5, O = −2

23. b) and c)

25. a) no reaction
  b) no reaction
  c) $3\,Mg_{(s)} + Al_2(SO_4)_{3(aq)} \longrightarrow 3\,MgSO_{4(aq)} + 2\,Al_{(s)}$
  d) $Fe_{(s)} + Pb(NO_3)_{2(aq)} \longrightarrow Fe(NO_3)_{2(aq)} + Pb_{(s)}$
  e) $Sn_{(s)} + 2\,HCl_{(aq)} \longrightarrow SnCl_{2(aq)} + H_{2(g)}$

27. a) $AS_2O_{3(s)} + 2\,Cl_{2(g)} + 5\,H_2O_{(\ell)} \longrightarrow$
  $2\,H_3AsO_{4(aq)} + 4\,HCl_{(aq)}$
  b) $3\,CO_{(g)} + K_2Cr_2O_{7(aq)} + 4\,H_2SO_{4(aq)} \longrightarrow$
  $3\,CO_{2(g)} + Cr_2(SO_4)_{3(aq)} + K_2SO_{4(aq)} + 4\,H_2O_{(\ell)}$
  c) $3\,Se_{(s)} + 4\,HNO_{3(aq)} \longrightarrow 3\,SeO_{2(s)} + 4\,NO_{(g)} + 2\,H_2O_{(\ell)}$
  d) $4\,PH_{3(g)} + 8\,O_{2(g)} \longrightarrow P_4O_{10(s)} + 6\,H_2O_{(\ell)}$

29.

	Oxidation	Reduction
a)	$2\,Al \longrightarrow 2\,Al^{3+} + 6\,e^-$	$3\,S + 6\,e^- \longrightarrow 3\,S^{2-}$
b)	$2\,K \longrightarrow 2\,K^+ + 2\,e^-$	$I_2 + 2\,e^- \longrightarrow 2\,I^-$
c)	$2\,Fe \longrightarrow 2\,Fe^{3+} + 6\,e^-$	$3\,Cl_2 + 6\,e^- \longrightarrow 6\,Cl^-$
d)	$4\,Na \longrightarrow 4\,Na^+ + 4\,e^-$	$O_2 + 4\,e^- \longrightarrow 2\,O^-$
e)	$2\,Rb \longrightarrow 2\,Rb^+ + 2\,e^-$	$2\,H_2O + 2\,e^- \longrightarrow 2\,OH^- + H_2$

31. a) $Br_2 + 2\,e^- \longrightarrow 2\,Br^-$
  b) $Fe^{2+} \longrightarrow Fe^{3+} + e^-$
  c) $ClO_2^- + 4\,H^+ + 4\,e^- \longrightarrow Cl^- + 2\,H_2O$
  d) $S_2O_4^{2-} + 8\,OH^- \longrightarrow 2\,SO_4^{2-} + 4\,H_2O + 6\,e^-$

33. a) $OCl^- + H_2O + 2\,e^- \longrightarrow Cl^- + 2\,OH^-$
  b) $AsO_3^{3-} + 3\,H_2O + 3\,e^- \longrightarrow As + 6\,OH^-$
  c) $S^{2-} + 8\,OH^- \longrightarrow SO_4^{2-} + 4\,H_2O + 8\,e^-$
  d) $N_2H_4 + 4\,OH^- \longrightarrow N_2 + 4\,H_2O + 4\,e^-$

35. a) $2\,S_2O_4^{2-} + 3\,O_2 + 4\,OH^- \longrightarrow 4\,SO_4^{2-} + 2\,H_2O$
  b) $2\,Cr(OH)_3 + IO_3^- + 4\,OH^- \longrightarrow 2\,CrO_4^{2-} + I^- + 5\,H_2O$
  c) $Ag_2O + CH_2O + OH^- \longrightarrow 2\,Ag + CHO_2^- + H_2O$
  d) $4\,MnO_4^- + 3\,N_2H_4 \longrightarrow 4\,MnO_2 + 3\,N_2 + 4\,H_2O + 4\,OH^-$
  e) $S_2O_3^{2-} + 4\,OCl^- + 2\,OH^- \longrightarrow 2\,SO_4^{2-} + 4\,Cl^- + H_2O$
  f) $8\,MnO_4^- + I^- + 8\,OH^- \longrightarrow 8\,MnO_4^{2-} + IO_4^- + 4\,H_2O$

37. $Au_{(s)} + 4\,Cl^-_{(aq)} + 3\,NO_3^-_{(aq)} + 6\,H^+_{(aq)} \longrightarrow$
  $AuCl_4^-_{(aq)} + 3\,NO_{2(g)} + 3\,H_2O_{(\ell)}$

39. $2\,CrI_{3(aq)} + 64\,KOH_{(aq)} + 27\,Cl_{2(g)} \longrightarrow$
  $2\,K_2CrO_{4(aq)} + 6\,KIO_{4(aq)} + 54\,KCl_{(aq)} + 32\,H_2O_{(\ell)}$

41. $I_{2(aq)} + H_3AsO_{3(aq)} + H_2O_{(\ell)} \longrightarrow H_3AsO_{4(aq)} + 2\,HI_{(aq)}$;
  $[I_2] = 0.198$ mol·L^{-1}

27. a) Anode: $Ti_{(s)} \longrightarrow Ti^{2+}_{(aq)} + 2\,e^-$ $\mathscr{E}° = +1.75$ V
Cathode: $Co^{2+}_{(aq)} + 2\,e^- \longrightarrow CO_{(s)}$ $\mathscr{E}° = -0.28$ V
$\mathscr{E}°_{cell} = +1.47$ V

b) Anode: $H_{2(g)} \longrightarrow 2\,H^+ + 2\,e^-$ $\mathscr{E}° = 0.00$ V
Cathode: $Au^+_{(aq)} + e^- \longrightarrow Au_{(s)}$ $\mathscr{E}° = +1.69$ V
$\mathscr{E}°_{cell} = +1.69$ V

c) Anode: $Ni_{(s)} \longrightarrow Ni^{2+}_{(aq)} + 2\,e^-$ $\mathscr{E}° = +0.23$ V
Cathode: $Ag^+_{(aq)} + e^- \longrightarrow Ag_{(s)}$ $\mathscr{E}° = +0.80$ V
$\mathscr{E}°_{cell} = +1.03$ V

29. Zn

31. a) Anode: $Zn_{(s)} \longrightarrow Zn^{2+}_{(aq)} + 2\,e^-$
Cathode: $Cl_{2(g)} + 2\,e^- \longrightarrow 2\,Cl^-_{(aq)}$

b) Anode: $Na \longrightarrow Na^+ + e^-$
Cathode: $S + 2\,e^- \longrightarrow S^{2-}$

33. Anode: $NiO_{(s)} + 2\,OH^-_{(aq)} \longrightarrow NiO_{2(s)} + H_2O_{(\ell)} + 2\,e^-$
Cathode: $FeO_{(s)} + H_2O_{(\ell)} + 2\,e^- \longrightarrow Fe_{(s)} + 2\,OH^-_{(aq)}$

35. Magnesium is higher in activity series than iron, therefore:
Oxidation (anodic sites): $Mg_{(s)} \longrightarrow Mg^{2+}_{(aq)} + 2\,e^-$
Reduction (cathodic sites): $\frac{1}{2}\,O_{2(g)} + H_2O_{(\ell)} + 2\,e^- \longrightarrow 2\,OH^-$

37. a)

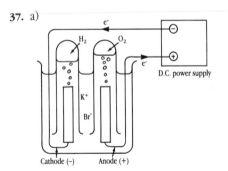

b) Anode: $2\,Br^-_{(aq)} \longrightarrow Br_{2(aq)} + 2\,e^-$
Cathode: $2\,H_2O_{(\ell)} + 2\,e^- \longrightarrow H_{2(g)} + 2\,OH^-_{(aq)}$

39. 0.191 A

41. $\mathscr{E}°_{cell} = +0.03$V; $\Delta G° = -3$ kJ; $K_c = 3$

43. 7.2 hours

45. a) (H_2O_2 has a slightly more favourable oxidation potential.)

47. a) $2\,H_2O_2 + 4\,H^+ + 4\,e^- \longrightarrow 4\,H_2O$
and i) $2\,H_2O \longrightarrow O_2 + 4\,H^+ + 4\,e^-$
or ii) $2\,H_2O_2 \longrightarrow 2\,O_2 + 2\,H^+ + 2\,e^-$

b) $K_c = 3 \times 10^{-37}$ if i) used
$K_c = 1 \times 10^{-37}$ if ii) used

c) The reaction rate is very slow at low temperatures, which implies the activation energy for the reaction is very high.

49. 11.7 min

21. a) $^{18}_{9}F$ b) $^{4}_{2}He$ c) $^{0}_{-1}e$ d) $^{210}_{81}Tl$ e) $^{0}_{+1}e$

23. $^{238}_{92}U \longrightarrow {}^{234}_{90}Th + {}^{4}_{2}He$
$^{234}_{90}Th \longrightarrow {}^{234}_{91}Pa + {}^{0}_{-1}e$
$^{234}_{91}Pa \longrightarrow {}^{234}_{92}U + {}^{0}_{-1}e$
$^{234}_{92}U \longrightarrow {}^{230}_{90}Th + {}^{4}_{2}He$
$^{230}_{90}Th \longrightarrow {}^{226}_{88}Ra + {}^{4}_{2}He$
$^{226}_{88}Ra \longrightarrow {}^{222}_{86}Rn + {}^{4}_{2}He$
$^{222}_{86}Rn \longrightarrow {}^{218}_{84}Po + {}^{4}_{2}He$
$^{218}_{84}Po \longrightarrow {}^{214}_{82}Pb + {}^{4}_{2}He$

25. 0.50 mg

27. 5.0×10^{11} J

29. 2.86×10^{-11} kg (or 2.86×10^{-8} g)

31. a) $^{1}_{0}n$ b) $^{1}_{1}p$ (or $^{1}_{1}H$) c) $^{7}_{4}Be$

33. $^{99}_{43}Tc \longrightarrow {}^{0}_{-1}e + {}^{99}_{44}Ru$

35. a) natural decay, beta particle
b) transmutation, fusion (as atomic number increased)
c) natural decay, positron
d) transmutation, fusion
e) transmutation, fission

37. $^{10}_{5}B + {}^{2}_{1}H \longrightarrow {}^{11}_{6}C + {}^{1}_{0}n$

39. $^{235}_{92}U \longrightarrow {}^{231}_{90}Th + {}^{4}_{2}He$
$^{231}_{90}Th \longrightarrow {}^{231}_{91}Pa + {}^{0}_{-1}e$
$^{231}_{91}Pa \longrightarrow {}^{227}_{89}Ac + {}^{4}_{2}He$
$^{227}_{89}Ac \longrightarrow {}^{227}_{90}Th + {}^{0}_{-1}e$
$^{227}_{90}Th \longrightarrow {}^{223}_{88}Ra + {}^{4}_{2}He$
$^{223}_{88}Ra \longrightarrow {}^{219}_{86}Rn + {}^{4}_{2}He$
$^{219}_{86}Rn \longrightarrow {}^{215}_{84}Po + {}^{4}_{2}He$
$^{215}_{84}Po \longrightarrow {}^{211}_{82}Pb + {}^{4}_{2}He$
$^{211}_{82}Pb \longrightarrow {}^{211}_{83}Bi + {}^{0}_{-1}e$
$^{211}_{83}Bi \longrightarrow {}^{207}_{81}Tl + {}^{4}_{2}He$
$^{207}_{81}Tl \longrightarrow {}^{207}_{82}Pb + {}^{0}_{-1}e$

17. B

19. a) and c); b) and d); f) and g)

21.
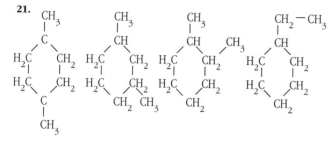

23. a) 2-methylpentane
    d) ethylcyclopentane
b) 2,3-dimethylhexane
    e) 3,5,5,7-tetramethylnonane
c) 3,3,5-trimethylheptane

25. a) $CH_3-CH-CH_2-CH_2-CH_2-CH_3$
      |
      CH_3

b) $CH_3-CH_2-CH-CH_2-CH-CH_2-CH_3$
           | |
           CH_3 CH_3

c)
$$H_2C-CH_3$$
$$H_2C-CH_3$$

d)
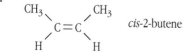

27. $C_{10}H_{22}$

29. a) 2-butene
    d) 2,6-dimethyl-2-heptene
b) 3-ethyl-2-pentene
    e) 5,7,7-trimethyl-2-octene
c) 2-methyl-2-pentene

31.

cis-2-butene

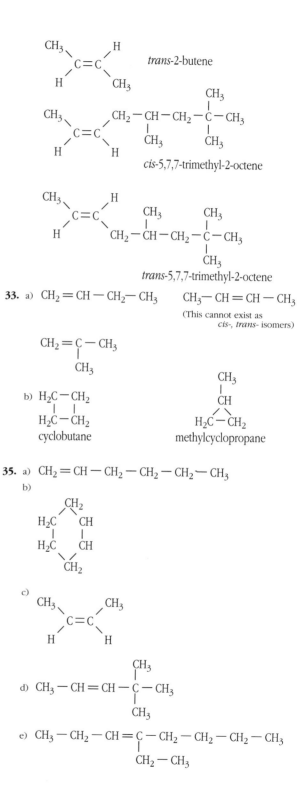

trans-2-butene

cis-5,7,7-trimethyl-2-octene

trans-5,7,7-trimethyl-2-octene

33. a) $CH_2=CH-CH_2-CH_3$ $CH_3-CH=CH-CH_3$

(This cannot exist as
cis-, *trans*- isomers)

$CH_2=C-CH_3$
     |
     CH_3

b) H_2C-CH_2
    H_2C-CH_2
    cyclobutane

methylcyclopropane

35. a) $CH_2=CH-CH_2-CH_2-CH_2-CH_3$

b)

c)
CH_3 CH_3
   C=C
 H   H

d) $CH_3-CH=CH-C-CH_3$
              |
             CH_3

e) $CH_3-CH_2-CH=C-CH_2-CH_2-CH_2-CH_3$
                  |
               CH_2-CH_3

37. a) $CH_2 = CH - CH = CH_2 + 2\ Br_2 \longrightarrow$

$$CH_2Br - CHBr - CHBr - CH_2Br$$

b) $3\ CH_2 = CH - CH_2 - CH_3 + 2\ KMnO_4 + 4\ H_2O \longrightarrow$

$$3\ CH_2 - CH - CH_2 - CH_3 + 2\ MnO_2 + 2\ KOH$$
$$\quad\ \ |\quad\ \ |$$
$$\quad\ \ OH\quad OH$$

39. a) 2-butyne   d) 4-methyl-1-pentyne

     b) 4,4-dimethyl-2-pentyne   e) 2,2,5,5-tetramethyl-3-hexyne

     c) 3-methyl-1-pentyne

41. a) $CH_3 - C \equiv C - CH_2 - CH_3$

b) $CH \equiv C - CH_2 - CH_2 - CH - CH_3$
$$\qquad\qquad\qquad\qquad\ \ |$$
$$\qquad\qquad\qquad\qquad\ CH_3$$

c)
$$\qquad\qquad\quad CH_3$$
$$\qquad\qquad\quad |$$
$$CH_3 - C \equiv C - C - CH_3$$
$$\qquad\qquad\quad |$$
$$\qquad\qquad\quad CH_3$$

d)
$$\qquad\qquad CH_2 - CH_3$$
$$\qquad\qquad |$$
$$CH \equiv C - C - CH_2 - CH_2 - CH_2 - CH_2 - CH_3$$
$$\qquad\qquad |$$
$$\qquad\qquad CH_2 - CH_3$$

e)
$$\qquad\qquad CH_3$$
$$\qquad\qquad |$$
$$CH \equiv C - C - CH_3$$
$$\qquad\qquad |$$
$$\qquad\qquad CH_3$$

43. $CH \equiv C - CH_2 - CH_2 - CH_3$

$CH \equiv C - CH - CH_3$
$$\qquad\qquad |$$
$$\qquad\qquad CH_3$$

$CH_3 - C \equiv C - CH_2 - CH_3$

45. a)

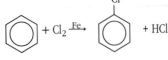 + Cl$_2$ $\xrightarrow{Fe}$ + HCl

b)

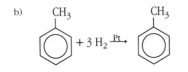 + 3 H$_2$ $\xrightarrow{Pt}$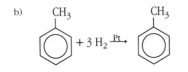

47. $CH \equiv C - CH_2 - CH_3$ $CH_3 - C \equiv C - CH_3$
     alkyne   alkyne

     $CH_2 = CH - CH = CH_2$ $CH_2 = C = CH - CH_3$
     alkene (alkadiene)   alkene (alkadiene)

$$\qquad\qquad\qquad\qquad\qquad\qquad CH_3$$
$$\qquad\qquad\qquad\qquad\qquad\qquad |$$
$$HC = CH\qquad\qquad\qquad\qquad\ C$$
$$\ |\qquad |\qquad\qquad\qquad\qquad / \backslash$$
$$H_2C - CH_2\qquad\qquad HC = CH$$
$$\ \ \text{cycloalkene}\qquad\quad \text{cycloalkene}$$

(None can exist as geometric isomers.)

49. a) $2\ C_8H_{18(\ell)} + 25\ O_{2(g)} \longrightarrow 16\ CO_{2(g)} + 18\ H_2O_{(\ell)}$

     b) $1.2 \times 10^3\ L$

Chapter 15

19. a) 3   b) 4

21. a) $2\ CH_3OH \xrightarrow{H_2SO_4} CH_3 - O - CH_3 + H_2O$

b) $3\ CH_3OH + 4\ MnO_4^- + 4\ H^+ \longrightarrow$

$$3\ HCO_2H + 4\ MnO_2 + 5\ H_2O$$

(Permanganate usually oxidizes alcohols to the corresponding carboxylic acid.)

c)
$$\qquad\qquad\qquad\qquad CH_3$$
$$\qquad\qquad\qquad\qquad |$$
$$CH_3 - CH_2 - C - CH_2OH + HCl \longrightarrow$$
$$\qquad\qquad\qquad\qquad |\qquad\qquad\qquad\qquad CH_3$$
$$\qquad\qquad\qquad\qquad CH_3\qquad\qquad\qquad\quad |$$
$$\qquad\qquad\qquad CH_3 - CH_2 - C - CH_2Cl + H_2O$$
$$\qquad\qquad\qquad\qquad\qquad\qquad\qquad |$$
$$\qquad\qquad\qquad\qquad\qquad\qquad\qquad CH_3$$

d) $CH_2 - CH_2 - CH_2 - CH_2 \xrightarrow{H_2SO_4}$
$$\ |\qquad\qquad\qquad\qquad |\qquad CH_2 = CH - CH = CH_2 + 2\ H_2O$$
$$\ OH\qquad\qquad\qquad\ OH$$

23. a) $CH_3 - O - CH_3$ methoxymethane

     b) $CH_3 - CH_2 - OH$ ethanol

25.

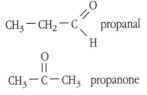

$CH_3 - CH_2 - C \overset{\displaystyle O}{\diagdown_H}$ propanal

$$\qquad\quad O$$
$$\qquad\quad ||$$
$$CH_3 - C - CH_3$$ propanone

27. a) $CH_3 - CH_2 - CH_2 - CH_2 - CH_2 - OH$ 1-pentanol

b) $CH_3 - CH_2 - \underset{\underset{OH}{|}}{CH} - CH_2 - CH_3$ 3-pentanol

29. a) 5-methylhexanoic acid   b) 2,2-dimethylpropanoic acid

31. a) ethyl propanoate   b) propyl propanoate

33. carboxylic acids:

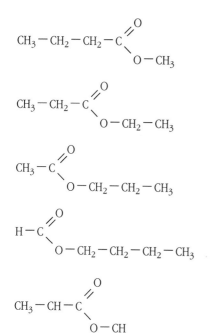

esters:

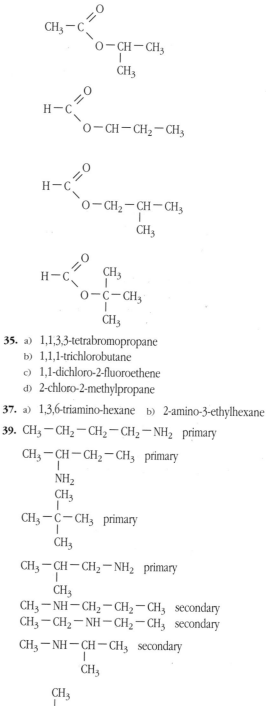

35. a) 1,1,3,3-tetrabromopropane
b) 1,1,1-trichlorobutane
c) 1,1-dichloro-2-fluoroethene
d) 2-chloro-2-methylpropane

37. a) 1,3,6-triamino-hexane   b) 2-amino-3-ethylhexane

39. $CH_3 - CH_2 - CH_2 - CH_2 - NH_2$ primary

$CH_3 - \underset{\underset{NH_2}{|}}{CH} - CH_2 - CH_3$ primary

$CH_3 - \underset{\underset{CH_3}{|}}{\overset{\overset{CH_3}{|}}{C}} - CH_3$ primary

$CH_3 - \underset{\underset{CH_3}{|}}{CH} - CH_2 - NH_2$ primary

$CH_3 - NH - CH_2 - CH_2 - CH_3$ secondary
$CH_3 - CH_2 - NH - CH_2 - CH_3$ secondary

$CH_3 - NH - \underset{\underset{CH_3}{|}}{CH} - CH_3$ secondary

$CH_3 - \underset{\underset{CH_2 - CH_3}{|}}{\overset{\overset{CH_3}{|}}{N}}$ tertiary

41.

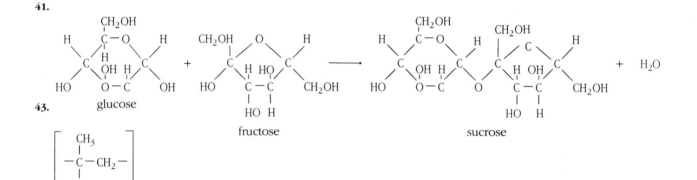

glucose   fructose   sucrose

43.

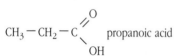

45. 3.92 g·L^{-1} (about five times the density of air)

47. a) physical: boiling point—ethanol will have a much higher boiling point than methoxymethane;
chemical: reaction with dichromate or permanganate ion—ethanol will be oxidized, resulting in a colour change; methoxymethane will be unchanged

b) physical: boiling point—butanoic acid will have a higher boiling point than ethyl ethanoate;
chemical: reaction with the base form of an indicator (such as litmus) —butanoic acid will give the acid colour to the indicator (for example, blue litmus will turn red); there will be no reaction with ethyl ethanoate

c) physical: boiling point—propanol will have a higher boiling point than propanone;
chemical: reaction with dichromate or permanganate ion—propanol will be oxidized resulting in a colour change; propanone will not be oxidized

49. A   CH$_3$—CH—CH$_3$ 2-propanol
            |
            OH

B   CH$_3$—CH$_2$—CH$_2$—OH   2-propanol

C   CH$_3$—C—CH$_3$ 1-propanone
            ||
            O

D

CH$_3$—CH$_2$—C$\overset{\displaystyle O}{\underset{\displaystyle OH}{}}$ propanoic acid

51. butane 272 K; ethoxyethane 307 K; butanone 352 K; 1-butanol 390 K

Index

Key words are indicated by **boldface** references; tables and figures are indicated by (t) and (f) respectively; colour plates are indicated by the letter P.

Photo Credits

AC Spark Plug 6.30; AIP Neils Bohr Library 2.2, 2.7, 5.33, 7.24, 13.5, 13.8; Aldrich Chemical Co., Inc. 10.20b); Alltech Associates 8.43; Allured Publishing Corp. 8.9; Dr. John Anderson, University of North Carolina 8.29; AP/Wide World Photos 9.16a), 13.22, 13.26, 15.19; L'Institut de l'amiante 3.25; Barnaby's Picture Library 8.21; Lois Bateman, Biology Dept., Sir Wilfred Grenfell College 14.17; Beckmann Instruments Inc. 9.19; Belgian Tourist Office 2.23; The Berkshire Museum 12.7; Bettmann Newsphotos 1.4; The Bettman Archive 4.40, 8.11; Boreal Laboratories 6.5; Burndy Library 1.11, 1.13, 4.35; Cadet Cleaners 8.4; Canadian Bank Note Co., Ltd. 12.24, 12.25; Canadian Jewellers Institute 3.16b), 3.24a), b), c); Canapress Photo Service 2.13, 2.31, 6.9, 9.15, 9.16b), 10.1, 12.13, 13.24; Central Electricity Generating Board 3.11a); Reed Clarke 14.14; Cominco Limited 11.18; Cordon Art-Baarn-Holland 2.35, 5.1; Corning Glass Works 9.18; Cosa Instruments Corp. 10.7; C.I.L. Inc. 5.16; C.W. Hill Photography Ltd. 15.24; Dr. V. Daniels, British Museum 11.19; Fraser Day 4.11, 6.27, 6.46a), 8.14, 8.39, 9.1, 9.2, 10.13; Defense Meteorological Satellite Program/National Snow and Ice Data Center 5.25; A.L. Devries, University of Illinois 8.40; Dionne Photography 10.19; Dover Publications, Inc. 2.15; Du Pont Canada 15.25, 15.26; E.I. du Pont de Nemours and Co. 15.27; Eastman Kodak Company 11.22; Edgar Fahs Smith Collection 9.3, 14.1; Thomas Eisner, Cornell University 15.15; Field Museum of Natural History 7.9; Fisher Scientific 11.10; Four by Five Photography, Inc. 5.13, 7.5; Dudley Foster, Woods Hole Oceanographic Institute 8.22; Fundamental Photographs 1.1; GE Aerospace 4.13; GE Research and Development Centre 4.14, 4.16; Geographical Visual Aids 1.2; Geological Survey of Canada 3.16a), 3.23a); The Geology Museum 14.25; Gesellschaft Für 13.16; Dr. Paul A. Giguère, Université Laval 9.7; Ralph Ginzburg 15.9; R.J. Gillespie, University of McMaster 3.1; Grant Heilman Photography 2.26; Henold and Walmsley, *Chemical Principals, Properties and Reactions*; Addison-Wesley Publishing Company 9.10; R. Hessler, Scripps Institution of Oceanography 11.16; John Hus 7.23; IMC Fertilizer, Inc. 1.6; Imperial Oil Limited 14.13; Inco 11.17; Jeremy Jones Photography © Addison-Wesley Publishers Limited 1.5, 4.20, 4.30, 4.41, 4.43, 5.7a), b), 6.1, 6.6, 6.7, 6.10a), b), 6.21, 6.33, 6.44, 6.46b), 7.1, 7.2, 7.18, 8.6, 8.18, 8.26, 8.32, 8.33, 9.4, 9.9, 9.10, 9.22, 10.6, 10.14, 10.18, 11.5, 11.9, 11.14, 11.15, 12.8, 13.17, 14.8, 15.7, 15.8, 15.11; Jet Propulsion Laboratory 14.11; John Wiley and Sons Inc. per A. Silverman 7.11; Brian Kellett 15.4; Ken Kimble and Co. Ltd. 7.10; The Keystone Collection 6.28; Dr. Jena K. Khodadad, Rush-Presbyterian-St. Luke's Medical Centre 8.41; Julius Kirschner, American Museum of Natural History 8.27; Lab Safety Supply Co. 13.7; Lavalin Inc. 5.26; Dr. Peter Lea, University of Toronto 7.15; Lo He Weitner-Graf 4.36; Lockheed-California Company 6.42; Lisa Lowry 15.21; Donna Cantor Maclean 12.22; Magnum Photos 7.20; Mark Edwards Picture Library 5.29; Andrew J. Martinez 6.8; Mary Evans Picture Library 11.11; Masterfile 6.45, 8.8; Johnson Matthey/AESAR 2.41; McGill University Archives 13.1; McKim Advertising 5.2; Don Meiwald 1.2, 2.1, 5.22, 6.11, 8.37, 11.4, 14.2, 15.2, 15.18; Meteorological Research Flight 3.11b); Metropolitan Toronto Police 11.20; Miller Services 4.1; Dr. B.T. Mossman, Chemical and Engineering News 3.26; MRC Dunn Nutrition Unit, Cambridge 5.24; The Museum of Modern Art 15.13; Nasa 6.43; Nasa/Lewis Research Centre 12.2; National Archives of Canada 5.5; National Library of Medicine 15.6; National Optical Astronomy Observatories 13.15; National Osteoporosis Foundation 8.28; National Research Council 13.14; New York Public Library 5.8a); Nicolet X-ray Instruments 2.36; Notman Photographic Archives, McGill University 13.3; Dr. G.A. Olah, University of Southern California 10.20a); Ontario Hydro 5.28; Orgo-Thermit Inc. 11.13; Richard Palmer 6.35c); Parr Instrument Co. 5.23; Peter Arnold Inc. 12.18; Photo Researchers, Inc. 4.3, 4.52, 8.25; Pioneer Electronics 6.2; Professor John Polanyi 6.35a), b); Potash Corporation of Saskatchewan 8.23, 8.24; Princeton University, Plasma Physics Lab 13.18; Wayne Purchase 1.3, 6.26; Rintje Raap 9.13, 9.20,•10.3, 11.1, 12.1, 12.2, 12.19; Reed Clarke 14.14; The Royal Institution 12.30; Royal Ontario Museum 2.25; Royal Society of Chemistry 2.40; The Royal Society 14.27; Chris Schwarz, *Edmonton Journal* 15.20; Scintrex 14.19; Scripps Institution of Oceanography 8.36; Dr. C.V. Senoff 11.8; Robert Sherbow/*People Weekly* © 1980 Time Inc. 8.42; Spectra Physics 14.20; Sumitoma Electric Industries Ltd. 4.17a), b); S.S.C. photo centre: Duncan Cameron 5.3; Faber 2.27; Ted Grant 11.2; George

Hunter 8.20; Chris Lund 4.8; Mia & Klaus 12.26; Terry Pearce 4.9; Tony Scammell 12.15; 5.27; The Tate Gallery 6.49; Texas A & M University 8.35; TexasGulf Inc. 6.31; Toshiba of Canada Ltd. 5.5; Travel Alberta 4.7; University of Utah Library 6.15; UPI Bettman Newsphotos 1.4, 2.38; U.S. Council for Energy Awareness 13.25; U.S.S.R. Embassy, Press Office 13.20; Van Den Berghs and Jurgens Ltd. 14.22; W.C.I. Canada 4.34; Ward's Natural Science 3.19, 3.23b); *The Whig Standard* 12.14; Kimberly Willis, University of California at Los Angeles 5.6; Sir Geoffrey Wilkinson 14.12;

COLOUR PLATES: Association of Cape Cod P14 (bottom); Atomic Energy of Canada Ltd. P26 (top left), P27 (right), P28 (left, bottom right), P29 (bottom left, bottom right); Australian Nuclear Science and Technology Organisation P31 (top left, top right); Bowen Plus Associates P12 (top right); The British Museum P23 (bottom right); British Nuclear Fuels plc P29 (top left, top right); Professor R.R. Brooks, Massey University P18 (top left, top right, bottom right); Calgary Chamber of Commerce P34 (top left); Canadian Petroleum Association P37 (top left); Chemical Design Ltd. P5, P6 (top right, bottom), P7 (bottom left, bottom middle, bottom right), P8 (top left, top right); Computer Graphics Laboratory of the University of California at San Francisco P3 (bottom right); Copper Development Association P22 (top right, bottom left, bottom right) P23 (bottom left); Department of Fisheries and Oceans P12 (top left), P13 (top right); Digital Instruments, Inc. P8 (bottom left, bottom right); *Discover Magazine*, Familiy Media, Inc. P15 (bottom); Du Pont P39 (bottom right); Edmon Scientific P40 (top left, bottom left); Education Service of the Plastics Industry P38, P39 (top left, top right, bottom right), P40 (top right, bottom right); Fishery Products International P9, P10 (bottom right), P11; FMC Corporation P13 (top right); Furuno Electric Co., Ltd. P10 (bottom left); Gessellshchaft fur P28 (top right); Harbour branch Oceanographic Institution, Inc. P15 (top); Inco Limited P19 (bottom right), P20 (right); Jeremy Jones Photography P14 (top right, top left), P24 (bottom); Marine Institute, St. John's P10 (top right, top left); Meridian Instruments Inc. P4; Molecular Design Ltd. P1; National Archives of Canada P33 (bottom left); National Capital Commision P22 (top left); Nicolet X-ray Instruments P3 (top left, top right, bottom right), P6 (top left); Noranda Minerals, CCR Division P23 (top), P24 (top); Dr. Uwe Oehler, University of Guelph P2; Ontario Hydro P25 (top right), P26 (bottom), P27 (top left, middle left, bottom left), P30 (top left, right); Petro Canada P35 (top left, top right), P36 (top left), P37 (top right, bottom); The Petroleum Resources Communication Foundation P33 (top, bottom right), P34 (bottom left, bottom right), P35 (bottom), P36 (bottom right); Provincial Archives of Alberta P34 (top right); Dr. Conor Reilly, Queensland Institute of Technology P18 (bottom left); Kenneth L. Rinehart P16 (bottom); Paul J. Scheuer, University of Hawaii P16 (top); *Scientific American* P7 (top); S.S.C. photocentre: Bryce Flynn P19 (bottom left); Crombie McNeill P19 (top right); Pat Morrow P21; Karl Sommerer P20 (top left, middle left, bottom left); Syncrude Canada Ltd. P 36 (bottom left); Terra Nova Fishery Co., Ltd P13 (bottom right); Tom Stack & Associates P12 (bottom); Ward's Natural Science Ltd. P17; Westinghouse Hanford Co. P32 (top left, top right, bottom);

p. 55 excerpt from "Common Sense and The Universe" by S. Leacock courtesy of The Canadian Publishers, McClelland and Stewart, Toronto

Symbols, Units, and Abbreviations

α	alpha rays		ΔG_f°	free energy of formation
β	beta rays		g	gram
γ	gamma rays		(g)	gas
Δ	change in		Gy	gray
$\xrightarrow{\Delta}$	heat added to a reaction		H	enthalpy
δ^+, δ^-	partial charge		ΔH°	standard change in enthalpy
Π	osmotic pressure		ΔH_f°	standard enthalpy of formation
π	pi bond		h	hour
σ	sigma bond		J	joule
a	year		k	constant
A	ampere		K	Kelvin
(aq)	aqueous solution		K_a	acid dissociation constant
b.p.	boiling point		K_b	base dissociation constant
Bq	becquerel		k_b	boiling-point elevation constant
c	concentration (mol·L^{-1})		K_c	equilibrium constant (concentration)
C	coulomb		K_{eq}	equilibrium constant
°C	degree Celsius		k_f	freezing-point depression constant
Ci	curie		K_w	ion product constant for water
C_p°	molar heat capacity (constant pressure)		K_{sp}	solubility product constant
d	day		kg	kilogram
E	energy		kPa	kilopascal
E_a	activation energy		L	litre
$\mathscr{E}$	electromotive force		L.P.	lone pair
$\mathscr{E}^\circ$	standard (reduction) potential		(ℓ)	liquid
$\mathscr{E}^\circ_{ox}$	standard oxidation potential		m	moles per kilogram, mass (nuclear chemistry)
$^0_{+1}e$	positron		min	minute
$^0_{-1}e$	electron (nuclear chemistry)		mL	millilitre
e^-	electron (electrochemistry)		mol	mole
F	Faraday constant (charge)		m.p.	melting point
G	Gibbs free energy		^1_0n	neutron
ΔG	change in Gibbs free energy		n	number of moles (amount of substance)
ΔG°	standard change in free energy		P	pressure